£12.00

WITHDRAWN

GUIDE TO RESEARCH AND REFERENCE WORKS

ON SUB-SAHARAN AFRICA

Hoover Institution Bibliographical Series: XLVI

GUIDE TO RESEARCH AND REFERENCE WORKS
ON SUB-SAHARAN AFRICA

Edited by

Peter Duignan

Compiled by

Helen F. Conover

and

Peter Duignan

with the assistance of

Evelyn Boyce

Liselotte Hofmann

Karen Fung

Hoover Institution Press

Stanford University • Stanford, California

Standard Book Number 8179-2461-2
Library of Congress Catalog Card Number 76-152424
Printed in the United States of America

CONTENTS

PART III

SUBJECT GUIDE IN GENERAL

PART IV

AREA GUIDE
(BY FORMER COLONIAL POWER, REGION, AND COUNTRY)

PREFACE

The purpose of this volume is to describe African library and archival materials important in reference, research, and teaching. It aims to serve especially the librarian and the student. For the librarian it should be not only a reference source but also a guide to building an African collection. For the student it can be a beginning reference bibliography for the entire field of African studies.

The major categories of reference works defined by Constance Winchell's GUIDE TO REFERENCE BOOKS were sought out--that is, guides and manuals, bibliographies, indexes and abstracts, encyclopedias, dictionaries of special subjects, handbooks, annuals and directories, histories, biographical works, atlases, serial and series publications. Unfortunately, African studies does not have a good supply of all these kinds of reference works. So we have substituted scholarly specialized books and articles to fill in where reference works were unavailable. This makes the manual a cross between a guide to reference materials and an annotated reading list.

The coverage is Africa south of the Sahara, excluding Morocco, Algeria, Tunisia, Libya, and Egypt. There are four parts. Part I has three chapters: (1) centers, institutions, and records of research; (2) libraries and archives; and (3) publishers and bookdealers. Part II has eight chapters covering various forms of bibliographies: bibliographies of bibliographies, current bibliographies, retrospective bibliographies, acquisitions lists, serials lists, surveys of official publications, dissertations, and atlases and maps. Part III provides a subject guide to the literature of geography, history, politics and government, international relations, law, economics, sociology, demography, labor, education, religion and missions, anthropology, linguistics, arts and letters, communications, natural sciences, and medicine and health. For each subject there are at least two major divisions: bibliographies and reference works. For some subjects the topic is broken down into several subdisciplines; for example, economics is treated under four headings: general, statistics, agriculture, and mining. Part IV is an area guide to the regions and countries of Africa grouped under the former colonial powers. The division by colonial power seemed necessary and useful, for most materials on African states are those that were produced during the colonial period. Most chapters have three rubrics: bibliographies, serials, and reference works. Where there is no separate serial listing, individual titles of journals appear in the reference works section.

In the selection of references we have tried to encompass the needs of the undergraduate and graduate student as well as the librarian and teacher/researcher. Only a few titles could be suggested for each topic but they were chosen to lead to other important sources. We did not try to be exhaustive in listing bibliographies or finding aids, nor did we seek out obscure items; rather our purpose was to give illustrative examples of the kinds of material available. Works in English, French, German, Italian, Spanish, and Portuguese are cited, as well as a few in Slavic languages, Arabic, and Afrikaans.

Most entries are annotated. Those that are not were usually not available for examination or were included too late to be reviewed. In the annotations we have attempted to describe the scope and character of the work and, frequently, to critically evaluate it. Information about institutions and organizations and biographical data are often included (unfortunately, it proved impossible to keep up to date on groups and individuals). Works cited in the annotations are not necessarily of secondary importance; their placement was simply governed by our grudging acceptance of space limitations. The style of the bibliographical data follows, in a modified form, Library of Congress practices.

I should like to express my gratitude to Dr. W. Glenn Campbell, Director of the Hoover Institution, for sponsoring the production of this guide. The task took far longer than either I intended or the Institution expected. Even when the original two-year project extended into four and finally six years, the Institution's Research and Publications Committee remained cheerfully supportive, as did the Publications Department, which supplied what must have seemed like battalions of copy editors, typists, indexers, and proofreaders. I am grateful, too, to the Center for Research in International Studies at Stanford University, which also gave a grant to support the project.

My special thanks go to Mrs. Evelyn Boyce, Miss Liselotte Hofmann, and Miss Karen Fung. During the long period of gestation and ultimate birth Mrs. Boyce and Miss Hofmann were constant in their encouragement, zealous in their enthusiasm, and ever willing to suggest dozens of new entries, complex organizational changes, and exotic new forms of entries. Mrs. Boyce, in addition to much copy editing, also typed part of the manuscript and checked entries for accuracy. Miss Hofmann did everything from typing to annotating to rechecking entries and seeing the manuscript through all phases of production into a book. Miss Fung with a falcon's eye uncovered new entries and annotated them. Then there was the copy editor whose nausea, we were happy to learn, was caused not by the manuscript but by an unpropitious pregnancy; and the one who over a skiing weekend managed to break one of her legs and all of our momentum. For the delays and improvements I owe much to every one of them.

I wish to thank also the many scholars and friends who read parts of the manuscript and made candid criticisms and suggestions: David Brokensha, Robert O. Collins, Jacques Depelchin, Leonard Doob, Renée Fox, William Friedland, Lewis Gann, Joseph Greenberg, Per Hassing, Robert L. Hess, Graham Irwin, William O. Jones, Raymond Kent, Martin Lowenkopf, Alan P. Merriam,

John Povey, A. Arthur Schiller, Alan Taylor, Benjamin E. Thomas, Immanuel Wallerstein, Brian Weinstein, Douglas L. Wheeler, Donald Wiedener, Frank Willett, and Julian Witherell. Mr. Reuben Musiker of Rhodes University Library, South Africa, provided most of the entries for the Southern Africa section.

Having decided back in 1964 to do a guide on African reference works, I sought out the world's premier African bibliographer, Miss Helen Conover. The basic organization and some modified entries derive from Miss Conover's AFRICA SOUTH OF THE SAHARA: A SELECTED, ANNOTATED LIST OF WRITINGS (1963). We collaborated on the first draft of the study and up to 1967 Miss Conover sent additional entries. The delay and the incomplete coverage after 1967 are my fault. If the volume has value it is largely due to Miss Conover's unparalleled knowledge and experience in the realm of African bibliography.

It has been difficult to complete this volume. No part could be considered closed as new titles kept appearing. But going back and updating proved to be a losing battle. In fact, ground was lost, and more material was missed than was discovered by trying to keep a guide of more than 3,000 entries current. A year's leave of absence in 1969-70 further weakened the coverage, so after six month's work in 1970 I simply closed the study. This means that Parts I and II were essentially closed in 1968 and only partially revised to include material for 1969-70; more revisions were added to Parts III and IV through 1970. In a sense, this volume is only a preliminary version--to be criticized and revised during the next two years; then a new edition will be issued. Still, with all its flaws, I hope the guide will prove of value and will stimulate others to do better. In any case, I end this work "with feelings of regret, not untempered by relief."

Peter Duignan

Hoover Institution
January 1971

PART I

GUIDE TO RESEARCH ORGANIZATIONS, LIBRARIES AND ARCHIVES,

AND THE BOOK TRADE

NOTE ON GENERAL LIBRARY TOOLS

Note: In research on Africa, it is axiomatic that one should make full use of general library tools. Besides the immediate approach of the card catalogues, there will be found in most large libraries published guides to a variety of forms of documentation (e.g., archives, government documents, maps, newspapers) and to subject fields (e.g., architecture, botany, medicine) in which materials useful for African studies may not be specified as such but will occur in a broader context. Such reference works are amply described in the following three standard library handbooks, American, British, and French:

1. Winchell, Constance M. GUIDE TO REFERENCE BOOKS. 8th ed. Chicago, American Library Association, 1967. xx, 741 p. (7,500 entries)

   First Supplement, 1965-1966. By Eugene Sheehy. Chicago, American Library Association, 1968. 122 p.

   The standard American authority to consult for general library tools. In this eighth edition, thousands of entries are explained in considerable and sufficient detail, and an index of authors, subjects, and selected titles provides quick access to all entries. The five parts are general reference works (with bibliographies treated first), the humanities, social sciences, history and area studies, and pure and applied sciences. Coverage in the main stops with 1964, though a few exceptions were made (e.g., UNION LIST OF SERIALS, 3d ed., 1965) where it seemed essential. The earlier seventh edition (1951; supplements, 1950-52, 1953-55, 1956-58, 1959-June 1962) was also prepared by Miss Winchell, formerly reference librarian of Columbia University, now retired.

   There are not many current national bibliographies for African countries, but since the majority of works on Africa are published in Great Britain, Western Europe, and the United States, a large proportion of new books can be most quickly identified in such comprehensive catalogues as the American CUMULATIVE BOOK INDEX, the BRITISH NATIONAL BIBLIOGRAPHY, the BIBLIOGRAPHIE DE BELGIQUE, BIBLIOGRAPHIE DE LA FRANCE, etc. Similarly, much of the periodical material can be spotted in the

BRITISH HUMANITIES INDEX, SOCIAL SCIENCES AND HUMANITIES INDEX (formerly
INTERNATIONAL INDEX), the Public Affairs Information Service BULLETIN,
the READERS' GUIDE TO PERIODICAL LITERATURE, and other general or specialized indexes to serials. For description of all such regular library
tools, the user may be referred to Winchell.

2. Walford, Albert J. GUIDE TO REFERENCE MATERIAL. 2d ed. London, Library
        Association, 1968, 1970. 2 v.

    This British counterpart to Winchell's seventh edition complemented
and in part duplicated Winchell, with somewhat different emphases as well
as concentration on British sources. References to Africa may be found
in the index under Africa, the name of the country, and the name of the
author (or title if there is no main author).

3. Malclès, Louise N. LES SOURCES DU TRAVAIL BIBLIOGRAPHIQUE. Genève, E.
        Droz, 1950-58. 3 v. in 4.

    The French standard guide to reference tools, Malclès is especially
helpful in regard to European documentation. Entries are classified
under broad categories with many subdivisions. Vol. I is devoted to
general bibliographies. Vols. II and III cover specialized sources.
Vol. II, in two parts, continuously paged, is on the sciences humaines
(prehistory, anthropology, literature, geography, philosophy, and the
language, literature, and history of the Slavic and Balkan countries and
the Near, Middle, and Far East); Vol. III is on the sciences exactes et
techniques (history of science, mathematics, physics, chemistry, zoology,
botany, medicine, etc.). For the last volume, G. Garnier and others collaborated. Chapter headings and many subheadings are followed by analytical comment, and though a few references are separately annotated, most
are grouped with a descriptive note. Each of the three volumes ends with
a complete index of authors and titles of anonymous works and a brief
table of contents.

CHAPTER 1

CENTERS, INSTITUTIONS, AND RECORDS OF RESEARCH

Note: In recent years there has been a substantial growth of institutions concerned with African studies and research. No comprehensive directory has been published, and new bodies come into existence so fast that no published record can for long be up to date. A few lists of institutions of specifically African interest have been issued, and some general world directories include groups relating to Africa. The names of those organizations that publish periodicals, as most do, usually appear in the indexes of lists of serials. Some large study centers keep card files of organizational names, to which constant additions are made as new institutions come to notice. Information about newly formed organizations is carried regularly in the news and notes sections of the leading Africanist journals. These same journals are also among the best sources for accounts of research in progress or completed. In this section we indicate available lists of organizations concerned with African studies, guides to research on Africa, and registers of individual researchers.

4. AFRICA: JOURNAL OF THE INTERNATIONAL AFRICAN INSTITUTE. 1928- London, Oxford University Press. Quarterly.

    For further description see no. 280. The "News and Notes" section is indispensable for reports on new institutions, conferences, programs of universities, and research and foundation activities. It is now available as an offprint (as is the "Bibliography of Current Publications").

5. AFRICAN SOCIAL RESEARCH. 1966- Manchester, Eng., published on behalf of the Institute for Social Research, University of Zambia, by the Manchester University Press (distributed in the United States by Humanities Press, New York 10010). Biannual.

    Formerly the RHODES-LIVINGSTONE JOURNAL: HUMAN PROBLEMS IN CENTRAL AFRICA. In its scholarly articles and book reviews the journal plans to widen its scope to cover social research in all Africa and even work being done elsewhere when the findings appear to be applicable to Africa, especially in sociology and social anthropology, psychology, economics, human geography and demography, history, and political science. An index is to be issued every five years.

6.   African Studies Association, New York. AFRICAN STUDIES BULLETIN.
          1958- 3 times a year. Published for the ASA by Hoover
          Institution, Stanford, Calif. 1965-66; by African Studies
          Center, Boston University, Boston, Mass., 1967-69; by African
          Studies Center, Michigan State University, Lansing, Mich; 1969-

          The African Studies Association was formed in Mar. 1957 at a
     conference in New York at which 35 Africanists were present. In
     1967 membership had grown to more than 1,400, almost 700 of them
     fellows. The first number of the AFRICAN STUDIES BULLETIN made its
     appearance in Apr. 1958. The Association has reported in its pages
     on advances in African studies, for example, efforts to foster
     teaching and research in the African field, to promote courses and
     programs in colleges and universities (the BULLETIN includes an
     annual list of American universities and the courses they offer,
     e.g., "African Studies in the United States," by Norman R. Bennett,
     v. 11, no. 1, April 1968: 83-127), to widen the scope of studies
     across disciplines, and to improve American library and archival
     resources. Reports of many conferences have been included, among
     them those under the auspices of the African Research Committee.
     A 24-page INDEX covering vols. 1-10 (1958-67), compiled by Norman
     R. Bennett and Marguerite Ylvisaker, was issued in 1968. The
     Association also issues each year a ROSTER OF FELLOWS. In 1970
     the name of the bulletin was changed to AFRICAN STUDIES REVIEW;
     henceforth substantive articles will be published.

          Contact with African colleauges has been recognized as of
     primary importance. As a result of this need the Research Liaison
     Committee was established by the Association in 1966 to serve as a
     central agency for information on the planning and conduct of
     research with regard to Africa and for issuance of further infor-
     mation through the ASA BULLETIN and through special reports (e.g.,
     A DIRECTORY OF STUDIES CENTERS AND RESEARCH INSTITUTES ABROAD:
     AFRICA, New York [1967?] 63 l.). A supplement was issued in 1968.
     A grant by the Ford Foundation was crucial in the formation of
     the Research Liaison Committee.

          The Association's Libraries-Archives Committee has been important
     in encouraging compilation of descriptions of archives and manuscript
     collections and guides and bibliographies on holdings. In the
     following pages of this guide many of these lists and descriptions
     in the BULLETIN are referred to; see also p. 86 on the Cooperative
     African Microfilm Project (CAMP).

7. African Studies Association, New York. AFRICAN STUDIES NEWSLETTER.
    v. 1, no. 1- 1968- New York. 6 or 9 times a year.

    Experimental issues of this leaflet were published in 1967 by the
Washington Liaison Committee, and the Research Liaison Committee began
issuing the NEWSLETTER regularly in 1968. It is sent automatically to
the membership of the Association and is devoted to announcements of
interest to Africanists, including the news and notes section formerly
published in the AFRICAN STUDIES BULLETIN. Among items are data on
institutions, conferences, meetings, seminars, U.S. Government action in
connection with Africa, foundation grants for study and research, positions available for teaching in or about Africa, African visitors in the
United States, and new or forthcoming publications of special import.
Beginning in the third issue, May-June 1968, the NEWSLETTER is publishing the record of research in progress previously issued by the U.S.
Office of External Research (see no. 40).

8. African Studies Association of the United Kingdom. BULLETIN. no. 1-
    1964- Birmingham. 3 times a year.

    Like the American AFRICAN STUDIES BULLETIN and the NEWSLETTER, this
journal is a prime source of information regarding institutions, centers
of research, and activities relating to African studies.

9. BULLETIN OF INFORMATION ON CURRENT RESEARCH ON HUMAN SCIENCES CONCERNING
    AFRICA. BULLETIN D'INFORMATION SUR LES RECHERCHES DANS LES SCIENCES
    HUMAINES CONCERNANT L'AFRIQUE. no. 1- 1963- Bruxelles, Centre
    International de Documentation Economique et Sociale Africaine
    (CIDESA).

    Annotated list of research in progress, irregularly issued. The
first two numbers (no. 1, 1963; no. 1, 1964) were entitled BULLETIN OF
INFORMATION ON THESES AND STUDIES IN PROGRESS OR PROPOSED. Beginning
with no. 2 of 1964, studies are classified according to the Dewey decimal
system (general, religion, social sciences, philology, etc.) instead of
the earlier alphabetical arrangement by author. Almost every issue begins with a list of works published prior to the current date, theses
completed, works scheduled for publication, etc. There are indexes of
institutions, authors, topics (by title words), and geographic distribution. The studies recorded are from universities and centers of learning
in England, Germany, France, Belgium, Australia, Africa, and, in a few
cases, the United States, etc.; there seems to be no attempt at complete
coverage.

    In Jozef Bogaert's SCIENCES HUMAINES EN AFRIQUE NOIRE: GUIDE BIBLIO-
GRAPHIQUE 1945-1965 (CIDESA, Enquêtes bibliographiques, no. 15, 1967)
(see no. 273) there are included lists of organizations characterized as
"Répertoires d'institutions scientifiques, de bibliothèques et de chercheurs" and "Répertoires de sociétés et d'organismes commerciaux, politiques, économiques et sociaux."

10. CANADIAN JOURNAL OF AFRICAN STUDIES. [Title also in French] no. 1-
    Mar. 1967- Montreal, published for the Committee on African
    Studies in Canada by Loyola College. Twice yearly.

    Supersedes the BULLETIN OF AFRICAN STUDIES IN CANADA (see no.
    105). Donald C. Savage is editor. The journal is continuing the
    BULLETIN'S bibliographical work, and the first issue had a critical
    bibliography on the Malagasy Republic by Professor Louis Molet.
    Articles (in English or French) by Canadian scholars on development
    of African studies and research in Canada are a feature.

11. Carnegie Corporation of New York. COMMONWEALTH PROGRAM TRAVEL GRANTS,
    1947-1962. By Stephen H. Stackpole. New York, 1963. 93 p.
    (Booklet no. 38)

    Arrangement by countries of nationals receiving grants; summaries
    by fields of studies and countries.

12. Dauphin, Joanne Coyle. "Belgian Centers of Documentation and Research
    on Africa." AFRICAN STUDIES BULLETIN, v. 8, no. 3, Dec. 1965:
    21-39.

    Signaling the many changes in "orientation and in nomenclature" of
    Belgian institutions concerned with Africa, this welcome list gives
    information on about 50 bodies.

13. Dauphin, Joanne Coyle. "French Provincial Centers of Documentation and
    Research on Africa." AFRICAN STUDIES BULLETIN, v. 9, no. 3, Dec.
    1966: 48-65.

    A checklist of more than 40 French institutions outside Paris.

14. Dauphin, Joanne Coyle, Agnès Rosset, and Brigitta Rupp. "Inventaire
    des ressources documentaires africanistes à Paris." RECHERCHE,
    ENSEIGNEMENT, DOCUMENTATION AFRICANISTES FRANCOPHONES: BULLETIN
    D'INFORMATION ET LIAISON, v. 1, no. 1, 1969.

    A survey of 129 French organizations, institutions, and scholarly
    and publishing associations concerned with African studies. It gives
    addresses, size of libraries (if any), interests, and major publica-
    tions. For further annotation, see no. 1616.

15. Desai, Ram. "The Explosion of African Studies in the Soviet Union."
    AFRICAN STUDIES BULLETIN, v. 11, no. 3, Dec. 1968: 248-257.

The most important centers for African studies are described on p. 249-251. The major part of the article is devoted to a review of Soviet publications in the African field.

16. DIRECTORY: FOREIGN AREA FELLOWS, 1952-1963, OF THE JOINT COMMITTEE OF THE AMERICAN COUNCIL OF LEARNED SOCIETIES AND THE SOCIAL SCIENCE RESEARCH COUNCIL, 1962-1963. Formerly administered by the Ford Foundation, 1952-1962. New York, Foreign Area Fellowship Program (444 Madison Ave., New York 10022), 1964. 301 p.

   Foreign Area Fellows--African Studies: p. 1-43. The listing records: in anthropology, 48; communications, 3; economics, 13; education, 2; fine arts, 4; geography, 7; history, 30; international relations, 1; language and literature, 1; law, 3; linguistics, 2; musicology, 2; philosophy and religion, 1; political science and government, 39; psychology, 2; sociology, 13 (171 in all). For each, the directory provides biographical information and bibliography of published and unpublished writings.

   This is the second edition of a directory first published in 1959 by the Ford Foundation: DIRECTORY OF FOREIGN AREA TRAINING FELLOWS, 1952-1959 (204 p.; African Studies: p. 1-20, 91 in all). A new directory is to be issued in 1969.

17. Dobson, W. A. C. THE CONTRIBUTION OF CANADIAN UNIVERSITIES TO AN UNDERSTANDING OF ASIA AND AFRICA: A BIBLIOGRAPHICAL DIRECTORY OF SCHOLARS. [Title also in French] Ottawa, National Commission for UNESCO, 1964. 70 p.

   This list--which is free on request--includes the publications of each scholar.

18. German African Society. MUSEUMS IN AFRICA: A DIRECTORY. New York, Africana Pub. Corp., 1970. 594 p.

19. Gessain, Monique. "Liste des chercheurs dans les états francophones de l'Afrique noire et Madagascar; Séminaire des Sciences Humaines, Département d'Afrique Noire, Musée de l'Homme." JOURNAL DE LA SOCIETE DES AFRICANISTES, v. 32, fasc. 1, 1962: 179-205.

   In this listing as of July 1962, 25 institutes and 700-800 researchers were named.

20. HANDBOOK ON AFRICA. New York, Foreign Policy Association, 1966. (INTERCOM, May-June 1966).

Compact guide for the average reader, comprising a description of African regional organizations, U.N. and affiliated agencies, embassies and missions of African countries in the United States, U.S. government agencies and voluntary organizations concerned with Africa, and informational materials available from each. There is also a section on resources for teaching African studies. A well-chosen and annotated bibliography is arranged by subject and region. This booklet is a revision and updating of two earlier numbers of INTERCOM, the bimonthly bulletin of the Foreign Policy Association: FOCUS ON AFRICA, v. 2, no. 4, May 1960, and the same title, v. 5, no. 3, 1963.

In 1968 publication of INTERCOM was transferred from the Foreign Policy Association to the Editorial Department, Center for War/Peace Studies, 218 E. 18th Street, New York 10003. In early 1969 the HANDBOOK ON AFRICA is out of print, so a new edition may be looked for in the near future.

21. Hewitt, Arthur R. GUIDE TO RESOURCES FOR COMMONWEALTH STUDIES IN LONDON, OXFORD, AND CAMBRIDGE, WITH BIBLIOGRAPHICAL AND OTHER INFORMATION. London, published for the Institute of Commonwealth Studies, University of London, by the Athlone Press, 1957. 219 p.

By the then secretary of the Institute and its librarian, this guide describes in detail the resources of the chief British centers for African studies. (For full description see no. 83). The third part (p. 183-203) names universities, research and advisory organizations, and other official and unofficial institutions and organizations. There is a comprehensive index. Although designed for students of British Commonwealth matters, some of the resources described furnish material for studies of all parts of Africa.

For further and current information on scholarly institutions relating to Africa, see issues of the BULLETIN OF THE AFRICAN STUDIES ASSOCIATION OF THE UNITED KINGDOM (no. 8) and SCOLMA DIRECTORY OF LIBRARIES AND SPECIAL COLLECTIONS ON AFRICA (no. 92).

22. Institut Africain de Genève. REPERTOIRE DES PRINCIPALES INSTITUTIONS S'INTERESSANT A L'AFRIQUE NOIRE. Genève, 1963. 1 v. unpaged, loose-leaf.

Survey of the leading European and American institutes, research centers, universities, publishing and documentation centers, libraries, archives, and museums interested in African affairs. Particular emphasis is given to institutions specializing in history, economics, political science, etc. Over 180 centers are surveyed, and information includes name and address of the institution, its director, and a résumé of the organization's activities, library facilities, and publication program. The loose-leaf format permits easy addition of

data on new institutions or revision to bring information up to date.
As of 1967, this work provided the most complete source available for
description of the chief learned bodies (outside of those within Africa)
concerned with African studies. It is inevitable that there are certain
inaccuracies.

23. International Conference on African Bibliography, Nairobi, Dec. 1967.
     SURVEY OF CURRENT BIBLIOGRAPHICAL SERVICES ON AFRICA. London,
     International African Institute, 1967. 1 v. various pagings.

     A working document for the International African Institute
conference, the results of questionnaires answered by directors of
bibliographical services dealing with Africa. Information given includes
address of organization, bibliographies issued, compiler, frequency, subscription cost, circulation figures, number of items, promptness of service (date of entries in current issue), scope of bibliography, and
whether abstracts or annotations are provided. There are over 60 organizations listed.

24. International Institute of Differing Civilizations [INCIDI]. INTER-
     NATIONAL GUIDE TO STUDY CENTERS ON CIVILIZATIONS AND THEIR
     PUBLICATIONS. [Title also in French] Brussels, 1955. 156 p.

     Centers of African studies in Europe, Africa, and throughout the
world are on p. 40-73; 58 centers are described, grouped by geographical location, with listings of their chief publications.

25. International Social Science Council. INSTITUTIONS ENGAGED IN ECONOMIC
     AND SOCIAL PLANNING IN AFRICA: DIRECTORY. Paris, UNESCO, 1967.
     155 p.

     An up-to-date listing of public, semipublic, and private insti-
tutions. The directory was prepared with the aid of CARDAN (Centre
d'Analyse et de Recherche Documentaires pour l'Afrique Noire).

26. JOURNAL OF MODERN AFRICAN STUDIES. 1963- Cambridge, Eng.; New York,
     Cambridge University Press. Quarterly.

     For description see no. 296. Section on Africana provides descrip-
tions of new African institutes and programs and surveys individual
country programs.

27. Rupp, Brigitta. INVENTAIRE DES REGISTRES DE LA RECHERCHE EN COURS
     DANS LE DOMAINE DES SCIENCES SOCIALES ET HUMAINES EN AFRIQUE
     NOIRE (MS. PRELIMINAIRE). Paris, CARDAN (Centre d'Analyse et de
     Recherche Documentaires pour l'Afrique Noire), Dec. 1966. 32 p.

28. Smith, Dorothy, comp. "Scientific Research Centers in Africa."
       AFRICAN STUDIES BULLETIN, v. 10, no. 3, Dec. 1967: 20-47.

       Contains recommendations for scientific research, traces its
     development under the colonial powers, and discusses the current
     status of some of the major African research centers, including a
     listing by country of research establishments (South Africa is ex-
     cluded). There is a bibliography and an abbreviations list.

29. Société des Africanistes. Centre de Documentation et d'Information.
       BULLETIN D'INFORMATION. no. 1- June 1964- Paris. Quarterly.

       The Society maintains in its documentation center card files
     of scientific institutions in Africa, of courses relating to Africa
     in French-speaking institutions, and of research in progress, as well
     as calendars of congresses and conferences, exhibitions, and other
     events of scholarly interest. These are recorded in the quarterly
     bulletin in sections of "Thèses et diplômes," "Fichier des chercheurs,"
     and under other rubrics.

30. Technical Assistance Information Clearing House. AFRICA TECHNICAL
       ASSISTANCE PROGRAMS OF U.S. NON-PROFIT ORGANIZATIONS, INCLUDING
       VOLUNTARY AGENCIES, MISSIONS, AND FOUNDATIONS: DIRECTORY, 1969.
       Edited by Jackie Horn. New York, American Council of Voluntary
       Agencies for Foreign Service, 1969. 336 p.

       This clearinghouse, founded in 1955, is operated by the American
     Council of Voluntary Agencies, under contract with U.S. AID, to serve
     as a center of information on the socioeconomic development programs
     abroad of U.S. nonprofit organizations. The directory is arranged in
     three parts. Part 1 presents organization profiles, giving for each
     group: address, phone number, executive officers, short description
     of program, countries of operation, and expenditures. Included are
     such groups as the Ford Foundation, Operation Crossroads Africa, the
     African-American Institute, and the Church World Service. Part 2
     contains country program information. Arrangement is by country,
     (the continent and the islands, excluding the United Arab Republic,
     are covered) then alphabetical by organization. Programs are broken
     down into those of operation and those of support. Under each organi-
     zation are described the types of assistance, medicine, social welfare,
     education, agriculture, and community development (for Nigeria emer-
     gency programs operating during the civil war are described). Part 3
     is a summary index in chart form of each organization and the assistance
     provided, arranged by Africa (general), then by country. There is also
     an organization index. A short list of African church-related groups,
     such as the Christian Council of Nigeria, is included in the directory.

31. Technical Assistance Information Clearing House. U.S. NON-PROFIT
       ORGANIZATIONS: VOLUNTARY AGENCIES, MISSIONS AND FOUNDATIONS
       PARTICIPATING IN TECHNICAL ASSISTANCE ABROAD, A DIRECTORY 1964.
       Edited by Dao N. Spencer. New York, American Council of Voluntary
       Agencies for Foreign Service, 1964. 759 p.

Supplement. Edited by Binnie Schroyer. 1965. 416 p.

The 1964 directory is the fifth edition, the number of agencies
listed having increased from about 60 in 1956 to 98 in the 1961 fourth
edition and in this volume to 242 groups "whose programs were current
and applicable and who met the deadline for submitting materials"--
160 voluntary agencies, 71 missions, 11 foundations. Programs are
current as of Feb. 1964. The first section of this large handbook
is an alphabetical set of "organization profiles." Part 2 lists
country programs, beginning with Africa (p. 263-335). The volume
ends with tabulated statistics by countries and agencies (Africa, p.
612-647).

32. Tropical African Studies Conference, Ibadan, 1964. A PRELIMINARY
REGISTER OF AFRICAN STUDIES AT UNIVERSITIES, RESEARCH CENTRES
AND OTHER INSTITUTIONS. [London?] International African Institute,
1964. 33 p. 33 cm. Mimeographed.

The register, prepared for the conference and compiled from a
questionnaire sent out at the end of 1963, was intended to provide an
outline of the organization and scope of teaching and research in
African studies. Data provided by the institutions answering the
inquiry include name, address, and status, committees, centers,
institutes, etc., concerned with African studies and, also, the
scope of teaching and research, indicated by abbreviations. A good
many institutions that failed to reply are given with name and address
only. Entries are by country, in alphabetical order within continents,
beginning with Africa; institutions from 28 countries of Africa south
of the Sahara are listed.

33. United Nations Educational, Scientific and Cultural Organization.
Secretariat. SOCIAL SCIENTISTS SPECIALIZING IN AFRICAN STUDIES.
[Title also in French] Paris, La Haye, Mouton & Co., 1963.
375 p. (Ecole Pratique des Hautes Etudes, 6th section; Sciences
économiques et sociales) (Monde d'outre-mer passé et présent,
4th series: Bibliographies et instruments de travail, 5)

International list of 2,072 Africanists, in alphabetical order,
based on data collected from 1959 through 1961 (information is kept
up to date by a card index in the Maison des Sciences de l'Homme).
Priority is given to specialists in the central disciplines in the
social sciences (e.g., economics, social and cultural anthropology,
sociology, psychology, political science, law), but such fields as
criminology and public administration are also included, as well as
humanistic sciences such as archaeology, folklore, musicology, and
linguistics. There is an index by subject fields and a geographic
index.

34. U.S. Congress. House. Committee on Foreign Affairs. Subcommittee on International Organizations and Movements. OVERSEAS PROGRAMS OF PRIVATE NON-PROFIT ORGANIZATIONS. Washington, U.S. Govt. Print. Off., 1965. 565 p. (89th Cong., 1st sess.)

Description of the work of welfare organizations, colleges, universities, etc.

35. U.S. Department of State. Bureau of Educational and Cultural Affairs. INTERNATIONAL EDUCATIONAL, CULTURAL AND RELATED ACTIVITIES FOR AFRICAN COUNTRIES SOUTH OF THE SAHARA. Washington, 1961. 321 p. Offset print.

A revision and updating of a survey brought out in light mimeographed pamphlet volumes in 1959: INTERNATIONAL EDUCATIONAL EXCHANGE AND RELATED EXCHANGES-OF-PERSONS FOR AFRICAN COUNTRIES SOUTH OF THE SAHARA. In two parts, the first "Total Programs," the second by individual countries. The volume covers in detail governmental, United Nations, and private agency activities, student exchanges, missions, business firms, and individual scholars doing research on Africa.

36. U.S. Department of State. Bureau of Intelligence and Research. GOVERNMENT RESOURCES AVAILABLE FOR FOREIGN AFFAIRS RESEARCH. Compiled by Linda Lowenstein. Washington, 1965. 56 p.

Directory of government facilities available to the academic research community, with detailed description of each, from the Agency for International Development (AID) to the U.S. Tariff Commission. The pamphlet is a revision of the major part of a 1963 report entitled RELATIONSHIP OF THE GOVERNMENT AND PRIVATE RESEARCH COMMUNITIES IN THE FIELD OF FOREIGN RELATIONS.

37. U.S. Department of State. Bureau of Intelligence and Research. External Research Staff. AFRICAN PROGRAMS OF U.S. ORGANIZATIONS: A SELECTIVE DIRECTORY. Compiled by Jacqueline S. Mithun. Washington, May 1965. 132 p.

Earlier reports were issued in 1958, 1960, and 1961. Here are listed: American colleges and universities (42) having (a) area studies and language training programs and (b) operational programs; foundations (30); religious and missionary organizations (224); business organizations (266); and private nonprofit organizations and institutions specifically concerned with African culture, education, and training (162). Also helpful are an index by African countries and a general index of organizational names. The comprehensiveness of this directory makes it mandatory for information on American interests in Africa.

38. U.S. Department of State. Bureau of Intelligence and Research. External Research Staff. LANGUAGE AND AREA STUDY PROGRAMS IN AMERICAN

UNIVERSITIES.   Compiled by Larry Moses. Washington, 1964. xi, 162 p.

Third edition, revising and updating AREA STUDY PROGRAMS IN AMERI-CAN UNIVERSITIES (1959) and LANGUAGE AND AREA STUDY PROGRAMS IN AMERICAN UNIVERSITIES (1962, 143 p.); 153 programs are described, those relating to Africa, p. 1-13. It is explained that the growth in the African area has slowed since the 1959 edition and that African programs are heavily weighted toward sociology and anthropology.

39.   U.S. Department of State. Bureau of Intelligence and Research. External Research Staff. RESEARCH CENTERS ON THE DEVELOPING AREAS. Prepared for the Agency for International Development. Compiled by Margaret M. Rhoades. Washington, Nov. 1964. 131 p. Offset print.

Foreign Area--Africa: p. 75-85.

A survey of research centers which are carrying out projects under contract to AID or under large foundation grants, with listing of their recent publications. Arrangement is General, by Foreign Area, then by disciplines. The index of institutions includes only 11 directly concerned with Africa, though some of the 78 listed for General Programs (by discipline) have pertinence for African studies.

For details of U.S. government agencies concerned with Africa, the latest issue of the U.S. GOVERNMENT ORGANIZATION MANUAL (Washington, U.S. Govt. Print. Off., annual) may be consulted. Addresses of the embassies and diplomatic staff of the African countries in Washington are given in the DIPLOMATIC LIST, published quarterly by the Department of State. These offices are generally equipped to provide information, with special information branches or cultural, educational, or press attachés. The quarterly FOREIGN SERVICE LIST, also issued by the State Department, contains similar data for American officers overseas.

The British Information Services have offices in both Washington and New York. The French Embassy, however, refers all research questions to its French Press and Information Service, 972 Fifth Ave., New York 10021.

A reminder of the usefulness of the telephone directories of New York, Washington, and other large cities for locating organizations may also be in order.

40.   U.S. Department of State. Office of External Research. AFRICA: A LIST OF CURRENT SOCIAL SCIENCE RESEARCH BY PRIVATE SCHOLARS AND ACADEMIC CENTERS. Washington, 1952-68. Annual. (External Research Lists)

The title of this list based on information provided to the External Research unit of the Bureau of Intelligence and Research by faculties, graduate students, and other scholars throughout America, has varied, as has the designation of the unit compiling the material. It was begun by the External Research Staff, later the External Research Division, as a semiannual, the first part in April listing research in progress, the second in October recording completed projects. In 1965 the Division became the Office of External Research, and the publication was changed to an annual, covering only unpublished material, with the title, AFRICA.... The general section was by discipline and subdivided into research "in progress" and "completed." The following sections, classed by region and country, had the same subdivision. The last issue appeared in June 1968, when the recording of research in progress was taken over by the AFRICAN STUDIES NEWSLETTER (see no. 7). The Office of External Research, through its section of Foreign Affairs Research (FAR), will continue to collect unpublished material to be kept for government use only.

The FAR Documentation Center has brought out a special report, AFRICA, Feb. 1969 (61 p.), outlining subjects and needs of government research, together with a bibliography of the Center's holdings on Africa, in subject arrangement.

41. U.S. Library of Congress. General Reference and Bibliography Division. SERIALS FOR AFRICAN STUDIES. Compiled by Helen F. Conover, African Section. Washington, 1961. 163 p. Offset print.

For full description see no. 396; see also other lists of serials in that section.

The Index of Organizations (p. 155-163) lists between 900 and 1,000 institutional names, exclusive of government departments. Business concerns, chambers of commerce, social welfare organizations, etc., are included as well as learned institutions, the criterion being whether the body in question has a publication program. A new edition, enlarged to well over twice its size, is to be published in 1970. It too will have a separate index of institutional names.

42. U.S. Library of Congress. International Organizations Section. INTERNATIONAL SCIENTIFIC ORGANIZATIONS: A GUIDE TO THEIR LIBRARY, DOCUMENTATION, AND INFORMATION SERVICES. Prepared under the direction of Kathrine O. Murra. Washington, 1962 [i.e., 1963]. xi, 794 p.

See index under Africa, also geographical breakdown under certain subjects, e.g., abstracting services, exchange of personnel, forests, etc. This guide goes far beyond the usual handbook, including for each body a full description of organization, data on conferences, lists of publications, and other valuable information.

43. Walraet, Marcel. DOCUMENTATION BELGE ET TIERS MONDE. Bruxelles, Bibliothèque Royale de Belgique, 1965. 71 p.

    Outlines chief Belgian sources of information in the form of printed materials regarding the developing countries of Asia, Africa, and Latin America. Among collections described are those of official scientific and administrative organizations, international bodies, universities, and private learned societies. The first appendix is a list of groups, with bibliographical references for each, and the second appendix gives periodicals in Belgium concerned in whole or in part with the Third World.

44. WISSENSCHAFT IN AFRIKA. Bonn, Deutsche Afrika-Gesellschaft, 1962. 168 p.

    List of principal research centers and scientific organizations in Africa, arranged by country. Although by the time it was published additions were needed, the brochure is useful. Many of the institutions named are government departments and offices, which have changed names and increased in number since independence.

45. WORLD OF LEARNING. 1947- London, Europa Publications, Ltd. Annual.

    In this general directory of universities, scholarly institutes, and museums throughout the world (for full description see Winchell) the coverage of institutions involving African studies is sufficient to warrant its inclusion here as a specific source. Data are given for the chief learned bodies in each African country, for research institutes devoted to African studies in Europe, Asia, and America, and for departments of African studies in the universities of the world. The approach for countries outside Africa is by name of institution only, the index not including subjects. Information is up to date and authoritative.

46. YEARBOOK OF INTERNATIONAL ORGANIZATIONS. ANNUAIRE DES ORGANISATIONS INTERNATIONALES. Brussels, Union of International Associations, biennial. 12th ed., 1968-69. 1220 p.

    Handbook and directory of international and regional organizations throughout the world. The 2,000-odd bodies are grouped as U.N. Family, European Community, official and governmental groups, and international nongovernmental institutions, the last arranged by subject fields. Indexes are to key words of subject fields, initials, and geographical units. About 50 institutions cited in recent editions are in Africa; the subject index also includes African interests.

    The Union gives continuing information on newly formed bodies in its monthly, INTERNATIONAL ASSOCIATIONS.

CHAPTER 2

LIBRARIES AND ARCHIVES

Note: Information on African libraries and archives and American and
European holdings of published and manuscript African material is scat-
tered through scores of journals and specialist publications. Some of
the most important sources are the AFRICANA NEWSLETTER (1962-64; Stanford,
Calif.); AFRICAN STUDIES BULLETIN (African Studies Association, New York);
BULLETIN of the African Studies Association of the United Kingdom (Birming-
Ham); AMERICAN ARCHIVIST (Menasha, Wis.); ARCHIVES, BIBLIOTHEQUES ET
MUSEES DE BELGIQUE (Bruxelles); ARCHIVES (journal of the British Records
Association, London); ARCHIVUM: REVUE INTERNATIONALE DES ARCHIVES (Paris);
GAZETTE DES ARCHIVES (Paris); LIBRARY LITERATURE (New York); and LIBRARY
SCIENCE ABSTRACTS (London). The Standing Conference on Library Materials
on Africa (London) produces a newsletter, LIBRARY MATERIALS ON AFRICA,
which has information on library holdings and acquisitions. Also useful
are SCAUL NEWSLETTER, (Dar es Salaam); SOUTH AFRICAN LIBRARIES (Pretoria);
UNESCO BULLETIN FOR LIBRARIES (Paris); and the former WALA NEWS, bulletin
of the West African Library Association, and its successors in 1964, the
bulletins of the Ghana Library Association and the Nigerian Library Association, respectively.

    The following section will list first general reference works and then
works for specific regions and countries--i.e., works relative to library
and archive collections in Western Europe, for example, will precede those
concerned with collections in specific countries. The section presents its
material by region and according to the following order: Western Europe,
the United States, Canada, and Africa.

EUROPE

47. GUIDE TO THE DIPLOMATIC ARCHIVES OF WESTERN EUROPE. Edited by Daniel
        H. Thomas and Lynn M. Case. Philadelphia, University of Penn-
        sylvania Press, 1959. 389 p.

Chapters by specialists on Western European archives provide
history of principal depositories, chronological scope, arrangements,
organization and condition of materials, and administration and use
of records. Attention is called to valuable collections on Africa in
Belgium, France, Germany, Great Britain, Italy, Portugal, Spain, and
the Vatican. See also Jenkins and Kirk, no. 111.

48. Guides to Materials for West African History in European Archives
     [series]. London, Athlone Press, University of London, 1962-

     The following in this series have been published:

a)   no. 1. MATERIALS FOR WEST AFRICAN HISTORY IN THE ARCHIVES OF
             BELGIUM AND HOLLAND. By Patricia Carson. 1962.
             86 p. (1,258 items)

             Additions to this work are provided by H. M.
             Feinberg in AFRICAN STUDIES BULLETIN, v. 10,
             no. 3, Dec. 1967: 48-53; and v. 12, no. 1,
             Apr. 1969: 81-89.

b)   no. 2. MATERIALS FOR WEST AFRICAN HISTORY IN PORTUGUESE ARCHIVES.
             By A. F. C. Ryder. 1965. 92 p. (997 items)

c)   no. 3. MATERIALS FOR WEST AFRICAN HISTORY IN ITALIAN ARCHIVES.
             By Richard Gray and David Chambers. 1965. 164 p.
             (1,480 items)

             Part 1 covers the Vatican archives and other archives
             in Rome, Part 2 the archives and libraries outside
             Rome.

d)   no. 4. MATERIALS FOR WEST AFRICAN HISTORY IN FRENCH ARCHIVES
             By Patricia Carson. 1968. 170 p. (2,723 items)

49. Huisman, A. J. W. LES MANUSCRITS ARABES DANS LE MONDE: UNE BIBLIOGRA-
     PHIE DES CATALOGUES. Leiden, E. J. Brill, 1967.

50. International Council on Archives (ICA); Conseil International des
     Archives (CIA). Guide to the Sources of African History outside
     of Africa [series]. Paris.

     This guide is the major archival survey under way in Europe and the
United States on Africa at the present time. For some years ICA, assisted by UNESCO, has been sponsoring this multivolume series. The
guides, which will be both comprehensive and detailed, have been commissioned for Africa-related materials in France, West Germany, Denmark,
Belgium, Holland, Switzerland, Italy, Spain, Portugal, the Vatican, and

the United States. Publication is planned for 1969-70. It is hoped that ICA can extend its coverage to every country possessing a significant amount of African sources--e.g., China, India, Brazil, and the Caribbean nations.

51. Leopard, Donald D. "Africa-related Materials in European Missionary Archives." AFRICAN STUDIES BULLETIN, v. 10, no. 2, Sept. 1967: 1-5.

    The article describes the type of material to be found in three archives in London (London Missionary Society for the Propagation of the Gospel, and Friends Foreign Missionary Association) and one in France (Société des Missions Evangéliques de Paris). Information on almost every aspect of African life can be found in such materials-- if sufficient effort is expended. Addresses are given for other organizations furnishing information on missionary activity in Africa.

52. McCall, Daniel F. A REPORT ON AFRICAN MATERIALS AND ACTIVITIES IN SOME EUROPEAN INSTITUTIONS. Boston, Boston University, 1967. 59 p. (Boston University Papers on Africa, no. 1)

    Description of holdings, and finding aids on Africa, of archives and museums in Austria, Denmark, France, Germany, Italy, Sweden, and Switzerland.

Belgium

53. Académie Royale des Sciences d'Outre-Mer (formerly Institut Royal Colonial Belge and Académie Royale des Sciences Coloniales). BULLETIN DES SEANCES. v. 1-25, 1930-54; n.s. v. 1- 1955- Bruxelles. illus., ports., maps.

    In the BULLETIN and Mémoires of the academy there have been frequent articles having to do with archives of Congolese history and administration.

    Roger Anstey in "Earlier and Later Congo," JOURNAL OF AFRICAN HISTORY (v. 2, no. 2, 1961: 324-326), discusses other papers appearing in the BULLETIN on Congo documentary material.

54. Belgium. Ministère des Affaires Africaines. Bibliothèque. CATALOGUE DE LA BIBLIOTHEQUE. By Th. Simar. Bruxelles, Vromant, 1922-

55. Belgium. Ministère du Congo Belge et du Ruanda-Urundi. DOCUMENT NOTTE: STANLEY AU CONGO, 1879-1884. Bruxelles, 1960. 206 p.

Facsimile report prepared by C. Notte, archivist of the Independent State of the Congo, from the administrative records of Stanley's two expeditions into the Congo.

56. Danse, Léon. "La bibliothèque centrale du Congo belge." ARCHIVES, BIBLIOTHEQUES ET MUSEES DE BELGIQUE, v. 24, no. 1, 1953: 28-35.

Abstract in LIBRARY SCIENCE ABSTRACTS, v. 5, no. 1, Jan.-Mar. 1954: no. 3387.

57. Fonds National de la Recherche Scientifique. INVENTAIRE DES MICROFILMS DE PAPIERS PRIVES RELATIFS A L'HISTOIRE DU CONGO CONSERVES A LA "SCHOOL OF ORIENTAL AND AFRICAN STUDIES" DE L'UNIVERSITE DE LONDRES ET AU "BRITISH MUSEUM." Bruxelles [1959?]. 18 l.

At the School of Oriental and African Studies letters microfilmed were drawn from the Mackinnon Papers (Jules Devaux, J. Hutton, Sir John Kirk, L. Lambert, H. M. Stanley, and Colonel Strauch). The British Museum material consists of some pages of the Gladstone and the Dilke Papers.

58. Fonds National de la Recherche Scientifique. INVENTAIRE DES MICROFILMS DES DOCUMENTS RELATIFS A L'HISTOIRE DE LA BELGIQUE ET DU CONGO CONSERVES AU "PUBLIC RECORDS OFFICE" A LONDRES, 1866-1903. Bruxelles [1959?]. 57 l.

The documents are mostly correspondence between the Foreign Office and British ministers abroad.

59. Fonds National de la Recherche Scientifique. INVENTAIRE DES MICROFILMS DES PAPIERS MOREL, SERIES A, B, E, F, G, H, I, SE RAPPORTANT A L'HISTOIRE DU CONGO ET CONSERVES A LA BRITISH LIBRARY OF POLITICAL AND ECONOMIC SCIENCE, LONDON SCHOOL OF ECONOMICS AND POLITICAL SCIENCE. Bruxelles [1961?]. 115 l.

The E. D. Morel Papers were assembled at the suggestion of Jean Stengers and on the advice of the organization's Commission Interuniversitaire du Microfilm. The two preceding inventories were also suggested by the Commission.

The three inventories were described in the AFRICANA NEWSLETTER, v. 1, no. 2 (Spring 1963): 16. A loan copy of the microfilms is available under certain conditions from the Cooperative African Microfilm Project (CAMP) of the Center for Research Libraries, Chicago.

60. Grieken, Emile van. LA BIBLIOTHEQUE DU MINISTERE DES AFFAIRES AFRI-
         CAINES: SON ROLE, SES COLLECTIONS ET SES OUVRAGES PRECIEUX.
         Bruxelles, 1962. p. 186-201. (Académie Royale des Sciences
         d'Outre-Mer, Commission d'Histoire, fasc. no. 82)

         Extract from the BULLETIN DES SEANCES of the Académie Royale des
     Sciences d'Outre-Mer, n.s. v. 8, no. 2, 1962. Listed are the most val-
     uable works in the library of the Ministry of African Affairs. Many
     are of the seventeenth century.

         In this and entries below the name of the institution is given as
     at the time of publication. Former names are Institut Royal Colonial
     Belge and Académie Royale des Sciences Coloniales.

61. Grieken, Emile van, and Madeleine van Grieken-Taverniers. LES ARCHIVES
         INVENTORIEES AU MINISTERE DES COLONIES. [Bruxelles, 1958] 69 p.
         (Académie Royale des Sciences d'Outre-Mer, Classe des sciences
         morales et politiques, Mémoires in-8°, n.s. v. 12, fasc. 2)

         Bibliography: p. 66-69.

         "Les archives de l'Etat indépendant du Congo" is by E. van Grieken,
     "La Commission d'Histoire du Congo et les archives historiques de l'In-
     stitut Royal Colonial Belge" by M. van Grieken-Taverniers.

62. Grieken-Taverniers, Madeleine van. "L'histoire de l'Etat indépendant
         du Congo et les archives du Ministère du Congo Belge et du Ruanda-
         Urundi." ARCHIVES, BIBLIOTHEQUES ET MUSEES DE BELGIQUE, v. 30, no.
         1, 1959.

63. Grieken-Taverniers, Madeleine van. INVENTAIRE DES ARCHIVES DES AFFAIRES
         ETRANGERES DE L'ETAT INDEPENDANT DU CONGO ET DU MINISTERE DES
         COLONIES, 1885-1914. Bruxelles, 1955. 125 p. (Académie Royale
         des Sciences Coloniales, Classe des sciences morales et politiques,
         Mémoires in-8°, n.s. v. 2, fasc. 2)

64. Heyse, Théodore. "L'Académie Royale des Sciences Coloniales et l'ancien
         Congo." ARCHIVES, BIBLIOTHEQUES ET MUSEES DE BELGIQUE, v. 29, no.
         1, 1958.

         On sources for history of the Congo.

65. Heyse, Théodore. "A propos d'un inventaire des archives des territoires
         du Congo et du Ruanda-Urundi." Académie Royale des Sciences
         Coloniales. BULLETIN DES SEANCES, n.s. v. 4, no. 2, 1958: 271-286.

66. Luwel, Marcel. "Inventaire des archives historiques du Musée Royal du Congo Belge à Tervuren." Institut Royal Colonial Belge. BULLETIN DES SEANCES, v. 25, no. 2, 1954: 799-821.

67. Luwel, Marcel. INVENTAIRE: PAPIERS JULES CORNET, GEOLOGUE (1865-1929). Tervuren, Musée Royal de l'Afrique Centrale, 1961. 100 p. Polycopie. (Inventaire des archives historiques, no. 1)

68. Vandewoude, E. "Les archives du personnel d'Afrique de 1877 à 1918." Institut Royal Colonial Belge. BULLETIN DES SEANCES, v. 25, no. 2, 1954: 615-651.

69. Walraet, Marcel. "Inventaires d'archives et publications de textes." Académie Royale des Sciences Coloniales. BULLETIN DES SEANCES, n.s. v. 3, no. 2, 1957: 359-373.

    Account of four years of activity of the Commission d'Histoire du Congo to produce an inventory of archives.

    See also MATERIALS FOR WEST AFRICAN HISTORY IN THE ARCHIVES OF BELGIUM AND HOLLAND, no. 48(a).

France

Note: See also no. 1616 for a directory of 129 organizations in Paris concerned with Africa.

70. ANNUAIRE INTERNATIONAL DES ARCHIVES. INTERNATIONAL DIRECTORY ON ARCHIVES. Paris, Presses Universitaires de France, 1956. 253 p. (ARCHIVUM, v. 5 for 1955)

    Published under the auspices of the Conseil International des Archives and with the financial assistance of UNESCO. Data given for each archive include name and address, conditions of use, reference services, facilities for reproduction of records, importance of repository, age and character of documents, etc. The arrangement is geographical, by country or region. In the Index locorum there are entries for many African countries. Any new edition of this title or comparable work by the Conseil should be a noteworthy contribution.

71. France. Direction des Bibliothèques de France. REPERTOIRE DES BIBLITHEQUES D'ETUDE ET ORGANISMES DE DOCUMENTATION. Publié sous l'égide de la Délégation Générale à la Recherche Scientifique et Technique. Paris, Bibliothèque Nationale, 1963. 3 v.

This edition of a useful reference tool (an earlier edition was published for UNESCO in 1950-51) lists 2,382 research collections and libraries in France in two volumes. Vol. III contains a small supplement and an extensive subject index which includes special collections by name and enables the user to find quickly the research libraries of special interest to him. Under the general heading of Africa more than 30 research collections are listed.

72. France. Ministère de la France d'Outre-Mer. Service des Archives, de la Bibliothèque et de L'Etat Civil. AFRIQUE. Paris [1962]. 1 v. (unnumbered leaves).

This large volume, inventory of the Africa holdings of the Archives of the Overseas Ministry of France, is organized first for Africa in general by subjects, i.e., explorations, diplomacy, personnel, with the date and contents of each file given; then there are breakdowns for the major regions (French West Africa, French Equatorial Africa) and for the countries within each region. The contents of each dossier are briefly described and the inclusive dates provided. Copies are held by Carlo Laroche in Paris and J. F. Maurel in Dakar. A few xerographic copies are also in existence.

73. Laroche, Carlo. "Les archives d'outre-mer et l'histoire coloniale française." REVUE HISTORIQUE, no. 206, Oct.-Dec. 1951: 213-253.

_____ (Laroche, Charles). "Les archives de l'expansion française outre-mer conservées en Métropole." GAZETTE DES ARCHIVES, n.s. no. 55, 1966: 235-252.

The author is chief conservator of the Section Outre-Mer des Archives Nationales, having previously been chief archivist of the former Archives du Ministère de la France d'Outre-Mer. In addition to these two analytical articles, he has written a number of brief descriptions of the current state of the archives which have appeared in the GAZETTE DES ARCHIVES: n.s. no. 4, 1948: 14-20; no. 23, Jan. 1958: 77-79; no. 28, 1960: 32-33.

74. Taillemite, Etienne. "Les archives de la France d'Outre-Mer." GAZETTE DES ARCHIVES, n.s. no. 22, 1957: 6-22.

General information on the archives of the Ministry, with special attention to working tools and to archival enterprises carried out in the Ministry and in overseas territories of recent years.

See also MATERIALS FOR WEST AFRICAN HISTORY IN FRENCH ARCHIVES, no. 48(d).

75. Vajda, Georges. INDEX GENERAL DES MANUSCRITS ARABES MUSULMANS DE LA
    BIBLIOTHEQUE NATIONALE DE PARIS. Paris, Editions du Centre National
    de la Recherche Scientifique, 1953. 743 p. (Publications de l'
    Institut de Recherche et d'Histoire des Textes, no. 4)

    Contains some Arabic documents pertaining to Africa.

76. Note: Other guides surveying African material are:

    a) Paris. Bibliothèque Nationale. Département des Manuscrits.
       CATALOGUE DES MANUSCRITS ETIOPIENS. Paris, Impr. Nationale,
       1954. 287 p.

    b) _____. _____. Département des Manuscrits. CATALOGUE DES
       MANUSCRITS ETIOPIENS (GHEEZ ET AMHARIQUE) DE LA BIBLIOTHEQUE
       NATIONALE. By Hermann Zotenburg. Paris, 1877. 287 p. (500
       entries)

    c) _____. _____. Département des Manuscrits. CATALOGUE DES
       MANUSCRITS ETIOPIENS DE LA COLLECTION GRIAULE. Edited by
       Sylvain Grébaut [Vols. I-III] and Stefan Strelcyn [Vol. IV].
       Paris, Institut d'Ethnologie, 1938-54. 4 v. in 3. facsims.
       (2,500 entries) ([Vol. I, III] Université de Paris, Travaux et
       mémoires de l'Institut d'Ethnologie, 29, 30; [Vol. II] Miscel-
       lanea africana Lebaudy, Cahier no. 3)

    d) _____. _____. Département des Manuscrits. CATALOGUE DES
       MANUSCRITS ETIOPIENS DE LA COLLECTION MANDON-VIDAILHET. By
       Marius Chaîne. Paris, E. Leroux, 1913. xiv, 70 p. (400
       entries)

Germany

Note: Articles on German African holdings occasionally appear in ARCHI-
VALISCHE ZEITSCHRIFT, DER ARCHIVAR, and ARCHIVMITTEILUNGEN. There is no
comprehensive guide to the German archival material of official provenance
relating to Germany's African colonies. The material of metropolitan origin
is to be found mainly in the Deutsche Zentralarchiv in Potsdam and Merseburg,
East Germany, but the Bundesarchiv in Bonn also has valuable holdings. Some
of these have been microfilmed. (See the excellent description of the various
German archival holdings in the essay by Hartmut Pogge von Strandmann, "The
German Empire in Africa and British Perspectives: A Historiographical Essay,"
especially p. 757-765, in BRITAIN AND GERMANY IN AFRICA, nos. 550 and 3027).
In addition, researchers will find material in such basic works as J. Lepsius,
A. Mendelssohn-Bartholdy, and F. Thimme, DIE GROSSE POLITIK DER EUROPAISCHEN
KABINETTE, 1871-1914: SAMMLUNG DER DIPLOMATISCHEN AKTEN DES AUSWARTIGEN AMTES
(Berlin, Deutsche Verlagsgesellschaft für Politik und Geschichte, 1922-27,
40 v.).

Archival material produced by the German colonial authorities is also found in various parts of Africa. The Archives Depot of South West Africa at Windhoek is administered by the South African archival service. It contains holdings of the Zentral-Bureau, of various other departments such as the Bergbauamt (mining department), of different Bezirksämter (districts), as well as private and semiofficial papers of German and of indigenous leaders, etc. Material relating to German colonialism is also found in the Cape Archives Depot and the Transvaal Archives Depot. These records are partially described in the appendix to J. H. Esterhuyse, SOUTH WEST AFRICA 1880-1894: THE ESTABLISHMENT OF GERMAN AUTHORITY IN SOUTH WEST AFRICA (Cape Town, C. Struik, 1968), p. 246-251, which also has an extensive bibliography concerning South West Africa.

The records of the German East African Government are to be found in Dar es Salaam, Tanzania, but require a good deal of additional work if they are to be fully usable. West African material is found, for instance, in the Bibliothèque Nationale at Lomé, Togo, and in various other locations. Much of this material still needs to be retrieved and properly processed.

Material of value to students of German colonialism should also consult relevant records in the British Public Record Office, in the National Archives of France and of the United States (for instance, Consular Reports), as well as sources of private provenance. These include, among others, mission societies, political organizations and so forth, to which more detailed reference is made in Pogge von Strandmann's essay cited above. American material of value to the investigation of German colonialism is also mentioned in HANDBOOK OF AMERICAN RESOURCES FOR AFRICAN STUDIES (no. 101).

The best surveys of German African related materials have been done in the United States as a result of the acquisition of captured German Foreign Ministry Archives (see next entry).

77. American Historical Association. Committee for the Study of War Documents. A CATALOGUE OF FILES AND MICROFILMS OF THE GERMAN FOREIGN MINISTRY ARCHIVES, 1867-1920. Washington, 1959. xliv, 1290 columns.

Continued by:

U.S. Department of State. Historical Office. A CATALOG OF FILES AND MICROFILMS OF THE GERMAN FOREIGN MINISTRY ARCHIVES, 1920-1945. Compiled and edited by George O. Kent. Stanford, Calif., Hoover Institution, Stanford University, 1962-66. 3 v. (Hoover Institution Publications)

The defeat of Germany in 1945 has made available to scholars archival collections of the greatest importance. Most of the captured collections were shipped to England or the United States, where they were microfilmed

and indexed before the new German government could request their
return. Among the materials are the archives of the German Foreign
Ministry (Auswärtiges Amt), to which these two guides refer. For
those specializing in African affairs the first-named catalogue has
almost a hundred columns (cols. 726-812) of primary sources.

Reference should also be made to other guides listing African
material. The GUIDE TO CAPTURED GERMAN DOCUMENTS, edited by Fritz
T. Epstein (Air University, 1952), cites an I.G. Farben report on the
foreign trade of the Congo, dated June 1940 (p. 41). During World
War II the German Foreign Ministry published a volume of VOLKER-
RECHTLICHE DOKUMENTE UBER AFRIKA (1942) using papers from the Belgian
and French foreign ministry archives. An INDEX OF MICROFILMED RECORDS
OF THE GERMAN FOREIGN MINISTRY AND THE REICH'S CHANCELLERY COVERING
THE WEIMAR PERIOD, prepared by Ernst Schwandt for the Committee on War
Documents of the American Historical Association and published by the
National Archives and Records Service (Washington, 1958), contains some
files about Africa.

78. Facius, Friedrich, Hans Boom, and Heinz Boberach, eds. DAS BUNDESAR-
     CHIV UND SEINE BESTANDE: UBERSICHT. Boppard am Rhein, H. Bold,
     1961. xvi, 211 p. facsims. (Schriften des Bundesarchivs, no.
     10)

The Archives of the Federal German Republic are not as rich in
German archival material as those of East Germany, but they do contain
a good deal of material, especially derived from consular sources.
Some of this has been microfilmed and is available abroad. See Pogge
von Strandmann's essay (no. 3027), p. 757, footnote 32; the same work
also mentions various private German sources in West Germany.

79. Lötzke, Helmut, and Hans Stephan Brather, eds. UBERSICHT UBER DIE
     BESTANDE DES DEUTSCHEN ZENTRALARCHIVS, POTSDAM. Berlin, Rütten
     and Loening, 1957. 232 p. illus. (Schriftenreihe des Deutschen
     Zentralarchivs, no. 1)

Bibliography: p. 219-223.

The main holdings concerning German colonial activities are to
be found in the Central Archives of the German Democratic Republic
(East Germany) in Potsdam and Merseburg. The survey gives information
concerning files dealing with the colonies, but there is no similar
guide for the archives in Merseburg as yet. The files concerning the
Kolonialrat (a central advisory body on which economic interest groups
were also represented) have been microfilmed. The material in question
covers the period 1890-1906, and microfilms are available both at the
Hoover Institution, Stanford University, and at Rhodes House, Oxford.

80. Markov, P. "West African History in German Archives." JOURNAL OF
    THE HISTORICAL SOCIETY OF NIGERIA, v. 2, no. 4, Dec. 1963: 602-
    605.

    Outlines the holdings in the German Federal Republic (the
    Bundesarchiv at Koblenz and the local archives of Hamburg, Bremen, and
    Emden) and in the German Democratic Republic (the archives at Merse-
    burg, the Geographische Gesellschaft in Gotha, and the second central
    archives at Potsdam).

81. Mommsen, Wolfgang, ed. DIE SCHRIFTLICHEN NACHLASSE IN DEN ZENTRALEN
    DEUTSCHEN UND PREUSSISCHEN ARCHIVEN. Koblenz, 1955, xxxiv, 139 p.
    (Schriften des Bundesarchivs, no. 1)

    Contains descriptions of various important private papers belonging
    to deceased German politicians.

Great Britain

82. Note: Excellent guides to British (and German) archives, unpublished
    and published sources, books and monographs have appeared in the follow-
    ing works:

    a) THE CAMBRIDGE HISTORY OF THE BRITISH EMPIRE, Vol. III. Cambridge,
       Eng., Cambridge University Press, 1959. p. 769-907.

    b) Gifford, Prosser, and William Roger Louis, eds. BRITAIN AND
       GERMANY IN AFRICA: IMPERIAL RIVALRY AND COLONIAL RULE. New
       Haven, London, Yale University Press, 1967. p. 709-795.

    c) Harlow, Vincent, and E. M. Chilver, eds. HISTORY OF EAST AFRICA,
       Vol. II. Oxford, Clarendon Press, 1965. p. 700-736.

    THE CAMBRIDGE HISTORY OF THE BRITISH EMPIRE, Vol. III, is espe-
    cially useful in surveying official records and parliamentary papers.
    The HISTORY OF EAST AFRICA, Vol. II, provides data on collections in
    Great Britain, Kenya, Tanganyika, and Zanzibar. Both studies list
    titles of parliamentary papers on Africa.

83. Hewitt, Arthur R. GUIDE TO RESOURCES FOR COMMONWEALTH STUDIES IN
    LONDON, OXFORD, AND CAMBRIDGE, WITH BIBLIOGRAPHICAL AND OTHER
    INFORMATION. London, published for the Institute of Common-
    wealth Studies, University of London, by the Athlone Press,
    1957. 219 p.

    By the then secretary of the institute and its librarian, this
    guide describes in detail the resources of the chief British centers for

African studies. In the first part Hewitt covers public and private archives, papers of chartered companies and other companies, parliamentary papers and official publications, periodicals and newspaper holdings in libraries, theses and research in progress, bibliographies and works of reference. A second part describes individual collections, and the third part (p. 183-203) names universities, research and advisory organizations, and other official and unofficial institutions and organizations. There is a comprehensive index. Although designed for students of British Commonwealth matters, some of the resources described furnish material for studies of all parts of Africa. Hewitt cites existing guides, registers and inventories to collections. Until J. D. Pearson, librarian of the School of Oriental and African Studies, publishes his guide to British African collections Hewitt's volume will remain one of the most useful descriptions yet produced of any country's African-related materials.

Official guides and inventories include the following:

84. Great Britain. Foreign Office. INDEX TO THE CORRESPONDENCE OF THE FOREIGN OFFICE OF GREAT BRITAIN FOR THE YEARS 1920-1938. London, Public Record Office. 77 v.

The confidential period for the archives of the Foreign Office was amended in 1969 from 50 years to 30 years, thus opening to scholars significant material covering the interwar years. The actual documents exist only in the Public Record Office in London, but photocopies can be ordered provided the index number is quoted.

A list of the archives of the Foreign Office from 1782 (the date of the establishment of the Office as a separate department of state) to 1878 had been published previously in the Public Record Office's series Lists and Indexes, no. LII. A supplementary list covering 1879 to 1905 had been published in 1964 in the Public Record Office's Lists and Indexes, Supplementary Series, no. XIII. The total period for indexes now in print to British Foreign Office correspondence is 1879-1905, 1920-1938. Publication plans are being formulated for an index of the period 1906 to 1919. As the open date for the confidential period is advanced annually, indexes subsequent to 1938 will be published.

85. Great Britain. Public Record Office. GUIDE TO THE CONTENTS OF THE PUBLIC RECORD OFFICE: Vol. I, LEGAL RECORDS, ETC.; Vol. II, STATE PAPERS AND DEPARTMENTAL RECORDS. Rev. and extended to 1960 from the Guide by the late M. S. Giuseppi. London, H. M. Stationery Off., 1963. 249, 410 p.

Africa-related materials are found almost entirely in Vol. II, in the records of the Colonial Office (p. 52-92), the Commonwealth Relations Office (p. 93-97), and the Foreign Office (p. 123-164). All records are arranged by region or country, with separate classes for each. The Colonial Office and the Commonwealth Relations Office material is classed by Original Correspondence, Registers of Correspondence, Entry Books, Colonial Acts, Sessional Papers (of colonial assemblies or councils), Government Gazettes, and Miscellanea. The Foreign Office records are classed under General Correspondence, Treaties, Embassy and Consular Archives, Archives of Commissioners, Confidential Print, and Private Collections. Each volume has two indexes, one for persons and places, another for subjects.

86.   Great Britain. Public Record Office. LIST OF COLONIAL OFFICE
        CONFIDENTIAL PRINT TO 1916. London, H. M. Stationery Off., 1965.
        179 p. (PRO Handbooks, no. 8)

The section on Africa (p. 5-85) has over a thousand numbered items in 116 volumes of selected correspondence, memoranda, reports, and other documents which range from a single page to several hundred pages.

87.   Great Britain. Public Record Office. Lists and Indexes [series].
        London.

The Public Record Office has available various Search Room lists-- (a) Colonial Office, (b) Foreign Office--and xerographic copies of these and other Search Room finding lists can be supplied on request. The following volumes in the Lists and Indexes series are essential for Africa:

a)   no. 36. LIST OF COLONIAL OFFICE RECORDS. 1911.

b)   no. 52. LIST OF FOREIGN OFFICE RECORDS TO 1878. 1929.

c)   no. 53. ALPHABETICAL GUIDE TO WAR OFFICE AND OTHER MILITARY
               RECORDS PRESERVED IN THE P.R.O. 1931.

d)   no. 13 in the Supplementary Lists and Indexes. LIST OF FOREIGN
               OFFICE RECORDS (1879-1913?). [1966?] 8 v. Vols. I-IV,
               General Correspondence; Vol. V, Various Classes; Vols.
               VI-VIII (?), Embassy and Consular Archives.

Other lists are in preparation, including those for the Board of Trade, War Office, Admiralty, and State papers.

See also:

        Pugh, Ralph B. THE RECORDS OF THE COLONIAL AND DOMINIONS
        OFFICES. London, H. M. Stationery Off., 1964. 118 p.
        (Public Record Office Handbooks, no. 3). Valuable mate-
        rial is also found in the LIST OF CABINET PAPERS, 1880-

1914. (P.R.O. Handbooks, no. 4, London, 1964) and LIST
OF PAPERS OF THE COMMITTEE OF IMPERIAL DEFENCE (1888-
1914). (P.R.O. Handbooks, no. 6, London, 1964)

Some important non-official guides and inventories would include:

88. Church Missionary Society, London. Archives. INDEX LISTS. Microfilm
    ed. [1960?]

    Listed are papers of the West Africa (Sierra Leone) Mission, 1803-
1914, the Yoruba Mission, the Niger Mission, and the Nyanza Mission, as
well as those of other missions, e.g., Tanganyika, Northern Nigeria,
Ruanda, East Africa, and South Africa. Entries cover letters and journals from missionaries and government officials, minutes of committee
meetings, correspondence, treaties, petitions, proclamations, and ordinances. Included are papers of Samuel Crowther, Thomas B. Macauley,
William Balfour Baikie, and Alexander M. Mackey. Microfilm copies of
this material are available from the Center for Research Libraries,
Cooperative African Microfilm Project (CAMP), Chicago.

89. Oxford University. Committee for Commonwealth Studies. Colonial
    Records Project. ANNUAL REPORT.

    The Colonial Records Project has since 1963 been trying to col-
lect the diaries, papers, correspondence, etc., of people who have
lived and worked in Africa in any capacity be it as missionary, merchant, government official, or traveler. In 1965 the Project had
approached 3,200 possible contributors, and 6,000 additional names
still remained. The 1966 report listed more than 400 additions to
the Rhodes House Library of Oxford. Notes on acquisitions are issued
irregularly and are listed at the end of each annual report. The
Project is producing name lists, lists of papers received, and inventories or registers of papers and collections. It is hoped from these
individual registers to bring out a full descriptive catalogue of all
the Project's archival and manuscript materials.

90. Oxford University. Rhodes House Library. ACCESSIONS OF NOTE
    RECEIVED.

    These lists, irregularly issued, of manuscripts or copies of manu-
scripts received, provide a most important bibliographic source of
information.

91. Oxford University. Rhodes House Library. MANUSCRIPT COLLECTIONS OF
    AFRICANA IN RHODES HOUSE LIBRARY, OXFORD. Compiled by Louis B.
    Frewer. [Oxford, Published by the Bodleian Library] 1968. 100 p.

Founded in 1928 Rhodes House Library had steadily been acquiring African archival materials, but the Oxford Colonial Records Project flooded the library with over 1500 collections (75% of them dealing with Africa).

Arrangement of this guide is by territory and alphabetically by the name of the collection. Shelf-numbers for open material have been provided with 1258 archives cited.

92. Standing Conference on Library Materials on Africa (SCOLMA). LIBRARY MATERIALS ON AFRICA: NEWSLETTER. 1962- London. Irregular.

This bulletin is largely concerned with descriptions of library and archival collections on Africa. Among individual holdings described in the first several volumes are the following:

a) Colonial Office and Commonwealth Office Library. v. 1, no. 2, 1963: 2-6.

Good account of these two offices whose collections represent perhaps the most important source for official material on the parts of Africa formerly under British control.

b) Rhodes House Library, Oxford. v. 1, no. 4, 1964: 3-6.

This survey of African archival and manuscript collections shows the richness and variety of the holdings of Rhodes House and indicates the wide scope of materials dealing with the British Empire, i.e., films of private collections in South Africa or the United States.

c) Afro-Asian Social Studies Centre, Cambridge. v. 2, no. 1, 1964: 5.

d) University of London:

Institute of Education, Department of Education in Tropical Areas Library. v. 2, no. 2, Oct. 1964: 6.

School of Oriental and African Studies Library. v. 2, no. 3, Jan. 1965: 7-10.

The four preceding articles were reprinted in AFRICAN STUDIES BULLETIN, v. 8, no. 2, Sept. 1965: 86-95.

e) Institute of Commonwealth Studies Library. v. 3, no. 3, Mar. 1966: 2-3.

f) International African Institute Library. v. 4, no. 1, July 1966: 17-19.

g) Africa Institute Library, Pretoria. v. 4, no. 2, Jan. 1967: 6-7.

93. Standing Conference on Library Materials on Africa. THE SCOLMA
    DIRECTORY OF LIBRARIES AND SPECIAL COLLECTIONS ON AFRICA.
    2d ed. Compiled by Robert Collison. London, Crosby Lockwood;
    Hamden, Conn., Shoe String Press, 1967. 92 p.

    Expanding on the information in the 1963 edition and listing some
    15 additional libraries, this is a very useful directory of about 155
    libraries, archives, institutes, government depositories, etc., in the
    United Kingdom which hold Africa-related materials. It supplements
    Hewitt's GUIDE TO RESOURCES FOR COMMONWEALTH STUDIES (1957; see no. 83),
    but the analyses, except in a few cases, are not as informative as
    Hewitt. (Still, one could wish for such directories for each country
    of Europe and Africa.) Arrangement is alphabetical by towns. Data
    for each collection are generally confined to address, telephone number,
    name of director and/or librarian, hours, brief description of holdings,
    conditions of access to materials, and relevant publications issued. An
    index is included.

94. Other inventories of archives and manuscript collections in Great
    Britain are:

    a) British Museum. Department of Oriental Printed Books and Manu-
        scripts. CATALOGUE OF THE ETHIOPIC MANUSCRIPTS IN THE BRITISH
        MUSEUM ACQUIRED SINCE 1847. By William Wright. London, 1877.
        xiii, 366 p. (408 entries)

    b) THE CAMBRIDGE HISTORY OF THE BRITISH EMPIRE, Vol. III. Cambridge,
        Eng., Cambridge University Press, 1959.

        See p. 769-907, particularly Part 1, "Collections of Manuscripts
        and Public and Private Archives, and Official Papers and Publica-
        tions."

    c) Durham, Eng. University. School of Oriental Studies. Sudan
        Archives. HAND-LIST OF ARABIC MANUSCRIPTS AND LITHOGRAPHS
        WITH ACCESSIONS SINCE 1963. Compiled by Richard Hill. 3d
        draft. Durham, 1966. 78 l.

    d) Hill, Richard. "The Sudan Archive, School of Oriental Studies,
        University of Durham, England." AFRICANA NEWSLETTER, v. 1,
        no. 4, 1963: 40-41.

    e) Scotland. Record Office. MATERIAL RELATING TO AFRICA IN THE
        SCOTTISH RECORD OFFICE. Edinburgh [1965?]. 7 l.

    f) Wright, Stephen G., comp. CATALOGUE OF ETHIOPIAN MANUSCRIPTS IN
        THE CAMBRIDGE UNIVERSITY LIBRARY. Cambridge, Eng., Cambridge
        University Press, 1961. 75 p.

    g) The three-volume inventory of British government and private
        collections dealing with the Belgian Congo (see nos. 57-59).

<u>Portugal</u>

<u>Note</u>: The archives for Portugal's overseas territories--Arquivo Histórico Ultramarino, Palácio da Ega, Calçada da Boa Hora, 30, Lisbon (formerly known as the Arquivo Histórico Colonial)--contain the papers of the important overseas council from 1643 to 1833 as well as the papers of the colonial offices which succeeded the council. For the history of Portuguese diplomatic affairs and involvement with other nations in Africa these archives are indispensable. So little is known about Portuguese archives that we have provided more details than for the other colonial powers.

95. "Documenting Portuguese Africa: Archives, Libraries, and Institutes."
    AFRICANA NEWSLETTER, v. 1, no. 3, 1963: 19-24.

A brief description of the main archives, libraries, and institutes--14 in Lisbon and 2 in other cities of Portugal, 6 in Angola, Mozambique, and Portuguese Guinea. Also cited are sources in Rhodesia, England, Germany, and the United States. See also MATERIALS FOR WEST AFRICAN HISTORY IN PORTUGUESE ARCHIVES, no. 48(b).

The following archives, in addition to the Arquivo Histórico Ultramarino (mentioned above), contain pertinent material:

a) Arquivo e Biblioteca do Ministério dos Negócios Estrangeiros,
        Largo do Rilvas, Lisbon.

    For the period since 1851 the foreign office keeps its own archives. Material is classified chronologically by origin and stored in classified sections: correspondence of the Portuguese and foreign diplomatic missions and of Portuguese consulates and ministries; correspondence on the Lourenço Marques railway and on boundary questions; correspondence of overseas province governors; and documents on Portuguese Guinea, Portuguese sovereignty in Zambezia, and the Boer War.

b) Arquivo Histórico Militar, Museu Militar, Largo dos Caminhos
        de Ferro, Lisbon.

    One section of the archives deals with overseas expeditions, campaigns, and colonial wars. The material is organized chronologically by subject.

c) Arquivo Nacional da Torre do Tombo (the National Archive of
        Portugal), Palácio de São Bento, Lisbon.

    The Torre do Tombo is the most important archive in Portugal. It holds millions of records, many of which have not been fully inventoried. For the diplomatic history of

Portugal in Africa the most valuable source is the Historical
Archives of the Portuguese Foreign Office now housed in the
Torre do Tombo.

Among the 717 boxes of materials (from approximately 1756
to 1851) are: correspondence of Portuguese and foreign diplomatic missions and consulates (Correspondência das Caixas);
internal records of the foreign office; letters of cardinals
and princes; records relating to slavery, the slave trade,
and the suppression of the slave trade; miscellaneous petitions,
investigating commissions, and international treaties and conventions.

Diplomatic correspondence and instructions from 1641 to 1705
are also preserved in the National Archives.

d)   Biblioteca e Arquivo da Assembleia Nacional, Lisbon.

Contains government records of the proceedings of the
National Assembly.

e)   Biblioteca da Academia das Ciências, Rua da Academia das
      Ciências, 19, Lisbon.

Has papers of religious orders and of diplomatic affairs.
Especially valuable are the letter books dealing with Africa.

f)   Biblioteca da Ajuda, Palácio Nacional da Ajuda, Lisbon.

Valuable library for diplomatic history of Portugal; for
example, it has the correspondence of the governors of India
and Africa from 1500 on.

g)   Biblioteca Geral da Universidade de Coimbra, Coimbra.

Has manuscripts and letter books dealing with Africa.

h)   Biblioteca Nacional, Largo da Biblioteca Nacional, Lisbon.

The National Library has large amounts of materials
(books, manuscripts, and documents) dealing with diplomatic
affairs of the Portuguese in Africa. A catalogue of the
collection has been printed.

i)   Biblioteca Pública Municipal, Oporto.

One of the best libraries in Portugal; valuable for
documents relating to Africa and diplomatic history. A
catalogue has been printed.

Countries other than Portugal with Portugese African material:

j) In 1949-50, Professor Eric Axelson microfilmed on 2,782 feet of film more than 14,750 documents dealing with the Portuguese in East and Central Africa. The great majority of the documents were found in Portugal, but important Portuguese materials were also found in Paris, London, Rome, and Madrid. The film is now deposited in the Archives of Rhodesia in Salisbury. The documents are the basis for a series being edited jointly by the National Archives and Father Antonio da Silva Rego of the Centro de Estudos Políticos e Sociais da Junta de Investigações do Ultramar. The Portuguese text and an English translation will be printed. See no. 2109, DOCUMENTS ON THE PORTUGUESE IN MOZAMBIQUE AND CENTRAL AFRICA, 1497-1840.

Axelson found material in:

London, British Museum, miscellaneous maps and manuscripts (40 ft. of film);

Madrid, Biblioteca Nacional, a few rare books and documents were found in Madrid, most notably an account of the Portuguese penetration from the west coast of Africa to the interior (32 ft.);

Rome, Sta. Sabina, Dominican library and the Sacra Congregazione de Propoganda Fide have some manuscripts and early printed books, such as FONTANA MONUMENTA DOMINICANA (1575) (40 ft.);

Paris, Bibliothèque Nationale, assorted maps, manuscripts, and documents (70 ft.).

k) London: British Museum.

Miscellaneous maps and manuscripts, large book and government document collection dealing with the Portuguese in Africa. For example, British Consular and Diplomatic Reports from 1855 are excellent sources of information on Portuguese Africa.

l) London: Kings College, University of London, Strand, W.C.2, has a Portuguese library which has extensive material on colonial history.

m) London: Government Records. The Public Record Office, Colonial Office and Foreign Office Libraries.

n) The American Historical Association. Committee for the Study of War Documents. A CATALOGUE OF FILES AND MICROFILMS OF THE GERMAN FOREIGN MINISTRY ARCHIVES, 1867-1920. Washington, D. C., 1959.

o) Germany (Democratic Republic). Deutsches Zentralarchiv, Potsdam. UBERSICHT UBER DIE BESTANDE DES DEUTSCHEN ZENTRALARCHIVS POTSDAM. Berlin, Rütten & Loening, 1957. (Schriftenreihe des Deutschen Zentralarchivs, no. 1)

p) Hinsley, F. H., and M. H. Ehrmann. A CATALOGUE OF SELECTED FILES OF THE GERMAN NAVAL ARCHIVES. London, The Admiralty, 1957. Microfilmed at the Admiralty, London, for the University of Cambridge and the University of Michigan.

q) George O. Kent, ed. A CATALOG OF FILES AND MICROFILMS OF THE GERMAN FOREIGN MINISTRY ARCHIVES, 1920-1945. Vol. I. Stanford, Calif., Hoover Institution, 1962.

Spain, Italy, and Turkey

Note: Little appears to have been published about collections in Spain, Italy, or northern European countries.

From 1882 to 1912 Italy's colonial affairs were handled by a special department within the Foreign Office. In 1912 the Ministry of Colonies became an independent body. In 1937 it became the Ministry of Italian Africa, which continued to operate until 1943. Today its successor is known as the Comitato per la Documentazione dell'Opera dell'Italia in Africa. There is a vast collection in the Archivio Storico dell'ex Ministerio dell'Africa Italiana (ASMAI) in Rome.

Professor Robert I. Hess in his work ITALIAN COLONIALISM IN SOMALIA (see no. 3119), p. 214-15, explains that ASMAI contains some 80,000 documents dealing with all phases of Italian interest and administration. During the Second World War, however, a good deal of material was lost through repeated evacuations, and the sources of the Fascist era in Somalia are sparse. Certain documents are still classified as "confidential," "highly confidential" or "secret." The sources include the correspondence of colonial governors and officials with metropolitan authorities; confidential correspondence of trading companies and exploratory societies; reports of travelers and government investigators; copies of diplomatic correspondence; minutes of cabinet meetings and a great deal of related material. The colonial archives of Somalia were not available to the author. He states that during the British occupation from 1941 to 1950, all documents not destroyed by the Italian authorities were methodically confiscated and shipped to London, where they are not yet available to scholars.

See also no. 48(c), MATERIALS FOR WEST AFRICAN HISTORY IN ITALIAN ARCHIVES.

96. Martin, B. G. "Turkish Archival Sources for West African History." AFRICAN STUDIES BULLETIN, v. 10, no. 3, Dec. 1967: 59-65.

This brief survey contains useful bibliographic material and suggestions for research. It reports also on archives in North Africa.

97. Val, María Asunción. "El archivo y biblioteca de la Dirección General de Plazas y Provincias Africanas, posible base para un centro de documentación de Africa." REVISTA DE ARCHIVOS, BIBLIOTECAS Y MUSEOS (Madrid), v. 65, 1958: 123-128.

NORTH AMERICA

United States

Note: United States links with Africa have been close not only because of the slave trade but also because Americans, as explorers and missionaries, frontiersmen and soldiers, tobacco farmers and mining engineers, played a role in the history of the continent. Yet the history of American involvement in Africa to be found in a variety and quantity of archival and manuscript materials is inadequately known. Because of the extent of American commercial, missionary, philanthropic, scientific, and governmental contacts with Africa since 1619 the resources are many.

98. "ASA Guide to Archival and Manuscript Materials Relating to Africa in the United States." AFRICAN STUDIES BULLETIN, v. 7, no. 2, May 1964: 1-2.

Announcement of the program for production of a guide to cover the broad range of Africa-related archives and manuscript materials in the United States. The African Studies Association has undertaken this project with a Ford Foundation grant over a three-year period. The National Archives and Records Service will assume joint responsibility with ASA for the conduct of the project, which is to be directed by Morris Rieger of the NARS staff. The guide will become the U.S. national volume of the projected "Guide to the Sources of African History outside of Africa" sponsored by the UNESCO-affiliated International Council on Archives. An article by Mr. Rieger, "Africa-related Papers of Persons and Organizations in the United States," appears in the AFRICAN STUDIES BULLETIN, v. 8, no. 3, Dec. 1965: 1-11; it illustrates preliminary findings of the project in the area of private (i.e., nongovernmental) papers and emphasizes their wide variety and distribution. See also his "Preliminary Report on Materials in the National Archives Relating to Africa," AFRICAN STUDIES BULLETIN, v. 2, no. 2, Apr. 1959: 1-13.

99. Collins, Robert O., and Peter Duignan. AMERICANS IN AFRICA: A PRELIMINARY GUIDE TO AMERICAN MISSIONARY ARCHIVES AND LIBRARY MANUSCRIPT

COLLECTIONS ON AFRICA. Stanford, Calif., Hoover Institution, Stanford University, 1963. 96 p. (Hoover Institution, Bibliographical Series, no. 12)

Surveys 52 missionary archives and 48 library and society manuscript collections with material on Americans in Africa. It includes supplements on American missionary-sending societies for Africa and a territorial survey of mission groups, as well as an index. This guide is largely superseded by the much-increased list in the HANDBOOK OF AMERICAN RESOURCES FOR AFRICAN STUDIES (see no. 101).

100. Hamer, Philip M., ed. A GUIDE TO ARCHIVES AND MANUSCRIPTS IN THE UNITED STATES. New Haven, Conn., Yale University Press, 1961. xxxii, 775 p.

Useful for locating African material in the United States, though unfortunately entries do not always indicate an African relationship.

101. HANDBOOK OF AMERICAN RESOURCES FOR AFRICAN STUDIES. By Peter Duignan. Stanford, Calif., Hoover Institution, Stanford University, 1967. 218 p. (Hoover Institution, Bibliographical Series, no. 29)

This compilation, brought closely up to date as of early 1966, supersedes AMERICANS IN AFRICA...(no. 99) as well as articles in the former AFRICANA NEWSLETTER and the AFRICAN STUDIES BULLETIN describing library collections and archives in America. Descriptions of African holdings are given for 95 library and manuscript collections, 108 church and missionary libraries and archives, 95 art and ethnographic collections, and 4 business archives. A long article describes material in the National Archives dealing with Africa. There is an index.

102. Haywood, Carl. "American Contacts with Africa: A Bibliography of the Papers of the American Whalemen." AFRICAN STUDIES BULLETIN, v. 10, no. 3, Dec. 1967: 82-95.

Lists personal journals and official logbooks of American whalemen who visited Africa and adjacent islands during the nineteenth century. Arrangement is by location of documents in the United States.

103. Macmillan, Gary D. AN INFORMAL INDEX TO DOCUMENTS IN THE U.S. NATIONAL ARCHIVES (U.S. DEPT. OF STATE RECORDS), PERTAINING TO LIBERIA 1852-1906, 1910-1929. Monrovia, 1968.

104. THE NATIONAL UNION CATALOG OF MANUSCRIPT COLLECTIONS, 1959-1961. Ann Arbor, Mich., J. W. Edwards, 1962. 1061 p.

1962. Hamden, Conn., Shoe String Press, 1964. 532 p.

INDEX, 1959-1962. Hamden, Conn., Shoe String Press, 1964. 732 p.

1963-1964. Washington, Library of Congress, 1965. 500 p.

1965 [AND] INDEX, 1963-1965. Washington, Library of Congress, 1966. 701 p.

Compiled by the Library of Congress from reports provided by American repositories. Many American collections with African material are cited. Indexes are full, in one alphabet of names, places, subjects, and historical periods.

Canada

105. BULLETIN OF AFRICAN STUDIES IN CANADA. [Title also in French] v. 1, no. 1- v. 3, no. 2. Edmonton, University of Alberta, 1963-64; Montreal, Loyola College, 1965-66. Twice yearly.

Published by the Committee on African Studies in Canada. Lists of documents and archives held in Canada appeared in its pages. It was succeeded by the CANADIAN JOURNAL OF AFRICAN STUDIES.

AFRICA

106. "African Archival Directory." AFRICANA NEWSLETTER, v. 1, no. 1, 1962: 16-18.

Lists name, address, director, and founding date of 26 archives in Africa. It brought up to date the Baxter survey (see below).

Surveys of African archives have appeared in the AFRICANA NEWS-LETTER, v. 1, nos. 1, 3, 4, 1963, and v. 2, no. 1, 1964. Brief descriptions of the organization and content of the archives of Cameroun, Gambia, Sierra Leone, the Rhodesias and Nyasaland, Madagascar, Réunion, and Senegal were given.

107. Baxter, T. W. ARCHIVAL FACILITIES IN SUB-SAHARAN AFRICA. Report prepared for CCTA. London, Commission for Technical Co-operation in Africa, 1959. 68 p. (Scientific Council for Africa South of the Sahara, Publication no. 78)

By the director of the former National Archives of Rhodesia and Nyasaland (now the National Archives of Rhodesia), this report begins with a list of 27 governmental archives in Africa south of the Sahara

and then continues with the replies of these archives to a questionnaire regarding their control, scope of holdings, techniques and
available finding aids, etc. It ends with an outline of prospects
for further interarchival cooperation and the recommendations of the
Inter-African Conference on Social Science at Bukavu in 1955 regarding
conservation of archives.

108. Curtin, Philip D. "The Archives of Tropical Africa: A Reconnaissance."
        JOURNAL OF AFRICAN HISTORY, v. 1, no. 1, 1960: 129-147.

        Brief description of organization, problems, and holdings of
archives in former French West Africa, Senegal, Mauritania, Ivory
Coast, Cameroons, Guinea, Soudan, Togoland, Niger, Dahomey, former
French Equatorial Africa, Nigeria, Ghana, Sierra Leone, Gambia,
Zanzibar, Kenya, Tanganyika, Uganda, Sudan, Congo (Leopoldville),
Portuguese Guinea, Ethiopia, and Ruanda-Urundi.

109. Dadzie, Kwakuvi E. W. "Libraries, Bibliography and Archives in French-
        speaking Countries of Africa." UNESCO BULLETIN FOR LIBRARIES, v.
        15, no. 5, Sept.-Oct. 1961: 242-253.

        Mr. Dadzie is secretary-general of the International Association
for the Development of Libraries in Africa, known by its French initials,
AIDBA. Established in the late 1950s as the Association pour le Développement des Bibliothèques Publiques d'Afrique, the organization changed
its name to the present form in 1960, and national branches have been
set up in Senegal, Togo, and Mauritania. AIDBA issues a Bulletin, circulated to the membership. (Further information on AIDBA may be obtained from M. Dadzie, B. P. 166, Saint-Louis, Senegal.)

110. DIRECTORY OF ARCHIVES, LIBRARIES, AND SCHOOLS OF LIBRARIANSHIP IN
        AFRICA. REPERTOIRE DES ARCHIVES, BIBLIOTHEQUES ET ECOLES DE
        BIBLIOTHECONOMIE D'AFRIQUE. By E. W. Dadzie and J. T. Strickland.
        Paris. UNESCO, 1965. 112 p.

        The text of this valuable record, authorized by UNESCO's Inter-
national Advisory Committee on Bibliography, Documentation, and
Terminology in 1961, was completed in July 1963 on the basis of
questionnaires to which 508 institutions throughout the continent
returned answers. (Some variation in answers is understandable under
the circumstances.) Systematic information on each gives all necessary
detail--address, constitution, scope, special interests and collections,
etc. Each section is arranged by country; in the first, 36 archives are
described, in the second 8 library schools. The section on libraries
(464) is subdivided by character of institution: national libraries,
educational establishments, special libraries and documentation centers,
public libraries.

Archival data include foundation, staff, subjects covered, and
date of oldest record and series of records held. Details are provided on the existence of catalogues, inventories, guides, registers,
etc., and whether or not these were published and available or were
just for internal use. At least 23 archives indicated that they had
some guides or inventories, though most of these finding aids were
only for internal use. Two versions of the subject index are given,
one French, one English. The editors are respectively secretary-general
of the Association Internationale pour le Développement des Bibliothèques en Afrique and the former chief librarian of the Sierra Leone
Library Board.

A bibliographic guide to the use of African libraries is: France,
Ministère de la Coopération, INDICATIONS BIBLIOGRAPHIQUES A L'USAGE
DES BIBLIOTHEQUES AFRICAINES ET MALGACHES (Paris [1965?] 262 p.).

111. Jenkins, William, and Frederick Kirk, Jr. A PRELIMINARY REPORT ON A
        SURVEY OF THE PUBLIC RECORDS DEPOSITORIES OF AFRICA, THE LEVANT
        AND WESTERN EUROPE, 1963. Chapel Hill, Bureau of Public Records,
        University of North Carolina, 1966.

Included are reports about archives and libraries in Senegal,
Nigeria, South Africa, and Rhodesia.

112. "Library Development in Africa." UNESCO BULLETIN FOR LIBRARIES, v.
        15, no. 5, Sept.-Oct. 1961: 225-287.

Supplemented in v. 16, no. 1, Jan.-Feb. 1962: 47-48; v. 17, no.
2, Mar.-Apr. 1963: 98-102; v. 18, no. 4, July-Aug. 1964: 193.

Among the most important documents relating to libraries in
Africa, this special issue contains details of UNESCO projects, brief
surveys of library resources, and other articles, some here noted under
individual authors. The last 11 pages give information on libraries
and other institutions throughout the world having significant collections of Africana. Data on other collections are continued in the
subsequent issues listed.

The UNESCO BULLETIN FOR LIBRARIES (Paris), bimonthly, is also
useful for international coverage of reference works relating to
Africa.

113. Scientific Council for Africa South of the Sahara (CSA). DIRECTORY
        OF SCIENTIFIC AND TECHNICAL LIBRARIES IN AFRICA SOUTH OF THE
        SAHARA. [Title also in French] [London] Published under the
        sponsorship of the Commission for Technical Co-operation in
        Africa South of the Sahara, 1954. 71 p. (Publication no. 10)

The second revised edition of this directory contains data on
239 libraries outside the Republic of South Africa and 68 within the
Republic. For the countries outside South Africa, the large general
libraries of universities and municipalities are included. The list
was supplemented by Miss Hazel Mews in "Scientific Documentation in
Africa South of the Sahara," REVUE DE LA DOCUMENTATION, v. 26, Nov.
1959: 87-93.

CSA and CCTA, of which CSA was the scientific advisory body, are
now functioning as the scientific branch of the Organization of African
Unity. The publications, formerly issued by the Publications Bureau,
Watergate House, York Buildings, London, W.C.2, are available in the
United States from the International Publications Service, New York.

114. Standing Committee on African University Libraries. SCAUL NEWSLETTER.
Jan. 1965- Mimeographed.

Planned at the Leverhulme Conference on University Libraries in
Tropical Africa held at University College, Salisbury, Rhodesia,
Sept. 14-23, 1964, for publication once a term. No issues appeared
in 1966, however, because of unsettled conditions in Nigeria, where
a number of the staff were situated. Wilfred J. Plumbe, in Apr. 1967
librarian at the University of Malawi, Limbe, is the first editor;
Harold Holdsworth, librarian, University College, P.O. Box 9184, Dar
es Salaam, Tanzania, is the distributor. Articles in the first several issues dealt with such subjects as library education and training available at African universities, lists of exchange material
available, new publications and serials, and preservation of books.
The Mar. 1968 issue surveyed 14 African university libraries.

115. United Nations Educational, Scientific and Cultural Organization.
DEVELOPMENT OF PUBLIC LIBRARIES IN AFRICA: THE IBADAN SEMINAR.
Paris, 1954. 155 p. (UNESCO Public Library Manuals, 6)

_____. Seminar on the Development of Public Libraries in Africa,
2d, Enugu, Sept. 1962. "Final Report." UNESCO BULLETIN FOR
LIBRARIES, v. 17, no. 2, Mar.-Apr. 1963, Supplement.

The growth of libraries in Africa and other developing countries
has been a major concern of UNESCO. Groundwork for procedures and
projects was laid at the 1st Seminar on the Development of Public
Libraries held in Ibadan in 1953. The volume of its proceedings included as appendix a roundup of conditions of public libraries in
35 countries and territories of Africa as of that date. Progress
is recorded in the article on "Library Development in Africa" (see
no. 112), and statistics of library growth are given in the issues
of the UNESCO STATISTICAL YEARBOOK (see no. 917). A second Seminar
held in Enugu in 1962 discussed advances and continuing problems of

library development. It also gave attention to the question of training African librarians. Its final report has been followed by a number of articles and news bulletins in the UNESCO BULLETIN FOR LIBRARIES and other UNESCO-sponsored publications. The following may be of particular interest:

a) Gardner, Frank M. "UNESCO and Library and Related Services in Africa." UNESCO BULLETIN FOR LIBRARIES, v. 20, no. 5, Sept.-Oct. 1966: 212-218.

An account of seminars, school libraries, library demonstration projects, and other services to libraries instituted in Africa by UNESCO.

b) Gelfand, M. A. UNIVERSITY LIBRARIES FOR DEVELOPING COUNTRIES. Paris, UNESCO, 1967. 225 p.

c) Isnard, F. Lalande. "The Development of Libraries in Africa: Six Years after the Enugu Seminar." UNESCO BULLETIN FOR LIBRARIES, v. 22, no. 5, Sept.-Oct. 1968: 241-246.

A review of accomplishments during six years of UNESCO aid and advice, and assessment of problems and prospects.

d) "A Library Education Policy for the Developing Countries." UNESCO BULLETIN FOR LIBRARIES, v. 22, July-Aug. 1968: 173-188.

This article was a follow-up to the special issue on training of librarians in Africa and elsewhere (see Willemin, below). It contains the views of three specialists, including M. Bousso, director of the Dakar University Library School, and Danish and French library training officers, with a summing up by John Dean, director of the Institute of Librarianship at Ibadan.

e) Willemin, Silvère. "The Training of Librarians in Africa." UNESCO BULLETIN FOR LIBRARIES, v. 21, no. 6, Nov.-Dec. 1967: 291-300.

A paper in a special issue devoted to the training of librarians. It stresses need of professional training, problems of recruitment, organization of studies and importance of planning, and describes the chief library training institutes in Africa. The author is head of the Swiss Union Catalogue in the National Library of Berne.

116. U.S. Library of Congress. General Reference and Bibliography Division. AFRICAN LIBRARIES, BOOK PRODUCTION, AND ARCHIVES: A LIST OF REFERENCES. Compiled by Helen F. Conover, African Section. Washington, 1962. 64 p.

In three sections, each beginning with general tools and then subdivided by region. Coverage of material up to the 1960's was good, especially for libraries.

117. Varley, Douglas H. "Conference of University Libraries in Tropical Africa." UNESCO BULLETIN FOR LIBRARIES, v. 19, no. 2, Mar.-Apr. 1965: 73-76.

Account of proceedings of the Leverhulme Inter-universities Conference on the Needs and Problems of University Libraries in Tropical Africa, held in Salisbury in Sept. 1964. There were representatives of 21 universities and colleges of Africa south of the Sahara, as well as observers from various other countries. A list of 18 working papers which formed the basis of the discussion is appended.

118. Varley, Douglas H. THE ROLE OF THE LIBRARIAN IN THE NEW AFRICA. London, Oxford University Press, 1963. 24 p.

The author of this short paper has served both as editor of SOUTH AFRICAN LIBRARIES and as librarian of the University College of Rhodesia.

* * * * *

Note: The following short selection of books, papers, and articles must be considered as no more than illustrative of material that can be found regarding the libraries and particularly the archives of the individual countries of Africa; it is arranged by region, with subgrouping by subregion and country. Leads to further research are often given in the bibliographical references included in such authoritative country studies as those mentioned in Part IV of the present guide.

There are frequent regional library meetings in Africa, details of which are to be found in the African library journals or the announcements section of the UNESCO BULLETIN FOR LIBRARIES. The papers of a conference held under the auspices of the Scandinavian Institute of African Studies at Norrköping, Sweden, in 1965 have been published by the Institute: LIBRARY WORK IN AFRICA, edited by Anna-Britta Wallenius (Uppsala, 1966, 75 p.). The 1965 meeting was attended by leading African librarians. Papers presented covered library services and training in Ghana, Zambia, East Africa, Uganda, and Tanganyika, and adult education.

The International Conference on African Bibliography, Nairobi, Dec. 1967, whose proceedings were published in 1970 by Frank Cass, was also of interest in connection with African libraries and archives and training for African librarians, as well as various bibliographical and collecting problems. (See no. 275.)

West Africa

119. Alagoa, E. J. "Preliminary Inventory of the Records of the United
      States Diplomatic and Consular Posts in West Africa, 1856-1935."
      JOURNAL OF THE HISTORICAL SOCIETY OF NIGERIA (Ibadan), v. 2, no.
      1, Dec. 1960: 78-104.

      Records described are from Record Group 84 in the U.S. National
Archives, Records of the Foreign Service Posts of the Department of
State; they are papers from consular offices in Liberia (legation
records at Monrovia also), the Gold Coast, Sierra Leone, Senegal,
Gambia, and Lagos, Nigeria. At the end is a "Select List of Signif-
icant Documents" which occur among them. The essay also appears in
HANDBOOK OF AMERICAN RESOURCES.... (no. 101).

120. Destaing, E. "Notes sur les manuscrits arabes de l'Afrique occidentale."
      REVUE AFRICAINE, v. 55, 1911: 64-99, 216-248, 484-522; v. 56,
      1912: 267-300, 447-469; v. 57, 1913: 139-162.

121. Hiskett, M. "Material Relating to the State of Learning among the
      Fulani before Their Jihād." BULLETIN OF THE SCHOOL OF ORIENTAL
      AND AFRICAN STUDIES, v. 19, pt. 3, 1957: 551-578.

      This article, a large part of which consists of the text and trans-
lation of a century-old Arabic manuscript, contains excellent bibliographic information on Arabic manuscripts of West Africa.

122. Ibadan. University. Institute of African Studies. Centre of Arabic
      Documentation. RESEARCH BULLETIN, v. 1, no. 1- July 1964-
      Ibadan, Nigeria. Semiannual (v. 1, 3 issues).

      A leading source for information on Arabic manuscripts, texts, and
archives dealing with West Africa, including data on private library
collections and location of Arabic manuscripts in Europe and Africa.
In the first issue was an article by K. Mahmud, "The Arabic Collection
of Ibadan University Library." The July 1965 issue reported on a
conference on Arabic documents which was held at the University of
Ghana, Feb. 26-27, 1965. Professor V. Monteil, director of IFAN,
Dakar, spoke of the current state of Arabic documentation in Senegal
and other states of former French West Africa. Professor Ivor Wilks
described the Arabic collection (over 500 works at the University of
Ghana (see also no. 138). Dr. Ivan Hrbek of Prague reported he was
working on an inventory of all Arabic sources relating to Africa.
"Arabic Source Material and Historiography in Sokoto to 1864: An
Outline" was contributed by D. M. Last in the Jan. 1965 issue and
"Arabic Manuscripts in the National Archives, Kaduna" in July 1966.
Subsequent issues continue to carry articles on this subject.

123. Institut Fondamental d'Afrique Noire, Dakar. CATALOGUE DES MANU-
          SCRITS DE L'I.F.A.N. By Thierno Diallo et al. Dakar, IFAN,
          1966. 155 p. (Catalogues et Documents, no. 20)

      A catalogue of six collections of documents on peoples and
regions of West Africa. The manuscripts are in the Arabic, Peul,
and Voltaic languages, but most have been translated into French.

124. Monteil, Vincent. "Les manuscrits historiques arabo-africains
          (bilan provisoire)." BULLETIN DE L'I.F.A.N., v. 27, ser. B,
          nos. 3-4, July-Oct. 1965: 531-542; "Les manuscrits historiques
          arabo-africains (II)," v. 28, ser. B, nos. 3-4, July-Oct. 1966:
          668-675; "Les manuscrits historiques arabo-africains (III),"
          v. 29, ser. B, nos. 3-4, July-Oct. 1967: 599-603.

      The first article deals with Ghana, Nigeria, East Africa, and
French-speaking Africa, the second with Nigeria, Cameroun, Chad,
Senegal, Mali, and Niger, and the third with Mali, Niger, and Nigeria.

125. WALA NEWS. Ibadan, West African Library Association, 1953-64. Semi-
          annual.

      The West African Library Association, an organization of the
librarians of English-speaking West Africa, was formed in 1953 and
brought out two issues of a journal, WEST AFRICAN LIBRARIES. The
Association held an inaugural conference in Lagos in Sept. 1954, at
which John Harris of the Ibadan University College Library was elected
president and the name of the journal was changed to WALA NEWS. It
appeared regularly twice a year until 1964, when the regional character of the organization had so declined that it split into separate
bodies, and WALA NEWS was superseded by the GHANA LIBRARY JOURNAL and
NIGERIAN LIBRARIES, bulletin of the Nigerian Library Association.
The latter, edited in the beginning by John Harris, augments three
issues a year with supplementary mimeographed newsletters.

Former French West Africa

126. Charpy, Jacques. "Les archives de l'Afrique occidentale française."
          ABCD--ARCHIVES, BIBLIOTHEQUES, COLLECTIONS, DOCUMENTATION, no.
          12, Nov.-Dec. 1953: 317-322.

      The writer, director of the Service des Archives of French West
Africa, published in 1958 a volume of documents, LA FONDATION DE
DAKAR (1845-1857-1869) (see no. 1811).

127. Faure, Claude. LES ARCHIVES DU GOUVERNEMENT GENERAL DE L'AFRIQUE
          OCCIDENTALE FRANCAISE. Paris, E. Larose, 1922. 57 p.

      Publication of the Comité d'Etudes Historiques et Scientifiques
of the Gouvernement Général de l'AOF, the predecessor of IFAN.

128. French West Africa. Service des Archives. LES ARCHIVES DU GOUVERNE-
          MENT GENERAL DE L'A.O.F. EN 1954: ORGANISATION ET FONCTIONNE-
          MENT DU DEPOT D'ARCHIVES ET DE LA BIBLIOTHEQUE ADMINISTRATIVE.
          Rapport annuel, 1954. Dakar, 1955. 67 p. plans. Mimeographed.

129. French West Africa. Service des Archives. REPERTOIRE DES ARCHIVES.
          Sér. A- 1954- Rufisque.

      Prepared under the direction of Jacques Charpy.

      Sér. A, E, H à T, issued by the Haut Commissariat de la
          République en Afrique occidentale française; Sér. B,
          D, F, and G, by the Gouvernement Général de l'Afrique
          occidentale française.

      Sér. A-B. By Claude Faure and Jacques Charpy. 2 v.
      Sér. A. ACTES OFFICIELS, 1817-1895. 1958. 18 p.
      Sér. B. CORRESPONDANCE GENERALE, 1779-1895. 1955. 70 p.

      Sér. C. [Not published in 1968.]

      Sér. D. AFFAIRES MILITAIRES, 1763-1920. 1956. 90 p.

      Sér. E. CONSEILS ET ASSEMBLES, 1819-1920. 1958. 37 p.

      Sér. F. AFFAIRES ETRANGERES, 1809-1921. 1955. 57 p.

      Sér. G. POLITIQUE ET ADMINISTRATION GENERALE, 1782-1920. 1954-
          55. 9 pts. in 1 v.

      Sér. H-T. AFFAIRES SOCIALES, JUDICIAIRES, ECONOMIQUES ET
          FINANCIERES, 1782-1920. 1958. 213 p.

130. Johnson, G. Wesley, Jr. "The Archival System of Former French West
          Africa." AFRICAN STUDIES BULLETIN, v. 8, no. 1, Apr. 1965: 48-58.

      Account of the central archives of AOF in Dakar as well as other
archives and associated research institutes in Senegal, Mauritania,
Mali, Upper Volta, Niger, Dahomey, Ivory Coast, and Guinea, based on
visits made by the writer in late 1964.

131. Verdat, Marguerite. BREVES INSTRUCTIONS A L'USAGE DES BIBLIOTHECAIRES-
ARCHIVISTES DANS LES CERCLES DE L'A.O.F., SUIVIES DU CADRE DE
CLASSEMENT DES ARCHIVES DE L'A.O.F. Rufisque, Impr. du Gouverne-
ment Général [n.d.]. 29 p.

Publication of the Institut Français d'Afrique Noire.

The official archives of former French Africa formed the Section
Outre-Mer of the Service des Archives Nationales located at the former
Colonial Ministry (27 rue Oudinot, Paris 7).

See also nos. 128 and 129.

Western Sudan

132. Brockelmann, Carl. GESCHICHTE DER ARABISCHEN LITTERATUR. Zweite den
Supplementbänden angepasste Auflage. Leiden, E. J. Brill, 1943-
49. 2 v. Supplementband. Leiden, E. J. Brill, 1937-42. 3 v.

Islamic literature predominates in this monumental work, which
includes chapters on Egypt, North Africa, and the Maghreb, as well as
smaller sections on East Africa, Abyssinia, and the Sudan. The first
edition came out in 1898-1902 (2 v., Berlin, E. Felber).

133. Hunwick, J. O. "Arabic Manuscript Material Bearing on the History of
the Western Sudan." Supplement to BULLETIN OF NEWS OF THE
HISTORICAL SOCIETY OF NIGERIA, v. 7, no. 2, Sept. 1962: 9 p.

134. Kensdale, W. "Field Notes on the Arabic Literature of the Western
Sudan." JOURNAL OF THE ROYAL ASIATIC SOCIETY, pts. 3 and 4,
1955: 162-168; pts. 1 and 2, 1956: 78-80; pts. 1 and 2, 1958:
53-57.

Important bibliographic information on Arabic manuscripts may
be found in this material.

135. Smith, H. F. C. "Arabic Manuscript Material Bearing on the History
of the Western Sudan: A List (Published in the 1950's) of Books
Written by the Khalifa Muhammad Bello." Supplement to BULLETIN
OF NEWS OF THE HISTORICAL SOCIETY OF NIGERIA, v. 3, no. 4, Mar.
1959: 4 p.

_____. "Source Material for the History of the Western Sudan."
JOURNAL OF THE HISTORICAL SOCIETY OF NIGERIA, v. 1, no. 3, 1958:
238-247.

Both the JOURNAL and the BULLETIN OF NEWS of the Historical
Society of Nigeria provide interim publication of material such as
that above (see also no. 147) which is to be integrated into an
eventual HANDLIST OF ARABIC MANUSCRIPTS BEARING ON THE HISTORY OF
THE WESTERN SUDAN, a project of the Department of History of the University of Ibadan in cooperation with the Nigerian National Archives.

Gambia

136. Gailey, Harry A., Jr. "African Archives: Gambia." AFRICANA NEWS-
     LETTER, v. 1, no. 3, 1963: 38-39.

   "A Note on the Gambian Archives," also by Gailey, was published
in the AFRICAN STUDIES BULLETIN of Dec. 1968 (v. 11, no. 3: 312-313).
He reports that since 1963 "the Gambia government has acted to pre-
serve and catalogue the materials which prior to independence had been
so carelessly handled."

137. Gambia. REPORT ON THE PUBLIC RECORDS OF THE GAMBIA, APRIL, 1966. By
     J. M. Smyth. Bathurst, 1966. 8 p. (Sessional Paper no. 10 of
     1966)

   Gambia organized a Public Record Office in 1965, and this report
details progress in collecting and organizing the P.R.O. The largest
group of records are those of the Colonial Secretary--routine, confed-
erated, and secret. Numerous departmental records were uncovered but
have not been transferred. Handlists of records have been prepared
(approximately 50).

Ghana

138. Boyo, (al-Hajj) Osmanu Eshaka, Thomas Hodgkin, and Ivor Wilks, comps.
     CHECK LIST OF ARABIC WORKS FROM GHANA. Legon, Institute of
     African Studies, University of Ghana, Dec. 1962. 12 l.

   A provisional list of material (originals, photographic reproductions, or microfilms) held by the Institute of African Studies.
Revised lists, with additional acquisitions, are issued periodically
and may be obtained from the Institute upon request.

139. De Chantal, J. "Institute of Public Administration Library, Achimota,
     Ghana." CANADIAN LIBRARY, v. 20, Nov. 1963: 121-122.

140. Evans, Evelyn J. A. A TROPICAL LIBRARY SERVICE: THE STORY OF GHANA'S
     LIBRARIES. London, Andre Deutsch, 1964. xvii, 174 p.

The GHANA LIBRARY JOURNAL is published by the Ghana Library Board, which Miss Evans describes in this book.

141. Ghana. National Archives. REPORT. 1950- Accra, Govt. Printer. Annual.

Begun as the Gold Coast National Archives report. These reports have been abstracted or listed in ARCHIVES (London): 10th report for 1959 in v. 5, no. 26, Michaelmas 1961: 119; 11th for 1960-61, v. 6, no. 29, Lady Day 1963: 63; 12th for 1961-62, v. 6, no. 31, Apr. 1964: 195; 13th for 1962-63, v. 7, no. 33, Apr. 1965; 14th for 1963-64, v. 7, no. 36, Oct. 1966: 252.

142. Rieger, Morris. "Gold Coast: Archives Reports, 1950-57." AMERICAN ARCHIVIST, v. 22, Apr. 1959: 243-245.

Account and description of the National Archives of Ghana (formerly Gold Coast) established in 1950; organic legislation in 1955.

143. Wolfson, Freda. "Historical Records on the Gold Coast." London. University. Institute of Historical Research. BULLETIN, v. 24, no. 70, 1951: 121-240.

Guinea

144. Guinea. Institut National de Recherches et de Documentation. PREMIER REPERTOIRE DES ARCHIVES NATIONALES DE GUINEE: SER. A-N, 1720- 1935. By Damien d'Almeida. Conakry, 1962. 224 p. (Mémoires, no. 1)

This is the first calendar of part of the archives, covering Sér. A, Actes officiels, 1720-1935; Sér. B, Correspondance générale, 1890- 1935; Sér. D, Administration générale, 1907-1932; Sér. E, Affaires politiques, 1896-1936; Sér. N, Affaires militaires, 1907-1919. Other parts will follow.

Ivory Coast

145. Delrieu, Suzanne. "Ivory Coast Central Library: A UNESCO Pilot Project." UNESCO BULLETIN FOR LIBRARIES, v. 18, Sept. 1964: 201- 206.

By a UNESCO expert who helped to establish the project.

Liberia

146. Foley, David M. "Liberia's Archival Collection." AFRICAN STUDIES
     BULLETIN, v. 11, no. 2, Sept. 1968: 217-220.

     A brief survey of Liberia's rich store of archival materials.
     The author stresses that with persistence the serious researcher
     can gain access, despite occasional government discouragement, to
     this virtually unrecognized collection.

Mali

147. Smith, H. F. C. "Arabic Manuscript Material Bearing on the History
     of the Western Sudan: The Archives of Segu." Supplement to
     BULLETIN OF NEWS OF THE HISTORICAL SOCIETY OF NIGERIA, v. 4,
     no. 2, 1959.

     See no. 135 for annotation.

Mauritania

148. Heymowski, Adam. "Organizing the National Library of Mauretania in
     Nouakchott." UNESCO BULLETIN FOR LIBRARIES, v. 20, no. 2, Mar.-
     Apr. 1966: 98-99.

     Description of present holdings (French works on Africa, general
     reference works, Arabic works) and of plans for expansion. The Mauri-
     tanian section of the Centre de l'IFAN at Saint-Louis, Senegal, is
     considered part of the young National Library. A preliminary list has
     been compiled of all manuscripts by Mauritanian authors in private
     collections.

Nigeria

Note: WALA NEWS (see no. 125) in 1964 became NIGERIAN LIBRARIES, bulletin
of the Nigerian Library Association and chief organ for information about
libraries in Nigeria.

149. Arif, Aida S., and Ahmad M. Abū Hakima. DESCRIPTIVE CATALOGUE OF
     ARABIC MANUSCRIPTS IN NIGERIA [IN THE] JOS MUSEUM AND LUGARD
     HALL LIBRARY, KADUNA. London, Luzac and Co., 1965. 216 p.

A briefly annotated title listing of more than 1,000 manuscripts, with names of authors supplied wherever possible. Dates are omitted. Subjects covered are history, religion, language (Arabic grammar), poetry, astronomy, astrology, mathematics, folklore, prose, geography, education, sociology, logic, and law.

150. Bivar, A. D. H. "Arabic Documents of Northern Nigeria." BULLETIN OF THE SCHOOL OF ORIENTAL AND AFRICAN STUDIES, v. 22, pt. 2, 1959: 324-349. plates.

_____., and M. Hiskett. "The Arabic Literature of Nigeria to 1804: A Provisional Account." BULLETIN OF THE SCHOOL OF ORIENTAL AND AFRICAN STUDIES, v. 25, pt. 1, 1962: 104-148. plates.

The first article, based on photographs of nineteenth-century Arabic official letters, emphasizes the importance of distinguishing between original official documents and various transcripts made from them. The second article serves as an introduction to Arabic literature composed in Nigeria and contiguous areas in the period before the Fulani JIHAD. Both articles, but particularly the second one, offer valuable bibliographical material on Arabic manuscripts.

151. Dike, Kenneth Onwuka. REPORT ON THE PRESERVATION AND ADMINISTRATION OF HISTORICAL RECORDS AND THE ESTABLISHMENT OF A PUBLIC RECORD OFFICE IN NIGERIA. Lagos, Govt. Printer, 1954. 27 p.

Following this report by Nigeria's leading historian, the Record Office was established. It has been superseded by the National Archives (see no. 164).

152. Gwam, L. C. A BIBLIOGRAPHY OF THE NATIONAL ARCHIVES LIBRARY, IBADAN: Part 1, AFRICANA; Part 2, GENERAL WORKS. Ibadan, 1964. 2 v. 94 1, 165 l.

153. Gwam, L. C. "First Permanent Building of the Nigerian National Archives." AMERICAN ARCHIVIST, v. 26, Jan. 1963: 67-74.

154. Gwam, L. C. A HANDLIST OF FOREIGN OFFICIAL PUBLICATIONS IN THE NATIONAL ARCHIVES LIBRARY. Ibadan, 1964. unpaged.

155. Gwam, L. C. A HANDLIST OF NIGERIAN OFFICIAL PUBLICATIONS IN THE NATIONAL ARCHIVES HEADQUARTERS, IBADAN. Ibadan, 1964. 188 l.

Supersedes two provisional volumes published in 1961.

156. Gwam, L. C. "Introduction to the Nigerian National Archives." WALA NEWS, v. 4, Dec. 1961: 59-69.

The author was until his untimely death in 1965 director of the National Archives of Nigeria. In his charge was the extensive project of recording the voluminous archival material held in Ibadan and in other official archives (Enugu, Kaduna, Lagos, etc.). For titles of individual records, see no. 164.

157. Harris, John. "National Library Development in Nigeria." WALA NEWS, v. 4, Dec. 1961: 53-58.

158. Horrocks, S. H. THE REGIONAL CENTRAL LIBRARY AT ENUGU, EASTERN NIGERIA: AN ASSESSMENT. Paris, UNESCO, 1962. 55 p. illus. Published also in French.

A summarization of this study of a UNESCO pilot project, which was presented as a main paper at the UNESCO Seminar at Enugu in Sept. 1962, was published with illustrations in the UNESCO BULLETIN FOR LIBRARIES, v. 16, no. 5, Sept.-Oct. 1962: 244-246. plates.

159. Kensdale, W. E. N. "The Arabic Manuscripts Collection of the Library of the University College of Ibadan, Nigeria." WALA NEWS, v. 2, June 1955: 21-25. photo.

160. Kensdale, W. E. N. A CATALOGUE OF THE ARABIC MANUSCRIPTS PRESERVED IN THE UNIVERSITY LIBRARY, IBADAN. Ibadan, Ibadan University Library, 1955. 38 p.

161. Kirk-Greene, A. H. "A Preliminary Note on the Sources for Nigerian Military History." JOURNAL OF THE HISTORICAL SOCIETY OF NIGERIA, v. 3, no. 1, 1964: 129-147.

162. Lagos. University. Library. DIRECTORY OF LAGOS LIBRARIES. Compiled in the University of Lagos Library; edited by Elizabeth M. Moys and C. C. Momah. Lagos, Dobbs Ferry, N.Y., Oceana Publications, 1965. xiii, 62 p.

Founding date, address, name of librarian, type of library, hours open, admission, are among the data given for the Lagos libraries.

163. Lagos. University. Library. UNILAG: QUARTERLY NEWS BULLETIN. v. 1, no. 1- Jan. 1964- Yaba, Lagos.

Processed bulletin, which gives news of progress and includes lists of various sorts. A projected union catalogue of legal materials in Nigerian libraries had not yet appeared by 1967.

164. Nigeria. National Archives. REPORT. 1954/55- Lagos, Ibadan. Annual.

The Nigerian Record Office was established in Lagos in 1954, and the first three reports were issued under its name. In 1961 the fourth annual report (for 1959-60) appeared. The first under independence, it was considered a landmark. (It was abstracted in ARCHIVES [London], v. 5, no. 26, Michaelmas 1961: 120. The fifth and sixth annual reports were abstracted in v. 6, nos. 30 and 31.) THE SEVENTH REPORT OF THE WORK OF THE NATIONAL ARCHIVES OF NIGERIA, 1962-63 was published by the Federal Ministry of Information, Lagos, in 1964. The National Archives Headquarters was eventually located in Ibadan, with L. C. Gwam as director until his death in 1965. Work is continuing on lists and inventories of several of the archival record groups. A full listing as of 1965 appears in the Library of Congress's OFFICIAL PUBLICATIONS OF NIGERIA (1966). By 1967, publications included the following:

a) Adedipe, G. A. K. A SPECIAL LIST OF RECORDS ON LAND AND SURVEY, NIGERIAN SECRETARIAT RECORD GROUP. Ibadan, 1963. 23 l.

b) _____. A SPECIAL LIST OF RECORDS ON INTERNATIONAL AFFAIRS, NIGERIAN SECRETARIAT RECORD GROUP. Ibadan, 1965. 62 l.

c) _____. A SPECIAL LIST OF RECORDS ON INTER-STATE AFFAIRS IN THE NIGERIAN SECRETARIAT RECORD GROUP. Ibadan, 1965. 99 l.

d) _____. A SPECIAL LIST OF RECORDS ON THE ARMY, IN THE NIGERIAN SECRETARIAT RECORD GROUP. Ibadan, 1965. 79 p.

e) _____. A SPECIAL LIST OF RECORDS ON THE POLICE FORCE, FROM THE NIGERIAN SECRETARIAT RECORD GROUP. Lagos, 1965. 22 l.

f) Akinfemiwa, Akintunde. A SPECIAL LIST OF RECORDS ON "THE ORIGINS AND DEVELOPMENT OF THE NIGERIAN MEDICAL AND SANITARY SERVICES," 1861-1960, FROM THE NIGERIAN SECRETARIAT RECORD GROUP. Ibadan, 1964. 123 l.

g) _____. A SPECIAL LIST OF RECORDS ON THE SUBJECT OF PUBLIC WORKS, FROM THE NIGERIAN SECRETARIAT RECORD GROUP. Lagos, 1965. 106 l.

h) Alagoa, E. J. SERIES INVENTORY OF THE RECORDS OF THE PROVINCIAL OFFICE, ONITSHA--"ONPROF," 1896-1955. Enugu, 1961. 19 l.

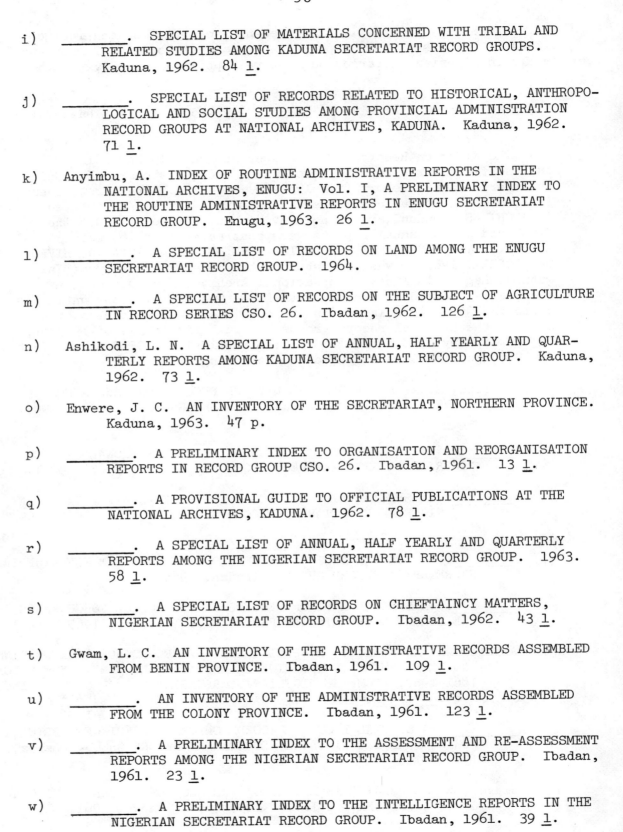

i) _____. SPECIAL LIST OF MATERIALS CONCERNED WITH TRIBAL AND RELATED STUDIES AMONG KADUNA SECRETARIAT RECORD GROUPS. Kaduna, 1962. 84 l.

j) _____. SPECIAL LIST OF RECORDS RELATED TO HISTORICAL, ANTHROPO-LOGICAL AND SOCIAL STUDIES AMONG PROVINCIAL ADMINISTRATION RECORD GROUPS AT NATIONAL ARCHIVES, KADUNA. Kaduna, 1962. 71 l.

k) Anyimbu, A. INDEX OF ROUTINE ADMINISTRATIVE REPORTS IN THE NATIONAL ARCHIVES, ENUGU: Vol. I, A PRELIMINARY INDEX TO THE ROUTINE ADMINISTRATIVE REPORTS IN ENUGU SECRETARIAT RECORD GROUP. Enugu, 1963. 26 l.

l) _____. A SPECIAL LIST OF RECORDS ON LAND AMONG THE ENUGU SECRETARIAT RECORD GROUP. 1964.

m) _____. A SPECIAL LIST OF RECORDS ON THE SUBJECT OF AGRICULTURE IN RECORD SERIES CSO. 26. Ibadan, 1962. 126 l.

n) Ashikodi, L. N. A SPECIAL LIST OF ANNUAL, HALF YEARLY AND QUAR-TERLY REPORTS AMONG KADUNA SECRETARIAT RECORD GROUP. Kaduna, 1962. 73 l.

o) Enwere, J. C. AN INVENTORY OF THE SECRETARIAT, NORTHERN PROVINCE. Kaduna, 1963. 47 p.

p) _____. A PRELIMINARY INDEX TO ORGANISATION AND REORGANISATION REPORTS IN RECORD GROUP CSO. 26. Ibadan, 1961. 13 l.

q) _____. A PROVISIONAL GUIDE TO OFFICIAL PUBLICATIONS AT THE NATIONAL ARCHIVES, KADUNA. 1962. 78 l.

r) _____. A SPECIAL LIST OF ANNUAL, HALF YEARLY AND QUARTERLY REPORTS AMONG THE NIGERIAN SECRETARIAT RECORD GROUP. 1963. 58 l.

s) _____. A SPECIAL LIST OF RECORDS ON CHIEFTAINCY MATTERS, NIGERIAN SECRETARIAT RECORD GROUP. Ibadan, 1962. 43 l.

t) Gwam, L. C. AN INVENTORY OF THE ADMINISTRATIVE RECORDS ASSEMBLED FROM BENIN PROVINCE. Ibadan, 1961. 109 l.

u) _____. AN INVENTORY OF THE ADMINISTRATIVE RECORDS ASSEMBLED FROM THE COLONY PROVINCE. Ibadan, 1961. 123 l.

v) _____. A PRELIMINARY INDEX TO THE ASSESSMENT AND RE-ASSESSMENT REPORTS AMONG THE NIGERIAN SECRETARIAT RECORD GROUP. Ibadan, 1961. 23 l.

w) _____. A PRELIMINARY INDEX TO THE INTELLIGENCE REPORTS IN THE NIGERIAN SECRETARIAT RECORD GROUP. Ibadan, 1961. 39 l.

x) _____. A PRELIMINARY INVENTORY OF THE ADMINISTRATIVE RECORDS ASSEMBLED FROM ONDO PROVINCE. 1963. 64 l.

y) _____. A PRELIMINARY INVENTORY OF THE ARCHIVES OF THE NIGERIAN SECRETARIAT, LAGOS.

z) _____. A SPECIAL LIST OF RECORDS ON THE SUBJECT OF EDUCATION IN RECORD SERIES CSO. 26. 1961. 56 l.

aa) Mbah, V. C. J. A PRELIMINARY INDEX TO THE INTELLIGENCE REPORTS IN THE ENUGU SECRETARIAT RECORD GROUP. Enugu, 1962. 15 l.

ab) Nwaguru, J. E. N. AN INVENTORY OF THE ADMINISTRATIVE RECORDS FROM THE OLD CALABAR PROVINCE. Lagos, 1965. 102 l.

ac) Nwaobi, J. O. A SPECIAL LIST OF RECORDS ON AGRICULTURE, FISHERY & VETERINARY IN THE KADUNA SECRETARIAT RECORD GROUP. 1964.

ad) Ododo, Kate. A SPECIAL LIST OF RECORDS ON FORESTRY FROM THE NIGERIAN SECRETARIAT RECORD GROUP. Ibadan, 1963. 87 l.

ae) _____. A SPECIAL LIST OF RECORDS ON VETERINARY [SCIENCE] AND THE FISH INDUSTRY IN THE NIGERIAN SECRETARIAT RECORD GROUP CSO. 9-CSO. 26. Ibadan, 1963. 43 l.

af) Onuoha, Kate. A SPECIAL LIST OF RECORDS ON THE NIGERIAN RAILWAY IN THE CSO RECORD GROUP 11-21. Ibadan, 1964. 3 v.

ag) _____ and A. O. Evborokhai. A SPECIAL LIST OF RECORDS ON LAND CASES IN THE OYO PROVINCIAL RECORD GROUP. 1964.

ah) Waniko, S. S. A DESCRIPTIVE CATALOGUE OF THE EARLY PAPERS OF THE SECRETARIAT, NORTHERN PROVINCES, KADUNA: NATIONAL ARCHIVES RECORD GROUP S.N.P., SERIES 10. Kaduna, 1961. 57 l.

ai) _____ and M. S. D. Ilyasu. A DESCRIPTIVE CATALOGUE OF EARLY LUGARD-SULTAN OF SOKOTO CORRESPONDENCE, INCLUDING A DESCRIPTION OF 131 ARABIC LETTERS FOUND IN SOKOTO IN 1903. Kaduna, 1961. 24 l.

165. Nigeria. National Archives Headquarters, Ibadan. A SUBJECT CATALOG OF THE NATIONAL ARCHIVES LIBRARY, IBADAN, Pt. 1- no. 1- 1964/65-

166. Nigerian Library Association. Northern Division. NORTHERN NIGERIA LIBRARY NOTES. no. 1- May 1964- Zaria, The Division, Ahmadu Bello University.

No. 1, in mimeographed form, contained 61 pages.

167. Northern Region of Nigeria. Library. [Catalogue of] HOLDINGS.
        Kaduna, 196-. 55 1. 33 cm.

        Author list of holdings. Official documents of the Northern
Region are heavily represented.

168. Waniko, S. S. ARRANGEMENT AND CLASSIFICATION OF NIGERIAN ARCHIVES.
        Lagos, Nigerian Archives Service, 1958. 21 p.

                                Senegal

169. Johnson, G. Wesley. "Archival Materials of Senegal." AFRICANA
        NEWSLETTER, v. 2, no. 1, 1964: 74-76.

170. Seguin, Louis. "The Regional Centre for the Training of Librarians
        at Dakar." UNESCO BULLETIN FOR LIBRARIES, v. 18, no. 3, May-
        June 1964: 101-104.

        The center was inaugurated on Nov. 4, 1963, with 20 students--
two Senegalese, the rest holding fellowships from other francophone
African states. This survey is by the UNESCO expert who assisted in
setting up the training school. A brief note on the center appeared
in the LIBRARY OF CONGRESS INFORMATION BULLETIN, Dec. 9, 1963: 655.

171. Senegal. Archives Nationales. REPERTOIRE DES ARCHIVES. By J.-F.
        Maurel.

        The archival collections of the former colony of Senegal have
now been transferred from Saint-Louis to Dakar, and M. Maurel is
preparing an index for them.

172. Senegal. Archives Nationales. Centre de Documentation. BULLETIN
        BIBLIOGRAPHIQUE DES ARCHIVES DU SENEGAL. no. 1- Jan. 1963-
        Dakar. Quarterly.

                            Sierra Leone

173. Gailey, Harry. "African Archives: Sierra Leone." AFRICANA NEWS-
        LETTER, v. 1, no. 3, 1963: 39.

174. Sierra Leone. CATALOGUE OF ARCHIVES, THE PROPERTY OF THE GOVERNMENT
        OF SIERRA LEONE, DEPOSITED AT FOURAH BAY COLLEGE, SIERRA LEONE,

WEST AFRICA. [Freetown? 1952?] 33 p.

A typescript inventory of the holdings of the archives has been prepared by Mrs. Gladys Sheriff.

175. Sierra Leone. Library Board. REPORT. 1959- Freetown, Library
       Board, 1961-

176. Sierra Leone. Library Board. SIERRA LEONE PUBLICATIONS: A LIST OF
       BOOKS AND PAMPHLETS IN ENGLISH RECEIVED BY THE SIERRA LEONE
       LIBRARY BOARD UNDER THE PUBLICATIONS (AMENDMENT) ACT. 1962-
       1964/65. Freetown, Library Board, 1963-66.

This listing of official, semiofficial, and other publications in English received by the Library Board has now become a NATIONAL BIBLIOGRAPHY (see no. 1509).

177. Strickland, John T. "Library Development in Sierra Leone." LIBRARY
       WORLD, v. 64, July 1962: 3-9.

The Sierra Leone Government Library Board here described was formed in 1959. A brief account of it was published also in the UNESCO BULLETIN FOR LIBRARIES, v. 16, no. 3, May-June 1962: 157-158.

Equatorial Africa

Former French Equatorial Africa
(Afrique équatoriale française)

178. Glénisson, Jean. "Les archives de l'A.E.F.: Lettre de Brazzaville."
       GAZETTE DES ARCHIVES, n.s. no. 22, July 1957: 23-30.

By the former chief archivist of the Gouvernement Général de l'AEF.

A reference has been noted in the bibliography accompanying Guy Lasserre's study, LIBREVILLE: LA VILLE ET SA REGION (GABON, A.E.F.); ETUDE DE GEOGRAPHIE HUMAINE (see no. 2019), to a mimeographed inventory of documents by Jean Glénisson, LES SOURCES DE L'HISTOIRE D'A.E.F.: INVENTAIRE SOMMAIRE DES ARCHIVES DE LA MINISTERE DE LA FRANCE D'OUTRE-MER CONCERNANT L'A.E.F. (Brazzaville, 1953, 96 p.).

179. Institut d'Etudes Centrafricaines, Brazzaville. Bibliothèque.
       CATALOGUE DE LA BIBLIOTHEQUE DE L'I.E.C. By Jeanine Lambert.

Montpellier, Impr. Charité, 1951. 152 p. (Mémoires, no. 4)

Supplement no. 1, 1953- 232 p.

About 5,000 entries are listed.

Cameroun

180. Gardinier, David E. "African Archives: Cameroun." AFRICANA NEWS-
        LETTER, v. 1, no. 3, 1963: 37-38.

Congo (Former Belgian Congo)

181. Congo, Belgian. Force Publique. CATALOGUE DE LA BIBLIOTHEQUE DE
        LEOPOLDVILLE. Léopoldville, Force Publique, 1953. 488 p.

182. Depasse, Charles. LES BIBLIOTHEQUES PUBLIQUES AU CONGO. Bruxelles,
        Editions Universitaires, 1948. 32 p. illus.

    Extract from ZAIRE, v. 2, Mar. 1948: 277-302.

    Short historical account beginning with legislation in 1898.
Included are statistics of public libraries for Europeans and Congolese
and data on research and mission libraries and books and pamphlets for
African readers.

Eastern Africa and the Horn

East Africa

Note: See also BRITAIN AND GERMANY IN AFRICA (no. 550) and HISTORY OF EAST
AFRICA, Vols. I and II (no. 2427), for information on archives and library
collections in this region.

183. Belton, E. J. DIRECTORY OF EAST AFRICAN LIBRARIES. Kampala, Uganda,
        Makerere College Library, 1961. 76 p. (Makerere Library
        Publications, no. 1)

    A thorough survey of all libraries existing at the time in East
Africa. It contains entries for over 90 specialized and larger general
libraries.

184. Charman, D., and M. Cook. "The Archive Services of East Africa."
     ARCHIVES: THE JOURNAL OF THE BRITISH RECORDS ASSOCIATION,
     v. 8, 1967: 70-80.

185. East African Library Association. BULLETIN. no. 1- Jan. 1962-
     Kampala, Published for the Association by Makerere College
     Library. Quarterly.

     An organ for information on East African libraries.

186. Hockey, S. W. DEVELOPMENT OF LIBRARY SERVICES IN EAST AFRICA: A RE-
     PORT SUBMITTED TO THE GOVERNMENTS OF EAST AFRICA. Nairobi, 1964.
     42 p.

     The 1960 report with a new introduction. The author was appointed
to East Africa in June 1960 as Libraries Development Organizer by the
British Council.

187. Hockey, S. W. "Library Resources in English-speaking Countries of
     East Africa." UNESCO BULLETIN FOR LIBRARIES, v. 15, no. 5,
     Sept.-Oct. 1961: 232-236. illus.

188. Larsen, Knud. "The East African School of Librarianship." UNESCO
     BULLETIN FOR LIBRARIES, v. 18, no. 3, May-June 1964: 105-109.

     By a UNESCO expert who helped to establish this school, opened
at Makerere University on Jan. 6, 1964.

                              Ethiopia

189. Danton, J. P. "Libraries in the Land of the Lion of Judah." LIBRARY
     JOURNAL, v. 87, May 1, 1962: 1732-1736.

190. Eldon, Rita. "The National Library of Ethiopia." ETHIOPIA OBSERVER,
     v. 1, Oct. 1957: 369-370.

     A description of the first public library in Ethiopia, founded
shortly after the liberation.

191. Pankhurst, Richard. "The Foundations of Education, Printing, News-
     papers, Book Production, Libraries and Literacy in Ethiopia."
     ETHIOPIA OBSERVER, v. 6, no. 3, 1962: 241-290.

Includes the names of many organizations and individual scholars.

192. Wright, Stephen. "Book and Manuscript Collection in Ethiopia,"
        JOURNAL OF ETHIOPIAN STUDIES, v. 2, no. 1, Jan. 1964: 11-24.

        An interesting article on the Ethiopian attitude towards books,
the development of printing and publishing, and the history and
current status of book and manuscript collections.

        The author in collaboration with Stephen G. Wright has compiled
a CATALOGUE OF ETHIOPIAN MANUSCRIPTS IN THE CAMBRIDGE UNIVERSITY
LIBRARY (Cambridge, Eng., University Press, 1961, 75 p.).

193. Wright, Stephen G., comp. ETHIOPIAN INCUNABULA FROM THE COLLECTIONS
        IN NATIONAL LIBRARY OF ETHIOPIA AND THE HAILE SELLASSIE I
        UNIVERSITY. Addis Ababa, 1967. 107 p.

Kenya

194. Kenya. Government Archives. ARCHIVES MICROFILMING PROGRAMME. Sec.
        I. Nairobi, Mar. 1964. 75 l. fold map. 33 cm. Mimeographed.

        An inventory of provincial and district annual and quarterly
reports held in the Kenya Government Archives--the first section of
a projected program to make available on film records from the beginning of colonial rule to 1962. Two other syllabuses will be
published listing the political record books of provinces and districts and miscellaneous early records and diaries, but these will
be available only to 1939. Each section is to be preceded by an
introduction dealing with the form and content of the documents.
The general introduction in Sec. I is by Derek Charman, government
archivist seconded from England as technical adviser on archives to
the Kenya government.

195. Nairobi. University College. Library. LIBRARY ACCESSIONS LIST.
        1958- Nairobi. Monthly.

196. Syracuse University. Maxwell Graduate School for Citizenship and
        Public Affairs. Program of Eastern African Studies. A
        CATALOGUE OF THE KENYA NATIONAL ARCHIVE COLLECTION ON MICRO-
        FILM AT SYRACUSE UNIVERSITY. Compiled by Nathan W. Fedha
        and John B. Webster. Syracuse, N.Y., 1967. 1 v. (Occasional
        Bibliography, no. 6)

        _____. A GUIDE TO THE KENYA NATIONAL ARCHIVES, TO THE MICROFILMS
          OF THE PROVINCIAL AND DISTRICT ANNUAL REPORTS, RECORD BOOKS, AND

HANDING-OVER REPORTS; MISCELLANEOUS CORRESPONDENCE; AND
INTELLIGENCE REPORTS. Compiled by Robert C. Gregory, Robert
M. Maxon, and Leon P. Spencer. Syracuse, N.Y., 1968. 452 p.
(Eastern African Bibliographical Series, no. 3)

The second entry is a detailed annotated guide to the 157 reels
of microfilm (negative and positive) which Syracuse University purchased from the Kenya National Archives. Coverage includes Secretariat
circulars and debates of the Legislative Council and the National Assembly. Also given are accounts of administrative reorganizations, a list
of ethnic groups, and indexes for province and district, personalities
and organizations, and miscellaneous correspondence (subject index).
The work concerns mainly the period 1900 to 1965, but the period covered varies with the type of material, some of which goes back as far
as the 1880's.

Sudan

197. Holt, Peter M. "Mahdist Archives and Related Documents." ARCHIVES
(London), v. 5, no. 28, Sept. 1962: 193-200.

A brief historical account of Mahdist manuscripts and a survey
of their scope and present distribution. Some of these materials or
copies of them are to be found outside the Sudan, as, for example,
those described by Richard Hill in "The Sudan Archive, School of
Oriental Studies, University of Durham, England," AFRICANA NEWSLETTER,
v. 1, no. 4, 1963: 40-41.

198. Plumbe, Wilfred J. "Sudan Libraries." SOUTH AFRICAN LIBRARIES, v.
18, Oct. 1950: 2, 51-56.

Abstract in LIBRARY SCIENCE ABSTRACTS, v. 1, no. 4, Oct.-Dec.
1950: no. 382.

199. Sewell, P. H. "The Development of Library Service in Sudan." UNESCO
BULLETIN FOR LIBRARIES, v. 15, no. 2, Mar.-Apr. 1961: 87-90.

Tanzania (Tanganyika and Zanzibar)

200. Dar es Salaam. University College. Library. LIBRARY BULLETIN AND
ACCESSIONS LIST. 1961- Dar es Salaam. Monthly, 1961-Feb. 1965;
fortnightly (irregular), Mar. 1965- Stenciled.

64

201. Dar es Salaam. University College. Library. LIST OF MANUSCRIPTS
IN THE EAST AFRICAN SWAHILI COMMITTEE COLLECTION. Dar es
Salaam, Mar. 1964. 25 p. (Library Bulletin, no. 24)

Annotated list, mainly of Swahili texts but including also some
historical and bibliographical works in European languages. A similar list appeared in SWAHILI, v. 35, no. 1, Mar. 1965: 99-115.

202. Dar es Salaam. University College. Library. THE PAPERS OF HANS
CORY IN THE LIBRARY OF THE UNIVERSITY COLLEGE, DAR ES SALAAM.
Dar es Salaam, 1968. 53 p.

A government sociologist and linguist, Cory wrote and collected
much valuable material on all aspects of traditional life.

203. Hill, Patricia J. SHELF LIST AND INDEX TO SECRETARIAT ARCHIVES
(EARLY SERIES) 1919-1927. Dar es Salaam, National Archives
of Tanzania, 1966. 104 p.

Covers 1,539 files and contains provincial, district, and departmental annual reports, information on medical, economic, political,
military, legal, educational matters.

204. Tanganyika Library Service. TANGANYIKA LIBRARY SERVICE NEWS. 1963-
Dar es Salaam. Irregular. Stenciled.

205. Tanzania. National Archives. ANNUAL REPORT OF THE NATIONAL ARCHIVES
OF TANZANIA FOR THE YEAR 1964-1965. Dar es Salaam, Govt.
Printer, 1966. 19 p.

This first annual report lists surveys of archives and gives a
summary of archive holdings available for study.

206. Wright, Marcia. "The Tanganyika Archives." AMERICAN ARCHIVIST, v.
28, n. 4, Oct. 1965: 511-520.

An article on the National Archives which, since its formation in
June 1962 at Dar es Salaam, has been collecting a wide variety of
historical records--official (including both German and British colonial periods), missionary, and commercial--as well as the private
papers of important persons or families.

207. Zanzibar. Archives and Museum Department. REPORT. 1956- Zanzibar,
Govt. Printer. Annual.

The Zanzibar Archives were approved in 1955 and combined with the Peace Memorial Museum. The 1957-58 reports were reviewed by Morris Rieger in AMERICAN ARCHIVIST, v. 24, Jan. 1961: 99. A brief note on the National Archives of Zanzibar appeared in the UNESCO BULLETIN FOR LIBRARIES, v. 18, no. 5, Sept.-Oct. 1964: 244.

208. Zanzibar. Museum. Reference Library. CATALOGUE OF ZANZIBAR MUSEUM REFERENCE LIBRARY, 1955. By Beit-el-Amani. Zanzibar, Govt. Printer, 1955. 49, 3 p.

Uganda

209. English, Patrick T. "Archives of Uganda." AMERICAN ARCHIVIST, v. 18, July 1955: 225-230.

210. Makerere University College. Library. LIBRARY BULLETIN AND ACCESSIONS LIST. 1954- Kampala. Every 2 months. Stenciled.

211. Teso, Uganda (District). Office of the District Commissioner. INDEX LIST TO THE ARCHIVES OF THE OFFICE OF THE DISTRICT COMMISSIONER, TESO DISTRICT. Soroti, 1960. 106 p.

212. Trowell, Kathleen M., comp. A HANDBOOK OF THE MUSEUMS AND LIBRARIES OF UGANDA. Kampala, Uganda Museum, 1957. 16 p. (Uganda Museum, Occasional Paper no. 3)

213. UGANDA LIBRARY BULLETIN. v. 1, no. 1- Mar. 1966- Kampala, Uganda Library Service (P.O. Box 4262).

South-Central Africa

Rhodesia, Zambia, and Malawi
(The Rhodesias and Nyasaland)

214. Baxter, T. W., ed. GUIDE TO THE PUBLIC ARCHIVES OF RHODESIA: Vol. I, 1890-1923. Rev. ed. Salisbury, National Archives of Rhodesia, 1969. 262 p.

A revision of the 1956 edition, A GUIDE TO THE PUBLIC RECORDS OF SOUTHERN RHODESIA UNDER THE REGIME OF THE BRITISH SOUTH AFRICA COMPANY, 1890-1923 (no. 224).

The introduction contains a historical survey of European activities and a history of national archival development. The main section consists of description of the archives of each department. There is an index. Vol. II will cover archives from 1923 to 1940.

215. Baxter, T. W., and L. H. Gann. "The National Archives of Rhodesia and Nyasaland." AFRICANA NEWSLETTER, v. 1, no. 4, 1963: 31-40.

216. Burke, Eric. "Records Management in the Central African Archives." Society of Archivists. JOURNAL, v. 1, Apr. 1956: 62-66.

Abstract in LIBRARY SCIENCE ABSTRACTS, v. 7, no. 2, Apr.-June 1956: no. 5909.

217. DIRECTORY OF LIBRARIES IN THE FEDERATION OF RHODESIA AND NYASALAND. Salisbury, University College of Rhodesia and Nyasaland, Library, 1960. 42 p. (Library Occasional Paper no. 1)

Processed pamphlet describing 103 libraries in the Federation, including a number of institutions of learning and government offices. There are subject and geographical indexes.

218. Edwards, J. "National Archives of Rhodesia and Nyasaland." LIBRARY WORLD, v. 62, Sept. 1960: 53-58.

219. "Librarianship in the Central African Federation." Special issue of LIBRARY WORLD, v. 64, Oct. 1962.

Among articles included are the following:

a) "Library Services in the Rhodesias: Twelve Years After." By D. H. Varley. p. 92-95.

b) "Southern Rhodesia National Free Library Service." By Norman Johnson. p. 96-100. illus.

c) "The National Archives of Rhodesia and Nyasaland." By T. W. Baxter. p. 101-105. illus.

d) "The Oldest Public Library in Rhodesia." By E. Worsley. p. 106-107, 109-111. illus.

220. "Public Libraries in the Federation of Rhodesia and Nyasaland." UNESCO BULLETIN FOR LIBRARIES, v. 15, no. 5, Sept.-Oct. 1961: 238-241; v. 16, no. 4, July-Aug. 1962: 213-214.

221. Rhodesia. National Archives. A CALENDAR OF THE HISTORICAL MANU-
        SCRIPTS COLLECTION OF THE NATIONAL ARCHIVES OF RHODESIA.

        The Historical Manuscripts Collection consists of material of
nonofficial provenance--political papers, records of commercial
companies, missionary material, papers of clerical organizations,
African associations, and other private bodies, and papers of individual settlers and Africans. Entries for each group of papers contain a biographical sketch of the person or a historical note on the
institution, whichever is appropriate; a general description of the
papers (origins, dates covered, approximate volume, etc.); a selective
calendar of the material in question; and editorial notes. This
calendar is now (1969) being prepared for publication.

222. Rhodesia, Southern. Central African Archives. REPORT BY THE CHIEF
        ARCHIVIST. Aug. 31, 1947-June 30, 1954. Salisbury. illus.

        Included are the following:

        1. CENTRAL AFRICAN ARCHIVES IN RETROSPECT AND PROSPECT:
              A REPORT...FOR THE TWELVE YEARS ENDING 31 AUGUST
              1947. 1947. 118 p.

        2. A REPORT . . . FOR THE PERIOD 1 SEPTEMBER 1947 TO 31 DECEMBER
              1948. 1949. 102 p.

        3. ARCHIVES IN A NEW ERA: A REPORT . . . FOR THE PERIOD 1
              JANUARY 1949 TO 30 JUNE 1954. 1955. 81 p.

        On July 1, 1954, the Central African Archives became a body of
the Federation of Rhodesia and Nyasaland. See the entries that follow.

223. Rhodesia and Nyasaland. Central African Archives. THE COMING OF AGE
        OF THE CENTRAL AFRICAN ARCHIVES. [Glasgow?] 1956. 40 p. illus.

224. Rhodesia and Nyasaland. Central African Archives. A GUIDE TO THE
        PUBLIC RECORDS OF SOUTHERN RHODESIA UNDER THE REGIME OF THE
        BRITISH SOUTH AFRICA COMPANY, 1890-1923. Salisbury, 1956. xxxviii,
        282 p. illus.

        By the National Archives Act of 1958 the name of the Central
African Archives was changed to National Archives of Rhodesia and
Nyasaland. This is one of the best guides to any African archives.

        A most comprehensive publication, it arranges the records according
to their archival groups as determined by their departmental provenance.
The groups are further subdivided into classes, and these into series
of related materials. The guide is supplemented by detailed historical

notes on the history and functions of the various departments and public bodies. It is fully indexed. The information given in the guide is supplemented by an even more detailed typescript inventory, which is locally available, and which covers each single archival unit. Between them, they provide the most detailed description of any large group of records in Africa.

The post-1923 records are now being described. They mostly become available to public inspection when they are 30 years old. This provisional inventory may later be published.

225. Rhodesia and Nyasaland. National Archives. ARCHIVES IN A GROWING SOCIETY: A REPORT BY THE DIRECTOR FOR THE PERIOD 1 JULY 1954 TO 30 JUNE 1962. Salisbury, 1963. 105 p. illus.

226. Rhodesia and Nyasaland. National Archives. LIST OF PUBLICATIONS DEPOSITED IN THE LIBRARY OF THE NATIONAL ARCHIVES, 1961. Salisbury, 1963. 17 p.

1962. Salisbury, 1964. 16 p.

The first two issues of an annual list contained publications of all three territories. In 1964 the list contained only Southern Rhodesia items. The latest issue is called the RHODESIA NATIONAL BIBLIOGRAPHY.

227. Wilding, N. W. "Salisbury, Southern Rhodesia, Queen Victoria Memorial Library." LIBRARY ASSOCIATION RECORD, v. 65, Dec. 1963: 526-529.

228. Zambia. GUIDE TO THE PUBLIC ARCHIVES OF ZAMBIA: Vol. I, 1895-1940. Compiled by I. M. Graham and B. C. Halwindi. Lusaka, National Archives, 1970.

Angola

229. Angola. Arquivo Histórico. BOLETIM DO ARQUIVO HISTORICO E DE BIBLIOTECA DO MUSEU DE ANGOLA. 1959- Luanda.

Most issues contain texts of documents; indexed in ARCHIVUM.

230. ARQUIVOS DE ANGOLA: PUBLICACAO TRIMESTRAL. no. 1- May 1933- Luanda.

Published by the Museu de Angola. Frequent collections of texts of documents appear; indexed in ARCHIVUM.

231. Instituto de Investigação Científica de Angola. Arquivo Histórico
     de Angola. ROTEIRO TOPOGRAFICO DOS CODICES: NUCLEO ANTIGO DA
     SECRETARIA GERAL; NUCLEO DO GOVERNO DE BENGUELA; NUCLEO GERAL.
     Luanda, Imprensa Nacional de Angola, 1966. 183 p.

         A major archival tool to locate and describe the government re-
     cords of Angola. The period from 1600 to 1920 is covered, but most
     entries are from 1800 on. A chronological index and subject and geo-
     graphical indexes are included. The work is part of a continuing pro-
     gram to prepare inventories to the records held at the Arquivo Histórico
     de Angola. Many of these inventories appear in ARQUIVOS DE ANGOLA (see,
     for example, the issue of July-Dec. 1959). See M. A. Samuels, "Report
     of Historical Research in Angola," AFRICAN STUDIES BULLETIN, v. 11, no.
     3, 1968: 245-247, for description of archives in Luanda and elsewhere
     in Angola.

232. Salvadorini, Vittorio. "Biblioteche e archivi d'Angola." BOLLETINO
     DELLA ASSOCIAZONE DEGLI AFRICANISTI ITALIANI, v. 2, no. 3-4,
     July-Dec. 1969: 16-30.

Mozambique

Note: The Arquivo Histórico de Moçambique, Lourenço Marques, under the
Direcção dos Serviços de Instrução of Mozambique, contains many historical
archives and has a library of over 8,000 volumes.

233. Montez, Caetano. "Inventário de fundo do seculo XVIII do Arquivo
     Histórico de Moçambique." MOCAMBIQUE, DOCUMENTARIO TRIMESTRAL,
     nos. 72-79, 1952-54; no. 81, 1955: 135-150.

234. Pinto, Frederico da Silva. ROTEIRO HISTORICO-BIOGRAFICO DA CIDADE DE
     LOURENCO MARQUES. Lourenço Marques, 1965. 204 p.

Southern Africa

Lesotho (Basutoland)

235. CATALOGUE OF THE BASUTOLAND GOVERNMENT ARCHIVES. Prepared Nov. 1962.
     74 p. Available from the Bursar, Pius XII College, P.O. Roma,
     Basutoland.

The archives contain such valuable material as (1) census reports from 1891; (2) papers, letters, and circulars of the Resident Commissioner's office, 1884-1917; (3) correspondence of the Governor's agents, 1871-84, of the High Commissioner from 1884 to 1917, and general from 1917 to 1931; (4) council proceedings; (5) district correspondence; (6) diaries, letter books, Pitso books, police correspondence, etc.

South Africa

Note: South Africa has the most extensive and the most widely used archival system in Africa. The South African archival system is administered as an organic whole. The Union Archives at Pretoria administer the bulk of the records amassed since the creation of the Union of South Africa in 1910. The Transvaal archives are likewise at Pretoria; the Cape archives are at Cape Town, the Natal archives are at Pietermaritzburg; and the Orange Free State archives are at Bloemfontein. The archives of South West Africa are located at Windhoek; they are administered separately, but come under the authority of the South African Chief Archivist.

236. Botha, Carol. A CATALOGUE OF MANUSCRIPTS AND PAPERS IN THE KILLIE CAMPBELL AFRICANA COLLECTION RELATING TO THE AFRICAN PEOPLES. Johannesburg, Department of Bibliography, Librarianship and Typography, University of the Witwatersrand, 1967. 85 p.

237. Botha, Colin Graham. CAPE ARCHIVES AND RECORDS. Cape Town, C. Struik, 1962. 331 p. (COLLECTED WORKS, v. 3)

This has a useful historical account, especially chap. v, "The Public Archives of South Africa, 1652-1910," p. 113-211. Appendix 5 (p. 205-207) of this chapter gives a list of publications relating to documents in the Cape Archives; appendix 6 (p. 208-209) contains another useful list, "Transcripts of Documents in Europe in the Cape Archives." An earlier publication of this chapter appeared in 1928 with the same title (Cape Town, Cape Times, Ltd., 108 p.).

238. Cape of Good Hope. Archives. A BRIEF GUIDE TO THE VARIOUS CLASSES OF DOCUMENTS IN THE CAPE ARCHIVES FOR THE PERIOD 1652-1806. By C. Graham Botha, in charge of Cape Archives. Cape Town, Cape Times, Ltd., 1918. 85 p. 4 facs.

239. Cape of Good Hope. Archives. LISTS AND INVENTORIES AVAILABLE IN THE CAPE DEPOT. Cape Town, n.d. 9 p.

A brief mimeographed checklist of material housed in the Archives. Similar lists exist for the other Archives Depots as well.

240. Johannesburg. University of the Witwatersrand. Library. GUIDE TO
     THE ARCHIVES AND PAPERS. Johannesburg, 1967. 60 p.

241. Kieser, A. SOUTH AFRICA'S ARCHIVES. Johannesburg, Hayne and Gibson,
     1958. 10 p. (Fact Paper no. 58, May 1958)

242. Long, Una. AN INDEX TO AUTHORS OF UNOFFICIAL, PRIVATELY-OWNED MANU-
     SCRIPTS RELATING TO THE HISTORY OF SOUTH AFRICA, 1812-1920, BEING
     THE RESULT OF TWO YEARS' RESEARCH. Cape Town, University of Cape
     Town, 1947.

     Edition limited to 200 copies; very scarce and important work.

243. Musiker, Reuben. GUIDE TO SOURCES OF INFORMATION IN THE HUMANITIES.
     Potchefstroom, Potchefstroom University in collaboration with
     the South African Library Association, 1962. 100 p.

     A directory of libraries and special collections in nonscientific
     and nontechnical fields. Special attention has been paid to libraries
     of Africana. The material is alphabetically arranged, with subject
     and geographical indexes. See also Musiker's SPECIAL LIBRARIES: A
     GENERAL SURVEY, WITH PARTICULAR REFERENCE TO SOUTH AFRICA (Metuchen,
     N.J., Scarecrow Press, 1970, 215 p.).

244. Quinn, Gerald D., and Otto H. Spohr, comps. HANDLIST OF MANUSCRIPTS
     IN THE UNIVERSITY OF CAPE TOWN LIBRARIES. Edited by R. F. M.
     Immelman. Cape Town, University of Cape Town Libraries, 1968.
     81 p. ports., facsims.

245. Robinson, H. M. "South African Library Scene." LIBRARY WORLD, v. 64,
     May 1963: 292-296.

246. S.A. ARGIEFBLAD. S.A. ARCHIVES JOURNAL. no. 1- 1959- Pretoria.
     Annual.

     The first number, issued by the Archives of South Africa, includes
     articles in Afrikaans and English on the history and development of
     archival agencies and work in South Africa. No. 2 and subsequent
     issues appear as the official organ of the newly organized South
     African Association of Archivists.

247. South Africa. Archives. ANNUAL REPORT OF THE DIRECTOR OF ARCHIVES.
     Pretoria, The Archives.

     These annual reports are very comprehensive. They give detailed
information about archives staff, work performed, preparation of documents for binding and microfilms, research and supply service, public
use of the Archives, the archives depots, publications, and schedule
of fees. The REPORT for 1962 gives as Annexure 2 (p. 41-46) the full
text of the Archives Act no. 6 of 1962, which provides for the custody,
care, and control of archives in South Africa and South-West Africa.
The REPORT for 1963 gives as Annexure 1 (p. 51-62) the archives regulations. Both reports include organization charts of the Archives,
showing at a glance the structure of the establishment.

248. South Africa. Archives. LIST OF ARCHIVES PUBLICATIONS PUBLISHED
     OFFICIALLY AFTER 1925. Pretoria, The Archives, 1964. 9 p.
     mimeographed.

     A full list of archives publications giving author, title, and
price of each publication. It includes a full contents list of
ARCHIVES YEARBOOK FOR SOUTH AFRICAN HISTORY (Vols. I-XXVI, 1938-63),
and has details of South African archival records for each province.

249. Note: A useful series of popular, descriptive, well-illustrated
     articles on the various archives depots appeared in the following
     issues of the periodical LANTERN (Pretoria, South African Association
     for the Advancement of Knowledge and Culture):

     a)   South African archives. General article, v. 7, Dec. 1957:
               126-133 (in Afrikaans, with English summary); article
               on government archives, v. 9, Mar. 1960: 294-301 (in
               Afrikaans, with English summary).

     b)   Cape. v. 7, Mar. 1958: 248-261 (in Afrikaans, with English
               summary).

     c)   Natal. v. 8, Mar. 1959: 268-279 (in English).

     d)   Orange Free State. v. 8, Dec. 1958: 154-161 (in Afrikaans,
               with English summary).

     e)   Transvaal. v. 9, Dec. 1959: 142-153 (in English).

250. South African Council for Scientific and Industrial Research. DIRECTORY
     OF SCIENTIFIC RESOURCES IN SOUTH AFRICA. Pretoria, The Council,
     1961- loose-leaf binder.

A work planned for continuous revision and comprising the following sections: 1, Scientific research organizations in South Africa-- a list of scientific institutes, government departments, museums, etc., giving nature of research and special facilities; 2, Guide to sources of scientific, technical, and medical information in South African libraries--the scientific counterpart of R. Musiker's GUIDE TO SOURCES OF INFORMATION IN THE HUMANITIES; 3, Scientific and technical societies in South Africa--with addresses, objects, publications, etc.; 4, Scientific and technical periodicals published in South Africa; 5, Acronyms.

Sections 1, 2, and 3 of this directory supersede the South African entries in the Scientific Council for Africa South of the Sahara, DIRECTORY OF SCIENTIFIC AND TECHNICAL LIBRARIES IN AFRICA SOUTH OF THE SAHARA (1954) and DIRECTORY OF SCIENTIFIC INSTITUTES, ORGANISATIONS, AND SERVICES IN AFRICA SOUTH OF THE SAHARA (1954).

251.   SOUTH AFRICAN LIBRARIES.   1933-   Pretoria, South African Library
       Association.   Quarterly.

       Edited by Dr. P. A. Coetzee, Department of Library Science, University of Pretoria. The chief organ for news of libraries in South Africa, this quarterly includes articles and notes, bibliographical notices and book reviews. Cumulated indexes are issued every two years.

252.   South African Library Association. DIRECTORY OF SCIENTIFIC, TECHNICAL
       AND MEDICAL LIBRARIES IN THE UNION OF SOUTH AFRICA.   Edited by
       Hazel Mews and P. E. Krige. Pretoria, South African Council for
       Scientific and Industrial Research, 1949. 1 v. unpaged.

       The Association also publishes an annual report, which contains additional information on libraries.

253.   South African Public Library, Cape Town. QUARTERLY BULLETIN. KWAR-
       TAALBLAD. v. 1- Sept. 1946- Cape Town. illus.

       In this journal (title has varied), a major source for bibliographies of South African publications (see also in area section), appear as well news notes and articles of library interest. See also AFRICANA NEWS AND NOTES, and C. Pama, ed., THE SOUTH AFRICAN LIBRARY: ITS HISTORY, COLLECTIONS AND LIBRARIANS (Cape Town, Balkema, 1968, 216 p.).

Malagasy Republic (Madagascar) and the Mascarenes

Malagasy Republic

254. "Les archives de Madagascar." BULLETIN DE MADAGASCAR, no. 150, Nov. 1958: 973-974.

255. Decary, Raymond. "Chronique de l'histoire coloniale: Madagascar (1950-1955)." REVUE D'HISTOIRE DES COLONIES, v. 43, no. 150, 1956: 82-119.

    In the first chapter the author lists many documents of special importance preserved in the Archives of the Gouvernement Général in Tananarive.

256. Deschamps, Hubert J. "Conceptions, problèmes et sources de l'histoire de Madagascar." JOURNAL OF AFRICAN HISTORY, v. 1, no. 2, 1960; 249-256.

    Includes account of existing archives.

257. Molet, Louis. "Les manuscrits arabico-malgaches." REVUE DE MADAGASCAR, v. 30, Jan. 1957: 53-61.

258. Sicard, Fernand. "Les archives de Madagascar." COMPTES RENDUS MENSUELS DES SEANCES DE L'ACADEMIE DES SCIENCES D'CUTRE-MER, v. 25, no. 8, 1965: 420-431.

    A report, followed by a panel discussion, on how the archives of the Malagasy Republic have been and are being collected, classified, and utilized.

259. "Tananarive, Madagascar." BULLETIN DES BIBLIOTHEQUES DE FRANCE, v. 6, Apr. 1961: 190.

    Note on the Bibliothèque Universitaire de Tananarive, which on the occasion of a visit by French statesmen, Feb. 1961, published a mimeographed brochure describing its development since its opening in Jan. 1960. The staff, all Malagasy, at that time numbered 17.

260. Valette, Jean. GUIDE DES SOURCES DE L'HISTOIRE RELIGIEUSE ANTERIEURE
        A 1896: INVENTAIRE DE LA SERIE HH (CULTES). Tananarive, Malagasy
        Republic, Service des Archives et de la Documentation, 1962. 31
        p.

        Prepared by the archivist of the Malagasy Republic, this guide
is an inventory of material on Protestant and Catholic missions up
to 1896. Included is the correspondence addressed by the missionaries
to the government, with an indication of the number of pieces and the
dates. The Protestant missions concerned are the London Missionary
Society, the Society of the Propagation of the Gospel, the Friends'
Foreign Mission Association, and the Norske Mission or Mission
Norvégienne. The Catholic missions are the Société de Jésus, Frères
des Ecoles Chrétiennes, and Soeurs de St. Joseph Cluny.

261. Valette, Jean. "Les instruments de travail aux archives de la
        République malgache." AFRICANA NEWSLETTER, v. 2, no. 1, 1964:
        70-72.

        Lists the various typed summaries and inventories available on
Jan. 1, 1964, for material (some of it going back to the 1820's) deposited at the Archives. For two guides already published, see the
preceding and following entries.

262. Valette, Jean. INVENTAIRE DE LA SERIE MI DES ARCHIVES DE LA
        REPUBLIQUE MALGACHE. Tananarive, Impr. Nationale, 1963. 16 p.

        Reprinted from the BULLETIN DE MADAGASCAR, no. 201, Feb. 1963:
163-176.

        Useful guide to the recently microfilmed collections deposited
at the National Archives of the Malagasy Republic after an intensive
search for foreign source materials conducted by the archivist, Jean
Valette. The inventory contains such items as photocopies from archives
in Mauritius pertaining to Madagascar, 1767-1848; microfilms of the
correspondence of General Gallieni, deposited at the Bibliothèque
Nationale in Paris; microfilms of documents on Madagascar preserved
at the Bibliothèque Centrale des Archives du Ministère de la Marine
de France; microfilms of documents relating to Madagascar before 1789
deposited at the Archives du Ministère des Affaires Etrangères de
France as well as certain political correspondence for the period
1816-85 from the same collections. In addition to these sources,
the guide lists manuscripts from the British Museum and the National
Archives of the United States of America concerning Madagascar.

263. Valette, Jean. "La Série C des archives de la République malgache."
        BULLETIN DE MADAGASCAR, no. 232, Sept. 1965: 804-806.

Mascarenes

264. Béchet, Roger O., ed. INVENTAIRE DES REGISTRES PAROISSIAUX DE L'ILE
DE FRANCE (ILE MAURICE) COMPAGNIE DES INDES, 1722-1767. Port
Louis, General Print. and Stationery Co., 1951-55. 3 v.

Bibliographical footnotes.

265. Lartin, U. "Archives de la Réunion." AFRICANA NEWSLETTER, v. 2, no.
1, 1964: 72-74.

Inventories, some published, of the archival holdings are listed,
as are a few other publications of the archives. Journals and reviews
of the nineteenth and twentieth centuries are also held.

266. Lougnon, Albert. DOCUMENTS CONCERNANT LES ILES DE BOURBON ET DE
FRANCE PENDANT LA REGIE DE LA COMPAGNIE DES INDES: REPERTOIRE
DE PIECES CONSERVEES DANS DIVERS DEPOTS D'ARCHIVES DE PARIS.
Nérac, Impr. G. Couderc, 1953. xxxvi, 202 p.

Review in AMERICAN ARCHIVIST, v. 20, Jan. 1955: 81-82.

267. Mauritius. Archives Department. BIBLIOGRAPHY OF MAURITIUS, 1502-
1954, COVERING THE PRINTED RECORDS, MANUSCRIPTS, ARCHIVALIA
AND CARTOGRAPHIC MATERIAL. By A. Toussaint, Chief Archivist.
Port Louis, Esclapon, 1956. xvii, 884 p.

The active interest of Mr. Toussaint has resulted in exceptionally
complete recording of Mauritian archives, as shown in this work and in
the items below.

268. Mauritius. Archives Department. REPORT. 1950- Port Louis, Govt.
Printer. Annual.

Previously issued as REPORT of the Archives Branch.

269. Pérotin, Yves. "The Archives of Réunion: A Workshop Opened for
Historical Research." AMERICAN ARCHIVIST, v. 17, July 1954:
257-261.

270. Toussaint, Auguste. "The Mauritius Archives." INDIAN ARCHIVES, v. 6,
          Jan.- Dec. 1952: 13-20.

          Abstract in LIBRARY SCIENCE ABSTRACTS, v. 4, no. 4, 1953: no.
      3311.

271. Toussaint, Auguste. REPERTOIRE DES ARCHIVES DE L'ILE DE FRANCE
          PENDANT LA REGIE DE LA COMPAGNIE DES INDES, 1715-1768. Nérac,
          Impr. G. Couderc, 1956. 44 p. (Mauritius Archives Publication
          Fund Publication, no. 3)

CHAPTER 3

PUBLISHERS AND BOOKDEALERS

Nowhere is the expansion of African studies during the present decade
more evident than in the publication and sale of books. In the late 1950's
only a handful of firms in England, France, Belgium, and South Africa (and
fewer in the United States) specialized in Africana, either as publishers
or booksellers. Most prominent publishing houses, among them practically
all American publishers, offered only occasional African titles. Catalogues
of Africana for sale came from a few bookshops which kept large stocks of
current and older material or dealt in collector sales. Such catalogues
gave authors' names, titles, and prices, but not publishers. Few publishers
sent out their own lists of works on Africa.

Today all major publishers, many small commercial houses, and, most
conspicuously, the university presses offer numerous African titles, and
the Africanist librarian receives a steady stream of announcements. The
United States, if not taking over the lead from Great Britain, is at least
catching up; many books appear simultaneously in the two countries. Germany,
Scandinavia, Russia, India, and other nations are entering into the Africana
publishing game. So many publishers in the United States are bringing out
their more popular works in paperbound editions that a separate reprint from
the R. W. Bowker PAPERBACKS IN PRINT listing African titles has several times
been issued. A fast-growing number of publishers are entering the reprint
field. The extent of output on Africa is well reflected in two booksellers'
catalogues now being published serially: AFRICAN QUARTERLY, by Kegan Paul,
Trench, Trubner in London, and AFRICANA CATALOGUE, from International University Booksellers, Inc., in New York. In the following pages some of the
currently better-known firms are listed; the choice could be expanded in-
definitely.

In the United States, catalogues of Africana have been sent out recently
by several booksellers, among them:

Cellar Book Shop, 18090 Wyoming, Detroit, Michigan 48221

El Cascajero, 506 West Broadway, New York, N.Y. 10012

East and West Shop, 132 East 61st Street, New York, N.Y. 10021

Humanities Press, 303 Park Avenue S., New York, N.Y. 10010

Lawrence Verry, Inc., 16 Holmes Street, Mystic, Connecticut 06355
     Distributors for Struik, Johannesburg.

The International University Booksellers, Inc. (101 Fifth Avenue, New York, N.Y. 10003) launched its quarterly catalogue series with AFRICANA CATALOGUE NO. 1: NEW BOOKS PUBLISHED JANUARY 1967-OCTOBER 1968, compiled by Hans M. Zell (1968, 161 p.). The new Africana Center of I.U.B. plans a reprinting and publishing program, as well as this catalogue, which is designed to serve as an extensive bibliographic guide as well as a sales catalogue. It includes works in foreign languages, notably in French, and writings by African authors. The list is in two parts, the first by subject, the second in geographical arrangement, with author index.

Prominent noninstitutional publishers are:

     International Publications Service, 303 Park Avenue South, New
          York, N.Y. 10010

          Brings out American editions of works published abroad,
     including various guidebooks and directories and the monographic
     publications of the OAU Scientific, Technical and Research Commis-
     sion (formerly CCTA/CSA).

     Oceana Publications, Inc., Dobbs Ferry, N.Y. 10522

          This firm acquires retrospective and new works on Africa,
     serials, documents, papers, etc., through representatives in
     Africa and issues reprints and its own publications.

     Frederick A. Praeger, Inc., 111 Fourth Avenue, New York, N.Y.
          10003

          Issues periodically lists of original contributions and
     American editions of books from British publishers; has paperback
     series.

Most of the larger publishers include a few books on Africa in their yearly output.

Among university publishing organizations, those issuing African materials with regularity are:

Boston University Press (African Research Studies and individual studies)

University of California Press

Hoover Institution Press, Stanford University

Johns Hopkins Press

Northwestern University Press (Northwestern University African Studies)

Stanford University Press

University of Wisconsin Press

African studies are not lacking on the lists from Columbia, Harvard, Princeton, Yale, Indiana University, University of North Carolina, University of Michigan, and most other large universities. Advance notices of their forthcoming works are sent regularly to libraries and individual African specialists. (Forthcoming titles are also to be seen in the quarterly announcement issues of PUBLISHERS' WEEKLY.)

A CURRENT BIBLIOGRAPHY ON AFRICAN AFFAIRS published monthly by the African Bibliographic Center in Washington (see no. 292) carries a listing by publisher of forthcoming books. In addition, in its Special Bibliographic Series the Center has issued lists entitled A CURRENT VIEW OF AFRICANA. These are arranged by publishing houses in the United States and abroad, with full bibliographical information on the offerings of each over a specified period (the first for Jan.-July 1964, the second 1965-66). The lists have author, title, and subject indexes, and entries are briefly annotated. The 1966 publication also has at the end of each entry a notation such as "Recommended for specialized collections" and the like.

The nonprofit educational organization, Franklin Publications, which prepared the reports BOOKS IN NIGERIA AND EAST AFRICA (New York [1961?] 26 l.), BOOKS FOR GHANA AND NIGERIA (New York, 1962, 33 l.), BOOKS IN WEST AFRICA (New York, 1963, 44 p.), and BOOKS IN EAST AFRICA (New York, 1964, 25 p.), does not publish books for Africa, but helps develop local book industries, its programs carried out entirely by nationals of the countries in Asia and Africa where it operates.

In the United Kingdom a notable catalogue is sent out serially each quarter by Kegan Paul, Trench, Trubner & Co., 43 Great Russell Street, London, W.C.1: AFRICA QUARTERLY, 1963-. The publishers, who have specialized in the sale of new and old Africana, announce this as "a bibliographical guide to important new publications of all countries relating to the contemporary African scene, giving [as well] particulars of an extensive selection from our stock of scarce and early material on the history and peoples of the African continent." The list is divided into two parts, "New Publications" first, then the older works from the dealer's stock. Entries are by title and author, with prices, but no publishers' names.

Catalogues of Africana come from many other booksellers, some of whom are also publishers. These include:

B. H. Blackwell, Ltd., 48-51 Broad Street, Oxford

Eric M. Bonner, 74 Belsize Park Gardens, London, N.W.3

W. & G. Foyle, Ltd., 119-25 Charing Cross Road, London, W.C.2

Susil Gupta, Antiquarian Booksellers, 12 Blakehall Crescent, London, E.11

Hammersmith Bookshop, Ltd., Liffords Place, High Street Barnes, London, S.W.13

W. Heffer & Sons, Ltd., 3-4 Petty Cury, Cambridge

Arthur Probsthain, 41 Great Russell Street, London, W.C.1

Charles J. Sawyer, Ltd., 12/13 Grafton Street, London, W.1

James Thin, 54-59 South Bridge, Edinburgh

Among British publishers contributing largely to the African field, pride of place goes to the Oxford University Press (offices also in New York), which prints, in addition to its own works, the more substantial scholarly contributions of several learned institutions—the International African Institute, the Royal Institute of International Affairs, the Institute of Race Relations, the Nigerian Institute of Social and Economic Research, etc. The Oxford University Press also handles British editions of many books from the American university presses, brought out simultaneously in both countries. It has recently launched the New Africa Series, addressed particularly to African elites. Cambridge University Press is publishing the JOURNAL OF MODERN AFRICAN STUDIES and other important Africana. Manchester University Press is handling the weightier publications of the Institute for Social Research of the new University of Zambia at Lusaka (the Institute was until late 1964 the Rhodes-Livingstone Institute). Chatto and Windus (the Oppenheimer Series), and Longmans, Green have for many years specialized in texts for an on Africa. Macmillan (simultaneously in New York), P. Alan, Gollancz, Faber & Faber, Hutchinson, Roy (who is bringing out reprints, as is Frank Cass also), and many other well-known British publishers increasingly have items of African interest on current lists. Among paperbacks, reprints and inexpensive editions of recent books are numerous, and some originals come out in paperback, including the notable Penguin African Series. A good idea of the scope of publishing on Africa can be gained from reviews and notices in the TIMES LITERARY SUPPLEMENT and especially from the more comprehensive BRITISH NATIONAL BIBLIOGRAPHY. Advance notices appear in the special announcement issues of the weekly BRITISH BOOKS.

In France, catalogues of Africana addressed to collectors have come intermittently from Librairie Orientale (H. Samuelian, 51, rue Monsieur-le-Prince, Paris 6), Librairie du Camée (3, rue de Valence, Paris 5), Hachette (79 boul. Saint-Germain, Paris 6), which is also a large publisher on Africa, notably in the guidebook field, Jean Polak Librairie (8, rue de l'Echaudé, Paris 6), Librairie "La Vieille Taupe" (1, rue des Fossés Saint-Jacques, Paris 5), and Présence Africaine (42 rue Descartes, Paris 5; 17, rue de Chaligny, Paris 12). Présence Africaine is both book dealer and publisher, concerned particularly with its own editions (see no. 298).

French publishers offering sizable lists of titles on Africa include also Payot (with a well-known introductory survey series, "Que sais-je?" as well as distinguished popular books; 106, boul. Saint-Germain, Paris 6); the Presses Universitaires de France (108, boul. Saint-Germain, Paris 6), publishers for the Sorbonne and other institutions of learning, which has a large corner on doctoral dissertations and professorial studies; the Mouton & Co. branch in Paris (45, rue de Lille, Paris 7; publications of Ecole Pratique des Hautes Etudes and the series Monde d'outre-mer passé et présent); the Librairie Générale de Droit et de Jurisprudence (20, rue Soufflot, Paris 5), which has the same function in its fields; the official Direction de la Documentation (part of Secrétariat Général du Gouvernement; publication arm, La Documentation Française, 31, quai Voltaire, Paris 7) and Office de la Recherche Scientifique et Technique Outre-Mer (ORSTROM; 20, rue Monsieur, Paris 7); Berger-Levrault (series Mondes d'outre-mer, etc.; 5, rue Auguste Comte, Paris 6); Diloutremer (specializing in documentation and guidebooks; 100, rue de Richelieu, Paris 2); and many others. The third part of the BIBLIOGRAPHIE DE LA FRANCE, the loose-leaf ANNONCES, is a source for news of current and forthcoming French books; the monthly BIBLIO is also useful; and reviews of more general works appear in the monthly BULLETIN CRITIQUE DU LIVRE FRANCAIS, and more selectively in the shorter English edition, RECENT FRENCH BOOKS. (See Winchell, no. 1, for descriptions of these general library tools.)

In Belgium the catalogue issued periodically by Pierre Hubaut (15, rue de l'Industrie, Brussels 4) was outstanding. A difficulty encountered here, however--one general to bookshop catalogues not giving publishers--is that individual titles in extensive series (such as the Mémoires of the Académie Royale des Sciences d'Outre-Mer) are not clearly identified; without close vigilance the librarian may therefore find that he has ordered items already coming on subscription. The problem looms large with Hubaut because the great majority of scientific studies of the Congo appear in the series of the officially sponsored institutions. An exception is CRISP, the Centre de Recherche et d'Information Socio-Politiques (35, rue du Congrès, Brussels 1), whose own independent publications are among the most important Belgian contributions to the African scene. Hubaut died in 1968 and his stock has been acquired by Drijver & Koolemans, Amsterdam. Another bookshop of increasing importance, Le Livre Africain (40, rue du Champ de Mars, Brussels 5), is the Belgian counterpart of Présence Africaine and, like it, handles works from liberal and African groups and writers. It issues a monthly bulletin, LE LIVRE AFRICAIN, in which, besides news, books, and pamphlets, there are frequent announcements of small nationalist journals just beginning.

In Holland, catalogues come from Mouton & Co. (P.O. Box 1132, The Hague; also in Paris), Martinus Nijhoff (9 Lange Voorhout, P.O. Box 269, The Hague), C. P. J. van der Peet (33-35 Nieuwe Spiegelstraat, Amsterdam), and Gé Nabrink (Korte Korjespoortesteeg 8, Amsterdam; AFRICA: CATALOGUE OF AN IMPORTANT COLLECTION OF OLD AND MODERN BOOKS AND PERIODICALS, 1965, 97 p.; Catalogue no. 163). All specialize in rare Africana.

In _Spain_ and _Portugal_ the largest publishers offering works on Africa are the official presses of the Instituto de Estudios Africanos and its parent body, the Consejo Superior de Investigaciones Científicas (Madrid), and the Junta de Investigaçãos Geográficas do Ultramar and the Agência Geral do Ultramar, Divisão de Publicaçãos et Biblioteca (both in Lisbon). A Portuguese bookshop presenting frequent lists of new and old books on Africa is R. B. Rosenthal (Rua do Alecem, 47-4, Lisbon 2). There are also O Mundo do Livro (Largo da Trinidade 13, Lisbon 2) and Livraria Castro e Silva (Rua de Rosa 31, Lisbon 2).

Notable antiquarian dealers in _Germany_ whose interests include Africa are F. A. Brockhaus (Räpplenstrasse 20, Stuttgart), Klaus Renner (Haar bei München), and Otto Harrassowitz (Taunusstrasse 5, Wiesbaden).

In _Africa_, catalogues are chiefly from government printers or the national or regional literature bureaus (see under Official Publications) or from the learned institutions, who often print the list of their publications on the endpapers of each new work. The conspicuous exception is South Africa, and notably the Cape Town bookseller C. Struik (Wale and Loop Streets, P.O. Box 1144). This house has for some years issued a monthly AFRICA BOOKS BULLETIN, as well as catalogues of Africana which include a wide selection of works published in the rest of English-speaking Africa and also British and American titles currently in stock. In early 1965 Struik brought out a comprehensive catalogue, AFRICA BOOKS: CATALOGUE OF SOUTH AFRICAN PUBLICATIONS, in two brochures, listing 762 items exclusive of government publications. His BULLETIN gives a good many advance notices of forthcoming material, particularly from South Africa and Rhodesia. He also has his own publishing firm. An enterprise called Africa Books, begun in Maseru, then moved to Rondebosch, Cape Province, has now been taken over by Struik. Its periodic mimeographed lists of available material included many official documents of early years.

Other South African bookdealers who specialize in rare Africana and from time to time issue lists of their stock are:

Frank R. Thorold, Raines Building, 54 Eloff Street, P.O. Box 241,
    Johannesburg
Africana Antiquarians (Pty.), Ltd., P.O. Box 455, Port Elizabeth

A new firm, African Universities Press, Lagos, has been set up by the British publisher André Deutsch. His aim is to provide inexpensive editions of books in English and vernacular languages. East Africa's only independent general publishing firm is the East African Publishing House opened in 1965. The EAPH has published over 100 books ranging from academic studies to primary school readers in various languages. Their program aims at publishing low-cost quality books and at encouraging indigenous authors (see its Modern African Library Series). Among other well-known bookshops in African cities are Clairafrique in Dakar, which handles the publications of IFAN, the University Bookshop in Ibadan, Librairie de Madagascar in Tananarive (B.P. HO2), the Educational Supply Association (ESA), S. J. Moore's Bookshop in Nairobi, and the Uganda Bookshop (also press) in Kampala.

Missionary presses publish material other than Bible translations or religious tracts, e.g., grammars, word lists, and vernacular histories and literary works. Many missionary presses also run bookshops. Notable among these are the Church Missionary Society (CMS), the Methodist Book Depot, the Presbyterian Book Depot, the Sudan Interior Mission (SIM), and the Librairie Évangélique du Congo, Kinshasa, Congo.

There are a few guides to the book trade to which reference may be made. Perhaps the most useful one yet published is THE ACQUISITION OF AFRICANA: A BRIEF REVIEW OF SOME COMMERCIAL SOURCES, compiled by Alan R. Taylor and others (Bloomington, Indiana University Library, 1968, 17 p.). In this leaflet Mr. Taylor surveyed bookstores in the United States and abroad which specialize in Africana. A much extended revision is being prepared in 1969, probably to be published by the African Bibliographic Center.

The following references may also be useful:

a) "Book Dealers in Africa." AFRICANA NEWSLETTER, v. 1, no. 2, Spring 1963: 24-28.

   A preliminary listing of names and addresses of book-dealers in 38 African countries.

b) NcNiff, Philip J., comp. A LIST OF BOOK DEALERS IN UNDER-DEVELOPED COUNTRIES. Chicago, Resources and Technical Services Division, American Library Association, 1963. 40 <u>1</u>.

   Compiled for the Policy and Research Committee, Acquisitions Section, as an aid for libraries developing acquisitions programs in Africa, the Far East, etc. It is based on surveys of the experience of libraries with major programs in each of the areas covered.

c) Panofsky, Hans E. "Acquisition of Library Materials from Africa." LIBRARY RESOURCES AND TECHNICAL SERVICES, v. 7, no. 1, Winter 1963: 38-46.

   Includes bibliography.

d) PUBLISHERS' WORLD: YEARBOOK. 1965- New York, Bowker.

   The first edition of this big volume contains country-by-country lists of booksellers and publishers throughout the world, arranged by continent and beginning with Africa. Additional features of African interest in the work include essays on publishing in Nigeria and other African countries and a listing of libraries.

In addition, names and addresses of publishers, especially official and institutional publishers, and of bookshops in Africa and Europe are included in the helpful reports made by Africanist librarians after buying trips abroad. Mr. Panofsky's article falls into this category. There have been a succession of reports on PUBLICATION SURVEY TRIP(s) from the African Section of the Library of Congress: to West and South Africa by Conrad C. Reining, 1962; to Central and East Africa, also by Dr. Reining, 1963; to West Africa and France by Julian W. Witherell, 1964; to Equatorial and West Africa, France and Belgium by Dr. Witherell, 1965; to West, Central, and Southern Africa by Sharon B. Lockwood, Dec. 1966; to West Africa, Ethiopia, France and Portugal by Dr. Witherell, May 1968; to West Africa, Equatorial Africa, Tunisia, France and Belgium by Samir M. Zoghby, July 1968. Each report has been more voluminous than the last, increasing from 18 pages in 1962 to 61 pages in 1968. These lists were not published for general circulation, but a few copies have been made available by the African Section. Reports of the same nature were written by Miss Dorothy Harmon of the UCLA Library, AFRICAN ACQUISITIONS TRIP, MARCH-MAY 1963, and by Eugene de Benko of Michigan State University. The latter's outstanding REPORT ON A LIBRARY ACQUISITION TRIP TO AFRICA, JUNE-SEPTEMBER 1966 contains valuable tips on bookdealers, lists and addresses of political organizations, and a bibliography of "Market Literature." It was prepared as a report to the Midwest Universities Consortium for International Activities, Inc. (MUCIA), but copies may be obtained from Michigan State University Library, East Lansing (42 p. and supplements). See also Sigfred Taubert, AFRICAN BOOK TRADE DIRECTORY, 1970 (Munich, Verlag Dokumentation, 1970, 319 p.).

Reprints

The significance for African studies of the older sources is reflected in current interest in reprints. Many classics of African voyages and explorations long out of print are now appearing in modern editions, from Leo Africanus and al-Bakri to Mary Kingsley. There are new editions of important studies from the pre-World War II period. The most valuable publications of the International African Institute are being reprinted.

In South Africa and Rhodesia pioneer journals and records are being reproduced in several handsome series. Commercial houses as well as university presses in England and America are joining in the effort to bring within reach important out-of-print material. Frank Cass & Co., Ltd. (8-10 Woburn Walk, London, W.C.1; U.S. distributors: Barnes & Noble, Inc., 105 Fifth Avenue, New York, N.Y. 10003), is issuing the Cass Library of African Studies, and the 1968 list describes 216 available or forthcoming works. Its Travels and Narratives series has 69 books for the nineteenth century, with 18 even earlier (from 1591 through the 1600's) and one for the twentieth century, while most of the 24 in the Missionary Researches and Travels series are of nineteenth-century origin also. The 104 works in the General Series are mainly publications of the first half of the twentieth century. Many of the volumes include new introductions by scholars in the relevant field. Routledge & Kegan Paul, Ltd., and Frederick A. Praeger, Inc., recently began publishing a valuable reprint series, Travellers and Explorers (see no. 559).

Gregg International Publishers, Ltd. (Westmead, Farnborough, Hants, England; Gregg Press, Inc., 171 East Ridgewood Avenue, Ridgewood, N.J. 07450), is reissuing needed works for the African linguistics field. In 1967 the first number in the African Heritage series, edited by G. Shepperson, appeared: CHRISTIANITY, ISLAM AND THE NEGRO RACE, by Edward W. Blyden (Edinburgh, University Press, xviii, ix, 407 p.); a reprint of WEST AFRICAN COUNTRIES AND PEOPLES, BRITISH AND NATIVE, by James Africanus Beale Horton, is also planned. The Johnson Reprint Corporation (111 Fifth Avenue, New York, N.Y. 10003) is issuing African titles in a new series, Landmarks in Anthropology, as well as reprinting older journals. Kraus Reprints in New York also offers journal titles. Valuable African works have been reissued in Collection U.N.E.S.C.O. d'oeuvres représentatives, Série africaine, including important Arabic documents dealing with the Western Sudan region (see no. 1654).

A helpful account of reprint projects, "Windfall for African Studies: Some Forthcoming Reprints," by John Ralph Willis, was published in the AFRICANA NEWSLETTER, v. 2, no. 2, 1964: 32-36. In the Dec. 1968 issue of the AFRICAN STUDIES BULLETIN Joan Ellis of the Foreign Area Materials Center contributed a 34-page list of "Reprints of Books and Journals on Africa" (v. 11, no. 3: 329-362). The last two pages contain a list of reprint publishers. A sequel, "Books and Documents on Africa in Microform," appeared in the Apr. 1969 issue of the BULLETIN. For further announcements of reprints, as for other news relating to African studies, the Africanist journals are to be consulted.

Microfilms

The standard library tool for lists of microfilms is SUBJECT GUIDE TO MICROFORMS IN PRINT (Washington, D.C., Microcard Editions, 1962/63-). It is an author-title list but has an index of subjects, in which African is included. There is also the Library of Congress NATIONAL REGISTER OF MICROFORM MASTERS (Sept. 1965-), a supplement to the NATIONAL UNION CATALOG and compiled with the cooperation of the American Library Association and the Association of Research Libraries; its aim is to provide a complete national record of microform masters from which libraries may acquire prints.

A microfilm program in the United States is being sponsored by the Libraries-Archives Committee of the African Studies Association and is described in the AFRICAN STUDIES BULLETIN, v. 8, no. 1, Apr. 1965: 77-79, "Cooperative African Microfilm Project (CAMP)." Under this plan a cooperative fund has been established. Among the projects is the microfilming of African newspapers, older government documents, journals, political ephemera, and archives. The conditions of subscription and specific projects under way are explained in the article.

The reproduction of newspapers and official gazettes on microfilm is also noted in the sections on bibliographies of serials (see nos. 371 and 398) and bibliographies of official publications (see no. 408). A large-scale project for micropublication of an extensive collection of basic books and serials on Africa is currently under way in Europe. The marketing and administration center is the Inter Documentation Company AG, Poststrasse 9, Zug, Switzerland; the central processing unit is now the Research Publications NV, Rijnsburgerweg 177, Leiden, the Netherlands (this was begun as the International Documentation Centre AB, Tumba, Sweden). Camera units are maintained in Stockholm, Helsinki, London, Paris, and Leiden. Catalogues and bibliographies are a part of the project. The filming of Congolese material in Belgium and the Congo is already well started.

PART II

BIBLIOGRAPHIES FOR AFRICA IN GENERAL

CHAPTER 4

BIBLIOGRAPHIES OF BIBLIOGRAPHIES

272. Note: The Grey bibliography mentioned below (no. 277) is unique in its completeness and has stood for many years as the standard work. African bibliographies are included with bibliographical work in all other fields in several well-known guides, all fully described by Winchell, for example:

    a) Besterman, Theodore. A WORLD BIBLIOGRAPHY OF BIBLIO-
          GRAPHIES AND OF BIBLIOGRAPHICAL CATALOGUES,
          CALENDARS, ABSTRACTS, DIGESTS, INDEXES, AND THE
          LIKE. 4th ed., rev. and greatly enl. throughout.
          Lausanne, Societas Bibliographica, 1965-66. 5 v.

          Earlier editions, 1939-40, 1947-49, 1955-56. The fourth
          edition has more than 117,000 bibliographies, classified
          under almost 16,000 headings and subheadings. Over 55,000
          are in English; there are 70 in Afrikaans. An index takes
          up Vol. V.

    b) BIBLIOGRAPHIC INDEX. v. 1- 1937- New York, H. W. Wilson
          Co. Semiannual and cumulative annual volume.

    c) BIBLIOGRAPHICAL SERVICES THROUGHOUT THE WORLD, 1950-1959.
          Compiled by R. L. Collison. Paris, UNESCO, 1961.
          228 p. Also annual reports.

273. Bogaert, Jozef. SCIENCES HUMAINES EN AFRIQUE NOIRE: GUIDE BIBLIOGRA-
      PHIQUE (1945-1965). Bruxelles, Centre de Documentation Econo-
      mique et Sociale Africaine (CEDESA), 1966. 226 p. (Enquêtes
      bibliographiques, no. 15)

    The compiler has brought together what he considers the most
important sources and reference works dealing with Black Africa--
over 1,500 entries. Books, monographs, journals, articles, and

government publications are included. Entries have information on author, title, source of the article, place of publication, publisher, date, and pages, and a number of them are briefly annotated. Part 1 consists of general bibliographies and lists, among them bibliographies of bibliographies, national bibliographies, retrospective bibliographies, bibliographies of periodicals, bibliographies of theses, and lists of encyclopedias, annuals, atlases, and tourist guides. Part 2 is arranged by subject--e.g., philosophy, psychology, religion, missions; social sciences (including economics, anthropology and sociology, politics and government, international relations, law, education); linguistics; arts and literature; history, archaeology, archives; geography. There are three helpful indexes: one on individual and corporate authors and titles (without specific authors), p. 188-212; a geographical index, p. 213-217; and a subject index, p. 218-225.

Bogaert was librarian for six years at Lovanium University, Leopoldville (Kinshasa), before going to the University of Louvain at Courtrai. He was the compiler of an earlier bibliography, LES SCIENCES HUMAINES ET L'AFRIQUE NOIRE AU SUD DU SAHARA: GUIDE BIBLIOGRAPHIQUE (Léopoldville, Editions de l'Université Lovanium, 1964, 79 p.).

274. Cambridge. University. African Studies Centre. BIBLIOGRAPHY OF AFRICAN BIBLIOGRAPHIES. Compiled by Anthea Garling. Cambridge, Eng., 1968. 138 p. Mimeographed. (Occasional Papers, no. 1)

This compact bibliography, covering references from the earliest times to 1966, is derived from relevant titles in Besterman's work (see no. 272a), the Centre's own current bibliographical catalogue, and bibliographical cards provided by CARDAN. Arrangement is by country under regional headings and alphabetical by author within each country. Though the work contains some misinformation, some older references of questionable values, and suffers from a high proportion of typographical errors, it nevertheless constitutes a valuable reference tool.

275. International Conference on African Bibliography, Nairobi, Dec. 1967. THE BIBLIOGRAPHY OF AFRICA: PROCEEDINGS AND PAPERS OF THE INTERNATIONAL CONFERENCE ON AFRICAN BIBLIOGRAPHY, NAIROBI, 4-8 DEC. 1967. London, Cass, 1970. 362 p.

The documents of this important conference include bibliographies prepared in advance of the meeting, as well as discussion of the aims and techniques of bibliographical efforts in and concerning Africa. The SURVEY OF CURRENT BIBLIOGRAPHICAL SERVICES ON AFRICA prepared as a working paper has already been referred to (see no. 23).

The gathering also includes papers on retrospective bibliographies, current bibliographic services, manuscript and archival collections, ephemeral materials, national bibliographies, etc.

276. Matthews, Daniel G. "African Bibliography Today: Selected and Current Bibliographical Tools for African Studies, 1967-68." CURRENT BIBLIOGRAPHY ON AFRICAN AFFAIRS, n.s. no. 1, Nov. 1968: 4-17.

A short "commentary" on the present state of African bibliography is followed by a classed list of 100-odd titles, all recent bibliographies of significance. In his discussion of background the author comments on the International Conference on African Bibliography in Nairobi in 1967.

277. South African Public Library, Cape Town. A BIBLIOGRAPHY OF AFRICAN BIBLIOGRAPHIES COVERING TERRITORIES SOUTH OF THE SAHARA. 4th ed., rev. to Nov. 1960 by A. M. Lewin Robinson. Cape Town, The Library, 1961. 79 p. (Grey Bibliographies, no. 7)

A most important bibliographical source, first compiled in Oct. 1942. Entries are limited to bibliographies of some length and substance. Arrangement is according to the Universal Decimal Classification, with several modifications. The bibliography is supplemented in the QUARTERLY BULLETIN of the South African Public Library (1946-, Cape Town, The Library).

Other important bibliographical sources for primary material are the Bibliographical Series of the University of Cape Town School of Librarianship and the student projects of the University of the Witwatersrand Department of Bibliography, Librarianship, and Typography. The July 1966 catalogue of the University of Cape Town Bibliographical Series lists 288 bibliographies on a variety of subjects, including many in the African studies field. These are listed in the current national bibliographies and in the Grey Bibliographies, no. 7. A new edition is in preparation (1969).

CHAPTER 5

CURRENT BIBLIOGRAPHIES

Note: Sources for current and continuing information on new writings about
Africa are almost inexhaustible. There are a few serial bibliographies devoted to Africa, and practically all significant reviews and journals in
the African field give more or less space to book reviews and notices. The
numerous general bibliographical and book reviewing organs are often more
ready library tools than the Africanist serials, and in view of the quantity
of writing now appearing on Africa, they reward attention. Abstracting services are few except in special fields; here the approach is usually by
discipline, e.g., agriculture, economic aid, library science, etc., and most
tools of this nature are not specifically for Africa but cover the tropics,
underdeveloped countries, or the world scene. In this section only the most
useful serials covering the whole field of African studies are named.

278. For analysis of the general current bibliographies and book review
        services, reference may be made to Winchell (no. 1). A brief
        listing by country might suggest:

   For the United States:

   a)   AMERICAN BOOK PUBLISHING RECORD. New York, Bowker. Monthly.

          A monthly cumulation from the Weekly Record listing of
          PUBLISHERS' WEEKLY; arranged by subject (Dewey decimal
          classification). It includes books printed and published
          abroad and distributed in the United States. There are two
          indexes, one by author and one by title and subject.

   b)   CUMULATIVE BOOK INDEX. New York, H. W. Wilson Co. Monthly
          and cumulated.

          Approach is by author and subject.

   c)   FORTHCOMING BOOKS. 1966- New York, Bowker. Every 2 months.

          Each bimonthly issue gives a comprehensive listing

of all books planned for publication in the coming five months. Author and title sections are separate.

d)   Public Affairs Information Service. BULLETIN. New York, Public Affairs Information Service. Weekly and cumulative.

Books, pamphlets, documents, and periodicals in the social sciences, including references in English and other languages. Arrangement is by subject, with abundant cross references.

e)   PUBLISHERS' WEEKLY. New York, Bowker.

Bibliographical information based on Library of Congress data with annotations added; arranged by author with Dewey decimal classification indicated. Besides the Weekly Record there is a Forecasts section. Three times a year one of the issues is an announcement number.

f)   READERS' GUIDE TO PERIODICAL LITERATURE. New York, H. W. Wilson Co. Semimonthly and cumulative.

Approach is by author and subject. Articles are from general and nontechnical periodicals only.

g)   SOCIAL SCIENCES AND HUMANITIES INDEX (formerly INTERNATIONAL INDEX). New York, H. W. Wilson Co. Quarterly and cumulative.

Index of periodical material only; subject approach.

h)   SUBJECT GUIDE TO BOOKS IN PRINT. New York, Bowker. Annual.

Over 35 bibliographies of this nature are cited in the Preface of the Hoover Institution list, UNITED STATES AND CANADIAN PUBLICATIONS AND THESES ON AFRICA, in the issue for 1966 (see no. 305).

For Great Britain:

i)   BRITISH NATIONAL BIBLIOGRAPHY. London. Weekly; quarterly and annual cumulations.

This magnificent national bibliography is so complete and so promptly current that it seems unnecessary to mention other lists; it is arranged according to a modified Dewey decimal classification. Each issue has an author and title index except that the one in the last issue of each month (identifiable by its green front cover) gives authors, titles, and subjects for the whole month.

j) BRITISH HUMANITIES INDEX. London. 1962-   Quarterly with
annual cumulations.

Covers periodical literature.

For <u>France</u>:

k) BIBLIOGRAPHIE DE LA FRANCE. Paris, Au Cercle de la Librairie.
Weekly, with annual indexes.

Part 1. BIBLIOGRAPHIE OFFICIELLE.

Record of publications received by copyright deposit
in the Bibliothèque Nationale, with entries established
by that institution according to the rules of library
cataloguing. Because the record is held till the works
have passed through the cataloguing process, the BIBLIO-
GRAPHIE OFFICIELLE is often several months behind. A more
prompt listing of new "trade" books can be found in the third
part, ANNONCES, which carries the publishers' blurbs for
their new and forthcoming productions. Quicker notices may
also be found in the monthly list for the book trade, BIBLIO
(Paris, 1933-, annual cumulation), which is arranged in
dictionary catalogue style by name of author and title and
under key word of subject; all works in French, wherever
published, are included.

The <u>Belgian</u>, <u>German</u>, <u>Italian</u>, <u>Portuguese</u>, and <u>Spanish</u> national catalogues
are all also in subject classification; they are useful as buying guides for
libraries acquiring Africana, but for the individual researcher they are not
very rewarding except the Belgian, which is of interest chiefly for the Congo,
as the small number of works on Africa which they record may be identified
more easily in the Africanist journals of those countries.

279. As to book reviews, the following might be noted among general library
tools (the works under review in all are usually limited to "trade"
books from leading publishers, and for critiques of scholarly works
reviews will probably be found only in the specialist journals):

For the <u>United States</u>, the standard publication is the BOOK REVIEW
DIGEST (New York, H. W. Wilson Co.), monthly and with half-yearly,
annual, and five-year cumulations. The cumulated numbers have indexing by subject. The BOOK REVIEW DIGEST not only provides a brief description of each work but also lists reviews to be found in the chief
newspapers and periodicals. In 1965 the BOOK REVIEW INDEX (Detroit,
Gale Research Co.), monthly with quarterly and annual cumulations, was
begun. Arrangement is alphabetical by author, with title of work, and
thereunder a list of periodicals and newspapers having reviews.

For Great Britain, the BRITISH BOOK NEWS (London, monthly) is a selected, annotated list of "best books" arranged in Dewey decimal classification, with indexes by author and title and a separate annual index cumulation. However, items of African interest are few. A larger selection of Africana is reviewed critically, sometimes at considerable length, in the TIMES LITERARY SUPPLEMENT (weekly, with annual index). Approach to this is by author only.

For France, the standard book review service, again of "trade books," is the BULLETIN CRITIQUE DU LIVRE FRANCAIS (Paris, Association pour la Diffusion de la Pensée Française, 1945-, monthly), which is in classed arrangement, with index of authors. An abridged edition is brought out in English: RECENT FRENCH BOOKS (quarterly). It includes reviews of many French trade books on Africa.

The German book review serial, DEUTSCHE BIBLIOGRAPHIE: DAS DEUTSCHE BUCH, unfortunately contains very few references to works on Africa. Before ceasing publication at the end of 1965, the monthly NEUES AFRIKA, organ of Afrika-Verein, Hamburg, covered a number of works in a short book review section.

280. AFRICA: JOURNAL OF THE INTERNATIONAL AFRICAN INSTITUTE. 1928- London, Oxford University Press. Quarterly.

See also no. 4.

"Bibliography of Current Publications," a classified list of several hundred titles of books and pamphlets, periodical articles, and documents, fills about 10 or more pages in each issue. Among the classes are ethnography, anthropology, and sociology, history, religion, language and linguistics, economic development, government, law, the arts and literature, and education. Each issue of AFRICA carries around 20 book reviews, often signed or initialed by specialists. These usually relate to the Institute's special interests of ethnology, which involves a broad area of social anthropology, and linguistics.

Two other periodicals with the same title--AFRICA, monthly review published by the Instituto de Estudios Africanos in Madrid, and AFRICA, the bimonthly review of the Istituto Italiano per l'Africa in Rome-- also carry book reviews and a listing of contents of current periodicals with international coverage, but they give more attention than in other organs to publications of their respective countries.

281. AFRICA REPORT. v. 1, no. 1- July 5, 1956- Washington, D.C., African-American Institute. Monthly (11 numbers a year); from 1966-, 9 numbers a year, Oct.-June, and annual index.

Leading American journal devoted to African affairs. For full description see no. 565. The bibliographical sections vary from issue to issue, but during the year most major American books on Africa are noticed, with some reviewed at length by specialists and others appearing in the "Received" lists. The bibliographical works reviewed or listed probably total around 300 a year. A discographical review by Alan Merriam on African music is published in each issue. The journal carries a few advertisements, predominantly of publishers; a number of university presses briefly describe their current Africana offerings.

282. AFRICAN ABSTRACTS: QUARTERLY REVIEW OF ARTICLES APPEARING IN CURRENT PERIODICALS. 1950- London. Quarterly.

Published by the International African Institute with the assistance of UNESCO. The Ford Foundation also gave support from 1956 to 1966. With the Jan. 1967 issue the name BULLETIN ANALYTIQUE AFRICANISTE was dropped, and AFRICAN ABSTRACTS is now entirely in English. A separate French edition, ANALYSES AFRICANISTES, is published by the Centre d'Analyse et de Recherche Documentaires pour l'Afrique Noire (CARDAN). Both editions contain exactly the same material. Around 200 abstracts appear in each issue, in geographical arrangement; the subject of each is indicated by a number in brackets, according to a key given at the front. The serials abstracted are listed on the inside back cover. A separate index is issued each year.

283. AFRICAN AFFAIRS: JOURNAL OF THE ROYAL AFRICAN SOCIETY. 1901- London.

For full description see no. 1204.

Book review section, with signed or initialed comment, and current bibliography of books and documents, in geographical arrangement. Most works cited are in English; many publications of African countries are included. Recent issues have a bibliography of articles on African appearing in non-Africanist journals.

284. AFRICAN NOTES. 1963- Ibadan, Institute of African Studies, University of Ibadan. 3 times a year.

Each issue from 1964 through Apr. 1966 contained a 22- to 52-page addendum of selected references to current periodicals held in the University Library, the listing being compiled by Margaret Amosu, with J. M. Cameron as co-compiler in 1964, J. M. Crossey in 1966.

285. AFRICAN URBAN NOTES. v. 1, no. 1- Apr. 1966- Milwaukee, Department of Political Science, University of Wisconsin-Milwaukee, Apr. 1966-Mar. 1967; Los Angeles, Department of Political Science, University of California, Apr. 1967- Irregular.

For annotation see no. 834. This newsletter occasionally issues bibliographical supplements, some of which are not confined to the subject of African urbanization.

286. AFRIQUE CONTEMPORAINE: DOCUMENTS D'AFRIQUE NOIRE ET DE MADAGASCAR. 1962- Paris, La Documentation Française. 6 times a year.

Prepared at the Centre d'Etudes et de Documentation sur l'Afrique et l'Outre-Mer. This important journal (see no. 1545) includes reviews or notices of a broad international selection of books.

287. Cambridge. University. African Studies Centre (Sidgwick Ave., Cambridge). [Index of current publications on Africa] 1961-

The card file prepared by this center covered author and title entries for books, government documents, theses, conference proceedings, unpublished material, and articles selected from several hundred periodicals. The cards, classed according to the Universal Decimal Classification, were sent on exchange to interested institutions in Europe and elsewhere, who supplied titles. In 1966 this service was merged with that of CARDAN (see below).

A comparable card file service is carried on by the Fondation Nationale des Sciences Politiques, 27, rue Guillaume, Paris 7. Their photoreproduced cards, also in decimal classification, carry brief annotations describing content and have reportedly been supplied periodically since the early 1960's. Hitherto they have not been readily available in the United States.

288. Centre d'Analyse et de Recherche Documentaires pour l'Afrique Noire (CARDAN). BIBLIOGRAPHIE FRANCAISE SUR L'AFRIQUE AU SUD DU SAHARA, 1968. Paris, 1969. 143 p. (v. 1, no. 4)

Modeled after the annual list of publications on Africa published in the United States (see no. 305). This French-language list makes the fourth such national survey. Like the other annuals it is valuable both as a reference tool and as an acquisitions tool for books and articles published in French on Africa south of the Sahara. The 584 entries are annotated. An annex lists Africanist periodicals published in France (86).

289. Centre d'Analyse et de Recherche Documentaires pour l'Afrique Noire. FICHES ANALYTIQUES/FICHES SIGNALETIQUES: SCIENCES HUMAINES AFRICANISTES. 1965- Paris. Quarterly; from 1967- 3 times a year. Processed.

FICHES ANALYTIQUES:SCIENCES SOCIALES ET HUMAINES was originally an abstracting service issued quarterly and providing around 2,000 filing cards a year on the principal new books and on articles in periodicals on sub-Saharan Africa in the social sciences. The cards, eight to a sheet, ready for cutting and filing, carried summaries of the items analyzed, often running to two or more cards. Indexes (geographical, ethnic-linguistic, author) and lists of works analyzed and of periodicals covered were usually provided in each issue as well as an annual subject index.

In 1966 the FICHES ANALYTIQUES and the bibliographical cards of the Cambridge African Studies Centre (CAS) were consolidated into one joint service, to become the FICHES ANALYTIQUES/FICHES SIGNALETIQUES: SCIENCES HUMAINES AFRICANISTES, with several thousand cards issued annually. The cards with bibliographical information only (on green stock) are published separately and are numbered in an F.S. sequence; they are, in general, geographical, ethnic-linguistic, and author indexes and lists of periodicals and of series and collective works covered. The cards having abstracts (on white stock) are numbered in the CARDAN-F.A. sequence, and for each issue there are author, ethnic-linguistic, geographical, and subject indexes as well as lists of periodicals covered and of works analyzed. In all CARDAN and CAS between them probably encompass some 800 periodicals. There are separate annual subject indexes, for the FICHES SIGNALETIQUES on green stock and for the FICHES ANALYTIQUES on white stock. Because of the complicated classification system that is used, a 24-leaf pamphlet KEY-WORDS USED BY C.A.R.D.A.N. AND C.A.S. was issued in Feb. 1966.

Another CARDAN-CAS publication began in 1966 with FICHES D'OUV-RAGES, 1964: SCIENCES HUMAINES AFRICANISTES (on green stock), in which book-length works are listed alphabetically; there are subject, geographical, and ethnic-linguistic indexes.

A detailed explanation of CARDAN, its services and publications, was written by its Director, René Bureau, and translated for American readers by John B. Webster: "The Center for Analysis and Documentary Research for Black Africa," AFRICAN STUDIES BULLETIN, v. 10, Dec. 1967: 66-81.

290. Centre d'Analyse et de Recherche Documentaires pour l'Afrique Noire.
INVENTAIRE DES REGISTRES DE LA RECHERCHE AN COURS DANS LE DOMAINE DES SCIENCES SOCIALES ET HUMAINES EN AFRIQUE NOIRE. Paris, 1966. 32 l.

A preliminary reference guide to current research in the social sciences and humanities in sub-Saharan Africa derived from CARDAN's extensive bibliographic files and from reports received from African research institutes, universities, and libraries. The annotated list

of 65 monographs and periodicals carrying information on current research projects is preceded by brief notes on major regional research
centers and their various journals and reports.

291. CULTURAL EVENTS IN AFRICA. Dec. 1964- London, Transcription Centre.
      Monthly.

          Gives summary of cultural events in Africa and elsewhere; covers
      art, drama, literature, gives brief reviews of new writing. Usually
      an issue includes a transcribed interview with an African artist or
      writer. Tapes can be purchased from the center (6 Paddington Street,
      London W.1).

292. A CURRENT BIBLIOGRAPHY ON AFRICAN AFFAIRS. Apr. 1962-Dec. 1967; n.s.
      Jan. 1968- New York, Greenwood Periodicals for African Biblio-
      graphic Center, Inc., Washington, D.C. Bimonthly 1963-67; monthly
      Jan. 1968- Cumulated annual issue.

          Editor-in-chief, Daniel G. Matthews. This useful documentation
      service lists books, pamphlets, documents, articles in various journals,
      and analytics from collective works published generally within a three-
      year period. In the 12 monthly issues of 1968, 2,606 titles, consecu-
      tively numbered, were given in subject and country classifications in
      each issue. Those in the general section include a liberal selection
      of works relating to the broader study of developing areas without
      specific reference to Africa. Material in Western European languages
      and Russian is well covered, the latter with translation of titles.
      Some entries have short annotations, and there is an author index.
      Preceding the classified list are three special features: "Commentary,"
      with original bibliographies and bibliographical articles as well as
      information on the Center's own activities and items of general interest
      to subscribers (summer programs, reprints, advance notices on publications,
      etc.); "Forthcoming Publications" of American and British publishers,
      each entry usually bearing a brief indication of the subject matter;
      and an "Annotated Book Review Section," the review ending with a note
      such as "Recommended for general collections" or the like. The 1966
      format consisted of a processed pamphlet of 30-40 pages. Publication
      was taken over in mid-1967 by Greenwood Periodicals, Inc., which issues
      it as a printed booklet. A new monthly series began with v. 1, no. 1,
      Jan. 1968.

          The African Bibliographic Center publishes a Special Bibliographic
      Series of bibliographies relating to specific aspects of Africana.
      Covering a wide range of subject fields, these have been of varying
      size. Several are of outstanding significance: e.g., AFRICAN ECONOMIC
      AFFAIRS, 1965-1966 (no. 7, 1966) and AFRICAN AFFAIRS FOR THE GENERAL
      READER, 1960-1967 (no. 4, 1967, and supplement, no. 3, 1968). A number
      of them are mentioned in later sections of this Guide. In 1969 the

entire series is being brought out by the Negro Universities Press
(211 E. 43d Street, New York, N.Y. 10017), in 6 volumes clothbound
in 4. Vols. I, II, and III, reprints of the numbers issued in 1963,
1964, and 1965, are together in binding. Vols. IV and V, for 1966
and 1967, are again reprints, and Vol. VI contains three original
lists of 1968. Future numbers will be issued as separates. The
Center also prepares a shorter series of Current Reading Lists on
individual topics of current significance: e.g., THE BEAT GOES ON
(African dance and music); THE ALPHABET GAME (acronyms of Africa-
connected organizations). These are issued separately. Services of
the Center are expanding steadily, and the entire bibliographic enterprise merits attention from libraries and institutions concerned with
Africa. See also no. 276.

293. Delhi University. Library. DOCUMENTATION LIST: AFRICA. v. 1- 1962-
      Delhi, India. Quarterly.

An excellent index to articles on Africa in periodicals held in
the library. The Apr.-June issue of 1964, v. 3, no. 2, has 50 mimeographed pages and covers 109 periodicals, about 90 percent of which
relate specifically to Africa. The list begins with a schedule of
classification, after which appear the classified list of titles (in
v. 3, no. 2, p. 1-38) and a subject index. The Oct.-Dec. 1964 issue
includes both a subject and an author index.

The library of the Indian Council for Africa in New Delhi issues
a similar index which, since the issue of Jan. 1968, v. 5, no. 1, has
also been titled DOCUMENTATION LIST: AFRICA (previous title, 1964-67,
MONTHLY INDEX OF IMPORTANT ARTICLES AND EDITORIALS ON AFRICA). Entries
are arranged alphabetically by author or title under each country and
under a few subject headings, with occasional notes of comment. Some
60 periodicals are analyzed each month.

294. Deutsche Afrika-Gesellschaft. Wissenschaftlicher Ausschuss. AFRIKA-
      BIBLIOGRAPHIE: VERZEICHNIS DES WISSENSCHAFTLICHEN SCHRIFTTUMS IN
      DEUTSCHER SPRACHE AUS DEN JAHREN 1960/1961. Compiled by Rudolf
      Thoden. Bonn, Kurt Schroeder, 1963-64. 2 pts. 83, 182 p.

      1962. Compiled by Rudolf Thoden. 1964. 148 p.

      1963. Compiled by Rudolf Thoden. 1965. 134 p.

      1964. Compiled by Elisabeth Greschat. 1966. 131 p.

These annual lists, showing the greatly increased German interest
in Africa, are issued by the leading study center in West Germany and
give books and periodical articles in all major fields relating to
Africa as they were published in the German language for the years covered.

295. GENEVE-AFRIQUE: ACTA AFRICANA. 1962- Genève. Quarterly.

Numerous short book reviews.

296. JOURNAL OF MODERN AFRICAN STUDIES: A QUARTERLY SURVEY OF POLITICS,
      ECONOMICS AND RELATED TOPICS IN CONTEMPORARY AFRICA. 1963-
      Edited by David and Helen Kimble. Cambridge, Eng.; New York,
      Cambridge University Press.

A distinguished periodical, with contributions by leading Africanists and specialists in many fields. The section of news and notes,
"Africana," presents in each issue informal statements on the work of
a few institutes and centers of African studies, "brief reports on
recent conferences; occasional accounts of important research in progress; information about a wide variety of groups and associations
existing in or concerned with Africa; and any other items of professional interest to students of Africa." A similar journal published
every quarter in Hamburg by the Deutsche Institut für Afrika-Forschung
is AFRIKA SPECTRUM. Each issue contains an extensive analysis of the
contents of official gazettes, book reviews, and review articles as
well as articles on contemporary events.

297. JOURNAL OF NEGRO EDUCATION: A QUARTERLY REVIEW OF PROBLEMS INCIDENT
      TO THE EDUCATION OF NEGROES. 1932- Lancaster, Pa., Lancaster
      Press, Published for the College of Education, Howard University,
      Washington, D.C.

The long bibliographical sections in this journal, which is
primarily concerned with the American Negro, are in two parts, the
second of which lists new books, pamphlets, and periodical articles
on the Negro in Africa. A substantial number of titles is given in
each issue.

Also of interest may be mentioned the INDEX TO SELECTED PERIODICALS
(1950-), compiled quarterly by the library of Central State College,
Wilberforce, Ohio, and published by G. K. Hall (Boston). While the
items indexed relate primarily to the Negro in America, the cumulated
annual index by author and subject usually includes a few articles
about Africa. As these contributions are not listed in other guides
to periodical literature, the work is worth consulting when available.

298. LE LIVRE AFRICAIN. v. 1, no. 1- Jan. 1959- Bruxelles (40, rue du
      Champ de Mars). Monthly.

The organ of Amis de Présence Africaine, this is in part a catalogue for the varied literary, political, and social publications of
Présence Africaine, many of them by African writers. LE LIVRE AFRICAIN

is a useful source for information regarding pamphlets and serials not often mentioned elsewhere.

299. MIDDLE EAST JOURNAL. 1947- Washington, D.C., Middle East Institute. Quarterly.

This scholarly journal carries regular sections of chronology, book reviews, and a "Bibliography of Periodical Literature," which is also issued separately. The coverage includes Egypt, North Africa, Sudan, Ethiopia, and Somalia.

300. Royal Anthropological Institute. INDEX TO CURRENT PERIODICALS RECEIVED IN THE LIBRARY. 1963- London. Quarterly.

This index contained over 5,000 entries in the first volume. Each issue is arranged under the rubrics of general works, Africa, America, Asia, East India, Oceania and Australia, and Europe. Under each major heading entries are further subdivided under general works, physical anthropology, archaeology, cultural anthropology and ethnology, and linguistics.

301. Société des Africanistes. JOURNAL. 1931- Paris. 2 issues a year.

An extensive bibliographical section (around 50 pages) in this important journal, which is in many respects comparable to that of the International African Institute, AFRICA, is carried annually in one of the two issues each year. It is classified according to disciplines and takes in more fields of interest than does AFRICA; also included are references to European writings that have not always reached the Institute in London. It is sometimes one or even two years behind AFRICA in its citations. An index to Vols. I-XXXV (1931-65) of the JOURNAL appeared in Vol. XXXVI, no. 2, 1966.

302. SOVIET PERIODICAL ABSTRACTS: ASIA, AFRICA, AND LATIN AMERICA. v. 1, no. 1- May 1961- New York, Soviet Society. Quarterly.

Formerly titled SELECTIVE SOVIET ANNOTATED BIBLIOGRAPHIES. The purpose of these abstracts of Soviet literature is to give an idea of Soviet ideology regarding social and political development in the underdeveloped countries; therefore the content is heavily weighted with statements of anti-imperialist dogma. The articles abstracted are from current issues of NARODY AZII I AFRIKI and occasional other journals and daily press. The section on Africa, arranged under general and country headings, is substantial.

303. Standing Conference on Library Materials on Africa (SCOLMA). UNITED
KINGDOM PUBLICATIONS AND THESES ON AFRICA, 1963. Cambridge, Eng.,
Heffer, 1966. 94 p.

1964. Cambridge, Eng., Heffer, 1966. 89 p.

1965. Cambridge, Eng., Heffer, 1967. 92 p.

This annual listing was begun by SCOLMA as a record of theses
only (see no. 419). It has now been enlarged to include published
books and articles. The general section is divided into subject
headings (from agriculture to wildlife and hunting); the second
section is arranged by country and region (for 1965, entries are
listed first by region and thereunder by country). Both sections
utilize book and article subdivisions. Each volume has as well a
section "References to Africa in Hansard," compiled by Malcolm McKee,
a supplement to THESES ON AFRICA, and an index of authors. The 1965
issue also lists and maps and has an appendix comprised of corrections
and additions to THESES ON AFRICA. The number of items, exclusive of
supplementary material, is 1,260 for 1963, 1,073 for 1964, and 1,137
for 1965.

304. U.S. Library of Congress. General Reference and Bibliography Division,
African Section. [Card files]

With the Library's tremendous worldwide acquisitions program,
many of the books, pamphlets, and documents received undergo some delay
in the cataloguing process before they are made available for public
use. However, preliminary catalogue cards are issued shortly after
reception of the works for the collections.

The African Section maintains several card files as supplements
to the public catalogues. These files, indexed by subject and region,
include citations to periodical articles, sub-Saharan ethnic groups,
and material from African literary reviews. In early 1969, the file
on periodical literature included more than 51,000 citations to articles
appearing in major serials during the past five years. The card services
of CARDAN (see no. 289) and CIDESA (see no. 829) form the basis of the
index. The Section's card files are accessible to readers on Monday
through Friday from 9:00 A.M. to 5:15 P.M. G. K. Hall plans to publish
the L.C. card files.

305. UNITED STATES AND CANADIAN PUBLICATIONS AND THESES ON AFRICA IN 1966.
Compiled by Liselotte Hofmann. Stanford, Calif., Hoover
Institution, Stanford University, 1970. 300 p. (Hoover Institution
Bibliographical Series, no. 38)

This is the seventh issue of this annual survey which prior to the
volume for 1965 was titled UNITED STATES AND CANADIAN PUBLICATIONS ON

AFRICA . . . . The first issue was published in 1962 (covering 1960) by the African Section of the Library of Congress; subsequent issues have been the responsibility of the Hoover Institution. The surveys for 1961, 1962, and 1963 were edited by Peter Duignan; Hilary Sims compiled the edition for 1962; Liselotte Hofmann has been the compiler since 1963.

The survey provides as complete a list as possible of books, pamphlets, documents, essays in collective works, periodical articles of more than news value, and (beginning with the volume for 1965) doctoral theses on Africa south of the Sahara. Arrangement is first by subject and then by region and country, with further division into books and articles. Included in each volume is an index of authors, and, for the 1966 survey, a subject and geographic index has also been provided. There were 1,111 numbered items cited for 1960; 1,369 for 1961; 1,215 for 1962; 1,572 for 1963; 1,883 for 1964; 2,312 for 1965; and 2,755 for 1966.

CHAPTER 6

RETROSPECTIVE BIBLIOGRAPHIES

General

Note: This group represents monographic bibliographies for Africa in general,
covering diversified subject fields. Several of them include, or because of
date are limited to, the older literature, before or of the nineteenth and
early twentieth centuries (Gay, Paulitschke, Royal Commonwealth Society Catalogue, and Work); the others emphasize more recent writing. There is, of
course, much duplication in all. See also the excellent lists of books on
the colonial period in no. 82: THE CAMBRIDGE HISTORY OF THE BRITISH EMPIRE,
Vol. III; BRITAIN AND GERMANY IN AFRICA; and HISTORY OF EAST AFRICA, Vols. I
and II.

306. Africa Bibliography Series: Ethnography, Sociology, Linguistics and
        Related Subjects. (Based on the bibliographical card index of
        the International African Institute.) Compiled by Ruth Jones.
        London, International African Institute, 1958- (Series A)

        Volumes are WEST AFRICA, 1958, 116 l.; NORTH-EAST AFRICA, 1959,
51 l.; EAST AFRICA, 1960, 62 l.; and SOUTH-EAST CENTRAL AFRICA AND
MADAGASCAR, 1961, 53 l. (see nos. 970, 1257, 2097, and 2370).

        These lists, which analyze periodical holdings of the International
African Institute as well as books and documents, relate primarily to
anthropological studies but in so broad a sense that they deserve reference as general sources.

        Series B of Africa Bibliography, issued by the Institute, are on
specific subjects. (see nos. 1073 and 1078).

307. AFRIKA SCHRIFTTUM: BIBLIOGRAPHIE DEUTSCHSPRACHIGER WISSENSCHAFTLICHER
        VEROFFENTLICHUNGEN UBER AFRIKA SUDLICH DER SAHARA. [Title also

in English and French] Vol. I, Text. Edited by George T. Mary.
Wiesbaden, Franz Steiner Verlag GmbH, 1966. 688 p.

An excellent catalogue of German scholarly works (books, articles,
and dissertations) on sub-Saharan Africa from the 1870's to 1962. The
subjects covered are geography, ethnology, linguistics, theology, education, tropical medicine, zoology, and botany. Arrangement is alphabetical by author under each topic, and essential keywords in English
and French are appended as marginal notes alongside each entry (except
in the section on theology and education). A second volume comprising
an index has apparently been prepared but not yet published.

308. American Historical Association. GUIDE TO HISTORICAL LITERATURE. New
        York, Macmillan, 1961. 962 p.

"Africa," by Vernon McKay: p. 745-769. Annotated selection of
545 fundamental works for a study of African history, by the head of
the African studies program of the Johns Hopkins University School of
Advanced International Studies. Dr. McKay's interpretation of history
is broad, including geography, anthropology, and the social sciences.
The volume of which the Africa chapter forms part is successor to the
well-known handbook of the same title edited by G. M. Dutcher and
others in 1931 (see Winchell for description).

309. American Universities Field Staff. A SELECT BIBLIOGRAPHY: ASIA, AFRICA,
        EASTERN EUROPE, LATIN AMERICA. New York, 1960. 534 p.

Supplement, 1961, 75 p; 1963, 66 p.; 1965, 80 p.

"Africa," compiled by L. Gray Cowan and Edwin S. Munger: p. 193-
253. This chapter in a bibliography prepared specifically for college
study and general reading is arranged in regional sections, subdivided
in part by subject. It comprises around 750 items, most of them with
brief descriptive annotations. The work has author and title indexes.
Distributed to university libraries by the American Universities Field
Staff, Inc., 366 Madison Ave., New York, N.Y. 10017. Supplements are
being issued at two-year intervals.

310. Cartry, Michel, and Bernard Charles. L'AFRIQUE AU SUD DU SAHARA:
        GUIDE DE RECHERCHES. Paris, Centre d'Etude des Relations
        Internationales, Fondation Nationale des Sciences Politiques,
        1962. 85 l. Processed. (Sér. D, Textes et documents, no. 3,
        Apr. 1962)

This guide for advanced study is in four parts: 1, Généralités
(introduction and reference works, geography, demography, economics,
history, societies and civilization); 2, Contexte traditionnel et

changements sociaux (ethnology and sociology); 3, La vie politique
(general problems, including documentary sources, political forces,
organizations and political influence, problems); 4, Idéologies.
The selection of 700-800 references to books and articles is broken
down into numerous sections and subsections, explained in a detailed
table of contents (there is no index). Within the groupings, works--
sometimes only one or two--are apparently listed according to the
compilers' judgment of significance. Only a few conspicuous individual
works are annotated, though there are long explanatory notes for most
categories. The text is in French, but the citations include many
English works and some in German.

311. Cercle Français du Livre. L'AFRIQUE [BIBLIOGRAPHIE]. New ed. Paris
[1965?] 208 p.

Gives author, title, and price (in francs) only. Most items are
in French. Works listed are in the fields of geography (including
zoology and botany), sociology and ethnology, linguistics, economics,
politics, constitutions, legislation, religion, arts (architecture,
sculpture, archaeology, and music), and literature. Studies on Afro-
Americans and publications of the Ministère de la Coopération are also
listed. There is an author and title index.

312. Copenhagen. Kongelige Bibliotek. NYERE AFRIKA-LITTERATUR, MARTS 1962.
København, 1962. 63 p. map. Processed.

Supplement. 1963. 78 p.

A selection of almost a thousand modern books on Africa in European
languages, in regional arrangement. The book list is followed by a
title list of over 150 periodicals or series, as well as a few unnumbered
pages with additional works--all extensively supplemented in 1963.

313. Fontán Lobé, Juan. BIBLIOGRAFIA COLONIAL: CONTRIBUCION A UN INDICE
DE PUBLICACIONES AFRICANAS. Madrid, Dirección General de
Marruecos y Colonias, 1946. 669 p.

This sizable bibliography of books, documents, and periodical
articles arranged alphabetically by author represents the 17,000 cards
assembled for his own library by Sr. Fontán Lobé, former director of
the Spanish colonial service and at one time Governor-General of Guinea,
for many years an authority on Africa. His collection included almost
all the notable works in European languages, with many volumes of the
nineteenth century, and a larger representation of Spanish and Portuguese
writings than most of the other standard bibliographies of Africana.
An index includes geographical names, subjects (several hundred numbers
follow the heading for administration), and names of collaborators and
translators.

314. Gay, Jean. BIBLIOGRAPHIE DES OUVRAGES RELATIFS A L'AFRIQUE ET A
           L'ARABIE: CATALOGUE METHODIQUE DE TOUS LES OUVRAGES FRANCAIS
           ET DES PRINCIPAUX EN LANGUES ETRANGERES TRAITANT DE LA GEOGRAPHIE,
           DE L'HISTOIRE, DU COMMERCE, DES LETTRES & DES ARTS DE L'AFRIQUE
           & DE L'ARABIE. Amsterdam, Meridian Publishing Co., 1961. 312 p.

       Reprint of a celebrated bibliography first published at San Remo,
   1875. Coverage is of writings before that date.

315. INDEX ISLAMICUS, 1906-1955: A CATALOGUE OF ARTICLES ON ISLAMIC SUBJECTS
           IN PERIODICALS AND OTHER COLLECTIVE PUBLICATIONS. Compiled by
           J. D. Pearson. Cambridge, Eng., W. Heffer, 1958. 897 p.

       SUPPLEMENT, 1956-1960. 1962. 316 p.

       SUPPLEMENT, 1961-1965. 1967. 342 p.

       Indexes more than 26,000 articles devoted to all aspects of Islamic
   studies. Classification is by subject, some with geographical breakdown, and by region. Included are a significant number of entries dealing with Islam in Africa south of the Sahara, so this catalogue should
   not be ignored by Africanists. It is especially valuable because before the 1930's there were few good surveys of African periodical
   literature. Further supplements at five-year intervals are planned.

316. International African Institute. SELECT ANNOTATED BIBLIOGRAPHY OF
           TROPICAL AFRICA. Compiled under the direction of Daryll Forde.
           New York, Twentieth Century Fund, 1956. various pagings (about
           490 p.) Mimeographed.

       Some 20 specialists were involved in the preparation of this ex-
   tensive research bibliography. The separately paged sections are:
   A, Geography; B, Ethnography, sociology, and linguistics; C, Government and administration; D, Economics; E, Education; F, Missions; G,
   Health. Within the sections arrangement is by major geographical
   areas, with subject subheadings. References are to books and periodical
   articles, with considerable variation in standards of choice and in
   treatment by the individual compilers. Annotations are scanty, though
   a good many headings have introductory notes. Material includes some
   writings of the nineteenth and early twentieth centuries as well as
   more recent studies. There are unfortunately no indexes.

317. Mylius, Norbert. AFRIKA BIBLIOGRAPHIE, 1943-1951. Wien, Verein
           Freunde der Völkerkunde, 1952. 237 p. Processed.

       A huge title list, containing 2,700 references to books and
   documents. Periodical articles are not included, but 250-odd periodicals
   are named in the introductory section, together with some 100 titles of

bibliographies. The references, which were selected as a supplement
to Wieschhoff (no. 322), are arranged by geographical regions and subdivided by subject--handbooks, travel, history and biography, arts,
sociology, law, culture, economics, colonies, politics, missions, etc.
Works cited are in Western European languages. There is no index.

318. Paulitschke, Philipp Viktor. DIE AFRIKA-LITTERATUR IN DER ZEIT VON
1500 BIS 1750: EIN BEITRAG ZUR GEOGRAPHISCHEN QUELLENKUNDE.
Wien, Brockhausen & Bräuer, 1882. 122 p.

Photo-litho reprint published by Kraus, New York, 1962, and
Meridian Publishing Co., Amsterdam, Holland, 1964.

Classified list of 1,212 titles of the early literature on Africa.

319. Royal Commonwealth Society, London. Library. SUBJECT CATALOGUE OF THE
LIBRARY OF THE ROYAL EMPIRE SOCIETY, FORMERLY ROYAL COLONIAL
INSTITUTE. By Evans Lewin. London, The Society, 1930-37. 4 v.

Vol. I. THE BRITISH EMPIRE GENERALLY AND AFRICA. (Africa, 582
p., separately paged.) Reprint, Dawson of Pall Mall, 1967.

The Royal Colonial Institute was established in the 1860's, publications of its proceedings beginning in 1869. (The name was changed
in the 1920's to Royal Empire Society; still later it became the Royal
Commonwealth Society, the present style.) Its outstanding library
collections--particularly rich in papers of the chartered companies
and British colonial documents--include most writings in English over
nearly a century, as well as notable works of other metropolitan powers.
This important catalogue was compiled by the librarian, Evans Lewin,
himself an authority on Africa. In his introduction he explains that
not all official material in the library could be included. The arrangement is geographical by country, with subject classes, and entries are
arranged chronologically. Besides books and pamphlets, the catalogue
includes articles in reviews and journals, papers read before learned
and other societies, and, despite Mr. Lewin's apology, a mass of
official documentation. There is an author index. For any historical
study of British Africa, this is a prime source.

In 1943 Mr. Lewin issued what amounts to a partial supplement,
ANNOTATED BIBLIOGRAPHY OF RECENT PUBLICATIONS ON AFRICA SOUTH OF THE
SAHARA, WITH SPECIAL REFERENCE TO ADMINISTRATIVE, POLITICAL, ECONOMIC
AND SOCIOLOGICAL PROBLEMS (London, The Society, 1943, 104 p.). The
annotations are slight, the compilation perhaps hasty under wartime
pressures.

320. U.S. Department of the Army. Headquarters. AFRICA: ITS PROBLEMS AND
    PROSPECTS; A BIBLIOGRAPHIC SURVEY. New ed. Washington, 1967.
    226 p. maps (part col., 2 fold., 1 in back pocket), charts.
    (DA Pamphlet, no. 550-5)

This is an updated edition of a 1962 publication (DA Pamphlet,
no. 20-62, 195 p.) which contained around 500 titles, largely for the
period 1960-62. The 1967 edition lists more than 900 classified and
annotated titles of books, documents, bibliographies appearing as parts
of larger works, and periodical articles (mainly U.S. publications for
the period 1962-66), as well as theses from American University. The
slant in both selection and annotation is toward strategic studies.
Appendixes include a summary of the armed forces of each country, a
checklist of Communist parties, 11 maps (one a National Geographic
1966 map), and a fact sheet on the independent states.

321. U.S. Library of Congress. General Reference and Bibliography Division.
    AFRICA SOUTH OF THE SAHARA: A SELECTED, ANNOTATED LIST OF
    WRITINGS. Compiled by Helen F. Conover, African Section.
    Washington, 1963 [i.e., 1964]. 354 p.

This substantial compilation, designed as a basic guide for
advanced research, was selected from the entire body of writing on
Africa South of the Sahara identifiable through reference sources in
the Library of Congress as well as in its large collections. It re-
vises and greatly extends earlier bibliographies published in 1952
and 1957 and now out of print. The items (2,173 numbered, 600-700
more titles in notes) are classified under 30-odd subjects for Africa
in general, and then by region and country, with smaller subject subdivisions. Practically all works mentioned have been examined and are
given annotations descriptive of content. There is a combined author-
subject index, with detailed geographical breakdown under major subjects.
A special effort was made in each category to stress available bibliographies, particularly those in serial form, in the hope that the study
would extend the range of source material well beyond the limitations
of one compilation and thus not become obsolete too quickly.

The out-of-print bibliographies referred to above are as follows:

a) U.S. Library of Congress. European Affairs Division.
    INTRODUCTION TO AFRICA: A SELECTIVE GUIDE TO BACKGROUND
    READING. Prepared by Helen F. Conover. Washington,
    University Press of Washington, 1952. 237 p.

    A guide for the general reader.

b) U.S. Library of Congress. General Reference and Bibliography
    Division. AFRICA SOUTH OF THE SAHARA: A SELECTED,

ANNOTATED LIST OF WRITINGS, 1951-1956. Compiled by Helen F. Conover. Washington, 1957. 269 p. Processed.

c) U.S. Library of Congress. General Reference and Bibliography Division. NORTH AND NORTHEAST AFRICA: A SELECTED, ANNOTATED LIST OF WRITINGS, 1951-1957. Compiled by Helen F. Conover. Washington, 1957. 182 p. Processed.

Because of the increased American interest in the 1950's concerning Africa--as well as increased writing activities, particularly of a scholarly nature--the two-part revision and supplement to the 1952 list not only is much larger than the original but is intended for a more informed audience. In addition to the numbered items (over 600 for Africa south of the Sahara), almost half again as many are referred to in notes. The list on North and Northeast Africa included the Sudan, Ethiopia, and the Horn of Africa.

322. Wieschhoff, Heinrich A. ANTHROPOLOGICAL BIBLIOGRAPHY OF NEGRO AFRICA. New Haven, American Oriental Society, 1948. xi, 461 p. (American Oriental Series, no. 23)

By the former editor of the University of Pennsylvania series of handbooks during World War II, later an official at the United Nations and technical adviser with Dag Hammerskjöld on the mission in the Congo in which both lost their lives in Sept. 1961. Mr. Wieschhoff's bibliography, prepared from a working card catalogue, was to be followed by a second subject bibliography, even more comprehensive, which was never issued. The entries in this "Tribal Index" are in alphabetical order under the names of tribes, with many cross references for tribal names and their synonyms. Works cited are in all fields related to anthropology, including travelers' accounts, history, geography, etc., and are broken down as they apply to individual tribes. Besides books and pamphlets, articles are selected from over 200 scholarly periodicals and journals of learned societies, which are listed at the beginning (p. vii-xi).

323. Work, Monroe N. BIBLIOGRAPHY OF THE NEGRO IN AFRICA AND AMERICA. New York, H. W. Wilson, 1928. xxi, 698 p.

Reprint, New York, Octagon Books, 1965.

Part 1, The Negro in Africa: p. 1-247.

Comprehensive bibliography of the older literature on Negro Africa arranged in 19 classes, covering history, ethnology and linguistics, slavery, governments and colonization, race problems, Christian missions, etc. The last grouping (p. 242-247) is made up of bibliographies. Ref-

erences include titles of books, pamphlets, and periodical articles in
English and other Western European languages.

Library Catalogues

Note: The card files of the major libraries holding African collections constitute a continuing source for bibliography, and this is the first recourse
of anyone studying in a large center. Several libraries have recently issued
catalogues of their Africana collections, which differ from the monographic
publications cited above in that, whether classed by subject or not, they
are inclusive rather than of a studied selection. The catalogues published
by G. K. Hall in Boston consist of photographic reproductions of card files.
The first of these compilations, Boston University's CATALOG OF AFRICAN
GOVERNMENT DOCUMENTS AND AFRICAN AREA INDEX, is described under Official
Publications (no. 403).

324. American Geographical Society of New York. RESEARCH CATALOGUE. Boston,
     G. K. Hall, 1962. 15 v.

     Map supplement. 1962. 16 p.

     Parts pertinent to African studies are: Vols. I-II, General
(topics 1-9); Vol. XI, Africa (regional nos. 25-35); Vol. XV, Tropics
(regional no. 52). For additions to this catalogue see nos. 422 and
464.

     In 1923 the library began a classified catalogue with regional and
systematic classification based on geographical regions and individual
countries. Subjects other than geography are covered. In addition to
references to books, government documents, and pamphlets there are cards
for essays in books and articles in journals received by the library.
Since 1938 this most valuable source of retrospective bibliography has
been kept up to date by CURRENT GEOGRAPHICAL PUBLICATIONS. An INDEX
TO MAPS IN BOOKS AND PERIODICALS was issued in 1968 by G. K. Hall,
Boston, in 10 volumes (see no. 461).

325. Great Britain. Colonial Office. Library. CATALOGUE OF THE COLONIAL
     OFFICE LIBRARY, LONDON. Boston, G. K. Hall, 1964. 15 v. 37 cm.

     Books, pamphlets, reports, some official publications, and period-
ical titles and articles, with imprints from the mid-seventeenth century,
are covered. It is a union catalogue and therefore has material on
Commonwealth countries after independence and on some non-Commonwealth
countries. Pre-1950 accessions are given first, then post-1950 accessions.
Vols. I-VI are by author or title, VII-XIII by subject, and XIV-XV in
classified order (post-1950 only, in the Library of Congress system).

African material may be found under Africa and the country name; many subjects (as agriculture, education) have subdivisions for Africa.

326. Harvard University. Library. AFRICA: CLASSIFICATION SCHEDULE, CLASSI-
        FIED LISTING BY CALL NUMBER, ALPHABETICAL LISTING BY AUTHOR OR
        TITLE, CHRONOLOGICAL LISTING. Cambridge, Mass., Harvard University
        Press, 1965. 1 v. in 4 pts. Classification schedule unpaged
        [82], 302, 204, 196 p. (Widener Library Shelflist, no. 2)

        This shelflist, produced by computer technology, provides a new
approach to the collections in the Widener Library; it can also be used
as a general bibliography on Africa, though the compilers warn of imper-
fections in their first efforts. The classification schedule is essentially geographical, with subject subdivisions, except for African
literatures, which are arranged according to languages. The second and
main part lists all the works in Widener so classified, with author,
title, and place and date of publication available at a glance. The
alphabetical listing by author or title (if anonymous), including
journals, and a chronological list by year of publication are useful.

327. Harvard University. Peabody Museum of Archaeology and Ethnology.
        Library.

        CATALOGUE ... AUTHORS. Boston, G. K. Hall, 1963. 26 v.

        CATALOGUE ... SUBJECTS. Boston, G. K. Hall, 1963. 27 v.

        In the Authors volumes, reference to the many works relating to
Africa must be made by individual name. In the Subjects set, Vol. I
begins with some place names (these are see references) and then come
Abyssinia, Africa (p. 4-356), Algeria (p. 424-455), etc. The average
is 21 titles to the page; consequently under the heading Africa alone
there are some 7,000 to 8,000 items.

328. Howard University. Library. The Moorland Foundation. A CATALOGUE
        OF THE AFRICAN COLLECTION. Compiled by students in the Program
        of African Studies, edited by Dorothy B. Porter. Washington, D.C.,
        Howard University Press, 1958. 398 p.

        Classified list of 4,865 books and pamphlets, with supplementary
lists of periodicals and newspapers (Howard has a notable collection
of the latter). There is an author index.

329. London. University. Institute of Education. CATALOGUE OF THE
        COLLECTION OF EDUCATION IN TROPICAL AREAS. Boston, G. K. Hall,
        1964. 3 v.

        A large proportion of the works cited relates to Africa.

330. London. University. School of Oriental and African Studies. Library.
LIBRARY CATALOG. Boston, G. K. Hall, 1963. 28 v.

   In Vols. I-VIII the library holdings are listed by author, in Vols.
IX-XIII by title. Vol. XIV is Subjects: General; Vol. XV, Subjects:
Africa.

331. New York. Public Library. Schomburg Collection. DICTIONARY CATALOG
OF THE SCHOMBURG COLLECTION OF NEGRO LITERATURE AND HISTORY.
Boston, G. K. Hall, 1962. 9 v. 8473 p. 37 cm.

   Supplement. 2 v. 1967.

   The catalogue includes books, pamphlets, and periodicals concerning
the Negro in Africa, America, and elsewhere. Authors, titles, and subjects (classified by the Dewey decimal system) are entered in a single
alphabet.

332. Northwestern University. Library. CATALOGUE OF THE AFRICAN COLLECTION.
Boston, G. K. Hall, 1962. 2 v.

   Author-title catalogue of over 20,000 works. The collection is
especially strong in languages, linguistics, and ethnography.

333. Paris. Musée de l'Homme. Bibliothèque. CATALOGUE SYSTEMATIQUE DE LA
SECTION AFRIQUE, BIBLIOTHEQUE DU MUSEE DE L'HOMME, PARIS. Boston,
G. K. Hall, 1970. 2 v.

   Catalogue of a major library for African ethnographic materials
(over 8,000 items).

334. Royal Commonwealth Society, London. Library. SUBJECT CATALOGUE ....
By Evans Lewin. London, The Society, 1930-37. 4 v.

   For annotation see no. 319.

335. Tenri Library, Tenri, Japan. AFRICANA: CATALOGUE OF BOOKS RELATING TO
AFRICA IN THE TENRI CENTRAL LIBRARY. Tenri, Japan, 1960-64. 2 v.
431, 283 p. plates. (Tenri Central Library Series, nos. 24, 27)

   The first volume of this handsome catalogue consists mainly of
some 3,000 titles, 3,300 volumes. Most of the books cited are of the
first half of the twentieth century, up to 1940. They are arranged by
region, then in decimal classification. The second volume shows more

recently acquired material (items 3124-4915), much of it relating to Egypt and Ethiopia, which have special interests. There are indexes of personal names and titles.

336. United Nations. Economic Commission for Africa. Library. BOOKS ON AFRICA IN THE UNECA LIBRARY. Addis Ababa, Sept. 1962. 318 p. Mimeographed. (E/CN.14/LIB/SER.A/3)

    Catalogue of 2,031 entries, the majority of which are publications of African governments. They are arranged by region and groups of countries (including some Western countries), with author, title, and subject indexes.

    Catalogues have been issued by a number of other large libraries in Africa. These, however, are of uncertain value as sources of Africana, for they are heavily weighted with general material.

Special Bibliographies

Note: The kinds of bibliographies that may be described as "special" are many and diverse. One consists of bibliographies on Africa written in particular languages, such as Russian or German, or emanating from countries of Communist ideology. Another kind appears in the steady flow of general reading lists on Africa compiled for special audiences--staff use, special study groups, teachers, etc.; many of these may be noted in the BIBLIOGRAPHIC INDEX and other library indexes of bibliographical publications (see above, at be-ginning of Current Bibliographies). The following titles are given as a sampling of such special material.

337. African-American Institute. Council. FILM CATALOGUE. New York, 1968. 34 l.

    Useful listing with prices of available films on many aspects of African cultures and peoples.

338. African Bibliographic Center, Washington, D.C. AFRICAN AFFAIRS FOR THE GENERAL READER: A SELECTED AND INTRODUCTORY BIBLIOGRAPHICAL GUIDE, 1960-1967. Compiled for the Council of the African-American Institute; prepared under the general editorship of Daniel G. Matthews. New York, Council of the African-American Institute, 1967. 210 p. Loose-leaf. (Special Bibliographic Series, v. 5, no. 4)

Supplement, 1968.

A basic checklist of current resources for elementary, secondary, college, and public libraries. Emphasis is on English-language materials, and a significant number of selections published in Africa are listed. Following a guide to periodicals (divided first into annotated entries and then by subject), the main part of the bibliography lists books, pamphlets, and occasional articles arranged by subject and then by region and country, with brief annotations or scope notes accompanying many of the references. Of the 1,737 entries given, a sizable number were previously listed in the Center's A CURRENT BIBLIOGRAPHY ON AFRICAN AFFAIRS (see no. 292). In addition to indexes by title and author, there is a special index of sources for elementary and secondary schools.

339. African Bibliographic Center, Washington, D.C. CONTEMPORARY AFRICAN
        WOMEN: AN INTRODUCTORY BIBLIOGRAPHICAL OVERVIEW AND A GUIDE TO
        WOMEN'S ORGANIZATIONS, 1960-1967. New York, Negro Universities
        Press, 1969. 59 p. (Special Bibliographic Series, v. 6)

        Compiled by the African Bibliographic Center for the Women's
Africa Committee of the African-American Institute. The bibliographical
section begins with "African Women in Periodicals," then classes entries
under "General," "Clothing and Dress," "Education," "Labor and Employment," "Politics and Government," "Social Studies," and by regions of
Africa. The guide to women's organizations names women's groupings in
Africa (by country), selected African teacher organizations, and
women's organizations in America having African interests. There is
an index of authors for the bibliographical sections. The list is
included in the published volume of the series for 1968.

340. Akademiia Nauk SSSR. Institut Afriki. BIBLIOGRAFIIA AFRIKI [Biblio-
        graphy of Africa]. Moskva, 1964-

        Issued by the Africa Institute in collaboration with the Funda-
mental Library of Social Sciences of the Academy. Vol. I (276 p.)
contains 2,506 numbered entries for the more important books, pamphlets,
and collections of articles on Africa which have appeared in Russian,
including translations, from the late 1700's to 1961. The material is
in classed arrangement, with index by author, editor, translator, and
title. Supplementary sections list 101 doctoral dissertations, 183
works of fiction and art, and 103 maps. The editors state in the preface that a second volume covering periodical literature will be published later.

        The American index to Russian periodical articles which include
Africa, SOVIET PERIODICAL ABSTRACTS, is mentioned above (no. 302), in
the section Current Bibliographies.

341. Akademiia Nauk SSSR. Institut Afriki. LIST OF BOOKS, PAMPHLETS AND
ARTICLES ON AFRICA PUBLISHED IN THE USSR IN 1962. Compiled by
S. Abramova. Moscow, 1963. 126 p.

Includes translated works and book reviews. Many of the references
to books have lengthy annotations.

342. American Library Association. Children's Services Division. AFRICA:
AN ANNOTATED LIST OF PRINTED MATERIALS SUITABLE FOR CHILDREN.
Selected and annotated by a joint committee of the American
Library Association, Children's Services Division and the African-
American Institute. [New York] Information Center on Children's
Cultures, United States Committee for UNICEF, 1968. 76 p.

343. American Library Association. Young Adult Services Division. AFRICAN
ENCOUNTER: A SELECTED BIBLIOGRAPHY OF BOOKS, FILMS, AND OTHER
MATERIALS FOR PROMOTING AN UNDERSTANDING OF AFRICA AMONG YOUNG
ADULTS. Prepared by a committee of the YASD, ALA; Esther J. Walls,
chairman. Chicago, American Library Association, 1963. 69 p.

Should be useful to librarians and teachers among others. Included
are such works as Basil Davidson's LOST CITIES OF AFRICA (1959), Albert
Luthuli's LET MY PEOPLE GO (1963), and Ulli Beier's ART IN NIGERIA
(1960).

344. Beyer, Barry K., ed. AFRICA SOUTH OF THE SAHARA: A RESOURCE GUIDE FOR
SECONDARY SCHOOL TEACHERS. Pittsburgh, Pa., Project Africa,
Carnegie-Mellon University, 1968. 210 p.

As courses on Africa in secondary schools multiply, selections
of appropriate literature become of increasing importance. This practical aid has as Part 1 a survey of literature on teaching African
studies in the secondary schools, with guidelines and some references
to texts. Part 2 is a classified bibliography, with sections on materials for teachers and for students, including film strips, slides,
tapes, programmed courses, and other audio-visual and written materials.
It is concluded by a list of addresses of publishers.

345. Engelborghs-Bertels, Marthe. "Articles publiés par les pays à régime
communiste." Académie Royale des Sciences d'Outre-Mer (Bruxelles),
BULLETIN DES SEANCES, n.s. v. 8, no. 4, 1962: 600-606.

_____. "L'Afrique et les pays communistes." ARSOM, BULLETIN DES
SEANCES, n.s. v. 9, no. 4, 1963: 662-680; v. 10, no. 2, 1964:
263-293.

By a specialist in Chinese studies at the Centre d'Etude des Pays de l'Est. These lists of articles and other material emanating from Communist sources are usually arranged in two sections, one concerning decolonization and Afro-Asian solidarity, the other on Africa in general and then specific African countries. In addition, "L'Afrique et les pays communistes" has sections covering non-Communist commentary on relations of Communist countries with Africa. Translations are noted where available; items are annotated at some length.

346. Glazier, Kenneth M., comp. AFRICA SOUTH OF THE SAHARA: A SELECT AND ANNOTATED BIBLIOGRAPHY, 1958-1963. Stanford, Calif., Hoover Institution, Stanford University, 1964. 65 p. (Hoover Institution Bibliographical Series, no. 16)

Selection of 150 important books with annotations and quotations from book reviews; designed for college and public libraries and as a reading guide for teachers. It is arranged alphabetically by author, with title and subject indexes. A new edition covering 1964-68 has been prepared.

347. Holdsworth, Mary. SOVIET AFRICAN STUDIES, 1918-1959: AN ANNOTATED BIBLIOGRAPHY. Oxford, Distributed for the Royal Institute of International Affairs by the Oxford University Press, 1961. 2 pts. in 1 v. 80, 76 p. Mimeographed. (Chatham House memoranda)

This work, by a specialist in Soviet studies, is practically an essay on Soviet writing regarding Africa, arranged in classed bibliographical form. Some 500 items, books, articles, reports, etc., are commented on, many of them to the extent of a page or more. There are author and subject indexes.

Miss Holdsworth's bibliography was supplemented two years later in the following:

Central Asian Research Centre, London. SOVIET WRITING ON AFRICA, 1959-1961: AN ANNOTATED BIBLIOGRAPHY. London, Distributed for the Royal Institute of International Affairs by the Oxford University Press, 1963. 93 p.

Less extensively annotated than the earlier work, this list contains 433 references to books and articles, similarly in classed arrangement. Most of the Russian titles are followed by an English translation. The coverage includes works of 1959 not cited by Holdsworth and writings of 1960 and 1961.

Further references are carried in the Central Asian Research Centre's MIZAN (1959-), a monthly bulletin including book notes and bibliography. The proportion on Africa is small compared to that for Asia.

348. Hungarian Academy of Sciences. HUNGARIAN PUBLICATIONS ON ASIA AND
     AFRICA, 1950-1962: A SELECTED BIBLIOGRAPHY. Compiled by Eva
     Apor and Ildiko Ecsedy. Budapest, Akadémiai Kiadó, 1963. 106
     p.

     Africa: p. 93-97, five pages of titles of Hungarian works on
Africa.

349. Institut za Izucavanje Radnickog Pokreta. GRADA ZA OPSTU BIBLIO-
     GRAFISKU DOKUMENTACIJU ZA IZUCAVANJE MEDUNARODNOG RADNICKOG
     POKRETA: Vol. II, AFRIKA I AZIJA, 4. Beograd, 1965. 146 l.
     Processed.

     The part on Africa (l. 7-51) has both a general and a country sec-
tion. Under each section entries are grouped by type of work (e.g.,
atlases, bibliographies, periodicals) and by subject.

350. Italiaander, Rolf. AFRICANA: SELECTED BIBLIOGRAPHY OF READINGS IN
     AFRICAN HISTORY AND CIVILIZATION. Holland, Mich., Hope College,
     1961. 101 l. Processed.

     Classified listing of a large number of recent titles, with a
very few annotations, prepared for student use. It does not have an
index.

351. Kozmiński, Macief, and Jan Milewski. BIBLIOGRAFIA POLSKICH PUBLIKACJI
     NA TEMAT AFRYKI. Warsaw, Polski Institut Spraw Miedzynarodowych,
     1965. 2 v.

     A bibliography of Polish publications on African subjects put out
by the Polish Institute of International Affairs.

352. Loewenthal, Rudolf. RUSSIAN MATERIALS ON AFRICA: A SELECTIVE BIBLIO-
     GRAPHY. Washington, Office of Intelligence Research, U.S. Depart-
     ment of State, 1958. 24 p. (External Research paper 133.2, Mar.
     1958)

     One of a series of bibliographies on Asia and Africa that had
appeared in the journal DER ISLAM (West Berlin) in 1957-58. The author
was then teaching at the Institute of Languages and Linguistics in the
Georgetown University School of Foreign Service. His 314 entries, without annotation but with translated titles, are for books and periodical
articles (emphasis on the latter). Arrangement is by region
and there is an index of personal and place names.

353. Matthews, Daniel G. "The Soviet View of Africa: A Select Guide to
        Current Resources for Study and Analysis." CURRENT BIBLIOGRAPHY
        ON AFRICAN AFFAIRS, v. 6, no. 4, Aug. 1967: 5-12.

        The first "Commentary" carried in the CURRENT BIBLIOGRAPHY, this
well-informed bibliographical essay discusses the background of Soviet
African studies and analyzes periodical resources, follcwing with a
classified selection of the more important recent works in Russian
and in English relating to Soviet African interests.

354. Moscow. Publichnaia Biblioteka. Nauchnometodicheskii Ctdel Biblio-
        tekovedeniia i Bibliografii. STRANY AFRIKI: REKOMENDATEL'NYI
        UKAZATEL' LITERATURY. Moskva, 1961. 108 p.

        A list of recommended books on Africa by the compilers at the
State Library of the USSR. Most, but not all, are in Russian.

355. Price, Arnold H. "Recent German-Language Publications on Africa."
        QUARTERLY JOURNAL OF THE LIBRARY OF CONGRESS, v. 22, Apr. 1965:
        148-156.

        Helpful bibliographical essay reviewing the more significant of
the large number of books and periodicals on Africa published in
Germany during the past 10 years or so.

356. Ragatz, Lowell, and Janet Evans Ragatz, comps. A BIBLIOGRAPHY OF
        ARTICLES, DESCRIPTIVE, HISTORICAL AND SCIENTIFIC, ON COLONIES
        AND OTHER DEPENDENT TERRITORIES, APPEARING IN AMERICAN GEO-
        GRAPHICAL AND KINDRED JOURNALS: Vol. I, THROUGH 1934, compiled
        by Lowell Ragatz; Vol. II, 1935 THROUGH 1950, compiled by Janet
        Evans Ragatz. 2d ed. Washington, D.C., Education Research
        Bureau, 1951. 2 v. 214, 149 p.

        Lists articles published from the 1870's through 1950. References
relevant to Africa appear in a general section, in a section devoted to
Africa, in sections on the Belgian, British, French, former German
colonial, Italian, Portuguese, and Spanish empires, and in sections on
U.S. spheres of influence (Liberia) and on jointly held regions (Anglo-
Egyptian Sudan).

357. Rosenblum, Paul, comp. CHECKLIST OF PAPERBOUND BOOKS ON AFRICA (IN
        PRINT NOV. 1967). Albany, State Education Dept., University of
        the State of New York, 1967. 59 p. Offset print.

        Distributed in cooperation with the African Studies Association.
The material is classed in around 20 broad subject headings, followed

by a list of addresses of publishers. Besides the usual fields, the classifications include "Juvenile and Young Adults" and "Maps and Pictures." Some 950-1,000 titles are listed, largely limited to American imprints or books distributed by American publishers. Earlier editions were issued in 1963 (in print Dec. 1962, compiled by Agatha Cowan, 12 p.), 1964 (in print Feb. 1964, 24 p.) and 1965 (in print Sept. 1965, 34 p.). The list is taken from the latest edition of PAPERBOUND BOOKS IN PRINT, published in monthly and cumulative form by R. Bowker Co., New York.

358. Strauch, Hanspeter F. "La contribution des auteurs suisses à la connaissance de l'Afrique: Etude bibliographique. Deuxième partie: De la fin de la première guerre mondiale jusqu'à nos jours." GENÈVE-AFRIQUE, v. 8, no. 1, 1969: 60-87.

The first part of the bibliography appeared in v. 7, no. 2, 1968, of GENÈVE-AFRIQUE. Arrangement is alphabetical by author.

359. U.S. Information Agency. Library. USIA LIBRARY RESOURCES ON AFRICA. Compiled and edited by Joseph L. Dees. Washington, Research and Reference Service, USIA, 1962. 158 p. Processed.

Designed for use by the USIA staff, this is "an annotated selection of 400 books from the Library's holdings on Africa, indexed according to region and country and coded as to principal subjects, together with a description of newspapers, periodicals, and documentary and other materials available in or through the Library."

360. U.S. Joint Publications Research Service. Translations on Africa [series]. Washington, Department of Commerce.

A good explanation of the Joint Publications Research Service, by Rita Lucas and George Caldwell, appeared in the Mar. 1964 issue of COLLEGE AND RESEARCH LIBRARIES (p. 103-110). This service was established in 1957 to fill the needs of certain federal agencies for English-language translations of books, newspaper and periodical articles, etc. At first only scientific and technical material was involved, but subsequently the social sciences were included. JPRS is under the direction of the Office of Technical Services, Department of Commerce, by whom pamphlets are sold (through the Clearinghouse for Federal Scientific and Technical Information, Adams Drive, 4th and 6th Streets, S.W., Washington, D.C. 20443, or Springfield, Va. 22151). Sets of the social science reports by subject and by geographical area are reproduced in microfilm and sold by Readex Microprint Corporation, 5 Union Square, New York 10003. (They can also be bought in rather limited and expensive microfilm reproduction from the Library of Congress or from the Research and Microfilm Publications, Inc.) Titles pertaining to Africa are usually listed in the MONTHLY CATALOG OF UNITED STATES GOVERNMENT PUBLICATIONS only as "Translations on Africa" and may be found under Joint Publications Research Service and in the index under Africa. In the 1964 cumulated annual index (in the December issue of the MONTHLY CATALOG) there are entries of almost a hundred "Translations on Africa" by JPRS; in 1967 the single issue for July has 22. Subject matter ranges widely over countries and political, economic, and social conditions; most of the translations are from journals and newspapers (see, for example, the item below, no. 363, by Julian W. Witherell). Length of translations varies from under 10 to 100 or more pages. In Dec. 1968 JPRS made available its full set of the Translations on Africa series at cost ($100.00).

Other services of JPRS include an index of the French newspaper LE MONDE, which corresponds to the NEW YORK TIMES or the London TIMES. This was begun in 1958, with index of July 1-31, and came out at intervals for a year or more. By 1960 it had become regular. It is published within one or two months after the period indexed. (LE MONDE began publication of an annual index in 1967 with LE MONDE: INDEX ANALYTIQUE 1965, 759 p.) There is a similar index of LA STAMPA and LA STAMPA SERA, morning and evening Turin newspapers by the JPRS.

See also the monthly BIBLIOGRAPHY-INDEX TO CURRENT U.S. JPRS TRANSLATIONS: INTERNATIONAL DEVELOPMENTS, AFRICA, LATIN AMERICA, NEAR EAST, INTERNATIONAL COMMUNIST DEVELOPMENTS (New York, Prepared by Research and Microfilm Publications, Inc., and published by CCM Information Sciences, Inc., 1970-). Each index is divided into two sections: social science; scientific-technical. Within each section references (accompanied by the JPRS document number) are arranged under country. The service began with no. 1, July-Sept. 1962, was called INTERNATIONAL DEVELOPMENTS: A BIBLIOGRAPHY . . . , and was published by Research Microfilms of Annapolis, Maryland.

There is also a semi-annual subject index, SUBJECT-INDEX TO U.S. JOINT PUBLICATIONS RESEARCH SERVICE TRANSLATIONS. This began publication with the index for Jan.-June 1966.

361. U.S. MONTHLY CATALOG OF UNITED STATES GOVERNMENT PUBLICATIONS. Jan. 1895- Washington, Superintendent of Documents, Govt. Print. Off.

The title of this publication has varied over the years. The diversity of documentation on Africa recorded in the MONTHLY CATALOG and in the annual cumulated index (in December issue) is surprising, as well as being invaluable. Besides the JPRS translations in the entry above, there are occasional short releases or informational booklets from the Bureau of Public Affairs of the Department of State and lists of research from its External Research Staff. The Department of Agriculture has several branches which issue reports on general

or particular agricultural subjects (it issues an individual catalogue
of its publications, as do the Department of Commerce, the Department
of State, and other government agencies). There are also a certain
number of congressional papers. In addition, documents that relate
to Africa or individual countries may upon occasion appear under other
headings; for example, under Foreign Service Institute in the index,
the entry "basic language courses" may include African languages (e.g.,
Fula, Shona, Swahili, etc.).

362. Venys, Ladislav, comp. A SELECT BIBLIOGRAPHY OF SOVIET PUBLICATIONS ON
       AFRICA IN GENERAL AND EASTERN AFRICA IN PARTICULAR, 1962-1966.
       Syracuse, N.Y., 1968. 125 l. (Syracuse University. Maxwell
       Graduate School of Citizenship and Public Affairs. Program of
       Eastern African Studies. Occasional Bibliography, no. 11)

       Supplement 1, 1967-1968. Syracuse, N.Y., 1968. (Occasional
            Bibliography, no. 14)

       Supplement 2, 1968-1969. Syracuse, N.Y., 1969. (Occasional
            Bibliography, no. 16)

363. Witherell, Julian W. "Articles on African Affairs Translated by
       J.P.R.S." AFRICAN STUDIES BULLETIN, v. 6, no. 1, Mar. 1963:
       22-37.

       A classified listing of titles of 163 articles which have been
translated into English from the original Russian, Chinese, French,
German, etc., by the Joint Publications Research Service, primarily
for use in official research. Most of the items relate to politics
and propaganda, though there are a few on ethnological and economic
matters. In this list the political articles on Africa in general
are grouped by the country in which they were written--Chinese
(Communist) Viewpoint, French Viewpoint, Guinean Viewpoint, etc.;
the largest group is Soviet Viewpoint.

CHAPTER 7

ACQUISITIONS LISTS

364. <u>Note</u>: Major accessions lists on libraries in the United States are
given below. For accessions lists from libraries in other countries,
the following might be noted as of significance for Africana:

<u>United Kingdom</u>

a) Great Britain. Office of Commonwealth Relations. Library.
        SELECTIVE LIST OF ACQUISITIONS. v. 1, no. 1- Apr.-May
        1949- London. Bimonthly. Mimeographed.

        Begun by the Office of Commonwealth Relations with title
        DIGEST OF BOOKS AND PAMPHLETS; later enlarged to include acces-
        sions of the Colonial Office Library. This is an extensive rec-
        ord of new publications, including not only official reports and
        papers but also titles of books, pamphlets, and new periodicals,
        some in French and other languages. Classification is by region.

b) London. University. Institute of Commonwealth Studies.
        Library. SELECT LIST OF ACCESSIONS. Quarterly.

c) London. University. School of Oriental and African Studies.
        Library. MONTHLY LIST OF TITLES ADDED TO THE CATALOGUE.
        1951-

d) Oxford University. Institute of Commonwealth Studies. LIBRARY
        ACCESSIONS. Quarterly.

e) Royal Commonwealth Society, London. LIBRARY NOTES, WITH LIST OF
        ACCESSIONS. Monthly. (n.s. no. 139, July 1968)

        The 1968 issues cover the history of the library.

<u>Belgium</u>

f) Belgium. Ministère des Affaires Etrangères et du Commerce
        Extérieur. CATALOGUE DES ACQUISITIONS. Bruxelles. Annual.

(1963, 183 p.)

Printed catalogue in decimal classification, including about
1,500 entries and an author index. There are monthly mimeographed supplements. This supersedes the CATALOGUE DES ACQUISITIONS
of the Ministère des Affaires Africaines, Bibliothèque.

France

g) France. Direction des Archives. Archives Nationales. Section
Outre-Mer. Bibliothèque. "Livres reçus au cours de l'année
1962." BULLETIN DES NOUVELLES ACQUISITIONS DE LA BIBLIO-
THEQUE, no. 18, Mar. 1963. 47 p.

Has 700-odd entries, in two groups, by subject and by region;
some titles are repeated. Imprint is given but not paging.

h) Paris. Musée de l'Homme. Bibliothèque. LISTE DES ACQUISITIONS.

Scandinavia

i) Uppsala, Sweden. University. Nordiska Afrika Institutet.
AFRICANA I NORDISKA VETENSKAPLIGA BIBLIOTEK. Semiannual.

A union list, giving acquisitions of 16 libraries in Denmark,
Norway, and Sweden; subject classification.

Africa

j) Bibliothèque du Congo, Léopoldville. LISTE DES ACQUISITIONS DE
LA BIBLIOTHEQUE DU CONGO. Monthly (irregular).

It is not known whether this has been discontinued.

k) Ghana. University. LIBRARY BULLETIN. v. 1- (n.s. 1963-)
Legon. Quarterly.

List of books catalogued during the last three months. Most
of them are general works, without special African interest, but
the last few pages give titles in the Africana Library.

l) Institut Fondamental d'Afrique Noire, Dakar. LISTE DES ACQUISITIONS.

Lists of periodicals and newspaper acquisitions are issued
regularly.

m) Instituto de Angola, Luanda. BOLETIM ANALITICO. Monthly. (no.
2, Nov. 1964)

n) Instituto de Angola, Luanda.   BOLETIM BIBLIOGRAFICO.
    Monthly.

    Two lists showing acquisitions, the first annotated, the
second a title list, in which are given a section of books and
pamphlets and then an analysis of current issues of periodicals.
Like the Ghana LIBRARY BULLETIN, these consist mostly of general
works, without special application to Africa.

o) United Nations. Economic Commission for Africa. Library. NEW
    ACQUISITIONS IN THE UNECA LIBRARY. NOUVELLES ACQUISITIONS
    DE LA BIBLIOTHEQUE DE LA CEA. v. 1, no. 1- Oct. 1962-
    Addis Ababa. Monthly. Mimeographed.

    This large monthly acquisitions list has four sections: 1,
works on Africa in general and on other regions of the world; 2,
works arranged by specific countries, including France, the United
Kingdom, and the United States as well as African and some Middle
Eastern countries; 3, publications on subject themes, arranged
by appropriate subject; 4, publications by UNESCO, divided into
two groups, by country and by subject. Although a large proportion
of the works cited are governmental documents and reports, the
library is by no means limited to official materials.

p) U.S. Library of Congress. National Program for Acquisitions
    and Cataloging. ACCESSIONS LIST: EASTERN AFRICA. v. 1, no.
    1- Jan. 1968- Nairobi, Library of Congress Office. Quarterly.

    A most valuable source for publications throughout East Africa,
the Horn and the various offshore islands.

365. Joint Committee on African Resources.   JOINT ACQUISITIONS LIST OF
      AFRICANA. 1962- Compiled by the African Department, Northwestern
      University Library. Evanston, Ill., Northwestern University
      Library. Quarterly. Processed.

    A very full bibliography of various kinds of publications on Africa
south of the Sahara as currently acquired by a group of libraries having
large holdings of Africana. The Joint Committee is a subcommittee of
two organizations, the Association of Research Libraries' Farmington
Plan African Committee and the African Studies Association's Libraries-
Archives Committee. The contributing libraries (21 in July 1967), including the Library of Congress, send the titles of their acquisitions
to Northwestern University, where they are assembled into an alphabetical
title list, with symbols showing library locations. Because some libraries continue to build up their collections with retrospective buying,
a certain number of the books, pamphlets, and documents listed are not
of very recent date, but in the main only those published in the last
five years are included. A number of the entries from the Library of
Congress represent preliminary cataloguing (see no. 304). The Joint

Committee list, which has averaged over 700 titles per issue, is extremely valuable in that the libraries concerned are buying, as heavily as possible, publications from Africa itself. Although many of these are of slight or ephemeral value, they are indicative of the advance of African publishing. The list covers, or in several cases has replaced, accessions lists previously issued by university libraries. Prepared by a microscopic photographic process, the list is hard to use except for those with keen eyesight.

366. Michigan State University. Libraries. International Library. AFRICANA: SELECT RECENT ACQUISITIONS. East Lansing. Bimonthly.

367. U.S. LIBRARY OF CONGRESS CATALOG. BOOKS: SUBJECTS. 1950- Washington, U.S. Govt. Print. Off. Jan.-Mar., Apr.-June, July-Sept., and annual and 5-year cumulations.

For full description see Winchell (no. 1). The large acquisitions of Africana catalogued in the Library of Congress collections appear under the subject headings Africa (in 1965 volume, p. 59-70) and other place names and also under topical breakdowns, e.g., Agriculture--Africa.

In the monthly and cumulative issues of the NATIONAL UNION CATALOG . . . AUTHOR LIST, which in 1953 replaced the LIBRARY OF CONGRESS AUTHOR CATALOG, the approach is of course by author. The LIST now includes titles reported by other American libraries.

368. Yale University. Library. African Collection. ACCESSIONS LIST. v. 1, no. 1, 1967- New Haven, Conn. Monthly.

CHAPTER 8

LISTS OF SERIALS

Note: There have recently been issued a number of lists of serials relating
in whole or in substantial part to Africa, some the record of individual
library holdings, others attempts to cover the field as widely as possible.
This form of material is peculiarly intractable so far as bibliographical
control is concerned. Not only in countries of Africa, where many serials
are temporary results of mission presses or of individual enthusiasm, but
even in Western centers magazines, journals, bulletins, and newsletters are
lavishly established, flourish for a few issues, and then with any adverse
wind, whatever its direction, are gone; if they survive, they change their
names and dispositions without regard for librarians. Consequently any rash
bibliographer trying to compile a comprehensive list of serials, particularly
if he wants to give dates and holdings, lays himself open to unlimited
opportunities for error. This brief comment may be interpreted by way of
apology for the inadequacies of the compilations noted below. The few named
are general in their subject coverage for Africa; lists relating to specialized periodicals--e.g., those on the Congo, missionary periodicals, etc.--
are noted in later sections. Separate listings of serials are also included
in the aforementioned bibliographies of Mylius and Wieschhoff and the Howard
University catalogue (nos. 317, 322, and 328).

Brief listings of the serial publications of African countries are
given in a number of surveys and handbooks, e.g., EUROPA YEARBOOK (see no.
459). The national press guides are occasionally helpful, especially when
a specific periodical is being sought. Not enough Africanist periodicals
are published in America to make the N.W. Ayer & Son's DIRECTORY: NEWSPAPERS
AND PERIODICALS of much use, but the French ANNUAIRE DE LA PRESSE FRANCAISE
ET ETRANGERE ET DU MONDE POLITIQUE often provides answers. It is in classed
arrangement with title index, and many French serials relating to Africa are
brought together in one category, Outre-Mer. In addition, there are at the
end sections for serials published overseas, including French-speaking African
countries, with a separate title index. The comparable British WILLING'S
PRESS GUIDE (London, annual) is in straight alphabetical arrangement for
serials appearing in London, then by regions or cities, including a short
listing of overseas periodicals by countries; it has neither subject nor
title indexes.

369. For titles of periodicals the following general library tools are available:

    a)   BRITISH UNION-CATALOGUE OF PERIODICALS. 1955-58. London. (4 v., and SUPPLEMENT TO 1960, published in 1962)

          Alphabetical listing of over 140,000 serial publications with indication of holdings in 440 British libraries. Includes publications of institutions (under name of institution) and of international conferences, nonadministrative official publications, etc. Approach is by title (the earliest form) or institutional name.

          In 1964 appeared the first annual volume entitled BRITISH UNION-CATALOGUE OF PERIODICALS INCORPORATING WORLD LIST OF SCIENTIFIC PERIODICALS: NEW PERIODICAL TITLES, which records new titles for the period in and after 1960. The WORLD LIST OF SCIENTIFIC PERIODICALS will in effect be continued in these separate annual volumes of the BUCOP.

    b)   NEW SERIAL TITLES: A UNION LIST OF SERIALS COMMENCING PUBLICATION AFTER DEC. 31, 1949. Jan. 1953- Washington, U.S. Library of Congress. Monthly and cumulative. (1950-60 cumulation in 2 v.)

          The continuing supplement to UNION LIST OF SERIALS. Arrangement is alphabetical by title or name of issuing institution. Official material is included. Symbols indicate holdings in American libraries.

          A classed subject arrangement, separately published, was begun in 1955; its classes are by discipline and are not especially useful for African studies.

    c)   ULRICH'S INTERNATIONAL PERIODICALS DIRECTORY: A CLASSIFIED GUIDE TO A SELECTED LIST OF CURRENT PERIODICALS, FOREIGN AND DOMESTIC. New York, Bowker, 1932-

          With the 11th edition (1965-66, 1110 p.) the publication became two volumes: I, scientific, technical, and medical periodicals (p. 1-484), and II, arts, humanities, business, and social sciences (p. 485-1110). The entries data on beginning dates, inclusion of book reviews and bibliography, etc. Each volume has an index and key to subjects, the one in Vol. II covering both volumes.

370. ADVERTISING & PRESS ANNUAL OF AFRICA (EXCLUDING NORTH AFRICA): THE BLUE BOOK OF ADVERTISING IN AFRICA. 1949- Edited by Percy A. Blooman, F. M. Botha, and G. H. Blooman. Cape Town, National Publishing Co. 1967 ed. 410 p.

Gives general advertising and press information, including market facts (by country), classified and geographical lists of newspapers and periodicals, national advertisers and agents, subscription and advertisement rates, who's who in advertising, etc., current within the year; title varies. It has the most comprehensive listing of newspapers and periodicals within Africa. Publications of learned societies, universities, and mission presses are not covered.

371. AFRICANA NEWSLETTER. 1962-64. Edited by Peter Duignan. Stanford, Calif., Hoover Institution, Stanford University. Quarterly, then semiannually. 2 v. (Integrated in 1965 into AFRICAN STUDIES BULLETIN)

Among the primary interests of the AFRICANA NEWSLETTER were African newspapers and holdings in specified libraries, and serial publications of the countries of Africa. The following articles and notes appeared in the two volumes of the NEWSLETTER:

v. 1, no. 2, Spring 1963:

"Newly Acquired African Newspapers in Selected American Libraries": p. 4-5.

"The Press of Ghana and Liberia": p. 5-7.

"Cameroon Newspapers, before and after Independence": p. 8-12.

"The African Nationalist and Radical Press of Southern Africa": p. 12-13.

"African Newspapers Available on Microfilm": p. 14-15.

This article shows 33 African newspapers being microfilmed at the Library of Congress and the Mid-West Library Center (now the Center for Research Libraries), as well as 27 available in microfilm from Microfile, Ltd., in Johannesburg, South Africa.

v. 1, no. 3, Summer 1963:

"Serial Publications of Portugal and Portuguese Africa": p. 16-19.

"The Press of Nigeria": p. 40-45.

"African Newspapers on Microfilm [in England]": p. 52.

v. 1, no. 4, Winter 1963:

"Periodicals of Kenya, Tanganyika, Uganda, and the Sudan": p. 42-52.

"Nigerian Newspapers [on Microfilm] at University College,
Ibadan": p. 63-64.

v. 2, no. 1, 1964:

"Serials of Cameroun, Dahomey, Togo, Mali, Ethiopia, and
the Somali Republic": p. 33-41.

v. 2, no. 2, 1964:

"African Serials: Angola, Central African Republic, Ivory
Coast, Malagasy Republic, Rwanda, Sierra Leone":
p. 41-47.

"South African Newspapers and Periodicals Available on
Microfilm, Sept. 1963": p. 48-51.

Over 60 newspaper and periodical titles, with dates
covered and agency from which microfilms are available;
compiled by the State Library in Pretoria.

Later contributions on African newspapers and serials appear
from time to time in the AFRICAN STUDIES BULLETIN.

372. Ainslie, Rosalynde. THE PRESS IN AFRICA: COMMUNICATIONS PAST AND
PRESENT. London, V. Gollanz, 1966. 256 p.

Covers the press, radio, and television, with emphasis on the
situation in English-speaking Africa. There are sections on West,
Southern, East, and North Africa, French-speaking Africa, Zambia,
and the Congo (Kinshasa), and on news agencies, the colonial legacy,
and freedom of the press. A concluding chapter discusses the conditions for the development of the mass media and the need for them
to be truly African. A list of African broadcasting stations, news
agencies, and daily newspapers as of Dec. 1965 is given. There is
an index. See also no. 378, Feuereisen and Schmacke, DIE PRESSE IN
AFRIKA (München, 1968).

373. Centre d'Analyse et de Recherche Documentaires pour l'Afrique Noire.
REPERTOIRE DES PERIODIQUES DEPOUILLES. Paris, Maison des Sciences
de l'Homme.

The REPERTOIRE of Nov. 1965 has 30 pages of serial titles.

374. Committee for Inter-African Relations. REPORT ON THE PRESS IN WEST
AFRICA. Ibadan, 1960. 133 p. map. Mimeographed.

Prepared for the International Seminar on "Press and Progress in
West Africa," University of Dakar, May 31 to June 4, 1960, organized in

collaboration with the University of Dakar, the University College of Ghana, Legon, and the University College, Ibadan, Nigeria.

375. Dakar. Université. ETAT DES PERIODIQUES CONSERVES A LA BIBLIOTHEQUE DE L'UNIVERSITE. Dakar, 1962. 67 l. Processed.

Supplement. 1963. 3, 10 l.

This and similar lists of periodicals held in individual African libraries represent general serials rather than those of the country.

376. De Benko, Eugene, and Patricia Butts. RESEARCH SOURCES FOR AFRICAN STUDIES: A CHECKLIST OF RELEVANT SERIAL PUBLICATIONS BASED ON LIBRARY COLLECTIONS AT MICHIGAN STATE UNIVERSITY. East Lansing, African Studies Center, Michigan State University, 1969. 384 p.

This list of over 2,000 serial titles is useful not only as a guide to the collection at Michigan State but also as a reference tool for interlibrary loan or for filling in incomplete holdings. It complements SERIALS FOR AFRICAN STUDIES (no. 396) and the next entry.

377. Duignan, Peter, and Kenneth M. Glazier, comps. A CHECKLIST OF SERIALS FOR AFRICAN STUDIES, BASED ON THE LIBRARIES OF THE HOOVER INSTITUTION AND STANFORD UNIVERSITY. Stanford, Calif., Hoover Institution, Stanford University, 1963. 104 p. (Hoover Institution Bibliographical Series, no 13)

The compilers have listed some 1,220 periodicals and almost 200 newspapers, the latter in country arrangement. The periodicals include many official bulletins, annuals, and reports--Stanford's Documents Division is an official depository for UN documents and receives general statistical annuals, bulletins, and reports from most countries of Africa; in addition, it was long an official depository for British government documents. The substantial serial holdings of the Food Research Institute are chiefly in the fields of agriculture, food and nutrition, agricultural economics, and other research needs.

378. Feuereisen, Fritz, and Ernst Schmacke, eds. DIE PRESSE IN AFRIKA: EIN HANDBUCH FUR WIRTSCHAFT UND WERBUNG. [Title also in English] München, Verlag Dokumentation, 1968. 251 p.

This bilingual manual on the press in Africa, designed for use in commerce and advertising, lists every important newspaper and periodical issued in Africa (excluding Egypt). For each country, introductory notes (data on size, population, government, language, currency, religion, imports and exports, etc.) are followed by information on the press presented in tabulated form: title, political leaning, address, circulation, language, frequency, kind of readers, number and size of pages, printing method, tariff, and fixed days for advertisements. There is also a summary of international newspapers and periodicals distributed in Africa, a geographical index (with indications of publications issued in each place), and a title index.

379. Ghana. University College, Legon. Library. LIST OF PERIODICALS IN THE LIBRARY. Legon, 1961. 168 p.

   As with most other listings of holdings of African libraries, the items named are not principally Africana but rather are of general, scientific, technical, or other educational nature.

380. Hewitt, Arthur R. UNION LIST OF COMMONWEALTH NEWSPAPERS IN LONDON, OXFORD, AND CAMBRIDGE. London, Published for the Institute of Commonwealth Studies, University of London, by the Athlone Press, 1960. 101 p.

   In offset print, legal-size paper. Arrangement is alphabetical by country and territory of origin, with title index. In the table of contents 18 African countries are included.

381. Hutton, James, ed. PERIODICALS IN THE LIBRARIES OF THE FEDERATION OF RHODESIA AND NYASALAND. Published with the aid of grants made by the Government of the Federation of Rhodesia and Nyasaland and the Government of Southern Rhodesia. Salisbury, University College of Rhodesia and Nyasaland, 1962. 238 l. loose-leaf.

382. Institut Français d'Afrique Noire. CATALOGUE DES PERIODIQUES D'AFRIQUE NOIRE FRANCOPHONE (1858-1962) CONSERVES A IFAN. Compiled by Marguerite Thomassery. Dakar, IFAN, 1965. 117 p. (Catalogues et documents, no. 19)

   A valuable list of almost 600 serials and government document series held by IFAN at Dakar. Included are files of rare newspapers produced by Africans since 1900. There are four indexes: geographic and analytical; chronological; organizations; directors, editors, and authors.

383. Institut Royal des Sciences Naturelles de Belgique. LISTE DES PERIODIQUES AFRICAINS DE LA BIBLIOTHEQUE. [Title also in Dutch] Bruxelles, 1960. 48 p.

   List of 223 serials, mostly bulletins, mémoires, and other series issued by universities and learned societies or other institutions, official and unofficial, in Africa. The emphasis is on publications relating to the natural sciences, but enough are of general coverage to warrant mention here.

384. Khartoum. University College. Library. SUDANESE UNION-CATALOGUE OF PERIODICALS. Khartoum, 1961. 116, 12 l.

Holdings of 19 libraries are listed. The "Appendix" (12 l. at end) is a separate listing in Arabic of the Arabic titles.

385. Kwame Nkrumah University of Science and Technology. Library. LIST OF PERIODICALS CURRENTLY RECEIVED. Kumasi, 1964. 51 p.

386. Maison des Sciences de l'Homme. Service d'Echange d'Informations Scientifiques. LISTE MONDIALE DES PERIODIQUES SPECIALISES, ETUDES AFRICAINES. WORLD LIST OF SPECIALIZED PERIODICALS, AFRICAN STUDIES. Etablié avec la collaboration du CARDAN. Paris, Mouton, 1969. 214 p. (Publications série C, Catalogues et inventaires 3)

Lists 492 periodicals concerning Africa south of the Sahara and dealing with the social sciences. The list is arranged by country of publication, then divided into three categories: category A, periodicals concerned solely with sub-Saharan Africa; category B, those with a significant part devoted to African subjects; category C, those concerned with African studies like category A, but which are information bulletins rather than research studies. Each entry gives standard abbreviation of title, name and address of editor and publisher, frequency, indexes provided, date of first issue, and either a description of one issue or an annotation.

387. Paris. Bibliothèque Nationale. Département des Périodiques. INVENTAIRE DES PERIODIQUES ETRANGERS RECUS EN FRANCE PAR LES BIBLIOTHEQUES ET LES ORGANISMES DE DOCUMENTATION EN 1960-61. [3d ed.] Paris, Bibliothèque Nationale, 1962. 636 p. (Direction des Bibliothèques de France, Inventaire permanent des périodiques étrangers en cours)

In the first edition (1955) over 1,800 bodies reported some 21,000 notices. Approach is by title only, and few African titles are noted.

388. Paris. Musée de l'Homme. Bibliothèque. LISTE DES PUBLICATIONS
      PERIODIQUES RECUES REGULIEREMENT. Paris.

      This list has been issued at intervals. The holdings of the
library are in the field designated as "sciences humaines," going
well beyond the usual definitions of anthropology into practically
all disciplines except the natural sciences. The periodicals received,
many on exchange from other learned institutions, come from all parts
of the world. They are entered alphabetically by title or institution.

389. PERIODICALS IN EAST AFRICAN LIBRARIES: A UNION LIST. 3d ed. Morgan-
      town, West Virginia University Library, 1969. 465 p.

      An annual edition of this publication was planned (1st ed., 1965).
Data, on forms provided, are sent in by the cooperating libraries to
the West Virginia University Library, Morgantown, for computerizing--
until such facilities become available in East Africa. Arrangement
is alphabetical by title, except for bulletins, journals, and similar
publications of societies and associations which are entered under the
name of the organization. A symbol indicates where the periodical may
be found, and interlibrary loan is thus made possible. For the present
the list covers only periodicals currently received; at some future
time complete holdings may be included. In the 1969 edition there are
over 3,000 entries.

390. "La presse en Afrique au sud du Sahara." AFRIQUE (Paris), no. 19,
      Dec. 1962: 35-53; no. 26, July 1963: 32-49.

      A roundup of newspapers and journals published in both English-
and French-speaking countries of Africa, with analytical description
of each. The first article, in the section of this useful monthly
called "Le dossier d'Afrique," takes in West Africa and Madagascar.
The second issue carries parts on the press in East Africa and South
Africa and, finally, general reflections on the African press and its
future development. In an evaluative listing of this sort, the very
ephemeral and inconsequential periodicals are of course excluded. For
West Africa the vernacular press is not noticed, but the section on
Madagascar includes dailies.

391. Ruth Sloan Associates, Washington, D.C. THE PRESS IN AFRICA. Edited
      by Helen Kitchen. Washington, 1956. 96 p.

      Analytical tables of the principal newspapers and periodicals,
country by country, with accompanying comment on the state of the
press. Included are publications in the vernacular. The work is
now much outdated but has useful historical data.

392. SITUATION DE LA PRESSE DANS LES ETATS DE L'UNION AFRICAINE ET MALGACHE,
     GUINEE, AU MALI, AU TOGO. By Jacqueline Gras. Paris, La
     Documentation Française, 1963. 175 p. (Travaux et recherches,
     no. 17)

     For each country of French-speaking Africa are given general
statistics (area, population, principal cities, official and local
languages, political parties, radio stations, etc.), a history of the
press, and present-day data including a list of daily newspapers and
periodical publications.

393. Standing Conference on Library Materials on Africa (SCOLMA). PERIODICALS
     PUBLISHED IN AFRICA. pt. 1- June 1965- London. Irregularly
     issued. Processed. (Supplement to LIBRARY MATERIALS ON AFRICA,
     v. 3, no. 1, May 1965-)

     These lists give both current periodicals and those which have
ceased publication. Included are government periodicals and annuals
but not government department reports. Excluded also are daily and
Sunday commercial newspapers. Countries are separately paged, each
part totaling around 40-60 pages. The first four parts have covered
French-speaking Africa, North Africa (except Egypt), Northeastern
Africa, Liberia, and most of the islands adjacent to Africa (part 4,
July 1966).

394. UNION LIST OF SERIALS IN LIBRARIES OF THE UNITED STATES AND CANADA.
     3d ed. Edited by Edna Brown Titus. New York, H. W. Wilson Co.,
     1965. 5 v. 4649 p.

     This revision, in preparation for several years at the Library
of Congress, records the holdings of 956 libraries in serials published
through 1949. There are 156,449 entries plus 70,538 cross-references
making a grand total of 226,987. NEW SERIAL TITLES continues the
coverage from Jan. 1, 1950. Approach is by name of periodical or
issuing institution; symbols indicate library holdings.

395. United Nations. Economic Commission for Africa. Library. PERIODICALS
     RECEIVED IN THE UNECA LIBRARY. Addis Ababa, Oct. 1961. 113 p.
     Mimeographed. (E/CN.14/LIB/SER.A/1)

     The UNECA Library listed 829 periodicals received, a large propor-
tion of which were African in origin, with many others relating primarily to African interests. The entries are arranged in three parts:
Nongovernmental (415 items), Governmental (292 items), UN and specialized
agencies (122 items). Part 2, Governmental, is broken down by country
(77; of these, 52 are African entities) and includes most official
gazettes, statistical bulletins, etc. There is a title index to the

first two parts as well as a detailed subject index. The first supplement was issued in 1962. A CHECKLIST OF SERIALS CURRENTLY RECEIVED IN THE ECA LIBRARY, JUNE 1968 was issued in 1968 (77 p.).

396. U.S. Library of Congress. General Reference and Bibliography Division. SERIALS FOR AFRICAN STUDIES. Compiled by Helen F. Conover, African Section. Washington, 1961. 163 p. Offset print.

This list, which has 2,080 numbered entries of serial titles, was designed to record as many as possible of the worldwide periodical publications relating to Africa and having more than ephemeral interest. Locations are given for holdings in the Library of Congress and some 40 American libraries, with dates where possible. (An effort--not wholly successful--was made to establish beginning and ending dates for all titles.) Many of the publications have not been found in American libraries but represent titles taken from European sources. The sources are listed in an appendix, p. 145-147; most of them are specialized, some are manuscript lists lent by other libraries. The list has two indexes, one by subject or type (e.g., fortnightly journals), the other of institutions publishing serials. Almost a thousand institutions are named, exclusive of official government agencies in African or other countries. Their names may be found in alphabetical order, under the name of the country, within the text. Official reports of departments have been omitted; also omitted are the many geological and meteorological serial publications of African governments, pamphlet series, and newspapers (for these, see next item). A revised edition of this list, which has been in preparation for two years or more, was scheduled for publication in late 1970. It follows the same general plan and arrangement but contains 4,670 entries (SUB-SAHARAN AFRICA: A GUIDE TO SERIALS).

397. U.S. Library of Congress. Serial Division. AFRICAN NEWSPAPERS IN SELECTED AMERICAN LIBRARIES. 3d ed. Compiled by Rozanne M. Barry. Washington, 1965. 135 p.

List of current and retrospective holdings of African newspapers in 33 selected American libraries as of the spring of 1964. This edition supersedes a list with the same title published in 1962 and giving holdings of 20 libraries, which in turn superseded a list of 1956 reporting on only 8 libraries. The present work lists 708 African newspapers, 283 of them new titles since the last edition, and includes both hard copy and positive microfilms. Dates of holdings are inclusive for each library. Since many African newspapers are indistinguishable in format from weekly periodicals, it is difficult to make a clear distinction, and a good many titles that appear as newspapers in other libraries are classed by the Library of Congress as periodicals; these are so indicated in the notation on holdings.

398. U.S. Library of Congress. Union Catalog Division. NEWSPAPERS ON
        MICROFILM. 6th ed. Compiled under the direction of George A.
        Schwegmann. Washington, 1967. xv, 487 p.

     The first part of this long list is for America, the second part
(p. 231-305) for foreign countries, in alphabetical arrangement by
name of country. The table of contents indicates material from 37
African countries.

399. Wallenius, Anna-Britta, comp. PERIODICA I NORDISKA AFRIKAINSTITUTETS
        BIBLIOTEK. Uppsala, Nordiska Afrikainstitutet, 1966. 21 1.
        Processed.

     A list of about 400 periodicals, most having direct concern with
Africa.

400. Yale University. Library. A PARTIAL LISTING OF THE PERIODICAL HOLDINGS
        OF THE STERLING LIBRARY...RELEVANT TO THE STUDY OF AFRICA. New
        Haven, Conn., 1963. 52 1. Offset print.

     Some 400-500 periodicals are listed, with dates of the holdings
in the Sterling Library. Quite a number go back to the nineteenth
century.

     See also the Howard University CATALOGUE (no. 328), which includes
a separate listing of periodicals and newspapers.

CHAPTER 9

OFFICIAL PUBLICATIONS

Note: In many African countries reports of government agencies, legislative
papers, and other documents are mimeographed in very limited editions, and
copies are often extremely hard to come by. Sometimes the government printer
issues a list of documents in stock. More often, the chief source of information regarding current official publications is the country's official
gazette, in which documents are sometimes announced as they appear and in
which from time to time are given lists of materials available from the
government printer. In these lists documents are usually difficult to identify, as their titles are not set down in strict obedience to library rules.

401. General library tools for official documents include, besides the
         entries under names of countries in such comprehensive works as
         the NATIONAL UNION CATALOG, NEW SERIAL TITLES, etc., the following:

SERIAL PUBLICATIONS OF FOREIGN GOVERNMENTS, 1815-1931. Edited by
     Winifred Gregory. New York, H. W. Wilson Co., 1932. 720 p.

     See under individual African countries.

402. BIBLIOGRAPHIE DE LA FRANCE: Supplément F, PUBLICATIONS OFFICIELLES.
         Paris, Au Cercle de la Librairie. Irregular (5-7 numbers a year).

     This list of official French documents included those of the over-
seas possessions (in alphabetical arrangement by country). Like the
British Ministry of Overseas Development's TECHNICAL CO-OPERATION
(successor to the Colonial Office's MONTHLY LIST), since 1958 the
entries have greatly diminished in number, with a few appearing only
occasionally for Outre-Mer.

     Another listing, more prompt but less complete, is the semimonthly
BIBLIOGRAPHIE SELECTIVE DES PUBLICATIONS OFFICIELLES FRANCAISES (1952-),
published by La Documentation Française, which is the publishing arm of

the official Direction de la Documentation. This bibliography includes a listing of the various series put out by La Documentation Française, e.g., the Notes et études documentaires, in which there are valuable background surveys of individual African countries or questions. These are not limited to former French Africa; for instance, the best recent brochure on Spanish possessions in Africa was in this series (see no. 2843).

403. Boston University. Libraries. CATALOG OF AFRICAN GOVERNMENT DOCUMENTS AND AFRICAN AREA INDEX. 2d ed., rev. and enl. Compiled by Mary Darrah Herrick. Boston, G. K. Hall, 1964. 471 p.

One of the photoprinted reproductions of library cards published by G. K. Hall, this shows the large collections in the Boston University libraries of official publications of African governments. The program of African studies at Boston University has been slanted toward politico-economic and administrative affairs, and great efforts have been made to acquire the documents of the African countries on the largest possible scale. A set of cards for these documents is kept closely up to date. The second part of this publication lists the subject headings under which African materials are to be found in the libraries. A preliminary edition of 124 pages (99, 25) was published in 1960.

404. Duke University. Library. A LIST OF SELECTED OFFICIAL PUBLICATIONS AND SERIALS OF THE BRITISH COMMONWEALTH IN THE DUKE UNIVERSITY LIBRARY. Durham, N.C., 1959. 83 l. Processed.

405. Great Britain. Colonial Office. Library. MONTHLY LIST OF OFFICIAL COLONIAL PUBLICATIONS. v. 1, no. 1-v. 16, no. 12. June 1948- Dec. 1963. London. 33 cm. Mimeographed.

Until the 1960's the MONTHLY LIST was the fullest available record of official publications for a large part of Africa and for other over- seas possessions of the United Kingdom, and it is now an indispensable source for retrospective study of the countries of Africa formerly British. In several sections, the listing is alphabetical by countries. Part 1A cites typescripts and other papers prepared in the colonies but not for sale; Part 1B lists colonial government publications, and 1C colonial legislation. Part 2 has publications of H.M. Stationery Office and the intelligence services of the Commonwealth Economic Committee. Part 3 lists government gazettes, and a maps section includes those listed in the Directorate of Overseas Surveys supplement.

The Ministry of Overseas Development took over some of the functions of the Colonial Office, and its publication TECHNICAL CO-OPERATION: A MONTHLY BIBLIOGRAPHY (see below) with an irregular supplement covers

much of the material formerly in the MONTHLY LIST. The Colonial Office
as such ceased to exist in Aug. 1966, when it was merged with the
Commonwealth Relations Office to form the Commonwealth Office.

406. Great Britain. Ministry of Overseas Development. Library. TECHNICAL
      CO-OPERATION: A MONTHLY BIBLIOGRAPHY. v. 1, no. 1- Jan. 1964-
      London.

      Supplement. no. 1- Apr. 1964- Irregularly issued.

      This bibliography is published by the office which has taken over
many of the functions of the Colonial Office and certain of those of
other branches of the British government; it was established in 1961
as the Department of Technical Co-operation and in Oct. 1964 became
the Ministry of Overseas Development. The list follows to some extent
the arrangement of the Colonial Office's MONTHLY LIST. In Part 1 are
unpublished reports of the Ministry and the Commonwealth Office and
bulletins and reports from foreign institutes and organizations. Part
2 has official publications of various Commonwealth governments, Part
3 the relevant publications of H.M. Stationery Office and the intelligence services of the Commonwealth Economic Committee. Part 4 is the
map additions list of the Directorate of Overseas Surveys. The supplement carries information relating to bills and subsidiary legislation
of the Commonwealth countries (information on main legislation is included in the issues of TECHNICAL CO-OPERATION).

407. Landskron, William A., comp. OFFICIAL SERIAL PUBLICATIONS RELATING TO
      ECONOMIC DEVELOPMENT IN AFRICA SOUTH OF THE SAHARA: A PRELIMINARY
      LIST OF ENGLISH-LANGUAGE PUBLICATIONS. Cambridge, Massachusetts
      Institute of Technology, 1961. 44 p.

408. New York. Public Library. NATIONAL AND LOCAL GAZETTES MICROFILMING
      PROGRAM. New York, 1962. 37 <u>1</u>.

      List of 236 national and local gazettes available on microfilm
as of the end of 1961. A number of gazettes of African countries are
included.

409. United Nations. Economic Commission for Africa. Library. ANNUALS
      RECEIVED IN THE UNECA LIBRARY. Addis Ababa, Jan. 1962. 194 p.
      Mimeographed. (E/CN.14/LIB/SER.A/2)

      The foreword states that the UNECA library has reasonably complete
holdings of the yearbooks and annual reports listed from 1958 onward.
The vast preponderance of them are published in or relate to Africa.
They are in three groups: Nongovernmental annuals (180 titles); Governmental annuals, including departmental reports, general and by country

144

and region, with classed subdivision (962 titles); and annuals of the UN and specialized agencies (118 titles).

See also UNECA lists of books and periodicals in the library (nos. 336, 395) and its monthly list of acquisitions (no. 364[o]).

410. U.S. Library of Congress. General Reference and Bibliography Division. [Official publications of the countries of Africa] 1959-

The African Section of the Library of Congress began a series of lists of the official publications of African countries in 1959 with NIGERIAN OFFICIAL PUBLICATIONS, 1869-1959: A GUIDE. This was followed by listings of government documents of most other countries of Africa south of the Sahara, a number of which were in print by 1968 (see under individual countries or regions). The lists are by no means restricted to holdings in the Library of Congress and other American libraries but have been compiled with the aid of all available library tools, including the French and British lists mentioned above, leaflets of publications in print from government printers, citations from official gazettes and legislative proceedings (papers laid on the table), etc. In general, they are restricted to publications on the national or regional level. Arrangement is usually by issuing agency; all have author and subject indexes.

411. Witherell, Julian W. "Government Printers in Africa." AFRICANA NEWS-LETTER, v. 1, no. 3, 1963: 45-48.

Addresses of some 50 government printers in Africa, from whom the majority of official publications are to be obtained.

CHAPTER 10

DISSERTATIONS

Note: The most important general library tool to be consulted is DISSERTA-
TION ABSTRACTS (Ann Arbor, Mich., 1952-, monthly), which since July 1961 has
had author and subject indexes in each issue. (For details see Winchell.)
The issues from 1961 only are worth consulting, since the Library of Congress
list (see below, no. 421) covered the earlier numbers and the predecessors,
MICROFILM ABSTRACTS (1938-51) and DOCTORAL DISSERTATIONS ACCEPTED BY AMERICAN
UNIVERSITIES (1933-55).

     For references to French dissertations, the extensive lists in the
BIBLIOGRAPHIE DE LA FRANCE: Supplément D, THESES, are a helpful source. In
1966 the Faculté de Droit et des Sciences Economiques of the Université de
Paris issued unpaged lists of theses and memoirs (in preparation, defended,
or on file) on African subjects in the fields of law, political science, and
economics for 1964, 1965, and 1966.

     In this connection, see also the External Research Lists issued by the
U.S. Department of State (no. 40).

412. Amosu, Margaret, comp. NIGERIAN THESES: A LIST OF THESES ON NIGERIAN
          SUBJECTS AND OF THESES BY NIGERIANS. Ibadan, Ibadan University
          Press, 1965. 36 p.

          As NIGERIAN BOOKS is the first national bibliography in Africa,
     so this is among the first African thesis lists. There are almost
     500 entries, as well as author and subject indexes.

413. Centre d'Analyse et de Recherche Documentaires pour l'Afrique Noire
          (CARDAN). INVENTAIRE DE THESES ET MEMOIRES AFRICANISTES DE LANGUE
          FRANCAISE SOUTENUS DEPUIS 1966: PREMIERE SERIE. By Brigitta Rupp
          and Agnès Rosset. Paris, 1969. 93 l. (v. 1, no. 2)

          Covers 464 theses and mémoires registered from Jan. 1, 1966,
     through May 1969, including those from Belgium, Switzerland, and

Senegal. It continues the listing through 1965 which appeared in the
Société des Africanistes, BULLETIN D'INFORMATION, no. 5, June 1965, and
no. 6, Sept. 1965. Arrangement is by the geographical area covered by
the thesis. The work is in "fiche" form which may also be arranged by
subject. There are separate indexes for author and subject.

Also issued by CARDAN are INVENTAIRE DE THESES ET MEMOIRES AFRI-
CANISTES DE LANGUE FRANCAISE EN COURS: DEUXIEME SERIE: THESES DE 3E
CYCLE (v. 1, no. 3, 1969, 124 p.) and INVENTAIRE ...: PREMIERE SERIE:
THESES D'ETAT ET D'UNIVERSITE (v. 2, no. 1, 1969, 104 p.), both by
Brigitta Rupp and Agnès Rosset.

414. Deutsche Afrika-Gesellschaft. DEUTSCHE DISSERTATIONEN UBER AFRIKA:
        EIN VERZEICHNIS FUR DIE JAHRE 1918-1959. Compiled by Jochen
        Köhler. Bonn, K. Schroeder, 1962. 1 v. unpaged. (Deutsche
        Afrika-Gesellschaft, Bonn, Veröftlichungen)

Inspired by the comparable Library of Congress publication, below
(no. 421), this list comprises 795 numbered entries, arranged by geographical area, with a separate section of linguistic studies. Indexes
by author and subject are included.

415. Dinstel, Marion, comp. LIST OF FRENCH DOCTORAL DISSERTATIONS ON AFRICA,
        1884-1961. Boston, G. K. Hall for Boston University Libraries,
        1966.

This work contains almost 3,000 listings; author, area, and subject
indexes are by Mary Darrah Herrick.

416. London. University. Institute of Historical Research. HISTORICAL
        THESES ON AFRICAN SUBJECTS COMPLETED IN THE UNIVERSITIES OF GREAT
        BRITAIN. London, 1961. 20 l.

There are 169 entries, arranged by region.

417. Paris. Université. Faculté de Droit et des Sciences Economiques.
        THESES ET MEMOIRES AFRICANISTES SOUTENUS ET DEPOSES: ANNEE 1967.
        Paris [1968]. 33 l.

418. Potchefstroom University for Christian Higher Education. Department of
        Librarianship. UNION CATALOGUE OF THESES AND DISSERTATIONS OF THE
        SOUTH AFRICAN UNIVERSITIES, 1942-1958. Compiled by S. I. Malan.
        Potchefstroom, The University, 1959. xii, 216 p. 2 fold. tables.

Annual supplement, 1959-

The work is arranged systematically under broad subject headings, with an author index. Locations are given and published theses are indicated.

The period prior to 1942 is covered in A.M.L. Robinson, CATALOGUE OF THESES AND DISSERTATIONS ACCEPTED FOR DEGREES BY THE SOUTH AFRICAN UNIVERSITIES, 1918-1941 (Cape Town, The Author, 1943, 155 p.; available from Potchefstroom University Library).

419. Standing Conference on Library Materials on Africa. THESES ON AFRICA ACCEPTED BY UNIVERSITIES IN THE UNITED KINGDOM AND IRELAND. Cambridge, Eng., Heffer, 1964. 74 p.

The second study by SCOLMA on African material in British institutions, this supplements the DIRECTORY OF LIBRARIES AND SPECIAL COLLECTIONS ON AFRICA, issued in 1963. There are listed 1,142 theses and dissertations prepared for advanced degrees at 22 major British and Irish universities between 1920 and 1962 (coverage for 1962 is incomplete). Entries are arranged by region or country and field of study, and there are separate indexes to authors and "tribes and peoples." Information on the availability of theses and dissertations at each institution is included. Coverage for 1963 and 1964 was published in 1966 as UNITED KINGDOM PUBLICATIONS AND THESES ON AFRICA (see no. 303).

420. United Nations Educational, Scientific and Cultural Organization. THESES DE SCIENCES SOCIALES: CATALOGUE ANALYTIQUE INTERNATIONAL DE THESES INEDITES DE DOCTORAT, 1940-1950. Paris, 1952. 236 p.

Many theses having to do with Africa, from many countries and in various subject fields, are included in this long listing of titles supplied by representatives in member states. The tables and index include the broad subject classification by which entries are arranged, an alphabetical index of detailed subject matter, and a geographical index through which the items relating to Africa may be identified.

421. U.S. Library of Congress. General Reference and Bibliography Division. A LIST OF AMERICAN DOCTORAL DISSERTATIONS ON AFRICA. Prepared by the African Section. Washington, U.S. Govt. Print. Off., 1962. 69 p.

This alphabetical listing of doctoral dissertations on Africa presented in universities of the United States and Canada attempted a comprehensive record from the late nineteenth century through the academic year 1960/61. It was prepared by means of a page-by-page examination of records of theses of individual universities (the many sources used are listed at the end of the bibliography) and of the general library lists cited above. A preliminary version was published in the AFRICAN STUDIES BULLETIN (v. 4, no. 1, Mar. 1961) with a request

to Africanists to send in addenda and corrections; these were incorporated in the final version.

The list has been supplemented in the following work compiled by
Doris M. Cruger: A LIST OF AMERICAN DOCTORAL DISSERTATIONS ON AFRICA,
COVERING 1961/62 THROUGH 1964/65; FRANCE, COVERING 1933/34 THROUGH
1964/65; ITALY, COVERING 1933/34 THROUGH 1964/65 (Ann Arbor, Mich.,
University Microfilms Library Services, 1967, 36 p., xerography).

A bibliography of theses derived from Vol. 26 of DISSERTATION
ABSTRACTS (1965/66) is presented by B. C. Bloomfield in "American
Theses on Africa," LIBRARY MATERIALS ON AFRICA, v. 4, no. 3, Apr. 1967:
13-19. Organization is alphabetical by author under a general section
and under sections on North, West, Central, East, and Southern Africa.
Dates of theses range from the late 1950's to 1966, but the majority
of entries are dated 1965.

U.S. and Canadian doctoral dissertations are also listed in the
annual UNITED STATES AND CANADIAN PUBLICATIONS AND THESES ON AFRICA
(see no. 305, retitled volume for 1965).

CHAPTER 11

ATLASES AND MAPS

422. Note: General bibliographic sources which include sections listing
maps of Africa are as follows:

a) BIBLIOGRAPHIE CARTOGRAPHIQUE INTERNATIONALE. 1950- Paris,
      A. Colin. Annual.

     Compiled by the Comité National Français de Géographie
with the cooperation of the International Geographical Union,
UNESCO, and the Centre National de la Recherche Scientifique.
The twelfth annual volume, 1960 (1962, 687 p.), cites 2,566
maps, 141 for Africa.

b) British Museum. CATALOGUE OF PRINTED MAPS, CHARTS AND PLANS.
      London, 1967. 15 v.

     This updates to the end of 1964 the CATALOGUE OF PRINTED
MAPS first published in two volumes in 1885.

c) CURRENT GEOGRAPHICAL PUBLICATIONS. 1938- New York, American
      Geographical Society. Monthly except July and Aug.

     Continuation of the RESEARCH CATALOGUE of the Society
(see no. 324). Maps in books and individual maps are cited
as well as writings on cartography. For further description
see no. 464. The British version is called NEW GEOGRAPHICAL
LITERATURE AND MAPS, published by the Royal Geographical Society.

d) U.S. Library of Congress. Copyright Office. CATALOG OF COPY-
      RIGHT ENTRIES: Part 6, MAPS AND ATLASES. Washington.
      Semiannual.

     The arrangement of this list of maps published in America
is by name of copyright claimant, but there is a geographical
index.

423. Dahlberg, Richard E., and Benjamin E. Thomas. "An Analysis and Bibliog-
      raphy of Recent African Atlases." AFRICAN STUDIES BULLETIN, v. 5,

no. 3, Oct. 1962: 23-33.

The bibliography cites 92 atlases examined by the authors at the Library of Congress, the American Geographical Society, and the University of California at Los Angeles.

424. Dahlberg, Richard E., and Benjamin E. Thomas. "Map Resources on Africa." AFRICAN STUDIES BULLETIN, v. 5, no. 1, Mar. 1962: 1-8.

The authors describe the common types of maps (political, topographic, aerial, resources-inventory, nautical, etc.), indicate their availability, and conclude with 24 references that will provide further information.

425. Gray, Richard. "Eclipse Maps." JOURNAL OF AFRICAN HISTORY, v. 6, 1965: 251-262.

426. Johannesburg. Public Library. EXHIBITION OF DECORATIVE MAPS OF AFRICA UP TO 1800. 4-16 AUG. 1952. DESCRIPTIVE CATALOGUE. Johannesburg, 1952. 77 l.

427. Ogunsheye, F. Adetowun. "Maps of Africa--1500-1800: A Bibliographic Survey." NIGERIAN GEOGRAPHICAL JOURNAL, v. 7, no. 1, June 1964: 34-42, plus maps.

428. Rumeau, A. "Topographic Mapping of Africa." In United Nations Educational, Scientific and Cultural Organization, A REVIEW OF THE NATURAL RESOURCES OF THE AFRICAN CONTINENT. Paris, UNESCO, 1963 (distributed by International Documents Service, Columbia University Press, New York): 19-49. (Natural Resources Research, no. 1)

Accompanying the essay written by the director of the Institut Géographique National, Paris, on the evolution of African topographic mapping between 1949 and 1959 are a bibliography (p. 30-35) and an inventory of topographical maps of the African continent at the end of 1959 (p. 35-47). The material concludes with two maps, the first on the status of topographic mapping of the African continent on Jan. 1, 1949, the second at the end of 1959. The survey was limited to maps published since 1930, on scales comprised between 1:10,000 and 1:250,000.

429. Scientific Council for Africa South of the Sahara (CSA). CARTES TOPOGRAPHIQUES DE L'AFRIQUE AU SUD DU SAHARA. TOPOGRAPHICAL MAPS OF AFRICA SOUTH OF THE SAHARA. [Rev. ed.] London, CCTA (Commission for Technical Co-operation in Africa South of the Sahara), 1955. 40 p. (Publication no. 15)

_____. CARTOGRAPHIE DE L'AFRIQUE AU SUD DU SAHARA: CARTES SPECIALES.
MAPS OF AFRICA SOUTH OF THE SAHARA: SPECIAL SUBJECT MAPS. Part 2.
70 p. (Publication no. 17)

These two catalogues form the revision of a single list, MAPS OF
AFRICA SOUTH OF THE SAHARA, which was issued at Bukavu, then the site
of CCTA/CSA, in Apr. 1953 (122 p.; Publication no. 4). That work had
been based on a provisional list of maps prepared by Dr. R. J. Harrison
Church of the London School of Economics and Miss Rodd of University
College, Ibadan, augmented by information from many institutions and
departments in and outside of Africa. It omitted obsolete material
and historical maps and gave only samples of maps included in books,
but it attempted to record "all maps believed to be useful." Arrangement was by political divisions rather than geographic areas. For each
region or country there were listed, first, topographical maps or series
of maps and then the special maps in systematic subject classification.

In the revision, the first part is limited to topographical maps,
and the special maps--town plans and cadastral maps and maps of geology,
climatology and hydrology, soils, vegetation and forests, agriculture
and animal husbandry, entomology, medicine, population and tribal
boundaries, administrative and political boundaries, and communications--
are in the second part. For CCTA/CSA, Africa south of the Sahara included Somaliland and offshore islands in the Indian Ocean but omitted
Ethiopia and the Sudan. CCTA/CSA has become the Organization of
African Unity's Scientific, Technical and Research Commission.

Nonserial publications of CCTA/CSA have been published by its
Publications Bureau, Watergate House, York Buildings, London, W.C.2.
When any are out of print, microfilm reproductions may be ordered from
the Bureau.

430. Tooley, Ronald Vere. THE PRINTED MAPS OF THE CONTINENT OF AFRICA AND
REGIONAL MAPS SOUTH OF THE TROPIC OF CANCER 1500-1900. London,
Map Collectors' Circle, 1966- Contents: pt. 1, 1500-1600; pt. 2,
1500-1600: Regional Maps South of the Tropic of Cancer. (Map
Collectors' Series, no. 29-)

431. U.S. Library of Congress. Map Division. A LIST OF GEOGRAPHICAL ATLASES
IN THE LIBRARY OF CONGRESS, Vol. VI. Compiled by Clara Egli LeGear.
Washington, U.S. Govt. Print. Off., 1963. lxxii, 681 p.

Africa: p. 426-475 (titles 10085-10169).

The atlases of Africa cited with annotations in this comprehensive
work relate to regions rather than to the general picture of Africa,
except for the volumes of reproductions of early maps, Prince Yusul
Kamal's MONUMENTA CARTOGRAPHICA AFRICAE ET AEGYPTI (Cairo, 1926-51, 5 v.

in 16). A "unique and magnificent contribution to the history of
cartography," the MONUMENTA comprise the most comprehensive collection
of source materials ever assembled, including facsimiles of maps from
pre-Ptolemaic antiquity to the present age. An annotation describes
Prince Kamal's work at great length.

PART III

SUBJECT GUIDE FOR AFRICA IN GENERAL

CHAPTER 12

GENERAL REFERENCE WORKS

432.   AFRICA ANNUAL 1968.   Compiled by E. M. Crossley.   London, Foreign
       Correspondents Ltd., 1968.   202 p.

          Arranged by region and country, the annual gives for each
       country a short paragraph on geography and climate, area and popu-
       lation, history, the constitution, addresses of diplomatic missions,
       agriculture, industry, development, foreign trade, communications,
       education, etc., and finally a directory of businesses, including
       banks and printers.

433.   AFRICA 1968:   A REFERENCE VOLUME ON THE AFRICAN CONTINENT.   Pre-
       pared by JEUNE AFRIQUE and published as a special annual issue.
       Paris, 1968-   376 p.   col. maps, tables.   Annual.

          This handsome pioneer volume issued by JEUNE AFRIQUE in col-
       laboration with a number of specialists is packed with current in-
       formation and statistics.   There are sections on general economic,
       political, geographic, social, and cultural facts about Africa in
       1967.   The major section (p. 121-335) offers a profile (accompanied
       by a map) of each African country--demography, political structure,
       educational system, economy, and major projects--in an abbreviated
       format similar to that of the WORLDMARK ENCYCLOPEDIA OF THE NATIONS.
       A useful chronology of principal events of the year and lists and
       maps showing major African organizations and multinational organi-
       zations are provided in the last portion of the volume.   Advertising
       is included.

434.   Africa Research Limited.   AFRICA ANNUAL SURVEY AND DOCUMENTS. v. 1,
       1968-   Exeter, England.   (Editors: Colin Legum and John
       Drysdale).

Replaces the Documentation Service as this annual volume will contain a substantial section on documentation (Part 3). Part 1 deals with "Current Issues," Part 2 "Country by Country Review."

435. AFRICA'S NGO'S (NON-GOVERNMENTAL ORGANIZATIONS). Geneva, International Council of Voluntary Agencies, 1968. 299 p.

An English and French directory of 1,839 organizations arranged alphabetically by name under each country on the continent. Primarily listed are the social welfare type of agencies such as girl guide associations, Catholic Relief Services, Red Cross groups, and youth clubs, but some research groups (e.g., Senegal's Institut de Science Economique Appliquée) are also described. Major representatives of religious denominations and of trade unions are included, while government-connected bodies, profit-making organizations, cooperatives, and purely indigenous bodies with no connection to a national coordinating body are generally omitted. In some cases only the name and address are given for an organization. There are two indexes, one by activities, one by affiliations to international nongovernmental organizations. The latter also serves as an abbreviations and address list.

436. Afrika-Verein Hamburg-Bremen. AFRIKA-HANDBUCH FUR WIRTSCHAFT UND REISE: Vol. I, NORD-, WEST- UND ZENTRAL-AFRIKA; Vol. II, NORDOST-, OST- UND SUD-AFRIKA. Issued by the Afrika-Verein e V., Hamburg (Peter Colberg, Martin Kramer); edited by Kurt Eitner. Hamburg, Uebersee-Verlag, 1967-68. 430, 456 p. col. illus., col. maps (2 fold, in back pockets), col. plans, charts.

In each of the two volumes of this excellent guidebook, a brief general section covers geography, history, peoples, languages, and cultures. This is followed by a regional and country section which first gives climatic data for each region and then supplies, for each country in the region, wide-ranging information (including recent relevant literature), a guide to major cities, and abundant details on the economy. A place-name index and a list of major African and Africa-related organizations--by acronym and full name-- are provided in each volume. Advertising is included.

437. ANNEE AFRICAINE 1966- Paris, Editions A. Pedone, 1968. (1968 ed., 662 p.)

An annual survey of Africa prepared in association with specialists from the Centre d'Afrique Noire (CEAN) of the University of Bordeaux, the Centre des Hautes Etudes Administratives sur l'Afrique et l'Asie Modernes (CHEAM) in Paris, and the African section of the Centre d'Etudes des Relations Internationales (CERI) of the Fondation National des Sciences Politiques in Paris. The first part of each

volume covers international (including inter-African) relations;
the second and main part gives for each country a summary of events
followed by a chronology.

438. L'ANNEE POLITIQUE ET ECONOMIQUE AFRICAINE, 1968. Dakar, Société
      Africaine d'Edition, 1968. 1 v. (At head of title: Pierre
      Biarnès, Philippe Decraene, Philippe Herreman.)

     The volume is divided by regions, i.e., West Africa, Equatorial
Africa. Then for each country in that region the following information is given: basic data about the country, a chronology of important events of the year, a political summary, and an economic
survey. The states of North Africa are included.

439. Buell, Raymond Leslie. THE NATIVE PROBLEM IN AFRICA. New York,
      Macmillan, 1928. 2 v. maps, tables.

     Reprint, London, Frank Cass, 1965.

     Bibliography: v. 2, p. 983-1049.

     This monumental work by an American expert on foreign affairs
has served as a basis for all subsequent investigations. It was prepared following 15 months of field work and study of all available
documents, which are listed by region in a 66-page bibliography. For
each of the British, French, and Belgian territories south of the
Sahara and for free Liberia, Dr. Buell surveyed analytically history,
government, labor conditions, racial questions, and colonial policy,
with the aim of determining how and to what extent the governments
concerned were solving the problems raised by the impact of industrial civilization on subsistence societies.

440. Deutsche Afrika-Gesellschaft, Bonn. Die Länder Afrikas [series].
      Bonn, K. Schroeder, 1958-

     A series of short monographs covering Africa country by country.
These provide data concerning the geography, history, population,
political structure, cultural life, and economic position of the
various states. Supplementing this information are short bibliographies, maps, and an index. By 1968, monographs had been issued on
34 countries and regions.

441. Deutsche Afrika-Gesellschaft, Bonn. Wissenschaftlicher Ausschuss.
      DEUTSCHE AFRIKAWISSENSCHAFT: STAND UND AUFGABEN. Edited by
      Herbert Abel. Köln, 1962. 172 p.

158

The lectures, given at a conference of the German Africa
Society, concern the present state and future tasks of African
studies in Germany. They deal with soil studies, botanical studies
and ecology, forestry, zoology, agricultural research, geology,
grography, veterinary studies, medicine, economics, modern history
and political science, prehistory, ethnology and African languages.

442. Encyclopedia Africana. Accra, Ghana.

An ambitious undertaking for an Encyclopedia Africana was begun
under the auspices of the Ghana Academy of Sciences, with the late
Dr. W. E. B. Du Bois the first director. In 1961 a Secretariat was
set up in Accra, with Dr. W. A. Hunton as secretary, and specialists
from all parts of Africa and Europe were asked to collaborate;
regional committees were established, and scholars at many institutions were asked to lend their services. A periodic information
report was issued by the Secretariat, outlining progress and plans
(no. 7, Dec. 1963). The project ran into difficulties, however, and
Dr. Hunton's residence permit was not renewed in late 1966. Professor
I. N. Ofusu-Appiah became the new director, and once more in 1967 work
on the projected ten volumes was reported under way, with the first
volume (on biographies) planned for 1969.

443. Friedrich-Ebert-Stiftung. Forschungsinstitut. AFRIKA BIOGRAPHIEN.
     Hannover, Verlag für Literatur und Zeitgeschehen GmbH, 1967-
     ports., maps. Loose-leaf.

Issued in loose-leaf binder with separate pagination for each
country section (supplementary pages to be inserted).

Biographical dictionary of leading African personalities in the
fields of business, literature, government (including diplomacy and
the military), labor, law, education, journalism, religion, and
traditional life (i.e., chiefs). By June 1968, 21 countries had been
covered. Arrangement is by country with no apparent order within
country sections, but there is a name index to the biographies. The
biographies, accompanied by a photograph in most cases, list the
following: curriculum vitae, position, address, birthdate, birth-
place, ethnic origin, religion, family status, languages spoken,
publications, foreign travel, party membership, hobbies, and honors.

444. Fung, Karen. "Index to 'Portraits' in WEST AFRICA, 1948-1966."
     AFRICAN STUDIES BULLETIN, v. 9, no. 3, Dec. 1966: 103-120.

There is great need for systematic gathering of African biographical data in all forms, and this index is the first step in a
Hoover Institution project to locate and film such biographical information.

445. Hailey, William Malcolm Hailey, 1st baron. AN AFRICAN SURVEY: A
        STUDY OF PROBLEMS ARISING IN AFRICA SOUTH OF THE SAHARA. Issued
        under the auspices of the Royal Institute of International
        Affairs. Rev. 1956. London, New York, Oxford University Press,
        1957. 1676 p.

        An encyclopaedic reference book, the most comprehensive of its
        kind regarding Africa south of the Sahara. For a full description of
        this work, which covers most fields of modern knowledge, see AFRICA
        SOUTH OF THE SAHARA . . . (no. 321), p. 4, or see Winchell (no. 1).
        Hailey, a senior British civil servant with extensive experience of
        high office in India and of academic life, produced the first version
        of his book in 1938 with the help of a distinguished group of re-
        searchers. This pioneer work was also described at length at the
        time by Lord Harlech and various collaborators in LORD HAILEY'S
        AFRICAN SURVEY, SURVEYED FOR THE ROYAL AFRICAN SOCIETY BY THE RIGHT
        HON. LORD HARLECH . . . , edited by F. H. Melland and published as a
        supplement to the Society's JOURNAL for Jan. 1939 (London, New York,
        Macmillan, 1938, 70 p.). See also Kimble (no. 477).

446. International Congress of Africanists, 1st, Accra, Dec. 11-18, 1962.
        PROCEEDINGS. Edited by Lalage Bown and Michael Crowder. London,
        Longmans, Green, 1964. 368 p.

        Collection of 29 interesting papers presented at this long-
        planned and well-attended congress by scholars of many lands and of
        varying ideologies. The papers were presented in nine sections:
        history; languages; social and economic problems; literature, art,
        and music; social and political institutions; science and technology;
        education; and psychology. An unusually large proportion of them are
        conceived in terms general to Africa rather than in relation to indi-
        vidual groups or regions.

447. Junod, Violaine I., ed., assisted by Idrian N. Resnick. THE HAND-
        BOOK OF AFRICA. New York, New York University Press, 1963.
        472 p. illus.; appendix and map.

        Gives information on each of the 50-odd political units of
        Africa. The format is that of fact sheets: short geographical and
        historical sketches, followed by data on government, population,
        society (education, health, social welfare, etc.), and economy. Long
        bibliographical notes are chiefly of official sources from which data
        are taken. Five appendixes summarize colonial policies in Africa,
        list regional groupings as of 1961, analyze British and French aid
        to African development and the trade and marketing systems of the
        metropolitan powers with dependencies, and give tables of measures
        and currencies.

448. Kitchen, Helen, ed. A HANDBOOK OF AFRICAN AFFAIRS. New York,
         Published for the African-American Institute by Frederick A.
         Praeger, 1964. xiii, 311 p. maps, charts.

      This concise handbook is made up from articles originally
published in AFRICA REPORT, primarily the "country profiles" from
the issue of Nov. 1963, which form Part 1, "A Country-by-Country
Political Guide" (p. 1-185). The section ends with a table of
universities of Africa. Part 2 is a survey of "The Armies of
Africa," prepared for AFRICA REPORT by George Weeks of the United
Press International. Part 3, "The Organization of African Unity,"
includes the OAU charter and other materials relating to the
founding conference in May 1963. Part 4 reprints three essays on
"Contemporary African Poetry and Prose." The volume ends with a
group of nine sketch maps of the various regions of Africa.

449. Legum, Colin, ed. AFRICA: A HANDBOOK TO THE CONTINENT. Rev. and
         enl. ed. New York, Praeger, 1966. xii, 558 p. plates, maps,
         tables.

      Articles by British and American specialists comprise the two
sections of this reference guide. Focus of the first section is on
the countries, in regional or other groupings; for each country there
is a general sketch, succint statements on political development and
the economic situation, basic data of the almanac type, and a bibliography. In the second part are essays on international attitudes
toward Africa, African art and literature, changing cultural patterns,
religion, and economics and the role of the United Nations. The first
edition was published in 1962 (New York, Praeger, 553 p.). There are
also English editions.

      For readers who have only two hours in which to learn about
Africa, a reviewer in WEST AFRICA describes as the best concise guide
a little book by Davidson Nicol, AFRICA: A SUBJECTIVE SURVEY (London,
Longmans, Green, 1964, 96 p.). This consists of five lectures delivered at the University of Ghana by the author, principal of
Fourah Bay College in Sierra Leone. The lectures offer a perspicacious
analysis of the political, social, and cultural situation of the continent.

450. Lystad, Robert A., ed. THE AFRICAN WORLD: A SURVEY OF SOCIAL RE-
         SEARCH. Edited for the African Studies Association. New York,
         Praeger, 1965. xvi, 575 p.

      Chapter notes and bibliographies, p. 493-560.

      An explanation of the fundamental problems of the disciplines
and the possibilities of interdisciplinary stimulus and integration;

analyzes and defines research problems, raises theoretical problems, and interrelates the findings of the various disciplines. The 18 essays by leading British and American scholars preceded by the editor's introduction examine agriculture, anthropology, biology, demography, economics, education, folklore and literature, geography, history, law, linguistics, medicine, music and the dance, prehistory, political science, psychology, sociology, and the visual arts. There are tables, notes, bibliographies, a map, an index of contents and a general index. A paperback edition has appeared.

451. McEwan, Peter J. M., and Robert B. Sutcliffe, eds. MODERN AFRICA. New York, Crowell, 1965. xii, 444 p. maps.

First published in Great Britain (Methuen, 1965) with the title THE STUDY OF AFRICA. Excerpts from the writings of almost forty African specialists describe the physical environment, traditional background (social structure, value systems, tribal government, economic activity), and contemporary scene (African nationalism, politics and government, economic change and development, social change, and social problems). A concluding section examines Africa's role in world affairs. Besides helpful introductions to the various divisions of the work, the editors have provided introductory notes that give continuity to the readings. Appendixes supply statistics on population, area, gross national product, etc., as well as data on economic assistance to African countries. There is an index.

452. Markov, Walter, ed. ETUDES AFRICAINES, AFRICAN STUDIES, AFRIKA-STUDIEN--DEM II. INTERNATIONALEN AFRIKANISTENKONGRESS IN DAKAR GEWIDMET. Herausgegeben im Auftrage der Sektion für Asien-, Afrika- und Lateinamerikawissenschaften an der Karl-Marx-Universität Leipzig. Leipzig, Karl Marx Universität, 1967. 237 p.

A collection of 16 studies dedicated by the East German delegates to the 2d International Congress of Africanists in Dakar in Dec. 1967. Included are essays (in German or English) on the function of national languages in Africa, on the South-West African leader Jacob Morenga, on "government schools" in the African colonies under German imperialism (1884-1914), and on sociological aspects of rural development in Mali. There appears also an essay by Jean Suret-Canale on the village community in tropical Africa.

453. MEYERS HANDBUCH UBER AFRIKA. Mannheim, Bibligraphisches Institut, 1962. 779 p. illus., maps (2 fold. col. in pocket), tables.

Bibliography: p. 738-745.

A hugh reference work, covering the continent and its peoples in general and setting forth a country-by-country survey of economic and human geography.

454. THE MIDDLE EAST AND NORTH AFRICA, 1967-68. 14th ed. London,
       Europa Publications, 1967. 984 p.

    The first edition appeared in 1948 with the title THE MIDDLE
EAST. Not until the 11th edition of 1964 was the scope expanded
to include 11 North African territories. In the present volume are
Algeria, Chad, Ethiopia, French Somaliland, Libya, Mali, Mauritania,
Morocco, Niger, Somalia, Spanish North Africa, the Sudan, Tunisia,
and the United Arab Republic. Other sections treat "The Year's
Developments in the Arab World," "Oil in North Africa," U. N. ac-
tivities in North Africa, the African Development Bank, the Organi-
sation Commune Africaine et Malgache, and the Union Douanière
Economique de l'Afrique Centrale.

    Each country section includes an economic and statistical sur-
vey, a list of government ministers and diplomatic representatives,
and a directory of political parties. Additionally, one finds data
on banking, transport, tourism, educational institutions, etc.
Short bibliographies follow each country section.

455. OWENS' COMMERCE AND TRAVEL AND INTERNATIONAL REGISTER, 1970: AFRICA,
       MIDDLE EAST AND FAR EAST WITH INTERNATIONAL TRADE LISTS. London,
       Pan-African Commercial Directory Ltd., 1970. 1088 p. illus.,
       maps. Annual.

    Supplement: OWENS' COMMODITY INDEX, 1970.

    Useful economic and commercial surveys of countries, with valuable
lists of banks, hotels, businesses, etc.

456. Sovetskaia Entsiklopediia, Gosudarstvennoe Nauchnoe Izdatel'stvo,
       Moscow. AFRIKA: ENTSIKLOPEDICHESKII SPRAVOCHNIK. Editor in
       chief: I. I. Potekhin. Moskva, Sovetskaia Entsiklopediia, 1963.
       2 v. illus., maps. (Entsiklopedii, slovari, spravochniki)

    This "Encyclopedic Handbook," published under the auspices of the
Institut Afriki of the Akademiia Nauk SSSR, gives broad coverage to
natural conditions, peoples, history, economics, and culture of Africa.
A "Brief Description" translated from the journal of the Akademiia Nauk
SSSR was issued in the JPRS Translations on Africa series (see no. 360),
Mar. 25, 1964 (2 p., 4 l.).

457. THE STATESMAN'S YEAR-BOOK. 1864- London, Macmillan; New York, St.
       Martin's Press. Annual. (1967-68 ed., 1736 p.)

    The concise volume of concentrated historical and statistical
information about the countries of the world is closely up to date
regarding government and politics of all nations. The useful index
includes place names for practically all important regions and cities.

458. U. S. Joint Publications Research Service. GLOSSARY OF ABBREVI-
         ATIONS RELATING TO AFRICAN AFFAIRS. Washington, 1966. 91 p.
         Processed.

      Abbreviations are listed alphabetically, each being followed by
the name of the organization for which it stands. The English name
for organizations in other languages is also given. So many general
abbreviations are included that the glossary might even be used as a
guide to abbreviations for international affairs.

459. WORLDMARK ENCYCLOPEDIA OF THE NATIONS. Editor and publisher, Moshe
         Y. Sachs. Vol. II, AFRICA, edited by Louis Barron. New York,
         Worldmark Press, 1963. 344 p.

      This encyclopedia, supplying concise information and statistics
on all countries of the world, was first published in two volumes in
1960. Arrangement was alphabetical by country. In a revised five-
volume edition, the chapters on African countries are brought together in one volume, arranged alphabetically, Algeria to Zanzibar.
For each there is systematic treatment in almanac style, including
illustration in color of the flag and text of the national anthem.
There are political and physical maps on inside cover pages, double
spread. Statistics are of 1960-61, political data into 1963.

      Comparable information appears in THE EUROPA YEARBOOK: Vol. II,
AFRICA, THE AMERICAS, ASIA, AND AUSTRALASIA (London, Europa Publications, Ltd., annual), in which African nations are included in
alphabetical arrangement with those of other countries outside Europe.
The yearbook is slanted toward business interests, including a directory section and commercial data.

CHAPTER 13

GEOGRAPHY

Atlases and Maps

See also Chapter 11 and the section "History--Atlases and Maps" in Chapter 14.

460. Afrika-Instituut. AFRICA: MAPS AND STATISTICS. no. 1-10, July
        1962-Apr. 1965. Pretoria, Africa Institute. 35 cm.

A statistical atlas with text in English and Afrikaans, pub-lished in ten issues with continuous paging. Statements of extreme simplification accompany statistical tables and maps, scale of which varies from 1:30,000,000 to 1:60,000,000. The range of information is continent-wide. Sources are given in bibliographies on inside cover pages. The separate parts are as follows:

    no. 1.   POPULATION. July 1962: p. 1-13.
    no. 2.   VITAL AND MEDICAL ASPECTS. Oct. 1962: p. 15-33.
    no. 3.   CULTURAL AND EDUCATIONAL ASPECTS. Jan. 1963: p. 34-52.
    no. 4.   TRANSPORT AND COMMUNICATION. Apr. 1963: p. 53-78.
    no. 5.   ENERGY RESOURCES, PRODUCTION AND CONSUMPTION. July
                1963: p. 79-94.
    no. 6.   AGRICULTURE AND FORESTRY. Oct. 1963: p. 95-124.
    no. 7.   LIVESTOCK FARMING AND FISHING. Jan. 1964: p. 125-148.
    no. 8.   MINING, INDUSTRY AND LABOUR. Apr. 1964: p. 149-171.
    no. 9.   TRADE, INCOME AND AID. Oct. 1964: p. 173-194.
    no. 10.   POLITICAL DEVELOPMENT. Apr. 1965: p. 195-220.
                Contains supplementary material consisting of the
                introduction (slightly revised) to the series, all
                the bibliographies listed, and an index to the
                entire atlas.

461. American Geographical Society. INDEX TO MAPS IN BOOKS AND PERIODICALS. Boston, G. K. Hall, 1968. 10 v. 35 cm.

    A commendable reference work, especially useful because maps which appear in monographic or serial publications are rarely entered in other cartobibliographies. Making up the large volumes are photo-reproductions of some 160,000 cards from the catalogue maintained by the Society's Map Department. Arrangement is alphabetical by subject and geographical-political division, with entries listed chronologically under each geographical division.

462. Philip (George) & Son, Ltd. PHILIPS' MODERN COLLEGE ATLAS FOR AFRICA. Edited by Harold Fullard. 9th ed. London, 1968. 136, 32 p.

    World atlas with special application to Africa, prepared with needs of African as well as non-African students in mind. Of the 136 pages of maps, well over a third (p. 24-73) relate to regions and countries of Africa. The scales vary according to space allotted to the region, from 1:1,500,000 to 1:8,000,000.

463. The Times, London. THE TIMES ATLAS OF THE WORLD. Edited by John Bartholomew. Mid-century ed. Vol. IV, SOUTHERN EUROPE AND AFRICA . . . WITH AN INDEX-GAZETTEER. London, The Times Pub. Co., 1956. 96 col. plates; 50-p. index. 49 cm.

    One of the best general atlases of Africa.

Bibliographies

Note: In most geographical works no clear distinction is made between physical, human, and economic geography, and for geographical studies nearly all nonspecialized bibliographies are applicable. The two bibliographies mentioned below are designed primarily for the use of geographers; they include African material within a wider framework. Journals of the geographical institutions of the West are also largely pertinent for African material; institutions within Africa are predominantly regional. In the Library of Congress list SERIALS FOR AFRICAN STUDIES, over 40 periodicals are indexed under geography.

464. CURRENT GEOGRAPHICAL PUBLICATIONS. 1938- New York, American Geographical Society. Monthly except July and Aug.

    A continuation of the Society's RESEARCH CATALOGUE (see no. 324). Each issue of this valuable publication contains a section on Africa--general and by region and country--listing references to books, pamphlets, government documents, periodical articles, and essays in composite works. African maps are noted in a separate section on atlases. A cumulative annual index has sections by subject, author, and region. Useful British tools are as follows: GEOGRAPHICAL ABSTRACTS (1960- London, London School of Economics, quarterly) and the GEOGRAPHICAL ABSTRACTS, INDEX 1966, which provides a valuable computer-produced listing of 40,000 entries.

465. International Geographical Union. Special Commission on the Humid Tropics. A SELECT ANNOTATED BIBLIOGRAPHY OF THE HUMID TROPICS. [Title also in French.] Compiled by Theo L. Hills. Montreal, Geography Department, McGill University, 1960. xiii, 238 p.

A substantial part of this bibliography is concerned with Africa (p. 69-144). Arrangement is by region and country, with subdivisions by discipline. The selection, though covering general aspects, is slanted toward the use of the geographer.

466. Sommer, John W. BIBLIOGRAPHY OF AFRICAN GEOGRAPHY, 1940-1964. Hanover, N. H., Geography Department, Dartmouth College, 1965. 139 p. (Geography Publications at Dartmouth, no. 3)

The 1,724 numbered items are divided into four parts: human, economic, and physical geography, each with a number of subdivisions, and general Africana. References derive from English and French periodical literature (primarily scholarly geographical journals). There is an author index.

467. Val, María Asunción del. CATALOGO DE LA EXPOSICION DE LIBROS ESPAÑOLES SOBRE GEOGRAFIA Y VIAJES EN AFRICA. Madrid, Consejo Superior de Investigaciones Científicas, Instituto de Estudios Africanos, 1948. 120 p.

There are 575 numbered entries covering works in Spanish on geography, travel, and exploration in Africa. A list of general works is followed by regional subdivisions. Also included are sections on Spanish explorers in the nineteenth century, expeditions to Guinea, periodicals which frequently have material on geography and voyages in Africa, and bibliographies consulted. There is an alphabetical index of authors and anonymous works.

468. Wright, John K., and Elizabeth T. Platt. AIDS TO GEOGRAPHICAL RESEARCH. 2d ed. New York, Columbia University Press, for the American Geographical Society, 1947. xii, 331 p. (American Geographical Society Research Series, no. 22)

In this valuable work (see Winchell for full description), all general tools for geographical study are described. A regional section is devoted to Africa (p. 255-269).

Reference Works

469. Automobile Association of South Africa. TRANS-AFRICAN HIGHWAYS: A ROUTE BOOK OF THE MAIN TRUNK ROADS IN AFRICA. 4th ed. Johannesburg, 1958. 539 p. maps (1 fold. in pocket).

Earlier editions of this volume, which relates to the whole continent, appeared in 1929, 1949 (408 p.), and 1952 (480 p.). It carries sketch maps and detailed route descriptions of highways, including comment on facilities available at each stop. A full index of place names follows appendixes of practical information for motorists. Road guides are also published by regional automobile associations in East Africa, former French West Africa, and elsewhere.

470. Church, R. J. Harrison, and others. AFRICA AND THE ISLANDS. New York, Wiley, 1964. xiv, 494 p. illus., maps. (Geographies: An Intermediate Series)

Includes bibliographies.

In this work Professor Church was aided by three specialists, John I. Clarke, P. J. H. Clarke, and H. J. R. Henderson. Part 1, "Africa as a Whole," covers outlines of history, the physical environment, and human geography (peoples, modes of life). Part 2 consists of regional studies--Northwest Africa, Northeast Africa, West Africa, West Central Africa, East Africa, Southern Africa, the African Islands. The same factors treated in the first section are analyzed for each region. The conclusion discusses present political, social, and economic characteristics and trends. Many chapters are followed by reading lists. Other good geographical studies are:

> Carlson, Lucile. AFRICA'S LANDS AND NATIONS. New York, McGraw-Hill, 1967. 398 p. illus., map.
>
> Bibliography: p. 380-384.
>
> De Blij, Harm J. A GEOGRAPHY OF SUBSAHARAN AFRICA. Chicago, Rand McNally, 1964. 435 p. illus., maps.

471. Fitzgerald, Walter. AFRICA: A SOCIAL, ECONOMIC, AND POLITICAL
          GEOGRAPHY OF ITS MAJOR REGIONS. 10th ed. rev. by W. C. Brice.
          London, Methuen, 1967. xii, 503 p. maps, tables.

      Includes bibliographies.

      Standard advanced manual of the geography of Africa, originally
published in 1934. The tenth edition, revised by a former student
of the late Professor Fitzgerald, is updated, rather unevenly, to
about 1963. The physical environment, history, and societies of
Africa as a whole are discussed first. More than three-fourths
of the book is then devoted to regional studies--South Africa,
East Africa, Madagascar, Central Africa, West Africa, the Barbary
States, the Nile Valley, and Abyssinia and its borderlands. While
the treatment of physical geography and of history stands up well,
as a text on social, economic, and political geography the work
suffers by comparison with a number of recent African geography
texts. The extensive bibliographies include mostly older British
and French works and apparently have not been updated since the
ninth edition of 1961.

472. FOCUS. v. 1, no. 1- Oct. 1950- New York, American Geographical
          Society. Monthly except July and Aug.

      Each six-page issue is devoted to a country, region, or resource,
with emphasis on the interplay of physical, economic, and social
factors, as well as historical influences. During the 1960-67 period
good country surveys of Africa appeared as follows: 1960--Ghana,
South West Africa; 1961--Congo (Leopoldville), Gabon, Liberia,
Mauritania; 1962--Congo (Brazzaville), Tanganyika; 1963--High Com-
mission Territories of Southern Africa, Rwanda and Burundi; 1964--
Senegal, Nigeria, Uganda; 1965--Ethiopia, Ivory Coast, Niger; 1966--
Cameroon, Kenya, Sudan; 1967--Guinea, Mali, South Africa, South West
Africa; 1968--Malawi.

473. Gourou, Pierre. THE TROPICAL WORLD: ITS SOCIAL AND ECONOMIC CON-
          DITIONS AND ITS FUTURE STATUS. 4th ed. Translated by S. H.
          Beaver and E. D. Laborde. London, Longmans, 1966. xii, 196 p.
          illus., maps, tables. (Geographies for Advanced Study)

      Using examples drawn from Africa, Asia, Latin America, and the
West Indies, the author discusses the tropical areas in terms of
population density, diseases, soils, agriculture, stock raising, food
supply problems, industrial possibilities, problems of densely populated areas, problems arising from European intervention, and future
prospects. The fourth edition has been virtually rewritten to reflect
advances in agriculture, medicine, and technology as well as political
changes since publication of the third edition in 1961.

474. Hance, William A. THE GEOGRAPHY OF MODERN AFRICA. New York,
     Columbia University Press, 1964. xiv, 653 p. illus., maps,
     charts, tables.

     A comprehensive survey of the economic development of Africa.
     After introductory chapters giving the background of physical setting,
     population and peoples, and describing the present political scene,
     treatment is by regions and countries, varied in accordance with the
     particular features important to the economy of each.

475. Hodder, B. W., and D. R. Harris, eds. AFRICA IN TRANSITION: GEO-
     GRAPHICAL ESSAYS. London, Methuen, 1967. xii, 378 p. maps,
     diagrs., charts, tables.

     Includes bibliographies.

     The authors of the essays, all lecturers of geography at the
     University of London, have contributed authoritative studies on the
     historical, economic, political, and physical geography of Africa.
     The book is divided into regional sections--North, Northeast, East,
     West, Equatorial, and Southern Africa. Valuable as a supplement to
     geography textbooks, the volume might well serve also as a background
     to African studies for the general reader.

476. Jarrett, Harold Reginald. AFRICA. 2d ed. London, Macdonald &
     Evans, 1966. 510 p. front., illus., maps. (New Certificate
     Geography Series, Advanced Level)

     Includes bibliographies.

     A textbook on the geography of the entire continent and the
     islands. The work begins with a survey of the physical and climatic
     characteristics, then establishes the racial, cultural, and economic
     background, and concludes with regional descriptions. Each chapter
     is followed by study questions and a short bibliography. There is an
     index.

     The author has also written OUTLINE GEOGRAPHY OF AFRICA (London,
     Methuen, 1962, 248 p.) for the secondary school certificate level.

477. Kimble, George H. T. TROPICAL AFRICA. New York, Twentieth Century
     Fund, 1960. 2 v. illus., port., maps (1 fold. col.).

     Bibliographical footnotes.

     A broad geographical study of Africa, in which many scholars
     collaborated. The list of 46 contributors of working papers is given
     opposite the title page. Dr. Kimble, the geographer, served as
     director and put together the final text, which, though massive in

its assemblage of facts, is eminently readable. The first volume
covers the continent in terms of physical and economic geography.
The second opens with an account of "The Old Order" and goes through
the factors of social and political change to "The Price of Growth"
and "The Shape of Things." In general, the Africa reflected is that
of the mid-1950's, although some sources used for the appendix of
"Selected Territorial Data" were of 1959. An adaptation from the
original study is: George H. T. Kimble and Ronald Steel, TROPICAL
AFRICA TODAY (St. Louis, Webster Publishing Co., 1966, 138 p., illus.
[part col.], col. maps).

A pamphlet by Dr. Kimble in the Foreign Policy Association Head-
line Series, TROPICAL AFRICA: PROBLEMS AND PROMISES (New York, 1961,
62 p., no. 147), serves in part as a précis of the full-length work.

See also: Alfred T. Grove, AFRICA SOUTH OF THE SAHARA (London,
Oxford University Press, 1967, 275 p., illus., maps; bibliography:
p. 260-265).

478. Kirchherr, Eugene C. ABYSSINIA TO ZONA AL SUR DEL DRAA: AN INDEX
        TO THE POLITICAL UNITS OF AFRICA IN THE PERIOD 1951-1967; A
        LISTING OF FORMER AND CURRENT PLACE NAMES WITH SUPPLEMENTARY
        NOTES AND MAPS. Kalamazoo, Institute of International and Area
        Studies and School of Graduate Studies, Western Michigan Uni-
        versity, 1968. 32 p. maps (1 fold.). (Monographic Series on
        Cultural Changes, no. 2)

This convenient reference work is of considerable help in disen-
tangling the toponymic confusion generated by political transitions
in Africa in the post-1950 period. A systematic and comprehensive
guide to countries, territories, and regions is provided by the alphabetical index. Supplementing this are notes and maps clarifying the
sequence of the changing names on the present-day map of Africa.

479. Meyer, Hans H., ed. DAS DEUTSCHE KOLONIALREICH: EINE LANDERKUNDE
        DER DEUTSCHEN SCHUTZGEBIETE. Leipzig, Verlag des Bibliographischen
        Instituts, 1909-10. 2 v. plates, maps.

The standard geography of the German colonial empire, treated in
great detail by individual colonies: Vol. I, East Africa, Cameroon;
Vol. II, Togo, German Southwest Africa, and the South Seas. The many
photographs, color plates, and maps are a significant feature of this
impressive older work. For further comment see no. 3042.

480. MEYERS KONTINENTE UND MEERE; DATEN, BILDER, KARTEN: AFRIKA.
        Bearb. von Werner Jopp. Mannheim, Bibliographisches Institut,
        Geographisch-Kartographisches Institut Meyer, 1968. 380 p.
        illus. (part col.), maps (part col.). (Meyers Kontinente
        und Meere, v. 1)

        Includes bibliographies.

        First in an eight-volume series which will cover the world.
First part consists of sections on geology, geography, climate,
vegetation, soils, tribes, history (includes a tribal map listing
985 groups, an explorers-kingdoms map, and a colonial rule map),
and geographical regions (North Africa, Northeast Africa, West
Africa, East Africa, Central Africa, Southern Africa and Madagascar).
This is followed by the main encyclopaedic section which lists the
various geographical features of Africa in alphabetical order. Each
country is fairly extensively described--physical features, population,
economy, trade, communications, constitution, and history--and each
survey concludes with a mini-bibliography. In the back of the book
are listed in alphabetical order: tribes of each country followed
by the geographical features described in the encyclopaedia. A
colored geographical map (scale: 1:15,000,000) is located in a back
pocket. Also in the back pocket is a chart of the legends for the
maps on geology, geomorphology, climate, vegetation, soils, and economic activities.

481. Migliorini, Elio. L'AFRICA. Torino, Unione Tipografico-Editrice
        Torinese, 1955. 821 p. illus., plates, fold. col. maps.

        Includes bibliographies.

        An impressive volume covering all Africa in physical, social,
and politico-economic geography. Arrangement, after a general
section, is by region. The folded, colored maps, supplemented
generously by subject sketch maps, are of high quality and value.
The author is director of the Institute of Geography at the University of Naples.

        While American and British geographers now tend to treat regions
or continents in independent studies of moderate length, continental
writers continue the tradition of multivolume sets of world geography.
The great French GEOGRAPHIE UNIVERSELLE edited by P. Vidal de la
Blache and L. Gallois reached its fifteenth and final volume after
the war (Paris, A. Colin, 1927-48), though those devoted to Africa
south of the Sahara, Vol. XI, Part 2, AFRIQUE OCCIDENTALE, by
Augustin Bernard (p. 285-529), and Vol. XII, AFRIQUE EQUATORIALE,
ORIENTALE ET AUSTRALE, by Fernand Maurette (398 p.) appeared in 1939
and 1938 respectively. Little attention is paid in these to political
and economic factors, the stress being on physical and human geography.

An even more lavish publishing venture is the GEOGRAFIA UNIVERSALE
ILLUSTRATA: LA FISIONOMIA ATTUALE DEL MONDO CONSIDERATA NELL'ASPETTO
FISICO, ANTROPICO ED ECONOMICO, edited by Robert Almagià (Torino,
Union Tipografico-Editrice Torinese). Vol. V, L'AFRICA, by Elio
Migliorini, was announced in 1960. Vol. II of the GEOGRAPHIE UNIVER-
SELLE LAROUSSE, edited by Pierre Deffontaines, is AFRIQUE, ASIE
PENINSULAIRE, OCEANIE (Paris, Larousse, 1959, 391 p.).

482. Mountjoy, Alan B., and Clifford Embleton. AFRICA: A GEOGRAPHICAL
        STUDY. With a contribution by W. B. Morgan. London, Hutchinson
        Educational, 1965 [i.e., 1966]. 688 p. illus., maps, tables,
        diagrs. (Hutchinson Advanced Geographies)

      A textbook partly derived from the Honours course given at the
University of London and intended for university freshmen and sixth-
form students. Three introductory sections cover the physical basis,
historical and political evolution, and human geography. These are
followed by detailed surveys of Northwest Africa, the Sahara, the Nile
Basin and Horn of Africa, East Africa, Malagasy, the Zambezi-Limpopo
lands, and South, Southwestern, Equatorial, and West Africa. Each
section includes a reading list. A concluding chapter deals with
problems of the tropical environment, population pressure, and agrarian and economic problems. There is an index.

483. Stamp, Laurence Dudley. AFRICA: A STUDY IN TROPICAL DEVELOPMENT.
        2d ed. New York, Wiley, 1964. 534 p. illus., maps.

      A considerably revised and updated edition of an excellent geog-
raphy text first published in 1953 by the director of the World Land
Use Survey. Professor Stamp presents the physical, economic, and
human geography of the continent as a whole in the first part of the
volume and then provides surveys of countries and regions in the second part. The work concludes with summaries of vital and economic
statistics for each country (p. 499-519) and an index. Also useful is
Leonard Suggate, AFRICA (9th ed. rev.; London, Harrap, 1968, 525 p.).

484. U.S. Department of the Interior. Office of Geography. [Official
        Standard Names Approved by the U.S. Board on Geographic Names]
        Washington, U.S. Govt. Print. Off., 1955-

      Series of gazetteers for individual countries in which most
parts of Africa have now been covered. Gazetteer no. 1, issued in
1955, was on British East Africa; later revisions have covered the
separate independent nations. The gazetteers are issued in oblong
format and offset print. See individual countries in Part IV for
titles.

485. U.S. Hydrographic Office. SAILING DIREC TIONS. Washington, U.S. Govt. Print. Off.

> H.O. Publication no. 105. SOUTHWEST COAST OF AFRICA, CAPE PALMAS TO THE CAPE OF GOOD HOPE. 4th ed. 1951. xxvi, 314 p. illus., maps.
>
> H.O. Publication no. 134. WEST COASTS OF SPAIN, PORTUGAL, AND NORTHWEST AFRICA AND OFF-LYING ISLANDS. 6th ed. 1952. xxvi, 410 p. maps.
>
> H.O. Publication no. 156. SOUTHEAST COAST OF AFRICA, CAPE OF GOOD HOPE TO RAS HAFUN. 4th ed. 1951. xxvi, 268 p. illus., maps.
>
> H.O. Publication no. 161. SOUTH INDIAN OCEAN, MADAGASCAR AND THE ISLANDS WEST OF LONGITUDE 90° EAST. 4th ed. 1952. xxvi, 454 p. maps.

The volumes for Africa in the SAILING DIRECTIONS sequence (begun in 1916 as the AFRICA PILOT), of which the above are examples, are in loose-leaf binders allowing for supplementary material and include folded maps and charts. New editions are based on all available sources, among them the recent volumes and supplements of the British Hydrographic Office AFRICA PILOT. The first chapter of each volume contains general remarks and information on buoyage, lifesaving stations, signals, regulations, wind and weather, currents, and routes. Then come detailed chapters describing shore features and sailing conditions point to point along the coast. There are appendixes listing principal ports, with particulars of depths, meteorological tables, and an index of place names.

486. Weeks, George. "Wings of Change: A Report on the Progress of Civil Aviation in Africa." AFRICA REPORT, v. 10, no. 2, Feb. 1965: 14-40.

A lengthy report by a United Press International specialist on Africa provides a country-by-country guide for all interested in this modern mode of travel to and within the continent. For 49 countries he lists civil airline carriers, airports, and kinds of aircrafts and their number of weekly flights. The article includes a map of Soviet-block air routes to Africa, a chart of aircraft in African service (with number of seats, engine type, and country of manufacture), a double-page chart of African air carriers (with tabulated information regarding them), and a smaller table of non-African airlines with scheduled service in Africa. In a foreword the editors warn readers that "the civil airline picture is changing very rapidly in Africa," and they claim only "to have captured the kaleidoscope in one single moment of time."

CHAPTER 14

HISTORY

GENERAL

Atlases and Maps

487.   Boyd, Andrew, and Patrick van Rensburg.   AN ATLAS OF AFRICAN AFFAIRS.
           With maps by W. H. Bromage. New York, Praeger, 1962. 133 p.
           maps.

           An explanatory guide to the fast-changing map of Africa, offering
       background information, the atlas was prepared with "the plain newspaper
       reader" in mind. The 50 sketch maps are "general" (population, regions
       and barriers, a few relating to history, the new political scence as
       of late 1962, United Nations activity, Pan-Africanism and regional
       unity, education, health, minerals, transport, power development) and
       "sectional." They are explained succinctly on facing pages. The
       atlas is available in hard-cover and paperback editions.

488.   Fage, J. D.   AN ATLAS OF AFRICAN HISTORY. London, E. Arnold, 1958.
           64 p. 62 maps.

           Reprint, 1962.

           The first work of its kind for Africa, with 62 sketch maps in
       diagrammatic form illustrating stages of African history from the eve
       of the Muslim Arab invasions to the present. Captions vary from thumb-
       nail sketches of the historic situation to keys to symbols that are
       used to indicate, for example, the spread of Christian missions. See
       also Harry Gailey, Jr., THE HISTORY OF AFRICA IN MAPS (Chicago,
       Denoyer-Geppert Co., 1967, 96 p.).

489. Healy, Allan M., and E. R. Vere-Hodge. THE MAP APPROACH TO AFRICAN
     HISTORY. London, University Tutorial Press, 1959. 64 p. 28 maps.

     Prepared by two secondary school teachers, this is a much simpli-
fied presentation of African history in 28 sketch maps with facing
explanatory text.

490. Horrabin, James Francis. AN ATLAS OF AFRICA. New York, Praeger,
     1960. 126 p. 50 maps. (Books That Matter)

     Collection of 50 maps with facing pages of interpretation that
summarize knowledge needed for understanding of current news. The
first 22 maps are grouped as "Background" and explain history from
the ancient world to the present. Part 2 is "Today," illustrating
issues, regions, and trends. Part 3 is "Tomorrow" and touches
problems of linguistics, settlement, economic development, and the
like.

Bibliographies

Note: The few books here mentioned are selected as well-balanced modern
presentations covering the entire range of the history of Africa, from
its dawn to the present era. In these works so many aspects are involved
(archaeology, anthropology, economic and political development, mission
activities, etc.) that bibliographical sources cannot be delimited, with
the result that the titles in Part II, Retrospective Bibliographies, are
generally applicable. The American Historical Association's GUIDE TO HIS-
TORICAL LITERATURE (see no. 308), in particular, is designed to serve the
historian. A few bibliographies relating to specific periods of history
are noted in the subsections below.

491. Curtin, Philip. AFRICAN HISTORY. New York, Macmillan Company, 1964.
     55 p.

     This useful bibliographical essay on all phases of African history
evaluates books and traces misconceptions and errors of various periods
of writing about Africa.

492. Meyer-Heiselberg, R. BIBLIOGRAFI OVER AFRIKANSK HISTORIE: NYERE
     LITTERATUR OM SYD FOR SAHARA. Undsendt af UNESCO-Skoleprojektet.
     [Copenhagen?] 1963. xi, 88 l.

     An annotated guide to the history of sub-Saharan Africa, with
emphasis on the precolonial era. An introductory essay covers the
more recent literature. Entries are in various languages and include
general handbooks, works arranged by subject and by area and country,
and a list of periodicals. There is an author index.

493. Paris. Institut Pédagogique National. Service de Recherches
     Pédagogiques pour les Pays en Voie de Développement. BIBLI-
     OGRAPHIE PRATIQUE SUR L'HISTOIRE DE L'AFRIQUE. Compiled by
     Henri Moniot. Paris, 1963. 55 p. (Documentation pédagogique
     africaine, no. 6)

     A partially annotated guide to French (and a few English) works
on the history of sub-Saharan Africa. Included are journals, non-
historic studies on various subjects, general histories, and works on
pre- and protohistory, on West and Central Africa and other regions,
on Madagascar, and on the colonial period.

Reference Works

494. AFRICAN HISTORICAL STUDIES. Edited by Norman R. Bennett. v. 1, no. 1-
     1968- Brookline, Mass., African Studies Center, Boston University.
     Twice a year.

     This new journal, which includes archaelogy in its coverage, pre-
sents about five essays in each issue. In addition, it carries a
solid section of book reviews and a "News and Notes" section.

495. Balandier, Georges. DICTIONNAIRE DES CIVILISATIONS AFRICAINES. [Sous
     la direction de Georges Balandier et Jacques Maquet] Paris,
     Fernand Hazan, 1968. 448 p. illus.

     A copiously illustrated volume, of chief interest to those con-
cerned with art, prehistory, history, anthropology. Emphasis is on
the cultures of West Africa. Each article is signed by the initials
of its author. Contributors, all of whom are French Africanists,
include Pierre Alexandre, Marguerite Dupire, Michel Leiris, Raymond
Mauny, Paul Mercier, and Denise Paulme.

496. Boubou Hama. ENQUÊTE SUR LES FONDEMENTS ET LA GENÈSE DE L'UNITÉ
     AFRICAINE. Paris, Présence Africaine, 1966. 560 p. plates, maps
     (1 fold. in back pocket).

     By a teacher and government adviser who is a devotee of geo-
graphic determinism, this is an intelligent, but not dispassionate,
account of the historical, geographical, ethnological, and political
factors involved in the genesis of African unity. A large portion
of the book is concerned with West African civilization. This leads
the author to a discussion of various types of African unity in the
past, the assault of the continent and its consequences, the "mental
universe" of Africa, the chance for African unity today, independent
Niger, and the destiny of Africa.

497. Butler, Jeffrey, ed. BOSTON UNIVERSITY PAPERS IN AFRICAN HISTORY,
Vol. I. Boston, Boston University Press, 1964. 270 p. tables.

Bibliographical footnotes.

_____. BOSTON UNIVERSITY PAPERS ON AFRICA: Vol. II, AFRICAN
HISTORY. Boston, Boston University Press, 1966. 337 p. maps,
tables.

Bibliographical footnotes.

Following publication of the first volume, the title of this
series was modified to reflect the wider scope of future volumes,
i.e., not only history but also political affairs (see no. 605) and
interdisciplinary subjects. Both volumes derive largely from faculty
seminars held by the African Studies Center at Boston University.

The 10 papers in Vol. I are mainly concerned with the colonial
period in specific areas of Africa, but also include such articles
as "Historical Inferences from Linguistic Research in Sub-Saharan
Africa," by Joseph Greenberg, and "European Sources for Tropical
African History," by Graham Irwin.

Vol. II consists of eight papers devoted wholly or in part to
activities of non-African groups and individuals in Africa during
the colonial period and three papers concerned with earlier periods,
i.e., Creighton Gabel's "Prehistoric Populations of Africa" and two
papers by Ronald Cohen on Bornu.

498. Collins, Robert O., ed. PROBLEMS IN AFRICAN HISTORY. Englewood
Cliffs, N. J., Prentice-Hall, 1968. 374 p.

A collection of readings on African history suitable for an
introductory class. This anthology reaches back to select from out-
of-print works of the nineteenth and twentieth centuries and to
select special chapters from specialized books. Major problems dealt
with are: Africa and Egypt, Bantu origins and migrations, Nilotic
origins and migrations, the historian and stateless societies,
African states, trade in precolonial Africa, and the African slave
trade. The names of prominent scholars in the fields of African
culture, linguistics, religion and politics appear in the list of
contributors.

Collins is Professor in the Department of History, University
of California, Santa Barbara.

499. Cornevin, Robert. HISTOIRE DE L'AFRIQUE. Paris, Payot, 1962-
        (Bibliothèque historique)

        The author, a former chief administrator of France Overseas, is
now director of the Centre d'Etude et de Documentation sur l'Afrique
et l'Outre-Mer in Paris and has written a number of comprehensive
histories of Africa. The first part of this work appeared in 1962:
DES ORIGINES AU XVIe SIECLE (453 p., maps). The second volume is
subtitled L'AFRIQUE PRECOLONIALE: 1500-1900 (1966, 638 p., maps),
and Marianne Cornevin collaborated. A third volume on colonization,
decolonization, and problems of the new independent Africa is to
come. There are chapter bibliographies (p. 441-447 in Vol. I, p.
601-625 in Vol. II).

        Before the appearance of the second volume Professor Cornevin,
in collaboration with his wife, Marianne Cornevin, brought out for
a more popular audience an updated edition of an earlier book,
HISTOIRE DE L'AFRIQUE DES ORIGINES A NOS JOURS (Paris, Payot, 1964,
423 p,; Petite bibliothèque Payot). The first edition appeared in
1956 (401 p.). In this volume, too, North and Northeast Africa are
included.

500. Davidson, Basil. AFRICA: HISTORY OF A CONTINENT. With photographs
        by Werner Forman. New York, Macmillan, 1966. 320 p. illus.
        (part col.), maps, plans.

        Bibliography: p. 315-317.

        This survey, extending from prehistoric times to the mid-1960's,
is particularly notable for its splendid illustrations (more than
240 black-and-white photographs, 42 colored plates, and 13 maps).
Of eight chapters, the seventh deals rather fleetingly with the period
of conquest and colonial rule. The last chapter is a brief discussion
of the growth of nationalism, emergence of independent states, and
problems of economic and social transition. An index is included. A
less expensive edition entitled AFRICA IN HISTORY has appeared.

501. Davidson, Basil, ed. THE AFRICAN PAST: CHRONICLES FROM ANTIQUITY TO
        MODERN TIMES. Boston, Little, Brown, 1964. xix, 392 p.

        Selection of extracts from writings of all sorts--letters, books,
speeches, etc.--from Egyptian antiquity to the immediate present. Mr.
Davidson has set them in a commentary which illuminates the entire
course of African history.

502. Fage, J. D., ed. AFRICA DISCOVERS HER PAST. New York, Oxford
     University Press, 1969. 112 p.

     This volume of essays looks at current methods of research
into African history, and shows what kind of results these methods
are achieving. The comparative value of oral, documentary, and
archaeological sources is analyzed, and developments in the writing
of history in different regions of Africa are examined.

503. International African Seminar, 4th, Dakar, 1961. THE HISTORIAN IN
     TROPICAL AFRICA. Edited by J. Vansina, R. Mauny, and L. V.
     Thomas. London, Ibadan, Accra, Published for the International
     African Institute by Oxford University Press, 1964. 428 p.
     2 maps.

     Proceedings of the fourth seminar organized by the Inter-
national African Institute. (Earlier volumes were SOCIAL CHANGE IN
MODERN AFRICA, 1961, and AFRICAN AGRARIAN SYSTEMS, 1963.) The first
hundred pages contain French and English versions of an excellent
introductory summary of the techniques and problems of the ethno-
historian in Africa. Following this are 17 specialists' papers on
linguistics, archaeology, oral tradition, ethnohistory, process
history, and historical aspects of specific peoples or states such
as the Hausa or Akwapim state. There are references at the end of
most chapters.

504. JOURNAL OF AFRICAN HISTORY. v. 1, no. 1- May 1960- London, Cambridge
     University Press.

     Edited by R. A. Oliver and J. D. Fage. Two issues a year
appear in 1960 and 1961, and three in 1962. It now has four issues
a year. The journal is designed to represent the highest scholarly
standards in its contributions to the broad field of African history.

505. London. University. School of Oriental and African Studies.
     HISTORY AND ARCHAEOLOGY IN AFRICA: REPORT OF A CONFERENCE
     HELD IN JULY 1953 AT THE SCHOOL OF ORIENTAL & AFRICAN STUDIES.
     Edited by R. A. Hamilton. London, 1955. 99 p. maps.

     "A list of the conference papers...[with] bibliographical
notes": p. 84-96.

     This conference, organized at the School of Oriental and African
Studies, was the first international gathering bringing together
British, French, and African scholars concerned with the African past
before the period of European administration. Its purpose was to
stimulate the collection and preservation of materials for the unwritten history of the African peoples. The two main sources of this

history, oral tradition and archaeology, formed the subject matter of the papers, a selected few of which are reproduced in this volume. A second conference was held at the School of Oriental and African Studies on July 16-18, 1957. Its proceedings were published by the school in 1959: HISTORY AND ARCHAEOLOGY IN AFRICA, edited by D. H. Jones (London, 58 p.). At that meeting a panel was set up to explore the practicability of publishing an international journal of African history. This was accomplished in 1960 with the launching of the JOURNAL OF AFRICAN HISTORY (see above). A third conference was held in Aug. 1961; its resolutions were reported in AFRICA, v. 31, Oct. 1961: 579-580.

A number of regional or national conferences on African history have been held in recent years, notably in Nigeria, Ghana, East Africa, and the Federation of Rhodesia and Nyasaland. They are reported regularly in the "Notes and News" section of the International African Institute journal, AFRICA.

506. McCall, Daniel F. AFRICA IN TIME-PERSPECTIVE: A DISCUSSION OF HISTORICAL RECONSTRUCTION FROM UNWRITTEN SOURCES. Boston, Boston University Press; Legon, Ghana University Press, 1964. xvii, 175 p.

"Notes" and bibliography: p. 160-169.

Based on an anthropologist's lectures at the University of Ghana, this is a survey and discussion of sources of history from archaeology, linguistics, oral traditions, ethnology, art, and physical sciences and an analysis of techniques for interdisciplinary cooperation in historical research. The approaches are not limited to African history.

507. McEwan, P. J. M., ed. Readings in African History [series]. New York, Oxford University Press, 1968. 3 v.

Vol. I, AFRICA FROM EARLY TIMES TO 1800. xxiv, 436 p. maps.

Vol. II, NINETEENTH-CENTURY AFRICA. xxiv, 468 p. maps.

Vol. III, TWENTIETH-CENTURY AFRICA. xxiv, 517 p. maps.

A series of documents on African history. The editor has selected contrasting passages from recognized authorities on the most significant events and movements in the history of the continent. Vol. I contains 41 selections, while Vols. II and III contain 45 and 50 selections, respectively. Each volume includes an editorial introduction, a chronological table, and an index.

508. Oliver, Roland A., and J. D. Fage. A SHORT HISTORY OF AFRICA.
     Baltimore, Md., Penguin Books, 1962. 279 p. (Penquin African
     Library, AP 2)

     Includes bibliography.

     A concentrated survey of Africa's history from prehistoric times
     to the present, by the editors of the JOURNAL OF AFRICAN HISTORY.

509. Rotberg, Robert I. A POLITICAL HISTORY OF TROPICAL AFRICA. New
     York, Harcourt, Brace & World, 1965. xvi, 440 p. illus., ports.,
     maps.

     Bibliography: p. 373-421.

     A narrative history of tropical Africa's political development
     from earliest times to 1965, intended to serve as an introduction and
     guide. Lightly blended into the account is an analysis of Africa's
     social systems and cultural patterns. Since the author attempts to
     synthesize the full sweep of tropical African history, only the con-
     cluding 24 pages of the text are devoted to "The Triumph of
     Nationalism, 1940-1965." Maps are liberally strewn throughout the
     work. The very useful and extensive bibliography is divided into
     historical periods. An analytical index is included.

510. Sík, Endre. THE HISTORY OF BLACK AFRICA. Translated by Sándor Simon.
     Budapest, Akadémiai Kiadó, 1966- 2 v. ([398], 323 p.).
     plates, maps.

     A survey of the history of sub-Saharan Africa from a non-
     Western viewpoint. The author believes that the history of Black
     Africa illustrates the theses of Marx, Lenin, and Stalin. African
     history is divided into five periods--that preceding European intru-
     sions (up to the end of the fifteenth century), the age of primi-
     tive accumulation (or the period of the slave trade), the epoch of
     conquest and partitioning, the age of imperialism, and the emergence
     of independent states. The account ends on the eve of World War II.
     Bibliographies follow each chapter. Vol. I of the French edition
     was first published in 1961, Vol. II in 1964. A third volume is to
     appear. Although outdated, Sík's books are useful Marxist surveys.

511. Vansina, Jan. THE ORAL TRADITION: A STUDY IN HISTORICAL METHODOLOGY.
     Chicago, Aldine, 1964. 226 p.

     A survey of the techniques of gathering African traditions and
     oral history and how to use and to interpret this information.

512. Westermann, Diedrich. GESCHICHTE AFRIKAS: STAATENBILDUNGEN
SUDLICH DER SAHARA. Köln, Greven-Verlag, 1952. xi, 492 p.
illus., ports., maps.

Bibliography: p. 455-470.

The late Dr. Westermann, emeritus professor of African languages
at the University of Berlin and a founder and director of the International African Institute, was German's foremost Africanist of the
first half of the twentieth century. This history of state building
in Africa south of the Sahara was begun in 1939. It is a standard
reference work, representing the sum total of scholarship to that
date. The manuscript was twice destroyed in air raids during the war,
and the work was finished only in 1950. In chronicling the rise,
decline, and fall of 64 African kingdoms south of the Sahara the
author treated European contacts and domination merely as episodes in
the story of independent peoples. The volume includes good illustrations, a long bibliography, and comprehensive indexes of place,
tribal, and personal names.

513. Wiedner, Donald L. A HISTORY OF AFRICA SOUTH OF THE SAHARA. New
York, Random House, 1962. 578 p. illus., maps.

Bibliography: p. 531-549.

This history, which covers the African past and analyzes present
problems, is readable and useful, though not above criticism by some
Africanists.

PREHISTORY (PROTOHISTORY) AND THE PERIOD UP TO 1700

Atlas

514. Clark, John Desmond, comp. ATLAS OF AFRICAN PREHISTORY. Chicago,
University of Chicago Press, 1967. 62 p. 50 maps (part col.).

Includes bibliographies.

Deals with prehistoric Africa and Africa during antiquity. The
scale of the maps, which are in portfolio, is 1:20,000,000 and
1:38,000,000.

Bibliographies

515. Council for Old World Archaeology. COWA BIBLIOGRAPHY: CURRENT
PUBLICATIONS IN OLD WORLD ARCHAEOLOGY. Cambridge, Mass.

The bibliographical accompaniment to an analytical series, COWA
SURVEY: CURRENT WORK IN OLD WORLD ARCHAEOLOGY (1957-), with which it
is bound under separate paging. There are 22 regional area reports
in the series; those relating to sub-Saharan Africa are: Area 11,
West Africa; Area 12, Equatorial Africa; Area 13, South Africa; Area
14, East Africa. African bibliographies appeared in 1959, 1962, and
1965; entries are annotated.

516. Mauny, R. "Contribution à la bibliographie de l'historie de l'Afrique
noire des origines à 1850," BULLETIN DE L'I.F.A.N., v. 28, ser.
B, nos. 3-4, July-Oct. 1966: 927-965.

A valuable bibliographical essay on sources for African history.
The article is divided into four parts: the geographic and chronologic
sphere; printed sources (periodicals and bibliographies); the humanities
(geography, ethnology, sociology, anthropology, and linguistics); and
primary sources (covering the Africa of antiquity, the Middle Ages of
Africa, and precolonial tropical Africa).

517. Ternaux-Compans, Henri. BIBLIOTHEQUE ASIATIQUE ET AFRICAINE, OU
CATALOGUE DES OUVRAGES RELATIFS A L'ASIE ET A L'AFRIQUE QUI ONT
PARU DEPUIS LA DECOUVERTE DE L'IMPRIMERIE JUSQU'EN 1700.
[Réimpression de l'édition Paris, 1841]. Amsterdam, B. R. Grüner,
1968. 350 p.

Reference Works

518. Alimen, Henriette. THE PREHISTORY OF AFRICA. Translated by Alan
Houghton Brodrick. London, Hutchinson, 1957. xviii, 438 p.
illus., maps, tables.

Includes bibliographies.

This work came out in the French edition in 1955 and serves
as a synthesis and summary of then existing knowledge regarding
geologic ages and remains of prehistoric man in Africa. Included
are many comparative tables, maps, drawings, and plates (28, some
in color) of artifacts and rock drawings. The work has now been
largely superseded by John Desmond Clark, THE PREHISTORY OF AFRICA
(New York, Praeger, 1970, 320 p.).

519. ANTIQUITES AFRICAINES. v. 1- 1967- Paris, Centre National de la
     Recherche Scientifique. Annual.

520. Cornevin, Robert. HISTOIRE DES PEUPLES DE L'AFRIQUE NOIRE. Paris,
       Berger-Levrault, 1960. 715 p. illus., plates, maps, geneal.
       tables. (Mondes d'outre-mer, Série: Histoire)

     A valuable and complex study of prehistoric and pre-European
history. The first of three parts is on African historiography and
origins in general, the second on the ancient kingdoms of West Africa,
the third on East, Central, and Southern Africa. Bibliographical
references (p. 671-686) are arranged by chapter.

521. Davidson, Basil. THE LOST CITIES OF AFRICA. Boston, Little, Brown,
       1959. 366 p. illus.

     London ed., Gollancz, has title OLD AFRICA REDISCOVERED.

     Includes bibliographies.

     This history by a well-known writer on African affairs covers
the 15 or 20 "proto-historic" centuries before the written records of
European trade and penetration began. Addressed to a popular audience,
it takes into account almost two decades of rapid advances in scholarly
research regarding the claims for the origin of man in East Africa,
the kingdoms of antiquity in Northeastern Africa and of the western
Sudan in the Middle Ages, the less well identified societies of Central
Africa known only through art remains, and the civilizations of East
and Southeast Africa, culminating in the great stone ruins of Zimbabwe.
Critics have charged the writer with romantic overenthusiasm in his
interpretations of tribal life.

522. Davidson, Basil, and the Editors of Time-Life Books. AFRICAN KINGDOMS.
       New York, Time, Inc., 1966. 192 p. illus. (part col.), col.
       maps. (Great Ages of Man)

     In this lavishly illustrated narrative of early African history
Davidson draws on anthropology and archaeology to aid historical
analysis. Each chapter is accompanied by a pictorial essay. The
opening chapter on early cities is followed by chapters on the civilizations of the Nile with a pictorial essay on the rock paintings of
Tassili n'Ajjer, traditional tribal life with an essay on the Nuba
wrestlers of the Sudan, the early "merchant empires"--the kingdoms of
Benin and the Ashanti--with an essay on Benin, traditional religions
with an essay on the rock-hewn churches of Lalibela in Ethiopia, and
the arts, with emphasis on sculpture. The final chapter traces the
changes in traditional societies and stresses Africa's cultural impact
on the Western world. A chronology of African civilizations and an
index are included.

523. Ibn Batuta, 13)4-77. TRAVELS, A.D. 1325-1354. Translated, with revisions and notes from the Arabic text edited by C. Defrémery and B. R. Sanguinetti, by H. A. R. Gibb. Cambridge [Eng.], Published for the Hakluyt Society at the Cambridge University Press, 1958-62. 2 v. illus., maps. (Hakluyt Society Works, 2d ser., nos. 110, 117)

    The early Arabic sources for African history are being increasingly studied for evidences of the medieval empires of sub-Saharan Africa. This fourteenth-century traveler visited the Emperor of Mali. Modern texts in English or French translation are also available for the works of the eleventh- and twelfth-century geographers, al-Bakri and Idrisi, who describe the ancient Ghana.

524. Labouret, Henri. AFRICA BEFORE THE WHITE MAN. Translated by Francis Huxley. New York, Walker and Co., 1963 [c. 1962]. 138 p. maps. (Sun Book)

    Bibliography: p. 127-129.

    A brief study of precolonial African societies by the former director of the International Institute of African Languages and Civilizations. An introduction on African prehistory is followed by chapters on the formation of societies and their way of life, the empires of the Western Sudan, the hegemonies of the Central Sudan, the Sudanese states of the Peuls, the states and principalities of the coast, and Ethiopia. Technically, the book is marred by erroneous page references.

    The work was first published in 1946 as L'AFRIQUE PRECOLONIALE (Paris, Presses Universitaires de France).

525. Leakey, Louis S. B. THE PROGRESS AND EVOLUTION OF MAN IN AFRICA. London, New York, Oxford University Press, 1961. 50 p. illus.

    In his set of lectures at Edinburgh University in 1935-36, published as STONE AGE AFRICA: AN OUTLINE OF PREHISTORY IN AFRICA (London, Oxford University Press, 1936, 218 p.), Professor Leakey summarized his theory that man originated in East Africa during the glacial epoch. This was before his epoch-making discovery, in the late 1950's, in the Olduvai gorge in Tanganyika, of the remains of Zinjanthropus, a tool-making creature who is dated as over one and a half million years old. Only lectures regarding the latest finds have been published. The volume here mentioned contains two short addresses.

In 1965-67 Professor Leakey had in progress a work entitled
OLDUVAI GORGE, 1951-1961, planned as two volumes. The first volume,
on geology, ecology, and climate, includes an account of the potassium-
argon dating techniques used.

526. Lhote, Henri. THE SEARCH FOR THE TASSILI FRESCOES: THE STORY OF THE
        PREHISTORIC ROCK-PAINTINGS OF THE SAHARA. Translated from the
        French by Alan Houghton Brodrick. New York, E. P. Dutton, 1959.
        236 p. col. illus.

Story of the expedition led by the author, which made dramatic
archaeological finds in the Ahaggar mountains of the Sahara. The rock
paintings, of which careful tracings, here reproduced in color, were made,
bear striking evidence of the routes of culture migrations in prehistoric Africa.

527. Oliver, Roland, ed. THE DAWN OF AFRICAN HISTORY. London, Oxford Uni-
        versity Press, 1961. 103 p. maps.

A collection of talks on the BBC Third Programme, summarizing the
known or deduced pre-European history of the different regions of
Africa. The scholars represented have themselves contributed to original
research; they include Thomas Hodgkin, Gervase Mathew, D. H. Jones, J. D.
Fage, C. R. Boxer, J. Vansina, and W. M. Macmillan. In his conclusions
the editor emphasizes the geographical causes of Africa's isolation and
the political achievement against overwhelming odds.

528. Oliver, Roland, ed. THE MIDDLE AGE OF AFRICAN HISTORY. Maps drawn by
        Regmarad. London, Oxford University Press, 1967. 105 p. maps.

This work, like the preceding entry, records a series of talks
broadcast by the BBC. All the short essays concern precolonial Africa,
and most of them expand upon material presented in the earlier volume.
Among the contributors are Nehemia Levtzion, A. Adu Boahen, Alan Ryder,
David Birmingham, Brian M. Fagan, and Bethwell Ogot. An anlytical
index is included.

529. Pan-African Congress on Prehistory. PROCEEDINGS. 1st- 1947-

Professor Leakey was the moving spirit of the first Pan-African
Congress on Prehistory, convened in Nairobi in 1947, and he edited the
PROCEEDINGS (published by Blackwell, Oxford, 1952, 239 p.). The sec-
ond Congress was held in Algiers in 1952 (PROCCEDINGS published by Arts
et Métiers Graphiques, 18, rue Séguier, Paris 6), and the third in
Livingstone, Northern Rhodesia, in 1955 (PROCEEDINGS, edited by J.
Desmond Clark and Sonia Cole, London, Chatto & Windus, 1957, 440 p.).
The fourth Congress took place in Leopoldville in Aug. 1959 (ACTES,
Tervuren, Musée Royal de l'Afrique Centrale, 1962, 505 p., Annales,

Ser. in-8, Sciences humaines, 40). The fifth Congress met in Tenerife, Canary Islands, in 1963 (papers not published by early 1970). All papers are in highly technical archaeological language.

530. Pericot García, Luis, and Miguel Tarradell. MANUAL DE PREHISTORIA AFRICANA. Madrid, Instituto de Estudios Africanos, Consejo Superior de Investigaciones Científicas, 1962. 345 p. illus.

By a noted Spanish archaeologist who has contributed many papers in the various congresses on prehistory. The introduction examines great geographical developments (climatic changes and fauna of the Quaternary period). Part 1 is Paleolithic and Mesolitic Cultures, Part 2 Neolithic Cultures. Bibliographical references are by chapter, p. 313-334.

SIXTEENTH CENTURY TO MODERN TIMES
(EXPLORATION, COLONIAL ERA)

Bibliographies

531. Bridgman, Jon, and David E. Clarke. GERMAN AFRICA: A SELECT ANNOTATED BIBLIOGRAPHY. Stanford, Calif., Hoover Institution, Stanford University, 1965. (Hoover Institution Bibliographical Series, no. 19)

Some 900 titles on German involvement in Africa. There are sections on general works, German East Africa, German Southwest Africa, Togo and Cameroon, British Confidential Prints, serials, and newspapers.

532. Cox, Edward G. REFERENCE GUIDE TO LITERATURE OF TRAVEL. Seattle, University of Washington Press, 1935. 3 v. Vol. I, OLD WORLD.

Africa: p. 354-401.

This important bibliography covers exhaustively the works of travelers and of exploration from the sixteenth century to 1800. It begins, for Africa, with Johannes Boemus, THE DESCRIPTION OF THE CONTREY OF APHRIQUE, 1554, and ends with Lady Anne Barnard at the Cape, 1797-1802. The arrangement of entries is chronological.

533. Frank, Z., and S. Stancioff. "Bibliographie sur l'histoire de l'Afrique et la colonisation européenne de sources principalement soviétiques." Académie Royale des Sciences d'Outre-Mer, BULLETIN DES SEANCES, v. 8, no. 4, 1962: 658-691; v. 9, no. 2, 1963: 265-302; no. 4, 1963: 751-79?; no. 5, 1963: 1017-1050; v. 10, no. 2, 1964: 186-220.

A classified title list of works, mostly in Russian, prepared by
two specialists at the Centre d'Etudes des Pays de l'Est in Brussels.
It is currently appearing in three issues a year of the ARSOM BULLETIN,
presented by M. M. Walraet.

534. Griffin, Appleton Prentiss Clark. LIST OF BOOKS, WITH REFERENCES TO
      PERIODICALS, RELATING TO THE THEORY OF COLONIZATION, GOVERNMENT
      OF DEPENDENCIES, PROTECTORATES, AND RELATED TOPICS. 2d ed.
      Washington, Library of Congress, 1900. 156 p.

535. Kayser, Gabriel. BIBLIOGRAPHIE D'OUVRAGES AYANT TRAIT A L'AFRIQUE EN
      GENERAL DANS SES RAPPORTS AVEC L'EXPLORATION ET LA CIVILISATION DE
      CES CONTREES. Bruxelles, 1887. 176 p.

536. Martineau, Alfred, ed. BIBLIOGRAPHIE D'HISTOIRE COLONIALE (1900-1930).
      Paris, Société de l'Histoire des Colonies Françaises, 1932. 667 p.

      This massive bibliography which cites the chief sources relating
to acquisition and administration of colonial possessions throughout
the world--British, Belgian, Dutch, German, Italian, Portuguese, and
Spanish, as well as French--has for each colony an introductory essay
on the sources of bibliography and then a reading list of several
pages. Compilers were specialists.

537. Ragatz, Lowell. A BIBLIOGRAPHY FOR THE STUDY OF AFRICAN HISTORY IN
      THE NINETEENTH AND TWENTIETH CENTURIES. Washington, D.C.,
      Paul Pearlman, 1943. 47 p.

      A good selection, arranged by region and country, and including
books, documents, and significant periodical material.

Reference Works

538. Anene, Joseph C., and Godfrey N. Brown, eds. AFRICA IN THE NINETEENTH
      AND TWENTIETH CENTURIES: A HANDBOOK FOR TEACHERS AND STUDENTS.
      Ibadan, Ibadan University Press; London, Nelson, 1966. xviii,
      555 p. illus., plates, maps (part col.), plans, diagrs.

      A companion volume to A THOUSAND YEARS OF WEST AFRICAN HISTORY
edited by J. F. A. Ajayi and I. Espie. Designed essentially for
African students, it incorporates many of the papers delivered at
the Workshop on the Teaching of African History held at the University
of Ibadan in Mar. 1965. Among the diversity of topics covered in
Parts 1, 2, and 7 are: the teacher and archaeology in sub-Saharan
Africa, tropical African art, slavery and the slave trade, the
chartered companies and the scramble for Africa, external influence

on African society, the emergence of a new elite, and Pan-
Africanism and nationalism. Parts 3, 4, 5, and 6 deal with North
Africa and Ethiopia, West Africa, South Africa, and East and Central
Africa, respectively. Each chapter ends with study questions and
a short bibliography. An analytical index is included.

539. Bennett, Norman R., and George E. Brooks, Jr., eds. NEW ENGLAND
MERCHANTS IN AFRICA: A HISTORY THROUGH DOCUMENTS, 1802 to 1865.
[Brookline, Mass.] Boston University Press, 1965. xxxiv, 576 p.
illus., maps. (Boston University, African Research Studies, no. 7)

Collections in the Peabody Museum and Essex Institute, Salem,
Mass., provide the bulk of the documents reproduced, and those selected
bring out the main areas of trade, the people involved, merchandise
traded, etc. An introduction fills in the historical background;
tables in an appendix give comparative statistics (U.S., France,
Hamburg, U.K., British India, etc.) for the years 1861-65. Salem was
able to hold its prominent place in commerce from America to Africa
because the size of its sailing vessels was at that time adequate to
conditions along the African east and west coasts.

540. Berque, J.   DE L'IMPERIALISME A LA DECOLONISATION. Paris, Les Editions
de Minuit, 1966. 504 p.

541. Brunschwig, Henri. L'AVENEMENT DE L'AFRIQUE NOIRE. Paris, A. Colin,
1963. 248 p. maps, table. (Collection "Sciences politiques")

Bibliography: p. 225-233.

A description of Black Africa's slow evolution toward active
participation in international life. Brunschwig begins with a brief
discussion of the isolation of Africa during precolonial times and then
gives an account of the anti-slavery movement (1772-1815), the continuance of slavery and the attempts at colonization (1817-43), the
civilization of Africa from 1840 to 1880, the Africa of ivory, South
Africa, the stages and rhythms of trade, Pierre de Savorgnan de
Brazza and his explorations, the impact of late nineteenth-century
colonialism, and the genesis of the new nations. A synoptic table
(1771-1900) and an index of proper names are included.

542. THE CAMBRIDGE HISTORY OF THE BRITISH EMPIRE. General eds., J. Holland
Rose, A. P. Newton, and E. A. Benians. Cambridge, Eng., University Press, 1929-

For description, especially of the excellent bibliographical
sections, see no. 1227.

543. Collins, Robert O., ed. PROBLEMS IN THE HISTORY OF COLONIAL AFRICA,
          1860-1960. Englewood Cliffs, N.J., Prentice-Hall, 1970. xiii,
          389 p. map.

      Useful book of readings for courses in African history and poli-
tics during the colonial period. See also his book of readings, THE
PARTITION OF AFRICA: ILLUSION OR NECESSITY? (New York, J. Wiley, 1969,
239 p., maps).

544. Davidson, Basil. BLACK MOTHER: THE YEARS OF THE AFRICAN SLAVE TRADE.
          Boston, Little, Brown, 1961. 311 p. illus.

      Includes bibliography.

      Mr. Davidson here continues his presentation of African history
for the general audience (see his LOST CITIES OF AFRICA, no. 521). He
examines the connections of Africa and Europe from the fifteenth to
nineteenth centuries through commerce and its development into the
slave trade. Quoting extensively from contemporary sources, he en-
deavors to show that in the earliest contacts the races met on a basis
of equality, for the "feudal" societies of Africa were understandable
to Europeans still not emancipated from their own feudal traditions
into the full era of commercialism, but that in the latter age the subordination of all other values to the profit motive resulted in the
appalling horrors of the traffic in slaves and its concomitant European assumption of African inferiority.

545. Diop, Cheikh Anta. L'AFRIQUE NOIRE PRE-COLONIALE: ETUDE COMPAREE
          DES SYSTEMES POLITIQUES ET SOCIAUX DE L'EUROPE ET DE L'AFRIQUE
          NOIRE, DE L'ANTIQUITE A LA FORMATION DES ETATS MODERNES. Paris,
          Présence Africaine, 1960. 213 p. illus. (part col.), maps.
          (Collection Présence Africaine)

      This work and one by Endre Sík, THE HISTORY OF BLACK AFRICA (see
no. 510), describe the first contacts of Africa and Europe from a
Marxist viewpoint. They make large use of early source materials,
including Arabic.

546. Donnan, Elizabeth, ed. DOCUMENTS ILLUSTRATIVE OF THE HISTORY OF THE
          SLAVE TRADE TO AMERICA. Washington, D.C., Carnegie Institution,
          1930-35. 4 v. fold. map. (Publication no. 409)

      Reissued. New York, Octagon Books, 1965.

      Both printed and manuscript sources have been used in this massive
work on the slave trade to the Thirteen Colonies, to the West Indies,
and to Spanish America. Vol. I covers the years 1441-1700, Vol. II the
eighteenth century, Vol. III is on New England and the Middle Colonies,
Vol. IV the Border Colonies and the Southern Colonies.

547.	Edinburgh. University. Centre of African Studies. THE THEORY OF
	IMPERIALISM AND THE EUROPEAN PARTITION OF AFRICA: PROCEEDINGS
	OF A SEMINAR HELD IN THE CENTRE OF AFRICAN STUDIES, UNIVERSITY
	OF EDINBURGH, 3rd AND 4th NOVEMBER, 1967. Edinburgh, 1968.
	187 p.

	A series of papers dealing with the background of imperialism and
subjects as varied as the imperial idea and English fiction, the origins of the Congo Free State, French militarism and the Western Sudan,
the search for an Anglo-German understanding before the years immediately
preceding World War I, opposition to slavery and its impact on the partition, the role of the "man on the spot," and Victorian views about
Africa and imperialism. An historiographical essay by Eric Stokes,
IMPERIALISM AND THE SCRAMBLE FOR AFRICA (Salisbury, Historical Association of Rhodesia and Nyasaland, 1963, 15 p.) is also quite useful.

548.	Ganiage, Jean, Hubert Deschamps, and Odette Guitard, with the collab-
	oration of André Martel. L'AFRIQUE AU XXᵉ SIÈCLE. Paris, Sirey,
	1966. 908 p. maps (part fold. col.), tables. (L'histoire du
	XXe Siècle)

	Bibliography: p. 863-867.

	This massive volume includes in its broad scope not only major
historical events but also the geographic sociological, demographic,
political, economic, and cultural framework of developments on the
African continent from 1900 to 1965. Ganiage's study of North Africa
takes up roughly a third of the book, with Martel contributing some
30 pages on the Saharan region. The next section (p. 303-517), by
Deschamps, covers West, Central, and Northeastern Africa, and the
last section (p. 521-867), by Guitard, is devoted to Southern and
East Africa and includes the volume's only bibliography. There is an
index.

549.	Gann, Lewis H., and Peter Duignan. BURDEN OF EMPIRE: AN APPRAISAL OF
	WESTERN COLONIALISM IN AFRICA SOUTH OF THE SAHARA. New York,
	Published for the Hoover Institution by Praeger, 1967. xii, 434 p.
	maps. (Hoover Institution Publications)

	Bibliography: p. 399-417.

	The authors discuss different theories of imperialism and their
application to the realities of colonialism in Africa. They seek to
evaluate the impact of colonial rule on the indigenous people and to
reinterpret the process of decolonization. They believe that despite
its many failings colonial empire in Africa was one of the most
"efficacious engines of cultural diffusion in world history." Their
work is based on extensive reading in both African and European history
and also has a comparative dimension.

550. Gifford, Prosser, and William Roger Louis, eds., assisted by Alison
         Smith. BRITAIN AND GERMANY IN AFRICA: IMPERIAL RIVALRY AND
         COLONIAL RULE. New Haven, London, Yale University Press, 1967.
         xvii, 825 p. maps.

         Bibliography: p. 709-795.

         The most up-to-date work in English on British and German colonial
policy. It is distinguished by the high standard of the majority of
the 24 contributions, by the advantage of the comparison introduced
through juxtaposition of British and German colonial theory and practice, and by the original research that went into many of the essays.
The first part, titled "Imperial Rivalry," deals with Germany's role in
the scramble, Anglo-German rivalry and Anglo-German collaboration in
the colonial field, and the "repartition" of Africa occasioned by World
War I. The second part, titled "Colonial Rule," comprises essays on
various aspects of colonial administration, missionary policy, African
responses to European rule, the policies of trusteeship and of indirect
rule, and related topics. The third part is an excellent historiographical essay, with detailed notes on archival sources (p. 709-774),
an extensive listing of works (p. 774-795), lists of senior British and
German officials, and other relevant information. There is an index
and five (too few) maps. A similar volume is planned for Britain and
France.

551. Hallett, Robin. THE PENETRATION OF AFRICA: EUROPEAN EXPLORATION IN
         NORTH AND WEST AFRICA [Vol. I] to 1815. New York, Praeger, 1965.
         xxii, 458 p. illus., maps.

         Chapters on the African setting in the eighteenth century (land,
people, the states of northern and western Africa, African ideas about
Europe) are followed by sections on Europe's knowledge of Africa; the
widening of contacts through trade, curiosity, and the interest of
great men (e.g., Sir Joseph Banks); the antislavery movement; activities of the African Association and early explorers; the roots of imperialism; and the African Association, 1802-15, and further exploration.

552. Italy. Comitato per la Documentazione dell'Opera dell'Italia in Africa.
         L'ITALIA IN AFRICA: SERIE STORICO-MILITARE. Roma, Istituto Poli-
         grafico dello Stati, 1960-64. 5 v.

         See no. 3082(f) for annotation.

553. Lucas, Sir Charles. THE PARTITION AND COLONIZATION OF AFRICA. Oxford,
         Clarendon Press, 1922. 228 p. fold. map.

         A set of lectures by a noted Oxford historian of the British
Empire who had formerly been head of the Dominions Department of the

Colonial Office. The first two chapters give prenineteenth-century background; then nine talks expound with exemplary clarity the phases of the European penetration, rivalries, and wars in Africa. The last chapter assesses the results of World War I on the map of Africa and speculates on problems of the future, as "millions of natives [become] year by year less unsophisticated and possessed of more race consciousness and more self-respect."

The nineteenth-century standard history is Sir John Scott Keltie's PARTITION OF AFRICA (1st ed., 1893; 2d ed., rev., 1895). It was further revised and edited by Professor Albert Galloway Keller of Yale and published with the title AFRICA in the History of Nations series edited by Henry Cabot Lodge (New York, P. F. Collier & Son, Memorial ed., 1928, 335 p.).

Documentation on the diplomatic aspects of the European take-over of Africa is provided in one of the Peace Handbooks series prepared by the British Foreign Office, Historical Section: PARTITION OF AFRICA (London, H. M. Stationery Off., 1920, 82 p.; Handbooks, no. 89). The appendix gives texts of the bilateral agreements and treaties of Great Britain with the other European powers concerning African colonies, 1890-1904.

The involvement of the European powers in Africa was treated importantly later in William L. Langer's basic works on European diplomatic history, EUROPEAN ALLIANCES AND ALIGNMENTS, 1871-1920 (1931; 3d ed., Knopf, 1950; reprinted 1960, 510 p.) and THE DIPLOMACY OF IMPERIALISM, 1890-1902 (1935; 2d ed., Knopf, 1950; reprinted 1962, 797 p.).

554. Neill, Stephen Charles. COLONIALISM AND CHRISTIAN MISSIONS. New York, McGraw-Hill, 1966. 445 p.

   Bibliography: p. 426-429.

   There are chapters on the history of slavery in Africa, the colonial policies in Africa of Portugal, Britain, France, Belgium, and Germany, and the effects of these policies on missions under their jurisdiction.

555. Oliver, Roland. SIR HARRY JOHNSTON & THE SCRAMBLE FOR AFRICA. New York, St. Martin's Press, 1958 [c. 1957]. 368 p. illus.

   A satisfactory telling of history through the medium of biography. In 10 years of intensive study of African history, says Mr. Oliver, "no one personality has more constantly crossed my path" than Johnston, whose career as naturalist, explorer, civil servant, administrator, and historian extended to most parts of Black Africa. Johnston's own works, including THE COLONIZATION OF AFRICA (1899) and THE OPENING UP OF AFRICA (1911), as well as regional histories, linguistics, and zoological writings, are among the most important source works of his period.

Note: Other biographies, although of less than continent-wide application, are noted in regional or topical sections of the present work.

556. Oliver, Roland, and Anthony Atmore. AFRICA SINCE 1800. Cambridge, Eng., University Press, 1967. 304 p. maps.

Bibliography: p. 284-297.

A narrative history of the continent from 1800 to early 1966. The precolonial and colonial periods receive almost equal attention and more than two-thirds of the book is devoted to them. The latter part of the work succinctly covers the emergence of independent states and the perpetuation of white dominance in Southern Africa. The text is largely regional in format, but the continent as a whole is treated in chapters on the partition, on political, economic, social, and religious developments during colonial rule, on the interwar years, World War II, and the postwar period, and on independent Africa in the modern world. Adding to the cohesiveness of the account are 36 maps. An expository bibliography deals first with several broad topics and then with each main region.

557. Perham, Margery, and J. Simmons, eds. AFRICAN DISCOVERY: AN AN-THOLOGY OF EXPLORATION. London, Faber & Faber, 1946. 280 p. plates, ports., maps.

Reprint in paperback, Evanston, Ill., Northwestern University Press, 1963.

List of books: p. 274-277.

These generous extracts from the works of British explorers of Africa cover the period from 1769 to 1873. They are arranged in order in which the writers arrived in Africa--James Bruce, Mungo Park, Clapperton and Lander, Livingstone (his first journey in Africa), Baikie, Burton, Speke, Baker, Livingstone and Stanley. There are introductions by Miss Perham and Mr. Simmons. Miss Perham, formerly director of the Institute of Colonial Research, now Official Fellow of Nuffield College at Oxford, outlines the purpose and character of the anthology; Mr. Simmons briefly sketches the geography of the continent and the explorers. Each of the selections is preceded by a few paragraphs of details regarding the career of the traveler. The bibliography names the chief works by these men and biographies or other sources of information about them.

Fuller selections from the works of British explorers have been published in volumes for West Africa (edited by Cecil Howard, 1952) and East Africa (selected by Charles Richards and James Place, 1960).

558. Rieger, Morris. "United States Consular Agencies in Africa, 1789-1939." AFRICANA NEWSLETTER, v. 2, no. 2, 1964: 36-41.

   Table of consular agencies giving locality, territory, level at outset, inclusive dates. A preliminary contribution to the National African Guide Project (see no. 98).

559. Travellers and Explorers [series]. London, Routledge & Kegan Paul; New York, Praeger, 1965-

   A new series which in some respects is a continuation of the old Broadway Travellers Series of the 1920's. The general editor is Robin Hallett. The series, which will not be restricted to travellers of any one continent or century, is designed to make some of the great works of the past available in new editions that will appeal both to the general reader and to the scholar. Some works published are:

a)   Lander, Richard Lemon, and John Lander. THE NIGER JOURNAL OF RICHARD AND JOHN LANDER. Edited and abridged with an introduction by Robin Hallett. 1965. 317 p. illus., maps. Bibliography: p. 302-304.

b)   Burton, Sir Richard. FIRST FOOTSTEPS IN EAST AFRICA. Edited with an introduction and additional chapters by Gordon Waterfield. 1966. xii, 320 p. illus., maps, ports. Bibliographical references.

c)   Burton, Sir Richard. MISSION TO GELELE, KING OF DAHOMEY. Edited with an introduction and notes by C. W. Newbury. 1966. 372 p. illus., maps. Bibliographical references.

560. Ward, W. E. F. EMERGENT AFRICA. London, George Allen and Unwin, 1967. 231 p. (20th Century Histories, no. 3)

   History of Africa from 1800 to 1964, suitable for secondary schools and possibly for undergraduate libraries; somewhat oversimplified in presentation. Emphasis is on the role of the European.

MODERN ERA

Note: Although there is a constant flood of books on present-day Africa which are amply recorded in the Current Bibliographies noted above (see Part II), the present in African history is so kaleidoscopic that it can hardly be reflected in a book, since between the time of the author's conclusion and the release in print, situations are apt to undergo radical change. The handbooks and surveys listed above must be supplemented for the study of today's history by periodical literature and the daily press. Periodical indexes and newspaper indexes are helpful here. Among the latter, those of the London TIMES and the NEW YORK TIMES are of long standing and are familiar to all library users. A SUBJECT INDEX OF THE CHRISTIAN SCIENCE MONITOR (Boston) was begun in 1960 and is published monthly with semiannual cumulations. The WALL STREET JOURNAL INDEX (Dec. 1957-) is mainly but not exclusively concerned with business and financial matters. The U.S. Joint Publications Research Service (JPRS) issues an index of LE MONDE, and LE MONDE itself began publication of an annual index in 1967 with LE MONDE: INDEX ANALYTIQUE 1965 (759 p.).

Other general library tools are the documentation services, FACTS ON FILE (New York), and KEESING'S CONTEMPORARY ARCHIVES (London). For descriptions of these and also of the newspaper indexes, see Winchell (no. 1).

The index of the Library of Congress list SERIALS FOR AFRICAN STUDIES (see no. 396) may be consulted for titles of more information and documentation services relating to Africa. The items which follow are a select few among the many serials devoted to present-day Africa.

Serials

561. AFRICA DIARY. v. 1, no. 1- July 1/7, 1961- Edited by Hari Sharan Chhabra. New Delhi, Africa Publications. Weekly, with quarterly and annual indexes. Loose-leaf.

A weekly record of events in Africa. Abstracted from the international press. Countries are in alphabetical order, and there is a general section for Africa as a whole. An airmail edition reaches American libraries within the week.

562. AFRICA DIGEST. v. 1- July 1952- London, Africa Bureau. Monthly, 1952-Oct. 1955; bimonthly, Nov./Dec. 1955-

Country-by-country summary of outstanding developments; based on newspaper accounts.

563. AFRICA 196-. 1960- London. Fortnightly.

Confidential newsletter published by Chas. Lanson, 5/33 Rutland, London, S.W.7. This was begun as AFRICA 1960, the year changing in the title to correspond with the calendar. Content is analysis and forecast, particularly of politico-economic developments.

564. AFRICA QUARTERLY. Apr./June 1961- New Delhi [Indian Council for
      Africa].

          The quarterly journal of the Indian Institute for African
      Affairs, this excellent review carries, besides specialist articles
      on many aspects of political, social, and economic life of Africa, a
      quarterly chronicle, a list of books received, and an extensive
      bibliography in each issue.

565. AFRICA REPORT. v. 1, no. 1- July 5, 1956- Formerly edited by
          Helen Kitchen, now by Aaron Segal. Washington, D.C., African-
          American Institute. Monthly (11 numbers a year); from 1966-
          9 numbers a year, Oct.-June, and annual index.

          This journal, which is the foremost American organ for authori-
      tative reportage on and interpretation of the present African scene,
      carries articles and news notes on the politics, economics, social
      life and cultural life of Africa as a whole and of individual countries.
      Of particular interest on current developments are the following: the
      issues of Nov. 1961 and Nov. 1963, which contain a country-by-country
      situation report (brought together in Mrs. Kitchen's HANDBOOK OF
      AFRICAN AFFAIRS--see no. 448), the Dec. 1966 issue with a chart--
      "The 39 Independent States of Africa"--in which a column includes the
      major political changes during 1965-66, and the section "News in Brief,"
      a monthly chronology of major events country by country begun in May
      1964. The Fact Sheet Series, printed on the back cover and tabulating
      data on particular questions, last appeared in the August 1965 issue.
      The journal formerly had 11 issues a year until in 1966 the size of
      the magazine was increased from around 40 pages to about 60, with no
      issues in July, August, and September. A separate annual index is
      published.

566. AFRICA RESEARCH BULLETIN. v. 1, no. 1- Jan. 1964- Exeter, Eng.

          Published in two series:

      ECONOMIC, FINANCIAL, AND TECHNICAL. (Yellow pages, maps)

      POLITICAL, SOCIAL, AND CULTURAL. (White pages)

          An extensive service in two parts summarizing current developments
      in Africa and issued by John Drysdale's Africa Research Ltd., 1 Parlia-
      ment St., Exeter, Eng. The consecutively numbered loose-leaf pages
      are perforated for insertion in a binder, the first series on yellow
      paper, the second on white. Cover pages list contents and give an in-
      dex of countries surveyed; an inside page cites newspaper and official
      sources from which data are abstracted, with symbols which are put
      after each abstract of quotation. Cumulative and annual indexes are
      issued. The price of the combined series is $105 ($75 for African
      research institutes), postage included.

567. AFRICA: SEMI-WEEKLY INTERAFRICAN NEWS SURVEY. Paris, Agence France-
     Presse. 2 issues a week. Mineographed.

     English-language edition covering African news; title changed in
1965 from AFRICA SOUTH OF THE SAHARA. The rapidly prepared pages
numbering 30 or more are in geographical (usually regional) arrangement following a "general information" section. Information given has
sometimes been at variance with that found in other news sources.

568. AFRICAN CHRONICLER: A DIARY OF WEEKLY EVENTS IN AFRICA. v. 1- 1963-
     Accra, Ghana.

     A weekly news summary, more in the style of KEESING'S CONTEMPO-
RARY ARCHIVES than of the usual chronology. The selection is arranged
by country, with an indication of the source--radio, press, etc. No. 8
(July 3/9, 1963) of the first volume includes a full-page profile of
President Nasser of the UAR. Pan-Africanism and anticapitalism receive
attention.

569. AFRICAN RECORDER: A FORTNIGHTLY RECORD OF AFRICAN EVENTS WITH INDEX.
     v. 1, no. 1- Jan. 1/14, 1962- M. Henry Samuel, executive editor.
     New Delhi (6 Dr. Rajendra Prasa Road). Loose-leaf.

     Summaries of events are entered under country (the countries
arranged alphabetically), with an added section for events relating to
"Africa outside Africa." Semiannual and annual indexes are planned.

570. AFRIKA: GERMAN REVIEW OF POLITICAL, ECONOMIC AND CULTURAL AFFAIRS IN
     AFRICA AND MADAGASCAR. June 1960- Pfaffenhofen/Ilm, Afrika
     Verlag in collaboration with German Africa Society, Bonn. illus.
     6 numbers a year.

     This English edition was begun in collaboration with Afrika-
Verlag, Hamburg. (The German edition, NEUES AFRIKA, 1959-1965, originally titled AFRIKA: MONATSSCHRIFT FUR POLITIK, WIRTSCHAFT UND KULTUR
IM NEUEN AFRIKA, was the organ of Afrika-Verein.) Deutsche Afrika-
Gesellschaft, Bonn, also collaborated for a time in the publication of
the English AFRIKA. It reports on many aspects of contemporary African
affairs, and it has carried a section on books and publications.

571. AFRIKA HEUTE. 1957- Edited for the Deutsche Afrika-Gesellschaft by
     Oskar Splett. Bonn, L. Röhrschied. illus. Bimonthly and annual
     yearbook.

     The annual yearbook of the leading society for African studies in
West Germany represents an excellent symposium of articles on many aspects

of African affairs by noted and competent writers, chosen on an international scale, among them African leaders. Appendixes include bibliography, chronology, a brief almanac of products by country, various tables, and directories of groups concerned with Africa. The bimonthly journal, bearing the same title as the yearbook, is largely devoted to current news.

572. BULLETIN DE L'AFRIQUE NOIRE. 1957- Paris, EDIAFRIC. Weekly.

News-service processed leaflet, published at 57, avenue d'Iéna, Paris 16. The emphasis is on French-speaking countries, but coverage is given to all Africa south of the Sahara. A fortnightly supplement, PERSPECTIVE AFRICAINE, treats of economics and finances. Lengthy special issues have appeared since 1964, most of them devoted to the economies of French-speaking West and Equatorial Africa (see, for example, nos. 760, 1579, 1608, 1609, and 1895).

573. CAHIERS D'ETUDES AFRICAINES. 1960- Paris. Quarterly.

This distinguished review is the French counterpart of the JOURNAL OF MODERN AFRICAN STUDIES and like that periodical presents essay-length articles on all the so-called "human sciences." It is published by Mouton for the Ecole Pratique des Hautes Etudes, Université de Paris, 6e Section: Sciences Economiques et Sociales. Concern is primarily--but far from exclusively--with French-speaking Africa.

574. CHRONOLOGIE POLITIQUE AFRICAINE. v. 1, no. 1- Jan./Feb. 1960-
     Paris, Fondation Nationale des Sciences Politiques. Bimonthly.

Chronological survey of political developments throughout Africa, prepared by the Centre d'Etude des Relations Internationales, in the Section Afrique au Sud du Sahara, under the direction of Professor Georges Balandier. It consists of a section "Problèmes généraux (conférences africaines, etc.)" and four regional sections (West, Central, East, and Southern Africa) with country subdivisions.

575. Foreign Broadcast Information Service. DAILY REPORT, FOREIGN RADIO
     BROADCASTS. 1947- Washington, D.C.

Section 1, Middle East, Africa, and Western Europe.

The daily monitoring and translation of international radio broadcasts is of special interest for any study of the immediate situation. The broadcasts in the section for Africa include radio comment on African affairs from Western Europe, the Soviet Union, China, and other parts of the world, as well as domestic African broadcasting services. Content is largely political. These daily reports are accessible in a few large libraries. The Library of Congress is microfilming them, so that in mid-1964 there was a microfilm for 1947-63.

The comparable British series by the British Broadcasting Corporation is the SUMMARY OF WORLD BROADCASTS, prepared by the Monitoring Service, issued in regional parts since 1947; it was begun in 1939 as DIGEST OF FOREIGN BULLETINS and has had various titles. Part 4 is on the Middle East and Africa.

576. Institute of Current World Affairs. Letters and Reports [African series]. New York (366 Madison Ave., New York 10017). illus. Irregular.

Sets of informal letters written to the director of the Institute, Richard H. Nolte, by correspondents who have been given institute fellowships for study and research in Africa. Although labeled "Not for Publication," these letters of penetrating analysis are not shut off from general circulation.

577. Institute of Race Relations. NEWSLETTER. no. 1- Jan. 1961- London. Monthly.

A monthly booklet summarizing events in race relations throughout the world, and particularly in Africa and Britain. The Institute also publishes a quarterly journal, RACE (v. 1, no. 1- Nov. 1959-, printed by Oxford University Press), and occasional pamphlets on race questions.

578. JOURNAL OF MODERN AFRICAN STUDIES: A QUARTERLY SURVEY OF POLITICS, ECONOMICS AND RELATED TOPICS IN CONTEMPORARY AFRICA. v. 1, no. 1- Mar. 1963- Edited by David and Helen Kimble. Cambridge, Eng., University Press.

This significant scholarly journal, of 100-150 pages per issue, carries authoritative articles on the present scene in Africa, a "review article," which is a critique of writings in some special field, substantial reviews of 10 or more new books, and an interesting section on "Africana" (see no. 296).

579. REMARQUES AFRICAINES: REVUE PANAFRICAINE DE DOCUMENTATION. 1959- Bruxelles. Every 2 weeks.

Originally titled REMARQUES CONGOLAISES, its most recent name more nearly reflects the scope of coverage.

580. WEST AFRICA. 1917- London. illus. Weekly.

   Although the title indicates a limited geographic coverage, this
long-established weekly magazine touches on most events in the continent
south of the Sahara. For any study of the west coast from Mauritania
to Angola it is indispensable. Among regular features, there appears
in each issue a full-page biographical "profile" of a prominent person,
usually an African. There are three or four reviews of new books each
week.

CHAPTER 15

POLITICS AND GOVERNMENT

General Library Aids

581. The Africanist serials most important for studies of political develop-
        ments have already been noted under the History section, Modern
        Era. Contributions on African affairs appear in many general
        political science journals. Among those frequently useful, for
        both articles and book notices, are the following:

    a) AMERICAN POLITICAL SCIENCE REVIEW. 1906- Menasha, Wis.,
          Washington [etc.], American Political Science Association.
          Quarterly.

        Classified bibliographies of books and of selected
      periodical articles include sections for Africa.

    b) FOREIGN AFFAIRS. 1922- New York, Council on Foreign
          Relations. Quarterly.

        The section "Recent Books on International Relations" has
      regional classification. There is also a documentary "Source
      Material" section.

    c) INTERNATIONAL AFFAIRS. 1922- London, Royal Institute of
          International Affairs. Bimonthly.

        The book review section has regional breakdown, including
      Africa.

    d) REVUE FRANCAISE DE SCIENCE POLITIQUE. v. 1, no. 1- Jan./
          June 1951- Paris, Presses Universitaires de France.
          Quarterly.

        Published by the Fondation Nationale des Sciences Politiques
      and the Association Française de Science Politique. Includes long
      sections of "Notes bibliographiques" and "Informations bibliog-
      raphiques," in which many works on Africa are noted.

Bibliographies of world coverage in the field of political science
include the following:

e) FOREIGN AFFAIRS BIBLIOGRAPHY, 1952-1962. Edited by H. L. Roberts.
    New York, Bowker, 1964. 750 p.

    The latest compilation of the notable bibliographies carried
in the issues of FOREIGN AFFAIRS. Earlier cumulations have been
issued for the periods 1919-32, 1932-42, and 1942-52. The arrangement is in broad subject categories, with subdivision by country
and cross references.

    In the quarterly issues, the FOREIGN AFFAIRS bibliography
has, first, several broad subject divisions and then sections by
continents or regions. In recent years one may note a great increase in the number of works on Africa selected for these brief
evaluative notices. Following the book notes is a listing of
source materials--documents of U.S., UN, and other governments and
also pamphlets.

f) INTERNATIONAL BIBLIOGRAPHY OF POLITICAL SCIENCE. BIBLIOGRAPHIE
    INTERNATIONALE DE SCIENCE POLITIQUE. v. 1- 1952- Paris,
    UNESCO, 1954-61; London, Stevens & Sons, 1962-63, and
    Travistock Publications, 1963- Annual. (International
    Bibliography of the Social Sciences)

    Prepared by the International Committee for Social Sciences
Documentation under the auspices of the International Political
Science Association with the financial support of UNESCO; edited
by Jean Viet. Vol. VIII, covering the works of 1959 (published
in 1961) was the latest issued by UNESCO. It appeared in their
Documentation in the Social Sciences series. Vol. XIV for 1964
was published in 1965. The arrangement of this extensive international coverage of writings in political science follows a
complicated subject scheme: political thought, government and
public administration (including political systems, economic and
social functions of government, instruments of government, local
government), governmental process (including political parties
and political behavior), international relations, and area studies
each subdivided into many topical aspects. A number of the classes
have further division by country. There are author and subject
indexes; the latter index includes countries, with topical
breakdown, and country breakdown under some topics.

g) INTERNATIONAL POLITICAL SCIENCE ABSTRACTS. DOCUMENTATION
    POLITIQUE INTERNATIONALE. v. 1- 1951- Paris, UNESCO,
    1951-54; Oxford, Basil Blackwell, 1955- Quarterly.

    The subject index includes a few references in each issue to
Africa and African countries--a comparatively small selection from

more than a hundred periodicals in the international field of
political science. The principal use of this serial for African
studies lies in the abstracts of individual articles, which provide a reliable guide to the contents of some of the most conspicuous contributions in periodical form relating to African
politics.

582. McGowan, Patrick J. AFRICAN POLITICS: A GUIDE TO RESEARCH RESOURCES,
      METHODS AND LITERATURE. Syracuse, N.Y., 1970. 85, 45 <u>l</u>.
      (Syracuse University. Maxwell Graduate School of Citizenship and
      Public Affairs. Program of Eastern African Studies. Occasional
      Paper, no. 55)

A most valuable bibliographical reference book for students of
African politics. The first of two parts cites references and guides,
handbooks, and bibliographies--both of general and of African interest;
the second part lists a select number of items on political change in
Africa. Although the annotations are brief, McGowan comes close to
providing a Winchell for African studies. He describes many bibliographies and bibliographical tools and provides information on libraries,
catalogues, special collections, and various lists for locating material.
Since it is a draft edition there are many misprints.

583. RURAL AFRICANA: RESEARCH NOTES ON LOCAL POLITICS AND POLITICAL ANTHRO-
      POLOGY. no. 1- 1967- East Lansing, African Studies Center,
      Michigan State University.

Excellent continuing source on research and bibliographic matters.
Some issues are devoted to a single topic, e.g., "Ethiopia."

Bibliographies

584. Alderfer, Harold F. A BIBLIOGRAPHY OF AFRICAN GOVERNMENT, 1950-1966.
      Lincoln University, Pa., Lincoln University Press, 1967. 2d and
      rev. ed. 163 p.

Entries, in English or French, cover the entire continent. Following a general section, arrangement is by region and then by country,
with book and article subdivisions. Under "books" are included unpublished manuscripts, government documents, pamphlets, conference proceedings, doctoral dissertations, and chapters from larger works. There is
an author index. The Institute of African Government of Lincoln University plans to update this bibliography with supplements.

585. Boston University. African Studies Program. Development Research Center. BIBLIOGRAPHIE SELECTIVE D'OUVRAGES DE LANGUE FRANCAISE SUR LES PROBLEMES GOUVERNEMENTAUX ET ADMINISTRATIFS (NOTAMMENT EN AFRIQUE). SELECT BIBLIOGRAPHY OF FRENCH-LANGUAGE WORKS ON GOVERNMENTAL AND ADMINISTRATIVE PROBLEMS (WITH SPECIAL ATTENTION TO AFRICA). Edited by Edouard Bustin. Boston, Nov. 1963. 36 p.

_____. A SELECTIVE BIBLIOGRAPHY OF BOOKS, ARTICLES AND DOCUMENTS ON THE SUBJECT OF AFRICAN ADMINISTRATIVE PROBLEMS. [Title also in French] Prepared under contract for the Agency for International Development by Wilbert J. Le Melle. Boston, 1964. 51 p.

The first of these two bibliographies, which is more or less preliminary to the second, was prepared specifically for the needs of institutions in French-speaking Africa. It includes much material on governmental and administrative problems in general as well as those with special reference to Africa. Arrangement is by technical subject headings, e.g., "Personnel Management and Training."

The second bibliography follows the same pattern, though it includes works in English as well as French and applies more widely to the new African nations.

586. Carnell, Francis. THE POLITICS OF THE NEW STATES: A SELECT ANNOTATED BIBLIOGRAPHY WITH SPECIAL REFERENCE TO THE COMMONWEALTH. London, Published for the Institute of Commonwealth Studies by Oxford University Press, 1961. xvi, 171 p.

Prepared with an eye to African users, this bibliography includes general studies of political practices with specific references on the government and politics of the new states of Asia and Africa, chiefly but not exclusively the English-speaking nations of the Commonwealth. Among section subject headings are approaches to the study of politics, colonial policies of the powers, international colonial problems, Commonwealth relations, leaders and elites, trade unions, Communism, foreign aid, constitutions, transfer of power, political parties, etc. Under a number of these headings there are subheads by country. Some items are briefly annotated. Besides the index of authors there is an index of places.

587. Conover, Helen F., comp. NON SELF-GOVERNING AREAS WITH SPECIAL EMPHASIS ON MANDATES AND TRUSTEESHIPS: A SELECTED LIST OF REFERENCES. Washington, Library of Congress, 1947. 2 v.

588. Engelborghs-Bertels, Marie. LES PAYS DE L'EST ET LA DECOLONISATION PAR-
          TICULIEREMENT EN AFRIQUE: BIBLIOGRAPHIE. Bruxelles, 1962. 62 p.
          (Académie Royal des Sciences d'Outre-Mer, Classe des sciences mo-
          rales et politiques, Mémoires in-8°, n.s. v. 28, fasc. 2, Histoire)

          Annotated list of articles in journals of the Soviet bloc coun-
     tries regarding colonialism, anticolonialism, and national liberation.
     Arrangement is by countries of publication, with subdivision by African
     countries. Titles in Eastern European languages and Chinese are given
     in French translation. The annotations in many cases are essentially
     abstracts.

589. Hanna, William John, and Judith Lynne Hanna. POLITICS IN BLACK AFRICA:
          A SELECTIVE BIBLIOGRAPHY OF RELEVANT PERIODICAL LITERATURE. East
          Lansing, Mich., African Studies Center, Michigan State University,
          1964. 139 p. Offset print.

          Prepared for undergraduate courses as a set of core readings on
     African political systems. The list of articles in English and French
     is arranged in 17 categories: tradition and change, communication,
     towns and urbanization, economy, etc. Items total 1,283, with index
     of names. See also Hertefelt (no. 969).

590. Ibadan. University. Institute of African Studies. PAN-AFRICANISM AND
          NEGRITUDE: A BIBLIOGRAPHY. Compiled by Joanna M. Cameron.
          Ibadan [1965?] 16 p. Processed.

591. Karal, Gulgan. AFRICAN LEGAL AND CONSTITUTIONAL MATERIALS: AN
          ANNOTATED BIBLIOGRAPHY. Prepared under the direction of J. C. N.
          Paul. Los Angeles, University of California, 1969. 125 p.

592. Liniger-Goumaz, Max. L'EURAFRIQUE: BIBLIOGRAPHIE GENERALE. Genève,
          Editions du Temps, 1970. 160 p.

          Lists 1,300 articles and books covering European relations with
     Africa, particularly the Common Market and colonization. There are
     author, chronological, and geographical/subject indexes.

593. Malengreau, Guy. PROBLEMES POLITIQUES DE L'AFRIQUE: BIBLIOGRAPHIE
          SOMMAIRE. With the collaboration of P. Demunter. Louvain,
          Institut d'Etude des Pays en Développement, 1967-68. 58 l.

          _____. SUPPLEMENT A LA BIBLIOGRAPHIE SUR LES PROBLEMES POLITIQUES
          DE L'AFRIQUE. Louvain, Institut d'Etude des Pays en Développement,
          1968-69. 8 l.

Books, articles, and theses arranged by subjects such as political anthropology, colonization, decolonization, administration, ideologies, elections, armies, trade unions, elites, Pan-Africanism, the UN in the Congo, and nationalism.

594. Martin, Jane. A BIBLIOGRAPHY ON AFRICAN REGIONALISM. Boston, Development Program, African Studies Center, Boston University, 1969. 121 p.

595. Perham, Margery. COLONIAL GOVERNMENT: ANNOTATED READING LIST ON BRITISH COLONIAL GOVERNMENT, WITH SOME GENERAL AND COMPARATIVE MATERIAL UPON FOREIGN EMPIRES, ETC., WITH AN INTRODUCTION. London, Published for Nuffield College by the Oxford University Press, 1950. xvii, 80 p. (Nuffield College Colonial Reading Lists, no. 1)

The author has been director of the Institute of Colonial Studies as well as a long-time Fellow of Nuffield College. She is among the best-known writers on Africa. As the title indicates, this list is not limited to British colonial administration but includes references on French, Belgian, and other colonial systems.

596. Smith, Whitney. "Bibliography of Materials on African Political Symbols." AFRICANA NEWSLETTER, v. 2, no. 2, 1964: 26-31.

A useful annotated bibliography of books and articles on flags and other symbols of the countries of Africa. The first few titles cited are reference works in the field of vexillology (history of flags)--FLAGS OF THE WORLD, etc. Then are listed references by individual country, in alphabetical order. The author is connected with the Flag Research Center in Boston, where most of the works cited are available.

Reference Works

597. Adams, T. R. GOVERNMENT AND POLITICS IN AFRICA SOUTH OF THE SAHARA. 3d ed., rev. Princeton, N.J., Princeton University Press, 1965. 176 p. illus., map.

598. Adu, Amishadai L. THE CIVIL SERVICE IN NEW AFRICAN STATES. New York, Praeger, 1965. 242 p. (Books That Matter)

Study of the development of public administration in the new English-speaking states of Africa. The author is a high-ranking administrator, former head of the preindependence Gold Coast civil service, later secretary-general of the East African Common Services

Organization, now regional representative of the UN Technical
Assistance Board for East Africa. In these offices he has been
intimately involved with programs of Africanization.

599. AFRIKANISCHE KOPFE. Bonn, Deutsche Afrika-Gesellschaft. no. 1- June
        1962- Irregular. Loose-leaf.

        Biographical directory of African leaders, issued in sets of 24
sheets, one sheet to each individual subject. An alphabetical name
list for the cumulated leaves, which are in country arrangement, is
followed by a geographical list, on pink stock, provided with each
number. The sketches, sometimes showing minor inaccuracies, are in
essay form and include portraits. Except for a very few political
leaders of the European community in Southern Africa, the subjects are
Africans.

600. Alderfer, Harold F. PUBLIC ADMINISTRATION IN NEWER NATIONS. New
        York, Praeger, 1967. 206 p.

601. Andreski, Stanislav. THE AFRICAN PREDICAMENT: A STUDY IN THE
        PATHOLOGY OF MODERNISATION. London, Joseph, 1968. 237 p.

        Bibliographical footnotes.

        Critical examination of political and social conditions in the
new states of Africa.

602. L'ANNEE POLITIQUE AFRICAINE. By Pierre Biarnès, Philippe Decraene,
        and Philippe Herreman. Dakar, Société Africaine d'Edition,
        1963- Annual. (1967 ed., 1967, 148 p.)

        An annual publication on contemporary African affairs by three
political journalists who cover African for LE MONDE. The volumes are
issued so promptly that year-end developments may be slighted; each
volume, however, not only provides useful data and analyses but also
contributes a historical setting for current African political events.

603. Apter, David E. THE POLITICS OF MODERNIZATION. Chicago, University
        of Chicago Press, 1965. 481 p.

        Professor Apter is concerned with fundamental aspects of moderni-
zation. He discusses "modernizing" rather than developing societies,
and modernization as an earlier stage in development than industrialization. He discusses the role of tradition, ideology, stratification,
the political party as a modernizing system and its alternatives.

His book is particularly interesting because it suggests several
frameworks upon which to organize data in a useful way for the
comparative political analysis of countries in the process of modernization.

604. Bustin, Edouard. GUIDE DES PARTIS POLITIQUES AFRICAINS: INVENTAIRE
        DE 300 PARTIS RECENSES DANS 45 PAYS AFRICAINS. Léopoldville,
        Editions CRISP-IPC, 1962. 80 p.

      Extract from ETUDES CONGOLAISES, no. 7, 1962.

      Brief descriptions of origin, leadership, and ideology of each
party, arranged alphabetically. The guide has an index of parties by
countries.

605. Butler, Jeffrey, and A. A. Castagno, eds. BOSTON UNIVERSITY PAPERS ON
        AFRICA: TRANSITION IN AFRICAN POLITICS. New York, Published for
        the African Studies Center of Boston University by Praeger, 1967.
        342 p. tables. (Praeger Special Studies in International Politics
        and Public Affairs)

      Bibliographical footnotes.

      A series of 12 papers largely derived from a faculty seminar on
African politics at Boston University's African Studies Center during
1963-65. Most of the studies concern specific countries or regions,
and the collection offers wide-ranging points of emphasis: political
parties and political theory, legal and constitutional development,
"machine politics" in local government, the relationship between religion and politics, and trade unions and trade unionism.

606. Carter, Gwendolen M., ed. AFRICAN ONE-PARTY STATES. Contributors:
        Charles F. Gallagher, Ernest Milcent, L. Gray Cowan, Virginia
        Thompson, J. Gus Liebenow, and Margaret L. Bates. Ithaca, N.Y.,
        Cornell University Press, 1962. 501 p.

      Includes bibliographies.

      The countries selected for these substantial studies on the trend
toward one-party rule are Tunisia, Senegal, Guinea, the Ivory Coast,
Liberia, and Tanganyika.

607. Carter, Gwendolen M., ed. FIVE AFRICAN STATES: RESPONSES TO DIVER-
        SITY--THE CONGO, DAHOMEY, THE CAMEROUN FEDERAL REPUBLIC, THE
        RHODESIAS AND NYASALAND, SOUTH AFRICA. Ithaca, N.Y., Cornell
        University Press, 1963. 643 p. maps.

Includes bibliographies.

A group of papers analyzing the evolution of states in which diverse tribal and racial elements play a dominant part in political developments. Contributors are Edouard Bustin, Virginia Thompson, Victor T. Le Vine, Herbert J. Spiro, and Thomas Karis.

608. Carter, Gwendolen M., ed. NATIONAL UNITY AND REGIONALISM IN EIGHT AFRICAN STATES: NIGERIA, NIGER, THE CONGO, GABON, CENTRAL AFRICAN REPUBLIC, CHAD, UGANDA, ETHIOPIA. Ithaca, N.Y., Cornell University Press, 1966. xiii, 565 p. maps.

Includes bibliographies.

The third and final volume of essays on individual African states edited by Miss Carter. Her introduction is followed by essays which give a broad political, economic, and historical account of the country concerned. Richard L. Sklar, C. S. Whitaker, Jr., Virginia Thompson, John A. Ballard, Donald Rothchild, Michael Rogin, and Robert L. Hess contribute essays. The essays on the four equatorial states (the "Congo" refers to Congo-Brazzaville) and that on Niger are especially useful since they survey countries about which there is a paucity of material in English. A bibliography follows each essay, the one for Nigeria being unusually extensive (14 p.). There is a concluding chapter by Carter and Hess.

609. Carter, Gwendolen M., ed. POLITICS IN AFRICA: 7 CASES. New York, Harcourt, Brace & World, 1966. 283 p. maps (1 fold.). (Harbrace Casebooks in Political Science)

Includes bibliographies.

A casebook approach to contemporary African politics. The cases covered are the Sanniquellie Conference of 1959, by J. Gus Liebenow; the Mali Federation, 1959-60, by William J. Foltz; the Sekondi-Takoradi strike in Ghana, 1961, by St. Clair Drake and Leslie A. Lacy; the ordeal of Chief Awolowo, Nigeria, 1960-65, by Richard Sklar; Katanga, 1960-63, by Crawford Young; East African Federation, 1963-64, by Donald Rothchild; and the case of Anderson Ganyile of Basutoland, by Jeffrey Butler. Each case is followed by study questions and a selected bibliography.

610. Coleman, James S. "Politics of Sub-Saharan Africa." In Almond, Gabriel A., and James S. Coleman, eds. THE POLITICS OF THE DEVELOPING AREAS. Princeton, N.J., Princeton University Press, 1960: p. 247-368.

Monograph-length essay in a volume of comparative analysis of political systems in Asia, Africa, and Latin America. Professor Coleman focused his discussion on the great diversity of African traditional and evolving political systems and on the racial and tribal pluralism which complicates the establishment of new governments. He includes tables of population, degree of commercialization, political groups, types of elites, etc.

611. Coleman, James S., and Belmont Brice, Jr. "The Role of the Military in Sub-Saharan Africa." In Johnson, John J., ed. THE ROLE OF THE MILITARY IN UNDERDEVELOPED COUNTRIES. Princeton, N.J., Princeton University Press, 1962: p. 359-405.

Published also by African Studies Center, University of California at Los Angeles, as its African Studies Paper no. 3.

The volume in which this paper appears resulted from a RAND Corporation conference of Aug. 1959, revised with data through 1960. The authors of the paper for Africa examine the military legacy of the colonial powers and the national military situation, buildup, and policies in the new nations. (See also later survey in Helen Kitchen, ed., A HANDBOOK OF AFRICAN AFFAIRS, no. 448.)

A brief bibliography on this subject was issued by the External Research Staff of the Department of State as its External Research Paper no. 147: ROLE OF THE MILITARY IN LESS DEVELOPED COUNTRIES, JAN. 1958-FEB. 1964: A SELECTED BIBLIOGRAPHY, by Nancy Blankenstein (1964, 11 p.). In a British work, ARMY AND NATION IN SUB-SAHARAN AFRICA (London, Institute for Strategic Studies, 1965, 16 p.; Adelphi Papers, no 21), M. J. V. Bell attempts to assess the role of military forces in furthering or hampering the growth and stability of new African nations. See also no. 624.

612. Coleman, James S., and Carl G. Rosberg, eds. POLITICAL PARTIES AND NATIONAL INTEGRATION IN TROPICAL AFRICA. Berkeley, Los Angeles, University of California Press, 1964. 730 p.

Select bibliography: p. 692-709.

Sixteen papers by experts in the political development of modern African states, focused on the part played in the new societies by political parties. The first group of essays study the one-party tendency, the "pragmatic-pluralistic pattern" as exemplified in Senegal, the Ivory Coast, Sierra Leone, and Cameroun, and the "revolutionary-centralizing trend" in Guinea, Mali, and Ghana, followed by analyses of the control of nonparty groups--voluntary associations, trade unions, traditional rulers, and students. In Part 2, "Parties and National

Integration," there are discussed the transformation of historic oligarchies, Liberia and Zanzibar, and the expansion in political scale--Somali Republic, Congo (Leopoldville), and Nigeria. The long chapter of conclusions by the editors offers certain generalizations regarding the political group structure of the new Africa and its role in nation building. See also Coleman, ed., EDUCATION AND POLITICAL DEVELOPMENT (no. 900).

613. Cox, Richard. PAN-AFRICANISM IN PRACTICE: AN EAST AFRICAN STUDY, PAFMECSA, 1958-1964. Written under the auspices of the Institute of Race Relations. London, New York, Oxford University Press, 1964. 95 p. map.

For description see under East Africa, no. 2410.

614. Currie, David P., ed. FEDERALISM AND THE NEW NATIONS OF AFRICA. Chicago, Chicago University Press, 1964. 440 p.

Study of federal structures as they are evolving in the new African groupings, by contributors to a symposium held in Feb. 1962 at the Chicago Law School Center for Legal Research (New Nations). The speakers included African political leaders as well as Western political economists. Their papers are divided into four groups: 1, African problems in historical perspective; 2, Federalism and economic advancement; 3, Federalism and human rights; 4, Federalism and international legal relations. Each group is followed by the text of the panel discussion.

615. Decraene, Philippe. TABLEAU DES PARTIS POLITIQUES DE L'AFRIQUE AU SUD DU SAHARA. Paris, Fondation Nationale des Sciences Politiques, Centre d'Etude des Relations Internationales, 1963. 137 l. (Sér. C, Recherches, no. 8, May 1963)

A valuable brochure, in two parts, the first an analysis of the development and role of political parties in sub-Saharan Africa, the second a country-by-country inventory of the principal parties. In the latter, data on each party include an outline and dates of history, present status, program, and names of leaders. The index, p. 124-135, lists the parties by their initials.

616. Egyptian Society of International Law. CONSTITUTIONS OF THE NEW AFRICAN STATES: A CRITICAL SURVEY. Alexandria, 1962. 107 p. (ITS Brochure no. 17)

Analytical compilation of essential features, but not full texts, of the constitutions of the new states of Africa south of the Sahara, prepared with the aid of a Ford Foundation grant. There are included the states of Africa, the Congo-Leopoldville Republic, and the East African colonies and territories. The appendix contains texts of the Casablanca Charter, the Charter for the Union of African States, the conclusions of the 1961 African Conference on the Rule of Law, and other documents.

617. Emerson, Rupert. FROM EMPIRE TO NATION: THE RISE TO SELF-ASSERTION OF ASIAN AND AFRICAN PEOPLES. Cambridge, Mass., Harvard University Press, 1960. 466 p.

This study of the rise of nationalism and the problems of the emerging states includes a bibliography of 35 pages.

618. Foreign Affairs. AFRICA: A FOREIGN AFFAIRS READER. Edited by Philip W. Quigg. New York, Praeger, 1964. 352 p.

Reproducation of 24 articles selected from the hundred or so published in FOREIGN AFFAIRS between Apr. 1925 and Oct. 1963 (omitting any on North Africa). The authors are leaders in government, politics, and thought, from Lord Lugard on native administration in 1926 to Tom Mboya on the place of labor in the independent state in 1963. The focus is on political and social problems, touching only incidentally on economic development.

619. Fortes, Meyer, and E. E. Evans-Pritchard. AFRICAN POLITICAL SYSTEMS. London, Published for the International Institute of African Languages & Cultures by the Oxford University Press, H. Milford, 1940. xxiii, 301 p. maps, geneal. tables, diagrs.

Reprint in paperback ed., Oxford University Press, 1961.

A group of short surveys by prominent anthropologists, a number of the essays being taken from longer works by the same writers. The peoples studied are representative of the major political groupings of Africa. The writers vary in treatment, some concentrating on traditional patterns, others on the changes made under European rule.

A complementary work, TRIBES WITHOUT RULERS: STUDIES IN AFRICAN SEGMENTARY SYSTEMS, edited by John Middleton and David Tait (London, Routledge & Kegan Paul, 1958, 234 p.), relates largely to tribes of the southern Sudan and East Africa. These two books, which may be classed as either anthropology or political science, exemplify the interdisciplinary nature of many African studies.

620. Friedland, William H., and Carl G. Rosberg, Jr., eds. AFRICAN SOCIALISM. Stanford, Calif., Published for the Hoover Institution on War, Revolution, and Peace by Stanford University Press, 1964. 313 p. (Hoover Institution Publications)

Bibliographical references included in "Notes" (p. 279-300); Bibliography: p. 301-306.

The editors introduce this symposium with an essay on "The Anatomy of African Socialism." Then seven political scientists and economists (including Professor Potekhin; the others are American and British) attempt definitions, and four other writers analyze national socialist programs in Ghana, Guinea and Senegal, Mali, and Tanganyika. The appendixes contain statements on socialism by African leaders.

621. Friedrich-Ebert-Stiftung. Forschungsinstitut. PROBLEME DES AFRIKANISCHEN SOZIALISMUS. Hannover, 1966. 159 1. (Studien und Berichte)

A collection of working papers. Colin Legum writes on African socialism, nationalism, and Pan-Africanism; Jacques Janvier on African socialism and geographical factors and on the relations between the parties of French-speaking Africa and foreign parties; René Dumont on African socialism and agricultural development; Wilhelm Wehner on African socialism and trade unions; and Albert Tevoedjre on Africa facing the problems of socialism and foreign aid.

622. Geiss, Imanuel. PANAFRIKANISMUS: ZUR GESCHICHTE DER DEKOLONISATION. Frankfurt am Main, Europäische Verlagsanstalt, 1968. 489 p. maps.

Bibliography: p. 457-474.

A major work by a student of the German historian Fritz Fischer, who has previously worked on trade unionism in Africa as well as German history. Geiss first of all defines Pan-Africanism, and links it to the "Triangle of trade" in the Atlantic, and to American slavery. He subsequently discusses what he calls "proto-Pan-Africanism"; the settlements of Liberia and Sierra Leone; Methodism and early nationalism on the Gold Coast; emigration from the USA; early demands for equal rights; and independent African churches. The second section of the book relates to the formulation of Pan-African thought between 1900 and 1945 both in the New World and in Africa. It covers, among other subjects, the role played by men such as Garvey and Du Bois; Pan-African thought in France and the French colonies; Pan-Africanism in Great Britain; and the impact of the Second World War, and of the Fifth Pan-African Congress in Manchester, 1945. The writer concludes with a general appraisal of Pan-Africanism in history. There is a detailed bibliography covering archival sources, private collections, and published works. The work, by its thorough coverage, supersedes valuable previous accounts such as Thomas Hodgkin's (no. 627) or Colin Legum's (no. 631).

623. Gonidec, P. F. COURS D'INSTITUTIONS PUBLIQUES AFRICAINES ET MALGACHES.
     Paris, Les Cours de Droit, 1968. 354 p.

     Bibliographical footnotes.

     Lectures of Professor Gonidec of the Faculté de Droit et des
     Sciences Economiques of the University of Paris. The volume is in
     four parts: political development from precolonial times to the present;
     various ideologies held by African leaders; unity and federal states
     and multinational groupings; and foreign relations of African states.
     See also Michel Jeol, DROIT PUBLIC AFRICAIN: INSTITUTIONS POLITIQUES,
     ADMINISTRATIVES ET JUDICIAIRES (Paris, Editions Berger-Levrault, 1967,
     408 p.).

624. Gutteridge, William F. MILITARY INSTITUTIONS AND POWER IN THE NEW
     STATES. New York, Praeger, 1965. 182 p.

     Examines the nature and role of the armed forces in some of
     the independent African states and the influence they exert both at
     home and in international relations.

     Another study, THE AFRICAN MILITARY BALANCE (London, Institute
     for Strategic Studies, 1964, 15 p.; Adelphi Papers, no. 12), by
     Neville Brown and the author, includes statistical data by country on
     population, total armed forces (army, air force, navy, police), and
     defense budget. The study also carries tables on comparative military
     strengths by groups and regions (Commonwealth countries, French Community,
     North Africa, East Africa, etc.).

625. Hamrell, Sven, ed. REFUGEE PROBLEMS IN AFRICA. Uppsala, Scandinavian
     Institute of African Studies, 1967. 123 p.

     The Uppsala Seminar on Central and Southern African refugees, held
     in 1966, was concerned with the unsettled refugees in Africa whose
     number is the largest in the world apart from the Palestinians and
     Vietnam's "internal" refugees from war. The seminar was particularly
     interested with the "political" refugees, i.e., those exiled on account
     of their political views and actions. See also by the same institute
     the interesting discussions of AFRICAN BOUNDARY PROBLEMS, edited by
     Carl G. Widstrand (1969, 202 p.).

626. Hazlewood, Arthur, ed. AFRICAN INTEGRATION AND DISINTEGRATION:
     CASE STUDIES IN ECONOMIC AND POLITICAL UNION. Issued under the
     auspices of the Oxford University Institute of Economics and
     Statistics and the Royal Institute of International Affairs.
     London, New York, Oxford University Press, 1967. xii, 414 p.
     plates, maps, tables.

     Bibliography: p. 397-402.

     For description see no. 751.

627. Hodgkin, Thomas. NATIONALISM IN COLONIAL AFRICA. London, F. Muller, 1956. 216 p. illus.

_____. AFRICAN POLITICAL PARTIES: AN INTRODUCTORY GUIDE. Harmonds-worth, Middlesex, Penguin Books [1962, c.1961]. 217 p. (Penguin African Series, WA 12)

Two works widely hailed as authoritative surveys of the politics of the developing countries of Africa. The author made extensive use of sources on African politics, sociology, and history in French and other languages as well as English. In NATIONALISM IN COLONIAL AFRICA he compared in tabular form the self-contradictions of French, British, and Belgian policies, examined the institutions of African nationalism and the ideologies behind them, and foresaw accurately what would be the results of the chain reactions of nationalism in the territories then considered calm in their colonial status.

AFRICAN POLITICAL PARTIES, issued in a paperback edition, is a concise and valuable guide that sketches the setting, origins, types of of political parties, party organizations, activities, and objectives, with a conclusion of generalized "hypotheses" regarding them. A bibli-ography of sources is followed by an appendix listing the major parties from 1945 to 1960.

628. International Institute of Differing Civilizations, 33d Study Session, Palermo, 1963. LES CONSTITUTIONS ET INSTITUTIONS ADMINISTRATIVES DES ETATS NOUVEAUX: COMPTE RENDU DE LA 33ME SESSION D'ETUDES DE INCIDI, TENU A PALERMO DU 23 AU 27 SEPTEMBRE 1963. [Title also in English] Bruxelles, Institut International des Civilisations Différentes (INCIDI), 1965. 886 p.

Among the 33 regional reports in this comprehensive account, those for sub-Saharan Africa cover the Congo (Kinshasa), the Ivory Coast, Dahomey, Ghana, Upper Volta, Kenya, Malagasy Republic, Nigeria (two reports), Rwanda, Senegal, Sierra Leone, Sudan, Tanganyika, and Uganda. There are also papers on specific constitutional and administrative problems, of which five are on Africa, as well as four general reports and discussions dealing with legal, political, economic, and social matters. The text is in French and English.

629. Kitchen, Helen, ed. A HANDBOOK OF AFRICAN AFFAIRS. New York, Pub-lished for the African-American Institute by Praeger, 1964. xiii, 311 p. maps, charts.

For description, see no. 448.

630. Lavroff, Dimitri G., and Gustave Peiser, eds. LES CONSTITUTIONS AFRI-CAINES. Paris, Pedone, 1961- (Collection du Centre de Recherches, d'Etudes et de Documentation sur les Institutions et la Législa-tion Africaines)

Vol. I. L'AFRIQUE NOIRE FRANCOPHONE ET MADAGASCAR. 1961. 277 p.

Vol. II. ETATS ANGLOPHONES. 1964. 392 p.

Vol. I contains, for each country of French-speaking Africa, an explanatory comment on the evolution of constitutional principles and the new constitution, then the full text in French. Presumably the second volume (not available for examination) does the same for the English-speaking countries, with text of constitutions probably also in French.

There is a Russian work, edited by Iosif Levin, KONSTITUTSII GOSUDARSTV AFRIKI (v. 1, Moscow, Izdatel'stvo Inostrannoi Literatury, 1963, 748 p.). Whether this contains texts of constitutions and commentary is not known to the compilers of the present guide; only the title of the work is known.

631. Legum, Colin. PAN-AFRICANISM: A SHORT POLITICAL GUIDE. Rev. ed.
      New York, Praeger, 1965. 326 p. fold. map.

References: p. 309-315.

An authoritative explanation of the ideas and programs of Pan-Africanism, expanded from the 1961 annual address of the African Bureau, delivered by Mr. Legum. "Fission and Fusion," chap. viii in the new edition, is a record of developments in 1962-64. A chapter by Mrs. Legum on trade unions, "Africa's Divided Workers," is more comprehensive than in the first edition (1962, 296 p., map). About half the text in both editions consists of appendixes of documents (called by the author the most useful part); four new ones, among them the Charter of the Organization of African Unity, are added, and a few have been dropped.

A solid and comprehensive study of this subject was published in German in 1964: Hanspeter F. Strauch, PANAFRIKA: KONTINENTALE WELT-MACHT IM WERDEN? ANFANGE, WACHSTUM UND ZUKUNFT DER AFRIKANISCHEN EINIGUNGSBESTREBUNGEN (Zürich, Atlantis Verlag, 416 p.). Peter Duignan's "Pan-Africanism: A Bibliographic Essay," in AFRICAN FORUM (v. 1, no. 1, Summer 1965, p. 105-107), surveys the Pan-African movement through the periods 1900-1945, 1945-58, and 1958-65. See also no. 590.

632. Lee, John Michael. AFRICAN ARMIES AND CIVIL ORDER. New York, Pub-
      lished for the London Institute for Strategic Studies by Praeger,
      1969. 198 p. map.

Bibliography: p. 187-190.

Probably the best existing work concerning the impact of armies on African society, a relatively neglected subject. The book deals with the colonial inheritance, problems of independence, and the wider role of the military within the political community. The author covers police as well as military problems. He provides unusual material concerning the ethnic composition of the army, the changing nature of the officer corps, military training, and the like.

The writer has previously written COLONIAL DEVELOPMENT AND GOOD GOVERNMENT: A STUDY OF THE IDEAS EXPRESSED BY THE BRITISH OFFICIAL CLASSES IN PLANNING DECOLONIZATION 1939-1964 (Oxford, Clarendon Press, 1967, 311 p., tables, diagrs.).

633. Mackenzie, William J. M., and Kenneth Robinson, eds. FIVE ELECTIONS IN AFRICA: A GROUP OF ELECTORAL STUDIES. Oxford, Clarendon Press, 1960. 496 p. illus., maps.

Bibliographical footnotes.

Papers examining the pioneer elections in which the characteristically Western device of the electoral system was used in African society: the Western Region of Nigeria in 1956, the Eastern Region in 1957, Sierra Leone in 1957, Senegal in 1957, Kenya in Mar. 1957.

The same theme and the same elections were treated within a broader context by T. E. Smith in his ELECTIONS IN DEVELOPING COUNTRIES: A STUDY OF ELECTORAL PROCEDURES USED IN TROPICAL AFRICA, SOUTH-EAST ASIA, AND THE BRITISH CARIBBEAN (London, Macmillan; New York, St. Martin's Press, 1960, 278 p.).

634. Macmillan, William M. THE ROAD TO SELF-RULE: A STUDY IN COLONIAL EVOLUTION. London, Faber & Faber, 1959. 296 p. illus.

Includes bibliography.

A historical study of the process of change from colonial rule to independent government. The author, a South African historian, had been director of colonial studies at the University of St. Andrews from 1947 to 1954. His examination of African evolution is limited to British Africa.

635. Mason, Philip. COMMON SENSE ABOUT RACE. London, Gollancz, 1961. 173 p. (The Common Sense Series)

By the director of the Institute of Race Relations, a foremost spokesman on the subject. This book, in a series for the general reader, discusses and refutes the arguments of racial differentiation and inferiority and examines specific instances of race relations arising from "conquest and fusion" in African societies, notably the "classical example" of an insoluble dilemma in South Africa. A selected bibliography cites the most valuable literature on racism.

636. Organization of African Unity. BASIC DOCUMENTS AND RESOLUTIONS. Addis Ababa, Published by the Provisional Secretariat, 1964. 79 p.

This brochure gives the text of the Charter of OAU; resolutions of the first Conference of Independent African Heads of State and Government, May 1963; resolutions and recommendations of the first ordinary session of the Council of Ministers, Dakar, Aug. 2-11, 1963, and functions and regulations of the Secretariat; resolutions of the first and second extraordinary sessions of the Council, Addis Ababa, Nov. 15-18, 1963 (on the Algerian-Moroccan differences), and Dar es Salaam, Feb. 12-15, 1964 (on the revolt in Tanganyika and the Ethiopia-Somalia boundary dispute); and resolutions and recommendations of the second ordinary session, Lagos, Feb. 24-29, 1964.

The second Conference of Heads of State met in Addis Ababa in July 1964. It set headquarters definitely in that city and appointed Diallo Telli, Guinea's ambassador to the United Nations since 1958, as secretary-general. The third meeting was held in Accra, Oct. 1965. There have been a number of meetings of the Foreign Ministers, several in connection with the conflict in the Congo.

An account of the beginning of OAU, THE ADDIS ABABA CHARTER, by Professor Boutros Boutros-Ghali of the University of Cairo, was published as no. 546 of INTERNATIONAL CONCILIATION (New York, Carnegie Endowment for International Peace, Jan. 1964, 62 p.).

637. Organization of African Unity. OAU REVIEW. v. 1, no. 1- May 1964- Addis Ababa.

The first issue of the review of OAU began with the statement of purpose on the first anniversary of the founding of the organization. Next were explanations of the five specialized commissions functioning for OAU--Economic and Social Commission; Educational and Cultural Commission; Health, Sanitation, and Nutrition Commission; Defense Commission; Scientific, Technical, and Research Commission--and their sessions in 1963 to Feb. 1964 were recorded in an "Informal Report." (There was no report on the Liberation Committee, which was appointed later in 1963 and is concerned with measures to be taken in aid of nationalist movements in territories still dependent. Other commissions are formed as occasion demands, e.g., the Ad Hoc Committee on Conciliation in the Congo.)

The OAU REVIEW also contained a calendar of events and announcements of coming conferences. The journal was unfortunately suspended, but in late 1967 there was a report that publication might be resumed in 1968.

In 1965 it was decided by the Foreign Ministers of OAU that the UN Economic Commission on Africa would be considered their technical adviser on economic development. From the beginning of OAU, CCTA/CSA had been pronounced the adviser on scientific matters, and on Jan. 1, 1965, CCTA/CSA was formally incorporated in the OAU Scientific, Technical, and Research Commission as its agent for scientific and technical research. (It is hoped that CCTA/CSA, which had been allowed to run down for lack of OAU support, will revive in the coming years.)

638. Padmore, George. PAN-AFRICANISM OR COMMUNISM? THE COMING STRUGGLE
        FOR AFRICA. London, D. Dobson; New York, Roy Publishers, 1956.
        463 p. illus., ports.

Bibliographical footnotes.

Standard work on the history of Pan-Africanism by a foremost spokesman. The late author has given a straightforward account of nationalist movements in West Africa, East and Central Africa, and Liberia and of the Pan-African movement, its launching by the American Negro leader W. E. B. Du Bois, its international congresses, and leaders in the individual countries who follow its aims. In his re-review of Communist attempts to influence African movements, Padmore analyzed the policy of Communism as false and cynical.

A more recent survey of this subject is by Philippe Decraene, a French Africanist--LE PANAFRICANISME (Paris, Presses Universitaires de France, 1959, 126 p., maps; 3d ed., rev. and corr., 1964, 128 p., maps). There is also a pamphlet issued by the British Central Office of Information in 1964, PAN-AFRICANISM (53 p.; R.5512/64).

639. Peaslee, Amos J. CONSTITUTIONS OF NATIONS. Rev. 3d ed. in 4 v. Pre-
        pared by Dorothy Peaslee Xydis. The Hague, Nijhoff. Vol. I,
        AFRICA. 1965. 1108 p. illus., maps.

For 36 countries, from Algeria to Zambia, the new edition of this famous compilation gives first a summary and then the full text of each constitution.

640. Reuters News Agency. THE NEW AFRICANS: A GUIDE TO THE CONTEMPORARY
        HISTORY OF EMERGENT AFRICA AND ITS LEADERS. Written by fifty
        correspondents of Reuters News Agency, edited by Sidney Taylor.
        London, Hamlyn, 1967. 504 p. illus.

Biographical dictionary of African leaders, many with photographs; information is mainly on events of political significance to their careers. Primary arrangement is by country, from Botswana to Zambia, with biographies alphabetically therein. Independent Africa only is covered; each country section begins with a short general description. There is an index.

641. Rotberg, Robert I., and Ali A. Mazrui, eds. PROTEST AND POWER IN
      BLACK AFRICA. New York, Oxford University Press, 1970. 1274 p.
      maps.

      Bibliography: p. 1197-1213.

      The most comprehensive anthology of its kind. The editors,
assisted by thirty-one contributors, cover the most variegated forms
of resistance to colonial conquest, rebellions against imperial
governance, as well as a large number of political, economic, and
literary expressions of discontent, all of which are interpreted as
forms of anticolonial resistance. The book also deals with post-
colonial rebellions against African rule, problems of plural societies,
socialism and Pan-Africanism as forms of protest, and so forth. A
"postlude" attempts to formulate a theory of protest. The book concentrates throughout on factors making for change rather than on those
making for stability.

642. Segal, Ronald, in collaboration with Catherine Hoskyns and Rosalynde
      Ainslie. POLITICAL AFRICA: A WHO'S WHO OF PERSONALITIES AND
      PARTIES. New York, Praeger, 1961. 475 p. map. (Books That
      Matter)

      The most useful and comprehensive biographical directory as yet
available in English. The author, formerly editor of the now defunct
AFRICA SOUTH IN EXILE, admits in the preface that his information is
more complete for South Africa, Kenya, and Nigeria than for former
French Africa and other territories where contacts were scanty. Part
1 consists of biographical sketches of political figures in alphabetical order, varying in length from a short paragraph to two or three
pages. Part 2, p. 291-475, is a country-by-country report on political
parties, their actions and their status. In some cases information is
given into 1961. A condensed version, AFRICAN PROFILES, was published
in the paperback Penguin African Library (Baltimore, Penguin Books,
1962, 352 p.).

643. Sithole, Ndabaningi. AFRICAN NATIONALISM. 2d ed. London, Oxford Uni-
      versity Press, 1968. 196 p. frontis.

      A greatly revised version of the first edition of 1959, the
latter having been intended as a "justification" of African nationalism.
In the new edition the author, a Black Rhodesian minister, treats the
subject somewhat differently--because he feels that nationalism has

"justified itself by its own achievements" and because he has, since
writing the original version, been active in the liberation movement.
The first of the work's four parts is largely autobiographical, the
second deals with factors contributing to the rise of African nationalism, the third concerns the nature of white supremacy, and the fourth
discusses nationalism's problems consequent upon Africa's sovereign
independence.

644. Spiro, Herbert J., ed. PATTERNS OF AFRICAN DEVELOPMENT: FIVE COM-
         PARISONS. Englewood Cliffs, N.J., Prentice-Hall, 1967. 144 p.
         (Spectrum Book)

         Bibliographical footnotes.

         An introduction by the editor is followed by studies based on
    papers presented at the 8th meeting of the African Studies Association
    in Philadelphia, Oct. 1965: "Some Reflections on Constitutionalism
    for Emergent Political Orders," by Carl J. Friedrich; "Nationalism in
    a New Perspective: The African Case," by Ibrahim Abu-Lughod; "The
    Challenge of Change: Japan and Africa," by Claude E. Welch, Jr.; "Bor-
    rowed Theory and Original Practice in African Politics," by Ali A.
    Mazrui; and "Repetition or Innovation?" by Herbert J. Spiro.

645. Thomas, Charles M. AFRICAN NATIONAL DEVELOPMENTS. 2d ed. Maxwell
         Air Force Base, Ala., Documentary Research Division, Aerospace
         Studies Institute, Air University, 1967. 196 p. Processed.
         (Air University Documentary Research Study, AU-295-65-ASI)

         An orderly fund of information on each country on the continent,
    presented in narrative style. The short individual surveys cover cur-
    rent political status and recent developments in internal politics,
    political and diplomatic relations with neighbors, position in African
    political associations and in larger international organizations, sig-
    nificance of foreign aid, fiscal position, economic and industrial
    bases, and various sociological factors of import for the political
    future and international position of the country concerned.

646. Thomas, L. V. LE SOCIALISME ET L'AFRIQUE: Vol. I, ESSAI SUR LE
         SOCIALISME AFRICAIN; Vol. II: L'IDEOLOGIE SOCIALISTE ET LES
         VOIES AFRICAINES DE DEVELOPPEMENT. Paris, Le Livre Africain,
         1966.

         Bibliographical footnotes.

647. Wallbank, Thomas W., ed. DOCUMENTS ON MODERN AFRICA. Princeton, N.J.,
         D. Van Nostrand, 1964. 192 p. (Anvil Books, no. 72)

For student use, this little volume is a sampling of the huge
quantity of documentation available on the political history of
modern Africa. The first four items relate to the opening of Africa,
items 5-20 explain colonial rule through the interwar years, and items
21-31 are for the postwar period and the coming of independence. The
last 17 items relate to special problems and trends. Notes of explanation precede the documents.

648. Wallerstein, Immanuel. AFRICA: THE POLITICS OF UNITY; AN ANALYSIS OF
      A CONTEMPORARY SOCIAL MOVEMENT. New York, Random House, 1967.
      xi, 274 p. map.

A Columbia University sociologist follows the development of conflicts and policies in the various supranational organizations. The
book is an interpretation of the major political developments in Africa
between 1957 and 1965 from the perspective of a major social movement
on the continent, the movement toward African unity. It is the thesis
of this book that this movement represented the strongest indigenous
force on the continent during this period, though, as later events
have proved, not a force strong enough to achieve its objectives.

649. Welch, Claude E., Jr. SOLDIER AND STATE IN AFRICA: A COMPARATIVE
      ANALYSIS OF MILITARY INTERVENTION AND POLITICAL CHANGE. Evanston,
      Northwestern University Press, 1970. 320 p.

      Bibliography: p. 302-309.

A series of case studies primarily concerned with Francophone
Africa--Dahomey, Upper Volta, Algeria, and Congo (Kinshasa). There
is an essay on Ghana and an essay on "The Military and Political Change
in Africa." A chronology, a glossary of acronyms, and a bibliography
add to the value of the book.

CHAPTER 16

INTERNATIONAL RELATIONS

Reference Works

650.   AFRICA AND WORLD ORDER. Edited by Norman J. Padelford and Rupert
          Emerson. New York, Praeger, 1963. 152 p. map.

          Bibliography: p. 137-152.

          Collection of articles which formed a special issue of INTER-
     NATIONAL ORGANIZATION (v. 15, Spring 1962), the quarterly of the
     World Peace Foundation, and which constitutes a guide to the
     political groupings of Africa with data to mid-1961. The last
     article, a review of African unification movements, includes a
     table of African groupings in major organizations and conferences;
     it has a supplementary summary of political and regional groupings.
     The 25-page classified selected bibliography gives references on
     these groupings.

          Comparable data for an additional year and a half were printed
     in tabulated form on the back cover (the "Fact Sheet" series) of
     the June 1963 AFRICA REPORT.

          Individual conferences are noticed in many of the African
     news journals. See also CHRONOLOGIE POLITIQUE AFRICAINE (no. 574)
     and WORLD LIST OF FUTURE INTERNATIONAL MEETINGS (consult Winchell
     for description).

651.   Akademiia Nauk SSSR. Institut Afriki. AFRIKA 1956-1961. [Edited
          by I. I. Potekhin.] Moskva, Izd-vo Vostochnoi Lit-ry, 1961.
          252 p. illus., maps.

          A survey of political, economic, and cultural developments over
     the years 1956-61 as seen from Moscow. Emphasis is on relations
     with the USSR, and statistics are included on African trade with
     the Soviet Union. An English translation has been prepared by the
     Joint Publications Research Service (Translations on Africa, no. 851,
     1963, 357 p.). See also no. 771.

652.   American Assembly. THE UNITED STATES AND AFRICA. Rev. ed., edited
          by Walter Goldschmidt. New York, Praeger, 1963. xvi, 298 p.
          maps, diagrs., tables.

          Originally prepared as background reading for participants in
       the Thirteenth American Assembly, May 1958. See also Zartman, INTER-
       NATIONAL RELATIONS IN THE NEW AFRICA (no. 1317).

          Analysis of political, economic, and social developments in
       modern Africa and of American interests in Africa. An appendix in-
       cludes factual details of American relations with Africa.

653.   Brzezinski, Zbigniew K., ed. AFRICA AND THE COMMUNIST WORLD. Stanford,
          Calif., Published for the Hoover Institution on War, Revolution,
          and Peace by Stanford University Press, 1963. xii, 272 p. map
          (on lining papers). (Hoover Institution Publications)

          Bibliographical references in notes: p. 233-264.

          A useful review of political and economic activities of Communist
       countries in Africa, with contributions by specialists--Alexander
       Dallin for the Soviet Union, Richard Lowenthal for China, etc.

          A more recent but sometimes factually inaccurate study is: Fritz
       Schatten, COMMUNISM IN AFRICA (New York, Praeger, 1966, 352 p.; Praeger
       Publications in Russian History and World Communism, no. 174).

654.   Collotti Pischel, Enrica, and Chiara Robertazzi. L'INTERNATIONALE
          COMMUNISTE ET LES PROBLEMES COLONIAUX, 1919-1935. Paris, La
          Haye, Mouton 1968. 584 p. (Matériaux pour l'histoire du
          socialisme international. 2. sér.: Essais bibliographiques, 2)

          An annotated bibliographic survey of communist writings on
       colonialism published officially by the Communist International
       between 1919 and 1935.

655.   Emerson, Rupert. AFRICA AND UNITED STATES POLICY. Englewood Cliffs,
          N.J., Prentice-Hall, 1967. 117 p. map, tables. (America's
          Role in World Affairs Series)

          Bibliographical footnotes.

          A succinct analysis of relations between the governments, rather
       than the peoples, of sub-Saharan Africa and the United States. Intro-
       ductory material is followed by a discussion of a century of Afro-
       American relations, and the major portion of the volume is then devoted
       to U.S. interests and activities in Africa. An index is included.

656. Geiger, Theodore. THE CONFLICTED RELATIONSHIP: THE WEST AND THE
TRANSFORMATION OF ASIA, AFRICA AND LATIN AMERICA. New York,
Published for the Council on Foreign Relations by McGraw-Hill,
1967. xiv, 303 p. (Atlantic Policy Studies)

Bibliography: p. 300-303.

Mr. Geiger, chief of international studies at the National
Planning Association, has also co-authored with Winifred Armstrong
THE DEVELOPMENT OF AFRICAN PRIVATE ENTERPRISE (Washington, D.C.,
National Planning Association, 1964, 158 p., map; bibliography:
p. 154-156; Planning Pamphlet no. 120). The present book, intended
for both the specialist and the layman, includes chapters on Western
attitudes and expectations, the encounter of the West with Asia and
Africa, the nature and outcome of the transitional process in Asia
and Africa, and their limitations.

657. Hamrell, Sven, and Carl Gösta Widstrand, eds. THE SOVIET BLOC,
CHINA AND AFRICA. Uppsala, Scandinavian Institute of African
Studies, 1964. 173 p.

Bibliographical footnotes.

Seven papers delivered at an international seminar arranged
by the Institute in Uppsala in 1963 appear here (some in slightly re-
vised form): "Pan-Africanism and Communism," by Colin Legum; "Soviet
Policy towards Africa," by David L. Morison; "Chinese Policy towards
Africa," by W. A. C. Adie; "Communism in North Africa," by Walter
Laqueur; "Communism in Tropical Africa," by Franz Ansprenger; "Soviet
and Chinese Programmes of Technical Aid to African Countries," by
Kurt Müller; and "The Sino-Soviet Split and Its Repercussions in
Africa," by Richard Lowenthal. In conclusion Sven Hamrell presents a
report on the discussions.

658. Hovet, Thomas. AFRICA IN THE UNITED NATIONS. Evanston, Ill., Northwestern University Press, 1963. xiii, 336 p. map, diagrs.
(African Studies, no. 10)

A study of the group influence of Africa in the UN, based largely
on an analysis of voting behavior in the General Assembly, 1946-62.
Tables of votes, 1946-62, and the subjects of resolutions voted on are
included in appendixes.

As the greater part of the UN material relating to Africa is in
economic and social fields, UN reference works are noted in the Economics section (Chapter 18) of the present guide.

659. McKay, Vernon. AFRICA IN WORLD POLITICS. New York, Harper & Row, 1963.
     468 p.

     "List of sources": p. 429-454.

     Described by the author as "a narrative of contemporary history
since 1945," this work has four parts dealing with the impact of the
United Nations on Africa; Pan-African, Afro-Asian, and Eurafrican
movements; Africa's relations with India and the Soviet Union; and
American policy in Africa.

660. McKay, Vernon, ed. AFRICAN DIPLOMACY: STUDIES IN THE DETERMINANTS OF
     FOREIGN POLICY. New York, Published for the School of Advanced
     International Studies, Johns Hopkins University, by Praeger, 1966.
     xiii, 210 p.

     The book is the result of a June 1965 symposium held at Johns
Hopkins. Seven participants, including the editor, present chapters
on international conflict patterns, national interest and ideology,
economic, military, cultural, and political determinants, and external pressures. A final chapter pinpoints African foreign policy
problems on which further research is needed. See also Zartman,
INTERNATIONAL RELATIONS IN THE NEW AFRICA (no. 1317).

661. Mazrui, Ali A. THE ANGLO-AFRICAN COMMONWEALTH: POLITICAL FRICTION
     AND CULTURAL FUSION. Oxford, New York, Pergamon Press, 1967.
     163 p. (Commonwealth International Library, Commonwealth
     Affairs Division)

     Bibliographical footnotes.

     An interesting study of the impact of Africa on the British
Commonwealth and vice versa. Mazrui's comments are in two sections,
"History and Politics" and "Culture and Thought," including chapters
on the European Economic Community and on the influence of Shakespeare
on African political thought. A third section consists of seven appendixes of speeches and writings, mainly of African leaders and
British administrators, on race and Pan-Africanism vis-à-vis the
Commonwealth, the English language in African politics and culture,
etc.

662. Mendiaux, Edouard. L'AFRIQUE SERA CHINOISE. Bruxelles, Editions
     Sineco [1965?]. 328 p.

     An apprehensive appraisal of Chinese Communist penetration in
Africa. Topics included are the Sino-Soviet conflict, two Afro-Asian
conferences (Algiers and Winneba, Ghana), and the Chinese role in North
Africa, Mali, Guinea, Ghana, the Afro-Malagasy Union, Burundi, the two

Congos, Tanzania, East Africa (Uganda, Kenya, Somalia, Sudan, Ethiopia),
Portuguese Africa, Zambia, Malawi, Rhodesia, and South Africa. The
book contains extracts of declarations, speeches, and propaganda items
from Peking and also reproduces materials previously published in
journals.

An analytical study of Chinese influence in Africa, and one which
offers a less ominous view, is L'AFRIQUE DE PEKIN: CONTRIBUTION A
L'ETUDE DES RELATIONS SINO-AFRICAINS, 1964-1966. by Pierre Mertens and
Paul F. Smets (Bruxelles, Impr. Amibel, 1966, 116 p.; bibliography: p.
105-114).

663. Morison, David L. THE U.S.S.R. AND AFRICA. Issued under auspices of
       the Institute of Race Relations and the Central Asian Research
       Centre. London, New York, Oxford University Press, 1964. 124 p.
       map.

A concise study of Soviet views of Africa as ascertained from
Soviet writing, much of which, says the author in his preface, "seems
to be virtually self-generating," having little to do with African
views of the Soviet Union. Soviet aims and attitudes are analyzed
and African studies in Russia described. The helpful appendix presents in compact form "Soviet Views on Africa Country by Country"
(Algeria-Zanzibar, p. 75-124).

664. Nielsen, Waldemar A. AFRICAN BATTLELINE: AMERICAN POLICY CHOICES IN
       SOUTHERN AFRICA. New York, Published for the Council on Foreign
       Relations by Harper & Row, 1965. 144 p.

By the president of the African-American Institute, this book,
brought out for the Council on Foreign Relations in its series of
Policy Books, is a discussion of specific danger areas in South and
South-West Africa, the High Commission Territories, Rhodesia,
Portuguese Africa, and the Congo. Also considered are implications
for the United States, and the roles of UN and of Communist influence.

665. Northwestern University, Evanston, Ill. Interdisciplinary Committee
       on African Studies. UNITED STATES FOREIGN POLICY: AFRICA. Pre-
       pared at the request of the Committee on Foreign Relations, U.S.
       Senate, by the Program of African Studies, Northwestern University.
       Washington, U.S. Govt. Print. Off., 1959. 84 p. map. (U.S. Con-
       gress, Senate, Committee on Foreign Relations, A Study, no. 4)
       At head of title: Committee print, 86th Cong., 1st sess.

Bibliographical footnotes.

One of an influential series of studies authorized by the Senate
Committee on Foreign Relations in 1958, reviewing conditions and trends

in the world and policies and programs of the United States. This
volume, presented by Dr. Melville J. Herskovits, begins with a
summary of the position of the United States in relation to the
changing African scene and is followed by a succinct statement of
conclusions and recommendations for American policy toward Africa.
The body of the text expands the points made.

666. Permanent Organization for Afro-Asian Peoples' Solidarity. Perma-
        nent Secretariat. AFRO-ASIAN PEOPLES' SOLIDARITY MOVEMENT:
        PRINCIPLES, STRUCTURE, FRIENDLY ORGANIZATIONS. Cairo [1962 or
        1963]. 269 p.

      This international body, resulting from the Bandung Conference,
has headquarters in Cairo and is "anti-imperialist" in motivation.
Among its other publications have been a few numbers of three periodicals: AFRO-ASIAN BULLETIN (monthly, 1958-), AFRO-ASIAN QUARTERLY
(1959-), and AFRO-ASIAN WOMAN (1959?-).

667. U.S. Congress. Senate. Committee on Appropriations. REPORT ON U.S.
        FOREIGN OPERATIONS IN AFRICA. By Allen J. Ellender. Mar. 23,
        1963. Washington, U.S. Govt. Print. Off., 1963 803 p. map,
        tables. (88th Cong., 1st sess., Senate Doc. no. 8, Committee
        print)

      One of a series of reports by members of Congress relating to
study missions, etc., concerned with Africa south of the Sahara.
Other material of similar nature may be identified through the annual
index of the MONTHLY CATALOG OF UNITED STATES GOVERNMENT PUBLICATIONS.
This is the source also for publications of the Department of State,
USIA, AID, Bureau of Foreign Agriculture, Bureau of Foreign Commerce,
and many other government agencies having connection with African
affairs. Notable is the long series of translations on Africa by the
Joint Publications Research Service (see no. 360).

      A review of congressional connections with African affairs, in-
cluding notation of the various reports, was published in AFRICA REPORT,
Aug. 1964: "The U.S. Congress and Africa," by Stanley Meisler (v. 9,
no. 8, p. 3-7). Other documents on American economic aid to Africa are
noted in the Economics section of the present guide.

668. Wingenbach, Charles. THE PEACE CORPS--WHO, HOW, AND WHERE. 2d ed.
        New York, John Day, 1963. 188 p.

      The original edition and THE COMPLETE PEACE CORPS GUIDE, by Roy
Hoopes, both appeared in 1961, written with official blessing to
correct ideas about the Peace Corps, then in its early stages. The
second edition of Mr. Wingenbach's book is more up to date and includes
a number of letters from the field. The Hoopes work had a new edition
in 1966.

CHAPTER 17

<u>LAW</u>

<u>Bibliographies</u>

669. African Law Association in America, Inc. BIBLIOGRAPHY OF AFRICAN
      LAW. Compiled by A. Arthur Schiller. New York, 1965-

      Various issues of the Association's NEWSLETTER were used to
publish preliminary drafts of the African law bibliography. French
Africa appeared first in 1965, then South Africa, Italian Africa,
German Africa, Portuguese and Spanish Africa, then sections on individual countries. The bibliography is a most useful and full listing
of all aspects of African law, especially valuable for the colonial
period. There are usually sections on: bibliographies, legislative
enactments, compilations of law, treatises and monographs, gazettes
and government reports. The three parts are to be completed and
replaced by LAW BOOKS RECOMMENDED FOR LIBRARIES, No. 39: African
Law, Association of American Law Schools (to be published in 1970
by Fred B. Rothman & Co., South Hackensack, N.J.).

670. AFRICAN LAW BIBLIOGRAPHY, 1947-1966. Addis Ababa, Centre for
      African Legal Development, Faculty of Law, Haile Sellassie
      I University; Bruxelles, Centre pour le Développement Juridique
      Africaine, Institut de Sociologie, Université Libre de Bruxelles
      [1968].

      Consisting of titles of all books and articles on African law
available at the Law Library of Haile Sellassie I University,
this bibliography is being issued in two forms: separate cardboard
sheets holding four perforated cards, with an entry on each card;
book form (at the end of 1968). There are an estimated 6,000
entries, titles being listed first by subject and thereunder by
country.

671. AFRICAN LAW STUDIES. First Issue, June 1969- New York, African Law
        Center, Columbia University. 3 issues a year.

        Contains articles of bibliographical and methodological nature
intended to serve as tools for research in African law. A preliminary
issue appeared in Jan. 1969. The journal aims to cover aspects of
African law not noticed in other established journals.

672. Afrika-Studiecentrum, Leiden. DOCUMENTATIEBLAD. Jan. 1967- Monthly.

        Abstracts of articles (in the original language) dealing with
political, social, and economic sciences.

673. BIBLIOGRAPHY OF AFRICAN LAW. London, School of Oriental and African
        Studies, University of London, 1961-

        This bibliography, being prepared as the first step in the Re-
statement of African Law project directed by Professor Antony N. Allott,
is designed to cover published and unpublished material on the customary
laws of Commonwealth African countries. A draft of the first part,
EAST AFRICA, was issued in typescript in 1961 (see under East Africa, no.
2363). A draft on GHANA has also appeared.

674. Blaustein, Albert P. "African Legal Periodicals: A Bibliography."
        LAW LIBRARY JOURNAL, v. 59, 1966: 93-96.

        An offprint is available.

675. Gilissen, John. INTRODUCTION BIBLIOGRAPHIQUE A L'HISTOIRE DU DROIT
        ET A L'ETHNOLOGIE JURIDIQUE. BIBLIOGRAPHICAL INTRODUCTION TO
        LEGAL HISTORY AND ETHNOLOGY. Bruxelles, Ministère de l'Education
        Nationale et de la Culture, 1963-

        To date, three volumes with loose-leaf parts. These volumes in-
clude Bantu law in South Africa, modern law in South Africa, and law
in Ethiopia-Eritrea, Somaliland, and Madagascar.

676. INDEX TO PERIODICAL ARTICLES RELATED TO LAW. v. 1- 1958- Stanford,
        Calif., Law Library, Stanford University. Quarterly.

        Surveys periodicals containing articles on African law. The
index does not, however, include titles covered by the INDEX TO LEGAL
PERIODICALS and the INDEX TO FOREIGN LEGAL PERIODICALS. A one-volume,
six-year cumulation (1958-1964) has been issued.

677. A LEGAL BIBLIOGRAPHY OF THE BRITISH COMMONWEALTH OF NATIONS: Vol. VII,
     THE BRITISH COMMONWEALTH EXCLUDING THE UNITED KINGDOM, AUSTRALIA,
     NEW ZEALAND, CANADA, INDIA AND PAKISTAN. Compiled by Leslie F.
     Maxwell. 2d ed. London, Sweet and Maxwell, 1964. 459 p.

     African section: p. 1-188.

     New edition of a volume first published in 1949 (BRITISH
COLONIES, PROTECTORATES AND MANDATE TERRITORIES). It has a large general section and is then broken down by regions, islands, and countries
(and by provinces, territories, or regions within specific countries).
Articles, books, gazettes, reports, collections of statutes, ordinances,
sessional papers, subsidiary legislation, etc., are covered, and there
is a full index. An additional source for details of reports and periodicals is to be found in A COMPLETE LIST OF BRITISH AND COLONIAL LAW RE-
PORTS AND LEGAL PERIODICALS by W. H. Maxwell and C. R. Brown (3d ed.,
1937, with supplements thereafter).

678. Meek, Charles K. COLONIAL LAW: A BIBLIOGRAPHY WITH SPECIAL REFERENCE
     TO NATIVE AFRICAN SYSTEMS OF LAW AND LAND TENURE. London, Pub-
     lished for Nuffield College by Oxford University Press, 1948. xiii,
     58 p.

     Old standard bibliography by a leading British authority on land
law and tenure in the colonies.

679. United Nations Educational, Scientific, and Cultural Organization.
     CATALOGUE DES SOURCES DE DOCUMENTATION JURIDIQUE DANS LE MONDE.
     A REGISTER OF LEGAL DOCUMENTATION IN THE WORLD. Paris, 1953.
     362 p.

     This excellent guide to legal documentation in all countries is
unfortunately far out of date, particularly so where Africa is concerned. The index of places includes the names of many African
countries but as dependencies under Great Britain, France, and the
other metropolitan powers of preindependence. For each country there
are summarized legislation, the constitution, principal laws, collections of laws, jurisprudence, centers of legal activities and libraries,
periodicals and reviews. Even though it relates to another era, it
may offer helpful suggestions, especially where legal institutions have
continued through the change of governments.

Reference Works

Note: See also the collections of national constitutions noted in Chapter
15 (nos. 616, 630, and 639) and the Sweet & Maxwell's Law in Africa Series
and Butterworth's African Law Series.

680. AFRICAN LAW DIGEST. Jan. 1966- New York, African Law Center,
     Columbia University. Quarterly.

     Official publication of the African Law Association in America,
edited by Cliff F. Thompson. The journal carries digests of current
legislation and administrative regulations of English- and French-
speaking states and reviews law journals of East, Central, and West
Africa. Included are a notes section and a useful index and cross-
classification. Xerox copies of items mentioned in the journal are
available.

681. AFRICAN LAW STUDIES. June 1969- New York, African Law Center,
     Columbia University.

     See no. 671 for annotation.

682. Afrika-Instituut (Netherlands). THE FUTURE OF CUSTOMARY LAW IN
     AFRICA. L'AVENIR DU DROIT COUTUMIER EN AFRIQUE. Symposium-
     colloque, Amsterdam, 1955. Organized by the Afrika-Instituut,
     Studiecentrum, Leiden, in collaboration with the Royal Tropical
     Institute, Amsterdam. Leiden, Universitaire Pers Leiden, 1956.
     xvii, 305 p.

     Bibliography: p. 273-305.

     Papers on the law of indigenous societies in Africa as
exercised through the native courts and local jurisdictions in the
former Belgian, British, and French territories. Past development,
present conditions, and future possibilities under spreading
detribalization were discussed.

683. Alliot, Michel. COURS D'INSTITUTIONS PRIVEES AFRICAINES ET
     MALGACHES. Paris, Les Cours de Droit, 1965-66. 351 p.

     A series of lectures prepared in the traditional French
manner for a course in African law at the Paris Faculty of Law.

684. Allott, Antony N. ESSAYS IN AFRICAN LAW, WITH SPECIAL REFERENCE
     TO THE LAW OF GHANA. London, Butterworth, 1960. xxviii,
     323 p. (Butterworth's African Law Series, no. 1)

     This volume begins a new series which will presumably reappraise
the law of all Africa, certainly of all English-speaking Africa. Dr.
Allott, reader in African law in the University of London School of
Oriental and African Studies, is editor of the JOURNAL OF AFRICAN LAW.
The three parts of his study deal in historical and analytical terms
with (1) the general common law of British Africa, received from the

metropole; (2) customary law, its fundamental characteristics, its possible unity among laws of the innumerable tribes, and its native administration; and (3) a special case study of Ghana, particularly in relation to conflicts of customary law. Dr. Allott also edited the record of preceedings of a conference held in London from Dec. 28, 1959, to Jan. 8, 1960, under the chairmanship of Lord Denning, formerly Lord Chief Justice. The volume was published with the title THE FUTURE OF LAW IN AFRICA (London, Butterworth, 1960, 58 p.).

A Conference on Local Courts and Customary Law in Africa was held in Dar es Salaam in Sept. 1963, and a Conference on Integration of Customary and Modern Legal Systems in Africa was held under the auspices of the University of Ife Institute of African Studies at Ibadan, Aug. 24-29, 1964.

Most of the subsequent volumes in Butterworth's African Law Series are concerned with individual countries and will be noted in later sections.

685. Allott, Antony N., ed. JUDICIAL AND LEGAL SYSTEMS IN AFRICA. London, Butterworth, 1962. xiii, 226 p. diagrs. (Butterworth's African Law Series, no. 4)

A thorough compilation, covering systems of the entire continent in digest form. For the most part, the institutions reported are little changed from those of preindependence days.

686. Anderson, James N. D. ISLAMIC LAW IN AFRICA. London, H.M. Stationery Off., 1954. 409 p. (Colonial Research Publication, no. 16)

Bibliographical footnotes.

Survey prepared for the Colonial Office by the professor of Oriental laws in the University of London. His interest was in several interactions: of Islamic law--the Shari'a--and the customary law of the various Muslim societies of British Africa and of the native law and Islamic law and institutions. Appendixes include surveys of the Sudan and of the law as affecting immigrant Muslims, tables of ordinances and cases, and a glossary. There is a full index.

687. Baade, Hans Wolfgang, ed., and Robinson O. Everett, associate ed. AFRICAN LAW: NEW LAW FOR NEW NATIONS. Dobbs Ferry, N.Y., Oceana Publications, 1963. 119 p. (Library of Law and Contemporary Problems)

Bibliographical footnotes.

The essays presented are: "African Legal Studies--A Survey of the Field and the Role of the U.S.," by Denis Cowen; "Personnel Problems in the Administration of Justice in Nigeria," by Sir Adetokunbo Ademola; "The Evolution of Ghana Law since Independence," by William Burnett Harvey; "Customary Law in the New African States," by Lloyd Fallers; "The Future of Islamic Law in British Commonwealth Territories in Africa; by J. N. D. Anderson; and "United Nations Law in Africa: The Congo Operation as a Case Study," by Thomas Franck.

688. Columbia University. School of Law. SYLLABUS FOR THE SEMINAR IN AFRICAN LAW, COLUMBIA UNIVERSITY SCHOOL OF LAW. By A. Arthur Schiller. New York, 1961. 1 v. various pagings. Mimeographed.

In this outline of the course, Part 1 deals with basic information, e.g., indigenous and nonindigenous law, organization of the courts, problems of culture conflict. The second part is bibliographical, with lists of secondary writings and primary source materials. The last part comprises cases and materials dealing with the substance of African law, including conflicts in the diverse legal systems and the variety of courts.

689. Gluckman, Max, ed. IDEAS AND PROCEDURES IN AFRICAN CUSTOMARY LAW. London, International African Institute, 1969. 361 p.

Studies presented and discussed at the Eighth International African Seminar at the Haile Sellassie I University, Addis Ababa, Jan. 1966.

690. Gonidec, P.-F. LES DROITS AFRICAINS: EVOLUTION ET SOURCES. Paris, Librairie Générale de Droit et de Jurisprudence, 1968. 278 p. (Bibliothèque africaine et malgache, Droit et sociologie politique, v. 1)

691. Gower, L. C. B. INDEPENDENT AFRICA: THE CHALLENGE TO THE LEGAL PROFESSION. Cambridge, Mass., 1967. 154 p.

Based on lectures given at Harvard University by the former Dean of the Law Faculty at the University of Lagos, this volume examines the legal inheritance and problems of former British Africa. Gower discusses the pre- and postindependence periods and concludes with comments on the legal profession. An analytical index is included.

692. Hutchinson, Thomas W., ed., in association with James N. Roethe and others. AFRICA AND LAW: DEVELOPING LEGAL SYSTEMS IN AFRICAN COMMONWEALTH NATIONS. Madison, Milwaukee, and London, University of Wisconsin Press, 1968. 181 p.

Bibliographical footnotes.

A volume based on the Fall 1966 issue of the WISCONSIN LAW REVIEW.
An introduction by A. Arthur Schiller is followed by a long essay
(p. 3-74) by Robert B. Seidman, "Law and Economic Development in Independent, English-speaking Sub-Saharan Africa." The remaining four
essays are "Land Law in Kenya," by Ann P. Munro; "Post-Nkrumah Ghana:
The Legal Profile of a Coup," by William B. Harvey; "Law and Society in
Ghana," by S. K. B. Asante; and "The Sources of Law in the New Nations
of Africa: A Case Study from the Republic of the Sudan," by Cliff F.
Thompson. There is an analytical index.

693. JOURNAL OF AFRICAN LAW. v. 1, no. 1- Spring 1957- Edited by Antony
        N. Allott. London, Butterworth. 3 issues a year.

Designed as an organ for the discussion of general principles
that might emerge from objective study, criticism, and comparison of
the diverse legal systems operative in Africa--the heterogeneous
tribal laws, the variant forms of Islamic law, the British common law,
the codes imported from France, Belgium, and the other colonial powers.
The journal was founded in 1957, as a result of the Amsterdam conference
(see Afrika-Instituut, no. 682 above) at which extensive airing had
been given to the confusion of law in Africa.

694. Kuper, Hilda, and Leo Kuper, eds. AFRICAN LAW: ADAPTATION AND
        DEVELOPMENT. Published under the auspices of the African Studies
        Center, University of California, Los Angeles. Berkeley and Los
        Angeles, University of California Press, 1965. 275 p.

Bibliography: p. 261-266.

An introduction by the editors is followed by 10 studies: "The
Sociological Framework of Law," by M. G. Smith; "Land Law in the
Making," by Philip and Iona Mayer; "Justice and Judgment among the
Southern Ibo under Colonial Rule," by Daryll Forde; "A Traditional
Legal System: The Kuba," by Jan Vansina; "Reasonableness and Respon-
sibility in the Law of Segmentary Societies," by Max Gluckman; "The
Adaptation of Muslim Law in Sub-Saharan Africa," by J. N. D. Anderson;
"L'évolution de la législation dans les pays africains d'expression
française et à Madagascar," by Gabriel d'Arboussier; "The Evolution
of Law and Government in Modern Africa," by T. O. Elias; "The Adaptation
of Customary Family Law in South Africa," by Leslie Rubin; and "The
Future of African Law," by Antony N. Allott.

695. M'Baye, Keba, ed. LE DROIT DE LA FAMILLE EN AFRIQUE NOIRE ET A
        MADAGASCAR. Etudes préparées à la requête de l'UNESCO. Paris,
        G. P. Maisonneuve et Larose, 1968. 295 p.

696. Milner, Alan, ed. AFRICAN PENAL SYSTEMS. London, Routledge & Kegan
         Paul, 1969. 501 p.

      Essays by 16 contributors who survey the penal systems of 14
African states and then discuss in detail specific problems in the
development and operation of the systems.

697. Poirier, Jean, ed. ETUDES DE DROIT AFRICAIN ET DE DROIT MALGACHE.
         Paris, Editions Cujas, 1965. 529 p. (Etudes malgaches, 16)

698. Tunc, André, ed. LES ASPECTS JURIDIQUES DU DEVELOPPEMENT ECONOMIQUE.
         LEGAL ASPECTS OF ECONOMIC DEVELOPMENT. Paris, Librairie
         Dalloz, 1966. 206 p.

      Prepared for UNESCO by French- and English-speaking authorities,
this collection of studies is devoted to an analysis of changes which
the present legal systems should undergo in order to meet development
needs.

699. Verhelst, Thierry. MATERIALS ON LAND LAW AND ECONOMIC DEVELOPMENT
         IN AFRICA. Preliminary ed., not for publication. Prepared under
         the joint auspices of the School of Law and the African Studies
         Center, University of California, Los Angeles. Los Angeles,
         1968. 605 p.

      Collection of materials (laws, legislation, articles) on land law
and economic development with regard to customary law, law during the
colonial period, and postindependence reforms. French-speaking former
British territories of Africa are covered.

700. Virginia Legal Studies. THE LEGAL SYSTEMS OF AFRICA SERIES. General
         editor: Kenneth R. Redden. Charlottesville, Va., The Michie
         Company, 1969-

      New series. Thus far only the volume on Ethiopia has been pub-
lished. A volume dealing with French-speaking Africa is in press (1969).

CHAPTER 18

ECONOMICS

(INCLUDING DEVELOPMENT PLANNING)

GENERAL

Guides to Organizations for Economic
and Technical Assistance
and Development

Note: See also nos. 30 and 31.

701.   ANNUAIRE DES ENTERPRISES ET ORGANISMES D'OUTRE-MER. Paris, René
          Moreux (190, blvd. Haussmann). Annual. 58e année. 1967.
          500, 1096 p.

          The scope is limited to organizations and undertakings serving
          the former French territories, and arrangement is in the main geo-
          graphical. Included are official and professional organizations of
          overseas countries; organizations for cooperation with overseas
          countries, French, international, and foreign; private enterprises,
          governmental organizations, mixed economy (financial, transport,
          multi-industry; Afrique de nord, Cameroun, Congo, etc.); and
          industrial traders of overseas countries. There are indexes.

702.   Centre for Labour and Social Studies. DIRECTORY OF NON-GOVERNMENTAL
          EUROPEAN ORGANIZATIONS OFFERING ASSISTANCE IN THE DEVELOPING
          COUNTRIES, 1964. Rome, 1964. 202 p.

          A guide to the European-based organizations--more than 1,800--
          concerned with world development. There is a brief listing of the

program, publications, and officers of each organization. No
attempt is made to evaluate these organizations. See also
INSTITUTIONS ENGAGED IN ECONOMIC AND SOCIAL PLANNING IN AFRICA:
DIRECTORY PREPARED FOR UNESCO BY THE INTERNATIONAL SOCIAL SCIENCE
COUNCIL AND THE CENTRE D'ANALYSE ET DE RECHERCHE DOCUMENTAIRES
POUR L'AFRIQUE NOIRE (MAISON DES SCIENCES DE L'HOMME) (Paris,
UNESCO, 1967, 155 p.).

703. MULTINATIONAL ECONOMIC ORGANIZATIONS IN AFRICA: A SUMMARY DESCRIP-
        TION. 4th ed. Prepared by staff of Deputy Director for Economic
      Affairs, AFI Bureau of African Affairs, Department of State.
      Washington, D.C., 1968. 46 p. maps.

      For each organization described, the following information is
given: members, brief history, aims, structure, headquarters city
(but no address). There is a guide to abbreviations for organizations' names. Twelve shaded maps of Africa illustrate membership
in the various economic groups.

704. Organisation for Economic Co-operation and Development (OECD). Devel-
        opment Enquiry Service. Paris (91, blvd. Exelmans, Paris 16).

      This international center provides documentation in all fields of
economic development for the emerging countries. The Development
Enquiry Service acts as a clearinghouse, with the help of many national and international reference services. Upon request it supplies
informational material, including bibliographies. See, for instance,
under Guinea, no. 1700.

705. Overseas Development Institute, London. DEVELOPMENT GUIDE: A DIREC-
        TORY OF DEVELOPMENT FACILITIES PROVIDED BY NON-COMMERCIAL
        ORGANIZATIONS IN BRITAIN. London, G. Allen & Unwin, 1962.
      unpaged (about 250 p.).

      A total of 198 organizations are described systematically as to
research, publications, educational services, information, recruitment, orientation, financial assistance, etc. Most bodies are of
worldwide scope, e.g., the Medical Research Council and Save the
Children Fund. Not many relate to Africa. See also Organisation for
Economic Co-operation and Development, CATALOGUE OF SOCIAL AND ECO-
NOMIC DEVELOPMENT RESEARCH INSTITUTES AND PROGRAMMES (Paris, 1968,
411 p.).

706. U.S. Congress. House. Committee on Foreign Affairs. ACTIVITIES OF
        PRIVATE U.S. ORGANIZATIONS IN AFRICA. Hearings ... 87th Cong.,
      1st sess. Washington, U.S. Govt. Print. Off., 1961. 280 p.

      Statements of industrial firms, directors of missionary work, and
organizations for African-American relations. See also nos. 30 and 31.

Atlas

707. OXFORD REGIONAL ECONOMIC ATLAS: AFRICA. Prepared by P. H. Ady and
        the Cartographic Department of the Clarendon Press, with the
        assistance of A. H. Hazlewood. Oxford, Clarendon Press, 1965.
        60, 164 p. maps, tables.

        This impressive volume edited by two British specialists in Afri-
can economics is in three parts: economic commentary; maps, thematic
and regional; and gazetteer. The first part consists of concentrated
notes grouped under population, agriculture, minerals and mines, manufacturing industries, sources of energy and power, transport, and foreign trade. It is illustrated with many statistical talbes. In the
second part, the 112 pages of highly colored maps are both thematic,
illustrating about 100 topics from airways to zinc, and regional,
including climate, geology, population, etc. The gazetteer (p. 115-
164) is perhaps the most exhaustive available, containing about 15,000
place names.

Bibliographies

Note: The listings of works on economics in such general reference sources
as the bibliographical sections of the ANNALS of the American Academy of
Political and Social Science (books only) and the AMERICAN ECONOMIC REVIEW
(books, periodical articles, dissertations) are disappointing with regard
to Africana, for although they include most notable writings on African economics, there is no geographical approach, and all titled must be examined
to select those relating to Africa. Rather more useful is the American Economic Association's comprehensive INDEX OF ECONOMIC JOURNALS (Homewood,
Ill., Irwin, 1961-62, 5 v.), which covers the years from 1886 to 1959 and
analyzes the contents of 89 journals in various languages. The arrangement
is by a detailed subject classification scheme--23 classes with 700 sub-
classes; certain of the headings, e.g., "General Contemporary Economic Conditions," have geographical breakdowns. Under the subhead cited, there are
in Vol. V (1950-59) some 30 entries for Africa. The more helpful feature
is the author index in each volume, which may be consulted to identify contributions by known Africanists. Among general library tools, the Public
Affairs Information Service BULLETIN should always be consulted, both under
specific branches of economics and under Africa and geographical divisions.

        Two other significant bibliographies are those prepared by Jean Viet,
an expert of the International Committee for Social Sciences Documentation:
ASSISTANCE TO UNDER-DEVELOPED COUNTRIES: AN ANNOTATED BIBLIOGRAPHY [title
also in French] (Paris, UNESCO, 1957, 83 p.; Reports and Papers in the
Social Sciences, no. 8) and INTERNATIONAL CO-OPERATION AND PROGRAMMES OF
ECONOMIC AND SOCIAL DEVELOPMENT: AN ANNOTATED BIBLIOGRAPHY [title also in
French] (Paris, UNESCO, 1962, 107 p.; Reports ..., no. 15). Both are

universal in scope and arranged in subject classes, without geographical approach. Annotations are in English for works in that language, in French for other languages. In view of the classed arrangement and lack of geographical index, the usefulness of such works lies chiefly in methods. This is true also of general studies of developing areas, including such authoritative works as Professor Georges Balandier's LE "TIERS-MONDE": SOUS-DEVELOPPEMENT ET DEVELOPPEMENT (new ed. rev. and brought up to date by Alfred Sauvy, Paris, Presses Universitaires de France, 1961, 393 p.; Institut National d'Etudes Démographiques, Travaux et documents, Cahier no. 39).

708. African Bibliographic Center, Washington, D.C. AFRICAN ECONOMIC AFFAIRS: A SELECT BIBLIOGRAPHICAL SURVEY, 1965-66. Washington, 1966. 46 p. (Special Bibliographic Series, v. 4, no. 7)

A list of references over a two-year period, including books, documents of governments and international organizations, and articles selected from a variety of specialist journals, many of them published in Europe and Africa. The editors plan to have continuing supplements. There are over 500 entries, in two sections, general and geographical. The first is in subject subdivision--agriculture, economic policy, planning, conditions and development, finance, foreign economic assistance, etc.--the second by region and country. There is an index of authors.

The African Bibliographic Center publishes A CURRENT BIBLIOGRAPHY OF AFRICAN AFFAIRS (see no. 292), as well as the Special Bibliographic Series. A number of other selected title lists on economic subjects have been issued in that series, e.g., A SELECT BIBLIOGRAPHICAL LISTING ON TECHNICAL ASSISTANCE IN AFRICA, 1961-62 (1963, 11 p.; v. 1, no. 2).

709. Antwerp. Institut Universitaire des Territoires d'Outre-Mer. DEVELOPING COUNTRIES: BIBLIOGRAPHIC COMPENDIUM (CO-OPERATION--ECONOMIC DEVELOPMENT PLANNING). [Title also in Dutch and French] Antwerp, 1964. 157 p.

A selection of about a thousand titles of books, papers, and articles relating to economic development in the so-called Third World. Most are of recent date, 1958-63; in classed arrangement according to the International Decimal System, without distinction by country. There is an author index, as well as a short listing of organizations and journals concerned with developing countries.

710. Bremer Ausschuss für Wirtschaftsforschung. BIBLIOGRAPHIE DER ENTWICKLUNGSPLANE UND -VORHABEN. 11th ed. Bremen, Apr. 1965. 63 l.

A listing of works (mainly periodical articles) on development plans and prospects for various continents and regions. Most entries are in German or English, a few in French. The section on Africa (p. 41-54) lists general works and then entries by country.

711. Centre de Documentation Economique et Sociale Africaine (CEDESA).
      Enquêtes bibliographiques [series]. Bruxelles, 1959-

      For full description see no. 829. In addition to the entry for
      Guy Smet below (no. 722), the following in the series are primarily
      concerned with economic questions:

      a) no. 4.   PROBLEMES FONCIERS ET REGIME DES TERRES: ASPECTS ECO-
                   NOMIQUES, JURIDIQUES ET SOCIAUX. By Théodore
                   Heyse. Bruxelles, 1960. 163 p.

      b) no. 6.   LE PROBLEME DES ROUTES EN REGIONS INTERTROPICALES,
                   SPECIALEMENT L'AFRIQUE. By J. Nuyens. Bruxelles,
                   1961. 133 p.

      c) no. 11. EXPLOITATION, UTILISATION ET POTENTIEL ECONOMIQUE
                   LOCAUX DES BOIS D'AFRIQUE INTERTROPICALE: AS-
                   PECTS JURIDIQUES, SOCIAUX, ECONOMIQUES ET TECH-
                   NIQUES. By Paul Verhaegen. Bruxelles, 1964.
                   3 v. (630 p.). tables.

                        An extensive bibliographic study of litera-
                   ture in English, French, German, etc., on the
                   African lumber industry. The first two brochures
                   list 2,211 references, in alphabetical order by
                   author. The smaller third volume contains several
                   indexes and glossaries.

712. Commission for Technical Co-operation in Africa South of the Sahara
      (CCTA/CSA). INVENTORY OF ECONOMIC STUDIES CONCERNING AFRICA
      SOUTH OF THE SAHARA: AN ANNOTATED READING LIST OF BOOKS, ARTI-
      CLES AND OFFICIAL PUBLICATIONS. [Title also in French] Contendo
      uma relação de títulos em português. London, 1960. xi, 301 p.
      (Publication no. 30, Joint Project no. 4)

      Supplement no. 1. 1962. 159 p.

          A useful bibliography, edited by Miss Peter Ady of St. Anne's
      College, Oxford, with the aid of national correspondents. The period
      covered is largely from 1945 through 1956, though there are a few
      references of 1957 and 1958. Nearly all the 1,377 entries are anno-
      tated (in French or English). A section for general works is followed
      by works arranged by area or country, with subdivision by country
      where appropriate and with subject subclassifications for all. The
      supplement, also edited by Miss Ady, follows the same general format,
      but not all the areas are subdivided by country. All of the 896
      entries are annotated except those pertaining to Portuguese Africa.
      Each of these two volumes contains an author index.

713.   Friedrich-Ebert-Stiftung. Forschungsinstitut. Literatur über
        Entwicklungsländer: Eine Zusammenstellung des wichtigsten
        Schrifttums deutscher, englischer, französischer und russischer
        Sprache (1950-1959-) [series]. Hannover, Verlag für Literatur
        und Zeitgeschehen, 1961- (Schriftenreihe: A. Sozialwissen-
        schaftliche Schritfen)

        Gocd bibliographic surveys of books, reports, and periodical
articles on developing countries in Asia and Africa. In each volume
the first part concerns general questions, the second deals with
Africa as a whole, the third covers Asia, and the fourth is devoted
to individual countries in Africa and Asia, arranged in alphabetical
order. Each volume contains both an author index and an index of
periodicals used in the compilation of the work. The first four
volumes were issued under the Forschungsinstitut's earlier name,
Forschungsstelle.

        By 1968 the following volumes had appeared:

        Vol. I.   EINE ZUSAMMENSTELLUNG DES WICHTIGSTEN SCHRIFTTUMS
                     DEUTSCHER, ENGLISCHER UND FRANZOSISCHER SPRACHE,
                     1950-1959. Bearbeitet in Zusammenarbeit mit dem
                     Institut Selbsthilfe und Sozialforschung, Köln.
                     1961. 702 p.

        Vol. II.   EINE ZUSAMMENSTELLUNG DES WICHTIGSTEN SCHRIFTTUMS
                     RUSSISCHER SPRACHE, 1950-1959. Bearbeitet in
                     Zusammenarbeit mit dem Institut Selbsthilfe und
                     Sozialforschung, Köln. 1961. 88 p.

        Vol. III.   EINE ZUSAMMENSTELLUNG DES WICHTIGSTEN SCHRIFTTUMS
                     DEUTSCHER, ENGLISCHER UND FRANZOSISCHER SPRACHE,
                     1960. Bearbeitet von Ingrid Heidermann. 1963.
                     373 p.

        Vol. IV.   EINE ZUSAMMENSTELLUNG DES WICHTIGSTEN SCHRIFTTUMS
                     RUSSISCHER SPRACHE, 1960. Bearbeitet von Eva Braun
                     und Miroslaw Petruszek. 1963. 112 p.

        Vol. V.   EINE ZUSAMMENSTELLUNG DES WICHTIGSTEN SCHRIFTTUMS
                     DEUTSCHER, ENGLISCHER UND FRANZOSISCHER SPRACHE,
                     1961. Bearbeitet von Vera Lamberg. 1966. 455 p.

        Vol. VI.   EINE ZUSAMMENSTELLUNG DES WICHTIGSTEN SCHRIFTTUMS
                     RUSSISCHER SPRACHE, 1961. Bearbeitet von Miroslaw
                     R. Petruszek. 1966. 135 p.

        Vol. VII.   EINE ZUSAMMENSTELLUNG DES WICHTIGSTEN SCHRIFTTUMS
                     DEUTSCHER, ENGLISCHER UND FRANZOSISCHER SPRACHE, 1962.
                     Bearbeitet von G. Dommick-Herdina. 1967. 495 p.

714. Great Britain. Ministry of Overseas Development (formerly Department of Technical Co-operation). Library. TECHNICAL CO-OPERATION: A MONTHLY BIBLIOGRAPHY. v. 1, no. 1- Jan. 1964- London, The Ministry.

   SUPPLEMENT. no. 1- Apr. 1964- Irregularly issued.

   Bibliography largely limited to official publications of the Commonwealth nations but including reports and bulletins from a few foreign organizations and institutes concerned with technical aid to developing countries. The Department of Technical Co-operation was established in 1961 to administer certain functions formerly performed by the Colonial Office, the Commonwealth Relations Office, and the Foreign Office. In late 1964, with the advent of the Labor Government, it was transformed into the Ministry of Overseas Development (with Mrs. Barbara Castle the first minister).

   A description of the Department of Technical Co-operation was published by H. M. Stationery Office in July 1961 (TECHNICAL ASSISTANCE FROM THE U.K. FOR OVERSEAS DEVELOPMENTS, 43 p.; Misc. no. 1, 1961, Cmnd. 1308); see also OVERSEAS DEVELOPMENT: THE WORK OF THE NEW MINISTRY (London, H. M. Stationery Off., Aug. 1965; Cmnd. 2736).

715. Hazlewood, Arthur, comp. THE ECONOMICS OF DEVELOPMENT: AN ANNOTATED LIST OF BOOKS AND ARTICLES PUBLISHED 1958-1962. London, Published for the Institute of Commonwealth Studies, Oxford University, by Oxford University Press, 1964. 104 p.

   A sequel to THE ECONOMICS OF "UNDER-DEVELOPED" AREAS. It is confined to English-language publications from early 1958 to the end of 1962 (732 numbered items).

716. Hazlewood, Arthur, comp. THE ECONOMICS OF "UNDER-DEVELOPED" AREAS: AN ANNOTATED READING LIST OF BOOKS, ARTICLES, AND OFFICIAL PUBLICATIONS. 2d enl. ed. London, Published for the Institute of Commonwealth Studies by Oxford University Press, 1959. xii, 156 p.

   Reprint of the first edition (1954; p. 1-89) with an additional section of 67 pages, including separate indexes. Classifications are by subject--national income, consumption and investment, population and labor, etc. For reference to parts of Africa the indexes of places must be consulted, where under each place name there is a subject breakdown.

   A succinct overall study, THE ECONOMY OF AFRICA, by Mr. Hazlewood (London, Oxford University Press, 1961, 90 p.; New Africa Library), is specially addressed to the new African reader and is a helpful introduction in this field.

717. Institut d'Etudes Politiques de Bordeaux. Centre d'Etude d'Afrique
        Noire. Bibliothèque. ETUDES D'ECONOMIE AFRICAINE. By Yves
        Péhaut and J. M. Fonsegrive. Paris, Editions A. Pedone, 1970.
        198 p. (Série Afrique noire, no. 1)

        Not available for examination.

718. INTERNATIONAL BIBLIOGRAPHY OF ECONOMICS. BIBLIOGRAPHIE INTERNATIONALE
        DE SCIENCE ECONOMIQUE. v. 1- 1952- Paris, UNESCO, 1955-61;
        London, Stevens & Sons, 1962-63, and Tavistock Publications,
        1963- Annual. (International Bibliography of the Social Sciences)

        Prepared by the International Committee for Social Sciences Docu-
        mentation (with the financial support of UNESCO) and covering broadly
        the international field of writing in all branches of economics. (Vols.
        I-VIII were published by UNESCO in the Documentation in the Social
        Sciences series.) The arrangement is by subject classes, but indexes
        for authors and subjects (geographical areas and countries are also
        listed) provide ready reference to African material. Included is a
        long list of periodicals, with abbreviations by which they are noted
        in the citations.

719. Landskron, William A. OFFICIAL SERIAL PUBLICATIONS RELATING TO
        ECONOMIC DEVELOPMENT IN AFRICA SOUTH OF THE SAHARA: A PRELIM-
        INARY LIST OF ENGLISH-LANGUAGE PUBLICATIONS. Cambridge, Center
        for International Studies, Massachusetts Institute of Technology,
        1961. 44 l.

        This list, which covers a broad range of subjects relating to
        economic development, cites the latest issues of official and a few
        unofficial serial reports known to have been received in the United
        States by Dec. 1960. Most items are dated from 1958 to 1960. Before
        the listing begins, a preliminary page names 25 African states and
        territories for which no English-language periodicals are known to
        exist (included are the states of former French Africa).

        For unofficial serials relating to African economics, see the
        UN Economic Commission for Africa list PERIODICALS RECEIVED IN THE
        UNECA LIBRARY (no. 395) and the list in the INTERNATIONAL BIBLIOG-
        RAPHY OF ECONOMICS (above).

720. Neville-Rolfe, Edmund. ECONOMIC ASPECTS OF AGRICULTURAL DEVELOPMENT
        IN AFRICA: A SELECTIVE ANNOTATED READING LIST OF REPORTS AND
        STUDIES CONCERNING 40 AFRICAN COUNTRIES DURING THE PERIOD 1960-
        1969. Oxford, University of Oxford (Agricultural Economics Re-
        search Institute), 1969. xi, 257 p.

721. ReQua, Eloise G., and Jane Statham. THE DEVELOPING NATIONS: A GUIDE
TO INFORMATION SOURCES CONCERNING THEIR ECONOMIC, POLITICAL,
TECHNICAL AND SOCIAL PROBLEMS. Detroit, Gale Research Co., 1965.
339 p. map (on lining paper). (Management Information Guide,
v. 5)

A bibliographical collection of English-language materials drawn
from scholarly books, documents of governments and international organizations, and periodicals. All these well-annotated sources have been
selected from the holdings of the Library of International Relations at
Chicago. Included is a section devoted to African economic development
(p. 171-179). Agencies and institutions administering development are
described, addresses of publishers and of periodicals cited are listed,
and there are author and title indexes.

722. Smet, Guy. CONTRIBUTION A L'ETUDE DE LA PROGRESSION ECONOMIQUE DE
L'AFRIQUE. Bruxelles, Centre de Documentation Economique et
Sociale Africaine, 1960. 217 p. (Enquêtes bibliographiques, no.
5)

Over 1,500 slightly annotated references to books, pamphlets,
official documents, and articles chosen from a four-page list of
periodicals. Arrangement is alphabetical by author, with a complicated plan of analytical and geographic classificaton by number referring to the entries. Material analyzed runs through the first half
of 1959.

723. Tamuno, Olufunmilayo G., comp. CO-OPERATION FOR DEVELOPMENT: A
BIBLIOGRAPHY ON INTER-STATE RELATIONS IN ECONOMIC, TECHNICAL
AND CULTURAL FIELDS IN AFRICA, 1950-1968. Ibadan, Nigerian
Institute of Social and Economic Research, 1969. 113 p.

Lists 876 items, including periodical articles, government documents, and research papers. Emphasis is on economic, rather than
political, cooperation. Such organizations as OCAM, the African Development Bank, and UDEAC are covered. Arrangement is by subject
(e.g., agriculture, educational and cultural co-operation, finance,
science and technology, transportation and communication and then by
geographic area. There is an author index.

724. United Nations. Dag Hammarskjöld Library. UNITED NATIONS DOCUMENTS
INDEX. v. 1- Jan. 1950- New York. Monthly, with annual
cumulated index.

Comprehensive current list of all documents and publications of
the United Nations and specialized agencies except restricted materials

and internal papers. Arrangement each month is by issuing agency, and entries give full titles, document numbers, dates, and paging. A general index on colored stock is included in each issue and cumulated at the end of the year, furnishing complete coverage of references to persons, places, agencies, and subjects. The number of references on Africa has increased a hundredfold since 1950; during the first five years they were almost entirely limited to documents relating to the trust territories. These can be identified in the UN Department of Public Information volume TEN YEARS OF UNITED NATIONS PUBLICATIONS, 1945 TO 1955: A COMPLETE CATALOGUE (New York, 1955, 217 p.). For the publications of the League of Nations relating to Africa, Hans Aufricht's THE WORK OF THE LEAGUE, 1920-1947 (New York, Columbia University Press, 1951, 682 p.) may be consulted.

For those lost in the intricacies of United Nations documentation, a helpful general work is by Brenda Brimmer, L. R. Wall, Waldo Chamberlin, and Thomas Hovet, A GUIDE TO THE USE OF U.N. DOCUMENTS (Dobbs Ferry, N.Y., Oceana Publications, 1962, 272 p.; New York University Library, Occasional Paper no. 3).

725. United Nations. Dag Hammarskjöld Library. UNITED NATIONS DOCUMENTS INDEX: CUMULATIVE CHECKLIST. v. 1- 1950- New York. Annual.

The 14th edition of the CUMULATIVE CHECKLIST, covering publications of late 1962 and 1963, was issued in 1964 (245 p.). Unlike the INDEX, the volume omits the specialized agencies and is arranged for the full year by the issuing agency. It has no general index. The material on Africa most readily identifiable is that emanating from the Economic and Social Council, Economic Commission for Africa (p. 185-205). Here several thousand entries appear. They include: General series; Information series; Limited series; Meeting records; Economic Committee; Social Committee; Committee on Programme of Works and Priorities; Committee of Nine on the Establishment of an African Development Bank; Seminar on Population Problems (Cairo, 1962); Conference of African Statisticians (3d session); Technical Meeting on Balance of Payments Statistics (ECA/IMF, Rabat, 1963); Working Group of Experts on Foreign Trade Statistics (Addis Ababa, 1963); Working Group on Problems of Estimating Capital Formation (Addis Ababa, 1963); UN Regional Cartographic Conference for Africa (Nairobi, 1963); Conference of Finance Ministers on the Establishment of an African Development Bank (Khartoum, 1963); Meeting of Experts on Housing Problems in Africa (Addis Ababa, 1963); African Institute for Economic Development and Planning; Standing Committee on Industry and Natural Resources (1st session); Meeting of Experts on Iron and Steel in West Africa (Monrovia, 1963); Meeting of Experts on the Integration of Social Development Plans with Over-all Development Planning (Addis Ababa, 1963); Standing Committee on Trade; Expert Panel on Transit Traffic in West Africa; Statistical Bulletins; Standing Committee on Social Welfare and Community Development; Seminar on Social Work Training in Africa (Lusaka, 1963); Workshop on Urban Problems (Lagos, 1963).

726. United Nations. Economic Commission for Africa. Bibliographical
        Series. Addis Ababa, 1961-

        See Part II above, BOOKS ON AFRICA IN THE UNECA LIBRARY, NEW
ACQUISITIONS IN THE UNECA LIBRARY, PERIODICALS RECEIVED IN THE UNECA
LIBRARY, and ANNUALS RECEIVED IN THE UNECA LIBRARY (nos. 336, 364[o],
395, and 409). Although coverage in the UNECA Library goes far beyond
a single field, the emphasis is on economic aspects.

727. United Nations. Economic Commission for Africa. BIBLIOGRAPHY: ECO-
        NOMIC AND SOCIAL DEVELOPMENT PLANS OF AFRICAN COUNTRIES. [Title
        also in French] [New York?] May 1968. 40 p. (E/CN.14/LIB/
        SER.C/4)

        A comprehensive list of the official documentation on economic
and social development planning in Africa, consisting mainly of
preparatory studies and reports, outlines, draft plans and final
plans, periodical progress reports, summaries, and relevant documents.
Arrangement is chronological under country.

728. United Nations. Economic Commission for Africa. LIST OF ECA DOCU-
        MENTS DISTRIBUTED UP TO 1 APRIL 1964. Limited Series. New York,
        1964. 82 p. (E/CN.14/DOC/1)

        This list, in English only, is for limited distribution.

Reference Works

729. Ady, Peter, and Michel Courcier. SYSTEMS OF NATIONAL ACCOUNTS IN
        AFRICA. For the Commission for Technical Co-operation in Africa
        South of the Sahara in co-operation with O.E.E.C. Paris,
        Organisation for European Economic Co-operation, 1960. 232 p.

        The OEEC/UN standardized system of accounts is based on national
concepts of income, consumption, etc., and the French system uses domestic concepts of the same elements. In this work an attempt is made
to draw up a system reconciling the data of the two.

730. "The African Development Bank." JOURNAL OF MODERN AFRICAN STUDIES,
        v. 2, no. 3, Nov. 1964: 442-443.

        A note by Joseph Mubiru in the "Africana" section giving an ex-
planation of the bank, which was approved by the Conference of African
Finance Ministers in their meeting at Khartoum, July 31-Aug. 4, 1963,

and which came into existence on Sept. 10, 1964. The Board of Governors held their inaugural meeting in Lagos in November and decided to have the bank's headquarters in Abidjan. Any independent African state, including the African islands, is eligible for membership. The capital authorized was $250 million (the Board of Governors may increase the amount), divided into 25,000 shares, half paid up, half callable, to which each member government subscribes.

Two printed documents of the United Nations regarding the African Development Bank were published by the United Nations in 1964: AGREEMENT ESTABLISHING THE AFRICAN DEVELOPMENT BANK: PREPARATORY WORK, INCLUDING SUMMARY RECORDS OF THE CONFERENCE OF FINANCE MINISTERS, prepared by the executive secretary of the Economic Commission for Africa (New York, 258 p.; E/CN.14/ADB/28), and the text of the AGREEMENT ESTABLISHING THE AFRICAN DEVELOPMENT BANK (New York, 38 p.; E/CN.14/ADB/36).

A useful visual summarization is given in a Fact Sheet on the back cover of AFRICA REPORT, v. 10, no. 3, Mar. 1965. A three-part article, "Money and Banking in Africa," which includes tables, a map, and a chart of African currencies, appeared in the May 1966 issue of AFRICA REPORT (v. 11, no. 5, p. 45-56). See also Robert Badouin, LES BANQUES DE DEVELOPPEMENT EN AFRIQUE, in section on French-speaking Africa (no. 1571).

731. Afro-Asian Organization for Economic Cooperation. AFRO-ASIAN ECONOMIC REVIEW. 1959- Cairo (Cairo Chamber of Commerce Building). Monthly.

Bulletin carrying factual reports on economic matters of general interest (e.g., GATT, European Common Market) and local news and events. The organization was established at a conference in Cairo, Dec. 8-11, 1958, with 38 countries of Asia and Africa attending. African countries then represented were Algeria, Cameroons, Liberia, Libya, Ethiopia, Ghana, Somalia, Sudan, and Togoland. In the introduction to the PROCEEDINGS (Cairo, 1959) the UAR minister described the group as "another embodiment of the Bandung spirit." At a second conference in Cairo, April 30-May 3, 1960, Morocco and Tunisia were also members and Nigeria an associate member. A third conference was held in New Delhi in Dec. 1961, and a fourth in Karachi in Dec. 1963. The organization publishes Occasional Papers; the first was ECONOMIC UNDERSTANDING AND FOREIGN INVESTMENT: A SURVEY AND SOME SUGGESTIONS (Cairo, 1960, 25 l.). It also issues fact sheets of BASIC INFORMATION ON AFRO-ASIAN COUNTRIES, including statistical tables.

Note: In May 1959 a symposium on an Afro-Asian common market (Colloque sur le Projet d'un Marché Commun Afro-asiatique) was held in Brussels. Its ACTES (272 p.) became its first publication.

The Division de l'Information Outre-Mer of the European Common
Market in Brussels issues statistical publications on trade with
African countries, particularly the francophone member states of
UAMCE.

732. Arkhurst, Frederick S. AFRICA IN THE SEVENTIES AND EIGHTIES: ISSUES
        IN DEVELOPMENT. New York, Praeger, Published in cooperation with
        The Adlai Stevenson Institute of International Affairs, 1970. 420
        p. tables, appendix. (Praeger Special Studies)

Project Africa's political and economic situation in the decades
ahead. Topics covered by experts in their field are: politics; law;
requirements for economic development, the political and administrative
setting for rural development; education in middle Africa; trade and
aid; and economic integration. Included are a Nigerian case study in
agricultural development and a projection of population growth and its
effects in tropical Africa.

733. Banque Centrale des Etats de l'Afrique de l'Ouest. UNE COMMUNAUTE
        ECONOMIQUE OUEST AFRICAINE? Paris, 1968. 200 p. (B.C.E.A.O.
        bibliographie no. 1)

Lists 984 entries for books, articles, and chapters from composite works concerning economic integration in Africa. The partially
annotated entries are arranged by topics covering economic integration
and unity in Europe, South America, Southeast Asia, and the Middle East
as well as Africa. Specific African organizations dealt with include
the OAU, UN Economic Commission for Africa, OCAM, UDEAC, African Development Bank, and the OERS. Transportation studies and publications on
industrial development are also listed. In addition, there is a guide
to organizational abbreviations, an address directory of interstate
organizations for regional economic cooperation, and an index of authors.

734. Benveniste, Guy, and William E. Moran, Jr. HANDBOOK OF AFRICAN ECONOMIC
        DEVELOPMENT. New York, Published for the Stanford Research In-
        stitute by Praeger, 1962. xi, 178 p. tables. (Books That Matter)

Study of ways in which Western aid to African countries can best
be used in coordination with efforts of the countries themselves. Factors of expanded multilateral action and of governmental assistance in
men, money, foreign investments, and trade are examined in general aspects and in specific cases, including analysis of proposals made bi-
laterally and in international councils of European and African powers.
The writers stressed the need for long-term aid geared to careful and
coordinated planning on the part of the recipient countries and strongly
advocated the creation of new international bodies. Tables include
statistics of trade with and aid to Africa in the postwar period.

735. Bohannan, Paul J., and George Dalton, eds. MARKETS IN AFRICA.
         Evanston, Ill., Northwestern University Press, 1962. 762 p.
         maps, tables, diagrs. (African Studies, no. 9)

         Bibliography: p. 739-753.

         Papers written by professional anthropologists, economists, and
geographers on the role of markets, money uses, and external trade in
the nonindustrial economies of 28 societies south of the Sahara.

         For the benefit of general students of economic anthropology and
economic development, MARKETS IN AFRICA: EIGHT SUBSISTENCE ECONOMIES
IN TRANSITION, a new selection edited and with an introduction by the
authors of the original work, has been published in paperback format
in cooperation with the American Museum of Natural History (Garden
City, N.Y., Doubleday, 1965, xiii, 372 p., maps, tables, diagrs;
Anchor Book; Natural History Library). The original bibliography has
been retained.

736. Brokensha, David, ed. ECOLOGY AND ECONOMIC DEVELOPMENT IN TROPICAL
         AFRICA. Berkeley, Institute of International Studies, University
         of California, 1965. 268 p. plate, maps, tables, diagrs., graphs.
         (Research Series no. 9)

         Bibliographical footnotes.

         A series of papers which represent an interdisciplinary approach
to the study of sub-Saharan Africa (excluding South Africa). The
editor's introduction is followed by 13 studies which range from J.
Desmond Clark's "Culture and Ecology in Prehistoric Africa" to
Bernard W. Riley's "Mineral Resources" to Priscilla Copeland Reining's
"Land Resources of the Haya," but in which four recurring themes are
evident: i.e., climate and water; health, nutrition, and population
growth; nationalism; and the application of science.

737. Commission for Technical Co-operation in Africa (CCTA/CSA). METHODO-
         LOGIE DES ENQUETES SUR LES BUDGETS FAMILIAUX. [Paris?] 1964-65.
         6 v. forms. Processed. (Projet conjoint no. 9; CSA publication
         no. 95)

         A study of methodology for home economy surveys in sub-Saharan
Africa. Coverage is as follows: Vol. I, East Africa, Rhodesia and
Nyasaland, Nigeria, South Africa, Ghana (210 p.); Vol. II, Cameroun,
Congo (Brazzaville) (182 p.); Vol. III, Gabon, Madagascar (235 p.);
Vol IV, Ivory Coast, Upper Volta (211 p.); Vol. V, Mali, Niger (140 p.);
Vol. VI, Senegal, general synthesis of the project (130 p.).

738. Conference on Economic Development for Africa, Addis Ababa, 1961.
ECONOMIC DEVELOPMENT FOR AFRICA SOUTH OF THE SAHARA: PROCEEDINGS
OF A CONFERENCE HELD BY THE INTERNATIONAL ECONOMIC ASSOCIATION.
Edited by E. A. G. Robinson. London, Macmillan; New York, St.
Martin's Press, 1964. 743 p.

The conference, at which some 26 papers were read, was one of the
more important among the many meetings held in recent years and was
attended by leading authorities on African economics. Among contributors
were Professors S. H. Frankel, P. T. Bauer, and W. F. Stolper. Most
aspects of African economic development were covered in general or
specific terms.

739. Conference on Public Policy, 3d, Dar es Salaam, 1964. PROBLEMS OF
FOREIGN AID: PROCEEDINGS OF THE CONFERENCE ON PUBLIC POLICY
SPONSORED BY THE UNIVERSITY COLLEGE, DAR ES SALAAM, TANZANIA,
NOVEMBER 1964. London, Nairobi, Published for the Institute of
Public Administration by Oxford University Press, 1965. 289 p.
diagrs. (Institute of Public Administration, Study no. 3)

A collection of 22 papers, supplemented by reports from four
study groups. East Africa is the focus of each of nine papers presented by Paul G. Clark, B. van Arkadie and P. Ndegwa, Peter Newman,
Michael Roemer, Philip Bell, A. R. Jolly, Lionel Cliffe, Roger Scott,
and Henry Bienen. Other African-related papers are those by Vladimir
Martynov on Soviet aid to newly liberated countries, David Carney on
basic prerequisites for foreign aid to Africa, and Edward Rubin on
manpower and aid in Tanzania.

740. Du Jonchay, Ivan. L'INDUSTRIALISATION DE L'AFRIQUE: HISTORIQUE,
ENERGIE, MATIERES PREMIERES, INDUSTRIES, TRANSPORTS, MAIN-
D'OEUVRE ET INFRASTRUCTURE, FINANCES. Paris, Payot, 1953.
344 p. illus., maps. (Bibliothèque géographique)

Encyclopedic treatment, by subject, heavily reinforced by tables
of statistics and maps at the end of the volume. The lack of an index
is somewhat alleviated by a full table of contents.

A previous French survey of economic development of all Africa
by René Laure, LE CONTINENT AFRICAIN AU MILIEU DU SIECLE: PERSPEC-
TIVES ET PROBLEMES DE LA MISE EN VALEUR ECONOMIQUE (Paris, Charles-
Lavauzelle, 1952, xv, 433 p., maps, tables), is in the form of sections
on general factors, followed by paragraph résumés of the situation in
individual territories.

741. The Economist. Intelligence Unit, London. THREE-MONTHLY ECONOMIC
     REVIEW. 1952- London.

     Title varies; also appears as QUARTERLY ECONOMIC REVIEW. These
are series of statistical surveys of individual countries, summarizing
latest data in large processed pamphlets which end with tables of economic activity. Among 70-odd areas covered, a number are useful for
keeping abreast of the latest economic information on Africa.

742. Farer, Tom J., ed. FINANCING AFRICAN DEVELOPMENT. Cambridge,
     Massachusetts Institute of Technology Press, 1965. 245 p. map,
     diagrs., tables.

     Thoughtful and critical analyses, by former M.I.T. Fellows in the
Africa Program, of financial problems that face African countries in
working out their economic development--Tanganyika, Ghana, Nigeria,
Kenya, and Uganda among them.

743. FOUNDATION FOR MUTUAL ASSISTANCE IN AFRICA SOUTH OF THE SAHARA [FAMA].
     London, Joint Secretariat, CCTA/CSA, 1959. 4 p.

     Leaflet explaining the Foundation, which was formed in Feb. 1958
as an auxiliary to CCTA/CSA to promote technical aid in Africa--its
functions to find out about offers of and requests for assistance and
to arrange bilateral agreements over and above existing programs. Its
periodic reports are available from CCTA/CSA headquarters.

744. France. Commission Jeanneney. FRENCH AID: THE JEANNENEY REPORT;
     AN ABRIDGED TRANSLATION OF LA POLITIQUE DE COOPERATION AVEC LES
     PAYS EN VOIE DE DEVELOPPEMENT. London, Overseas Development
     Institute, 1964. 51 p.

     The Jeanneney Commission, under Dr. Jean-Marcel Jeanneney, was
set up by the French government in 1963 to examine the whole problem
of French aid. This translation gives the gist of the report, which
supported the French program as morally right and politically sound.

745. France. Ministère de la Coopération. CINQ ANS DE FONDS D'AIDE ET
     DE COOPERATION, 1959-1964: RAPPORT SUR LA COOPERATION FRANCO-
     AFRICAINE. By Raymond Triboulet. Paris, 1964. 71 p. tables.

     Defense and restatement of French policy, defining the scope and
orientation of the very large-scale French aid. It has been directed
chiefly, but not entirely, to the countries "d'expression française."

746. Gaud, Michel. LES PREMIERES EXPERIENCES DE PLANIFICATION EN AFRIQUE
        NOIRE. Paris, Editions Cujas, 1967. 483 p. charts, graphs,
        tables.

        Bibliography: p. 435-443.

        The first section deals with political and administrative
        structures of planning, the second with the techniques and processes
        of formulating a plan, the third with characteristics of specific
        plans, namely, those of Cameroun, Congo (Brazzaville), Dahomey, Guinea,
        Madagascar, Mali, Mauritania, Niger, Senegal, Togo, Ethiopia, Ghana,
        Kenya, Nigeria, Sierra Leone, Somalia, Sudan, and Tanzania.

747. Germany (Federal Republic). Bundesstelle für Aussenhandelsinformation.
        Wirtschaftlicher Aufbau in Afrika [series]. Köln, 1964- illus.,
        tables.

        A series of brief essays from the Federation Office of Information
        on Foreign Trade concerning economic reconstruction in Africa. There
        are specific topics (e.g., Ghana's Seven-Year Plan) as well as short
        monographs on various economic aspects of particular countries, in-
        cluding Cameroun, Chad, Central African Republic, Guinea, Ivory Coast,
        Libya, Malawi, Mali, Rhodesia, Sierra Leone, Somalia, Tanzania, Togo,
        Uganda, and Zambia. The country studies average around 70 pages and
        have statistical tables as well as photos.

748. Green, Reginald Herbold, and K. G. V. Krishna. ECONOMIC CO-OPERATION
        IN AFRICA: RETROSPECT AND PROSPECT. Based on the International
        Seminar on Economic Co-operation in Africa held at University
        College, Nairobi, Dec. 1965. Nairobi, London, Published for
        University College, Nairobi, by Oxford University Press, 1967.
        160 p.

        Bibliography: p. 120-122.

        Summing up by Green and Krishna of the discussions and papers at
        the seminar (see also no. 751 below). The authors discuss economic
        integration in terms of its aims and potential, its institutional
        framework, and its status as of 1965, and also cover the dynamics of
        the building of economic unions and the role of foreign influence in
        assisting or impeding African economic integration. See also Green
        and Ann Seidmann, UNITY OR POVERTY? THE ECONOMICS OF PAN-AFRICANISM
        (Har   worth, Eng., Penguin, 1968, 364 p.).

749. Hance, William Adams. AFRICAN ECONOMIC DEVELOPMENT. Rev. ed. New York, Published for the Council on Foreign Relations [by] Praeger, 1967. 326 p. maps.

Bibliography: p. 303-309.

The author is Professor of Economic Geography at Columbia University. His book is concerned with the theme of economic development as seen through case studies of various countries (Liberia) or of various sectors of African economies, such as agriculture (Gezira scheme) or industrial development (Volta River Project).

750. Harlander, Hildegard, and Dorothea Mezger. ENTWICKLUNGSBANKEN UND -GESELLSCHAFTEN IN AFRIKA: GRUNDDATEN ZU 95 AFRIKANISCHEN FINANZIERUNGS-INSTITUTIONEN. München, Welforum Verlag, 1969. 211 p. (Afrika-Studien. Sonderreihe Information und Dokumentation, v. 2)

This comprehensive work describes 95 financial institutions in Africa, including state banks, development corporation, and so forth. The authors provide data on the address, date of foundation, legal status, terms of reference, capital, organizational framework, economic policy, and various activities. The work is extremely thorough and accurate. There is appended material, including a table of abbreviations and a list of publications put out by the African section of the IFO-Institut (including a list of bibliographies).

751. Hazlewood, Arthur, ed. AFRICAN INTEGRATION AND DISINTEGRATION: CASE STUDIES IN ECONOMIC AND POLITICAL UNION. Issued under the auspices of the Oxford University Institute of Economics and Statistics and the Royal Institute of International Affairs. London, New York, Oxford University Press, 1967. xii, 414 p. plates, maps, tables.

Bibliography: p. 397-402.

Four of the chapters were presented as papers at the Dec. 1965 International Seminar on Economic Co-operation in Africa held in Nairobi (see no. 748, above). Economic unions in Equatorial Africa, East Africa, and between Senegal and Gambia are covered by, respectively, Peter Robson, Arthur Hazlewood, and Robson (again). The political unions of Nigeria, the Central African Federation, the union of British Somaliland and Italian Somalia, and the union of French and British Cameroon are covered by James O'Connell, Hazlewood, I. M. Lewis, and Edwin Ardener, respectively. Roland Julienne discusses integration in French-speaking Africa and Catherine Hoskyns analyzes the influence of Pan-Africanism on the continent as a whole during 1957-66. Events are described up to the end of 1966. There is an appendix on the 1967 Treaty for East African Co-operation and an index.

752. Herskovits, Melville J., and Mitchell Harwitz, eds. ECONOMIC TRANS-
     ITION IN AFRICA. Evanston, Ill., Northwestern University Press,
     1964. xviii, 444 p. (Northwestern University African Studies,
     no. 12)

     Bibliography: p. 409-425.

     Papers of a Conference on Indigenous and Induced Elements in the
     Economics of Sub-Saharan Africa held at Northwestern University in
     Nov. 1961.

753. Hilling, D., and Hoyle, B. S., eds. SEAPORTS AND DEVELOPMENT IN
     TROPICAL AFRICA. New York, Praeger, 1970. 294 p. 15 photos,
     36 drawings.

     Fourteen essays, based on up-to-date information, which stress
     the important features that distinguish Africa's ports from those serv-
     ing countries with more advanced economic systems. Ports covered in-
     clude those of Ghana, Nigeria, Dahomey, Gabon, Congo (Brazzaville),
     and many others. Case studies are presented by professional geographers
     with first-hand knowledge of the ports they discuss.

754. Jucker-Fleetwood, Erin Elver. MONEY AND FINANCE IN AFRICA: THE EX-
     PERIENCE OF GHANA, MOROCCO, NIGERIA, THE RHODESIAS AND NYASALAND,
     THE SUDAN, AND TUNISIA FROM THE ESTABLISHMENT OF THEIR CENTRAL
     BANKS UNTIL 1962. London, George Allen & Unwin; New York,
     Praeger, 1964. 335 p. illus., tables, graphs, map.

     Bibliography: p. [322]-330.

     A detailed study of the monetary and financial problems of emerging
     African countries. The author begins with an analysis of conditions
     for economic growth, considers the African social, political, and eco-
     nomic background, and then examines the central banks, various other
     financial intermediaries, monetary policy, and modern development plans.
     There are several appendixes and an index.

755. Kamarck, Andrew M. THE ECONOMICS OF AFRICAN DEVELOPMENT. New York,
     Praeger, 1967. 292 p. (Praeger Series on International Economics
     and Development)

     The author discusses the economic and financial position of Africa
     in the world, mineral development, obstacles to industrialization, the
     effect of foreign investment and aid, economic plans, and the relation
     between economic forces, politics, and foreign policy; he also forecasts
     future economic development. The latest statistics given are for 1964.
     There are bibliographies.

756. Kanarek, Jehudi J. ISRAELI TECHNICAL ASSISTANCE TO AFRICAN COUNTRIES. Genève, African Institute, 1969. 115 p.

757. Kirdar, Uner. THE STRUCTURE OF UNITED NATIONS ECONOMIC-AID TO UNDER-DEVELOPED COUNTRIES. The Hague, M. Nijhoff, 1966. xxiv, 361 p.

    Bibliography: p. 348-356.

    Based on the author's Ph.D. thesis for the University of Cambridge, this book examines only those specialized agencies of the UN which finance economic development. The study was undertaken from a legal point of view, but its analysis and arguments take account of economic and political factors. There are three sections: technical assistance, financing of economic development, and retrospect and prospect of international economic aid.

758. Luchaire, François. L'AIDE AUX PAYS SOUS-DEVELOPPES. Paris, Presses Universitaires de France, 1966. 123 p. (Que sais-je? Le point des connaissances actuelles, no. 1227)

    Chapters on the reasons for economic aid, the problems of aid, and aid from international organizations and individual countries.

759. Marcus, Edward, and Mildred R. Marcus. INVESTMENT AND DEVELOPMENT POSSIBILITIES IN TROPICAL AFRICA. New York, Bookman Associates, 1960. 286 p.

    Survey of potentialities of the immense natural resources of tropical Africa north of the Republic of South Africa and south of the Sahara and examination of problems of their development, focused on the attraction of capital from Western Europe and the United States. Much of the information is based on investigations made at first hand by the two economist-writers during a study tour in 1958-59. Their discussion covers many factors which present difficulties for the investor.

760. MEMENTO DE L'ECONOMIE AFRICAINE AU SUD DU SAHARA, 1965. Paris, EDIAFRIC, 1965. 473 p. (BULLETIN DE L'AFRIQUE NOIRE, numéro special, no. 354)

    Comprehensive economic survey, in two parts, the first of French-speaking Africa (Rwanda and Malagasy Republic included), the second of English-speaking countries. For each there is systematic information on agriculture, fisheries, forestry, mines, industries, foreign commerce, budget, development plans, foreign aid programs, business organizations public and private, and stations and centers of research. There are appendixes of statistical tables. A few advertisements are scattered throughout.

761. Millikan, Max F., and Donald L. M. Blackmer, eds. THE EMERGING
      NATIONS: THEIR GROWTH AND UNITED STATES POLICY. A study from
      the Center for International Studies, Massachusetts Institute of
      Technology. Boston, Little, Brown, 1961. 171 p.

      Bibliography: p. 161-168.

      An extensive revision of a document submitted by the Center for
International Studies of MIT to the Senate Committee on Foreign Re-
lations (UNITED STATES FOREIGN POLICY: ECONOMIC, SOCIAL AND POLITICAL
CHANGE IN THE UNDERDEVELOPED COUNTRIES AND ITS IMPLICATIONS FOR UNITED
STATES POLICY, Washington, U.S. Govt. Print. Off., 1960, 98 p.; 86th
Cong., 2d sess., Committee print). This is an "interdisciplinary"
analysis in which experts in several branches of the social sciences--
economists, political scientists, sociologists, psychologists--shared.
An appendix gives summary tables of suggested levels of international
aid for individual countries. These are derived from a study by
Professor P. N. Rosenstein-Rodan, "International Aid for Underdeveloped
Countries," REVIEW OF ECONOMICS AND STATISTICS, May 1961. The book
ends with a selected bibliography on underdeveloped areas and international assistance.

762. Neumark, S. Daniel. FOREIGN TRADE AND ECONOMIC DEVELOPMENT IN AFRICA:
      A HISTORICAL PERSPECTIVE. Stanford, Calif., Food Research Insti-
      tute, Stanford University, 1964. 222 p. maps. (Miscellaneous
      Publications, no. 14)

      Bibliographic references at the end of chapters.

      Well-balanced summary of historic aspects--early contacts, European
settlement, slave trade, colonial development of transportation, mining,
agricultural exports, etc.--and of international trade and economic
development at present.

763. Okigbo, P. N. C. AFRICA AND THE COMMON MARKET. Evanston, Ill.,
      Northwestern University Press, 1967. 183 p.

      The author was a negotiator sent from Nigeria to determine what re-
lationship his country would have to the European Economic Community.
Included are the historical background of the EEC, the 1963 Yaoundé
Convention, the background and terms of Nigerian association, possibilities for an African Common Market, and future prospects for Africa
with respect to the EEC.

764. Overseas Development Institute, London. ANNUAL REPORT. London. (3d
      ed., 1964)

The function of this institute, set up in 1960 and financed by the Ford Foundation and British industrial and commercial enterprises (William Clark, director), is to stimulate and guide public discussion of development problems in newly developing areas. It performs reference services, organizes meetings, and publishes research studies. The British aid system is the subject of the major study to date, which is coming out in six booklets on separate aspects. (See also translation of the Jeanneney Report on French aid, no. 744.)

765.   OXFORD REGIONAL ECONOMIC ATLAS: AFRICA. Prepared by P. H. Ady and the Cartographic Department of the Clarendon Press, with the assistance of A. H. Hazlewood. Oxford, Clarendon Press, 1965. 60, 164 p. maps, tables.

For description see no. 707.

766.   PARALLELES. no. 1- Feb. 1968- Genève, SESAF. Quarterly.

SESAF (Société Anonyme pour les Echanges entre la Suisse et l'Afrique) is an organization incorporated in 1966 for the purpose of promoting Afro-Swiss trade, maintains a library, carries out market research and other studies, and in 1966-67 published six issues of HANDELSBULLETIN MIT INFORMATIONEN UBER AFRIKA FUR DIE SCHWEIZ. This bulletin has now been replaced by PARALLELES and SESAF INFORMATIONS, issued bimonthly, on trade with Africa. Each issue of PARALLELES presents a survey either of one African country or of a branch of Swiss industry in Africa, in addition to a column, open to African contributors, commenting on some aspect of African economics.

767.   Reader, D. H. "A Survey of Categories of Economic Activities among the Peoples of Africa." AFRICA (London), v. 34, Jan. 1964: 28-45.

Based on a review of the documentation of tribal economies made for the South African National Institute for Personnel Research. A bibliography and tables are included.

768.   Rivkin, Arnold. AFRICA AND THE EUROPEAN COMMON MARKET: A PERSPECTIVE. Denver, University of Denver, 1964. 61 p. (Social Science Foundation and Department of International Relations, Monograph Series in World Affairs, no. 2).

In this paper delivered in an inter-university faculty seminar series in Feb. 1964, Dr. Rivkin, then director of the African program at MIT, outlined the background of Africa after the formation of the OAU at Addis Ababa in 1963, which was a triumph for the former Monrovia bloc. He then explained, first, the terms of the Treaty of Rome, Mar.

1957, which set the association of (then) French and Belgian African territories with the EEC--the "highwater mark of the 'Eurafrica' movement"--and, second, the post independence convention of association, the Yaoundé Convention of Dec. 20, 1962. The monograph includes extensive tables of aid given, a description of new institutions, and a summary of attitudes of African states and prospects for an African Common Market.

The text of the Yaoundé Convention was published by the EEC at Luxembourg in 1963: CONVENTION D'ASSOCIATION ENTRE LA COMMUNAUTE ECONOMIQUE EUROPEENNE ET LES ETATS AFRICAINS ET MALGACHES ASSOCIES A CETTE CONVENTION ET DOCUMENTS ANNEXES (129 p.). For later information, recourse must be had to current economic journals and such organs for African news as WEST AFRICA.

769. Sawyer, Carole A. COMMUNIST TRADE WITH DEVELOPING COUNTRIES: 1955-65. New York, Praeger, 1966. 126 p. tables. (Praeger Special Studies in International Economics and Development)

Bibliography: p. 121-126.

The author, a U.S. government economist, aims to evaluate the claims of Communist countries about their trade with developing economies and seeks an economic rather than a political explanation for this trade. All the countries of Africa except South Africa are included in her general discussion. The book begins with an analysis of the doctrinal background and then covers commodity patterns, the economic rationale of the trade, communist aid and expansion of trade, foreign trade problems, and prospects. Statistical tables give data for 1955 and 1960-64.

770. Scientific Council for Africa. COLLOQUE SUR LES ROUTES. SYMPOSIUM ON ROADS, ABIDJAN, 1963. London, CCTA, 1963. 209 p. maps, charts. (CSA Publication no. 90)

This symposium upon a primary aspect of technical development in Africa includes papers and recommendations of the experts on technical problems of road building.

771. Stokke, Baard Richard. SOVIET AND EASTERN EUROPEAN TRADE AND AID IN AFRICA. New York, Praeger, 1967. xx, 326 p. (Praeger Special Studies in International Economics and Development)

Bibliography: p. [297]-317.

A work concerned with economic facts and analysis without political commentary. Economic relations during the decade 1955/56-1965/66 are covered.

772. Union Africaine et Malgache de Coopération Economique. ETUDE MONO-
     GRAPHIQUE DE TRENTE ET UN PAYS AFRICAINS. Paris, Compagnie
     Générale d'Etudes et Recherches pour l'Afrique (COGERAF), 1964.
     4 v. maps, tables, graphs.

     Includes bibliographies.

     Prepared with the assistance of specialists from the Ministère
     de la Coopération. An introduction provides a comparison of 31
     countries of sub-Saharan Africa on a demographic, sociological, and,
     especially, economic basis. Each country is then surveyed separately,
     with emphasis on economic aspects.

773. United Nations. Conference on the Application of Science and Tech-
     nology for the Benefit of the Less Developed Areas, Geneva, 1963.
     SCIENCE AND TECHNOLOGY FOR DEVELOPMENT. New York, United Nations,
     1963-64. 8 v.

     Report for the public on the conference, for which 1,839 papers
     were submitted and discussed in 93 sessions covering all phases of
     development. These volumes summarize in nontechnical language the
     contents of papers and talks. Vol. VIII, PLENARY PROCEEDINGS, is a
     reference volume, including the list of papers and index. Many
     papers were issued separately. Among those relating specifically to
     Africa were LES SERVICES STATISTIQUES EN AFRIQUE, by A. Ficatier
     (Genève, 1963), and UN PROGRAMME INTERNATIONAL DE DOCUMENTATION
     ECONOMIQUE ET SOCIALE AFRICAINE, by J. Cuyvers (Genève, 1963).

774. United Nations. Department of Economic and Social Affairs. INDUSTRIAL
     ESTATES IN AFRICA. New York, United Nations, 1965. 52 p. plans.
     (ST/CID/5)

     This is the fourth in a UN series of studies and reports on prob-
     lems relating to industrial estates. Contents include a "Report of
     the U.N. Seminar on Industrial Estates in the Region of the Economic
     Commission for Africa," a study of "Planning, Design and Construction
     of Industrial Estates with Particular Reference to Africa," and a sur-
     vey of industrial estate plans and projects by country reflecting de-
     velopments as of early 1965. An important conclusion of the seminar
     is that industrial estates, through their promotion of small-scale
     industries, "may facilitate a breakthrough of the indigenous entrepreneur
     into industrial activities."

775. United Nations. Economic Commission for Africa. ECONOMIC BULLETIN FOR
     AFRICA. v. 1, no. 1- Jan. 1961- Addis Ababa, Published for the
     Secretariat of the Economic Commission for Africa. Irregular.
     (E/CN.14/62, 202-)

In the first issue of the year (in 1963 only one issue was published), this official journal of ECA is in two parts. Part A covers
current economic trends, with general surveys of world trends and their
impacts on the countries importing raw materials, of recent trends in
African trade, and of trends in export commodities of the African region.
Part B contains special articles on various aspects of economic life
and a survey of development in individual countries. The back inside
cover is a statistical map of Africa. There is a separate brochure of
statistics. The single issue of the third volume, Jan. 1963, has at
the end a list of UNECA publications, with some description of each.
See also the monthly STATISTICAL BULLETIN FOR AFRICA.

776. United Nations. Economic Commission for Africa. ECONOMIC CONDITIONS
      IN AFRICA IN RECENT YEARS. 1968. 202 p. (E/CN.14/435)

777. United Nations. Economic Commission for Africa. ECONOMIC SURVEY OF
      AFRICA: Vol. I, WESTERN SUB-REGION; REPUBLIC OF SOUTH AFRICA.
      New York, 1966- xi, 230 p. tables. (E/CN.14/370)

      Bibliographical footnotes.

      This report updates the 1959 publication, ECONOMIC SURVEY OF
AFRICA SINCE 1950, issued by the UN's Department of Economic and
Social Affairs, and also studies the period treated there in greater
detail. Furthermore, the report provides abundant information on
current economic development problems, plans, and prospects. Future
volumes will deal with North, East, and Central Africa (as those regional divisions are defined by the UN). For further annotation on
the first volume, see nos. 1311 and 2957. See also no. 792.

778. United Nations. Economic Commission for Africa. REPORT. 1st session,
      Dec. 29, 1958-Jan. 6, 1959- New York. (E/CN.14/-)

      This and other reports issued as supplements to the OFFICIAL
RECORDS of the Economic and Social Council (probably issued also in
Addis Ababa).

      UNECA has headquarters in Addis Ababa, where most of its many re-
ports and other documents are prepared, though some are published in
New York. The fourth session was held from Feb. 19 to Mar. 3, 1962,
and a two-page list of its documents and resolutions appears in the
UNITED NATIONS REVIEW of May 1962 (p. 49-50). These include many
special studies and reports, usually in mimeographed pamphlet form.
Among the more substantial are the following:

a) REPORT OF THE FACILITIES AVAILABLE FOR THE TRAINING OF
   AFRICANS IN ECONOMICS, STATISTICS AND RELATED FIELDS
   OF STUDY. Prepared by UNESCO...Dec. 7, 1959. 35, 11,
   36, 2, 8, 5 p. (includes appendixes). (E/CN.14/35)

b) THE IMPACT OF WESTERN EUROPEAN INTEGRATION ON AFRICAN TRADE
   AND DEVELOPMENT. Dec. 7, 1960. 101 p. (E/CN.14/72)

c) INTERNATIONAL ECONOMIC ASSISTANCE TO AFRICA. Nov. 16, 1960.
   35 p. (E/CN.14/88)

d) ECONOMIC AND SOCIAL CONSEQUENCES OF RACIAL DISCRIMINATORY
   PRACTICES. Jan. 6, 1962. 216 p. plus corr. 1. diagrs.
   (E/CN.14/132)

e) THE CO-OPERATIVE MOVEMENT IN AFRICA. Jan. 15, 1962. 208 p.
   (E/CN.14/133)

f) REPORT OF THE CONFERENCE ON INDUSTRIAL COORDINATION IN WEST
   AFRICA. Oct. 30, 1964. 11 p. plus annexes. (E/CN.14/324)

g) SURVEY OF MONETARY INSTITUTIONS IN AFRICA. 1964. 88 p. plus
   annexes. (E/CN.14/STC/AMA2)

779. United Nations. Economic Commission for Africa. A SURVEY OF ECO-
      NOMIC CONDITIONS IN AFRICA, 1960-1964. New York, 1968. 242 p.
      graphs, tables. E/CN.14/401)

    First of a projected annual survey; the last such overview was
ECONOMIC SURVEY OF AFRICA SINCE 1950 (United Nations, Dept. of Economic and Social Affairs, New York, 1959, E/CN.14/28). Parts 1 and 2
cover such facets of economic and social development as population,
agriculture, industry, transportation, trade, health, education, and
labor. Part 3 presents a social study of development planning in
Africa.

780. United Nations. Office of Public Information. THE UNITED NATIONS AND
      AFRICA: A COLLECTION OF BASIC INFORMATION ON THE ECONOMIC AND
      SOCIAL ACTIVITIES OF THE UNITED NATIONS AND RELATED AGENCIES IN
      AFRICA. New York, United Nations, distributed by the United
      Nations Office of Public Information, External Relations Division,
      1962. 262 p. tables, maps.

    Issued in Feb. 1962.

    The introduction by Mekki Abbas, executive secretary of the UN
Economic Commission for Africa, is followed by an explanation of the
functions and organizations of the Commission. Next are detailed and

statistically supported reports of UN programs for technical cooperation
and of programs carried out by the 11 related agencies. A section is
given to UN civilian operations in the Congo, and another to international economic assistance to Africa. The appendixes give various
tabulated country-by-country surveys, a list of addresses of UN and related agency officers and representatives, and a glossary interpreting
initials used to designate organizations and programs.

781. United Nations Educational, Scientific and Cultural Organization. IN-
      STITUTIONS ENGAGED IN ECONOMIC AND SOCIAL PLANNING IN AFRICA:
      DIRECTORY. Prepared for UNESCO by the International Social Science
      Council and the Centre d'Analyse et de Recherche Documentaires
      pour l'Afrique Noire; prepared under the responsibility of Michèle
      Cser. Paris, 1967. 155 p.

The directory aims for world-wide coverage, but the regions best
represented are North America, Western Europe, and Israel. The 300 private and public institutions included are listed alphabetically under
country where located. For each organization data generally given include address, telephone, type, founding date, purpose, officers, and
details concerning projects.

782. U.S. Agency for International Development. FY [FISCAL YEAR] PROJECTS,
      BY COUNTRY AND FIELD OF ACTIVITY, 1962. Washington, 1963. 108 p.
      (Statistics and Reports Division, W-132)

For other reports of U.S. Economic relations with Africa, see current numbers of the MONTHLY CATALOG OF UNITED STATES GOVERNMENT PUBLI-
CATIONS.

783. U.S. Bureau of International Commerce. AFRICA: SALES FRONTIER FOR U.S.
      BUSINESS. Washington, U.S. Dept. of Commerce, 1963. 121 p. (A
      supplement to INTERNATIONAL COMMERCE)

Bibliography: p. 115-120.

Chapters on economic policies for a changing Africa present U.S.
business interests (tables), AID program and its implications, export
outlook contrasts in selected countries, the Soviet bloc economic of-
fensive, Ghana (a case study), African regional groupings, and private
investment outlook contrasts in selected countries. In the appendixes
there are tables and maps.

Note: For the help of Western business interests in Africa there
is a wide variety of slight but useful material. The Bureau of International Commerce of the U.S. Department of Commerce regularly issues
reports in its World Trade Information Service. A checklist of avail-

able titles in Dec. 1962 includes well over a hundred on Africa and
the separate countries. This listing is reproduced in an article in
the AFRICAN STUDIES BULLETIN, v. 5, no. 3, Oct. 1962, by the Department's
director of the Africa Division of the Bureau of International Programs,
Bernard Blankenheimer. Among the series for each country are ESTABLISH-
ING A BUSINESS IN [ ], ECONOMIC DEVELOPMENTS IN [ ], PREPARING SHIPMENTS
TO [ ], and LIVING CONDITIONS IN [ ]. A comparable British series is
issued by the Board of Trade in London, HINTS TO BUSINESS MEN VISITING
[ ], little pamphlets of elementary information regarding travel, trade,
credits, etc. The Austrian Bundeskammer der Gewerblichen Wirtschaft has
a series of booklets of OESTERREICHS AUSSENHANDEL which relate to individual countries of Africa and give the same sort of data. An Italian
series, GUIDA PER L'ESPORTATORE ITALIANO IN [GHANA, etc.], consists of
leaflets containing the same practical notes.

For current news of African business and economics the WALL STREET
JOURNAL INDEX may prove helpful. There are notes on current economic
developments in the issues of AFRICA REPORT; the Fact Sheet on the back
cover (until its disappearance after Aug. 1965) sometimes tabulated
useful information, e.g., Jan. 1963, "Currencies of the Independent
African States." See also no. 566 for details on all aspects of economics.

For individual African countries newsletters and reports published
by various national and local Chambers of Commerce are of importance.
Some of these are noted in the area sections.

784. U.S. Congress. House. AFRICA BRIEFING. Hearings before the Sub-
      committee on Africa, 88th Cong., 1st sess., Feb. 27, 1963. Wash-
      ington, U.S. Govt. Print. Off., 1963. 20 p.

Statement of the Assistant Secretary of State for Africa, the Hon.
G. Mennen Williams, with supporting statistics. The statement, presented every session, affords a concentrated picture of American economic and political relations with Africa.

In the huge volume of Hearings on Foreign Operations appropriations
before the House Appropriations Committee (88th Cong., 1st sess., 1963,
Part 3, ECONOMIC ASSISTANCE PROGRAM: GENERAL STATEMENT--AFRICA--EUROPE--
FAR EAST, 1963, 1132 p.), material on Africa can be identified through a
detailed index.

For other U.S. reports and papers on Africa, see the MONTHLY CATALOG
OF UNITED STATES GOVERNMENT PUBLICATIONS.

STATISTICS

Bibliography

785. United Nations. Economic Commission for Africa. BIBLIOGRAPHY OF
          AFRICAN STATISTICAL PUBLICATIONS, 1950-1965. [Title also in
          French] [Addis Ababa?] Dec. 1966. 256 p. Processed.
          (E/Cn.14/LIB/SER.C/2)

      The second issue (the first was put out in Apr. 1962) of this
valuable listing of official documents, serials, and reports from
African countries, including some significant unofficial publications
on African statistics on all subjects. Entries are listed by region
and by country (Algeria to Zambia). Each publication is given a broad
subject classification and reference number.

Reference Works

786. Afrika-Instituut. AFRICA: MAPS AND STATISTICS. no. 1-10, July 1962-
          Apr. 1965. Pretoria, Africa Institute. 35 cm.

      See no. 460.

787. Harvey, Joan M. STATISTICS AFRICA, SOURCES FOR MARKET RESEARCH.
          Beckenham, Kent, Eng., CBD Research Ltd., 1970. 175 p.

      Arranged alphabetically by country with the first section on
Africa as a whole. Each country section contains the address of the
central statistical office and other organizations which produce statistics, with a description of each organization and also of the libraries
housing statistical information. The principal bibliographies of statistics and the major statistical publications are arranged under the
following topics: general, production, external trade, internal distribution, population, standard of living. Each statistical publication
cited is annotated.

788. Inter-African Conference on Statistics. [Publications] London, CCTA/
          CSA, 195-

      The first meeting of the Inter-African Conference on Statistics
was held in Salisbury in 1951, the second in Lourenço Marques in 1957.
A semiannual BULLETIN was begun in 1955, published in Lisbon.

789. International Association for Research in Income and Wealth, Conference, Addis Ababa, 1961. AFRICAN STUDIES IN INCOME AND WEALTH. Edited by L. H. Samuels. London, Bowes & Bowes; Chicago, Quadrangle Books, 1963. xviii, 433 p. diagrs., tables.

Includes bibliographies.

Sixteen papers by statisticians and economists on the practical problems of income accounting in Africa.

790. Martin, Geoffrey J. AFRICA IN STATISTICS. n.p., 1961. 49 p. (Department of Geography, Eastern Michigan University, Spring 1961)

A compilation of data from various sources, which are not quoted. Pages are divided by country, and data are given on such widely diversified subjects as medical care facilities, percentage illiteracy, number of telephones, vegetation, geology, and the number of African students in the United States. There is no commentary, just tables, with figures of 1957-60.

791. United Nations. Economic Commission for Africa. AFRICAN STATISTICS. Addis Ababa, 1963. 46 p. (E/CN.14/202, Annex 1)

This Jan. 1963 issue of the ECA ECONOMIC BULLETIN FOR AFRICA is a compilation of the most recent statistics available at date of issuance. Statistical information is a regular feature of the BULLETIN.

792. United Nations. Economic Commission for Africa. FOREIGN TRADE STATISTICS OF AFRICA: Series A, DIRECTION OF TRADE; Series B, TRADE BY COMMODITY. [Title also in French] New York, 1962- (E/CN.14/STAT/SER.A [and] B)

Series A, no. 9. 1967. 92 p. map.

Series B, no. 11. 1967. 302 p. map.

In Series A, figures are listed for imports of each country by country of origin and figures for exports by country of destination. Series B gives cumulative half-yearly data on African commodity trade by regions and countries of provenance and destination.

793. United Nations. Statistical Office. 1964 SUPPLEMENT TO THE WORLD TRADE ANNUAL: TRADE OF THE INDUSTRIALIZED NATIONS WITH EASTERN EUROPE AND THE DEVELOPING NATIONS: Vol. III, AFRICA. New York, Walker and Co., 1965. xlii, 703 p.

Separate import and export data for 49 geographical entities are provided at each of the levels of commodity detail of the UN Standard International Trade Classification (SITC). Data are based on statistics for 1964 reported by 23 industrial countries. Their statistics have been rearranged to bring together figures for countries in regions for which current data are not available.

794. United Nations. Statistical Office. STATISTICAL YEARBOOK. ANNUAIRE STATISTIQUE. 1948- New York, 1949-

17th issue, for 1965. 1966. 747 p.

Summary of international statistics covering population, agriculture, mining, manufacturing, trade, finance, social statistics, education, etc., with tables as closely up to date as possible and often going back to prewar figures. Sources are given for the information if other than the Statistical Office. The tabulated figures are in subject classes, with country breakdown for most. There is a separate country index.

795. U.S. Agency for International Development. Office of Program and Policy Coordination. Statistics and Reports Division. A.I.D. ECONOMIC DATA BOOK: AFRICA. Washington [distributed by Clearinghouse for Federal and Scientific and Technical Information] 1967. 1 v. various pagings. maps. (AID 3/00/03089)

AGRICULTURE

Note: Material on the physical aspects of agriculture is also cited in sections of Chapter 29.

Bibliographies

796. De Benko, Eugene. "Agricultural Change and Rural Development in Sub-Saharan Africa: A Bibliography." RURAL AFRICANA, no. 3, Fall 1967: 38-67.

Arrangement is alphabetical by author, in two sections, the first covering books, monographs, and government publications, the second periodical articles. Publications in French, German, and English are listed.

797. Lebrun, J., and P. C. Lefèvre. FERTILITE DES SOLS ET ELEMENTS DE
       SOCIOLOGIE RURALE EN AFRIQUE AU SUD DU SAHARA. Bruxelles, CEDESA,
       1964. 182 p. (Enquêtes bibliographiques, no. 10)

       Some 1,400 references to books, serials, series, and periodical
articles on African agriculture. Entries are on cards on recto only,
suitable for filing.

798. Lefèvre, P. C. ALIMENTATION DES POPULATIONS AFRICAINES AU SUD DU
       SAHARA. Bruxelles, CEDESA, 1965. xiv, 221 p. (Enquêtes
       bibliographiques, no. 13)

       _____. LES PAYSANNATS EN AFRIQUE AU SUD DU SAHARA. Bruxelles,
       CEDESA, 1965. 215 p. (Enquêtes bibliographiques, no. 12)

       Both of these books are based on the library collections of the
Institut National pour l'Etude Agronomique de Congo (INEAC) in Brussels.
Arrangement is alphabetical by author and most of the entries are for
periodical articles, although a few books are included, and most are
annotated. The first book lists 985 entries on the food of African
populations south of the Sahara. The 844 references in the second book
concern farming and agriculture in sub-Saharan Africa, covering such
topics as agricultural systems, social and economic improvements,
mechanization of farming, agricultural credit, and crop diseases. Each
book contains subject and geographic indexes as well as a list of periodicals analyzed.

799. U.S. Library of Congress. General Reference and Bibliography Division.
       AGRICULTURAL DEVELOPMENT SCHEMES IN SUB-SAHARAN AFRICA: A BIBLI-
       OGRAPHY. Compiled by Ruth S. Freitag. Washington, U.S. Govt.
       Print. Off., 1963. xii, 189 p.

       An extensively annotated bibliography, prepared for the African
Section with the assistance of a panel of consultants. The introduction,
by Miss Freitag and Dr. Walter Deshler, gives a full outline of the subject, which is broad enough to cover most general writings on agriculture
in Africa. This work has been commended as a model of subject bibliography.

Reference Works

800. AGRICULTURAL ECONOMICS BULLETIN FOR AFRICA. no. 1- Sept. 1962-
       Addis Ababa, ECA-FAO Joint Agriculture Division. Irregular.

       Joint publication of the United Nations Economic Commission for
Africa and the Food and Agriculture Organization of the United Nations,
to appear "at intervals during the year" in English and French editions.

The object of the BULLETIN is "to spread the experiences of African countries in the field of agricultural development, as widely as possible, throughout the continent." It includes articles of monograph length, short notes on individual experiments, and a list of future meetings.

801. Allan, William. THE AFRICAN HUSBANDMAN. New York, Barnes & Noble, 1965. 505 p.

This is a study on the agricultural economies of Africa. It is divided in four parts: Part I, "The Basis of African Land Use," sets out the relation between the African husbandman and the soil and vegetation of his countryside. Part II examines husbandry systems in Africa. Part III discusses hunters and herdsmen. Part IV, "Change and Development," considers patterns of population distribution and land tenure. The book concludes with a chapter on "New Horizons" in which the author sets out the enormous needs and aspirations of the new African nations, and considers the extent to which African agriculture can contribute to them.

802. Biebuyck, Daniel, ed. AFRICAN AGRARIAN SYSTEMS: STUDIES PRESENTED AND DISCUSSED AT THE SECOND INTERNATIONAL AFRICAN SEMINAR AT LOVANIUM UNIVERSITY, LEOPOLDVILLE, 1960. London, International African Institute, 1963. Reprinted 1966. 407 p. maps.

803. De Wilde, John C., and others. EXPERIENCES WITH AGRICULTURAL DEVELOPMENT IN TROPICAL AFRICA: Vol. I, THE SYNTHESIS; Vol. II, THE CASE STUDIES. Baltimore, Published for the International Bank for Reconstruction and Development by the Johns Hopkins Press, 1967. 254, 466 p. maps, tables, diagrs.

Bibliographical footnotes.

A valuable contribution by Mr. de Wilde, formerly acting director of the Economic Staff of the World Bank, assisted by Peter F. M. McLoughlin, André Guinard, Thayer Scudder, and Robert Maubouché. Since agriculture tends to trail other sectors of the economy in tropical Africa, yet continues to absorb the majority of the population and will probably long remain the basis of the economy, the writers evaluate in Vol. I the factors involved in securing successful agricultural development. Topics of discussion as illustrated by chapter headings, are: principal features of African agriculture; the state of knowledge (the natural milieu and research); the rural society; labor, land, intensification, and farm economics; implements and machinery; land tenure and land use; agricultural extension, training, and education; credit, marketing, and cooperatives. Vol. II presents case studies of five areas in Kenya, two in Mali, two in Uganda, and one each in Tanzania, Upper Volta, Chad, and the Ivory Coast. Each volume includes an index.

804. Dumont, René. L'AFRIQUE NOIRE EST MAL PARTIE. Paris, Coll. Esprit "Frontière ouverte," 1962. 286 p.

Eng. tr. FALSE START IN AFRICA. New York, Praeger, 1966. 288 p.

This widely noticed book by a French agronomist and political scientist, though applicable chiefly to francophone countries, has implications for agricultural economics in most of sub-Saharan Africa. The author attacks the waste and prestige expenditures of the new cadres of African bureaucracy and urges vigorous agricultural development as the best use of natural resources.

805. Food and Agriculture Organization of the United Nations. FAO AFRICA SURVEY: REPORT ON THE POSSIBILITIES OF AFRICAN RURAL DEVELOPMENT IN RELATION TO ECONOMIC AND SOCIAL GROWTH. New York, 1961. xvi, 235 p. charts, maps, tables; bibliog. footnotes. (Conference C 61/15) Rome, 1962. xiv, 168 p. fold. map, tables.

A survey by an international team of experts, who visited 33 countries (omitting 22 others) and studied available reports. Special reports were prepared for seven countries, and Ghana supplied a review of agricultural development plans. These materials are the substance of this general survey, in three parts: 1, "The Setting"; 2, "Technical Change and the Balanced Use of Resources"; 3, "Some Problems of Rural Development." The last chapter draws conclusions regarding administrative, financial, and technical phases of rural development.

806. FOOD RESEARCH INSTITUTE STUDIES. v. 1, no. 1- Feb. 1960- Stanford, Calif., Food Research Institute, Stanford University. 3 times a year.

New title, 1968-, FOOD RESEARCH INSTITUTE STUDIES IN AGRICULTURAL ECONOMICS, TRADE, AND DEVELOPMENT.

The Food Research Institute, established in 1921, has been engaged in studies of African food and agricultural economics since 1953, and has issued numerous books and pamphlets. Its journal of scholarly research frequently carries monograph-length articles (also available as reprints) on economic aspects of food in Africa. Among them are the following:

a)   v. 1, no. 2, 1960. "Economic Man in Africa." By William O. Jones. p. 107-134.

b)   v. 2, no. 1, Feb. 1961. "Food and Agricultural Economies of Tropical Africa: A Summary View." By William O. Jones. p. 3-20.

c)   v. 2, no. 2, May 1961. "The Food Economies of Urban Middle Africa:
      The Case of Ghana." By Thomas T. Poleman. p. 121-175.

d)   v. 2, no. 3, Nov. 1961. "Urban Food Expenditure Patterns in Tropical
      Africa." By Hiromitsu Kaneda and Bruce F. Johnston. p. 229-
      275.

e)   v. 3, no. 1, Feb. 1962. "Consumption of Exotic Consumer Goods as
      an Indicator of Economic Achievement in Ten Countries of
      Tropical Africa." By William O. Jones and Christian Mérat.
      p. 35-60.

f)   v. 3, no. 2, May 1962. "Agricultural Change in Uganda, 1945-1960."
      By G. B. Masefield. p. 87-124.

g)   v. 3, no. 3, Nov. 1962. "An Agroclimatic Mapping of Africa." By
      Merrill K. Bennett. p. 195-216.

h)   v. 4, no. 1, Feb. 1963. "Agricultural Change in Ruanda-Urundi,
      1945-1960." By Philippe P. Leurquin. p. 39-89.

i)   v. 4, no. 2, 1963-64. "African Agricultural Development in Southern
      Rhodesia, 1945-1960." By R. W. M. Johnson. p. 165-223.

j)   v. 5, no. 1, 1965. "Patterns of Bread Consumption in Nigeria."
      By Peter Kilby. p. 3-18.

k)   v. 5, no. 2, 1965. "Environment, Technical Knowledge, and Economic
      Development in Tropical Africa." By William O. Jones. p. 101-
      116.

l)   v. 5, no. 2, 1965. "Agricultural Change in the Belgian Congo:
      1945-1960." By V. Drachoussoff. p. 137-200.

m)   v. 5, no. 3, 1965. "Agricultural Change in Nyasaland: 1945-1960."
      By R. W. Kettlewell. p. 220-285.

n)   v. 6, no. 2, 1966. "Typology in Development Theory: The Land Sur-
      plus Economy (Nigeria)." By Gerald K. Helleiner. p. 181-194.

o)   v. 6, no. 2, 1966. "Agricultural Change in Northern Rhodesia/
      Zambia: 1945-1965." By S. M. Makings. p. 195-247.

p)   v. 6, no. 3, 1966. "Rice Marketing in Eastern Nigeria." By
      Delane E. Welsch. p. 329-352.

q)   v. 7, no. 2, 1967. "The Nigerian Palm Oil Industry." By Peter
      Kilby. p. 177-203.

r) v. 8, no. 1, 1968. "Agricultural Change in Kenya: 1945-1960."
By L. H. Brown. p. 33-90.

s) v. 8, Supplement, 1968. "Economics of Smallholder Farming in
Rhodesia: A Cross-Section Analysis of Two Areas." By
Benton F. Massell and R. W. M. Johnson. p. 1-74.

807. Gaudy, M. MANUEL D'AGRICULTURE TROPICALE (AFRIQUE TROPICALE ET EQUATO-
RIALE). Paris, Maison Rustique, 1959. 443 p. illus., map, diagrs.

Handbook for students in African agricultural schools and for
officials of the agricultural services. The work covers systems and
possible improvements in African agriculture, problems of soil conservation, irrigation and drainage, mechanization, and rural economy.

808. Harroy, Jean Paul. AFRIQUE, TERRE QUI MEURT: LA DEGRADATION DES SOLS
AFRICAINS SOUS L'INFLUENCE DE LA COLONISATION. 2d ed. Bruxelles,
M. Hayez, 1949. 557 p. fold. map.

"Principaux ouvrages cités": p. 549-557.

Among important older studies of soil exhaustion and erosion in
Africa is this brilliant work by the Belgian director of a foundation
promoting scientific study of the national parks of the Belgian Congo,
later Governor of Ruanda-Urundi and director of IRSAC (Institut pour la
Recherche Scientifique en Afrique Centrale). Of his seven lucidly presented sections, two are devoted to the transformation of African life
and agriculture under colonization and two to possible remedial measures
and their application through science, education, and government direction.

809. Johnston, Bruce F. THE STAPLE FOOD ECONOMIES OF WESTERN TROPICAL AFRICA.
Stanford, Calif., Stanford University Press, 1959. 315 p. illus.,
maps. (Stanford University, Food Research Institute, Studies in
Tropical Development)

Authoritative work by an economist of the Food Research Institute,
which excels in the study of food economics. The broad region covered
by Dr. Johnston in his examination of the most important food crops includes Angola and the Belgian Congo together with the territories of
former French and British West Africa. The physical environment is considered, as well as the geographical distribution of the major crops;
economic factors; social, cultural, and historical influences, the place
of the foods in African diets, and prospects for changes and increasing
production.

810. Jones, William O. MANIOC IN AFRICA. Stanford, Calif., Stanford Uni-
         versity Press, 1959. 315 p. illus., maps. (Stanford University,
         Food Research Institute, Studies in Tropical Development)

      References at end of chapters.

      In this study of the starchy foodstuff--known also as cassava--which
   is a major supplier of food and feed calories to the tropical world,
   Dr. Jones has limited his account to African uses of manioc. He gives
   interesting coverage to background on land, climate, and people and a
   history of the introduction and spread of manioc as it became a staple
   of diet in the Congo, Guinea, and East Africa. There are references
   at the end of chapters and a section of notes.

811. Joshi, N. R., and others. TYPES AND BREEDS OF AFRICAN CATTLE. Pre-
         pared by N. R. Joshi, E. A. McLaughlin, and Ralph W. Phillips.
         Rome, Food and Agriculture Organization of the United Nations,
         1957. 297 p. tables, illus. (FAO Agricultural Studies, no. 37)
         Issued also in French.

      Bibliography: p. 291-297.

      Information on indigenous types and breeds of African cattle im-
   portant as to numbers and differentiation. It is explained that tribal
   migrations and nomadic movements have tended to produce many intermediate
   types. There are five main types, described in detail with regard to
   characteristics, measurements, numbers, milk production, etc.

812. Phillips, John F. V. AGRICULTURE AND ECOLOGY IN AFRICA: A STUDY OF
         ACTUAL AND POTENTIAL DEVELOPMENT SOUTH OF THE SAHARA. New York,
         Praeger, 1960. 423 p. map, tables. (Books That Matter)

      Bibliography: p. 397-412.

      _____. THE DEVELOPMENT OF AGRICULTURE AND FORESTRY IN THE TROPICS.
      London, Faber & Faber, 1961. 212 p.

      The writer, a "forester, conservationist, agriculturalist and
   ecologist," was formerly at the University College of Ghana. The scope
   of his study of African agriculture and ecology is, as set forth in the
   first chapter, "no more than a preliminary recording of some salient
   points" regarding hazards and potentials in agricultural and related
   development, classification of ecological units, and suggestions as to
   how development might proceed. The contents are in five sections. The
   first gives the ecological basis and background of problems inherent in
   African climate, vegetation and soils, wild life, and domesticated animals. The next two parts discuss the bioclimatic regions of the forest

and the great wooded savannah. The fourth surveys human and animal health and economics and planning. The last section offers conclusions and suggestions for "saving Africa unnecessary disappointment" in its development schemes for agriculture.

In the second work Professor Phillips directs his attention to applications of agricultural development and discusses the problems of Africa in comparison with those of the rest of the tropical world.

813. Shantz, Homer L. AGRICULTURAL REGIONS OF AFRICA. Published in ECO-
      NOMIC GEOGRAPHY, Clark University, Worcester, Mass. With 297
      photographs (by the author unless otherwise cited). Santa
      Barbara, Calif., H. L. Shantz [1944?]. 327 p. illus. (incl. maps).

Nine articles from ECONOMIC GEOGRAPHY, v. 16-19, 1940-43.

_____. VEGETATION AND SOILS OF AFRICA. New York, National Research
      Council and American Geographical Society, 1923. 263 p. illus.,
      maps.

Dr. Shantz, a distinguished American plant physiologist, began his studies of African agriculture in connection with the American Commission to Negotiate Peace in 1918-19, and he went on special details to Africa to study crops in 1919-20 and 1924. The 1923 volume, with C. F. Marbut as collaborator, is an authoritative study.

The nine articles in ECONOMIC GEOGRAPHY form a valuable introductory survey for the layman. The first two papers (Jan. and Apr. 1940) are on "Basic Factors," the figures not later than 1931; tables of statistics are scattered through the text. The succeeding articles describe vegetation and potential productivity of the land (Oct. 1940, July and Oct. 1941), present and potential productivity (July and Oct. 1942), and, finally, "Regional Distribution and Character of Land Use" (Jan. and July 1943). Much is of sufficiently general character to have remained valid in spite of changes in the intervening period. In his chapter on potentials Dr. Shantz reckoned that Africa has 11 percent of the world's forest land, a third of the world's grazing land, and 28 percent of the total potential cropland area of the world.

814. THE SOIL RESOURCES OF TROPICAL AFRICA: A SYMPOSIUM OF THE AFRICAN
      STUDIES ASSOCIATION OF THE UNITED KINGDOM. Edited by R. P. Moss.
      London, Cambridge University Press, 1968. 226 p.

815. SOLS AFRICAINS. AFRICAN SOILS. v. 1- 1951- Paris, Inter-African
      Bureau for Soils and Rural Economy. 3 times a year.

This affiliate of CCTA/CSA (see Library of Congress, INTERNATIONAL SCIENTIFIC ORGANIZATIONS, for full description) has an extensive library, containing over 100,000 subject index cards. Since the early 1950's it has issued INDEX CARDS: SELECTED CURRENT BIBLIOGRAPHY, a biweekly series of 32 index cards for the principal articles received. Besides the scientific journal SOLS AFRICAINS, the Bureau publishes a MONTHLY ANALYTICAL BULLETIN (v. 1-, 1951), with alternate title BIBLIOGRAPHICAL BULLETIN; this carries abstracts and accessions lists.

The Inter-African Soils Conference, sponsored by this bureau and by CCTA/CSA, held meetings at Goma, Belgian Congo, in 1948, Leopoldville in 1954, and Dalaba, Guinea, in 1959. The COMPTES RENDUS has been published by CSA (third conference, 1959, CSA Publication no. 50, 924 p.).

Related to the Inter-African Bureau for Soils and Rural Economy is the Inter-African Pedological Service, with headquarters at Yangambi, Republic of the Congo (Leopoldville). It is working on a map of soils of Africa.

816. Stamp, L. Dudley, ed. A HISTORY OF LAND USE IN ARID REGIONS. Paris, UNESCO, 1961. 388 p. maps, diagrs. (Arid Zone Research, no. 17)

Includes bibliographies.

Chapters by specialists, each concluding with bibliography. The first section is general, on climatic change since the Pliocene, by K. W. Bulzer (p. 31-56). Sections relating to Africa are "Land Use in the Sahara-Sahel Region," by Théodore Monod and Charles Toupet (p. 239-254), and "Land Utilization in the Arid Regions of Southern Africa" (Part 1, South Africa, by W. J. Talbot, p. 299-331; Part 2, South West Africa, by Richard F. Logan, p. 331-338). The last chapters, on public health problems, have country breakdowns.

817. Tempany, Harold A., and D. H. Grist. AN INTRODUCTION TO TROPICAL AGRICULTURE. London, New York, Longmans, Green, 1958. 347 p. illus.

The late Sir Harold Tempany was agricultural adviser to the Secretary of State for the Colonies. This book, written in collaboration with a former agricultural economist of Malaya, is general for tropical regions. It is in three parts, the first on the tropical background of climate, soils, types of vegetation, etc., the second on agricultural practices, and the third on economic conditions of marketing and transport, land tenure and use, and finance and credit.

Longmans, Green has followed this work with a Tropical Agriculture series. The volumes in this series cover Africa and the rest of the tropical world and present full, thorough discussions of specific agricultural products. To date there have been published RICE, by D. H. Grist

(1959); BANANAS, By N. W. Simmonds (1959); BEEKEEPING IN THE TROPICS, by F. G. Smith (1960); INTRODUCTION TO ANIMAL HUSBANDRY, by G. Williamson and W. J. A. Payne (1960); and COCOA, by Duncan H. Urquhart (1961). The last named is the second edition of a work first published in 1955 by the Director of Agriculture for Ghana. The other books are of equal authority as to authorship and coverage. They are prepared "with the active encouragement" of the Colonial Advisory Council of Agriculture, Animal Health and Forestry.

818. U.S. Department of Agriculture. Economic Research Service. [Publications of the African and Middle East Analysis Branch, Regional Analysis Divison] Washington.

The African and Middle East Analysis Branch was a part of the Foreign Agricultural Service until Apr. 1961, when it was transferred to the newly formed Economic Research Service (ERS). Its publications on Africa, formerly issued in the FAS-M series and occasionally in the more substantial Foreign Agricultural Report series, now appear in the ERS-Foreign series. The majority of these publications apply to a single country or region, and they vary in extent from processed "Notes" to full-scale surveys of the agricultural economies of specific countries. The following publications are cited as of general or regional interest rather than being limited to one country:

a) AGRICULTURAL DEVELOPMENTS IN ANGOLA, BRITISH EAST AFRICA, RHODESIA AND NYASALAND, AND ZANZIBAR--THEIR EFFECTS ON U.S. FARM EXPORTS. By Robert C. Moncure. 1958. 81 p. illus. (Foreign Agriculture Report no. 111)

b) CITRUS INDUSTRY OF SOUTHERN AFRICA. By J. Henry Burke. 1957. 89 p. illus., fold. map, tables. (Foreign Agriculture Report no. 103)

c) COTTON PRODUCTION IN AFRICA: TRENDS AND PROSPECTS. By Horace G. Porter and Thomas R. Richmond. Feb. 1960. 40 p. illus. (Foreign Agriculture Report no. 117)

d) THE OUTLOOK FOR WHEAT AND FLOUR IMPORTS IN TROPICAL AFRICA. By Bruce F. Johnston. 1959. 34 p. (FAS-M-48)

e) PLANTING AND HARVESTING SEASONS FOR AFRICA AND WEST ASIA. By Ione L. Bauman. 1960. 60 p. tables. (FAS-M-90)

f) AFRICA'S TOBACCO INDUSTRY. By John B. Parker. 1963. 118 p. illus. (Foreign Agriculture Report no. 123)

819. Webster, B. N. INDEX OF AGRICULTURAL RESEARCH INSTITUTIONS AND STATIONS IN AFRICA. [n.p.] Food and Agriculture Organization of the United Nations, [19 ?]. 217 p.

MINING

See also Geology in Chapter 29.

Reference Works

820. De Kun, N. A. THE MINERAL RESOURCES OF AFRICA. Amsterdam, Elsevier,
         1965. 740 p. illus., maps.

         Bibliography: p. 683-695.

         A large, important study. The first part is on industrial develop-
    ment and mineral economics (African production value and distribution
    by groups of minerals, history and development of mining, in general and
    by regions); Part 2 is economic geology, broken down by mineral groups.
    The first appendix gives conversion factors, the second a list of com-
    panies, individuals, and organizations engaged in mineral and related
    industries.

821. Furon, Raymond. LES RESSOURCES MINERALES DE L'AFRIQUE: GEOLOGIE ET
         MINES, LA PRODUCTION AFRICAINE DANS LE MONDE, LA PRODUCTION
         REGIONALE, LES NOUVEAUX PROBLEMES. 2d ed. Paris, Payot, 1961.
         284 p. maps, diagrs. (Bibliothèque économique)

         The first edition of Professor Furon's survey of mineral resources
    came out in 1944. The second edition is extensively revised and modern-
    ized, with a general and historical introduction, a classification and
    allocation of individual mineral products, discussion of their regional
    importance, and a concluding section on prospects and problems for the
    future.

         See also his GEOLOGY OF AFRICA, no. 1135.

822. Krenkel, Erich. GEOLOGIE UND BODENSCHATZE AFRIKAS. 2. stark veränderte
         Aufl. Leipzig, Geest und Portig, 1957. xv, 597 p. illus., maps,
         diagrs.

         Bibliography: p. 573-597.

         Second edition of a survey of African geology and mineral resources
    first published in 1925. Revision is extensive, and the bibliography is
    brought up to date.

823. Munger, Averill H., and E. Placidi. PETROLEUM DEVELOPMENTS AND GEN-
ERALIZED GEOLOGY OF AFRICA AND THE MIDDLE EAST. Los Angeles,
Munger Map Book Co., 1960. 115 p. (chiefly maps).

Base maps of African and Middle East areas showing water-well
locations, well drilling, oil wells, gas wells, suspended or idle wells,
pipelines, etc. Transparent map overlays with base maps are in sepia and
locate oil and gas fields and outline the general geological formations
of the areas. Only a small number of the maps relate to sub-Saharan
Africa.

824. Pelletier, R. A. MINERAL RESOURCES OF SOUTH-CENTRAL AFRICA. Cape
Town, New York, Oxford University Press, 1964. 277 p. figs.,
maps.

This survey, by a geologist with long experience in mineral explorations, a former president of the Geological Society of South Africa,
begins with the early geological and mining history of the whole region
and then gives systematically by territory the physical features, geological features, mineral statistics, and description of individual
mineral deposits. Areas covered are the South African Republic, Northern
Rhodesia and Nyasaland, Congo Republic, Ruanda-Urundi, Portuguese possessions (Angola, Mozambique), and East Africa (Tanganyika, Kenya,
Uganda).

825. United Nations Educational, Scientific and Cultural Organization. RE-
VIEW OF GEOLOGY AND MINERAL INVESTIGATION IN AFRICA. By Frank
Dixey; prepared for the Economic Commission for Africa. Paris,
UNESCO, 1959. 77, 6, 25 p. (E/CN.14/30, Dec. 10, 1959)

Published by UNESCO in a series of surveys of resources, this report is the work of a distinguished British scientist, for many years
director of geological research in Nyasaland. It provides a résumé of
current geological knowledge in general, covering geological surveys,
departments of mines, governmental interest in prospecting and mining,
mining companies, universities, scientific societies and research organizations, international collaboration, interterritorial and foreign
technical aid, etc. The author outlines the present state of mineral
investigation and development, as well as the search for new mineral
deposits. The report ends with recommendations. A list of geological
research organizations and a bibliography of geological maps make up
two appendixes.

An earlier work of somewhat the same nature by Mr. Dixey was
COLONIAL GEOLOGICAL SURVEYS, 1947-56: A REVIEW OF PROGRESS (London,
H.M. Stationery Off., 1957, 129 p., illus., maps).

826. U.S. Bureau of Mines. MINERALS YEARBOOK 1969: Vol. IV, AREA REPORTS: INTERNATIONAL. Washington, 1970. 979 p. tables.

This annual publication, issued since 1933 and expanding from one to three volumes, added a fourth volume beginning with the 1963 edition to review world mineral production, consumption, and trade on a country-by-country basis. For 1963 the mineral industry of over 30 African countries is surveyed by Thomas G. Murdock, Thomas C. Denton, and Taber de Polo (p. 829-1162). In Vol. IV for 1964 (1966, 1350 p.) a general review of the African situation is followed by surveys of 46 African countries presented by eight contributors, the most prominent being William C. Henkes (p. 747-1021).

827. Woodtli, Robert. LE POTENTIEL MINERAL AFRICAIN. Lausanne, Centre de Recherches Européennes, Ecole des H.E.C. [Hautes Etudes Commerciales], Université de Lausanne, 1961. 302 p. (L'Europe et l'Afrique, v. 1)

Bibliography: p. 295-302.

Compendium of detailed information on mineral resources of Africa by an eminent Swiss geologist. The book is in two parts, with brief general introductions and conclusions. Part 1, of about 170 pages, classifies individual minerals and names the chief African deposits; the arrangement is alphabetical, from "abrasifs" to "zirconium et halmium." The second part (p. 197-274) specifies resources of the African states, also in alphabetical order. In his conclusion Dr. Woodtli examines the place of Africa in world mineral production, as a whole and by region, and speculates on the future role of the European in mineral development. He considers that as "counselor" the white man will be needed for many years to come.

CHAPTER 19

SOCIOLOGY

Bibliographies

828.   AFRICAN URBANIZATION: A READING LIST OF SELECTED BOOKS, ARTICLES
            AND REPORTS. Compiled by the Department of Social Anthropology,
            University of Edinburgh. London, International African Institute,
            1965. 27 p. (Africa Bibliography, Series B)

        This guide to research on urban problems and urbanization in Africa
        south of the Sahara lists almost a thousand works with scope mainly demo-
        graphic, economic, and sociological. Main sections are bibliographies,
        Africa in general, and West, Central, Southern, and East Africa. Each
        region has a general category followed by component countries and further
        subdivision into cities and towns (alphabetical index to the last also
        included).

829.   Centre de Documentation Economique et Sociale Africaine (CEDESA).
            Enquêtes bibliographiques [series]. Bruxelles, 1959-

        CEDESA, Belgian center for documentary services relating to eco-
        nomic and social studies of Africa, was created in Dec. 1957 and in 1958
        began an extensive distribution of file cards with annotated entries in
        classed decimal arrangement. As a result of the cooperation of scholars
        and libraries abroad the Centre International de Documentation Economique
        et Sociale Africaine (CIDESA) came into being in 1961 and thereafter
        issued the file cards; CIDESA also produces the BULLETIN D'INFORMATION
        SUR LES RECHERCHES DANS LES SCIENCES HUMAINES CONCERNANT L'AFRIQUE (1963-;
        see no. 9). The CEDESA Enquêtes bibliographiques series is usually the
        work of individual compilers and deals with special subjects of social
        or economic significance. Among those in the field of sociology are the
        following:

        a)   no. 1. LE PROBLEME DE LA DELINQUANCE JUVENILE. By M. L. Kerremans-
                Ramioulle. Bruxelles, 1959. 63 p. (1,027 entries)

b) no. 3. LE PROBLEME DE L'HABITAT RURAL EN AFRIQUE NOIRE. By Paul Verhaegen. Bruxelles, 1960. 73 p. (433 entries)

c) no. 7. BIBLIOGRAPHIE DE LA CONDITION DE L'AFRICAINE EN AFRIQUE NOIRE. By F. Plisnier-Ladame. Bruxelles, 1961. 241 p. (1,418 entries)

d) no. 8. ASPECTS ECONOMIQUES ET SOCIAUX DE L'INDUSTRIALISATION EN AFRIQUE. By P. Dethine. Bruxelles, 1961. 136 p. (726 entries)

e) no. 9. L'URBANISATION DE L'AFRIQUE NOIRE: SON CADRE, SES CAUSES ET SES CONSEQUENCES ECONOMIQUES, SOCIALES ET CULTURELLES. By Paul Verhaegen. Bruxelles, 1962. xiii, 387 p. (2,544 entries)

f) no. 15. SCIENCES HUMAINES EN AFRIQUE NOIRE: GUIDE BIBLIOGRAPHIQUE (1945-1965). By Jozef Bogaert. Bruxelles, 1966. 226 p. (1,494 entries)

830. Centre de Recherche et d'Information Socio-Politiques. BIBLIOGRAPHIE SUR LES CLASSES SOCIALES EN AFRIQUE. Compiled by B. Verhaegen. Bruxelles, 1965. 70 l. Processed. (Travaux africains, Dossier documentaire, no. 2)

An annotated list of 364 articles and books dealing with various aspects and problems of social classes in Africa. Most citations are of material published since 1960. Following an introduction and eight chapters on general literature about social classes are separate chapters on Algeria, Egypt, Guinea, and the former Belgian Congo. There is an author index.

831. Comhaire, J. L. L., comp. URBAN CONDITIONS IN AFRICA: SELECT READING LIST ON URBAN PROBLEMS IN AFRICA. New and rev. ed. London, Published for the Institute of Colonial Studies by Oxford University Press, 1952. xi, 48 p.

The first edition of this list, edited by Dr. Margery Perham, was issued in 1947. It was revised to reflect the great increase in literature on the subject in five years, and the new list is no. 3 of the distinguished series of reading lists upon colonial questions prepared for the Institute of Colonial Studies. Like the others of the series, it might be cited as a model for subject bibliography relating to Africa.

832. Deregowska, Eva Loft, comp. SOME ASPECTS OF SOCIAL CHANGE IN AFRICA SOUTH OF THE SAHARA, 1959-66: A BIBLIOGRAPHY. [Lusaka?] Institute for Social Research, University of Zambia, 1967. 93 p. Processed. (Communication no. 3)

A bibliography of 640 numbered entries arranged by subject (e.g., conflict, social stratification, elites, acculturation, religion, women, labor, town life, legal change, nationalism, psychological aspects), plus an appendix citing current and retrospective bibliographies. References are to periodical articles, books, and conference papers in English, French, and German. Included are author and country indexes and a list of journals analyzed.

Reference Works

833. Abidjan. Université. Institut de Géographie Tropicale. Institut
        d'Ethno-sociologie. BULLETIN D'INFORMATION ET DE LIAISON. no. 1-
        1967- Abidjan. Irregular.

834. AFRICAN URBAN NOTES. v. 1, no. 1- Apr. 1966- Milwaukee, Department
        of Political Science, University of Wisconsin-Milwaukee, Apr.
        1966-Mar. 1967; Los Angeles, Department of Political Science, Uni-
        versity of California, Apr. 1967- Irregular.

        An informal newsletter on conferences, research, courses, disser-
tations, and publications of interest to students and scholars concerned
with African urbanization. George Jenkins is the issue editor, with
Ruth Simms Hamilton and Ed Soja (replacing Remi Clignet) as co-editors
in late 1967. Occasionally an issue is devoted to a specific topic,
e.g., a special issue on Nigeria (Apr. 1967) and one on geography (May
1967). By June 1968 seven bibliographical supplements had appeared,
among them A HISTORICAL BIBLIOGRAPHY OF THE CITY OF DURBAN, by M. W.
Swanson (no. 1, Nov. 1966, 12 p); UNEMPLOYMENT, by Peter C. W. Gutkind
(nos. 2 and 5, Feb. and Dec. 1967, 5 and 4 p.; no. 6, Apr. 1968, 4 p.);
A PRELIMINARY CHECKLIST OF NIGERIAN BIOGRAPHICAL AND AUTOBIOGRAPHICAL
CHAPBOOKS IN ENGLISH, by Bernth Lindfors (no. 4, Nov. 1967, 13 p); and
ELISABETHVILLE, by Bruce Fetter (no. 7, June 1968, 33 p.), which includes commentative notes.

835. Banton, Michael. RACE RELATIONS. London, Tavistock, 1967. 434 p.

        Bibliography: p. 394-415.

        An excellent and timely study of race relations the world over,
but with emphasis on Africa and the United States. Banton discusses
the history of thinking on race from the time of Aristotle, race as a
role determinant, cultural symbiosis, caste and conquest, the concept
and roots of prejudice, ethnic differences, slavery in the new world,
growth of African prophetic movements, tribal relations in Africa with
particular reference to British Africa, stereotypes, and social distance.
Three of the chapters are produced from the author's WHITE AND COLOURED
(London, Jonathan Cape, 1959).

836. L'ENFANT AFRICAIN: L'EDUCATION DE L'ENFANT AFRICAIN EN FONCTION DE SON
MILIEU DE BASE ET DE SON ORIENTATION D'AVENIR. Paris, Editions
Fleurus, 1960. 484 p. (Bureau International Catholique de
l'Enfance, Collection Etudes et documents)

Bibliography: p. 464-484.

The report of a conference on child welfare held under the auspices
of the Bureau at Yaoundé, Cameroun, in 1957 and attended by 400 European
and African missionaries, priests, nuns, doctors, and teachers. Twelve
chapters summarize the material gathered from responses to a preliminary
questionnaire and from papers and discussions upon various aspects of
the life, education, and well-being of the African child. The text of
the questionnaire, a synthesis of 800 pages of documentation, and a bibliography of about 1,500 references are given as appendixes.

837. Gray, Robert F., and P. H. Gulliver, eds. THE FAMILY ESTATE IN AFRICA:
STUDIES IN THE ROLE OF PROPERTY IN FAMILY STRUCTURE AND LINEAGE
CONTINUITY. London, Routledge & Kegan Paul, 1964. 265 p. diagrs.
(1 fold.).

Includes bibliographies.

A series of essays concerning family life in seven societies of
Eastern and Central Africa. The contributors (Robert F. Gray, E. V.
Winans, Robert A. LeVine, Igor Kopytoff, Alfred and Grace Harris,
Eileen Jensen Krige, and P. H. Gulliver) focus on the family's attach-
ment to property and resources and on the developmental aspect (time
dimension). Gray has provided a 33-page introduction.

838. Hunter, Guy. THE NEW SOCIETIES OF TROPICAL AFRICA: A SELECTIVE STUDY.
Issued under the auspices of the Institute of Race Relations,
London. London, New York, Oxford University Press, 1962. xviii,
376 p. illus., fold. maps, tables.

Bibliography: p. 348-360.

The result of a project undertaken in 1959 and placed under the
direction of Mr. Hunter, who traveled widely in Africa and interviewed
over a thousand people. Although he was alone responsible for the final
text, it was based on the work of many writers and on papers done especially for this purpose by local study groups in Africa. The chapters
cover the historical growth of modern economies and changing culture,
present rural and urban society, growth of industry, labor problems, education and manpower, evolving political systems, and, last, "The Quality
of African Society."

839. Inter-African Conference on Housing and Urbanization, 2d session, Nairobi, Jan. 1959. REPORT. London, CCTA, 1959(?). 267 p. diagrs. (Scientific Council for Africa South of the Sahara Publication no. 47)

Report of a conference under CSA auspices, including summaries of papers. More important for research purposes is an accompanying paper, DIRECTORY OF RESEARCH AND OTHER ORGANIZATIONS PROVIDING INFORMATION ON HOUSING IN AFRICA SOUTH OF THE SAHARA (London, 1960; CSA Publication no. 72).

840. International African Institute. SOCIAL IMPLICATIONS OF INDUSTRIALIZATION AND URBANIZATION IN AFRICA SOUTH OF THE SAHARA. Paris, UNESCO, 1956. 743 p. illus., maps, diagrs., tables. (Tensions and Technology Series)

Under the auspices of UNESCO an International Conference on the Social Impact of Industrialization and Urban Conditions in Africa South of the Sahara was organized by the International African Institute and held at Abidjan in Sept.-Oct. 1954. This volume represents the results. The first two parts comprise an introduction by the director of the Institute, Professor Daryll Forde, explaining the conference and its field of study, and a survey by Miss Merran McCulloch of about 30 then recent and current field studies on the social effects of economic developments in tropical Africa, ending with a chapter of comparisons and conclusions. Part 3 is the report of a sample study made by a field research team on social effects of urbanization in Stanleyville, Belgian Congo (preliminary report by V. G. Pons, N. Xydias, and P. Clément). Part 4 contains papers presented at the conference, five on West Africa, five on East Africa, three on the Belgian Congo, and three on Southern Africa.

841. International African Seminar, 1st, Makerere College, 1959. SOCIAL CHANGE IN MODERN AFRICA: STUDIES PRESENTED AND DISCUSSED. Edited by Aidan Southall. London, New York, Published for the International African Institute by the Oxford University Press, 1961. xi, 337 p.

Reprint, 1965.

Includes bibliographies.

The great increase in research on African contemporary social and cultural life has been accompanied by the establishment of a number of research centers and frequent assemblages held under the auspices of various organizations seeking to pool their insights. In the notable seminar of which the present volume is the report, leading scholars from most countries of black Africa took part. There were papers on general themes--e.g., anthropological problems arising from the African industrial revolution and papers relating to specific issues or areas.

842. International African Seminar, 6th, University of Ibadan, 1964. THE
         NEW ELITES IN TROPICAL AFRICA: STUDIES PRESENTED AND DISCUSSED.
         Edited with an introduction by P. C. Lloyd. London, Published
         for the International African Institute by the Oxford University
         Press, 1966. 390 p. tables, diagrs.

         Includes bibliographies.

         Participants who contributed papers and took part in discussions
    were 18 social anthropologists. Their topics included description and
    history, educational systems and social mobility, the structure of elite
    families, modern and traditional associations, and concepts in relation
    to the contemporary situation. Lloyd has written a book on a related
    subject, AFRICA IN SOCIAL CHANGE: CHANGING TRADITIONAL SOCIETIES IN
    THE MODERN WORLD (Baltimore, Penguin Books, 1967, 362 p.), focusing on
    West Africa (see no. 1299).

    International Children's Centre, Paris. ETUDE DES CONDITIONS DE VIE DE
         L'ENFANT AFRICAIN EN MILIEU URBAIN ET DE LEUR INFLUENCE SUR LA
         DELINQUANCE JUVENILE: ENQUETE ENTREPRISE A MADAGASCAR, AU CAMEROUN
         ET EN COTE D'IVOIRE DE 1954 A 1957. Paris, 1959. 175 p. maps,
         charts, tables. (Travaux et documents, no. 12)

         Bibliography: p. 165-173.

         Thorough sociological study presented statistically with many
    tables, graphic charts, maps, and case histories. The bibliography cen-
    ters on juvenile delinquency in Africa and other underdeveloped areas.

         For other conferences on the problems of African childhood, see
    numbers of the WORLD LIST OF FUTURE INTERNATIONAL MEETINGS.

844. International Institute of Differing Civilizations. WOMEN'S ROLE IN
         THE DEVELOPMENT OF TROPICAL AND SUB-TROPICAL COUNTRIES. Brussels,
         1959. 543 p.

         Report of the 31st meeting, Brussels, Sept. 17-20, 1958. At this
    session of the influential organization known as INCIDI, representatives
    from 18 countries were present, and papers were on a high level of author-
    itativeness. After the opening speeches, the first 254 pages are given
    over to reports from Africa, beginning with that by Sister Marie André
    du Sacré Coeur on French West Africa. Then follow reports by spokesmen
    for the Ivory Coast, Liberia, Nigeria, Somalia, the Portuguese provinces
    in Africa, the Belgian Congo, Ruanda, Rhodesia and Nyasaland, Uganda,
    Madagascar, the Union of South Africa (by Muriel Horrell of the S.A.
    Institute of Race Relations), Egypt, and the Sudan. The remainder of
    the volume is taken up with reports from Asia and Latin America.

845. Maistriaux, Robert. LA FEMME ET LE DESTIN DE L'AFRIQUE: LES SOURCES
     PSYCHOLOGIQUES DE LA MENTALITE DITE "PRIMITIVE." Elisabethville,
     CEPSI, 1964. 534 p. diagrs., tables. (Collection de mémoires,
     no. 16)

     Bibliography: p. 515-525.

     After methods of research employed in the investigation are out-
     lined, subsequent parts describe the African woman in an urban milieu
     (Elisabethville)--beliefs and customs on marriage, wedded life, children,
     religion, Christianity, etc.--and education from birth on, including
     the effect of economic and social factors in the development of the
     African child. The fourth part discusses the psychological origins of
     the mentality called "primitive," and a final part presents a synthesis
     and conclusions.

846. Miner, Horace, ed. THE CITY IN MODERN AFRICA. London, Pall Mall, 1967.
     xi, 364 p. maps, tables.

     Bibliography: p. 337-352.

     Based on papers presented by distinguished American and British
     social scientists at the Conference on Methods and Objectives of Urban
     Research in Africa, held in Warrenton, Va., Apr. 1965. Representative
     essays are: "Africa and the Theory of Optimum City Size," by Joseph
     J. Spengler; "Urbanization and Economic Growth: The Cases of Two White
     Settler Territories," by William J. Barber; "Father-Child Relationships
     and Changing Life-Styles in Ibadan, Nigeria," by Robert A. Levine,
     Nancy H. Klein, and Constance R. Owen; and "Kampala-Mengo," by Aidan
     Southall. An index is included.

847. Miner, Horace, ed. SOCIAL SCIENCE IN ACTION IN SUB-SAHARAN AFRICA.
     New York, Society for Applied Anthropology, 1960. p. 97-168.
     double map, tables, diagrs. (HUMAN ORGANIZATION, v. 19, Fall 1960)

     This special issue of the journal of the Society for Applied An-
     thropology "was planned as a contribution to the American discovery of
     Africa," its purpose to acquaint American scholars recently entering
     the field with some of the European tradition of African studies and
     resultant activities. The first four papers examine British (by Lucy
     Mair), French (Georges Balandier), Belgian (Joseph Nicaise), and Soviet
     (Christopher Bird) research in the social sciences in Africa. The
     articles that follow are by English and American scholars on particular
     subjects--slums and family life, labor migration, etc.

848. Paulme, Denise, ed. WOMEN OF TROPICAL AFRICA. Translated by H. M.
Wright. London, Routledge & Kegan Paul, 1963. 308 p.

Bibliography: p. 231-293.

Six exceptionally interesting essays, by women ethnologists, are
based on field experience of the last 10 years. The introduction,
generalizing on the theme of the work, the status, and ways of life of
women in Africa, is by the editor, a well-known anthropologist now with
the Division des Aires Culturelles in the Ecole Pratique des Hautes
Etudes. The analytical bibliography is classified by subject. FEMMES
D'AFRIQUE NOIRE, the French original, was published by Mouton, Paris,
in 1960 (280 p.; Le monde d'outre-mer passé et présent, 1st ser.,
Etudes, no.9). See also no. 992.

849. Phillips, Arthur, ed. SURVEY OF AFRICAN MARRIAGE AND FAMILY LIFE.
London, New York, Published for the International African Institute by Oxford University Press, 1953. xli, 462 p. fold. map.

Includes bibliographies.

The survey came to fruition through a suggestion made to the International Missionary Council by Lord Hailey in 1946. The editor, then
reader in administration of colonial law at the University of London,
wrote the introductory essay. Part 1, "African Marriage and Social
Change," is by Dr. Lucy P. Mair; Part 2, "Marriage Laws in Africa,"
by Dr. Phillips; Part 3, "Christian Marriage in African Society,"
by the Rev. Lyndon Harries, now at the University of Wisconsin. Each
part has its own scholarly footnotes, bibliography, and index; included
also are a list of tribes referred to (Part 1) and tables of statutes
and cases (Part 2).

A short summary of the SURVEY OF AFRICAN MARRIAGE AND FAMILY LIFE
was published by the International Missionary Council as no. 1 of their
series of Research Pamphlets: AFRICAN MARRIAGE, by Thomas Price (London,
SCM Press, 1954, 56 p.) The conflicts of Christian practices and principles with the tribal marriage customs--particularly with polygamy and
bride price--are the main points of discussion. See also no. 992.

850. RURAL AFRICANA. no. 1- Mar. 1967- East Lansing, African Studies
Center, Michigan State University. 3 times in academic year.

A research bulletin on local politics, political anthropology,
rural development, and other related topics in tropical Africa. Reports on research findings and commentary on current rural problems
are emphasized; new publications and periodical literature, book reviews, and conference news are included. See also no. 834, AFRICAN
URBAN NOTES.

851. Société Africaine de Culture. ECONOMIE ET CULTURE (TRAVAUX DE LA
       SOCIETE AFRICAINE DE CULTURE, PARIS, UNESCO, 20-21 OCTOBRE 1962).
       Paris, Présence Africaine, 1965. 241 p.

       A reproduction of the papers presented and discussed at the
   society's 1962 meeting. Among the topics are culture and politics,
   the elite and community innovation, the Guinea experience, education
   in economics, and nationalism and the nation.

852. United Nations. Economic Commission for Africa. DIRECTORY OF REGIONAL
       SOCIAL WELFARE ACTIVITIES. Compiled by the Social Development
       Section. New York, Oct. 1964. 114 p. fold. map. (E/CN.14/SWSA/1)

       The directory has been compiled to supply information for each of
   the African countries on national social welfare agencies and services
   provided as well as the social welfare activities of the ECA and other
   UN agencies in the region.

       Among other ECA publications on social welfare in Africa are the
   following:

   a)   PATTERNS OF SOCIAL WELFARE ORGANIZATION AND ADMINISTRATION IN
            AFRICA. 1965. 83 p. map. (E/CN.14/SWSA/2)

   b)   SOCIAL WORK TRAINING IN A CHANGING AFRICA. 1965. 86 p.
            (E/CN.14/SWTA/41)

   c)   TRAINING FOR SOCIAL WORK IN AFRICA. 1965. 54 p. (E/CN.14/SWSA/3)

853. United Nations. Economic Commission for Africa. HOUSING IN AFRICA.
       [Addis Ababa?] 1965. 221 p. col. map (back pocket), tables.
       (E/CN.14/HOU/7/Rev.)

       Part 1 reviews the housing situation and discusses the construction
   industry, financing, and the use of space in grouped housing. Part 2
   is an analysis of housing problems; topics include the elaboration of a
   housing policy, development of the building materials industry, physical
   and town planning, improvement of productivity in the building industry,
   and the need for research documentation and training.

854. United Nations. Secretariat. PROGRESS OF THE NON-SELF-GOVERNING
       TERRITORIES UNDER THE CHARTER: Vol. III, SOCIAL CONDITIONS. New
       York, 1961. 251 p. (ST/TRI/Ser.A/15/v.3)

       Review of general development in social conditions of dependent
   territories throughout the world, covering race relations, social welfare, social security legislation, community development, freedom of

association and industrial relations, cooperative societies, demographic conditions and population trends, health services and activities, nutrition. This is one of five volumes: the first a general review, Vol. II on economic conditions, Vol. IV on educational developments; Vol. V summaries for individual territories. A cumulative index is to be published separately. The progress report covers the period from 1946 to 1957, and thus most of Africa south of the Sahara (former British colonies except Ghana, former French territories, the Belgian Congo, Portuguese and Spanish territories) is included. Official sources are given for almost all the data.

855. Wallerstein, Immanuel. SOCIAL CHANGE: THE COLONIAL SITUATION. New York, Wiley, 1966. 674 p.

Book of readings (articles or chapters from books by specialists) on various social, political, and economic phenomena evolving out of the interaction of colonial rule and African societies. Covers subjects such as nationalism, labor migration, and changes in traditional authority.

856. Ziégler, Jean. SOCIOLOGIE DE LA NOUVELLE AFRIQUE. Paris, Gallimard, 1964. 380 p. (Collection Idées, no. 59)

The author, who is personally committed to revolutionary ideals, first discusses the general problem of class struggles in Africa. He subsequently deals with three case histories--Ghana, Congo (Leopoldville), and the United Arab Republic--during the later 1950's and early 1960's. He tries to analyze the power structure of these countries and to explain their inability to solve certain pressing political, social, and economic problems that beset their respective societies.

CHAPTER 20

DEMOGRAPHY

Bibliographies

857. France. Institut National de la Statistique et des Etudes Economiques.
        Service de Coopération. BIBLIOGRAPHIE DEMOGRAPHIQUE (1945-1964):
        TRAVAUX PUBLIES PAR L'I.N.S.E.E. (SERVICE DE COOPERATION), LES
        SERVICES DE STATISTIQUE DES ETATS AFRICAINS D'EXPRESSION FRANCAISE
        OU DE MADAGASCAR ET LE MINISTERE DE LA COOPERATION. Paris, 1965.
        36 l.

        The first part lists handbooks, studies, and bibliographies; the
    second covers the former French African territories and regions and
    includes entries on nonindigenous populations. The last part is arranged
    by country.

858. France. Institut National de la Statistique et des Etudes Economiques.
        Service de Coopération. BIBLIOGRAPHIE DES ETUDES DEMOGRAPHIQUES
        RELATIVES AU PAYS EN VOIE DE DEVELOPPEMENT: OUVRAGES PARUS DEPUIS
        1945, MISE A JOUR LE 1er JUILLET 1961. Paris, 1961. 110 p.

        Most useful for French-speaking countries but includes a certain
    amount of material for "pays d'expression anglaise." Arrangement is
    by country.

        See also nos. 1533 and 1534.

859. POPULATION INDEX. v. 1- 1935- Princeton, N.J., School of Public
        Affairs, Princeton University, and the Population Association of
        America. Quarterly.

        Annotated bibliography of book and periodical literature on all
    phases of population problems, worldwide. The arrangement is by class,
    but annual cumulated indexes by author and country provide complete
    guidance to the literature of African demography.

860. Texas. University. Population Research Center. INTERNATIONAL POPU-
LATION CENSUS BIBLIOGRAPHY: AFRICA. Austin, Bureau of Business
Research, College of Business Administration, University of Texas,
1965- 1 v. (loose-leaf). (Census Bibliography no. 2)

Part of a project of the Population Research Center to compile a
universal bibliography of census reports. It is arranged alphabetically
by country, and thereunder entries are in chronological order. A title
is given and then an English translation of the title. Coverage is
limited to population censuses, but other types of census reports are
given if they were included in the population census.

861. U.S. Library of Congress. Census Library Project. POPULATION CENSUSES
AND OTHER OFFICIAL DEMOGRAPHIC STATISTICS OF AFRICA (NOT INCLUDING
BRITISH AFRICA): AN ANNOTATED BIBLIOGRAPHY. Prepared by Henry J.
Dubester. Washington, 1950. 53 p.

_____. POPULATION CENSUSES AND OTHER OFFICIAL DEMOGRAPHIC STATISTICS
OF BRITISH AFRICA: AN ANNOTATED BIBLIOGRAPHY. Prepared by Henry
J. Dubester. Washington, 1950. 78 p.

Full coverage of published official material to 1949. For supplementary census reports see the Library of Congress series on Official
Publications of African Countries (no. 410).

See also no. 864 below.

Reference Works

862. Blanc, Robert. HANDBOOK OF DEMOGRAPHIC RESEARCH IN UNDER-DEVELOPED
COUNTRIES. n.p., n.d. 115 p. diagrs. (Scientific Council for
Africa South of the Sahara Publication no. 36)

Translation of a paper in French, issued in a limited mimeographed
edition as Publication no. 36 of CSA in 1958 or 1959. The English handbook was given out to participants at the Seminar on Population Problems
held in Cairo (see no. 865 below).

863. Caldwell, John C., and Chukuka Okonjo, eds. THE POPULATION OF TROPICAL
AFRICA. New York, Columbia University Press, 1968. xiii, 457 p.
maps, tables.

Bibliographical footnotes.

This worthy reference work comprises a record of almost all of the
proceedings of the First African Population Conference, which was held

at the University of Ibadan, Jan. 3-7, 1966, and was sponsored by the University in cooperation with the Population Council. The 46 papers published here represent the first major attempt at a definition and analysis of tropical Africa's population problems. Caldwell provides an introduction to each of the volume's two main parts. Part 1 examines the demographic situation and has five subsections: censuses; vital statistics; correction of sex-age distributions; estimation of fertility, mortality, and natural increase; and movement of population, density, and urbanization. In Part 2, devoted to population growth and economic development, subsections cover governmental population policy, family planning programs and attitudes toward family planning, and training and aid. An analytical index is included.

Another new work on African population is Robert F. Stevenson's provocative POPULATION AND POLITICAL SYSTEMS IN TROPICAL AFRICA (New York, London, Columbia University Press, 1968, xiii, 306 p.; bibliography: p. 263-293). Its aim is to demonstrate that there is in Africa, as on other continents, a positive relationship between the complexity of a political system and the density of population (i.e., states are generally more densely populated than nonstates). Basically, the work constitutes a reanalysis of the introduction to the collective volume AFRICAN POLITICAL SYSTEMS (see no. 619) and a refutation of the claim made therein (and subsequently widely accepted) that no demonstrable relationship of this type exists. See also William Brass et al., THE DEMOGRAPHY OF TROPICAL AFRICA (Princeton, N.J., Princeton University Press, 1968, 539 p.), a textbook for demographers.

864. Lorimer, Frank. DEMOGRAPHIC INFORMATION ON TROPICAL AFRICA. Boston, Boston University Press, 1961. 207 p. map.

   Includes bibliographies.

   The result of a study carried out under the auspices of the African Studies Program at Boston University and the Population Council of New York. The author made, also, his own investigations in statistical offices and research centers in Africa. It is a review and analysis of the whole course of population studies for Africa, beginning with a general consideration of methodology and then examining by regions the development of demographic information. Tables and bibliographies of census reports and other population studies are interspersed. In the introductory chapter there are listings (with explanation) of the chief bibliographies and manuals of African demographic statistics and of the conferences on population held by CCTA and other international bodies.

865. Seminar on Population Problems in Africa, Cairo, Oct. 29-Nov. 10, 1962. REPORT. Cairo, United Nations, Economic and Social Council, 1962. 58 p. and annexes. (E/CN.14/186; E/CN.9/CONF.3/1)

The document of an important seminar held under UNECA auspices, beginning with a summary of conclusions and recommendations, followed by a summary of discussions. The annexes contain texts of the most important addresses and statements, lists of participants and observers, the program, and, finally, a long list of documents (E/CN.14/ASPP/L.1-17; E/CN.14/ASPP/INF.1; E/CN.14/ASPP/G.1-7), which had been prepared as preliminary papers for the conference. Among these was the HANDBOOK by Robert Blanc, noted above (no. 862), as well as a paper entitled FERTILITY, MORTALITY, INTERNATIONAL MIGRATION AND POPULATION GROWTH IN AFRICA (42 p.; E/CN.14/ASPP/L.2; E/CN.9/CONF.3/L.2).

866.   United Nations. Economic Commission for Africa. SIZE AND GROWTH OF URBAN POPULATION IN AFRICA. [New York?] 1968. 47 p. (E/CN.14/ CAS.6/3)

CHAPTER 21

LABOR

Bibliographies

867. African Bibliographic Center, Washington, D.C. LE TIERS MONDE: A
      SELECT AND PRELIMINARY BIBLIOGRAPHIC SURVEY OF MANPOWER IN
      DEVELOPING COUNTRIES, 1960-1964. Compiled by Daniel G.
      Matthews. Washington, 1965. 30 p. Processed. (Special
      Bibliographic Series, Labor in Africa, v. 3, no. 5)

868. African Bibliographic Center, Washington, D.C. TRADE UNIONS IN
      AFRICA: A SELECT BIBLIOGRAPHY, 1960-1962. Washington, 1962.
      7 p. Processed. (Special Bibliographic Series, Labor in
      Africa, v. 1, no. 1)

869. Friedland, William H. UNIONS, LABOR AND INDUSTRIAL RELATIONS IN
      AFRICA: AN ANNOTATED BIBLIOGRAPHY. Ithaca, N.Y., Center for
      International Studies, Cornell University, 1965. 159 p.
      (Cornell Research Papers in International Studies, no. 4)

      This excellent bibliography begins in unorthodox fashion with
      subject and geographic indexes (p. 7-16) and continues with 683
      numbered and descriptively annotated entries in alphabetical order
      by author or title. The subject index has about 40 headings cover-
      ing general surveys, bibliography, child labor, collective bargaining,
      conditions of work, conventions of the ILO, diet, disputes and
      strikes, etc. The compiler explains the chief sources in his intro-
      duction.

870. Panofsky, Hans E. A BIBLIOGRAPHY OF LABOR MIGRATION IN AFRICA SOUTH
      OF THE SAHARA. Evanston, Ill., University Library, Northwestern
      University, 1961. 28 l.

Compiled by the curator of Africana of the Northwestern University Library and focused on a limited phase of the labor question, although a number of general works on labor in Africa are included. The arrangement is regional, with author index. The work has extensive coverage of books and periodical materials in English and European languages up to mid-1961 and includes slight annotations and indication of reviews or précis in AFRICAN ABSTRACTS. This bibliography was reproduced in the Inter-African Labour Institute report cited below (no. 877).

871. United Nations. Economic Commission for Africa. SELECTED BIBLIOGRAPHY: MANPOWER AND TRAINING PROBLEMS IN ECONOMIC AND SOCIAL DEVELOPMENT. [New York?] July 1967. 45 p. (E/CN.14/LIB/SER.C/3)

Books, articles, and documents are listed by subject, including general works, manpower (planning and utilization, labor and management, employment and unemployment), education and training (education, general; education, planning; training), bibliographies, and reference works (general and periodicals). Supplements are planned.

872. U.S. Bureau of Labor Statistics. BIBLIOGRAPHY ON LABOR IN AFRICA, 1960-1964. Washington, 1965. 121 p. (Bulletin no. 1473)

Entries are arranged alphabetically by country (the United Arab Republic and the smaller countries and islands are excluded) and then according to six headings: political, economic, and social; employment, unemployment, and labor force; industrial relations; labor legislation and administration; labor organizations; wages, hours, and working conditions. Periodical articles, chapters of larger works, and government publications as well as books and monographs are given. There are also sections listing guides, bibliographies, and periodicals and one covering Africa in general.

873. THE UNIVERSITY OF MICHIGAN INDEX TO LABOR UNION PERIODICALS: A MONTHLY SUBJECT INDEX TO MATERIALS FROM A SELECTED LIST OF NEWSPAPERS AND JOURNALS PUBLISHED BY MAJOR LABOR UNIONS. 1960- Ann Arbor, Bureau of Industrial Relations, School of Business Administration, University of Michigan. Annual cumulation.

Useful for survey of African trade-union literature.

Reference Works

874. Beling, Willard A., ed. THE ROLE OF LABOR IN AFRICAN NATION-BUILDING. New York, Praeger, 1968. 204 p. (Institute of World Affairs, v. 41, Proceedings)

875. Davies, Ioan. AFRICAN TRADE UNIONS. Middlesex, Eng., Baltimore, Md., Penguin Books, 1966. 256 p. (Penguin African Library, AP19)

    Bibliography: p. 233-244.

    Davies, a lecturer in sociology at the University of Essex, covers labor policies of Britain, France, and Belgium, industrialization and racial policies in South Africa, and the growth of trade unions in Africa. A glossary and an index are included.

876. Inter-African Labour Institute. BULLETIN. v. 1- 1953- London, Commission for Technical Cooperation in Africa. Quarterly.

    Text in English and French.

    The Institute was set up in 1948 as the permanent organ of the Inter-African Labour Conference, which operated under the aegis of CCTA. The BULLETIN provides broad coverage of important aspects of African labor in its articles and also carries bibliographical notes which include texts of labor legislation. It reports on the sessions of the Inter-African Labour Conference (see below, 6th, 1961) and regional conferences (1st, Lagos, Dec. 1960).

877. Inter-African Labour Institute. MIGRANT LABOUR IN AFRICA SOUTH OF THE SAHARA: PROCEEDINGS UNDER ITEM II OF THE AGENDA OF THE SIXTH INTER-AFRICAN LABOUR CONFERENCE, ABIDJAN, 1961, AND OTHER RELEVANT PAPERS. London, CCTA, 1962. 338 p. (Scientific Council for Africa South of the Sahara Publication no. 79)

    Contains the report, conclusions, and recommendations of the sixth session of the Inter-African Labour Conference; the questionnaire issued to the member governments and the answers received; six important articles published in the years 1959-61 in the Inter-African Labour Institute BULLETIN; and a bibliography compiled by Hans E. Panofsky. There is an index of authors and editors.

    The Institute also prepares monographic studies--e.g., THE HUMAN FACTORS OF PRODUCTIVITY IN AFRICA: A PRELIMINARY SURVEY (2d ed., Brazzaville, 1960, 156 p., diagrs.)--announcement of which may be found in the BULLETIN.

878. International Labor Office. AFRICAN LABOUR SURVEY. Geneva, 1958. xiv, 712 p. map, tables. (Studies and Reports, n.s. no. 48)

    Bibliography: p. 695-707.

The drafts of this survey, which had been authorized by the ILO
in 1956, were examined by its Committee of Experts on Social Policy
in Non-metropolitan Territories in late 1957; the final text was prepared under supervision of the director general, its primary purpose
to provide a point of departure for future work in Africa south of
the Sahara. All possible aspects bearing on labor are covered. Each
chapter ends with a summary of conclusions, and the final chapter
gives the general conclusions of the Committee of Experts, which in
1958 was replaced by a separate ILO African Field Office, for liaison
with the Economic Commission for Africa, and an African Advisory
Committee. Appendixes are texts of ILO documents of standards and
recommendations, citation of principal labor legislation of the
countries of Africa, miscellaneous tables of statistics, and a bibliography.

879. MANPOWER AND UNEMPLOYMENT RESEARCH IN AFRICA: A NEWSLETTER. v. 1,
        no. 1- Apr. 1968- Montreal, Centre for Developing-Area Studies,
        McGill University.

        The first issue of this mimeographed newsletter, which is to appear
at least twice a year (Apr. and Nov.), was edited by Peter C. W.
Gutkind, Peter Carstens, and André Lux. Its main intent is to serve as
a "house organ" for the increasing number of researchers who are
studying unemployment as a "core" problem. In its pages current
research, information, and bibliographical material will be made
readily available to researchers as well as to governments. The chief
focus will be on Africa, but material will not be restricted to that
continent; occasionally an issue will be devoted to a special theme.
The first issue included three working bibliographies by Peter Gutkind,
which originally appeared in AFRICAN URBAN NOTES.

880. Meynaud, Jean, and Anisse Salah Bey. TRADE UNIONISM IN AFRICA: A
        STUDY OF ITS GROWTH AND ORIENTATION. Translated by Angela
        Brench. London, Methuen, 1967.   242 p.

        Bibliography: p. 161-163.

        Survey of the evolution of African trade unionism to the mid-
1960's, with emphasis on its political significance. Part 1 analyzes
socioeconomic conditions and outside influences which led to establishment of the first trade unions in the primarily agricultural African
countries. Part 2 examines the rise of the unions under colonial
administration and their role in the national liberation movements.
Part 3 discusses the development of Pan-African trade unionism and
the participation of the African unions in the International Labor
Organization. A glossary gives brief descriptions of the situation
in each country and of the major trade-union organizations. The book
concludes with a biographical section on seven African trade-union

leaders, a 54-page documentary appendix, and an index.

The work was originally published as LE SYNDICALISME AFRICAIN:
EVOLUTION ET PERSPECTIVES (Paris, Payot, 1963, 260 p.; Etudes and
documents Payot).

881. Orde-Brown, G. St. J. THE AFRICAN LABOURER. London, Published for
       the International Institute of African Languages and Cultures
       by Oxford University Press, H. Milford, 1933. 240 p. map.

      Reprint, New York, Cass, 1968.

      Pioneer study of the problems of African labor, by a former labor
commissioner in Tanganyika who was subsequently a representative in the
International Labor Organization and an adviser on colonial labor to
the British Colonial Office. Part 1 concerns the background of
tribal African society and the first impact of foreign influences,
the incentives offered the African for wage earning, forced labor,
methods and conditions of recruiting and labor contracts, living and
social conditions of laborers, etc. Part 2 contains a country-by-
country summary of labor legislation, and Part 3 cites international
draft conventions relative to African labor.

882. U.S. Bureau of International Labor Affairs. DIRECTORY OF LABOR
       ORGANIZATIONS, AFRICA. Rev. ed. Washington, 1966. 2 v. (loose-
       leaf). map, tables.

      This revision of the second edition (1962) gives information on
the history, structure, composition, officers, membership, publications,
and international affiliations of labor organizations in Africa as of
May 15, 1966. There are 51 chapters, each devoted to a country (Vol. I
covers from Algeria to Nigeria; Vol. II, Portuguese Guinea to Zambia).
Narratives accompanying each chapter summarize important factors
affecting labor in the country. Included are political, economic, and
social data. There is a section on regional labor organizations.
Four appendixes list, respectively, the names of labor organizations,
names of labor officials, international trade secretariats, and U.S.
Department of Labor directories and monographs on foreign and international trade-union organizations. Supplementary material is kept
current by the Bureau.

883. U.S. Bureau of Labor Statistics. LABOR DIGESTS ON COUNTRIES IN AFRICA.
       Washington, 1966. 1 v. various pagings. (Bulletin no. 1539)

CHAPTER 22

EDUCATION

Bibliographies

884. African Bibliographic Center, Washington, D.C. COMMUNIST BLOC
          EDUCATIONAL ASSISTANCE AND CULTURAL EXCHANGES WITH AFRICAN
          COUNTRIES, 1965-1966. Compiled by Daniel G. Matthews.
          Washington, 1966. 19 l. Processed. (Special Bibliographic
          Series, v. 4, no. 5)

     Bibliography: l. 15-19.

     Lists treaties and agreements (for cultural and scientific
exchanges, etc.) between the Communist countries and African
countries and lists, furthermore, the subjects studied by African
students. Included also are several directories: of Communist bloc
institutions which have trained foreign students, of Communist bloc
ministers of education, foreign affairs, and culture, of chairmen of
state committees, and of commissions for cultural relations with
foreign countries.

885. African Bibliographic Center, Washington, D.C. PRELIMINARY EDUCATIONAL
          SURVEY OF AFRICA: A SELECT CURRENT READING LIST (1963-1966).
          Parts 1 and 2. Washington, 1966. 11, 13 p. Processed. (Current
          Reading List Series, v. 4, nos. 5-6)

     See note on this center, no. 292. Prompt listing of books,
official documents, pamphlets, and articles on education, each part
divided into a general and a regional section; alphabetically arranged
by author.

886. Brembeck, Cole S., and John P. Keith. EDUCATION IN EMERGING AFRICA:
          A SELECT AND ANNOTATED BIBLIOGRAPHY. East Lansing, College of

Education, Michigan State University [1962?]. 153 p. (Education
in Africa Series, no. 1)

     Classified by subject: administration and control; education and
change; educational planning; fundamental and adult education; teachers,
teaching, and students; vocational, technical, and special education;
and bibliographies in African education. Under each heading there
appear only a few references, chosen to cover all aspects of the topic;
an annotation so extensive as to form an abstract of the book or article
accompanies each reference. The work constitutes rather a study of
subject matter, illustrated by writings, than a proliferation of titles.

887. Couch, Margaret. EDUCATION IN AFRICA: A SELECT BIBLIOGRAPHY. London,
      Institute of Education, University of London.

          Part 1. BRITISH AND FORMER BRITISH TERRITORIES IN AFRICA. 1962.
              121 p. (Education Libraries Bulletin, Suppl. 5)

          Part 2. FRENCH-SPEAKING TERRITORIES (FORMER FRENCH AND BELGIAN
              COLONIES); PORTUGUESE AND SPANISH TERRITORIES; ETHIOPIA
              AND ERITREA; LIBERIA; AND GENERAL AFRICAN REFERENCES, 1962-
              1964. 1965. xii, 116 p. (Education Libraries Bulletin,
              Suppl. 9)

     The first part is taken from the catalogue of the Department of
Education in Tropical Areas Library and includes material to the end
of 1961 (it does not include South Africa). Arrangement is by country
with such subdivisions as bibliography, general, primary, etc. Part 2
lists books, articles, and reports available in the United Kingdom,
arranged first by country and then chronologically.

888. Drake, Howard. A BIBLIOGRAPHY OF AFRICAN EDUCATION SOUTH OF THE
          SAHARA. Aberdeen, University Press, 1942. 97 p. (University
          of Aberdeen Anthropological Museum Publication no. 2)

     Standard work providing extensive coverage of pre-World War II
material on the subject.

889. Hanson, John W., and Geoffrey W. Gibson. AFRICAN EDUCATION AND
          DEVELOPMENT SINCE 1960: A SELECT AND ANNOTATED BIBLIOGRAPHY.
          East Lansing, Institute for International Studies in Education
          and African Studies Center, Michigan State University, 1966.
          325 p.

     The 1,587 items listed cover books and articles in English, French,
and German. Entries are arranged by subject and thereunder by country.
They include works not specifically on education. Some helpful cross-

referencing has been included; there is an author index. Addresses
of serials and journals frequently cited are given in an appendix.

890. Leyder, Jean. L'ENSEIGNEMENT SUPERIEUR ET LA RECHERCHE SCIENTIFIQUE
          EN AFRIQUE INTERTROPICALE. Bruxelles, CEDESA, 1959-60. 2 v.
          67, 220 p. (Enquêtes bibliographiques, no. 2)

     One of the bibliographical series put out by this research center
(see no. 829). It contains 1,025 entries.

891. London. University. Institute of Education. CATALOGUE OF THE
          COLLECTION OF EDUCATION IN TROPICAL AREAS. Boston, G. K. Hall,
          1964. 3 v.

     Many of the works cited relate to Africa.

892. Nussbaum, Mary Johnston, comp. A SELECTED BIBLIOGRAPHY FOR LITERACY
          WORKERS (WITH SPECIAL REFERENCE TO AFRICA). Rev. and enl. ed.
          Hartford, Conn., Hartford Seminary Foundation, 1965. 133 l.
          (Hartford Studies in Linguistics, no. 16)

     Useful for literacy workers everywhere. Entries are arranged
under headings such as teaching adults, teaching reading, writing for
new literates, and literacy campaigns and programs. Some entries are
annotated. There are author, title, and country indexes, a periodical
list, and a list of agencies and organizations.

893. Parker, Franklin, comp. AFRICAN EDUCATION: A BIBLIOGRAPHY OF 121 U.S.A.
          DOCTORAL DISSERTATIONS. Washington, D.C., World Confederation of
          Organizations of the Teaching Profession, 1965. 48 p.

     Some of the dissertations listed are followed by abstracts taken
from DISSERTATION ABSTRACTS. Many entries concern studies undertaken
in Egypt. Arrangement is by author, and there is a subject index.

894. United Nations Educational, Scientific and Cultural Organization.
          Regional Center for Educational Information and Research in
          Africa, Accra, Ghana. INDEX TO AFRICAN EDUCATIONAL JOURNALS.
          INDEX DES REVUES PEDAGOGIQUES AFRICAINES. Accra, June 1967-

895. Yates, Barbara A. "A Bibliography on Special Problems in Education
          in Tropical Africa." COMPARATIVE EDUCATION REVIEW, v. 8, Dec.
          1964: 307-319.

_____. "Educational Policy and Practice in Tropical Africa: A
General Bibliography." COMPARATIVE EDUCATION REVIEW, v. 8, Oct.
1964: 215-228.

Useful, up-to-date bibliographical articles in the journal published
at Teachers College, Columbia University, and simultaneously at Oxford.
The COMPARATIVE EDUCATION REVIEW is significant as a source for information on African education.

Reference Works

896. African Education Commission. EDUCATION IN AFRICA: A STUDY OF WEST,
      SOUTH AND EQUATORIAL AFRICA. Conducted by the African Education
      Commission under the auspices of the Phelps-Stokes Fund and
      foreign mission societies of North America and Europe; report
      prepared by Thomas Jesse Jones, chairman. New York, Phelps-Stokes
      Fund, 1922. xxviii, 323 p. illus., maps.

      Abridged ed., 1962.

      _____. EDUCATION IN EAST AFRICA. . . . Thomas Jesse Jones, chair-
      man. New York, Phelps-Stokes Fund, 1925. xxviii, 416 p. illus.

      Abridged ed., 1962.

      The Phelps-Stokes Commission on African Education sent represen-
      tatives in the early 1920's to study the entire field of education in
      Africa south of the Sahara. The reports marked an important step in
      American interest in African development. As a direct result, the
      Jeanes schools were begun in East and Central Africa in 1925. Named
      after a Philadelphia philanthropist who left a fund for such purposes,
      these institutions trained African teachers and their wives to take
      charge of village schools and community improvement. An abridged
      edition of the two Phelps-Stokes reports, with introduction by Leonard
      J. Lewis, was published by the Oxford University Press in London, Sept.
      1962 (5, 213 p.).

897. "African Education South of the Sahara." JOURNAL OF NEGRO EDUCATION,
      v. 30, no. 3, Summer 1961: 173-364.

      The yearbook number devoted to African education has four sections:
      1, Common problems arising in the process of nation-building (articles
      on current political status, crucial problems, history and culture,
      urbanization, white settlers, etc.); 2, Some special educational problems
      (Ethiopia, South Africa and apartheid, Liberia and mass education, etc.);
      3, Some problems of implementation (role of the UN, stake of the United
      States, future of missionary enterprise, problems of teacher supply);
      4, Some major educational problems: a critical summary. The last is by

Karl Bigelow and Horace Mann Bond, who summarize, respectively, the Conference of African States on the Development of Education in Africa, held in Addis Ababa in May 1961, and the foregoing contributions to the yearbook. Among other symposia on the all-important subject of education in developing countries are two which appeared in 1965: EDUCATION AND NATION-BUILDING IN AFRICA, edited by L. Gray Cowan, James O'Connell, and David G. Scanlon (New York, Praeger, 403 p.), and EDUCATION AND ECONOMIC DEVELOPMENT, edited by C. Arnold Anderson and Mary Jean Bowman (Chicago, Aldine, 429 p.).

The journal carries in at least one issue a year an extensive bibliography of books, pamphlets, and articles on Africa, including many references to works concerned with education.

898. American Council on Education. Africa Liaison Committee. INVENTORY OF AMERICAN AID TO EDUCATION IN AFRICA. A listing, by geographical area in Africa, of 1961-62 educational assistance projects supported by funds from public and private agencies in the United States; prepared by Gwendolyn Groomes. Washington, D.C., Oct. 1962. 236 p.

A survey of aid for scholarships and other educational programs to bring African students to America and to help staff and students at African institutions. Included are statistical data on grants by foundations, private agencies, and government and also on university enrollment and staff. After a section for Africa in general, arrangement is by country.

899. Ashby, Eric, in association with Mary Anderson. UNIVERSITIES: BRITISH, INDIAN, AFRICAN: A STUDY IN THE ECOLOGY OF HIGHER EDUCATION. Cambridge, Mass., Harvard University Press, 1966. 558 p.

References and Notes: p. [377]-448; bibliography: p. 527-540.

A valuable history and analysis of the "export" of British university models overseas from the early nineteenth century to 1965. In Parts 1 and 2 Sir Eric establishes the historical background of European universities and discusses the founding of universities in Ireland, Australia, and (at some length) in India. Part 3 (almost two-thirds of the text) is confined to educational strategy in tropical Africa and the founding of universities there. Included is a section on the development of academic freedom and autonomy in Britain and Africa and a section comparing non-British patterns of higher education in Africa, i.e., the "Bantu" colleges in South Africa, Haile Sellassie I University, Lovanium University, and the universities in French-speaking Africa. Appended are 75 pages of documentary material. There is an analytical index.

An excellent essay on higher education in Africa by Sir Eric, based on a lecture series at Harvard in Apr. 1964, was published with the title AFRICAN UNIVERSITIES AND WESTERN TRADITION (Cambridge, Mass., 1964, 113 p.).

900. Coleman, James S., ed. EDUCATION AND POLITICAL DEVELOPMENT. Princeton, N.J., Princeton University Press, 1965. 620 p.

Contains articles by 18 economists, sociologists, and political scientists, including the editor, and is supplemented by a specially prepared "Bibliographic Guide to Education and Political Socialisation." The studies cover countries at four different stages of development: advanced, semi-advanced, partially developed, and underdeveloped. For the most part the articles take advantage of first-hand research, using modern sociological and general statistical techniques; they also refer to other published works. The work of coordinating and reviewing is undertaken by Professor Coleman in a series of articles which serve as introductions to the four groups of studies.

901. Columbia University. Teachers College. Institute of International Studies. Center for Education in Africa. African Education Series. New York, 1967-

In each monograph of this series social science, history, or psychology will be applied to the study of problems in African education. About three monographs a year are to be published. The first three to appear are: LANGUAGE, SCHOOLS, AND GOVERNMENT IN CAMEROON, by Hugh Vernon-Jackson; DIVERGENCE IN EDUCATIONAL DEVELOPMENT: THE CASE OF KENYA AND UGANDA, by Sheldon Weeks; and POLITICAL SOCIALIZATION IN THE NEW NATIONS OF AFRICA, by Penelope Roach.

902. Conference of African States on the Development of Education in Africa, Addis Ababa, May 15-25, 1961. FINAL REPORT. Paris, UNESCO and UN Economic Commission for Africa, 1961. 64, 27, 127 p.

Organized and convened by the UN Economic Commission for Africa and UNESCO, this conference brought together representatives of 63 governments (39 participants, 24 observers, including the United States) and delegates from UN and international nongovernmental agencies. The chairman was the Minister of Education and Welfare of Ghana, A. J. Dowuona-Hammond. The final report contains summaries of the plenary sessions--an inventory of educational needs, education as a basic factor in economic and social development, patterns of international cooperation for developing African education--and the reports of several commissions concerned with financing, educational planning, technical and vocational training, and adult education. These occupy 64 pages. Next, 27 separately numbered pages give the "Outline of a

Plan for African Educational Development" (also issued separately),
largely concerned with financing and ending with 80 recommendations
for long-term (1961-80) and short-term (1961-66) plans. The last and
longest section consists of annexes, including addresses and selected
background papers.

A follow-up meeting of ministers of education of African countries
engaged in the implementation of the Addis Ababa Plan was held in Paris,
March 26-30, 1962, under the auspices of UNESCO. Its FINAL REPORT was
issued as a UNESCO Document (Paris, 1962, 223 p., tables; UNESCO/ED/191).

903. Conference on the Development of Higher Education in Africa, Tananarive,
        1962. THE DEVELOPMENT OF HIGHER EDUCATION IN AFRICA: REPORT...
        3-12 SEPTEMBER 1962. Paris, UNESCO, 1963. 339 p.

The final volume emanating from the conference devotes its first
90 pages to the report. Sections cover the role of planning, staffing,
financing, choice of curriculum, inter-African cooperation, international aid and cooperation, and, at the end, conclusions and recommendations. A second part consists of statistics on staffing,
financing, etc., a descriptive list of institutions, figures on students
overseas, and a glossary of terms. In the third part there are printed
the major addresses of the conference, by the assistant director general
of UNESCO, the Vice-President of the Malagasy Republic, and the
minister of education in Tananarive.

904. Du Sautoy, Peter. THE PLANNING AND ORGANIZATION OF ADULT LITERACY
        PROGRAMMES IN AFRICA. Paris, UNESCO, 1966. 127 p. (Manuals
        on Adult and Youth Education, 4)

Bibliography: p. 125-127.

A guide to the solution of some common problems in the development of adult literacy programs at national and local levels in Africa.
The author was formerly director of Social Welfare and Community
Development in Ghana. Among his topics are motivation, legislation,
finance, publicity, language, teaching methods, audio-visual aids,
teachers, and supervision and evaluation.

905. Elliott, William Yandell, ed. EDUCATION AND TRAINING IN THE DEVELOPING
        COUNTRIES: THE ROLE OF U.S. FOREIGN AID. New York, Praeger,
        1966. 399 p.

Largely concerned with education and training as factors in
national growth and with the roles of the U.S. government, the university, the foundation and private enterprise in educational aid abroad.
Articles relating particularly to Africa are: "Education for Attitudes

in Nigeria," by W. R. Charleston; "Teacher Training for Nigeria and the Ashby Report," by Judson T. Shaplin; and "Developing Human Resources: A New Approach to Educational Assistance in Africa," by Arnold M. Zack.

906.   Greenough, Richard. AFRICA PROSPECT: PROGRESS IN EDUCATION. Paris, UNESCO, 1966. 111 p. illus., map.

A sequel to the author's booklet AFRICA CALLS, written following the May 1961 Addis Ababa conference on education. Covering nine countries which Greenough visited in 1965, the book deals with primary education in Madagascar, teacher training in Nigeria, higher education in East Africa, the literacy campaign in Mali, adult education in Senegal, audio-visual education in Ghana, textbook publication and news services in Cameroun, and the UNESCO educational building center in Khartoum.

907.   International Institute for Educational Planning. African Research Monographs. Paris, 1966-

Established in mid-1963 by UNESCO in cooperation with the World Bank, the French government, and the Ford Foundation, the Institute is a world center for research and advanced training in educational planning. Its aim is to aid member states of UNESCO in their social and economic development efforts through the increase of expertise in educational planning. In 1965, research teams, consultants, and local experts began to examine the practical problems of starting educational planning in newly independent African nations. By June 1967, 14 monographs had been published, covering francophone Africa, East Africa, the Ivory Coast, Nigeria, Senegal, Tanzania, and Uganda, and another two were in preparation.

908.   LANGUAGE IN AFRICA. Edited by John Spencer. Papers of the Leverhulme Conference on Universities and the Language Problems of Tropical Africa, held at University College, Ibadan, 1961-62. Cambridge, Eng., University Press, 1963. 167 p.

Series of specialist papers on language teaching in universities and on political, social, and educational aspects of language. Specially treated are the problems of multilingualism and the role of vernaculars. (See also Chapter 26.)

909.   Maes, Pierre G. AFRIQUE STATISTIQUES SCOLAIRES (JUIN 1963-DECEMBRE 1964). Paris, UNESCO, 1965. 94 p. Processed.

Contains charts and questionnaires, together with recommendations made by Mr. Maes to the ministries of education of the Central African

Republic, the Ivory Coast, Guinea, Upper Volta, Kenya, Mali, Mauritania, Senegal, Sierra Leone, Somalia, and Chad.

910. Moore, Gerald, ed. AFRICAN LITERATURE AND THE UNIVERSITIES. Ibadan, Published for the Congress for Cultural Freedom by Ibadan University Press, 1965. 148 p.

For annotation, see no. 1056.

911. Pan-African Catholic Education Conference, Leopoldville, Aug. 16-23, 1965. CATHOLIC EDUCATION IN THE SERVICE OF AFRICA: REPORT OF THE PAN-AFRICAN CATHOLIC EDUCATION CONFERENCE. Brussels, Regional Secretariat for Africa and Madagascar, Catholic International Education Office, 1966. 532 p.

Includes bibliographies.

A general account of the conference, studies prepared for the conference, debates and statements, reports of conference commissions on higher education, resolutions, and speeches. A short chapter deals with the activities of UNESCO in the field of education in sub-Saharan Africa, including Madagascar.

912. Ruth Sloan Associates, Washington, D.C. THE EDUCATED AFRICAN: A COUNTRY-BY-COUNTRY SURVEY OF EDUCATIONAL DEVELOPMENT IN AFRICA. Edited by Helen Kitchen. New York, Praeger, 1962. xvii, 542 p. illus., maps. (Books That Matter)

Bibliographical footnotes.

A "functional reference survey," and a source book of lasting value. It represents a notable accomplishment, namely, the collection and synthesis of factual and statistical information on all phases of education in almost 50 countries of Africa, presented to the editors in working papers by about 30 area specialists. The material is ordered according to region and country; for each country there are thumbnail statistics, the briefest possible bit of historical background, an outline of the history of education, a statement (with statistics) of the present situation, and plans and prospects for the future. It supersedes a compilation of 1955, RESOURCES AND NEEDS FOR TRAINING FACILITIES FOR AFRICANS IN BRITISH AFRICA, ETHIOPIA AND LIBERIA (Washington, 1955, 250 l., diagrs.).

913. Sasnett, Martena Tenney, and Inez Hopkins Sepmeyer. EDUCATIONAL SYSTEMS OF AFRICA: INTERPRETATIONS FOR USE IN THE EVALUATION OF ACADEMIC CREDENTIALS. Berkeley, University of California Press,

1967 [c. 1966] xliv, 1550 p. maps, tables, charts.

Bibliography: p. 1510-1550.

A valuable sourcebook for interpreting school, college, and university credentials of students from Africa. All phases of education are covered, including preprimary schooling and vocational, technical, and teacher training. Forty-four educational patterns of Africa (excluding Egypt) are described. Each national study is prefaced with a brief historical survey and a chart illustrating the ages at which students enter different levels of education. Entrance requirements, length of programs, and degrees awarded are listed. Appendixes include sections on the University of Cambridge Local Examinations Syndicate, the University of London General Certificate of Education Examinations, the West African Examinations Council, the French Baccalauréat examination, placement recommendations by the Council of Evaluation of Student Foreign Credentials, and a study of African students selected through the African Scholarship Program of American Universities (ASPAU).

914. Scanlon, David G., ed. CHURCH, STATE, AND EDUCATION IN AFRICA. New
       York, Teacher College Press, Teachers College, Columbia University,
       1966. 313 p.

Seven essays on the past, present, and future status of church-state relations with regard to education in Ethiopia, the two Congos (Leopoldville and Brazzaville), Uganda, Ghana, Nigeria, and South Africa. The authors are, respectively, Richard Pankhurst, Richard Dodson, Gerard Lucas, Roland Hindmarsh, Nicholas O. Amin, David B. Abernethy, and A. P. Hunter, with commentary by J. J. Fourie.

915. "Staffing of African Universities and International Co-operation:
       Report of an International Conference Organized by the German
       Foundation for Developing Countries in Co-operation with the
       Netherlands Universities Foundation for International Co-operation,
       Berlin, 2-4 May 1966." HIGHER EDUCATION AND RESEARCH IN THE
       NETHERLANDS, v. 10, no. 3, 1967: 77 p.

Recommendations and some observations on the conference precede the texts of eight working papers. Topics covered are the development of African universities since the Tananarive Conference, the development of French-language universities since 1962, academic standards and the university's function, staff problems and solutions at the University of Khartoum, recruitment and position of foreign staff in English-language and in French-language African universities, and international cooperation with regard to development of African universities.

916. United Nations Educational, Cultural and Scientific Organization.
         FELLOWSHIPS FOR AFRICANS. BOURSES DESTINEES AUX AFRICAINS.
         Paris, 1961. 51 p. (IES/5)

         A supplement to the 13th edition of the handbook STUDY ABROAD,
this is a round-the-world listing of organizations, universities, and
governments that offer scholarships to African students. There are
indexes of donor countries and recipient countries. The introduction
advises that the full annual handbook gives more complete information
about opportunities in specified fields of study.

         A handbook OVERSEAS STUDENTS IN BRITAIN, prepared by the London
Conference on Overseas Students, was published by the British Council
(rev. ed., London, 1964, 44 p., tables).

917. United Nations Educational, Cultural and Scientific Organization.
         STATISTICAL YEARBOOK. ANNUAIRE STATISTIQUE, 1965. Paris, 1966.
         612 p.

         In accordance with its major world interest, UNESCO assumes much
responsibility for the promotion of education in the developing
countries; in particular, the gathering of statistics has become its
function. This world survey, with some 600 pages of tables, covers
all aspects of education. The tables are in four main groups--
population, education, libraries and museums, and communications
(publishing, press, film, radio, and television). These are subdivided minutely, each heading having further division by continent;
thus the tables for Africa, country by country, stand first in each
category. Under many headings (for instance, education, Table 12,
secondary education--institutions, teachers, and pupils, 1950, 1955,
1960-64) 56 administrative entities are presented, including Ifni,
St. Helena, and the Seychelles. With such a wide scope it is not
surprising that some of the statistical information is from the early
1960's. For much of Africa, however, these are the latest available
figures having any pretense at reliability.

918. Widstrand, Carl Gösta, ed. DEVELOPMENT AND ADULT EDUCATION IN AFRICA.
         Uppsala, Scandinavian Institute of African Studies, 1965. 97 p.

         Papers of a seminar held in Oct. 1963, with contributions by
several experts, edited by the director of the Institute. Experiments
in adult education in various regions form much of the subject matter.

919. World Confederation of Organizations of the Teaching Profession. SURVEY
         OF THE STATUS OF THE TEACHING PROFESSION IN AFRICA. Washington,
         D.C., 1962. 148 p.

Based on a field survey made by a Commission on Educational
Policy for Africa of the WCOTP. Fairly full sections for each
country review such problem areas as low salaries, lack of new
candidates, and uneven standards, as well as many evidences of
progress in educational methods. The report was prepared by a
Gambian education officer, S. H. M. Jones.

CHAPTER 23

RELIGION AND MISSIONS

Bibliographies

920.   BIBLIOGRAFIA MISSIONARIA. v. 1- 1933- Comp. dal Giovanni Rommer-
          skirchen, Giovanni Dindinger. Roma, Unione Missionaria del
          Clero in Italia. Annual (1951, pub. 1952).

          A classified bibliography of books and periodical material on
       Catholic missions throughout the world, with author and subject
       indexes. The regional arrangement includes a long section on Africa.

921.   Coldham, Geraldine Elizabeth. A BIBLIOGRAPHY OF SCRIPTURES IN
          AFRICAN LANGUAGES. London, British and Foreign Bible Society,
          1966. 2 v.

          A revision of the African sections of the Darlow and Moule
       "Historical Catalogue of Printed Editions of the Holy Scripture,"
       with additions to 1964.

922.   Dejeux, J., and R. Caspar. "Bibliographie sur le dialogue islamo-
          chrétien." HOMMES ET MIGRATIONS: DOCUMENTS, no. 681, Feb. 7,
          1967.

923.   INDEX ISLAMICUS, 1906-1955: A CATALOGUE OF ARTICLES ON ISLAMIC
          SUBJECTS IN PERIODICALS AND OTHER COLLECTIVE PUBLICATIONS.
          Compiled by J. D. Pearson. Cambridge, Eng., W. Heffer, 1958.
          897 p.

          SUPPLEMENT, 1956-1960. 1962. 316 p.

          SUPPLEMENT, 1961-1965. 1967. 342 p.

See no. 315 for annotation.

924. INTERNATIONAL REVIEW OF MISSIONS. v. 1, no. 1- Jan. 1912- Geneva, New York. Quarterly.

Formerly the organ of the International Missionary Council, the review is now published by the Commission on World Mission and Evangelism of the World Council of Churches. Each issue has a "Bibliography on World Mission and Evangelism," in eight sections, which include a number of works on Africa.

925. Mitchell, Robert Cameron, and Harold W. Turner, comps., with the assistance of Hans-Jürgen Greschat. A COMPREHENSIVE BIBLIOG- RAPHY OF MODERN AFRICAN RELIGIOUS MOVEMENTS. Evanston, Ill., Northwestern University Press, 1966. 132 p.

A bibliographical survey of non-Islamic African religious move- ments which arose in connection with the West's impact on African societies. Items in various languages are listed (English, French, and German predominate). The 1,313 entries, most of which are annotated and some of which extend into 1966, include periodical articles, books, dissertations, and sections of books. Arrangement is by the following categories: theory, Africa general, West Africa, Central Africa, Middle Africa, and Southern Africa (each region is subdivided by country). There is an index of authors and one of ethnic groups. Supplements appear in JOURNAL OF RELIGION IN AFRICA.

926. New York. Missionary Research Library. DICTIONARY CATALOG. Boston, G. K. Hall, 1968. 17 v.

Several American missionary boards combined the resources of their libraries in 1914 to form the Missionary Research Library, which now houses more than 100,000 books, pamphlets, periodicals, reports, and archival materials. In the DICTIONARY CATALOG emphasis is on Protestant overseas missions, but works on Catholic missionary theory and activities are not slighted. Coverage includes the theory and practice of missions, histories of missionary societies, missionary biographies, and material on the cultures of African, Asian, and Latin American countries to which the missions have gone. Author entries include periodical articles. In Vol. XVII are listed the Library's holdings of nineteenth-century missionary magazines, some 800 currently received periodicals, and reports of churches, missions, and Christian institutions.

The Library's irregular OCCASIONAL BULLETIN often contained listings or other data of interest for studies of the mission field

in Africa. Published in 1961 as one of its issues is CURRENT
PERIODICALS IN THE MISSIONARY RESEARCH LIBRARY: ALPHABETICAL LIST
AND INDEXES, compiled by John T. Ma (2d and rev. ed., 38 l.). In
1961 the Library also issued a CUMULATIVE INDEX OF DOCTORAL DISSER-
TATIONS AND MASTERS' THESES ON FOREIGN MISSIONS AND RELATED SUBJECTS,
compiled by Laura Person (46 l.); although this classed list has no
regional breakdown, the subject index (p. 39-46) shows quickly which
items are of import for Africa. A guide to biographical information
on missionaries to all parts of the world appears in the Library's
MISSIONARY BIOGRAPHY: AN INITIAL BIBLIOGRAPHY (1965, 151 p.). Its
2,155 entries derive from books, pamphlets, articles, and obituaries.
Arrangement is alphabetical by title, and there is an index of authors,
compilers, and editors.

927. Streit, Robert, and Johannes Dindinger. BIBLIOTHECA MISSIONUM.
        Münster i. W., Aachen, 1916-63. 22 v. in 64.

        Tremendous bibliographical enterprise covering the literature
of Catholic missions throughout the world from earliest times to the
present day. The volumes have been issued by various publishing
concerns, but the monastery of Aachen in Münster has been the central
point. The literature is set down by continents and periods. Vols.
XV-XX cover writings on African missions from 1053 to 1940.

928. Walls, A. F., ed. BIBLIOGRAPHY OF THE SOCIETY FOR AFRICAN CHURCH
        HISTORY--I. 94 p. (Reprint from JOURNAL OF RELIGION IN AFRICA,
        v. 1, fasc. 1, 1967)

        Listed are 425 works related to African church history which
have appeared since 1961. The items, in fifteen languages, include
books, periodical articles, unpublished papers, popular books,
juvenillia, and newspaper articles. General arrangment is alphabetical by country, with a special section on biography. Annual
publication is a goal. There is an index of names.

Reference Works

929. All-Africa Conference of Churches. BULLETIN. no. 1- Oct. 1963-
        Kitwe, Zambia, African Literature Centre (P.O. Box 1319). illus.

        First issue, 60 p. Three issues are noted in AFRICA, Apr. 1964.

        An assembly of the All-Africa Church Conference was held in Ibadan,
Nigeria, in Jan. 1958, with over 200 representatives of Protestant
clergy present, more than half of them African. Its report was published by the International Missionary Council with the title THE

CHURCH IN CHANGING AFRICA (New York, 1958, 106 p.). A related conference, the Urban African Consultation, was held at Nairobi in Mar. 1961 (REPORT, 1962, 755 p.). The second assembly took place at Kampala, Apr. 20-30, 1963 (report published as DRUMBEATS FROM KAMPALA, London, United Society for Christian Literature, 1964), and a third was tentatively scheduled for 1967. The BULLETIN carries news on church conferences, etc.

930. Barrett, David B. SCHISM AND RENEWAL IN AFRICA: AN ANALYSIS OF SIX THOUSAND CONTEMPORARY RELIGIOUS MOVEMENTS. Nairobi, Oxford University Press, 1968. 363 p.

Begins with a detailed examination of the Luo tribe of Kenya, and then surveys 300 African tribes. This study probes the movements of renewal, protest, and dissidence within the Protestant and Catholic churches in thirty-four African nations over the last hundred years. By means of a cross-cultural methodology, it is shown that movements of renewal and independence emerge spontaneously from a well-defined background of social and religious tension, the strength of which can be assessed.

931. Beetham, Thomas Allan. CHRISTIANITY AND THE NEW AFRICA. London, Pall Mall Press; New York, Praeger, 1967. 206 p. maps. (Library of African Affairs)

Bibliography: p. 183-186.

A discussion of the future role of Christianity in Africa by a Methodist minister who was with Wesley College in Kumasi, Ghana, from 1928 to 1948. His emphases are English-speaking Africa and the Protestant religion. The author traces the coming of Christianity, evaluates the weaknesses and strengths of the Church at national independence, and weighs the challenges facing the Church and the Christian community, e.g., nationalism, Islam, traditional religion, secularism, and communism. Appendix III is a brief history of the All-Africa Conference of Churches. See also R. Pierce Beaver, ed., CHRISTIANITY AND AFRICAN EDUCATION: THE PAPERS OF A CONFERENCE AT THE UNIVERSITY OF CHICAGO (Grand Rapids, W. B. Eerdmans Pub. Co., 1966, 233 p.); and Adrian Hastings, CHURCH AND MISSION IN MODERN AFRICA (New York, Fordham University Press, 1967, 263 p.).

932. Benz, Ernst, ed. MESSIANISCHE KIRCHEN, SEKTEN UND BEWEGUNGEN IM HEUTIGEN AFRIKA. Leiden, E. J. Brill, 1965. 128 p.

Bibliography: p. 105-127.

A collection of six studies on the messianic churches, sects, and movements in modern Africa. Ernst Dammann writes on the conceptions of Christ in separatist sects; Katesa Schlosser on the secular reasons for membership in separatist churches of South and South West Africa; O. F. Raum on the politico-religious leadership among the Xhosa in the nineteenth and the twentieth centuries; H..W. Turner on the catechism in independent West African churches; and H.-J. Greschat on witchcraft and church separatism in Central Africa. Greschat also provides a preliminary bibliography on the subject of the messianic churches, sects, and movements, listing some 350 titles of various types of works in several languages.

933. Brelvi, Mahmud. ISLAM IN AFRICA. Lahore, Institute of Islamic
        Culture, 1964. xxxvi, 657 p. illus., maps.

Includes bibliographies at chapter ends and a list of sources (p. 602). A great deal of the material is based on the personal knowledge of the author, a Muslim. The preface has a thumbnail history of Africa from earliest times to the present. The book proper, comprised of 54 chapters and a conclusion, begins with the introduction of Islam to Africa. There are chapters on sections of Africa (2, Islam in North Africa; 10, East Africa; 14, British East Africa; and so on), each one followed by chapters on the of the region countries. Three appendixes give a selective chronology of the major events of African history; a list of African countries and territories, 1962, with area, population, etc.; and the estimated Muslim population of the world, 1962, by country or territory. The book concludes with a section of maps and an index.

934. Burridge, William. DESTINY AFRICA: CARDINAL LAVIGERIE AND THE MAKING
        OF THE WHITE FATHERS. London, Dublin, G. Chapman, 1966. 195 p.
        front.

The author, a White Father, recounts the life and work of Cardinal Lavigerie, who founded the White Fathers and the White Sisters and opened Roman Catholic missions in East, Central, and West Africa (after the Holy Ghost Fathers). Emphasizing religious rather than historical aspects, the book discusses the Cardinal's religious principles, his concept of missionary spirituality, his role as spiritual director to individuals, and his methods of conversion and of missionary training.

935. Catholic Church. Pius XII, Pope, 1939-58. THE FUTURE OF AFRICA: THE
        ENCYCLICAL, FIDEI DONUM, OF POPE PIUS XII. Apr. 21, 1957. London,
        Sword of the Spirit, 1957. 24 p.

This message is the foundation of present-day Roman Catholic activity in Africa. Addressed particularly to those working in the mission field, it called for "particular heed to the accession of new peoples to the responsibilities of political freedom."

936. Colloque sur les Religions, Abidjan, Ivory Coast, 1961. COLLOQUE SUR
     LES RELIGIONS, ABIDJAN, 5/12 AVRIL, 1961. Paris, Présence
     Africaine, 1962. 240 p.

     Eighteen studies by Africanists and clergymen on "The Contribution
of Religions to the Cultural Expression of the African Personality"
presented at a conference sponsored by the Société Africaine de Culture.
The studies fall into four main sections--animism, Islam, Protestantism,
and Roman Catholicism--each of which is accompanied by a panel discussion
in summary. Representative topics are the structure of African religions, by Melville J. Herskovits; Islam and Black Africa, by Amadou
Hampaté Bâ; Quakerism and the African personality, by Olumbe Bassir;
and the Bantu and Christ, by Placied Tempels.

937. De Mestral, Claude. CHRISTIAN LITERATURE IN AFRICA. London,
     Distributed by the Christian Literature Council, 1959. 84 p.

     Useful survey of fundamentals (the readers, the literature),
administrative matters (church leaders and missionary boards), and
matters of production and distribution (literature committees,
Christian bookshops, Christian presses). The last three sections
contain lists of addresses; the bookshops and presses are of Protestant
sects only.

938. Deschamps, Hubert. LES RELIGIONS DE L'AFRIQUE NOIRE. Paris, Presses
     Universitaires de France, 1954. 128 p. maps. ("Que sais-je?"
     no. 632)

     A succinct two-part survey describing traditional beliefs and
new religions (Christianity, prophetism, and new cults) in black
Africa.

939. Froelich, Jean Claude. LES MUSULMANS D'AFRIQUE NOIRE. Paris, Editions
     de l'Orante, 1962. 406 p. maps, tables (Lumière et nations)

     Bibliography: p. 361-366.

     Impressive general study of Islam in sub-Saharan Africa by a
former administrator of France Overseas. A distinguished ethnologist,
Froelich is now director of studies in the Centre des Hautes Etudes
sur l'Afrique et l'Asie Modernes (CHEAM: earlier name, Centre des
Hautes Etudes d'Administration Musulmane). He covers comprehensively
and succinctly the Islamization of black Africa, east and west, in
ancient and recent times and the colonial period. He then describes
the character of Islam--its aspect of conciliation of pagan and
Christian, its appeal to the animist, to the ignorant, and to the
learned, its mysticism, and the Brotherhoods. He concludes with an

analysis of modern tendencies of laicism and reform and prospects
for the future. Appendixes include various doctrinal creeds, a
lexicon of vernacular terms, tables on numbers of Muslims, Christians,
and pagans by country (p. 360), and a chronology of Islamization in
black Africa (p. 371-389).

940. Gatewood, R. D. SOME AMERICAN PROTESTANT CONTRIBUTIONS TO THE WELFARE
OF AFRICAN COUNTRIES IN 1963. New York, National Council of the
Churches of Christ in the U.S.A., Dec. 1964. 88 p.

Tabulated statistics of manpower and money devoted to missions in
Africa by Protestant churches in America.

941. Groves, Charles Pelham. THE PLANTING OF CHRISTIANITY IN AFRICA. London,
Lutterworth Press, 1948-58. 4 v., maps. (Lutterworth Library,
v. 26, Missionary Research Series, no. 12)

Bibliographical footnotes.

Published under the auspices of the Department of Missions, Selly
Oak Colleges, Birmingham, this is the definitive history in English
of Christian missionary work in Africa, Protestant and Catholic,
written by a professor of missions in the Selly Oak Colleges. Vol. I
goes to 1840; Vol. II covers 1840-78; III, 1878-1914; IV, 1914-54.

An excellent older work is J. Du Plessis, THE EVANGELISATION OF
PAGAN AFRICA: A HISTORY OF CHRISTIAN MISSIONS TO THE PAGAN TRIBES OF
CENTRAL AFRICA, published under the auspices of the University of
Stellenbosch (Cape Town and Johannesburg, Juta, 1930, 408 p., fold.
map; bibliography: p. 357-389).

942. International African Seminar, 5th, Zaria, Nigeria, 1964. ISLAM IN
TROPICAL AFRICA: STUDIES PRESENTED AND DISCUSSED AT THE FIFTH
INTERNATIONAL AFRICAN SEMINAR, AHMADU BELLO UNIVERSITY, ZARIA,
JANUARY 1964. Edited with an introduction by I. M. Lewis.
London, Published for the International African Institute by the
Oxford University Press, 1966. 470 p. front., maps.

Includes bibliographies.

Contributions on the history and sociology of the Muslim
communities of sub-Saharan Africa from the seventh century to the
present by leading experts in the field. Four of the selections are
in French, the rest in English; each is accompanied by a summary in
the other language. In Part 1 the editor reviews the penetration of
Islam into tropical Africa and sociological aspects of the interaction
between Islamic and non-Islamic institutions; a five-page bibliography
is included. Part 2 consists of 19 special studies on the subjects of
expansion of Islam and Islamic belief and practice in Senegal, Mali,

the Ivory Coast, Ghana, Nigeria, Sudan, the Somali Republic, Kenya, and Tanzania. There is an index.

943. International African Seminar, 7th, Accra, 1965. CHRISTIANITY IN
      TROPICAL AFRICA: STUDIES PRESENTED AND DISCUSSED AT THE SEVENTH
      INTERNATIONAL AFRICAN SEMINAR, UNIVERSITY OF GHANA, APRIL 1965.
      Edited by C. C. Baëta. London, Published for the International
      African Institute by the Oxford University Press, 1968. xiii,
      449 p.

      Bibliographical footnotes.

      Eighteen wide-ranging studies (in English or French, with summary
   in the other language) on the general theme of issues and problems
   most directly relevant to Christianity in tropical Africa. Arrangement
   is in three parts: "Historical Perspective," "The Analytical Perspective,"
   and "Trends and Prospects in African Christianity." The Rev. Professor
   Baëta has provided an introduction to each part, summing up the salient
   points of the discussions elicited by the papers. An index is included.

944. JOURNAL OF RELIGION IN AFRICA/RELIGION EN AFRIQUE. 1967- Leiden,
      E. J. Brill. 3 times a year.

      A journal devoted to the study of the forms and history of reli-
   gion within the African continent, especially south of the Sahara.
   Bibliographical material and instrumenta studiorum are regular features.
   For example, v. 1, fasc. 3, 1968, carried as Supplement I a "Bibliography of Modern African Religious Movements."

      See also THE BULLETIN OF THE SCOTTISH INSTITUTE OF MISSIONARY
   STUDIES (v. 1, no. 1, 1968- Edinburgh, University of Edinburgh, 3
   times yearly). It gives good coverage of Africa.

945. Leopard, Donald D. "Africa-related Materials in European Missionary
      Archives." AFRICAN STUDIES BULLETIN, v. 10, no. 2, Sept. 1967:
      1-5.

      For annotation see no. 51.

946. Monteil, Vincent. L'ISLAM NOIRE. Paris, Editions du Seuil, 1964.
      368 p. plates, maps (1 fold.). (Collection Esprit "Frontière
      ouverte")

      Bibliography: p. 337-349.

A broad survey of Islam in black Africa--its origins, its
characteristics, its expansion, its cultural, political, and social
impact and implications. Monteil concludes that Islam clearly
continues to expand (one quarter of the population of black Africa
are Muslims), to be dynamic, and, for the time being, "irresistible."
Three indexes are included, one of proper names, one of titles, castes,
CONFRERIES, and vernacular terms, and one of authors cited.

947. Mulago, Vincent. UN VISAGE AFRICAIN DU CHRISTIANISME: L'UNION VITALE
         BANTU FACE A L'UNITE VITALE ECCLESIALE. Paris, Présence Africaine,
         1965. 263 p. (Culture et religion)

       Bibliography: p. 245-259.

       A commentary on ecclesiastical unity vis-à-vis the unity of
communities and individuals among the Bantu--the author's aim being
the encouragement of Bantu participation in and contribution to the
Roman Catholic Church. The volume offers considerable discussion
of all aspects of Bantu life.

948. Mullin, Joseph. THE CATHOLIC CHURCH IN MODERN AFRICA: A PASTORAL
         THEOLOGY. London, G. Chapman, 1965. 256 p.

       Bibliography: p. 244-247.

       The author describes the forces at work in the African cultural
revolution. One of his main concerns is to integrate the rich African
inheritance of cultural and religious values into a future way of life.
The four parts cover general background, the theological structure of
the local church, the priest's sacred activities (baptism, eucharist,
etc.), and his apostolic activities.

       Another recent book on Catholicism in Africa is: Adrian Hastings,
CHURCH AND MISSION IN MODERN AFRICA (New York, Fordham University
Press, 1967, 263 p.).

949. Neill, Stephen Charles. COLONIALISM AND CHRISTIAN MISSIONS. New York,
         McGraw-Hill, 1966. 445 p.

       Bibliography: p. 426-429.

       For annotation see no. 554.

950. New York. Missionary Research Library. DIRECTORY OF NORTH AMERICAN
         PROTESTANT FOREIGN MISSIONARY AGENCIES. 4th ed. New York, 1960.
         78 p. (MRL Directory Series, no. 11)

One of a series of directories kept current by the Missionary
Research Library. Scope of the coverage is world wide. Others are
the DIRECTORY OF CHRISTIAN COLLEGES (1961, 38 p.) and an extensive
DIRECTORY OF PROTESTANT MEDICAL MISSIONS.

951. Pan-African Catholic Education Conference, Leopoldville, Aug. 16-23,
       1965. CATHOLIC EDUCATION IN THE SERVICE OF AFRICA: REPORT. . . .
       Brussels, Regional Secretariat for Africa and Madagascar,
       Catholic International Education Office, 1966. 532 p.

       For annotation see no. 911.

952. PERSONNALITE AFRICAINE ET CATHOLICISME. Paris, Présence Africaine,
       1963. 296 p. illus.

       Papers presented to a seminar called to discuss the role of the
Catholic Church and understanding African cultural nationalism.

953. Rencontres Internationales de Bouaké, Oct. 1962. LES RELIGIONS
       AFRICAINS TRADITIONNELLES. Paris, Editions du Seuil, 1965.
       202 p.

       A collection of eight papers delivered at a colloquium organized
by the Cultural Center of the Benedictine Monastery of Bouaké, Ivory
Coast. Denise Paulme's essay poses the question, "What do we know
about African religions?," Amadou Hampaté Bâ writes on animism in
the African savanna, Jacques Maquet on knowledge of traditional
religions, Hans Himmelheber on the system of religion among the Dan,
Pierre Verger on whether the traditional African religions are
compatible with actual forms of existence, William Bascom on African
religion in the New World, Luc de Heusch on possession and shamanism,
and Michel Leiris on African religious statuary. Discussions follow
each paper.

954. Schlosser, Katesa. PROPHETEN IN AFRIKA. Braunschweig, A. Limbach
       Verlag, 1949. 426 p. map. (Kulturgeschichtliche Forschungen,
       v. 3)

       Bibliography: p. 410-422.

       An ambitious work, identifying leaders of the dissident sects
which have arisen widely both among Christian converts and in Islamic
Africa. The list of prophets recorded, each through citation of
published sources of information, begins in the eighth century when
the first wave of Islam brought forth opposing prophets of the old
indigenous religions of Africa. These are followed through Northwest

Africa, the Sahara, Gambia, South and East Africa, and the Upper
Nile. Then come Islamic prophets, from the eighth century through the
time of the Mad Mullah in Somaliland. Last are discussed the prophets
leading splinter movements from the Christian missions, prophets who
often represented nationalistic as well as religious dissension, like
Harris in Guinea and Kimbangu in the Congo.

Studies on individual prophets and sects are noticed in the
regional sections of the present guide. Dr. Schlosser has herself
written a good book on indigenous churches in South Africa, EINGE-
BORENENKIRCHEN IN SUD- UND SUD-WEST-AFRIKA (Kiel, Mühlau, 1958,
355 p.).

955. Silva Rego, Antonio da. CURSO DE MISSIONOLOGIA. Lisboa, Agência
Geral do Ultramar, 1956. xlv, 700 p. fold. maps.

At head of title: Centro de Estudos Políticos e Sociais da
Junta de Investigações du Ultramar.

Bibliography: p. xxvii-xlv.

A history of Roman Catholic missions in general and Portuguese
missions in particular. Included is a chapter on comparative religions
with ten pages devoted to Bantu religion. Among the chapters on
Portuguese missions are seven on Africa--North Africa, São Tomé and
Príncipe, Portuguese Guinea, Cape Verde Islands, Congo, Angola,
Mozambique, and Ethiopia. There are several appendixes, a chronology
(1455-1955), and an index of proper names and place names.

956. Society for African Church History. BULLETIN. v. 1, no. 1- Apr.
1963- Nsukka, Nigeria. Semiannual, 1963-64; annual, 1965-

The Society for African Church History was founded in 1962 in
Freetown, Sierra Leone, as an international and interdenominational
organization. The president is Professor Groves, and vice-presidents
are Professor Baëta, Professor Dike, Dr. M'Tinkulu, and Bishop
Sundkler. The BULLETIN carries articles on church history (e.g.,
"Foreign Missions in Ethiopia, 1828-1868," "Christian African Participation in the 1906 Zulu Rebellion"). It also carries news of
the publication of recent works by members or the publication of
local church histories, and other news items. A French edition is
published in Yaoundé, Cameroun, under the auspices of the Faculté de
Théologie Protestante.

957. Sundkler, Bengt. THE CHRISTIAN MINISTRY IN AFRICA. Uppsala, Swedish
Institute of Missionary Research, 1960. 346 p. illus. (Studia
missionalia Upsaliensia, no. 2)

Includes bibliographical footnotes.

This extensive general study of the native African ministry was
written at the request of the International Missionary Council. The
author is a Swedish scholar and missionary who, after experience in
Zululand and Tanganyika, was named research secretary of the Council.
He traveled widely in Africa gathering the material for his survey. He
examines the development, mostly recent, of African leadership in both
Protestant and Catholic churches, the role of the pastor in the new
Africa, and his relations with his co-workers. Almost half the text
describes the training of ministers, including the patterns and trends
of African theological thought. In an appendix is a list of the theo-
logical schools, other than Roman Catholic, in the whole of Africa.
See also his outstanding BANTU PROPHETS IN SOUTH AFRICA (no. 2954).

958. Trimingham, John Spencer. ISLAM IN THE SUDAN. London, New York, Oxford
       University Press, 1949. 280 p. maps (1 fold. col.).

       Reissue, New York, Barnes & Noble, 1965.

       _____. ISLAM IN ETHIOPIA. London, New York, Oxford University
       Press, 1952. xv, 299 p. maps (part fold. col.).

       Reissue, New York, Barnes & Noble, 1965.

       _____. ISLAM IN WEST AFRICA. Oxford, Clarendon Press, 1961.
       262 p. map, diagr.

       _____. A HISTORY OF ISLAM IN WEST AFRICA. London, Glasgow, New
       York, Published for the University of Glasgow by the Oxford
       University Press, 1962. 262 p. maps, tables.

       _____. ISLAM IN EAST AFRICA. Oxford, Clarendon Press, 1964. 198 p.
       maps (1 fold.).

       _____. THE INFLUENCE OF ISLAM UPON AFRICA. New York, Praeger,
       1968. 170 p. maps. (Arab Background Series)

       Includes bibliography.

       The best-known English studies of Islam in Africa are by a clergy-
man who is also a sociologist and Arabic scholar. Dr. Trimingham was
in the Sudan as secretary of the Church Missionary Society in the late
1940's. He published his first booklet, THE CHRISTIAN APPROACH TO ISLAM
IN THE SUDAN, in 1948 (Oxford University Press, 73 p.). The following
year came his full-length study of Islam in the Sudan. In this he
analyzed the conflict between the dogmatic conception of religion, the
Shari'a, and the mystic Sufistic interpretation which had inspired the

Mahdist movement. In the same work he examined the present-day impact of the West upon the Islamic way of life. Dr. Trimingham then turned to Ethiopia. A short pamphlet, THE CHRISTIAN CHURCH AND MISSIONS IN ETHIOPIA, was published in a survey series by the World Dominion Press (see no. 2639n). ISLAM IN ETHIOPIA continues the author's main work, a definitive study of Islam in Africa south of the so-called Middle East (see no. 2639). This work was carried further in ISLAM IN WEST AFRICA, which similarly deals with the present age and the effects of cultural change. The second volume on West Africa is a historical study of Islam, going back to the medieval states of the Sudan before, during, and after the Mohammedan invasion. The chronological tables in the appendix run from the Soninke state of Wagadu in A.D. 750-800 to the French conquest of Guinea in 1902. The author is now lecturer in Arabic at the University of Glasgow.

959. U.S. CATHOLIC OVERSEAS MISSIONARY PERSONNEL. Washington, D.C., Mission Secretariat. Annual.

1962 ed., xxiii, 122 p.

Not available for examination.

CHAPTER 24

ANTHROPOLOGY

960. Note: There are a number of general tools for anthropological studies
which the researcher may wish to use, although the content specific to
Africa is too scant to warrant their listing here. The following might
be noted as examples:

a) CURRENT ANTHROPOLOGY: A WORLD JOURNAL OF THE SCIENCES OF MAN.
v. 1- Jan. 1960- Chicago. 5 issues a year.

Sponsored by the Wenner-Gren Foundation for Anthropological
Research, Inc.

b) INTERNATIONAL DIRECTORY OF ANTHROPOLOGICAL INSTITUTIONS. Edited
by William L. Thomas and Anna M. Pikelis. New York, Wenner-
Gren Foundation for Anthropological Research, Inc., distributed by the American Anthropological Association, 1953.
468 p.

c) INTERNATIONAL DIRECTORY OF ANTHROPOLOGISTS. 3d ed. Melville J.
Herskovits, editor; Barbara Ames, editorial assistant.
Washington, D.C., Division of Anthropology and Psychology,
National Research Council, 1950. 210 p.

Maps

961. Froelich, Jean-Claude. CARTE DES POPULATIONS DE L'AFRIQUE NOIRE.
Paris, La Documentation Française, 1955. col. map. 76 x 111 cm.,
fold. (Carte no. 71)

Scale: about 1:5,000,000.

_____. NOTICE ET CATALOGUE. Paris, La Documentation Française,
1955. xxx, 113 p.

Bibliography: p. xiii-xxvii.

A valuable tribal map. The accompanying text (NOTICE ET CATALOGUE) explains the map and contains a "répertoire alphabétique des populations" and listing of peoples in big cities and along important water courses. The tribes are entered by the best-known names, with indication of other names, and locations on the map (1,540 peoples numbered and located). The coverage takes in all West Africa from Mauritania to Angola, including Rwanda and Burundi as well as the former Belgian Congo. A long bibliography gives basic reference works and works consulted.

962. Hunter, C. Bruce. TRIBAL MAP OF NEGRO AFRICA: MAP N AND TRIBAL KEY. New York, American Museum of Natural History, 1956. 61 p. fold. col. map, 87 x 72 cm., 1:11,3000,000. (Man and Nature Publications)

Bibliography: p. 57-59.

On this large map, 1,016 tribes are located, with explanation in the text.

Another useful tribal map is that folded in the back cover of Murdock (no. 990).

Bibliographies

Note: See also nos. 29, 280, and 300.

963. AFRICAN ABSTRACTS. BULLETIN ANALYTIQUE AFRICANISTE. 1950- London. Quarterly.

Reviews and abstracts of ethnological, social, and linguistic studies appearing in current periodicals. It is published by the International African Institute with the assistance of UNESCO. A list of periodicals, most of them journals of learned societies from which contributions are abstracted, is given in each issue. The list constitutes a satisfactory register of both serials and institutions for anthropological study of Africa.

964. Andor, L. E. APTITUDES AND ABILITIES OF THE BLACK MAN IN SUB-SAHARAN AFRICA, 1784-1963: AN ANNOTATED BIBLIOGRAPHY. With an introduction by W. Hudson. Johannesburg, National Institute for Personnel Research, South African Council for Scientific and Industrial Research, 1966. 174 p.

A nonselective catalogue of books, pamphlets, monographs, confidential reports, and articles concerned mainly with the Bantu-speaking African. Annotations are in the form of abstracts. The

486 references in Part 1, on intellectual functions, are given in chronological units (1784 to 1963). The 35 entries in Part 2, on personality characteristics, cover the period 1950-63. Author and subject indexes are given for Part 1 only.

965. BIBLIOGRAPHIE ETHNOGRAPHIQUE DE L'AFRIQUE SUD-SAHARIENNE. 1932-
    Tervuren, Belgium, Musée Royal de l'Afrique Centrale. Annual.

Extensive annotated bibliography of books and periodical articles in ethnological fields relating to the Congo and to most of sub-Saharan Africa. The first volume covered literature from 1925 to 1930; coverage in later volumes is usually year by year (except after World War II). The title was originally BIBLIOGRAPHIE ETHNOGRAPHIQUE DU CONGO BELGE ET DES REGIONS AVOISINANTES. The adjective BELGE was dropped with the volume for 1959, published in 1961, and the new title was adopted with the volume for 1960, appearing in 1962. Earlier names of the Museum are Musée du Congo Belge and Musée Royal du Congo Belge. For some years the bibliography has been edited by Olga Boone. The 1964 volume (published in 1966) contains 577 pages, with around four annotated entries to the page. The arrangement is alphabetical by author, with an index of subjects, names of peoples, and countries. Increasingly over the years attention has been given to writings on the "neighboring regions," and subjects have been widened to include art, geography, law, literature, music, and philosophy.

966. Brokensha, David. APPLIED ANTHROPOLOGY IN ENGLISH-SPEAKING AFRICA.
    Lexington, University of Kentucky, 1966. 31 p. (Monograph
    No. 8, 1966.

Most useful survey of the theory and practices of applied anthropology. Part 1 is a bibliographical essay reviewing the major works by regions and subjects. Part 2 is a bibliography of important books and articles classed by subjects, i.e., health, labor.

967. Gibson, Gordon D., et al. "A Bibliography of Anthropological
    Bibliographies: Africa." CURRENT ANTHROPOLOGY, v. 10, Dec. 1969:
    527-566.

Covers archaeology, ethnography, social anthropology, culture history, prehistory, folklore, and linguistics, as well as the related disciplines of history, economics, political science, sociology, geography, and medicine. Arrangement is by topic and by region and country. There are author and subject indexes.

968. Hambly, Wilfrid D. SOURCE BOOK FOR AFRICAN ANTHROPOLOGY. Chicago,
         Field Museum of Natural History, 1937. 953 p. maps, figs.
         (Anthropological Series, Publication nos. 394 and 396)

       Bibliography: p. 728-866.

         This huge volume by the curator of African ethnology of the Field
       Museum is an attempt "to bring together a summary of all the most
       important facts that are known about Africa," on the basis of significant
       anthropological publications. Part 1, a synthesis of studies, covers
       outlines of physiography and nature, history, prehistory, physical
       anthropology, dress and ornament, psychology, languages and literature,
       and the culture area concept. Part 2 comprises basic elements of
       Negro culture, social organization, religion, and economic life and
       the European period. There is a long bibliography of the authors and
       works quoted, as well as a big general index and a bibliographical
       index. So ambitious a work naturally evoked much criticism; in
       addition, it has been outdated in many features by later research, so
       that now its chief value is as bibliography.

         A supplemental BIBLIOGRAPHY OF AFRICAN ANTHROPOLOGY, 1937-1949
       was published by the Museum in 1952 (Fieldiana, Anthropology, v. 37,
       no. 2, p. 155-292). A long list of periodicals from which references
       have been cited begins the bibliography (p. 161-173).

969. Hertefelt, Marcel d'. AFRICAN GOVERNMENTAL SYSTEMS IN STATIC AND
         CHANGING CONDITIONS: A BIBLIOGRAPHIC CONTRIBUTION TO POLITICAL
         ANTHROPOLOGY. Tervuren, Musée Royal de l'Afrique Centrale,
         1968. xxiv, 178 p.

       Bibliography: p. xxii-xxiv.

970. International African Institute. Africa Bibliography Series:
         Ethnography, Sociology, Linguistics, and Related Subjects.
         London, 1958- (Series A)

         A series based on the bibliographical card index of the Inter-
       national African Institute, compiled by Ruth Jones, librarian, with
       the assistance of a panel of consultants. Many of the entries have
       appeared in the quarterly bibliographies published in the journal of
       the Institute, AFRICA, since 1929, and the more notable periodical
       contributions have been summarized in AFRICAN ABSTRACTS, issued by
       the Institute in cooperation with UNESCO since 1950. Volumes published
       as of early 1969 are uniformly of folio size, in offset print: WEST
       AFRICA (1958, 116 l.), NORTH-EAST AFRICA (1959, 51 l.), EAST AFRICA
       (1960, 62 l.), SOUTH-EAST CENTRAL AFRICA AND MADAGASCAR (1961, 53 l.).
       They include books, periodical articles, and documents arranged by
       country and subject and under the main subjects, ethnography and

linguistics, by tribal groupings. Each part has an index of names of ethnic sections and languages.

Besides these comprehensive bibliographies and the above-mentioned current lists in AFRICA and AFRICAN ABSTRACTS, there are notable chapter bibliographies in the Institute's series, Ethnographic Survey of Africa (no. 980). Useful reading lists will also be found in a number of the studies described in this section. The various series are being reprinted.

971. INTERNATIONAL BIBLIOGRAPHY OF SOCIAL AND CULTURAL ANTHROPOLOGY. BIBLIOGRAPHIE INTERNATIONALE D'ANTHROPOLOGIE SOCIALE ET CULTURELLE. v. 1- 1955- Paris, UNESCO, 1958-61; London, Stevens & Sons, 1962-63, and Tavistock Publications, 1963- Annual. (International Bibliography of the Social Sciences)

Prepared by the International Committee for Social Sciences Documentation with the financial support of UNESCO. Vol. X, appearing in 1966, covers the works of 1964. Vols. I-V, published by UNESCO, were in the Documentation in Social Sciences series. Articles--from an international roster of more than a thousand periodicals--are arranged in a detailed scheme of subject classification. There are author and subject indexes. Some subjects have geographical breakdown (e.g., archaeology, arts and architecture, literature, religion), and there are references to geographical areas and individual countries including the continent of Africa.

972. Liniger-Goumaz, Max. PYGMEES ET AUTRES RACES DE PETITE TAILLE (BOSCHIMANS, HOTTENTOTS, NEGRITOS, ETC.): BIBLIOGRAPHIE GENERALE. Genève, Editions du Temps, 1968. 335 p.

See also F. Plisnier-Ladame, LES PYGMEES (Bruxelles, CIDESA, 1970, 255 p.

973. Royal Anthropological Institute. INDEX TO CURRENT PERIODICALS RECEIVED IN THE LIBRARY. v. 1, no. 1- May 1963- London. Quarterly.

Classed listing of articles in the periodicals received during the quarter (400-500). The six sections--general; Africa; America; Asia; Europe; East Indies, Oceania, Australia--are subdivided into physical anthropology, archaeology, cultural anthropology, ethnography, and linguistics. A separate annual index is to be published. In the first three issues of 1963 almost 600 references relate to Africa.

974. Wieschhoff, Heinrich A. ANTHROPOLOGICAL BIBLIOGRAPHY OF NEGRO AFRICA. New Haven, American Oriental Society, 1948. xi, 461 p. (American Oriental Series, no. 23)

By the former editor of the University of Pennsylvania series of
handbooks during World War II, later an official at the United Nations
and technical adviser with Dag Hammerskjöld on the mission in the Congo
in which both lost their lives in Sept. 1961. The bibliography,
prepared from a working card catalogue, was intended to precede a
second subject bibliography, even more comprehensive, which was never
issued. The entries in this "Tribal Index" are in alphabetical order
under the names of tribes, with many cross references for tribal names
and their synonyms. Works cited are in all fields related to anthropology, including travelers' accounts, history, geography, etc., and
are broken down as they apply to individual tribes. Besides books
and pamphlets, articles are selected from over 200 scholarly periodicals
and journals of learned societies, which are listed at the beginning
(p. vii-xi).

975. Work, Monroe N. BIBLIOGRAPHY OF THE NEGRO IN AFRICA AND AMERICA.
New York, H. W. Wilson, 1928. xxi, 698 p.

Reprint, New York, Octagon Books, 1965.

See no. 323 for annotation.

Reference Works

Note: For important anthropological journals see nos. 29, 280, and 300.
See also Chapter 17 for items on law in traditional society.

976. Baumann, Hermann, and Diedrich Westermann. LES PEUPLES ET LES
CIVILISATIONS DE L'AFRIQUE, SUIVI DE LES LANGUES ET L'EDUCATION.
Traduction française par L. Homburger. Paris, Payot, 1948.
605 p. illus. (Bibliothèque scientifique)

Bibliography: p. 521-552.

The German original of this basic work, in which the anthropologist
Professor Baumann collaborated with the philologist Professor Westermann,
was published in 1939, with a second edition in 1943. In the latter a
third part concerning the European impact on African society was by
Dr. Richard Thurnwald, but this is omitted in the French translation,
which is by the director of African linguistic studies at the Ecole
Pratique des Hautes Etudes. Dr. Baumann's part (p. 11-437), considered
authoritative by many European ethnologists, is a broad analysis of
cultural cycles and regional ethnography in sub-Saharan Africa.

977. Biasutti, Renato. LE RAZZE E I POPOLI DELLA TERRA. Con la collabo-
razione dei professori Matteo Bartoli [et al.]. 3. ed. riv. e

aggiornata. Torino, Unione Tipografico-Editrice Torinese, 1959.
4 v. (about 2500 p.) illus., col. plates, maps, diagrs. Vol.
III, AFRICA.

Includes bibliographies.

Handsomely illustrated compilation of data regarding the findings
of anthropological study, prepared with the collaboration of Professors
Ernesta Cerulli, Lidio Cypriani, and other leading Italian Africanists.
A general survey of African prehistory and of present-day races and
cultures is followed by chapters analyzing the physical anthropology
of African peoples by region, each chapter ending with bibliography.
A comprehensive index of tribal names is, unfortunately, in Vol. IV
of this encyclopedic Italian work, along with that of peoples of the
rest of the world.

978. Bishop, Walter W., and J. Desmond Clark, eds. BACKGROUND TO EVOLUTION
IN AFRICA. Chicago, London, University of Chicago Press, 1967.
935 p. illus., maps.

This book is the result of a symposium sponsored by the Wenner-
Gren Foundation for Anthropological Research and held at Burg Wartenstein, Austria, in 1965. The symposium reviewed Quarternary and Later
Tertiary research of the past ten years. The discoveries made call
for revised concepts concerning the origin and evolution of animal
species, vegetation patterns, and landscape features and of man himself
and his culture. The application of geophysical data to the study of
the Quaternary demands methodological reappraisals of the relevant time
spans and revised geometry of the stratigraphical setting. This is a
major work, thoroughly furnished with maps, sketches, tables, bibliographical information, and an index. It should prove indispensable to
specialists.

979. Case Studies in Cultural Anthropology [series]. Edited by George
Spindler and Louise Spindler. New York, Holt, Rinehart and
Winston, 1960-

Although designed for students, the series provides insight into
human social life in many diverse areas. A number of African studies
are included:

a)   Beattie, John. BUNYORO, AN AFRICAN KINGDOM. 1960. 86 p.
        illus., port., map.

b)   Cohen, Ronald. THE KANURI OF BORNU. 1967. 115 p. illus.,
        map.

c)   Kuper, Hilda. THE SWAZI, A SOUTH AFRICAN KINGDOM. 1963. 87 p.
        illus., map.

d) Middleton, John. THE LUGBARA OF UGANDA. 1965. 96 p. illus.,
map.

e) Uchendu, Victor Chikezie. THE IGBO OF SOUTHEAST NIGERIA. 1965.
xiii, 111 p. illus., port., map.

980. Ethnographic Survey of Africa [series]. Edited by Daryll Forde. London,
International African Institute, 1950-

The French series, Monographies ethnologiques africaines, is
published for the Institute by Presses Universitaires de France, Paris
(see no. 1670).

The volumes in this series are generally considered the most
comprehensive sources of information on the peoples of Africa, based on
extensive research in published material as well as on original field
studies. Each volume presents a concise summary of an African people
or group of peoples, covering location, natural environment, economy,
crafts, social structure, political organization, and religious beliefs
and cults. Each contains a bibliography and a specially drawn map.
A number of the individual volumes are now out of print, and there
are plans to make revisions in some of them before the proposed reprinting.

Subseries include Western Africa (English and French series);
North-eastern Africa; East Central Africa; West Central Africa; Belgian
Congo (prepared with the cooperation of the Musée Royal du Congo
Belge, now the Musée Royal de l'Afrique Centrale, and published also
in its series, Monographies ethnographiques); Southern Africa; and
Madagascar (a related French series). The full list of surveys published
in English or French in the various subseries is given in a list of its
publications issued each year by the International African Institute.
Many individual volumes are cited in regional sections of the present
guide. See also the excellent volumes in the African Bibliography
Series (no. 970).

981. Evans-Pritchard, E. E. THE POSITION OF WOMEN IN PRIMITIVE SOCIETIES
AND OTHER ESSAYS IN SOCIAL ANTHROPOLOGY. New York, Free Press,
1965. 260 p. illus.

Includes bibliographies.

An interesting collection of lectures and essays. Three general
studies are: "The Comparative Method in Social Anthropology," "The
Position of Women in Primitive Societies and in Our Own," and "Some
Collective Expressions of Obscenity in Africa." The major part of
the book is concerned with customs of the Azande, the Nuer, the Dinka,
and the Anauk peoples of the Southern Sudan, and of the Nandi and Luo
peoples of Kenya.

982. Fortes, Meyer, and E. E. Evans-Pritchard. AFRICAN POLITICAL SYSTEMS. London, Published for the International Institute of African Languages & Cultures by the Oxford University Press, H. Milford, 1940. xxiii, 301 p. maps, geneal. tables, diagrs.

Reprint in paperback ed., Oxford University Press, 1961.

See no. 619 for annotation.

983. Frobenius, Leo. MONUMENTA AFRICANA: DER GEIST EINES ERDTEILS. Frankfurt am Main, Frankfurter Societäts-Druckerei, 1929. 526 p. illus., plates (part fold.), fold. charts. (Erlebte Erdteile, v. 6)

Half-title: "Veroffentlichungen des Forschungsinstitutes für Kulturmorphologie."

984. Gibbs, James L., Jr., ed. PEOPLES OF AFRICA. New York, Holt, Rinehart and Winston, 1965. 594 p. illus.

Includes bibliographies.

Excellent compilation of African ethnological studies. It consists of descriptions of 15 tribal groups by anthropologists who have done field research in their areas and who have as a rule written fuller works on these tribes. The cultures described are representative of the major types of sub-Saharan Africa. Included are a guide to pronunciation of African words and a very full index.

985. Gluckman, Max. POLITICS, LAW AND RITUAL IN TRIBAL SOCIETY. Oxford, Basil Blackwell, 1965. 339 p. plates, maps.

Bibliography: p. 315-324.

A discussion of the forms of social organization among pre-literate, preindustrial peoples of Africa, with occasional reference to such societies outside of Africa. In seven chapters Gluckman examines the systematic interdependence which has evolved in these societies: data and theory, property rights and economic activity, stateless societies and the maintenance of order, the state and civil strife, dispute and settlement, mystical disturbance and ritual adjustment, and custom in stability and change. A descriptive list of the principal societies analyzed and a good index are included.

986. Holas, Bohumil. L'HOMME NOIR D'AFRIQUE. Dakar, Institut Français d'Afrique Noire, 1951. 105 p. illus., 48 plates, map. (Initiations africaines, no. 8)

Bibliography: p. 89-101.

Treatise by a French Africanist which is in the nature of a general handbook of African anthropology. Dr. Holas begins with a brief outline of human paleontology, physical anthropology, and anthropometry and devotes the bulk of his text to systematic description of the principal ethnic groups of Africa south of the Sahara, specifying over 150 tribes.

A basic primer, RACES OF AFRICA, by Charles G. Seligman, professor of ethnology at the University of London, came out in 1930. A third edition, with revised reading list, was published by the Oxford University Press in 1957 (236 p., illus.; Home University Library of Modern Knowledge, no. 144). Professor Seligman's racial groupings, based on physical criteria, are now questioned by many anthropologists.

987. Howell, Francis, and François Bourlière, eds. AFRICAN ECOLOGY AND
        HUMAN EVOLUTION. London, Methuen, 1964. 666 p. illus., maps.
        (Viking Fund Publications in Anthropology, no. 36)

Background papers (with bibliographies) and discussion transcription of a symposium sponsored by the Wenner-Gren Foundation for Anthropological Research at Burg Wartenstein, Austria, July 10-22, 1961. The symposium hoped to integrate studies on the biological-behavioral evolution of the higher primates with studies on the paleoecology and the mammalian ecology of sub-Saharan Africa. Topics of papers included observations on the ecology of some large African mammals, aspects of the Pleistocene paleogeography of the Chad basin, baboon ecology and human evolution, adaptive radiation in the australo-pithecines, and the origin of man.

988. International Congress of Anthropological and Ethnological Sciences.
        PROCEEDINGS.

        1st   London, 1934. 340 p.
        2d   Copenhagen, 1938. 397 p.
        3d   Brussels, 1948. 277 p.
        4th   Vienna, 1952. 3 v.
        5th   Philadelphia, 1956. (MEN AND CULTURES: PAPERS. 810 p.)
        6th   Paris, 1960. (Vol. II, ETHNOLOGIE. Paris, Musée de
                l'Homme, 1962. 664 p. illus.)
        7th   Moscow, Aug. 3-10, 1964.
        8th   Tokyo and Kyoto, 1968. 239 p.

In the volumes on ethnology at the 5th and 6th Congresses, about half the papers presented were printed (about 120 in each volume). Of these, less than a tenth were specifically on Africa.

989. Johannesburg. Public Library. Strange Collection. AFRICAN NATIVE
        TRIBES: RULES FOR THE CLASSIFICATION OF WORKS ON AFRICAN
        ETHNOLOGY IN THE STRANGE COLLECTION OF AFRICANA, WITH AN INDEX
        OF TRIBAL NAMES AND THEIR VARIANTS. Johannesburg, 1956. xxvii,
        142 l.

        Handbook giving classification numbers (Dewey) used in the
collection. Prefatory leaves d, e, and f give sources, and leaves
ii-xxvii the geographic class numbers. On the 142 leaves are listed
the African tribes, in alphabetical arrangement, followed by geographic numbers--e.g., aBulu (6755), which refers back to p. xiii
and locates the tribe in the Belgian Congo, Eastern Province. There
are about 13,000 names of tribes, including variant names.

990. Murdock, George P. AFRICA: ITS PEOPLES AND THEIR CULTURE HISTORY.
        New York, McGraw-Hill, 1959. xiii, 456 p. illus., maps (1 fold.
        in pocket).

        Includes bibliographies.

        A compendium of African ethnological data. In the first few
chapters Professor Murdock summarizes the general topics of geography,
race, language, economy, society, government, and history for the
whole continent; then follow systematic surveys by cultural areas.
Each regional section begins with a numbered list of the tribes in
groups of essentially identical language and culture, and each chapter
ends with a selective reading list. There is an index of about 5,000
tribal names, and, in a pocket inside the back cover, a large folded
map of the chief culture areas.

        Professor Murdock of Yale University had been associated with
the large project of Human Relations Area Files (HRAF) which brought
together in card form systematic data on all peoples of the world.
The material for Africa was a main source for this work. In 1959 a
collection was made available by Yale University, AFRICAN CULTURAL
SUMMARIES--a box containing reproductions of about 2,000 5 x 8 cards
of data on African tribes. The collection is held by a limited number
of libraries. For a description of Africa-related work of HRAF see
"News and Notes," AFRICA, July 1968, p. 341-343.

991. Ottenberg, Simon, and Phoebe Ottenberg, eds. CULTURES AND SOCIETIES
        OF AFRICA. With a general introduction, commentaries, and notes.
        New York, Random House, 1960. 614 p. plates.

        Bibliography: p. 565-598.

        Selections chosen to fill the need for a collection of readings
on Africa suitable for use in courses in anthropology in American

universities. The articles, all by well-known specialists, date from
1940 to the present. They follow an introductory survey of Africa
and its peoples by the editors. There are six groups of papers, some
general, some relating to individual areas or tribes. Most of the
essays are followed by references for further reading, and there is a
long classified bibliography.

992. Radcliffe-Brown, Alfred R., and Daryll Forde, eds. AFRICAN SYSTEMS
        OF KINSHIP AND MARRIAGE. London, New York, Published for the
        International African Institute by the Oxford University Press,
        1950. 399 p. illus., maps.

        Reprint in paperback edition, 1960.

        Symposium by nine eminent anthropologists who illustrate,
through study of a representative selection of native tribes in
Africa south of the Sahara, the main varieties of kinship organization.
The long introduction by Professor Radcliffe-Brown is a definitive
essay on existing knowledge and theory regarding kinship systems.

CHAPTER 25

TRADITIONAL RELIGION AND THOUGHT

Note: See also Chapter 23.

Bibliography

Note: For bibliographies, aside from those in works here listed, see the
bibliographic entries in Chapter 24.

993. Zaretsky, Irving I., comp. BIBLIOGRAPHY ON SPIRIT POSSESSION AND
         SPIRIT MEDIUMSHIP. Berkeley, Department of Anthropology,
         University of California, 1966. xvi, 106 p. Processed.

         A valuable listing of ethnographic sources (books, monographs,
     and articles) on spiritualism and the occult sciences in Africa, with
     focus primarily on sub-Saharan Africa. Most of the entries are
     annotated. Arrangement is alphabetical by author, and an ethnic group
     index is included.

Reference Works

994. Dammann, Ernst. DIE RELIGIONEN AFRIKAS. Stuttgart, Kohlhammer, 1963.
         302 p. map. (Religionen der Menschheit, v. 6)

         Bibliography: p. 281-288.

         This volume of a series of comprehensive syntheses of world
     religions is offered as "a survey for all those who require an initial
     introduction into the religions of Africa." Dealing with many aspects
     of religious origins, past concepts and rites, foreign religions,
     changes and present forms of African religion, it has detailed footnotes

and a full bibliography. Though learned and well documented, it is
not likely to prove the definitive work on the subject.

995. Froelich, Jean-Claude. ANIMISMES: LES RELIGIONS PAIENNES DE L'AFRIQUE
        DE L'OUEST. Paris, Editions de l'Orante, 1964. 253 p. maps.

        Bibliography: p. 233-238.

        Written by an authority on the subject, to answer the nonspecialist's
question as to what animism is; since the answer varies according to
the region, only that part of Africa west of Chad and south of the
Sahara is treated.

996. International African Institute. AFRICAN WORLDS: STUDIES IN THE
        COSMOLOGICAL IDEAS AND SOCIAL VALUES OF AFRICAN PEOPLES. Edited
        by D. Forde. London, New York, Oxford University Press, 1954.
        xvii, 243 p. diagrs., tables.

        Reprint, 1960; paperback reprint, 1963.

        This set of concise studies of the relationship of religious
myth and social practice as exemplified by typical African peoples is
one of the best-known works on African religion. The introduction by
Professor Forde, director of the Institute, explains the general frame
of reference--analysis of the world outlook of each people as expressed
in beliefs, ritual, and secular practice. The nine separate essays
are by distinguished ethnologists and social anthropologists who have
studied at first hand the societies of which they write; all are
provided with scholarly footnotes and reading lists.

        A later significant contribution on this theme was made at the 3d
International African Seminar, held in Salisbury, Dec. 1960. The
studies presented were published in 1965: Meyer Fortes and G. Dieterlen,
eds., AFRICAN SYSTEMS OF THOUGHT (London, Oxford University Press for
the International African Institute, 392 p.).

997. Joset, Paul E. LES SOCIETES SECRETES DES HOMMES-LEOPARDS EN AFRIQUE
        NOIRE. Paris, Payot, 1955. 276 p. illus. (Bibliothèque
        historique)

        Bibliography: p. 260-276.

        In a style which because of its subject matter can hardly fail to
seem sensational, the author of this study of the notorious "leopard-
men" societies examined records of trials and other evidence, analyzing
the basis of the secret society in religion and magic, its political
implications, ritual practices, and significances cf cannibalism.
There is a long bibliography of source materials.

998. Parrinder, Edward Geoffrey. AFRICAN TRADITIONAL RELIGION. 2d rev.
ed. London, S.P.C.K., 1962. 156 p. illus. (Seraph)

First published in 1954 in Hutchinson's University Library, World
Religions.

A general account of the old beliefs of the "incurably religious"
people of Africa which are still held by the majority of Africans and
underlie the veneer of new faiths accepted by the educated. The
author, a former missionary and professor of religious studies in
Ibadan University, is a recognized authority on African, religious
beliefs (see his WEST AFRICAN RELIGION, no. 1304). An interesting
study, WITCHCRAFT, by Dr. Parrinder, was brought out by Penguin
Books, Harmondsworth, in 1950 (208 p.; Pelican Books, A409; new ed.,
1963). In it he compares African witchcraft to the witch lore of
Europe, finding major similarities.

999. Smith, Edwin W., ed. AFRICAN IDEAS OF GOD: A SYMPOSIUM. 2d ed.,
revised and re-edited by E. G. Parrinder. London, Edinburgh
House Press, 1961. 308 p. map.

The introductory essay by the late Dr. Smith, a general survey
of the subject, is followed by a group of analyses of the religious
beliefs of the tribes with which the writers have worked. The
contributors are well-known missionary anthropologists of South-West
Africa, the Belgian Congo, and East and West Africa. The essay on
the Luo peoples of Uganda is by H. B. Thomas, formerly of the Civil
Service, the only layman of the group. The peoples studied are Bantu
and Negro tribes (except Bushmen) and the writing is nonacademic.
The first edition was published in 1950.

1000. Tempels, Placied. BANTU PHILOSOPHY. Translated into English from
LA PHILOSOPHIE BANTOUE, the French version by A. Rubbens of Fr.
Tempels' original work. Colin King, translator. Paris, Présence
Africaine, 1959. 123 p. illus. (Collection Présence Africaine)

First French edition, 1949.

This celebrated monograph by a Catholic missionary priest in the
Belgian Congo is described as a "revolutionary" study of the soul of
the Bantu; it tries to prove that his religious creed is not sheer
incoherent animism but is based on a solidly built set of abstract
ideas which constitute a complete philosophical system. Father Tempels
argued that a new approach is needed for the European missionaries and
ethnologists if their "mission civilisatrice" is to produce évolués
"in the noble sense of the word"--something which the civilization of
money values has failed to do. The brochure is well presented, with
dramatic full-page plates of Bantu carving.

CHAPTER 26

LINGUISTICS

Note: See also area sections for further references.

Bibliographies

Note: Bibliographical sources for the study of African languages and
linguistics are numerous and extensive, particularly for the early period,
when missionaries and colonial officers, making contacts for the first time
with unstudied tribes, were prolific in their written attempts at grammar
and vocabularies and in their translations of Scripture. Long bibliographies are included in such important linguistic studies as Cust's in
1883 or Sir H. H. Johnston's in 1919-22. THE CATALOGUE OF BANTU, KHOISAN
AND MALAGASY IN THE STRANGE COLLECTION OF AFRICANA in the Johannesburg
Public Library (edited by Anna H. Smith, Johannesburg, 1942, 232 p.)
contains 1,671 numbered entries. One regional section alone of the
bibliography compiled in 1937 by Russian linguists runs to over 30 pages.

Among the most useful sources are the various publications of the
International African Institute, which was founded in 1926 under the name
International Institute of African Languages and Cultures. The quarterlies
AFRICA and AFRICAN ABSTRACTS are in part bibliographical, with language a
major concern. The Africa Bibliography Series based on the bibliographical
card index of the Institute has linguistics as one of its three subject
classifications. BIBLIOGRAPHIE LINGUISTIQUE DE L'ANNEE [--] (English title
also; 1949-, Utrecht, Spectrum, annual) includes a section on the languages
of Negro Africa; it is published by the Permanent International Committee
of Linguists with financial assistance from UNESCO. The volumes of the
Handbook of African Languages series contain long bibliographies of the
languages covered, and the references in a good many of the volumes of the
Ethnographic Survey of Africa include linguistics.

The recently established JOURNAL OF AFRICAN LANGUAGES is an important
source. Other scholarly journals which, both in articles and in bibliographical sections, count linguistics among their primary interests are

340

AFRICAN STUDIES (formerly BANTU STUDIES, published at the University of the Witwatersrand); AFRIKA UND UBERSEE: SPRACHEN, KULTUREN; and the JOURNAL of the Société des Africanistes (Paris, 1931-).

Notable regional institutions devoted to language studies are the Institute of Swahili Research and the West African Language Committee. Such regional bodies as the East African Literature Bureau and the Bureau of Ghana Languages, which are publishing texts in the vernacular in increasing numbers, issue occasional lists of their stock. Lists from government information services include their publications in the vernacular. The current bibliography, NIGERIAN PUBLICATIONS, has a separate listing of works in African languages, as does the South African bibliography, AFRICANA NOVA.

The references that follow are in part bibliographical; see especially the entries for Cole, Doke, the Handbook of African Languages series. See also Spaandonck no. 2381, for wholly bibliographical material on Swahili. See also Angela Molnos, LANGUAGE PROBLEMS IN AFRICA, A BIBLIOGRAPHY (1946-1967) AND SUMMARY OF THE PRESENT SITUATION, WITH SPECIAL REFERENCE TO KENYA, TANZANIA AND UGANDA (Nairobi, East African Research Information Centre, 1969, 62 p.). There are 561 entries including books, articles, parts of composite works, and conference papers. Scope of the work, which is not limited to East Africa but covers other African areas, is sociolinguistics, not pure linguistics. Subjects are "language use, language teaching, the evolution of the language situation, descriptions of linguae francae, reciprocal influences of languages in contact, problems of transcription and translation, modernization and standardization of African languages, language policies."

1001. Murphy, John D. A BIBLIOGRAPHY OF AFRICAN LANGUAGES AND LINGUISTICS. Washington, D.C., Catholic University of America, 1969. 147 p.

Reference Works

1002. AFRICAN LANGUAGE STUDIES. no. 1- 1960- Edited by Malcolm Guthrie. London, School of Oriental and African Studies, University of London. Annual.

The first number of this significant new series contains thirteen articles on the structure of African languages by leading scholars. Succeeding issues maintain the high standard.

1003. Akademiia Nauk SSSR. Institut Iazyka i Myshelniia. TRUDY . . . , v. 10, AFRICANA. Moskva, 1937. 198 p.

Transactions of the Section of African Languages of the Marr Institute of Language and Thought, v. 9.

Part 3, Sec. 1, The South-eastern Bantu.

Includes papers, some by Western authors, as well as book reviews and a long "Bibliography of African Languages," edited by I. L. Sneguireff and N. V. Yushmanov (p. 163-196), listing books received by Marr Institute.

1004. Alexandre, Pierre. LANGUES ET LANGAGE EN AFRIQUE NOIRE. Paris, Payot, 1967. 171 p. (Bibliothèque scientifique)

Bibliography: p. 167-169.

A timely, essentially nontechnical analysis of the problems stemming from the linguistic confusion in independent black Africa and of their significance for Africa's political, cultural, and social future. The author devotes a large part of his book to a detailed discussion of current theories of African language classification; he also provides a synopsis of the most important African languages (location, number of speakers, classification, etc.), traces the historical development of African-language research, and comments on the social significance of oral literature.

1005. Cole, Desmond T. "African Linguistic Studies, 1943-1960." AFRICAN STUDIES (Johannesburg), v. 19, no. 4, 1960: 219-229.

A valuable bibliographical essay, offering comparative analysis of the most important modern works on classification of African languages and area studies, particularly of the Bantu area.

1006. Cust, Robert Needham. A SKETCH OF THE MODERN LANGUAGES OF AFRICA. Accompanied by a language map. London, Trübner, 1883. 2 v. 30 ports., 2 maps (in pockets). (Trübner's Oriental Series)

The first, and for many years the only, overall study in English of African languages. The writer followed the classification of African languages made by the Viennese philologist and ethnologist Friedrich Wilhelm Müller (ETHNOGRAPHIE GENERALE, 1873) into six divisions: Semitic family, Hamitic group, Nuba-Fula group, Negro group, Bantu family, and Hottentot-Bushman group. Cust's two-volume work describes the great variety of source material already available and locates the most reliably identifiable languages on a map which forms the first appendix. Other appendixes include a 50-page "Bibliographical Table of Languages, Dialects, Localities, and Authorities" (covering 438 languages and 151 dialects), a list of translations of the Bible, and various indexes of languages and dialects, authors quoted, etc.

1007. Doke, Clement M. BANTU: MODERN GRAMMATICAL, PHONETICAL, AND LEXICO-
GRAPHICAL STUDIES SINCE 1860. London, Published for the
International African Institute by P. Lund, Humphries, 1945.
119 p.

_____. BANTU LINGUISTIC TERMINOLOGY. London, New York, Longmans,
Green, 1935. 237 p.

Two works on Bantu linguistics by the former professor of Bantu
philology at the University of the Witwatersrand, Johannesburg. His
classification of Bantu languages into seven zones, four subzones,
and subsidiary groups and dialect clusters is presented in the first
named, which is essentially a bibliographical study. From 1931 to
1953 Professor Doke was joint editor of AFRICAN STUDIES (formerly
BANTU STUDIES) published by the University. A reprint with additions
of his long article of 1943, "The Growth of Comparative Bantu
Philology," appeared in that journal in 1960 (v. 19, no. 4, p. 193-
218).

1008. France. Centre National de la Recherche Scientifique. CLASSIFICATION
NOMINALE DANS LES LANGUES NEGROAFRICAINES. Paris, 1967. 400 p.
(Colloques internationaux. Sciences humaines)

1009. Greenberg, Joseph H. THE LANGUAGES OF AFRICA. Bloomington, Indiana
University, 1963. 171 p. (INTERNATIONAL JOURNAL OF AMERICAN
LINGUISTICS, v. 29, no. 1, pt. 2; Research Center in Anthro-
pology, Folklore, and Linguistics of Indiana University,
Publication no. 25)

_____. STUDIES IN AFRICAN LINGUISTIC CLASSIFICATION. New Haven,
Conn., Compass Pub. Co., 1955. 116 p. maps (1 fold.).

Reprinted from the SOUTHWESTERN JOURNAL OF ANTHROPOLOGY for the
Language and Communication Research Center, Columbia University, and
the Program of African Studies, Northwestern University.

In seven papers published in the SOUTHWESTERN JOURNAL OF ANTHRO-
POLOGY in 1949-50 Professor Greenberg offered an entirely new
classification of African languages, based not on typological criteria
but on rigorous lexical and morphological comparison. His terms were
made more explicit in an eighth paper published in 1954 (SJA, v. 10,
no. 4). The first tabulation offered 6 major genetic language
families and 10 lesser ones. In 1954 the author revised the list,
reducing the number of independent families to 12. These eight
papers make up the reprint of 1955. A summary by Professor William
E. Welmers ("Note on the Classification of African Languages,"
LINGUISTIC REPORTER, v. 1, no. 2, May 1959; supplement no. 1) indicates
that Greenberg is now inclined to reduce his families to 4 which
Welmers labels Afro-Asiatic, Sahara-Savannah, Niger-Congo, and Macro-

Khoisan. Professor Greenberg has further simplified his classifications in the revised study, THE LANGUAGES OF AFRICA, published in
1963.

Controversy regarding classification of African languages is by
no means over. See, for example, an article in CURRENT ANTHROPOLOGY,
Feb. 1964, by Harold K. Schneider, "Confusion in African Linguistic
Classification," with replies by Dr. Greenberg and George P. Murdock
(v. 5, no. 1, p. 56-57). But the data being accumulated by Dr.
Greenberg and students in West Africa put the burden of proof now on
his opponents.

For a recent analytical study and general synthesis of languages
in sub-Saharan Africa see Pierre Alexandre's LANGUES ET LANGAGE EN
AFRIQUE NOIRE (no. 1004).

1010. Guthrie, Malcolm. THE CLASSIFICATION OF THE BANTU LANGUAGES. London,
        New York, Published for the International African Institute by
        the Oxford University Press, 1948. 91 p. map (fold. col. in
        pocket).

Inventory and classification of Bantu languages and dialects,
much of it based on data gathered by Dr. Guthrie himself in little-
known areas. This was expanded in his volume THE BANTU LANGUAGES
OF WESTERN EQUATORIAL AFRICA in the Handbook of African Languages
series (below). For comment on both see the article by Cole, cited
above.

1011. Handbook of African Languages [series]. London, New York, Published
        for the International African Institute by Oxford University
        Press, 1948-

This series was planned "to provide a systematic and critical
study of the incidence, distribution and interrelations of the
different African languages and dialects, as well as of the numbers
speaking the several languages and dialects, and the extent of
literacy among these different groups." It includes bibliographies
of publications relating to the various language groups--linguistic
studies, grammars, dictionaries, and textbooks. The following are
among the handbooks published:

a) LA LANGUE BERBERE. By André Basset. 1952. 71 p. map, diagrs.

b) LANGUAGES OF WEST AFRICA. By D. Westermann and M. A. Bryan.
        1952. 201 p. map.

c) THE NON-BANTU LANGUAGES OF NORTH-EASTERN AFRICA. By A. N.
        Tucker and M. A. Bryan. 1956. 228 p. maps.

d) THE BANTU LANGUAGES OF AFRICA. Compiled by M. A. Bryan. 1959. 170 p. map.

e) THE CLASSIFICATION OF THE BANTU LANGUAGES. By Malcolm Guthrie. 1948. 91 p. map.

f) THE BANTU LANGUAGES OF WESTERN EQUATORIAL AFRICA. By Malcolm Guthrie. 1953. 94 p. map.

g) THE SOUTHERN BANTU LANGUAGES. By Clement M. Doke. 1954. 302 p. map.

Also issued by the International African Institute are the following:

h) LINGUISTIC SURVEY OF THE NORTHERN BANTU BORDERLAND, vol. I. By A. Jacquot, I. Richardson, G. van Bulck, Peter Hackett, A. N. Tucker, and M. A. Bryan. 1956. 146 p. maps.

_____, vol. II. By Irvine Richardson. 1956. 95 p.

_____, vol. III. By G. van Bulck.

_____, vol. IV. By A. N. Tucker and M. A. Bryan. 1957. 89 p. maps.

1012. Johnston, Sir Harry H. A COMPARATIVE STUDY OF THE BANTU AND SEMI-BANTU LANGUAGES. Oxford, Clarendon Press, 1919-22. 2 v.

Bibliography: v. 1, p. 784-815.

In this impressive work, still one of the landmarks of African linguistic studies, the famous explorer and writer gave illustrative vocabularies of over 200 languages and dialects. The first volume includes an annotated bibliography of his sources.

1013. JOURNAL OF AFRICAN LANGUAGES. v. 1, pt. 1- 1962- London, Macmillan, 1962-65; Hertford, Mimram Books, Ltd., 1965- 3 pts.

A scholarly linguistic journal originally sponsored jointly by Michigan State University and the School of Oriental and African Studies of the University of London, later by Michigan State University alone. The first editor was Professor Jack Berry, then of the School of Oriental and African Studies; Irvine Richardson became editor with Vol. III, Part 3 (1964). The roll of assistant editors and editorial consultants includes leading philologists of Europe, the United States, and Africa. Each part carries five or more papers of high professional level. Recent issues also have a bibliographical list ("Bibliographia"), reviews, and notices.

A comparable periodical though of more limited range is the
JOURNAL OF WEST AFRICAN LANGUAGES (see no. 1264). Also limited to
West African languages and limited to a much more modest scale is the
new RESEARCH NOTES (Mar. 1967-) of the Department of Linguistics and
Nigerian Languages of the University of Ibadan. Available data are
presented in the form of word lists, folk tales, grammatical notes,
and the like.

1014. Meinhof, Carl. AN INTRODUCTION TO THE STUDY OF AFRICAN LANGUAGES.
          Translated by Alice Werner. London, Dent; New York, Dutton,
          1915. 169 p.

       Professor Meinhof, of the Kolonial-Institut in Hamburg, was one
of Europe's foremost authorities on African languages. J. Lukas, in
an obituary article in the journal founded and edited by Meinhof,
ZEITSCHRIFT FUR EINGEBORENEN-SPRACHEN (now AFRIKA UND UBERSEE), gave
a 40-page list of his writings--including book reviews--on African
languages (many, but not all, on Bantu languages), religion, etc.
The above book is largely concerned with phonetics.

1015. Spaandonck, Marcel van, comp. PRACTICAL AND SYSTEMATICAL SWAHILI
          BIBLIOGRAPHY: LINGUISTICS, 1850-1963. Leiden, E. J. Brill,
          1965. xxiv, 61 p.

       For annotation see no. 2381.

1016. SWAHILI: JOURNAL OF THE INSTITUTE OF SWAHILI RESEARCH. v. 36- Mar.
          1966- Edited by W. H. Whiteley. Dar es Salaam, Institute of
          Swahili Research, University College. Semiannual.

       See no. 2401 for description.

1017. U.S. Department of State. Foreign Service Institute. Basic Course
          Series [of African languages]. Washington, U.S. Govt. Print.
          Off., 1962-

       A program of African language studies is being carried on by
the Foreign Service Institute in Washington. It is planned to
include languages of sub-Saharan Africa, plus Amharic. Textbooks
for general use in a Basic Course Series are being published, among
them Chinyanja (1965, 351 p.), Fula (1965, 489 p.), Hausa (1963,
399 p.), Igbo (1962, 498 p.), Kirundi (1965, 526 p.), Kituba (1963,
470 p.), Lingala (1963, 293 p.), Moré (1966, 340 p.), Shona (1965,
519 p.), Swahili (1963, 560 p.), Twi (1963, 224 p.), and Yoruba
(1963, 343 p.).

347

1018. U.S. Library of Congress. General Reference and Bibliography
Division. FOREIGN LANGUAGE-ENGLISH DICTIONARIES. Washington,
1955. 2 v. Vol. I, SPECIAL SUBJECT DICTIONARIES. Vol. II,
GENERAL LANGUAGE DICTIONARIES.

This seems to be the most comprehensive list of dictionaries,
including those of as many African languages as possible, although
longer lists for individual languages will be found in the bibliographies included in the Handbook of African Languages series and
other linguistic studies relating to individual languages or groups
of languages. In Vol. II, GENERAL LANGUAGE DICTIONARIES, there are
cited 1,465 items, dictionaries or grammatical works including
vocabularies. Arrangment is under the accepted name of the language,
with cross-references under alternate names (e.g., Ashanti, see Twi).
Of the total, at least a third (400-500) of the titles relate to
African languages.

1019. Westermann, Diedrich. DIE SUDANSPRACHEN: EINE SPRACHVERGLEICHENDE
STUDIE. Hamburg, L. Friederichsen, 1911. 222 p. map.
(Abhandlungen des Hamburgischen Kolonialinstituts, Bd. 3)

_____. DIE WESTLICHEN SUDANSPRACHEN UND IHRE BEZEIHUNGEN ZUM
BANTU. Berlin, de Gruyter, 1927. 313 p. (Beiheft zu den
Mitteilungen des Seminars für orientalische Sprachen, Jahrg.
29)

_____. "Les langues et l'éducation." In Baumann, Hermann, and
Diedrich Westermann. LES PEUPLES ET LES CIVILISATIONS DE
L'AFRIQUE, SUIVI DE LES LANGUES ET L'EDUCATION. Traduction
française par L. Homburger. Paris, Payot, 1948. 605 p. illus.
(Bibliothèque scientifique)

Major contributions to the general field of African linguistics
by the famous German scholar.

Simple popularizations of Westermann's five-way division of
African languages (Semitic, Hamitic, Negro, Bantu, Hottentot-
Bushman) were written by Dr. Alice Werner: THE LANGUAGE FAMILIES
OF AFRICA (2d ed., London, Society for Promoting Christian Knowledge,
1951, 149 p., map, tables) and STRUCTURE AND RELATIONSHIP OF AFRICAN
LANGUAGES (London, New York, Longmans, Green, 1930, 61 p.)

1020. Westermann, Diedrich, and Ida C. Ward. PRACTICAL PHONETICS FOR
STUDENTS OF AFRICAN LANGUAGES. London, Published for the
International Institute of African Languages and Cultures by
Oxford University Press, H. Milford, 1933. xvi, 227 p. illus.

3d impression, 1957. xvi, 169 p. illus. Bibliography: p. 158-160.

This book has been for many years a basic text of students of African languages. The authors begin with a consideration of the difficulties of learning a new language and explain phonetic alphabets and orthography, the organs of speech, classification of vowel and consonant sounds, and phonemes. Then they turn to the specifically African sounds, classifying the various types of vowels and consonants and explaining syllables, stresses, etc. Over 50 pages are given to phonetic summaries of 10 languages. There is a subject index, as well as an index of about 70 languages, broken down by subject.

A pamphlet guide, A PRACTICAL ORTHOGRAPHY OF AFRICAN LANGUAGES, issued by the International Institute of African Languages and Cultures (now International African Institute) as its Memorandum 1 in 1927 (16 p.) and revised in 1930, set down the standard phonetic system advocated by the Institute. Another of the Memoranda Series (no. 14, 1937), PRACTICAL SUGGESTIONS FOR LEARNING AN AFRICAN LANGUAGE IN THE FIELD, by Ida C. Ward, which was issued as a supplement to AFRICA, v. 10, no. 2, has been reprinted by the Institute (1960, 39 p.).

CHAPTER 27

<u>ARTS AND LETTERS</u>

GENERAL

1021. <u>Note</u>: In several recent books by Africans evaluating traditional culture and the effect of contacts with the West, literature by and about the African is a central theme. Among notable studies are:

  a) Abraham, William E. THE MIND OF AFRICA. Chicago, University of Chicago Press, 1962. 206 p. (The Nature of Human Society)

  b) Jahn, Janheinz. MUNTU: AN OUTLINE OF THE NEW AFRICAN CULTURE. Translated by Marjorie Grene. New York, Grove Press, 1961. 267 p. illus.

  c) Mphahlele, Ezekiel. THE AFRICAN IMAGE. London, Faber & Faber; New York, Praeger, 1962. 240 p.

<u>Bibliographies</u>

<u>Note</u>: See also under regions and countries in Part IV.

1022. ARTS, HUMAN BEHAVIOR, AND AFRICA. New York, African Studies Association, 1962. 70 p. (AFRICAN STUDIES BULLETIN, v. 5, no. 2, May 1962)

     Special issue of the bulletin of the African Studies Association, devoted to essays on various aspects of the arts in Africa and including helpful selected bibliographies. The latter relate to music (by Alan P. Merriam, p. 35-40), art (by Roy Sieber, p. 40-42), oral

literature (by Daniel J. Crowley, p. 43-44), dance (by Nadia
Chilkovsky, p. 45-47), architecture (by Douglas Fraser, p. 47-49),
theater and drama (by Herbert L. Shore, p. 49-53), and "Fiction by
African Authors: A Preliminary Checklist" (by Dorothy B. Porter,
p. 54-66).

Reference Works

1023. AFRICAN ARTS/ARTS D'AFRIQUE. v. 1, no. 1- Autumn 1967- Los Angeles,
      African Studies Center, University of California. illus.
      (part col.). Quarterly.

      This handsome new quarterly is devoted to the traditional and
contemporary arts of Africa, its purpose being "to record the art
of the African past, to provide an outlet for the contemporary
African artist, and to stimulate the creative arts in Africa."
Contributions are in English or French.

1024. Belinga, Eno. LITTERATURE ET MUSIQUE POPULAIRE EN AFRIQUE NOIRE.
      Paris, Editions Cujas, 1965. 258 p. illus., music.

1025. Congrès International des Ecrivains et Artistes Noirs, 1st, Paris,
      Sept. 1956. CONTRIBUTIONS. Paris, Présence Africaine, 1958.
      363 p. ports. (PRESENCE AFRICAINE, n.s. no. 14-15, June-Sept.
      1957)

      ————. 2d, Rome, Mar.-Apr. 1959. RESPONSABILITES DES HOMMES
      DE CULTURE. Paris, Présence Africaine, 1959. 368 p. (PRESENCE
AFRICAINE, n.s. no. 27-28, Aug.-Nov. 1959)

      The first International Congress of Negro Writers and Artists
was called by Alioune Diop, founder and editor of the journal
PRESENCE AFRICAINE, which is the chief organ of French-speaking
African intellectuals. It was well attended by Negro writers from
many parts of Africa and from the United States. The second Congress,
three years later, was given still more attention. Papers contributed
at both sessions were concerned with the manifestations of African
culture: in 1956, with literature, art, theater, dance, etc., but
also with political expression, particularly the expression of race
and culture conflicts; in 1959, with the concept of négritude, with
the re-creation of African history, African philosophy, and, in
general, the assertion of the African personality in the arts and
social sciences.

      The influence of African art and music on the Western world was
the main theme of a conference, the International Congress of African

Culture, held in Salisbury, Rhodesia, in Aug. 1962. About 70 delegates from Africa, the Americas, Europe, and the West Indies were invited to give papers.

The first World Festival of Negro Arts, designed to illustrate the contribution of Negro culture to world civilization, took place in Dakar, Senegal, in Apr. 1966. The opening address was by President Léopold Sédar Senghor. For almost four weeks poetry, plays, dances, musical programs, and exhibitions of contemporary and traditional painting, sculpture, and handicrafts were presented by 24 nations, including 14 countries of black Africa. Fifty-one photographs of art works loaned by IFAN appear in "Catalogue des oeuvres d'art prêtées par l'IFAN au Musée Dynamique du premier Festival Mondial des Arts Negrès (avril 1966)," NOTES AFRICAINES, no. 110, Apr. 1966: 36-71.

1026.   JOURNAL OF THE NEW AFRICAN LITERATURE. Spring 1966- Stanford, Calif. illus. Semiannual.

Retitled JOURNAL OF THE NEW AFRICAN LITERATURE AND THE ARTS, Fall 1966.

Writings on modern African literature, music, the fine arts, and the performing arts, including African dance, appear in the journal's pages. Articles, by both new and established authors, may be in English, French, Portuguese, or African languages, along with English translations for the last two. The editor and publisher is Joseph O. O. Okpaku.

LITERATURE

Note: In addition to African literature series being published outside of Africa (see nos. 1040, 1046, and 1059), publishers in Africa are also launching such series in an attempt to stimulate creative writing. For example, the series Modern African Library of the East African Publishing House, Nairobi, offers original works in English, mainly by East African writers. Five titles had appeared by early 1968, e.g., NO BRIDE PRICE, by David Rubadiri, and PROMISED LAND, by Grace Ogot. In Nigeria, as a result of the encouragement of creative talent by the Mbari Clubs, Ife University Press is publishing the Mbayo Series.

Bibliographies

1027.   Abrash, Barbara. BLACK AFRICAN LITERATURE IN ENGLISH SINCE 1952: WORKS AND CRITICISM. New York, Johnson Reprint Corp., 1967. xiv, 92 p.

A worthy contribution to African literature studies in the United
States. Listed first are bibliographies and works of criticism (books
and journal articles, the latter arranged by subject). Mrs. Abrash
then lists the major African authors alphabetically, citing their
full-length works, reviews of these works, short stories, anthologies
in which the author's work appears, and critical articles on his
work. She concludes with a list of selected periodicals and an index
to authors of creative and critical writings. References include
some children's books as well as relevant essays and autobiographies;
a few plays which have been performed but not published are also
cited. Adding to the value of this bibliography is John Povey's
excellent introduction, a concise summary of modern African literature.
A revision is in process.

1028. Amosu, Margaret. A PRELIMINARY BIBLIOGRAPHY OF CREATIVE AFRICAN
        WRITING IN THE EUROPEAN LANGUAGES. Ibadan, University of
        Ibadan, 1964. 35 p.

        Special supplement to AFRICAN NOTES, bulletin of the Institute
of African Studies. Arrangement is by African country and then by
author. There is an author index.

1029. Baratte, Thérèse, comp. BIBLIOGRAPHIE: AUTEURS AFRICAINS ET
        MALGACHES DE LANGUE FRANCAISE. Paris, Office de Coopération
        Radiophonique (OCORA), 1965. 50 p.

        A country-by-country listing concerned with writers in French-
speaking Africa south of the Sahara. The subjects covered are
literature, education, medicine, theater, art, politics, and economics. Entries are arranged alphabetically by author and there is
an author index.

1030. INDEX TO COMMONWEALTH LITTLE MAGAZINES. 1964/65- New York, Johnson
        Reprint Corp. Every other year.

        An author-subject index of English-language magazines published
in Commonwealth or ex-Commonwealth countries; reviews are included.
The 1964-65 issue was compiled by Stephen H. Goode. Africa-related
magazines indexed are BLACK ORPHEUS, OKYEAME (Institute of African
Studies, University of Ghana), TRANSITION, the Association for African
Literature in English BULLETIN, THE NEW AFRICAN, and JOURNAL OF COM-
MONWEALTH LITERATURE. A retrospective index to 1900 is planned.

1031. Jahn, Janheinz. A BIBLIOGRAPHY OF NEO-AFRICAN LITERATURE FROM AFRICA,
        AMERICA, AND THE CARIBBEAN. New York, Praeger, 1965. xxxv,
        359 p.

        Editorial matter in English, French, and German.

The African material (p. 4-129) is arranged by region following
the listing of anthologies on Africa as a whole: Western, Central,
Eastern, and Southern Africa. The German edition is titled DIE
NEOAFRIKANISCHE LITERATUR: GESAMTBIBLIOGRAPHIE VON DEN ANFANGEN BIS
ZUR GEGENWART (Düsseldorf, Diederichs, 1965, xxxv, 359 p.). See also
Bernth Lindfors, "Additions and Corrections to Janheinz Jahn's
BIBLIOGRAPHY OF NEO-AFRICAN LITERATURE (1965)," AFRICAN STUDIES
BULLETIN, v. 11, no. 2, Sept. 1968: 129-148.

1032. JOURNAL OF COMMONWEALTH LITERATURE. 1965- Leeds, University of
          Leeds.   Semiannual.

     Edited by Arthur Ravenscroft. It has the most current bibliogra-
phy of anything in its purview. See also no. 291, Transcription
Centre's monthly CULTURAL EVENTS IN AFRICA, for new publications of
African literature.

1033. Mercier, Roger. "Bibliographie africaine et malgache: Ecrivains
          noirs d'expression française." REVUE DE LITTERATURE COMPAREE,
          v. 37, no. 1, 1963: 145-171.

     List of over 360 books and articles in French by Africans on
Africa, covering anthologies, poetry, novels, the arts, legends,
essays, and history.

1034. Padmore Research Library in African Affairs, Accra, Ghana. A SELECT
          BIBLIOGRAPHY OF FOLKLORE, LEGENDS AND TRADITIONS OF AFRICAN
          PEOPLES. By D. E. M. Oddoye. Accra, Ghana Library Board,
          1963. 25 p. (Bibliography Series, Special Subject Bibliography
          no. 2, May 1963)

     Two to three hundred well-chosen entries from the published
folk literature of all Africa. Begun with Ghanaian material alone,
it was expanded to cover the whole African field.

1035. Ramsaran, J. A. NEW APPROACHES TO AFRICAN LITERATURE: A GUIDE TO
          NEGRO-AFRICAN WRITING AND RELATED STUDIES. Ibadan, Ibadan
          University Press, 1965. 177 p.

     A slim volume in which the first two sections are devoted to
Africa (p. 5-93: oral literature--vernacular and translation--and
modern African literature). Both sections consist largely of book
lists. There is both an author and a title index.

1036. SCHONE SCHRIFTEN AUS AFRIKA: EIN VERZEICHNIS VON WERKEN ZEITGENOSSISCHER AFRIKANISCHER AUTOREN. Bonn, Deutsche Afrika-Gesellschaft, 1962. 83 p.

A listing of present-day African writers and their literary works. On p. 9-54 are covered in one alphabet writers of the continent and their books in English, French, and African languages. Next are separate alphabetical listings of writers in Arabic, with translation of titles in German, of writers from Madagascar and Réunion, and those from the Caribbean. The last list is of anthologies and collections of tales. A "Landesregister" groups the writers by country.

A monthly newsletter, CULTURAL EVENTS IN AFRICA, edited by Diana Speed, was launched by the Transcription Centre, London, with the issue of Dec. 1964. It gives lists of new plays, novels, and other writings, news of new journals, literary criticism, biographical notes, and other material of cultural interest (see no. 291).

Reference Works

1037. AFRICAN FOLKTALES & SCULPTURE. Folktales selected and edited by Paul Radin, with the collaboration of Elinore Marvel. Introd. to the tales by Paul Radin. Sculpture selected with an introd. by James Johnson Sweeney. New York, Pantheon Books, 1952. xxi, 355 p. plates, map. (Bollingen Series, no. 32)

2d rev. ed. 1964.

A luxurious publication, in which a fine selection of folktales from many parts of Africa (p. 25-320) is followed by an album of reproductions of African sculpture. The tales, with introduction by the anthropologist Paul Radin, are in four groups: "The Universe and Its Beginnings," "The Animal and His World," "The Realm of Man," and "Man and His Fate." They are followed by an epilogue, a list of sources, and a glossary. The striking full-page plates of sculptures in bronze and wood are preceded by an introductory essay by James Johnson Sweeney, who had directed the exhibition of African Negro art at the Museum of Modern Art in New York in 1935.

A Russian collection of African folklore is edited by the leading ethnologist, D. A. Ol'derogge: SKAZKI NARODOV AFRIKI (Tales of the African peoples) (Moscow, State Publishing House for Artistic Literature, 1959, 319 p., illus.). It is in regional arrangement, with subdivision by tribes, and is sparsely illustrated with line drawings.

1038. AFRICAN LITERATURE TODAY. no. 1- 1968- London. (Heinemann
        Educational Books)

        Supersedes the BULLETIN of the Association for African Literature
in English (see no. 1041). Its object is to be a forum for the examination of the literature of Africa. It carries articles, book re-
reviews, and bibliographies.

1039. African Writers of Today [television series]. New York, National
        Educational Television, in collaboration with the Transcription
        Centre, London.

        A series of television interviews held by the South African
journalist and writer Lewis Nkosi with prominent African writers,
which was featured on NET stations and affiliates in the United States
in the summer of 1964. The filmed series, on 16mm and 35mm cinefilm,
can be borrowed through the usual sources. The July 1964 issue of
AFRICA REPORT has slightly abridged transcripts of several units
of this series (p. 7-21). On the back cover is a Fact Sheet listing
"Novels by African Writers--A Partial Bibliography."

        Russian interest in the new African writers is evidenced in a
recent article by I. D. Nikiforova and J. V. Palievskaya, "Novye
gorizonty afrikanskoy literatury" (New horizons of African literature)
in NARODY AZII I AFRIKI: ISTORIIA, EKONOMIKA, KUL'TURA (Moscow),
no. 5, 1963. p. 135-140.

1040. African Writers Series. London, Heinemann Educational Books, 1962-

        This commendable series makes available a wide range of African
writing (fiction, nonfiction, poetry, and drama) and includes both
original works and reprints of well-known works. Chinua Achebe is
the editorial adviser. Over 70 of these paperback books had appeared
by 1970.

1041. Association for African Literature in English. BULLETIN. v. 1,
        no. 1- 1964-67. Fourah Bay College, University of Sierra
        Leone, Freetown.

        The first issue of this journal for review and criticism of
African writing was edited by Professor Creighton of the University
of Sierra Leone. Subsequent issues were edited by his successor in
the English Department there, Professor Eldred Jones. Contributions
came from "listening posts" established by connections throughout
English-speaking Africa. The journal was superseded by AFRICAN
LITERATURE TODAY (see no. 1038).

1042. Beier, Ulli, ed. INTRODUCTION TO AFRICAN LITERATURE: AN ANTHOLOGY
    OF CRITICAL WRITING FROM "BLACK ORPHEUS." Evanston, Ill.,
    Northwestern University Press, 1967. 272 p.

    Bibliography: p. 265-270.

    This interesting volume, edited by the co-editor of BLACK
    ORPHEUS, is divided into four parts: the oral traditions (Yoruba
    [Ijálá], Ewe, Akan, Hausa, and Swahili poetry and Luo songs), poetry,
    the novel, and drama. In addition to critiques of the works of
    individual poets and novelists, there are included such essays as
    Gerald Moore's "The Negro Poet and His Landscape," Robert July's
    "The African Personality in the African Novel," O. R. Dathorne's
    "African Writers of the Eighteenth Century," and an essay by Lewis
    Nkosi on the mediocre quality of black South African fiction. The
    drama section covers Yoruba theater and the playwrights Wole Soyinka
    and J. P. Clark. Margaret Amosu has contributed a bibliography of
    critical writing.

1043. BLACK ORPHEUS: A JOURNAL OF AFRICAN AND AFRO-AMERICAN LITERATURE.
    no. 1- Sept. 1957- Ibadan. 3 times a year.

    Published by the Ministry of Education of the Western Region
    of Nigeria and devoted to African literature and arts, especially
    but not exclusively in West Africa. The co-editor is Ulli Beier,
    who was one of the founders of the Mbari Club in Ibadan for African
    writers and artists. The Mbari Club has a small publishing house,
    from which it is issuing new African literature.

    A selection of 16 stories, edited by Ulli Beier, was published
    with the title BLACK ORPHEUS: AN ANTHOLOGY OF AFRICAN AND AFRO-
    AMERICAN PROSE (London, Longmans; New York, Mc-Graw-Hill, 1964, 156
    p.).

1044. Brench, A. C. THE NOVELIST'S INHERITANCE IN FRENCH AFRICA: WRITERS
    FROM SENEGAL TO CAMEROON. London, Oxford University Press,
    1967. 146 p.

    Bibliography: p. 135-146.

    _____. WRITING IN FRENCH FROM SENEGAL TO CAMEROON. London, Oxford
    University Press, 1967. 153 p.

    Bibliography: p. 142-153.

    Selections of untranslated extracts in the second volume com-
    plement essays in the first volume. Each volume has an introduction,
    a bibliography, and a biographical note for each author.

1045. Cartey, Wilfred. WHISPERS FROM A CONTINENT: THE LITERATURE OF
           CONTEMPORARY BLACK AFRICA. New York, Random House, 1969.
           397 p. illus.

1046. Classiques africains [series]. Paris, Juilliard, 1963-

           The first volume in this series, edited by the Institut d'
       Ethnologie de l'Université de Paris, is Eric de Dampierre, ed.,
       POETES NZAKARA, Vol. I (222 p., plates), with an introduction in
       French and poems in French and Nzakara. Vols. 3 and 4 of the series
       comprise the two-volume work edited by Pierre F. Lacrois, POESIE
       PEULE DE L'ADAMAWA, with poems in French and Fulah. Vol. 5, edited
       by A. I. Sow, is a bilingual volume of Peul poetry, collected at
       Fouta Djalon, LA FEMME, LA VACHE ET LA FOI (1966, 373 p.).

1047. Drachler, Jacob, ed. AFRICAN HERITAGE: INTIMATE VIEWS OF THE BLACK
           AFRICANS FROM LIFE, LORE, AND LITERATURE. New York, Crowell-
           Collier Press, 1963. 286 p.

           An interesting anthology. Part 1, "African Voices," contains
       well-chosen examples of oral literature (tales and songs), written
       literature in African languages, and African literature in European
       languages. Part 2 illustrates "Afro-American Responses"--Aimé Césaire,
       Langston Hughes, etc.--and Part 3, "Through the Eyes of Others,"
       includes some striking passages from European novelists and other
       writers on Africa.

1048. Eliet, Edouard. PANORAMA DE LA LITTERATURE NEGRO-AFRICAINE, 1921-
           1962. Présence Africaine, 1965. 263 p.

           A sensitive study of forty years of Negro-African literary
       developments. The introduction includes a discussion of Etienne
       Lero and of the concept of négritude. Part 1 covers poetry,
       specifically that of Rabearivelo, Senghor, Césaire, Fodéba,
       Rabemananjara, and Diop. Part 2 deals with the novel and the works
       of Maran, Dadié, Oyono, Beti, Roumain, Alexis, and Laye. The
       concluding Part 3 covers essays and critiques and the writings of
       Césaire and Fanon. Eliet uses a literary approach to African
       writings in contrast to Kesteloot's (see no. 1055) more historical
       approach.

1049. Gleason, Judith Illsley. THIS AFRICA: NOVELS BY WEST AFRICANS IN
           ENGLISH AND FRENCH. Evanston, Ill., Northwestern University
           Press, 1965. xix, 186 p. illus. (Northwestern University
           African Studies, no. 14)

           Bibliography: p. 178-186.

A discussion of the influence of colonial rule precedes consideration of some 25 novels, 17 originally of French expression, 8 in English, mainly West African.. These are grouped into novels of the African past, novels about village life, novels of the cities, and finally novels of psychic conflict in which traditional Africa and imperial Europe play symbolic parts.

1050. Hughes, Langston, ed. AN AFRICAN TREASURY: ARTICLES, ESSAYS, STORIES, POEMS, BY BLACK AFRICANS. New York, Crown Publishers, 1960. 207 p.

Selection from African writings in newspapers, magazines, etc., chosen by the American Negro author, who had judged a short-story contest for the Johannesburg magazine of African circulation, DRUM. The contributions are grouped according to their form--articles, miscellanea (including newspaper columns, folktales, and proverbs), essays, stories, and poetry. There are biographical notes on authors.

1051. Hughes, Langston, ed. POEMS FROM BLACK AFRICA. Bloomington, Indiana University Press, 1963. 158 p. illus. (UNESCO Collection of Contemporary Works)

Grouped as "oral traditionals" and then by individual poets. Bibliographical notes are included. Countries listed are Ethiopia, Southern Rhodesia, Sierra Leone, Madagascar, Ivory Coast, Nigeria, Kenya, Gabon, Senegal, Nyasaland, Mozambique, South Africa, Congo, Ghana, and Liberia.

1052. Hughes, Langston, and Christiane Reygnault, eds. ANTHOLOGIE AFRICAINE ET MALGACHE. Paris, Seghers, 1966. 317 p. (Collection Mélior)

A new edition of a volume first published in 1962 (Paris, Marabout) with the subtitle NOUVELLES, ESSAIS, TEMOIGNAGES, POEMES. The editors' aim is to bring together works which they consider most representative of the African personality, even though the writers may not figure prominently in the black African literature scene.

1053. Irele, Abiole. "Négritude: Literature and Ideology." JOURNAL OF MODERN AFRICAN STUDIES, v. 3, no. 4, Dec. 1965: 499-526.

An interesting discussion of négritude, which the author describes as the cultural parallel of Pan-Africanism. A four-page bibliography is included.

See also Thomas Melone's DE LA NEGRITUDE DANS LA LITTERATURE NEGRO-AFRICAINE (Paris, Présence Africaine, 1962, 139 p.; bibliography: p. 135-137), a compassionate discussion of the genesis and development of négritude in Negro-African literature.

1054. Jahn, Janheinz. GESCHICHTE DER NEOAFRIKANISCHEN LITERATUR: EINE EINFUHRUNG. Düsseldorf, Köln, Diederichs, 1966. 285 p.

Includes bibliographical references.

An introduction to the history of modern African literature, including early African writers, Afro-American literature, oral traditions, Afro-Arab literature, the literature of the Southern Bantu, Negro music, the ideology of négritude, and other related aspects.

1055. Kesteloot, Lilyan. LES ECRIVAINS NOIRS DE LANGUE FRANCAISE: NAISSANCE D'UNE LITTERATURE. Bruxelles, Institut de Sociologie, Université Libre de Bruxelles, 1963. 340, 3 p. (Etudes africaines)

Bibliography: p. 331-340.

A detailed, well-documented history and analysis of the origins, evolution, and present state of the works of French-speaking black writers in Africa, the West Indies, and the United States. Interwoven throughout the book are the cultural, sociological, and political factors influencing these writers. Special attention is given to the works of Léon Damas, Aimé Césaire, and Léopold Senghor, and to the origins and influence of the journal PRESENCE AFRICAINE. There is an index of authors and journals.

1056. Moore, Gerald, ed. AFRICAN LITERATURE AND THE UNIVERSITIES. Ibadan, Published for the Congress for Cultural Freedom by Ibadan University Press, 1965. 148 p.

Papers from the Dakar Conference on French African Literature held at the University of Dakar, Mar. 1963, and the Freetown Conference of African Literature and the University Curriculum held at Fourah Bay College, Apr. 1963. The conference was to encourage the introduction of African literature into the university curriculum and eventually to secondary and primary schools.

1057. Moore, Gerald, and Ulli Beier, eds. MODERN POETRY FROM AFRICA. Harmondsworth, Middlesex; Baltimore, Md., Penguin Books, 1963. 192 p. (Penguin African Library, AP7)

Well-noticed recent anthology.

Another recent anthology has been compiled and edited by John Reed and Clive Wake, A BOOK OF AFRICAN VERSE (London, Heinemann, 1964, 119 p.).

1058. Mphahlele, Ezekiel, ed. AFRICAN WRITING TODAY. Baltimore, Penguin
Books, 1967. 347 p. (Penguin Book 2520)

A cross section of recent African prose and poetry in English,
French, and Portuguese (the last two in translation) drawn from 16
countries. The works of white Africans and non-Africans like Joyce
Cary are not included, Mphahlele's aim being to bring out the distinctive literary themes and styles of black African writing. He
presents new and unfamiliar work of some of the more celebrated
writers (though several well-known authors are not represented) and
also introduces a number of newer authors whose writings either have
not appeared in print before or have not yet enjoyed wide circulation,
even in Africa. Bibliographical notes on the authors are included.

1059. Oxford Library of African Literature [series]. London, Oxford
University Press, 1963-

A series on the indigenous prose and poetry of Africa, edited
by E. E. Evans-Pritchard, W. H. Whiteley, and Godfrey Lienhardt.
The volumes have English translation of text or texts, introductory
essay and notes, and either full vernacular text or specimens.

Twelve works had appeared by 1968, among them being the
following:

a) Andrzejewski, B. W., and I. M. Lewis. SOMALI POETRY: AN
INTRODUCTION. 167 p. plates.

b) Babalola, S. A. THE CONTENT AND FORM OF YORUBA IJALA. 395 p.

c) Mbiti, John. AKAMBA STORIES. 240 p.

d) Morris, H. F. THE HEROIC RECITATIONS OF THE BAHIMA OF ANKOLE.
xii, 143 p. map.

e) Whiteley, W. H., comp. A SELECTION OF AFRICAN PROSE. I,
TRADITIONAL ORAL TEXTS. xv, 200 p. II, WRITTEN PROSE.
185 p.

1060. Pageard, Robert. LITTERATURE NEGRO-AFRICAINE: LE MOUVEMENT
LITTERAIRE CONTEMPORAIN DANS L'AFRIQUE NOIRE D'EXPRESSION
FRANCAISE. Paris, Le Livre Africain, 1966. 138 p.

Bibliography: p. 119-120; bio-bibliography: p. 121-128.

A literary history of African writers in French-speaking black
Africa during the colonial period, 1920-46, the period of the
French Union, 1946-48, and the era of independent nations, 1958-64.

The second part of the book covers African literature by type, including chapters on political and social works, theories of African personality, oral tradition and ethno-history, modern histories, the novel, the short story, theater, and poetry. Biographical sketches are given, and there are both author and title indexes.

1061. Ramsaran, J. A. NEW APPROACH TO AFRICAN LITERATURE: A GUIDE TO NEGRO-AFRICAN WRITING AND RELATED STUDIES. Ibadan, Ibadan University, 1965. 177 p.

Essays on oral and traditional literature in the various regions of Africa, on modern writing in Western languages and vernaculars, and on Caribbean and American literature. Each essay is followed by a book list.

1062. RESEARCH IN AFRICAN LITERATURES. no. 1- 1970- Austin, Texas. 2 times a year.

Published by the African and Afro-American Research Institute, University of Texas. It treats all aspects of oral and written literature. Book reviews and a notes section are included.

1063. Rive, Richard, ed. MODERN AFRICAN PROSE: AN ANTHOLOGY. Illustrated by Albert Adams. London, Heinemann Educational Books, 1964. xv, 214 p. illus. (African Writers Series, no. 9)

Reprint, 1965.

A collection of hard-to-find African writings in English. It ignores experimental work of West Africans, and selections are of conventional and often uninteresting writing.

1064. Rutherfoord, Peggy, ed. AFRICAN VOICES: AN ANTHOLOGY OF NATIVE AFRICAN WRITING. New York, Vanguard Press, 1960. 208 p.

First published in 1958 under the title DARKNESS AND LIGHT.

An excellently varied anthology of stories, poems, tales, and essays, grouped by the regions from which they come. Some are the products of well-known new writers, some are translations by Europeans or Africans from traditional song or legend, and some are as told by informants. At the end are biographical notes about the writers.

1065. Senghor, Léopold Sédar, ed. ANTHOLOGIE DE LA NOUVELLE POESIE NEGRE ET MALGACHE DE LANGUE FRANCAISE, PRECEDEE DE "ORPHEE NOIR" PAR JEAN-PAUL SARTRE. Paris, Presses Universitaires de France, 1948. xliv, 227 p. (Colonies et empires, 5th ser., Art et littérature)

By the celebrated French African poet and apostle of négritude-- also political leader up to independence for Senegal and currently President of that country--this anthology includes the most famous poems by blacks and Malagasy brought up in the French culture, with bio-bibliographical sketches of the authors. The volume has as its introduction the essay by Jean-Paul Sartre, "Orphée noir" (Black Orpheus), which introduced the concept of négritude to the French literary world.

Among the more recent anthologies and biographical studies are two volumes by Armand Guibert, LEOPOLD SEDAR SENGHOR (Paris, Seghers, 1961, 215 p., ports.; bibliography: p. 205-211; Poètes d'aujourd'hui, 82), and LEOPOLD SEDAR SENGHOR: L'HOMME ET L'OEUVRE (Paris, Présence Africaine, 1962, 175 p., illus.); an anthology with commentary by Robert Mercier and Monique and Simon Battestini, L. S. SENGHOR, POETE SENEGALAIS (Paris, F. Nathan, 1965, 63 p.; Classiques du monde, Littérature africaine, 3); and a volume of Senghor's works selected and translated by John Reed and Clive Wake, PROSE AND POETRY (London, Oxford University Press, 1965, 181 p.; bibliography: p. 173-182).

1066. Tibble, Anne Northgrave, ed. AFRICAN-ENGLISH LITERATURE: A SHORT SURVEY AND ANTHOLOGY OF PROSE AND POETRY UP TO 1963. New York, October House, 1965. 304 p.

Bibliography: p. 292-302.

The author and compiler of this work, which combines critical essays on African writing and writers, datelines the book "School of Education, Leicester University." She is extraordinarily well read in African literature and comments interestingly on the history of written and oral story and song, on languages, and on traditional and modern writing in both English- and French- speaking Africa, giving fairly full précis and appraisals of works of most of the new authors in South, East, and West Africa. These essays make up less than half the book. In the remainder are extracts from a wide selection of novels, plays, and poetry of all major figures in the African literary scene--a fascinating collection. The book ends with an extensive bibliography of writings by African authors.

1067. TRANSITION: A JOURNAL OF THE ARTS, CULTURE AND SOCIETY. v. 1, no. 1- Nov. 1961- Kampala (P.O. Box 20026). Irregular.

A sophisticated literary magazine, including contributions by
African and European writers--fiction, poetry, articles on literary
or sociocultural subjects, book reviews, art. The editor is Rajat
Neogy, and Christopher Okigbo is editor for West Africa. Format
and content are distinguished.

1068. Traoré, Bakary. LE THEATRE NEGRO-AFRICAIN ET SES FONCTIONS SOCIALES.
Paris, Présence Africaine, 1958. 159 p. (Enquêtes et études)

By a Senegalese author and teacher, himself involved in the
African theater movement. He examines here in sociological terms
the origins of African dramatic forms in dance, miming, song, and
traditional drama and the forms and tendencies of modern theater.
A part of the book was presented as a paper at the first International
Congress of Negro Writers and Artists (see no. 1025).

1069. Tucker, Martin. AFRICA IN MODERN LITERATURE: A SURVEY OF CONTEMPORARY
WRITING IN ENGLISH. New York, Frederick Ungar, 1967. xii, 316 p.

Bibliography: p. 263-309.

A basic book on literary history and literary criticism. Tucker
surveys literature in English about Africa by treating American,
English, and African writers as part of African literature. The long
bibliography comprises a selected reading list of modern African
literature through 1966.

1070. Wästberg, Per, ed. THE WRITER IN MODERN AFRICA. Uppsala, Scandinavian
Institute of African Studies, 1969. 123 p.

A literary conference held in 1967 and attended by 24 African
writers and 24 Scandinavian authors. Included are outstanding
contributions by Wole Soyinka and Albert Menni on the dangers of
romantic preoccupation with the past and on the need to see Africa
as it really is today--threatened by disintegration.

1071. Wauthier, Claude. THE LITERATURE AND THOUGHT OF MODERN AFRICA: A
SURVEY. Translated by Shirley Kay. London, Pall Mall Press,
1966; New York, Praeger, 1967. 323 p. (Library of African
Affairs)

Bibliography: p. 286-295.

This revised version of the original French edition, L'AFRIQUE
DES AFRICAINS: INVENTAIRE DE LA NEGRITUDE (Paris, Editions du Seuil,
1964, 314 p.; Collection "L'histoire immédiate"), is updated to 1966

with regard to major political events. Wauthier, a correspondent of
Agence France Presse specializing in African affairs, discusses the
works of some 150 African writers and intellectuals as he traces the
parallel development of cultural revival and the demand for independence. The main substance of the book covers the literature up
to May 1963 and is confined to former colonial Africa. Part 1 is
concerned with writings in the linguae francae (pidgin, creole, etc.)
and with African folklorists and historians. In Part 2 the literature
of revolt against colonialism is considered, and in Part 3 themes of
the new Africa. The bibliography cites over 300 works, mostly by
Africans. There is a name index and a subject and title index.

MUSIC

Bibliographies

1072. African Bibliographic Center, Washington, D.C. THE BEAT GOES ON:
        A SELECTED GUIDE TO RESOURCES ON AFRICAN MUSIC AND DANCE, 1965-
        1967. Washington, 1968. 14 p. (Current Reading List Series,
        v. 6, no. 2)

1073. International African Institute. A SELECT BIBLIOGRAPHY OF MUSIC IN
        AFRICA. Compiled by L. J. P. Gaskin under the direction of K. P.
        Wachsmann. London, 1965. 83 p. (Africa Bibliography, Series B)

        Valuable and handsome guide to the literature of music in Africa,
    compiled and published with the aid of a Ford Foundation grant. There
    are nearly 3,500 numbered items, in an arrangement primarily geo-
    graphical. Main sections are general (not specifically African but of
    value to the student in the African field), Africa general, African
    music (p. 7-35), musical instruments (p. 36-51), and the dance (p.
    52-59), followed by catalogues, bibliographies, and periodicals.
    There is an index of authors as well as a geographical and ethnic
    index.

        Numerous references to music in Africa appear in ETHNOMUSICOLOGY
    AND FOLK MUSIC: AN INTERNATIONAL BIBLIOGRAPHY OF DISSERTATIONS AND
    THESES, compiled by F. Gillis and Alan P. Merriam (Middletown, Conn.,
    Published for the Society of Ethnomusicology by Wesleyan University
    Press, 1966, 148 p.), and in ETHNOMUSICOLOGY: JOURNAL OF THE SOCIETY
    FOR ETHNOMUSICOLOGY, 1953-. See also B. A. Anang's AN ANNOTATED
    BIBLIOGRAPHY OF MUSIC AND DANCE IN ENGLISH-SPEAKING AFRICA (Legon,
    Institute of African Studies, University of Ghana, 1967, 47 p.).

1074. Merriam, Alan P. "An Annotated Bibliography of African and African-
        derived Music since 1936." AFRICA: JOURNAL OF THE INTERNATIONAL

AFRICAN INSTITUTE, v. 21, no. 4, Oct. 1951: 319-329.

An extension of the Varley bibliography (below), including references to books and periodical sources published through 1950. Entries are listed alphabetically by author in two sections. Sec. I lists references the compiler had personally checked; Sec. II lists references obtained from various other sources. See also this author's contribution in the AFRICAN STUDIES BULLETIN (above, no. 1022).

Dr. Merriam is a contributing editor on music to AFRICA REPORT, in which he reviews new publications and recordings of African music. He has prepared a discography of African music records entitled AFRICAN MUSIC ON L. P.: AN ANNOTATED DISCOGRAPHY.

1075.   U.S. Library of Congress. Music Division. AFRICAN MUSIC: A BRIEFLY ANNOTATED BIBLIOGRAPHY. Compiled by Darius L. Thieme. Washington, 1964. xxvi, 55 p. map.

In this valuable bibliography which updates the earlier compilations of Varley and Merriam, Mr. Thieme has listed 84 books, mostly published since 1950, of which 22 are devoted entirely to African music, while the rest include significant discussions. Also listed are 513 articles on African music, appearing in 144 periodicals and serials (named on p. xvii-xxv). The majority of these have been published since 1950, but a selection of significant older titles is included. There are an author index, an index of tribal names, and an index of linguistic areas, relating to a map on the end page which shows approximate localities of Bantu linguistic zones.

1076.   Varley, Douglas H., comp. AFRICAN NATIVE MUSIC: AN ANNOTATED BIBLIOGRAPHY. London, Royal Empire Society, 1936. 117 p. (Royal Empire Society Bibliographies, no. 8)

The literature on music among the tribes of Africa is widely scattered in general studies of ethnological, geographical, and anthropological nature. This comprehensive bibliography brings together the titles of many books and articles from journals in these fields. Its arrangement is geographical, by territory, with large general sections; the subject matter includes native music and musical instruments. It is restricted to music of peoples south of the Sahara.

Reference Works

<u>Note</u>: The bibliographies just listed, as well as Merriam's continuing list in AFRICA REPORT (see no. 1074, above), are so recent and comprehensive that repetition here of the reference works they name is made unnecessary.

1077. AFRICAN MUSIC: JOURNAL OF THE AFRICAN MUSIC SOCIETY. v. 1, no. 1-
        1954- Roodepoort, Transvaal. Annual.

        Superseding the earlier NEWSLETTER, this journal has an annual
issue of around a hundred pages giving musical scores, illustrations,
bibliographic references, book and record reviews, etc. Although
Bantu music predominates, coverage is general for Africa south of
the Sahara. Vol. I, no. 4 (1957), and Vol. II, no. 1 (1958), include
a list of the 100 long-playing records of African native music issued
by the International Library of African Music.

        Records of African music are steadily increasing in popularity
and will be found listed in catalogues of commercial firms. A
section for African folk music and songs is included in the monthly
SCHWANN LONG PLAYING RECORD CATALOG (Boston, W. Schwann).

                        ART AND SCULPTURE

Bibliographies

1078. International African Institute. A BIBLIOGRAPHY OF AFRICAN ART.
        Compiled by L. J. P. Gaskin under the direction of Guy Atkins.
        London, 1965. 120 p. (Africa Bibliography, Series B)

        It would be hard to be overenthusiastic regarding this fine new
bibliography, both as to content and format. The latter is that of
a well printed and bound book, made possible because of a generous
grant from the Ford Foundation. The arrangement is superbly clear.
A contents list cites a preliminary list of countries (in regional
groups), an introduction, and seven main categories. The first,
general, has five subheads--encyclopedias; ethnographical works;
African art, primitive art; technology, crafts, the artist; African
art today. The second category, a regional classification, has for
each region, as appropriate, the subdivisions figures and masks;
buildings and furniture; clothing and adornment; rock art; techniques;
utensils, tools and weapons, miscellaneous; African art today. Under
the foregoing categories are listed almost 4,200 titles on all aspects
of African art. This straight bibliography is followed by five guide
lists: catalogues and guides to museums, exhibitions, and collections;

bibliographies of Africana likely to be of use to the student;
special numbers of periodicals; periodicals consulted; and abbreviations. These additional entries (excluding the abbreviations)
bring the total to 5,359. There are three indexes--author, geographical and ethnic, subject. In all respects the work sets a near-
impeccable standard for subject bibliography.

Reference Works

Note: These titles are selected as broadly covering one or more aspects of
art through large parts of Africa. Besides works of this nature, there
appear constantly catalogues of collections of African art accompanied by
analytical text. A number of such catalogues are mentioned in the bibliographies of works here cited and in the bibliography on art in the
AFRICAN STUDIES BULLETIN (see no. 1022, above). The Museum of Primitive
Art (New York City) has produced several special catalogues on African art.

1079. L'ART DE L'AFRIQUE NOIRE. Besançon, France, 1958. 70 p. 57 plates.

     Catalogue of art objects mainly from museums and collections in
France gathered for the Festival Artistique held July 12-Oct. 5, 1958,
at the Palais Granvelle, Besançon. Arrangement is geographical and
then ethnographic (Soudan--Bambara, Dogon, etc.). There are 512
numbered items, including masks, Benin bronzes, sculptures, and
cloth. A two-page bibliography is given.

1080. L'ART NEGRE. Paris, Présence Africaine, 1966. 169 p. illus., plates.

     Includes bibliography.

     A collection of numerous and diverse studies on African art and
artisans by renowned specialists. The volume is a reimpression of a
special issue of PRESENCE AFRICAINE published in 1951, with some new
articles added.

1081. Beier, Ulli. CONTEMPORARY ART IN AFRICA. New York, Praeger, 1968.
     188 p. 110 illus. (part col.).

     An account of the development of African art during the past
decade stressing the social context from which it emerged as well as
the sources from which the artists have drawn. Mr. Beier includes
illustrations of the work of nearly every artist mentioned.

     From the early 1950's to 1961 Ulli Beier taught and conducted
artists' workshops in Nigeria. He is the founder-editor of the
magazine BLACK ORPHEUS.

1082. Bodrogi, Tibor. ART IN AFRICA. Translated by András Deák. New York,
       McGraw-Hill, 1968. 131 p. illus. (part col.), plates (part
       col.), maps.

       Bibliography: p. 97-101.

       A well-organized work, handsomely prepared. After an introduc-
       tory survey of African art, the author groups what he regards as some
       of the more important art styles in categories based on regional and
       political units--i.e., the Western Sudan, the Atlantic Coast and the
       Forest Belt, the Guinea Coast, from the Niger to the Congo, and the
       Congo. Detailed descriptions are provided for each of the 191 unpaged
       black-and-white plates which conclude the volume (all the art objects
       pictured are housed by museums in Budapest, Dresden, Leipzig, and
       Prague). While the text is sound, the plates are of poor quality.

1083. Brown, Evelyn S. AFRICA'S CONTEMPORARY ART AND ARTISTS: A REVIEW OF
       CREATIVE ACTIVITIES IN PAINTING, SCULPTURE, CERAMICS AND CRAFTS
       OF MORE THAN 300 ARTISTS WORKING IN THE MODERN INDUSTRIALIZED
       SOCIETY OF SOME OF THE COUNTRIES OF SUB-SAHARAN AFRICA. New
       York, Division of Social Research and Experimentation, Harmon
       Foundation, 1966. 136 p. 40 illus.

       A useful handbook and directory on modern African art. For each
       country a brief review of art history is given as well as notes on
       galleries, art centers, and prominent artists. An index of artists
       is included.

1084. California. University. AFRICAN ARTS: AN EXHIBITION AT THE ROBERT
       H. LOWIE MUSEUM OF ANTHROPOLOGY OF THE UNIVERSITY OF CALIFORNIA,
       BERKELEY, APRIL 6/OCTOBER 22, 1967. Berkeley, University of
       California Printing Dept., 1967. 90 p. illus.

       Outstanding catalogue of one of the major exhibitions of African
       art held in the United States. There are detailed and informative
       notes on 190 items photographed. Slides of the exhibit are on sale
       from the Lowie Museum.

1085. Elisofon, Eliot. THE SCULPTURE OF AFRICA: 405 PHOTOGRAPHS. Text by
       William Fagg; preface by Ralph Linton; design by Bernard Quint.
       New York, Praeger, 1958. 256 p. illus., map (on lining papers).
       36 cm. (Books That Matter)

       Bibliographical notes: p. 252-254.

       Handsome folio art album containing 405 photographs, a large pro-
       portion of them full-page reproductions, arranged in three groups

according to the regions from which they come: Western Sudan, the Guinea coast, and the Congo. Each group is preceded by a short interpretative essay--stated not to be "encyclopaedic"--by Mr. Fagg, then assistant keeper of the Department of Ethnography of the British Museum. The introduction, a significant discussion of primitive art, is by the late Professor Ralph Linton of the Department of Anthropology of Yale University. Mr. Elisofon is a research fellow in primitive art at the Peabody Museum, Harvard.

1086. Fagg, William Buller. AFRICAN TRIBAL IMAGES: THE KATHERINE WHITE RESWICK COLLECTION. Cleveland, Cleveland Museum of Art, 1968. 1 v. (unpaged). illus., maps.

This is the catalogue of the Katherine White Reswick Collection, well illustrated, well described. Included are photographs of masks in use. There is a bibliography.

1087. Fagg, William Buller. AFRICAN TRIBAL SCULPTURES. London, Methuen, 1967. 2 v. plates, maps. (The Little Library of Art, 82)

1088. Fagg, William Buller. THE ART OF CENTRAL AFRICA: TRIBAL MASKS AND SCULPTURES. New York, New American Library by arrangement with UNESCO, 1967. 24 p. col. plates.

_____. THE ART OF WESTERN AFRICA: TRIBAL MASKS AND SCULPTURES. London, Collins in association with UNESCO, 1967. 24 p. col. plates. (Fontana UNESCO art books, U24)

These two paperbacks contain 32 fine color plates in each volume, and an excellent text.

1089. Fagg, William Buller. TRIBES AND FORMS IN AFRICAN ART. New York, Tudor Publishing Co., 1965. 122 p. 122 plates.

This quarto volume, with exceptionally handsome full-page plates of art objects, mostly wood sculpture, shows one example each of the art of 122 tribes of West, Central, and Southern Africa. Fagg assembled the photographs from museum collections in Europe and Africa to illustrate the "separateness" of tribal styles. His introduction and the notes on pages facing the photographs stress his thesis that the artist can easily communicate with members of his own tribe through his style. It would have been possible, he says, to extend the list to 300 or even 400 tribal names, each attached to a distinct style. Fagg expresses the fear that in the efforts of national leaders to do away with political tribalism this artistic "tribality" may be lost. This concept of "tribality" is questioned by other experts.

1090. Fagg, William Buller, and Margaret Plass. AFRICAN SCULPTURE. London,
           Studio Vista; New York, E. P. Dutton, 1964. 157 p. illus.
           (Dutton Vista Pictureback)

       Pocket-size book containing some 200 photographs and providing
one of the best available introductions to African art. The authors,
respectively the deputy keeper of ethnography at the British Museum
and a well-known collector of African art, contribute a text of comment
on the photographs, which are for the most part of previously unrecorded
objects. The art of each tribe is considered as a separate entity,
"as coherent and consistent as the tribal religion and philosophy
which largely inspired it." An index of tribes is included.

1091. Gessain, R., and others. "The Role of Museums in Contemporary Africa."
           MUSEUM (Paris, UNESCO), special issue, v. 18, no. 3, 1965: 118-
           188.

1092. Gerbrands, Adrianus Alexander. ART AS AN ELEMENT OF CULTURE,
           ESPECIALLY IN NEGRO AFRICA. Leiden, Medelingen vat het
           Rijksmuseum voor Volkenkunde 12, 1957. unpaged.

       Despite its title, this is one of the most important books on
African art. Although not based on his own field work, Gerbrands'
book surveys the field work of others, often from unpublished ms.
sources; also, it summarizes a good deal of work otherwise available
only in German or French. It is oriented towards understanding the
role of art and of the artist in traditional African society.

       See also René S. Wassing, AFRICAN ART: ITS BACKGROUND AND
TRADITIONS (New York, Abrams, 1968, 285 p.), which has 240 fine
black-and-white plates and 24 color plates. The text of this work,
however, is not particularly valuable because of over-generalization,
which is the mistake of most of the books of its kind with the
exception of Gebrands'.

1093. Himmelheber, Hans. NEGERKUNST UND NEGERKUNSTLER. Mit Ergebnissen
           von sechs Afrika-Expeditionen des Verfassers. Braunschweig,
           Klinckhardt & Biermann, 1960. 436 p. illus. (Bibliothek
           für Kunst- und Antiquitätenfreunde, v. 40)

       Bibliography: p. 415-527.

       By an ethnologist and physician, who made six expeditions in
Africa. The author's particular interest is to examine for himself
works of art and the identity of artists. The 386 illustrations are
in large part his own photographs in situ. He first examines the
forms of art and the character, techniques, and style of the artists
and then turns to a detailed survey of sculpture by regions and

tribes. The bibliography is arranged similarly.

The significance of masks in African religious and secular life is described in Himmelheber's LES MASQUES AFRICAINS, translated by S. Wallon (Paris, Presses Universitaires de France, 1960, 47 p., illus.; Collection Mementos illustrés).

1094. Krieger, Kurt. WEST-AFRIKANISCHE PLASTIK I. Berlin, Museum für Volkerkunde, 1965. 143 p. 272 plates, fold. map.

Bibliography: p. 135-140.

Illustrates and describes 272 sculpture from the whole of Africa (despite the title) in the Museum für Volkerkunde.

1095. Krieger, Kurt, and Gerdt Kutscher. WESTAFRIKANISCHE MASKEN. Berlin, Museum für Volkerkunde, 1960.

Illustrates and describes 80 masks from all parts of Africa in the Museum collection.

1096. Kultermann, Udo. NEW ARCHITECTURE IN AFRICA. Translated from the German by Ernst Flesch. New York, Universe Books, 1963. 26 p. 180 p. of illus., plans.

The introductory essay of this book of fine photographs of new buildings, public and private, throughout Africa includes a country-by-country statement on trends in modern architecture, beginning with North Africa and so by east-west belts through the continent. Only present-day building is described, with much interest in architectural firms and individual architects. There is no comment upon or illustration of the traditional. The photographs are without captions except for the name of the architect and identification of the building.

1097. Laude, Jean. LES ARTS DE L'AFRIQUE NOIRE. Paris, Hachette, 1966. 384 p. illus., maps. (Le livre de poche)

Includes bibliography.

An excellent paperback edition, though the plates are small.

1098. Leiris, Michel, and Jacqueline Delange. AFRIQUE NOIRE: LA CREATION PLASTIQUE. Paris, Gallimard, 1967. 457 p. illus., plates (part col.), maps (col., 1 fold.). (L'universe des formes, v. 11)

Bibliography: p. 387-[406].

This volume on the plastic arts of black Africa is itself a
work of art. Virtually each page of the three parts devoted to
illustrative material contains one or more well-chosen and excellent
plates accompanied by a running text. The volume has four parts: an
introduction to African art; the plastic activities in black Africa
(body adornment and masks, habitats, and figurative art); peoples
and arts (Western Sudan, Atlantic Coast, Congo, East Africa, and
South Africa), along with a concluding statement; and a fourth part
comprised of reference material. The first two parts and the conclusion are the work of Mr. Leiris, director of research at the
Centre National de la Recherche Scientifique; the third part and the
documentary material are the contributions of Mme Delange, director
since 1961 of the Département d'Afrique Noire of the Musée de
l'Homme. The bibliography is alphabetical by author, with the most
important works marked with an asterisk. The 444 illustrations and
plates are given comprehensive documentation in the 40-page
"Documentation iconographique." An unusual and useful 24-page
"Dictionnaire-index" indexes peoples, places, terms, etc., by
presenting for each item brief descriptive material preceding the
page references.

A complementary work by Mme Delange, also published in 1967 by
Gallimard, is ARTS ET PEUPLES DE L'AFRIQUE NOIRE: INTRODUCTION A
L'ANALYSE DES CREATIONS PLASTIQUES (xxii, 279 p., plates, fold. map;
bibliography: p. 219-249; Bibliothèque des sciences humaines).
This is one of the best surveys now in print. Another collaboration
by the authors is the text accompanying illustrations of African art
in a work prepared by the Société des Amis du Musée de l'Homme:
CHEFS-D'OEUVRE DU MUSEE DE L'HOMME (Paris, Caisse Nationale des
Monuments Historiques, 1965, 232 p., photos [part col.]).

1099. Leuzinger, Elsy. AFRICA: THE ART OF THE NEGRO PEOPLES. Translated
        by Ann E. Keep. New York, McGraw-Hill, 1960. 247 p. illus.
        (part col.), 4 maps. (Art of the World, the Historical,
        Sociological and Religious Backgrounds, Non-European Cultures).

        Bibliography: p. 228-232.

A broad study of African art in relation to historical,
sociological, and religious backgrounds, illustrated with 63 color
plates and 144 figures, with sources named. Chapters are devoted to
country and people, religion, sociology, material and technique, and
form and then take up eight style regions. The appendixes include
maps, tables of culture, bibliography, and glossary. A list of plates
and figures, with sources, precedes the text.

1100. Leuzinger, Elsy. AFRICAN SCULPTURE, A DESCRIPTIVE CATALOGUE.
           Translated by Ann E. Keep. [At head of title: Museum Rietberg
           Zürich.] Zürich, Atlantis Verlag, 1963. 326 p. illus., map.

       This work is a detailed catalogue, well illustrated and very
       informative, of a selection of 215 pieces in the Rietberg Museum.

1101. Mveng, E. L'ART D'AFRIQUE NOIRE: LITURGIE COSMIGUE ET LANGAGE RELI-
           GIEUX. Paris, Mame, 1964. 159 p. illus. (part col.), diagrs.
           (Point omega, 1)

       Bibliography: p. 155-157.

       An analysis of the relationship between the language of Negro-
       African prayer and the "language" of African art.

1102. Paris. Musée de l'Homme. ARTS CONNUS ET ARTS MECONNUS DE L'AFRIQUE
           NOIRE: COLLECTION PAUL TISHMAN. Paris, 1966. 1 v. (unpaged).
           plates.

       Includes bibliographies.

       The 135 plates in this volume are described in French and Eng-
       lish. Jacqueline Delange has provided an introduction.

1103. Paulme, Denise. AFRICAN SCULPTURE. Translated by Michael Ross.
           New York, Viking Press, 1962. 160 p. illus. (A Studio Book)

       _____, and Jacques Brosse. PARURES AFRICAINES. Photographs by
           M. Huet [et al.]. Paris, Hachette, 1956. 91 p. illus. (part
           col.).

       The author, former director of the Département d'Afrique Noire
       of the Musée de l'Homme, had begun her studies of Africa under the
       noted anthropologist Marcel Griaule. Her AFRICAN SCULPTURE sets the
       art in its social setting but is not well illustrated. The original
       French edition appeared in 1956 (LES SCULPTURES DE L'AFRIQUE NOIRE,
       Paris, Presses Universitaires de France, 130 p., 32 plates). A
       companion volume of striking photographs, many in color, depicts
       ceremonial costumes, masks, and cicatrizations of many African tribes.
       Most of the pictures are from West and Equatorial Africa, with a few
       from South West Africa, Mozambique, and the Sudan.

1104. Plass, Margaret. "African Negro Sculpture." UNIVERSITY MUSEUM
           BULLETIN (Philadelphia), Dec. 1957. 79 p.

Descriptive catalogue of the large collection of West and Central African masks, bronzes, etc., in the Museum's collections.

This is one of the larger catalogues describing collections of individual art museums in America. There is a detailed account of these museums and their African art collections and catalogues in the HANDBOOK OF AMERICAN RESOURCES FOR AFRICAN STUDIES (see no. 101).

1105. Robbins, Warren M. AFRICAN ART IN AMERICAN COLLECTIONS. L'ART AFRICAIN DANS LES COLLECTIONS AMERICAINES. Written with the assistance of Robert H. Simmons; translated into French by Richard Walters. New York, Praeger, 1966. 237 p. 354 illus.

Compilation of photographs of treasures of African art held by American collectors and in American museums. The author, director and founder of the Museum of African Art, Washington, D.C., contributes an introduction surveying the development and styles of African sculpture. The text is given in English and French.

1106. Symposium on the Artist in Tribal Society, London, 1957. THE ARTIST IN TRIBAL SOCIETY: PROCEEDINGS OF A SYMPOSIUM HELD AT THE ROYAL ANTHROPOLOGICAL INSTITUTE. Edited by Marian W. Smith. London, Routledge & Kegan Paul, 1961. xiii, 150 p. illus. (Royal Anthropological Institute, Occasional Publications, no. 15)

Bibliography: p. 137-146.

The papers and discussions of an international cross section of anthropologists and art historians, including such prominent spokesmen as Sir Herbert Read, E. R. Leach, and William Fagg. An American edition of this work was published by the Free Press of Glencoe (New York, 1961).

1107. Trowell, Kathleen Margaret. AFRICAN DESIGN. New York, Praeger, 1960. 78 p. 77 plates. (Books That Matter)

2d ed. 1966. 78 p. 78 plates (2 col.).

_____. CLASSICAL AFRICAN SCULPTURE. London, Faber and Faber, 1954. 103 p. 48 plates.

2d ed. 1964.

By the art director in the Uganda Museum, Kampala, these two works are descriptive of the art of sub-Saharan Africa in general. The first covers in text and plates a variety of media: textile design, basketwork, beadwork, hides and leather work, body painting,

carving of calabashes, wood, metal, and pottery. The second,
earlier work is a more extended essay on the history and culture
of Africa, particularly West Africa, as interpreted in figures and
masks of wood and bronze. In the revised edition of 1964 there are
over 120 photographs; the text has been somewhat revised, and the
bibliography brought up to date.

1108. Trowell, Kathleen Margaret, and Hans Nevermann. AFRICAN AND OCEANIC
          ART. New York, H. N. Abrams, 1968. 263 p. illus. (part col.),
          col. maps. (Panorama of World Art)

        A very brief text liberally illustrated with color photographs
of the best-known pieces of African sculpture.

1109. Wingert, Paul S. THE SCULPTURE OF NEGRO AFRICA. New York, Columbia
          University Press, 1950. 96 p. illus., plates, map.

        Bibliography: p. 83-96.

        Essay by the then assistant professor of art and archaeology at
Columbia University, treating African sculpture under four major
regions, West Africa, Cameroon, Central Africa, and East Africa. It
is accompanied and illustrated by 118 excellent plates and includes a
long bibliography.

CHAPTER 28

COMMUNICATIONS
(PRESS, RADIO, TELEVISION, AND FILM)

Bibliographies

1110. Comité International du Film Ethnographique et Sociologique. PREMIER
        CATALOGUE SELECTIF INTERNATIONAL DE FILMS ETHNOGRAPHIQUES SUR
        L'AFRIQUE NOIRE. Paris, UNESCO, 1967. 408 p.

        Full descriptions and, in some cases, brief critiques of films
on Africa are given in this outstanding catalogue. Africa in general
is covered first, and then a country-by-country survey is presented.
Jean Rouch contributes the introduction as well as a concluding
essay on the situation and trends of the cinema in Africa, and Amadou
Hampaté Bâ comments on "Le dit du cinéma africain." Four indexes are
included: films, subjects, ethnic groups, and film directors.

1111. Moyne, Claudia W., comp. A LIST OF FILMS ON AFRICA. Brookline,
        Mass., Development Program, African Studies Center, Boston
        University, 1966.

        Though not a complete listing of available films on Africa
(films by foreign producers are excluded if not rentable in the United
States), this is a useful guide with good annotations.

        A survey of 311 commercially issued films about sub-Saharan
Africa, arranged by subject, is the rather uneven inventory AFRICAN
FILM BIBLIOGRAPHY 1965, arranged by Warren D. Stevens in cooperation
with the Educational Media Council (Bloomington, Ind., Committee of
Fine Arts and the Humanities, African Studies Association, 1966, 31 p.;
Occasional Papers, no. 1). The aim of a 34-page FILM CATALOGUE published by the Council of the African-American Institute, New York,
in 1968, is to emphasize "Africa today, omitting or eliminating films
which present the Continent and its people in a patronizing way or as
an isolated curiosity."

376

Africa has become in recent years a favorite location for film
makers. In each quarterly issue of the Library of Congress CATALOG:
MOTION PICTURES AND FILM STRIPS, Africa appears as a main subject
heading, with many entries. Another general library guide worth
mention is the EDUCATIONAL MEDIA INDEX, published by McGraw-Hill for
the Educational Media Council (v. 1-14, 1964), in which are listed
many documentary films on Africa.

Reference Works

1112. ADVERTISING & PRESS ANNUAL OF ALL AFRICA: THE BLUE-BOOK OF ADVERTISING
      IN AFRICA, 1968. 422 p. Johannesburg, National Publishing Co.,
      1968.

      Press guide to newspapers and periodicals, radio, TV, cinema;
outdoor advertising, advertising agents, advertisers and advertising
organizations, together with a who's who in advertising and publishing.

1113. Ainslie, Rosalynde. THE PRESS IN AFRICA: COMMUNICATIONS PAST AND
      PRESENT. London, V. Gollanz, 1966. 256 p.

      For description of this book, which also covers radio and
television, see no. 372.

1114. Bebey, Francis. LA RADIODIFFUSION EN AFRIQUE NOIRE. Issy-les-
      Moulineaux (Seine), Editions Saint-Paul, 1963. 191 p.

      Includes bibliography.

      By a Camerounian radio specialist, this study gives a brief
sketch of the history of radio broadcasting in Africa and discusses
the differences in the French- and English-language broadcasts and
the role of broadcasting in civilizations geared to oral communication. The author's conclusion is that Africans rather than Europeans
must determine program content.

      A special nonprofit organization for designing and taping
cultural programs for African radio stations was opened in 1962, the
Transcription Centre, 38 Dover St., London, W.1. It publishes a
processed newsletter, CULTURAL EVENTS IN AFRICA (no. 17, Apr. 1966),
which contains notes on drama, radio programs, art exhibits, and
other cultural events, in company with a few reviews and announcements
of forthcoming books.

1115. Deutsche Afrika-Gesellschaft. COMMERCIAL RADIO IN AFRICA. Bonn,
      German Africa Society, 1970. 307 p.

1116. Feuereisen, Fritz, and Ernst Schmacke, eds. DIE PRESSE IN AFRIKA:
      EIN HANDBUCH FUR WIRTSCHAFT UND WERBUNG. [Title also in
      English] München, Verlag Dokumentation, 1968. 251 p.

      A useful bilingual handbook on the African press. For full
annotation, see no. 378.

1117. France. Direction de la Documentation. LA RADIODIFFUSION ET LA
      TELEVISION EN AFRIQUE NOIRE FRANCOPHONE ET A MADAGASCAR. Paris,
      1963. 28 p. (Notes et études documentaires, no. 2986, Apr.
      1963)

      See general note on this series, no. 1587.

1118. Huth, Arno. COMMUNICATIONS MEDIA IN TROPICAL AFRICA: REPORT. Pre-
      pared for the International Cooperation Administration.
      Washington, 1961. 171 p. tables.

      Study of the operations of radio, press, and cinema in 15
countries of Africa, with recommendations for improvement of programs.

1119. Linden, Fred van der. LE PROBLEME DE L'INFORMATION EN AFRIQUE:
      JOURNAUX EUROPEENS, AGENCES DE PRESSE, PUBLICATIONS AFRICAINES,
      CINEMA, TELEVISION, RADIO. Bruxelles, 1963. 62 p. (Académie
      Royale des Sciences d'Outre-Mer, Classe des sciences morales et
      politiques, n.s. v. 27, fasc. 4)

      Includes bibliography.

1120. Schramm, Wilbur Lang. MASS MEDIA AND NATIONAL DEVELOPMENT: THE
      ROLE OF INFORMATION IN THE DEVELOPING COUNTRIES. Stanford,
      Calif., Stanford University Press, 1964. xiv, 333 p.

      Bibliography: p. 311-327.

      Discussions in general, based on UNESCO efforts and having
little special pertinence to Africa. There are chapters on the role
of information in national development, the flow of information in
the world, how mass media are developed, what mass communication can
do and what it can help to do in national development, mass media
in the great campaigns, commercial research as an arm of economic and
social development, and building the mass media.

1121. United Nations Educational, Scientific and Cultural Organization.
      WORLD COMMUNICATIONS: PRESS, RADIO, FILM, TELEVISION. 4th
      rev. ed. Paris, 1964. 380 p.

Country-by-country survey of communication facilities, including Africa, with statements of press, radio, and film services for each.

A UNESCO-sponsored conference on this theme for Africa was held in Paris in 1962. Its report was published as Meeting of Experts on Development of Information Media in Africa, DEVELOPING INFORMATION MEDIA IN AFRICA: PRESS, RADIO, FILM, TELEVISION (Paris, Mass Communication Techniques Division, UNESCO, 57 p.; Reports and Papers on Mass Communication, no. 37). The conference discussed techniques for development of the various services, and nothing like the foregoing survey of existing facilities was included in the report. An African LF/MF (long frequency/medium frequency) Broadcasting Conference took place in Madrid, Sept. 7-26, 1964.

1122. United Nations Educational, Scientific and Cultural Organization. WORLD PRESS: NEWSPAPERS AND NEWS AGENCIES. New York, UNESCO Publications Center, 1964. 159 p.

Contains a useful section on Africa giving for each country information on the number of daily newspapers, total daily circulation, and various other statistics, along with data on news agencies and, also, general comments. The names of newspapers and periodicals are not listed.

CHAPTER 29

NATURAL SCIENCES

GENERAL

Note: In this section, the chief emphasis is on works involving nature and the physical sciences, with much lesser emphasis upon man's part in the development of nature. For material on agriculture and mining, for example, see Chapter 18.

Bibliographies and Serials

1123. Note: Bibliographies of all-African coverage in the general field of natural sciences are those included in the reference works named below, notably in the UNESCO review of natural resources (no. 1128) and in the two volumes by Worthington (nos. 1129 and 1130). Organizations of intercontinental scope are the CCTA/CSA and its affiliates, now merged in the Organization of African Unity (OAU).

Although 40 serials are indexed under science in the Library of Congress SERIALS FOR AFRICAN STUDIES, only the now-discontinued bulletin of CCTA/CSA, SCIENCE-AFRIQUE, applies to all Africa. Others are regional, though often of broad extent, like BULLETIN A, SCIENCES NATURELLES of the Institut Fondamental d'Afrique Noire or the scientific publications series of the Académie Royale des Sciences d'Outre-mer in Brussels. See also the LISTE DES PERIODIQUES AFRICAINS DE LA BIBLIOTHEQUE (title also in Dutch), Institut Royal des Sciences Naturelles de Belgique, Service de Documentation de Sciences Naturelles (Bruxelles, 1960, unpaged). Practically all 223 African periodicals received by the Library of the Institut Royal des Sciences Naturelles in Brussels are publications of learned institutions devoted to the natural sciences.

Reference Works
_____

1124.   Commission for Technical Co-operation in Africa South of the Sahara.
            INTER-AFRICAN SCIENTIFIC AND TECHNICAL CO-OPERATION, 1948-1955.
            London, Commission for Technical Co-operation in Africa South
            of the Sahara [CCTA] and Scientific Council for Africa South
            of the Sahara [CSA], 1956? xv, 294 p. maps.

         This comprehensive report was issued after eight years' work by
the inter-African organizations, which were formed to provide long-
term programs of technical and scientific conferences and exchanges
of technical and research information and specialists. (For full
description of the former CCTA, its scientific advisory body, CSA,
and affiliates, see Library of Congress, INTERNATIONAL SCIENTIFIC
ORGANIZATIONS, 1962.)

         The report details conferences held, projects, and recommenda-
tions of the bodies from 1948, when the idea was first proposed, to
1955. The first chapters describe the organization of CCTA/CSA
(established in 1950) and the scope and accomplishment of the bureaus
set up under it, which represent "a network of technical co-operation
covering practically every field of technical activity in Africa
south of the Sahara." The list of bureaus and committees is followed
by an index of technical conferences held, in five groups: natural
resources, health, organization of production, social welfare, and
statistics. The final page gives the list of CSA publications. A
bimonthly information bulletin, SCIENCE-AFRIQUE, was issued by CCTA/
CSA from 1956 to 1961.

         The original members of CCTA, Belgium, France, Portugal, the
United Kingdom, Southern Rhodesia, and South Africa, had by 1964
given way to a completely African membership, with the United Kingdom,
France, and Belgium permitted to come to conferences as observers.
In 1962 there were 29 member nations, the Republic of South Africa
had been ejected, and North African countries were admitted; "South
of the Sahara" was dropped from the name. Headquarters were moved
from London to Lagos, though in 1963/64 publishing was still being
carried out by the Joint Secretariat in London. In Jan. 1965 CCTA/
CSA was transformed into the scientific and technical branch of OAU,
the Scientific, Technical, and Research Commission.

1125.   International Conference on the Organization of Research and Training
            in Africa in Relation to the Study, Conservation and Utilization
            of Natural Resources, Lagos, Nigeria, July 28 to Aug. 6, 1964.
            FINAL REPORT OF THE LAGOS CONFERENCE, 28 JULY TO 6 AUGUST 1964.
            Paris, UNESCO, in association with UNECA, 1964. 102 p.

  a)   _____. OUTLINE OF A PLAN FOR SCIENTIFIC RESEARCH AND TRAINING IN
            AFRICA. 1964. 25 p.

b) _____. LAGOS CONFERENCE: SELECTED DOCUMENTS. 1965. 214 p.

c) _____. SCIENTIFIC RESEARCH IN AFRICA: NATIONAL POLICIES, RESEARCH INSTITUTIONS. 1966. 214 p.

In the FINAL REPORT all the decisions and recommendations of the conference are presented, along with a detailed report of the debates. A list of abbreviations of institutional and organizational names is given in Appendix VIII. The decisions and recommendations are also issued separately as the OUTLINE.

The SELECTED DOCUMENTS consist of introductory material prepared by specialists to serve as a guide to the conference discussions.

The first part of SCIENTIFIC RESEARCH contains statements made by delegates of each country with regard to research on natural resources. Part 2 consists of a survey on the scientific and technical potential of African countries and includes a listing, by country, of scientific and technical research institutions in Africa.

1126. National Academy of Sciences, Washington, D.C. RECOMMENDATIONS FOR STRENGTHENING SCIENCE AND TECHNOLOGY IN SELECTED AREAS OF AFRICA SOUTH OF THE SAHARA. Prepared for the International Cooperation Administration. Washington, National Academy of Sciences, National Research Council, 1959. 108, 12 p. map.

Bibliography: 12 p. at end.

The "Harrar Report" (executive director, Dr. J. G. Harrar of the Rockefeller Foundation) was an attempt to draw up guidelines for technical-assistance planning in Africa, with the collaboration of many specialists in African studies and applied sciences. Educational needs were consistently stressed. Although the study was limited to countries in which English is generally spoken, recommendations applied in the main to sub-Saharan Africa.

1127. Scientific Council for Africa South of the Sahara (CSA). REPORT OF THE SECRETARY-GENERAL TO THE 13TH MEETING OF THE SCIENTIFIC COUNCIL, MUGUGA, 1962. [n.p.] CCTA, 1962. 148 p.

Distributed by the Publications Bureau, Watergate House, York Buildings, London, W.C.2.

In three parts: general questions (the Council, the Commission, FAMA, training of personnel); natural resources (activities in conservation, climatology, pedology, etc.); social, economic, and technical activities (in public health, linguistics, and other social sciences, education, etc.). There are five useful appendixes: 1,

Meetings held under CCTA/CSA/FAMA auspices, June 1961-June 1962;
2, Meetings (prospective), 1962-64; 3, Other meetings at which CCTA
was represented, June 1961-June 1962; 4, Publications; 5, List of
joint projects.

1128. United Nations Educational, Scientific and Cultural Organization.
      A REVIEW OF THE NATURAL RESOURCES OF THE AFRICAN CONTINENT.
      Paris, 1963. 437 p. illus., maps. (Natural Resources Research,
      no. 1)

      Distributed by International Documents Service, Columbia
University Press, New York.

      The contents are as follows:

      1. Topographic mapping of Africa, by A. Rumeau; bibli-
          ography; inventory of topographic maps at the end of
          1959.

      2. Geology, applied geology (mineral resources), and
          geophysics in Africa, by F. Dixey; geological libraries
          of African territories; bibliography; scientific
          personnel; geological research organizations operating
          in Africa; review of geological mapping; location of
          chief mineral resources.

      3. The seismicity of Africa, by G. P. Gorstkov; charts;
          bibliography.

      4. Climate and meteorology in Africa: a, Africa north of
          the Tropic of Cancer, by M. F. Taha; b, Africa south
          of the Tropic of Cancer, by H. O. Walker (footnote
          references, no bibliography).

      5. Hydrology in Africa, by J. Rodier; bibliography.

      6. The soils of Africa, by F. Fournier; bibliography;
          scientific periodicals.

      7. African flora: a, Flora of Africa north of the Sahara,
          by M. Drar; bibliography; b, Flora of Africa south of
          the Sahara, by J. Loechlin; bibliography; herbaria
          holding important collections of African plants.

      8. African fauna: a, Taxonomy, ecology, and zoogeography,
          by F. Khalil; bibliography; b, Economic aspects of
          entomology, by W. F. Jepson; c, Freshwater biology,
          by G. Marlier; bibliography; d, Marine biology and
          biology applied to the fishing industry, by E. Postel;

bibliography; e, Conservation and management of game
stock, by F. Bourlière; bibliography; specialized
reviews relating to the conservation of wildlife;
official and private organizations concerned with
wildlife conservation; national parks and equivalent
reserves.

Appendix I, Abbreviations; II, Member states, international
organizations, governmental and private organizations
and experts consulted by the UNESCO Secretariat.

Map showing location of the chief mineral resources of
Africa (double-page spread, inside back cover).

This comprehensive survey is an essential guide to study of the
natural sciences in Africa. In several branches the bibliographies
included form the most satisfactory listings available for coverage
of Africa as a whole.

1129. Worthington, Edgar B. SCIENCE IN AFRICA: A REVIEW OF SCIENTIFIC
RESEARCH RELATING TO TROPICAL AND SOUTHERN AFRICA. London,
New York, Oxford University Press, 1938. xiii, 746 p. maps,
diagrs.

Bibliography: p. 626-691.

The bibliography in this pioneer work is arranged by chapters:
surveys and maps, geology, meteorology, soil science, botany,
forestry, zoology, fisheries, entomology, agriculture, health and
medicine, and anthropology. A list of authorities who assisted in
the review is included.

1130. Worthington, Edgar B. SCIENCE IN THE DEVELOPMENT OF AFRICA: A REVIEW
OF THE CONTRIBUTION OF PHYSICAL AND BIOLOGICAL KNOWLEDGE SOUTH
OF THE SAHARA. London, Commission for Technical Co-operation
in Africa South of the Sahara, 1958. xix, 462 p. illus., maps
(1 fold. col.).

Bibliography: p. 421-435.

Survey by the first secretary-general of CCTA/CSA, 1950-55. It
covers research for all Africa recorded in Dr. Worthington's earlier
book, SCIENCE IN AFRICA, and work accomplished or projected under the
aegis of CCTA and affiliated international organizations. The
appendixes give lists of abbreviations, of the principal inter-African
meetings from 1948 to 1956, and of scientific bodies and services.

GEOLOGY

Maps

1131. United Nations Educational, Scientific and Cultural Organization.
GEOLOGICAL MAP OF AFRICA. Published in collaboration with the
Association for African Geological Surveys. New York, Columbia
University Press, 1964.

The first edition of the GEOLOGICAL MAP OF AFRICA was published in 1939 by the International Geological Congress. It has
been completely revised in the new edition sponsored by UNESCO
and consists of nine maps, 27" by 41", in full color, with legends,
key, and explanatory booklet. The scale is 1:5,000,000. The
first azimuthal projection map, it gives a full survey of subsur-
face resources. The nine maps cover West Africa, Eastern Mediter-
ranean, Red Sea, Western Atlantic, Central Africa, Eastern Africa,
South Atlantic (the islands only), South and South-West Africa, and
the Indian Ocean and Madagascar. The captions are in English and
French.

Bibliographies

1132. Geological Society of America. BIBLIOGRAPHY AND INDEX OF GEOLOGY
EXCLUSIVE OF NORTH AMERICA. v. 1- 1933- Washington. Annual
(biennial, 1941/42-1945/46).

The most comprehensive library tool for geological literature.
Arrangement is alphabetical, but in the index there are entries for
Africa and individual African countries. The compilation is several
years behind.

1133. Orcel, J., and S. Gaillère. BIBLIOGRAPHIE MINERALOGIQUE DE LA FRANCE
ET DE SES ANCIENS TERRITOIRES D'OUTRE-MER DE 1913 A 1963. Paris,
Librairie Scientifique et Technique Albert Blanchard, 1964.
204 p.

1134. United Nations. Economic Commission for Africa. GEOLOGICAL BIBLIOGRA-
PHY OF AFRICA. BIBLIOGRAPHIE GEOLOGIQUE DE L'AFRIQUE. New York,
1963. 169, 114 p.

Supplements chap. ii of UNESCO's A REVIEW OF THE NATURAL RESOURCES
OF THE AFRICAN CONTINENT (see no. 1128). The first 169 pages were
included as bibliography in that work, covering books and periodical

articles to 1959; Part 2, Annexes, adds references to 1963, similarly divided into monographic publications--books, official reports, etc.-- and articles. Both table of contents and index are lacking in this otherwise valuable and extensive work.

Reference Works

1135. Furon, Raymond. GEOLOGY OF AFRICA. Translated by A. Hallam and L. A. Stevens. New York, Hafner Pub. Co., 1963. 377 p. illus., maps.

Translation of the standard survey of African geology by Professor Furon of the Académie des Sciences d'Outre-Mer in Brussels, a leading geologist who has specialized in the study of Africa. The text used is that of the second edition (Paris, Payot, 1960, 400 p.; Bibliothèque scientifique; 1st ed., 1950). It begins with a general survey of stratigraphy of the continent, followed by 25 chapters on individual regions, exclusive of North Africa. Abundant footnote references, updated for the second edition, take the place of a bibliography.

Professor Furon's companion work, LES RESSOURCES MINERALES DE L'AFRIQUE, as well as other works on applied geology, is noticed in the Mining section in Chapter 18.

1136. Haughton, Sidney H. THE STRATIGRAPHIC HISTORY OF AFRICA SOUTH OF THE SAHARA. New York, Hafner Pub. Co., 1963. 365 p. maps.

See also Pan-African Congress on Prehistory, PROCEEDINGS (1952; no. 529), Part 1 of which contains papers on geology, paleontology, and climatology.

CLIMATOLOGY, HYDROLOGY, METEOROLOGY

Atlases and Maps

1137. Thompson, B. W. THE CLIMATE OF AFRICA. Nairobi, London, New York, Oxford University Press, 1965. 15 l., 132 maps. 46 x 52 cm. Separate leaves bound together.

By the director of the East African Meteorological Department, this atlas of black-and-white maps is intended as a contribution toward development of Africa and also "to assist in the training of the new generation of African meteorological personnel." The 15-page

introduction covers techniques. The maps show total radiation, bright
sunshine, rainfall, screen temperature, relative humidity, pressure
and wind, upper temperature, and upper dew points.

1138. Witwatersrand. University. African Climatology Unit. CLIMATOLOGICAL
       ATLAS OF AFRICA. Compiled under the direction of Stanley P.
       Jackson, with the collaboration and assistance of the African
       Regional Association of the World Meteorological Organisation
       and the cartographic services of member governments of the
       Commonwealth. Lagos, CCTA/CSA, 1961. 8 l., 55 fold. col. maps.
       62 cm.

       This handsome volume, with text in English, French, and Portuguese,
has maps for Africa as a whole and by five regions, most of them
1:500,000,000 in scale. Shown are mean annual rainfall, monthly
distribution of mean rainfall, mean monthly rainfall, mean daily
maximum and minimum temperatures, and humidity mixing ratio.

Bibliographies

1139. METEOROLOGICAL AND GEOASTROPHYSICAL ABSTRACTS. v. 1- Jan. 1950-
       Lancaster, Pa., American Meteorological Society. Monthly.

       _____. Index.

       "An experimental subject, author, and keyword index to titles
of articles in periodicals and serials listed in METEOROLOGICAL AND
GEOASTROPHYSICAL ABSTRACTS," second experimental issue, v. 2, no. 1,
Jan. 1962. This index volume includes geographic locations, with
references for Africa and individual African regions and countries.

1140. South Africa. Weather Bureau. BIBLIOGRAPHY OF REGIONAL METEOROLOGICAL
       LITERATURE: Vol. I, SOUTHERN AFRICA, 1486-1948. Pretoria,
       1949. 412 p.

       The only available bibliography of more than single-country or
region coverage relating specifically to African weather, the
compilation includes works on British East Africa, Rhodesia and
Nyasaland, Angola and Mozambique, Madagascar, South Africa, and offshore islands--i.e., from a half to a third of the continent. It
comprises 3,000-odd entries: individual papers and reports and items
taken from over 200 journals.

1141. United Nations Educational, Scientific and Cultural Organization.
       BIBLIOGRAPHIE HYDROLOGIQUE AFRICAINE. BIBLIOGRAPHY OF AFRICAN
       HYDROLOGY. Edited by J. Rodier. Paris, 1963. 166 p.

       This bibliography greatly expands the short list of references
given by M. Rodier with his contribution on hydrology in the UNESCO
REVIEW OF THE NATURAL RESOURCES OF THE AFRICAN CONTINENT. He covers
in it the chief works of the last 30 years. The arrangement is:
All Africa--1, Precipitations and general climatic data; 2, Evaporation;
3, Runoff, hydrological balance: rivers, streams, and lakes; 4, Ground-
water, infiltration, soil moisture; 5, Solid transports (i.e., erosion).
Under these five subject heads there are references for individual
countries, "going from West to East across a succession of rough
climatic belts traversing the continent, and belts being considered
in turn from North to South." Meteorological references are included.
In the part for all Africa almost no works of general survey nature
are noted except for sections on Africa in the publications of world
coverage by the British Meteorological Office and the U.S. Weather
Bureau.

Reference Works

1142. Aubréville, André. CLIMATS, FORETS ET DESERTIFICATION DE L'AFRIQUE
       TROPICALE. Paris, Société d'Editions Géographiques, Maritimes et
       Coloniales, 1949. 351 p. illus., maps.

       Bibliography: p. 345-351.

       An ecological study by the inspector general of French colonial
forests and waterways, covering tropical forests in general and those
of Africa in particular. He treats the causes of climates of the
great natural regions and then gives systematic classification of
climates and forest formations of tropical and subtropical areas of
Africa. The last part examines the problem of the advancing desert.
A "climatological and phytogeographical" bibliography is arranged by
region.

       See also the Agriculture section in Chapter 18.

1143. Inter-African Conference on Hydrology, Nairobi, 1961. PAPERS AND
       COMMUNICATIONS. London, CCTA, 1961. 585 p. maps, diagrs.,
       profiles, tables, all part fold. (CSA Publication no. 66)

       Includes bibliographies.

       These are technical papers.

1144. Kendrew, Wilfred G. THE CLIMATES OF THE CONTINENTS. 5th ed. Oxford, Clarendon Press, 1961. 608 p. illus., maps, tables.

Bibliography: p. 581-586.

A standard handbook, including tables of precipitation, climatic means, temperature charts, etc. The first section is introductory (28 p.). Part 2 is on Africa (p. 29-146); general features are summarized and then there is detailed analysis by region.

1145. Knox, Alexander. THE CLIMATE OF THE CONTINENT OF AFRICA. Cambridge, Eng., University Press, 1911. xii, 552 p. 13 maps.

Old standard work, not as yet superseded in a single handy volume.

1146. Rodier, J. REGIMES HYDROLOGIGUES DE L'AFRIQUE NOIRE A L'OUEST DU CONGO. Paris, ORSTOM, 1964. 137 p.

BIOLOGY

Note: Three affiliates of CCTA/CSA relating to biological sciences, the Inter-African Bureau for Animal Health and Production, the Inter-African Bureau for Soils and Rural Economy, and the Inter-African Phytosanitary Commission, are concerned with development rather than with scientific biology and fall more properly under agriculture. Publications in these branches are included in the monthly BIBLIOGRAPHY OF AGRICULTURE, published by the U.S. Department of Agriculture. This is a comprehensive, worldwide listing of substantive agricultural books, reports, pamphlets, and articles. Unfcrtunately, it has no geographical index, and approach must be by subject, under which a breakdown by country is often indicated in the general index.

Bibliography

1147. BIOLOGICAL ABSTRACTS: A COMPREHENSIVE ABSTRACTING AND INDEXING JOURNAL OF THE WORLD'S LITERATURE IN THEORETICAL AND APPLIED BIOLOGY, EXCLUSIVE OF CLINICAL MEDICINE. Published (beginning with the literature of 1926) with the cooperation of individual biologists, biological industries, and biological journals generally. 1926- Philadelphia, University of Pennsylvania Press. Monthly.

The cumulated index volumes of this general reference tool have a separate geographical index in which Africa and individual African

locations are named. Flora and fauna and other branches of biological
studies are comprehensively covered.

See also the UNESCO REVIEW OF THE NATURAL RESOURCES OF THE
AFRICAN CONTINENT (no. 1128).

Reference Works

1148. Great Britain. Colonial Office. THE WILD RESOURCES OF EAST AND
CENTRAL AFRICA: A REPORT FOLLOWING A VISIT TO KENYA, UGANDA,
TANGANYIKA, NORTHERN AND SOUTHERN RHODESIA AND NYASALAND IN
FEBRUARY AND MARCH, 1960. By Dr. E. B. Worthington. London,
H.M. Stationery Off., 1961. 26 p. (Colonial no. 352)

This report by Dr. Worthington as deputy director general
(scientific) of Nature Conservancy, a British government office
established in 1949, relates specifically only to those parts of
Africa south of the Sahara still under British authority at the
time, but it is widely applicable to the rest of the subcontinent.
His thesis is that the extremely varied and rich wild flora and
fauna of Africa constitute "a cultural and scientific asset of
priceless value" and that increasing efforts must be made by
international bureaus and governments, particularly the new independent
governments, to conserve their wild resources. The hardest problem,
he warns, is that of influencing African public opinion to regard
wild life as an asset rather than a nuisance.

A comparable report of a mission accomplished for UNESCO in
July-Sept. 1960 was made by Sir Julian Huxley, THE CONSERVATION OF
WILD LIFE AND NATURAL HABITATS IN CENTRAL AND EAST AFRICA (Paris,
UNESCO, 1961, 113 p.; bibliography: p. 110-113). The writer's
conclusions are more specific than those expressed by Dr. Worthington
and end with 46 points on which urgent study is recommended.

BOTANY

Map

1149. Association pour l'Etude Taxonomique de la Flore d'Afrique Tropicale.
VEGETATION MAP OF AFRICA SOUTH OF THE TROPIC OF CANCER. CARTE
DE LA VEGETATION DE L'AFRIQUE AU SUD DU TROPIQUE DU CANCER.
Explanatory notes by R. W. J. Keay; translated by A. Aubréville.
London, Oxford University Press, 1959. 24 p. fold. col. map
(in pocket).

Bibliography: p. 20-24.

Large map colored to show the plant communities of the various regions of Africa, accompanied by notes explaining in technical terms the types of vegetation in Africa south of the Sahara. The author and the translator are both noted botanists.

Reference Works

1150.   FLORA OF TROPICAL EAST AFRICA. Editors: W. B. Turrell and E. Milne-
        Redhead. London, Crown Agents for the Colonies, 1952-63. 37 v.
        illus., maps.

1151.   Food and Agriculture Organization. Plant Production and Protection
        Division. THE GRASS COVER OF AFRICA. By J. M. Rattray, Crop
        Production and Improvement Branch. Rome, Food and Agriculture
        Organization of the United Nations, 1960. 168 p. fold. col.
        map. (FAO Agricultural Studies, no. 49)

        Bibliography: p. 136-144.

        A technical study in phytogeography, including a large map with
colors to indicate the types of grasses indigenous to regions of
Africa. The appendixes include index of types, geographical
distribution, bibliography, and index of botanical names.

        This is one of the more general of the numerous FAO publications
having to do with Africa. For any complete listing of FAO documents,
the UNITED NATIONS DOCUMENTS INDEX should be consulted.

1152.   Hutchinson, John, and J. M. Dalziel. FLORA OF WEST TROPICAL AFRICA,
        THE BRITISH WEST AFRICAN COLONIES, BRITISH CAMEROON, THE FRENCH
        AND PORTUGUESE COLONIES SOUTH OF THE TROPIC OF CANCER TO LAKE
        CHAD, AND FERNANDO PO. Prepared at the Herbarium, Royal Botanic
        Gardens, Kew, under the supervision of the Director. London,
        Crown Agents for Overseas Governments and Administrations, 1954-
        63. 2 v. in 4. illus.

        Includes bibliographies.

        An earlier issue of this work was supplemented by J. M. Dalziel,
THE USEFUL PLANTS OF WEST TROPICAL AFRICA, BEING AN APPENDIX TO THE
FLORA OF WEST TROPICAL AFRICA (London, Published under the authority
of the Secretary of State for the Colonies by the Crown Agents for the
Colonies, 1948 [c. 1937], xii, 612 p.).

1153. Inter-African Phytosanitary Commission, London. [Information sheets
       and documents.]

       The Commission, devoted to the study of plant pathology, uses the
       collections of the Commonwealth Institute of Entomology and the Common-
       wealth Mycological Institute at Kew. For description see Library of
       Congress, INTERNATIONAL SCIENTIFIC ORGANIZATIONS (no. 42).

1154. Monod, Théodore. LES GRANDES DIVISIONS CHOROLOGIQUES DE L'AFRIQUE:
       RAPPORT PRESENTE A LA REUNION DE SPECIALISTES SUR LA PHYTOGEO-
       GRAPHIE, YANGAMBI, 29 JUILLET-8 AOUT 1956. Londres [Commission
       de Coopération Technique en Afrique au Sud du Sahara], 1957.
       146 p. illus., fold. map. (Scientific Council for Africa
       South of the Sahara Publication no. 24)

       Bibliography: p. 127-137.

       A very learned paper by the director of the then Institut
       Français d'Afrique Noire, constituting "a descriptive explanation
       and definition of the phytogeographic territories of the continent
       on the upper levels of the floristic hierarchy (Regions and Domains)"
       and comparing the patterns thus established with the findings of
       zoologists. Includes a long bibliography. He defines "chorological"
       as "the study of the dispersion and distribution of living beings,"
       interpreted in this paper in botanical terms.

1155. United Nations Educational, Scientific and Cultural Organization.
       STUDY OF TROPICAL VEGETATION: PROCEEDINGS OF THE KANDY
       SYMPOSIUM. [Title also in French] Paris, 1958. 226 p.
       (Humid Tropics Research)

       The symposium was held in Kandy, Ceylon, Mar. 19-21, 1956.
       Only two of the papers dealt specifically with African areas (British
       West Africa and West Africa).

1156. United Nations Educational, Scientific and Cultural Organization.
       TROPICAL SOILS AND VEGETATION: PROCEEDINGS OF THE ABIDJAN
       SYMPOSIUM. [Title also in French] Paris, 1961. 115 p. illus.,
       charts. (Humid Tropics Research)

       Not available for examination. The symposium was jointly
       organized by UNESCO and the Commission for Technical Cooperation in
       Africa South of the Sahara and held Oct. 20-24, 1959, in Abidjan.

1157.   Watt, John Mitchell, and Maria G. Breyer-Brandwijk. THE MEDICINAL
        AND POISONOUS PLANTS OF SOUTHERN AND EASTERN AFRICA. 2d ed.
        Edinburgh, E. & S. Livingstone, 1962. xii, 1457 p. illus.
        (part col.).

        Bibliography: p. 1147-1198.

        Thoroughly revised; the first edition of this handbook was
        published in 1932.

                            ZOOLOGY

Reference Works

1158.   Bannerman, David Armitage. THE BIRDS OF WEST AND EQUATORIAL AFRICA.
        Edinburgh, Oliver & Boyd, 1953. 2 v. xiii, 1526 p.

        Handbook with full descriptions in clear, simple language and
        with technical data; illustrated with drawings and color plates of
        all species. The two-volume edition is condensed from an eight-
        volume work by this leading British ornithologist, BIRDS OF TROPICAL
        WEST AFRICA (London, Crown Agents for the Colonies, 1930-51). A
        portion of the handbook has been further condensed for a popular
        audience in a volume of the Penguin Books series, LARGER BIRDS OF
        WEST AFRICA (Harmondsworth, Middlesex; Baltimore, Md., 1958, 195 p.).

1159.   Copley, Hugh. THE GAME FISHES OF AFRICA. London, H. F. & G.
        Witherby, 1952. 276 p. illus.

        Designed as a standard reference book, a companion volume to the
        time-honored work of Richard Lydekker, THE GAME ANIMALS OF AFRICA
        (2d ed., rev. by J. G. Dollman, London, Ward, 1926, 483 p.).

        A good series of illustrated handbooks on animals by Charles
        T. Astley Maberly has been published by H. Timmins in Cape Town,
        ANIMALS OF RHODESIA (1959, 211 p.), ANIMALS OF SOUTHERN AFRICA (1959,
        211 p.), and ANIMALS OF EAST AFRICA (1960, 211 p.), as well as a
        more recent volume from Nelson in Johannesburg, THE GAME ANIMALS OF
        SOUTHERN AFRICA (1963, 292 p.).

1160.   Isemonger, Richard M. SNAKES OF AFRICA. London, New York, Nelson,
        1962 [i.e. 1963, c. 1962]. 236 p. illus.

        Field handbook constituting a guide to snakes of Southern,
        Central, and Eastern Africa.

1161.   Mackworth-Praed, Cyril W., and Claude H. B. Grant. BIRDS OF EASTERN
        AND NORTH EASTERN AFRICA. 2d ed. London, New York, Longmans,
        Green, 1957-60. 2 v. (African Handbook of Birds, ser. 1,
        v. 1-2)

        Reprint, with additions, of the first edition of this authori-
tative ornithological handbook which was published in 1952-55. The
various species of birds are catalogued with brief descriptions and
diagrams and illustrated in black-and-white drawings and color plates.
The two large volumes have, respectively, 806 and 1113 pages, with
full unpaged indexes of scientific and popular names.

1162.   Mackworth-Praed, Cyril W., and Claude H. B. Grant. BIRDS OF THE
        SOUTHERN THIRD OF AFRICA. London, Longmans, Green, 1963. 747 p.
        (African Handbook of Birds, ser. 2, v. 2).

1163.   Skaife, Sydney H. AFRICAN INSECT LIFE. London, New York, Longmans,
        Green, 1953. 387 p. illus.

        By a South African entomologist, this book is written "in
language as simple as is consistent with scientific accuracy." The
work is primarily intended for farmers, gardeners, and householders
who cope with African insect friends and foes. Arrangement is
systematic by orders, from lowest to highest--primitive insects,
cockroaches, to bees and wasps, ants. Illustrated with drawings
and photographs. The few color plates are mostly of the more amiable
insects, moths and butterflies.

CHAPTER 30

MEDICINE AND HEALTH

Bibliographies

1164.   Frank, M. K., comp. BIBLIOGRAPHY OF EAST AFRICAN LITERATURE ON
         BILHARZIASIS (INCLUDING THAT OF MALAWI, RHODESIA, SUDAN AND
         ZAMBIA) PRESENTS MATERIAL PUBLISHED BETWEEN 1933 AND 1964.
         Mwanza, Tanzania, East African Institute for Medical Research,
         1965. 16 p. 35 cm.

         Selected list of references to books, reports, and articles on
         bilharziasis in various African countries, with the first of two
         parts devoted to East Africa. Under each country, arrangement is
         alphabetical by author. An expanded edition is planned.

1165.   Klingelhofer, E. L. A BIBLIOGRAPHY OF PSYCHOLOGICAL RESEARCH AND
         WRITINGS ON AFRICA. Dar es Salaam, University College, University
         of East Africa, 1967. 31 p. Mimeographed.

         Lists mainly articles but also includes books, conference pro-
         ceedings, dissertations, and mimeographed papers covering the period
         from as early as 1895 to 1966. Arrangement is by subject, and most
         entries are in English. The work updates J. Hopkins' "Bibliographie
         des recherches psychologiques conduites en Afrique," REVUE DE
         PSYCHOLOGIE APPLIQUEE (v. 12, no. 3, 1962, p. 201-213), and Leonard
         Doob's bibliography for his essay "Psychology" in THE AFRICAN WORLD
         (p. 543-549; see no. 450).

1166.   Langlands, B. W., comp. BIBLIOGRAPHY OF THE DISTRIBUTION OF DISEASE
         IN EAST AFRICA (COMPLETE TO 1963). Kampala, Makerere University
         College, 1965. 184 p. (Makerere Library Publication no. 3)

Chiefly a listing of medical geographic articles and papers. References under each geographical entity--East Africa, Kenya, Uganda, Tanganyika, Zanzibar, and Ruanda-Urundi--are first listed in a general section and according to type of disease (alphabetically arranged). Except for the East African section, entries are then further broken down into administrative subsections. An index of diseases and an author index are included.

1167. World Health Organization. CATALOGUE OF WORLD HEALTH ORGANIZATION
          PUBLICATIONS, 1947-1958. Geneva, 1959. 78 p.

        Listing of titles and prices of all WHO publications up to the end of 1958, in three parts. The first part groups by subject certain nonperiodical publications and some important numbers of technical periodicals, with descriptive annotations. The second part describes periodical publications and gives titles of articles and papers in periodicals and series, cross-referenced to the annotated entries in Part 1. Part 3 has official (i.e., administrative) publications of WHO. Many are concerned with Africa, e.g.: J. F. Brock and M. Autret, KWASHIORKOR IN AFRICA (Geneva, 1952, 78 p., illus.; WHO Monograph Series, no. 8).

1168. World Health Organization. PUBLICATIONS OF THE WHO, 1947-1957: A
          BIBLIOGRAPHY. Geneva, 1958. 128 p.

        1958-1962: A BIBLIOGRAPHY. Geneva, 1964. 125 p.

        The 10-year list of WHO publications and the first supplement, covering five years, include articles in the BULLETIN of the WHO, the WHO CHRONICLE, other WHO serials and monograph series, Public Health Papers, Official Records, etc. There are author and country indexes. Each edition has in the country index about a hundred entries for Africa and individual countries.

1169. WORLD MEDICAL PERIODICALS. LES PERIODIQUES MEDICAUX DANS LE MONDE.
          [Title also in Spanish and German] 3d ed. Prepared by C. H.
          A. Fleurent. New York, World Medical Association, 1961. 407 p.

        Comprehensive guide to periodicals of all countries relating to medicine, pharmacy, dentistry, veterinary medicine, hospitals, medical equipment, etc.--more than 5,800 titles in all. There are two indexes, by country (including Algeria, Angola, etc., in Africa) and by subject (bilharziasis, malaria, tropical medicine, etc.). The arrangement is alphabetical by title, and institutional publications are set down as ANNALS, BULLETIN, JOURNAL, with name of institution, often in abbreviated form, following. The usefulness for African medicine will probably be more through subject than by country.

Reference Works

1170. Bala Mbarga, Henri. GUIDE AFRICAIN DE LA SANTE: MANUEL D'HYGIENE. Paris, Librairie Hatier, 1964. 111 p. illus.

1171. BULLETIN OF HYGIENE. 1926- London, Bureau of Hygiene and Tropical Diseases. Monthly.

This has superseded the Sanitation supplements of the TROPICAL DISEASES BULLETIN. Both journals give considerable emphasis to Africa.

1172. Carothers, John C. THE AFRICAN MIND IN HEALTH AND DISEASE: A STUDY IN ETHNOPSYCHIATRY. Geneva, World Health Organization, 1953. 177 p. diagr. (World Health Organization Monograph Series, no. 17)

Bibliography: p. 173-177.

By a former colonial medical officer and consultant in mental health to WHO. This technical study, full of statistics, drew on the author's own experience and that of many other authorities to examine African psychology against the background of the environment, physical anthropology, and other factors. Dr. Carothers included comparative consideration of the psychology and psychiatry of the Negro in the United States.

1173. Colbourne, Michael James. MALARIA IN AFRICA. London, Ibadan, etc., Oxford University Press, 1966. 115 p. map, tables, diagrs. (Students' Library)

A survey for medical students and laymen which discusses the causes and effects of malaria, its treatment and eradication. The author, a WHO adviser on malaria eradication, was Government Malariologist in Ghana from 1952 to 1955 and is now head of the Department of Social Medicine and Public Health, University of Singapore.

For a history of malaria in nineteenth-century Africa and its effects on European exploration, see RIVERS OF DEATH IN AFRICA, by Michael Gelfand (London, Oxford University Press, 1964, 100 p., maps). See also Prothero's MIGRANTS AND MALARIA (below, no. 1182), and, for a technical, specialized study, MALARIA IN TANZANIA, by David F. Clyde (London, Oxford University Press, 1967, 167 p.).

1174. Gelfand, Michael. THE SICK AFRICAN: A CLINICAL STUDY. 3d ed. Cape
Town, Juta, 1957. 866 p. illus.

Bibliography: p. 793-842.

A handbook on diseases most common to the people of Africa--
"destined," said a reviewer in AFRICAN AFFAIRS at the time of its
first publication (1944), "to lie upon the table of doctors, nuns,
priests, medical missionaries, colonial administrators, in fact,
every white man and woman working in Equatorial Africa who has to
treat the sick African." The preliminary chapters discuss popular
fallacies regarding tropical diseases and tribal psychology: the
African fear of hospitals, their conviction that some illnesses
are caused by witchcraft. Following chapters describe and analyze
individual diseases and give directions for their treatment, in a
style as little technical as possible. Most of Dr. Gelfand's other
studies relate specifically to the Rhodesias and Nyasaland, although
a 1964 book is entitled MEDICINE AND CUSTOM IN AFRICA (Edinburgh, E.
and S. Livingstone, 174 p.).

1175. Harley, George Way. NATIVE AFRICAN MEDICINE: WITH SPECIAL REFERENCE
TO ITS PRACTICE IN THE MANO TRIBE OF LIBERIA. Cambridge, Mass.,
Harvard University Press, 1941. xvi, 294 p.

Bibliography: p. 255-263.

By a noted medical missionary who is also an anthropologist
richly experienced in West African culture. The body of his study
is an analysis of the medicine and magic of the Mano tribe of
Liberia, among whom he had worked for years, and he ends with a
clear exposition and definition of fetishism. A supplementary
section, "Native Medical Practice in Africa as a Whole," draws on
the findings of other scholars, indicated in a long bibliography
of sources.

1176. Inter-African Bureau for Animal Health and Production. BULLETIN OF
EPIZOOTIC DISEASES OF AFRICA. v. 1, 1953- Muguga, P.O. Kikuyu,
Kenya.

This affiliate of CCTA/CSA was formerly called Inter-African
Bureau for Epizootic Diseases (1951-59). Its library does abstracting
and indexing and has information services. For full description see
Library of Congress, INTERNATIONAL SCIENTIFIC ORGANIZATIONS (no. 42).

A Study Group on Animal Diseases of the U.S. National Academy of
Sciences visited Africa in 1964 to survey animal health programs
sponsored by CCTA, particularly Project 15 on rinderpest. The report,
prepared under contract to AID, was scheduled for 1965 publication.

1177. International Children's Centre. JOURNEES AFRICAINES DE PEDIATRIE.
Dakar, 12-16 April 1960. Reports. Paris, 1961. 256 p. illus.

A number of recent conferences have related to African children.
This one was concerned with questions of health and childhood diseases.

1178. Kiev, Ari, ed. MAGIC, FAITH, AND HEALING: STUDIES IN PRIMITIVE
PSYCHIATRY TODAY. New York, Free Press of Glencoe, 1964. 475 p.
illus.

This is a collection of excellent papers, woven together by a
preface written by the editor. Not all of the essays are about
African societies, but several of them (6 essays out of a total of
19, including the preface and epilogue) are concerned with African
phenomena. These are written by Raymond Prince, Michael Gelfand,
Victor W. Turner, Michael G. Whisson, John Dawson, and T. Adeoye
Lambo. Bibliographical references are included.

1179. King, Maurice, ed. MEDICAL CARE IN DEVELOPING COUNTRIES, A PRIMER
ON THE MEDICINE OF POVERTY.... London, Oxford University Press,
1966. 537 p.

This book consists of 30 papers, most of them presented to a conference on "Health Centres and Hospitals in Africa" held at Makerere
University College. It is of value to more than medical specialists.

1180. Latham, Michael. HUMAN NUTRITION IN TROPICAL AFRICA: A TEXTBOOK
FOR HEALTH WORKERS, WITH SPECIAL REFERENCE TO COMMUNITY HEALTH
PROBLEMS IN EAST AFRICA. Rome, FAO, 1965. 268 p. illus.,
tables. Distributed by Columbia International Service, New York.

1181. New York. Missionary Research Library. DIRECTORY OF PROTESTANT
MEDICAL MISSIONS. Compiled by Arthur W. March. New York,
1959. 134 p.

In this long list there is first a statistical survey by
continent and country, Africa leading, with the name of each mission
followed by figures of size, number of patients, doctors, nurses,
and other pertinent data. Next is given a separate index of leprosy
missions in Africa and Asia.

1182. Prothero, R. Mansell. MIGRANTS AND MALARIA. London, Longmans, 1965.
142 p. illus., maps.

Includes bibliographies.

This book on medical geography, by a sometime consultant to the World Health Organization, is concerned with the influence of all human factors on malaria and its eradication in Africa. Prothero describes malaria at some length and explains the significance of population mobility in Africa. The bulk of the book deals with the situation in the Sudan, Horn of Africa, East and South-Central Africa, and Morocco. An index is included.

1183. TROPICAL DISEASES BULLETIN. 1912- London, Bureau of Hygiene and Tropical Diseases. Monthly.

This abstracting/indexing journal is very useful for African material.

1184. Trowell, Hubert C. NON-INFECTIVE DISEASE IN AFRICA: THE PECULI-ARITIES OF MEDICAL NON-INFECTIVE DISEASES IN THE INDIGENOUS INHABITANTS OF AFRICA SOUTH OF THE SAHARA. London, E. Arnold, 1960 [on cover: Baltimore, Williams & Wilkins]. 481 p. illus.

Includes bibliography.

Technical study of diseases common among Africans but seldom found elsewhere. "Examples are endomyocardial fibrosis, idiopathic cardiomyopathy, siderosis, porphyria, primary carcinoma of the liver, kwashiorkor and some of the haemoglobinopathies." The author is a clinician with 29 years' experience in East Africa as well as work in other parts of Africa south of the Sahara.

1185. United Nations. Economic Commission for Africa. DIRECTORY OF REGIONAL SOCIAL WELFARE ACTIVITIES. 2d ed. 1967. 124 p. (E/CN.14/SWSA/1/Rev.)

1186. World Health Organization. REVIEW OF THE SECOND DECADE OF PUBLIC HEALTH WORK IN AFRICA. Brazzaville, W.H.O. Regional Office for Africa, 1968. 68 p.

PART IV

AREA GUIDE

(BY FORMER COLONIAL POWER, REGION, AND COUNTRY)

INTRODUCTION TO PART IV

In this part of the guide we suggest bibliographies, serials, and reference works by colonial power, by separate areas and countries. A few titles from the earlier parts are sometimes repeated if especially meaningful, but in general the references for Africa as a whole must be consulted for their application to individual regions. In the case of official documents, for instance, it seemed unnecessary to name for each country the gazettes (except the former French territories), statistical publications, development plans, legislative debates, etc., which are recorded not only in the Library of Congress series of official documents now published for most countries but also in the inclusive lists cited in the bibliographies of Chapter 9. Similarly, newspapers and journals of individual countries are for the most part omitted here, since they are listed by country in the various bibliographies in Chapter 8. Information on libraries, archives, and manuscript collections dealing with each colonial power and specific regions and countries will be found in Part I.

Following the geographic headings below we give numbers of items in other parts of the bibliography that have specific reference to the region or country in question. See especially no. 669, Schiller's BIBLIOGRAPHY OF AFRICAN LAW, which covers each colonial power and most colonies.

Although it is, in a sense, repetitious, we have included separate sections on former German Africa and Italian Africa.

CHAPTER 31

FORMER BRITISH AFRICA

Note: A large body of writing, mostly prior to 1960, deals with the former
African territories of the British Empire and Commonwealth without specific
country or regional application. The present section offers a few outstanding examples cf this literature.

     The most useful single reference tool for study of former British
Africa is still A. R. Hewitt's GUIDE TO RESOURCES FOR COMMONWEALTH STUDIES
(see no. 83). See also, in earlier sections, nos. 2, 82, 84-94, 196, 319,
325, 330, 364, 369, 586, and 634.

     Official gazettes of the countries formerly under British administra-
tion are primary sources for any research. In general, legislation goes into
effect only when the text of the law, ordinance, decree, proclamation, etc.,
is published in the gazette. Gazettes also carry news items of governmental
acticn, announcements of official publications, and much other information
regarding administration. The supplements are often long reports on particular questions of economic and social conditions and developments.

     Since the gazettes for the English-speaking countries are fully re-
corded in a number of bibliographies--the MONTHLY LIST cited below (no. 1191),
the Library of Congress lists of official publications of each country, the
UNECA list (no. 364[o]), and the AFRICAN LAW DIGEST (no. 680, for current
legislation)--mention of them is omitted in the following sections. Likewise
omitted are the statistical bulletins and budgets which have been regular
publications of each government before and since independence, as well as the
many development plans which are covered in current bibliographies (see
Chapter 5).

Bibliographies

1187. Brokensha, David. APPLIED ANTHROPOLOGY IN ENGLISH-SPEAKING AFRICA.
       Lexington, Society for Applied Anthropology, University of
       Kentucky, 1966. 31 p. (Monograph no. 8)

Bibliography: p. 18-31.

A compact survey, with emphasis on the application of social anthropology to government planning. The main part of the text is in four sections--regional surveys, topics of study, other applications, and conclusion. The bibliography, which is divided into 18 subject headings, lists works published mainly from 1955 to 1966.

1188. Coleman, James S. "A Survey of Selected Literature on the Government and Politics of British West Africa." AMERICAN POLITICAL SCIENCE REVIEW, v. 49, Dec. 1955: 1130-1150.

Although events have movqd far beyond anything forecast in Professor Coleman's bibliographical essay, it is meaningful in its indications of methodology of research. Many of the sources he mentions apply to East and Southern Africa as well as West Africa.

1189. Couch, Margaret, ed. EDUCATION IN AFRICA: A SELECT BIBLIOGRAPHY: Part 1, BRITISH AND FORMER BRITISH TERRITORIES IN AFRICA. London, Institute of Education, University of London, 1962. 121 p. (EDUCATION LIBRARIES BULLETIN, Suppl. 5)

Bibliography on education in former British territories in Africa, excluding the Republic of South Africa. Selected from the catalogue of one of the Institute of Education libraries, it contains material listed to the end of 1961. Entries to both books and articles are arranged by country and subdivided by subject headings. An author index is included.

1190. Ford, Percy, and Grace Ford. A GUIDE TO PARLIAMENTARY PAPERS: WHAT THEY ARE, HOW TO FIND THEM, HOW TO USE THEM. Oxford, B. Blackwell, 1955. 79 p.

A vade mecum to aid in finding one's way through the complexities of British parliamentary papers. Part 1 describes papers relating to Parliament's business and proceedings (procedure papers, journals, debates, standing committee debates) and papers giving Parliament information for consideration (bills, reports of committees and royal commissions, departmental papers, command and non-parliamentary papers). Part 2 explains indexes, collections, sets, consolidated lists, and other aids in finding material. Part 3 discusses use of reports, etc.

1191. Great Britain. Colonial Office. Library Reference and Research Section. MONTHLY LIST OF OFFICIAL COLONIAL PUBLICATIONS. June 1948- London. 33 cm. Mimeographed.

Until the 1960's the MONTHLY LIST was the fullest available
record of official publications for a large part of Africa and for
other overseas possessions of the United Kingdom, and it is an
important source for retrospective study of the formerly British
countries of Africa. The list is divided into sections and arranged
alphabetically by country. Part 1A cites typescripts prepared in
the colonies and not for sale. Part 1B is the full list of publications from the colonies available from the Crown Agent for the
Colonies or elsewhere, and of publications of the Colonial Office.
Part 2 is a separate listing of government gazettes, with the more
significant supplements cited.

1192. Great Britain. Ministry of Overseas Development. PUBLIC ADMINIS-
           TRATION: A SELECT BIBLIOGRAPHY. London, 1964. Mimeographed.

       2d Supplement, 1966.

1193. Great Britain. Parliament. House of Commons. GENERAL INDEX TO
           THE ACCOUNTS AND PAPERS, REPORTS OF COMMISSIONERS, ESTIMATES,
           &C, &C, PRINTED BY ORDER OF THE HOUSE OF COMMONS OR PRESENTED
           BY COMMAND, 1801-1852. London, H.M. Stationery Off., 1853.
           1080 p. (Reprinted 1938)

           _____. GENERAL INDEX TO THE ACCOUNTS AND PAPERS . . . 1852-1899.
           London, 1909.

           _____. GENERAL INDEX TO THE BILLS, REPORTS AND PAPERS PRINTED BY
           ORDER OF THE HOUSE OF COMMONS AND TO THE REPORTS AND PAPERS
           PRESENTED BY COMMAND, 1900-1948/49. London, 1960. 893 p.

       In these general 50-year indexes, there are subject headings
for Africa, with cross-references to individual countries. Very
little relevant material is cited in the first index, but the indexes
covering 1852 to 1948/49 are rich with sources for historical studies
of the British African territories. These and other indexes to
British official publications are described in the general guides
to reference tools, Walford and Winchell (see nos. 1 and 2). For
those of particular usefulness in African studies, see Hewitt (no.
83).

1194. Great Britain. Parliament. House of Lords. A GENERAL INDEX TO
           THE SESSIONAL PAPERS PRINTED BY ORDER OF THE HOUSE OF LORDS
           OR PRESENTED BY SPECIAL COMMAND, 1801-1859. London, H.M.
           Staionery Off., 1938. 992 p. (1st ed., 1860)

       1859-1870. London, G. E. Eyre and William Spottiswoode, 1872.
           368 p.

       1871-1884/5. London, Hansard, 1890. 544 p.

Headings include African colonies, African states, slave trade,
and individual place names. The general indexes for 1859-70 and
1871-85 have not been reissued to date.

1195. Great Britain. Stationery Office. GOVERNMENT PUBLICATIONS. 1936-
        London. Monthly with annual cumulations and five-year indexes.

        The systematic listing of official British publications from
the H.M. Stationery Office began with a MONTHLY LIST OF PARLIAMENTARY
PAPERS in 1881, to which was added a QUARTERLY LIST in 1894; there
were also MONTHLY AND QUARTERLY LISTS OF OFFICIAL AND PARLIAMENTARY
PUBLICATIONS (more inclusive) from 1897 to 1921. In 1922 they were
superseded by the MONTHLY LIST OF GOVERNMENT PUBLICATIONS, with semiannual cumulations, and the annual CONSOLIDATED LIST OF PARLIAMENTARY
AND STATIONERY OFFICE PUBLICATIONS. In Jan. 1936 these two were combined with the MONTHLY CIRCULAR: A SELECTION FROM RECENT PUBLICATIONS
to form the present catalogue. Arrangement in all is by issuing
agency, with numbered listing of command papers, etc. The monthly
catalogues have no indexes, and items concerning Africa must be
looked for by agency. In the annual volume and the five-year indexes,
entries are by subject, including place names.

        The H.M. Stationery Office also has a set of SECTIONAL LISTS for
separate agencies or groups of agencies. No. 34 is COLONIAL OFFICE,
containing a list of papers by subject, etc., from 1925--complete
lists of the colonial numbered series, the Colonial Research Studies,
the Colonial Research Publications, the Colonial Advisory Council of
Agriculture, Animal Health and Forestry publications, and Fishery
publications. This has presumably been revised and updated.

1196. Hewitt, Arthur R. UNION LIST OF COMMONWEALTH NEWSPAPERS IN LONDON,
        OXFORD, AND CAMBRIDGE. London, Published for the Institute of
        Commonwealth Studies, University of London, by the Athlone Press,
        1960. 101 p. Offset print. Legal size.

        Listing of newspapers of Commonwealth countries in London, Oxford,
Cambridge, and other centers. The arrangement is geographical, and
the table of contents lists 18 African countries. Holdings of the
receiving libraries are given.

1197. Horne, A. J. THE COMMONWEALTH TODAY: A SELECT BIBLIOGRAPHY OF THE
        COMMONWEALTH AND ITS CONSTITUENT COUNTRIES. London, Library
        Association (7 Ridgement St., Store St.), 1965. 107 p. (Library
        Association, Special Subject List no. 45)

        Listing of 720 books published in recent years and still in print.
Works on Britain are not included. Arrangement is geographical by
continent and country, with subclassification by subject.

1198. Meek, Charles K. COLONIAL LAW: A BIBLIOGRAPHY WITH SPECIAL REFERENCE
       TO NATIVE AFRICAN SYSTEMS OF LAW AND LAND TENURE. London, Pub-
       lished for Nuffield College by Oxford University Press, 1948.
       xiii, 58 p.

       This reading list, compiled by a leading British authority on
African land law, is restricted to the territories under U.K. administration at the time of compilation.

1199. OVERSEAS OFFICIAL PUBLICATIONS: QUARTERLY BULLETIN OF OFFICIAL PUB-
       LICATIONS RECEIVED BY THE ROYAL EMPIRE SOCIETY AND ISSUED IN THE
       OVERSEAS BRITISH EMPIRE OR RELATING THERETO. v. 1-5, Apr. 1927-
       Jan. 1932. London, Royal Empire Society, 1927-32.

       Unofficial listing of official documents of the British Empire,
most of which came into the library of the Society, now the Royal
Commonwealth Society.

       See also T. R. Reese, THE HISTORY OF THE ROYAL COMMONWEALTH
SOCIETY, 1868-1969 (London, Oxford University Press, 1968, 280 p.).

1200. Oxford. University. Institute of Colonial Studies. Nuffield College
       Colonial Reading Lists.

       a) COLONIAL ADMINISTRATION: GENERAL. By Margery Perham. 1947.
           Rev. ed. with title COLONIAL GOVERNMENT: ANNOTATED READING
           LIST ON BRITISH COLONIAL GOVERNMENT, WITH SOME GENERAL AND
           COMPARATIVE MATERIAL UPON FOREIGN EMPIRES, ETC. 1950.
           80 p. (See no. 595.)

       b) COLONIAL ECONOMICS. Compiled by Penelope A. Bower. With a
           supplementary list added in July 1949 by Professor S. Herbert
           Frankel. 1949. 42 p.

       c) URBAN CONDITIONS IN AFRICA: SELECT READING LIST ON URBAN
           PROBLEMS IN AFRICA. New and rev. ed. Compiled by J. L. L.
           Comhaire. 1952. 48 p. (See no. 831.)

       These three lists were prepared in 1947-48 before the Nuffield
College program of colonial studies headed by Dame Perham was replaced
by the Institute of Colonial Studies; they focused on the British
colonial system.

1201. Temperley, Harold, and L. M. Penson. A CENTURY OF DIPLOMATIC BLUE
       BOOKS, 1814-1914. Cambridge, Eng., University Press, 1938.
       xvi, 600 p.

A record, by year, of bills, sessional papers, and command papers, covering the entire published diplomatic activity of the British government. The index is by country with whom the diplomatic traffic took place, and by subject, including place names (Africa and individual countries). It was succeeded by Vogel (no. 1203).

1202. UNION LIST OF COMMONWEALTH AND SOUTH AFRICAN LAW: A LOCATION GUIDE TO COMMONWEALTH AND SOUTH AFRICAN LEGISLATION, LAW REPORTS AND DIGESTS HELD BY LIBRARIES IN THE UNITED KINGDOM, MAY 1963. London, Institute of Advanced Legal Studies, 1963. xi, 129 p.

Publications nos. 1 and 2 of the Institute cover earlier lists: A SURVEY OF LEGAL PERIODICALS HELD IN BRITISH LIBRARIES (London, 1949, 52 p.) and UNION LIST OF COMMONWEALTH LAW LITERATURE IN LIBRARIES IN OXFORD, CAMBRIDGE AND LONDON (London, 1952, various pagings: South Africa E.1-17; Colonies, including East Africa, Kenya, etc., G.1-49).

1203. Vogel, Robert. A BREVIATE OF BRITISH DIPLOMATIC BLUE BOOKS, 1919-1939. Montreal, McGill University, 1963. xxxv, 474 p.

This successor to Temperley and Penson follows the same arrangement but is considerably fuller with regard to Africa. In the subject index there appears at once Abyssinia, shortly thereafter Africa, and then individual countries by name.

Serials

Note: There have been so many serials published in Great Britain dealing with Africa that only a few can be mentioned here. The various lists mentioned at the beginning of Part IV provide full coverage. In addition, the British established a network of government and non government serials in every colony. Some of these titles appear in the region and country sections.

1204. AFRICAN AFFAIRS: JOURNAL OF THE ROYAL AFRICAN SOCIETY. v. 1, no. 1-Oct. 1901- London. plates, ports., maps. Quarterly.

Published until July 1944 as JOURNAL OF THE ROYAL AFRICAN SOCIETY; Vols. I-XLV published in London and New York by Macmillan, 1901-46. Separately paged supplements accompany some numbers. Reviews and bibliography of new books and documents are included.

Membership of the Society includes Britain's leading Africanists and former colonial administrators. Many of the articles are addresses presented before the Society on current conditions in African countries and are followed by highly informed discussion. Until recently an introductory section by the editor formed a commentary on events of the quarter. Contributions are largely concerned with the former British territories.

1205. BULLETIN OF THE SCHOOL OF ORIENTAL AND AFRICAN STUDIES. 1917- London. 3 times a year.

1206. CAMBRIDGE HISTORICAL JOURNAL. 1923-57. Cambridge, London. Continued as HISTORICAL JOURNAL, 1958- London, New York. 4 times a year.

1207. COLONIAL OFFICE JOURNAL. 1907-10. London. Continued as COLONIAL JOURNAL, 1907-1920. London.

1208. COMMONWEALTH AND EMPIRE REVIEW. 1901-44. London. Monthly.

1209. CORONA: THE JOURNAL OF HER MAJESTY'S OVERSEAS SERVICE. 1949-1962. London, H.M. Stationery Office. Monthly.

1210. EMPIRE. 1938-49. London, Fabian Society. Superseded by VENTURE, 1949- London. Monthly.

1211. GEOGRAPHICAL JOURNAL. 1893- London, Royal Geographical Society. 4 times a year.

1212. IMPERIAL INSTITUTE JOURNAL. 1895-1902. London, Imperial Institute. Superseded by BULLETIN, 1903-48. London.

1213. INTERNATIONAL REVIEW OF MISSIONS. 1912- Geneva. Quarterly.

    See no. 924 for annotation.

1214. JOURNAL OF LOCAL ADMINISTRATION OVERSEAS. v. 1- Jan. 1949- London, H.M. Stationery Off. Quarterly.

    This journal, concerned with practical problems of government in Africa, primarily English-speaking Africa, was earlier titled DIGEST OF AFRICAN LOCAL ADMINISTRATION, then JOURNAL OF AFRICAN ADMINISTRATION, and was formerly edited by the African Studies Branch of the Colonial Office. It was taken over by the Department of Technical Co-operation (now Ministry of Overseas Development) in 1962.

1215.   JOURNAL OF MODERN AFRICAN STUDIES. 1963- Cambridge, Eng.; New York,
            Cambridge University Press. Quarterly.

            See no. 296 for annotation. See also no. 504 for JOURNAL OF
        AFRICAN HISTORY.

1216.   NINETEENTH CENTURY, A MONTHLY REVIEW. 1877-1900. Continued in NINE-
            TEENTH CENTURY AND AFTER. 1901-50. London.

1217.   PROCEEDINGS OF THE ROYAL COMMONWEALTH SOCIETY. 1869-1909. London.
            Continued in UNITED EMPIRE. (See no. 1224.)

1218.   PROCEEDINGS OF THE ROYAL GEOGRAPHICAL SOCIETY. 1855-78; n.s. 1879-92.
            Superseded GEOGRAPHICAL MAGAZINE. Superseded by GEOGRAPHICAL
            JOURNAL. 1893-

1219.   PROCEEDINGS OF THE ROYAL SOCIETY OF EDINBURGH. 1832-1939/40. Edin-
            burgh. Irregular.

1220.   RACE: THE JOURNAL OF THE INSTITUTE OF RACE RELATIONS. 1959- London.
            Quarterly.

1221.   THE ROUND TABLE: A QUARTERLY REVIEW OF THE POLITICS OF THE BRITISH
            COMMONWEALTH. 1910- London.

1222.   SCOTTISH GEOGRAPHICAL MAGAZINE. 1885- Edinburgh. 3 times a year.

1223.   United Africa Company, Ltd. STATISTICAL AND ECONCMIC REVIEW. 1948-
            London. Semiannual.

            See no. 1266 for annotation.

1224.   UNITED EMPIRE. 1910-58. London. Superseded JOURNAL ... and PROCEED-
            INGS OF THE ROYAL COLONIAL INSTITUTE, 1869-1909. Superseded by
            COMMONWEALTH JOURNAL, 1958-

1225.   WEST AFRICAN REVIEW. 1922-62. London. Monthly.

Reference Works
<u>   </u>

1226. BRITISH COMMONWEALTH YEAR BOOK. Edited by Ronald S. Russell. London,
       MacGibbon & Kee. (10th ed., 1962/63, 614 p., illus., tables)

       Compendium of general and statistical information on the nations
of the Commonwealth, including English-speaking Africa (except the
Republic of South Africa). This yearbook was begun in 1952 (then published by Newman Neame for the Empire Economic Union) as COMMONWEALTH
CO-OPERATION: THE EMPIRE AND COMMONWEALTH YEAR BOOK; the title was
later changed to EMPIRE AND COMMONWEALTH YEAR BOOK. The present form
was adopted in 1960/61, when a new publisher took it over. Arrangement is by country, with emphasis on commercial interests.

       A broad coverage of geographical, historical, political, eco-
nomic, and social aspects of each country was presented in a volume
of almost a thousand pages issued by Europa Publications in 1956 and
1958 with the title THE BRITISH COMMONWEALTH. The last issue, in 1959
when it ceased publication, was entitled COMMONWEALTH YEAR BOOK (London, 1150 p., tables, bibliographies).

1227. THE CAMBRIDGE HISTORY OF THE BRITISH EMPIRE. General eds.: J. Hol-
       land Rose, A. P. Newton, and E. A. Benians. Cambridge, Eng.,
       University Press, 1929-

       Vol. II. THE GROWTH OF THE NEW EMPIRE, 1783-1870. 1940. (Bib-
       liography: p. 885-1004)

       Vol. III. THE EMPIRE-COMMONWEALTH, 1870-1919. 1959. (Bibliog-
       raphy: p. 769-907)

       Vol. VIII. SOUTH AFRICA, RHODESIA AND THE PROTECTORATES. 1936.
       (2d ed., edited by Eric A. Walker, 1963; bibliography: p. 917-1017)

       In Vols. II and III, the treatment of African history occupies
only a small portion of the text, but the bibliographies are of outstanding importance, especially in Vol. III. Part 1 surveys collections
of manuscripts in public and private archives, and official papers and
publications. Select lists of parliamentary papers and parliamentary
debates are included. Part 2 contains two sections--general bibliographies and special bibliographies. In the former are listed bibliographies and guides, periodicals, collected historical records, general
histories and descriptive works, and biographies. Under special
bibliographies are listed manuscripts as well as the above categories
of material for each unit: colonial policy and administration in
general, 1870-1921; the opening of tropical Africa, 1870-1914; imperial
finance, trade, and communications, 1870-1914; international relations
and colonial affairs, 1869-1914; the British Empire and the United
States, 1870-1914; imperial defence, 1870-1914; the Empire at war,
1914-18; the British Empire and the peace treaties, 1918-19; international law and colonial questions, 1870-1914; and the Colonial Office.

1228. COLONIAL OFFICE LIST. 1862-1940; 1946- [1947 not published] London,
       H.M. Stationery Off. Annual.

       This handbook, which has now been published for more than a full
century (1966 ed., 334 p.), formerly had as its subtitle the words
"comprising historical and statistical information respecting the
colonial empire, list of officers serving in the colonies, etc., and
other information." The first section gives history and functions
of the Colonial Office in London, its staff, its subject departments,
and associations, institutions, and committees concerned with colonial
affairs. Next are sections on individual colonies, with information
on area, population, history, economic situation, etc., former governors,
present cabinet, and civil establishment. These are followed by a
directory of colonial officials, with biographical data and record of
services. The volume ends with a bibliography, a list of "Parliamentary
and Non-Parliamentary Papers of Colonial Interest Published during
[the past year]," as well as periodicals, in two groupings, by subject
and by country.

       With the COLONIAL OFFICE LIST of 1948 a separate MAP SUPPLEMENT
was issued, containing 38 maps, most of them folded to a size uniform
with the list.

1229. THE COMMONWEALTH RELATIONS OFFICE YEARBOOK. v. 1- 1951- London,
       H.M. Stationery Off. (1966 ed., 658 p.)

       This work largely replaces the COLONIAL OFFICE LIST for African
countries. Until 1966 it was titled THE COMMONWEALTH RELATIONS
OFFICE LIST and included biographical notes on staff members (in the
early 1960's only senior members); these notes now appear in THE
DIPLOMATIC SERVICE LIST and are not duplicated in the YEARBOOK.

       The 1966 edition has sections on Ghana, Nigeria, Sierra Leone,
Tanzania, Uganda, Kenya, Malawi, Zambia, Gambia, and Southern Rhodesia.
For each country there is a brief description, history, and account
of constitutional development, followed by lists of government officials,
ministries and government departments, and diplomatic representatives
overseas and in the country concerned. The section on Nigeria is
additionally divided into regions and has a small glossary of official
titles. National flags are shown in color. Brief chapters are allotted
for the East African Common Services Organization and the Central
African Joint Services. There is an index.

1230. Conference on African Education, Cambridge, Eng., 1952. AFRICAN
       EDUCATION: A STUDY OF EDUCATIONAL POLICY AND PRACTICE IN BRITISH
       TROPICAL AFRICA. Edited by W. E. F. Ward. Oxford, University
       Press (available from the Crown Agents for the Colonies, London),
       1953. 187 p.

Significant publication resulting from the work of two study groups sponsored by the Nuffield Foundation and the Colonial Office, 1951-52, and the ensuing conference at Cambridge in Sept. 1952. The reports were based on six months' visits by teams of three or four educational specialists, who examined thoroughly the entire educational systems of West Africa and of East and Central Africa, and their special problems and needs.

A summary in popular style of the work of the 1952 conference was written by John McLeod Campbell, AFRICAN HISTORY IN THE MAKING (London, Edinburgh House Press, 1955, 120 p.). A slightly later work by F. H. Hilliard, A SHORT HISTORY OF EDUCATION IN BRITISH WEST AFRICA (London, New York, T. Nelson, 1957, 186 p., illus. [Nelson's Education Handbooks], is a survey of a portion of this field which was greatly increasing in importance during the final years before independence.

1231. De Smith, S. A. THE NEW COMMONWEALTH AND ITS CONSTITUTIONS. London, Stevens, 1964. 312 p.

In writing this general survey of constitutional developments in the newly self-governing and independent countries of the Commonwealth, the author admits that some of the facts he sets in the present tense will have "passed into constitutional history" before the date of publication. His analysis of the constitutional forms which have accompanied political change relates largely to the new countries of Africa.

1232. Elias, Taslim Olawale. BRITISH COLONIAL LAW: A COMPARATIVE STUDY OF THE INTERACTION BETWEEN ENGLISH AND LOCAL LAWS IN BRITISH DEPENDENCIES. London, Stevens, 1962. 323 p.

_____. THE NATURE OF AFRICAN CUSTOMARY LAW. Manchester, Manchester University Press, 1956. 318 p.

By a well-known African jurist who rose to the position of Attorney General of Nigeria. These two works are confined to the countries formerly under British control.

1233. Great Britain. Colonial Office. [Annual reports on the colonies.] London, H.M. Stationery Off.

Series begun in the nineteenth century, with varying titles and providing an authoritative general survey of the current situation and background of each of the British colonial possessions; suspended in 1940 and begun again with the reports for 1946. They are published annually or, in some cases, biennially, in uniform booklets having about 50 to over 100 pages, with a few pages of photographs and a folded map. The arrangement of contents is systematic, with slight variations: Part 1, general review of the year's developments; Part 2, brief factual and statistical paragraphs on socioeconomic aspects; Part 3, geography, history, administration, etc., and various bibliographies. Appendixes have texts of special documents and statistical tables.

The reports on the trust territories (Tanganyika, Togoland, and British Cameroons) were submitted first to the League of Nations and then to the General Assembly of the United Nations and followed a rather different pattern, concentrating on social and economic advances.

1234. Great Britain. Colonial Office. COLONIAL RESEARCH. 1944/45- London. Annual.

Includes the overall report of the Colonial Research Council and individual reports of its branches. In 1959/60 these were the Committee for Colonial Agricultural, Animal Health, and Forestry Research; Colonial Economic Research Committee; Colonial Fisheries Advisory Committee; Colonial Medical Research Council; Colonial Pesticides Committee; Colonial Road Research Committee; Colonial Social Science Research Council; Tsetse Fly and Trypanosomiasis Committee; and the report of the director, Anti-Locust Research Centre. A final section summarizes research matters not covered by the specialist advisory bodies.

1235. Great Britain. Colonial Office. DIGEST OF COLONIAL STATISTICS. 1952- London, H. M. Stationery Office. Bimonthly.

1236. Great Britain. Colonial Office. Colonial Research Publications [series].

_____. Colonial Research Studies [series]. no. 1, 1950-

Significant monographs on many aspects of colonial research. Titles will be found in the official bibliographies and in most listings of important works of each year.

The pamphlets now issued by the Central Office of Information (alternately British Information Services) are background surveys for a general public.

1237. Great Britain. Colonial Office. AN ECONOMIC SURVEY OF THE COLONIAL TERRITORIES. 1932, 1933, 1935-37, 1951. London, H. M. Stationery Off. maps (part fold.). (Colonial)

Begun as an annual review, this overall statistical report on British colonial possessions was published in one volume until 1938, when the war caused its suspension. The only postwar edition, 1951, appeared in 1952 in seven volumes of 100 to 200 legal-size pages each. Those relating to Africa are I, THE CENTRAL AFRICAN AND HIGH COMMISSION TERRITORIES: II, THE EAST AFRICAN TERRITORIES; III, THE WEST AFRICAN TERRITORIES...WITH ST. HELENA. The country sections give systematic coverage of economic life and conditions, with summarization of general background including geography and population, political structure, principal economic legislation, communications and transport, and surveys of productive activities, finance and trade, and development. Many statistical tables and folded maps showing production areas were included. Vol. VII, evenly divided into 100 pages of text and 100 pages of tables of exports, analyzed principal products throughout the colonial territories.

Coordinated reports on the economics of the English-speaking countries of Africa, as well as the rest of the former empire, are now issued by the British Central Office of Information, Reference Division, as reference pamphlets.

1238. Great Britain. Foreign Office. BRITISH AND FOREIGN STATE PAPERS, with which is incorporated Hertslet's COMMERCIAL TREATIES. London, H.M. Stationery Off., 1841-

These volumes contain texts of treaties, correspondence about foreign affairs, and many documents of historical interest, including texts of constitutions and organic laws of foreign countries. The Foreign Office handled the British territories in Africa from about 1885 to 1905, so that these years are of particular interest. The volumes of Hertslet's COMMERCIAL TREATIES, each covering a number of years, were published for H.M. Stationery Office from 1827 to 1922, ceasing with the last index volume, v. 31 (London, Harrison & Sons, 1925). After 1922 the commercial treaty information was included with the BRITISH AND FOREIGN STATE PAPERS, beginning with v. 116 of the latter in 1923. The PAPERS are well indexed, volume by volume, and there are several GENERAL INDEXES (the first covering 1373-1853, later ones for 10 to 20 or more years).

There is also the FOREIGN OFFICE TREATY SERIES (London, H.M. Stationery Off., 1892-), numbered and indexed as a separate set. These and numerous other British official series of interest for Africa are fully described by Hewitt (see no. 83).

A companion work to Hertslet's COMMERCIAL TREATIES and the FOREIGN OFFICE TREATY SERIES, relating to the partition of Africa, is Sir Edward Hertslet's THE MAP OF AFRICA BY TREATY (3d ed., rev. and completed to the end of 1908, London, Printed for H.M. Stationery Off. by Harrison & Sons, 1909, 3 v. and portfolio of maps).

1239. Great Britain. Ministry of Overseas Development. OVERSEAS DEVELOP-
      MENT: THE WORK OF THE NEW MINISTRY. London, H.M. Stationery
      Off., Aug. 1965. 74 p. (Cmnd. 2736)

    White paper presented by the minister, then Mrs. Barbara Castle,
surveying the present economic scene in the developing countries in
Africa and elsewhere and the part played by British aid. The conclusion is that, in spite of UN efforts for more liberal trade policies,
the decline in prices of commodities--e.g., cocoa--has cut export
earnings of the producer countries, making aid more necessary than
ever.

1240. Hailey, William M. Hailey, 1st baron. NATIVE ADMINISTRATION IN THE
      BRITISH AFRICAN TERRITORIES. London, H.M. Stationery Off.,
      1950-53. 5 v.

    At head of title: pt. 1-4, Colonial Office; pt. 5, Commonwealth
Relations Office.

    Lord Hailey's AFRICAN SURVEY (see no. 445) appeared first in
1938. In 1941 he reported on journeys in the British colonies during
the two previous years, examining administration under wartime conditions. After an inspection in 1947-48 he found the situation so
changed that he rewrote his report, the first four volumes of which
(East Africa, Central Africa, West Africa, General Survey) appeared
in 1950-51; the fifth, on the High Commission Territories, appeared
in 1953. The work is little concerned with political or constitutional
development but is a detailed statement of administrative systems in
the colonies under review, including the administration of justice
through native tribunals and changes in land law and customary law--
the whole forming a handbook for administrative officers in the
Colonial Office.

1241. Henige, David. COLONIAL GOVERNORS FROM THE FIFTEENTH CENTURY TO THE
      PRESENT: A COMPREHENSIVE LIST. Madison, University of Wisconsin
      Press, 1970. 461 p.

    All colonies of Africa are covered fully for each colonial power.

1242. Jeffries, Sir Charles, ed. A REVIEW OF COLONIAL RESEARCH, 1940-1960.
      London, H.M. Stationery Off., 1964. 238 p. (Great Britain,
      Department of Technical Co-operation, Overseas Research
      Publication no. 6)

    Summarization of research carried on with financial assistance
from British public funds, chiefly under the Colonial Development
and Welfare Fund but including also some enterprises of nongovernmental

bodies such as the Locust Research Control. Among fields covered are the social sciences, economics, health and medicine, agriculture, building and roads, forestry, animal products, etc.

1243. Kirkman, W. P. UNSCRAMBLING AN EMPIRE: A CRITIQUE OF BRITISH COLONIAL POLICY, 1956-1966. London, Chatto & Windus, 1966. 214 p. maps.

Kirkman, a correspondent for the London TIMES, 1960-64, analyzes what he regards as the British Government's lack of a definite, well-conceived policy of disengagement in Africa, South Arabia, Malaysia, and the Caribbean. More than half of his book is devoted to Africa, with emphasis on Ghana, Nigeria, Kenya, Uganda, Rhodesia, and Zambia, and on the failure of the Federation of Rhodesia and Nyasaland. An index is included.

1244. Kirkwood, Kenneth. BRITAIN AND AFRICA. London, Chatto & Windus; Baltimore, Md., Johns Hopkins Press, 1965. 235 p. (Britain in the World Today, no. 6)

Survey and analysis of the entire range of British connections and relationships with African countries, from the earliest contacts to the present Commonwealth "partnership."

1245. Kuczynski, Robert René. DEMOGRAPHIC SURVEY OF THE BRITISH COLONIAL EMPIRE. London, New York, Oxford University Press, 1948. 4 v. tables.

Includes bibliographies.

A comprehensive survey of demographic statistics prior to World War II, prepared under the auspices of the Royal Institute of International Affairs. The first volume deals with West Africa, with a full account from the beginnings through 1946 and statistics for each country on census taking, total population, composition of African and non-African population, birth and death registration, fertility, mortality, and population growth. The second volume covers the same material for the High Commission Territories, Central and East Africa, Mauritius, and the Seychelles. Many of Mr. Kuczynski's figures and conclusions have been disputed by population specialists.

See also no. 861.

1246. Lee, J. M. COLONIAL DEVELOPMENT AND GOOD GOVERNMENT: A STUDY OF THE IDEAS EXPRESSED BY THE BRITISH OFFICIAL CLASSES IN PLANNING DECOLONIZATION, 1939-1964. Oxford, Clarendon Press, 1967. 311 p. diagrs.

Bibliography: p. 286-290.

The author successively discusses the principles of good government as understood by the British governing classes; the framework
for development in its social and political aspects; the foundations
of good government, including education for social advance and democratic practice; Great Britain's rejection of international supervision;
the transfer of power; and British commitments overseas in general,
including the question of foreign aid and the lessons of colonial
development. A bibliographical note gives data on the published works
of British policy makers and administrators. Also included are diagrams illustrating the numbers of social scientists in British Africa
in 1950, Colonial Service recruitment, 1920-60, Colonial Office
organization in 1950, colonial development resources, 1955-60, and
an analysis of the background, education, and careers of colonial
governors, 1940-60.

1247. London. University. Institute of Commonwealth Studies. Commonwealth
        Papers [series]. London, Athlone Press, 1954-

A series of which a number are devoted to Africa. Typical is
No. 9, T. E. Smith and J. G. C. Blacker, POPULATION CHARACTERISTICS
OF THE COMMONWEALTH COUNTRIES OF TROPICAL AFRICA (1963, 72 p.;
bibliographical footnotes).

1248. Lugard, Lord. THE DUAL MANDATE IN BRITISH TROPICAL AFRICA. Edinburgh,
        Blackwood and Sons, 1922. Reprint, London, Frank Cass, 1965.

Basic work explaining the famous administrator's concepts of
indirect rule in governing Africa.

1249. Newbury, Colin W. THE WEST AFRICAN COMMONWEALTH. Durham, N.C., Duke
        University Press, 1964. xiv, 106 p. (Duke University Common-
        wealth-Studies Center, Publication no. 22)

Bibliography: p. [99]-102.

A study of the problems of self-government in Ghana, Nigeria,
Sierra Leone, and Gambia, and of the significance of voluntary membership in the Commonwealth. In the three chapters comprising this slim
volume, Dr. Newbury traces the "evolution of British government in
West Africa," discusses the "educated elite and traditional chiefs in
the transfer of power," and comments on "current perspectives."

1250. Newbury, Colin W., ed. BRITISH POLICY TOWARDS WEST AFRICA: SELECT
        DOCUMENTS, 1786-1874. Oxford, Clarendon Press, 1965. xxviii,
        656 p. maps (1 fold.)

Bibliographical footnotes.

An excellent sourcebook dealing with the period just before the "scramble." Many of the 433 extracts are from state papers either hitherto unpublished or not readily available. The editor provides both a general introduction and brief comments at the beginning of each chapter. Parts 1, 2, and 3 concern exploration and survey, legitimate trade, and the slave trade. The relations between Britain and the West African states are brought out in 145 pieces in Part 4, which is arranged in chronological order under each region. Part 5 covers company and crown administration. An index is included.

1251.   Overseas Development Institute, London. BRITISH AID: Part 1, SURVEY
           AND COMMENT: Part 3, EDUCATIONAL ASSISTANCE. London, 1963.
           63, 125 p.

Two of the informative pamphlets issued by this organization, which was established to study the entire range of progress in and aid to the newly developing countries, in Africa and elsewhere (see no. 764).

1252.   Perham, Margery. LUGARD. London, Collins (distributed in America
           by Essential Books), 1956-60. 2 v. illus., ports., maps, facsims.

Includes bibliographies.

These two volumes by one of England's foremost colonial scholars trace every phase of the career of the famous administrator who established the twentieth-century British concept of indirect rule in native administration.

British colonial policy during the second quarter of the twentieth century is discussed by Dame Perham in her recent contribution, COLONIAL SEQUENCE, 1930 TO 1949: A CHRONOLOGICAL COMMENTARY UPON BRITISH COLONIAL POLICY ESPECIALLY IN AFRICA (London, Methuen [distribution in America by Barnes & Noble, New York], 1967, xxv, 351 p., maps, tables).

1253.   Simpson, Donald H., ed. BIOGRAPHY CATALOGUE OF THE LIBRARY OF THE
           ROYAL COMMONWEALTH SOCIETY. London, Royal Commonwealth Society,
           1961. 511 p.

The first section lists biographical writings on individual men and women born in, or actively connected with, countries of the Commonwealth and on Britains concerned with colonial affairs. Full names, dates of birth and death, and a brief description are given for as many names as possible, with titles of books and articles of a bio-

graphical nature and bibliographies. The second section (register)--
collective biography and country indexes--is by area and country.
Each begins with works of collective biography, both biographical
dictionaries and collections of articles by one or more writers. The
arrangement of these entries is chronological by date of publication,
with continuing series at the end. These details are followed by
lists of the names relating to the country or region. There is an
extensive section on Africa. The author index includes editors,
translators, writers of introductions, etc.

CHAPTER 32

WEST AFRICA (ENGLISH-SPEAKING)

Note: The entries below relate, as a whole or in substantial part, to West
Africa, both English- and French-speaking. See also the following numbers
in earlier sections: 119-125, 809, 1152, 1158, 1188, 1249, 1250, and 1252.

Bibliographies

1254.   Brasseur, Paule. "Introduction bibliographique aux arts plastiques
            de l'Ouest africain." NOTES AFRICAINES, no. 110, Apr. 1966:
            73-80.

1255.   Food and Agriculture Organization of the United Nations. WEST AFRICAN
            PILOT STUDY OF AGRICULTURAL DEVELOPMENT, 1960-65: BIBLIOGRAPHY.
            Prepared with the help of the Centre for African Studies,
            Cambridge University. [Cambridge, Eng.?] 1965. xi p. (WIPA/W.
            Afr. 65/4, May 17, 1965)

            Covers general works, basic statistical sources, and country
        studies.

1256.   Guides to Materials for West African History in European Archives
            [series]. London, University of London, Athlone Press, 1962-

            See no. 48 for list of guides already published.

1257.   International African Institute. WEST AFRICA: GENERAL, ETHNOGRAPHY,
            SOCIOLOGY, LINGUISTICS. Compiled by Ruth Jones, librarian,
            with the assistance of a panel of consultants. London, 1958.
            116 l. 33 cm. (Africa Bibliography Series, Ethnography,
            Sociology, Linguistics and Related Subjects)

Based on the bibliographical card index of the International African Institute. For note on series, see nos. 316 and 970.

1258. Mauny, Raymond. "Bibliographie de la préhistoire et de la protohistoire de l'Ouest africain." BULLETIN DE L'INSTITUT FONDAMENTAL D'AFRIQUE NOIRE, v. 29, ser. B, no. 3-4, July-Oct. 1967: 879-917.

Compiled by Mauny over the last 20 years, this is a valuable updating and expansion of Pierre Laforgue's bibliographies of 1925 and 1936 on West African pre- and protohistory.

1259. Rydings, H. A. THE BIBLIOGRAPHIES OF WEST AFRICA. Ibadan, Nigeria, Published on behalf of the West African Library Association by the Ibadan University Press, 1961. 36 p. tables.

Critically annotated bibliographical essay by the former deputy librarian of the University College of Ghana, now librarian of the University of Hong Kong. He comments comparatively here on the chief general African bibliographies, serial bibliographies, and selective lists and then on bibliographical sources for the individual countries of West Africa in English, French, and Portuguese. Besides bibliographical publications, he includes valuable reading lists in leading country studies. He ends with a tabulated survey of the 50 items covered.

1260. Simms, Ruth P. URBANIZATION IN WEST AFRICA: A REVIEW OF CURRENT LITERATURE. Evanston, Ill., Northwestern University Press, 1965. xv, 109 p. tables.

A concise survey of post-1950 publications, containing some 60 pages of text and 50 of slightly annotated bibliography. The bibliographical section contains more than 300 references to books and articles on African urbanization.

Serials

1261. Note: The roster of professional and learned society journals concerned with West Africa, particularly English-speaking West Africa, has included the following, some of which are now nationalized:

a) West African Institute for Oil Palm Research. JOURNAL. no. 1- Sept. 1953- Benin City, Nigeria. Irregular.

b) WEST AFRICAN JOURNAL OF BIOLOGICAL CHEMISTRY. v. 1, no. 1- Apr. 1957- London. Quarterly.

Edited at the University of Ibadan, Nigeria.

c) WEST AFRICAN JOURNAL OF EDUCATION. v. 1- Feb. 1957- Cambridge, Eng. Irregular.

d) WEST AFRICAN MEDICAL JOURNAL. v. 1, no. 1- Mar. 1952- Ibadan, Nigeria.

Published under the auspices of the Directors of Medical Services of Nigeria, Ghana, Sierra Leone, and Gambia.

e) West African Rice Research Station, Rokupr, Sierra Leone. REPORT. 1953- Freetown, Sierra Leone, Govt. Print. Dept. Annual.

f) West African Science Association. JOURNAL. v. 1, no. 1- Oct. 1954- London. Semiannual.

1262. Bank of West Africa, London. ANNUAL REPORT.

Includes a notable review of the year's economic developments in the English-speaking countries of West Africa.

See also the Economist Intelligence Unit digest THREE-MONTHLY ECONOMIC REVIEW for West African economic data.

1263. Bank of West Africa, London. ANNUAL REVIEW OF CONDITIONS IN GAMBIA, SIERRA LEONE, GHANA AND NIGERIA.

A booklet accompanying the annual report of the Bank, giving a detailed picture of local conditions.

1264. JOURNAL OF WEST AFRICAN LANGUAGES. v. 1, no. 1- Oct. 1963- Cambridge, Eng., University Press, in association with the Institute of African Studies, University of Ibadan. Semiannual.

A journal devoted to presentation of basic technical data on languages. The editor is Robert Armstrong of the University of Ibadan. Word tests, grammatical sketches, dialect comparisons, and illustrative texts are included.

In 1964 the journal issued the first in a series of monograph supplements, West African Language Monographs, edited by Joseph H. Greenberg and John Spencer and published by Cambridge University Press in connection with the West African Languages Survey.

1265. RESEARCH NOTES. Mar. 1967- Ibadan, Dept. of Linguistics and Nigerian
       Languages, University of Ibadan. Twice a year.

       This new journal makes available data and research notes on West
African languages, in the form of word lists, folktales, grammatical
notes, and the like.

1266. United Africa Company, Ltd. STATISTICAL & ECONOMIC REVIEW. v. 1, no.
       1- Mar. 1948- London. illus. (part col.), maps, diagrs.
       Semiannual.

       This subsidiary of Unilever leads in the palm-oil and other
industries of West Africa; its journal is a useful source for articles
of economic significance as well as statistics and other data on West
African trade.

1267. WEST AFRICA: A WEEKLY NEWSPAPER. v. 1- Feb. 3, 1917- London. illus.

       WEST AFRICA, published by the West African Graphic Co., 9 New Fetter
Lane, London, E.C.4, is an essential source for continuing information
about economic, political, and social affairs in both French-speaking
and British West Africa. For further annotation see no. 580.

1268. WEST AFRICA ANNUAL. 1962- Edited by L. K. Jakande. London, J. Clarke,
       1962; Lagos, John West, 1963- maps, tables. (1967 ed., 389 p.)

       A useful volume treating West Africa as a whole and then by
country. Paragraphs cover land and people, climate, population,
mineral resources, historical résumé, constitutional development,
synopsis of constitution, government, judiciary, public service,
police force, franchise, elections, local government, and similarly
in detail all economic, social, and cultural features, national symbols,
and many other aspects.

1269. WEST AFRICA BUSINESS DIRECTORY (INTERNATIONAL). Lagos, INA (Nigeria),
       Ltd. 1963-64 (6th year). 128 p. illus., ports.

       Earlier title, NIGERIA BUSINESS DIRECTORY (INTERNATIONAL). Among
subjects covered are geography and population, oil companies, technical
and engineering information, chambers of commerce, banking, the diplomatic corps, transport, railway statistics, hotels, and cocoa and
tobacco industries. There is an index to advertisers.

1270. THE WEST AFRICAN ARCHAEOLOGICAL NEWSLETTER. no. 1- Dec. 1964-
       Ibadan, Institute of African Studies, University of Ibadan.

A very useful newsletter published for private circulation only.
It contains up-to-date information on most recent discoveries and
excavations. Reports on the two conferences of West African archae-
ologists have also appeared.

1271. WEST AFRICAN DIRECTORY, 1967-8. London, Thomas Skinner, 1967. 656 p.
      illus., col. map with gazetteer (fold. in back pocket). Annual.

The sixth edition of this volume of facts and figures on West
African countries (excluding Mauritania) and the offshore islands.
Country topics include geography, climate, peoples, government, finance,
industry, agriculture, public and social services (education, postal
service, etc.), and trade and commerce, along with travel and tourist
information and a classified business directory. There are special
sections on shipping lines, air transport, and exporters to the coast.
A French-English glossary (p. 651-656) and an index to advertisers
(p. iii-vii) are included.

Reference Works

1272. Ajayi, J. F. Ade, and Ian Espie, eds. A THOUSAND YEARS OF WEST AFRI-
      CAN HISTORY: A HANDBOOK FOR TEACHERS AND STUDENTS. Ibadan,
      Ibadan University Press; London, Nelson, 1965. 543 p. maps,
      diagr.

Bibliography: p. 496-505.

1273. Behn, Hans Ulrich. DIE PRESSE IN WESTAFRIKA. Hamburg, Deutsches
      Institut für Afrika-Forschung, 1968. 267 p. (Hamburger Beiträge
      zur Afrika-Kunde, v. 8)

Bibliography: p. 261-267.

1274. Blake, John W. EUROPEAN BEGINNINGS IN WEST AFRICA, 1454-1578: A
      SURVEY OF THE FIRST CENTURY OF WHITE ENTERPRISE IN WEST AFRICA,
      WITH SPECIAL EMPHASIS UPON THE RIVALRY OF THE GREAT POWERS.
      London, New York, Published for the Royal Empire Society by
      Longmans, Green, 1937. 212 p. fold. map. (Imperial Studies,
      no. 14)

Selected bibliography: p. 193-203.

Standard work, based on examination of many primary sources.
Although the author laments the loss in the Lisbon earthquake of
1765 of a mass of documents, he has found a rich source in the British
High Court of the Admiralty records. He tells of much material to be

unearthed in Portuguese local archives.

1275. Campbell, M. J., T. G. Brierly, and L. F. Blitz. THE STRUCTURE OF
        LOCAL GOVERNMENT IN WEST AFRICA. The Hague, Published for
        the International Union of Local Authorities by M. Nijhoff, 1965.
        421 p. fold. map, tables, charts. (Publication of the Inter-
        national Union of Local Authorities, no. 84)

        Bibliography: p. 390-400.

        An excellent volume of concise information, containing consider-
        able basic statutory data which may not be readily available else-
        where to students of African government. The authors begin with a
        comparison of local government trends in West Africa and a discussion
        of the distinguishing features of English-speaking and of French-
        speaking West Africa. Each of the 14 countries is then treated
        separately. The text surveys the situation as of Jan. 1, 1964; an
        addendum presents relevant legislation passed later in 1964. A
        glossary of terms and an index are included.

1276. Centre des Hautes Etudes Administratives sur l'Afrique et l'Asie
        Modernes. CARTE DES RELIGIONS DE L'AFRIQUE DE L'OUEST: NOTICE
        ET STATISTIQUES. Paris. CHEAM, 1966. 135 p.

1277. Church, R. J. Harrison. WEST AFRICA: A STUDY OF THE ENVIRONMENT AND
        OF MAN'S USE OF IT. 6th ed. New York, Wiley, 1968. xxix,
        543 p. illus., plates, maps, tables, diagrs. (Geographies for
        Advanced Study)

        Includes bibliographies.

        A revised and updated edition of a basic work in anthropogeography.
        In Part 1 Professor Church deals with natural conditions, along with
        some of the human problems they impose. Part 2, devoted to resources
        and their development, includes an interesting analysis of population
        distribution and movements. Part 3 (p. 177-526) is a concise country-
        by-country analysis; a historical outline and commentary on future
        prospects are included in most of the country surveys.

1278. Cissoko, Sékéné Mody. HISTOIRE DE L'AFRIQUE OCCIDENTALE: VOL. I,
        MOYEN-AGE ET TEMPS MODERNES: VIIe SIECLE-1850. Paris, Présence
        Africaine, 1966.

        Bibliography: p. 327-330.

1279. Committee on Inter-African Relations. REPORT ON THE PRESS IN WEST
       AFRICA. Ibadan, Nigeria, Distributed by Director, Dept. of
       Extra-mural Studies, University College, 1960. xi, 133 p.
       illus., fold. map, tables. 33 cm.

     Prepared for an International Seminar on the Press and Progress
in West Africa held at the University of Dakar May 31 to June 4, 1960.
The interesting papers, which include lists and descriptions of newspapers, are "Position of the Press in French-speaking West Africa,"
by Father J. de Benoist; "Ghana Press," by K. B. Jones-Quartey; "Press
in Liberia," by Henry B. Cole; and "The Nigerian Press, 1929-59," by
Increase Coker.

1280. Cowan, L. Gray. LOCAL GOVERNMENT IN WEST AFRICA. New York, Columbia
       University Press, 1958. 292 p.

     By a professor of government at Columbia University, an American
expert on African political questions. In this study of the representative institutions coming into operation, especially those in
French territories under the loi-cadre, he focuses attention on the
problems of getting the new local authorities accepted by the unpre-
pared communities in which the traditional authority of the paramount
chief still exists and is frequently in conflict with that of the
government official. His data are of 1954-55.

1281. Crowder, Michael. WEST AFRICA UNDER COLONIAL RULE. London, Hutchinson,
       1968. xv, 540 p. maps (1 fold.), tables.

     Bibliographical footnotes.

     A massive survey of West Africa under British and French domination
by a scholar who since Jan. 1968 has been director of African Studies
at the University of Ife. Essentially, this incisive study provides
a comparative analysis of the different impacts of British and French
colonial rule and of the reactions of the West Africans to that rule.
Professor Crowder considers the history of the colonial period from
both the European and the African point of view and is frankly critical
of many aspects of the colonial administration. Discussion of Portuguese
Guinea is excluded and Togo is dealt with only fleetingly in this review
of West Africa's diverse administrative, political, economic, and social
histories. Appendixes include chronologies of governors and governors-
general. The substantial footnotes which follow each chapter give ample
evidence of the author's effort to synthesize in his study the more
important sources available on the 1885-1945 period. A good analytical
index is included.

1282.   Daniels, W. C. Ekow. THE COMMON LAW IN WEST AFRICA. London, Butter-
            worth, 1964. lvi, 424 p. (Butterworth's African Law Series, no.
            9)

        See note on this series under no. 684.

1283.   Davidson, Basil. A HISTORY OF WEST AFRICA TO THE NINETEENTH CENTURY.
            With F. K. Buah and the advice of J. F. Ade Ajayi. Maps by
            K. C. Jordan. Rev. version. Garden City, N.Y., Anchor Books,
            1966. xvi, 342 p.

        Bibliography: p. [327]-332.

        A popular introduction with a dating guide and a good bibliography.
    The work is a revision of Davidson's textbook THE GROWTH OF AFRICAN
    CIVILISATION: WEST AFRICA, 1000-1800 (London, Longmans, 1965). See
    also no. 1313 below.

1284.   Davies, Oliver. WEST AFRICA BEFORE THE EUROPEANS: ARCHAEOLOGY AND
            PREHISTORY. London, Methuen; New York, Barnes & Noble, 1967.
            xii, 364 p. illus., plates, maps.

        Bibliography: p. 323-327.

        A supplement to the author's QUATERNARY IN THE COASTLANDS OF
    GUINEA (1964) and the result of five years' additional fieldwork.
    The present work, extending from the Palaeolithic to the arrival of
    the Portuguese, has more general discussion and less detail; it is
    intended for well-informed readers and university students rather
    than specialists. Nigeria is not included. There is a geographical
    and a subject index.

1285.   Fage, John D. AN INTRODUCTION TO THE HISTORY OF WEST AFRICA. 3d ed.
            Cambridge, Eng., University Press, 1962. 232 p. illus.

        "Further Reading": p. 201-205.

        This is an authoritative story of West Africa from the earliest
    days of the trans-Saharan trade contacts to the present.

1286.   Forde, Daryll, and P. M. Kaberry, eds. WEST AFRICAN KINGDOMS IN THE
            NINETEENTH CENTURY. London, Published for the International
            African Institute by the Oxford University Press, 1967. xiv,
            289 p. front., maps, diagrs.

Includes bibliographies.

An introduction by the editors is followed by ten essays, each devoted to a West African kingdom. A bibliography and a map accompany each study, and there is an index.

1287. Hargreaves, John D. PRELUDE TO THE PARTITION OF WEST AFRICA. London, Macmillan; New York, St. Martin's Press, 1963. xi, 383 p. maps.

Bibliography: p. 350-368.

In this well-written history of nineteenth-century Africa, the valuable bibliography includes main sources and authorities used and unpublished. Published sources include published official or semi-official documentary collections, works by contemporaries containing primary material, bibliographies, works of reference and general histories, and modern studies of special topics. The unpublished sources mentioned are official British archives, archives of the government of Sierra Leone, official French archives, private collections of manuscripts in the United Kingdom, and unpublished theses.

1288. Howard, Cecil, ed. WEST AFRICAN EXPLORERS. London, New York, Oxford University Press, 1952. 598 p. (World's Classics, no. 523)

In his selections the editor has tried to cover each explorer's journey and achievement while avoiding repetition of routes traveled. Among the extracts are some from the works of the famous seventeenth- and eighteenth-century travelers Richard Jobson and William Bosman and the nineteenth-century Mungo Park, Major Denham, Captain Clapperton, Richard Lander, Sir Richard Burton, William Balfour Baikie, Dr. Henry Barth, and Mary Kingsley. The volume, printed on India paper, is pocket size, but its clear print is not hard to read. The list of sources, p. 26-27, cites the important original travel books.

The adventures and achievements of nineteenth-century West African explorers are related along with excerpts from their writings, in Hubert Jules Deschamps' interesting narrative, L'EUROPE DECOUVRE L'AFRIQUE: AFRIQUE OCCIDENTALE, 1794-1900 (Paris, Berger-Levrault, 1967, 284 p., illus., maps; bibliography: p. 267-274).

1289. Institut Fondamental d'Afrique Noire. INTERNATIONAL ATLAS OF WEST AFRICA. Prepared under the auspices of the Organisation of African Unity Scientific, Technical and Research Commission and with the assistance of the Ford Foundation. First instalment. Dakar, 1968. 29 p. In English and French.

Eighty maps with accompanying descriptive explanations illustrating climate and elevations of Africa in comparison with the rest of the world, seas and coasts of West Africa, annual and monthly rainfall, temperature, winds, humidity, zoogeography, and administrative and political boundaries.

There is a place-name gazetteer.

1290.   International Seminar on Inter-University Co-operation in West Africa, Freetown, Sierra Leone, 1961. THE WEST AFRICAN INTELLECTUAL COMMUNITY: PAPERS AND DISCUSSIONS. Ibadan, Nigeria, Published for the Congress for Cultural Freedom by Ibadan University Press, 1962. 356 p.

Leading figures in the intellectual community of West Africa include among their topics freedom of the universities, interuniversity cooperation, liaison between governments in presenting needs to foreign organizations, planning, exchange of students and teachers, and many other aspects of university education and exchanges.

Each year the number of conferences of this character increases. For current data, see the news and notes sections in AFRICA, etc., or the WORLD LIST OF FUTURE INTERNATIONAL MEETINGS.

1291.   International West African Conference. COMPTES RENDUS. 1945- illus., maps.

This international gathering of economists, sociologists, scientists, and other specialists from the countries of West Africa was begun at the instigation of the Institut Français d'Afrique Noire, and the first meeting was held in Dakar in 1945. The second session, 1947, was in Bissau, Portuguese Guinea; the third, 1949, in Ibadan, Nigeria; the fourth, 1951, in Santa Isabel, Spanish Guinea; the fifth, 1953, in Abidjan, Ivory Coast; the sixth, Aug. 1956, in São Tomé, Portuguese West Africa; the seventh, Apr. 1959, in Accra, Ghana. The papers are published by the hosts of the respective sessions. The papers of the 1947 session, for example, appeared in five volumes, 1950-52, issued by the Ministério das Colónias in Lisbon. Contributions are in the languages in which the papers were delivered, titles and editorial matter in the language of the hosts--COMPTES RENDUS, 1945; CONFERENCIA, 1947; etc. Volumes of the 1951 meeting appeared in 1953-54. Some of the papers include bibliographical references.

1292.   Irvine, Frederick Robert. WEST AFRICAN BOTANY. 2d ed., rev. London, Oxford University Press, 1956. 203 p. illus.

Standard work. See also his books on Ghana (nos. 1371, 1372).

1293. Jarrett, Harold Reginald. A GEOGRAPHY OF WEST AFRICA. New ed.,
          completely rev. and corrected. London, Dent, 1966. 229 p.
          maps, diagrs.

          Not available for examination. The fourth edition (1961, 173 p.)
       was an excellent compact text, especially suitable for school use.

          Another recently updated geography is the fifth edition, revised,
       of H. O. N. Oboli's AN OUTLINE GEOGRAPHY OF WEST AFRICA, written with
       editorial assistance from R. J. Harrison Church (London, Harrap, 1967,
       224 p., illus., maps, tables, diagrs.).

1294. Jordan, Robert S. GOVERNMENT AND POWER IN WEST AFRICA. With the
          editorial assistance of Caroline Ifeka and Michael A. Rebell.
          New York, Africana Pub. Corp., 1969. 336 p. maps.

          A useful and readable textbook for students of English-speaking
       West African governments. Part 1 covers the concept of contemporary
       government. Part 2 surveys the various political systems. Part 3
       discusses the processes of government, i.e., the administration. Part
       4 looks at political leadership, values, and behaviors and the political
       community. An appendix provides a chronological summary of the
       constitutional history of Sierra Leone, Gambia, Ghana, and Nigeria.
       There is an index.

1295. July, Robert W. THE ORIGINS OF MODERN AFRICAN THOUGHT: ITS DEVELOPMENT
          IN WEST AFRICA DURING THE NINETEENTH AND TWENTIETH CENTURIES.
          New York, Praeger, 1967. 512 p. plates, map.

          Bibliography: p. 481-493.

          A perceptive, well-written study of the confrontation of West
       Africa with Western Europe and America. Illustrations are provided
       from the lives of such West Africans as Africanus Horton, Olaudah
       Equiano, Gabriel Pellegrin, Bishop Samuel Ajayi Crowther, Edward W.
       Blyden, Bishop James Johnson, Blaise Diagne, and Casely Hayford.
       Westernization, as reflected for example in the founding and develop-
       ment of Sierra Leone, Gorée and St. Louis, and Liberia, is examined,
       and West African historiography and nationalist journalism are discussed.

1296. Kouassigan, Guy-Adjété. L'HOMME ET LA TERRE: DROITS FONCIERS
          COUTUMIERS ET DROIT DE PROPRIETE EN AFRIQUE OCCIDENTALE. Paris,
          Office de la Recherche Scientifique et Technique Outre-Mer,
          Berger-Levrault, 1966. 284 p. (L'homme d'outre-mer, n.s. no. 8)

          Bibliography: p. [267]-277.

A thoughtful, well-organized study of West Africa's customary land laws and property rights, which, in this region as in the rest of predominantly agrarian Africa, have left their mark on all traditional juridical institutions. The work is in two main parts. Part 1 treats the originality of customary land laws (the land as a collective, inalienable, sacred property and the complementary individual rights); Part 2 is concerned with the rapid and profound transformation of traditional land laws and property rights induced by European contact during the nineteenth century.

1297. Kuper, Hilda, ed. URBANIZATION AND MIGRATION IN WEST AFRICA. Published under the auspices of the African Studies Center, University of California, Los Angeles. Berkeley, Los Angeles, University of California Press, 1965. 227 p. maps.

Bibliography: p. 203-214.

A collection of papers originally presented at an interdisciplinary seminar in 1962. Included are "The Location and Nature of West African Cities," by Benjamin E. Thomas; "Some Thoughts on Migration and Urban Settlement," by John D. Fage; "Urbanism, Migration, and Language," by Joseph H. Greenberg; "Labor Migration among the Mossi of the Upper Volta," by Elliott P. Skinner; "Oshogbo--An Urban Community?" by William B. Schwab; "Urban Influences on the Rural Hausa," by Horace M. Miner; "Social Alignment and Identity in a West African City [Freetown]," by Michael Banton; "Migration in West Africa: The Political Perspective," by Immanuel Wallerstein; and "The Economics of the Migrant Labor System," by Elliot J. Berg. There is an index.

1298. Little, Kenneth Lindsay. WEST AFRICAN URBANIZATION: A STUDY OF VOLUNTARY ASSOCIATIONS IN SOCIAL CHANGE. London, Cambridge University Press, 1965. 187 p. maps.

Bibliography: p. 167-172.

The author categorizes voluntary associations as (1) tribal unions and syncretist cults and (2) various groups concerned with mutual benefit and recreation, the Christian religion, and Western cultural or social pursuits. Using West Africa as an example of a former "backward" area now undergoing considerable industrial and urban growth, he analyzes the role played by these associations in adapting traditional institutions and in integrating the changing social system.

1299. Lloyd, Peter C. AFRICA IN SOCIAL CHANGE: CHANGING TRADITIONAL SOCIETIES IN THE MODERN WORLD. Harmondsworth, Middlesex; Baltimore, Md., Penguin Books, 1967. 362 p. maps. (Penguin African Library, AP22)

435

Bibliography: p. 343-355.

Limiting his frame of reference to West Africa, the author focuses on the interaction between the new social groups (especially the Western-educated elites) and traditional society, the extent to which the patterns of Western industrial society are being reproduced, and the growth and present role of the new elites. The four parts of the work cover the historical background, the impact of the West, changing institutions, and, in conclusion, ideologies, tribalism, and conflicts. An appendix presents comparative data on the states discussed.

1300. Mauny, Raymond. GRAVURES, PEINTURES ET INSCRIPTIONS RUPESTRES DE L'OUEST AFRICAIN. Dakar, Institut Français d'Afrique Noire, 1954. 91 p. illus. (Initiations africaines, no. 11)

Inventory of prehistoric art of West Africa by an archaeologist and historian of IFAN. The sites covered are in the southern and western Sahara, mostly within the former AOF and Nigeria.

1301. Mauny, Raymond. TABLEAU GEOGRAPHIQUE DE L'OUEST AFRICAIN AU MOYEN AGE D'APRES LES SOURCES ECRITES, LA TRADITION ET L'ARCHAEOLOGIE. Dakar, Institut Français d'Afrique Noire, 1961. 587 p. illus., plates, maps. (Mémoires de l'IFAN, no. 61)

Bibliography: p. 547-575.

Likely to be the standard reference work on West African iron-age archaeology for many years to come. There are sections on sources, ecology of West Africa, economic geography, and human geography. The bibliography is a good one and an index is included.

1302. Migeod, Frederick W. H. THE LANGUAGES OF WEST AFRICA. London, K. Paul, Trench, Trubner, 1911-13. 2 v. fold. map, tables.

The writer, once an official in the Gold Coast, was an authority on the languages of the region, particularly Mende. This well-known pioneer work is a study of linguistic classification, grammar, syntax, and parts of speech including about 50 language specimens.

1303. November, András. L'EVOLUTION DU MOUVEMENT SYNDICAL EN AFRIQUE OCCIDENTALE. Paris, Mouton, 1965. 282 p. table. (Université de Genève, Institut Universitaire de Hautes Etudes Internationales, Thèse no. 154; Etudes et travaux de l'Institut Africain de Genève)

Bibliography: p. 254-257.

A doctoral thesis on the evolution of the trade-union movement in West Africa. In Part 1 the English-speaking countries (especially Ghana and Nigeria) and the French-speaking countries are considered separately. Part 2 deals with the Pan-African trade-union movement, and Part 3 with the relations of the international trade unions with those in Africa.

1304. Parrinder, Geoffrey. WEST AFRICAN PSYCHOLOGY: A COMPARATIVE STUDY OF PSYCHOLOGICAL AND RELIGIOUS THOUGHT. London, Lutterworth Press, 1951. 229 p. (Lutterworth Library, v. 37; Missionary Research Series, no. 17)

_____. WEST AFRICAN RELIGION: A STUDY OF THE BELIEFS AND PRACTICES OF AKAN, EWE, YORUBA, IBO, AND KINDRED PEOPLES. 2d ed., completely rewritten, rev. and enl. London, Epworth Press, 1961. xv, 203 p. map.

The writer, a former missionary and a recognized authority on West African religious beliefs, spent 10 years as lecturer in the Department of Religious Studies at Ibadan. The first edition (1949) of WEST AFRICAN RELIGION had been used as a doctoral thesis. The second edition brings the material up to date and includes coverage of the Ibo peoples as well as a final chapter on religious change. WEST AFRICAN PSYCHOLOGY is a comparative study of the concepts of the soul among West African tribes.

1305. Pedler, F. J. ECONOMIC GEOGRAPHY OF WEST AFRICA. London, New York, Longmans, Green, 1955. xii, 232 p. illus., maps, tables.

The writer proposed to establish through facts, analysis, and reasoning "the relationship of cause and effect in the work-a-day world of West Africa." His coverage includes questions of land and its use, domestic production and export crops, mining, manufacturing, transport, commerce, and the economic aspects of government. Statistical data were closely current at the time of writing; much of his factual material is still relevant.

1306. Post, Kenneth William John. THE NEW STATES OF WEST AFRICA. Rev. ed. Baltimore, Md., Penguin Books, 1968. 231 p. maps. (Penguin African Library, AP14)

Bibliography: p. 203-219.

Based on a course of lectures on the political systems of West Africa given at the University of Ibadan, where the author was teaching political science. Although very brief, it is a broad analysis of postindependence history of both French-speaking and English-speaking states, from Mauritania to Cameroun. The bibliography includes many political and governmental documents.

1307. Price, Joseph H. POLITICAL INSTITUTIONS OF WEST AFRICA. London, Hutchinson Educational, 1967. 266 p. fold. map, tables, diagrs.

Bibliography: p. [258]-260.

Describes the political situation in English-speaking West Africa, including Liberia, to Dec. 1966. Parts 1 and 2 consist of a political and constitutional history before and after 1945, with detailed examinations of the Ghana Constitution of 1960 and the Nigerian Constitution of 1960 and the Nigerian Constitution of 1963. The remainder of the book covers the judiciary, public services, public finance, and local government.

1308. Sadler, Sir Michael Ernest, ed. ARTS OF WEST AFRICA (EXCLUDING MUSIC). London, Published for the International Institute of African Languages and Cultures by the Oxford University Press, H. Milford, 1935. xi, 101 p. 32 plates on 16 l.

"Bibliography Relating to Indigenous Art in Tropical Africa": p. 97-101.

The authoritative essays in this compilation are by way of introduction to the 32 plates, each of which is described in a long note. The examples are mainly from collections in British museums.

1309. Seck, Assane, and Alfred Mondjannagni. L'AFRIQUE OCCIDENTALE. Paris, Presses Universitaires de France, 1967. 290 p. illus., maps. (Magellan; La géographie et ses problèmes, no. 21)

A physical, human, and economic geography of West Africa. Following a general discussion of the natural environment, population, and resources, a survey of each country is provided.

1310. Trimingham, John Spencer. THE CHRISTIAN CHURCH AND ISLAM IN WEST AFRICA. London, S.C.M. Press, 1955. 56 p. illus., map. (International Missionary Council Research Pamphlets, no. 3)

_____. A HISTORY OF ISLAM IN WEST AFRICA. Oxford, Clarendon Press, 1962. 262 p. fold. map, diagr.

See no. 958 for general comment on Dr. Trimingham's studies of Islam.

A recent scholarly analysis of the patterns of Islamization in the region now encompassing parts of Ghana, Upper Volta, Togo, and the Ivory Coast is presented in Nehemia Levtzion's MUSLIMS AND CHIEFS IN WEST AFRICA: A STUDY OF ISLAM IN THE MIDDLE VOLTA BASIN IN THE

PRE-COLONIAL PERIOD (Oxford, Clarendon Press, 1968, xxvi, 228 p., maps; bibliography: p. [204]-215; Oxford Studies in African Affairs). This interpretative study traces the history of Muslim communities of various ethnic origins and is based on oral traditions, local Arab sources, and European accounts.

1311. United Nations. Economic Commission for Africa. ECONOMIC SURVEY
OF AFRICA: Vol. I, WESTERN SUB-REGION: REPUBLIC OF SOUTH AFRICA.
New York, 1966- xi, 230 p. tables. (E/CN.14/370)

Bibliographical footnotes.

The section on West Africa (p. 1-170) presents detailed information, fortified by 94 statistical tables, on the economic growth and development of the 14 countries comprising that area. Part 1, on economic growth (1950-63), discusses physical environment and population, economic and social infrastructure, agriculture, industry, transport, foreign trade, and money, banking, and public finance. Part 2, devoted to planned development and structural change, focuses on agriculture, industry, manpower, capital formation and economic balance, and development problems and prospects.

1312. United Nations. Economic Commission for Africa. West African
Industrial Co-ordination Mission. REPORT. New York, 1964.
71 p. and annexes. (E/CN.14/246)

Bibliographical footnotes.

This survey, typical of ECA studies, has three parts with supporting statistics: Part 1, economic setting; Part 2, industrial development of large-scale industries (iron and steel, other metals, chemicals and fertilizers, cement, textiles); Part 3, development of small-scale industries. Another useful ECA report is TRANSPORT PROBLEMS IN RELATION TO ECONOMIC DEVELOPMENTS IN WEST AFRICA (New York, 1962, 68 p.; E/CN.14/63), also with bibliographical footnotes indicating sources; an earlier version of this report had the same title and same document number and was issued in Addis Ababa in 1960 (125 p. and tables).

For other ECA material concerned specifically with West Africa, see the preceding entry and the ECA bibliographies (nos. 726-728).

1313. Webster, James Bertin, and A. Adu Boahen. THE REVOLUTIONARY YEARS:
WEST AFRICA SINCE 1800. With a contribution by H. O. Idowu.
London, Longmans, 1967. xv, 343 p. illus., plates, maps,
diagrs. (Growth of African Civilisation, no. 2)

Bibliographical references.

A textbook which complements Davidson's history of West Africa to the nineteenth century (see no. 1283 above). Commendably equipped with 46 maps, the volume is divided into five main parts: states of the Western Sudan in the nineteenth century; coastal kingdoms in the nineteenth century; West Africa and Europe, 1800-1900; response and resistance to foreign rule; and return to independence. A series of questions for students and a list of "activities" to aid both students and teachers appear at the end of each chapter, in addition to suggestions for further reading.

A more specialized historical study by Boahen is BRITAIN, THE SAHARA, AND THE WESTERN SUDAN, 1788-1861 (Oxford, Clarendon Press, 1964, 268 p., maps [part fold.]; bibliography: p. [253]-257; Oxford Studies in African Affairs).

1314. Westermann, Diedrich, and Margaret A. Bryan. LANGUAGES OF WEST AFRICA. London, for International African Institute Oxford University Press, 1952. 215 p. fold. col. map (in pocket). (Handbook of African Languages, pt. 2)

Bibliography: p. 178-201.

See note on this series (no. 1011).

1315. Wilson, John. EDUCATION AND CHANGING WEST AFRICAN CULTURE. London, Oxford University Press, 1966. 113 p.

The author was a member of the Gold Coast Education Department, 1929-50, and later senior lecturer in the Department of Education in Tropical Areas of the Institute of Education, University of London. His topics include indigenous and early missionary education, education problems of new urban areas, quality in community education and in school education, and the implications for education of economic development. Illustrations are taken from the author's Ghanaian experience.

1316. Wraith, Ronald E. LOCAL GOVERNMENT IN WEST AFRICA. New York, Praeger, 1964. 184 p.

Detailed analysis of the structure and control of local government in Nigeria, Ghana, and Sierra Leone, along with some questions for the future. Emphasis is on the 1950-60 period, and the major portion of this compact work concerns Eastern and Western Nigeria and Ghana.

1317.   Zartman, I. William.   INTERNATIONAL RELATIONS IN THE NEW AFRICA.
        Englewood Cliffs, N.J., Prentice-Hall, 1966. xi, 175 p. map.
        tables, charts. (Spectrum Book)

        Bibliographical footnotes.

        A study of the development of foreign relations, 1956-65, among
the new states of North and West Africa. Following a discussion of
the party, the state, and pre- and postindependence alliances, Zartman
takes up the criteria for policy, examines infra-African policy and
its limits, and concludes with the developing nature of African
foreign policy, patterns of regional unity, and expected trends and
changes. An index is included.

GAMBIA

Bibliographies

1318.   Gailey, Harry A., Jr. "Bibliographic Essays: The Gambia." AFRICANA
        NEWSLETTER, v. 2, no. 1, 1964: 4-10.

        A short introduction and a list of books, government publications,
and articles in periodicals concerned with the Gambia. The 80-odd
entries are grouped in various categories--early travel accounts,
histories, anthropology and geography, etc. A few have brief
annotations. Some of the works cited are general for the region or
even broader geographical area and touch only briefly, though
meaningfully, on the Gambia.

1319.   Gamble, David P. BIBLIOGRAPHY OF THE GAMBIA. Bathurst, Govt. Printer,
        1967. 154 p. 33 cm.

        A mimeographed brochure revised and updated from his 1958 compi-
lation by a scholar who formerly conducted research on the Gambia for
the Colonial Office. Approximately 1,600 entries are classified and
arranged in chronological order under subheadings. Books, articles,
and some theses and processed and typescript items are included. A
section on government publications gives quite useful annotations on
the background of departmental annual reports. There is an author
index.

1320.   Kingdon, Donald. A CHRONOLOGICAL TABLE AND INDEX OF THE ORDINANCES
        OF THE COLONY OF THE GAMBIA, 1901-1908 (INCLUSIVE), AND OF THE
        RULES, REGULATIONS AND ORDERS PASSED AND MADE BY THE GOVERNOR-
        IN-COUNCIL, AND OF THE PROCLAMATIONS, ACTS OF PARLIAMENT, ORDERS

OF THE KING-IN-COUNCIL, TREATIES, ETC. PUBLISHED IN THE GAMBIA
GOVERNMENT GAZETTES, 1901-1908 (INCLUSIVE). London, Waterlow, 1909.
103 p. (3,000 entries)

1321. U.S. Library of Congress. General Reference and Bibliography Division.
       OFFICIAL PUBLICATIONS OF SIERRA LEONE AND GAMBIA. Compiled by
       Audrey A. Walker, African Section. Washington, 1963. xii, 92 p.

       Historical note on the Gambia: p. 58-61 (outline of political
history); publications: p. 62-84.

       One of the series of official publications of African states
compiled at the Library of Congress (see no. 410). In the section
on the Gambia, coverage is from the earliest British documents to
within two years of the independence date, Feb. 18, 1965.

Reference Works

1322. Deschamps, Hubert Jules. LE SENEGAL ET LA GAMBIE. 2d ed. Paris,
       Presses Universitaires de France, 1968. 125 p. maps.
       ("Que sais-je?" no. 597)

       Bibliography: p. [123]-125.

       See no. 1818 for annotation.

1323. Gailey, Harry A. HISTORY OF THE GAMBIA. London, Routledge, Kegan
       Paul, 1964. 244 p. fold. map.

       Bibliography and notes: p. 218-239.

       Presentation of "the political development of the area from a
casual appendage of Britain, through the crucial period of the 'scramble,'
to the modern position of the tiny enclave on the verge of independence."
About half the text concentrates on recent history, just prior to and
since World War II.

1324. Gambia Constitutional Conference, London, July 1964. FINAL REPORT.
       London, H.M. Stationery Off., 1964.

       In this report, announcing the decision for independence of the
Gambia in Feb. 1965, there are listed the changes which will be made
in the constitution of the new nation.

Although official documents relating to new constitutions have not as a rule been included, exception is made here since the Gambian constitution was not published recently enough to be included in the compilations of African constitutions mentioned in Part III (nos. 616, 630, and 639). It can presumably be located without too much difficulty in the British Parliamentary Papers indexes for 1964 and 1965.

1325. Gambia Oilseeds Marketing Board. REPORT. 1949/50- London. Annual.

Almost 90 percent of exports from the Gambia consist of peanuts, the sales of which are handled by this board.

1326. Gamble, David P. THE WOLOF OF SENEGAMBIA, TOGETHER WITH NOTES ON THE LEBU AND THE SERER. London, International African Institute, 1957. 110 p. illus., maps. (Ethnographic Survey of Africa, Western Africa, pt. 14)

Includes bibliographies.

For a general description of the systematic ethnological surveys in this series, see no. 980. Mr. Gamble's study is notable for its extensive list of references on the Wolof (in the Colonial Office report spelled "Wollof"). This list is in three sections: linguistic material, religious literature, and general bibliography. The notes on the Lebu and the Serer are similarly followed by bibliography. In 1949 Mr. Gamble prepared for the Colonial Office an account of Wolof agriculture and money economy, CONTRIBUTIONS TO A SOCIO-ECONOMIC SURVEY OF THE GAMBIA. A linguistic work by this author, GAMBIAN-FULA VERB LIST, was issued by the Research Department of the Colonial Office in 1958 (London, 43 p., processed).

The dominant tribe, the Mandingo, in Senegambia is treated in the French series Monographies ethnologiques africaines (see no. 1670).

1327. Gray, Sir John Milner. A HISTORY OF THE GAMBIA. Cambridge, Eng., University Press, 1940. 508 p. fold. map.

The standard scholarly history of the Gambia. The author, at the time the book was written Justice of the Supreme Court of the Gambia, made use of many early travel narratives that included references to the Gambia and of unpublished material in the Public Record Office and other university and mission archives. The book is documented with footnote references.

1328. United Nations. Department of Economic and Social Affairs. Commis-
          sioner for Technical Assistance. REPORT ON THE ALTERNATIVES FOR
          ASSOCIATION BETWEEN THE GAMBIA AND SENEGAL. New York, Mar. 16,
          1964. 97 p. Mimeographed. (Restricted; TAO/Gambia/Senegal/1)

          Prepared for the governments of the Gambia and Senegal by
       Hubertus J. Mook, Max Graessli, Henri Monfrini, and Hendrik Weisfelt.
       Legal, administrative, economic, and monetary and fiscal matters are
       considered, with a final chapter of conclusions and recommendations.

GHANA

Bibliographies

1329. Agyei, Christiana Opokua. REFERENCES TO THE POLITICAL HISTORY OF
          GHANA, 1928-1957: A SELECT INTRODUCTORY BIBLIOGRAPHY COMPILED
          IN PARTIAL FULFILMENT OF THE REQUIREMENTS FOR THE DIPLOMA IN
          LIBRARIANSHIP AND ARCHIVES. Legon, Balme Library, University
          College, 1966. xxxiv, 125 p.

1330. Cardinall, Allan W. A BIBLIOGRAPHY OF THE GOLD COAST. Issued as
          a companion volume to the Census Report of 1931. Accra,
          Govt. Printer, 1932. xix, 384 p.

          Classified, with author index. Blank pages for "Addenda" at
       end of each section.

          This justly celebrated bibliography, covering writing on the
       Gold Coast from 1496 to 1931 and much on West Africa in general, is
       described at length by Rydings in his THE BIBLIOGRAPHIES OF WEST
       AFRICA (see no. 1259). The compiler was a British colonial official
       of long experience in West Africa and the author of several semian-
       thropological books on peoples of the Gold Coast and Togo.

1331. Cochrane, T. W. PRELIMINARY BIBLIOGRAPHY OF THE VOLTA RIVER AUTHORITY
          PROGRAMME. Accra, Volta River Authority, 1968. 36 p. Mimeo-
          graphed.

1332. Ghana. Laws, statutes, etc. INDEX TO THE ACTS AND ORDINANCES WITH
          CHRONOLOGICAL TABLE, IN FORCE ON 31ST MARCH 1961. Accra, Govt.
          Printing Dept. [1961?]. 127 p.

1333. Ghana. Ministry of Agriculture. Reference Library. GHANA AGRICULTURE, 1890-1962: A BIBLIOGRAPHY OF CROP AND STOCK, CO-OPERATION AND FORESTRY, FOOD AND FISHERY. Compiled by S. N. Tetteh. Accra, 1962. 315 p. (Ministry of Agriculture Bulletin no. 3 [Draft])

Attempt at a full listing of all material published about Ghanaian agriculture from 1890 to 1962. Included are items written about other areas by Ghanaians or by people who came to Ghana.

1334. GHANA: A CURRENT BIBLIOGRAPHY--SEPTEMBER/OCTOBER 1967- Bibliography Series, v. 1, no. 1- Nov. 1967- Accra, Ghana Library Board Research Library on African Affairs. Every two months.

A new mimeographed series issued by the former Padmore Research Library on African Affairs. Early issues have been compiled by A. N. de Heer. Arrangement is alphabetical by author under broad subject headings; lists of government publications, new periodicals, and vernacular publications are appended. Annual cumulations are planned.

1335. GHANA NATIONAL BIBLIOGRAPHY, 1965. Compiled at the Ghana Library Board Research Library on African Affairs by E. Oko Oddoye and Teresa Gyedu. Accra, Ghana Library Board, 1968. 51 p.

The first separately published current national bibliography of Ghana. Listed are all official and nonofficial works published in Ghana or elsewhere written either by Ghanaians or by other nationals. Periodical articles, special periodical issues, music, and films are omitted, but these are to be included in subsequent issues. The first issue consists of four main parts: publications in English; publications in Ghanaian and other African languages; periodicals, school magazines, and other serial publications; and maps.

1336. Johnson, Albert F. A BIBLIOGRAPHY OF GHANA, 1930-1961. Evanston, Ill., Published for the Ghana Library Board by Northwestern University Press, 1964. xiii, 210 p.

A continuation of A. W. Cardinall's A BIBLIOGRAPHY OF THE GOLD COAST, listing titles of all monographic publications and selected periodical articles on the Gold Coast and Ghana during the formative years 1930-61. The list is intended to be comprehensive, including works of technical and scientific interest, translations, and pure literature, but vernacular texts have been omitted. A few items have slight annotations. The 2,608 titles, among them 357 government publications, are classified in broad subject groupings, and an author index is provided.

Designed as a continuation of Johnson's work is David Brokensha and S. I. A. Kotei, "A Bibliography of Ghana: 1958-1964," AFRICAN STUDIES BULLETIN, v. 10, no. 2, Sept. 1967: 35-79. Arrangement is by broad subject headings with various subdivisions, and some of the entries are in languages other than English. An extensive list of Nkrumah's speeches and writings is included. (See also under no. 1337 below.)

A preliminary bibliography compiled by Mr. Johnson was issued by the Ghana Library Board in 1961, BOOKS ABOUT GHANA: A SELECT READING LIST (32 p.). This contained about 300 titles covering the most significant and easily accessible works on the Gold Coast and Ghana, classified by subject, with author index. A separate section named the chief official publications--commissions and special reports, documents on the constitution, etc.

See also Cynthia Adams, A STUDY GUIDE FOR GHANA (Boston, African Studies Center, Boston University, 1967, 95 p.).

1337. Padmore Research Library on African Affairs. Bibliography Series. Accra, Ghana Library Board, 1962-65.

A set of special subject bibliographies prepared by this outstanding African library service. No. 3 is THE AKAN OF GHANA: A SELECT BIBLIOGRAPHY (1963, 17 p.). No. 4, about the father of Pan-Africanism, DR. W. E. B. DU BOIS, 1868-1963 (1964, 39 l., mimeographed), lists Dr. Du Bois' own works and almost 50 books about him. The final issue in the series is No. 5, SELECT ANNOTATED BIBLIOGRAPHY OF GHANA (1965, 47 p., mimeographed), which updates further Johnson's BIBLIOGRAPHY OF GHANA, 1930-1961. These three issues were all compiled by S. I. A. Kotei.

1338. Pitcher, G. M. BIBLIOGRAPHY OF GHANA, 1957-1959. Kumasi, Kumasi College of Technology Library, 1960. 177 l.

Restricted to books, articles, pamphlets, etc., which appeared just before the transition to and during the first two years of Ghana's national independence. Entries are classified under broad headings; some have brief annotations.

1339. Smalman Smith, Sir John. ANALYTICAL INDEX TO THE ORDINANCES REGULATING THE CIVIL AND CRIMINAL PROCEDURE OF THE GOLD COAST COLONY AND OF THE COLONY OF LAGOS. London, 1888. 119 p. (3,000 entries)

In addition to the many entries in this work, a later index of some 300 references appears in Stanley W. Morgan, A CHRONOLOGICAL TABLE AND AN ALPHABETICAL INDEX OF THE ORDINANCES OF THE GOLD COAST COLONY (London, 1895, xxiv p.). See no. 669 for lists of indexes and collections of laws, ordinances, etc.

1340. Witherell, Julian W., and Sharon B. Lockwood, comps. GHANA: A GUIDE TO
         RESEARCH PUBLICATIONS, 1872-1968. Washington, General Reference
         and Bibliography Division, Reference Department, Library of Con-
         gress, 1969. 110 p.

       Contains 1,283 entries and includes publications of the League of
Nations and the United Nations on British Togoland from 1920 to 1957.

       For material on labor see also U.S. Department of Labor, Bureau of
Labor Statistics, Division of Foreign Labor Conditions, A BIBLIOGRAPHY
OF LABOR IN GHANA, by Lester Trachtman (Washington, 1962, 9 p.).

Serials

1341. ECONOMIC BULLETIN OF GHANA. v. 1- 1957- Legon, Economic Society of
         Ghana. Quarterly.

1342. GHANA JOURNAL OF SCIENCE. v. 1- 1961- Legon, Ghana Science Associa-
         tion. Quarterly.

1343. GHANA NOTES AND QUERIES. v. 1- 1961- Legon, Historical Society of
         Ghana. Irregular.

1344. GHANA TODAY. v. 1- Mar. 1957- Accra, Information Division of the
         Ministry of External Affairs. Formerly every 2 weeks, now weekly.

       This information bulletin, begun in 1956 as GOLD COAST TODAY, is a
useful official source for current developments in Ghana.

       Among other official journals of Ghana are the following (since
the fall of Nkrumah in 1966 the situation of the press remains fluid
and some of the serials listed here may no longer be published):

a) ADVANCE. no. 1- 1954- Department of Social Welfare and Commu-
       nity Development. Quarterly.

b) GHANA FARMER. v. 1- Aug. 1956- Ministry of Agriculture. Quar-
       terly.

       First three issues titled NEW GOLD COAST FARMER.

c) GHANA REVIEW. v. 7, no. 1- 1967- Ghana Information Services.
       Monthly.

       Continuation of GHANA BUILDS (1961) and GHANA RECONSTRUCTS
(1961-66).

d) GHANA TEACHERS' JOURNAL. 1957- Ministry of Education. Quarterly.

Continuation of GOLD COAST EDUCATION (1952-55) and GOLD
COAST TEACHERS' JOURNAL (1955-57).

e) NEW GHANA. v. 1- Oct. 1957- Ghana Information Services.
Formerly semimonthly, now monthly.

Supersedes GOLD COAST WEEKLY REVIEW (1951-57) and GHANA
WEEKLY REVIEW (1957).

f) VOICE OF AFRICA: FREEDOM! v. 1-[6?] 1960-[65?] Bureau of
African Affairs. Monthly.

1345. GHANA YEAR BOOK: A DAILY GRAPHIC PUBLICATION. 1957- Accra, Graphic
Co. illus. Annual.

Published by this leading newspaper office from 1953 to 1956 as
GOLD COAST YEAR BOOK. It includes a general directory of the govern-
ment and organizations of Ghana, with a brief biographical section.
The 1964 edition had 344 pages, including advertising and a folded map.

1346. Historical Society of Ghana. TRANSACTIONS. 1952- Legon, Department of History, University of Ghana. Annual (irregular).

1347. THE LEGON OBSERVER. v. 1- 1966- Legon, Department of Political
Science, University of Ghana. Semimonthly.

Organ of the Legon Committee for National Reconstruction.

1348. RESEARCH REVIEW. Spring 1965- Legon, Institute of African Studies,
University of Ghana. 3 times a year.

Journal edited by Kwame Arhin and devoted to basic ethnographic
and historical data, manuscripts, oral tradition, etc.

1349. UNIVERSITY OF GHANA LAW JOURNAL. v. 1- 1964- Legon, Published for
the University by Sweet & Maxwell, London. Semiannual.

Reference Works

1350. American University, Washington, D.C. Foreign Areas Studies Division. AREA HANDBOOK FOR GHANA. Washington, 1962. xii, 533 p.

One of a series of country background studies being prepared
under contract with the Department of the Army. The extensive

coverage is of sociological, political, economic, and military background. Each section is followed by a seven- or eight-page bibliography of the main sources used.

1351.   Antubam, Kofi. GHANA'S HERITAGE OF CULTURE. Leipzig, Koehler & Amelang, 1963. 221 p. plates.

By a member of the Arts Council of Ghana and senior art master at Achimota School, this very rich collection of Ghanaian lore relates to values (religion, society, prayer, goodness and badness, disgrace, death, time, etc.), basic ideas of beauty, and heritage in universally known forms of art (sculpture, painting, literature, music and dance, poetry, etc.). A summary is followed by appendixes on modern development and the contributions of various individuals and groups.

GHANA RESURGENT (Accra, Waterville Pub. House, 1964, 248 p., illus.), by Michael Dei-Anang, is more about the art and history of Ghana and the meaning of "African personality" than about modern political history, although the author, a well-known Ghanaian poet, was an ambassador extraordinary and a key adviser on inter-African affairs to former President Nkrumah.

1352.   Apter, David E. GHANA IN TRANSITION. Rev. ed. New York, Atheneum, 1963. 432 p. illus., ports., map.

Case study of political institutional transfer published originally in 1955 with title THE GOLD COAST IN TRANSITION (Princeton, N.J., Princeton University Press, 355 p.). Much of the text, after a sketch of background, traditional system of politics, and the British policy of indirect rule, is devoted to the evolutionary changes between the constitution of 1950 and the Nkrumah constitution of 1954, which brought representative and responsible self-government, foreshadowing complete independence. In the new edition a chapter "Ghana as a New Nation" has been added, as well as appendixes giving the Ghana constitution, 1960, the program of the Convention People's Party, and the charter (1961) of the Union of African States: Ghana, Guinea, and Mali.

1353.   Austin, Dennis. POLITICS IN GHANA, 1946-1960. London, New York, Oxford University Press, 1964. xiv, 459 p. maps, tables.

Bibliography: p. 447-451.

In describing the Gold Coast's progress from "model colony" to republic the author first provides an introductory preview, followed by chapters on early years (1946-51), the Convention People's Party

in office (1951-54), the struggle for power (1954-56), and a concluding chapter on independence and succeeding years (1957-60).
Appendixes include the 1960 constitution.

1354.   Bennion, Francis A. R.   THE CONSTITUTIONAL LAW OF GHANA.   London,
        Butterworth, 1962.   xxxvi, 527 p.   (Butterworth's African Law
        Series, no. 5)

        For note on this series, see no.   684.

1355.   Birmingham, Walter, I. Neustadt, and E. N. Omaboe, eds.   A STUDY OF
        CONTEMPORARY GHANA: Vol. I, THE ECONOMY OF GHANA: Vol. II,
        SOME ASPECTS OF SOCIAL STRUCTURE.   London, Published for the
        Ghana Academy of Sciences by Allen & Unwin; Evanston, Ill.,
        Northwestern University Press, 1966-67.   472, 271 p.   col.
        plates, maps (part col.), tables, diagrs.

        Ambitious comprehensive study of Ghana's economy and social
        structure, designed for public servants, scholars, and teachers and
        students of secondary and university level.   The first volume covers
        the entire economic structure, including major features, policy, and
        planning.   The second volume, utilizing the 1960 population census
        of Ghana, deals with population--general characteristics, change,
        migration and urbanization, and prospects and policy.

1356.   Boateng, E. A.   A GEOGRAPHY OF GHANA.   2d ed.   Cambridge, Eng.,
        University Press, 1966.   xv, 212 p.   plates, maps, tables,
        diagrs.

        Bibliographical footnotes.

        Designed as an introductory text for students in West Africa
        by a Ghanaian geographer, this is a substantial revision of the
        first edition (1959), with essential material updated and much new
        factual information added.   The first part is a survey of the physical
        geography.   In Part 2 the author deals with various aspects of the
        economy and with population and settlements.   Part 3 consists of
        surveys of 12 geographical regions of Ghana.   There are 24 plates,
        and an index is included.

        Another text for African students is by an English author,
        David Thickens Adams, A GHANA GEOGRAPHY (2d ed., London, University
        of London Press, 1960, 192 p., illus., maps).

1357.   Bourret, Florence M.   GHANA: THE ROAD TO INDEPENDENCE, 1919-1957.
        3d ed.   Stanford, Calif., Stanford University Press, 1960.
        xiii, 246 p.   map, tables.

Bibliography: p. 221-231.

An informative study by an American nun and history professor,
first published with the title THE GOLD COAST: A SURVEY OF THE GOLD
COAST AND BRITISH TOGOLAND, 1919-1946 (Stanford, 1949, 231 p.).
Mother Bourret planned her twentieth-century political, economic, and
social history of the colony as a case study of the "day-by-day working
out" of British policy in bringing dependent territories into the
modern world. An updated edition, 1919-1951, was published in 1952,
and the present volume completes the survey with a chapter detailing
the political and constitutional changes of 1945-47 and Independence
Day. The work has footnote references and a useful bibliography,
including documents.

1358. Claridge, William W. A HISTORY OF THE GOLD COAST AND ASHANTI FROM
        THE EARLIEST TIMES TO THE COMMENCEMENT OF THE TWENTIETH CENTURY.
        2d ed. London, Frank Cass; New York, Barnes & Noble, 1964. 2
        v. 649, 638 p. maps (part fold. col.), geneal. table.

        Bibliography: v. 2, p. 577-581.

        This famous work, known particularly for its full treatment of
the Ashanti wars, first appeared in 1915. The second edition has a
new introduction by W. E. F. Ward.

1359. Diplomatic Press. TRADE DIRECTORY OF THE REPUBLIC OF GHANA, INCLUDING
        TRADE INDEX. 1959- London, Diplomatic Press and Publishing Co.
        illus., ports.

        The series of country directories now being published regularly
by the Diplomatic Press are compiled with the cooperation of public
relations services in the countries concerned. The title varies
slightly, i.e., the fifth edition (95 p.) is titled GHANA TRADE
DIRECTORY, 1967, INCLUDING CLASSIFIED TRADE INDEX (previous editions,
1959, 1960, 1961-62, 1964). It includes almanac-type information on
the country and government and a generous number of pages of advertising.
Earlier editions had biographical sections and material on education,
health services, and social welfare.

1360. Elias, Taslim Olawale. GHANA AND SIERRA LEONE: THE DEVELOPMENT OF
        THEIR LAWS AND CONSTITUTIONS. London, Stevens, 1962. xii,
        334 p. (The British Commonwealth, the Development of Its Laws
        and Constitution, v. 10)

        See note on Dr. Elias under Nigeria (no. 1468).

1361. Ethnographic Survey of Africa: Western Africa. London, International African Institute, 1950-52.

The volumes of the Ethnographic Survey relating to Ghana are by Madeline Manoukian, AKAN AND GA-ADANGME PEOPLES OF THE GOLD COAST (1950, 112 p.; Western Africa, pt. 1), TRIBES OF THE NORTHERN TERRITORIES OF THE GOLD COAST (1951, 102 p.; pt. 5), and THE EWE-SPEAKING PEOPLE OF TOGOLAND AND THE GOLD COAST (1952, 63 p.; pt. 6). Each has a bibliography of several pages.

The number of anthropological studies relating to Ghana is too large to permit mention of more than a few individual authors. Among the better known are M. J. Field, Meyer Fortes, Robert Lystad, and J. Goodie.

1362. Fage, John Donelly. GHANA. A HISTORICAL INTERPRETATION. Madison, University of Wisconsin Press, 1959. 122 p. illus., maps.

Bibliography: p. 89-115 (notes).

Very useful synthesis of Ghanaian history.

1363. Flint, John E. NIGERIA AND GHANA. Englewood Cliffs, N.J., Prentice-Hall, 1966. 176 p. (The Modern Nations in Historical Perspective)

See no. 1472 for annotation.

1364. Ghana. Census Office. 1960 POPULATION CENSUS OF GHANA. Accra, 1962- illus., ports., maps (part col.), tables.

_____. _____. SPECIAL REPORT: A. STATISTICS OF TOWNS WITH 10,000 POPULATION OR MORE; E. TRIBES IN GHANA. Accra, 1964- illus., maps.

_____. _____. ATLAS OF POPULATION CHARACTERISTICS. Accra, 1964. 29 p.

The 1960 census was the first complete census held in Ghana and the first to use modern census techniques although experts still question its accuracy. Its results are being published as indicated above. For the first entry five volumes, in addition to an ADVANCE REPORT OF VOLUMES III AND IV, had appeared by late 1967: Vol. I, THE GAZETTEER; Vol. II, STATISTICS OF LOCALITIES AND ENUMERATION AREAS; Vol. III, DETAILED DEMOGRAPHIC CHARACTERISTICS OF LOCAL AUTHORITIES, REGIONS, AND TOTAL COUNTRY; Vol. IV, ECONOMIC CHARACTERISTICS OF LOCAL AUTHORITIES, REGIONS, AND TOTAL COUNTRY; Vol. V, GENERAL REPORT. A sixth and final volume is to consist of a statistical summary.

1365.   Ghana. Information Services, New York. GHANA REBORN. New York,
        1966. 68 p. illus., map (on lining paper).

        Part 1 deals with the military revolt and takeover of Feb. 1966,
the economic and international policies of the National Liberation
Council, and the NLC's first 100 days of rule. Part 2 offers brief
facts on Ghana--e.g., history, natural resources, Volta River project,
education, and social welfare.

1366.   GHANA BUSINESS GUIDE 1968. Accra, Business Publications, 1968. 236 p.

        Revision and enlargement of the Accra Business Guide published
in 1964. Designed for manufacturers, traders, importers, exporters,
and other businessmen. It contains the annual report of the Bank of
Ghana, a report on the National Investment Bank, postal and telephone
information, information on import control and restricted imports, a
listing of registered importers, a list of the ministries and their
areas of jurisdiction, the Budget Statement for 1968-69 by A. A.
Afrifa, addresses of publishers of newspapers and journals, rail,
air, and bus transport information, trade statistics, bank addresses,
and information on taxation and labor legislation.

1367.   GHANA 1966. Accra, Anowuo Educational Publications, 1967. 157,
        [8] p.

        A day-by-day account of significant political, economic, social,
and other events in 1966. Members of various missions and delegations
visiting abroad are listed. There is an index of names.

1368.   Gold Coast. Vernacular Literature Bureau. ANNUAL REPORT. 1951/52-
        Accra, Govt. Print. Dept.

        This office has been superseded by the Bureau of Ghana Languages,
Accra. The Bureau produces basic literature for teaching illiterates,
texts for follow-up work, newspapers, advanced literature, and translations of government papers and commercial advertisements.

1369.   Harvey, William Burnett. LAW AND SOCIAL CHANGE IN GHANA. Princeton,
        N.J., Princeton University Press, 1966. xiii, 453 p.

        Bibliographical footnotes.

        Professor Harvey, who was Dean of the Faculty of Law at the
University of Ghana from 1962 to 1964, presents a perceptive study
of legal developments in Ghana, 1951-64, within the context of the
social pressures impinging upon the contenders for political power.

After providing a brief background, he traces the progress of
independence from the constitutions of 1951 and 1957 through the
constitution of 1960 and offers detailed analyses of relevant
legislation and executive action. Appendix 1 describes legal
education in Ghana, and Appendix 2 reprints the text of the 1960
constitution, government proposals concerning it, and selected
legislation. There is an index.

1370. Hill, Polly. THE MIGRANT COCOA-FARMERS OF SOUTHERN GHANA. New York,
        Cambridge University Press, 1963. xv, 265 p. illus., ports.,
        maps (3 fold.).

        Bibliography: p. 252-256.

        A preliminary survey of this study was issued by Oxford University
Press in 1956, THE GOLD COAST COCOA FARMER (139 p.). The new volume
has been widely hailed as an authoritative work; in the foreword
Professor Meyer Fortes writes that "the outstanding feature of this
book is the documentation and discussion of fundamental issues in the
economic history and the theoretical appreciation of the cocoa
industry in Ghana." The author does not follow the regular social-
survey technique but what she calls "hit-and-miss methods," carried
out in talks with many informants. The results may not always be
accurate facts but are history handed down by oral tradition. Each
chapter of discussion and theorizing is followed by one or more
appendixes giving historical notes, statistics, case studies, and
other interesting data. There are footnote references.

        For any study of the cocoa industry, reference should also be
made to the annual reports of the Ghana Cocoa Marketing Board and
to its quarterly magazine THE C.M.B. NEWSLETTER (1957-, Accra).
There are also reports of the West African Cacao Research Institute
at Tafo which was converted in 1964 into the Cocoa Research Institute
of the Ghana Academy of Sciences.

1371. Irvine, Frederick R. THE FISHES AND FISHERIES OF THE GOLD COAST.
        With illus. and an account of the fishing industry by A. P.
        Brown and classification and keys for the identification of the
        fishes by J. R. Norman and E. Trewavas. London, Published on
        behalf of the Government of the Gold Coast by the Crown Agents
        for the Colonies, 1947. 352 p. illus.

        Bibliography: p. 327-337.

        There are three classification indexes, one of English and Latin
names, one of Ga and Adangme names, and one of Fante, Ashanti, and
Twi names.

1372. Irvine, Frederick R. WOODY PLANTS OF GHANA, WITH SPECIAL REFERENCE
TO THEIR USES. London, Oxford University Press, 1961. xcv,
868 p. illus., 35 plates (part col.).

Bibliography: p. 790-793.

This was first published in 1930 under the title PLANTS OF THE
GOLD COAST. Another full-scale study of forestry in Ghana is by Charles
J. Taylor, SYNECOLOGY AND SILVICULTURE IN GHANA (Edinburgh, Published
on behalf of the University College of Ghana by Nelson, 1960, 418 p.,
illus., maps).

1373. Kimble, David. A POLITICAL HISTORY OF GHANA: THE RISE OF GOLD COAST
NATIONALISM, 1850-1928. Oxford, Clarendon Press, 1963. xviii,
587 p. ports., maps, tables.

The author, former director of the Institute of Extra-mural
Studies at the University College of Ghana, is editor of the JOURNAL
OF MODERN AFRICAN STUDIES. In this excellent, full-scale history of
the origins of nationalism in the former Gold Coast, he gives sources
in footnotes. His thesis is that Gold Coast nationalism is of relatively
early origin.

1374. Metcalfe, G. E., ed. GREAT BRITAIN AND GHANA: DOCUMENTS OF GHANA
HISTORY, 1807-1957. London, Published on behalf of the University
of Ghana by T. Nelson, 1964. xvii, 779 p. maps.

Documents were selected in order to illustrate the development
of British policy in Ghana, but this should be understood in its
West African and even global context. There are brief introductions
to each period (age of experiment, 1807-52; of laissez-faire, 1852-86;
of expansion, 1887-1918; of fulfillment, 1919-57). Appendixes include
lists of British governors and administrators and of Gold Coast government treaties, statistics on trade and revenue, and maps. There is
an index.

1375. National Tourist Corporation. OFFICIAL GUIDE BOOK OF GHANA. Compiled
and edited by E. T. Anim. Accra, 1969. 105 p.

1376. Nketia, J. H. Kwabena. AFRICAN MUSIC IN GHANA. Evanston, Ill.,
Northwestern University Press, 1963. 148 p. illus., maps,
music, tables. (African Studies, no. 11)

Bibliography: p. 110-113; songs: p. 115-146.

Discussion of the organization of folk music, musical types,
performing groups, instrumental resources, and many other aspects
of African music, by a leading Western-trained African scholar.
His useful bibliography includes a good selection of anthropological
studies of Ghana. Another volume by Mr. Nketia is FOLK SONGS OF
GHANA (London, Oxford University Press for the University of Ghana,
1963, 205 p.). The first of a series designed to provide source
material for performers, composers, and students of African music,
this work gives the text of songs in Akan, with musical accompaniment.

1377. Nkrumah, Kwame. CONSCIENCISM: PHILOSOPHY AND IDEOLOGY FOR DECOLONIZATION
AND DEVELOPMENT, WITH PARTICULAR REFERENCE TO THE AFRICAN REVOLU-
TION. London, Heinemann, 1964. 112 p.

a) _____. GHANA: THE AUTOBIOGRAPHY OF KWAME NKRUMAH. New York, T.
Nelson, 1957. 302 p. illus.

b) _____. HANDS OFF AFRICA! Some famous speeches by Dr. the Rt.
Hon. Kwame Nkrumah, P.C., M.P. (first President of the Republic
of Ghana); with a tribute to George Padmore written by Tawia
Adamafio, General Secretary of C.P.P. Accra, Kwabena Owusu-
Akyem, 1960. 62 p. illus.

c) _____. I SPEAK OF FREEDOM: A STATEMENT OF AFRICAN IDEOLOGY.
New York, Praeger, 1961. 291 p. illus. (Books That Matter)

d) _____. NEO-COLONIALISM: THE LAST STAGE OF IMPERIALISM. London,
Nelson, 1965. 280 p. (Bibliography: p. 260-262.)

All primary source material. Nkrumah's work NEO-COLONIALISM
displays many of the misconceptions and dogmas which contributed
to his downfall.

The biography by a West African newspaperman, Timothy Bankole,
KWAME NKRUMAH: HIS RISE TO POWER (Evanston, Ill., Northwestern
University Press, 1963, 191 p.), was first published in 1955 and has
been reprinted with three added chapters, "Osagyefo," "Nkrumah the
Man," and "Nkrumah and the African Personality." See also a neo-
Marxist interpretation of Nkrumah's rule by Bob Fitch and Mary
Oppenheimer, GHANA: END OF AN ILLUSION (New York, Monthly Review
Press, 1966, 130 p.).

1378. Nsarkoh, J. K. LOCAL GOVERNMENT IN GHANA. Accra, Ghana Universities
Press; New York, Oxford University Press, 1964. 309 p.

Survey of the fundamentals of the local government system in
Ghana, the first of its kind. There are appendixes of facts and
figures. A very brief list of sources is given on p. 232-233.

1379. Rattray, Robert Sutherland. ASHANTI. Oxford, Clarendon Press, 1923. 348 p.

Reprint, Kumasi, Basel Mission Book Depot, 1954.

a) _____. ASHANTI LAW AND CONSTITUTION. Oxford, Clarendon Press, 1929. 420 p.

Reprint, London, Oxford University Press, 1956.

b) _____. RELIGION AND ART IN ASHANTI. Oxford, Clarendon Press, 1927. 414 p.

Reprint, Kumasi, 1955.

c) _____. TRIBES OF THE ASHANTI HINTERLAND. Oxford, Clarendon Press, 1932. 2 v.

There are modern reprints of the three justly famous works by the authority on native languages and customs who as head of a new Anthropology Department in Ashanti submitted in 1921 as a confidential "Intelligence Report" to the Administration the detailed investigation of the beliefs and customs of that warlike people.

Another book by Captain Rattray is AKAN-ASHANTI FOLK-TALES (Oxford, Clarendon Press, 1930, 275 p.). This is a group of stories collected in the more remote villages and given as closely as possible in the words of the informants, with text on one side in the Akan language, on the other in English. Illustrations are by African artists.

1380. Reindorf, Carl C. THE HISTORY OF THE GOLD COAST AND ASANTE, BASED ON TRADITIONS AND HISTORICAL FACTS COMPRISING A PERIOD OF MORE THAN THREE CENTURIES FROM ABOUT 1500 to 1860. With a biographical sketch by C. E. Reindorf. 2d ed. Basel, Basel Mission Book Depot, 1951. xii, 349 p. illus., ports., map.

Reprint of a book published in 1889, which was a pioneer work by a native pastor of the Basel Mission in Christiansborg. His history was based very largely on the traditions he had heard in his youth. The introductory biography of the author is by his son. Important as a source work, the narrative abounds in translations of Ga anecdotes, sayings, and songs. See also Brodie Cruickshank, EIGHTEEN YEARS ON THE GOLD COAST OF AFRICA (1853, 2 v.; 2d ed., New York, Barnes & Noble, 1966, 2 v.).

1381.   Rubin, Leslie, and Pauli Murray.   THE CONSTITUTION AND GOVERNMENT OF
            GHANA.   London, Sweet & Maxwell, 1961.   xvi, 310 p.   tables.
            (Law in Africa Series, no. 1)

        Bibliography: p. 285-287.

            Much of this study is speculative, as the Ghana courts had not
        yet given decisions on various significant questions.   The text of
        the Constitution of Ghana is included (p. 250-266).

            Two other legal analyses in this Sweet & Maxwell series are by
        N. A. Ollennu: PRINCIPLES OF CUSTOMARY LAND LAW IN GHANA (1962, xxvi,
        272 p., plates, maps, tables, diagrs.; Law in Africa Series, no. 2);
        and THE LAW OF TESTATE AND INTESTATE SUCCESSION IN GHANA (1966, xxvii,
        322 p.; Law in Africa Series, no. 16).

1382.   Scott, David.   EPIDEMIC DISEASE IN GHANA, 1901-1960.   London, New
            York, Oxford University Press, 1965.   xviii, 208 p.   (Oxford
            Medical Publications)

        Includes bibliographies.

            Study by an epidemiologist formerly of the Ghana Ministry of
        Health, giving a full account of the development of public health
        services in the British colony and under the independent government.
        Data are from official statistics and reports, fortified by personal
        experience.   The account of measures to combat plague, yellow fever,
        smallpox, cerebrospinal meningitis, relapsing fever, and African
        trypanosomiasis and influenza is of wide application to the health
        problems of the continent.

1383.   Snell, Kenneth S.   GHANA DECIMAL CURRENCY.   Cambridge, Eng., University
            Press, 1964.   32 p.

            Ghana's new currency system is explained in this booklet by an
        assistant master in a primary school for the instruction of children.
        The basic unit of the new currency is the pesewa; the word is Fante
        for penny.   There is also the codi, Akan word for pound.   Exercises
        are given in conversion, simple interest, and exchange rates.

1384.   Volta River Preparatory Commission.   THE VOLTA RIVER PROJECT.   London,
            Published for the Governments of the United Kingdom and of the
            Gold Coast by H.M. Stationery Off., 1956.   3 v.   illus., maps,
            diagrs., tables.

        Includes bibliographies.

This scheme for the development of large-scale aluminum production had been outlined in a British Colonial Office White Paper of 1952 (Cmd. 8702), with an estimate for total general expenditure of £144 million. The Preparatory Commission was set up in 1953. Its report is given in the first volume (135 p. and large folded map); the second volume, with many tables, maps, and charts, contains appendixes on various effects and special problems (475 p.). The third volume, ENGINEERING REPORT, by Sir William Halcrow and Partners, contains 88 pages of text and many large folded sheets of plans, as well as a general bibliography including 65 items.

A monograph on THE GEOLOGY OF THE VOLTA RIVER PROJECT, by W. B. Tevendale (Accra, 1957, 119 p., illus.), was published as Bulletin No. 20 of the Ghana Geological Survey.

1385. Wallerstein, Immanuel. THE ROAD TO INDEPENDENCE: GHANA AND THE IVORY COAST. The Hague, Paris, Mouton, 1964. xiii, 200 p. tables, chart. (Le monde d'outre-mer, passé et présent, 1st ser., Etudes, 20)

Bibliography: p. 179-200.

For annotation see no. 1733.

1386. Ward, William Ernest. A HISTORY OF GHANA. 2d ed. rev. London, Allen & Unwin, 1958. 434 p. illus., ports., maps.

_____. A SHORT HISTORY OF GHANA. 7th ed. London and New York, Longmans, Green, 1957. xi, 275 p. illus., maps, geneal. table.

Professor Ward's SHORT HISTORY was first published while he was teaching at Achimota in 1935 and was addressed particularly to African students. It has gone through many editions and has become the standard modern text for political history, "of tribal movements, wars and treaties, and the rise and fall of states." The latest revision brings the story up to independence. The longer work, for a European audience, was first published in 1948 as A HISTORY OF THE GOLD COAST.

1387. Wight, Martin. THE GOLD COAST LEGISLATIVE COUNCIL. London, Published under the auspices of Nuffield College by Faber & Faber, 1947. 285 p. fold. map. (Studies in Colonial Legislatures, v. 2)

This is the second volume of the significant series edited by Margery Perham and now chiefly of historical value. Mr. Wight, an authority on colonial constitutions, also wrote the first general volume, DEVELOPMENT OF THE LEGISLATIVE COUNCIL, 1606-1945. His specialist study of the Gold Coast function of self-government began

with a review of historical and political development and then
analyzed the constitution of 1925, the Council set up by it, and
its working. He examined the postwar political situation of the
colony and concluded with a brief glance at the new constitution of
1946.

1388. Wills, J. Brian, ed. AGRICULTURE AND LAND USE IN GHANA. London,
        New York, Published for the Ghana Ministry of Food and Agriculture
        by the Oxford University Press, 1962. xviii, 503 p.
        tables, charts, maps.

        Bibliography: p. 445-494.

        Compendium of information available on background, state, and
    problems of agriculture and land use in Ghana, in three parts. The
    first part is on general conditions and patterns of rural land use;
    the second on special aspects, with particular emphasis on cocoa
    crops; the third on forestry and plant and animal husbandry. The
    work, intended as a textbook for officials, teachers, and research
    workers, was begun in 1954 and was finished by an official of the
    Ghana Soil and Land-Use Survey. Mr. Wills compiled the extensive
    "Bibliography of Agriculture, Land Use and Surrounding Conditions in
    Ghana and Adjacent Territories, 1930-1959."

LIBERIA

Bibliographies

1389. Holsoe, Svend E. "A Bibliography of Liberian Government Documents."
        AFRICAN STUDIES BULLETIN, v. 11, no. 1, Apr. 1968: 39-63; v. 11,
        no. 2, Sept. 1968: 149-194.

        A very useful bibliography which constitutes the first attempt
    to provide a comprehensive listing of various types of printed and
    duplicated Liberian government documents. Arrangement is by subject
    and by government agency. The compiler has indicated at which public
    libraries specific documents are available.

1390. Holsoe, Svend E. A STUDY GUIDE FOR LIBERIA. Boston, African Studies
        Center, Development Program, Boston University, 1967. 32 p.
        Includes bibliography.

        Annotated list of books, articles, and government documents.

1391. Solomon, Marvin D., and Warren L. d'Azevedo, comps. A GENERAL BIBLI-
        OGRAPHY OF THE REPUBLIC OF LIBERIA. Evanston, Ill., 1962.
        68 p. (Northwestern University Working Papers in Social Science,
        no. 1)

        The most up-to-date and comprehensive bibliography available
for Liberia. Entries are in four sections: the first, works arranged
by individual author; the second, title or corporate author entries;
the third, official documents; and the fourth, miscellaneous materials
such as maps and surveys. There are well over 2,000 entries, including
periodical references.

        See also works by Holas (no. 1402) and Huberich (no. 1403), below.

Serials

1392. LIBERIA ANNUAL REVIEW. v. 1- 1960/61- London, Monrovia, Consolidated
        Publications Co. illus., map.

        Promotional handbook covering government, economic, and social
life. The first volume included an 8-page report, "The Year in Review,"
with items selected from President Tubman's State of the Union message,
and a section entitled "Who's Who in Liberia." No later issues have
been noticed.

1393. LIBERIA: TRADE, INDUSTRY AND TRAVEL. 1957- Monrovia, Consolidated
        Publications Co. Quarterly.

1394. LIBERIAN HISTORICAL REVIEW. v. 1- 1964- Monrovia, Liberian Historical
        Society. Annual.

1395. LIBERIAN LAW JOURNAL. v. 1- 1965- Monrovia, University of Liberia.
        Biannual.

1396. LIBERIAN STUDIES JOURNAL. v. 1- 1968- Greencastle, Ind., African
        Studies Center, Depauw University. Biannual.

1397. UNIVERSITY OF LIBERIA JOURNAL. 1958- Monrovia, University Research
        Bureau. Semiannual.

        Title varies: 1958- UNIVERSITY OF LIBERIA RESEARCH BULLETIN.

Reference Works
_____

1398. American University, Washington, D.C. Special Operations Research
          Office. AREA HANDBOOK FOR LIBERIA. By T. D. Roberts and
          others. Washington, U.S. Govt. Print. Off., 1964. 419 p. maps.
          (Department of the Army Pamphlet no. 550-38)

          Like others of the series, this is an extensive background study
     of the country, covering sociology, politics, economics, and military
     considerations. Each section is followed by a bibliography of sources.

1399. Buell, Raymond Leslie. LIBERIA: A CENTURY OF SURVIVAL, 1847-1947.
          Philadelphia, University of Pennsylvania Press, University
          Museum, 1947. 140 p. (African Handbooks, edited by H. A.
          Wieschhoff, no. 7)

          Supplementing the extensive review of the Liberian situation in
     his general work, THE NATIVE PROBLEM IN AFRICA (see no. 439), Dr.
     Buell in this shorter book clearly expresses his criticism of the
     Liberian experiment in independent government, with particular ref-
     erence to the True Whig regimes of the interwar period. His appen-
     dixes give documents of Liberian agreements with the United States
     and with Firestone up to 1939. Another good survey is that by Nnamdi
     Azikiwe, LIBERIA IN WORLD POLITICS (London, Stockwell, 1934, 406 p.).

1400. Clower, Robert W., George Dalton, Mitchell Harwitz, and A. A. Walters,
          with the assistance of Robert P. Armstrong and others. GROWTH
          WITHOUT DEVELOPMENT: AN ECONOMIC SURVEY OF LIBERIA. Evanston,
          Ill., Northwestern University Press, 1966. xv, 385 p. maps,
          charts. (African Studies, no. 16)

          Bibliographical footnotes.

          The survey was conducted from Jan. 1961 to Aug. 1962 at the
     request of the government of Liberia and the U.S. Agency for Inter-
     national Development in order to suggest policies for development,
     and findings were reported to both governments in 1962. Primary
     production has grown, the authors have found, but this has not been
     matched by any development planning. The authors believe that basic
     reforms in traditional policies are needed to produce the necessary
     structural and social change. The first part of the book gives an
     overall view; the second examines the various concessions (rubber,
     iron ore, etc.), the labor situation, education, and foreign aid.
     The work offers a critical review of Liberian government.

1401. Fraenkel, Merran. TRIBE AND CLASS IN MONROVIA. London, Published
        for the International African Institute by the Oxford University
        Press, 1964. xii, 244 p. illus., maps.

        Bibliography: p. 238-241.

           A social anthropologist's study of the modern change in the
        society of Liberia's capital, where the old distinction between the
        "civilized" Americo-Liberians and the "tribal" peoples, Kru, Bassa,
        Vai, etc., is beginning to yield to "an embryonic social class
        structure" based on education and social standing rather than origins.

1402. Holas, Bohumil. MISSION DANS L'EST LIBERIEN (P.-L. DEKEYSER, B.
        HOLAS, 1948): RESULTATS DEMOGRAPHIQUES, ETHNOLOGIQUES ET
        ANTHROPOMETRIQUES. Dakar, IFAN, 1952. xiii, 566 p. illus.,
        40 plates. (Mémoires de l'Institut Français d'Afrique Noire,
        no. 14)

        Bibliography: p. 481-530.

           Report, in eight parts, of an expedition undertaken by two IFAN
        scientists. The first and longest part is "Itinéraire," containing
        systematic descriptions, in demographic detail village by village,
        of the tribal regions of eastern Liberia through which the authors
        traveled. Part 2 is physical anthropology, with tabled anthropo-
        metric observations; Part 3, linguistics; Part 4, religion and magic;
        Part 5, "intellectual manifestations," chiefly in arts and crafts.
        Part 6 is a comprehensive bibliography of Liberia, covering books,
        pamphlets, documents, periodical literature, and maps, in English,
        French, and other languages. Part 7 is given to indexes, general
        (subject and place name), vernacular terms, and personal names, and
        Part 8 is a separate section of plates, mostly of ethnological interest.

1403. Huberich, Charles H. THE POLITICAL AND LEGISLATIVE HISTORY OF LIBERIA.
        New York, Central Book Co., 1947. 2 v. 1734 p.

        Bibliography: v. 2, p. 1668-1703.

           The subtitle reads: "A documentary history of the constitutions,
        laws and treaties of Liberia from the earliest settlements to the
        establishment of the Republic, a sketch of the activities of the
        American colonization societies, a commentary on the constitution of
        the Republic and a survey of the political and social legislation
        from 1847 to 1944; with appendixes containing the laws of the colony
        of Liberia, 1820-1839, and Acts of the Government and Council, 1839-1847."
        Foreword is by Roscoe Pound. This exhaustive and heavily documented
        work, which places chief emphasis on legislative history, is more useful
        for reference than for reading. Its extensive bibliography covers
        printed material and manuscript collections in the United States.

A collection of several hundred volumes of manuscript materials relating to the American Colonization Society and the settlement of Liberia is held by the Library of Congress. See Staudenraus (no. 1412) and Duignan (no. 101) for description of other American collections on Liberia.

1404. Johnston, Sir Harry H. LIBERIA. New York, Dodd, Mead, 1906. 2 v. 1183 p.

Bibliography: v. 1, p. xiii-xvii.

Classic work on Liberia. The first volume deals comprehensively with the period of settlement, the slave trade, the establishment of the colony, and the first half-century of the Republic; the second volume with natural history (including an appendix on the flora of Liberia by Dr. Otto Stapf of the Kew Herbarium), anthropology, and linguistics.

1405. Keiser, Robert L. LIBERIA: A REPORT ON THE RELATIONS BETWEEN THE UNITED STATES AND LIBERIA. Washington, U.S. Govt. Print. Off., 1928. 371 p. (U.S. Department of State, Second Series B, no. 1, Liberia no. 1)

Study by a Foreign Service officer covering the official record of the 1926 agreement of the Firestone Rubber Co. with the Liberian government for a concession of a million acres of land and the arrangement of a loan of $5 million through the Finance Corporation of America to provide for the rehabilitation of the deeply embarrassed finances of Liberia--a loan which had been arranged in 1922 through the U.S. Treasury but had failed to be approved by the Senate. The work, restricted to material dealing specifically with American-Liberian relations, includes background on the foundation of the Liberian colonies, using for most of the record the actual text of documents. The appendixes are index-digests of documents and lists of papers and memoranda. A single introductory page (vii) gives sources.

1406. Liberia. Laws, statutes, etc. LIBERIAN CODE OF LAWS OF 1956, ADOPTED BY THE LEGISLATURE OF THE REPUBLIC OF LIBERIA, MARCH 22, 1956. Published under authority of the Legislature of Liberia and President William V. S. Tubman. Ithaca, N.Y., Cornell University Press, 1957. 3 v.

1407. Liberia. Supreme Court. LIBERIAN LAW REPORTS. v. 1- 1861/1907- New York (etc.).

Vol. XV, prepared for the Republic of Liberia by the Liberian Codification Project, Cornell University, under the direction of Milton

R. Konvitz (Ithaca, N.Y., Cornell University Press, 1967), contains cases adjudged by the Supreme Court of Liberia from the March term 1962 through the October term 1963. This and earlier volumes, all covering extended periods, have been edited and published in the United States. The subtitle varies: CASES ADJUDGED BY THE SUPREME COURT or DECISIONS OF THE SUPREME COURT.

1408. THE LIBERIAN YEARBOOK FOR 1962. Compiled and edited by Henry B. Cole. Monrovia, Liberian Review, 1962. 272 p. illus., ports., maps.

Second edition of a comprehensive handbook (1st ed., 1956). The 21 chapters cover in factual presentation all matters relating to Liberia--land and people, government and administration, economic, social, political, and cultural life. Lists of names and addresses of officials, business firms, and institutions of various kinds are included.

See also HANDBOOK AND DIRECTORY OF LIBERIA, published for the Chamber of Commerce in Monrovia by the Consolidated Publications Co. in 1963, 132 p.

1409. Liebenow, J. Gus. "Liberia." In Carter, Gwendolen M., ed. AFRICAN ONE-PARTY STATES. Ithaca, N.Y., Cornell University Press, 1962. p. 325-394.

Bibliography: p. 386-394.

An excellent brief survey, covering historical background, the economy, social structure, the political process, and contemporary issues. The bibliography is in essay form, with evaluative comment on works cited. See also Liebenow's LIBERIA: THE EVOLUTION OF PRIVI-LEGE (Ithaca, N.Y., Cornell University Press, 1969, xx, 247 p., maps).

1410. Marinelli, Lawrence A. THE NEW LIBERIA: A HISTORICAL AND POLITICAL SURVEY. With an introduction by Léopold Sédar Senghor. New York, Published for the Africa Service Institute of New York by Praeger, 1964. 244 p. map, ports.

A general study of Liberia, this is essentially a laudatory biography of President Tubman, with superficial treatment regarding other aspects of Liberian history.

An earlier history of somewhat the same nature is by the former superintendent of government printing of Liberia, Nathaniel R. Richardson, LIBERIA'S PAST AND PRESENT (London, Diplomatic Press & Pub. Co., 1959, 348 p., illus.). Included are biographical sketches, texts of documents and addresses, and a calendar of events from 1816 to 1952.

1411. Schwab, George. TRIBES OF THE LIBERIAN HINTERLAND. Cambridge, Mass.,
       Peabody Museum, 1947. 527 p. 111 plates. (Peabody Museum
       Papers, v. 31)

       The most comprehensive ethnographic survey available in English
of the little-studied tribes of Liberia, by an amateur anthropologist
and former missionary who had undertaken a mission financed by the
Peabody Museum in 1928. The work was edited with contributions of
additional material by Dr. G. Way Harley. Twenty-three tribes or
remnants of tribes are covered, with full technical ethnological
data on nine. There are two appendixes, one on languages, one a
glossary, and a long section of plates showing artifacts and physical
anthropology.

1412. Staudenraus, P. J. THE AFRICAN COLONIZATION MOVEMENT, 1816-1865.
       New York, Columbia University Press, 1961. 323 p.

       Includes bibliographies.

       Authoritative work, based largely on the archives of the American
Colonization Society in the Library of Congress. It is a historical
examination of American social thought regarding slavery and coloni-
zation rather than a history of the actual settlement in Liberia.
It includes detailed bibliography in the "Notes," p. 252-304, and a
"Bibliographical Essay," p. 305-310.

1413. Tubman, William V. S. PRESIDENT TUBMAN OF LIBERIA SPEAKS. Edited by
       E. Reginald Townsend. London, Consolidated Publications Co., 1959.
       301 p. illus.

       In the elections of 1943, William V. S. Tubman was chosen President
of Liberia, then in heavy economic difficultires. According to Mr.
Townsend, "A New Day was dawning. A New Nation was being born." The
volume, handsomely printed and illustrated, begins with the first
inaugural address of the durable President on Jan. 5, 1944, and
continues with his more important speeches through 1958.

1414. Tubman, William V. S. THE OFFICIAL PAPERS OF WILLIAM V. S. TUBMAN,
       PRESIDENT OF THE REPUBLIC OF LIBERIA, COVERING ADDRESSES, MESSAGES,
       SPEECHES, AND STATEMENTS 1960-1967. Edited by E. Reginald
       Townsend. London, Longmans, 1968. 687 p. illus., maps.

1415. U.S. Department of the Interior. Army Map Service. Geographic
       Names Division. LIBERIA: OFFICIAL STANDARD NAMES APPROVED BY
       THE UNITED STATES BOARD ON GEOGRAPHIC NAMES. Washington, 1968.
       61 p. map. (Gazetteer no. 106)

See note on series, no. 484.

1416. U.S. Operations Mission to Liberia. [Reports] Washington, 195-

    Issued by the International Cooperation Administration, etc.

    American cooperation in economic aid to Liberia has been intensified
since World War II, and many missions have made reports. Among the
more substantial are the following:

a) FOREST RESOURCES OF LIBERIA. Washington, 1951. 69 p. map,
        tables. (AGRICULTURE INFORMATION BULLETIN, no. 67)

b) FROM STRENGTH TO STRENGTH. Completion of tour report by Griffith
        J. Davis, audiovisual advisor. [Monrovia, Authority Govt.
        Print Off., 1953] 79 l. illus.

c) GOVERNMENT BUILDING ACTIVITIES IN LIBERIA, 1954-1956. Completion
        report by Fred V. Annis, architectural advisor. [Monrovia?
        1956?] 76 p. illus., maps.

d) THE MARINE FISHERIES PROGRAM IN LIBERIA. 1955- [n.p.] illus.
        Annual report.

e) RECONNAISSANCE SOIL SURVEY OF LIBERIA. Washington, 1951. 107 p.
        maps, diagrs., tables. (AGRICULTURE INFORMATION BULLETIN,
        no. 66)

f) THIRD REPORT ON FORESTRY PROGRESS IN LIBERIA, 1951-1959.
        Washington, 1961. 1 v. various pagings. illus., maps.

g) 12 YEARS OF MUTUAL COOPERATION, 1944-1957. Terminal report by
        Frank E. Pinder, chief agriculturist. [Washington, 1958?]
        35 l. illus., fold. map.

NIGERIA

Atlas

1417. Philip (George) and Son, Ltd. PHILIPS' ATLAS FOR EASTERN NIGERIA.
        Edited by Harold Fullard. London, 1964. 24 p. col. maps,
        col. plans.

    The atlas first presents maps of Eastern Nigeria--its physio-
graphy, climate, provinces, vegetation, and economy--and town plans
of Enugu, Port Harcourt, Lagos, and Onitsha. These are followed by

various maps of Nigeria as a whole, West Africa, the African continent, and other continents.

Bibliographies

1418.   Abimbola, S. O. INDEX TO NIGERIANA IN SELECTED PERIODICALS, 1966.
        Lagos, National Library of Nigeria, 1968. 39 p. (National
        library publication 11)

        Indexes 22 periodicals published in Nigeria or of Nigerian
interest (such as West Africa). Arrangement is a combined subject/
author listing of articles published in 1966. Book reviews are included. Hopefully this will be an annual publication.

1419.   Aboyade, 'Bimpe. "A Preliminary Bibliography of Nigerian Languages,
        Hausa, Yoruba and Igbo." AFRICAN NOTES (Ibadan), Special Supple-
        ment, v. 5, no. 1, 1968: i-xxvi.

        Lists 276 books, articles, government publications in English,
French, German and Russian from the nineteenth century to the 1960's.
Arrangement is by language and under each the following subject breakdown: general, manuals, dictionaries and vocabulary, orthography,
phonology, grammar, dialects. Excludes publications in the languages
as such.

1420.   African Bibliographic Center, Washington, D.C. PRELUDE--COUP D'ETAT--
        MILITARY GOVERNMENT: A BIBLIOGRAPHICAL AND RESEARCH GUIDE TO
        NIGERIAN POLITICS AND GOVERNMENT, JANUARY 1965 TO FEBRUARY 1966.
        Compiled by Daniel G. Matthews. Washington, 1966. 21 l.
        (Special Bibliographic Series, v. 4, no. 1)

        This timely bibliographical study includes a chronology of events,
lists of cabinet officers, and other informational data as well as a
selected bibliography of periodical articles, papers, and documents.

1421.   "African Ephemeral Materials: Three Collections on Nigeria."
        AFRICANA NEWSLETTER, v. 1, no. 4, Winter 1963: 17-25.

        Material held by the libraries of the University of California at
Los Angeles, the Hoover Institution, and Western Michigan University.

1422.   Ahmadu Bello University, Zaria, Nigeria. Institute of Administration.
        PUBLICATIONS OF THE GOVERNMENT OF THE NORTHERN REGION OF NIGERIA.
        Zaria. Mimeographed. 33 cm.

_____. _____. PUBLICATIONS PERTAINING TO NIGERIA IN THE
INSTITUTE LIBRARY. Zaria. Mimeographed. 33 cm.

Two bibliographical projects currently being carried on at the
University in Zaria.

1423. Akinyotu, Adetunji, comp. A BIBLIOGRAPHY ON DEVELOPMENT PLANNING IN
NIGERIA, 1955-1968. Ibadan, Nigerian Institute of Social and
Economic Research, 1968. 133 p.

Over 1,080 entries--books, pamphlets, articles, and government
documents--arranged by subject.

1424. Cole, Herbert M., and Robert Farris Thompson. BIBLIOGRAPHY OF YORUBA
SCULPTURE. New York, Museum of Primitive Art, 1964. 11 p.
(Primitive Art Bibliographies, no. 3)

Not an exhaustive bibliography but an aid to research. It surveys
book, pamphlet, and periodical literature. There are two parts: first,
sources on the Yoruba; second, general handbooks and exhibition
catalogues.

1425. Dipeolu, J. O. BIBLIOGRAPHICAL SOURCES FOR NIGERIAN STUDIES. Evanston,
Ill., Northwestern University, 1966. 26 p.

Most entries are annotated, some evaluatively. Arrangment proceeds
from general to topical (geography, agriculture and botany, anthropology,
etc.). Excluded are bibliographies which have been superseded by more
comprehensive or up-to-date ones.

1426. Harris, John. BOOKS ABOUT NIGERIA: A SELECT READING LIST. 4th ed.
Ibadan, Ibadan University Press, 1963. 52 p.

A useful classified and annotated reading list of 300 to 400
titles, including periodicals and official reports of the federal
and regional governments, compiled by the then librarian of the
University of Ibadan.

1427. Ibadan. University. Library. NIGERIAN PUBLICATIONS. 1950/52-
Ibadan, Ibadan University Press. Annual.

Until recently the only national bibliography published in black
Africa, this serial has continued annually since the 1950/52 volume,
with quarterly processed supplements. Before 1962 the publication
appeared under the university's earlier name, University College;

beginning with the 1961 edition the subtitle has been CURRENT NATIONAL
BIBLIOGRAPHY (early issues were subtitled A LIST OF WORKS RECEIVED
UNDER THE PUBLICATIONS ORDINANCE). Each issue carries a comprehensive
listing of books, pamphlets, and documents in English and African
languages published in the Federation. Since 1955 the issues include
a section of new and defunct serial titles supplementing a monograph
titled NIGERIAN PERIODICALS AND NEWSPAPERS, 1950-1955: A LIST OF THOSE
RECEIVED FROM APRIL 1950 TO JUNE 1955 UNDER THE PUBLICATIONS ORDINANCE,
1950 (1956, 23 p.). See also the Library's THESES AND DISSERTATIONS
ACCEPTED FOR HIGHER DEGREES, 1964-1968 (Ibadan, 1969, 13 l.).

1428. Ike, Adebimpe O. ECONOMIC DEVELOPMENT OF NIGERIA, 1950-1964: A
          BIBLIOGRAPHY. Nsukka, Library, University of Nigeria, 1966.
          129 p. Processed. (University of Nigeria Library Series, no. 1)

       Entries, some of which are annotated, are arranged by subject
according to the Library of Congress classification scheme. Topics
covered are population, economic conditions, economic planning, land,
agriculture, industry, minerals, labor, transportation and communication,
commerce and trade, and finance (including banking). For each topic
publications on the whole country are given first, with regions following. Geographical divisions are further subdivided into two sections:
books and pamphlets in one; periodical articles in another. Included
are official publications as well as books which do not deal primarily
with the subject but contain substantial sections on the Nigerian
economy. There are author and title indexes.

1429. Livingston, William S., ed. FEDERALISM IN THE COMMONWEALTH: A
          BIBLIOGRAPHICAL COMMENTARY. London, Published for the Hansard
          Society by Cassell, 1963. xviii, 237 p.

       A group of expert bibliographical essays, one of which is "Feder-
alism in Nigeria," by Grady H. Nunn (p. 173-192).

1430. Nigeria. Ministry of Works and Housing. Survey Division. CATALOG
          OF MAPS, JUNE 1968. Lagos, Federal Surveys, 1968. 109 p. maps.

1431. Nigeria. National Library. National Library Publication [series].
          no. 1- Lagos, 1966-

       a) SPECIAL LIBRARIES IN NIGERIA. 1966. 4 p.

       b) THE ARTS IN NIGERIA: A SELECTIVE BIBLIOGRAPHY. 1967. 5 p.

       c) SERIALS IN PRINT IN NIGERIA. 1967. 40 p.

       d) 18TH AND 19TH CENTURY AFRICANA IN THE NATIONAL LIBRARY OF
              NIGERIA. 1967. 6 p.

e)   INDEX TO SELECTED NIGERIAN PERIODICALS, 1965-

f)   A BIBLIOGRAPHY OF BIOGRAPHIES AND MEMOIRS ON NIGERIA. 1968.
      11 p.   (Publications, no. 9)

      Arrangement is alphabetical by author. Regular biblio-
graphical information is provided, but no page numbers are
given. Included are travel memoirs, autobiographies, biographies by Nigerians on individuals not directly connected with
Nigeria, and straight biographies.

      See also Nigeria, National Library, LAGOS PAST AND PRESENT: AN
HISTORICAL BIBLIOGRAPHY (Lagos, 1968, 42 p.; Occasional Publication,
no. 1).

1432. Nigerian Institute of Social and Economic Research. A LIST OF BOOKS,
       ARTICLES AND GOVERNMENT PUBLICATIONS ON THE ECONOMY OF NIGERIA,
       1967. Compiled by Johanna Visser. Ibadan, NISER, 1969. 84 p.
       Mimeographed.

      Brings up to date previous editions (the first, 1960-62, was
compiled by Juliet O. Kemp; the succeeding three, 1963-64, 1965, and
1966, were compiled by Johanna Visser). No analysis of the daily press
has been attempted. The 407 entries are arranged under 28 main headings. Included is a list of bibliographies and one of reading lists,
and there is an author index. The Institute issues other bibliographies;
for example, O. G. Tamuno, THE E.E.C. AND DEVELOPING NATIONS: A
BIBLIOGRAPHY (1967, 49 p.).

1433. O'Connell, James. "A Survey of Selected Social Science Research on
       Nigeria since the End of 1957." In Tilman, Robert O., and
       Taylor Cole, eds. THE NIGERIAN POLITICAL SCENE. Durham, N.C.,
       Duke University Press, 1962: 287-327.

      A useful bibliographical article on Nigeria which covers history,
political development, public administration, sociology, law, education,
economic development, and research up to 1962.

1434. Ogunsheye, Felicia Adetowun. A PRELIMINARY BIBLIOGRAPHY OF THE YORUBA
       LANGUAGE. Ibadan, Institute of Librarianship, University of
       Nigeria, 1963. 38 p.

      List of writings from 1840 to 1963 in or about the Yoruba language.

1435. Oni-Orisan, B. A., comp. A BIBLIOGRAPHY OF NIGERIAN HISTORY. Ibadan,
       University of Ibadan Library, 1968. 124 p. Mimeographed.

An attempt to list all known books, pamphlets and articles on Nigerian history. The work lists 1,502 items arranged under twelve headings. Supplements are to be issued.

1436. Perry, Ruth. A PRELIMINARY BIBLIOGRAPHY OF THE LITERATURE OF NATIONALISM IN NIGERIA. [London, International African Institute, 1956.] 38 p. Processed.

A well-known pioneer work by a librarian from the Hoover Institution at Stanford University who had studied under a Fulbright grant in Nigeria. Nine pages of this posthumously issued booklet are devoted to a review of the educational and literary aspects of Nigerian nationalism from the mid-nineteenth-century beginnings through its great upsurge during the 1950's. Her bibliography is limited to titles of works--mainly pamphlets--on politics, history, tribal laws and customs, biographies, and trade union publications printed by the private presses of Nigeria. Sixty-five percent of the almost 300 items listed are preserved in the library of the University College at Ibadan; the rest are in local and private collections.

1437. "The Press of Nigeria." AFRICANA NEWSLETTER, v. 1, no. 3, Summer 1963: 40-45.

Newspapers and periodicals, daily, weekly, monthly, and quarterly, published in Nigeria; 85 titles in all. Official serials are included. Fifty-three are entirely in English, with Hausa (11) and Yoruba (7) next. Publications of the Gaskiya Corporation in Zaria are in Hausa and eight other vernacular languages.

1438. THE PROGRESS OF NIGERIAN PUBLIC ADMINISTRATION, A REPORT ON RESEARCH. Compiled by D. J. Murray, J. Barbour, E. O. Kowe. Ife Institute of Administration, University of Ife, 1968. 238 p.

Lists 1,673 items published between Jan. 1, 1960 and Apr. 1968. Arrangement is by type of publication, i.e., books, articles, papers and reports, theses, government publications, research in progress; then by subjects: i.e., federal, regional and state governments; para-governmental bodies; local government; political and constitutional development. Subject coverage is quite broad, and there is an author index.

1439. Shaw, Thurstan, and Joel Vanderburg. A BIBLIOGRAPHY OF NIGERIAN ARCHAEOLOGY. Ibadan, Ibadan University Press for Institute of African Studies, University of Ibadan, 1969. 68 p.

Covers literature from the mid-nineteenth century to the mid-1960's. The first part is a subject arrangement of books, pamphlets, articles, and theses. The second part is an alphabetical listing by author of the same items listed in the first part. This work is of value to anyone interested in Nigerian art and archaeology, early history, and museums.

1440. U.S. Library of Congress. General Reference and Bibliography Division. NIGERIA: A GUIDE TO OFFICIAL PUBLICATIONS. Compiled by Sharon Lockwood, African Section. Washington, 1966. xii, 166 p.

A very full bibliography, much of it based on archival records from Nigerian sources. Over 2,450 numbered titles are given, many of those from before 1947 being unavailable in American libraries. There are four parts: (1) publications issued 1861-1914; (2) publications of the federal and regional governments, 1914-65, and of the Southern Cameroons, 1954-61; (3) British publications relating to Nigeria; and (4) League of Nations publications relating to Nigeria and UN publications on the trusteeship territory of the Cameroons. This compilation supersedes an earlier list compiled in 1959.

Serials

Note: Since the civil war of 1966-67 conditions in Nigeria as regards serials are unstable.

1441. Historical Society of Nigeria. JOURNAL. 1956- Ibadan. Annual.

Edited at the University of Ibadan, this scholarly journal contains significant contributions to historical research. It concentrates on, but is by no means confined to, Nigeria and West Africa.

A new historical magazine, TARIKH, began publication (by Longmans) in 1965 under the editorship of Dr. J. B. Webster of the History Department of the University of Ibadan. Articles, Pan-African in content, are to be of general interest, "pleasant and readable," addressed in particular to secondary school and undergraduate students. The articles are by experts in their respective fields.

The University of Ife also issues irregularly AFRICAN HISTORIAN.

1442. NIGERIA MAGAZINE. no. 1- 1934- Lagos, Federal Govt. illus. Quarterly.

Government-sponsored periodical, begun by the Education Department with the title NIGERIAN TEACHER, later changed to NIGERIA:
A QUARTERLY MAGAZINE OF GENERAL INTEREST. This is a distinguished
journal, handsomely illustrated, with issues often devoted to a
single theme or a special publication. The editor in 1970 is
T. O. A. Adebango.

1443. NIGERIA TRADE JOURNAL. v. 1- Jan. 1953- Lagos. illus. (part
        col.), maps. Quarterly.

        Published by the Federal Department of Commerce and Industry.

1444. NIGERIA YEAR BOOK. 1952- Lagos, Daily Times Publication. (1967 ed.,
        308 p.). illus. Annual.

        Directory and guide of the almanac type, including a political
who's who, a trade directory, and a register of the federal and
regional governments.

1445. NIGERIAN BAR JOURNAL. v. 1- 1958- Lagos, Nigerian Bar Association.
        Annual.

1446. NIGERIAN GEOGRAPHICAL JOURNAL. v. 1, no. 1- Apr. 1957- Ibadan.
        Irregular.

        Organ of the Nigerian Geographical Association, which, like a
number of other learned societies, has its headquarters at the
University of Ibadan.

1447. Nigerian Institute of Social and Economic Research. ANNUAL CONFERENCE
        PROCEEDINGS. 1952- Ibadan, The Institute, University of Ibadan.

        The latest report of this institute, formerly the West African
Institute of Social and Economic Research, appeared in 1963 (230 p.).

1448. NIGERIAN JOURNAL OF ECONOMIC AND SOCIAL STUDIES. no. 1- May 1959-
        Ibadan. 3 times a year.

        Publication of the Nigerian Economic Society, edited at University
College, Ibadan.

1449. NIGERIAN OPINION: A MAGAZINE OF THE NIGERIAN CURRENT AFFAIRS SOCIETY.
v. 1- 1965- Ibadan. Bimonthly.

1450. ODU: UNIVERSITY OF IFE JOURNAL OF AFRICAN STUDIES. v. 1- 1960-
Ibadan. Twice yearly. (Supersedes ODU: JOURNAL OF YORUBA AND
RELATED STUDIES, 1955-1960.)

1451. TARIKH: LEADERSHIP IN NINETEENTH-CENTURY AFRICA. 1965- London,
Published for the Historical Society of Nigeria by Longmans
of Nigeria Ltd. Semiannual.

1452. WEST AFRICAN PILOT. Lagos. Daily.

This newspaper, founded by Nnamdi Azikiwe in Nov. 1937 and
serving as the leading organ in the long nationalist struggle, is
perhaps still the most influential of Nigerian newspapers. A
complete file, in part filled out on microfilm, is held by the
Library of Congress. (For other newspaper titles, see nos. 397
and 398.)

Reference Works

1453. Awa, Eme O. FEDERAL GOVERNMENT IN NIGERIA. Berkeley, University
of California Press, 1964. 349 p.

Bibliography: p. 329-335.

A solidly informative study analyzing the provisions of the
Nigerian constitution and the working of governmental institutions.

1454. Awolowo, Obafemi. AWO: THE AUTOBIOGRAPHY OF CHIEF OBAFEMI AWOLOWO.
Cambridge, Eng., University Press, 1960. xii, 315 p. illus.

The personal story of the former head of the Western Region's
"loyal opposition" Action Group, covering the preindependence part
of his checkered career, is a primary source for the history of
Nigerian nationalism.

1455. Ayandele, E. A. THE MISSIONARY IMPACT ON MODERN NIGERIA 1842-1914:
A POLITICAL AND SOCIAL ANALYSIS. London, Longmans, 1966. 393 p.
plates, map.

Bibliography: p. 347-360.

See also J. F. Ade Ajayi, CHRISTIAN MISSIONS IN NIGERIA 1841-1891: THE MAKING OF A NEW ELITE (London, Longmans, 1965, 317 p.). Both works are excellent examples of the new African history written by Africans.

1456. Azikiwe, Nnamdi. ZIK: A SELECTION FROM THE SPEECHES OF NNAMDI AZIKIWE. Cambridge, Eng., University Press, 1961. 344 p. illus.

This selection of the speeches of the dynamic leader of Nigerian nationalism, formerly Premier of Eastern Nigeria, and Governor-General of the Federation of Nigeria from Oct. 1960, begins with his lectures as a graduate student in America in 1927 and offers the most celebrated examples of Zik's oratory through 1959. Among the topics are education, democracy, the color bar, finance and banking, the press and broadcasting, Moral Re-Armament, local government, the Church Missionary Society, and many aspects of anticolonial politics.

1457. Balewa, Sir Abubakar Tafawa. NIGERIA SPEAKS: COLLECTED SPEECHES, 1957-64. Selected by Sam Epelle. London, Longmans, Green, 1964. 178 p.

Collection of primary source material for recent history by the late premier of Nigeria. The editor has supplied a general introduction and notes for each speech.

1458. Bello, Sir Ahmadu. MY LIFE. Cambridge, Eng., University Press, 1962. 245 p.

The autobiography of the late Sardauna of Sokoto, political and spiritual leader of Northern Nigeria.

1459. Bivar, A. D. H. NIGERIAN PANOPLY: ARMS AND ARMOUR OF THE NORTHERN REGION. Lagos, Dept. of Antiquities, Federal Republic of Nigeria, 1964. 68 p. illus., 22 plates.

Bibliography: p. 43-44.

1460. Cohen, Ronald. THE KANURI OF BORNU. New York, Holt, Rinehart and Winston, 1967. 115 p. illus., map. (Case Studies in Cultural Anthropology)

Bibliography: p. 113-115.

After sketching the historical background of the Kanem-Bornu area, the study proceeds with an analysis of the Kanuri family and household, the life cycle, economic life, and political organization. The author spent approximately two years in Bornu in 1956-57, 1964, and 1965.

1461.   Coker, Increase Herbert Ebenezer. LANDMARKS OF THE NIGERIAN PRESS: AN OUTLINE OF THE ORIGINS AND DEVELOPMENT OF THE NEWSPAPER PRESS IN NIGERIA: 1859 TO 1965. Apapa, 1968. 126 p. facsims.

Includes bibliography.

History of the Nigerian press for popular audience but with valuable information on people and newspapers. There are lists of newspapers from 1859 to 1965.

1462.   Coleman, James S. NIGERIA: BACKGROUND TO NATIONALISM. Berkeley, University of California Press, 1958. xiv, 510 p. illus., ports., maps.

Bibliography: p. 481-496.

History of the emergence of the Nigerian nation from colony to full self-government, ending three years short of independence. The first part gives physical, cultural, and historical background, the second an analysis of the factors in the Western impact which led to social and political change. With Part 3, p. 169, Dr. Coleman turns to a detailed account of the beginnings and progress of the nationalist movement in the interwar years; in the last part, he carries it to the postwar achievement of the new era of self-government. The work is considered a notable contribution to scholarship on African affairs.

1463.   Crowder, Michael. A SHORT HISTORY OF NIGERIA. Rev. and enl. ed. New York, Praeger, 1966. 416 p. illus., ports, maps (1 fold.). (Books That Matter)

Bibliography: p. 379-389.

A narrative of Nigerian history, based largely on modern research and written as a clear account for the general reader. Much important new material is provided in this new edition of a work originally published in 1962. Appendixes include a summary of major events from independence to Dec. 1964 and several dynastic lists. There are end-notes and an excellent analytical index.

The older standard HISTORY OF NIGERIA by Sir Alan C. Burns was first published in 1929 and is largely confined to the period of

European control. In the latest revision (7th ed., New York, Barnes
& Noble, 1969, 366 p., maps) the account of political and social
change is brought up through the first years of independence.
Appendixes (p. 312-343) include text of treaties. References are
indicated in footnotes. See also J. C. Anene, SOUTHERN NIGERIA IN
TRANSITION 1885-1906: THEORY AND PRACTICE IN A COLONIAL PROTECTORATE
(Cambridge, Eng., University Press, 1966, 360 p., illus., map, tables;
bibliography: p. 340-346); and Saburi O. Biobaku, THE EGBA AND THEIR
NEIGHBOURS, 1842-1872 (Oxford, Clarendon Press, 1957, 128 p.; bibliography: p. 108-118).

1464.   Dike, Kenneth Onwuka. TRADE AND POLITICS IN THE NIGER DELTA, 1830-
            1885: AN INTRODUCTION TO THE ECONOMIC AND POLITICAL HISTORY OF
            NIGERIA. Oxford, Clarendon Press, 1956. 250 p. map, tables.
         (Oxford Studies in African Affairs)

         Bibliographical references in "Notes on the Sources": p. 224-230.

         This distinguished African historian, formerly professor, now
principal, at University College, Ibadan (which in 1962 became the
University of Ibadan), is also on the editorial board of the JOURNAL
OF AFRICAN HISTORY and a leading figure in African scholarship. His
book of 1956, based on his doctoral thesis at the University of London,
is a thoroughly documented study of the gradual supplanting of the
native governments of Nigeria by British administration. See also
G. I. Jones, THE TRADING STATES OF THE OIL RIVERS: A STUDY OF POLITICAL
DEVELOPMENT IN EASTERN NIGERIA (London, Oxford University Press, 1963,
263 p.).

1465.   Diplomatic Press. TRADE DIRECTORY OF THE FEDERAL REPUBLIC OF NIGERIA,
            INCLUDING CLASSIFIED TRADE INDEX. 1960- London, Diplomatic
            Press and Publishing Co. illus., ports., map.

         Useful reference work, the first editions of which appeared
under a slightly different title. The fourth edition (1965-66,
180 p.) has two sections; the first covers government and administration,
with register of government personnel, and many aspects of the economy,
and the second is a trade index, with classified list of firms. Advertisements appear lavishly throughout, and there is an index of advertisers. Earlier editions carried some biographical and cultural
material.

1466.   Eastern Region of Nigeria. Ministry of Information. KNOW YOUR
            LEGISLATORS: BIOGRAPHICAL NOTES, 1963. Enugu, Govt. Printer,
            1963. 118 p. ports.

Portraits and biographies of the governor, premier, ministers, provincial commissioners, parliamentary secretaries, and members of the House of Assembly and the House of Chiefs of Eastern Nigeria in 1963. Included is a section on the 1961 election and a list of election results by constituency.

1467. Eastern Region of Nigeria. Ministry of Information. NIGERIAN CRISIS, 1966. Enugu, Govt. Printer, 1966-67. 7 v.

A review (analyses, reports, and documents) of the turbulent and tragic events of 1966. The seven volumes are as follows:

v. 1. EASTERN NIGERIA VIEWPOINT. 1966. 68 p.

v. 2. THE PROBLEM OF NIGERIAN UNITY (THE CASE OF EASTERN NIGERIA). 1966. 50 p.

v. 3. NIGERIAN POGROM: THE ORGANIZED MASSACRE OF EASTERN NIGERIANS. 27 p. plates.

v. 4. THE AD HOC CONFERENCE ON THE NIGERIAN CONSTITUTION. 1966. 129 p.

v. 5. THE NORTH AND CONSTITUTIONAL DEVELOPMENTS IN NIGERIA. 1966. 40 p.

v. 6. THE MEETING OF THE SUPREME MILITARY COUNCIL AT ABURI, ACCRA, GHANA, 4-5 JANUARY 1967. 1967. 64 p.

v. 7. JANUARY 15: BEFORE AND AFTER. 1966. 91 p.

1468. Elias, Taslim Olawale. NIGERIA: THE DEVELOPMENT OF ITS LAWS AND CONSTITUTIONS. London, Stevens, 1967. xii, 491 p. tables. (British Commonwealth, The Development of Its Laws and Constitutions, v. 14)

Bibliographical footnotes.

An excellent volume on the legal and constitutional problems of Africa's most populous country. Dr. Elias provides a comprehensive analysis of the Federal legislature, executive, and judiciary, describes in some detail their historical evolution, and discusses the relations between the Federal and Regional authorities. He also deals amply with the economic and social aspects of Nigerian life and treats extensively not only the laws of the professions but also commercial and industrial laws. A table of statutes and one of cases are given, and there is an index.

NIGERIAN LAND LAW AND CUSTOM (3d ed. rev., London, Routledge & Kegan Paul, 1962, 386 p.), a work first published as Dr. Elias' LL.D. thesis at the University of London, has, since the second edition of 1953, been recognized as a standard study of the principles of Nigerian land tenure in the light of "the growing body of case law." The text is preceded by a table of cases and a table of ordinances and concludes with bibliography and index. A second book, THE NIGERIAN LEGAL SYSTEM (2d ed. rev., London, Routledge & Kegan Paul, 1963, xxxvii, 386 p.), was originally titled GROUNDWORK OF NIGERIAN LAW (1954, xxx, 374 p.) and was intended as a textbook for fellow countrymen who, like the author, take law degrees abroad and return to practice in Nigeria. Dr. Elias became Attorney General of Nigeria in 1960. See also Oluwole I. Odumosu, THE NIGERIAN CONSTITUTION: HISTORY AND DEVELOPMENT (London, Sweet & Maxwell, 1963, 407 p.). For an excellent administrative survey see I. F. Nicolson, THE ADMINISTRATION OF NIGERIA, 1905-1960: MEN, METHODS AND MYTHS (Oxford, Clarendon Press, 1969, 326 p.).

1469. Ethnographic Survey of Africa: Western Africa. London, International African Institute.

For the general note on this series, see no. 980. The following surveys relating to Nigeria summarize ethnological findings to the time of their publication, and each has tribal maps and three or four pages of bibliographical data.

a)   3.   THE IBO AND IBIBIO-SPEAKING PEOPLES OF SOUTH-EASTERN NIGERIA. By Daryll Forde and G. I. Jones. 1950. 80 p.

b)   4.   THE YORUBA-SPEAKING PEOPLES OF SOUTH-WESTERN NIGERIA. By Daryll Forde. 1951. 102 p.

c)   7.   THE PEOPLES OF THE PLATEAU AREA OF NORTHERN NIGERIA. By Harold D. Gunn. 1953. 111 p.

d)   8.   THE TIV OF CENTRAL NIGERIA. By Laura Bohannan and Paul Bohannan. 1953. 100 p.

e) 10.   PEOPLES OF THE NIGER-BENUE CONFLUENCE. Nupe, by Daryll Forde; Igbira, by Paul Brown; Igala and Idoma-speaking Peoples, by Robert G. Armstrong. 1955. 160 p.

f) 12.   PAGAN PEOPLES OF THE CENTRAL AREA OF NORTHERN NIGERIA. By Harold D. Gunn. 1956. 146 p.

g) 13.   THE BENIN KINGDOM AND THE EDO-SPEAKING PEOPLES OF SOUTH-WESTERN NIGERIA. By R. E. Bradbury. 1957. 212 p.

h) 15.   PEOPLES OF THE MIDDLE NIGER REGION OF NORTHERN NIGERIA. By Harold D. Gunn and F. P. Conant. 1960. 136 p.

1470. Ezera, Kalu. CONSTITUTIONAL DEVELOPMENTS IN NIGERIA: AN ANALYTICAL
       STUDY OF NIGERIA'S CONSTITUTION-MAKING DEVELOPMENTS AND THE
       HISTORICAL AND POLITICAL FACTORS THAT AFFECTED CONSTITUTIONAL
       CHANGE. 2d ed. Cambridge, Eng., University Press, 1964. xvi,
       315 p. maps.

       Bibliography: p. 301-309.

       Clear, factual analysis of the constitutional history of Nigeria,
first published in 1960. A new chapter, "Independent Nigeria, 1960-
63" (p. 262-300) has been added. Dr. Ezera, now at the University of
Nigeria, studied in America (Lincoln University and Harvard), was a
research student at Nuffield College, and received his doctorate at
Oxford.

1471. Fagg, William B. NIGERIAN IMAGES: THE SPLENDOR OF AFRICAN SCULPTURE.
       Photos. by Herbert List. New York, Praeger, 1963. 124 p. 144
       plates, map.

       Bibliography: p. 10.

       An authoritative account of the great works of Benin, Ife, and
later Nigerian sculpture by the assistant keeper of the British
Museum's Department of Ethnography. His text is accompanied by a
section of impressive plates.

1472. Flint, John E. NIGERIA AND GHANA. Englewood Cliffs, N.J., Prentice-
       Hall, 1966. 176 p. (Modern Nations in Historical Perspective)

       Explains, in terms of historical events and experiences that pre-
dated the coming of the white man, the vivid contrasts existing between these two representative African nations--including differences
in government, political, and social ideals, size, wealth, and relative
status among other African states. Focusing on the precolonial past,
the author discusses the Negro colonization of West Africa, tracing
the growth of black empires in the medieval period and describing the
effects of the slave trade, Christianity, and Islam on the formation
of Nigeria and Ghana today. Then, in a perceptive interpretation of
the more recent impact of colonialism and African nationalism, the
author explores the broader themes of society, politics, and culture
in present-day Nigeria and Ghana.

1473. Food and Agriculture Organization of the United Nations. AGRICULTURAL
       DEVELOPMENT IN NIGERIA, 1965-1980. Rome, 1966. xx, 512 p. maps.

       Prepared by the FAO at the request of the Federal Government of
Nigeria. Detailed programs for cocoa, rubber, and palm production are

given special attention. The importance of diversification and of the growth of processing industries is stressed, as well as the need to improve the quality of diet, mainly by increasing the supply of high-protein foods.

1474.   Heussler, Robert. THE BRITISH IN NORTHERN NIGERIA. London, Oxford University Press, 1968. xxi, 210 p.

Includes bibliography.

1475.   Hodgkin, Thomas L. NIGERIAN PERSPECTIVES: AN HISTORICAL ANTHOLOGY. London, Oxford University Press, 1960. xviii, 340 p. illus. (West African History Series)

Bibliographical footnotes.

Called by reviewers "indispensable," this selection of documents is concerned with the precolonial history of Nigerian peoples. The extracts are from European and Arabic sources, recorded oral tradition, local chronicles, etc., were chosen to illustrate the past of five major regions--Kanem-Bornu, the Hausa States, the Oyo Empire and Yoruba successor states of the nineteenth century, the Kingdoms of Benin and Warri, and the Delta States and Iboland.

1476.   Hogben, Sidney John, and Anthony H. M. Kirk-Greene. THE EMIRATES OF NORTHERN NIGERIA: A PRELIMINARY SURVEY OF THEIR HISTORICAL TRADITIONS. London, Oxford University Press, 1966. xxvii, 638 p. illus., maps (1 fold. col.), geneal. tables.

Bibliography: p. [593]-603.

A reorganized and extensively expanded version of Hogben's THE MUHAMMADAN EMIRATES OF NIGERIA (1930). Part 1 (p. 3-146), by Hogben, presents a broad historical survey of the Western Sudan. Part 2, by both authors, is comprised of individual histories of 37 Northern Nigerian traditional states--the emirates deriving from the Hausa states and from the Bornu and Sokoto empires and those deriving independently. Included are a glossary, notes on European travelers in the Sudan and Sahara, 1875-1880, and a list of Northern Nigerian chiefs.

1477.   International Bank for Reconstruction and Development. THE ECONOMIC DEVELOPMENT OF NIGERIA: REPORT OF A MISSION ORGANIZED BY THE INTERNATIONAL BANK FOR RECONSTRUCTION AND DEVELOPMENT AT THE REQUEST OF THE GOVERNMENTS OF NIGERIA AND THE UNITED KINGDOM. Baltimore, Johns Hopkins Press, 1955. xxii, 686 p. maps, diagrs., tables.

A study prepared in connection with technical aid by a mission
of experts on agriculture, money and banking, transportation, mineral
resources, roads, and water resources and power who made a full survey
in late 1953. The first part of the report embodies recommendations
for organization and financing of a five-year development program.
Part 2 consists of technical reports on specific phases, and Part 3
of appendixes giving mainly statistical data. Many maps, charts,
and tables appear throughout the volume. There are a few footnotes
indicating statistical sources.

1478. Keay, R. W. J. AN OUTLINE OF NIGERIAN VEGETATION. 2d ed. Lagos,
        Govt. Printer, 1953. 55 p. illus., fold. col. map.

        Bibliography: p. 39-43.

1479. Kirk-Greene, Anthony H. M., ed. THE PRINCIPLES OF NATIVE ADMINISTRATION
        IN NIGERIA: SELECTED DOCUMENTS, 1900-1947. London, Oxford
        University Press, 1965. 248 p.

        There is a foreword by Margery Perham; Mr. Kirk-Greene, formerly
a civil administrator, has provided a scholarly introduction (p. 1-42).
Documents run from the first in 1903, the address at Sokoto by Lugard,
to the last in 1947, the local government dispatch by Arthur Creech
Jones, Colonial Secretary.

1480. Leighton, Alexander H., T. Adeoye Lambo, Charles C. Hughes, Dorothea
        C. Leighton, Jane M. Murphy, and David B. Macklin. PSYCHIATRIC
        DISORDER AMONG THE YORUBA: A REPORT FROM THE CORNELL-ARO MENTAL
        HEALTH RESEARCH PROJECT IN THE WESTERN REGION, NIGERIA. Ithaca,
        N.Y., Cornell University Press, 1963. 413 p. illus., map., diagrs.,
        tables.

        Bibliography: p. 395-403.

        This book is a report on "the result of an attempt to estimate
types and prevalence of psychiatric disorder and to explore sociocultural
influences in a selected number of rural villages and one urban center
among the Yoruba of Nigeria." One of its major authors, T. Adeoye
Lambo, is a Nigerian psychiatrist.

1481. Mackay, Ian K. BROADCASTING IN NIGERIA. Ibadan, Ibadan University
        Press, 1964. 159 p. illus., ports., maps, diagrs.

        Bibliography: p. 105-108.

A description and appraisal of broadcasting in Nigeria by the
last expatriate director-general of the Nigerian Broadcasting Corporation (described as the largest broadcasting organization in Africa).
Mr. Mackay points out the significant role of broadcasting as a social
force in Nigeria, offers a plan for the future, and concludes his
account with 50 pages of appendixes.

1482. Mercier, Paul. CIVILISATIONS DU BENIN. Paris, Société Continentale
d'Editions Moderns Illustrées, 1962. 365 p. illus., plates
(part col.), maps. (Connaissance de l'Afrique)

For annotation see no. 1692.

1483. NATIONAL DIRECTORY OF NIGERIA. 3d ed. London, UNIMEX, 1964. 303 p.
illus., maps.

A commercial directory, beginning with slight general information
and followed by a business directory, first in an alphabetical list,
then a classified list. Last are tables of commercial intelligence.

1484. Nederlands Adviesbureau voor Ingenieurswerken in het Buitenland.
RIVER STUDIES AND RECOMMENDATIONS ON IMPROVEMENT OF NIGER AND
BENUE. Amsterdam, North-Holland Pub. Co., 1959. 1000 p. illus.,
maps.

Bibliography: p. 981-989.

_____. RIVER CHARTS OF THE NIGER FROM BURUTU TO JEBBA AND THE
BENUE FROM LOKOJA TO GARUA: NIGER AND BENUE INVESTIGATION,
FINAL REPORT, 1959. The Hague, NEDECO, 1959. 64 p. of maps.
36 x 67 cm.

The first reference consists of the report of a mission by 14
Dutch engineers (Netherlands Engineering Consultants [NEDECO]) to
investigate the possibilities of improving shipping conditions on
the Niger and Benue Rivers. The work is divided into six parts:
introduction and summary; the investigation; the rivers (general
description, physiography, geology, hydrological cycle, etc.);
transport and navigation; defects of navigability; and suggestions
for improving the rivers' navigability. There is a glossary, and
an index is included in the back pocket.

1485. Nigeria. THE NIGERIA HANDBOOK. London, Published by the Crown
Agents for the Colonies on behalf of the Government of Nigeria,
1953. 339 p. illus. (part col.), tables, maps (incl. 6 fold.
col. in pocket).

484

Bibliography: p. 272-288.

This formerly indispensable work, containing essays, statistics, and tabular data on all aspects of the country and its life, is now of use mainly for historical research.

1486.   Nigeria. Commission on Post-School Certificate and Higher Education.
        INVESTMENT IN EDUCATION: REPORT. Lagos, Federal Ministry of
        Education, 1960. 140 p.

The so-called Ashby Report, named after the chairman of the Commission, Sir Eric Ashby of Cambridge University. The first of two parts is general and contains recommendations aimed at meeting Nigeria's needs for educated manpower up to 1980, with university development planned to ensure an enrollment of at least 7,500 students by 1970 and substantial growth during the next decade. The second part consists of special reports on high-level manpower needs, the sixth form and examinations, teacher training, technical and commercial education, agricultural education, universities, and new educational techniques.

A HANDBOOK OF EDUCATION, NIGERIA, 1960, edited by J. E. Adetoro, was issued as an independence-year souvenir (Oshogbo, Printed for the Schools and General Publication Services by Tanimehin-Ola Press, 1960, 280 p.). The handbook gives an outline of the history of educational development in southern and northern Nigeria, an explanation of educational development in southern and northern Nigeria, an explanation of educational systems, and a directory, with catalogue information regarding institutions of learning.

The Ministry of Education, Eastern Region of Nigeria, issued in 1964 the EDUCATION HANDBOOK, 1964, revised to July 31, 1964 (Enugu, Govt. Printer, 60 p.), which outlines the policy of education in the Eastern Region in 1963 and presents education laws and regulations of various dates.

1487.   Nigeria. Federal Ministry of Commerce and Industry. HANDBOOK OF
        COMMERCE AND INDUSTRY IN NIGERIA. 5th ed. Lagos, 1962. 398 p.

Volume of useful information for businessmen, first issued in pamphlet form in 1952. The present edition is loose-leaf to permit additions and revision. It includes surveys and statistics of economic and governmental life, useful addresses, tables, maps, and miscellaneous commercial facts. This office also issued an INDUSTRIAL DIRECTORY: A LIST OF MAJOR MANUFACTURING PLANTS IN NIGERIA (1962, 35 p.), which includes some 700 plants.

1488. Nigeria. National Economic Council. Joint Planning Committee.
ECONOMIC SURVEY OF NIGERIA, 1959. Lagos, Federal Govt. Printer,
1959. 132 p. plate, col. maps, tables.

Valuable assemblage of statistics and summary articles regarding
the position and outlook of the economy of Nigeria as of mid-1958,
with a review of economic development since 1945.

An earlier survey of somewhat the same nature, made by the Near
Eastern and African Division of the U.S. Bureau of Foreign Commerce,
was published in 1957: INVESTMENT IN NIGERIA: BASIC INFORMATION FOR
UNITED STATES BUSINESSMEN (prepared by Bernard Blakenheimer and others;
Washington, U.S. Govt. Print. Off., 182 p.).

For other official documents of Nigeria, see the Library of
Congress bibliography, no. 1440.

1489. Nigerian Broadcasting Corporation. EMINENT NIGERIANS OF THE NINE-
TEENTH CENTURY: A SERIES OF STUDIES ORIGINALLY BROADCAST BY
THE NIGERIAN BROADCASTING CORPORATION. By K. O. Dike, J. C.
Anene, and others. Cambridge, University Press, 1960. 97 p.

Following an introduction on Nigeria in the nineteenth century
by Professor Dike, 12 biographies are presented, ranging from King
William Dappa Pepple to Samuel Ajayi Crowther to Oba Overami of
Benin. Contributors include Saburi Biobaku, T. C. Eneli, H. F. C.
Smith, Robin Hallett, and Peter Lloyd.

1490. Nigerian Institute of Social and Economic Research. RESEARCH FOR
NATIONAL DEVELOPMENT. Ibadan, NISER, 1966. 138 p. Processed.

A survey of recent, current, and proposed research concerning
Nigerian economic and social development. It updates the first NISER
inventory published in Apr. 1965 and is part of a series scheduled to
be issued twice a year. Studies are arranged by type of research
organization--i.e., government departments, companies, and universities in Nigeria, institutions abroad, and international organizations.
Included are an abbreviations list and indexes of subjects and institutions. A bibliography of relevant published material and an index
of research institutions are to be published in conjunction with this
inventory.

1491. Nigerian Opinion (periodical). NIGERIA 1965: CRISIS AND CRITICISM:
SELECTIONS FROM NIGERIAN OPINION. Ibadan, Ibadan University
Press, 1966. 130 p.

NIGERIAN OPINION, a monthly magazine founded by the Nigerian Current Affairs Society and intended for the Nigerian reading public, is concerned with analysis of and commentary on political, economic, and social issues. In these selections from the first volume (1965), topics covered are the politics of development, rule and justice, competition for power, change and the constitution, economics, health and welfare, and problems of education.

1492.   Nigerian Tourist Association. GUIDE TO HOTELS AND CATERING IN NIGERIA, 1965. Lagos, NTA (P.O. Box 299, 47 Marina) [1965?].

Besides full information on hotels and rest houses in cities and towns, this guide has sections on transportation, currency and customs, places of entertainment, sightseeing, etc.

1493.   Northern Region of Nigeria. THE INDUSTRIAL POTENTIALITIES OF NORTHERN NIGERIA. Kaduna, 1963. 284 p. plates, fold. maps, diagrs., tables.

This report, compiled by the Ministry of Trade and Industry, is based on an industrial and economic survey made in 1962 by Sir Alexander Gibb & Partners in association with Industrial and Process Engineering Consultants (Great Britain) and sponsored by the Government of Northern Nigeria and the United Kingdom Department of Technical Co-operation. The work, in five parts totaling 46 chapters, begins with a description of Nigerian economy in general and goes on to a detailed analysis of Northern Nigerian prospects. There are also nine appendixes ending with a one-page bibliography (p. 284).

1494.   Nwabueze, Benjamin Obi. THE MACHINERY OF JUSTICE IN NIGERIA. London, Butterworth, 1963. xxi, 309 p. (Butterworth's African Law Series, no. 8)

See note on this series, no. 684.

1495.   OFFICIAL NIGERIA CATHOLIC DIRECTORY, 1967. Lagos, African Universities Press, 1967. 130 p.

1496.   Onyemelukwe, Clement Chukwukadibia. PROBLEMS OF INDUSTRIAL PLANNING AND MANAGEMENT IN NIGERIA. London, Longmans; New York, Columbia University Press, 1966. 330 p. tables, diagrs.

Bibliography: p. 319-322.

By the chief electrical engineer and head of the system operations
department of the Electricity Corp. of Nigeria. Included are background
information and surveys of government and industrialization, financing,
fuel and energy resources, industrial organization, industrial relations,
research and development, and manpower development.

1497. Owen, John, comp. DIRECTORY OF VOLUNTARY ORGANISATIONS IN WESTERN
      NIGERIA. Ibadan, Nigerian Institute of Social and Economic
      Research, 1966. 65 p. Processed.

      Lists organizations (including professional associations and
government-sponsored organizations) alphabetically and gives the
following information: address, secretary, date established, membership, branches, source of funds, organization, and activities.

1498. Sklar, Richard L. NIGERIAN POLITICAL PARTIES. Princeton, N.J.,
      Princeton University Press, 1963. xi, 578 p.

      Bibliography: p. 535-559.

      A detailed study of the development of the multiparty system
during the last years of British rule. The author has set his
analysis in narrative form, beginning with the rise of political
parties. Sec. 2 covers studies in power and conflict; Sec. 3, party
structure and social structures. An appendix lists party officials
and executive council members. The long and valuable bibliography
is arranged by forms of material.

1499. Stapleton, G. Brian. THE WEALTH OF NIGERIA. 2d ed. Ibadan, Oxford
      University Press, 1967. xii, 264 p. maps, tables.

      Bibliography: p. [252]-260.

      A factual analysis of the problems of Nigerian economic develop-
ment and a view on possible solutions. The first 12 chapters deal
essentially with the situation up to 1958 and include a discussion
of agricultural and industrial resources, population, public services,
national income as compared with that of other countries, integrated
development, and trade. The last chapter is devoted to development
since independence.

1500. Temple, O. NOTES ON THE TRIBES, PROVINCES, EMIRATES AND STATES OF THE
      NORTHERN PROVINCES OF NIGERIA. Compiled from Official Reports.
      2d ed. 1922.

      Reprint: London, Frank Cass 1965. 595 p.

Classic older study of the Northern Provinces. See also Murray
Last, THE SOKOTO CALIPHATE (London, Longmans, 1967, 280 p.; bibliography: p. 236-262); and M. G. Smith, GOVERNMENT IN ZAZZAU: 1800 TO
1950 (London, Oxford University Press, 1960, 371 p., maps; bibliography: p. 356-357).

1501. Weiler, Hans N., ed. ERZIEHUNG UND POLITIK IN NIGERIA. EDUCATION
          AND POLITICS IN NIGERIA. 1. Aufl. Freiburg im Breisgau, Verlag
          Rombach, 1964. 294 p. (Freiburger Studien zu Politik and
          Soziologie)

        Bibliography: p. 273-292.

        Collective study of the relationship between education and politics
in Nigeria, with contributions by well-known scholars. Among others,
Phoebe and Simon Ottenberg write on Ibo education and social change;
James O'Connell on the state and organization of elementary education;
Hugh H. Smythe on the educational foundation of Nigerian politicians;
Willfried Feuser on universities. Articles by English writers are
followed by summaries in German, those in German by summaries in
English. There are 12 pages of selected educational statistics.

1502. WHO'S WHO IN NIGERIA: A BIOGRAPHICAL DICTIONARY. 1st ed. Lagos,
          Nigerian Print. & Pub. Co., 1956. 278 p. ports.

        A DAILY TIMES publication, with biographies of more than 1,500
prominent people.

        From time to time the information services of the federal or
regional governments publish a who's who of legislative members, e.g.:

a)   WHO'S WHO OF THE FEDERAL HOUSE OF REPRESENTATIVES. Lagos, 1958.
        124 p. illus., ports.

b)   WHO'S WHO, WESTERN NIGERIA LEGISLATURE. Ibadan, Govt. Printer
        [1959?]. 53 p.

c)   WHO'S WHO, NORTHERN REGION OF NIGERIA LEGISLATURE. Kaduna,
        1961. 107 p. ports.

d)   WHO'S WHO IN MIDWESTERN NIGERIA LEGISLATURE. Compiled by
        Peter M. Ayeni. 1st ed. 81 p. ports. Benin City, 1964.

1503. Willett, Frank. IFE IN THE HISTORY OF WEST AFRICAN SCULPTURE. New
          York, McGraw-Hill, 1967. 232 p. 13 color plates, 110 mono-
          chrome plates, 41 line drawings, map. (New Aspects of Archaeology,
          edited by Sir Mortimer Wheeler)

Bibliography: p. 216-226.

At Ife in Western Nigeria in 1938 a unique group of bronze or brass sculptures, more similar to European styles than to any other African artwork, was discovered, later to be supplemented by finds of terracotta and stoneworks. The author, formerly archaeologist to the Federal Government of Nigeria and curator of the Ife Museum and now professor of African art at Northwestern University, discovered many of these sculptures himself. He presents an authoritative account of their origins and purpose, basing his description not only on the actual artworks but also on oral tradition and archaeology. The cultural setting and chronological sequence of one of the most extraordinary phases of African art history are established as Willett traces the record of the art of Ife. Many of the pieces photographed appear here for the first time in a published work, and all illustrations are accompanied by concise descriptions.

SIERRA LEONE

Atlases

1504. Clarke, John Innes, ed. SIERRA LEONE IN MAPS. London, University
           of London Press, 1966. 119 p. maps, tables, diagrs.

       Bibliography: p. 115-119.

       Fifty-one maps with brief accompanying texts illustrating the physical, social, and economic geography of Sierra Leone. Among the subjects treated are economic history, chiefdoms, ethnic groups, languages, education, transport, and external trade. The result of a collaboration by past and present members of the Department of Geography, Fourah Bay College, University College of Sierra Leone, the volume is an outstanding piece of work.

1505. Sierra Leone. Surveys and Lands Division. ATLAS OF SIERRA LEONE.
           2d ed. London, E. Stanford, 1966. 16 p. col. maps.

       Contains maps of climatic conditions, physical features, and political divisions, and a map of Freetown. Smaller maps show agricultural products, mineral deposits, the towns of Bonthe, Bo, and Magburaka, medical facilities, tribal distribution, etc. A gazetteer is included.

Bibliographies

1506. Hair, P. E. H. "A Bibliographical Guide to Sierra Leone, 1460-1650"
       and "1650-1800"; "A Check-list of British Parliamentary Papers
       on Sierra Leone." SIERRA LEONE STUDIES, n.s. no. 10, June 1958:
       62-72; no. 13, June 1960: 41-49; no. 19, July 1966: 146-150.

       "A Bibliography of the Mende Language"; "Notes on the Discovery
       of the Vai Script, with a Bibliography"; "Susu Studies and
       Literature, 1799-1900." SIERRA LEONE LANGUAGE REVIEW, no. 1,
       1962: 218-226; no. 2, 1963: 36-49; no. 4, 1965: 38-53.

       Comprehensive guide to sources for studies of Sierra Leone which
       is being published serially. The arrangement is in general chrono-
       logical.

1507. Luke, Harry C. A BIBLIOGRAPHY OF SIERRA LEONE, PRECEDED BY AN ESSAY
       ON THE ORIGIN, CHARACTER AND PEOPLES OF THE COLONY AND
       PROTECTORATE. 2d, enl. ed. London, Oxford University Press,
       1925. 230 p. plates, fold. map.

       An authoritative bibliography, with wide coverage almost to
       date of publication, prefaced by an interesting essay which is one
       of the best introductions to Sierra Leone. The author was Colonial
       Secretary.

       It is reported that Mr. G. J. Williams, director of the Department
       of Geography at Fourah Bay College, will publish a supplement to Luke's
       bibliography, covering the period 1925-66 and including periodicals.
       Regular supplements are planned.

1508. Pinkett, F. F. CHRONOLOGICAL AND ALPHABETICAL INDEX OF THE ORDINANCES
       OF SIERRA LEONE. Rev. ed. London, Waterlow & Sons, 1900.
       129 p. (3,000 entries)

1509. Sierra Leone. National Library. NATIONAL BIBLIOGRAPHY OF SIERRA
       LEONE. Freetown, [1967?].

       Annual list of titles deposited in the National Library. Only
       works in English are given.

1510. U.S. Library of Congress. General Reference and Bibliography Division.
       OFFICIAL PUBLICATIONS OF SIERRA LEONE AND GAMBIA. Compiled by
       Audrey A. Walker, African Section. Washington, 1963. xii, 92 p.

Another excellent bibliography in the Library of Congress series of guides to the documents of African governments. Included are materials issued by the British government on the country in question. An introductory essay outlines governmental history for each. Entries are listed alphabetically by author and title, and there is an index to authors and subjects.

1511. Zell, Hans M., comp. and ed. A BIBLIOGRAPHY OF NON-PERIODICAL LITERATURE ON SIERRA LEONE, 1925-66. Freetown, Fourah Bay College Bookshop, University College of Sierra Leone, 1966. 44, [2] p. Processed.

Intended only as a provisional checklist, with a comprehensive annotated bibliography planned for later publication. The bibliography supplements Luke's bibliography and that issued by the U.S. Library of Congress (both cited above) as well as the bibliographies of the Sierra Leone Library Board. The 253 entries include books, chapters from comprehensive works, reports, and theses (British and American) but not Sierra Leone government publications. Arrangement is by subject and includes poetry, plays, and fiction by Sierra Leoneans but no vernacular literature. There is an author index. All titles (except for the theses) are available from the Fourah Bay College Bookshop.

Reference Works

1512. Cox-George, N. A. FINANCE AND DEVELOPMENT IN WEST AFRICA: THE SIERRA LEONE EXPERIENCE. London, D. Dobson, 1961; New York, Humanities Press, 1962. 333 p.

Bibliography: p. 317-321.

_____. REPORT ON AFRICAN PARTICIPATION IN THE COMMERCE OF SIERRA LEONE...AND THE GOVERNMENT STATEMENT THEREON. Freetown, Govt. Print. Dept., 1958. 64 p. diagr., tables.

The first-named work, a version of the Sierra Leonean author's doctoral thesis at the University of London in 1956 (THE FINANCIAL SYSTEM OF A WEST AFRICAN COLONY IN RELATION TO ECONOMIC DEVELOPMENT, 466 p., microfilm), provides a complete analysis of the economic and financial history of the former British dependency. The 1958 report, which is related to the drive for Africanization of the Civil Service, was prepared at the request of the Sierra Leone government while Mr. Cox-George was in the Department of Economics at Fourah Bay College.

An earlier work officially commissioned by the government of Sierra Leone was prepared by Professor Daniel T. Jack, an expert on international trade: ECONOMIC SURVEY OF SIERRA LEONE (Freetown, Govt. Print. Dept., 1958, 75 p.).

1513.   Elias, Taslim Olawale. GHANA AND SIERRA LEONE: THE DEVELOPMENT OF
THEIR LAWS AND CONSTITUTIONS. London, Stevens, 1962. xii,
334 p. (The British Commonwealth, the Development of Its Laws
and Constitution, v. 10)

See note on Dr. Elias under Nigeria (no. 1468).

1514.   Fyfe, Christopher. A HISTORY OF SIERRA LEONE. London, Oxford
University Press, 1962. 773 p. fold. maps.

"Guide to Sources": p. 621-639.

This impressive history has a brief introduction on the period from the fifteenth-century Portuguese discovery of Sierra Leone to the founding of the colony in 1787 (which is treated in the complementary work by Kup mentioned below) and then covers chronologically and in great detail all affairs of the colony and protectorate to about 1900. The author had been temporary Government Archivist in Sierra Leone, and his sources (itemized on p. 621-639, with "References" on p. 640-723) include a vast array of documents and newspapers. A greatly simplified version, A SHORT HISTORY OF SIERRA LEONE, adapted to school use, was issued in a paperback by Longmans, Green (London, 1962 and 1967, xiii, 193 p. illus., maps). Another book edited by Professor Fyfe, SIERRA LEONE INHERITANCE, published in 1964 (London, Oxford University Press, 352 p.) is a collection of documents illustrating the country's history--not, the author indicates, a history illustrated by documents. Texts in English are given in original form. Those in other languages--French, Portuguese, etc.-- are translated.

For the earliest period of Sierra Leone's connection with Europe, there is an excellent work by A. P. Kup, A HISTORY OF SIERRA LEONE, 1400-1787 (Cambridge, Eng., University Press, 1961, 211 p., illus.). It is based on Portuguese and other precolonial source materials and ends where Dr. Fyfe's account begins.

1515.   Goddard, Thomas N. A HANDBOOK OF SIERRA LEONE. London, G. Richards,
1925. 335 p. illus., map.

Prepared by the Colonial Secretary in Freetown, this handbook of governmental information was sponsored by the Sierra Leone government. It is still useful for quick reference on the earlier history of the country and its administration.

1516. Kilson, Martin. POLITICAL CHANGE IN A WEST AFRICAN STATE: A STUDY
         OF THE MODERNIZATION PROCESS IN SIERRA LEONE. Cambridge, Mass.,
         Harvard University Press, 1966. 301 p. illus., ports., maps.

         Bibliography: p. 293-296.

         This excellent, critical analysis of the political process in
Sierra Leone emphasizes the significance of groups and their interrela-
tions. Comparisons with other African political systems are given.
While Dr. Kilson traces developments in Sierra Leone over the whole
period from 1863 to the present time, most of the book is taken up
with the years between the Second World War and 1961, the year Sierra
Leone achieved independence. A major analysis of modernization in
Sierra Leone, much of it applies to Africa in general. See also
Kenneth L. Little's THE MENDE OF SIERRA LEONE: A WEST AFRICAN PEOPLE
IN TRANSITION (rev. ed., London, Routledge & Kegan Paul; New York,
Humanities Press, 1967, 307 p., illus., map; bibliography: p. 292-294);
and Arthur T. Porter's CREOLEDOM: A STUDY OF THE DEVELOPMENT OF FREE-
TOWN SOCIETY (London, Oxford University Press, 1963, 151 p., illus.,
ports., maps; bibliography: p. 142-146).

1517. Lewis, Roy. SIERRA LEONE: A MODERN PROTRAIT. London, H.M. Stationery
         Off., 1954. 263 p. illus., maps. (Corona Library)

         Although addressed to a popular audience, this was written by a
specialist and based on thorough study of source materials as well as
field work.

1518. McCulloch, Merran. THE PEOPLES OF SIERRA LEONE PROTECTORATE. London,
         International African Institute, 1950. 102 p. (Ethnographic
         Survey of Africa. Western Africa, pt. 2)

         Reissue, 1964, with title PEOPLES OF SIERRA LEONE. 102 p. fold.
            map. ("Supplementary Bibliography," 4 p., inserted.)

         Bibliography: p. 95-98.

         Like other parts of the Ethnographic Survey, the study is intended
as a quick reference source, bringing together scattered information
regarding the tribes of the area in question and outlining their
ethnic and cultural position.

1519. Saylor, Ralph Gerald. THE ECONOMIC SYSTEM OF SIERRA LEONE. Durham,
       N.C., Published for the Duke University Commonwealth-Studies
       Center by Duke University Press, 1967. 231 p. map. (Duke
       University Commonwealth-Studies Center, pub. no. 31)

       Bibliography: p. 209-225.

1520. SIERRA LEONE STUDIES. no. 1- June 1918- Irregular. n.s. no. 1-
       Dec. 1953- Freetown. Twice a year.

       Reactivated in Jan. 1966 under the editorship of Michael Crowder,
       after a lapse of more than two years. Early editors were John Har-
       greaves, A. P. Kup, and A. T. Porter. By arrangement with the govern-
       ment of Sierra Leone, it is now the journal of the Sierra Leone
       Society and is produced by the Institute of African Studies of Fourah
       Bay College, the University College of Sierra Leone. Articles may be
       on any Sierra Leonean topic.

1521. SIERRA LEONE YEARBOOK. Freetown, Daily Mail. Annual.

       Handbook of information about the government, administration,
       and welfare services of Sierra Leone, including a who's who of
       leading Sierra Leoneans and Europeans. A short classified trade
       directory is included (on 8 inserted gray pages in the 1963 ed.;
       176 p. illus.--advertisements). There is a minimum of information
       about the country's economic life.

1522. U.S. Department of the Interior. Office of Geography. SIERRA LEONE:
       OFFICIAL STANDARD NAMES APPROVED BY THE UNITED STATES BOARD ON
       GEOGRAPHIC NAMES. Washington, U.S. Govt. Print. Off., June
       1966. 125 p. map. (8,800 names) (Gazetteer no. 101)

       See note on series, no. 484.

CHAPTER 33

FORMER FRENCH AFRICA

Note: The only countries of the former vast empire of France in Africa still
under French sovereignty are the overseas territories of French Somaliland
(now called French Territory of the Afars and the Issas), the Comoro Islands,
and the overseas department of Réunion. For all francophone Africa, however,
the great body of literature has been and still is in French and is published
in Paris. The quantity of significant writing and publishing regarding
Africa may be gauged by a glance at the LIVRES DE L'ANNEE, the yearly catalogue of the Librairie Française, under the heading "Afrique" and under the
names of the individual countries, or, even more impressively, at the 10-year
indexes (latest, TABLES DECENNALES--TITRES, 1956-1965).

    Because of the importance of official journals for any research and
contrary to our practice for the English-speaking countries, the individual
journaux officiels of some of the new states of francophone Africa are cited
in various sections that follow.

Atlas

1523. Grandidier, Guillaume, ed. ATLAS DES COLONIES FRANCAISES, PROTECTORATS
          ET TERRITOIRES SOUS MANDAT DE LA FRANCE. Paris, Société d'Editions
          Géographiques, Maritimes et Coloniales, 1934. 236 p. illus.,
          maps (159 col. maps on xxxix double plates), tables, diagrs.
          Large folio, loose-leaf, issued in parts; various pagings.

          This monumental library atlas begins with an essay on the for-
       mation of the colonial empire. Next are the maps, by region and
       country, with insets of geological, climatic, and other special maps,
       interspersed with text which is a full synopsis of physical geography,
       as well as detailed description of major cities, brief indications of
       ethnology, etc. North Africa has the first 48 pages and 13 folded
       maps, AOF 28 pages and 5 folded maps, AEF and Cameroun 20 pages and 5
       folded maps, and Madagascar, Réunion, and other islands 28 pages and

6 folded maps. The remainder cover French possessions outside Africa.
The alphabetical index gives place names by section (e.g., AOF and AEF,
p. 15-30; Madagascar, p. 31-38).

Bibliographies

Note: These bibliographies, whose content covers all French-speaking Africa,
are extensively supplemented in the regional bibliographies mentioned in the
sections below. The comprehensive library guide to French writing is the
BIBLIOGRAPHIE DE LA FRANCE, Part 1, BIBLIOGRAPHIE OFFICIELLE (see Part II
of the present guide, Current Bibliographies). Some bibliographies are included in the periodicals listed under the subsection Serials below.

1524. Ballard, John A. "Politics and Government in Former French West and
        Equatorial Africa: A Critical Bibliography." JOURNAL OF MODERN
        AFRICAN STUDIES, v. 3, no. 4, Dec. 1965: 589-605.

        An evaluation of major contributions, 1955-65, to the study of
former French African territories during the colonial period and
since independence.

1525. Baratte, Thérèse, comp. BIBLIOGRAPHIE: AUTEURS AFRICAINS ET
        MALGACHES DE LANGUE FRANCAISE. Paris, Office de Coopération
        Radiophonique (OCORA), 1965. 50 p.

        For annotation, see no. 1029.

1526. Boston University. African Studies Program. Development Research
        Center. BIBLIOGRAPHIE SELECTIVE D'OUVRAGES DE LANGUE FRANCAISE
        SUR LES PROBLEMES GOUVERNEMENTAUX ET ADMINISTRATIFS (NOTAMMENT
        EN AFRIQUE). [Title also in English] Edited by Edouard Bustin.
        Boston, Nov. 1963. 36 p.

        This bibliography, described in Part III (no. 585), is chiefly
concerned with French-speaking Africa.

1527. Boston University. Libraries. LIST OF FRENCH DOCTORAL DISSERTATIONS
        ON AFRICA, 1884-1961. Compiled by Marion Dinstel; with indexes
        by Mary Darrah Herrick. Boston, G. K. Hall, 1966. 336 p.

        Reproduction of almost 3,000 cards, with author, area, and subject
indexes. The titles are, naturally, for the most part studies of French
African possessions, though occasional dissertations are concerned with
other parts of Africa.

1528. Centre d'Analyse et de Recherche Documentaires pour l'Afrique Noire
and Club des Lecteurs d'Expression Française. AFRIQUE NOIRE
D'EXPRESSION FRANCAISE: SCIENCES SOCIALES ET HUMAINES: GUIDE
DE LECTURE. Edited by M. C. Jacquey and F. Niellon. Paris,
CARDAN, CLEF [1968?]. 301 p. maps.

A worthy contribution to reference material on French-speaking
West and Equatorial Africa. Most references are annotated and many
derive from publications of the Banque Centrale des Etats d'Afrique
de l'Ouest, Musée Royale de l'Afrique Centrale, Centre d'Etude et de
Documentation sur l'Afrique et l'Outre-Mer, Fondation Nationale des
Sciences Politiques, etc. This is exclusively a guide to French-
language publications (including many processed items), except where
the basic character of a work or the absence of an equivalent publication in French warrants inclusion of a study in English or German.
There are two main parts with many subdivisions: global studies and
country studies. The former includes works on Africa as a whole and
covers bibliographies, general works, geography, history, cultural
anthropology, politics, law, social questions, and economics. A
very helpful inclusion in the second part is that of an ethnographic
map for each country. There is an author index. The concentration
on French-language publications mars somewhat the usefulness of this
bibliography since important works in other languages are often
omitted. Moreover there are some unnecessary duplications. More
serious limitations, however, are the high number of typographical
errors, the frequent lack of complete bibliographical data, and
occasionally erroneous information. But even though it can be
faulted, this is a highly recommended bibliography, invaluable for
research on the areas treated.

1529. Favitski de Probobysz, Cmdt. de. REPERTOIRE BIBLIOGRAPHIQUE DE LA
LITTERATURE MILITAIRE ET COLONIAL FRANCAISE DEPUIS CENT ANS.
Liège, Thone, 1935. 363 p.

1530. France. Archives Nationales. Section Outre-Mer. NOTICE BIBLIOGRA-
PHIQUE DES PRINCIPAUX OUVRAGES FRANCAIS RECENTS INTERESSANT LES
TERRITOIRES FRANCAIS D'OUTRE-MER, LE SAHARA, ET LES ETATS AFRI-
CAINS D'EXPRESSION FRANCAISE. Edited by G. de Forges. Paris,
1961. 61 p.

1531. France. Direction de la Documentation. L'AFRIQUE A TRAVERS LES
PUBLICATIONS DE LA DOCUMENTATION FRANCAISE: BIBLIOGRAPHIE,
1945-1961. [Etablie par Madame Coisel] Paris, La Documentation
Française, 1961. 107 p. (Travaux et recherches, no. 14)

Listing of pamphlets, articles, maps, documents, etc., on Africa
that have appeared in the several series of La Documentation Française,

the more substantial of which are Notes et études documentaires,
Documentation française illustrée, and Cahiers français. Arrangement
is first by region or country (56 headings) and under that by year.
There are perhaps 1,500 titles.

1532. France. Direction de la Documentation. BIBLIOGRAPHIE SELECTIVE DES
        PUBLICATIONS OFFICIELLES FRANCAISES. 1952- Paris, La
        Documentation Française. Semimonthly.

        The most immediate record of French official publications, in-
cluding those for France overseas and, since 1960, a few issued by
the governments of French-speaking African states. Entries are by
issuing offices in Part 1. A separate enclosure, Part 2, is "Bulletin
des Sommaires"; this lists the contents of the various series of La
Documentation Française, notably the Notes et études documentaires,
which are background pamphlets, including country studies in which
the French-speaking states of Africa are covered.

1533. France. Institut National de la Statistique et des Etudes Economiques.
        Paris.

        A valuable service by the French government before and after
independence which provided bibliographies, and censuses, demographic and economic studies.

        France. Institut National de la Statistique et des Etudes Economiques.
        Service de Coopération. BIBLIOGRAPHIE DEMOGRAPHIQUE, 1945-1962:
        LISTE DES TRAVAUX DEMOGRAPHIQUES PUBLIES PAR LE SERVICE DE
        COOPERATION DE L'I.N.S.E.E. ET LES SERVICES DE STATISTIQUES DES
        ETATS AFRICAINS D'EXPRESSION FRANCAISE, OU REALISES AVEC LEUR
        COLLABORATION. Paris, 1963. 33 1.

        France. Institut National de la Statistique et des Etudes Economiques.
        Service de Coopération. BIBLIOGRAPHIE DEMOGRAPHIQUE (1945-1964):
        TRAVAUX PUBLIES PAR L'I.N.S.E.E. (SERVICE DE COOPERATION), LES
        SERVICES DE STATISTIQUES DES ETATS AFRICAINS D'EXPRESSION
        FRANCAISE OU DE MADAGASCAR ET LE MINISTERE DE LA COOPERATION.
        Paris, 1965. 36 1.

        See also nos. 857 and 858.

1534. France. Institut National de la Statistique et des Etudes Economiques.
        BULLETIN BIBLIOGRAPHIQUE. Paris. Bimonthly. (no. 124, Mar.-
        Apr. 1967)

        An abstracting service, providing fairly full abstracts (500 words
or more) of articles from the principal economic reviews and books in
French and other languages regarding France and overseas. Arrangement

is by subject classes, largely of economic significance. The African coverage is limited to French-speaking countries.

The Institut issues a periodically revised list of its PUBLICA-TIONS, which includes a section for Outre-Mer in which are noted the many statistical annuals, bulletins, and special reports prepared in past years and in some cases still being published as official French documents. The Institut's SITUATION DES ENQUETES STATISTIQUES ET SOCIO-ECONOMIQUES DANS LES ETATS AFRICAINS ET MALGACHE AU 1ER JANVIER 1965 (90 p.) is a comprehensive guide to surveys and reports issued (by various agencies) or in progress, 1955-65; Guinea is not covered.

1535. Le Melle, Wilbert J. A SELECTIVE BIBLIOGRAPHY OF BOOKS, ARTICLES AND DOCUMENTS ON THE SUBJECT OF AFRICAN ADMINISTRATIVE PROBLEMS. [Title also in French] Boston, Development Research Center, African Studies Program, Boston University, 1964. 51 p.

The states of former French Africa receive special emphasis.

1536. Martineau, Alfred, ed. BIBLIOGRAPHIE D'HISTOIRE COLONIALE (1900-1930). Paris, Société de l'Histoire de Colonies Françaises, 1932. 667 p.

See no. 536 for full annotation. For French colonies in Africa, Afrique occidentale française is by Georges Hardy (p. 331-341, includ-ing about 60 references), Afrique équatoriale française by Georges Bruel (p. 311-332, 160 to 170 references), and Madagascar by André You (p. 365-374, almost 150 references). See also A. Lebel, L'AFRIQUE OCCI-DENTALE DANS LA LITTERATURE FRANCAISE DEPUIS 1870 (Paris, 1925, 279 p.).

1537. Mercier, Roger. "Bibliographie africaine et malgache: Ecrivains noirs d'expression française." REVUE DE LITTERATURE COMPAREE, v. 37, no. 1, 1963: 145-171.

For annotation see no. 1033.

1538. Robinson, Kenneth E. "Survey of the Background Material for the Study of Government in French Tropical Africa." AMERICAN POLITICAL SCIENCE REVIEW, v. 50, no. 1, Mar. 1956: 170-198.

Bibliographical article of lasting value for any serious research on former French Africa. The references are selected from the author-itative literature, largely in French, over the preceding quarter-century, with special emphasis on French legislative sources. Profes-sor Robinson's evaluative analyses cover the chief bibliographical works, French official publications, specialized periodicals, books and articles on French Africa in general, and then in separate sec-tions, French West Africa, French Equatorial Africa, and Madagascar.

1539. Société des Africanistes. JOURNAL. 1931- Paris.

        An outstanding bibliographic section is carried each year.
See no. 301 for description.

1540. Thomassery, Marguerite. CATALOGUE DES PERIODIQUES D'AFRIQUE NOIRE
        FRANCOPHONE (1858-1962) CONSERVES A L'IFAN. Dakar, Institut
Français d'Afrique Noire, 1965. 117 p. (Catalogues et
documents, no. 14)

        A listing of all serials and some series publications such as
Etudes sénégalaises and Etudes soudanaises published in French-speaking
Africa (excluding Madagascar) and held at the IFAN library in Dakar.
Arrangement is alphabetical by title or, for official publications, by
issuing agency; there is a separate listing of budgets. Serials total
584, and 21 budgets are listed. There are an abbreviations index, a
geographical index (by area and country, subdivided into official
and nonofficial publications, with subjects under each), a chronological index, and an index of publishers arranged by field (economic,
scientific, etc.), and an editor-director-manager index.

1541. U.S. Library of Congress. Division of Bibliography. FRENCH COLONIES
        IN AFRICA: A LIST OF REFERENCES. Compiled by Helen F. Conover.
Washington, 1942. 89 p.

        A useful list of books and articles (1,265 items) for the period
before 1942.

Serials

Note: The following titles represent a small selection among the many
periodicals published in French-speaking Africa and in France. For fuller
listings see the bibliographies in the List of Serials in Part II, especially
nos. 373, 382, 386, 387, and 392.

1542. Académie des Sciences Coloniales. COMPTES RENDUS DES SEANCES: COM-
        MUNICATIONS. 1922/23-1941. Paris. Irregular. Continued in
COMPTES RENDUS DES SEANCES, 1941-46; COMPTES RENDUS MENSUELS DES
SEANCES, 1947-57.

        Continued under the Académie's new name (see next entry).

1543. Académie des Sciences d'Outre-Mer. COMPTES RENDUS MENSUELS DES
        SEANCES. 1957- Paris.

        See also preceding entry.

1544. AFRIQUE. 1961-66. Paris. illus. Monthly.

This handsomely illustrated magazine was of particular importance for the French-speaking countries of Africa, although it gave coverage to the entire continent.

1545. AFRIQUE CONTEMPORAINE: DOCUMENTS D'AFRIQUE NOIRE ET DE MADAGASCAR.
       1962- Paris, La Documentation Française. 6 times a year.

A valuable documentary review, published under the direction of Professor Robert Cornevin at the Centre d'Etudes et de Documentation sur l'Afrique et l'Outre-Mer (31, quai Voltaire, Paris 7). It carries texts of important documents, a diary of events, and analyses of articles in African newspapers, reports of congresses, etc., and many book reviews.

1546. L'AFRIQUE D'EXPRESSION FRANCAISE ET MADAGASCAR. 1960- Paris, Europe
       France Outremer. illus., maps.

The first special issue with this title in a journal emphasizing African affairs came out in Oct. 1960, and there has been an annual spring edition since 1962. Every edition provides an up-to-date country-by-country guide (with a map for each country) to the political and economic status of French-speaking Africa (including North Africa, French Somaliland, Réunion, and the Comoro Islands), to groups and organizations (with index of abbreviations), and to links with the Common Market. The seventh edition appeared in Apr. 1967 (EUROPE FRANCE OUTREMER, no. 447, 272 p.).

1547. AFRIQUE-DOCUMENTS. 1954- Dakar. Bimonthly.

Published from 1954 to Feb. 1960 as SAVOIR POUR AGIR: BULLETIN DU CENTRE CULTUREL DANIEL BROTTIER. It is a significant politico-social journal, (Catholic in orientation) including articles, texts of occasional documents, and a section of chronology, "Ephémérides de l'Ouest africain." A supplement, DOSSIERS AFRICAINS, is published from time to time, e.g., no. 1, MEDECINE SOCIALE AU SENEGAL, by Drs. M. Sankalé and P. Pène.

A chronology is also carried quarterly in the review of the Centre de Hautes Etudes Administratives sur l'Afrique et l'Asie Modernes (CHEAM), L'AFRIQUE ET L'ASIE (1948-, Paris).

1548. BULLETIN DE L'AFRIQUE NOIRE. 1957- Paris, EDIAFRIC. Weekly.

Press summaries of events in French-speaking Africa. For annotation see no. 572.

1549.   CAHIERS D'ETUDES AFRICAINES. no. 1- Jan. 1960- Paris, Mouton.
            Quarterly.

            This journal, edited by the Ecole Pratique des Hautes Etudes
        at the University of Paris (6^e Section, Sciences Economiques et
        Sociales), is spoken of as the French counterpart of the JOURNAL OF
        MODERN AFRICAN STUDIES. Its essays and notes, on a high level of
        scholarship and authoritativeness, are concerned with the ethnology,
        sociology, history, and economic and cultural aspects of all of
        modern Africa, in particular with the French-speaking countries.
        There are occasional articles in English.

1550.   Chambre de Commerce, d'Agriculture et d'Industries [des pays de
            l'Afrique noire]. BULLETIN...

            In most capital cities of the French-speaking states there is
        an active Chamber of Commerce and/or Agriculture and Industry,
        officially supported, from which emanate reports and bulletins of
        various sizes and frequencies, all valuable for statistical and
        other business information regarding the country. The names vary--
        for instance, in Douala, Cameroun, the Chambre d'Agriculture, de
        l'Elevage et des Forêts issues a well-printed and illustrated slick-
        paper pamphlet, and the Chambre de Commerce et d'Industrie has a
        50-page printed magazine. In Abidjan, Ivory Coast, the Chambre
        d'Agriculture et d'Industrie sends out a mimeographed CIRCULAIRE
        HEBDOMADAIRE D'INFORMATION, while the Chambre de Commerce de la
        Côte d'Ivoire issues a large pamphlet in offset print, including
        statistical tables and texts of documents. For listing see the
        UNECA list of serials in its library (no. 395) and the Library of
        Congress SERIALS (no. 396).

1551.   CHRONIQUES D'OUTRE-MER: ETUDES ET INFORMATIONS. Jan. 1951-58.
            Paris, La Documentation Française, Editions de la Présidence
            du Conseil. illus., ports., maps. Monthly. Superseded by
            CHRONIQUES DE LA COMMUNAUTE, 1959-.

1552.   COMMUNAUTES ET CONTINENTS: NOUVELLE REVUE FRANCAISE D'OUTRE-MER.
            n.s. v. 1- 1959- Paris. Quarterly.

            The organ of the Comité Central Français pour l'Outre-Mer
        (41, rue de la Bienfaisance, Paris 8), published first as the
        BULLETIN of the Comité, then from 1950 to 1958 (42 année-) as LA
        NOUVELLE REVUE FRANCAISE D'OUTRE-MER. Its contents often include
        addresses made by members.

1553.   DOSSIER ON FRENCH TROPICAL AFRICA. 1960- By Raymond Lefèvre.
            Asinières (Seine). Loose-leaf.

A serial consisting of groups of "cards" (slips, 6 1/2" x 8"), usually about 30 a month, giving biographical data regarding statesmen in the countries of French-speaking Africa, occasionally a few in English-speaking countries. The pink sheets, each with the name of an individual at the top, are interspersed with white cards showing government organizations.

1554. EUROPE FRANCE OUTREMER. 1923- Paris. illus. Monthly.

This important monthly was published until 1958 with the title FRANCE OUTREMER. Beginning as an illustrated feature magazine, the subject content has constantly increased in significance. Most issues are now devoted to a single theme or country, with a number of specialist articles. Beginning in 1960, a spring issue--smaller in format than the regular review though thicker--has constituted a handbook of French-speaking Africa (see no. 1546).

1555. France. JOURNAL OFFICIEL DE LA REPUBLIQUE FRANCAISE. Paris, Impr. des Journaux Officiels.

The highly centralized nature of French government is exemplified nowhere to better advantage than in the JOURNAL OFFICIEL, the component parts of which include practically all legislative material. Among these parts are DEBATS PARLEMENTAIRES of the Assemblée Nationale, the Conseil de la République, and the former Assemblée de l'Union Française (these all are daily during sessions); DOCUMENTS PARLEMENTAIRES of these bodies; LOIS ET DECRETS (texts of laws, decrees, orders, etc.--daily), with monthly and annual tables; and TEXTES D'INTERET GENERAL, a selection from the LOIS ET DECRETS published weekly and in special numbers. Of limited relevance for Africa since independence of the territories, this is a primary source for historical study.

Among other tools relating to the French administration and useful in studies of former French Africa are the following:

a) BOTTIN ADMINISTRATIF ET DOCUMENTAIRE. Paris, Société Didot-Bottin. (166th year, 1963) Table alphabétique des noms.

b) ENCYCLOPEDIE PERMANENTE DE L'ADMINISTRATION FRANCAISE. Paris. 30 nos. a year. Loose-leaf.

Includes LES DOCUMENTS A JOUR (current--replaced as they become outdated) and LES DOCUMENTS PERIMES (archives). The leaves are numbered 1-1400, and as one is withdrawn, it is replaced by another carrying the same number followed by a letter (e.g., 15, 15A, 15B). There are periodic TABLES DE MATIERES ANALYTIQUES ET ALPHABETIQUES. At present there is little of importance relating to the independent states of former French Africa.

c)   France. REPERTOIRE PERMANENT DE L'ADMINISTRATION FRANCAISE.
            Paris, La Documentation Française. (22nd ed., Jan. 1963)

        Government manual.

1556. France. Ministère de la France d'Outre-mer. ANNUAIRE DU MINISTERE
        DE LA FRANCE D'OUTRE-MER ET DU MINISTERE D'ETAT CHARGE DES
        RELATIONS AVEC LES ETATS ASSOCIES. Paris.

1557. France. Ministère de la France d'Outre-mer. BULLETIN OFFICIEL.
        Paris. Monthly.

        Published from 1887 by the Ministère des Colonies; from 1946-59
by the Ministère de la France d'Outre-Mer. The Agence Générale des
Colonies also issued a monthly BULLETIN, 1908-[1934?] Paris, which
superseded FEUILLE DE RENSEIGNEMENTS.

1558. France. Office de la Recherche Scientifique et Technique Outre-Mer
        (ORSTOM). RAPPORT D'ACTIVITE DE L'OFFICE. Paris. illus.
        Annual.

        ORSTOM is an official research institution which sponsors
technical and scientific research projects in the countries formerly
part of overseas France. During its first few years (1949-54) it
issued a helpful record of these researches, COURRIER DES CHERCHEURS
(no. 10, 1953-54, Paris, 1956); in 1957 it began a serial SCIENCES
HUMAINES OUTRE-MER. A new series, Cahiers O.R.S.T.O.M.: Sciences
humaines, was begun in 1963. The results of ORSTOM projects are
published in part in mimeographed form, for limited distribution;
one valuable series is printed for ORSTOM by Berger-Levrault, L'homme
d'outre-mer (see, for example, under Cameroun, the work by Tardits,
no. 1955). Important monographs have appeared on most countries
of former French Africa. Some other major ORSTOM works include:

a)   BULLETIN SCIENTIFIQUE. no. 1- 1951- Nogent-sur-Marne
            (Seine).

b)   LISTE BIBLIOGRAPHIQUE DES TRAVAUX, ANNEES 1958 A 1962. Seine,
            1964. 2 v.

c)   L'OFFICE DE LA RECHERCHE SCIENTIFIQUE ET TECHNIQUE OUTRE-MER
            ET LES RECHERCHES SCIENTIFIQUES ET TECHNIQUES EN VUE DU
            DEVELOPPEMENT ECONOMIQUE ET SOCIAL EN AFRIQUE ET A
            MADAGASCAR. Paris, 1962. 45 p.

d)   ORGANISATION, ACTIVITES, 1944-1955. Paris, 1955. 182 p.

1559. MARCHES TROPICAUX ET MEDITERRANEENS. 1945- Paris. Weekly.

        This useful magazine reviewing commercial interests of France
and French-speaking countries overseas was begun with the title
MARCHES COLONIAUX; in 1956 it was changed to MARCHES TROPICAUX DU
MONDE and in 1959 to the present form. The average issue runs from
40 to 50 pages, but each year there are several special issues,
varying from some 150 to over 200 pages and each devoted to a single
theme, country, or region--e.g., LE MARCHE DE LA COTE D'IVOIRE,
June 15, 1963 (issued also in English); LE MARCHE MALGACHE, July 20,
1963; LE MARCHE CAMEROUNAIS, Apr. 25, 1964, and Oct. 22, 1966; and
LE MARCHE D'AFRIQUE EQUATORIALE, Oct. 30, 1965. Other special
numbers comprise a full statistical survey, LE MARCHE AFRICAIN ET
MALGACHE: the seventh edition, no. 1168, Mar. 30, 1968, had about
150 pages, with articles in 35 categories and abundant statistical
tables, graphs, and charts.

        The publisher of MARCHES TROPICAUX ET MEDITERRANEENS is René
Moreux, who also issues the ANNUAIRE DES ENTREPRISES ET ORGANISMES
D'OUTRE-MER (see no. 1568 below), and a monthly devoted to problems
of industrialization and equipment, INDUSTRIES ET TRAVAUX D'OUTRE-
MER.

1560. NATIONS NOUVELLES. nos. 1-7, 1962-Jan./Feb. 1964; n.s. no. 1,
        Oct. 1964- Cotonou, Dahomey; Yaoundé, Cameroun. illus.
        Quarterly.

        The review of the Organisation Commune Africaine et Malgache
(OCAM); originally issued by the Union Africaine et Malgache, early
designation of this African states grouping, which has had various
changes of name; journal also in English. The new series (no. 1,
Oct. 1964-) is in continuation of the REVUE TRIMESTRIELLE (nos. 1-6,
Dec. 1962-June 1964, issued by the Organisation Africaine et Malgache
de Coopération Economique) and supersedes this publication.

        An article interpreting the African organization appeared in
AFRICA REPORT, v. 10, no. 3, Mar. 1965: Victor T. Le Vine, "New
Directions for French-speaking Africa?" (p. 7-11).

1561. PENANT: RECUEIL GENERAL DE JURISPRUDENCE, DE DOCTRINE ET DE
        LEGISLATION D'OUTREMER [COLONIALE ET MARITIME]. 1891- Paris.
        Monthly.

        A basic source for the study of Africa.

1562. PRESENCE AFRICAINE: REVUE CULTURELLE DU MONDE NOIR. no. 1- Nov.-
        Dec. 1947- n.s. Trimestrielle, 1953- Paris.

The review PRESENCE AFRICAINE, edited by M. Alioune Diop, and the several series of books and pamphlets published under the auspices of Présence Africaine form the chief organs for the elites of French-speaking Africa. Contributions are largely by African writers, and the contributors during the decade of the 1950's included the foremost nationalist intellectuals. Typical books are Césaire's DISCOURS SUR LE COLONIALISME and Tevoedjre's L'AFRIQUE REVOLTEE. Numbers of the review are often on a single theme, e.g., LES ETUDIANTS NOIRS PARLENT (Paris, 1953; PRESENCE AFRICAINE, no. 14). Catalogues of all publications are available from the Librairie Présence Africaine, 42, rue Descartes, Paris 5.

1563.   REVUE FRANCAISE D'HISTOIRE D'OUTREMER. 1913- Paris, Société de
          l'Histoire des Colonies Françaises. Quarterly, 1913-27;
          Bimonthly, 1928-33; Quarterly, 1934-

          Title varies: 1913-31, REVUE DE L'HISTOIRE DES COLONIES
FRANCAISES; 1932-1958, REVUE D'HISTOIRE DES COLONIES.

          A most important journal for the study of France in Africa.

1564.   REVUE FRANCAISE D'OUTRE-MER. 1897- 1914- 1928- Paris, Union Coloniale
          Française. Frequency varied.

1565.   REVUE JURIDIQUE ET POLITIQUE D'INDEPENDANCE ET COOPERATION. 1947-
          Paris. Quarterly.

          Title varies: v. 1-12, 1947-1958, REVUE JURIDIQUE ET POLITIQUE
DE L'UNION FRANCAISE; v. 13-17, 1959-1963, REVUE JURIDIQUE ET
POLITIQUE D'OUTRE-MER.

Reference Works

1566.   ADMINISTRATION ET DIPLOMATIE D'AFRIQUE NOIRE ET DE MADAGASCAR, 1962.
          Paris, Europe-Outremer et EDIAFRIC, 1962. 391 p. (Includes
          advertising.)

          Directory and who's who for the French-speaking states of West and Equatorial Africa (as in this volume, 15 including Madagascar). The volume is limited to composition and personnel of the national governments and of inter-African organizations in which the states participate.

1567.   AFRIQUE NOIRE [ET] OCEAN INDIEN: GUIDE ECONOMIQUE. Limoges, Annuaires
            Noria, 1963. 641 p. illus., fold. maps. (Includes advertising.)

        With the 1963 edition this commercial directory service brought
together in one volume two earlier Annuaires Noria--AFRIQUE NOIRE
and OCEAN INDIEN. The present large guide covers the 14 republics
of Black Africa as well as Malagasy Republic, Réunion, and Mauritius
(Ile Maurice). The notes for each country survey the general situation
and economic life and have summaries in English, German, and Italian.
They are followed by lists of firms and products.

1568.   ANNUAIRE DES ENTREPRISES ET ORGANISMES D'OUTRE-MER, 1968. Paris, René
            Moreux (190, blvd. Haussmann), 1967. 1042 p. (59th year)

        This business yearbook concerning French-speaking countries now
includes Les organismes officiels et professionnels des pays d'outre-
mer; Les organismes de coopération avec les pays d'outre-mer; Les
entreprises privées, les sociétés d'état et d'économie mixte; and
Industriels fournisseurs des pays d'outre-mer. There are indexes.

1569.   ANNUAIRE DES ETATS D'AFRIQUE NOIRE: GOUVERNEMENTS ET CABINETS
            MINISTERIELS, PARTIS POLITIQUES. 2d ed. Paris, EDIAFRIC,
            1962. 443 p. illus., ports. (Includes advertising.)

        Who's who of politics in 14 French-speaking African states.
The gay cover bears the flags of the countries covered (West and
Equatorial Africa). At the beginning are lists of directors of the
political parties, the national orders, and composition of the governments, with analytical tables of presidential and ministerial functions.
The bulk of the text (p. 121-403) is devoted to biographies of leading
officials of the governments, country by country, and of inter-African
organizations. Indexes of personal names and abbreviations are on
green pages at the end.

1570.   ANNUAIRE PARLEMENTAIRE DES ETATS D'AFRIQUE NOIRE: DEPUTES ET CONSEILLERS
            ECONOMIQUES DES REPUBLIQUES D'EXPRESSION FRANCAISE, 1962. Paris,
            Annuaire Afrique, 1962. 332 p. illus., ports. (Includes
            advertising.)

        Complementary to, and in part repeating, the information in the
EDIAFRIC ANNUAIRE, above. (The Annuaire Afrique address is the same
as that of EDIAFRIC, 57, avenue d'Iéna, Paris 16.) The present volume
contains 1,100 brief biographies of the political personnel and
administrative service officers of the 14 republics formerly associated
with France. The presidents of the republics, the governments, the
national assemblies, economic and social councils, cabinet ministers,
administration and public services, diplomatic representatives, and

political parties are listed. There are indexes of names and abbreviations.

1571. Badouin, Robert. LES BANQUES DE DEVELOPPEMENT EN AFRIQUE. Paris,
          Pedone, 1964. 271 p. (Collection du Centre de Recherches,
          d'Etudes et de Documentation sur les Institutions et les
          Législations Africaines, no. 5)

       By a former professor of law and economic sciences at Dakar,
now at the Université de Montpellier. The first part analyzes the
history, role, organization, and functions of the various development
banks, and the second reviews documents regarding banks of the 15
individual countries of francophone Africa.

1572. Blanchet, André. L'ITINERAIRE DES PARTIS AFRICAINS DEPUIS BAMAKO.
          Paris, Plon, 1958. 209 p. (Tribune libre, no. 31)

       This account of the preindependence parties in French Africa
has been rapidly outdated by events but remains a source for background study especially for 1957-58. It includes a "Petit bottin
politique de l'Afrique noire," with names and brief biographical
notes on some 30 leaders in early 1958. The author, a journalist,
is LE MONDE'S expert on Africa.

       Another reliable study, INTRODUCTION A L'ETUDE DES PARTIS
POLITIQUES DE L'AFRIQUE FRANCAISE (Paris, Librairie Générale de
Droit et de Jurisprudence, 1959, 196 p.) by Léo Hamon, was reprinted
from the authoritative journal, REVUE JURIDIQUE ET POLITIQUE DE
L'UNION FRANCAISE. A second part, by the same author, was published
in 1961: LES PARTIS POLITIQUES AFRICAINS (Paris, 51 p.). Another
important and complementary book is by Ernest Milcent, L'A.O.F.
ENTRE EN SCENE (Paris, Editions Témoignage Chrétien, 1958, 190 p.).

1573. LES 500 [CINQ CENT] PREMIERES SOCIETES D'AFRIQUE NOIRE. Paris,
          EDIAFRIC-La Documentation Africaine [1969?]. 348 p. (Numéro
          spécial du BULLETIN D'AFRIQUE NOIRE)

       Covers former French Africa. The first section lists 500
businesses, industries, and banks in order of their capital. It gives
addresses, year established, and serves as an index to the second
section where each organization is fully described. The second
section is divided by country. Under each country section there
are two subsections, first a listing of the country's organizations,
by capital, then a full description of each organization arranged
alphabetically by name.

1574. Decraene, Philippe. TABLEAU DES PARTIS POLITIQUES DE L'AFRIQUE
        AU SUD DU SAHARA. Paris, Fondation Nationale des Sciences
        Politiques, Centre d'Etude des Relations Internationales,
        1963. 137 l. (Sér. C, Recherches, no. 8, May 1963)

        See no. 615 for annotation. Another work by Decraene is LE
PANAFRICANISME (see no. 638).

1575. Delavignette, Robert. L'AFRIQUE NOIRE FRANCAISE ET SON DESTIN.
        Paris, Gallimard, 1962. 207 p.

        Discussion of problems of decolonization by one well qualified
to speak. As a former Governor-General of French West Africa, and
from 1947 to 1951 Director of Political Affairs of the Ministry of
France Overseas, Professor Delavignette has been among France's
leading colonial thinkers. One of his important books is the 1948
SERVICE AFRICAIN, first published in English translation for the
International African Institute as FREEDOM AND AUTHORITY IN FRENCH
WEST AFRICA (London, New York, Oxford University Press, 1950,
152 p.).

1576. Deschamps, Hubert J. LES METHODES ET LES DOCTRINES COLONIALES DE
        LA FRANCE, DU XVIe SIECLE A NOS JOURS. Paris, A. Colin, 1953.
        222 p. illus. (Collection Armand Colin, no. 281, Section
        d'histoire et sciences économiques)

        Bibliographie sommaire: p. 214-218.

        By a former colonial governor, now professor of African history
at the Sorbonne, who has written many books enunciating the enlightened
views of liberal French thought. This short account includes in its
chapters on the period from 1880 to 1940 comment by the foremost
spokesmen of French colonial theory who foresaw an end to empire.
A selected bibliography is arranged by period, the last covering
the years 1940-50. See also his THE FRENCH UNION ... (Paris, Berger-
Levrault, 1956, 256 p., illus., maps; bibliography: p. 249-251).

        Among Professor Deschamps' later works is LES INSTITUTIONS POLI-
TIQUES DE L'AFRIQUE NOIRE (Paris, Presses Universitaires de France,
1962, 126 p.; "Que sais-je?" no. 549).

1577. Dumon, Frédéric. LA COMMUNAUTE FRANCO-AFRO-MALGACHE: SES ORIGINES,
        SES INSTITUTIONS, SON EVOLUTION, OCTOBRE 1958-JUIN 1960.
        Bruxelles, Institut de Sociologie Solvay, 1960. 294 p. (Etudes
        d'histoire et d'ethnologie juridiques, 2)

        Annexe 10: "Les constitutions des Etats membres de la Communauté"
(p. 176-291).

1578. Dumont, René. AFRIQUE NOIRE, DEVELOPPEMENT AGRICOLE: RECONVERSION
       DE L'ECONOMIE AGRICOLE--GUINEE, COTE D'IVOIRE, MALI. Paris,
       Presses Universitaires de France, 1961. 212 p. (Cahiers "Tiers
       monde," Problèmes des pays sous-développés)

       The author, a distinguished agronomist and political scientist,
is a member of the Fonds d'Aide et de Coopération (FAC) that has replaced FIDES. In this work, published in a scholarly economic series,
he spells out in detail the plans that with outside financial help
might revolutionize agricultural production in the three countries
studied. His other much-noticed book of 1962, L'AFRIQUE NOIRE EST MAL
PARTIE (published in English as FALSE START IN AFRICA) is discussed in
Chapter 18 (no. 804).

       An earlier work of somewhat the same character is by a professor
of geography at the Sorbonne, Charles Robequain, LES RICHESSES DE
LA FRANCE D'OUTRE-MER: STRUCTURE ECONOMIQUE ET PROBLEMES HUMAINS
(Paris, Payot, 1949, 221 p., illus., maps; Bibliothèque géographique).
The author here surveys on a broad scale the economic structure and
status of the overseas territories, evaluating products and their
development always in terms of their relation to the well-being of
the native populations and urging more scientific and ethnological
research in colonial planning.

1579. LES ELITES AFRICAINES, 1970-71. Paris, EDIAFRIC, 1970. 298 p.
       (Numéro spécial du BULLETIN DE L'AFRIQUE NOIRE)

       Very brief biographies arranged alphabetically by surname of
individuals from French-speaking Africa (Cameroun, Central African
Republic, Congo-Brazzaville, Ivory Coast, Dahomey, Gabon, Upper
Volta, Mali, Mauritania, Niger, Senegal, Chad, Togo).

1580. ENCYCLOPEDIE AFRICAINE ET MALGACHE. Paris, Larousse, 1964-65. 26
       fasc., 544 p. illus., maps (part col.), music.

       An encyclopedia devoted primarily to French-speaking Africa.
The work, which includes a 16-page atlas, has been issued in 26
fascicles, each of which is available as a separate unit. The first
seven fascicles comprise a general section (geography, history of
the world, history of Africa, literature and grammar, arithmetic
and geometry, anatomy and health, ethics). The remaining 19 provide
the following regional and country surveys: North Africa (Algeria,
Tunisia, and Morocco), Burundi, Cameroun, Central African Republic,
Republic of the Congo (Brazzaville), Democratic Republic of the
Congo (Kinshasa), Ivory Coast, Dahomey, Gabon, Guinea, Upper Volta,
Malagasy Republic and Somalia, Mali, Mauritania, Niger, Rwanda,
Senegal, Chad, and Togo.

1581.   ENCYCLOPEDIE COLONIALE ET MARITIME. Edited by Eugène Guernier
        and G. Fromont-Guieysse. Paris, Encyclopédie de l'Empire
        Français, 1944-51.

        Basic reference work with separate folio volumes devoted to each
of the French overseas territories, published in 15 parts during the
between-war years. A revised postwar edition was begun in 1944 with
Vol. II, TUNISIE (4th ed.). Parts relating to French sub-Saharan
Africa are Vol. IV, AFRIQUE OCCIDENTALE FRANCAISE (1947, 2 v.); Vol.
V, AFRIQUE EQUATORIALE FRANCAISE ET COTE FRANCAISE DES SOMALIS (1950);
Vol. VI, CAMEROUN-TOGO (1951, 583 p.); and Vol. VII, MADAGASCAR ET
REUNION (1947, 2 v.). Edited by two distinguished geographers and
written by competent specialists, among them high-ranking colonial
administrators, each volume presents a comprehensive set of essays
on physical, economic, and human geography, history, administrative
organization, and arts and culture of the territory in question,
including statistics and extensive bibliographies. Volumes have
been issued under various main titles, in addition to the above
title: ENCYCLOPEDIE DE L'EMPIRE FRANCAIS, ENCYCLOPEDIE DE L'UNION
FRANCAISE, ENCYCLOPEDIE DE L'AFRIQUE FRANCAISE.

        A new edition of this encyclopedia, not available for examination,
appeared under the title ENCYCLOPEDIE DE L'AFRIQUE FRANCAISE (Paris,
Editions de l'Union Française, 1952-53). Relevant volumes listed
are: AFRIQUE EQUATORIALE FRANCAISE (1953, 608 p.); AFRIQUE OCCIDENTALE
FRANCAISE (1953, 2 v., 820 p.); CAMEROUN-TOGO (1952, 550 p.);
MADAGASCAR, REUNION (1953, 2 v., 776 p.).

        Another series of more popular surveys of the states formerly
under French control, Pays africains, was published by the Société
d'Editions Géographiques, Maritimes et Coloniales. Among volumes in
this series are the following:

a)   LA COTE D'IVOIRE. By Emmanuel Avice. 1951. 94 p. illus.,
        maps. (Bibliography: p. 93-94.)

b)   LE DAHOMEY. By A. Akindélé and C. Aguessy. 1955. 126 p.
        maps, table. (Bibliography: p. 123-124.)

c)   LA GUINEE FRANCAISE. By Maurice Houis. 1953. 94 p. plates,
        maps. (Bibliography: p. 93-94.)

d)   LE NIGER. By E. Séré de Rivières. 1952. 94 p. plates, maps.
        (Bibliography: p. 92-94.)

e)   LE SENEGAL: DAKAR. By E. Séré de Rivières. 1953. 127 p. plates,
        maps. (Bibliography: p. 126-127.)

1582.   ETAT ACTUEL ET PERSPECTIVES DE LA RECHERCHE SCIENTIFIQUE FRANCAISE
EN AFRIQUE ET A MADAGASCAR (COLLOQUE ORGANISE PAR LA "SOCIETE
ALLEMAND POUR L'AFRIQUE" A COLOGNE LES 2-4 JANVIER 1964). Paris,
La Documentation Française, 1964. 84 p.

Includes papers by Pierre Alexandre on the state of French
African linguistic research in 1963, Lionel Balout on pre-proto-
historic archaeology, Raymond Mauny on French African historic
research, Marcel Merle on French research in African political
science, Paul Pélissier on French geographical research in tropical
Africa, Marcel Vaucel on French medical research and the state of
public health in tropical Africa, B. Geze on geology, and G. Leduc
on economic studies.

1583.   ETATS AFRICAINS D'EXPRESSION FRANCAISE ET REPUBLIQUE MALGACHE. 2d ed.
Paris, René Julliard, 1964. 329 p.

A handbook offering "as precise as possible a summary of political and administrative organization of the young states" and describing their common organizations and those which furnish aid; the first
edition was published in 1962. The 1964 edition is divided into four
parts: the first systematically covers 14 states (including Mali and
Togo but not Guinea); the second, the principal organizations of
interstate cooperation (Union Africaine et Malgache, Air-Afrique,
Office Inter-Etats du Tourisme Africain, and others); the third,
organizations of economic and financial aid; and the fourth, French
bureaus, institutes, and the like concerned with technical assistance
(agricultural production, communications, railroads, etc.).

1584.   France. Armée. Etat-Major. LES ARMEES FRANCAISES D'OUTRE-MER.
Paris, Impr. Nationale, 1931-32. 21 v. illus., plates (part
col.), maps (part fold.).

Prepared for the Exposition Coloniale Internationale de Paris in
1931. This superlative multi-volume set gives the military history
of the colonial possessions (9 v.), the service history of the colonial troops and their organizations, etc. (10 v.), and describes
colonial leaders and heroes (2 v.). For example, Vol. VI is on the
military history of French West Africa. See also no. 1611.

1585.   France. Bureau pour le Développement de la Production Agricole
Outre-Mer. [Publications] Paris.

Variety of valuable studies on various aspects of agriculture in
African countries.

1586.   France. Direction de la Documentation. LA COOPERATION ENTRE LA
         FRANCE ET L'AFRIQUE NOIRE D'EXPRESSION FRANCAISE. Paris, La
         Documentation Française, 1966. 47 p. (Notes et études docu-
         mentaires, no. 3330, Oct. 26, 1966)

         See general note on this series in next entry.

         Part 1 of this issue covers administrative, juridical, and finan-
cial machinery (organizations, legislation, etc.) concerned with aid;
Part 2 gives the general characteristics of aid and a review by sectors (e.g., administrative, educational, cultural, military, agricultural).

1587.   France. Direction de la Documentation. Notes et études documentaires
         [series]. Paris, La Documentation Française.

         This series has valuable background surveys of individual Afri-
can countries or questions. They are not entirely limited to former
French Africa but occasionally include background material on other
parts of Africa. The Notes and études documentaires are listed in
the semimonthly BIBLIOGRAPHIE SELECTIVE DES PUBLICATIONS OFFICIELLES
FRANCAISES, along with the other series put out by La Documentation
Française and the Direction de la Documentation.

1588.   France. Direction de la Documentation. [Les nouvelles républiques
         d'Afrique] Paris, 1960-61. (Notes et études documentaires)

         A set of surveys of most of the new states of former French
Africa was issued in this official documentary series in 1960 and
1961. The coverage is systematic: a general glance at geography,
history, ethnography, and demography, an outline of political and
administrative institutions, of economic and financial affairs, and
of cultural and social evolution, a conclusion covering prospects,
and, in an appendix, the text of the new constitution. For series
numbers, see under individual countries.

         A more popular set of statements for American readers regarding
the former French African countries is in a series of illustrated
booklets, THE REPUBLIC OF [...]: HOUR OF INDEPENDENCE, obtainable
from the Service de Presse et d'Information of the French Embassy in
New York. These are largely translations of a series in French, La
documentation française illustrée, which produced brochures for each
country in the year of independence.

1589.   France. Direction de la Documentation. LA RADIODIFFUSION ET LA
         TELEVISION EN AFRIQUE NOIRE FRANCOPHONE ET A MADAGASCAR. Paris,
         1963. 28 p. (Notes et études documentaires, no. 2986, Apr.
         1963)

1590.   France.   Institut National de la Statistique et des Etudes Econo-
            miques.   Paris.

            See nos. 1533 and 1534.

1591.   France.   Ministère de la Coopération.   [Various series and publica-
            tions]   Paris.

            A most valuable series of books, statistics, budgets, country
        studies, development plans, and economic surveys have been issued
        by departments or bureaus of this ministry.   Most development plans
        for individual African countries are produced in cooperation with
        this ministry.

1592.   France.   Ministère de la Coopération.   ATTITUDES ET OPINIONS DES
            FRANCAIS SUR L'AFRIQUE ET LA COOPERATION FRANCO-AFRICAINE.
            Paris, 1962.   2 v.   illus.

1593.   France.   Ministère de la Coopération.   CINQ ANS DE FONDS D'AIDE ET
            DE COOPERATION, 1959-64:   REPORT SUR LA COOPERATION FRANCO-
            AFRICAINE.   By Raymond Triboulet.   Paris, 1964.   71 p.   tables.

            See no. 745 for annotation.

1594.   France.   Ministère de la Coopération.   L'ENSEIGNEMENT SUPERIEUR EN
            AFRIQUE NOIRE D'EXPRESSION FRANCAISE ET A MADAGASCAR.   n.p.,
            1965.   1 v.   various pagings.

1595.   France.   Ministère de la Coopération.   ETUDE MONOGRAPHIQUE DE TRENTE
            ET UN PAYS AFRICAINS.   Paris, 1965.   4 v.   illus.

1596.   France.   Ministère de la Coopération.   RAPPORT D'ACTIVITE.   Paris.
            [Irregular?]

1597.   France.   Ministère de la Coopération.   Direction de la Coopération
            Culturelle et Technique.   Division d'Information.   GUIDE PRA-
            TIQUE SUR LES REPUBLIQUES: FEDERALE DU CAMEROUN, CENTRAFRICAINE,
            DU CONGO, DE COTE D'IVOIRE, DU DAHOMEY, GABONAISE, DE GUINEE,
            DE HAUTE-VOLTA, MALGACHE, DU MALI, ISLAMIQUE DE MAURITANIE, DU
            NIGER, DU SENEGAL, DU TCHAD, DU TOGO, A L'USAGE DES AGENTS DE
            LA COOPERATION.   Paris, 1964.   222 p.   illus., col. maps.

Includes bibliographies.

A guide book to the geographic, social, economic, and political and administrative aspects of the French-speaking African nations. Brief data on education, medical services, the press, and communications are included. Each chapter concludes with tourist information and a short bibliography on the country concerned.

1598.   France. Ministère d'Etat. LA POLITIQUE DE COOPERATION AVEC LES PAYS EN VOIE DE DEVELOPPEMENT: RAPPORT DE LA COMMISSION D'ETUDE INSTITUEE PAR LE DECRET DU 12 MARS 1963. Avec annexes. Paris, La Documentation Française, 1964. 136, 284 p.

Important report analyzing the French policy of aid to developing countries and justifying its continuance. It was prepared under the direction of Professor Jeanneney and is generally cited as the Jeanneney Report. An English translation was published by the Overseas Development Institute in London (see no. 744).

A balance sheet of FAC, the successor of FIDES, was issued in 1964 by the Ministère de la Coopération, CINQ ANS DE FONDS D'AIDE ET DE COOPERATION, 1959-64, prepared by Raymond Triboulet (see no. 745). Earlier a brief survey of FIDES appeared in an English edition by the French Embassy's Service de Presse et d'Information, FRENCH AFRICA: A DECADE OF PROGRESS, 1948-1958; ACHIEVEMENTS OF FIDES, INVESTMENT FUND FOR ECONOMIC AND SOCIAL DEVELOPMENT IN FRENCH WEST AND EQUATORIAL AFRICA (New York, 1958, 40 p., col. maps and diagrs.). It included a short bibliography giving titles of pertinent official documents.

1599.   France. Office de la Recherche Scientifique et Technique Outre-Mer (ORSTOM). OFFICE DE LA RECHERCHE SCIENTIFIQUE ET TECHNIQUE OUTRE-MER: ORGANISATION, ACTIVITIES, 1944-1955. [Rapport présenté par Raoul Combes, directeur]. Paris, 1955. 182 p. illus., maps (part fold.).

Includes bibliography.

See also no. 1558.

1600.   France. Service des Statistiques d'Outre-Mer. OUTRE-MER 1958: TABLEAU ECONOMIQUE ET SOCIAL DES ETATS ET TERRITOIRES D'OUTRE-MER A LA VEILLE DE LA MISE EN PLACE DES NOUVELLES INSTITUTIONS. Paris, 1959. 862 p. maps, tables, diagrs., charts.

Complete statistical handbook. Many of the tables include figures for the year 1957/58. Part 1 gives overseas territories in the world setting; Part 2, territories, plus Togo and Cameroun, 1947-58; Part 3, an analysis by subject as of about 1958, with tabular breakdown for individual countries.

Earlier works of the same character from this office were L'ECONOMIE DE L'UNION FRANCAISE D'OUTRE-MER (Paris, Sirey, 1952-54, 2 v.), a reprint from the professional journal REVUE D'ECONOMIE POLITIQUE, and INVENTAIRE SOCIAL ET ECONOMIQUE DES TERRITOIRES D'OUTRE-MER, 1950 A 1955 (Paris, Impr. Nationale, 1957, 467 p., tables).

1601. Gonidec, P. F. CONSTITUTIONS DES ETATS DE LA COMMUNAUTE: TEXTES RECUEILLIS. Paris, Sirey, 1959. 185 p.

Texts of the constitutions of the new states which had opted for the French Community in the referendum of Sept. 1958. This specialist in the law of France overseas was responsible for two authoritative earlier works, both published by the Librairie Générale de Droit et de Jurisprudence: DROIT DE TRAVAIL DES TERRITOIRES D' OUTRE-MER (in collaboration with M. Kirsch, 1958, 743 p.; Bibliothèque de droit des territoires d'outre-mer, v. 1) and L'EVOLUTION DES TERRITOIRES D'OUTRE-MER DEPUIS 1946 (1958, 126 p.). A more recent study, issued by the same publisher, is Gonidec's volume of 30 lectures on labor laws and legislation in the French Community and Madagascar, COURS DE DROIT DU TRAVAIL AFRICAIN ET MALGACHE (1966, 288 p.). See also his COURS D'INSTITUTIONS PUBLIQUE AFRICAINES ET MALGACHE (Paris, Les Cours de Droit, 1967, 406 p.). For the latest texts of constitutions of the French African states, see the work by Lavroff and Peiser, below (no. 1604).

A collection of 21 essays by Belgian, British, French, and Malagasy specialists, published under the direction of Jean Poirier, ETUDES DE DROIT AFRICAIN ET DE DROIT MALGACHE (Paris, Editions Cujas, 1965, 529 p., maps, bibliographies; Etudes malgaches, 16), offers diverse juridical, sociological, and ethnological studies and analyses.

A new school of African law and economics was opened in the University of Paris (Sorbonne) in Mar. 1964, with a planned enrollment of 500 students in the academic year 1964/65 and several chairs-- overseas law, Moslem law, African and Malagasy economic affairs, African and Malagasy private institutions, and judicial ethnology.

1602. Gras, Jacqueline. SITUATION DE LA PRESSE DANS LES ETATS DE L'UNION AFRICAINE ET MALGACHE, EN GUINEE, AU MALI, AU TOGO. Paris, La Documentation Française, 1963. 175 p. (Travaux et recherches, no. 17)

A study going far beyond other records of the press in its inclusion not only of titles, addresses, and circulation data for

newspapers and periodicals of each country but also of helpful notes
on organization of the press, journalists, news services, etc.

1603. Labouret, Henri. PAYSANS D'AFRIQUE OCCIDENTALE. 5th ed. Paris,
Gallimard, 1941. 307 p. (Le paysan et la terre)

Bibliography: p. 290-294.

Standard work by one of France's outstanding and scholarly
colonial administrators.

1604. Lavroff, Dimitri G., and Gustave Peiser, eds. LES CONSTITUTIONS
AFRICAINES: Vol. I, L'AFRIQUE NOIRE FRANCOPHONE ET MADAGASCAR.
Paris, Pedone, 1961. 277 p. (Collection du Centre de Recherches,
d'Etudes et de Documentation sur les Institutions et la Législation
Africaines, no. 1)

See note no. 630.

Another authoritative study of the new French-speaking states
and their governments is by Jean Buchmann, L'AFRIQUE NOIRE INDEPENDANTE
(Paris, Librairie Générale de Droit et de Jurisprudence, 1962, 434 p.;
Comment ils sont gouvernés, v. 7). Texts of the constitutions have
been published by La Documentation Française in the series Notes et
études documentaires (no. 3175, Mar. 26, 1965, 52 p.).

1605. Leduc, Michel. LES INSTITUTIONS MONETAIRES AFRICAINES: PAYS FRANCO-
PHONES. Paris, Pedone, 1965. 397 p. (Collection du Centre de
Recherches, d'Etudes et de Documentation sur les Institutions
et les Législations Africaines, no. 6)

By a professor of economics at Dakar, this scholarly overall
study gives a full account of the history of the "banques d'émission"
and of the evolution of the franc zone, with changes in internal
financial structures of the French-speaking states and the integration
of the new institutions into world monetary systems. The second part
reviews the monetary institutions of Equatorial Africa and Cameroun,
French-speaking West Africa--with subsections on Mali and Guinea,
which stand apart from the regional monetary union--and Madagascar.
A short final chapter is on monetary institutions of the remaining
French-controlled countries, the Comoro Islands, Réunion, and French
Somaliland (now called the French Territory of the Afars and the Issas).

1606. Leroi-Gourhan, André, and Jean Poirier. ETHNOLOGIE DE L'UNION
FRANCAISE (TERRITOIRES EXTERIEURS). Paris, Presses Universitaires
de France, 1953. 2 v. 1083 p. plates, maps. (Pays d'outre-

mer, colonies, empires, pays autonomes, 6th ser., Peuples et civilisations d'outre-mer, v. 1-2)

Bibliography: v. 1, p. 441-468.

An encyclopedic study, the first volume on Africa, the second on Asia, Oceania, and America. Vol. I, AFRIQUE, begins with a general section, then treats the regions, and ends with an essay "Les sociétés négro-africaines." There is a long bibliography as well as statistical appendixes.

1607. Luchaire, François. DROIT D'OUTRE-MER ET DE LA COOPERATION. Paris, Presses Universitaires de France, 1966. 2d ed. 628 p. ("Themis": Manuels juridiques, économiques et politiques)

Includes bibliographies.

An updated edition of a work published in 1959 under the title DROIT D'OUTRE-MER. An introductory analysis of colonialism, decolonization, and underdevelopment is followed by a study of the laws of French territories and departments, laws of French-speaking African countries, and laws concerning financial, cultural, and technical aid.

1608. MEMENTO DE L'INDUSTRIE AFRICAINE, 1966. Paris, EDIAFRIC, 1966. 447 p. maps, tables. (BULLETIN DE L'AFRIQUE NOIRE, numéro spécial, no. 413)

Covering individually the same nations described in the next entry, this work sets forth the general conditions for industrialization, describes the industries of various sectors of the economy, gives lists of industrial societies and enterprises, and includes a section on the Union Douanière et Economique de l'Afrique Centrale (UDEAC). See also by EDIAFRIC: L'INDUSTRIE AFRICAINE EN 1969 (1969, 600 p.).

1609. MEMENTO STATISTIQUE DE L'ECONOMIE AFRICAINE, 1969. Paris, EDIAFRIC, 1969. 365 p. maps, tables. (BULLETIN DE L'AFRIQUE NOIRE, numéro spécial, no. 557)

This is the fifth edition of a special issue on African economies. The first two editions were devoted to francophone West and Equatorial Africa; the third to francophone and, more briefly, anglophone black Africa. The 1969 volume covers the economies of Cameroun, Central African Republic, Congo (Brazzaville), Ivory Coast, Dahomey, Gabon, Upper Volta, Mali, Mauritania, Niger, Senegal, Chad, and Togo. For

each country a geographical outline is followed by data on the various sectors of the economy, current budgets, development programs,
foreign commerce, and foreign aid, with ample statistical material
provided. A map accompanies each country study, and an index to
advertisers is included.

1610. Monographies ethnologiques africaines [series]. Paris, Published for
the International African Institute by Presses Universitaires de
France, 1954-

The French series of the Ethnographic Survey of Africa (see general notes, nos. 980 and 1670). The individual volumes for peoples
of French-speaking Africa are named under the separate regions and,
where possible, countries.

1611. Paris. Exposition Coloniale Internationale, 1931. [Publications]

Among the many publications prepared for the 1931 Exposition the
following are of lasting significance:

Exposition Coloniale Internationale de 1931. [Série géogra-
phique] Paris, Société des Editions Geographiques, Maritimes et Coloniales, 1931. 10 v.

Authoritative geographical studies. Those for Africa,
sponsored by the Gouvernements Généraux, are Le gouvernement
général de l'Afrique occidentale française; La Côte d'Ivoire;
Le Dahomey; La circonscription de Dakar dépendances; La Guinée;
La Haute-Volta; La Mauritanie; Le Niger; Le Sénégal; Le Soudan;
Territoires africains sous mandat de la France: Cameroun et
Togo; Afrique équatoriale française; and Madagascar.

France. Armée. Etat-Major. LES ARMEES FRANCIASES D'OUTRE-MER.
Paris, Impr. Nationale, 1931-32. 21 v. illus., plates
(part col.), maps (including 5 portolios of 63 fold. maps).

Vol. VI, HISTOIRE MILITAIRE DES COLONIES . . . AFRIQUE OCCI-
DENTALE FRANCAISE; Vol. VII, AFRIQUE EQUATORIALE FRANCAISE;
Vol. VIII, MADAGASCAR; Vol. IX, LA CONQUETE DU CAMEROUN ET
DU TOGO; Vol. X, LES UNIFORMES DES TROUPES DE LA MARINE ET
DES TROUPES COLONIALES ET NORD-AFRICAINES (by Albert Depré-
aux, 192 p., illus., col. plates).

See also no. 1584.

1612. Pierson-Mathy, Paulette. L'EVOLUTION POLITIQUE DE L'AFRIQUE: LA
COMMUNAUTE "FRANCAISE," LA REPUBLIQUE DE GUINEE, L'INDEPENDANCE

DE LA SOMALIE. Bruxelles, Institut Royal des Relations Internationales, 1961. 485 p. (CHRONIQUE DE POLITIQUE ETRANGERE,
v. 14, no. 1-3, Jan.-May 1961)

Bibliographical footnotes.

In this detailed and commendably documented study, the major
portion of the text deals with the Community: its organization, the
interstate regroupings, and the evolution of the African republics
(p. 7-237). About 50 pages each are then devoted to Guinea and
Somalia. The volume ends with 22 documents and an analytical index.

1613. LA POLITIQUE AFRICAINE EN 1969. Paris, EDIAFRIC-La Documentation
Africaine, 1969. 333 p. (Numéro spécial du BULLETIN DE L'AF-
RIQUE NOIRE).

Covers former French Africa excluding the Malagasy Republic.
For each country the volume gives major political events of the
year, including international relations and changes in office.
Regional organizations are also described. Biographies (some with
addresses) of political leaders, including mayors, are provided.

1614. Poquin, Jean J. LES RELATIONS ECONOMIQUES EXTERIEURES DES PAYS
D'AFRIQUE NOIRE DE L'UNION FRANCAISE, 1925-1955. Paris,
Librairie A. Colin, 1957. 297 p. (Centre d'Etudes Economiques,
Etudes et mémoires, 37)

1615. PRESIDENTS, ADMINISTRATEURS ET DIRECTEURS GENERAUX DES SOCIETES PUB-
LIQUES ET PRIVEES D'AFRIQUE NOIRE. PDG-AFRIQUE 1969. Paris,
EDIAFRIC-La Documentation Africaine [1969?]. 471 p. (Numéro
spécial du BULLETIN DE L'AFRIQUE NOIRE).

Covers former French Africa and France. Arrangement is by
country. At the beginning of each country section addresses and
officers of chambers of commerce and employers organization are
given. Then follow in alphabetical order by surname brief biographies, some with addresses, of key individuals in the country's economy. Data are given on 1,500 individuals, 2,500 businesses, 100
consular and professional groups, and the 13 states of francophone
Africa.

1616. RECHERCHE, ENSEIGNEMENT, DOCUMENTATION AFRICANISTES FRANCOPHONES:
BULLETIN D'INFORMATION ET DE LIAISON. v. 1, no. 1- 1969-
Paris, Centre d'Analyse et de Recherche Documentaires pour
l'Afrique Noire, Publié avec le concours du Centre National
de la Recherche Scientifique. Quarterly.

A francophone publication covering African studies in French-speaking Africa, Belgium, France, Switzerland, and Canada. Format will be in "fiches" which can be cut up for filing. A bristol paper edition will be produced if there is sufficient demand. Future issues will carry lists of thèses and diplômes, annotations of Africanist periodicals, reports of research projects and trips, and studies of documentary methods. The social sciences and humanities are the disciplines covered.

The first issue, "Inventaire des ressources documentaires africanistes à Paris," by Joanne Coyle Dauphin, Agnès Rosset, and Brigitta Rupp, comprises a directory of 129 organizations (libraries, research institutes, information centers) in Paris. Data given are sponsoring organization, address, amount and types of material in collection (maps, photographs, records, etc.), areas of specialty, publications, current projects, history of facilities, services, and access to public. There are indexes of abbreviations used, of series, and of periodicals cited, with separate lists for bibliographical bulletins, acquisitions lists, publications lists, and annual reports of organizations. There is also a subject and geographic index.

1617. REPERTOIRE DE L'ADMINISTRATION AFRICAINE. 1st ed. Paris, EDIAFRIC-La Documentation Africaine, 1969. 411 p. (Numéro spécial du BULLETIN DE L'AFRIQUE NOIRE)

Covers former French colonial Africa. For each country is given a roster of the chief political and civil service personnel; addresses of ministries are also supplied.

1618. Roberts, Stephen H. HISTORY OF FRENCH COLONIAL POLICY, 1870-1925. London, P. S. King, 1929. 2 v.

Reprint. New York, Archon Books, 1963. xvi, 741 p.

Bibliography: p. 685-736.

Standard work on French administrative theory and practice in France's dependent territories, by an Australian historian. Appendixes include a list of the chief colonial officers and an extensive bibliography.

An American reference work on the same lines, with more attention to France's acquisition of its overseas empire, is by Herbert I. Priestly, FRANCE OVERSEAS: A STUDY OF MODERN IMPERIALISM (New York, London, Appleton-Century, 1938, 463 p.).

1619. SOCIETES ET FOURNISSEURS D'AFRIQUE NOIRE ET DE MADAGASCAR: GUIDE
        ECONOMIQUE NORIA. Paris, La Documentation Africaine, 1968.
        787 p. Annual.

        An earlier title was ANNUAIRE ECONOMIQUE DES ETATS D'AFRIQUE
NOIRE: SOCIETES ET ORGANISMES PUBLICS ET PRIVES. This large
commercial directory covers the 14 countries of French-speaking
West and Equatorial Africa and Madagascar; information includes
the names of government officials concerned with economic affairs.
There are indexes of personal, society, and company names.

        La Documentation Africaine (like EDIAFRIC and Annuaire
Africain situated at 57, avenue d'Iéna, Paris 16) also publishes
a fortnightly, HOMMES ET ORGANISATIONS D'AFRIQUE NOIRE, 1959-,
which gives news of public and private institutions of the Black
African states. EDIAFRIC publishes the news service BULLETIN
DE L'AFRIQUE NOIRE (see no. 572).

1620. Soras, Alfred de. RELATIONS DE L'EGLISE ET DE L'ETAT DANS LES
        PAYS D'AFRIQUE FRANCOPHONE: VUES PROSPECTIVES. Tours, Mame,
        1963. 156 p. (Esprit et mission)

        A compact study of relations between the Catholic Church and
the State in French-speaking Africa, along with a consideration
of possible meeting points between the two forces in independent
Black Africa. For an anti-clercial view of the topic see François
Mejan, LE VATICAN CONTRE LA FRANCE D'OUTRE-MER (Paris, 1957).

1621. Suret-Canale, Jean. AFRIQUE NOIRE, OCCIDENTALE ET CENTRALE:
        Vol. I, GEOGRAPHIE, CIVILISATION, HISTOIRE. 2d ed. rev. Paris,
        Editions Sociales, 1961. 321 p. illus., maps. (La culture
        et les hommes)

        Vol. II, L'ERE COLONIALE (1900-1945). Paris, Editions Sociales,
        1964. 637 p. illus., maps, tables. (La culture et les hommes)

        The writer, a geographer who had taught in Senegal, studied
African history and problems from a Marxist point of view. Vol. I,
first published in 1958, is an outline of physical and human geography
and history up to 1900, heavily documented with footnotes and a long
bibliography (2d ed., p. 273-313). The second volume, published in
1964, brings the record up to 1945 and is centered on economic,
social, and political aspects. The bibliography, p. 601-616, does
not repeat works listed in Vol. I.

        Published in English as THE COLONIAL ERA IN FRENCH WEST AND
CENTRAL AFRICA 1900-1945 (London, C. Hurst, 1970, 550 p.).

1622.　UAM (Union Africaine et Malgache).　DOCUMENTATION:　OAMCE, UAMD,
　　　UAMPT, AIR-AFRIQUE.　Paris, Marcomer, 1963.　409 p.　illus.
　　　(Includes advertising.)

　　　Handbook of the former UAM and its subsidiary groups, OAMCE
(see no. 1560), Union Africaine et Malgache de Défense, Union
Africaine et Malgache des Postes et Télécommunications, and Air-
Afrique.　Included are texts of charters, details of organization,
and documents of the various conferences held between the founding
in 1960 and Mar. 1963.　Among the several appendixes are a biographical directory of officials (p. 309-340) and a list of abbreviations
for organizational names (p. 343-388).

　　　A new study by the former secretary-general of the UAM, Albert
Tevoedjre, is entitled PAN-AFRICANISM IN ACTION:　AN ACCOUNT OF THE
UAM (Cambridge, Mass., Center for International Affairs, Harvard
University, 1965, 88 p.; Occasional Papers in International Affairs,
no. 11).　The work is an analysis of the success and failure, crises,
and future of the UAM; appendixes cover the charter, finances,
conferences, organization, and excerpts from important resolutions.

CHAPTER 34

FORMER FRENCH WEST AFRICA

(AFRIQUE OCCIDENTALE FRANCAISE)

Atlas

1623. Institut Français [Fondamental] d'Afrique Noire (IFAN). INTERNATIONAL
ATLAS OF WEST-AFRICA. ATLAS INTERNATIONAL DE L'OUEST-AFRICAIN.
Dakar, 1965-

An impressive undertaking, which is appearing in separate folio
sheets, to be bound in a book of maps opening to a size of 21 x 30
inches. It was begun in 1964 under the auspices of CSA (now absorbed
by OAU/STRC--Organization of African Unity/Scientific, Technical and
Research Commission) and will comprise about 48 separate maps, prepared by a team of experts directed by Professor Théodore Monod.
The basic scale is 1:5,000,000 though a few of the maps--notably
those of relief and population--vary to 1:2,500,000. The first part
will contain maps of environment, situation of West Africa in relation
to the world, relief, geology, geomorphology, pedology, climate, and
density of population. Part 2 will include maps of history, languages
or civilization, industrial development, town planning, etc. Aerial
photographs have been extensively utilized.

Another IFAN work is CARTES ETHNO-DEMOGRAPHIQUES DE L'AFRIQUE
OCCIDENTALE, prepared by G. Brasseur and G. Savonnet, respectively,
for the northern and southern parts (Dakar, 1960), which is comprised
of 2 colored maps on 4 sheets accompanied by a 34-page text in folder.

For description of IFAN see no. 1644.

524

Bibliographies

Note: The following bibliographies for French-speaking West Africa are with few exceptions the only general bibliographies available for the individual countries. Under the country headings from Dahomey to Upper Volta, cross-reference is indicated to this subsection.

1624. Banque Centrale des Etats de l'Afrique de l'Ouest. NOTES D'INFORMATION
      ET STATISTIQUES. Paris. Monthly.

      Two bibliographical fascicles are included. See below, no. 1640.

1625. Blaudin de Thé, Bernard, ed. ESSAI DE BIBLIOGRAPHIE DU SAHARA
      FRANCAIS ET DES REGIONS AVOISINANTES. Edité avec le concours
      de l'Organisation Commune des Régions Sahariennes. 2d ed.
      Paris, Arts et Métiers Graphiques, Librairie C. Klinksieck,
      1960. 258 p.

      For commentary on this work, see no. 1760 under Mauritania.

1626. Bovy, L., Abbé. BIBLIOGRAPHIE DU MOUVEMENT SYNDICAL OUEST-AFRICAIN
      D'EXPRESSION FRANCAISE. Bruxelles, CEDESA, 1965. 113 p.
      (Enquêtes bibliographiques, no. 14)

      See no. 829, for note on the CEDESA series. The present work is
an extensive examination of literature on all phases of the labor
movement in French-speaking Africa. Most of the 518 entries are
annotated. Arrangement is alphabetical by author; there is a classified subject index.

1627. Brasseur, Paule, and Jean-François Maurel. LES SOURCES BIBLIOGRAPHIQUES
      DE L'AFRIQUE DE L'OUEST D'EXPRESSION FRANCAISE. Dakar, 1967.
      48 p. Processed.

      Although called "a preliminary survey," this monograph is the
essential and definitive bibliographical survey of the former French
West African Federation and the states that once made up AOF; The
authors (the distinguished bibliographer of Mali, Mme Brasseur, and
the outstanding archivist M. Maurel) survey first the federation-wide
learned societies (their history, series published, etc.), government
publications, and then essential sources by subject. Each country is
treated in the same manner. Hundreds of entries are analyzed and the
starting dates and change of titles and structure for learned societies, journals, and government series are given. Articles as well
as books and monographs are analyzed.

1628. Clozel, François. BIBLIOGRAPHIE DES OUVRAGES RELATIFS A LA
           SENEGAMBIE ET AU SOUDAN OCCIDENTAL. Paris, 1891. 60 p.
           (1,200 entries)

       Appeared serially in the REVUE DE GEOGRAPHIE, July-Dec. 1890,
Jan.-June 1891, and July-Dec. 1891.

1629. Joucla, Edmond A. BIBLIOGRAPHIE DE L'AFRIQUE OCCIDENTALE FRANCAISE.
           Avec la collaboration des services du Gouvernement Général de
           l'Afrique occidentale française et pour le Dahomey de M. Maupoil,
           administrateur des colonies. Paris, Société d'Editions Géo-
           graphiques, Maritimes et Coloniales, 1937. 704 p. (BIBLIO-
           GRAPHIE GENERALE DES COLONIES FRANCAISES, by G. Grandidier and
           E. Joucla)

       Basic for any study of French West Africa that involves back-
ground material, this huge bibliography appeared in an officially
sponsored series begun shortly before World War II. Joucla cites
almost 1,700 maps and charts of AOF. His references include books,
papers, official documents (without distinction from unofficial
material), and select periodical articles. The arrangement is
alphabetical, with several subject indexes.

1630. Lavergne de Tressan, Michel de. INVENTAIRE LINGUISTIQUE DE L'AFRIQUE
           OCCIDENTALE FRANCAISE ET DU TOGO. Dakar, IFAN, 1953. 240 p.
           9 fold. maps. (Mémoires, no. 30)

       Bibliography: p. 25-45.

       Comprehensive reference work, with detailed information as to
localities where the various languages of French West Africa are
spoken and estimates of number of speakers from the French census of
1950. The bibliography for each language or group of languages includes texts as well as ethnological books and articles. There is
an index of languages, dialects, and tribes.

1631. Martonne, Edouard de. INVENTAIRE METHODIQUE DES CARTES ET CROQUIS,
           IMPRIMES ET MANUSCRITS, RELATIFS A L'AFRIQUE OCCIDENTALE
           EXISTANT AU GOUVERNEMENT GENERAL DE L'A.O.F. A DAKAR. Laval,
           1926. xvi, 138 p. (1,250 entries)

1632. Mauny, Raymond. "Les recherches archéologiques et historiques en
           Afrique occidentale française, de 1952 à 1957: Bibliographie
           Ouest africain." BULLETIN DE L'IFAN, ser. B, v. 20, no. 1-2,
           Jan.-Apr. 1958: 291-302.

_____. "Les recherches archéologiques et historiques en Afrique occidentale d'expression française de 1957 à 1961." BULLETIN DE L'IFAN, ser. B, v. 24, no. 1-2, Jan.-Apr. 1962: 279-298.

_____. "Bibliographie de la préhistoire et de la protohistoire de l'Ouest africain." BULLETIN DE L'IFAN, ser. B, v. 29, no. 3-4, July-Oct. 1967: 879-917.

In each of these three articles the state of research is examined and a two-part bibliography is presented, the first being on archaeology, the second on tradition, legend, and history of the area within present French-speaking West Africa, including the Sahara, and the third on West Africa generally.

1633. Paris-Leclerc, L. TABLES CHRONOLOGIQUE AND ALPHABETIQUE DES ACTES METROPOLITAINS ET LOCAUX PROMULGES DANS LA COLONIE DU SENEGAL ET DEPENDANCES, LE SOUDAN FRANCAIS ET LES ETABLISSEMENTS FRANCAIS DE LA COTE OCCIDENTALE D'AFRIQUE. Melun, 1903. 872, lii p. (7,000 entries)

1634. Société d'Etudes et de Réalisations Economiques et Sociales dans l'Agriculture. ELEMENTS DE DOCUMENTATION SUR L'AFRIQUE OCCIDENTALE. Dakar, SERESA, 1959. 8 fasc. Processed.

Eight partially annotated bibliographies on the rural economy of former French West Africa, each fascicle and its entries being allotted the code number employed by the Service Mécanigraphique de l'AOF. Each fascicle has two main sections--"important documents" and "other documents"--with several subdivisions, and references are to processed materials issued by various technical services of the administrations, to printed works, and to periodical articles. The eight fascicles are: no. 1, SENEGAL, 60 l. (281 entries); no. 2, MAURITANIE, 44 l. (243 entries); no. 3, SOUDAN, 65 l. (277 entries); no. 5, COTE D'IVOIRE, 76 l. (250 entries); no. 6, HAUTE-VOLTA, 15 l. (87 entries); no. 7, DAHOMEY, 48 l. (238 entries); no. 8, NIGER, 21 l. (84 entries); no. 9, AFRIQUE OCCIDENTALE, 195 l. (886 entries). There is no fascicle on Guinea.

1635. Tuaillon, Jean Louis Georges. BIBLIOGRAPHIE CRITIQUE DE L'AFRIQUE OCCIDENTALE FRANCAISE. Paris, Lavauzelle, 1936. about 50 p.

Heavily annotated list prepared as a thesis by an artillery officer. Arrangement is by subject--history, juridical works, geography and maps, etc., with further breakdown under history. The works, mostly of the 1920's and 1930's, are arranged chronologically in each section. Besides the hundred or so critically reviewed books there is a "Bibliographie supplémentaire" in two parts: books and pamphlets (over 400 titles) and a short listing of important periodicals and articles in journals (p. 46-48).

1636. U.S. Library of Congress. General Reference and Bibliography Division. FRENCH-SPEAKING WEST AFRICA: A GUIDE TO OFFICIAL PUBLICATIONS. Compiled by Julian W. Witherell, African Section. Washington, 1967. xii, 201 p.

The guide is a greatly expanded revision of OFFICIAL PUBLICATIONS OF FRENCH WEST AFRICA, 1946-1958 (1960, 88 p.), compiled by Helen F. Conover, then also of the African Section. The new bibliography contains 2,431 entries listing published government records from the mid-nineteenth century through early 1967; locations of the items (in American and African libraries or bibliographic sources) are given. After publications on French West Africa are listed, arrangement is by country, and there are author and subject indexes. Included also are selected League of Nations and UN publications, French documents on the area before and after independence, and material issued by the Organisation Commune Africaine et Malgache (OCAM).

Serials

1637. AFRIQUE NOUVELLE. 1948- Dakar. Weekly.

The leading newspaper of French-speaking West Africa.

1638. ANNALES AFRICAINES. 1954- Dakar, Faculté de Droit et des Sciences Economiques, Université de Dakar. Annual.

Although articles tend to be concentrated on West Africa, there is an attempt to cover all of Africa and a variety of subjects: the Organisation Commune Africaine et Malgache, the marriage rights of women in the Ivory Coast, monetary systems in West Africa, a social security system for Africans.

1639. ANNUAIRE DES REPUBLIQUES DE L'OUEST AFRICAIN: COTE D'IVOIRE--DAHOMEY-- HAUTE-VOLTA--MAURITANIE--NIGER--SENEGAL--SOUDAN. 1960- Paris, Diloutremer; Dakar, Havas Afrique. illus., ports, maps, plans, diagrs.

Useful yearbook (1960, 450 p.), the first part carrying essays on notable aspects of West African affairs, the second giving systematic data about political, economic, and social life country by country, and the third explaining organization of the community. The section

on Dakar includes a business directory. Advertising is interspersed
throughout. Included are indexes of place names and advertisers.

1640.   Banque Centrale des Etats de l'Afrique de l'Ouest. NOTES D'INFOR-
        MATION ET STATISTIQUES. Paris. tables, graphs. Monthly.

        This extremely useful serial publication comes in the form of
separate leaflets in an overall cover. The fascicles are in part
articles on specific financial and economic questions, in part
bibliographic. The two bibliographical fascicles are printed in the
form often used by French services--reproductions of catalogue cards
adapted for clipping and filing. The first section contains cards
for books and articles on general subjects, slanted toward economics;
the second, "Répertoire législatif," has analytic cards for all
important laws of the various states. The fascicles "Indicateurs
économiques" and "Statistiques" have many graphs and tables.

        The Banque Centrale also publishes occasional monographic studies,
e.g., COMPTES ECONOMIQUES: TOGO, 1956-1957-1958 (Paris, 1961, 278 p.)
and SIGLES OUEST AFRICAINS D'HIER ET D'AUJOURD'HUI: CONTRIBUTION A
L'ENTENDEMENT DE L'AFRIQUE DE L'OUEST (1959, 104 p.; outdated but useful, including acronyms for French and British institutions, companies,
etc.).

1641.   Banque Centrale des Etats de l'Afrique de l'Ouest. RAPPORT D'ACTIVITE.
        Paris. illus., tables, charts. Annual.

        The report for 1966 had grown to 211 pages and includes almost
70 tables in presenting the wide-ranging material. Agriculture,
mineral resources, foreign aid, exports of coffee, cocoa, cotton,
etc., are among numerous topics reported upon.

1642.   French West Africa. JOURNAL OFFICIEL DE L'AFRIQUE OCCIDENTALE
        FRANCAISE. nos. 1-3049. 1905-59. Gorée, 1905-40; Rufisque,
        1941-59. tables. Weekly

        The journaux officiels of the French-speaking states of Africa,
like the French models, include all legislation in addition to
official information in many fields. Lois, décrets, etc., do not go
into effect until their publication in the JOURNAL OFFICIEL. For
other official publications of the former AOF see the Library of
Congress bibliography above, no. 1636.

1643.   GUID'OUEST AFRICAIN. 1948- Paris, Diloutremer; Dakar, Agence de
        Distribution de Presse. illus. Annual.

A sketchy and journalistic annual report, published from 1948 to 1955/56 with the title GUID'A.O.F. The 1967-68 issue (472 p.) includes maps, indexes of place names and of abbreviations of organizations, banks, etc. (e.g., FIDES, ORSTOM, BIAO), and a list of advertisers. A general section precedes the country-by-country listing.

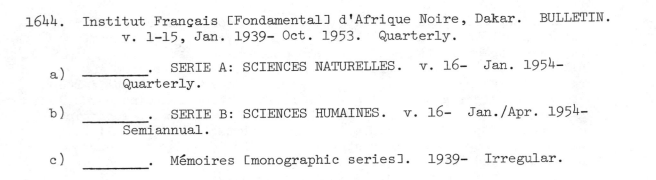

1644. Institut Français [Fondamental] d'Afrique Noire, Dakar. BULLETIN. v. 1-15, Jan. 1939- Oct. 1953. Quarterly.

a) _____. SERIE A: SCIENCES NATURELLES. v. 16- Jan. 1954- Quarterly.

b) _____. SERIE B: SCIENCES HUMAINES. v. 16- Jan./Apr. 1954- Semiannual.

c) _____. Mémoires [monographic series]. 1939- Irregular.

d) _____. NOTES AFRICAINES. 1939- Quarterly.

The renowned research institute of French West Africa was created in 1936 and activated in 1938 with the appointment of Dr. Théodore Monod as director. In 1960 it was incorporated as an institute in the University of Dakar. A sketch of IFAN's history for its 25th birthday was published in NOTES AFRICAINES, no. 90, Apr. 1961. Since 1966 the name has appeared as Institut Fondamental d'Afrique Noire, preserving the familiar acronym but discarding the neocolonial label. Over the years IFAN has undertaken learned studies in practically all disciplines relating to the region--botany, zoology, oceanography, ethnology, archaeology, anthropology, sociology, linguistics, geography; only geology is excluded, as coming within the province of the Direction des Mines. The monographic series Mémoires, which was begun in 1939, has included distinguished contributions in all these fields. A few recent volumes in the human sciences are separately analyzed in the present guide. Besides the Mémoires, there is the monographic series Initiations et études africaines (variant title, Initiations africaines), shorter papers usually in more popular vein than the Mémoires; there is also the series Catalogues et documents (nos. 1-14 titled Catalogues), describing the various collections of natural and ethnological materials gathered by IFAN and preserved in its museums in Dakar and local branches. The BULLETIN of IFAN, a journal of scholarly contributions in the various disciplines, often of monograph length, is now published in two sections, SER. A: SCIENCES NATURELLES, and SER. B: SCIENCES HUMAINES. The full list of IFAN publications is given on the inside of the front and back covers of each issue. The bulletin of information and correspondence, NOTES AFRICAINES, is also published quarterly, and this too carries on its back-cover pages the full list of IFAN'S publications.

Until independence the chief scholarly institutions in the states of French West Africa were the local Centres IFAN (or Centrifans) in the individual capitals. Most centers began a series of studies-- ETUDES GUINEENES, ETUDES DAHOMEENNES, etc.--some of which have continued since 1960 in the same or changed style. They are named in the country sections that follow.

Reference Works

1645. Adloff, Richard. WEST AFRICA: THE FRENCH-SPEAKING NATIONS, YESTERDAY AND TODAY. New York, Holt, Rinehart and Winston, 1964. 361 p.

Bibliography: p. 349-351.

This is a popular book valuable to a wide audience as a quick reference work. It sketches the historical and political background and analyzes succinctly the present international position of the new states of the former AOF.

1646. AFRIQUE OCCIDENTALE FRANCAISE [ET LE] TOGO. Paris, Hachette, 1958. ccxliv, 542 p. maps (part fold. col.). (Les guides bleus)

Bibliography: p. ccxxiv-ccxxxi.

Still useful for most matters aside from politics is this Baedeker-like guide to the countries of the former AOF and Togo, with a preliminary section on airlines, shipping, railroads, and roads and detailed descriptions of localities. The introductory essays on West Africa, its geography, economy, history and pre-history, missions, peoples, arts and crafts, languages, and flora and fauna, are by prominent scholars, headed by Professor Théodore Monod of IFAN.

1647. Béart, Charles. JEUX ET JOUETS DE L'OUEST AFRICAIN. Dakar, IFAN, 1955. 2 v. 888 p. illus., ports., maps. (Mémoires, no. 42)

Bibliography: v. 2, p. 847-866.

A unique ethnological study of the games and playthings of both children and adults in West Africa, particularly former French West Africa. The two large volumes, involving a detailed analysis of each game or toy, are lavishly illustrated.

1648. Bourcart, Robert. LE GRAND CONSEIL DE L'AFRIQUE OCCIDENTALE FRANCAISE. 2d ed. Paris, Encyclopédie d'Outre-Mer, 1956. 242 p.

Bibliography: p. 227-229.

Discussion of the formation, functions, powers, and economic role of the assembly in French West Africa which gave many Africans their first political experience.

1649. Bovy, Lambert. LA NATURE DU MOUVEMENT SYNDICAL OUEST-AFRICAIN D'EXPRESSION FRANCAISE. Bruxelles, Académie Royale des Sciences d'Outre-Mer, 1967. 194 p. (Académie Royale . . . , Classe des sciences morales et politiques, n.s. 35, no. 2)

Bibliography: p. 187-194.

In four sections. First part contains background on French-speaking West Africa, the major social, economic, political facts. The second part is a history of the trade-union movement in French-speaking West Africa from its origins on the eve of World War II up to 1963. Part 3 concerns labor legislation, national and international, before and after independence and the influence of the International Labor Organization. Part 4 considers the trade-union movement as revealed through statements of its leaders.

1650. Brench, Anthony Cecil. THE NOVELISTS' INHERITANCE IN FRENCH AFRICA: WRITERS FROM SENEGAL TO CAMEROON. London, Nairobi, Oxford University Press, 1967. 146 p.

1651. Capet, Marcel F. TRAITE D'ECONOMIE TROPICALE: LES ECONOMIES D'A.O.F. Paris, Librairie Générale de Droit et de Jurisprudence, 1958. 348 p. illus., fold. map.

A survey of the economic situation on the eve of independence.

1652. Chailley, Marcel. LES GRANDES MISSIONS FRANCAISES EN AFRIQUE OCCIDENTALE. Dakar, IFAN, 1953. 145 p. illus., ports., maps, tables. (Initiations africaines, no. 10)

Bibliography: p. 135-137.

Recital of French exploration in West Africa, from the first establishment in Senegal in 1639 (Saint-Louis in 1659, Gorée in 1677) to the 28,000-kilometer inspection by air, from the Sahara to Dakar, to Zinder and the AEF, by a 28-plane air squadron under General Vuillemin in 1933. There are indexes of geographical and personal names, illustrations, and maps. The bibliography cites the original sources.

1653. Chailley, Marcel. HISTOIRE DE L'AFRIQUE OCCIDENTALE FRANCAISE,
      1638-1959. Paris, Editions Berger-Levrault, 1968. 580 p.
      (Mondes d'Outre-Mer, Série: Histoire)

      The first section contains introductory material on geography,
religion, the influence of the past on the present, the Africa "life
style," traditional political systems, arrival of the Europeans.

      The remaining six sections relate the history of French West
Africa from the first French settlement in 1638 in Senegal to the
dissolving of the A.O.F. in 1959.

1654. Collection U.N.E.S.C.O. d'oeuvres représentatives. Série africaine.
      Documents arabes relatifs à l'histoire du Soudan. Paris.

      In this series are reissued important Arabic documents dealing
with the Western Sudan region. Among them are the following:

      Abderrahman es-Sadi. TARIKH ES-SOUDAN. Edited and translated
         by O. Houdas with the collaboration of Edm. Benoist.
         Paris, Librairie d'Amérique et d'Orient, A. Maisonneuve,
         1964. xix, 540, 333 p. (Publications de l'Ecole des
         Langues Orientales Vivantes, 4th ser., v. 13)

         In French and Arabic, with notes and index; first published
      1898-1900. The manuscript was completed around 1655.

      Mahmoud Kāti. TARIKH EL-FETTACH, OU CHRONIQUE DU CHERCHEUR
         POUR SERVIR A L'HISTOIRE DES VILLES, DES ARMEES ET DES
         PRINCIPAUX PERSONAGES DU TEKROUR. Translated by O. Houdas
         and M. Delafosse. Paris, Librairie d'Amérique et d'Orient,
         1964. xx, 361, 183 p. map. (Publications de l'Ecole des
         Langues Orientales Vivantes, 5th ser., v. 10)

         In French and Arabic, with notes and index; first published
      1913-14. The manuscript was begun in 1519 and completed by one
of Mahmoud Kāti's grandsons, Ibn el-Mohktar, around 1665.

1655. COUTUMIERS JURIDIQUES DE L'AFRIQUE OCCIDENTALE FRANCAISE. Paris,
      Larose, 1939. 3 v. (Publications du Comité d'Etudes Historiques
      et Scientifiques de l'AOF, sér. A, nos. 8-10)

      Bibliography: v. 1, p. 43-54.

      Comprehensive study on customary law of the French colonies of
West Africa, the first volume devoted to Senegal, the second to the
Sudan, the third to Mauritania, Niger, the Ivory Coast, Dahomey, and
French Guinea.

1656. Dakar. Chambre de Commerce. SYNTHESE DE LA SITUATION ECONOMIQUE DE
L'EX-AFRIQUE OCCIDENTALE FRANCAISE DURANT LA PERIODE DE 1948 A
1958. Dakar, 1959. 7 v. 1455 l. tables. Mimeographed.

The seven volumes cover Problèmes de structure, Productions,
Transports et communications, Economie générale, Investissements et
mise en valeur, and Balance des comptes. A particular subject often
covers more than one volume.

1657. Deloncle, Pierre E. L'AFRIQUE OCCIDENTALE FRANCAISE: DECOUVERTE,
PACIFICATION, MISE EN VALEUR. Paris, Editions Ernest Leroux,
1934. 461 p.

General introduction to the conquest of West Africa by the French,
published under the auspices of the Gouvernement Général of French
West Africa.

1658. Deschamps, Hubert. L'EUROPE DECOUVRE L'AFRIQUE: AFRIQUE OCCIDENTALE,
1794-1900. Paris, Berger-Levrault, 1967. 284 p.

Bibliography: p. 267-274.

1659. Dia, Mamadou. REFLEXIONS SUR L'ECONOMIE DE L'AFRIQUE NOIRE. 2d ed.
Paris, Présence Africaine, 1961. 210 p. (Enquêtes et études)

The noted Senegalese economist Mamadou Dia was Prime Minister
of the new state from 1958 to Dec. 1962, when he was arrested and
imprisoned after an abortive coup d'état. In this thoughtful essay,
first published in 1952, he advocated a coordinated socialist organization of African economy free from European pressures. The second
edition reprints the original together with several later addresses,
including a speech before the General Assembly of the United Nations
in 1960. In 1957 Dia published a second influential work on general
economic theory, L'ECONOMIE AFRICAINE: ETUDES ET PROBLEMES NOUVEAUX
(Paris, Presses Universitaires de France, 119 p.), and in the next
year a particularized study, CONTRIBUTION A L'ETUDE DU MOUVEMENT
COOPERATIF EN AFRIQUE NOIRE (Paris, Présence Africaine, 1958, 62 p.).
A politico-economic study, stressing positive neutralism for Africa,
was also published in an English translation by Mercer Cook, AFRICAN
NATIONS AND WORLD SOLIDARITY (New York, Praeger, 1961, 145 p.).

1660. French West Africa. Comité d'Etudes Historiques et Scientifiques.
Publications. 1921- Paris, Larose.

This group, which preceded IFAN as a center for scholarly research regarding the AOF, produced a variety of valuable monographs.

See, for example, COUTUMIERS JURIDIQUES DE L'AFRIQUE OCCIDENTALE
FRANCAISE (no. 1655).

1661. Gautier, E. F. L'AFRIQUE NOIRE OCCIDENTALE: EQUISSE DES CADRES
        GEOGRAPHIQUES. Paris, 1935. 188 p. illus., map. (Publications
        du Comité d'Etudes Historiques et Scientifiques de l'Afrique
        Occidentale Française, Série A, no. 4)

        Richly illustrated and with numerous maps, this is an important
study on the geography, ethnography, and history of former French
West Africa.

1662. Gautier-Walter, A. AFRIQUE NOIRE, TERRE INCONNU: LA CROISIERE NOIRE
        DE LA SANTE: RECIT DE LA MISSION OCEM-LAFORGE A TRAVERS L'A.O.F.;
        CHEF DE LA MISSION: RAYMOND SOUQUES. Avec préface de M. L. S.
        Senghor, député du Sénégal. Paris, 1951. 238 p. illus.

        Excellent and important study of the state of health and the
numerous medical problems in former French West Africa.

1663. Goldwater, Robert. SENUFO SCULPTURE FROM WEST AFRICA. New York, Museum
        of Primitive Art (distributed by New York Graphic Society,
        Greenwich, Conn.), 1964. 126 p. illus., map.

        Readable and authoritative ethnographic study by the director of
the Museum of Primitive Art, New York, describing the functions of
sculpture among the Senufo people of Mali, Upper Volta, and the Ivory
Coast by means of 186 excellent photographs and drawings of masked
dancers, sculptors at work, and carvings in use in everyday life.
His factual approach, in sharp contrast to most African art studies,
compares with Marcel Griaule's pioneer work, MASQUES DOGONS (see no.
1748). The older French, German, and Flemish sources have been
surveyed; bibliography, map, index, notes and sources, and appendix
on contemporary Senufo work are excellent.

        See Chapter 27 for other works including material on French West
Africa.

1664. Gouilly, Alphonse. L'ISLAM DANS L'AFRIQUE OCCIDENTALE FRANCAISE.
        Paris, Larose, 1952. 318 p. fold. map.

        Bibliography: p. 285-287.

        The author, a French authority on Islam, first describes the
country and people of the semiarid Sahelian zone where the Muslim
nomads of the "white" north have met, clashed, and mingled with the

sedentary animist blacks. The work is then divided into four main
parts: the history of Islamization in West Africa from the eleventh
through the nineteenth century; the religious brotherhoods; the
effects of Islamization (corruption of the Muslim creed through
animist accretions, influence of Islam on black African ways of
life); and French policy toward Islam.

See also the work by Froelich, no. 939.

1665. Goyat, Michel. GUIDE PRATIQUE DE L'EMPLOYEUR ET DU TRAVAILLEUR EN
        AFRIQUE OCCIDENTALE. Dakar, Editions Clairafrique; Paris,
        Présence Africaine. 1960. 798 p. illus.

A treatise on labor legislation and practice.

1666. Great Britain. Naval Staff. Naval Intelligence Division. FRENCH
        WEST AFRICA: Vol. I, THE FEDERATION; Vol. II, THE COLONIES.
        Oxford, Oxford University Press, 1939-44. (Geographical Hand-
        book Series B.R. 512a)

Useful surveys.

1667. Hargreaves, John D. WEST AFRICA: THE FORMER FRENCH STATES. Englewood
        Cliffs, N.J., Prentice-Hall, 1967. 183 p. maps. (Spectrum
        Book: Modern Nations in Historical Perspective Series)

Bibliography: p. 169-173.

The author, professor of history at the University of Aberdeen
and formerly senior lecturer in history at Fourah Bay College, Sierra
Leone, has contributed the best survey of the area yet to appear in
English. His book covers the early history to the postindependence
period of Senegal, Mali, Guinea, Mauritania, Ivory Coast, Upper
Volta, Dahomey, Niger, and Togo.

1668. Mauny, Raymond. TABLEAU GEOGRAPHIQUE DE L'OUEST AFRICAIN AU MOYEN
        AGE D'APRES LES SOURCES ECRITES, LA TRADITION ET L'ARCHEOLOGIE.
        Dakar, IFAN, 1961. 587 p. illus., maps (part fold.), plans.
        (Mémoires, no. 61)

Bibliography: p. 547-575.

A study of West African history between the Arab invasions and
the era of Portuguese discoveries, based on largely unfamiliar source
material which is itemized in the bibliography. The author, formerly
director of archaeological research for IFAN, presented this work as
his thesis for the doctorat d'état-ès-lettres at the Sorbonne in 1959.

His secondary thesis was LES NAVIGATIONS MEDIEVALES SUR LES COTES SAHARIENNES ANTERIEURES A LA DECOUVERTE PORTUGAISE (1434) (Lisboa, Centro de Estudos Históricos Ultramarinos, 1960, 151 p., illus., maps). Mauny is now professor of African history at the Sorbonne.

1669. May, Jacques M.   THE ECOLOGY OF MALNUTRITION IN WEST AFRICA AND
       MADAGASCAR. New York, Hafner Pub. Co., 1968. xiii, 433 p.
       maps, tables. (Studies in Medical Geography, no. 8)

An important contribution to the better understanding of the population and nutritional problems of 10 African countries--Senegal, Guinea, Ivory Coast, Togo, Dahomey, Cameroun, Niger, Mali, Upper Volta, and Madagascar. An index is included.

1670. Monographies ethnologiques africaines [series]. Paris, Published for
       the International African Institute by Presses Universitaires
       de France, 1954-

In the French series of the Ethnographic Survey (see no. 980), the volumes studying tribes of the states of former French West Africa are particularly hard to place in individual countries, where the Sudanic, Mande, and Voltaic peoples are mingled without respect to boundaries. The following numbers relate to some of these groups:

a)   1. LES BAMBARA. By Viviana Paques. 1954. xiii, 100 p.
        illus., fold. map. (Bibliography: p. [113]-119.)

b)   2. LES SONGHAY. By Jean Rouch. 1954. 100 p. illus., fold.
        map. ("Essai de bibliographie analytique": p. [68]-
        95.)

c)   3. LES CONIAGUI ET LES BASSARI (GUINEE FRANCAISE). By Monique
        de Lestrange. 1955. 86 p. illus., maps (1 fold.),
        diagrs., tables. (Bibliography: p. [77]-82.)

d)   4. LES DOGON. By Montserrat Palau-Marti. 1957. xii, 122 p.
        illus., fold. maps. (Bibliography: p. [97]-109.)

e)   5. LES SENOUFO (Y COMPRIS LES MINIANKA). By Bohumil Holas.
        1957; reissued 1966. 183 p. maps, tables. (Bibliog-
        raphy: p. 173-177.)

f)   6. LE GROUPE DIT PAHOUIN (FANG, BOULOU, BETI). By Pierre
        Alexandre and Jacques Binet. 1958. 152 p. fold. map,
        tables. (Bibliography: p. [137]-148.)

        English ed.: THE GROUP CALLED PAHOUIN. . . . Trans-
           lated by Isabella Athey. New Haven, Conn., Human
           Relations Area Files, 1959. 185 p. illus., maps.
           (Bibliography: p. 173-181.)

538

1671. Morgenthau, Ruth Schachter. POLITICAL PARTIES IN FRENCH-SPEAKING
WEST AFRICA. New York, Oxford University Press, 1964. xxii,
445 p. maps, tables.

Reprint, 1967, with corr.

Bibliography: p. 359-376.

A detailed study of the growth of political parties in the
states of former French West Africa. The major emphasis is on
politics, but the first chapter explains the African social setting,
and there are long sections on the economy. The region as a whole
is treated in an analysis of French policy and African institutions
and of the part given to West Africans in the French Parliament;
then long chapters discuss the political developments in Senegal,
the Ivory Coast, Guinea, and Mali, with briefer consideration of
Upper Volta, Niger, Dahomey, and Mauritania. The last chapter
examines the trend toward one-party states. Useful appendixes
detail administrators and politicians and tabulate other political,
social, and economic data. The bibliography includes much primary
source material.

1672. Panis, J. C. LE CHEMIN DE FER DE LA MEDITERRANEE AU NIGER. Bruxelles, Editions de Vischer, 1956. 138 p. fold. map.

Bibliography: p. 131-134.

Dissertation by a Belgian colonial administrator reviewing and
analyzing the question of the trans-Saharan railway, at that time
projected as the Mer-Niger, to run from Morocco into Algeria and
south through Mauritania and the Sudan, to meet the West African
transportation system now operating under the Office du Niger, from
the dam at Sansanding to the railway line at Bamako. The bibliography lists papers, articles, speeches, etc.; there are few books
on the subject, though the proposal goes back to the late nineteenth
century, well before the Chemin de Fer Transsaharien study group was
set up under the French Ministry of Public Works in 1928. In the
mid-1960's there was talk of again considering the plan.

For a lively, if brief, discussion of this subject and a full
bibliographic survey, see Max Liniger-Goumaz, "Transsaharien et
transafricain: Essai bibliographique," GENEVE-AFRIQUE, v. 7, no. 1,
1968: 70-84.

1673. PERSONNALITES PUBLIQUES DE L'AFRIQUE 1969: COTE D'IVOIRE, DAHOMEY,
HAUTE-VOLTA, MALI, MAURITANIE, NIGER, SENEGAL, TOGO. Paris,
EDIAFRIC, 1968. 450 p. (Numéro spécial du BULLETIN DE L'AF-
RIQUE NOIRE).

Presents biographical facts on approximately 3,000 prominent
individuals from French-speaking West Africa. Arrangement is
alphabetical by last name under each country. Data generally
include date and place of birth, academic degrees, past positions,
present position, and address. There is no index.

1674. Richard-Molard, Jacques. AFRIQUE OCCIDENTALE FRANCAISE. 3d ed.,
        rev. Paris, Berger-Levrault, 1956. 252 p. illus. (L'Union
        française)

        Bibliography: p. 227-234.

        A highly praised introductory survey by the late chief of the
Geographical Section of IFAN; original edition, 1949. The preface
by Professor Monod, director of IFAN, speaks of it as the most satisfactory up-to-date synthesis for the layman of the many special
studies on French West Africa, interpreted through the understanding
eye of the geographer.

1675. Spitz, Georges. L'OUEST AFRICAIN FRANCAIS: A.O.F. ET TOGO. Paris,
        Société d'Editions Géographiques, Maritimes et Coloniales,
        1947. 508 p. illus. (Terres lointaines)

        By a former colonial governor, this is an excellent survey
intended for a general public as well as for students. It covers
country and people, history, administrative and political structure,
social welfare, economic development, and wartime history. The
French West African countries are considered as a unit, and there
is a separate section on Togo.

1676. Sy, Seydou Madani. RECHERCHES SUR L'EXERCICE DU POUVOIR POLITIQUE
        EN AFRIQUE NOIRE (COTE D'IVOIRE, GUINEE, MALI). Paris, A.
        Pedone, 1965. 230 p. (Collection du Centre de Recherches,
        d'Etudes et de Documentation sur les Institutions et la
        Législation Africaines, 7)

        Bibliography: p. 215-225.

        Doctoral thesis of a Senegalese prepared for the University of
Dakar. Part 1 deals with the economic and social infrastructure,
the place of traditional society, and the new elites. Part 2 covers
constitutional organs and the preeminence of the executive in the
constitutional system. Part 3 concerns the political party, the
preeminence of constitutional bodies over party institutions in the
Ivory Coast, collaboration between constitutional bodies and party
institutions, and the subordination of the former to the latter in
Mali.

1677.   Thompson, Virginia McLean, and Richard Adloff. FRENCH WEST AFRICA.
        Stanford, Calif., Stanford University Press, 1957. 626 p.
        illus., maps, tables.

        Bibliography: p. 599-614.

        Detailed, analytical survey by two experts; indispensable as
source material for any research on the French-speaking countries
of West Africa. The useful bibliography includes books, pamphlets,
documents, and significant periodical material.

        A concise pamphlet by Philip Neres summarizing political history
was published several years later under the auspices of the Institute
of Race Relations: FRENCH-SPEAKING WEST AFRICA--FROM COLONIAL STATUS
TO INDEPENDENCE (London, Oxford University Press, 1962, 101 p., illus.).

1678.   Wade, Abdoulaye. ECONOMIE DE L'OUEST AFRICAIN (ZONE FRANC): UNITE ET
        CROISSANCE. Paris, Présence Africaine, 1964. 371 p. tables.
        (Enquêtes et études)

        Bibliography: p. 357-366.

        By a scholar on the staff of the Faculty of Law and Economic
Sciences at the University of Dakar. This work is developed from
a thesis at the University of Grenoble in 1959, and the data studied
are largely pre-independence.

                              DAHOMEY

Bibliographies

1679.   "Serials of Cameroun, Dahomey [etc.]." AFRICANA NEWSLETTER, v. 2, no.
        1, 1964: 33-41.

        See no. 371.

        For Dahomey (p. 35) there are listed 13 newspapers and periodicals,
all in the French language.

1680.   Silva, Guillaume da. "Contribution à la bibliographie du Dahomey."
        ETUDES DAHOMEENNES, n.s. v. 3, no. 12, Jan. 1969. 1969 p.

        Entire issue consists of Da Silva's article listing authors G-Z.
The bibliography is based on the collection of the Institut de Recherches
Appliquées du Dahomey, the former IFAN center. Listed by author are

articles, monographs, newspaper articles, and government publications.
There is an index of broad subjects such as agriculture, ethnology,
history. Some 2,400 entries are given. Authors A-F appeared in v. 2,
no. 12 but this issue was not available for examination.

Reference Works

1681. Akindélé, Adolphe, and Cyrille Aguessy. CONTRIBUTION A L'ETUDE DE
       L'HISTOIRE DE L'ANCIEN ROYAUME DE PORTO-NOVO. Dakar, IFAN,
       1953. 168 p. (Mémoires, no. 25)

       "Bibliographie sommaire": p. 163-168.

       Monograph by two African scholars relating to the general and
particular history of the former kingdom of Porto-Novo, now the
capital of Dahomey, including details on the selection and coronation
of the king and other aspects of court and governmental life, as well
as a list of kings and chiefs from 1688 to 1941, with notes on their
reigns. It is based on a work written in Yoruba by Akindélé
Akinsowon, father of one of the authors, and published in 1914 under
the title IWE ITAN AJASE. The long section on family and religious
customs contains poetic translations of funeral chants. Appendixes
give a list of native words and a select bibliography.

       There is also a survey by these two writers in the Pays africains
series, no. 6, LE DAHOMEY (Paris, Editions Maritimes et Coloniales,
1955, 126 p., plates, map, tables). This may be compared with the
official survey of the colony at the beginning of the present century,
issued by the Gouvernement Général de l'A.O.F. for the Colonial
Exposition of Marseilles, LE DAHOMEY (Corbeil, E. Crété, 1906, 351 p.,
illus.). See also the chapter on Dahomey by Virginia Thompson in
Carter's FIVE AFRICAN STATES, no. 607.

1682. Argyle, William Johnson. THE FON OF DAHOMEY: A HISTORY AND ETHNO-
       GRAPHY OF THE OLD KINGDOM. Oxford, Clarendon Press, 1966.
       210 p. map, diagrs. (Oxford Monographs on Social Anthropology)

       Bibliography: p. 201-207.

       A well-documented account. Argyle first traces the founding,
growth, and decline of the old kingdom. The bulk of the book is
then devoted to political, military, judicial, economic, and religious
aspects of the kingships, local government lineage, marriage and
divorce, cooperative institutions, and cults.

1683. Cornevin, Robert. HISTOIRE DU DAHOMEY. Paris, Berger-Levrault, 1962.
       568 p. illus., ports., maps. (Mondes d'outre-mer, Histoire)

Bibliography: p. 533-556.

An authoritative history, based on archaeological evidence and
oral records as well as archives and published sources. The long
bibliography is arranged by chapters.

A more recent work by Professor Cornevin is LE DAHOMEY (Paris,
Presses Universitaires de France, 1965, 128 p., maps; "Que sais-je?"
no. 1176), a compact survey of Dahomey's past and present. Part 1
deals with the natural environment and the peoples; Part 2 with the
precolonial period. The third and longest part is devoted to the
colonial period, the coming of independence, the economy, religion,
and social and cultural evolution.

1684. Cotonou. Chambre de Commerce et d'Industrie. NOTE HEBDOMADAIRE.
      Weekly. Mimeographed.

The government-supported Chamber of Commerce, which serves as
an official agency for promotion of trade and industry, has issued
this bulletin for many years.

An additional source of information on the economy is the report
of the Banque Dahoméenne de Développement in Cotonou, titled BDD.

1685. Dahomey. JOURNAL OFFICIEL DE LA REPUBLIQUE DU DAHOMEY. 1958/59-
      Porto-Novo. Semimonthly.

In Nov. 1958 the journal of the new republic superseded the
former JOURNAL OFFICIEL DU DAHOMEY, which had been published under
various titles since 1890.

Further official serials of importance for research are the
BULLETIN QUOTIDIEN DE L'INFORMATION, a mimeographed sheet issued
by the government-sponsored Agence Dahoméenne de Presse, and the
monthly BULLETIN ECONOMIQUE ET STATISTIQUE, issued by the Ministère
des Finances et des Affaires Economiques et du Plan. Other government agencies carrying out research and issuing reports are the
Service du Développement Rural, the Ministère de l'Education Nationale
et de la Jeunesse, the Imprimerie Nationale, the Archives Nationales
(which has an excellent collection on the colonial administration of
Dahomey), the Direction de l'Information, and the Institut de Recherches
Appliquées du Dahomey, all still located in the old capital of Porto-
Novo.

For government documents of the past see the Library of Congress
OFFICIAL PUBLICATIONS OF FRENCH WEST AFRICA (no. 1636), and for
periodicals, the "Serials of Cameroun, Dahomey [etc.]" (no. 1679).

1686.   ETUDES DAHOMEENNES.   v. 1- 1948-58; n.s. 1963/64- Porto-Novo.
        illus., maps. Irregular.

        The publication of the former Centre IFAN Dahoméenne, a schol-
        arly journal sometimes in monographic form. Since independence the
        center has become the Institut de Recherches Appliquées du Dahomey
        (IRAD) and is issuing the ETUDES DAHOMEENNES in a new series (latest
        Apr. 1966). A new series of Mémoires brought out its first number
        in 1964.

1687.   France. Direction de la Documentation. LA REPUBLIQUE DU DAHOMEY.
        Paris, La Documentation Française, 1966. 41 p. (Notes et
        études documentaires, no. 3307, July 8, 1966)

        See general note on this series of background country studies,
        no. 1587.

1688.   Herskovits, Melville J. DAHOMEY, AN ANCIENT WEST AFRICAN KINGDOM.
        New York, J. J. Augustin, 1938. 2 v. 402, 407 p. illus.,
        101 plates (part. col.), on 52 l.

        References: v. 2, p. [373]-376.

        Standard anthropological study of Dahomey by the late Professor
        Herskovits, who was one of America's foremost Africanists.

1689.   Lombard, Jacques. STRUCTURES DE TYPE "FEODAL" EN AFRIQUE NOIRE:
        ETUDE DES DYNAMISMES INTERNES ET DES RELATIONS SOCIALES CHEZ
        LES BARIBA DU DAHOMEY. Paris, La Haye, Mouton, 1965. 544 p.
        illus., maps, geneal. tables. (Le monde d'outre-mer passé
        et présent, 1st ser., Etudes, 26)

        Bibliography: p. [535]-540.

        An interesting study in which the author attempts to show that
        while colonization was the most important factor in the social
        transformation of an African society, it was neither the only nor
        the first to contribute to modifications. Lombard discusses the
        cultural diversity and tribal unity of Bariba society, then analyzes
        the hierarchy and its politico-social organization. Finally, he
        focuses on the reactions and adjustments of the Bariba to colonization
        and on the renewal of initiative and the birth of a ruling bourgeoisie,
        concluding with comments on conflicts and social cohesion in an old
        "feudal" society.

1690. Marty, Paul. ETUDES SUR L'ISLAM AU DAHOMEY: LE BAS DAHOMEY, LE HAUT DAHOMEY. Paris, E. Leroux, 1926. 295 p. illus., fold. map. (Collection de la REVUE DU MONDE MUSULMAN)

The first section, on lower Dahomey, reviews ethnic groups, beliefs and rites, and the Islamic community. In the second section, on upper Dahomey, focus is on ethnic groups, Islamic circles, unwritten law, social institutions, animism, and "witch-doctoring." There are 12 appendixes. For note on Marty, see no. 1753.

1691. Maupoil, Bernard. LA GEOMANCIE A L'ANCIENNE COTE DES ESCLAVES. Paris, Institut d'Ethnologie, 1943; reissued 1961. xxii, 690 p. illus. (1 col.), plates, diagrs. (Université de Paris, Travaux et mémoires de l'Institut d'Ethnologie, 42)

"Bibliographie africaine de Fa": p. [xvii]-xxvii.

This very detailed examination of the old Dahomean system of divination known as fa is at the same time an interesting anthropological study of the former Slave Coast.

1692. Mercier, Paul. CIVILISATIONS DU BENIN. Paris, Société Continentale d'Editions Modernes Illustrées, 1962. 365 p. illus., plates (part col.), maps. (Connaissance de l'Afrique)

A handsomely illustrated, popularized account of the Benin civilization in the Bight of Benin (former Slave Coast) area, with emphasis on the Dahomean portion. The author successively covers origins, history, kings, hierarchies, cities and places, arts, religion, aspects of sociology and anthropology, material life, adaptations, and exiles.

1693. Polanyi, Karl, in collaboration with Abraham Rotstein. DAHOMEY AND THE SLAVE TRADE: AN ANALYSIS OF AN ARCHAIC ECONOMY. Seattle and London, University of Washington Press, 1966. xiii, 204 p. maps. (American Ethnological Society, Monograph 42)

Bibliography: p. 195-200.

The last scholarly work of the noted economic anthropologist and economic historian who died in 1964. Polanyi traces the origins and historical and geographical background of one of the great West African kingdoms, explains the patterns of the economy with due emphasis on the role of social institutions, and discusses the gold trade, colonialism, and, especially, the slave trade and their impact on the economy. He includes an incisive analysis of the complexities of the Dahomeans' trade with the French and the British--complexities arising from the fact that only the Europeans had a fully monetized economy.

1694. Serreau, Jean. LE DEVELOPPEMENT A LA BASE AU DAHOMEY ET AU SENEGAL. Paris, Librairie Générale de Droit et de Jurisprudence, 1966. 358 p. tables. (Bibliothèque d'économie politique, v. 7)

Bibliography: p. 319-323.

A study of the economic development of the essentially agricultural countries of Dahomey and Senegal. The first part deals with the obstacles to and favorable factors in their development during 1959-60. Part 2 covers the first four-year plan of Senegal, rural animation and education for development, centers of rural development, techniques for rural communities, and the cooperative economic basis of a developing socialist society. Part 3 discusses the development of Dahomey and its four-year plan, the village as the basis for development, and the cooperative experiment.

1695. Tardits, Claude. PORTO-NOVO: LES NOUVELLES GENERATIONS AFRICAINES ENTRE LEURS TRADITIONS ET L'OCCIDENT. Paris, Mouton, 1958. 128 p. (Le monde d'outre-mer, passé et présent, 1st ser., Etudes, no. 7)

Sociological study of the changes in Dahomean society in urbanized centers as contrasted with traditional mores. The writer based his research in part on replies to a questionnaire.

1696. U.S. Department of the Interior. Office of Geography. DAHOMEY: OFFICIAL STANDARD NAMES APPROVED BY THE UNITED STATES BOARD ON GEOGRAPHIC NAMES. Washington, U.S. Govt. Print. Off., May 1965. 89 p. map. (6,250 names) (Gazetteer no. 91)

See note on series, no. 484.

GUINEA

Bibliographies

1697. Du Bois, Victor D. GUINEA: THE YEARS BEFORE WORLD WAR II: AN HISTORICAL SKETCH AND A BIBLIOGRAPHIC INDEX OF 112 TITLES. New York, American Universities Field Staff, 1962. 20 p.

1698. Lalande-Isnard, Fanny. "Ouvrages publiés en Guinée du 2 octobre
         1958 au 31 décembre 1963." RECHERCHES AFRICAINES (Conakry),
         no. 1-4, Jan.-Dec. 1964: 167-169.

         Publications concerning the Parti Démocratique de Guinée and
those of the Ministère de l'Education Nationale, des Finances, du
Plan, du Travail, etc., are listed, all of more than 49 pages.

         The journal plans to publish in its first issue each year a
national bibliography covering publications of the preceding year.

1699. Mengrelis, Thanos. BIBLIOGRAPHIE GENERALE DE LA REGION DE N'ZEREKORE.
         Conakry, Institut National de Recherches et Documentation, 1964.
         55 p.

         Not available for examination.

1700. Organisation de Coopération et de Développement Economiques. Centre
         de Développement. BIBLIOGRAPHIE SUR LA GUINEE. BIBLIOGRAPHY
         ON GUINEA. Paris [1965?] 46 l. (CD/D/Bibl./2)

         Emphasis is mainly on economic, political, and sociological
matters. Listed by subject are books, monographs, government publications, chapters from composite works, and articles. A list of
Guinea periodicals concludes the work.

Reference Works

1701. Ameillon, B. LA GUINEE: BILAN D'UNE INDEPENDANCE. Paris, F.
         Maspero, 1964. 205 p. (Cahiers libres, no. 58-59)

         In 1958 Guinea alone chose independence from France. Chapters
on the aftermath consider Guinea itself, Guinea and France, the
economy, relations with other countries, and socialism.

1702. American University, Washington, D.C. Special Operations Research
         Office. AREA HANDBOOK FOR GUINEA. Prepared by Foreign Areas
         Studies Division. Washington, 1961. xii, 534 p. maps.

         Prepared under contract with the Department of the Army. The
carefully presented factual information is in four sections, on
sociological, political, economic, and military background. Bibliographies of seven or eight pages follow each section. See also
L. G. Cowan, "Guinea," in Carter, AFRICAN ONE-PARTY STATES (no.
606).

1703. Charles, Bernard. GUINEE. Photos. by Marc Riboud. Lausanne,
          Editions Rencontre, 1963. 224 p. illus. (L'atlas des
          voyages)

       Combination of travel narrative and photograph album, reflec-
       ting current conditions in the new republic.

1704. France. Direction de la Documentation. LA REPUBLIQUE DE GUINEE.
          Paris, La Documentation Française, 1965. 42 p. map. (Notes
          et études documentaires, no. 3202, June 21, 1965)

       See general note on this series, no. 1587.

1705. Guinea. JOURNAL OFFICIEL DE LA REPUBLIQUE DE GUINEE. 1958-
          Conakry, Impr. Nationale "Patrice Lumumba." Semimonthly.

       Superseded the JOURNAL OFFICIEL DE LA GUINEE FRANCAISE, which
       had been published since 1901. For other official publications
       before independence, see the Library of Congress OFFICIAL PUBLI-
       CATIONS OF FRENCH WEST AFRICA (no. 1636).

       Government agencies now issuing their own publications for
       general distribution include the Ministère de l'Information et du
       Tourisme, the Ministère de l'Education Nationale, and the Banque
       Centrale de la République de Guinée. Besides the JOURNAL OFFICIEL,
       the Imprimerie Nationale issues a daily, HOROYA, the journal of the
       Parti Démocratique de Guinée.

       The Agence Guinéenne de Presse issues a BULLETIN QUOTIDIEN, a
       fairly extensive mimeographed leaflet in legal size.

1706. GUINEE: PRELUDE A L'INDEPENDANCE. Paris, Présence Africaine, 1959.
          175 p.

       This report of the Conférence des Commandants de Cercle in-
       cludes the opening address by Governor Ramadier, an address by
       President Sékou Touré, a report of the Minister of Finance and of
       the Commandant de Cercle de Labé, and a section "Naissance de la
       République de Guinée."

       The conference here referred to, held in Conakry in 1957, pre-
       ceded Touré's repression of the chefferies and led to his personal
       control of the country which brought about the vote of no in 1958.

       A combined issue for Dec. 1959 and Jan. 1960 of the serial
       PRESENCE AFRICAINE was devoted to "Guinée indépendante."

1707. Holas, Bohumil. LE CULTE DE ZIE: ELEMENTS DE LA RELIGION KONO (HAUTE GUINEE FRANCAISE). Dakar, IFAN, 1954. 275 p. illus. (Mémoires, no. 39)

"Ouvrages cités": p. 231-242.

Important contribution to anthropological studies of Guinea.

Another volume relating to Guinean tribes is in the French series of the International African Institute, Monographies ethnologiques africaines: Monique de Lestrange, LES CONIAGUI ET LES BASSARI (GUINEE FRANCAISE) (1955, 86 p., illus., maps; bibliography: p. [77]-82).

1708. Marty, Paul. L'ISLAM EN GUINEE: FOUTA-DIALLON. Paris, E. Leroux, 1921. 588 p. illus., maps, geneal. tables. (Collection de la REVUE DU MONDE MUSULMAN)

The author first provides a historical background and then discusses Islamic communities and groups, the Moorish influence, Islamic doctrine and religion, education, juridical institutions, social customs, rites and practices, and survivals from the past. There are 34 appendixes, including maps. For note on Marty, see no. 1753.

1709. RECHERCHES AFRICAINES: ETUDES GUINEENNES. n.s. no. 1- Jan. 1959- Conakry, Institut National de Recherches et de Documentation, République de Guinée. Quarterly.

This new serial, launched under the direction of M. Jean Suret-Canale, has superseded the former ETUDES GUINEENNES of the Centre IFAN du Guinée, the volumes of which were published irregularly from 1947 to 1955.

The Institut, one of the major research centers in French-speaking West Africa, also issues an irregular publication, Mémoires. The first number is an index to the archives of French Guinea for the period 1720-1935, compiled by the former archivist, Damien d'Almeida: PREMIER REPERTOIRE DES ARCHIVES NATIONALES DE GUINEE: SER. A-N, 1720-1935 (1962, 224 p.). The archives are housed in the Institut, which has a library of over 8,000 catalogued items, several hundred rare books and pamphlets on the slave trade, and a limited number of official documents of the Republic.

1710. Suret-Canale, Jean. LA REPUBLIQUE DE GUINEE. Paris, Editions Sociales, 1970. 431 p. maps, plates.

549

Bibliography: p. 401-422.

A major survey by the leading Marxist geographer-historian of West Africa.

1711. Touré, Sékou. L'action politique du Parti démocratique de Guinée
          [series]. Conakry, Impr. Nationale "Patrice Lumumba," 1958-
          illus. (v. 10, 1963)

          _____. EXPERIENCE GUINEENNE ET UNITE AFRICAINE. Paris, Présence
          Africaine, 1959. 566 p. (Leaders politiques africains)

          _____. TOWARD FULL RE-AFRICANISATION (POLICY AND PRINCIPLES OF
          THE GUINEA DEMOCRATIC PARTY). Paris, Présence Africaine,
          1959. 108 p.

          The speeches, weekly press conferences, and other papers of
          President Touré in L'action politique du Parti démocratique de
          Guinée are published in large volumes of offset print. The 1959
          volume was brought out in these editions by Présence Africaine, and
          the 1961 work combines the first two volumes of the series. For
          more detailed publishing data on the series through Vol. X, see
          Lalande-Isnard's bibliography (above, no. 1698). Vol. X (1963,
          812 p.), titled LA REVOLUTION GUINEENNE ET LE PROGRES SOCIAL, con-
          tains two reports by Touré, the first presented at the PDG's
          second Conférence Nationale des Cadres, Kissidougou, Nov. 21-24,
          1960, the second (p. 159-721) presented in his capacity as Secre-
          tary-General of the PDG's Bureau Politique National, Conakry, Aug.
          14-17, 1961. The last portion of the volume discusses Guinea's
          political and administrative structure and includes Touré's ad-
          dress to the June 1963 conference of the Organization of African
          Unity in Addis Ababa, in addition to other OAU documents. Other
          volumes have appeared, to Vol. XVI, but were not available to the
          compilers.

1712. U.S. Department of the Interior. Office of Geography. GUINEA:
          OFFICIAL STANDARD NAMES APPROVED BY THE UNITED STATES BOARD
          ON GEOGRAPHIC NAMES. Washington, U.S. Govt. Print. Off., Apr.
          1965. 175 p. map. (12,400 names) (Gazetteer no. 90)

          See note on series, no. 484.

IVORY COAST

Bibliographies

1713. Organisation de Coopération et de Développement Economiques. Centre
        de Développement. ESSAI D'UNE BIBLIOGRAPHIE SUR LA COTE D'IVOIRE.
        By N. Novacco. Paris, 1964. 122 l.

        The bibliography is divided into monographs and articles and
        under these are two alphabetical listings, one by author, the other
        (for anonymous works) by title. There is no subject approach.
        Most of the 254 monographs and 407 articles deal with socioeco-
        nomic problems in the Ivory Coast. One of the four appendixes lists
        French organizations which have done work in the Ivory Coast.

1714. Schwartz, A. ETUDES DE SCIENCES HUMAINES EN COTE D'IVOIRE: ESSAI
        DE BIBLIOGRAPHIE. Paris, ORSTOM, 1964. 47 l. (Sciences
        humaines)

        A systematic listing of works (including articles) arranged in
        three chronological sections under each main subject heading and sub-
        division (i.e., publications issued before 1945, from 1945 to
        1960, and from 1960 through early 1964). The seven main headings
        are general works, history, demography, economy, sociology, eth-
        nology, and linguistics.

Reference Works

1715. American University, Washington, D.C. Special Operations Research
        Office. AREA HANDBOOK FOR THE IVORY COAST. Prepared by the
        Foreign Areas Studies Division. Washington, U.S. Govt. Print.
        Off., Dec. 1962. xii, 485 p. maps, diagrs.

        Another in the series of country handbooks prepared under con-
        tract with the Department of the Army. Comprehensive background
        information is given on social, economic, and political institutions
        and on national security in four main sections, each of which is
        followed by an extensive bibliography (up to 12 pages). A glossary
        is included.

1716. Amin, Samir. LE DEVELOPPEMENT DU CAPITALISME EN COTE D'IVOIRE. Paris,
        Editions de Minuit, 1967. 330 p. maps, diagrs., tables. (Grand
        documents, 28)

Bibliography: p. 309-321.

Covers population and employment, growth of agricultural production, regional and social division of rural income, growth of industrial production and transportation, social division of urban income, volume, efficiency, and financing of investments (1950-65), public finance, and balance of payments. The good bibliography is divided into main subject headings with subclassifications.

1717. Amon d'Aby, F. J. LA COTE D'IVOIRE DANS LA CITE AFRICAINE. Paris, Larose, 1951. 606 p. illus.

By the government archivist of the Ivory Coast, a well-known African playwright. In this book he has given background history and analysis of political, economic, and cultural progress in the country under French administration, particularly of the changes following the Conference of Brazzaville in 1944 and the formation of the French Union. His viewpoint is one of enthusiasm for the fusion of French and African culture.

Two of the author's later studies are LE PROBLEME DES CHEFFERIES TRADITIONNELLES EN COTE D'IVOIRE (Abidjan, 1957, 51 p.; Mémoires du CHEAM, no. 2778) and CROYANCES RELIGIEUSES ET COUTUMES JURIDIQUES DES AGNI DE LA COTE D'IVOIRE (Paris, Larose, 1960, 184 p., plates, fold. map).

1718. Atger, Paul. LA FRANCE EN COTE-D'IVOIRE DE 1843 A 1893: CINQUANTE ANS D'HESITATIONS POLITIQUES ET COMMERCIALES. Dakar, Faculté des Lettres et Sciences Humaines, Université de Dakar [Macon, Impr. Protat Frères], 1962. 204 p. maps. (Publications de la Section d'Histoire, no. 2)

Bibliography: p. 11-18.

In this study of the early French administration the lengthy bibliography lists archives, documents, and printed sources for nineteenth-century history.

1719. Development and Resources Corporation, New York. A PROGRAM FOR GEOLOGICAL AND MINERALS DEVELOPMENT, JANUARY 1961-DECEMBER 1963: A REPORT TO THE MINISTER OF FINANCE, ECONOMIC AFFAIRS AND PLANNING, REPUBLIC OF THE IVORY COAST. New York, 1961. 1 v. fold. maps.

1720. Etudes éburnéennes. no. 1- Abidjan (etc.), Institut Francais d'Afrique Noire, Centre de Côte d'Ivoire, 1950- illus. Irregular.

This scholarly series, usually monographic (e.g., no. 8, consisting of Marguerite Dupire, PLANTEURS AUTOCHTONES ET ETRANGERS EN BASSE-COTE D'IVOIRE ORIENTALE, and Edmond Bernus, KONG ET SA REGION, Abidjan, 1960, 324 p.), was suspended with independence. The Institut has been replaced by a new research organization, the Centre des Sciences Humaines, which has a collection of about 6,000 books, pamphlets, and periodicals on Africa. As of 1969, publication of the Etudes had not been resumed.

1721. France. Direction de la Documentation. LA REPUBLIQUE DE COTE D'IVOIRE. Paris, La Documentation Française, 1965. 51 p. map, tables. (Notes et études documentaires, no. 3308, July 12, 1966)

See general note on this series, no. 1587.

1722. Holas, Bohumil. ARTS DE LA COTE D'IVOIRE. 2d ed. Paris, Presses Universitaires de France, 1966. 121 p. illus., 220 plates.

Bibliography: p. 115-119.

_____. COTE D'IVOIRE: PASSE, PRESENT, PERSPECTIVES. Paris, P. Geuthner, 1963. 101 p. plates, map.

_____. LES TOURA: ESQUISSE D'UNE CIVILISATION MONTAGNARDE DE COTE D'IVOIRE. Paris, Presses Universitaires de France, 1962. 234 p. illus., plates.

Bibliography: p. 227-229.

Three volumes selected from among the numerous studies by this scholar, director of the Centre des Sciences Humaines de la Côte d'Ivoire. The first work cited is a revised and corrected edition of the author's CULTURES MATERIELLES DE LA COTE D'IVOIRE (1960, 90 p.). The plastic arts and the works of artisans described and illustrated all reveal an inherently religious quality.

The second work comprises a general survey of the physical geography, peoples, prehistory and archaeology, history, institutions and administrative organization, economy, religion and rituals, culture, tourist resources, and prospects for development. Sixty unpaged plates appear at the end of the book.

LES TOURA is a detailed account of the customs, beliefs, cults, and rituals of a people of the highland region northeast of the city of Man. Included are discussions of the physical environment, ethnic composition, language, and social structure. There is an extensive glossary of vernacular terms. Holas's LES SENUFO (Y COMPRIS LES

MINIANKA) was first published in 1957 and reissued in 1966 in the Monographies ethnologiques africaines series (see no. 1670).

1723. Ivory Coast. ANNUAIRE NATIONAL DE LA COTE D'IVOIRE. 1963- Abidjan, B.P. 1265. (1965 ed., 276 p., maps)

Presents information on administrative organization, the diplomatic corps, cults and religions, investments and industries, the economy, agriculture and exports, tourism, and history.

1724. IVORY COAST: FACTS AND FIGURES, 1966. Abidjan, Ministry of Information, 1966. 131 p.

A useful reference book containing information on the history, geography, the land and people, the economy and cultural life of the Ivory Coast. Numerous pictures and tables. Provides surveys of press, literature, drama and the organization of the government and military.

1725. Ivory Coast. JOURNAL OFFICIEL DE LA REPUBLIQUE DE COTE D'IVOIRE. no. 1- Dec. 6, 1958- Abidjan. Weekly.

This JOURNAL OFFICIEL superseded that published semimonthly from 1895 to 1958 by the government of the former French colony.

The Imprimerie Nationale also publishes the annual BUDGET GENERAL and the DEBATS DE L'ASSEMBLEE NATIONALE. An annual volume of LOIS is issued in mimeographed form by the Assemblée's Services Législatifs.

Other government agencies issuing publications in the post-independence period are the Direction de la Statistique et des Etudes Economiques et Démographiques (BULLETIN MENSUEL DE STATISTIQUE, Supplément trimestriel, and other periodic reports, including statistical data for Upper Volta and Niger), the Ministère de l'Information (BULLETIN QUOTIDIEN DE L'INFORMATION of the Agence Ivoirienne de Presse), the Ministère de l'Agriculture et de la Coopération, and the Ministère de l'Education Nationale (monthly bulletin, EDUCATION ET TECHNIQUES).

The Chambre de Commerce and the Chambre d'Agriculture, both government supported, issue monthly bulletins, which are useful reviews of current economic conditions.

1726. Ivory Coast. Direction de la Statistique et des Etudes Economiques
et Démographiques. INVENTAIRE ECONOMIQUE ET SOCIAL DE LA
COTE-D'IVOIRE, 1947 A 1958. Abidjan, Ministère des Finances,
des Affaires Economiques et du Plan, Service de la Statistique,
1960. 283 p. maps (part. col.), diagrs., tables.

An impressive publication of the former colonial government, in
handsome makeup, with tables exhibiting all economic and social
factors. The previous edition was issued by the Service de la
Statistique Générale et de la Mécanographie under the title INVENTAIRE
ECONOMIQUE DE LA COTE-D'IVOIRE (1947 A 1956).

1727. Joseph, Gaston. COTE D'IVOIRE. Paris, Fayard, 1944. 254 p.

Bibliography: p. 207-213.

The Ivory Coast became a French colony by a decree of Mar. 10,
1893. This survey, combining history, ethnology, administration, and
economic and social aspects, was written as a 50-year balance sheet.

1728. Marty, Paul. ETUDES SUR L'ISLAM EN COTE D'IVOIRE. Paris, E. Leroux,
1922. 496 p. illus., plates, map. (Collection de la REVUE DU
MONDE MUSULMAN)

A thorough study of Islam and its influence and survival in
the Ivory Coast. Arrangement is by three regions--coastal, forest,
and savanna. Seventeen appendixes are included. For note on Marty,
see no. 1753.

1729. Meillassoux, Claude. ANTHROPOLOGIE ECONOMIQUE DES GOURO DE COTE
D'IVOIRE: DE L'ECONOMIE DE SUBSISTANCE A L'AGRICULTURE COM-
MERCIALE. Paris, La Haye, Mouton, 1964. 382 p. plates, maps
(part fold.), tables, diagrs., plans, geneal. tables. (Le
monde d'outre-mer, passé et présent, 1st ser., Etudes, 27)

Bibliography: p. [353]-356.

An excellent, extremely detailed study of the Gouro group of
peoples inhabiting the middle section of the Ivory Coast. This
well-illustrated work, interspersed with 17 maps, covers the
environment, peoples, villages, subsistence economy, alliances and
war, rapport between man and the land, precolonial trade, colonial
economy and forced labor, and commercial agriculture. Included are
an index and an alphabetical list of villages along with the tribal
names of their inhabitants.

555

1730. Rougerie, Gabriel. LA COTE D'IVOIRE. Paris, Presses Universitaires
        de France, 1964. 128 p. maps. ("Que sais-je?" no. 1137)

        A concise review of the physical and human geography and of the
economic problems and prospects of the country.

        Among other works on the Ivory Coast by this IFAN geographer
is LE PAYS AGNI DU SUD-EST DE LA COTE D'IVOIRE FORESTIERE (Paris,
Tournier, 1957, 242 p., illus.).

1731. Société d'Etudes pour le Développement Economique et Social.
        REPUBLIQUE DE COTE D'IVOIRE: REGION DE KORHOGO: ETUDE DE
        DEVELOPPEMENT SOCIO-ECONOMIQUE. Paris, ORSTOM, 1965. 9 v.
        maps.

        Nine reports and studies ranging from 52 to 268 pages, each
volume devoted to a specific category: pedology, demography,
sociology, agriculture, commerce and transportation, household
budgets, economic accounts (1963, 1970, 1975), propositions for
intervention, and synthesis.

1732. U.S. Department of the Interior. Office of Geography. IVORY COAST:
        OFFICIAL STANDARD NAMES APPROVED BY THE UNITED STATES BOARD ON
        GEOGRAPHIC NAMES. Washington, U.S. Govt. Print. Off., Mar.
        1965. 250 p. map. (17,700 names) (Gazetteer no. 89)

        See note on series, no. 484.

1733. Wallerstein, Immanuel. THE ROAD TO INDEPENDENCE: GHANA AND THE
        IVORY COAST. La Haye, Paris, Mouton, 1964. xiii, 200 p.
        tables, chart. (Le monde d'outre-mer, passé et présent, 1st
        ser., Etudes, 20)

        Bibliography: p. [179]-200.

        Study of social change under colonial rule in these two West
African states, with the basic thesis that there were more similarities than differences in development of the countries under,
respectively, British and French rule. Particular attention is given
to the rule of voluntary associations and to the relation of elite
groups to the rise of nationalism.

1734. Zolberg, Aristide R. ONE-PARTY GOVERNMENT IN THE IVORY COAST.
        Princeton, N.J., Princeton University Press, 1964. xiv, 374 p.
        maps, diagr., tables.

        Bibliography: p. 343-360.

A thorough doctoral study of the government of the Ivory Coast
since independence, under the Parti démocratique of President
Houphouet-Boigny. The long bibliography includes books, pamphlets,
and periodical articles, official documents, organizational reports
and proceedings, and titles of unpublished material. See also V.
Thompson, "Ivory Coast," in Carter, AFRICAN ONE-PARTY STATES, no.
606.

MALI (SOUDAN)

Note: Upon independence in Nov. 1958 the former French Sudan became the
République soudanaise. In 1959 it joined with Senegal to form the Federation
of Mali, which was dissolved in Aug. 1960. The country then took the name
Republic of Mali.

Bibliography

1735. Brasseur, Paule. BIBLIOGRAPHIE GENERALE DU MALI (ANCIEN SOUDAN
          FRANCAIS ET ANCIEN HAUT-SENEGAL-NIGER). Dakar, IFAN, 1964. 461
          p. fold. map. (Catalogue et documents, no. 16)

          Comprehensive model bibliography listing almost 5,000 titles,
       in subject classification, with index. A preliminary list of sources
       includes maps, periodicals, and bibliographies. See also no. 1760.

1736. Cutter, Charles H. "Mali: A Bibliographical Introduction." AFRICAN
          STUDIES BULLETIN, v. 9, no. 3, Dec. 1966: 74-87.

          This bibliographical essay covers the best and most important
       works concerning Mali and at the same time stresses materials in
       English and those that have appeared since publication of Brasseur's
       work.

1737. "Serials of Cameroun, Dahomey, Togo, Mali...." AFRICANA NEWSLETTER,
          v. 2, no. 1, 1964: 33-41.

          Seven newspapers and periodicals published in Mali are listed
       here (p. 37), with language, frequency, place of publication, and
       publisher given for each.

Reference Works

1738. Amin, Samir. TROIS EXPERIENCES AFRICAINES DE DEVELOPPEMENT: LE MALI,
           LA GUINEE ET LE GHANA. Paris, Presses Universitaires de France,
           1965. 236 p. tables. (Etudes "Tiers-Monde")

       In this study of the development of three West African economies,
Mali receives the most detailed treatment. A brief introduction to
the geography, natural resources, and political and social systems of
the three countries sets the scene. The first three chapters (p. 21-
129) are devoted to Mali--its structure and evolution during the
colonial period of 1928-59, its decolonization, and its 1961-66
development plan. The author then describes the economic development
of Guinea, 1959-63, and the recent and projected (to 1970) development of Ghana, and in a concluding section analyzes the significance
for West Africa of the experiences of the three countries.

1739. Beuchelt, Eno. MALI. Bonn, Kurt Schroeder, 1966. 153 p. maps
           (1 fold.), tables. (Die Länder Afrikas, v. 34)

       Bibliography: p. 143-146.

       A well-organized and concise survey of Mali. The text begins
with the physical and economic geography, continues with history,
peoples, political structure before and after independence, and
culture, and concludes with a long section on the economy.

1740. Dieterlen, Germaine. ESSAI SUR LA RELIGION BAMBARA. Paris, Presses
           Universitaires de France, 1951. 240 p. illus. (Bibliothèque
           de sociologie contemporaine)

       Mme. Dieterlen, a former student of Professor Marcel Griaule,
is one of the well-known French anthropologists. This work, based
on extensive field research in the region of Bamako, is a detailed
ethnological treatise on religious myths, beliefs, and practices of
a Sudanese tribe, the Bambara.

       Other anthropological studies of the Bambara include the Inter-
national African Institute volume in the Ethnographic Survey series,
LES BAMBARA, by Viviana Paques (see no. 1670[a]), Dominique Zahan's
SOCIETE D'INITIATION BAMBARA: LE N'DOMO, LE KORE (Paris, La Haye,
Mouton, 1960, 439 p., illus., plates, fold. maps, tables; Le monde
d'outre-mer, passé et présent, 1st ser., Etudes, 8), and two books
by Louis Tauxier, HISTOIRE DES BAMBARA (Paris, Paul Geuthner, 1942,
226 p., illus., map) and LA RELIGION BAMBARA (Paris, Geuthner, 1927).
Another work by this last anthropologist is his MOEURS ET HISTOIRE
DES PEULS (Paris, Payot, 1937, 422 p., plates, map; Bibliothèque
scientifique).

1741. L'ESSOR HEBDOMADAIRE. 1959- Bamako. Weekly.

Once considered the best news journal published in Mali, this
weekly was the organ of the Union Soudanaise-R.D.A.

1742. Etudes soudanaises. no. 1- Koulouba, Institut Français d'Afrique
        Noire, Centre du Soudan, 1953- Irregular.

Only three monographs were issued in this series, the first two
under the variant title Etudes soudaniennes (1953-54). The third was
a valuable study based on many sources other than European records by
a prominent African scholar, Amadou Hampaté Bâ, in collaboration with
Jacques Daget, L'EMPIRE PEUL DU MACINA: Vol. I, 1818-1853 (1955); it
was reissued for the Institut by Mouton, Paris (1962, 306 p., map;
Le monde d'outre-mer, passé et présent, 1st ser., Etudes, 15).

The IFAN Centre du Soudan has been replaced since independence
by the Institut des Sciences Humaines in Koulouba, which is intended
to serve as the legal depository for publications of the Malian
government. The Etudes series had not been continued as of late
1969.

The Archives Nationales are also located in the Institut's
headquarters; most of the thousands of documents are as yet un-
catalogued.

Reference Works

1743. Delafosse, Maurice. LES FRONTIERES DE LA COTE D'IVOIRE, DE LA COTE
        D'OR, ET DU SOUDAN. Paris, Masson, 1908. 256 p.

One of the many useful volumes by the great administrator-
historian-ethnographer Delafosse. A monument in French colonial
studies of the early twentieth century was HAUT-SENEGAL-NIGER
(SOUDAN FRANCAIS): SERIES D'ETUDES, 1-2 sér., published under the
direction of the Governor, M. F. J. Clozel (Paris, Larose, 1912,
5 v., illus., maps, plans; bibliographical footnotes). The first
series was by Maurice Delafosse, LE PAYS, LES PEUPLES, LES LANGUES,
L'HISTOIRE (3 v.), the second series, GEOGRAPHIE ECONOMIQUE, by
Jacques Méniaud (2 v.).

1744. Foltz, William J. FROM FRENCH WEST AFRICA TO THE MALI FEDERATION.
        New Haven, London, Yale University Press, 1965. 235 p.

Bibliography: p. 215-228.

Scholarly study of the short-lived Mali Federation of Senegal
and the former Republic of the Soudan (later the Republic of Mali),
by a firsthand observer of West African politics immediately after
the breakup. Dr. Foltz's aim was to answer the questions of why
the Federation was formed and why it failed.

1745. France. Direction de la Documentation. LA REPUBLIQUE DU MALI.
        Paris, La Documentation Française, 1961. 65 p. (Notes et
        études documentaires, no. 2739, Jan. 13, 1961)

        See general note on this series, no. 1587.

        No comprehensive modern survey of Mali has come to our attention.

1746. Gallieni, Joseph S. MISSION D'EXPLORATION DU HAUT-NIGER: VOYAGE
        AU SOUDAN FRANCAIS (HAUT-NIGER ET PAYS DE SEGOU), 1879-1881.
        Paris, Hachette, 1885. 632 p.

        _____. GALLIENI PACIFICATEUR: ECRITS COLONIAUX DE GALLIENI.
        Selection and notes by Hubert Deschamps and Paul Chauvet.
        Paris, Presses Universitaires de France, 1949. 382 p. (Les
        classiques de la colonisation, no. 13)

        Classics of history of the Sudan from the French viewpoint.
        See note under Madagascar, no. 2049.

1747. Galloy, Pierre, Yvon Vincent, and Maurice Forget. NOMADES ET
        PAYSANS D'AFRIQUE NOIRE OCCIDENTALE: ETUDES DE GEOGRAPHIE
        SOUDANAISE PUBLIEES PAR LES SOINS DE XAVIER DE PLANHOL.
        Nancy, Faculté des Lettres et des Sciences Humaines, Université
        de Nancy, 1963. 242 p. illus., plates, maps (part fold.).
        (Annales de l'Est, Mémoire no. 23; also Publication no. 3 of
        the Institut de Géographie)

        Three anthropogeographic studies of the Middle Niger region:
        "Nomadisme et fixation dans la région des lacs du moyen Niger," by
        Galloy; "Pasteurs, paysans et pecheurs du Guimballa (partie centrale
        de l'erg du Bara)," by Vincent; and "Populations et genres de vie
        dans le Kounary (cercle de Mopti, Soudan)," by Forget.

1748. Griaule, Marcel. MASQUES DOGONS. Paris, Institut d'Ethnologie,
        1963. 2d ed. 896 p. illus. (part col.), plates, maps.
        (Travaux et mémoires de l'Institut d'Ethnologie, v. 33)

        Bibliography: p. [879]-882.

An important basic work, first published in 1938, on the elaborate
mythology of the Dogon by the late noted authority on Dogon cosmology.
An introduction briefly surveys the geography, economy, and culture
of the Bandiagara, Sanga, and Kassa regions. The volume is then
divided into five major parts which closely examine the rituals of
the Dogon masked societies and elucidate the symbolism of the masks.
Included are a lexicon and, commendably, 11 indexes. The volume
concludes with 32 unpaged plates.

A later study of Dogon mythology, in which the role of the
white fox receives exhaustive analysis, is Marcel Griaule and Germaine
Dieterlen, LE RENARD PALE: Vol. I, LE MYTHE COSMOGONIQUE: Fasc. 1,
LA CREATION DU MONDE (Paris, Institut d'Ethnologie, 1965, 544 p.,
illus. [part fold. col.], plates, fold. maps; bibliography: p. [517]-
525; Travaux et mémoires de l'Institut d'Ethnologie, v. 72).

Griaule's daughter, Geneviève Calame-Griaule, has written a
detailed work on the theory and mythology of the language of the
Dogon, its social phenomenology, and its relation to the plastic arts
and to music: ETHNOLOGIE ET LANGAGE: LA PAROLE CHEZ LES DOGON (Paris,
Gallimard, 1965, 593 p., illus., plates; bibliography: p. 557-561;
Bibliothèque des sciences humaines). Three excellent analytical
indexes are included.

The results of a sociological survey conducted in the Sanga
region are recorded in Denise Paulme's comprehensive work,
ORGANISATION SOCIALE DES DOGONS (SOUDAN FRANCAIS) (Paris, Domat-
Montchrestien, 1940, 603 p., illus., plates, maps, plans; bibliography: p. 571-587; Institut de Droit Comparé, Etudes de sociologie
et d'ethnologie juridique). A concise review of the economic, social,
cultural, and religious life of the Dogon is Montserrat Palau-Marti's
LES DOGON, an International African Institute volume in the Ethnographic Survey series (see no. 1670). For a psychoanalytical study
of the Dogon, see no. 1755 below.

1749. Grundy, Kenneth W. "Mali: The Prospects of 'Planned Socialism.'"
        In Friedland, W. H., and C. G. Rosberg, eds. AFRICAN SOCIALISM.
        Stanford, Calif., Stanford University Press, 1964: p. 175-193.

Good recent analysis of the politico-economic situation of Mali
in the early 1960's. See also Morgenthau and Hodgkin in Coleman and
Rosberg, POLITICAL PARTIES AND NATIONAL INTEGRATION IN TROPICAL
AFRICA (no. 612).

1750. Ligers, Ziedonis. LES SORKO (BOZO): MAITRES DU NIGER: ETUDE
        ETHNOGRAPHIQUE. Paris, Librairie des Cinq Continents, 1964-67.
        3 v. xvi, 200, 220 p.; xxiv, 175 p. plates.

A study of a people who live on islets of the Niger in the region of Mopti and whose mode of life and subsistence depends on fishing, harvesting, and hunting. In Vol. I Ligers describes in intricate detail the last two activities and in Vol. II the techniques, rituals, and taboos of the Sorko. Vol. III is devoted to the habitat of the people.

1751. Mali. JOURNAL OFFICIEL DE LA REPUBLIQUE DU MALI. Sept. 1960-
        Koulouba. Semimonthly.

        Supersedes the JOURNAL OFFICIEL DE LA FEDERATION DU MALI
        (Apr. 1959-Aug. 1960, Dakar, weekly) and the JOURNAL OFFICIEL DE LA
        REPUBLIQUE SOUDANAISE (Nov. 1958-Sept. 1960), which had replaced the
        JOURNAL OFFICIEL DU SOUDAN FRANCAIS (Koulouba, Impr. du Gouvernement,
        1921-58) and the JOURNAL OFFICIEL DU HAUT-SENEGAL-NIGER (1906-21).

        The Imprimerie Nationale, in the Bamako suburb of Koulouba,
        also publishes the BUDGET GENERAL and law codes. Statistical
        reports, including the BULLETIN MENSUEL DE STATISTIQUE (irregular)
        and the ANNUAIRE STATISTIQUE, are prepared by the Service de la
        Statistique Générale et de la Comptabilité Economique Nationale in
        Koulouba and usually released by the Chambre de Commerce de Bamako.

        For official publications before and after independence, see
        the Library of Congress OFFICIAL PUBLICATIONS OF FRENCH WEST AFRICA
        (no. 1636).

1752. Mali. Office Malien du Tourisme. LE GUIDE DE MALI. Bamako, 1968.
        147 p. illus., maps (1 fold.). ("Supplément de AFRIQUE-MAGAZINE")

1753. Marty, Paul. ETUDES SUR L'ISLAM ET LES TRIBUS DU SOUDAN. Paris, E.
        Leroux, 1920-21. 4 v. plates, ports., maps (part fold.),
        facsims., geneal. tables. (Collection de la REVUE DU MONDE
        MUSULMAN)

        Vol. I.   LES KOUNTA DE L'EST: LES BERABICH, LES IGUELLAD.
                   1920. 358 p. (Bibliography: p. [352]-354.)

        Vol. II.   LA REGION DE TOMBOUCTOU (ISLAM SONRAI): DIENNE,
                   LE MACINA ET DEPENDANCES (ISLAM PEUL). 1920.
                   334 p.

        Vol. III. LES TRIBUS MAURES DU SAHEL ET DU HODH. 1921. 475 p.

        Vol. IV.   LA REGION DE KAYES: LE PAYS BAMBARA, LE SAHEL DE
                   NIORO. 1920. 295 p.

These four volumes constitute a portion of Marty's extensive
and authoritative work on regional Islam--work which was officially
encouraged by the French who felt that Islam disrupted the religio-
social order of Africans and was a threat to French hegemony. An
account of the traditional religions vis-à-vis Islam and of France's
efforts to avoid a clash between the two forces is given in Jules
Brévié, ISLAMISME CONTRE "NATURISME" AU SOUDAN FRANCAIS: L'ESSAI
DE PSYCHOLOGIE POLITIQUE COLONIALE (Paris, E. Leroux, 1923, xvi,
320 p.).

1754. Monteil, Charles. "Les empires du Mali: Etude d'histoire et de
          sociologie soudanaises." BULLETIN DU COMITE D'ETUDES HISTORIQUES
          ET SCIENTIFIQUES DE L'A.O.F., v. 12, 1929: 291-447. map.

        Reprint: Paris, Maisonneuve et Larose, 1968. 160 p.

        Presents sources of information, a synopsis of the dynasties,
and the descriptions given by Arab writers, as well as an account
of the pilgrimage of Mansa Mussa and of the decline and ruin of the
empire.

1755. Parin, Paul, Fritz Morgenthaler, and Goldy Parin-Matthèy. DIE
          WEISSEN DENKEN ZUVIEL: PSYCHOANALYTISCHE UNTERSUCHUNGEN BEI
          DEN DOGON IN WESTAFRIKA. Zürich, Atlantis Verlag, 1963.
          527 p. illus., plates, maps, tables.

        Bibliography: p. 516-520.

        An arresting study of the Dogon by three enterprising Swiss
psychoanalysts who here bypass the traditional methods of ethnological research. The volume begins with an explanation of the
psychoanalytical methods used and then describes the Dogon and
their life, essentially summarizing the work of Griaule and other
French ethnologists. The bulk of the book is devoted to 13 psychoanalytical dialogues, a profile of a young Dogon man, 100 Rorschach
tests, and observations on the authors' findings and methods. The
work has also appeared in French translation: LES BLANCS PENSENT
TROP (Paris, Payot, 1966, 477 p.; Sciences de l'homme).

1756. Rouch, Jean. LES SONGHAY. Paris, Presses Universitaires de France,
          1954. 100 p. fold. map. (Monographies ethnologiques
          africaines, no. 2)

        "Essai de bibliographie analytique": p. 68-95.

        See note on this series, published for the International African
Institute (no. 1670). Rouch's excellent annotated bibliography is
accompanied by an author index.

Rouch, anthropologist and film director, is also the author of
LA RELIGION ET LA MAGIE SONGHAY (Paris, Presses Universitaires de
France, 1960, 325 p.) and of the second part (p. 121-259) of IFAN's
Mémoire no. 29: UN PEUPLE DE L'OUEST SOUDANIEN: LES DIAWARA, by
Gaston Boyer; CONTRIBUTION A L'HISTOIRE DES SONGHAY, by Jean Rouch
(Dakar, IFAN, 1953, 259 p., illus., plates, maps; bibliography: p.
[249]-252). Another interesting study of the Songhai is: Jean
Boulnois and Boubou Hama, L'EMPIRE DE GAO: HISTOIRE, COUTUMES ET
MAGIE DES SONRAI (Paris, A. Maisonneuve, 1954, 185 p., illus.,
fold. map).

1757. Snyder, Frank Gregory. ONE-PARTY GOVERNMENT IN MALI: TRANSITION
         TOWARD CONTROL. New Haven, London, Yale University Press,
         1965. 178 p. (Yale College Series, no. 4)

       Bibliography: p. 161-170.

       A detailed account of the history and structure of the Union
Soudanaise, the only political party in Mali. The author based
much of his material concerning this African political system on
interviews in 1963 with government and political leaders and on
party communiqués and documents. Part 1 traces the origins of the
party (1936-47), covering the period of the Popular Front and of
Vichy, World War II, and postwar political parties. Part 2, dealing
with the period 1947-64, describes the founding of the parti unique
and examines political ideology and perceptions. Part 3 consists
of an analysis of the party's problems and prospects. Six useful
appendixes take up 42 pages.

1758. Spitz, Georges. SANSANDING: LES IRRIGATIONS DU NIGER. Paris,
         Société d'Editions Géographiques, Maritimes et Coloniales,
         1949. 237 p. illus., fold. maps.

       _____. LE SOUDAN FRANCAIS. Paris, Editions Maritimes et
         Coloniales, 1955. 111 p. illus., maps. (Pays africains, no. 5)

       The first book gives a comprehensive account to that date of
the irrigation works undertaken by the Office of the Niger, written
just after the completion in 1947 of the great dam near Sansanding
in the Ségou region, now under the control of Mali. The second book
is an introductory survey, following the pattern of the Pays africains
series (see no. 1581n).

1759. U.S. Department of the Interior. Office of Geography. MALI: OFFICIAL
         STANDARD NAMES APPROVED BY THE UNITED STATES BOARD ON GEOGRAPHIC
         NAMES. Washington, U.S. Govt. Print. Off., Sept. 1965. 263 p.
         map.

       See note on series, no. 484.

MAURITANIA

<u>Note</u>: The Islamic Republic of Mauritania lies for most of its 418,000 square
miles within the vague boundaries of the western and southern Sahara, the
desert merging gradually into the semiarid lands of the interior. Therefore
a few works on the Sahara are included here. These apply equally to the
northern regions of Mali, Niger, and Chad, and cross-references from those
country sections have been indicated.

Bibliographies

1760. Blaudin de Thé, Bernard, ed. ESSAI DE BIBLIOGRAPHIE DU SAHARA
          FRANCAIS ET DES REGIONS AVOISINANTES. Edité avec le concours
          de l'Organisation Commune des Régions Sahariennes. 2d ed.
          Paris, Arts et Métiers Graphiques, Librairie C. Klinksieck,
          1960. 258 p.

        A comprehensive catalogue of books, documents, pamphlets, mono-
graphs, and articles in French and other Western languages. Edited
by an officer in the Service des Affaires Sahariennes, it combines
a reprint of an earlier bibliography of the Territoires du Sud de
l'Algérie, prepared by Lieutenant Moulias in 1923 and expanded by
Lieutenant Thinières in 1930 (p. 1-61, 2,372 entries arranged
chronologically under a variety of subjects) with his own compilation, parts of which had been published earlier. Commandant Blaudin
de Thé's scope is wider than that of the first compilers, and he has
brought together 9,301 references on the entire Saharan region, including Mauritania, upper Niger, and much of Mali and Chad. Entries
are arranged alphabetically by author in subclassifications under
four main sections--travel and exploration before the twentieth
century, natural sciences, humanities, and "varia," the last including means of communication, economic exploitation, miscellany
(travel narratives, general and regional studies, tourism, etc.),
and unpublished documents. An author index is included, as well as
an address list of French periodicals cited.

1761. Toupet, Charles. "Orientation bibliographique sur la Mauritanie."
          BULLETIN DE L'INSTITUT FRANCAIS D'AFRIQUE NOIRE, ser. B, v.
          31, no. 1-2, 1959: 201-239.

        An extensive bibliography, in subject classification, including
maps, bibliography, general works, six rubrics of natural sciences,
archaeology and history, Islam, linguistics, way of life, techniques
and art, economics, regional and tribal studies, and general literature.
A large proportion of the references are to articles in IFAN bulletins.
The titles are almost without exception in French; a few have brief
annotations.

Reference Works

1762. Briggs, Lloyd C. THE LIVING RACES OF THE SAHARA DESERT. Cambridge,
      Mass., Peabody Museum, 1958. xii, 217 p. illus., 69 plates,
      maps. (Papers of the Peabody Museum of Archaeology and
      Ethnology, Harvard University, v. 28, no. 2)

      "References": p. 203-212.

      _____. TRIBES OF THE SAHARA. Cambridge, Mass., Harvard University
      Press, 1960. xx, 295 p. illus., maps.

      Bibliography: p. 277-285.

      Two systematic anthropological studies of the peoples of the
      Sahara, Tuareg, Teda, Chaamba, and other tribes, by a research
      fellow at Harvard. The Tuareg and Teda peoples are widespread in
      the southern Sahara.

1763. Capot-Rey, Robert. L'AFRIQUE BLANCHE FRANCAISE: Vol. II, LE SAHARA
      FRANCAIS. Paris, Presses Universitaires de France, 1953.
      564 p. illus., maps. (Pays d'outre-mer, 4th ser., Géographie
      de l'Union française, no. 1)

      Bibliography: p. 495-541.

      Extensive and authoritative study of the Sahara, including
      Mauritania and regions of Mali, Niger, and Chad. The first part is
      a thorough presentation of physical geography, climatology, and
      geology; the second part is on human geography; and the third part
      reviews the work of France as to capital equipment and production
      and prospects for future development. The long classified bibli-
      ography contains 818 numbered items in addition to maps, periodicals,
      and collections; there is also an index of proper names.

      A succinct survey of the Sahara's physical, human, and economic
      geography appears as Part 5 (p. 419-510) of Jean Despois' GEOGRAPHIE
      DE L'AFRIQUE DU NORD-OUEST (Paris, Payot, 1967, 570 p., maps). The
      book's selective bibliography includes a section on the Sahara (p.
      532-539) arranged by region.

1764. Chambre de Commerce de Mauritanie. BULLETIN. Nouakchott. Biweekly.

      A mimeographed bulletin issued regularly. Distribution is
      largely to the membership.

1765. Cornet, Pierre. SAHARA, TERRE DE DEMAIN. Paris, Nouvelles Editions
       Latines, 1956. 270 p. illus., maps.

       A councillor of the French Union here sets forth in explicit
terms the plans for development of the Sahara, including the western
Sahara and such projects as the irrigation works of the Office of the
Niger and the proposed trans-Saharan railway. He ends with consideration of the projected French Saharan Region and its strategic
connection with the Fezzan. Two appendixes cite pertinent parliamentary and other official texts from 1952 to Oct. 1956, the
last being the law proposed by M. Houphouet-Boigny, then Minister
from the Ivory Coast, for the Organisation Commune des Régions
Sahariennes, to include Mauritania, the French Sudan (now Mali),
Niger, and Chad, together with Algeria.

       In 1961 a brochure in the Notes et études documentaires series
of the French Direction de la Documentation was devoted to LE CADRE
INSTITUTIONNEL DU DEVELOPPEMENT (Paris, 19 p.; no. 2801, July 31,
1961).

1766. Désiré-Vuillemin, Geneviève. CONTRIBUTION A L'HISTOIRE DE LA
       MAURITANIE DE 1900 A 1934. Dakar, Editions Clairafrique,
       1962. 412 p.

       Bibliography: p. 353-404.

       Only study of the important period of French dominance, written
from archival sources. Excellent bibliography and guide to archives
of West Africa and France with material on Mauritania.

1767. Etudes mauritaniennes. nos. 1-6. Saint-Louis, Sénégal, Institut
       Française d'Afrique Noire, Centre Sénégal-Mauritanie, 1948-55.
       Irregular.

       At least two of the series are worth mention as reference
sources: Mokhtar ould Hamidoun, PRECIS SUR LA MAURITANIE (1952, 69 p.;
no. 4), a geographical and ethnological introduction to the country,
and Ahmad ibn al-Amin al-Shinqiti, EL WASIT: LITTERATURE, HISTOIRE,
GEOGRAPHIE, MOEURS ET COUTUMES DES HABITANTS DE LA MAURITANIE, PAR
AHMED LAMINE ECH CHENGUITI, excerpts translated from the Arabic by
Mourad Teffahi (1953, 150 p.; no. 5).

       None of the series has been issued since independence, and the
library and archives of the IFAN Centre Mauritanie are still kept in
Saint-Louis du Sénégal.

1768.   France. Direction de la Documentation. LA REPUBLIQUE ISLAMIQUE
        DE MAURITANIE. Paris, La Documentation Française, 1960. 50 p.
        (Notes et études documentaires, no. 2687, July 29, 1960)

        See general note on this series, no. 1587.

1769.   France. Ministère de la Coopération. EDUCATION ET DEVELOPPEMENT
        EN MAURITANIE. By Marc Botti and Paul Vezinet. Paris, 1963.
        4 v.

        A study by an economist and an educator. The first volume
(93 p.) deals with the human environment, the educational system,
and employment, and states the general problems. The second volume
(97 p.) presents recommendations for general education, the third
(61 p.) recommendations for higher education and professional training. A synthesis of the report is provided in the concluding volume
(36 p.).

1770.   Furon, Raymond. LE SAHARA: GEOLOGIE, RESSOURCES MINERALES. 2d ed.,
        rev. Paris, Payot, 1964. 313 p. illus., maps. (Bibliothèque
        scientifique)

        Bibliographical footnotes.

        By a leading French specialist on geology and mineral resources,
this work is a completely revised and updated edition of Furon's
excellent basic survey which first appeared in 1957.

1771.   Gerteiny, Alfred G. MAURITANIA. New York, Praeger, 1967. xi, 243 p.
        map. (Praeger Library of African Affairs)

        Bibliography: p. 225-234.

        The first major publication in English on one of Africa's
least-known countries. Professor Gerteiny, basing his work on
extensive field and documentary research, ably handles a subject
that has heretofore been almost exclusively the concern of French
scholars. He first provides geographic and regional profiles and a
historical background, examines the society, customs, beliefs, and
language and literature of the Moors, and discusses the black
minorities. A review of the era of French colonialism and the
decolonization period follows, and the final portion of the volume
is devoted to political and administrative affairs, the economy,
and international relations. The book is loaded with Arabic words
and phrases, a situation somewhat alleviated by a 9-page glossary.
The good selective bibliography includes notes.

1772. Husson, Philippe. LA QUESTION DES FRONTIERES TERRESTRES DU MAROC.
         Paris, 1960. 128 p.

         Study by a French lawyer of the legal and political aspects of
the boundaries of Morocco with the western Sahara, both the Spanish
Sahara and Mauritania. The thorough examination of sources goes
through 1958 only, before Mauritanian independence and well before
the debated boundary question was brought before the United Nations
in Aug.-Nov. 1960.

1773. Jacques-Meunié, D. CITES ANCIENNES DE MAURITANIE: PROVINCES DU
         TAGANNT ET DU HODH. Paris, Librairie C. Klincksieck, 1961.
         195 p. illus., 80 plates, map, plans.

         "Sources non imprimées": p. 160; "Bibliographie": p. 161-
167.

         An interesting study devoted primarily to two distinctive forms
of architecture in two regions which thrived during the heyday of
the caravan trade. Mme. Jacques-Meunié also briefly describes the
country, the peoples and their social structures, and the ornaments
of women. Four glossaries are included, and the 80 plates which end
the work are unpaged.

1774. Marty, Paul. ETUDES SUR L'ISLAM ET LES TRIBUS MAURES: LES BRAKNA.
         Paris, E. Leroux, 1921. 399 p. illus., maps (part fold.),
         facsims., geneal. tables. (Collection de la REVUE DU MONDE
         MUSULMAN)

         _____. ETUDES SUR L'ISLAM MAURE: CHEIKH SIDIA, LES FADELIA,
         LES IDA OU ALI. Paris, 1916. 252 p. plates, facsims.
         (Collection de la REVUE DU MONDE MUSULMAN)

         _____. L'ISLAM EN MAURITANIE ET AU SENEGAL. Paris, 1915-16.
         483 p. 32 plates. (Collection de la REVUE DU MONDE MUSULMAN)

         By a renowned authority on Islam and on Mauritania, these three
works form part of his immense contribution to the study of Islam
in West Africa. The first book is a specific study of the Brakna
people of southwestern Mauritania. In the second specialized work
Marty presents a detailed account of Shaikh Sīdyā and his "way,"
of the Fadiliyya order and its followers, and of the Ida-ou-Ali
people and the Tijaniyya sect. The third study, very likely a
definitive one, covers not only the material of the second work but
extends the subject to Senegal, with a discussion of the Tijaniyya
sect among the Tukulors, Wolofs, and Mandingoes.

1775. Mauritania. JOURNAL OFFICIEL DE LA REPUBLIQUE ISLAMIQUE DE MAURITANIE.
       1959- Dakar. Semimonthly.

       Mauritania was the only AOF territory which had no official
gazette. Legislation for the 1920-58 period appeared in the JOURNAL
OFFICIEL DE L'AFRIQUE OCCIDENTALE FRANCAISE. As of 1967 the Mauritanian government had not built its own official printing press, and
the JOURNAL OFFICIEL and other official documents were printed in
Senegal.

       The Assemblée Nationale issues its debates in mimeographed form
following three annual sessions. Other legislative material, laws,
statutes, etc., are printed in Dakar, as is also the official newspaper, MAURITANIE NOUVELLE, issued by the Ministère de l'Information.

       The Ministère de l'Education Nationale issues a monthly teachers'
bulletin in mimeographed form, L'EDUCATEUR MAURITANIEN: JOURNAL DES
ENSEIGNANTS DE MAURITANIE. See also no. 1636 for other official
publications.

1776. LE MAURITANIEN: MAGAZINE ILLUSTRE. no. 1- Oct. 1962- Dakar.
       Monthly.

       Under the direction of the Senegalese writer S. N'Diaye, an
illustrated monthly was begun with an issue carrying a long article
on the economy of Mauritania as well as other prose, verse, and
pictorial features relating to Mauritanian life and thought.

1777. Monod, Théodore. MAJABAT AL-KOUBRA: CONTRIBUTION A L'ETUDE DE
       L'"EMPTY QUARTER" OUEST-SAHARIEN. Dakar, IFAN, 1958. 406 p.
       illus., 81 plates, maps (part fold.), profiles, 4 transparencies
       (in pocket). (Mémoires, no. 52)

       Bibliography: p. 389-392.

       A profound technical study of a barren region in the north of
Mauritania. Professor Monod, director of IFAN and an authority on
the western Sahara, made several expeditions on camelback in the
desert. He edited a technical report, CONTRIBUTIONS A L'ETUDE DU
SAHARA OCCIDENTAL (Paris, Larose, 1938-39, 2 v.; bibliography:
v. 2, p. 207-211), which was issued as Publications du Comité
d'Etudes Historiques et Scientifiques de l'Afrique Occidentale
Française (the predecessor of IFAN), Sér. A, no. 7, and Sér. B,
no. 5. These volumes are concerned with archaeological and geological finds.

1778. Pujos, Jérôme. CROISSANCE ECONOMIQUE ET IMPULSION EXTERIEURE: ETUDE SUR L'ECONOMIE MAURITANIENNE. Paris, Presses Universitaires de France, 1964. 314 p. maps, tables. (Etudes économiques internationales)

A valuable study of the economy of Mauritania. Pujos offers a constructive analysis of the imbalance created by the strong emphasis upon mineral exploitation in the sparsely populated north (and the concomitant influx of foreign technicians) and the tendency to neglect the traditional economic activities of the agricultural and pastoral south. The social and political aspects of this economic disequilibrium are carefully examined, and the problems involved in and means for fostering the growth and development of a more balanced economy are reviewed in great detail. The work is rounded out by ample tabulated statistics and six useful maps.

1779. Thomas, Marc-Robert. SAHARA ET COMMUNAUTE. Paris, Presses Universitaires de France, 1960. 298 p.

Bibliography: p. 285-292.

A treatise on legislation relative to the Sahara, a part of it concerned with the provisions of the Organisation Commune des Régions Sahariennes (OCRS), which has undertaken large cooperative projects in the southern Sahara as well as in the oil and iron-producing regions of Algeria.

1780. Treyer, Claude. SAHARA, 1956-1962. Paris, Société des Belles Lettres, 1966. 344 p. illus., maps (1 fold.), graphs, tables. (Publications de l'Université de Dijon, fasc. 37)

Bibliography: p. 325-333.

Part 1 consists of a general survey of geographical, demographical, political, and economic features. Part 2 deals with development of the Sahara's economic and social infrastructure by France from 1957 to 1962 with particular reference to the work of the Organisation Commune des Régions Sahariennes (OCRS). In Part 3 the development of petroleum and natural gas resources is examined, and Part 4 discusses the economic consequences of the Sahara's development for Africa and Europe.

1781. United Nations Educational, Scientific and Cultural Organization. NOMADES ET NOMADISME AU SAHARA. Paris, 1963. 195 p. plates, maps, tables. (Recherches sur la zone aride, 19)

571

"Bibliographie générale," by Renee Heyum: p. 185-195.

An excellent collaborative work by nine specialists, among them Claude Bataillon, Robert Capot-Rey, and Charles Toupet. The first part (traditional nomadism) is divided into seven chapters, as is the second part (nomadism and the modern world). A glossary of local terms is included. The valuable annotated bibliography lists references first under general works and then by region.

See also Jean Chapelle's NOMADES NOIRS DU SAHARA (no. 1979).

1782. U.S. Department of the Interior. Office of Geography. MAURITANIA: OFFICIAL STANDARD NAMES APPROVED BY THE UNITED STATES BOARD ON GEOGRAPHIC NAMES. Washington, U.S. Govt. Print. Off., June 1966. 149 p. map. (10,000 names) (Gazetteer no. 100)

See note on series, no. 484.

1783. Wellard, James. THE GREAT SAHARA. London, Hutchinson, 1964; New York, E. P. Dutton, 1965. 350 p. illus., plates, maps.

Bibliographical references included in "Notes": p. 334-343.

A highly readable history of the Sahara by a novelist. Though intended primarily for the layman, the book should also be of considerable interest for the beginning student of Africa. Wellard relies on conventional sources and on his own travel experiences as he vividly traces the Sahara's history from earliest times to the present. In his "Notes," he provides not the usual footnote material but rather a succinct bibliographical essay on the main sources relevant to each of his chapters.

NIGER

Bibliographies

1784. Niger. [Outline of Government Reports Issued since 1900, Containing Histories of Tribes and Cities, the Census, and Information on Education, Health, Religion, Etc.] Niamey [1967?]. 1 v. various pagings.

1785. Urvoy, Yves F. "Essai de bibliographie des populations du Soudan central (Niger française, nord de la Nigeria anglaise)." BULLETIN DU COMITE D'ETUDES HISTORIQUES ET SCIENTIFIQUES DE L'AFRIQUE OCCIDENTALE FRANCAISE, v. 19, 1936: 243-333.

Complements Urvoy's historical study (see no. 1802 below). See also nos. 1536 and 1627.

Reference Works

1786. Bonardi, Pierre. LA REPUBLIQUE DU NIGER: NAISSANCE D'UN ETAT. Paris, A.P.D., 1960. 99 p. illus.

Informative survey of the new country, in feature-article style. The author, a journalist and travel writer, gives full accounts of the government, development plans, etc.

1787. Chapelle, Jean. NOMADES NOIRS DU SAHARA. Paris, Plon, 1957. 449 p. illus., plates (1 col.), maps (1 fold. col.), tables. (Recherches en sciences humaines, 10)

Bibliography: p. 411-417.

For annotation see no. 1979.

1788. Clair, Andrée. LE NIGER: PAYS A DECOUVRIR. Paris, Hachette, 1965. 190 p. map, tables.

Bibliography: p. [187]-189.

A sympathetic description of Niger--its geography, history, and contemporary situation. See also his LE NIGER INDEPENDANT: FRATERNITE TRAVAIL, PROGRES (Paris, Editions A.T.E.O.S., 1966, 79 p.).

1789. Dupire, Marguerite. PEULS NOMADES: ETUDE DESCRIPTIVE DES WODAABE DU SAHEL NIGERIEN. Paris, Institut d'Ethnologie, 1962. 336 p. illus., plates, maps (part fold. col.), tables. (Travaux et mémoires de l'Institut d'Ethnologie, 64)

Bibliography: p. 329-331.

A detailed description of a nomadic people of the Bororo Peul group. An introduction includes a review of the physical characteristics and history and legends of the Bororo Peuls and a survey of other peoples of Niger. Attention then centers on the pastoral technique and economy, family life and customs, and various aspects of lineage among the Wodaabe.

1790. Etudes nigériennes. no. 1- Niamey, IFAN-CNRS (Centre Nigérien de Recherche Scientifique), 1953- Irregular.

This series, begun in 1953 by the IFAN Centre du Niger with two numbers in 1953 and 1955, is being continued with valuable contributions since independence. The new center is associated with the Musée de Niger. The Etudes are published in large processed brochures, illustrated lavishly with maps, charts, tables, and diagrams. Most are prepared at government request as working papers, some with assistance from ORSTOM or other French research organizations. Recent issues are mostly sociological studies; on the back page of each the full list of titles is given. Typical of recent production are no. 9, by Edmond Bernus, QUELQUES ASPECTS DE L'EVOLUTION DES TOUAREG DE L'OUEST DE LA REPUBLIQUE DU NIGER: RAPPORT PROVISOIRE (1963, 87 p.); no. 14, by Henri Raulin, ENQUETE SOCIO-ECONOMIQUE RURALE, 1961-1963 (1963, 142 p.); no. 15, by Nicole Echard, ETUDE SOCIO-ECONOMIQUE DANS LES VALLEES DE L'ADER-DOUTCHI-MAJYA (1964, 188 p.); and no. 19, by R. Rochette, DOUGEMA, DIOUNDIOU, KAMARA DEBE, VILLAGES DES DALLOLS MAOURI ET FOGHA: MONOGRAPHIES COMPAREES (1966, 111 p.).

1791. France. Direction de la Documentation. LA REPUBLIQUE DU NIGER. Paris, La Documentation Française, 1960. 50 p. (Notes et études documentaires, no. 2638, Feb. 26, 1960)

See general note on this series, no. 1587.

1792. France. Ministère de la Coopération. ETUDE DEMOGRAPHIQUE ET ECONOMIQUE EN MILIEU NOMADE. By F. Ganon, J. Ribet, and P. Verneuil. Paris, 1966. 2 v., 57, 201 p. maps, tables. Processed.

A 1962-64 survey which constitutes the first statistical survey of a nomadic population undertaken in Niger. The first volume, GENERALITES, METHODOLOGIE, is by Ribet and Ganon; the second, DEMOGRAPHIE, BUDGETS ET CONSOMMATION, by Ganon and Verneuil.

1793. Institut Français d'Afrique Noire. CONTRIBUTION A L'ETUDE DE L'AIR. Paris, Larose, 1950. 562 p. 142 figs., 22 plates, maps (1 fold.). Mémoires, no. 10)

Includes bibliographies.

A collection of studies on the ethnography and prehistory of the mountainous Aïr (Azbine) region of northwestern Niger inhabited by Tuaregs.

1794. Marty, Paul. L'ISLAM ET LES TRIBUS DANS LA COLONIE DU NIGER (2e SERIE). Paris, P. Geuthner, 1931. 102 p. map, tables, geneal. table.

A concise survey in which Marty first examines the Kaoaur-Tibesti region (now parts of Niger and Chad) and four of its major personalities and then discusses doctrines and legal obligations, education, and the influence of Islam on social and juridical institutions. For note on Marty, see no. 1753.

1795. Niger. JOURNAL OFFICIEL DE LA REPUBLIQUE DU NIGER. 1959- Niamey, Impr. Générale du Niger. Monthly.

Under the former colonial government, the JOURNAL OFFICIEL DU TERRITOIRE DU NIGER (variously titled), 1933-58, was printed for various periods by the government presses of other territories, i.e., in Ouagadougou, Porto Novo, Lomé, Koulouba, and Rufisque. The present journal is now printed by the small printing plant in Niamey which also produces the annual BUDGET and various other government publications.

The most important publishing body of the Niger government is the Service de la Statistique, which publishes the ANNUAIRE STATISTIQUE, an annual COMPTE ECONOMIQUE, COMMERCE EXTERIEUR, and BULLETIN DE STATISTIQUE (quarterly). The Service de l'Information et de la Presse issues the daily LE TEMPS DU NIGER and the weekly LE NIGER, which summarizes the news of LE TEMPS. The Ministère de l'Education Nationale has published LE NIGER: COURS DE GEOGRAPHIE (1966, 160 p.).

Niamey now has a national archives, and approximately 1,500 documents, some dating from the 1920's, are held in the library of the Bureau de la Documentation.

1796. Niger. Ministère de la Défense, de l'Information et de la Jeunesse. LE NIGER EN MARCHE. Niamey, 1964. 115 p. illus., maps.

Useful survey of the land, people, their institutions and economic development. Maps and pictures add to its value.

1797. NIGER: REVUE TRIMESTRIELLE. 1968- Niamey, Republic of Niger. Quarterly.

Provides articles and pictures on all aspects of Niger life. The President of the National Assembly is the director of the publication.

1798. PERSPECTIVES NIGERIENNES. 1966- Paris, Centre d'Information du
           Niger. Monthly.

1799. Séré de Rivières, Edmond. HISTOIRE DU NIGER. Paris, Berger-Levrault,
           1965. 24 plates, 8 maps. (Mondes d'outre-mer, Série histoire)

           Bibliography: p. 295-297.

           A survey of Niger's history from earliest times to the present
       by a former colonial officer who has served as a technical adviser to
       the Ministry of the Interior in Niamey. Part 1 describes the geo-
       graphical and ethnical background and external relations (trade and
       exploration). Part 2, divided into ethno-geographic zones, extends
       the account from the early medieval kingdoms through the nineteenth
       century. Part 3 covers the French occupation and administration, the
       coming of independence, and contemporary social and economic
       conditions and prospects. There is an index of names.

           The author contributed a brief survey of Niger as the second
       volume in the Pays africaines series: LE NIGER (Paris, Société
       d'Editions Géographiques, Maritimes et Coloniales, 1952, 94 p.,
       plates, maps; bibliography: p. 92-94).

1800. Thompson, Virginia. "Niger." In Carter, Gwendolen M., ed. NATIONAL
           UNITY AND REGIONALISM IN EIGHT AFRICAN STATES. Ithaca, N.Y.,
           Cornell University Press, 1966: p. 151-230.

1801. U.S. Department of the Interior. Office of Geography. NIGER:
           OFFICIAL STANDARD NAMES APPROVED BY THE UNITED STATES BOARD
           ON GEOGRAPHIC NAMES. Washington, U.S. Govt. Print. Off.,
           May 1966. 207 p. (14,700 names) (Gazetteer no. 99)

           See note on series, no. 484.

1802. Urvoy, Yves F. HISTOIRE DES POPULATIONS DU SOUDAN CENTRAL (COLONIE
           DU NIGER). Paris, Larose, 1936. 350 p. plates, maps.
           (Publications Comité d'Etudes Historiques et Scientifiques
           de l'Afrique Occidentale Française, ser. A, no. 5)

           A publication of the Comité which was the precursor of IFAN,
       this book by a French officer and ethnologist is a historical
       narrative of the tribes to the northeast of the Niger River.
       Captain Urvoy traces events from the fifteenth century to the 1930's.

SENEGAL

Atlas

1803. Senegal. Ministère du Plan. CARTES POUR SERVIR A L'AMENAGEMENT DU
    TERRITOIRE. Dakar, 1965. 42 p. 28 x 39 cm.

    Produced under the direction of P. Metge, this atlas of 39 maps
    (scale 1:2,000,000) covers a wide range of subjects: e.g., population
    density, rainfall, geology, pedology, hydrography, administration,
    production, distribution of income, social services.

Bibliographies

1804. Boulègue, Marguerite. "La presse au Sénégal avant 1939: Bibli-
    ographie." BULLETIN DE L'INSTITUT FRANCAIS D'AFRIQUE NOIRE,
    ser. B, v. 27, no. 3-4, July-Aug. 1965: 715-754.

    A comprehensive survey of 82 Senegalese periodicals, official
    publications, and bulletins of various societies issued before 1939.
    Mme. Boulègue provides a 7-page introduction and then lists and
    describes the journals in order of appearance, including data such
    as title, subtitle, change of title, editor, administration, format,
    periodicity, and libraries where available. Included are a chrono-
    logical and an alphabetical index.

1805. Dakar. Université. ETUDES AFRICANISTES ET TRAVAUX DE RECHERCHES.
    Dakar, 1966. 64 l.

    See also no. 1815.

1806. Johnson, G. Wesley. "Bibliographic Essays: Senegal." AFRICANA
    NEWSLETTER, v. 2, no. 1, 1964: 10-12.

    Short but interesting bibliographical essay with evaluative
    comment on the main sources for bibliography, history, ethnography,
    politics, economics, education, literature, and periodical literature.
    Many of the references are general for French West Africa rather than
    specifically relating to Senegal.

    See also nos. 1624-1636.

1807. Senegal. Archives Nationales. Centre de Documentation. ELEMENTS
        DE BIBLIOGRAPHIE SENEGALAISE, 1959-1963. Compiled by Laurence
        Porges. Dakar, 1964. 141 p.

        Bibliography of bibliographies and other reports and studies
on Senegal undertaken since independence. Groupings are by major
economic activities, the separate regions, and the scholarly research
bodies involved. References are to works in the Archive Centre de
Documentation at Dakar, including significant articles. The list may
be supplemented by reference to the monthly bibliography of holdings
issued by the Archives Nationales since 1962.

1808. Wane, Y. "Etat actuel de la documentation au sujet des Toucouleurs."
        BULLETIN DE L'INSTITUT DE L'AFRIQUE FRANCAISE NOIRE, ser. B,
        v. 25, no. 3-4, July-Oct. 1963: 457-477.

        A bibliography of the Tukulors, arranged under four main
headings--history, ethno-anthropology, economy, and archives.

Reference Works

1809. American University, Washington, D.C. Special Operations Research
        Office. AREA HANDBOOK FOR SENEGAL. Washington, Prepared by
        Foreign Areas Studies Division, Aug. 1963. xiv, 489 p. maps.

        Includes bibliographies.

        Background study in the country series; research and writing
completed on July 31, 1963. The four sections are on social,
political, and economic background and national security. There are
bibliographies at the end of the sections, and a glossary and an
analytical index are included.

1810. Brigaud, Félix. HISTOIRE TRADITIONNELLE DU SENEGAL. Saint-Louis,
        Sénégal, CRDS-Sénégal, 1962. 335 p. maps (1 fold.), tables.
        (Etudes sénégalaises, no. 9, Connaissance du Sénégal, fasc. 9)

        Bibliography: p. 313-335.

        _____. HISTOIRE MODERNE ET CONTEMPORAINE DU SENEGAL. Saint-
        Louis, Sénégal, CRDS-Sénégal, 1966. 149 p. maps (1 fold.),
        tables. (Etudes sénégalaises, no. 9, Connaissance du Sénégal,
        fasc. 11)

        Bibliography: p. [123]-146.

Two excellent volumes on the history of Senegal, by the
director of the Centre de Recherches et de Documentation Scientifique
du Sénégal (former Centre-IFAN). He brings together valuable material, much of it collected on various field trips around Senegal.

Brigaud has also contributed to other parts of the subseries,
Connaissance du Sénégal: fasc. 1 on geology (1960) and fasc. 2 on
hydrology (1961), both by Brigaud; fasc. 3 on climate, soils, and
vegetation (1965), by Brigaud and others; fasc. 5 on human geography
(1963), by J. Lombard; and fasc. 6 on economy (1967), by Brigaud.
Still to come are nos. 4, 7, 8, and 10, on fauna, political and
administrative structure, prehistory, and arts and letters. All are
expected to be on a high level of scholarship.

1811. Charpy, Jacques, ed. LA FONDATION DE DAKAR (1845-1857-1869). Paris,
      Larose, 1958. 596 p. plates (part col.), ports., fold. plans,
      fascims. (Collection des documents inédits pour servir à
      l'histoire de l'Afrique occidentale française, Recueil no. 1)

Bibliographical footnotes.

This large volume of documents is a publication of the former
Service des Archives du Haut-Commissariat en A.O.F., Dakar. The
editor has provided a brief introduction and excellent indexes: a
lengthy index to the founders of Dakar (with biographical data preceding page references) and both a chronological and a systematic
index to the documents.

1812. Crowder, Michael. SENEGAL: A STUDY OF FRENCH ASSIMILATION POLICY.
      Rev. ed. London, Methuen, 1967. 151 p. map, tables. (Studies
      in African History, no. 1)

Bibliography: p. 141-144.

This greatly revised edition of a work which first appeared in
1962 is an acute study of Senegal and its history, by a political
historian with long experience in West Africa. His central theme
in this concise account is that the French policy of assimilation
and the resultant high culture reached only a small elite, who now
in their doctrine of négritude have reacted, as has France, against
this policy. See also E. Milcent, "Senegal," in Carter, AFRICAN ONE-
PARTY STATES, no. 606.

1813. Dakar. Chambre de Commerce, d'Agriculture et d'Industrie. BULLETIN
      MENSUEL. 1925- Dakar.

579

The important Chambre de Commerce in French-speaking Africa's largest city also publishes a BULLETIN QUOTIDIEN, a periodic report, ECONOMIE DU SENEGAL (2d ed., July 1965, 248 p.), and an annual CONDENSE FISCAL DU SENEGAL.

1814. Dakar. Institut Pasteur. RAPPORT SUR LE FONCTIONNEMENT TECHNIQUE DE L'INSTITUT PASTEUR. Dakar, 1940-1957/59.

The findings of projects carried out in this major research body are reported in various French scientific journals, and the annual reports merely summarize the work. Since independence the RAPPORT is not issued for general distribution.

1815. Dakar. Université. ETUDES ET RECHERCHES AFRICANISTES. Dakar, 1967. 147 1.

A survey of African studies at the University of Dakar, describing activities of the various faculties and of institutes connected with the university (including works published by staff members and theses in preparation or submitted) and listing publications of the university as well as doctoral theses, etc., for 1966.

1816. Delbard, B. LES DYNAMISMES SOCIAUX AU SENEGAL: LES PROCESSUS DE FORMATION DE CLASSES SOCIALES DANS UN ETAT D'AFRIQUE DE L'OUEST. Dakar, Institut de Science Economique Appliquée, 1966. 158 1. tables.

Bibliography: 1. 153-158.

Economic, sociological, and ideological aspects of urban and rural social stratification in Senegal are analyzed, as well as the possibilities for overcoming class antagonisms in order to form a more progressive society.

1817. Delcourt, André. LA FRANCE ET LES ETABLISSEMENTS FRANCAIS AU SENEGAL ENTRE 1713 ET 1763: LA COMPAGNIE DES INDES ET LE SENEGAL: LA GUERRE DE LA GOMME. Dakar, IFAN, 1952. 432 p. fold. maps. (Mémoires, no. 17)

Bibliography: p. 27-37.

Extensive scholarly study of the first French settlements in Africa. A long bibliography of published and manuscript sources precedes the first chapter.

1818. Deschamps, Hubert Jules. LE SENEGAL ET LA GAMBIE. 2d ed. Paris, Presses Universitaires de France, 1968. 125 p. maps. ("Que sais-je?" no. 597)

    Bibliography: p. [123]-125.

    A compact survey of Senegal and Gambia--geography, peoples, history, and contemporary situation.

1819. Diop, Abdoulaye Bara. SOCIETE TOUCOULEUR ET MIGRATION: ENQUETE SUR L'IMMIGRATION TOUCOULEUR A DAKAR. Dakar, IFAN, 1965. 232 p. (Initiations et études africaines, no. 18)

    Bibliography: p. [225]-232.

    An analysis of the causes and consequences of the large-scale migration of the Tukulor from their native Senegal Valley to Dakar. Diop describes Tukulor society and its economy in the valley (Economic stagnation is the chief reason for the move to the city.) and probes the demographic, sociological, economic, and psychological conditions and problems stemming from Tukulor settlement in Dakar.

1820. Etudes sénégalaises. no. 1- Saint-Louis, Sénégal, Institut Français d'Afrique Noire, Centre Sénégal-Mauritanie, 1949- Irregular.

    This scholarly series has continued since independence. The first fascicle of Connaissance du Sénégal, part of the series, was issued in 1960. The Centre, since 1960 the Centre de Recherches et de Documentation Scientifique, has little connection with the headquarters of IFAN, now an institute of the University of Dakar (see no. 1644).

1821. Foltz, William J. FROM FRENCH WEST AFRICA TO THE MALI FEDERATION. New Haven, London, Yale University Press, 1965. 235 p.

    Bibliography: p. 215-228.

    See under Mali, no. 1744.

1822. France. Direction de la Documentation. LA REPUBLIQUE DU SENEGAL. Paris, La Documentation Francaise, 1961. 48 p. (Notes et études documentaires, no. 2754, Feb. 22, 1961)

    See general note on this series, no. 1587.

1823. France. Ministère de la Coopération. LES INDUSTRIES DU SENEGAL.
        Prepared by Jean Bernard Mas. Paris, 1965. 69 p. tables.

        The results of a 1963 inventory of Senegal's industries.
Description is in three parts: general survey; review by sector;
and tabular listings which include location of factories and workshops,
sales by type of product, local consumption, and import and export
data. Statistics apply to 1962.

1824. Gamble, David P. THE WOLOF OF SENEGAMBIA, TOGETHER WITH NOTES ON THE
        LEBU AND THE SERER. London, International African Institute,
        1957. 110 p. illus., maps. (Ethnographic Survey of Africa,
        Western Africa, pt. 14)

        See general note on this series (no. 980) and no. 1326.

1825. Groupe d'Etudes Dakaroises. DAKAR EN DEVENIR. Sous de direction de
        M. Sankalé, L. V. Thomas, P. Fougeyrollas. Paris, Présence
        Africaine, 1968. 519 p. illus.

        Includes bibliographies.

        A survey of social and economic conditions of Dakar and the
surrounding areas.

1826. Guyonnet, Marguerite. LA PRESSE AU SENEGAL JUSQU'A 1939. Dakar,
        1964. 340 <u>l</u>. Typescript. (Université de Dakar, Mémoire)

        Includes bibliography.

        Historical survey of the Senegalese press to 1939.

        A later period is covered in a doctoral thesis by Arlette
Fontaine, LA PRESSE AU SENEGAL, 1939-1960 (Dakar, Faculté des Lettres,
1967, 423 p.). A brief historical sketch, including a list of news-
papers held by the Bibliothèque Nationale, is provided by Roger
Pasquier in his article, "Les débuts de la presse au Sénégal,"
CAHIERS D'ETUDES AFRICAINES, no. 7, 1962: 477-490.

1827. Hardy, Georges. LA MISE EN VALEUR DU SENEGAL DE 1817 A 1854. Paris,
        Larose, 1921. xxxiii, 376 p. plates.

        Bibliography: p. xv-xxxiii.

        Study of the history of the oldest French colony of Africa
south of the Sahara, by a leading historian of the French overseas
empire. The work is based on almost 20 pages of source materials.

A survey introducing the colony in the preindependence postwar years was published in the Pays africains series: Edmond Séré de Rivières, LE SENEGAL: DAKAR (Paris, Editions Maritimes et Coloniales, 1953, 127 p., illus.; no. 4). A separate chapter is devoted to the French West African capital city, Dakar.

1828. Klein, Martin A. ISLAM AND IMPERIALISM IN SENEGAL: SINE-SALOUM, 1847-1914. Stanford, Calif., Published for the Hoover Institution by Stanford University Press, 1968. xvi, 285 p. maps, tables, diagrs. (Hoover Institution Publications)

Bibliography: p. [265]-277.

An important ethnohistorical monograph which, though concerned with a single region of Senegal, helps to elucidate much of contemporary African history. Professor Klein focuses on the two 400-year-old Serer states of Sine and Saloum (along with the adjacent Muslim Wolof state founded in 1861), offering an analysis of events in a region where three forces--the pagan African, the Muslim African, and the European Catholic--met. Extensive use was made of archival documents and oral tradition, as well as a wide range of scholarly works, in preparing this account of the Serer's resistance to change and of their transition from traditional authority to the French colonial system and to reformist Islam. A glossary is included.

1829. Lavroff, Dmitri Georges. LA REPUBLIQUE DU SENEGAL. Paris, Librairie Générale de Droit et de Jurisprudence, 1966. 257 p. fold. maps. (Collection "Comment ils sont gouvernés")

Bibliography: p. 251-254.

A useful work on the Senegalese government. Part 1 includes chapters on the formation of the Senegalese nation and contemporary Senegalese society. Part 2 deals with constitutional principles and civil liberties, the president of the republic, the national assembly, judicial powers, and the economic and social council. Part 3 covers the evolution of political parties, the Union Progressiste Sénégalaise, opposition parties, and the role of political parties in the operation of institutions.

1830. Lunel, Armand. SENEGAL. Photographs by Armand Deriez. Lausanne, Ed. Rencontres, 1966. 192 p. illus. (part col.), map. (Collection "L'atlas des voyages," v. 50)

A general-interest book on modern Senegal, written in a journalistic style and replete with excellent illustrations. The concluding section (p. 157-190) provides basic information in an encyclopedic format.

1831. Ly, Abdoulaye. LA COMPAGNIE DU SENEGAL. Paris, Présence Africaine,
            1958. 310 p. illus. (Enquêtes et études)

            Bibliography: p. 297-310.

            By a Senegalese intellectual, nationalist, and political leader,
       whose historical writings give fervent expression to anticolonialism.
       In this study of French commerce with West Africa at the time of
       Colbert and his immediate successors the author has made use of many
       little-known documents, some from departmental archives. In two
       previous studies he stressed French exploitation--political and
       economic in LES MASSES AFRICAINES ET L'ACTUELLE CONDITION HUMAINE
       (Paris, Présence Africaine, 1956, 254 p.; Enquêtes et études) and
       military in MERCENAIRES NOIRS: NOTES SUR UNE FORME DE L'EXPLOITATION
       DES AFRICAINS (Paris, Présence Africaine, 1957, 67 p.; Collection "Le
       colonialisme").

1832. Marty, Paul. ETUDES SUR L'ISLAM AU SENEGAL: Vol. I, LES PERSONNES;
            Vol. II, LES DOCTRINES ET LES INSTITUTIONS. Paris, E. Leroux,
            1917. 2 v. 412, 444 p. plates, facsims., maps. (Collection
            de la REVUE DU MONDE MUSULMAN)

            A monumental work by a noted authority on Islam. In the first
       volume Marty examines the influence of the Moorish shaikhs and des-
       cribes the Tijaniyya sect and its leaders among the Tukulors, Wolofs,
       and Mandingoes. The second volume is largely devoted to the Islamic
       doctrines and religious ethnics, the mosques, the schools of the
       Marabouts, rites and practices, and Islamization as reflected in
       juridical institutions, in social customs, and in the economic domain.
       For note on Marty, see no. 1753.

1833. Milcent, Ernest. AU CARREFOUR DES OPTIONS AFRICAINES: LE SENEGAL.
            Paris, Editions du Centurion, 1965. 223 p. plates, map.
            (Le poids du jour)

            Bibliography: p. 220-223.

            By a journalist who spent eight years in Senegal, this is a
       sympathetic account of the country's colonial history, road to
       independence, and choice of government, and of the problems confronting
       the new nation.

1834. Monteil, Vincent. ESQUISSES SENEGALAISES (WALO-KAYOR-DYOLOF-MOURIDES-
            UN VISIONNAIRE). Dakar, IFAN, 1966. 243 p. illus., maps
            (part fold.). (Initiations et études africaines, no. 21)

            Includes bibliographies.

584

A collection of five historical and socioreligious studies. In the first, a study of the Wolof kingdom of Walo (1186?-1855), Monteil introduces and comments upon a text by Amadou Wade. The remaining four essays deal, respectively, with the life of Lat-Dior, chief of the Cayor (1842-66), and the islamization of the Wolofs; the province of Dyolof and its last king, Al-Bouri N'Diaye; religious and socioeconomic aspects of the Muridiyya sect; and an analysis of the dreams, reveries, and visions of an anonymous Muslim visionary of Tukulor origin.

1835. Pélissier, Paul. LES PAYSANS DU SENEGAL: LES CIVILISATIONS AGRAIRES DU CAYOR A LA CASAMANCE. Saint-Yrieix (Haute Vienne), France, Impr. Fabrégue, 1966. 939 p. illus., plates, maps.

Bibliography: p. 911-918.

A monumental and definitive volume on the environment and life and livelihood of the Senegalese peasant. Pélissier painstakingly and compassionately describes the dialogue between the peasant and his milieu, illustrating how through the ages the peasant has shown exceptional ingenuity, patience, and flexibility in dealing with his environmental conditions. It is Pélissier's conclusion that Western-educated experts would do well to reconsider any plans to reform the remarkable cultural and technical pattern that has evolved. His observations derive both from his own intensive field work and from studies done by pedologists, agronomists, historians, sociologists, economists, and other specialists. While the physical geography of each region forms the basis of the study, ample stress is put on such factors as historical evolution, religion, customs, and institutions involved in the settlement and development of the land. The volume has three main sections: peoples and regions of the "peanut basin"; recent colonization and ancient enclaves in the Sudan zone; and landscapes and populations of the zone of the southern rivers. The numerous illustrations are excellent and there is a fine bibliography.

A detailed description of the tasks and problems of local officials and employees concerned with rural development is given in a mimeographed publication prepared for Senegal's Ministère du Plan et du Développement: Centre Africain des Sciences Humaines Appliquées, L'ADMINISTRATION LOCAL DU DEVELOPPEMENT RURAL AU SENEGAL, by Robert Descloitres, Jean Claude Reverdy, and Renald Volonte (Aix-en-Provence, 1964, 209 p.).

1836. Peterec, Richard J. DAKAR AND WEST AFRICAN ECONOMIC DEVELOPMENT. New York, London, Columbia University Press, 1967. 206 p. illus., maps, tables.

Bibliography: p. [197]-202.

An analysis of the response of the "colonial port" (not the city) of Dakar to recent political and economic changes in West Africa. Peterec, a professor of geography, first describes the physical and historic forces which conditioned the growth and development of the port, and then covers port facilities and traffic, the economic hinterland, and transportation links with the hinterland. In his concluding chapter he discusses the possible future role of this leading port in an independent West Africa. See also Guy Pfeffermann, INDUSTRIAL LABOR IN THE REPUBLIC OF SENEGAL (New York, Praeger, 1968, 325 p.).

1837. REVUE SENEGALAISE DE DROIT. 1967- Dakar, Association Sénégalaise d'Etudes et de Recherches Juridiques. Semiannual.

1838. Senegal. JOURNAL OFFICIEL DE LA REPUBLIQUE DU SENEGAL. 1959- Dakar, Impr. Nationale. Weekly.

The former JOURNAL OFFICIEL DU SENEGAL had been published in the French colonial capital of Saint-Louis and under various titles had been issued since 1856, originally being published in Rufisque.

The Imprimerie Nationale in Dakar publishes the major official publications, including the DEBATS PARLEMENTAIRES, the RECUEIL DE LEGISLATION ET DE JURISPRUDENCE, and ARRETS DE LA COUR SUPREME.

Mimeographed publications are issued by a number of government agencies, among them the Ministère de l'Economie Rurale, the Service de la Statistique, the Service des Pêches, the Ministère de l'Education Nationale et de la Culture, the Ministère de l'Information, and the Ministère du Plan et du Développement. The most complete listing available of Senegalese government documents, most of which can be obtained only from the issuing bodies, is a monthly accessions list, published by the Centre Documentaire of the Archives Nationales, LISTE DES OUVRAGES RECUS ET DES REVUES DEPOUILLEES.

1839. Senegal. RAPPORT GENERAL SUR LES PROSPECTIVES DE DEVELOPPEMENT DU SENEGAL. 3d ed. Dakar, 1963. 2 v.

Summary of a multivolume economic study prepared for the government in 1959-60 by the French economist Father Louis J. Lebret and his staff.

The Service de la Statistique of Senegal publishes a BULLETIN STATISTIQUE ET ECONOMIQUE MENSUEL and a monthly COMMERCE EXTERIEUR. For publications of the former colony, see the Library of Congress OFFICIAL PUBLICATIONS OF FRENCH WEST AFRICA (no. 1636).

1840. LE SENEGAL EN MARCHE: A L'AN 1 DE L'INDEPENDANCE SUR LA VOIE
           AFRICAINE DU SOCIALISME, 4 AVRIL 1961. Casablanca, Impri-
           meries Réunies, 1961. 210 p. illus., ports.

           Handsome brochure sponsored by the Ministère de l'Information,
    de la Radiodiffusion et de la Presse of Senegal. Contents are
    articles presenting political, economic, social, and cultural
    aspects of the new Senegal. The preface is by President Senghor;
    the lead article, "Réflexions sur l'indépendance du Sénégal et
    le socialisme africain," by Mamadou Dia.

1841. Senghor, Léopold Sédar. ON AFRICAN SOCIALISM. Translated and with
           an introduction by Mercer Cook. New York, Praeger, 1964. xv,
           173 p.

           Speeches enunciating the special socialistic theory of President
    Senghor, a combination of Marxism and Christianity with strongly
    spiritual and African nationalist overtones. They include his
    exposition of négritude. A French edition of Senghor's speeches
    was published by Présence Africaine in 1961, NATION ET VOIE AFRICAINE
    DU SOCIALISME (138 p.; Collection "Leaders politiques africains").

           The First World Festival of Negro Arts held in Dakar, Apr.
    1-24, 1966, occasioned wide reportage on Dr. Senghor, whose speech
    on opening the festival stressed negritude as its inspiration. A
    two-part article on the festival appears in the May 1966 issue of
    AFRICA REPORT: "Negritude: Words and Deeds," v. 11, no. 5, p. 57-62.
    For other works by and about Senghor, see no. 1065.

1842. Serreau, Jean. LE DEVELOPPEMENT A LA BASE AU DAHOMEY ET AU SENEGAL.
           Paris, Librairie Générale de Droit et de Jurisprudence, 1966.
           358 p. tables. (Bibliothèque d'économie politique, v. 7)

           Bibliography: p. 319-323.

           For annotation, see no. 1694.

1843. Thomas, Louis V. LES DIOLA: ESSAI D'ANALYSE FONCTIONNELLE SUR
           UNE POPULATION DE BASSE-CASAMANCE. Dakar, IFAN, 1959. 2 v.
           plates, music. (Mémoires, no. 55)

           Bibliography: v. 2, p. 797-809.

           This complete anthropological study is here cited because of
    its long bibliography, which includes recent work as well as earlier
    writings.

1844. Traoré, Bakary, Mamadou Lô, and Jean-Louis Alibert. FORCES
       POLITIQUES EN AFRIQUE NOIRE. Paris, Presses Universitaires
       de France, 1966. 312 p. (Travaux et recherches de la Faculté
       de Droit et des Sciences Economiques de Paris, Série "Afrique,"
       no. 2)

       Traoré traces the history of the political parties in Senegal
       since 1946 but also includes a brief introductory survey of the
       political stratification of traditional Senegal and the changes
       brought by colonial rule. Lô's study is devoted to the Union
       Progressiste Sénégalaise--its organization, doctrine of African
       socialism, position vis-à-vis opposition parties, and influence on
       administrative and economic structures. A documentary appendix
       lists the bylaws of the U.P.S. Alibert's work covers the organizations
       in opposition to the established governments in independent black
       Africa--the traditional opposition groups as well as the modern ones
       (army, trade unions, students, etc.). Each of the first two studies
       includes a short bibliography.

1845. U.S. Department of the Interior. Office of Geography. SENEGAL:
       OFFICIAL STANDARD NAMES APPROVED BY THE UNITED STATES BOARD
       ON GEOGRAPHIC NAMES. Washington, U.S. Govt. Print. Off.,
       Feb. 1965. 194 p. map. (13,600 names) (Gazetteer no. 88)

       See note on series, no. 484.

1846. Villard, André. HISTOIRE DU SENEGAL. Dakar, Ars Africae, 1943.
       264 p. illus., fold. maps.

       "Note bibliographique": p. 227-249.

       Standard history, dedicated to "the young Frenchmen of A.O.F.,
       European or African." The work ends with an annotated bibliography.

TOGO

Note: The former German colony of Togoland, which became a mandate under
the League of Nations and a trust territory under the United Nations, was
divided into two parts, the eastern section administered by France, the
western by the United Kingdom. A plebiscite in British Togoland in 1956
decided for union with Ghana, which went into effect upon independence in
1960. As a result the present Togo is the French-speaking eastern state
alone. In the older literature, especially in German works, the two parts
are generally considered as a unit. In addition, in some cases studies
relate to the two former German colonies of Togoland and Cameroons.

588

Bibliographies

1847. France. Office de la Recherche Scientifique et Technique Outre-Mer
          (ORSTOM). Institut de Recherches du Togo. LISTE DES TRAVAUX
          SCIENTIFIQUES, RAPPORTS ET PUBLICATIONS DES CHERCHEURS (CONCER-
          NANT LE TOGO). Paris, Sept. 15, 1962. 16 l. Mimeographed.

   Some 150 reports and publications are listed in subject classes,
including the physical sciences, sociology, and ethnology. The
Institut de Recherches du Togo in Lomé is an affiliate of ORSTOM
and publishes monographic research studies in the fields of hydrology,
geophysics, sociology, and nutrition. These are not generally
available for distribution but are held in the library of the Institut.

1848. Hintze, Ursula. BIBLIOGRAPHIE DER KWA-SPRACHEN UND DER SPRACHEN
          DER TOGO-RESTVOLKER. Berlin, Akademie-Verlag, 1959. 102 p.
          (Deutsche Akademie der Wissenschaften zu Berlin. Institut
          für Orientforschung. Veröffentlichung no. 42)

1849. U.S. Library of Congress. General Reference and Bibliography
          Division. OFFICIAL PUBLICATIONS OF FRENCH EQUATORIAL AFRICA,
          FRENCH CAMEROONS, AND TOGO, 1946-1958. Compiled by Julian W.
          Witherell, African Section. Washington, 1964. xi, 78 p.

   Togo: p. 39-41.

   See no. 1889 for annotation. See also nos. 1536 and 1627.

Reference Works

1850. Attignon, Hermann. GEOGRAPHIE DU TOGO. [Lome? 1965?] 89 l.
          illus., maps, tables.

   A concise survey of administrative divisions, physical environment, population, agriculture, cattle raising, fishing, forestry,
hunting, industry, and commerce.

1851. Banque Centrale des Etats de l'Afrique de l'Ouest. TOGO, 1960:
          FAITS ET CHIFFRES. Paris, 1960. 218 p. illus.

   Statistical survey of the newly independent republic. In the
bank's monographic series Etudes économiques ouest africaines, no.
3 was COMPTES ECONOMIQUES: TOGO, 1956-1957-1958 (Paris, 1961, 278 p.).

1852. Chazelas, Victor. TERRITOIRES AFRICAINS SOUS MANDAT DE LA FRANCE:
       CAMEROUN ET TOGO. Paris, Société d'Editions Géographiques,
       Maritimes et Coloniales, 1931. 240 p. plates.

       Prepared by the Administrator-in-Chief of the Colonies for the
       International Colonial Exposition at Paris in 1931 (see no. 1611).
       The quarto volume presented a significant survey of physical and
       human geography, history, and administration by France under the
       League of Nations mandate of the two colonies.

       A later survey of the colonies, then UN trust territories under
       French administration, was by Jean C. Froelich, CAMEROUN, TOGO:
       TERRITOIRES SOUS TUTELLE (Paris, Berger-Levrault, 1956, 217 p.,
       illus.; L'Union française).

1853. Coleman, James S. TOGOLAND. New York, Carnegie Endowment for
       International Peace, 1956. 91 p. (INTERNATIONAL CONCILIATION,
       no. 509, Sept. 1956)

       In the autumn of 1956 the question of terminating the trustee-
       ship of Togoland was to come up before the United Nations and pre-
       liminary choice was being offered to the people. This political
       review and analysis was written between the plebiscite in British
       Togoland in May 1956, which won the vote for union with the soon
       to be independent Gold Coast, and the referendum held in French
       Togoland in Oct. 1956.

1854. Cornevin, Robert. HISTOIRE DU TOGO. 2d ed. Paris, Berger-Levrault,
       1962. 437 p. illus., maps, tables. (Mondes d'outre-mer,
       Série: Histoire)

       Bibliographical notes by chapters: p. 401-406.

       The author of HISTOIRE DES PEUPLES DE L'AFRIQUE NOIRE (see
       no. 520) was commandant de cercle in Togo for eight years. His
       scholarship and intimate knowledge of the country is shown in this
       standard history, a third of which goes back to pre-European times.
       The book, which was published first in 1959, was given the Grand
       Prix of the Académie des Sciences d'Outre-Mer in 1960. Cornevin
       has also written a compact history, LE TOGO: NATION-PILOTE (Paris,
       Nouvelles Editions Latines, 1963, 159 p., illus., maps; Survol du
       monde), which covers geography, ethnography, economy, politics, and
       sociology. The book begins with prehistory and ends with a brief
       account of the revolt of early 1963. A more specialized study is
       his LES BASSARI DU NORD TOGO (Paris, Berger-Levrault, 1962, 156 p.,
       illus., maps; Mondes d'outre-mer, Série: Peuples). In it he makes
       use of much German source material, cited in chapter bibliographies.

1855. Debrunner, Hans W. A CHURCH BETWEEN COLONIAL POWERS: A STUDY OF
        THE CHURCH IN TOGO. Translated by Dorothea M. Barton.
        London, Lutterworth Press, 1965. 368 p. maps. (World
        Studies of Churches in Mission)

    Bibliography: p. 345-353.

1856. Etudes togolaises. v. 1, no. 1- Lomé, Institut Togolais des
        Sciences Humaines, Dec. 1965-

    The Institut was established in 1960. The first issue of its
    new series contained 110 pages and included several specialized
    socioreligious studies.

1857. France. RAPPORT DU GOUVERNEMENT FRANCAIS A L'ASSEMBLEE GENERALE
        DES NATIONS UNIES SUR L'ADMINISTRATION DU TOGO PLACE SOUS LA
        TUTELLE DE FRANCE. Paris, 1947-57. illus. Annual.

    A lavish publication with many maps, charts, and tables of
    statistics. The last presented, for the year 1957, has 374 pages.
    Emphasis is on economic and social advances, with special attention
    to French aid.

1858. Froelich, Jean Claude, Pierre Alexandre, and Robert Cornevin. LES
        POPULATIONS DU NORD-TOGO. With the collaboration of Pasteur
        J. Delord. Paris, Published for the International African
        Institute by Presses Universitaires de France, 1963. 199 p.
        maps, tables. (Monographies ethnologiques africaines)

    Bibliography: p. [187]-193.

    See general note on this series, nos. 980 and 1670.

    A more specialized study is Froelich's LA TRIBU KONKOMBA DU
    NORD-TOGO (Dakar, IFAN, 1954, 255 p., illus., plates, maps; Mémoires,
    no. 37).

1859. Great Britain. Colonial Office. REPORT...TO THE GENERAL ASSEMBLY
        OF THE UNITED NATIONS ON THE ADMINISTRATION OF TOGOLAND UNDER
        UNITED KINGDOM TRUSTEESHIP. 1920/21-1955. London. Annual.

    Begun as report to the League of Nations on the co-mandate.
    None was issued in 1939-46. The report of 1955 was the last pre-
    sented, since in the referendum of May 1956 British Togoland decided
    on union with Ghana.

1860. Kuczynski, Robert R. THE CAMEROONS AND TOGOLAND: A DEMOGRAPHIC
STUDY. London, New York, Oxford University Press, 1939.
xviii, 579 p.

"Sources quoted": p. 550-567.

Comprehensive technical work by a demographer connected with
the British Foreign Office, undertaken under the auspices of the
Royal Institute of International Affairs at the request of Lord
Hailey, director of the African Research Survey. Kuczynski treated
here with the utmost thoroughness all phases of population studies
of the former German territories of Togoland and the Cameroons and
their continuation under the French and British mandates of the
League of Nations.

1861. Manoukian, Madeline. THE EWE-SPEAKING PEOPLE OF TOGOLAND AND THE
GOLD COAST. London, International African Institute, 1952.
63 p. map. (Ethnographic Survey of Africa, Western Africa,
pt. 6)

See general note on this series (no. 980) and no. 1361.

1862. Metzger, O.F. UNSERE ALTE KOLONIE TOGO. Neudamm, Verlag J.
Neumann, 1941. 295 p. illus., maps.

Written by a former German colonial official, who had been
Governor of Togo during World War I, this book came out when German
hopes of recovering former colonies were high. It is a compendium
of information, emphasizing potential wealth in forest products,
palm oil, and agriculture.

1863. Müller, Julius Otto. PROBLEME DER AUFTRAGS-RINDERHALTUNG DURCH
FULBE-HIRTEN (PEUL) IN WESTAFRIKA: MOTIVATIONEN UND MEINUNGEN
IM HINBLICK AUF DIE ENTWICKLUNG DER BAUERLICHEN VIEHWIRTSCHAFT
AM BEISPIEL DER EWE UND ANDERER STAMME IN TOGO. Berlin, New
York, Springer-Verlag, 1967. xii, 124 p. maps. (Afrika-
Studien, no. 14)

Bibliography: p. 118-120.

An interesting study of the economic, social, and psychological
aspects of the symbiotic relationship between the pastoral Fulani
and Togo's agricultural Ewe, Kabre, Losso, and Moba peoples. The
Togolese peoples have long entrusted the herding of most of their
few head of cattle to the Fulani, West Africa's "cattle specialists."
The author has bolstered his analysis of this situation and of its
possible redirection with many interviews (in French) with members
of the Togolese groups.

1864.   Puig, François. ETUDES SUR LES COUTUMES DES CABRAIS [TOGO].
          Toulouse, Impr. Toulousaine, Lion et Fils, 1934. 204 p.
          fold. map.

       Anthropological study, focused on customary law of the Kabre,
one of the dominant peoples of Togo.

1865.   Togo. ANNUAIRE DU TOGO. [1962?-] Lomé, Service de l'Information
          et de la Presse.

       Coverage includes population and geography, political and
governmental structure, education, public health, economy,
communications, diplomatic relations, and tourism. The 1963-64
edition (1965, 208 p., illus., map) includes the constitution
of May 5, 1963, and the Charter of the Organization of African Unity.
The issuing agency was called Service de l'Information until 1962 or
1963.

1866.   Togo. JOURNAL OFFICIEL DE LA REPUBLIQUE TOGOLAISE. 1956- Lomé.
          Semimonthly.

       Superseded the JOURNAL OFFICIEL DE LA REPUBLIQUE AUTONOME DU
TOGO which, under earlier titles, was published monthly from 1920
to 1926, then semimonthly. The JOURNAL OFFICIEL is now produced
by the official printer, EDITOGO, which also prints some of the
brochures issued by the Service de l'Information et de la Presse.

       Most official publications are brought out in limited editions
in mimeographed form. Among these are the records of the Assemblée
Nationale, the DEBATS, ANNEXES, and PROCES-VERBAUX; a BULLETIN DE
PRESSE ET D'INFORMATION DE L'ASSEMBLEE NATIONALE ceased publication
in Jan. 1967.

       The Service de l'Information et de la Presse includes among
its publications a daily bulletin, TOGO-PRESSE, and ANNUAIRE DU
TOGO (see preceding entry); its serial TOGO-DOCUMENTATION was sus-
pended in 1963. The BULLETIN MENSUEL DE LA STATSTIQUE, published
by the Service de la Statistique et de la Comptabilité Economique
Nationale (until late 1965 or early 1966 called Service de la
Statistique Générale), continues the BULLETIN STATISTIQUE MENSUEL
DU TOGO, begun under the French administration in 1952. Among
other publications of the Service de la Statistique is a RECENSE-
MENT GENERAL (6 v., 196-), a detailed population study.

1867.   Togo. PLAN QUINQUENNAL DE DEVELOPPEMENT, 1966-1970. Lomé,
          République Togolaise; Bruxelles, Communauté Economique
          Européenne; Paris, Société d'Etudes pour le Développement

Economique et Sociale (SEDES); München, Institut für
Wirtschaftsforschung (IFO), 1965. 10 v. maps (part fold.),
tables, diagrs.

Cover title: PLAN DE DEVELOPPEMENT ECONOMIQUE ET SOCIAL,
1966-1970.

A comprehensive report prepared for the government of Togo and
financed by the European Economic Community. The details in the
initial, printed volume (Paris, Simag, 221 p.), on the PROJET VOTE
PAR L'ASSEMBLEE NATIONALE, are elaborated upon in the following nine
multigraphed volumes:

COMPTES ECONOMIQUES DU TOGO, 1962. SEDES. 134 p.

LE COMMERCE INTERIEUR. IFO. 99 p.

L'ARTISANAT TOGOLAIS. IFO. 35 p.

DEVELOPPEMENT ET ORGANISATION ADMINISTRATIVES. SEDES. 88 p.

SCOLARISATION, FORMATION DES CADRES, EMPLOI. SEDES. 159 p.

ANNEXES TECHNIQUES: DEVELOPPEMENT RURAL. SEDES. various
    pagings.

ANNEXES TECHNIQUES: INDUSTRIE. SEDES. 102 p.

FINANCES PUBLIQUES, BUDGET, FISCALITE. SEDES. 99 p.

ENQUETE SOCIOLOGIQUE: LE PAYSAN FACE AU DEVELOPPEMENT.
    By Julius Otto Müller. IFO. 192 p.

A more succinct report on Togo's economy and current development plan is given in the following multigraphed volume: France,
Ministère de la Coopération, ECONOMIE ET PLAN DE DEVELOPPEMENT,
REPUBLIQUE TOGOLAISE, 2d ed. (Paris, Oct. 1965, 105 p., maps
[part col.], tables, diagrs.; bibliography: p. 101-105)

1868. United Nations. Trusteeship Council. Visiting Mission to the Trust
       Territories in West Africa, 1949, 1952. SPECIAL REPORT ON THE
       EWE AND TOGOLAND UNIFICATION PROBLEM. New York, etc. 1950-52.
       2 v. (T/463; T/1105)

       _____. _____. Visiting Mission to the Trust Territories in
       West Africa, 1949, 1952, 1955. REPORT ON TOGOLAND UNDER FRENCH
       ADMINISTRATION. New York, etc. 1950-55. 3 v. fold. maps.
       (T/464; T/1108; T/1211)

_____. _____. _____. REPORT ON TOGOLAND UNDER UNITED
KINGDOM ADMINISTRATION. New York, etc. 1950-55. 3 v. fold.
maps. (T/465; T/1107; T/1210)

Title varies slightly; same issued from 1952 as Supplements to
the Official Records of the Trusteeship Council. The Visiting
Mission to Togoland, as to the Cameroons, made three inspection
trips, 1949, 1952, 1955. Their examination also included the
special consideration of the Ewe people of Togoland and the Gold
Coast, who were pressing for unification. The last visiting mission
recommended prompt self-determination. A plebiscite held in British
Togoland on May 9, 1956, resulted in a decision for union with Ghana
(Mar. 1957). In a referendum of Oct. 1956 (boycotted by the UN)
French Togoland voted to end the trusteeship status and, under
provisions of the loi-cadre, to become an autonomous state of the
French Community. The independent republic of Togo came into being
in Apr. 1960.

For official documentation on Togo as a trust territory of the
United Nations, see the UNITED NATIONS DOCUMENTS INDEX, 1950-58,
and for brief résumés, the YEARBOOK OF THE UNITED NATIONS.

1869. U.S. Department of the Interior. Office of Geography. TOGO:
OFFICIAL STANDARD NAMES APPROVED BY THE UNITED STATES BOARD
ON GEOGRAPHIC NAMES. Washington, U.S. Govt. Print. Off., Apr.
1966. 100 p. map. (7,000 names) (Gazetteer no. 98)

See note on series, no. 484.

1870. Westermann, Diedrich. DIE GLIDYI-EWE IN TOGO: ZUGE AUS IHREM
GESELLSCHAFTSLEBEN. Berlin, Walter de Gruyter, 1935. xv,
332 p. (Mitteilungen des Seminars für orientalische Sprachen
an der Universität Berlin, Beiband zum Jahrgang 38)

Professor Westermann's long and distinguished career as an
Africanist began with a dictionary of Ewe published in 1905, while
he was a missionary among the Ewe in Togoland. The anthropological
treatise on a particular tribe of the Ewe group was one among many
of his works on the Ewe.

UPPER VOLTA

Bibliographies

1871. African Bibliographic Center, Washington, D.C. UPPER VOLTA TODAY,
1960-1967. Washington, 1968. 37 p. (Special Bibliographic
Series, v. 6, no. 1)

Lists 320 books and articles on Upper Volta. Arrangement is by subject.

1872. Capron, J. "Bibliographie générale des Bwa," ETUDES VOLTAIQUES, n.s. no. 5, 1964: 201-205.

A linguistic and ethnographic listing of 68 books, monographs, articles, and unpublished works on the Bwa people.

1873. Izard, Françoise. BIBLIOGRAPHIE GENERALE DE LA HAUTE-VOLTA, 1956-65. Assisted by P. H. Bonnefond and M. d'Huart. Paris, C.N.R.S.; Ouagadougou, C.V.R.S., 1967. 300 p.

Major source for this period. It lists 1,541 entries arranged by subject.

1874. Izard, Michel. "Bibliographie générale des Mossi." ETUDES VOLTAIQUES, n.s. no. 3, 1962: 103-111.

Lists 215 books, monographs, articles, and unpublished works on the Mossi. See also nos. 1536 and 1627.

Reference Works

1875. Bassolet, François. EVOLUTION DE LA HAUTE-VOLTA DE 1898 A JANVIER 1966. Ouagadougou, Imprimérie Nationale, 1968. 133 p.

Not available for annotation.

1876. Colloque sur les Cultures Voltaïques, Sonchamp, Upper Volta, 1965. COLLOQUE SUR LES CULTURES VOLTAIQUES, SONCHAMP, 6-8 DECEMBRE 1965. Paris, Centre National de la Recherche Scientifique (CNRS); Ouagadougou, Centre Voltaïque de la Recherche Scientifique (CVRS), 1967. 188 p. Processed. (Recherches voltaïques, no. 8)

Virtually a verbatim transcription of a colloquium in which British and French ethnographers discussed various cultural aspects of Upper Volta.

1877. COURRIER CONSULAIRE DE LA HAUTE-VOLTA. no. 1- 1962(?)- Ouagadougou, Chambre de Commerce d'Agriculture et d'Industrie. Monthly.

Regarded as the best periodical publication of the republic.

1878. Dim Delobsom, A. A. L'EMPIRE DU MOGHO-NABA: COUTUMES DES MOSSI
      DE LA HAUTE-VOLTA. Paris, Domat-Montchrestien, 1932. 303 p.
      plates, map. (Institut de Droit Comparé, Etudes de sociologie
      et d'ethnologie juridiques, no. 2)

      A classic study, based on many non-European sources--from
archaeology, oral tradition, etc. A popular work by this West
African scholar won a literary prize for French West Africa: LES
SECRETS DES SORCIERS NOIRS (Paris, Librairie Emile Nourry, 1934,
298 p., illus.; Collection Science et magie, no. 5).

1879. France. Direction de la Documentation. LA REPUBLIQUE DE HAUTE-
      VOLTA. Paris, 1960. 64 p. (Notes et études documentaires,
      no. 2693, Aug. 19, 1960)

      See general note on this series, no. 1587.

1880. Labouret, Henri. LES TRIBUS DU RAMEAU LOBI. Paris, Institut
      d'Ethnologie, 1931. 507 p. illus., plates, maps, plans.
      (Université de Paris, Travaux et mémoires de l'Institut
      d'Ethnologie, 15)

      _____. NOUVELLES NOTES SUR LES TRIBUS DU RAMEAU LOBI: LEURS
      MIGRATIONS, LEUR EVOLUTION, LEURS PARLERS ET CEUX DE LEURS
      VOISINS. Dakar, IFAN, 1958. 295 p. maps. (Mémoires, no. 54)

      The 1931 monograph is a detailed anthropological study of the
Lobi peoples. Its paucity of linguistic material is well compensated
for in the 1958 publication.

1881. Recherches voltaïques. no. 1- 1965- Paris, Centre National de la
      Recherche Scientifique (CNRS); Ouagadougou, Centre Voltaïque de
      la Recherche Scientifique (CVRS). Irregular.

      A series devoted not only to research studies but also scheduled
to include archival documents and heretofore unpublished old texts.
Studies of the historical traditions of all the villages in the Mossi
country, according to administrative units, are being published.

      The series supersedes Etudes voltaïques (1950-59; n.s. 1960-64),
which was issued by the Centre IFAN-ORSTOM in Ouagadougou and presented monograph-length articles, e.g., Paul Barlet, "La Haute-Volta:
Essai de présentation géographique" (n.s. no. 3, 1962, p. 5-77), and
J. L. Boutillier, "Les structures foncières en Haute-Volta" (n.s. no.
5, 1964, p. 5-183). A series Notes et documents voltaïques is also
issued. Included are information on the Centre's activities and
short articles on Voltaic history, sociology, ethnology, archaeology,
and linguistics.

1882. Skinner, Elliott P. THE MOSSI OF THE UPPER VOLTA: THE POLITICAL
      DEVELOPMENT OF A SUDANESE PEOPLE. Stanford, Calif., Stanford
      University Press, 1964. 236 p. illus., map.

      Bibliography: p. 225-227.

      One of the few full-scale studies in English of Upper Volta,
this scholarly work is a political and anthropological analysis of
the only society of the western Sudan that has maintained almost to
the present time the traditional structure of government of the
medieval kingdoms. A glossary is included.

      Among recent French-language studies of the Mossi are:
Gomboudougou V. Kabore, ORGANISATION POLITIQUE TRADITIONNELLE ET
EVOLUTION POLITIQUE DES MOSSI DE OUAGADOUGOU (1966, 224 p., illus.),
and Michel Izard, TRADITIONS HISTORIQUES DES VILLAGES DU YATENGA:
Vol. I, CERCLE DE GOURCY (1965, 226 p., maps), which comprise,
respectively, no. 5 and no. 1 of the series Recherches voltaïques;
Yamba Tiendrebéogo, HISTOIRE ET COUTUMES ROYALES DES MOSSI DE
OUAGADOUGOU, edited by Robert Pageard (Ouagadougou, Larhallé
Naba, 1964, 205 p., illus. [part fold.]); and Françoise Izard-
Héritier and Michel Izard, LES MOSSI DU YATENGA: ETUDE DE LA VIE
ECONOMIQUE ET SOCIALE (Bordeaux, Institut des Sciences Humaines
Appliquées, 1959, 114 p., illus.). Gaston Canu provides an analysis,
evaluation, and presentation of Mossi tales, in light of their
sociocultural import, in his CONTES MOSSI ACTUELS: ETUDES ETHNO-
LINGUISTIQUE (Dakar, Faculté des Lettres et des Sciences Humaines,
Université de Dakar, 1966, 496 p., illus., map, lexicon).

1883. Société d'Etudes pour le Développement Economique et Social.
      DEVELOPPEMENT ECONOMIQUE EN HAUTE-VOLTA. Paris, SEDES, 1963.
      2 v. 124, 241 p., plus appendixes.

      The first volume elaborates on a growth model; the second is
devoted to indications for economic policy, comparing the economic
base of 1963 with the projected situation in 1978.

1884. U.S. Department of the Interior. Office of Geography. UPPER VOLTA:
      OFFICIAL STANDARD NAMES APPROVED BY THE UNITED STATES BOARD ON
      GEOGRAPHIC NAMES. Washington, U.S. Govt. Print. Off., Jan.
      1965. 168 p. map. (11,900 names) (Gazetteer no. 87)

      See note on series, no. 484.

1885. Upper Volta. JOURNAL OFFICIEL DE LA REPUBLIQUE DE HAUTE-VOLTA.
      1959- Ouagadougou. Weekly.

The JOURNAL OFFICIEL of the new republic was at first printed for the government by a press in Bobo-Dioulasso. The Imprimérie Nationale in Ouagadougou took over in 1964. The initial JOURNAL OFFICIEL DE HAUTE-VOLTA was issued 1919-32 and 1953-58; from 1948 to 1953 official acts of the territory appeared in the JOURNAL OFFICIEL DE LA COTE D'IVOIRE.

Among mimeographed publications issued by government agencies is the CARREFOUR AFRICAIN, a government information journal published by the Service de l'Information, not to be confused with the Rwanda journal, CARREFOUR D'AFRIQUE (see no. 2346). The Service houses part of the archives of the government. The Direction de la Statistique et des Etudes Economiques (called Service de la Statistique, 1960-61) issues a statistical periodical, BULLETIN MENSUEL DE STATISTIQUE. Reports of other government bodies, as well as legislative proceedings and laws of the Assemblée Nationale, are issued in limited quantity, mimeographed or in typescript.

CHAPTER 35

FORMER FRENCH EQUATORIAL AFRICA
(AFRIQUE EQUATORIALE FRANCAISE)

Note: The four states of former French Equatorial Africa (Central African
Republic, Chad, the Congo-Brazzaville, and Gabon) in 1959 formed the Union
Douanière Equatoriale (Equatorial Customs Union, franc zone). In 1961
Cameroun joined the UDE, which in Dec. 1964 changed its name to Union
Douanière et Economique de l'Afrique Centrale (UDEAC). It is especially
because of these ties that Cameroun is here considered a part of Equatorial
Africa rather than West Africa. A good overview of Equatorial Africa is
the essay by John A. Ballard in Carter, NATIONAL UNITY AND REGIONALISM
(no. 608). Especially useful are the publications of the Bureau pour le
Développement de la Production Agricole Outre-Mer, INSEE, and ORSTOM.
See also nos. 858, 1533, 1558, 1585, and 1587.

Bibliographies

1886. Bruel, Georges. BIBLIOGRAPHIE DE L'AFRIQUE EQUATORIALE FRANCAISE.
         Paris, Larose, 1914. 326 p. (Gouvernement Général de l'AEF)

         By an administrator for the colonies, and formerly the chief
    of the Geographic Service of the AEF, this is considered the
    authoritative bibliography of early material on French Central
    Africa. It contains over 7,000 references, 4,260 of which are for
    books, pamphlets, and signed periodical articles; the rest are
    content analyses of periodicals by year.

1887. French Equatorial Africa. Service de la Statistique Générale.
         BIBLIOGRAPHIE ETHNOGRAPHIQUE DE L'AFRIQUE EQUATORIALE FRANCAISE,
         1914-1948. By P. Sanner. Paris, Impr. Nationale, 1949. 107 p.

         By the director of the Service, now director of documentation
    of the Banque Centrale des Etats de l'Afrique de l'Ouest, this is

a list of 549 entries in the field of social or "human" sciences. Arrangement is in regional and subject classification with author index. This work supplements Bruel (preceding entry).

1888. Jacquot, André. CATALOGUE DES PUBLICATIONS ET RAPPORTS DU SERVICE DES SCIENCES HUMAINES (1949-67). Brazzaville, Office de la Recherche Scientifique et Technique Outre-Mer (ORSTOM), 1968. 91 p.

See no. 1995 for annotation.

1889. U.S. Library of Congress. General Reference and Bibliography Division. OFFICIAL PUBLICATIONS OF FRENCH EQUATORIAL AFRICA, FRENCH CAMEROONS, AND TOGO, 1946-1958. Compiled by Julian Witherell, African Section. Washington, 1964. xi, 78 p.

By examination of all available published sources, including French documentation, United Nations bibliographies, and listings in the journaux officiels and other publications of the governments concerned, the compiler has brought together over 400 titles of official publications of the AEF, its four former territories, and the two trust territories under French administration. Relatively few of the titles listed are held by American libraries.

Identification of official documents of these governments before World War II, other than those cited under special agencies as author, is almost impossible through the medium of published sources.

Reference Works

1890. AFRIQUE CENTRALE: LES REPUBLIQUES D'EXPRESSION FRANCAISE. Paris, Hachette, 1962. clxxxviii, 533 p. fold. map. (Les guides bleus)

"Indications bibliographiques": p. clxx-clxxiv.

This handbook in baedeker style--a guide established by Gilbert Houlet--has 188 pages of introductory essays written by specialists on various subjects (geography, economics, prehistory, etc.). These are followed by a section on the several means of transportation and then sections on the Congo, Gabon, Central African Republic, Chad, and Cameroun. A large folded road map is inserted at the end.

1891. Aubréville, André. FLORE FORESTIERE SOUDANO-GUINEENNE, A.O.F.--
CAMEROUN--A.E.F. Paris, Société d'Editions Géographiques,
Maritimes et Coloniales, 1950. 523 p. illus., maps.

A botanical guide to the forests which are a main resource of
wealth, particularly for the equatorial region. An earlier treatise
on forests and forest industries by M. Aubréville, the inspector
general of French colonial forests and waterways, is ETUDE SUR LES
FORETS DE L'AFRIQUE EQUATORIALE FRANCAISE ET DU CAMEROUN (Paris,
1948, 131 p.; Ministère de la France d'Outre-Mer, Direction de
l'Agriculture, de l'Elevage et des Forêts, Bulletin scientifique no.
2).

1892. Balandier, Georges. SOCIOLOGIE ACTUELLE DE L'AFRIQUE NOIRE:
DYNAMIQUE DES CHANGEMENTS SOCIAUX EN AFRIQUE CENTRALE. 2d ed.
Paris, Presses Universitaires de France, 1963. xii, 532 p.
illus., maps, tables. (Bibliothèque de sociologie contemporaine)

Bibliography: p. 521-524.

An important study (1st ed., 1955, xii, 510 p.) based on extensive
sociological research, which established its author as a foremost
authority on the sociology of developing areas. See also his
AMBIGUOUS AFRICA: CULTURES IN COLLISION (translated from the French
by Helen Weaver; New York, Pantheon Books, 1966, 276 p., illus., maps,
plans).

1893. Banque Centrale des Etats de l'Afrique Equatoriale et du Cameroun.
RAPPORT D'ACTIVITE. Paris. Annual.

_____. ETUDES ET STATISTIQUES.

These publications are comparable, on a smaller scale, to those
of the Banque Centrale des Etats de l'Afrique de l'Ouest (nos. 1640
and 1641). The ETUDES ET STATISTIQUES does not, however, include
documentation services.

1894. Bruel, Georges. L'AFRIQUE EQUATORIALE FRANCAISE: LE PAYS--LES
HABITANTS--LA COLONISATION--LES POUVOIRS PUBLICS. New ed.
Paris, Larose, 1935. 558 p. illus., 6 fold. col. maps.

An exhaustive geographic survey of AEF by this geographer and
bibliographer, epitomizing knowledge of the territory to the time
of its first publication in 1918. The 1935 edition, which has
slight changes to update it, mainly regarding colonial administration,
was subsidized by the Gouvernement Général de l'AEF et du Cameroun.

1895. Bulletin de l'Afrique Noire. PERSONNALITES PUBLIQUES DE L'AFRIQUE
           CENTRALE 1968. Paris, EDIAFRIC, 1968. 373 p. (Numéro spécial
           du BULLETIN DE L'AFRIQUE NOIRE)

       Biographical information on government/political figures from
Cameroun, Central African Republic, Congo-Brazzaville, Gabon, and
Chad. The amount of information provided for each person ranges
from birthdate, past and present positions and address to the
person's present position only.

1896. Cahen, Lucien, and N. J. Snelling. THE GEOCHRONOLOGY OF EQUATORIAL
           AFRICA. Amsterdam, North-Holland Pub. Co., 1966. 200 p.

       Includes bibliographies.

       Important experimental effort to chart language changes over
long periods of time in order to trace root languages, migrations,
and tribal mixing.

1897. Chemery, J. HISTOIRE DE LA MISE EN VALEUR MINIERE DES TERRITOIRES
           D'AFRIQUE CENTRALE. Paris, Bureau d'Etudes Géologiques et
           Minières Coloniales, 1960. 175 p. fold. map, tables. (Bureau
           d'Etudes Geologiques et Minières Coloniales, Publication no.
           21)

       Chemery's work covers an area of study for which information is
difficult to get.

1898. Documents pour servir à l'histoire de l'Afrique équatoriale
           française [series]. Paris, La Haye, Mouton, 1966-

       A collection issued by the Ecole Pratique des Hautes Etudes,
Sorbonne, 6th Section: Sciences économiques et sociale. The
documents being published in the collection are drawn exclusively
from public archives and will appear in three series: 1st ser.,
La correspondance des commandants particuliers du Gabon de 1843 à
1886; 2d ser., Le documents sur Brazza et la fondation du Congo
français (see no. 2022 below); 3d ser., Les textes essentiels
relatifs à la genèse de l'A.E.F.

1899. Dreux-Brézé, Joachim de. LE PROBLEME DU REGROUPEMENT EN AFRIQUE
           EQUATORIALE (DU REGIME COLONIAL A L'UNION DOUANIERE ET
           ECONOMIQUE DE L'AFRIQUE CENTRALE). Paris, Librairie Générale
           de Droit et de Jurisprudence, 1968. 211 p. (Bibliothèque
           africaine et malgache, Droit et sociologie politique, v. 2)

Bibliography: p. 205-207.

Traces in detail the development of economic integration among the former AEF states and Cameroun. The volume is in three main parts: French colonization and the administrative and political construction of Equatorial Africa; internal autonomy and regroupment; and independence and regroupment.

1900. Eboué, A. Félix. LA NOUVELLE POLITIQUE INDIGENE POUR L'AFRIQUE
        EQUATORIALE FRANCAISE. Paris, Office Français d'Edition,
        1945. 61 p. (La France des cinq parties du monde)

Short study by Governor Eboué, the black Governor-General of AEF, which served as a guide to the important Brazzaville Conference of 1944. It was previously published under the title POLITIQUE INDIGENE DE L'AFRIQUE EQUATORIALE FRANCAISE.

1901. France. AFRIQUE EQUATORIALE FRANCAISE. Paris. Annual.

An economic review; not available for inspection. The Library of Congress has some volumes for the period 1922-58.

1902. France. Agence de la France Outre-Mer. AFRIQUE EQUATORIALE FRAN-
        CAISE. Paris, 1950. 4 v.

Covers Gabon, Middle Congo, Ubangi-Chari, and Chad.

1903. French Equatorial Africa. JOURNAL OFFICIEL DE L'AFRIQUE EQUATORIALE
        FRANCAISE. 1904-58. Brazzaville, Impr. Officielle. Semi-
        monthly.

This journal, now superseded by the journaux officiels of the separate states, is a primary source for historical research. (Prior to 1910 it was called JOURNAL OFFICIEL DU CONGO FRANCAIS.)

1904. French Equatorial Africa. Haut Commissariat. L'A.E.F. ECONOMIQUE
        ET SOCIALE, 1947-1958. Paris, Editions Alain, 1959. 112,
        xxii p. illus. (part col.), maps, tables.

An official balance sheet stressing French contributions to the development of the territory on the eve of independence.

1905. French Equatorial Africa. Service de la Statistique Générale.
        ANNUAIRE STATISTIQUE: Vol. I, 1936-1950. Brazzaville, n.d.
        289 p. maps, diagrs., tables.

Very comprehensive economic statistics, including population
statistics, a map showing territorial organization, and another
giving density of population (by district) in the Middle Congo and
Gabon.

1906. Gamache, Pierre, ed. GEOGRAPHIE ET HISTOIRE DE L'AFRIQUE EQUATORIALE
            FRANCAISE: DOCUMENTATION. Paris, F. Nathan, 1949. 304 p.
            illus., ports., maps.

Basic introduction to the area, including selections from
various authors.

1907. Gide, André. TRAVELS IN THE CONGO. Translated from the French by
            Dorothy Bussy. 2d ed. Berkeley, University of California
            Press, 1962 [c. 1957]. 375 p. illus.

The American edition above (reprint of the 1929 Knopf edition)
comprises two books by this distinguished French literary figure,
VOYAGE AU CONGO and LE RETOUR DU TCHAD, published in Paris in 1927
and 1928. The account of his long trip in the French tropical
colony, with its challenging indictment of French exploitation and
inefficient administrative control, exerted a strong influence on
French opinion regarding colonial policy. In the June 10, 1950,
issue of FRANCE-ILLUSTRATION devoted to AEF, Gide, shortly before
his death, expressed the belief that most of the abuses which he
had criticized in 1927 had been corrected and that present-day
French policy, both public administration and private business, was
sincerely and intelligently directed to the welfare of the Africans.

1908. Gillet, J. F. LES ORGANISMES COMMUNS AUX QUATRE ETATS DE L'AFRIQUE
            EQUATORIALE. Brazzaville, 1963. 40 l. illus., charts. Offset
            print.

Review and explanation of the joint services--customs union,
communications, post and telegraph, research in geology and mining--
established by the four new francophone nations of Equatorial Africa,
the Central African Republic, Chad, Congo-Brazzaville, and Gabon.
The author is secretary-general of the Conference of Heads of State
(Conference of Prime Ministers under the French Community, 1959-60;
since then the respective four presidents).

1909. Guernier, Eugène, ed. AFRIQUE EQUATORIALE FRANCAISE. Paris,
            Encyclopédie Coloniale et Maritime, 1950.

See no. 1581.

1910. GUID'AFRIQUE EQUATORIALE. 1960/61- Paris, Diloutremer; Dakar,
          Havas Afrique illus., maps. Annual.

          Second edition, 1962/63, 169 p., including advertising. Almanac-
       style information regarding regions and localities, administrative
       setup, chief industries, etc., with lists of business addresses for
       the chief cities, Brazzaville, Pointe-Noire, Bangui, and Libreville.

1911. Guthrie, Malcolm. THE BANTU LANGUAGES OF WESTERN EQUATORIAL AFRICA.
          London, Published for the International African Institute by
          Oxford University Press, 1953. 94 p. fold. map in pocket.
          (Handbook of African Languages)

       "Sources" given at end of sections.

       This handbook includes linguistic groups from Cameroun to the
       Congo. For the general note on this series, see no. 1011.

1912. Institut d'Etudes Centrafricaines, Brazzaville. BULLETIN. v. 1-
          1945- Brazzaville.

       _____. Mémoires. no. 1- Brazzaville, 1948-

          The Institut is the leading center for scientific study of
       French-speaking Central Africa. Its BULLETIN (irregular; no. 19-20,
       1960) is largely devoted to monograph-length studies in the natural
       sciences. The Mémoires series includes history, social sciences,
       and linguistics. An example of the sociological studies is by
       Marcel Soret, DEMOGRAPHIE ET PROBLEMES URBAINS EN A.E.F.: POTO-POTO,
       BACONGO, DOLISIE (Montpellier, Impr. Charité, 1954, 134 p., tables;
       Mémoires, no. 7). See also CATALOGUE DE LA BIBLIOTHEQUE DE L'I.E.C.
       (MATIERES, AUTEURS ET PERIODIQUES), by Jeannine Lambert (Montpellier,
       Impr. Charité, 1951, 152 p.; Mémoire no. 4), and supplements, no. 1-
       Jan. 1, 1951/Mar. 31, 1953-.

1913. International Monetary Fund. SURVEY OF AFRICAN ECONOMICS: Vol. 1,
          CAMEROON, CENTRAL AFRICAN REPUBLIC, CHAD, CONGO (BRAZZAVILLE),
          AND GABON. 1968. 365 p.

1914. Maran, René. SAVORGNAN DE BRAZZA. Paris, Editions du Dauphin,
          1951. 246 p. illus.

          Biography by a West Indian writer who won the Prix Goncourt
       for his novel BATOUALA (an important anti-colonial book with over-
       tones of black resistance and négritude). The book covers Brazza's
       life and explorations from his first expedition up the Ogooué River
       into Central Africa in 1875 to his death in 1905. This edition

supersedes an earlier volume by Maran, BRAZZA ET LA FONDATION DE
L'A.E.F. (Paris, Gallimard, 1941). Henri Brunschwig is working on
a major biography of Brazza based on newly uncovered material.

1915.   REALITES ET GRANDS PROJETS EN AFRIQUE EQUATORIALE: REPUBLIQUE DU
         TCHAD, REPUBLIQUE DU GABON, REPUBLIQUE CENTRAFRICAINE,
         REPUBLIQUE DU CONGO. Monaco, P. Bory, 1961. 252 p. illus.
         (PERSPECTIVES D'OUTRE-MER, no. 42, Nov. 1961)

         In a magazine that featured articles on the economics of French-
speaking Africa, this large special issue explained at length the
present situation and plans for development of the extensive natural
resources of the four new republics.

         An earlier survey of the same nature, in a special issue of
the serial REALITES AFRICAINES, was LA MISE EN VALEUR DE L'A.E.F.
(Casablanca, Editions Fontana-Maroc, 1956, 358 p., illus., maps,
plans).

1916.   Thompson, Virginia, and Richard Adloff. THE EMERGING STATES OF
         FRENCH EQUATORIAL AFRICA. Stanford, Calif., Stanford University
         Press, 1960. xii, 595 p. illus., ports., maps.

         Notes (by chapters): p. 534-568; bibliography: p. 569-582.

         The indispensable work in English, providing a broad background
for study of the former French Equatorial Africa and its four states,
now independent republics--the Central African Republic, Chad,
Congo-Brazzaville, and Gabon. The authors glance hastily at history
and largely bypass any anthropological considerations, but few
phases of political, economic, and present-day social life have
escaped their careful analysis exhaustively documented with chapter
notes, bibliography, and index. At the time of its writing the four
states were members of the French Community.

1917.   Trézenem, Edouard. L'AFRIQUE EQUATORIALE FRANCAISE. 3d ed. Paris,
         Editions Maritimes et Coloniales, 1955. 208 p. illus.
         (Collection Terres lointaines, no. 1)

         Includes a 3-page bibliography.

         Third edition of a general survey of the AEF, previously published
with Bertrand Lembezat's CAMEROUN. The 1955 version was revised to
meet current conditions.

1918. Union Douanière Equatoriale (later the Union Douanière et Economique
       de l'Afrique Centrale). BULLETIN DES STATISTIQUES GENERALES.
       Jan. 1963- Brazzaville.

       Supersedes BULLETIN MENSUEL DE STATISTIQUE which from 1947 till
       independence was issued by the AEF's Service de la Statistique
       Générale (in 1959 called Bureau Centrale de la Statistique).

CAMEROUN

<u>Note</u>: See Note above, under Equatorial Africa. The Federal Republic of
Cameroun was formed in 1961, after the former trust territory of Southern
Cameroons under British administration voted by plebiscite to join the
Cameroun Republic (until 1960, the French trust territory of Eastern
Cameroun) in a bilingual federation. The former Northern Cameroons, British
administered, had rejected the federation and became an integral part of
Northern Nigeria in June 1961.

<u>Bibliographies</u>

1919. "Cameroun Ephemeral Materials." AFRICANA NEWSLETTER, v. 2, no. 1,
       1964: 13-17.

       "Three Collections on the Cameroun." AFRICANA NEWSLETTER, v. 1,
       no. 3, 1963: 8-16.

       Listings of several private collections of ephermera (party
       pamphlets, rare newspapers, constitutions, reports of congresses,
       trade-union literature, obscure government documents). Microfilms
       of the material are deposited in the Cooperative African Microfilm
       Project (CAMP) of the Center for Research Libraries, Chicago, Ill.,
       for borrowing by subscribers to a fund for filming rare African
       materials.

1920. Institut de Recherches Scientifiques du Cameroun. LISTE BIBLIO-
       GRAPHIQUE DES TRAVAUX PUBLIES PAR L'ANCIEN INSTITUT FRANCAIS
       D'AFRIQUE NOIRE, CENTRE CAMEROUN, ET PAR L'I.R.CAM, 1935-1964.
       Yaoundé [1965?] 19 p.

       _____. QUELQUES SOURCES BIBLIOGRAPHIQUES DU CAMEROUN. By Njikam
       Martin. Yaoundé [1967?] 11 <u>l</u>.

       The second reference cited is a list of important bibliographic
       material on Cameroun, of public and private Camerounian institutions
       offering research facilities, and of bibliographies in preparation.

1921. "Serials of Cameroun, Dahomey..." AFRICANA NEWSLETTER, v. 2, no. 1,
    1964: 33-41.

Twenty-five newspapers and periodicals, official and unofficial,
are listed here as currently published in Cameroun (p. 33-34). Six
are in African languages, two--from Western Cameroun--in English, and
two, including the JOURNAL OFFICIEL, in French and English. The
remainder are in French.

A longer list of "Cameroun Newspapers, before and after
Independence," was printed in AFRICANA NEWSLETTER, v. 1, no. 2, Spring
1963: 8-12. Perhaps the most important for anything other than
current local news is ABBIA: REVUE CULTURELLE CAMEROUNAISE, with text
in English and French (Yaoundé, no. 1, Feb. 1963-, illus., quarterly.).

Reference Works

1922. Billard, Pierre. LE CAMEROUN FEDERAL: Vol. I, ESSAI DE GEOGRAPHIE
    PHYSIQUE. Lyon, Impr. des Beaux-Arts, 1968. 291 p. illus.,
    maps (1 fold.), tables.

Bibliography: p. 265-268.

_____. LE CAMEROUN FEDERAL: Vol. II, ESSAI DE GEOGRAPHIE
HUMAINE ET ECONOMIQUE. Lyon, Impr. des Beaux-Arts, 1968. 399 p.
illus., tables.

Bibliography: p. 367-371.

Vol. I covers climate and topography in general and then describes
the mountainous regions--topography and vegetation, hydrography, and
flora and fauna. Vol. II covers the people, religion, agriculture,
cattle breeding and fishing, mineral resources, transportation
system, industries, banking, communications, political geography,
education, health facilities, sports, and tourism. Each volume
includes an index.

1923. Cabot, Jean, and Roland Diziain. POPULATION DU MOYEN LOGONE (TCHAD
    ET CAMEROUN). Paris, Office de la Recherche Scientifique et
    Technique Outre-Mer, 1955. 76 p. illus., plates, maps,
    diagrs., tables. (L'homme d'outre-mer, no. 1)

Sociodemographic analysis in the ORSTOM series. See no. 1558
for description.

1924. LE CAMEROUN: ASPECT GEOGRAPHIQUE, HISTORIQUE, TOURISTIQUE,
         ECONOMIQUE ET ADMINISTRATIF DU TERRITOIRE. Paris, Alépée,
         1953. 225 p. illus., ports., maps (1 fold.). (Les Documents
         de France)

       Older but still useful survey.

1925. Cameroun. ANNUAIRE NATIONAL, 1968. NATIONAL YEAR BOOK, 1968.
         Yaoundé, Les Quatre Points Cardinaux, 1968. xxi, 415, 60 p.
         illus. (part col.), maps (part col.), tables.

       A comprehensive source of information, in French and English,
  with data current to Apr. 1968 presented in seven main categories:
  government (text of constitution and data on the administration
  and the diplomatic corps); investments and industries; telephone
  directory (60 separately numbered green pages); economy; agriculture
  and exportation; professional directory; and tourism. A historical
  resumé is given in the preliminary pages. Advertising is included.
  This is apparently the second edition of the yearbook; the first
  appeared in 1963.

1926. Cameroun. JOURNAL OFFICIEL DE LA REPUBLIQUE FEDERALE DU CAMEROUN.
         Yaoundé, Impr. Nationale. Semimonthly.

       Supersedes the independent state's JOURNAL OFFICIEL DE LA
  REPUBLIQUE DU CAMEROUN, which was a continuation of the JOURNAL
  OFFICIEL DU CAMEROUN FRANCAIS (Yaoundé, 1916-; 45th year, 1960-).

       The monthly BULLETIN DE LA STATISTIQUE GENERALE, begun in 1950
  under the Service de la Statistique Générale of the French admin-
  istration of Cameroun, was continued under the republic through
  June 1962; in Jan. 1963 the Service de la Statistique Générale et
  de la Mécanographie began issuing RESUME DES STATISTIQUES DU CAMEROUN
  ORIENTAL: BULLETIN MENSUEL. For other government documents see the
  Library of Congress OFFICIAL PUBLICATIONS OF FRENCH EQUATORIAL
  AFRICA, FRENCH CAMEROONS, AND TOGO, 1946-1958 (no. 1889).

1927. Dugast, Idelette. INVENTAIRE ETHNIQUE DU SUD-CAMEROUN. Douala,
         IFAN, 1949. xii, 159 p. maps. (Mémoires de l'IFAN, Centre
         du Cameroun, Série: Populations, no. 1)

       Includes bibliographies.

       Ethnological analysis in systematic outline form, published
  as the first volume of a series of studies on population in Camerouns.
  The writer identifies divisions and subdivisions of many tribes:

pygmies, Duala, Bakundu, Bakoko and Basa, Bantu, Beti and Pahouins, Maka and Kozune, Soudano-Bantu, etc. Bibliographies and maps for each tribe are included at the end of sections, and there is a large map of the whole area.

1928. Dugast, Idelette. MONOGRAPHIE DE LA TRIBU DES NDIKI (BANEN DU CAMEROUN): Vol. I [subtitled VIE MATERIELLE]; Vol. II, VIE SOCIALE ET FAMILIALE. Paris, Institut d'Ethnologie, 1955-59. 2 v. (xxiv, (824); xx, (635 p.)). illus., maps (part fold.), geneal. tables, music. (Université de Paris, Travaux et mémoires de Institut d'Ethnologie, v. 58, 63)

Bibliography: v. 1, p. xi-xxiv; v. 2, p. vii-xx.

In Vol. I an introduction surveys the physical and human geography as well as the characteristics of the Ndiki, a people of southwestern Cameroun. The main part of the text covers first production and acquisitions and then consumption. Vol. II briefly discusses the geographic setting, history, social structures, and habitat, and then offers a detailed sociocultural study, along with two lengthy appendixes, one on language and the other on divination. Each volume includes an excellent bibliography and an analytical index.

1929. Ethnographic Survey of Africa: Western Africa. London, International African Institute.

For the general note on this series, see no. 980. The following two volumes relate to populations of Cameroun:

a) Part 9. PEOPLES OF THE CENTRAL CAMEROONS. Tikar, by Merran McCulloch; Bamum and Bamileke, by Margaret Littlewood; Banen, Bafia, and Balom, by Idelette Dugast. 1954. 174 p. fold. col. map, tables. Includes bibliographies.

b) Part 11. COASTAL BANTU OF THE CAMEROONS (THE KPE-MBOKO, DUALA-LIMBA AND TANGA-YASA GROUPS OF THE BRITISH AND FRENCH TRUSTEESHIP TERRITORIES OF THE CAMEROONS). By Edwin Ardener. 1956. 116 p. maps (1 fold.), tables. Bibliography: p. 109-111.

There are also two volumes on Cameroun in the Monographies ethnologiques africaines series:

c) LE GROUPE DIT PAHOUIN (FANG, BOULOU, BETI). By Pierre Alexandre and Jacques Binet. 1958. 152 p. fold. map. Bibliography: p. [137]-148.

d)   LES POPULATIONS PAIENNES DE NORD-CAMEROUN ET DE L'ADAMAOUA.
     By Bertrand Lembezat. 1961. 252 p. fold. map.
     Bibliography: p. 243-247.

1930. ETUDES CAMEROUNAISES. 1948-58. Yaoundé. illus., maps. Quarterly.

       Issued by the IFAN Centre du Cameroun, superseding an earlier
BULLETIN of the Société des Etudes Camerounaises; in turn superseded
in 1960 by RECHERCHES ET ETUDES CAMEROUNAISES (see below, no. 1951).

1931. France. RAPPORT DU GOUVERNEMENT FRANCAIS A L'ASSEMBLEE GENERALE
       DES NATIONS UNIES SUR L'ADMINISTRATION DU CAMEROUN PLACE SOUS
       LA TUTELLE DE LA FRANCE. Paris. illus., maps. Annual.

       Former annual publication presented to the United Nations by
France as an administering power, offering a survey of economic,
political, social, and educational status and progress in the trust
territory of the French Cameroons. The "Annexe statistique,"
containing tables and graphic charts, and the second appendix,
"Répertoire des principaux textes de lois et réglements généraux,"
fill almost half the large, well-illustrated volumes. Begun in
the 1920's under the League of Nations, the last submitted covered
the year 1957.

       Two background studies of the independent country were issued
in the authoritative series of the French Direction de la Documentation, Notes et études documentaires: LA REPUBLIQUE DU CAMEROUN
(Paris, 1961, 56 p.; no. 2746) and LE CAMEROUN SOUS TUTELLE
BRITANNIQUE A L'HEURE DE PLEBISCITE (Paris, 1961, 13 p.; no. 2756).

1932. Froelich, Jean C. CAMEROUN, TOGO: TERRITOIRES SOUS TUTELLE. Paris,
       Berger-Levrault, 1956. 217 p. illus., maps. (L'Union
       française)

       Bibliography: p. 209-212.

       Clear, scientific, well-balanced survey of the two trust
territories under French administration. The coverage is of country,
people, administration, economy, history, and culture.

       Earlier semiofficial surveys were LE CAMEROUN: ASPECT GEO-
GRAPHIQUE, HISTORIQUE, TOURISTIQUE, ECONOMIQUE ET ADMINISTRATIF
DU TERRITOIRE (Paris, Alépée, 1953, 225 p., illus., maps; Les
documents de France) and Bertrand Lembezat, LE CAMEROUN (3d ed.,
Paris, Editions Maritimes et Coloniales, 1954, 208 p., illus.;
Terres lointaines).

Victor Chazelas, Administrator-in-Chief of the Colonies, prepared for the International Colonial Exposition at Paris in 1931 TERRITOIRES AFRICAINS SOUS MANDAT DE LA FRANCE: CAMEROUN ET TOGO (Paris, Société d'Editions Géographiques, Maritimes et Coloniales, 1931, 240 p., plates).

1933. Gardinier, David E. CAMEROON: UNITED NATIONS CHALLENGE TO FRENCH POLICY. London, New York, Oxford University Press, 1963. 142 p.

Selective bibliography: p. 137-142.

Issued under the auspices of the Institute of Race Relations. This study of Cameroun under French administration during the trusteeship period, with slight background of earlier history, is concentrated on the period from 1946 to independence, Jan. 1, 1960. The Southern Cameroons are considered only insofar as they influenced events in the French territory.

1934. Garine, Igor de. LES MASSA DU CAMEROUN: VIE ECONOMIQUE ET SOCIALE. Paris, Presses Universitaires de France, 1964. 250 p. illus., maps, diagrs. (Institut International Africain, Etudes ethnographiques)

Bibliography: p. [231]-237.

A systematic study of the economic and social life of the Massa people of northeastern Cameroun. The work is divided into three parts: the natural, historical, and social setting; economic activities; and the traditional circulation of goods in relation to social organization and outside influences.

1935. Gonidec, P. F. LA REPUBLIQUE FEDERALE DU CAMEROUN. Paris, Berger-Levrault, 1969. 88 p. illus. (Encyclopédie politique et constitutionnelle, Série Afrique)

Bibliography: p. 83-86.

A brief, useful survey of politics and government.

1936. Great Britain. Colonial Office. THE CAMEROONS UNDER UNITED KINGDOM ADMINISTRATION: REPORT...TO THE GENERAL ASSEMBLY OF THE UNITED NATIONS ON THE ADMINISTRATION OF THE CAMEROONS UNDER UNITED KINGDOM TRUSTEESHIP. 1920/21-1961. London. H.M. Stationery Off. illus. Annual.

The strips of territory bordering on Nigeria known as Northern
Cameroons and Southern Cameroons were placed under British adminis-
tration after World War I as a co-mandate of the League of Nations.
Reports were issued annually to the League of Nations until World
War II, after 1946 to the United Nations. The final report was that
covering the year 1959 (London, 1961, 209 p., fold. maps).

1937. GUID'CAMEROUN, 1964. 3d ed. Paris, Diloutremer, 1964. 210 p. maps
          (1 col. fold.).

          Previously issued in 1959 and 1961. The guide first gives data
on administrative, political, judicial, and territorial administration, economy, education, public health, social organization,
transportation, the press, tourism, etc. The main portion of the
volume then covers each department of the country. Advertising is
included, and there is a place-name index.

1938. Guillard, Joanny. GOLONPOUI: ANALYSE DES CONDITIONS DE MODERNISATION
          D'UN VILLAGE DU NORD-CAMEROUN. Paris, La Haye, Mouton, 1965.
          502 p. illus., maps, tables.

          Bibliography: p. [15]-19.

          A thorough geographic, sociological, and economic study of rural
development in a village of the Tupuri people.

1939. Hurault, Jean. LA STRUCTURE SOCIALE DES BAMILEKE. Paris, Mouton,
          1962. 133 p. illus., maps (1 fold. col.), plans (part fold.
          col.), fold. geneal. tables, diagrs. (Le monde d'outre-mer
          passé et présent, 2e série: Documents, 1)

          A detailed examination of the social structure of the Bamileke
chefferies of Western Cameroun, covering habitat and agriculture,
system of kinship, family customs and common law, the chiefdom, and
districts. In appended sections the author describes the beliefs of
the people and reflects on the future of Bamileke institutions.

          For a comprehensive study of the traditional institutions of
the Bamileke, see E. K. Kwayeb, LES INSTITUTIONS DE DROIT PUBLIC
DU PAYS BAMILEKE (Paris, Librairie Générale de Droit et Jurisprudence, 1960, 200 p., illus., maps).

1940. Kuczynski, Robert R. THE CAMEROONS AND TOGOLAND: A DEMOGRAPHIC
          STUDY. London, New York, Oxford University Press, 1939.
          xviii, 579 p.

"Sources quoted": p. 550-567.

See no. 1860.

1941. Labouret, Henri. LA LANGUE DES PEULS OU FOULBE. Dakar, IFAN, 1952.
xii, 286 p. (Mémoires de l'IFAN, no. 16)

Bibliography: p. [ix]-xi.

"Lexique peul-français; Lexique français-peul": p. 245-286.

1942. Largeau, V. ENCYCLOPEDIE PAHOUINE. Paris, E. Leroux, 1911. 700 p.

This remains a source of rare information on the Pahouin people,
although it has been faulted--chiefly by Father H. Trilles, a noted
authority on the Fang. The major work of Trilles is LE TOTEMISME CHEZ
LES FAN (Münster i.W., Aschendorff, 1912, xvi, 653 p., illus., music;
Anthropos-Bibliothek, v. 1, fasc. 4).

Another comprehensive older work on the Pahouins is Günther
Tessmann, DIE PANGWE: VOLKERKUNDLICHE MONOGRAPHIE EINES WEST-
AFRIKANISCHEN NEGERSTAMMES: ERGEBNISSE DER LUBECKER PANGWE-EX-
PEDITION 1907-1909 UND FRUHERER FORSCHUNGEN 1904-1907 (Berlin,
Ernst Wasmuth A.-G., 1913, 2 v., illus., maps, music).

1943. Lebeuf, Jean Paul. L'HABITATION DES FALI MONTAGNARDS DU CAMEROUN
SEPTENTRIONAL: TECHNOLOGIE, SOCIOLOGIE, MYTHOLOGIE, SYMBOLISME.
Paris, Hachette, 1961. 607 p. illus. (part col.), maps,
diagrs. (Bibliothèque des Guides bleus)

Bibliography: p. 601-[604].

A detailed study of all aspects of the homes and home life of
the Fali people.

1944. Lecoq, Raymond. LES BAMILEKE: UNE CIVILISATION AFRICAINE. Paris,
Editions Africaines, 1953. 221 p. (chiefly illus.), fold.
map. (Présence africaine)

Pictorial monograph on a tribe known traditionally for its
sculpture. The author had worked among the Bamileke, developing
craft centers and encouraging the revival of the tribal arts here
studied.

1945. Lembezat, Bertrand. LE CAMEROUN. Paris, Nouvelles Editions Latines, 1964. 152 p. illus., map. (Survol du monde)

A compact survey of Cameroun--its geography, history, economy, evolution toward and attainment of independence in 1960, and events to 1964.

1946. Le Vine, Victor T. THE CAMEROONS, FROM MANDATE TO INDEPENDENCE. Berkeley, University of California Press, 1964. xi, 329 p. tables, maps.

Bibliography: p. 303-319.

A political history, which begins with a geographical and historical background and then goes on to analyze the rise of national politics in the interwar period, the constitutional changes after the war, and political parties and politics through the consolidation of East Cameroun and the British Cameroons in 1960. The last two chapters look at problems in the two parts of the Federal Republic. There are useful appendixes, references in notes, and a long bibliography.

1947. Mercier, A., and B. Paquier. DEVELOPPEMENT INDUSTRIEL AU CAMEROUN: Vol. I-II, RAPPORT PRELIMINAIRE 1964-65. Paris, Société d'Etudes pour le Développement Economique et Social, 1965. 2 v. 159, 328 p. maps, tables, graphs.

This two-volume report on all aspects of industrial development updates a 1960 document drawn up by SEDES and includes detailed data on existing industries.

1948. Mveng, Engelbert. HISTOIRE DU CAMEROUN. Paris, Présence Africaine, 1963. 533 p. plates, maps, tables.

Bibliography: p. 501-526.

General history, synthesizing all that is known on the Cameroun from prehistoric times through the reunification of the former British and French trust territories in 1961. The author is a Jesuit father deeply versed in the languages and folklore of the country. Unfortunately, he neglects British source material on the Northern Cameroons.

1949. Ngwa, J. A. AN OUTLINE GEOGRAPHY OF THE FEDERAL REPUBLIC OF CAMEROON. London, Longmans, 1967. 111 p. illus., maps, plan.

1950. Njoya, Sultan of the Bamun. HISTOIRE ET COUTUMES DES BAMUN.
Rédigées sous la direction du Sultan Njoya; traduction du
pasteur Henri Martin. Dakar, IFAN, 1952. 271 p. 5 facsims.
(Mémoires de l'IFAN, Centre du Cameroun, Série: Populations,
no. 5)

Reproduction in French translation of a manuscript text preserved in the palace of the Sultan of Bamun. The writing is in the
special characters of the Mun language, one of the two independently
developed alphabets of Black Africa. (The other is that of the
Vai of Liberia.) The text was transcribed into Latin script and
translated literally. It tells the history and traditions of the
Bamun people in the words of their elders, passing from kings to
customs and back again to kings and wars.

1951. RECHERCHES ET ETUDES CAMEROUNAISES. no. 1, 1960- Yaoundé, Institut
de Recherches Scientifiques du Cameroun. illus., plates, maps,
diagrs. Semiannual.

Journal of the Institut which succeeded the IFAN Centre du
Cameroun. An occasional special issue is devoted to a single full-
length study, e.g., René Bureau's ETHNO-SOCIOLOGIE RELIGIEUSE DES
DUALA ET APPARENTES (372 p., map, diagrs; bibliography: p. 11-13;
special issue, no. 7-8, 1962).

1952. Rudin, Harry R. GERMANS IN THE CAMEROONS, 1884-1914: A CASE STUDY
IN MODERN IMPERIALISM. New Haven, Yale University Press, 1938.
456 p. fold. map. (Yale Historical Publications, Studies, no. 12)

Bibliographical note: p. 427-437.

Prepared originally as a doctoral dissertation, this work
combines thorough documented research in published and archival
sources, many of them German, with on-the-spot investigations in
the Cameroons.

1953. Société d'Etudes pour le Développement Economique et Social.
ENQUETE SUR LE NIVEAU DE VIE A YAOUNDE. Yaoundé, Ministère
des Affaires Economiques et du Plan, 1965. 7 v. maps, tables,
graphs.

Seven provisional reports, ranging from 20 to 173 pages, on the
standard of living in Yaoundé (including the surrounding zone of
cacao plantations).

1954. Stoecker, Helmuth, ed. KAMERUN UNTER DEUTSCHER KOLONIALHERRSCHAFT: STUDIEN. Berlin, Rütten & Loening, 1960- illus., ports., maps. (Schriftenreiche des Instituts für Allgemeine Geschichte an der Humboldt-Universität Berlin, v. 5-)

Thorough scholarly study, heavily documented from archival and published sources in long footnote references.

1955. Tardits, Claude. CONTRIBUTION A L'ETUDE DES POPULATIONS BAMILEKE DE L'OUEST CAMEROUN. Paris, Berger-Levrault, 1960. 140 p. illus., maps. (L'homme d'outre-mer, n.s. no. 4)

Includes bibliography.

A work resulting from a survey of the chefferies in the prosperous agricultural regions of the Southern Cameroons, sponsored by the Office de la Recherche Scientifique et Technique Outre-Mer (ORSTOM).

1956. United Nations. Trusteeship Council. Visiting Mission to the Trust Territories in West Africa, 1949, 1952, 1955, 1958. REPORT ON THE CAMEROONS UNDER FRENCH ADMINISTRATION. New York. 4 v. maps.

_____. _____. _____. REPORT ON THE CAMEROONS UNDER UNITED KINGDOM ADMINISTRATION. New York. 4 v. maps.

The Visiting Missions examined political, social, and economic conditions in the Cameroons on four visits, 1949, 1952, 1955, and 1958, reporting to the Trusteeship Council, which passed the reports on to the General Assembly. For discussion of reports and for the many other UN documents relating to the Cameroons, including innumerable petitions, see the annual UNITED NATIONS DOCUMENTS INDEX under "Cameroons."

1957. U.S. Department of the Interior. Office of Geography. CAMEROON: OFFICIAL STANDARD NAMES APPROVED BY THE UNITED STATES BOARD ON GEOGRAPHIC NAMES. Washington, U.S. Govt. Print. Off., Mar. 1962. 255 p. map. (18,000 names) (Gazetteer no. 60)

See note on series, no. 484.

CENTRAL AFRICAN REPUBLIC
(UBANGI-SHARI)

Reference Works

Note: See also the essay by John A. Ballard in Carter, NATIONAL UNITY AND REGIONALISM IN EIGHT AFRICAN STATES (no. 608).

1958. Central African Republic. FORMATION ET CARACTERES DES CENTRES SECONDAIRES DANS LE CENTRE OUBANGUI. Paris, Bureau d'Etudes et Recherches du Plan, 1960. 66 p. map.

A demographic study, one of a series undertaken under French official auspices in the mid-1950's. A preliminary survey was made by Jean Paul Lebeuf and published as part of a report on urban centers in AEF: BANGUI (OUBANGUI-CHARI) (Paris, Editions de l'Union Française, 1954, 63 p.).

1959. Central African Republic. JOURNAL OFFICIEL DE LA REPUBLIQUE CENTRAFRICAINE. Oct. 1958- Bangui. Semimonthly.

Other official serials sometimes available for distribution include the DEBATS and DOCUMENTS ANNEXES AUX DEBATS of the Assemblée Législative, the BUDGET LOCAL, and the BULLETIN MENSUEL DE STATISTIQUE, published by the Service de la Statistique.

1960. Dampierre, Eric de. UN ANCIEN ROYAUME BANDIA DU HAUT-OUBANGUI. Paris, Plon, 1967. 620 pp. illus., plates. (Recherches en sciences humaines, 24)

1961. Eboué, A. Félix. LES PEUPLES DE L'OUBANGUI-CHARI: ESSAI D' ETHNOGRAPHIE, DE LINGUISTIQUE ET D'ECONOMIE SOCIALE. Paris, Publications du Comité de l'Afrique Française, 1933. 104 p. illus., music, maps, tables.

Governor Eboué served in his earlier career as an administrator in Ubangi-Shari. This book and a dictionary of one of the tribal languages resulted from his earliest study of the people of the country.

1962. France. Direction de la Documentation. LA REPUBLIQUE CENTRAFRI-CAINE. Paris, 1960. 49 p. (Notes et études documentaires, no. 2733, Dec. 19, 1960)

619

Background survey of general conditions, political and administrative institutions, economics and financial position, and cultural
and social evolution. The text of the constitution is given in an
appendix. (See general note on this series, no. 1587.)

1963. France. Institut National de la Statistique et des Etudes Economiques.
Service de Coopération. ENQUETE AGRICOLE EN REPUBLIQUE CENTRA-
FRICAINE, 1960-1961: RESULTATS DEFINITIFS. Edited by Marcel
Lafarge. Paris, Ministère de 1 Coopération; INSEE, 1965. 269 p.
maps, tables, diagrs.

Based on statistical surveys, this is a detailed, well-organized
inventory of Ubangi agriculture in the western and central regions
of the Central African Republic. The study points out the preponderance of the family type of enterprise, lack of diversification, soil-eroding farming techniques, limitations of traditional
equipment, and the disinterest in livestock-raising. This work is
a follow-up to INSEE's ENQUETE DEMOGRAPHIQUE EN REPUBLIQUE CENTRA-
FRICAINE, 1959-1960: RESULTATS DEFINITIFS, also edited by Lafarge
(Paris, 1964, 262 p.).

1964. Kalck, Pierre. REALITES OUBANGUIENNES. Paris, Berger-Levrault,
1959. 356 p. illus. (Mondes d'outre-mer, sér. Nations)

Bibliography: p. 329-343.

Well-balanced study of the country. Writing in 1958, the
author uses the name of the former colony, Ubangi-Shari (French,
Oubangui-Chari). The work is in three parts, with the first on
"precolonialism," a combination of history and anthropology. The
second part treats the French colonial territory, including a
table of population as of 1958, with concentration on the socioeconomic balance sheet. The last part, "L'Oubangui décolonisé,"
is an analysis of economic and social problems facing the new
government of the landlocked country. The book ends with a good
classified bibliography.

See also two older novels by a colonial official, René Maran:
BATOULA (Paris, A. Michel, 1921) and LE LIVRE DE LA BROUSSE (Paris,
A. Michel, 1934).

1965. LIVRE D'OR DE LA REPUBLIQUE CENTRAFRICAINE. Paris, Editions de
l'Afrique Nouvelle, 1964. 141 p. illus., plates (part col.),
maps.

General description, primarily comprised of illustrations and
plates, of the republic. Included are a biography of David Dacko
and brief profiles of government ministers, plus information on

geography, history, wildlife, the Jeunesse Pionniere Nationale,
the army, traditional art, mining, industry, agriculture, and the
Pygmies.

1966. Thomas, Jacqueline M. C. LES NGBAKA DE LA LOBAYE: LE DEPEUPLEMENT
      RURAL CHEZ UNE POPULATION FORESTIERE DE LA REPUBLIQUE CENTRA-
      FRICAINE. Paris, La Haye, Mouton, 1963. 495 p. plates, fold.
      maps, tables, diagrs. (Le monde d'outre-mer passé et présent,
      2d ser.: Documents, 11)

      Bibliography: p. 467-473.

      The Ngbaka (i.e., Ngbwaka) live largely west of the Ubangi
      River and north of the Lobaye River. In this volume the author
      examines various aspects of their social and demographic structures
      and offers a detailed analysis of rural depopulation (population
      mobility, demographic pressure in urban centers, problems of village
      life). Several biographies are presented in a concluding section.
      A lexicon is provided.

      Among the author's other works on these people is LE PARLER
      NGBAKA DE BOKANGA: PHONOLOGIE, MORPHOLOGIE, SYNTAXE (Paris, La
      Haye, Mouton, 1963, 307 p., map; Le monde d'outre-mer passé et
      présent, 1st ser.: Etudes, 22).

1967. Tucker, Archibald N. LE GROUPE LINGUISTIQUE ZANDE. Tervuren,
      Musée Royal du Congo Belge, 1959. 289 p.

1968. U.S. Department of the Interior. Office of Geography. CENTRAL
      AFRICAN REPUBLIC: OFFICIAL STANDARD NAMES APPROVED BY THE
      UNITED STATES BOARD ON GEOGRAPHIC NAMES. Washington, U.S.
      Govt. Print. Off., Apr. 1962. 220 p. map. (15,700 names)
      (Gazetteer no. 64)

      See note on series, no. 484.

1969. Vergiat, Antonin M. MOEURS ET COUTUMES DES MANJAS. Paris, Payot,
      1937. 323 p. illus. (Bibliothèque scientifique)

      _____. LES RITES SECRETS DES PRIMITIFS DE L'OUBANGUI. Paris,
      Payot, 1936. 210 p. illus. (Bibliothèque scientifique)

      Two scholarly, detailed anthropological studies of pagan
      Nigritic tribes of Equatorial Africa.

Another study of a tribe in the north of the Central African Republic is by John Hilberth, LES GBAYA (Uppsala, Uppsala University, 1962, 141 p.; Studia ethnographica Upsaliensa, no. 19).

CHAD

Bibliographies

1970. Appert, Monique. ESSAI DE BIBLIOGRAPHIE CONCERNANT LE TCHAD JUSQU'EN 1913. n.p., 1962. Mimeographed.

Has approximately 1,000 titles. No further information has been found.

1971. Lebeuf, J.-P. BIBLIOGRAPHIE DU TCHAD. Fort-Lamy, Institut National Tchadien pour les Sciences Humaines, 1968. 243 p. (Etudes et Documents Tchadiens, ser. A: 4)

Lists in alphabetical order over 2,000 items (printed or cyclostyled), books, articles, pamphlets, etc., dealing with Chad. Also cites records and films. Has a subject index.

Reference Works

Note: See also the essay by John A. Ballard in Carter, NATIONAL UNITY AND REGIONALISM IN EIGHT AFRICAN STATES (no. 608).

1972. Aerts, J. ECONOMIE D'OUTRE-MER: LA REPUBLIQUE DU TCHAD. Bruxelles, Institut Superieur du Commerce, 1965. 141 p.

Includes bibliography.

1973. ANNUAIRE DU TCHAD, 1958. Casablanca, Editions Fontana [1958?]. 161 p. illus. (part col.).

This presentation of Chad, "constituting a practical guide to its economy, organization, and structure," was prepared by the Chambre de Commerce, d'Agriculture et d'Industrie du Tchad in Fort-Lamy. It is an updating of a similar work brought out with the same title (the ANNUAIRE is misleading) in 1950-51, to celebrate the 50th anniversary of the French installation in Chad. The book is handsomely made up and illustrated, with both pictures and advertising partly in color. Coverage is general, including geography, history and archaeology, territorial organization, and economy, and there are chapters on the six largest cities.

The Chambre de Commerce also issues a weekly bulletin, INFORMATIONS ECONOMIQUES.

1974. Boisson, Jacques. L'HISTOIRE DU TCHAD ET DE FORT-ARCHAMBAULT. Paris, Editions du Scorpion, 1966. 249 p. maps.

A history of Chad, 1880-1966. The author traces the stages of French penetration, emphasizing the role of Fort-Archambault (created in 1899) in the region of the Sara people. The last two chapters bring economic and political developments up to 1966. There are 20 maps.

1975. Cabot, Jean. LE BASSIN DU MOYEN LOGONE. Paris, Office de la Recherche Scientifique et Technique Outre-Mer, 1965. 327 p. illus., fold. map. (Mémoires, 8)

Bibliography: p. [315]-324.

A study of the Logone Valley in southwestern Chad. Coverage includes natural environment, peoples and their traditional life, changes brought by colonization, realizations and perspective, and the psychological and political conditions for economic progress.

1976. Capot-Rey, Robert. BOURKOU ET OUNIANGA: ETUDE DE GEOGRAPHIE REGIONALE. Alger, Institut de Recherches Sahariennes, 1961. 182 p. plates, maps, plans, diagrs. (Mémoire, no. 5)

A study by the director of the Institut, leading authority on the Sahara. This monograph examines the present evolution and economic and human geography of the northern desert region of Chad.

1977. Chad. JOURNAL OFFICIEL DE LA REPUBLIQUE DU TCHAD. 1959- Fort-Lamy. Semimonthly.

Another publication of Chad, the BULLETIN MENSUEL DE STATISTIQUE, begun by the Service de la Statistique of the colonial government, is continued under the Service de la Statistique Générale of the republic. It is issued in mimeographed form.

1978. Chad. Ministère du Plan et de la Coopération. PREMIER PLAN
           QUINQUENNAL DE DEVELOPPEMENT ECONOMIQUE ET SOCIAL, 1966-1970.
           [Fort-Lamy, 1966?] 369 p. maps (part fold.), tables, diagrs.

       A thoroughgoing review of Chad's first five-year development
plan. The volume is divided into 10 main parts, each of which is
preceded by an outline of contents. A concluding section includes
a general recapitulation of the plan.

1979. Chapelle, Jean. NOMADES NOIRS DU SAHARA. Paris, Plon, 1957.
           449 p. illus., plates (1 col.), maps (1 fold. col.), tables.
           (Recherches en sciences humaines, no. 10)

       Bibliography: p. 411-417.

       A detailed study of the nomadic Toubou of northern Chad, a
people who also roam northeastern Niger and southwestern Libya--
their origins, history, population growth, environment, economic
activities, domestic life, life cycle, social organization, and
religion. An index of place names and peoples is included.

1980. France. Direction de la Documentation. LA REPUBLIQUE DU TCHAD.
           Paris, 1960. 67 p. (Notes et études documentaires, no.
           2696, Aug. 31, 1960)

       See general note on this series, no. 1587.

1981. Fuchs, Peter. TSCHAD. Bonn, Schroeder, 1966. 101 p. illus.,
           maps. (Die Länder Afrikas, v. 33)

       A complete monograph on Chad by an Austrian ethnologist.

       Fuchs is also the author of AFRICAN DECAMERON: FOLKTALES FROM
CENTRAL AFRICA, translated from the German edition of 1961 by Robert
Meister (New York, I. Oblensky, 1963, 203 p.), which presents tales
and oral traditions of peoples living in the Guera massif of Chad.

1982. Hugot, Pierre. LE TCHAD. Paris, Nouvelles Editions Latines, 1965.
           155 p. illus., map.

       A concise political, social, and economic survey of Chad from
its early history to the 1960's.

1983. Institut National Tchadien pour les Sciences Humaines. Etudes et
           documents Tchadiens [series]. 1967- Fort-Lamy.

The Institut was founded in Jan. 1961 as the Centre Tchadien pour les Sciences Humaines, and the name was changed to the present form in 1963. The director is the archaeologist and anthropologist Jean Paul Lebeuf. The Institut is at present engaged on an atlas, an archaeological map, a classification of ethnic groups, a codification of place names, and special ethnological studies.

1984. Kronenberg, Andreas. DIE TEDA VON TIBESTI. Horn-Wien, Verlag F. Berger, 1958. 160 p. 29 plates. (Wiener Beiträge zur Kulturgeschichte und Linguistik, Veröffentlichungen des Instituts für Völkerkunde der Universität Wien)

Bibliography: p. 148-154.

The Teda or Tibbu are an Islamized Negroid people of the Central Sahara who are scattered from the Fezzan southward to Lake Chad; their culture is in part nomadic, in part that of sedentary cultivators. The anthropologist-author had done fieldwork with the tribes and presents here a thorough and extensively documented account of rites, mores, clan structure, and culture history.

1985. Lebeuf, Annie M. D. LES POPULATIONS DU TCHAD (NORD DU 10e PARALLELE). Paris, Presses Universitaires de France, 1959. 130 p. illus. (Monographies ethnologiques africaines)

Bibliography: p. 119-124.

See note on the Monographies series, published for the International African Institute (nos. 980 and 1670). The present study covers the Saharan populations of northern Chad (Teda and Daza), those of the ancient kingdoms of Kanem, Kotoko, Boulala, Baguirmi, and Wadai (Ouadai), those termed Arabs, and regrouped peoples, whom the author classifies collectively as the Yedina, Kinga, and Dadjo.

1986. Lebeuf, Jean Paul, and A. Masson Detourbet. LA CIVILISATION DU TCHAD; SUIVI D'UNE ETUDE SUR LES BRONZES SAO, PAR RAYMOND LANTIER. Paris, Payot, 1950. 198 p. illus.

M. Lebeuf and his wife, the former Mlle. Masson Detourbet, are among the foremost scholars concerned with archaeological, anthropological, and sociological research on Chad. In 1962 he published a study of the remains of ancient civilizations, ARCHEOLOGIE TCHADIENNE: LES SAO DU CAMEROUN ET DU TCHAD (Paris, Hermann, 1962, 146 p., plates). Another of his works is a socio-demographic study, FORT-LAMY, TCHAD, A.E.F.: RAPPORT D'UNE ENQUETE PRELIMINAIRE DANS LES MILIEUX URBAINS DE LA FEDERATION (Paris, Editions de l'Union Française, 1954, 64 p., illus.).

Lebeuf's first expedition in search of the pre-Islamic Sao civilization below Lake Chad and along the Chari and Logone rivers was with the late director of the Musée de l'Homme, Marcel Griaule, whose book LES SAO LEGENDAIRES (Paris, Gallimard, 1943, 168 p.) is a classic of French Africanist archaeology.

1987. Le Cornec, Jacques. HISTOIRE POLITIQUE DU TCHAD DE 1900 A 1962. Paris, Librairie Générale de Droit et de Jurisprudence (R. Pichon et R. Durand-Auzias), 1963. 374 p. illus., maps, tables. (Bibliothèque constitutionnelle et de science politique, v. 4)

Bibliography: p. 321-329.

A detailed work on the political and legislative history of Chad, by a former administrator in the French territory. Expanded from a doctoral thesis, the book emphasizes the role of the chefferies in the political evolution of the country from its conquest by the French until independence.

1988. Le Rouvreur, Albert. SAHELIENS ET SAHARIENS DU TCHAD. Paris, Berger-Levrault, 1962. 467 p. illus., maps. (L'homme d'outre-mer, n.s. no. 5)

A broad study of the peoples of northern Chad and the neighboring semiarid regions of Niger, their country, history, ways of life, economic resources and needs, and development under French rule. The many tribes are grouped in two sets, the Sahelians (in semiarid country) and the Saharans (in true desert), and divided in each as sedentary, semisedentary, seminomad, and nomad. Among typical Sahelians are the Kanembou, Maba, and Kréda; among typical Saharans are the Kamadja, Téda-Tou, and Gaéda.

1989. Pias, J. LES SOLS DU MOYEN ET BAS LOGONE, DU BAS CHARI, DES REGIONS RIVERAINES DU LAC TCHAD ET DU BAHR EL GHAZAL. Paris, Office de la Recherche Scientifique et Technique Outre-Mer, 1963. 438 p.

Report of surveys of soils, geology, hydrology, vegetation, etc., of the river basins below Lake Chad, carried out by a scientific commission and basic to agricultural research and development in the region.

1990. Statistical Office of the European Communities. REPUBLIQUE DU TCHAD: ANNUAIRE, JAHRBUCH, YEARBOOK, 1962-1966. Bruxelles, 1968. 106 p. of tables (Associés: Statistique du commerce extérieur 1)

A statistical handbook on foreign commerce.

1991. Tubiana, Marie José. SURVIVANCES PREISLAMIQUES EN PAYS ZAGHAWA.
Paris, Institut d'Ethnologie, 1964. 228 p. illus., maps
(part fold.), geneal. tables. (Université de Paris, Travaux
et mémoires de l'Institut d'Ethnologie, v. 19)

Bibliography: p. 201-205.

A study of pagan beliefs and rituals persisting among the only
partially Islamized Zaghawa people.

The author has also collaborated with Joseph Tubiana on a
collection of 31 tales and two legends of the Zaghawa: CONTES
ZAGHAWA (Paris, Les Quatre Jeudis, 1962, 206 p., illus.).

1992. U.S. Department of the Interior. Office of Geography. CHAD:
OFFICIAL STANDARD NAMES APPROVED BY THE UNITED STATES BOARD
ON GEOGRAPHIC NAMES. Washington, U.S. Govt. Print. Off.,
May 1962. 232 p. map. (16,000 names) (Gazetteer no. 65)

See note on series, no. 484.

1993. Urvoy, Yves F. HISTOIRE DE L'EMPIRE DU BORNOU. Paris, Larose,
1949. 166 p. (Mémoires de l'IFAN, no. 7)

Authoritative study of the past civilizations of the western
Sudanic region, including a 12-page index of peoples and tribes
mentioned, many of whom are within the current boundaries of Chad.
(The present province of Bornu is in Northern Nigeria; the culture
area runs over into Niger also.)

CONGO-BRAZZAVILLE
(MIDDLE CONGO)

Bibliographies

1994. Bureau pour le Développement de la Production Agricole. REPERTOIRE
BIBLIOGRAPHIQUE: REPUBLIQUE DU CONGO-BRAZZAVILLE. Paris,
1965. 112 p. Processed.

Lists 867 works, including articles, arranged by subject
(economics, history, geography, culture, ethnosociology). There
is an author index.

1995. Jacquot, André. CATALOGUE DES PUBLICATIONS ET RAPPORTS DU SERVICE
       DES SCIENCES HUMAINES (1949-67). Brazzaville, Office de la
       Recherche Scientifique et Technique Outre-Mer (ORSTOM), 1968.
       91 p.

       A listing of published and unpublished books, articles, and
reports, etc., by 25 researchers and technicians associated with
the Centre ORSTOM at Brazzaville. Arrangement is alphabetical by
author, subject, and region. A most valuable series of monographs
is cited.

Reference Works

1996. Andersson, Efraim. CHURCHES AT THE GRASS-ROOTS: A STUDY IN CONGO-
       BRAZZAVILLE. Translated by Dorothea M. Barton. New York,
       Distributed in the U.S. by Friendship Press, 1968. 296 p.
       illus.

       Bibliography: p. 267-270.

1997. Balandier, Georges. DAILY LIFE IN THE KINGDOM OF THE KONGO FROM
       THE SIXTEENTH TO THE EIGHTEENTH CENTURY. Translated from the
       French by Helen Weaver. New York, Pantheon Books, 1968. 288 p.
       illus., plates, map.

       A well-written, popularized description of the ancient kingdom
of the Kongo after the arrival of the Portuguese. Balandier delves
into the religious, cultural, political, and economic life of the
people, discusses relations between the Africans and the Portuguese--
the ultimate disillusionment and conflict--and points out the
contemporary relevance of this historical study. The French
edition was published in 1965 by Hachette, Paris.

1998. Balandier, Georges. SOCIOLOGIE DES BRAZZAVILLES NOIRES. Paris,
       A. Colin, 1955. 274 p. illus. (Cahiers de la Fondation
       Nationale des Sciences Politiques, no. 67)

       Bibliography: p. 521-524.

       Analysis of Central African urbanization in the two centers
which have grown up around the small European capital city of the
former AEF.

       A recent study concerned with the situation of women in this
urban environment is J. F. Vincent's FEMMES AFRICAINES EN MILIEU
URBAIN (Paris, Office de la Recherche Scientifique et Technique

Outre-Mer, 1966, 287 p., illus.), based on surveys undertaken in the Brazzaville-Bacongo area. For another sociological work by Balandier, see his SOCIOLOGIE ACTUELLE DE L'AFRIQUE NOIRE (no. 1892), of which the third part (p. 285-487) is devoted to social changes among the Bakongo.

1999. Congo (Brazzaville). JOURNAL OFFICIEL DE LA REPUBLIQUE DU CONGO. no. 1- Oct. 1958- Brazzaville, Impr. Nationale. Semimonthly.

Among other official publications is the BULLETIN MENSUEL RAPIDE DE STATISTIQUE (1963-), issued by the Service National de la Statistique, des Etudes Démographiques et Economiques, and continuing a bulletin begun in 1957 under the agency's former name, Service de la Statistique.

2000. Devauges, Roland. LE CHOMAGE A BRAZZAVILLE EN 1957: ETUDE SOCIO-LOGIQUE. Paris, Office de la Recherche Scientifique et Technique Outre-Mer, 1958. 258 p. (Documents du Conseil Supérieur des Recherches Sociologiques Outre-Mer)

Sociological study of unemployment in the crowded African suburb of Poto-Poto near Brazzaville, based on questionnaires and interviews. This complements the earlier work of Balandier (no. 1998, above).

2001. France. Direction de la Documentation. LA REPUBLIQUE DU CONGO. Paris, 1960. 38 p. (Notes et études documentaires, no. 2732, Dec. 17, 1960).

Background study. See general note on this series, no. 1587.

2002. Lucas, Gerard. FORMAL EDUCATION IN THE CONGO-BRAZZAVILLE: A STUDY OF EDUCATIONAL POLICY AND PRACTICE. Stanford, Calif., Comparative Education Center, School of Education, Stanford University, 1964. 287 p. illus. (Education as an Instrument of National Policy in Selected Newly Developing Areas, Phase 3)

A comprehensive description and thoughtful evaluation of the Congo's educational system. Policy and practice both during the French colonial period and in the postindependence years are examined in detail.

2003. Sautter, Gilles. DE L'ATLANTIQUE AU FLEUVE CONGO: UNE GEOGRAPHIE DU SOUS-PEUPLEMENT, REPUBLIQUE DU CONGO, REPUBLIQUE GABONAISE. Paris, La Haye, Mouton, 1966. 2 v. (1103 p.). illus., plates,

maps (part fold., part col.). (Le monde d'outre-mer passé
et présent, 1st ser.: Etudes, 25)

Bibliography: p. 1031-1075.

In this minute examination of underpopulation in the Congo-
Brazzaville and Gabon, the first part (p. 15-201) is devoted to
the distribution of population and plans for a regional (geographic
and ethnic) investigation. The second part (p. 205-1028) concerns
regional development and economic adjustment in six areas: the
Congo basin (Likouala-Mossaka, Alima, Nkéni), Stanley Pool, Boko,
plain of Niari, southern lakes and Bas-Ogooué, and Woleu-Ntem. The
excellent bibliography is in three sections: an essay on sources,
a listing by region, and a listing by subject. Both an index of
proper names and a subject index are included.

2004. Savorgnan de Brazza, Pierre, comte. BRAZZA EXPLORATEUR: L'OGOOUE,
1875-1879. [Edited] by Henri Brunschwig, with the collaboration of
Jean Glénisson and others. Paris, La Haye, Mouton, 1966. 219 p.
fold. map. (Documents pour servir à l'histoire de l'Afrique
équatoriale française, 2d ser.: Brazza et la fondation du
Congo français, 1)

Bibliographical footnotes.

For annotation, see no. 2022.

2005. Soret, Marcel. LES KONGO NORD-OCCIDENTAUX. Avec la collaboration
d'André Jacquot pour les questions de linguistique. Paris,
Presses Universitaires de France, 1959. 144 p. illus.
(Monographies ethnologiques africaines)

Bibliography: p. 117-139.

One of the French series of the International African Institute's
Ethnographical Survey of Africa, this study is by a specialist on
demography and ethnology of Equatorial Africa. The peoples surveyed
in the monograph (following the pattern of the series, for which see
nos. 980 and 1670) are on both banks of the Congo, chiefly in the
former AEF. The sources in the long bibliography include Belgian
studies, but those of the French regions predominate. M. Soret has
also published several ethnic maps of AEF (Brazzaville, Secrétariat
Général de l'AEF, 1957).

2006. U.S. Department of the Interior. Office of Geography. REPUBLIC
OF CONGO (BRAZZAVILLE): OFFICIAL STANDARD NAMES APPROVED
BY THE UNITED STATES BOARD ON GEOGRAPHIC NAMES. Washington,
U.S. Govt. Print. Off., Mar. 1962. 109 p. map. (7,700 names)
(Gazetteer no. 61)

See note on series, no. 484.

2007. Vennetier, Pierre. GEOGRAPHIE DU CONGO-BRAZZAVILLE. Paris,
Gauthier-Villars, 1966. 169 p. illus., fold. map in front,
diagrs., tables. (Centre d'Enseignement Supérieur, Brazzaville, Publications)

Bibliography: p. 117-125.

Covered are structural geology, climate, hydrology, vegetation,
soils, population, habitat, traditional rural activities, modern
economic rural activities, commerce and industry, and problems of
development. Data given are generally current to 1964. The author
is director of research at the Office de la Recherche Scientifique
et Technique Outre-Mer (ORSTOM) and has had considerable research
experience in Congo-Brazzaville.

A more specialized study by Vennetier is his LES HOMMES ET
LEUR ACTIVITE DANS LE NORD DU CONGO-BRAZZAVILLE (Paris, ORSTOM,
1965, 296 p., illus., plates, maps; Cahiers de l'ORSTOM, Sciences
humaines, v. 2, no. 1).

2008. Wagret, Jean-Michel. HISTOIRE ET SOCIOLOGIE POLITIQUES DE LA
REPUBLIQUE DU CONGO (BRAZZAVILLE). Paris, Librairie Générale
de Droit et de Jurisprudence (R. Pichon et R. Durand-Auzias),
1963. 250 p. (Bibliothèque constitutionnelle et de science
politique, v. 3)

Bibliography: p. 227-231.

An authoritative work by a political scientist, covering
history and social development of the country from precolonial
days to postindependence (Sept. 1962 is the last date recorded,
after the riots in Libreville that led to the ouster of Abbé
Youlou as President). The volume is in two parts. The first,
following a brief introductory statement on the geopolitical
framework of the Congo, briefly sketches political history. The
second is on "political sociology." The latter three sections:
Congolese society, political parties, and parapolitical forces
(including separatist churches, labor unions, youth movements,
etc.). A 15-page who's who of political personnel ends the volume.

GABON

Bibliography

2009. Weinstein, Brian. "Gabon: A Bibliographic Essay." AFRICANA
NEWSLETTER, v. 1, no. 4, Winter 1963: 4-9.

Description of basic books, articles, and periodicals.

Reference Works

2010. Balandier, Georges. SOCIOLOGIE ACTUELLE DE L'AFRIQUE NOIRE:
DYNAMIQUE DES CHANGEMENTS SOCIAUX EN AFRIQUE CENTRALE.
Paris, Presses Universitaires de France, 1955. xii, 510 p.
illus., maps. (Bibliothèque de sociologie contemporaine)

Bibliography: p. 505-508.

For full annotation, see no. 1892. In Part 2 of this work
(p. 75-281) Balandier discusses social changes among the Fan
(Fang) people of Gabon.

2011. Botti, Marc, and Paul Vezinet. ENSEIGNEMENT AU GABON. Paris,
Société d'Etudes pour le Développement Economique et Social,
1965. 2 v. (351 p.).

Although the development of Gabon's educational system is
proceeding at a rapid pace, a number of obstacles are evident--
overcrowded classrooms, insufficient professional staff, etc.
The authors (one an economist, the other an educator) discusses
these problems and suggest some solutions.

2012. Charbonnier, François, ed. GABON, TERRE D'AVENIR. Paris,
Encyclopédie d'Outremer, 1957. 151 p. illus.

An informative popular survey. Following each descriptive
chapter (history, surface and vegetation, wild life, depopulation,
etc.) there is a well-chosen excerpt from one of the important
source works.

2013. Deschamps, Hubert Jules. QUINZE ANS DE GABON: LES DEBUTS DE
L'ETABLISSEMENT FRANCAIS, 1839-1853. Paris, Sociéte Française

d'Histoire d'Outre-Mer et librairie G. P. Maisonneuve et
Larose, 1965. 98 p. (Bibliothèque d'histoire d'outre-mer)
(Extract from LA REVUE FRANCAISE D'HISTOIRE D'OUTRE-MER,
1963, fasc. 180-181: p. 283-345; 1965, fasc. 186: p. 92-126.)

Bibliographical footnotes.

Survey of the early period of French settlement in Gabon.
Part 1 is a statement of sources; Part 2 presents a yearly chronology
of events from 1839 to 1853; and Part 3 discusses the people, the
French army and navy, public works, Protestant and Catholic missions,
slavery, and the economy.

2014. Deschamps, Hubert J. TRADITIONS ORALES ET ARCHIVES AU GABON:
CONTRIBUTION A L'ETHNO-HISTOIRE. Paris, Berger-Levrault,
1962. 172 p. illus., maps, tables. (L'homme d'outre-mer,
n.s. no. 6)

Bibliographies: p. 143-167.

Systematic review of the ethnohistory of the various peoples
and groups of Gabon according to the oral traditions given the
author by informants of each tribe. Insofar as possible the factors
explained are name and linguistic relationships, origins, slavery
and commerce, crafts, social institutions (a very sketchy outline),
and religion and magic. Other features are mentioned where and as
available. This survey fills 140 pages; then a second part (p. 143-
155) contains a listing of archives. An appendix (p. 161-167) is
a biobibliography of the grand old man of Gabonese literature, the
Abbé Raponda Walker (his books, papers in the vernacular, and
articles).

2015. France. Direction de la Documentation. LA REPUBLIQUE GABONAISE.
Paris, 1961. 56 p. (Notes et etudes documentaires, no. 2795,
July 10, 1961)

See general notes on this series, no. 1587.

2016. Gabon. JOURNAL OFFICIEL DE LA REPUBLIQUE DU GABON. 1959-
Libreville, Impr. Nationale.

Other official documents continued since independence include
the JOURNAL DES DEBATS, issued weekly during sessions, and the
BULLETIN MENSUEL DE STATISTIQUE of the Service des Statistiques.

2017. Gabon. Ministère de l'Information et du Tourisme. ANNUAIRE
NATIONAL 1966. Paris, Editions des Quatre Points Cardinaux,
1966. 184 p.

Provides basic data on the government, administrative organization, diplomatic corps, religion, economy, and tourism, and includes an "annuaire professionnel" of Libreville and Port Gentil.

A brochure explaining economic and social aspects and administrative organization at the beginning of the 1960's was issued by
the then Direction de l'Information: REALITES GABONAISES (Paris,
Diloutremer, 1960, 187 p., illus., maps, plans). An informative
booklet picturing Gabon's policy and economy was issued in an English
edition by the Gabon Chambre de Commerce, d'Agriculture, de
l'Industrie et des Mines, FLASH ON GABON (Libreville, 1962, 50 p.,
illus.). The Chambre de Commerce also publishes a REVUE MENSUELLE
and a mimeographed BULLETIN BIMENSUEL.

2018. Gabon. Ministère de l'Information et du Tourisme. GABON CONVER-
GENCE 80. Libreville, 1967. 219, [13] p. illus., plates,
col. maps, tables, diagrs., graphs.

Interwoven with a concise review of Gabon's past and present
economy is a forecast to 1980. The book begins with a comparison
of the economy with that of other developing countries, then discusses the economic sectors and the employment situation, evaluates
the economic effort of the Owendo-Belinga railroad, and concludes
with a prognostication for the Gabon of 1980. A resumé follows
each section and subsection of the book, and there is a small
glossary.

The current development plan is summed up by Gabon's Commissariat Général in RESUME DU PLAN DE DEVELOPPEMENT ECONOMIQUE ET
SOCIALE, PERIODE 1966-1971 (Monaco, Editions Paul Bory, 1966,
116 p., col. maps, tables, graphs), which constitutes a special
issue, edited by the Centre d'Information et de Documentation
Gabonaise, of ACTUALITES GABONAISES (no. 6-7, June-July 1966).
For an overview in English, see SURVEY OF ECONOMIC DEVELOPMENT IN
GABON (Washington, [U.S.] Joint Publications Research Service,
1968, 61 p., maps; Translations on Africa, no. 687), composed of
translations of selected excerpts from feature articles in EUROPE
FRANCE OUTREMER, no. 454, Nov. 1967.

2019. Lasserre, Guy. LIBREVILLE, LA VILLE ET SA REGION (GABON, A.E.F.):
ETUDE DE GEOGRAPHIE HUMAINE. Paris, A. Colin, 1958. 346 p.
illus., maps, diagr., tables. (Cahiers de la Fondation
Nationale des Sciences Politiques, no. 98)

Bibliography: p. 327-343.

This valuable study is in three parts. The first, "Présentation de Libreville," gives a geographical description of
the area, the European city, and African villages and a historical
account of the city's growth. The second part is on economic
activities--communications and links with the surrounding regions
and their rural societies, Libreville as the capital and port,
and the exploitation of the forests and wood industries. Last are
chapters on the European and African populations and the life of
Libreville and culture contacts therein.

2020. Neuhoff, Hans-Otto. GABUN: GESCHICHTE, STRUKTUR UND PROBLEME
       DER AUSFUHRWIRTSCHAFT EINES ENTWICKLUNGSLANDES. Berlin,
       New York, Springer-Verlag, 1967. xxii, 273 p. plates, maps,
       tables. (Afrika-Studien, no. 16)

       Bibliography: p. 216-246.

A detailed survey of Gabon's export commodities and of the
economic problems and prospects of this developing country.
Separate sections deal with the products of the land (cacao,
coffee, and palm oil), forests, and mountains (minerals), and a
good geographical background is provided. The extensive categorized
bibliography lists works through mid-1965.

2021. Sautter, Gilles. DE L'ATLANTIQUE AU FLEUVE CONGO: UNE GEOGRAPHIE
       DU SOUS-PEUPLEMENT, REPUBLIQUE DU CONGO, REPUBLIQUE GABONAISE.
       Paris, La Haye, Mouton, 1966. 2 v. 1103 p. illus., plates,
       maps (part fold., part col.). (Le monde d'outre-mer passé et
       présent, 1st ser.: Etudes, 25)

       Bibliography: p. 1031-1075.

       See no. 2003 for annotation.

2022. Savorgnan de Brazza, Pierre, comte. BRAZZA EXPLORATEUR: L'OGOOUE,
       1875-1879. [Edited] by Henri Brunschwig, with the collaboration
       of Jean Glénisson and others. Paris, La Haye, Mouton, 1966.
       219 p. fold. map. (Documents pour servir à l'histoire de
       l'Afrique équatoriale française, 2d ser.: Brazza et la fonda-
       tion du Congo français, 1)

       Bibliographical footnotes.

A valuable volume of previously unpublished archival material
on the first of Brazza's three explorations of the Ogooué River.
A brief biographical introduction, which emphasizes the French
government's unwillingness to finance Brazza's expedition, is
followed by two main parts. The first consists of Brazza's
communications (1874-78) with officials of the French navy concerning the organization of the expedition. Part 2 is comprised
of his lengthy report (dated Aug. 30, 1879) to the Ministère de
la Marine after his return to France. This last document, well
complemented with substantive and bibliographic footnotes, first
describes the regions explored and then gives an account of the
voyage during which the Ogooué basin and a part of the Congo basin
were explored. Included is an index with descriptive notes preceding
page numbers.

2023. Société d'Etudes pour le Développement Economique et Social. ETUDE
ECONOMIQUE DU CHEMIN DE FER OWENDO-BELINGA. Paris, SEDES,
1965. 14 v. maps, tables, graphs.

Prepared with the aid of a special United Nations fund, this
is the record of a full-scale economic survey undertaken to ascertain
the most practical route for the Owendo-Belinga railway. Each sector
of Gabon's economy is thoroughly covered, with projections to 1980.
Representative volumes are:

Vol. I.   ECONOMIE FORESTIERE: SITUATION DES EXPLOITATIONS
ET DES INDUSTRIES FORESTIERES EN 1962. By
P. Bellouard. 145 p.

Vol. II.   ECONOMIE FORESTIERE: PERSPECTIVE DE DEVELOPPEMENT.
by P. Bellouard. 160 p.

Vol. III.   ETUDE DU MARCHE DES BOIS TROPICAUX. By P. Bellouard.
258 p.

Vol. IX.   ECONOMIE DES TRANSPORTS. By J. H. Payen. 127 p.

Vol. XI.   EMPLOI ET FORMATION PROFESSIONNELLE. 296 p.

Vol. XIV.   SYNTHESE. 132 p.

2024. Trilles, H. LES PYGMEES DE LA FORET EQUATORIALE. Paris, Bloud &
Gay, 1932. xiv, 530 p. (Anthropos; collection internationale
de monographies ethnologiques, v. 3, fasc. 4)

"Index bibliographique": p. 517-521.

The text of a course given at the Institut Catholique de
Paris by the missionary anthropologist, Father Trilles. This
is one of the longest and most renowned studies of the Negrillos,
among whom the author worked in Gabon. (They also live in the
forests of Congo-Brazzaville.) The bibliographic index gives
titles only, the full references being in the voluminous footnotes.

2025. U.S. Department of the Interior. Office of Geography. GABON:
OFFICIAL STANDARD NAMES APPROVED BY THE UNITED STATES BOARD
ON GEOGRAPHIC NAMES. Washington, U.S. Govt. Print. Off.,
Mar. 1962. 113 p. map. (8,000 names) (Gazetteer no. 59)

See note on series, no. 484.

2026. Walker, André Raponda. NOTES D'HISTOIRE DU GABON. With an
introduction, maps, and notes by Marcel Soret. Montpellier,
Impr. Charité, 1960. 158 p. ports., maps. (Mémoires de
l'Institut d'Etudes Centrafricaines, Brazzaville, no. 9)

Includes bibliographies.

The first part of Abbé Walker's study is devoted to biographies
of several nineteenth-century Gabonese chiefs and kings; the second
to the history of some 15 tribes. Soret's helpful introduction
provides a classified grouping of the tribal peoples as well as a
chronological resumé of Gabonese history (1300-1929).

2027. Walker, André Raponda, and Roger Sillans. LES PLANTES UTILES
DU GABON. Paris, Lechevalier, 1961. 614 p. illus., plates,
map. (Collection "Encyclopédie biologique," no. 56)

"Rappel bibliographique": p. 153-154, 469-478.

Monumental inventory comprising all plants of the rich forests
of Gabon, over 8,000 species, with vernacular names as well as full
scientific descriptions, bibliography, tables, and indexes.

The first Mémoire published by the Institut d'Etudes Centrafricaines was on this subject: LES LEGUMINEUSES DU GABON, by Father
François Pellegrin (Brazzaville, 1948, 284 p., plates).

2028. Walker, André Raponda, and Roger Sillans. RITES ET CROYANCES DES
PEUPLES DU GABON: ESSAI SUR LES PRATIQUES RELIGIEUSES D'AUTRE-
FOIS ET D'AUJOURD'HUI. Paris, Présence Africaine, 1962. xx,
377 p. illus., plates, map, music. (Enquêtes et études)

Bibliography: p. 295-313.

A three-part description of Gabonese religious practices: the
agents and accessories of the rites, ritual practices, and initiation
rites. The bibliography lists both archival and printed sources.
There is a lengthy index.

2029. Weinstein, Brian G. GABON: NATION-BUILDING ON THE OGOOUE.
        Cambridge, Mass., and London, M.I.T. Press, 1966. xiv, 287 p.
        illus., map (on lining paper).

        Bibliography: p. 257-259.

        An examination of the forces acting on Gabon and its people
from without and from within, pushing the country both toward and
away from national consolidation. Following a brief analysis of
nation-building in general, Weinstein describes the motive force
in Gabonese nation-building (an account of the French and the Fan
people), and then considers national consolidation through shared
experience (the development of a national culture, history, and
belief system) and through decision-making. In concluding his
sympathetic account, he admits that there is no way to predict the
future, remarking that a former colonial governor estimated that it
would take at least a thousand years to form a developed nation,
whereas former President Mba stated that five years would be
sufficient. There is an excellent, briefly annotated bibliography.
For a more recent account of the politics and government of Gabon,
see Charles Darlington, AFRICAN BETRAYAL (New York, D. McKay Co.,
1968, 359 p., illus., map).

CHAPTER 36

OTHER FRENCH-SPEAKING AREAS

MALAGASY REPUBLIC (MADAGASCAR)

Atlas

2030. Association des Géographes de Madagascar. ATLAS DE MADAGASCAR.
     Tananarive, Bureau pour le Développement de la Production Agri-
     cole and Centre de l'Institut Géographique National à Madagas-
     car, 1969. illus., maps (part col.). 42 x 32 cm.

     A collection of 60 maps: one on location, 13 on human geography,
     16 on physical geography, 5 on industry and resources, 9 on rural
     matters, 9 on transportation and communication, 5 on miscellaneous
     aspects, one on regional divisions, and one on zones of development.

Bibliographies

2031. Duignan, Peter. MADAGASCAR (THE MALAGASY REPUBLIC): A LIST OF
     MATERIALS IN THE AFRICAN COLLECTIONS OF STANFORD UNIVERSITY AND
     THE HOOVER INSTITUTION ON WAR, REVOLUTION, AND PEACE. Stanford,
     Calif., Hoover Institution, Stanford University, 1962. 25 p.
     (Hoover Institution Bibliographical Series, no. 9)

     Helpful guide to some of the significant literature on Madagas-
     car, including French and Malagasy government documents and serials,
     newspapers, books and monographs, and microfilmed British documents
     (confidential prints of the Colonial Office and Foreign Office).
     Limited to the holdings of the Stanford University libraries, it
     contains 257 items, as well as an author and title index.

2032. Fleur, Guy. BIBLIOGRAPHIE DE MADAGASCAR. Paris, Fondation Nationale
des Sciences Politiques, 1962. 42 p. (Extract from REVUE FRAN-
CAISE DE SCIENCE POLITIQUE, v. 12, no. 4, Dec. 1962)

Systematic bibliography of works published on Madagascar since
1940.

A nine-page bibliography on Madagascar appears in SOUTH-EAST
CENTRAL AFRICA AND MADAGASCAR, a volume in the International African
Institute's African Bibliography Series (see no. 970).

2033. Grandidier, Guillaume. BIBLIOGRAPHIE DE MADAGASCAR. Paris, Comité
de Madagascar, etc., 1906-57. 3 v.

The listing in Vol. I of this comprehensive bibliography by a
French specialist on Madagascar covers the literature from the
earliest Portuguese records in 1506 to 1904; it is in two parts, the
first alphabetically arranged by author, the second by anonymous
works and periodical articles. Vol. II, issued as a volume of the
BIBLIOGRAPHIE GENERALE DES COLONIES FRANCAISES by G. Grandidier and
E. Joucla, was published in 1935 by the Société d'Editions Géographiques, Maritimes et Coloniales and covers writings from 1904 to
1933. A third volume, published in 1957 by the Institut de Recherche
Scientifique de Madagascar and covering writings from 1934 to 1955,
opens with a tribute to the author, who died in 1956. Vol. II is
arranged like Vol. I, but in Vol. III anonyms and authors' names are
together in alphabetical arrangement. All have author and subject
indexes, referring to the consecutively numbered references, which
in the three volumes amount to 23,003 items.

2034. Jaeglé, Eugène. ESSAI DE BIBLIOGRAPHIE: MADAGASCAR ET DEPENDANCES,
1905-1927. Tananarive, 1927. 213 p. illus.

Long list of titles, including many government publications, and
content analysis of journals (extract from the BULLETIN ECONOMIQUE DE
MADAGASCAR). The author was chief of the Bureau de Documentation of
Madagascar.

2035. Madagascar. Université. Bibliothèque. BIBLIOGRAPHIE ANNUELLE DE
MADAGASCAR. 1964- Prepared under the direction of Marie Simone
de Nucé and Juliette Ratsimandrava. Tananarive, Bibliothèque
Universitaire et Bibliothèque Nationale, 1966-

1964 ed., 262 p. (2,788 entries); 1965 ed. (1968), 221 p. (2,067
entries).

An excellent bibliography listing books, monographs, government
publications, journal and newspaper articles, and maps and atlases

published during the relevant year both in Madagascar and abroad, as well as processed materials and theses. Arrangement is by systematic (decimal) classification, with entries listed under some 300 headings. Book reviews are cited for some of the references. There is an index authors, titles of anonymous works, and new periodicals, plus, in the 1965 edition, an index of the classified headings.

2036. Molet, Louis. "Bibliographie critique récente sur Madagascar." CANADIAN JOURNAL OF AFRICAN STUDIES, v. 1, no. 1, Mar. 1967: 51-63.

A systematic and evaluative listing of some 130 important publications (excluding articles) on Madagascar, all of them French titles except for eight in a section on English works. Selected on the basis of their accessibility, the references cover the period from the 1940's on. Included is an index of authors.

2037. Paris. Bibliothèque Nationale. Département des Périodiques. PERIODIQUES MALGACHES: LISTE PROVISOIRE DES COLLECTIONS CON-SERVEES A LA BIBLIOTHEQUE NATIONALE, 1866-1960. By Germaine Razafintsalama. Paris, 1964. 106 l.

Alphabetical title list of periodicals from Madagascar held in the Bibliothèque Nationale. In all, 753 serials are listed, with, for most, title, address, periodicity, beginning date, and holdings in the library. The catalogue is preceded by a six-page subject classification by title (Presse politique et information, Sciences, etc.).

2038. U.S. Library of Congress. General Reference and Bibliography Division. MADAGASCAR AND ADJACENT ISLANDS: A GUIDE TO OFFICIAL PUBLICATIONS. Compiled by Julian W. Witherell, African Section. Washington, U.S. Govt. Print. Off., 1965. xiii, 58 p.

Contains 927 entries and numerous subentries covering publications of French administrations in Madagascar, the Comoro Islands, and Réunion, those of British administrations in Mauritius and Seychelles, selected documents issued by France and Great Britain relating to their respective territories, and official publications by individuals and government-sponsored organizations. The terminal date for entries in the Madagascar section is Oct. 1958 (the date of the establishment of the Malagasy Republic); for the other islands, entries have been continued to 1964. Official publications received by the Library of Congress are the basis of the bibliography, supplemented by information on the holdings of other American

libraries reporting to the NATIONAL UNION CATALOG and by titles
recorded in bibliographies issued by the governments of Madagascar,
Mauritius, France, and Great Britain. Under each dependency,
entries are arranged alphabetically by author and title, except
that census reports and material on development planning are grouped
by subject. An author and subject index is provided. Locations in
American libraries or sources of identification are cited for all
entries. This is the eleventh in the Library's series of guides to
documents of African governments.

Reference Works

2039. Académie Malgache, Tananarive. Mémoires. fasc. 1- Tananarive, G.
      Pitot de la Beaujardière, 1926- plates, maps, diagrs. Irregu-
      lar.

      The monographic volumes of the Mémoires series of the Académie
deal variously with history, sociology, anthropology, archaeology,
natural sciences, and other disciplines relating to Madagascar. The
inside cover pages of each number carry the full list of titles in
the series. A typical contribution is fasc. no. 40, by Louis Michel,
MOEURS ET COUTUMES DES BARA (1957, 192 p.). The Académie also has
a BULLETIN (1902-, annual [irregular]), in which proceedings and
the papers of the members appear, and in 1939 the COLLECTION DE
DOCUMENTS CONCERNANT MADAGASCAR ET LES PAYS VOISINS was begun.

2040. BULLETIN DE MADAGASCAR. no. 1- Jan. 1950- Tananarive, Impr.
      Nationale. illus., maps. Monthly.

      Originally published twice a month by the Service Général de
l'Information of the Haut Commissariat de la Republique Française à
Madagascar et Dépendances, now issued by the Direction de l'Information. The journal has grown from 48 pages to around a hundred per
issue. Malagasy life, from agriculture to linguistics to scientific
research, is given attention in scholarly articles, with occasional
emphasis on agricultural and economic subjects. Bibliographical
material is often included.

2041. Callet, François. HISTOIRE DES ROIS. Translation of TANTARAN'NY
      ANDRIANA by G. S. Chapus and E. Ratsimba. Tananarive, Académie
      Malgache, 1953-58. 4 v. (Académie Malgache, Collection de
      documents concernant Madagascar et les pays voisins, 4)

      A classic work of Merina idiom and an unequalled source of
oral tradition, according to Professor Raymond Kent.

2042. Chevalier, Louis. MADAGASCAR: POPULATIONS ET RESSOURCES. Paris, Presses Universitaires de France, 1952. 212 p. maps, tables. (Institut National d'Etudes Démographiques, Travaux et documents, cahier no. 15)

Bibliography: p. 208-212.

Much-quoted study by a population expert who went to Madagascar with a mission sent to consider the island as a possible place for settlement of European refugees. Use was made of local records of administrative districts and other unpublished sources in a careful and comprehensive assessment of demographic factors, resources, and agricultural techniques and limitations.

2043. Condominas, Georges. FOKON'OLONA ET COLLECTIVITES RURALES EN IMERINA. Paris, Berger-Levrault, 1961. 234 p. maps. (L'homme d'outre-mer, n.s. no. 4)

Bibliography: p. 231-234.

The ancient system of the clan community in the Malagasy villages had largely been broken up by the Merina despotism of the late eighteenth and nineteenth centuries and was being revived by the French authorities in the form of cooperatives following the constitution of 1946 and the loi-cadre of 1957. This intensive sociological study was made under auspices of ORSTOM. Approximately half the text is devoted to background history, the second half to present-day Merina society. The work is basic for the renovation of local life now being undertaken by the republic.

2044. Decary, Raymond. MOEURS ET COUTUMES DES MALGACHES. Paris, Payot, 1951. 280 p. illus. (Collection de documents et de témoignages pour servir à l'histoire de notre temps)

M. Decary, former chief colonial administrator in Madagascar, explains Malagasy ways and manners, illustrating them with his own drawings--family and social life, material culture, methods of work, industry and trade, games and amusements, customary law, sorcery and witch doctor medicine, religious ideas, and the prominent cult of the dead. The last chapter touches on social "evolution" in the half-century of European influence.

Among M. Decary's many other writings are the following:

a) L'ANDROY (EXTREME SUD DE MADAGASCAR): ESSAI DE MONOGRAPHIE REGIONALE. Paris, Société d'Editions Géographiques, Maritimes et Coloniales, 1930-33. 2 v.

A comprehensive study of the physical and human
geography, history, and civilization of the extreme south
of the island, inhabited by the most primitive of the cattle-
raising tribes, the last to come under French control.

b) LA FAUNE MALGACHE: SON ROLE DANS LES CROYANCES ET LES USAGES
        INDIGENES. Paris, Payot, 1950. 236 p. illus.
        Bibliothèque scientifique

    Bibliography: p. 231-234.

    An interesting combination of natural history and folklore.

c) L'HABITAT A MADAGASCAR. Pau, Impr. Marrimpouey Jeune, 1958.
        80 p. illus.

    A study of Malagasy house structure.

d) L'ILE NOSY BE DE MADAGASCAR: HISTOIRE D'UNE COLONISATION.
        Paris, Editions Maritimes et d'Outre-Mer, 1960. 225 p.

    A chapter in the early history of French occupation,
    written largely from study of unpublished documents in the
    archives of Madagascar and Paris.

2045. Deschamps, Hubert J. LES ANTAISAKA. Tananarive, Pilot de la
        Beaujardière, 1936. 220 p. illus., maps.

    Technical ethnological study of the Antaisaka people of the
    southeast coast of Madagascar, analyzing human geography, rites and
    customs, and the history of a tribe of primitive fishers, hunters,
    and rice farmers. Professor Deschamps, a former colonial governor
    of French Somaliland, is now at the University of Paris.

    M. Deschamps is the author as well of the following works on
    Africa:

    HISTOIRE DE MADAGASCAR. Paris, Berger-Levrault, 1960. 348 p.
        illus. (Mondes d'outre-mer)

        Bibliography: p. 317-325.

        Up-to-date and authoritative history from the obscure
    origins of the island to the immediate present of the Malagasy
    Republic.

    LES PIRATES A MADAGASCAR AU XVIIe ET XVIIIe SIECLES. Paris,
        Berger-Levrault, 1949. 244 p. (Histoires d'outre-mer,
        no. 1)

Interesting account of one of the picturesque episodes in the history of Madagascar, the pirate settlements of the seventeenth and eighteenth centuries.

Another of Professor Deschamps's more recent writings on Madagascar is LES MIGRATIONS INTERIEURES PASSEES ET PRESENTES A MADAGASCAR (Paris, Berger-Levrault, 1959, 278 p., illus., 30 maps; L'homme d'outre-mer, n.s. no. 1).

2046. ETUDES DE DROIT AFRICAIN ET DE DROIT MALGACHE. Collective work published under the direction of Jean Poirier. Paris, Editions Cujas, 1965. 529 p. maps, tables. (Etudes malgaches, 16)

Includes bibliographies.

Twenty-one diverse juridical, sociological, and ethnological studies by Belgian, British, French, and Malagasy specialists. Nine of the essays are devoted to the Malagasy Republic, and one includes a glossary of Malagasy words.

2047. Etudes malgaches. v. 1- Tananarive, Faculté des Lettres et des Sciences Humaines, Université de Madagascar, 1960- Irregular.

A solid series published by Editions Cujas, Paris, and including the subseries MADAGASCAR: REVUE DE GEOGRAPHIE, which is produced by the Faculté's Laboratoire de Géographie. By 1966, 16 volumes had appeared, most of them devoted to juridical or geographical studies.

2048. France. Direction de la Documentation. LES INVESTISSEMENTS ET LES PROBLEMES DE DEVELOPPEMENT DANS L'ECONOMIE DE LA REPUBLIQUE MALGACHE. Paris, 1960. 66 p. (Notes et études documentaires, no. 2707, Oct. 13, 1960)

_____. _____. LA REPUBLIQUE MALGACHE. Paris, 1960. 61 p. (Notes et études documentaires, no. 2737, Dec. 23, 1960).

Background surveys. See general note on this series, no. 1587.

2049. Gallieni, Joseph S. GALLIENI PACIFICATEUR: ECRITS COLONIAUX DE GALLIENI. Choix de textes et notes, par Hubert Deschamps et Paul Chauvet. Paris, Presses Universitaires de France, 1949. 382 p. maps.

Reports, papers, and speeches of the great general whose career in subduing, reconciling, and administering France's colonial empire included Senegal and Sudan (1876-88), Tonkin (1892-96), and, most notably, Madagascar (1896-1905). The material on Madagascar takes up more than half the text (p. 169-373).

A good account of Gallieni's work in Madagascar is that of General Jean Charbonneau, GALLIENI A MADAGASCAR (Paris, Nouvelles Editions Latines, 1950, 189 p.; Bibliothèque de l'Union française), based on documents and unpublished material gathered by Gallieni's daughter-in-law.

2050. Gendarme, René. L'ECONOMIE DE MADAGASCAR: DIAGNOSTIC ET PERSPECTIVES DE DEVELOPPEMENT. Paris, Editions Cujas, 1960. 209 p. illus., maps (1 fold. col.), charts, tables. (Etudes malgaches, no. 1)

Survey by a professor of the Institut des Hautes Etudes de Tananarive, providing a scientific basis for the work of the Centre d'Etudes Economiques which is planning for the economic development of the new republic. The first part presents the Malagasy position in world economy, features of underdevelopment, and fundamental handicaps, including those of a sociocultural and a political nature. The second part analyzes plans for development along all lines.

2051. Gennep, Arnold van. ...MADAGASCAR: ETUDE DESCRIPTIVE ET THEORIQUE. Paris, E. Leroux, 1904. 362 p.

See also his TABOU ET TOTEMISME A MADAGASCAR (Paris, 1904), still the best work of early anthropology.

2052. Grandidier, Alfred. COLLECTION DES OUVRAGES ANCIENS CONCERNANT MADAGASCAR. Edited by Alfred and Guillaume Grandidier. Paris, Comité de Madagascar, 1903-20. 9 v.

_____, et al. HISTOIRE PHYSIQUE, NATURELLE ET POLITIQUE DE MADAGASCAR. Paris, Impr. Nationale, 1875- (v. 39, 1955)

Great names connected with the study of Madagascar are those of the Grandidiers, père et fils. Alfred Grandidier, geographer and traveler, pioneered in explorations and mapping in the center and south of the Grand Island in 1865-70, read its ancient history, and studied its people. The monumental series of the HISTOIRE PHYSIQUE, carried on for many years after his death in 1921 with the cooperation of leading natural scientists, was edited with the aid of his son, Guillaume. The first volume, HISTOIRE DE LA GEOGRAPHIE (1875-92, 1 v. of text, 2 v. of maps), was by Alfred; Vol. IV, ETHNOGRAPHIE, was by Alfred and Guillaume (2 v. in 1908, v. 3 in 1917, v. 4, by Guillaume, in 1928). Vol. V, HISTOIRE POLITIQUE ET COLONIALE, was by Guillaume. The COLLECTION DES OUVRAGES ANCIENS, in the

editing of which father and son collaborated, brought together
texts of European travelers relative to Madagascar from 1500 to 1800.

2053. Grandidier, Guillaume. LE MYRE DE VILERS, DUCHESNE, GALLIENI:
QUARANTE ANNEES DE L'HISTOIRE DE MADAGASCAR, 1880-1920. Paris,
Société d'Editions Géographiques, Maritimes et Coloniales,
1923. 252 p.

Authoritative account of the French conquest, pacification, and
organization of Madagascar.

2054. Institut de Recherches Scientifiques de la République Malgache,
Tananarive. Mémoires: Sér. C, Sciences humaines. v. 1-
[Paris] 1952- illus., maps, diagrs.

This series of Mémoires of the prominent Institut (variant name:
Institut de Recherche Scientifique de Madagascar)--other series are
concerned with natural sciences--began with a careful statistical
study of the capital city, TANANARIVE: ETUDE D'ECONOMIE URBAINE, by
H. Fournier (1952, illus.; v. 1, fasc. 1, p. 29-157).

For a well-received, profusely illustrated general work in
French, see Claude Janicot's MADAGASCAR (Lausanne, Ed. Rencontre,
1964, 192 p., illus. [part col.], col. maps; L'atlas des voyages,
31).

2055. Kent, Raymond K. FROM MADAGASCAR TO THE MALAGASY REPUBLIC. New York,
Praeger, 1962. 182 p. illus. (Books That Matter)

Bibliography: p. 160-180.

Condensed general study, by an American scholar. It covers
geography and demography and goes on to history before the French
conquest in the 1880's and then the colonial period.

2056. Madagascar. Haut Commissariat de la République Française à Madagascar et Dépendances. ANNUAIRE STATISTIQUE DE MADAGASCAR: Vol. I,
1938-1951. Tananarive, 1953. 186 p.

A long-term statistical report. For other statistical material
see the Library of Congress list of official publications, no. 2038.

2057. MADAGASCAR A TRAVERS SES PROVINCES: ASPECT GEOGRAPHIQUE, HISTORIQUE,
TOURISTIQUE, ECONOMIQUE ET ADMINISTRATIF DU TERRITOIRE. Paris,
Alépée, 1954. 402 p. illus., ports., maps. (Les documents
de France)

Systematic survey from official sources of geography, history, economy, and administration of the five provinces, Tananarive, Fianarantsoa, Tamatave, Majunga, and Tuléar.

2058.   Malagasy Republic. ANNUAIRE NATIONAL DE LA REPUBLIQUE MALGACHE.
        Tananarive, B.P. 616, 1968. 313 p. illus. (part col.), ports.,
        maps (part col.).

        A directory in three sections. The first is made up of the
Annuaire administratif (including foreign diplomatic representation
in the republic). This is followed by a section on the economy
(répertoire corporatif, professionnel et syndical des principales
entreprises) and one on tourism and history. Advertising is included.

        A complementary volume is ANNUAIRE DU MONDE POLITIQUE, DIPLO-
MATIQUE ET DE LA PRESSE DE MADAGASCAR, 1965-1966 (Tananarive, Ed.
Madagasikara, 1965, 104 p.). See also the Annuaire Noria AFRIQUE NOIRE
[ET] OCEAN INDIEN (no. 1567).

2059.   Malagasy Republic. Commissariat Général au Plan. ECONOMIE MALGACHE:
        EVOLUTION, 1950-1960. Tananarive, Impr. Nationale, 1962. 277 p.
        illus., maps.

        A white book on the economic development of the Malagasy
Republic between 1950 and 1960. It covers all aspects of the economy:
commercial, agricultural, industrial, mines, energy, transportation,
investments, etc. There are numerous maps and charts.

        For a description of the republic's recent five-year development
plan, see the Commissariat's PLAN QUINQUENNAL, 1964-1968 (Tananarive,
Impr. Nationale, 1964, 253 p., tables).

2060.   Malagasy Republic. Institut National de la Statistique et de la
        Recherche Economique. INVENTAIRE SOCIO-ECONOMIQUE 1964-1968.
        Tananarive, 1969. 2 v.

2061.   Malagasy Republic. Service Géologique. LES RESSOURCES MINERALES
        DE MADAGASCAR. By Henri Besairie. Tananarive, Impr. Nationale,
        1960. 343 p. illus., ports., maps, tables. (Documentation,
        no. 151)

        Overall survey of the mineral wealth of Madagascar. An abbre-
viated version of this work was also published in the valuable series
Annales géologiques de Madagascar (1961, 116 p.; fasc. no. 30).

        For other official publications see the Library of Congress list,
no. 2038.

2062. Mannoni, Dominique O. PROSPERO AND CALIBAN: THE PSYCHOLOGY OF
        COLONIZATION. Translated by Pamela Powesland. New York,
        Praeger, 1956. 218 p. (Books That Matter)

        2d ed. (a reprint, with added Author's Note), 1964, 218 p.

        Bibliography: p. 210-214.

        A much-quoted psychoanalytical study which appeared in French
        in 1950 under the title PSYCHOLOGIE DE LA COLONISATION. The concept
        is general for colonial societies. Using the Prospero-Caliban and
        Crusoe-Man Friday relationships as symbols and Madagascar as case
        history, the author argues that the primitive emerging from the
        security of the old static, ancestor-worshiping society attaches
        himself as a dependent to the European; the latter, like Prospero,
        finds his own "inferiority complex" reassured by the colonial
        situation. He explains the revolution of 1947-48 as ultimately due
        to the threat of abandonment which the Malagasy felt in the postwar
        gestures toward fuller self-government initiated in the French
        Union.

2063. Massiot, Michel. LES INSTITUTIONS POLITIQUES ET ADMINISTRATIVES DE
        LA REPUBLIQUE MALGACHE. Tananarive, Ecole Nationale de
        Promotion Sociale, Université de Madagascar, 1967. 136 p.
        illus. (Guides d'initiation active au développement, 3)

        A study guide for teachers to assist development goals.

2064. Minelle, Jean. L'AGRICULTURE A MADAGASCAR: GEOGRAPHIE, CLIMATOLOGIE,
        GEOLOGIE, CONDITIONS D'EXPLOITATION DES SOLS, BOTANIQUE MALGACHE,
        PRODUCTIONS AGRICOLES, COLONISATION ET PAYSANNAT AUTOCHTONE,
        POSSIBILITES AGRICOLES, CONJONCTURE ET ECONOMIE AGRICOLE, STATIS-
        TIQUES AGRICOLES. Paris, Librairie M. Rivière, 1959. 379 p.
        illus., tables.

        Bibliography: p. 371-375.

        Basic study by a specialist in tropical agriculture who worked
        in Madagascar for 25 years as an agronomist and had firsthand knowl-
        edge of all regions.

2065. Oliver, Samuel Pasfield. MADAGASCAR: AN HISTORICAL AND DESCRIPTIVE
        ACCOUNT OF THE ISLAND AND ITS FORMER DEPENDENCIES. London,
        Macmillan, 1886. 2 v. 569, 562 p. illus.

        Bibliography: v. 2, p. 233-259.

        This large comprehensive work, written just after the Franco-

Malagasy war of 1885 by which the French took over the island, covers
history, topography, natural history, economy, administration, and
most other aspects of Madagascar as known in the precolonial period.
The long bibliography cites works in French and English from the
earliest travels to contemporary documents.

2066.   Pascal, Roger. LA REPUBLIQUE MALGACHE: PACIFIQUE INDEPENDANCE.
        Paris, Berger-Levrault, 1965. 202 p. plates, ports. (Mondes
        d'outre-mer, sér.: Histoire)

        Bibliography: p. 190-196.

        In his book on the Malagasy Republic's road to independence,
the author divided his discussion into three parts--causes, means,
and effects. The political situation in 1895, nationalism, and
anticolonialism; the Brazzaville conference (1944), loi-cadre, and
French heritage; the internal situation (political, legal, economic,
cultural) and external relations--all are given consideration in the
three parts. Problems, needs, and prospects are outlined in a
conclusion. Appended material includes the preamble to the Malagasy
constitution and the final resolution of the congress of Tamatave
(1958).

2067.   Le peuple malgache: Monographies ethnologiques. Directed by Hubert
        Deschamps. Paris, Presses Universitaires de France, 1959-

        A series complementary to the Monographies ethnologiques
africaines of the International African Institute. No. 1 is LES
MALGACHES DU SUD-EST: ANTEMORO, ANTESAKA, ANTAMBAHOAKA, PEUPLES
DE FARAFANGANA (ANTEFASI, ZAFISORO, SAHAVOAI, SAHAFATRA), by Hubert
Deschamps and Suzanne Vianès (xii, 118 p., 2 plates, maps). It is
written more in essay style than the Ethnographic Survey volumes but
covers the same ground. Sketch maps show the distribution and
migrations of peoples in southeastern Madagascar.

2068.   Rabemananjara, Jacques. NATIONALISME ET PROBLEMES MALGACHES. Paris,
        Présence Africaine, 1959. 219 p.

        By a French-educated poet and writer, one of the leaders of
the nationalist revolt, formerly Minister of State for the National
Economy and since 1965 Minister of Agriculture, Land and Food. In
this volume he discusses his country and its aims, political,
cultural, and religious. A long final section, "Rythmes malgaches:
Chants et danses folkloriques," contains his poems used in radio
programs. M. Rabemananjara's short poems appear in most anthologies
of African literature. Of his longer works, the poetic drama LES
BOUTRIERS DE L'AURORE, a tragedy of Malagasy history, is perhaps the
best known (published by Présence Africaine, Paris, 1957, 231 p.).

2069. Rajemisa-Raolison, Régis. DICTIONNAIRE HISTORIQUE ET GEOGRAPHIQUE
         DE MADAGASCAR. Fianarantsoa, Librairie Ambozontany, 1966.
         383 p. maps, illus.

       By a distinguished author and official of Madagascar. This
most useful reference book has numerous charts, maps, and illustrations and includes valuable biographic sketches.

2070. Ralaimihoatra, Edouard. HISTOIRE DE MADAGASCAR: Vol. I, DES
         ORIGINES A LA FIN DU XIXeme SIECLE; Vol. II, LE XXe SIECLE.
         Tananarive, Société Malgache d'Edition, 1965-66. 2 v. 227,
         108 p. illus., ports., maps, geneal. tables, facsims.

       An outline of Madagascar's history.

2071. LA REVUE DE MADAGASCAR. 1933- Tananarive, Impr. Nationale (origin-
         ally Impr. Officielle). illus. (part. col.), plates. Quarterly.

       Lavishly illustrated official review of general coverage,
issued by the Service Général de l'Information.

2072. Robequain, Charles. MADAGASCAR ET LES BASES DISPERSEES DE L'UNION
         FRANCAISE: COMORES, REUNION, ANTILLES ET GUYANE, TERRES
         OCEANIENNES, COTE DES SOMALIS, SAINT-PIERRE ET MIQUELON, ILES
         AUSTRALES, TERRE ADELIE. Paris, Presses Universitaires de
         France, 1958. 586 p. illus., maps. (Pays d'outre-mer,
         colonies, empires, pays autonomes, 4th ser: Géographie de
         l'Union française, no. 3)

       Bibliography: p. 541-572.

       Comprehensive work in an authoritative series of physical and
economic geographies.

2073. Sibree, James. FIFTY YEARS IN MADAGASCAR: PERSONAL EXPERIENCES OF
         MISSION LIFE AND WORK. London, G. Allen & Unwin, 1924. 359 p.

       British interest in Madagascar was largely connected with
missionary work, which began in 1820 and had remarkable success in
the early years and a spectacular period of martyrdom during the
persecutions of Queen Ranavalona from 1835 to 1861. Mr. Sibree
himself went out to Madagascar in 1863, after the country had been
opened again to Christians, with the assignment of building four
"martyr memorial churches"; the money had been raised in England
through the efforts of the pioneer missionary, the Rev. William
Ellis, whose HISTORY OF MADAGASCAR (1838) and THREE VISITS TO
MADAGASCAR (1859) introduced the country to the English public.

Mr. Sibree devoted his life to the Madagascar mission field and in the 1890's wrote a number of books on the history and natural history of the island.

A French missionary history explaining the Catholic side of Christian effort in Madagascar was by Father Pierre Lhande, MADAGASCAR (Paris, Plon, 1932, 265 p.).

2074.   Stratton, Arthur. THE GREAT RED ISLAND. New York, Scribner, 1964.
        368 p. illus., ports., map.

        Bibliography: p. 351-355.

        "Personalized biography" of Madagascar. Stratton presents in a chatty style some description, considerable history, and personal experiences.

2075.   Thébault, Eugène-Pierre. TRAITE DE DROIT CIVIL MALGACHE MODERNE:
        Vol. I, fasc. 1, LA CODIFICATION DU DROIT CIVIL MALGACHE: DIS-
        POSITIONS GENERALES DE CE CODE; LE NOM; LE DOMICILE; L'ABSENCE;
        LES ACTES D'ETAT CIVIL; COMMENTAIRE ET TEXTES; Vol. II, fasc. 2,
        LE MARIAGE, LE DIVORCE. Tananarive, Editions de Librairie de
        Madagascar, 1962-65. 2 fasc. 171, 230 p. (Les codes bleus
        malgaches)

        Includes bibliography.

        A comprehensive treatise on Malagasy civil law, updating the author's TRAITE DE DROIT CIVIL MALGACHE, published 1951-53. The new work is apparently comprised entirely of the two fascicles cited.

        Among Thébault's other contributions to Malagasy law studies is his editing of LA CONSTITUTION ET LES LOIS ORGANIQUES DE LA REPUB-LIQUE MALGACHE, ACCORDS ET CONVENTION CONSULAIRE FRANCO-MALGACHE: TEXTES MIS A JOUR AU 1er JANVIER 1964, 2d ed. (Tananarive, Editions de la Librairie de Madagascar, 1964, 147 p.; Les codes bleus mal-gaches). The Malagasy Republic's new law of obligations is treated in Jean Lacombe's lengthy THEORIE GENERALE DES OBLIGATIONS EN DROIT MALGACHE (Paris, Editions Cujas, 1967, 670 p.), intended primarily for judges, lawyers, and students.

2076.   Thompson, Virginia, and Richard Adloff. THE MALAGASY REPUBLIC:
        MADAGASCAR TODAY. Stanford, Calif., Stanford University Press,
        1965. xvi, 504 p. illus., ports., map.

        Bibliography: p. 485-494.

First comprehensive survey in English of developments in Madagascar since 1945. Part 1 covers Malagasy history and politics, colonial rule, the revolt of 1947, decolonization, and the post-independence period. Parts 2 and 3 treat typically internal developments in the fields of religion, education, economics, etc. A useful glossary, a list of abbreviations, and an index are included.

2077. U.S. Department of the Interior. Office of Geography. MADAGASCAR, REUNION AND THE COMORO ISLANDS: OFFICIAL STANDARD NAMES APPROVED BY THE UNITED STATES BOARD ON GEOGRAPHIC NAMES. Washington, U.S. Govt. Print. Off., May 1955. 498 p. (20,000 names) (Gazetteer no. 2)

See note on series, no. 484.

2078. Note: Some recent reviews which have not been examined but are being published:

a) ANNALES MALGACHES. 1963- Paris, Published for the Faculté des Lettres et Sciences Humaines, Université de Madagascar, by Editions Cujas.

b) CAHIERS DU CENTRE D'ETUDES DES COUTUMES. 1966- Tananarive, Centre d'Etudes des Coutumes, Faculté Droit et des Sciences Economiques, Université de Madagascar.

c) CIVILISATION MALGACHE. 1964- Tananarive, Faculté des Lettres et Sciences Humaines, Université de Madagascar.

d) TERRE MALGACHE/TANY MALAGASY. 1966- Tananarive, Ecole Nationale Supérieure Agronomique, Université de Madagascar. Semiannual.

REUNION, COMORO ISLANDS, FRENCH TERRITORY OF THE
AFARS AND THE ISSAS (FRENCH SOMALILAND)

Note: The islands in the Indian Ocean and the territory in the Horn of Africa, the only parts of the continent still under French administration, are frequently treated in conjunction with Madagascar, and not many books of reference character have been written on them individually. They are grouped here to avoid repetition of titles. Réunion, the former Ile Bourbon, has since 1946 been an overseas department of France, with three deputies elected to the French National Assembly and two senators to the Senate. The Comoro Islands, formerly administered from Madagascar, and the barren desert of French Somaliland (now called Territoire Française des Afars et des Issas) behind the important port and railroad center of Djibouti are overseas territories of France.

Bibliographies

2079.   France. Agence Economique des Colonies. Bibliothèque. COTE FRANCAISE
DES SOMALIS. 1 v. n.p., n.d.

Handwritten bibliographic listing by Roger Janvier and Christian
Dupont (colonial officials) of books, articles, and government
documents dealing with French Somaliland. Part 1 is alphabetically
arranged; part 2 has a topical or subject organization.

2080.   U.S. Library of Congress. General Reference and Bibliography
Division. MADAGASCAR AND ADJACENT ISLANDS: A GUIDE TO OFFICIAL
PUBLICATIONS. Compiled by Julian W. Witherell, African Section.
Washington, U.S. Govt. Print. Off., 1965. xii, 58 p.

For annotation, see no. 2038.

Reference Works

2081.   Aubert de la Rüe, Edgar. LA SOMALIE FRANCAISE. Paris, Gallimard,
1939. 162 p. illus. (Géographie humaine, v. 14)

"Bibliographie sommaire": p. 155-157.

The author, a literary man and expert photographer as well as
a geographer, was interested in meteorology, natural history, and
other physical sciences connected with country studies as well as
with description. This is one of the few books of general coverage
dealing exclusively with French Somaliland.

2082.   Chambre d'Agriculture de la Réunion. BULLETIN. Saint-Denis.

See note on Chambres de Commerce, etc., no. 1550.

2083.   Deschamps, Hubert J., Raymond Decary, and André Ménard. COTE DES
SOMALIS, REUNION, INDE. Paris, Berger-Levrault, 1948. 209 p.
plates, maps. (L'Union française)

Brief bibliographies at end of each section.

This general study of outlying French possessions is considered
among the most authoritative of recent works. Professor Deschamps
was for some years Governor of French Somaliland and is thoroughly
intimate with the country. M. Decary, the authority on Madagascar,
is also an expert on Réunion.

2084.   France. Direction de la Documentation. LA COTE FRANCAISE DES
           SOMALIS. Paris, 1961. 52 p. (Notes et études documentaires,
           no. 2774, Apr. 29, 1961)

           _____. _____. DJIBOUTI ET LE CHEMIN DE FER FRANCO-ETHIOPIEN.
Paris, 1945. (Notes et études documentaires, no. 122, Aug. 25,
1945)

           _____. _____. LA REUNION. Paris, 1967. 53 p. (Notes et
études documentaires, no. 3358, Jan. 27, 1967)

           For the general note on this series, see no. 1587.

           The first and third references above are basic background
surveys. The second provides official background information on the
Italo-French contest for control of the railroad from Djibouti to
Addis Ababa.

2085.   France. Institut National de la Statistique et des Etudes Economiques.
           ANNUAIRE STATISTIQUE DE LA REUNION. 1952/55- Paris, Impr.
           Nationale, 1956-

           For other official publications, see the Library of Congress
list (no. 2038).

2086.   LA FRANCE DE L'OCEAN INDIEN: MADAGASCAR, LES COMORES, LA REUNION,
           LA COTE FRANCAISE DES SOMALIS, L'INDE FRANCAISE. [By Raymond
           Decary and others] Paris, Société d'Editions Géographiques,
           Maritimes et Coloniales, 1952. 314 p. illus., maps. (Terres
           lointaines, no. 8)

           Includes bibliographies.

           Volume in a popular series of descriptions of French overseas
possessions. The first 225 pages, by Raymond Decary, are on
Madagascar and its island dependencies to the south, where the
Indian Ocean merges into the Antarctic--Saint-Paul and Amsterdam,
Kerguelen, Crozet, and, on the Antarctic continent, Terre Adélie.
The Comoro Islands are described by the administrateur supérieur,
Pierre Coudert (p. 227-242). The following chapter, by Hildebert
Isnard, is on Réunion (p. 243-276), and the next to last chapter
(p. 277-297) on French Somaliland, by a colonial official, Robert
Lemoyne.

2087.   GUIDE-ANNUAIRE DE LA COTE FRANCAISE DES SOMALIS. Djibouti,
           Djibouti-Publicité, 1959. ? p.

           This work, probably a business directory, is listed as a

reference source on French Somaliland in THE STATESMAN'S YEAR-BOOK of 1965-66. It does not appear in the BIBLIOGRAPHIE DE LA FRANCE for 1959-63 and does not seem to be available in American libraries.

2088. Lougnon, Albert. L'ILE BOURBON PENDANT LA REGENCE: DESFORGES-BOUCHER, LES DEBUTS DU CAFE. Paris, Larose, 1957. 371 p. maps, plans. (Bibliothèque d'histoire des Mascareignes)

Bibliography: p. 29-55.

Study of the eighteenth-century history of Réunion, based on exhaustive research in manuscript archives. After a short introduction on his general theme, the author devotes a chapter to a long classified bibliography of writings on Réunion, to which, however, he says his work owes little.

2089. MER ROUGE, AFRIQUE ORIENTALE: ETUDES SOCIOLOGIQUES ET LINGUISTIQUES--PREHISTOIRE--EXPLORATIONS--PERSPECTIVES D'AVENIR. Paris, Peyronnet, 1959. 342 p. illus. (Cahiers de l'Afrique et l'Asie, no. 5)

Bibliography: p. 336-339.

This scholarly work on the Red Sea region (southern Arabia, Ethiopia, and Somalia), with a preface by Professor Hubert J. Deschamps, contains three chapters on French Somaliland: "Les populations de la Côte française des Somalis," by R. Muller (p. 45-102); "Les Danakil du cercle de Tadjoura," by M. Albospeyre (p. 103-162); and "Le destin des Somalis," by R. Lamy (p. 163-212). A bibliography of some length includes Somalia and the former British Somaliland as well as French Somaliland.

A short section of official documents relating to French Somaliland is included in the Library of Congress list (see no. 2646, under Somalia).

2090. OCEAN INDIEN: MADAGASCAR, ILE DE LA REUNION, ILE MAURICE, COTE FRANCAISE DES SOMALIS. Monaco, 1959-62. (PERSPECTIVES D'OUTRE-MER, no. 30, Aug.-Sept. 1959; no. 36, Oct. 1960; no. 46-47, July-Aug. 1962)

Three special numbers of this illustrated review have been devoted since independence to the former and present French possessions in the Indian Ocean. Fully half of each issue consists of feature articles on Madagascar, but there are also useful economic and descriptive surveys of Réunion and the territory of the Somali Coast. For the latter, the 1959 issue ends with a hopeful article on "Tourisme en Côte française des Somalis."

2091. Poinsot, Jean-Paul. DJIBOUTI ET LA COTE FRANCAISE DES SOMALIS.
          Paris, Hachette, 1964. 127 p. chiefly illus. map.

       The illustrations are excellent. The text consists of an
   introduction, sections on the land and the inhabitants (including
   the Afar or Danakil and the Issa), and a final thumbnail sketch of
   the history from earliest times, with an appropriate group of
   illustrations for each part.

2092. Prosperi, Franco. VANISHED CONTINENT: AN ITALIAN EXPEDITION TO THE
          COMORO ISLANDS. Translated by David Moore. London, Hutchinson,
          1957. 232 p. illus.

       Translation of GRAN COMORA.

       Until 1946 the Comoro Archipelago was attached to the Gouverne-
   ment Général of Madagascar, and then it was put under separate
   administration. Since 1961 it has been an autonomous overseas
   territory of France. This account of an Italian zoological expedition is the only full-length work available in English regarding the
   Comoro Islands.

2093. Scherer, André. HISTOIRE DE LA REUNION. Paris, Presses Universi-
          taires de France, 1965. 128 p. map. ("Que sais-je?" no. 1164)

       An outline history divided into three main sections: the Com-
   pany of the Indies (1663-1767), the great epoch (1767-1862), and
   decline and revival (1863-1964).

2094. Thompson, Virginia, and Richard Adloff. DJIBOUTI AND THE HORN OF
          AFRICA. Stanford, Calif., Stanford University Press, 1968.
          246 p.

       Bibliography: p. 235-241.

       Part 1 gives a brief history of the area, of its people (Afars
   and Issas), and its politics and government. Part 2 covers
   religion, education, and culture, with sections on social welfare
   and communications. Part 3 discusses economic problems.

CHAPTER 37

FORMER BRITISH CENTRAL AFRICA

<u>Note</u>: This regional section treats the three countries referred to as
British Central Africa or, from 1953 to 1963, as the Federation of
Rhodesia and Nyasaland. The states concerned are now known as Malawi,
Zambia, and Rhodesia (the last is designated Zimbabwe by Black nation-
alist groups).

<u>Bibliographies</u>

2095. Burke, E. E. "Bibliography." <u>In</u> Central African Archives, THE
          STORY OF CECIL JOHN RHODES: SET OUT IN A SERIES OF HISTORICAL
          PICTURES AND OBJECTS TO COMMEMORATE THE CENTENARY OF HIS
          BIRTH. Bulawayo, Central African Rhodes Centenary Exhibi-
          tion, 1953. p. 131-192.

          This is the most complete bibliography on Rhodes now in
       existence. Part 1 is subdivided by periodicals bearing on Rhodes,
       substantial biographies, shorter studies and obituary notices.
       Part 2 lists the various works with reference to the various
       periods in Rhodes's life, starting with his family history, his
       early career in South Africa, his struggle for the "Road to the
       North," and his impact on South and Central Africa. Part 3 pro-
       vides material concerning Rhodes the man and his various interests.
       Part 4 gives details concerning his speeches and writings. Part
       5 records Rhodes in literature, and the last part shows "Rhodes
       in Memory," with details concerning such unusual media as films
       and memorabilia. Two appendixes list manuscript sources and
       academic dissertations.

2096. Cape Town. University. School of Librarianship. Bibliographical
          Series.

The bibliographical papers compiled as theses by students in the School of Librarianship are issued in stenciled form and contain a minimum of 150 titles; many are far longer. Microfilm copies are available from the University. The usual range of subjects relates to Southern Africa. Of recent years the following have been concerned with the Rhodesias and Nyasaland:

a) A BIBLIOGRAPHY OF AFRICAN EDUCATION IN THE FEDERATION OF RHODESIA AND NYASALAND, 1890-1958. By M. H. Rousseau. 1958. 29 p.

b) A BIBLIOGRAPHY OF THE FEDERATION OF THE RHODESIAS AND NYASALAND, UP TO JUNE 30TH, 1949. By D. L. Cox. 1949. 23 l.

c) CECIL JOHN RHODES. By Daphne W. Thomson. 1947. 29 l.

d) THE DEVELOPMENT OF SOUTHERN RHODESIA FROM THE EARLIEST TIMES TO THE YEAR 1900. By Olive Carpenter. 1946. 20 l.

e) THE ZAMBESI. By Jill Sherlock. 1963. 20 p.

f) ZIMBABWE CULTURE. By Patricia M. Stevens. 1950. 47 l.

2097. International African Institute. SOUTH-EAST CENTRAL AFRICA AND MADAGASCAR: GENERAL, ETHNOGRAPHY, SOCIOLOGY, LINGUISTICS. Compiled by Ruth Jones. London, 1961. 53 l. (Africa Bibliography Series)

See note on series, nos. 306 and 970. The section on Rhodesia and Nyasaland (p. 1-29) is an updated revision of R. M. S. Ng'ombe's A SELECTED BIBLIOGRAPHY OF THE FEDERATION OF RHODESIA AND NYASALAND (Lusaka, Rhodes-Livingstone Institute, 1957, 68 p.), which listed some 1,000 entries.

2098. Rhodesia and Nyasaland. National Archives. A SELECT BIBLIOGRAPHY OF RECENT PUBLICATIONS CONCERNING THE FEDERATION OF RHODESIA AND NYASALAND. Salisbury, Federal Information Dept., 1960. 13 p.

Useful classified listing of about 300 titles of books, pamphlets, documents, and periodicals, most of them published during the 1950's. The categories are general and descriptive; history and biography; politics and economic farming; geology, flora and fauna; anthropology and ethnography (including papers of the Rhodes-Livingstone Institute); some newspapers, periodicals, and journals; official periodical publications; government publications on special topics. A more complete list of the two last-named categories is given in the CATALOGUE OF OFFICIAL PUBLICATIONS issued by the Federal Information Department (1959, 40 p.).

The National Archives began in 1961 an annual LIST OF PUB-LICATIONS DEPOSITED IN THE LIBRARY OF THE NATIONAL ARCHIVES, the scope of which was later modified to cover only Rhodesian publi-cations (see no. 2156). A series of Occasional Papers of the National Archives was begun with a monograph in 1963 (no. 1 in the Federal Series), followed by another in 1965 (no. 1 in the New Series).

2099. Shepperson, George. "The Literature of British Central Africa: A Review Article." RHODES-LIVINGSTONE JOURNAL, no. 23, 1958: 12-46.

A detailed and discriminating account which stands out as a fine piece of historical writing in its own right. Additional bibliographical essays include George Shepperson, "British Cen-tral Africa," THE HISTORIOGRAPHY OF THE BRITISH EMPIRE-COMMON-WEALTH (Duke University Press, 1966, p. 237-247). See also Robert I. Rotberg, "Colonialism and After: The Political Liter-ature of Central Africa--a Bibliographic Essay," AFRICAN FORUM, v. 2, no. 3, 1967: p. 66-73.

2100. Taylor, A. R., and E. P. Dvorin. "Political Development in British Central Africa, 1890-1956: A Select Survey of the Literature and Background Materials." RACE, v. 1, no. 1, Nov. 1959: 61-78.

Concentrates on the movement for closer association. RACE is the quarterly journal of the Institute of Race Relations, London. See also no. 2118 for another survey by Taylor.

2101. U.S. Library of Congress. General Reference and Bibliography Division. THE RHODESIAS AND NYASALAND: A GUIDE TO OFFICIAL PUBLICATIONS. Compiled by Audrey A. Walker, African Section. Washington, 1965. 285 p.

The most extensive volume as yet prepared in the Library of Congress series of official publications of African governments, this includes the record of all English-speaking Central Africa. Documents of the Federation of Rhodesia and Nyasaland and earlier joint Central African agencies take up p. 1-46; Northern Rho-desia, p. 47-117; Southern Rhodesia, p. 118-193; Nyasaland, p. 194-228; British government, p. 229-253; British South Africa Company, p. 254-258. Entries total 1,889, and there is an author and subject index. The coverage is from earliest records (1889)

through 1963; material on the newly independent countries (1964)
of Malawi and Zambia is not included.

Reference Works

2102. Association of Rhodesia and Nyasaland Industries. ARNI REGISTER
       OF MANUFACTURERS, 1963/1964. Salisbury, 1963. 202 p.

       Lists of products and brands, names and addresses of manu-
       facturing industries in Northern Rhodesia, Southern Rhodesia, and
       Nyasaland, incorporating a survey of the economy of the region.

2103. Barber, William J. THE ECONOMY OF BRITISH CENTRAL AFRICA: A CASE
       STUDY OF ECONOMIC DEVELOPMENT IN A DUALISTIC SOCIETY. Stan-
       ford, Calif., Stanford University Press, 1961. 271 p.

       Examination of the contrasting economic systems of European
       settlers, with their cash and money crops, and the subsistence
       agriculture of the African tribesmen. The writer argues that the
       meeting point of the two, in the labor market, has meant below-
       subsistence wages for African workers.

       A number of other recent studies have centered on the same
       issue; among them are Phyllis Deane's COLONIAL SOCIAL ACCOUNTING
       (Cambridge, Eng., University Press, 1953, 360 p.; National Insti-
       tute of Economic and Social Research, Economic and Social Studies,
       no. 11); the UN Department of Economic and Social Affairs report,
       STRUCTURE AND GROWTH OF SELECTED AFRICAN ECONOMIES (New York, 1958,
       201 p.); and a book, ECONOMIC DEVELOPMENT IN RHODESIA AND NYASA-
       LAND (London, Dobson, 1954, 205 p.), by Cecil H. Thompson and
       Harry W. Woodruff, government economists in Salisbury, who argued
       for development through government finance in establishment of the
       Federation.

2104. Cairns, H. Alan C. PRELUDE TO IMPERIALISM: BRITISH REACTIONS TO
       CENTRAL AFRICAN SOCIETY 1840-1890. London, Routledge and
       Kegan Paul, 1965. 330 p.

       Bibliography: p. 303-324.

       Outlines the development of racial contacts in Central Africa
       before the British conquest. The work is based on archival research.

2105. CENTRAL AFRICAN CLASSIFIED DIRECTORY. Salisbury, Morris Pub. Co.
       (P.O. Box 1435). Annual.

This work, listed in the directory of newspapers and periodicals in the ADVERTISING AND PRESS ANNUAL OF AFRICA for 1967, is presumably a conventional trade directory. It is not available for examination, and the only indication of its importance is in its price, Ƚ3 10s. Another listing is a RHODESIA-ZAMBIA-MALAWI DIRECTORY (INCLUDING BOTSWANA AND MOZAMBIQUE), published annually in Bulawayo by Publications (Central Africa) Ltd., P.O. Box 1027 (58th ed., 1967, 1,067 p.).

2106. CENTRAL AFRICAN EXAMINER. v. 1-9, June 7, 1957-1966. Salisbury. illus., ports. Biweekly.

This liberal, reform-minded journal was valuable for political, economic, and social articles on the former Federation of Rhodesia and Nyasaland and on white-black relations.

2107. Central African Historical Association. Local Series. [196?]- Salisbury. Three times a year.

Valuable short pamphlets on historical subjects concerned primarily with Central Africa but occasionally dealing with neighboring territories. For example, see Douglas Wheeler, PORTUGUESE EXPANSION IN ANGOLA SINCE 1836. The Association also publishes PROCEEDINGS of its conferences.

2108. Colson, Elizabeth, and Max Gluckman, eds. SEVEN TRIBES OF BRITISH CENTRAL AFRICA. Reprinted with minor corrections. Manchester, Eng., Published on behalf of the Rhodes-Livingstone Institute, Northern Rhodesia, by Manchester University Press, 1959. xix, 409 p. illus., maps, geneal. table.

Includes bibliographies.

This symposium, an early result of the expanded research program of the Institute (see below) was published first in 1951 by the Oxford University Press. Dr. Colson, an American social anthropologist, edited it in conjunction with Dr. Gluckman, whom she had succeeded as director of the Institute in 1947 when the latter left to accept a lectureship at Oxford. The papers are studies of the leading tribes--Lozi, Tonga, Bemba, Ngoni, Nyakyusa, Yao, and Shona--by scholars whose field work was done under the auspices of the Institute. The studies are followed by short reading lists.

2109. DOCUMENTS ON THE PORTUGUESE IN MOZAMBIQUE AND CENTRAL AFRICA, 1497-1840. [Title also in Portuguese] Lisboa, National Archives of Rhodesia and Nyasaland and Centro de Estudos Históricos Ultramarinos, 1962-

These Portuguese documents with English translations on facing pages bear on the early background of Portuguese expansion as well as Portuguese penetration into the present Malawi, Zambia, and Rhodesia and northern Mozambique. The search for documents included archives and libraries in Europe and Goa. By 1966 five volumes through 1518 had appeared, with the work under the supervision of Professor A. da Silva Rego of the Higher Institute for Overseas Studies in Lisbon.

2110. Dotson, Floyd, and Lillian O. Dotson. THE INDIAN MINORITY OF ZAMBIA, RHODESIA, AND MALAWI. New Haven, Yale University Press, 1968. 444 p.

Bibliography: p. 410-426.

Concludes that while Indians are still in an intermediate economic position between Europeans and Africans, since independence they have become politically less influential and more insecure than either Europeans or Africans.

2111. Fortune, G. A PRELIMINARY SURVEY OF THE BANTU LANGUAGES OF THE FEDERATION. Lusaka, Rhodes-Livingstone Institute, 1959. 59 p. map. (Communications, no. 14)

Father Fortune, S.J., here names 36 language groups and dialect clusters of the Rhodesias and Nyasaland, giving data regarding distribution, number of speakers, etc.

2112. Gann, Lewis Henry, and Michael Gelfand. HUGGINS OF RHODESIA: THE MAN AND HIS COUNTRY. London, G. Allen & Unwin, 1964. 285 p. plates, ports.

Bibliography: p. 273-278.

A medico-political biography based on the private papers of Sir Godfrey Huggins (later Lord Malvern), Prime Minister of Southern Rhodesia, later of the Federation of Rhodesia and Nyasaland, 1933-56; the best existing historical account of this period.

2113. Gray, Richard. THE TWO NATIONS: ASPECTS OF THE DEVELOPMENT OF RACE RELATIONS IN THE RHODESIAS AND NYASALAND. Issued under the auspices of the Institute of Race Relations. London, New York, Oxford University Press, 1960. xvii, 373 p. maps.

Bibliography: p. 356-361.

Study on the history of Central Africa concerning contacts of the British settlers and government with the African tribes and political development from the end of World War I to the beginning of the Federation in 1953.

2114. Great Britain. Advisory Commission on the Review of the Constitution of the Federation of Rhodesia and Nyasaland. REPORT. Chairman, Lord Monckton. London, H.M. Stationery Off., 1960. 4 v. tables, map. (Cmnd. 1148-1151)

Vol. I includes a summary of conclusions and recommendations; Vol. II, a survey of developments since 1953; Vol. III, a consideration of possible constitutional changes; Vol. IV, a presentation of evidence.

2115. Hanna, Alexander John. THE BEGINNINGS OF NYASALAND AND NORTH-EASTERN RHODESIA, 1859-95. Oxford, Clarendon Press, 1956. 281 p. fold. maps.

Bibliography: p. 270-273.

_____ THE STORY OF THE RHODESIAS AND NYASALAND. London, Faber & Faber, 1960. 288 p. illus., ports, maps (1 col.), table.

Bibliography: p. 280-283.

By a historian of Central and East Africa, the first of the above-mentioned works is a carefully documented and scholarly study of British interests and activities--missionary, chartered company, and official--in state building. The second book is a spirited recital of Central African history in a series for the general public.

2116. Hole, Hugh Marshall. THE MAKING OF RHODESIA. London, Macmillan, 1926. illus., maps, appendixes. 402 p.

The early history of British colonization in Southern and Northern Rhodesia, written from the point of view of a senior official in the British South Africa Company's government, and based both on archival and on unpublished sources. Hole's book emphasizes diplomatic and military events in the older "imperial" school of colonial history.

2117. Johnston, Sir Harry H. BRITISH CENTRAL AFRICA: AN ATTEMPT TO GIVE SOME ACCOUNT OF A PORTION OF THE TERRITORIES UNDER BRITISH INFLUENCE NORTH OF THE ZAMBESI. With 6 maps and

223 illustrations reproduced from the author's drawings or from photographs. 2d ed. London, Methuen, 1898. xix, 544 p. illus., plates, maps.

This famous scholar-administrator who led the expeditions of the 1880's into Central Africa and laid the foundations for British control in Nyasaland, Uganda, and elsewhere, served as Commissioner in British Central Africa (Nyasaland and Northern Rhodesia) from 1891 to 1896. His book, the old standard work on the region, takes in geography, history, botany, zoology, anthropology, and languages.

2118. Leverhulme Inter-Collegiate History Conference, University College of Rhodesia and Nyasaland, Salisbury, 1960. HISTORIANS IN TROPICAL AFRICA: PROCEEDINGS OF THE LEVERHULME INTER-COLLEGIATE HISTORY CONFERENCE HELD AT THE UNIVERSITY COLLEGE OF RHODESIA AND NYASALAND SEPTEMBER 1960. Salisbury, University College of Rhodesia and Nyasaland, 1962. 425 p. 32 cm.

Thirty-one papers on various aspects of African history and ethno-history. Most of the contributions deal with nineteenth-century problems of Central and East Africa and with the European in Africa. Included is an excellent bibliographic essay by Alan Taylor, "Recent Trends in Central African Historiography," p. 387-400.

2119. Livingstone, David. LIVINGSTONE'S TRAVELS. Edited by James I. McNair, with geographical sections by Ronald Miller. London, Dent, 1954. xvi, 429 p. illus., ports., maps.

Generous extracts from Dr. Livingstone's three big books recording his explorations, MISSIONARY TRAVELS AND RESEARCHES IN SOUTH AFRICA (1857), THE ZAMBEZI AND ITS TRIBUTARIES (1865), LIVINGSTONE'S LAST JOURNAL (2 v., edited by Horace Waller, 1874), all published by John Murray, London. Four geographical sections are interspersed, explaining the African background, South and West Central Africa, the Lower Zambezi and Nyasaland, and the East African plateau. Brief appendixes are in the nature of extended notes.

Another modern edition is THE ZAMBEZI EXPEDITION OF DAVID LIVINGSTONE, 1858-1863, edited by J. P. R. Wallis and published as No. 9 of the Central African Archives, Oppenheimer Series (London, Chatto & Windus, 1956, 2 v., col. plates, map). The first volume contains a part of the Journals; the second continues the Journals, with letters and dispatches therefrom. Among the many lives of Livingstone, a notable biography emphasizing his role as explorer is by the geographer Frank Debenham, THE WAY TO ILALA: DAVID LIVINGSTONE'S PILGRIMAGE (London, New York, Longmans, Green, 1955, 336 p., illus., maps).

2120. Lockhart, John Gilbert, and C. M. Woodhouse. CECIL RHODES: THE COLOSSUS OF SOUTHERN AFRICA. New York, Macmillan, 1963. xiii, 525 p. illus., map.

Includes bibliographies.

A recent biography of the Empire Builder, but a more valuable earlier portrait was by Basil Williams, CECIL RHODES (London, Constable, 1938, 353 p., map; Makers of the Nineteenth Century).

2121. Mason, Philip. THE BIRTH OF A DILEMMA: THE CONQUEST AND SETTLE-MENT OF RHODESIA. Issued under the auspices of the Institute of Race Relations. London, New York, Oxford University Press, 1958. 366 p. illus.

Notes (by chapters): p. 331-342.

_____. YEAR OF DECISION: RHODESIA AND NYASALAND IN 1960. Issued under the auspices of the Institute of Race Relations. London, New York, Oxford University Press, 1960. 282 p. illus.

In the first of these two books the director of the Institute of Race Relations presents the sometimes violent history of Rhodesia from the earliest European contacts to the twentieth century--"an attempt to describe the impact on each other of peoples profoundly different and the results of that impact." This is the first part of a trilogy completed by Richard Gray's THE TWO NATIONS (see no. 2113 above) and Mr. Mason's second work, which is a history of the Federation, 1953-60, and an examination of the position in 1960.

2122. Ranger, T. O., ed. ASPECTS OF CENTRAL AFRICAN HISTORY. London, Heinemann Educational, 1968. 291 p. maps.

Papers prepared for a conference held at University College, Dar es Salaam, in 1967; specialist essays but most valuable.

2123. Rhodesia and Nyasaland. Central African Archives. Oppenheimer Series. Edited by J. P. R. Wallis [and others]. London, Chatto & Windus, 1945-56. illus., maps, plans, etc.

A series of reprints of the manuscript journals and other primary source materials relating to the early missionaries and pioneers in Central Africa (primarily Southern Rhodesia). Unless otherwise specified, they are edited by Mr. Wallis.

a) THE MATABELE JOURNALS OF ROBERT MOFFAT, 1829-1860. 1945. 2 v.

b) THE MATABELE MISSION: A SELECTION FROM THE CORRESPONDENCE OF JOHN AND EMILY MOFFAT, DAVID LIVINGSTONE, AND OTHERS, 1858-1878. 1945. 268 p.

c) THE NORTHERN GOLDFIELDS DIARIES OF THOMAS BAINES. 1946. 3 v.

d) GOLD AND THE GOSPEL IN MASHONALAND, 1888, BEING THE JOURNALS OF: 1, THE MASHONALAND MISSION OF BISHOP KNIGHT-BRUCE; 2, THE CONCESSION JOURNEY OF CHARLES DUNNELL RUDD. Edited respectively by Constance E. Fripp and V. W. Hiller. 1949. 246 p.

e) APPRENTICESHIP AT KURUMAN, BEING THE JOURNALS AND LETTERS OF ROBERT AND MARY MOFFAT, 1820-1828. Edited by I. Schapera. 1951. 308 p.

f) THE ZAMBESI JOURNAL OF JAMES STEWART, 1862-1863, WITH A SELECTION FROM HIS CORRESPONDENCE. 1952. 276 p.

g) THE BAROTSELAND JOURNAL OF JAMES STEVENSON-HAMILTON, 1898-1899. 1953. 246 p.

h) SOUTHERN AFRICAN DIARIES OF THOMAS LEASK, 1865-1880. 1954. 253 p.

i) THE ZAMBEZI EXPEDITION OF DAVID LIVINGSTONE, 1858-1863. 1956. 2 v. lvi, 462 p.

Another series based on the archives of the Rhodesian pioneers is the Robin Series, also published by Chatto & Windus. The first volume, edited by Edward C. Tabler, ZAMBEZIA AND MATABELELAND IN THE SEVENTIES (1960, 212 p., plates, ports., map), contains two narratives of 1875-1878. Mr. Tabler in an earlier book, THE FAR INTERIOR: CHRONICLES OF PIONEERING IN THE MATABELE AND MASHONA COUNTRIES, 1847-1879 (Cape Town, Balkema, 1955, 443 p.), gave a chronological account of the pioneers, including an 11-page bibliography of the printed and manuscript sources.

2124. Rhodesia and Nyasaland. Federal Information Department. HANDBOOK TO THE FEDERATION OF RHODESIA AND NYASALAND. Edited by W. V. Brelsford, Director of Information. London, Cassell, 1960. 803 p. plates (part col.), maps, charts, coat of arms, diagrs., tables.

Includes bibliographies.

Chapters by recognized experts cover all phases of land, life, and affairs of the three countries comprising the Federation. Some are followed by short reading lists. Institutions and organizations are listed in the chapters on education, social welfare, culture, etc., and similarly useful data appear in those on administrative organization. Appendixes include a chronology from 1498 to 1959, tables of statistics of population and income, lists of newspapers and periodicals, data on learned societies, and other miscellaneous information.

2125. Rhodes-Livingstone Institute, Lusaka, Northern Rhodesia. Communications [series]. nos. 1-29. Livingstone, Lusaka, 1943-65. Irregular. Mimeographed.

The Rhodes-Livingstone Institute in late 1964 became the Institute for Social Research of the new University of Zambia at Lusaka (see no. 2204). The reconstituted institute issues a Communications series of preliminary reports.

2126. Rhodes-Livingstone Institute, Lusaka, Northern Rhodesia. Rhodes-Livingstone Papers [series]. nos. 1-37. Livingstone, Lusaka, 1938-65.

The Rhodes-Livingstone Institute from its beginnings in 1937 has been among the major centers of Africa for research in the social sciences, and in addition to the Papers, usually under 100 pages, 16 books of greater length have appeared. The original site of the Institute was at Livingstone in Northern Rhodesia, and from there it moved in 1953 to Lusaka. The RHODES-LIVINGSTONE JOURNAL, called also HUMAN PROBLEMS IN BRITISH CENTRAL AFRICA (Manchester, Eng., Manchester University Press), totaled 38 numbers (1944-66); with no. 36 "British" was dropped from the title. The RLI also published, in mimeographed form, the proceedings of its annual conferences; among them were the following (see also no. 2132):

a) 13th Conference, Lusaka, 1959. FROM TRIBAL RULE TO MODERN GOVERNMENT. Edited by Raymond Apthorpe. 1959. 216 p.
b) 15th Conference, Lusaka, 1961. SOCIAL RESEARCH AND COMMUNITY DEVELOPMENT. Edited by Raymond Apthorpe. 1961. 173 p.
c) 16th Conference, Lusaka, 1962. THE MULTITRIBAL SOCIETY. Edited by Allie Dubb. 1962. 147 p. tables.

In late 1964 the Rhodes-Livingstone Institute became the Institute for Social Research of the new University of Zambia at Lusaka (see no. 2204). In the new setup a Communications series continues under the same name; the RLI Papers became the Zambian Papers; the journal has been renamed AFRICAN SOCIAL RESEARCH; and

the Conference Proceedings is replaced by a mimeographed BULLETIN,
to give news of the Institute and other information. A COMPLETE
LIST OF THE PUBLICATIONS OF THE FORMER RHODES-LIVINGSTONE INSTI-
TUTE (12 unnumbered pages, [1966?] has been issued by the Institute
for Social Research.

2127. RHODESIANA. no. 1- Salisbury, 1956- Annual.

Journal of the Rhodesiana Society, which began as the Rhodesian African Society (1956-57). The articles are largely of
historical and ethnological interest and relate to all Central
Africa.

2128. Rolin, Henri. LES LOIS ET L'ADMINISTRATION DE LA RHODESIE.
       Bruxelles, E. Bruylant, 1913. xlvii, 532 p. illus., maps.

Bibliography: p. xii-xix.

The standard work on administration in the two Rhodesias
under the British South Africa Company's regime; written from a
lawyer's point of view and yet to be superseded.

2129. Rotberg, Robert I. THE RISE OF NATIONALISM IN CENTRAL AFRICA: THE
       MAKING OF MALAWI AND ZAMBIA, 1873-1964. Cambridge, Mass.,
       Harvard University Press, 1965. xv, 362 p. illus., maps.

Bibliography: p. 329-340.

In this book the author, an historian, seeks to answer questions
concerning the realities of colonial rule and the nature of the
African response, the depth or shallowness of the roots of the
expressions of then current African nationalism (whether these
expressions indicated widespread grievances or merely manifested
the aspirations of a few educated Africans). The study is also
intended to portray the modern political history of the peoples of
Malawi and Zambia and to place the achievement of independence
within its immediate historical context.

2130. Smith, Edwin W. THE WAY OF THE WHITE FIELDS IN RHODESIA: A
       SURVEY OF CHRISTIAN ENTERPRISE IN NORTHERN AND SOUTHERN
       RHODESIA. London, World Dominion Press, 1928. 172, 20 p.
       tables, fold. maps.

This volume in the World Dominion Survey series is of special
interest because of the significant part played by missionary
enterprise in the Rhodesias after the pioneer missionary of
Bechuanaland, Robert Moffat (father-in-law of David Livingstone),

went in 1854 to visit the Matabele chieftains in what is now Rhodesia and in 1859 led the first party of white missionary settlers there. Dr. Smith devoted the first pages to a general account of the country and a brief historical sketch and then described each mission station and its work, ending with 20 pages of tabular statistics.

2131. Sowelem, R. A.   TOWARDS FINANCIAL INDEPENDENCE IN A DEVELOPING ECONOMY: AN ANALYSIS OF THE MONETARY EXPERIENCE OF THE FEDERATION OF RHODESIA AND NYASALAND, 1952-63. London, G. Allen & Unwin, 1967. 329 p. tables, graphs.

Bibliography: p. 324-327.

The short but significant life of the Bank of Rhodesia and Nyasaland is authoritatively analyzed in this account of the Federation's adaptation and establishment of financial institutions in an area previously wholly dependent on an externally controlled monetary system. In Part 1 Dr. Sowelem describes the emergence of the central bank, the development of commercial banking, and the creation of a London-type money market. He devoted Part 2 to a detailed examination of the economic background for these financial developments, the scope of monetary policy, and the impact of the establishment of a central bank.

2132. Stokes, Eric, and Richard Brown, eds.   THE ZAMBESIAN PAST: STUDIES IN CENTRAL AFRICAN HISTORY. Manchester, Eng. Manchester University Press, 1966. xxxv, 427 p. illus., maps (1 fold.), diagrs.

Includes bibliographies.

A collection of 16 studies on the history of Zambesia (Zambia, Malawi, Rhodesia, and parts of Mozambique and other adjacent areas) which are revised and/or expanded versions of papers given at the 17th Conference of the Rhodes-Livingstone Institute, May 1963. The studies are primarily concerned with the Bantu-speaking peoples and the sequence of their material culture and with the origins of the contemporary situation. Four of the papers utilize oral tradition, and topics range from a study of Zimbabwe archaeology to Nyasaland politics in the 1930's. In their introduction the editors focus on the diverse responses of the Zambesian peoples to European influence. Only six of the papers deal with the precolonial period, the majority being devoted to the "scramble" and its immediate aftermath. There is an analytical index.

2133. U.S. Department of the Interior. Office of Geography. RHODESIA AND NYASALAND: OFFICIAL STANDARD NAMES APPROVED BY THE

UNITED STATES BOARD ON GEOGRAPHIC NAMES. Washington, U.S.
Govt. Print. Off., Mar. 1956. 214 p. (17,000 names)
(Gazetteer no. 17)

See note on series, no. 484.

2134. Welensky, Sir Roy. WELENSKY'S 4000 DAYS: THE LIFE AND DEATH OF
THE FEDERATION OF RHODESIA AND NYASALAND. London, Collins,
1964. 383 p. ports., map.

Memoir by the powerful Rhodesian statesman who was Prime
Minister of the Federation of Rhodesia and Nyasaland from 1956
to its dissolution in 1963.

2135. WHO'S WHO OF RHODESIA, MAURITIUS, CENTRAL AND EAST AFRICA: SUP-
PLEMENT TO THE WHO'S WHO OF SOUTHERN AFRICA. Johannesburg,
Wootton & Gibson, 1960-1964; Johannesburg, Combined Pub-
lishers (Pty.), 1965- illus., ports.

Beginning with the 1960 edition, the last pages of the WHO'S
WHO OF SOUTHERN AFRICA (see no. 2961 for complete publication data)
have been numbered separately and issued also as a separate. Title
and coverage have varied. The 1968 edition of the separate, titled
as above, covers Rhodesia, Zambia, Malawi, Mozambique, Kenya, Tanzania, Uganda, Botswana, and Mauritius. Its 212 pages contain
roughly 2,000 biographical notes (many with portraits) and include
official guides for Rhodesia, Zambia, and Malawi.

Similarly, a separate section is devoted to Rhodesia, Zambia,
and Malawi in the well-known Union-Castle Mail Steamship annual
GUIDE TO SOUTHERN AFRICA: REPUBLIC OF SOUTH AFRICA, SOUTH-WEST
AFRICA, RHODESIA, ZAMBIA, MALAWI, ETC. (see no. 2915).

2136. Wills, A. J. AN INTRODUCTION TO THE HISTORY OF CENTRAL AFRICA.
2d ed. London, Oxford University Press, 1967. 412 p. maps.

Bibliography: p. 385-393.

A scholarly general history of the region comprising Malawi,
Rhodesia, and Zambia, written principally for students and teachers
of history in Central Africa but deserving of a wide audience. The
first three chapters survey the main features of the invasion of the
area by Stone Age and Iron Age peoples. The three chapters which
follow are devoted to the nineteenth century and include sections
on the slave trade, Livingstone, pioneer missions, and the European
advance into and occupation of the area. In the final three chapters the narrative extends from the turn of the century to Nov. 1965,
describing the consequences of European occupation, the attempt at

federation, and the end of the colonial phase. An analytical
index is included.

2137. YEAR BOOK AND GUIDE OF THE RHODESIAS AND NYASALAND, WITH BIOG-
GRAPHIES. Salisbury, Rhodesian Pubs., Ltd., 1937- illus.

This was a handy volume covering all aspects of country and
life; the 1962 edition, edited by Reginald Heath, had a hard cardboard cover and 350 pages, including advertising. There were no
reading lists. Presumably publication has ceased.

MALAWI (NYASALAND)

Note: Upon achieving independence, July 6, 1964, the former British
protectorate of Nyasaland took the name of Malawi. The new name is too
recent to be reflected in most writings concerning the country.

Bibliographies

2138. Malawi. National Archives. LIST OF PUBLICATIONS DEPOSITED IN
THE LIBRARY OF THE NATIONAL ARCHIVES 1965. Zomba, 1967.
12 p. Annual.

See also no. 2098.

2139. Syracuse University. Maxwell Graduate School of Citizenship and
Public Affairs. Program of Eastern African Studies. A
BIBLIOGRAPHY OF MALAWI. Compiled by Edward E. Brown and
others. Syracuse, N.Y., 1965. 161 p. (Syracuse University,
Eastern African Bibliographical Series, no. 1)

A title list, classed by subject, with author and title index.
The most comprehensive available record of writing on the past and
present of former Nyasaland. A supplement was issued in 1969 with
62 p.

2140. Tangri, Roger K. "Political Change in Colonial Malawi: A Bibliographical Essay." AFRICAN STUDIES BULLETIN, v. 11, no. 3,
Dec. 1968: 248-57.

See also the general bibliographic section of this chapter.

Reference Works

2141. Debenham, Frank. NYASALAND, THE LAND OF THE LAKE. London, H.M.
Stationery Off., 1955. xi, 239 p. plates, illus., fold.
maps. (Corona Library, no. 3)

"Books consulted": p. 231-232; "Further reading": p. 233-234.

One of a series sponsored by the Colonial Office, "to be
authoritative and readable, and to give a vivid yet accurate picture." This descriptive survey of Nyasaland is by a noted Cambridge geographer who had previously prepared a report on the
water resources of East and Central Africa. The territory, with
its tremendous water resources, is envisioned by the writer as
having the potentials of another Tennessee Valley Authority project.

2142. Gelfand, Michael. LAKESIDE PIONEERS: SOCIO-MEDICAL STUDY OF
NYASALAND, 1875-1920. Oxford, Basil Blackwell, 1964. 330 p.
plates, ports., fold. map.

Bibliography: p. 322-324.

This standard, but somewhat badly organized, work (like Dr.
Gelfand's comparable histories of the Rhodesias from the medical
point of view) is valuable with regard to social conditions, labor,
housing, and related aspects of socio-medical history.

2143. Jones, Griffith B. BRITAIN AND NYASALAND. London, G. Allen &
Unwin, 1964. 314 p. maps.

Notes by chapters: p. 266-303; references (classed):
p. 304-307.

An up-to-date study of the relationships between Great
Britain and the colony of Nyasaland, extending almost to the
moment of independence of the new state of Malawi. The references cited include many command papers leading to the change of
government.

2144. Malawi. A PORTRAIT OF MALAWI. Zomba, Govt. Press, 1964. 118 p.
illus., map.

Published on the occasion of Malawi independence, 1964.

A work produced in conjunction with the MALAWI, LAND OF PRO-
MISE: A COMPREHENSIVE SURVEY (Blantyre, Ramsay Parker Publi-
cations, 1966, 124 p., illus., maps part col.). FACTS FROM
MALAWI (Zomba, 1966, 72 p., illus., fold. map) is an overview

prepared by the Department of Information.

2145. Murray, S. S. THE HANDBOOK OF NYASALAND. 4th ed. London, Published for the Government of Nyasaland by the Crown Agents for the Colonies, 1932. xxxvii (advertising), 436 p.

A general descriptive and economic guide to the country, issued first in 1908, with later editions in 1910 and 1922.

2146. Nyasaland. Laws, statutes, etc. THE LAWS OF NYASALAND IN FORCE ON THE 1ST OF JANUARY 1957. Rev. ed. prepared . . . by Donald Kingdon. London, Waterlow, Govt. Printers, 1957. 6 v.

2147. NYASALAND JOURNAL. v. 1- 1948- Blantyre, Printed by the Church of Scotland Mission for the Nyasaland Society. Semiannual.

Now called SOCIETY OF MALAWI JOURNAL. The Nyasaland Society maintained a private library, promoted interest in literature, history, and scientific matters, and provided information about Nyasaland. The journal, contents of which reflect these interests, includes in each issue a list of books received in the Society library.

2148. Pike, John G. MALAWI: A POLITICAL AND ECONOMIC HISTORY. New York, Praeger, 1968. 248 p. maps, charts. (Praeger Library of African Affairs)

Bibliography: p. 225-232.

A review of physical factors serves as an introduction to a discussion of tribal migration into the area, the creation of a kingdom, the colonial situation, and the development of nationalism and independence. This is a basic introduction to Malawi by a former colonial official in that country.

2149. Pike, John G., and G. T. Rimmington. MALAWI: A GEOGRAPHICAL STUDY. London, Oxford University Press, 1965. xiv, 229 p. illus., maps (part fold.).

Includes bibliographies.

The work is in two parts: the first, by Pike, on physical geography (geology, climate and weather, soils and vegetation, etc.); the second, by Rimmington, on historical, social, and economic geography (including rural settlement patterns, major crops, natural resources and their development, export trade).

2150. Rhodesia and Nyasaland. Ministry of Economic Affairs. REPORT ON
AN ECONOMIC SURVEY OF NYASALAND, 1958-1959. Salisbury [1959?].
300 p. maps (part fold., part col.), charts, diagrs., tables.
34 cm. (Rhodesia and Nyasaland, C. Fed. 132)

Survey by a joint Federation and Nyasaland team under the
British economist Daniel T. Jack with R. J. Randall acting as his
deputy. The writers of the solid study found conclusive evidence
that Nyasaland economic development was being aided by federation.
Political considerations do not enter the report. A summary of
its conclusions and recommendations was issued by the Nyasaland
government (Zomba, 1960, 49 p.).

2151. SOCIETY OF MALAWI JOURNAL. Blantyre.

Before 1965 titled NYASALAND JOURNAL (see no. 2147).

2152. Tew, Mary. PEOPLES OF THE LAKE NYASA REGION. London, New York,
Published for the International African Institute by Oxford
University Press, 1950. 131 p. maps. (Ethnographic Survey
of Africa: East Central Africa, pt. 1)

Bibliography: p. 118-131.

For general note on the series, see no. 980.

Among other well-known anthropological studies of peoples
of Nyasaland are two books by Margaret Read: CHILDREN OF THEIR
FATHERS: GROWING UP AMONG THE NGONI OF NYASALAND (New Haven,
Conn., Yale University Press, 1960, 176 p.) and THE NGONI OF
NYASALAND (London, New York, Published for the International
African Institute by Oxford University Press, 1956, 212 p.).

2153. THIS IS MALAWI. 196- Blantyre, Department of Information. Monthly.

Useful publication covering most current aspects of life in
Malawi; strong on political and economic affairs.

2154. Van Velsen, Jaap. THE POLITICS OF KINSHIP: A STUDY IN SOCIAL
MANIPULATION AMONG THE LAKESIDE TONGA OF NYASALAND. Manchester, Eng., Published on behalf of the Rhodes-Livingstone Institute by Manchester University Press, 1964.
xxix, 338 p.

A study in social anthropology in the Rhodes-Livingstone series of Central African studies. In late 1964 the Rhodes-Livingstone Institute became the Institute for Social Research of the University of Zambia, Lusaka (see no. 2126).

RHODESIA (SOUTHERN RHODESIA)

Note: Southern Rhodesia changed its name to Rhodesia on Oct. 23, 1964, the date that Northern Rhodesia, on the eve of independence, renamed itself Zambia.

Having been a self-governing colony in the British Commonwealth since 1923, Rhodesia made a unilateral declaration of independence on Nov. 11, 1965. In 1969 its political status remained indeterminate.

Bibliographies

2155. Carpenter, Olive. THE DEVELOPMENT OF SOUTHERN RHODESIA FROM THE EARLIEST TIMES TO THE YEAR 1900: A BIBLIOGRAPHY. Cape Town, School of Librarianship, University of Cape Town, 1946. 20 l. (Bibliographical Series)

See note on series, above (no. 2096).

2156. Rhodesia. National Archives. RHODESIA NATIONAL BIBLIOGRAPHY: LIST OF PUBLICATIONS DEPOSITED IN THE LIBRARY OF THE NATIONAL ARCHIVES. 1967- Salisbury, 1968- Annual.

A continuation of the LIST OF PUBLICATIONS DEPOSITED IN THE LIBRARY OF THE NATIONAL ARCHIVES, which superseded the LIST of the National Archives of Rhodesia and Nyasaland upon dissolution of the Federation. Arranged alphabetically under subject headings are books, pamphlets, new serials, and official publications published in Rhodesia.

2157. Rhodesia and Nyasaland. University College. Department of Government. CATALOGUE OF THE PARLIAMENTARY PAPERS OF SOUTHERN RHODESIA, 1899-1953. By F. M. G. Willson and Gloria C. Passmore, assisted by Margaret T. Mitchell and Jean Willson. Salisbury, 1965. 484 p. (Source Book Series, no. 2)

For note on series, see no. 2176.

See also general bibliographic section of this chapter.

676

Reference Works

2158. Barber, James. RHODESIA: THE ROAD TO REBELLION. London, New
York, Published for the Institute of Race Relations, London,
by Oxford University Press, 1967. 338 p. illus., plates,
map.

Bibliography: p. 321-324.

The author was a temporary resident in Rhodesia during the
year following the unilateral declaration of independence. In this
book he offers a straightforward account and careful analysis of
the political and constitutional developments during the early
1960's which led to the UDI. Included are four appendixes and an
analytical index.

2159. Baxter, T. W., and R. W. S. Turner. RHODESIAN EPIC. Cape Town, H.
Timmins, 1966. 239 p. illus., ports., maps, facsims.

A pictorial history of Rhodesia from earliest times to the
granting of self-government in 1923. The National Archives of
Rhodesia, of which Mr. Baxter is director, provided most of the
illustrations. The volume begins with maps of the sixteenth to
nineteenth century, and after an excellent depiction of the drama
of peoples and events, ends with a brief section on modern urban
development. There is an index to illustrations.

2160. Caton-Thompson, Gertrude. THE ZIMBABWE CULTURE: RUINS AND REAC-
TIONS. Oxford, Clarendon Press, 1931. xxiv, 299 p. illus.,
63 plates on 48 l. (part fold.; incl. map, plans).

Bibliography: p. xix-xxii.

A celebrated study which has set the standard for recent
scholarship regarding Zimbabwe. See also nos. 2178 and 2188 below.

2161. Crawford, J. R. WITCHCRAFT AND SORCERY IN RHODESIA. London, Published for the International African Institute by the Oxford
University Press, 1967. xi, 312 p. plates, tables (1 fold.).

Bibliography: p. 303-305.

The author, a lawyer and currently legal draftsman for the
Botswana government, has written a thoughtful, carefully documented account of witchcraft in Rhodesia during the period 1956-
1962. He relied extensively on informants but used as his primary
source the judicial records of the Attorney-General of Rhodesia.

Following the introduction on his sources, in which he also discusses the Shona in the context of Rhodesian society, are four main
parts: evidence and confessions of wizardry, the nature of wizardry beliefs (with particular reference to the Shona), the allegation of wizardry, and the consequences of that allegation. The
volume should be of interest not only to social anthropologists
and historians but also to lawyers and administrators. Three
appendixes and an index are included.

2162. Day, John. INTERNATIONAL NATIONALISM: THE EXTRA-TERRITORIAL
RELATIONS OF SOUTHERN RHODESIAN AFRICAN NATIONALISTS. New
York, Humanities Press, 1967. 143 p. (Library of Political
Studies)

Bibliography: p. 137-141.

The problem of Rhodesia is one of the most distinctive, complicated, and publicized of all African problems. The Rhodesian
Nationalist Movement has tried to combine internal with international pressure for self-government. This is a concise history
of many aspects of the movement, and Day has attempted to estimate
the relative importance of internal and international activity.

See also Nathan M. Shamuyarira, CRISIS IN RHODESIA (New York,
A. Deutsch, 1965, 240 p.), a description of the nationalist movement in Rhodesia up to early 1965 by a ZANU leader, newspaper
editor, and university lecturer; and Ndabaningi Sithole, AFRICAN
NATIONALISM (2d ed., London, Oxford University Press, 1968, 196 p.),
an explanation of African nationalism in general by an active Rhodesian nationalist.

2163. Gann, Lewis Henry. A HISTORY OF SOUTHERN RHODESIA: EARLY DAYS TO
1934. London, Chatto & Windus, 1965. 354 p. fold. map.

Note on sources: p. 337-339; Selective bibliography: p. 341-348.

This is the standard work, compiled under the auspices of the
National Archives of Rhodesia and based on both "open" and "closed"
government and private records in Salisbury and elsewhere. Concentrating on European settlement and its political, social, and economic implications, the study supersedes the previous historical
literature on the subject. The history ends with the consolidation
of Sir Godfrey Huggins' rule in 1934. A second volume is planned.

2164. Gelfand, Michael. TROPICAL VICTORY: AN ACCOUNT OF THE INFLUENCE
OF MEDICINE ON THE HISTORY OF SOUTHERN RHODESIA, 1890-1923.
Cape Town, Juta, 1953. 256 p. illus., plates, ports., map.

Bibliography: p. 248-249.

A social as well as a medical history of the territory and its formative stage, written from a medical doctor's point of view; valuable on early labor conditions, housing, and related aspects.

Among other books by Dr. Gelfand are anthropological studies of the people of Mashonaland among whom he has worked: MEDICINE AND MAGIC OF THE MASHONA (Cape Town, Juta, 1956, 266 p., illus.); SHONA RITUAL (Cape Town, Juta, 1959, 217 p.); AFRICAN BACKGROUND: THE TRADITIONAL CULTURE OF THE SHONA-SPEAKING PEOPLE (Cape Town, Juta, 1965, 132 p., illus.), with a chapter by M. Hannan on the culture of the Shona as reflected in their language; and THE AFRICAN WITCH; WITH PARTICULAR REFERENCE TO WITCHCRAFT BELIEFS AND PRACTICE AMONG THE SHONA OF RHODESIA (Edinburgh, London, E. & S. Livingstone, 1967, xiv, 227 p., illus., plates, tables, diagrs.), illustrated by V. N. Barlow.

2165. Kuper, Hilda, and others. THE SHONA AND NDEBELE OF SOUTHERN RHO-
        DESIA. The Shona, by Hilda Kuper; the Ndebele, by A. J. B.
        Hughes and J. van Velsen. London, International African
        Institute, 1954. 131 p. fold. map, tables. (Ethnographic
        Survey of Africa: Southern Africa, pt. 4)

        Bibliographies: Shona, p. 37-40; Ndebele, p. 110-117.

        For general note on this series, see no. 980.

2166. Leys, Colin. EUROPEAN POLITICS IN SOUTHERN RHODESIA. Oxford,
        Clarendon Press, 1959. xi, 323 p. maps, diagrs., tables.

        Bibliography: p. 313-316; bibliographical footnotes.

        Searching examination of the foundations of European politics, structure of government, composition and living standards of the European population, interests and pressure groups, and the part played by political parties in Southern Rhodesia. The work was completed before the election of June 1958, which eliminated Prime Minister Garfield Todd and assured European control of the franchise, leading directly to the Emergencies of 1959. Election results are summarized in a short appendix. The bibliography includes a listing of the more notable constitutional and political documents.

2167. NADA. Nos. 1-40, 1923-63. n.s. no. 1- 1964- Salisbury. Annual.

        This magazine, originally subtitled SOUTHERN RHODESIA NATIVE AFFAIRS DEPARTMENT ANNUAL, is being continued, with new numbering

but with the same main title, by the Ministry of Internal Affairs.
The annual carries a wide variety of articles relating to the work
and experiences of the government agency and its charges. Emphasis
is largely on history and ethnology. A few book reviews are usually included.

2168. OUTPOST: MAGAZINE OF THE BRITISH SOUTH AFRICA POLICE. 1911-
        Salisbury, Published under authority of the Commissioner of
        Police. Monthly.

        The British South Africa Police began its career as a military
police force in 1890; its members took part in numerous campaigns,
and OUTPOST is therefore of interest for the country's military, as
well as its administrative and general history. The official organ
of the Rhodesian armed forces is now ASSEGAI: THE MAGAZINE OF THE
RHODESIAN ARMY (1961- Salisbury; monthly). This publishes information of local Rhodesian interest and also reprints articles from
other journals concerning general military problems.

2169. Palley, Claire. THE CONSTITUTIONAL HISTORY AND LAW OF SOUTHERN
        RHODESIA, 1888-1965, WITH SPECIAL REFERENCE TO IMPERIAL CON-
        TROL. Oxford, Clarendon Press, 1966. xxv, 872 p. tables,
        diagrs.

        Bibliography: p. 811-822.

        A massive compilation, based on a great wealth of sources.
It will remain the standard work on the subject for many years to
come. The author first traces the constitutional history of Southern Rhodesia since the beginnings of British rule. Subsequently
she analyzes the country's constitutional law, with special reference to the limitations on Southern Rhodesia's sovereignty. She
places considerable emphasis on the powers which--in her opinion--
the British Imperial government was traditionally able to wield in
Southern Rhodesia. She pays special attention to what she considers
to be the racially discriminatory character of Rhodesia's rule. An
addendum carries the story to the end of 1965 and deals with Rhodesia's unilateral declaration of independence. The book is furnished with numerous tables, a select bibliography, and a table of
statutes and cases as well as an index.

2170. Parker, Franklin. AFRICAN DEVELOPMENT AND EDUCATION IN SOUTHERN
        RHODESIA. Columbus, Ohio State University Press, 1960. 165 p.
        (International Education Monographs, no. 2)

        Bibliographical notes.

By an American educationalist who studied conditions in
Southern Rhodesia at first hand. He begins with a sketchy history focusing on African development and then gives a historical
review of African education and a discussion of its problems.
Appendixes analyze the present educational structure. Each
section is followed by bibliographical notes.

2171. Rhodesia. Prime Minister's Department. RELATIONS BETWEEN THE
        RHODESIAN GOVERNMENT AND THE UNITED KINGDOM GOVERNMENT,
        NOVEMBER, 1965-DECEMBER, 1966. Salisbury, 1966. 136 p.

        "Rhodesia and the United Nations" (mimeographed) in pocket.

        Contains "relevant parts" of the communiqué on the Common-
wealth Prime Ministers' conference held at Lagos, Jan. 1966, and
Rhodesia's commentary on this; an analysis of statements made by
the British Prime Minister subsequent to the Lagos conference and
of statements made by the Rhodesian Prime Minister; informal talks
between officials held Apr.-Aug. 1966; a Rhodesian communiqué on
the Commonwealth Prime Ministers' meeting, Sept. 1966; report on
the first visit to Salisbury by the Secretary of State for Commonwealth Affairs; a statement of the British government's terms for
a settlement in Rhodesia and the Rhodesian government's reply to
this; report on the second visit to Salisbury of the Secretary of
State; and report on the conference aboard the H.M.S. Tiger, Dec.
1966.

2172. Rhodesia. Scientific Council. DIRECTORY OF GOVERNMENT ORGANIZA-
        TIONS AND STATUTORY BODIES CONCERNED WITH SCIENTIFIC RESEARCH
        AND TECHNICAL SERVICES IN RHODESIA. Lusaka, 1969. 89 p.

2173. Rhodesia, Southern. OFFICIAL YEAR BOOK OF THE COLONY OF SOUTHERN
        RHODESIA. no. 1, 1924; no. 2, 1931; no. 3, 1932; no. 4, 1952.
        Salisbury, Rhodesian Print. and Pub. Co.

        The 1952 edition (xvi, 792 p., illus., maps) gives population
and other statistics, mainly up to 1950. There are full sections
on physiography, geology, climate, population and migration (including figures for the 1948 sample census of the native population), agriculture, irrigation, forestry, and mining and mineral
production.

2174. Rhodesia, Southern. Advisory Committee on the Development of
        Economic Resources. THE DEVELOPMENT OF THE ECONOMIC RESOURCES
        OF SOUTHERN RHODESIA WITH PARTICULAR REFERENCE TO THE ROLE OF
        AFRICAN AGRICULTURE. Salisbury, Govt. Printer, 1962. xxxvii,
        484 p. illus., maps, diagrs.

Bibliography: p. 477-479.

The so-called Phillips Report, by a committee under the chairmanship of Dr. John Phillips. The committee proposed a £34 million plan "for the saving of the natural resources, their amelioration and their steady development."

Two other special committee reports that were highly meaningful with regard to the African interests were the SECOND REPORT OF THE SELECT COMMITTEE ON RESETTLEMENT OF NATIVES (1960) and the REPORT OF THE URBAN AFFAIRS COMMISSION (1958; the so-called Plewman Report). For other official publications, see the Library of Congress bibliography mentioned above (no. 2101).

2175. Rhodesia, Southern. Department of Statistics. STATISTICAL YEAR BOOK OF SOUTHERN RHODESIA: OFFICIAL ANNUAL OF THE SOCIAL AND ECONOMIC CONDITIONS OF THE COLONY. 1924- Salisbury, Govt. Printer. tables. Irregular.

Prior to the formation of the Federation, this statistical yearbook was issued in 1924, 1930, 1938, 1947 (covered years 1938-46) and 1950. (A STATISTICAL HANDBOOK was also published in 1939 and 1945.) Well arranged and informative, it provided tabulated statistics on all phases of social and economic life. Under the Federation it was superseded by many publications issued by the Central African Statistical Office, notably the processed MONTHLY DIGEST OF STATISTICS OF RHODESIA AND NYASALAND. For full details, see the Library of Congress list (no. 2101).

2176. Rhodesia and Nyasaland. University College. Department of Government. Source Book Series. no. 1- Salisbury, Govt. Printer, 1963- illus.

For the second work in this series of University College publications (the institution was renamed University College of Rhodesia in 1966), see no. 2157, above. The first and third books in the series are as follows:

No. 1. SOURCE BOOK OF PARLIAMENTARY ELECTIONS AND REFERENDA IN SOUTHERN RHODESIA, 1898-1962. Edited by F. M. G. Willson and written and compiled by Gloria C. Passmore and Margaret T. Mitchell with the assistance of Jean Willson. Maps by R. F. Young. 1963. 255 p.

No. 3. HOLDERS OF ADMINISTRATIVE AND MINISTERIAL OFFICE 1894-1964 AND MEMBERS OF THE LEGISLATIVE COUNCIL 1899-1923 AND THE LEGISLATIVE ASSEMBLY 1924-1964. By F. M. G. Willson and Gloria C. Passmore, assisted by Margaret T. Mitchell. 1966. 77, 10 p.

2177. Rogers, Cyril, and C. Frantz. RACIAL THEMES IN SOUTHERN RHODESIA:
        THE ATTITUDES AND BEHAVIOR OF THE WHITE POPULATION. New Haven,
        Conn., Yale University Press, 1962. 427 p.

        Bibliography: p. 385-403.

        A psychologist and an anthropologist carefully measure the
        attitudes and behavior patterns of whites and survey the history of
        race relations. The work is valuable for understanding racial
        themes in all of Africa.

2178. Summers, Roger. INYANGA: PREHISTORIC SETTLEMENTS IN SOUTHERN
        RHODESIA. Cambridge, Eng., Published for the Inyanga Re-
        search Fund at the University Press, 1958. xviii, 335 p.
        illus., maps, plans.

        Includes bibliographies.

        _____. ZIMBABWE, A RHODESIAN MYSTERY. Johannesburg, London,
        Nelson, 1965. 120 p. illus.

        Bibliographical footnotes.

        The first work is a technical report, with sections contributed
        by several scholars, of archaeological investigations of Stone Age
        ruins and terraces in the Inyanga District. The work had been
        directed by the author when he was curator of the National Museum
        and chairman of the Monuments Commission, and by Keith Robinson,
        inspector for the Monuments Commission. The Research Fund was
        inspired by the late Dr. Neville Jones, author of the pioneering
        work, PREHISTORY OF SOUTHERN RHODESIA (Cambridge, Eng., University
        Press, 1949, 77 p.). The second book, intended for the general
        reader, begins with the "discovery" of Zimbabwe by Carl Mauch, then
        proceeds with an account of the myths surrounding the ruins, the
        first scientific investigations, the work of the Monuments Commiss-
        ion, recent archaeological research (1950-58), and anthropological
        research. For the Iron Age of Rhodesia see Fagan, no. 2911.

2179. Tow, Leonard. THE MANUFACTURING ECONOMY OF SOUTHERN RHODESIA:
        PROBLEMS AND PROSPECTS. Washington, D.C., National Academy
        of Sciences, National Research Council, 1960. 141 p. maps,
        diagrs, tables. (National Research Council, Division of
        Earth Sciences, Foreign Field Research Program, Report no.
        10; National Research Council Publication no. 850)

        Bibliography: p. 135-141.

2180. Young, Kenneth. RHODESIA AND INDEPENDENCE. London, Eyre & Spottiswoode; New York, Heineman, 1967. 567 p. maps.

British edition is subtitled A STUDY IN BRITISH COLONIAL POLICY.

A review of the events leading to the unilateral declaration of independence and its aftermath. The material is partially based on unpublished documents and private statements by leading participants in the Rhodesian episode. About half the text is devoted to the years 1965 and 1966. An opening background chapter and a beneficent profile of Ian Smith are included. In a final section the author, who is political adviser to the Beaverbrook newspapers and former editor of the YORKSHIRE POST, offers some personal opinions, substantiating the pro-UDI viewpoint manifested in the book's preceding pages. Included are a chronology of events, nine appendixes, and a select index.

2181. Yudelman, Montague. AFRICANS ON THE LAND: ECONOMIC PROBLEMS OF AFRICAN AGRICULTURAL DEVELOPMENT IN SOUTHERN, CENTRAL, AND EAST AFRICA, WITH SPECIAL REFERENCE TO SOUTHERN RHODESIA. Prepared under the auspices of the Center for International Affairs, Harvard University. Cambridge, Mass., Harvard University Press, 1964. xiv, 288 p. maps, tables.

Bibliographical footnotes.

The major problem of how to bring a predominantly agricultural society, producing largely for self-subsistence, into the market economy (with consequent increase in productivity) is the core of Dr. Yudelman's study. His emphasis is on Rhodesia, which, like South Africa and Kenya, is a "dual" society—one in which "European agriculture" and "African agriculture" coexist. Many of Dr. Yudelman's recommendations in this book (including the modification of certain strictures on allocation of land by race) were made to and endorsed by the government of Southern Rhodesia before the 1963 elections—in which the government party was rejected—and the dissolution of the Federation of Rhodesia and Nyasaland. An analytical index is included. See also no. 806.

ZAMBIA (NORTHERN RHODESIA)

Note: As this former British colony renamed itself Zambia only on Oct. 23, 1964, the day before gaining independence, literature has hitherto been on Northern Rhodesia.

Bibliographies

2182. Gifford, Prosser. "An Initial Survey of the Local Archival and
       Published Materials for Zambian History (1895-Independence
       1964)." AFRICAN SOCIAL RESEARCH, no. 1, June 1966: 59-84.

       An informative bibliographic essay on Zambian source materials.

2183. Parker, Franklin, comp. "African Education in Zambia (Formerly
       Northern Rhodesia): A Partial Bibliography of Magazine
       Articles, 1925-1963." AFRICAN STUDIES BULLETIN, v. 10,
       no. 3, Dec. 1967: 6-15.

       List of 148 articles, arranged chronologically.

       See also general bibliographic section in this chapter.

Reference Works

2184. Baldwin, Robert E. ECONOMIC DEVELOPMENT AND EXPORT GROWTH: A
       STUDY OF NORTHERN RHODESIA, 1920-1960. Berkeley and Los
       Angeles, University of California Press, 1966. 254 p.
       tables. (Publications of the Bureau of Business and Economic
       Research, University of California, Los Angeles)

       Bibliography: p. 222-245.

       An interesting analysis of the economic issues involved in
       the industrialization of Northern Rhodesia, this "first economic
       history" of the country serves as a supplement to Gann's HISTORY
       OF NORTHERN RHODESIA (see no. 2190). Baldwin discusses theories
       of development through export expansion, presents a survey of
       Rhodesian economic growth, and describes and appraises major
       aspects of the economy. He concludes that, like agriculture,
       significant industrial expansion must be directed at export mar-
       kets and that a well-trained labor force, rather than the existence
       of any special natural resource, must form the basis for export
       growth. A good analytical index is included, and the bibliography
       is excellent.

2185. Bancroft, Joseph A. MINING IN NORTHERN RHODESIA: A CHRONICLE OF
       MINERAL EXPLORATION AND MINING DEVELOPMENT. Arranged and
       prepared by T. D. Guernsey. Salisbury, British South Africa
       Co., 1961. 174 p. illus., ports., maps.

Available for free distribution from the company. The author is a geologist who has carried out surveys for the Canadian government.

2186. Brelsford, William V. THE TRIBES OF NORTHERN RHODESIA. 2d ed. Lusaka, Govt. Printer, 1965. 157 p. illus., ports., fold. col. map.

Bibliography: p. 147-149.

The writer had formerly been a district commissioner in Northern Rhodesia. This guide was prepared to replace the long out-of-print MEMORANDUM ON THE NATIVE TRIBES AND TRIBAL AREAS OF NORTHERN RHODESIA written in 1934 by J. Moffat Thomson, then Secretary of Native Affairs. Mr. Brelsford has made use of the extensive research and writing on many tribes since that time. His 22 chapters cover a great variety of tribes and tribal groups, going summarily into their history, ethnic composition, and tribal origins. A large folded map in brilliant colors shows tribes and language groups. Mr. Brelsford has also written a number of studies of individual tribes, some appearing in the publications of the Rhodes-Livingstone Institute (since 1964 the Institute for Social Research of the University of Zambia, Lusaka). The most substantial is FISHERMEN OF THE BANGWEULU SWAMPS: A STUDY OF THE FISHING ACTIVITIES OF THE UNGA TRIBE (Livingstone, 1946, 169 p., illus.; Rhodes-Livingstone Papers, no. 12). A work on the same area is Professor Frank Debenham's STUDY OF AN AFRICAN SWAMP: REPORT OF THE CAMBRIDGE UNIVERSITY EXPEDITION TO THE BANGWEULU SWAMPS, NORTHERN RHODESIA, 1949 (London, Published for the Government of Northern Rhodesia by H.M. Stationery Off., 1952, 88 p., illus.).

2187. Ethnographic Survey of Africa [series]. Edited by Daryll Forde. London, International African Institute, 1950-

For the general note on this series, see no. 980.

The following relate to tribes of Northern Rhodesia: East Central Africa, Part 2, one volume (1951 [1950], 100 p.) made up of BEMBA AND RELATED PEOPLES OF NORTHERN RHODESIA, by Wilfred Whiteley, and PEOPLES OF THE LOWER LUAPULA VALLEY, by J. Slaski; West Central Africa, Part 3, THE LOZI PEOPLES OF NORTH-WESTERN RHODESIA (1952, 62 p.), by V. W. Turner, and Part 4, THE ILA-TONGA PEOPLES OF NORTH-WESTERN RHODESIA (1953, 72 p.), by M. A. Jaspan. Because of the comparatively early date of these monographs, and particularly because of the important contributions to anthropological study of the territory made in publications of the Rhodes-Livingstone Institute (since 1964 the Institute for Social Research of the University of Zambia, Lusaka), there is later material available.

2188. Fagan, Brian, ed. A SHORT HISTORY OF ZAMBIA: FROM THE EARLIEST
         TIMES UNTIL A.D. 1900. London, Oxford University Press,
         1966. 164 p.

         Bibliography: p. 152-159.

         Whereas most books dealing with what is now Zambia have con-
cerned themselves with the period since the mid-nineteenth century,
this book concentrates on the prehistory and such subjects as
"Migrations from the Congo (A.D. 1500-1850)." The essays in this
first good, comprehensive history of the pre-1900 period are by
specialists.

2189. Gann, Lewis Henry. THE BIRTH OF A PLURAL SOCIETY: THE DEVELOPMENT
         OF NORTHERN RHODESIA UNDER THE BRITISH SOUTH AFRICA COMPANY,
         1894-1914. Manchester, Eng., Published on behalf of the Rhodes-
         Livingstone Institute by Manchester University Press, 1961
         [c. 1958]. xxi, 230 p. illus., fold. map at end.

         Bibliography: p. 192-210.

         The book was written to provide a historical background for
the major research program of the Rhodes-Livingstone Institute
(since 1964 the Institute for Social Research of the University
of Zambia, Lusaka). Not only are the European and political source
materials used but also the works of the anthropologists to show
"the African political systems and cultures . . . as contributing
in varying detail to the building of Northern Rhodesia, in the same
way as varied types of European." Dr. Gann covers background as
of 1894, the coming of the missionaries following Livingstone, the
beginnings of government and establishment of administration, and
the arrival of the settlers and their part in determining the
political patterns. The Northern Rhodesia plural society of 1914
which he analyzes in his last chapter reveals the complex interaction between the differing types of both European and African
societies.

2190. Gann, Lewis Henry. A HISTORY OF NORTHERN RHODESIA: EARLY DAYS TO
         1953. London, Chatto & Windus, 1964. xiv, 478 p. 3 fold.
         col. maps.

         Bibliography: p. 461-471.

         A magnificent history of Northern Rhodesia, compiled under the
auspices of the National Archives of Rhodesia, based on "open" as
well as "closed" government and private records in London, Lusaka,
and Salisbury. In this most comprehensive of works on the territory
(and one of the best on any African nation), the writer concentrates
on its political and social development under British rule.

2191. Gelfand, Michael. NORTHERN RHODESIA IN THE DAYS OF THE CHARTER: A MEDICAL AND SOCIAL STUDY, 1878-1924. Oxford, Blackwell, 1961. xvii, 291 p. plates, ports., fold. maps.

Bibliography: p. 278-283.

Written from a medical doctor's point of view but valuable also on early labor conditions and other related aspects.

2192. Gluckman, Max. THE JUDICIAL PROCESS AMONG THE BAROTSE OF NORTHERN RHODESIA. Manchester, Eng., Published on behalf of the Rhodes-Livingstone Institute by Manchester University Press, 1955. 386 p. illus., port., fold. maps.

Classic study of the judicial process of an African people by an anthropologist with legal training. The author emphasizes the concept of "reasonable men" in Lozi law.

2193. Great Britain. Commission on Financial and Economic Position of Northern Rhodesia. REPORT OF THE COMMISSION APPOINTED TO ENQUIRE INTO THE FINANCIAL AND ECONOMIC POSITION OF NORTHERN RHODESIA. A. Pim and S. Milligan, commissioners. London, H.M. Stationery Off., 1938. xi, 394 p. maps, tables. (Colonial Office, Colonial no. 145)

During the 1930's extensive economic surveys of colonial territories were carried out by special commissions for the Colonial Office. Sir Alan W. Pim headed a number of these, including the surveys of Zanzibar and the High Commission Territories, Kenya, and, last, in 1937, Northern Rhodesia. The detailed report is basic to later British surveys, including the so-called Bledisloe Report (Great Britain, Rhodesia-Nyasaland Royal Commission, REPORT, London, 1939, 283 p.; Comd. 5949), which examined the proposals for uniting the three territories. Its recommendations, like those of an earlier commission in 1927, were against political union but for a larger measure of economic federation, with creation of an Inter-territorial Council (set up in Mar. 1945).

In 1938 Sir Alan Pim gave the Beit lecture series at Oxford, later published by the Clarendon Press: THE FINANCIAL AND ECONOMIC HISTORY OF THE AFRICAN TROPICAL TERRITORIES (1940, 234 p.).

2194. Hall, Richard. ZAMBIA. London, Pall Mall Press, 1965; New York, Praeger, 1966. 357 p. maps. (Library of African Affairs)

American edition is subtitled STORY OF THE MAKING OF A NATION.

Bibliography: p. 315-320.

A lively and scholarly survey by the founder-editor of the
CENTRAL AFRICAN MAIL. Hall first describes the geographic and
cultural setting of Zambia's history and then discusses the
period of colonial rule, the rise of nationalism, the "genesis
and exodus" of federation, and the creation of the new state. A
lengthy concluding section is devoted primarily to the economy and
includes an analysis of the important role, economically and politically, of the Copperbelt. There are several appendixes. An otherwise excellent account is marred by a number of factual and typographical errors.

2195. Kaunda, Kenneth. ZAMBIA SHALL BE FREE: AN AUTOBIOGRAPHY. New
        York, Praeger, 1963. 202 p. illus. (Books That Matter)

        The leader of the United National Independence Party (UNIP)
of Northern Rhodesia, since 1964 President of Zambia, followed
the example of other African statesmen in writing his autobiography, which is also the history of the country's political and
constitutional development to independence.

        President Kaunda's recent views are recorded in ZAMBIA--
INDEPENDENCE AND BEYOND: THE SPEECHES OF KENNETH KAUNDA, edited
by Colin Legum (London, Nelson, 1966, xiii, 265 p.), a collection
which provides good source material on a type of African nationalism professedly directed toward nonviolence and practical politics.

2196. Kay, George. A SOCIAL GEOGRAPHY OF ZAMBIA: A SURVEY OF POPU-
        LATION PATTERNS IN A DEVELOPING COUNTRY. London, University
        of London Press, 1967. 160 p. illus., maps, diagrs.,
        tables.

        Bibliography: p. 151-154.

        A "preliminary account," according to the author. It begins
with a brief introduction to the physical environment (soils,
climate, vegetation) and continues with sections on the European
and African population, the Copperbelt, Lusaka, and Nkana-Kitwe.
There is a general index and an index of place names.

2197. Mulford, David C. ZAMBIA: THE POLITICS OF INDEPENDENCE, 1957-
        1964. London, Oxford University Press, 1967. xii, 362 p.

        Bibliography: p. 344-352.

        This scholarly study of Northern Rhodesia's transformation
from a Central African state under white minority rule into an
independent, African-governed Zambia is based on a notably rich,

and heretofore unexploited, fund of documentary evidence. Concentration is on the nationalist political parties--especially their evolution in relation to constitutional developments and elections and in relation to British administration of territorial politics.

2198. Rhodesia, Northern. THE NORTHERN RHODESIA HANDBOOK. Lusaka, Govt. Printer, 1953. 263 p. illus., maps.

Bibliography: p. 256-261.

Useful reference book with historical, economic, geographic, and political surveys. It provides basic data on people, trade and commerce, communications, and tourist facilities. Although it was superseded by the HANDBOOK TO THE FEDERATION OF RHODESIA AND NYASALAND (see no. 2124), it remains valuable as a compilation of older facts and figures.

2199. Rotberg, Robert I. CHRISTIAN MISSIONARIES AND THE CREATION OF NORTHERN RHODESIA, 1880-1924. Princeton, N.J., Princeton University Press, 1965. xi, 240 p. plates, maps.

Bibliography: p. 208-224.

Rotberg describes the role of the missionary during Northern Rhodesia's colonial period in establishing and strengthening Western influence, discusses the tension between Christian authority and secular power, and traces the beginnings of the educational system and of the indigenous church. Separatist churches are not covered, and Rotberg admittedly does not adequately "reflect African opinion of the day about missionaries." Appendixes include a chronology, missionary biographical sketches, and a good essay on sources. There is an analytical index.

2200. Taylor, John Vernon, and Dorothea A. Lehmann. CHRISTIANS OF THE COPPERBELT: THE GROWTH OF THE CHURCH IN NORTHERN RHODESIA. London, SCM Press, 1961. 308 p. map. (World Mission Studies)

Excellent survey.

See also Peter Bolink, TOWARDS CHURCH UNION IN ZAMBIA: A STUDY OF MISSIONARY CO-OPERATION AND CHURCH-UNION EFFORTS IN CENTRAL-AFRICA (Franeker, Holland, T. Wever, 1967, 430 p., maps; bibliography: p. 412-424).

2201. Zambia. Central Statistical Office. STATISTICAL YEAR-BOOK, 1968.
       Lusaka, 1969. 205 p.

2202. Zambia. Ministry of Lands and Mines. GAZETTEER OF GEOGRAPHICAL
       NAMES IN THE REPUBLIC OF ZAMBIA. Lusaka, 1966.

2203. Zambia. National Museums. Papers [series]. no. 1- 1967- London,
       Published on behalf of the National Museums of Zambia by Oxford
       University Press.

       Supersedes the Occasional Papers issued by the museum under
       its earlier names (Livingstone Museum and Rhodes-Livingstone
       Museum).

2204. Zambia. University. Institute for Social Research. [Publi-
       cations] Lusaka, 1966-

       In late 1964 the Rhodes-Livingstone Institute (see no. 2126)
       became the Institute for Social Research, first part of the new
       University of Zambia (opened to undergraduates in Mar. 1966) in
       Lusaka and the first element in a Centre for African Studies. The
       new institute currently emphasizes the fields of sociology, psy-
       chology, political science, and economics (including agricultural
       economics), and the earlier interests of the RLI in history, human
       geography, and demography are also to be extended. Like the RLI,
       the Institute will publish books, as well as the following:

       A Communications series continues with this name, but it has
       reverted to the original intention of providing a quick and eco-
       nomical outlet for preliminary reports by research workers. It
       appears in mimeographed form.

       a)   Communication no. 1. THE POPULATION OF A ZAMBIAN MUNICIPAL
            TOWNSHIP: A PRELIMINARY REPORT OF A 1964 SOCIAL SURVEY
            OF THE BROKEN HILL MUNICIPAL TOWNSHIPS. By Bruce Kapferer.
            1966. 66 p. map, tables (part fold.), diagr.

       b)   Communication no. 2. MAPS OF THE DISTRIBUTION AND DENSITY OF
            AFRICAN POPULATION IN ZAMBIA. By George Kay. 1967. 24 p.
            2 fold. maps (in pocket), tables. (A survey, not an
            atlas)

       c)   Communication no. 3. SOME ASPECTS OF SOCIAL CHANGE IN AFRICA
            SOUTH OF THE SAHARA, 1959-66: A BIBLIOGRAPHY. Compiled
            by Eva Loft Deregowska. 1967. 93 p. (See no. 832 for
            annotation.)

       The Zambian Papers, divided into Social Sciences and Natural
       Sciences, take the place of the RLI Papers, which were usually under

100 pages. They are being published for the Institute by the Manchester University Press.

d) Zambian Papers, no. 1. CO-OPERATION, LEADERSHIP AND VILLAGE
    STRUCTURE: A PRELIMINARY ECONOMIC AND POLITICAL STUDY
    OF TEN BISA VILLAGES IN THE NORTHERN PROVINCE OF ZAMBIA.
    By Bruce Kapferer. 1967. 77 p. plates, maps, tables,
    diagrs. (part fold.).

e) Zambian Papers, no. 2. THE INAUGURAL LECTURES OF THE UNIVER-
    SITY OF ZAMBIA. By Julius Nyerere, Davidson Nicol, and
    R. Cranford Pratt. 1967. 30 p. plates.

f) Zambian Papers, no. 3. A PHONEMIC ANALYSIS OF BEMBA: A PRE-
    SENTATION OF BEMBA SYLLABLE STRUCTURE, PHONEMIC CONTRAST
    AND THEIR DISTRIBUTION. By Mubanga E. Kashoki. 1968.
    40 p.

AFRICAN SOCIAL RESEARCH, edited by Alastair Heron and Ronald
Frankenberg, has replaced the RLI journal, HUMAN PROBLEMS IN CENTRAL
AFRICA. It is published twice yearly by the Manchester University
Press on behalf of the Institute. The first number appeared in
June 1966 (see no. 5).

The Conference Proceedings of the RLI have been discontinued.
In their stead the Institute for Social Research issues a mimeographed BULLETIN, edited by Alastair Heron, Ronald Frankenberg, and
Isabel Hancock, the first number of which appeared in 1966. Information not suitable for the journal AFRICAN SOCIAL RESEARCH and news
of the work of both university and institute are given in its pages.

2205. ZAMBIA [NORTHERN RHODESIA] JOURNAL. v. 1-6. 1950-65. Livingstone.
       illus., maps. Semiannual, then Irregular.

Published at the Rhodes-Livingstone Museum (now the Livingstone Museum) for the Northern Rhodesia Society; originally titled
the NORTHERN RHODESIA JOURNAL, editor W. V. Brelsford. The final
volume, under the new name, comprised three enlarged issues (380 p.),
plus the cumulative index (p. i-xxxvii) for the six volumes. Ethnology, history (specially early history), geography, natural history, and kindred sciences in their relation to Northern Rhodesia,
as well as aspects of mining, agriculture, fishing, and forestry,
were covered in the pages of this attractive journal; a section of
book reviews was also included.

CHAPTER 38

FORMER BELGIAN CONGO AND TRUST TERRITORIES

CONGO-KINSHASA (LEOPOLDVILLE)

Note: Until independence came suddenly to the former Belgian Congo in
June 1960, practically all writing relating to the colony, and to the
Belgian-administered trust territory of Ruanda-Urundi, was published in
Belgium. It was exhaustively catalogued, as is evident in the following
subsection of bibliographies. Since 1960 the increased international
concern over the country's unsettled government has been reflected in a
wide range of literature on the Democratic Republic of the Congo.

On June 30, 1966, the names of the chief Congolese cities were
changed to African forms in place of the French. Leopoldville has become
Kinshasa. Elisabethville is Lubumbashi; Stanleyville, Kisangani; Coquilhatville, Mbandaka. American newspaper datelines reflect these changes.

Atlases

2206. Académie Royale des Sciences d'Outre-Mer. ATLAS GENERAL DU CONGO
           ET DU RUANDA-URUNDI. Bruxelles, 1948-63. 34 pts. col. fold.
           maps.

       Monumental work covering all aspects of the former Belgian
       territories; issued in parts, each consisting of explanatory text
       of 7 to 30 folio pages (two editions, in French and Dutch) and one
       or more large-scale folded maps. The introductory part, "Avant-
       propos" (2d ed., 1954, 28 p., map), includes an index of place
       names, in which names of towns are followed by population statistics
       as of 1953-54. The other parts, accompanying maps covering all
       aspects of country and life, are by subject specialists.

2207. Comité Spécial du Katanga. ATLAS DU KATANGA. Bruxelles, 1929-

     Five parts of the atlas were published in 1952. Scale is 1:200,000.

2208. Rouck, René de. ATLAS GEOGRAPHIQUE ET HISTORIQUE DU CONGO BELGE ET DES TERRITOIRES SOUS MANDAT DU RUANDA-URUNDI. 4th ed. Bruxelles, 1954. 11 p. 13 col. maps. 36 cm.

     Forty-five maps and plans on 12 plates, with an alphabetic index of 5,972 names. The maps include physical geography, political and administrative divisions, history, economy, and plans of the seven chief cities.

Bibliographies

2209. Académie Royale des Sciences d'Outre-Mer. CATALOGUE. Bruxelles, Librairie Africaine Hubaut, Oct. 1, 1968. 36 p.

     The Institut Royal Colonial Belge was established in 1929; in 1954 its name was changed by royal decree to Académie Royale des Sciences Coloniales, and in Dec. 1959 to the present form. (By royal decree it was attached to the Ministère de l'Education Nationale et de la Culture on Oct. 1, 1962; another decree in 1964 put it under the official patronage of the King of the Belgians.) Its many publications, new series of which are dated from 1954, are listed in this periodically revised catalogue which includes items out of print as well as those in stock. The series contains many important works.

2210. Belgium. Ministère des Affaires Africaines [until 1960 Ministère du Congo Belge et du Ruanda-Urundi]. LISTE DES PUBLICATIONS. LIJST DER UITGAVEN. Bruxelles. (Latest received, June 1959, 135 p.)

     This periodically revised list covers official publications on the former Belgian colonies, including the many distinguished contributions in the fields of natural and human sciences that appear in the journals and monographic series of the government-sponsored organizations concerned with the Congo and Ruanda-Urundi. They are listed by agency or institution: the Direction de l'Agriculture of the Ministry with explanation of its serials, the outstanding BULLETIN AGRICOLE DU CONGO BELGE ET DU RUANDA-URUNDI and the related BULLETIN D'INFORMATION DE L'INEAC, followed by almost 30 pages of separate monograph titles; publications of other branches of the Ministry, including BULLETIN OFFICIEL and

BULLETIN ADMINISTRATIF, annual reports on administration, mapping
services, etc.; publications of the Institut National pour l'Etude
Agronomique du Congo (INEAC), of the Institut des Parcs Nationaux
du Congo Belge; the more general works issued by the Office de
l'Information et des Relations Publiques pour le Congo Belge et le
Ruanda-Urundi (INFORCONGO); the vast list of scientific publications
of the Musée Royal du Congo Belge (now Musée Royal de l'Afrique
Centrale); and the above-mentioned list of the Académie Royale des
Sciences d'Outre-Mer.

2211. Berlage, Jean. REPERTOIRE DE LA PRESSE DU CONGO BELGE (1884-1958)
        ET DU RUANDA-URUNDI (1920-1958). Bruxelles, Commission Belge
        de Bibliographie, 1959. 193 p. (Bibliographia belgica, no.
        43)

        Compilation of all periodicals issued in the Belgian African
territories, including many with terminal dates, numerous ephemeral
publications of mission presses in vernacular languages, etc. There
are 662 titles.

        In 1960 the Commissariat Générale à l'Information of the then
Belgian Congo issued a REPERTOIRE DE LA PRESSE AU CONGO ET AU
RUANDA-URUNDI, MIS A JOUR EN AVRIL 1960 (Léopoldville, 1960, 38 l.).
In addition, the Ministère de l'Education Nationale, Section
Bibliothèque, of the Congolese Republic has issued a REPERTOIRE DES
PERIODIQUES CONGOLAIS.

2212. BIBLIOGRAPHIE ETHNOGRAPHIQUE DE L'AFRIQUE SUD-SAHARIENNE [formerly
        ... DU CONGO BELGE ET DES REGIONS AVOISINANTES]. 1932-
        Tervuren, Musée Royal de l'Afrique Centrale. Annual.

        For annotation see no. 965.

        Although the "ethnographic" is signalized in the title of this
voluminous annual listing, the subject matter covers a number of
disciplines as well as a range of territory including much of Black
Africa. The selection of references is international in scope,
though Belgian literature is of course very well represented.

2213. BIBLIOGRAPHIE GENERALE DES ARTICLES ET OUVRAGES POLITIQUES SUR LA
        REPUBLIQUE DU CONGO-LEOPOLDVILLE (1959-1962). Léopoldville,
        1963. 132 p. (ETUDES CONGOLAISES, v. 4, Mar. 1963)

        Special number of the review ETUDES CONGOLAISES containing a
detailed bibliography on the political aspects of the Congo crisis
from 1959 through 1962. This bibliography supplements that published by the same review on the economic situation of the Congo,

1960-62 (v. 3, no. 9, 1962). The political bibliography contains short analyses of articles written about the Congo situation in official and unofficial publications of many countries and ideologies.

2214. Bustin, Edouard. A STUDY GUIDE FOR CONGO-KINSHASA. Boston, African Studies Center, Boston University, 1970. 167 p.

An excellent new bibliographic survey. For a useful listing of sources on education, see M. Boogaerts, "Education in the Congo: A Provisional Systematical Bibliography," CAHIERS ECONOMIQUES ET SOCIAUX, v. 5, no. 2, June 1967, p. 237-265.

2215. Heyse, Théodore. BIBLIOGRAPHIE DU CONGO BELGE ET DU RUANDA-URUNDI, 19-- Bruxelles, G. van Campenhout, 1946-53. (Cahiers belges et congolais, nos. 4-7, 9-12, 16-22)

Pamphlets of from about 40 to 70 pages listing by subject field writings on the Congo from 1939 to the date of publication. An article by Professor Heyse in ZAIRE of June 1948, "Le travail bibliographique colonial belge de 1876 jusqu'en 1933" (reprint, Bruxelles, Editions Universitaires, 1948, 20 p.), explains sources for earlier writings.

The separate titles are:

a) no. 4. (1939-1945): GEOLOGIE ET MINES.

b) no. 5. (1939-1946): REGIME FONCIER.

c) no. 6. (1939-1947): LITTERATURE, ARTS ORAUX INDIGENES.

d) no. 7. (1939-1947): AGRICULTURE . . . . In collaboration with J. Henrad.

e) no. 9. (1939-1948): TRANSPORTS, TRAVAUX PUBLICS, P.Y.Y., RADIO-DIFFUSION, FORCES HYDRO-ELECTRIQUES.

f) no. 10. (1939-1948): ECONOMIE GENERALE . . . .

g) no. 11. (1939-1949): BEAUX-ARTS, URBANISME, ARTS INDIGENES, CINEMA.

h) no. 12. (1939-1949): DOCUMENTATION GENERALE, HISTOIRE ET EXPANSION BELGE, BIOGRAPHIES, STANLEY, ARTICLES ET OUVRAGES GENERAUX.

i) no. 16. (1939-1950): POLITIQUE GENERALE, POLITIQUE INDIGENE, ENSEIGNEMENT, CULTES ET MISSIONS.

j) no. 17. (1939-1950): HYGIENE ET ASSISTANCE.

k) no. 18. (1939-1951): SCIENCES COLONIALES.

l) no. 19. (1939-1951): DOCUMENTATION GENERALE, BIBLI-
OGRAPHIES ET CENTRES D'ETUDE, EXPOSITIONS,
PRESSE ET PROPAGANCE.

m) no. 20. (1939-1951): DOCUMENTATION GENERALE, FOLKLORE,
PHILATELIE, SPORTS, TOURISME.

n) nos. 21-22. (1939-1951): L'AFRIQUE CENTRALE DANS LE
CONFLICT MONDIALE. (2 v.)

A separate list, published in the series Bibliographia belgica
(no. 64, 1961), was BIBLIOGRAPHIE DE H. M. STANLEY, 1841-1904.

2216. Heyse, Théodore. BIBLIOGRAPHIE JURIDIQUE DU CONGO BELGE ET DU RUANDA-
URUNDI, PERIODE 1939-51. Bruxelles, 1953. 26 pts. in 1 v.

2217. Heyse, Théodore. CONTRIBUTION AU PROGRES DES SCIENCES MORALES,
POLITIQUES ET ECONOMIQUES RELATIVES AUX TERRITOIRES D'OUTRE-
MER. Relevés bibliographiques I-III. Bruxelles, Commission
Belge de Bibliographie, 1957-1961. 3 v. (104, 206, 190 p.).
(Bibliographia belgica, 32, 57, 59)

Systematic bibliographies largely concerned with specific
studies on the Congo and Ruanda-Urundi. The first volume contains
1,064 entries, the second 783, and the third 811, and each volume
includes an author index.

2218. Heyse, Théodore. DOCUMENTATION GENERALE SUR LE CONGO ET LE RUANDA-
URUNDI, 1950-1953. Bruxelles, Commission Belge de Bibliographie,
1954. 31 p. (Bibliographia belgica, no. 4)

a) _____. DOCUMENTATION . . . 1953-1955. Bruxelles, G. van Campenhout, 1956. 56 p. (Cahiers belges et congolais, no. 26)

b) _____. DOCUMENTATION . . . 1955-1958. With the cooperation of
Jean Berlage. Bruxelles, Commission Belge de Bibliographie,
1958. 84 p. (Bibliographia belgica, no. 39)

c) _____. DOCUMENTATION . . . 1958-1960. With the cooperation of
Jean Berlage. Bruxelles, G. van Campenhout, 1960. 96 p.
(Cahiers belges et congolais, no. 34)

General listings supplementing the earlier special bibliographies.

2219. Heyse, Théodore. INDEX BIBLIOGRAPHIQUE COLONIAL: CONGO BELGE ET
           RUANDA-URUNDI; 1ere SERIE 1937-38, 2e SERIE 1938-39. Bruxelles,
           G. van Campenhout, 1939, 1940.

        Professor Heyse died on Jan. 10, 1963. In the ARSOM BULLETIN
DES SEANCES, no. 1, 1964, p. 137-155, there is a bibliography of his
writings, prepared by E. Van Grieken. Many of the titles are concerned with bibliographical studies of the Congo.

2220. Hoskyns, Catherine. "Sources for a Study of the Congo since
           Independence." JOURNAL OF MODERN AFRICAN STUDIES, v. 1, no. 3,
           Sept. 1963: 373-382.

        One of the bibliographical essays regularly carried in the
JOURNAL. The author is a specialist of the Royal Institute of
International Affairs.

2221. Hubaut, Pierre (former Librairie Africaine Hubaut) (15, rue de
           l'Industrie, Bruxelles 4). AFRIQUE: CONGO--AFRIQUE NOIRE:
           CATALOGUE. Bruxelles. (Catalogue no. 104, Apr. 1968, 24 p.)

        The catalogue of the late chief Belgian bookdealer carrying
African literature comes out several times a year with a long list
of new and older works available. Place of publication is given,
but no publisher's name. Included are many of the official series
of the Académie Royale des Sciences d'Outre-Mer and of the Musée
Royal de l'Afrique Centrale and the various monograph series of the
universities and institutions; they are not always easily identified.
The majority of the works have been concerned with the Congo, though
the list applied also to Africa in general and included books published in France and England as well as in Belgium.

2222. Lemarchand, René. "Selective Bibliographical Survey for the Study
           of Politics in the Former Belgian Congo." AMERICAN POLITICAL
           SCIENCE REVIEW, v. 54, Sept. 1960: 715-728.

        Bibliographical essay by a political scientist then with the
University of Lovanium in Leopoldville. The references are to
important works dealing with political developments in the Congo
and with their geographical and historical background. Sources
include the main official publications in addition to numerous
articles in leading periodicals and in the ENCYCLOPEDIE DU CONGO
BELGE.

2223. Liniger-Goumaz, Max. VILLES ET PROBLEMES URBAINS DE LA REPUBLIQUE DEMOCRATIQUE DU CONGO: BIBLIOGRAPHIE. Genève, Editions du Temps, 1968. 86 l.

Lists over 700 books, articles, theses in French, English, Russian, German. Arrangement is by topic: general works, cities and urban problems of Africa, urban problems of Congo-Kinshasa, then works on individual Congolese cities. Most publishers are omitted. An index is included.

2224. Monheim, Christian. CONGO-BIBLIOGRAPHIE. Antwerpen, Veritas, 1942. 211 p.

Supplement, 1944. 40 p.

A systematic bibliography on the Belgian Congo based on the catalogue of the Bibliothèque de l'Université Coloniale de Belgique. Following introductory geographic references, the 1942 volume of some 4,000 entries is divided into four main subject classifications --politics and administration, economy, history, and literature and the arts.

2225. Simar, T. "Bibliographie congolaise de 1895 à 1910." REVUE CONGOLAISE, v. 1, 1910. Printed as a separate in Brussels by Vroment, 1912. 61 p.

2226. Starr, Frederick. A BIBLIOGRAPHY OF CONGO LANGUAGES. Chicago, Department of Anthropology, University of Chicago, 1908. 97 p. (Bulletin no. 5) (678 entries)

2227. Tervuren, Belgium. Musée Royal de l'Afrique Centrale. BIBLIOGRAPHIE GEOLOGIQUE DU CONGO, DU RWANDA ET DU BURUNDI. v. 1- Tervuren, 1952-

Published in cooperation with the Commission de Géologie. Volumes are as follows: I, 1818-1924 (1955); II, 1925-34 (1953); III, 1935-44 (1952); IV, 1945-54 (1955); V, 1955-56 (1957); VI, 1957-58 (1959); VII, 1959-60 (1961); VIII, 1961-62 (1963). Publication through Vol. VI was under an early name of the Museum, Musée Royal du Congo Belge, and the bibliography title itself has varied somewhat. See also its CATALOGUE, no. 2263.

2228. Vandewoude, Emiel J. L. M. DOCUMENTS POUR SERVIR A LA CONNAISSANCE DES POPULATIONS DU CONGO BELGE: APERCU HISTORIQUE (1886-1933) DE L'ETUDE DES POPULATIONS AUTOCHTONES, PAR LES FONCTIONNAIRES

ET AGENTS DU SERVICE TERRITORIAL, SUIVI DE L'INVENTAIRE DES
ETUDES HISTORIQUES, ETHNOGRAPHIQUES ET LINGUISTIQUES CONSERVEES
AUX ARCHIVES DU CONGO BELGE. Léopoldville, Section Documentation des Archives du Congo Belge, 1958. 246 l. (Archives
du Congo belge, no. 2)

Beginning with an essay on the studies carried out by the agents
of the administration in the Congo during the years from the creation
of the Free State to 1933, this large processed volume lists 563
papers preserved in the archives. Many are notes of two or three pages,
others reports of considerable size. There are indexes of personal
names, places, and ethnic and linguistic terms and appendixes explaining official instructions for collecting and preserving the
material.

2229. Walraet, Marcel. BIBLIOGRAPHIE DU KATANGA: Fasc. I, 1884-1899.
Bruxelles, Institut Royal Colonial Belge, 1954. 136 p. map.
(Section des Sciences morales et politiques, Mémoires in-8°,
v. 32, fasc. 3, Série historique)

_____. BIBLIOGRAPHIE DU KATANGA: Fasc. II, 1900-1924. Bruxelles,
Académie Royale des Sciences Coloniales, 1956. 234 p. map.
(Classe des sciences morales et politiques, Mémoires in-8°, n.s.
v. 14, fasc. 1, Histoire)

_____. BIBLIOGRAPHIE DU KATANGA: Fasc. III, 1925-1949. Bruxelles,
Académie Royale des Sciences d'Outre-Mer, 1960. 280 p. map.
(Classe des sciences morales et politiques, Mémoires in-8°,
n.s. v. 23, fasc. 4)

A comprehensive systemative listing, with alphabetical arrangement by author or title under each section. Entries in the first
fascicle total 1,246, in the second 2,168, and in the third 2,934.
There is an author index for each fascicle, the one in Fasc. III
being cumulative for all three; Fasc. II also contains a chronological index.

2230. Wattel, Pierre. BIBLIOGRAPHIE DES MEMOIRES DE L'INSTITUT DES
TERRITOIRES D'OUTRE-MER. Bruxelles, Commission Belge de
Bibliographies, 1955. xi, 95 p. (Bibliographia belgica,
no. 11) (903 entries)

Includes a geographical index and an author index.

2231. Wauters, Alphonse-Jules. BIBLIOGRAPHIE DU CONGO, 1880-95: CATALOGUE
METHODIQUE DE 3,800 OUVRAGES, BROCHURES, NOTICES ET CARTES

RELATIFS A L'HISTOIRE, A LA GEOGRAPHIE ET A LA COLONISATION DU CONGO. With the collaboration of M. Ad. Buyl. Bruxelles, Administration du Mouvement Géographique, 1895. xlix, 356 p.

A bibliography of the early writings on the Congo, beginning with "Résumé chronologique des principaux faits de l'histoire du Congo," which has a 3-page essay on events from 1485 to 1815 and then dates of events from 1816 to 1895. Following are references in subject classification.

2232. Young, Crawford. "Materials for the Study of Islam in the Congo." CAHIERS ECONOMIQUES ET SOCIAUX, v. 4, no. 4, Dec. 1966: 461-464.

An informative bibliographic essay citing primary and secondary sources in English and French. Coverage extends from the nineteenth century, when Islam was introduced into the Congo, to the early 1960's.

Serials

2233. Académie Royale des Sciences d'Outre-Mer. Bruxelles.

The ARSOM series are:

a) BULLETIN DES SEANCES. MEDEDELINGEN DER ZITTINGEN. v. 1- 1930-54; n.s. v. 1- 1955-

Annual volumes, published in varying numbers of fascicles which range from under 500 to over 1,700 pages per volume. Ten-year indexes have been issued, 1930-39, 1940-49, 1950-59. The volumes contain valuable articles and reports. The first number, "Annuaire," of which year includes a list of periodicals received by the Academy.

b) Mémoires [monographs]:

Classe des sciences morales et politiques. Mémoires. Verhandelingen.

In-4°. v. 1- 1933- illus., maps.
In-8°. v. 1- 1933- illus., maps.

Classe des sciences naturelles et médicales. Mémoires. Verhandelingen.

In-4°. v. 1- 1931- illus., maps.
In-8°. n.s. v. 1- 1932- illus., maps.

Classe des sciences techniques. Mémoires. Verhandelingen.

In-4°. v. 1- 1930- illus., maps.
In-8°. n.s. v. 1- 1935- illus., maps.

The Academy also issues a set of Publications hors-série. The list of all titles in the CATALOGUE fills over 26 pages; these publications are also included in the official Belgian government list, below.

2234. AEQUETORIA: MISSION CATHOLIQUE. 1937- Coquilhatville, Congo.
       Quarterly.

Published by the Mission Catholique de Coquilhatville.

2235. BELGIQUE D'OUTRE-MER. 1945-60. Bruxelles. Monthly.

Leading popular journal, published from 1945-56 as LA REVUE COLONIALE BELGE, the numbering of which it continues (1945-60).

2236. Belgium. Ministère des Colonies. Office Colonial. BULLETIN DE
       L'OFFICE COLONIAL. 1910-40. Bruxelles. Monthly.

2237. BULLETIN AGRICOLE DU CONGO BELGE. 1910-61. Bruxelles. 4 times
       a year, Nov. 1910-52; 6 times a year, 1953-61.

2238. CAHIERS ECONOMIQUES ET SOCIAUX. ECONOMIC AND SOCIAL PAPERS. v. 1,
       no. 1- Oct. 1962- Léopoldville [Kinshasa], Institut de
       Recherches Economiques et Sociales (IRES), Université
       Lovanium. Quarterly.

The IRES (established 1955) attempts to continue the work of research organizations which functioned in the Congo before independence, and includes among its publications several series devoted to works on African (especially Congolese) economic, social, and political affairs. The aim of its journal is not only to study isolated features of the economic and social changes taking place in Africa but also to establish and interpret the emerging patterns and structures of the economic and social order in Africa generally. Articles are either in French or in English and are followed by a summary in the other language.

2239. CHRONOLOGIE DES EVENEMENTS RELATIFS AU CONGO. [1967?]- Bruxelles,
        Centre de Recherche et d'Information Socio-Politiques. Mimeo-
        graphed. Monthly.

        A useful documentation of Congolese events, classified under
        various headings for each day. This daily record, which runs to
        1,200-1,500 pages a year, has been maintained for some time by
        CRISP as a research instrument, and was only recently made available
        to scholars and specialized institutions.

2240. Congo, Belgian. BULLETIN OFFICIEL. AMTELIJK BLAD. 1908-60.
        Bruxelles. Monthly.

        Superseded BULLETIN OFFICIEL of the Congo Free State (1885-
        1908). Some numbers are accompanied by supplements. The bulletin
        was superseded in 1960 by MONITEUR CONGOLAIS, published in Kinshasa.

2241. Congo (Léopoldville). Université de l'Etat, Elisabethville, Katanga.
        PUBLICATIONS. v. 1- July 1961- illus., maps, diagrs.
        Irregular.

        Vol. II of this serial is titled L'INDUSTRIE KATANGAISE:
        REALISATIONS ET PERSPECTIVES: CONFERENCES AU COURS DES "JOURNEES
        DES INDUSTRIES KATANGAISES" ORGANISEES PAR L'UNIVERSITE . . . LES
        12, 13, ET 14 JUILLET 1961 (1961, 404 p., maps, diagrs., tables).

        In 1958, as criticism of the Belgian policy of education in
        the Congo came under international scrutiny, the Belgian Ministère
        du Congo Belge et du Ruanda-Urundi (later Ministère des Affaires
        Africaines) issued a brochure in English, UNIVERSITIES OF BELGIAN
        CONGO AND OF RUANDA-URUNDI (Brussels, 47 p., illus.). Much space
        is devoted to the Université de l'Etat in Elisabethville; this
        university and Lovanium University in Leopoldville were the only
        institutions of higher learning, aside from seminaries, in the
        Belgian territories.

2242. CONGO MISSION NEWS. 1913- Léopoldville. Quarterly.

        Journal of the Congo Protestant Council.

2243. ETUDES CONGOLAISES. no. 1- Mar. 1961- Léopoldville, Institut
        National d'Etudes Politiques (Institut Politique Congolais),
        and Bruxelles, Centre de Recherche et d'Information Socio-
        Politiques. Every 2 months.

Journal of political and social comments, published jointly by CRISP in Brussels and INEP in Leopoldville. Its regular sections are "Dossier" (a survey of the top question of the day), "Chronique," "Les livres," "Textes et documents," and "Revue de presse."

2244. FOLIA SCIENTIFICA AFRICAE CENTRALIS. v. 1, no. 1- Mar. 1955-
        Bukavu [etc.], IRSAC. Quarterly.

        Text in French and Dutch with summaries in English.

        Bulletin of information on current activities of the Institut pour la Recherche Scientifique en Afrique Centrale, with sections on biological, human, and physical sciences, giving brief accounts of work done and titles of new publications. The bulletin did not cease with independence, though combined nos. 2-3-4 (Dec. 31, 1960) of Vol. VI were printed in Europe.

2245. Institut National pour l'Etude Agronomique du Congo. BULLETIN
        D'INFORMATION. 1952-1961. Bruxelles.

2246. Institut National pour l'Etude Agronomique du Congo. Publication ...
        Hors-série. 1935-61. Bruxelles.

2247. Institut National pour l'Etude Agronomique du Congo. Publications.
        Série scientifique. 1935- Bruxelles.

2248. Institut National pour l'Etude Agronomique du Congo. Publications.
        Série technique. 1935- Bruxelles.

2249. Institut National pour l'Etude Agronomique du Congo. SPERMATOPHYTES.
        1948- Bruxelles.

2250. Institut National pour l'Etude Agronomique du Congo. Bureau
        Climatologique. Communication. 1950- Bruxelles.

2251. KONGO-OVERZEE: TIJDSCHRIFT VOOR EN OVER BELGISCH-KONGO EN ANDERE
        OVERZEESE GEWESTEN. 1934- Antwerpen. Every 2 months (except Aug., Sept.).

2252.   Notre Colonie (Société Coopérative). REVUE COLONIALE: ORGAN DE
          L'OFFICE BELGE DE COLONISATION AU CONGO. 1919-39. Bruxelles.
          Irregular.

2253.   PROBLEMES D'AFRIQUE CENTRALE. 1947-59. Bruxelles. Quarterly.

          Bulletin de l'Association des Anciens Etudiants de l'I.N.U.T.O.M.
    Title varies: 1947-50, BULLETIN.

2254.   PROBLEMES SOCIAUX CONGOLAIS. 1946- Lubumbashi, Centre d'Etude
          des Problèmes Sociaux Indigènes. Quarterly.

          Has valuable articles. The centre also publishes COLLECTION
    DE MEMOIRES irregularly.

2255.   REVUE BELGE DE GEOGRAPHIE. 1877- Bruxelles, Société Royale Belge
          de Geographie.

2256.   REVUE CONGOLAISE ILLUSTREE. 1929-66. Bruxelles, Association des
          Vétérans de l'Etat Independant du Congo. Monthly.

          Title changed to REVUE BELGO-CONGOLAISE ILLUSTREE with v. 33,
    no. 6, June 1962.

2257.   REVUE JUDICAIRE CONGOLAISE. 1962- Léopoldville. Every 3 months.

2258.   REVUE JURIDIQUE D'AFRIQUE CENTRALE. 1924-63. Elisabethville,
          Société d'Etudes Juridiques du Katanga. Bimonthly.

          Title varies. The journal was absorbed by REVUE JURIDIQUE DU
    CONGO: DROIT ECRIT ET DROIT COUTUMIER (1964-, Lubumbashi[?]).

2259.   Société Belge d'Etudes Coloniales. BULLETIN DE LA SOCIETE BELGE
          D'ETUDES COLONIALES. 1894-1919. Bruxelles. Bimonthly,
          1895-99; monthly, 1900-1919.

          Continued as CONGO: REVUE GENERALE DE LA COLONIE BELGE, 1920-
    40, then by ZAIRE, 1947-61 (see no. 2266).

2260.   Société Royale Belge de Géographie. BULLETIN. 1876- Bruxelles.

2261. Tervuren, Belgium. Musée Royal de l'Afrique Centrale. Annales.
        Série in 8°. Sciences historiques Annalen. Reeks in 8°.
        Historische Wetenschappen. no. 1- Tervuren, 1964-

        Supersedes in part its Annales, Série in 8°, Sciences historiques
et économiques. Among the other important series (Annales) produced
by the Museum are:

        1898-1934 Botaniques

        1947-   Sciences économiques

        1948-   Sciences géologiques

        1948-   Sciences zoologiques (Earlier series started in 1898.)

        1960-   Archives d'ethnographie

        1962-   Documentation économique

        See also CATALOGUE (no. 2263, below) and AFRIKA-TERVUREN,
1961- (quarterly), formerly CONGO-TERVUREN, 1955-61.

2262. Tervuren, Belgium. Musée Royal de l'Afrique Centrale. Annales.
        Série in 8°. Sciences humaines. Annalen. Reeks in 8°.
        Wetenschappen van de mens. no. 33- Tervuren, 1960-

        Nos. 1-32, 1951-60, published in 4 subseries: Anthropologie,
Ethnographique, Linguistique, Préhistoire. Almost sixty volumes of
this outstanding series had appeared by 1968.

2263. Tervuren, Belgium. Musée Royal de l'Afrique Centrale. CATALOGUE.
        Tervuren, 1966. 56 p.

2264. Tervuren, Belgium. Musée Royal de l'Afrique Centrale. Monographies
        ethnographiques. Ethnographische monographien. no. 1-
        Tervuren, 1954-

2265. LA VOIX DU CONGOLAIS. 1945- Léopoldville. Bimonthly, later
        monthly.

2266. ZAIRE: REVUE CONGOLAISE; CONGOLEESCH TIJDSCHRIFT. 1947-61.
        Bruxelles, Editions Universitaires. illus. Monthly except
        Aug. and Sept.

Important journal which superseded CONGO: REVUE GENERALE DE
LA COLONIE BELGE, published from 1920 to the outbreak of World War
II. Its bibliographical section was issued by the Ministère du
Congo Belge as a separate. The periodical was really terminated
with the independence of the Congo in 1960, although one issue
appeared in 1961.

Reference Works

2267. Académie Royale des Sciences d'Outre-Mer (ARSOM). BIOGRAPHIE
          COLONIALE BELGE. Bruxelles, Librairie Falk Fils, 1948-68.
          6 v. ports.

          Published by ARSOM under its earlier name, Institut Royal
Colonial Belge. The work is not confined to Belgians connected
with the Congo (e.g., Leopold II) but includes entries for Livingstone, Stanley, and others--more than 2,000 biographies in all.
All entries are signed, dated, and documented (normally with a
bibliography, sometimes with references as well). Each volume
has a separate alphabetic sequence of biographies of deceased
persons. Vol. IV and Vol. V both carry cumulative biographee
and author indexes to previous volumes as well as corrigenda and
addenda. With Vol. VI the title was changed to BIOGRAPHIE BELGE
D'OUTRE-MER.

2268. Académie Royale des Sciences d'Outre-Mer (ARSOM). LIVRE BLANC:
          RAPPORT SCIENTIFIQUE DE LA BELGIQUE AU DEVELOPPEMENT DE L'AF-
          RIQUE CENTRALE. [Title also in Dutch] Bruxelles, 1962-63.
          3 v. fold. col. map, tables.

          Vol. I, CLASSE DES SCIENCES MORALES ET POLITIQUES. 503, xx p.

          Vol. II, CLASSE DES SCIENCES NATURELLES ET MEDICALES. 436,
                xvi p.

          Vol. III, CLASSE DES SCIENCES TECHNIQUES. 183, xxxii p.

          A collective work reviewing the Belgian contribution to the
Congo and Rwanda and Burundi, undertaken by ARSOM after the former
colonies became independent countries. The many articles, in French
and Flemish, are by leading specialists in studies of the Congo.
Each volume is separately indexed, and there is a final alphabetical
index covering the whole work. The first volume contains an introduction by L. Guébels, president of ARSOM, and surveys of scientific
research problems by L. van den Berghe, of colonial congresses by
P. Coppens, of bibliography and documentation by Théodore Heyse,
and of archives by Mme. M. Van Grieken-Taverniers.

2269. American University, Washington, D.C. Special Operations Research
        Office. AREA HANDBOOK FOR THE REPUBLIC OF THE CONGO (LEOPOLD-
        VILLE). Prepared by Foreign Areas Studies Division. Washington,
        1962. xii, 657 p. maps, tables.

        Includes bibliographies.

        Country study prepared to provide basic factual background for
American officers in the Congo, with comprehensive information
presented objectively in short paragraphs. Sections are on sociological background, political background (through 1961), economic
background, and national security. Each section is followed by a
long bibliography.

2270. Andersson, Efraim. MESSIANIC POPULAR MOVEMENTS IN THE LOWER CONGO.
        Uppsala, Almqvist & Wiksells Boktr. (distributed by W. S.
        Heinman, New York), 1958. xiii, 287 p. illus., plates (part
        col.). (Studia ethnographica Upsaliensia, no. 14)

        Bibliography: p. xi-xiii.

        By a missionary who spent many years in Central Africa, this
is the most comprehensive account in English of Simon Kimbangu and
his cult with data on other "prophet movements" in French Equatorial
Africa.

2271. ANNUAIRE DE LA REPUBLIQUE DEMOCRATIQUE DU CONGO. 1965- Kinshasa,
        Agence Nationale de Publicite Congolaise, 1969- 524 p. illus.,
        col. maps, tables.

        A handsome volume covering political and administrative organi-
zation, basic economic data, perspective for industrialization,
legislation and regulations, and diverse practical information (pass-
ports and visas, customs regulations, commercial and industrial
enterprises, etc.). A telephone directory of subscribers and an
analytical index conclude the volume. Advertising is included.

2272. ANNUAIRE DES MISSIONS CATHOLIQUES AU CONGO BELGE ET AU RUANDA-
        URUNDI. 3d ed. Edited by the Rev. J. van Wing, S.J., and
        V. Goemé, S.J. Bruxelles, Edition Universelle, 1949. 671 p.
        maps.

        Includes history, current organization, locations, number of
converts, directory of priests, etc. The second edition was issued
in 1935.

2273. Anstey, Roger. KING LEOPOLD'S LEGACY: THE CONGO UNDER BELGIAN
RULE, 1908-1960. Issued under the auspices of the Institute
of Race Relations, London. London, New York, Oxford University Press, 1966. xiv, 293 p. illus., ports., plates,
map.

Bibliography: p. 265-272.

A sequel to Ruth Slade's KING LEOPOLD'S CONGO (see no. 2328),
this is a well-documented account of the origins, nature, and impact
of Belgian rule in the Congo. Two opening chapters describe what
Leopold's legacy comprised. The early period of Belgian rule is
then covered, followed by a discussion of the interwar years, with
focus on African administration and the pressures of customary
society, and on economic development and town growth. Following
a chapter on prophet movements, the latter half of the book deals
with the period 1940-60. An appendix consists of parts of Reverend
J. Van Wing's "Evolution of Ba-Kongo Custom," first published in
1927.

2274. Artigue, Pierre. QUI SONT LES LEADERS CONGOLAIS? 2d ed. Bruxelles,
Editions Europe-Afrique, 1961. 375 p. (Collection "Carrefours
africains")

Biographical sketches of Congolese personalities. A preliminary
edition came out in 1960 (139 p.; "Carrefours africains," no. 3).
The greatly enlarged revision contains more than 800 biographies.
They vary in length from 20 to several hundred words, including for
many individuals a carefully dated account of education and preindependence activities.

2275. Balandier, Georges. DAILY LIFE IN THE KINGDOM OF THE KONGO FROM
THE SIXTEENTH TO THE EIGHTEENTH CENTURY. Translated from the
French by Helen Weaver. New York, Pantheon Books, 1968. 288 p.
illus., plates, map.

See no. 1997 for annotation.

2276. Belgium. Ministère des Affaires Africaines. Direction de
l'Agriculture, des Forêts et de l'Elevage. VOLUME JUBILAIRE DU
BULLETIN AGRICOLE DU CONGO BELGE ET DU RUANDA-URUNDI, 1910-
1960. Bruxelles, 1960. 226 p. illus. (part col.), maps,
diagrs., tables.

Published by the Ministry under its earlier name, Ministère
du Congo Belge et du Ruanda-Urundi; text in French only.

Fiftieth anniversary volume of the official journal which has
been the main source of current information on Congolese agriculture.
The work, setting forth the history and accomplishments of Belgian
agricultural endeavor in the Congo, appeared almost simultaneously
with the independence proclamation.

2277.   Belgium. Ministère des Affaires Africaines. Direction des Etudes
        Economiques. LA SITUATION ECONOMIQUE DU CONGO BELGE ET DU
        RUANDA-URUNDI. 1950-59. Bruxelles, 1951-60. tables, charts.
        Annual. (1959 ed., 272 p., 84 tables)

        Yearly survey of the economy, relating to the Congo only from
1950 to 1954, then including Ruanda-Urundi. All features of economic
life are thoroughly covered in tabulated data from official and
private sources. For some years editions were issued also in English.

2278.   Belgium. Office de l'Information et des Relations Publiques pour
        le Congo Belge et le Ruanda-Urundi (INFORCONGO). BELGIAN CONGO.
        [v. 1 translated from the French by F. H. and C. Heldt, v. 2
        by Claire van Gelder]. Bruxelles, 1959-60. 2 v. 547, 187 p.
        illus., maps, tables.

        Bibliography: v. 2, p. 181-187.

        Faithful translation of the original French edition of 1958.
Vol. I is a digest of information on country and people, history,
political institutions, economic and social life, etc. Vol. II
contains statistics; this part was designed to be revised periodically.

2279.   Belgium. Office de l'Information et des Relations Publiques pour
        le Congo Belge et le Ruanda-Urundi. CONGO BELGE ET RUANDA-
        URUNDI: GUIDE DU VOYAGEUR. 4th ed. Bruxelles, 1958. 798 p.
        illus., maps.

        Formal guidebook, with itineraries and detailed regional
descriptions preceded by general articles. The first edition in
1949 and subsequent editions until 1956 were issued by the Belgian
Office du Tourisme du Congo Belge et du Ruanda-Urundi. Two editions
in English titled TRAVELLER'S GUIDE FOR THE BELGIAN CONGO AND
RUANDA-URUNDI were brought out in 1951 and 1956.

2280.   Bevel, Maurice Louis. LE DICTIONNAIRE COLONIAL (ENCYCLOPEDIE):
        EXPLICATION DE PLUS DE 8.000 NOMS ET EXPRESSIONS SE RAPPORTANT
        AUX DIVERSES ACTIVITES COLONIALES, DEPUIS L'EPOQUE HEROIQUE
        JUSQU'AUX TEMPS PRESENTS. 3d ed. Bruxelles, Guyot, 1955.
        202, 26 p. illus., port., maps (1 fold. col.).

Refers particularly to the Belgian Congo, giving in alphabetical order names of persons, places, and organizations and words and phrases connected with colonial activities. A supplement is included.

2281. Bilsen, A. A. J. van. L'INDEPENDANCE DU CONGO. Tournai, Casterman, 1962. 236 p.

By a Belgian specialist on the Congo, professor at the Institut Universitaire des Territoires d'Outre-Mer, who in 1960 acted as adviser to Kasavubu at the Brussels Round Table Conference and afterward in Leopoldville. His "Thirty-Year Plan for the Political Emancipation of Belgian Africa," published in 1955 (UN PLAN DE TRENTE ANS POUR L'EMANCIPATION POLITIQUE DE L'AFRIQUE BELGE, Antwerp), was at the time considered an impossibility at long range. The 1962 volume is a compilation of articles and documents issued during the last period of hurried preparation for independence, including writings to the spring of 1961, after Lumumba's downfall and death. It supplements an earlier work, VERS L'INDEPENDANCE DU CONGO BELGE ET DU RUANDA-URUNDI: REFLEXIONS SUR LES DEVOIRS ET L'AVENIR DE LA BELGIQUE EN AFRIQUE CENTRALE (Kraainem, 1958, 295 p.).

2282. Bouvier, Paule. L'ACCESSION DU CONGO BELGE A L'INDEPENDANCE: ESSAI D'ANALYSE SOCIOLOGIQUE. Bruxelles, Editions de l'Institut de Sociologie, Université Libre de Bruxelles, 1965. 392 p. tables. (Collection du Centre National d'Etudes des Problèmes Sociaux d'Industrialisation en Afrique Noire)

Bibliography: p. 365-378.

A sociological approach to decolonization in the Congo. Professor Bouvier's study is in five main parts: the social, economic, and political framework for emancipation; social factors involved in the behavior of various Belgian and Congolese groups; characteristics of the Congolese political movements; metropolitan reactions and Congolese counter-reactions (including a long section on the sociological components of the Brussels Round Table Conference); and events in the Congo from 1959 through 1962.

2283. Braekman, E. M. HISTOIRE DU PROTESTANTISME AU CONGO. Bruxelles, Editions de la Librairie des Eclaireurs Unionistes, 1961. 391 p. plates, maps, tables. (Collection "Histoire du Protestantisme en Belgique et au Congo belge," v. 5)

Bibliographical footnotes.

An outline history in which the author discusses the precursors of evangelization from the sixteenth to the late nineteenth century,

traces the development of Protestantism through 1959, and describes
Belgian missionary activities. Included are statistical data,
a chronological list of missionary societies and their stations,
and both an onomastic and a geographical index.

2284. Brausch, Georges. BELGIAN ADMINISTRATION IN THE CONGO. London,
        Oxford University Press, 1961. 92 p.

        An account of Belgian administration and decolonization by a
former Belgian official, who outlines the shifts of Belgian policy
preceding decolonization, shows how these were connected with
changes in metropolitan politics, and demonstrates how the morale
of the Belgian civil service was gradually eroded and finally
snapped.

2285. Bulck, G. van. LES RECHERCHES LINGUISTIQUES AU CONGO BELGE:
        RESULTATS ACQUIS, NOUVELLES ENQUETES A ENTREPRENDE. Bruxelles,
        G. van Campenhout, 1948. 767 p. fold. map. (Institut Royal
        Colonial Belge, Section des Sciences Morales et Politiques,
        Mémoires in-8°, v. 16)

        Synthesis of results of linguistic studies for the Congo by
a foremost authority on the subject. In 1949 Father van Bulck's
MANUEL DE LINGUISTIQUE BANTOUE was published as fasc. 3 of Vol.
XVII of this series. Many other papers on linguistics by him and
by his colleagues, G. Hulstaert and L. de Boeck, are to be found
in the indexes of the Mémoires of the Institut, now the Académie
Royale des Sciences d'Outre-Mer.

2286. Centre d'Information et de Documentation du Congo Belge et du
        Ruanda-Urundi. LISTE DES SOCIETES ET INSTITUTIONS COLONIALES
        AYANT UN SIEGE EN BELGIQUE ET AU CONGO BELGE OU AU RUANDA-
        URUNDI. Bruxelles, 1954. 74 p.

        The many publications of INFORCONGO (Centre d'Information et
de Documentation--CID--was earlier name) were for general
orientation purposes and included general reports, commercial
statistics, maps, customs requirements, directories, etc. This
directory shows the wealth of institutions concerned with the Congo
during the Belgian regime. Since independence some of them,
particularly the commercial bodies, are still in existence.

2287. Centre de Recherche et d'Information Socio-Politiques. CONGO 19--
        Bruxelles, 1960- (Les dossiers du CRISP)

Eight annual volumes have been issued in this Dossiers series:

a) CONGO 1959: DOCUMENTS BELGES ET AFRICAINS. 1960. 319 p. "Bibliographie politique sur le Congo en 1959": p. 303-309.

A second revised edition, edited by J. Gérard-Libois, was issued in 1961 (293 p.).

b) CONGO 1960. Edited by J. Gérard-Libois and Benoît Verhaegen. 1961. 2 v. 1115 p. map.

Bibliographical footnotes.

A supplement, ANNEXES ET BIOGRAPHIES (132 p.), also appeared in 1961.

c) CONGO 1961. Edited by Benoît Verhaegen. 1962. 691 p. tables.

Bibliographical footnotes.

d) CONGO 1962. Edited by J. Gérard-Libois and Benoît Verhaegen. 1963. 453 p. maps.

Bibliographical footnotes.

Issued jointly with the Institut National d'Etudes Politiques (INEP), Léopoldville.

e) CONGO 1963. Edited by Benoît Verhaegen, J. Beys, and P.-H. Gendebien. 1965. 456 p.

Bibliographical footnotes.

Issued jointly with INEP.

f) CONGO 1964: POLITICAL DOCUMENTS OF A DEVELOPING NATION. Edited by J. Gérard-Libois and J. Van Lierde. Introduction by Herbert F. Weiss. Princeton, N.J., Princeton University Press, 1966. xxiv, 591 p. maps.

Bibliographical footnotes.

g) CONGO 1965: POLITICAL DOCUMENTS OF A DEVELOPING NATION. Edited by J. Gérard-Libois and J. Van Lierde. Introduction by Herbert Weiss. Princeton, N.J., Princeton University Press, 1967. xvii, 507 p. illus., maps, tables.

Bibliographical footnotes.

h)   CONGO 1966. Edited by J. Gérard-Libois, B. Verhaegen, J.
         Vansina, and H. Weiss. Bruxelles, 1967. 543 p. maps,
         tables.

     Bibliographical footnotes.

     Issued jointly with INEP.

        CRISP, founded in 1958 by a group of Belgian scholars, jour-
nalists, and economists (and now including correspondents from
other European countries, the United States, and the Congo), has
undertaken this valuable sequence of annual documentary histories
of Congolese politics. In addition to the Dossiers, CRISP publishes
a number of special studies, a mimeographed bulletin, COURRIER
AFRICAIN, the bimonthly journal ETUDES CONGOLAISES (see no. 2243),
and the mimeographed monthly CHRONOLOGIE DES EVENEMENTS RELATIFS
AU CONGO (see no. 2239). In the series Les etudes du CRISP,
SECESSION AU KATANGA (by J. Gérard-Libois, 1963, 363 p.; English
ed., KATANGA SECESSION, translated by Rebecca Young, Madison,
University of Wisconsin Press, 1966, 377 p.), was issued jointly
with INEP (see no. 2303, below). Also in this series, in collab-
oration with INEP and the Institut de Recherches Economiques et
Sociales (IRES), Université Lovanium, Léopoldville, is REBELLIONS
AU CONGO, Vol. I (by Benoît Verhaegen, 1966, 568 p., map, bibliographies), a study based on documents and interviews.

        Among other volumes in the Dossiers series are two on political
parties in the Congo: A.B.A.K.O., 1950-1960: DOCUMENTS (edited
by Benoît Verhaegen, 1962, 367 p., illus., map) and PARTI SOLIDAIRE
AFRICAIN (P.S.A.): DOCUMENTS, 1959-1960 (edited by Herbert Weiss
and Benoît Verhaegen, 1963, 315 p., map, tables). LES PARTIS
POLITIQUES CONGOLAIS (by J. C. Willame, 1964, 156 l., map) has
appeared as the first volume of Dossiers documentaires in the
series Travaux africains.

2288. Chronique de Politique Etrangère (periodical). LA CRISE CONGOLAISE,
          1 JANVIER 1959- 15 AOUT 1960. Bruxelles, Institut Royal des
          Relations Internationales, 1960. (v. 13, no. 4-6, July-Nov.
          1960: 411-1012)

          _____. L'EVOLUTION DE LA CRISE CONGOLAISE DE SEPTEMBRE 1960 A
          AVRIL 1961. (v. 14, no. 5-6, Sept.-Nov. 1961: 565-1182)

          _____. L'O.N.U. AU CONGO, AVRIL 1961 A OCTOBRE 1962. (v. 15,
          no. 4-6, July-Nov. 1962: 339-1108)

          _____. CONCLUSION DE L'OPERATION DE L'O.N.U. AU CONGO, 1962-
          1963. (v. 17, no. 1, Jan. 1964, 126 p.)

Solid documentation on political developments in the Congo
before and since independence, in three sets of combined issues
plus a single issue of this leading Belgian journal of international affairs.

2289. Cleene, N. de. INTRODUCTION A L'ETHNOGRAPHIE DU CONGO BELGE ET
DU RWANDA-BURUNDI. 2d completed ed. Anvers, Editions de
Sikkel, 1957. 159 p. illus., maps. (Kongo-Overzee Biblio-
theek, no. 9)

Includes bibliographies.

Concentrated basic work on the populations of the former
Belgian territories by a professor at the Institut Universitaire
des Territoires d'Outre-Mer. He divides the peoples into three
classes--pygmies, agricultural peoples, and pastoral peoples--
and summarizes for each information on material, social, spiritual,
and political life. For the agricultural peoples there are separate
chapters on such aspects as intellectual life and esthetics.
Bibliographies follow each chapter; many of the references are to
the Mémoires of the Académie Royale des Sciences d'Outre-Mer.

A companion volume in this orientation series is by Amaat
F. S. Burssens, INTRODUCTION A L'ETUDE DES LANGUES BANTOUES DU
CONGO BELGE (Anvers, Editions de Sikkel, 1954, 152 p.; Kongo-
Overzee Bibliotheek, no. 8)

2290. CONGO BELGE. Genève, New York, Editions Nagel, 1958 [c. 1959].
256 p. maps. (Les guides Nagel)

Conventional travel guide.

2291. Congrès Scientifique du Cinquantenaire, Elisabethville, 1950.
COMPTES RENDUS. Bruxelles, Comité Spécial du Katanga, 1951.
7 v.

These volumes, published in commemoration of the 50th
anniversary of the Comité Spécial du Katanga, contain authoritative survey articles on all phases of scientific, geographical,
economic, and social life of the territory. Contributors include
all specialists on the Katanga.

The numerous scientific publications of the Committee are
issued in several monographic series: Sér. A, Geography, geology,
and mines; Sér. B, Natural history, etc. Titles will be found in
the annual RAPPORT DE L'EXERCICE (1920- ; v. 1 covers 1910-19).

2292. Cornet, René J. TERRE KATANGAISE: CINQUANTIEME ANNIVERSAIRE DU
COMITE SPECIAL DU KATANGA, 1900-1950. Bruxelles, 1950. 317
p. illus., maps.

Published in a deluxe edition for the 50th anniversary of the
Comité Spécial du Katanga and written by the son of the geologist
whose pioneer work led to discovery of Katanga's great mineral
wealth. The father's standard history, KATANGA, was issued in a
third edition by Cuypers, Brussels, in 1946. The present book,
lavishly illustrated with photographs and drawings, is a journalistic account, its author having been at the time editor of the
leading popular journal devoted to the Belgian Congo, the REVUE
COLONIALE BELGE.

2293. Cornevin, Robert. HISTOIRE DU CONGO, LEOPOLDVILLE-KINSHASSA:
DES ORIGINES PREHISTORIQUES A LA REPUBLIQUE DEMOCRATIQUE DU
CONGO. 2d ed., rev. and enl. With 19 maps and 54 photographs.
Paris, Berger-Levrault, 1966. 348 p. (Mondes d'outre-mer,
Série: Histoire)

Bibliography: p. 316-329.

By the director of CEDAOM (Centre d'Etudes et de Documentation
sur l'Afrique et l'Outre-Mer), who went to the Congo in the spring
of 1962 for a course of lectures and was able to observe at first
hand the international problems of the independent Republic. In
his introduction he comments that he had contemplated a study of
recent events only but that his lectures on Congolese history at
the National School of Law and Administration (ENDA) in Leopoldville made him realize that the Congolese are largely ignorant of
their own past. He has written a full-scale but simplified and
somewhat inaccurate history of the Congo from earliest times to
the present.

2294. De Craemer, Willy, and Renée C. Fox. THE EMERGING PHYSICIAN: A
SOCIOLOGICAL APPROACH TO THE DEVELOPMENT OF A CONGOLESE
MEDICAL PROFESSION. Stanford, Calif., Hoover Institution,
1968. 99 p.

Bibliography: p. 97-99.

An original and valuable approach via the study of a career
pattern as a key to understanding social change.

2295. Denis, Jacques. LE PHENOMENE URBAIN EN AFRIQUE CENTRALE. Bruxelles,
Académie Royale des Sciences Coloniales, 1958. 407 p. (Classe

des sciences morales et politiques, Mémoires in-8°, n.s. v. 19, fasc. 1)

Bibliography: p. 371-394.

Study by a Jesuit priest and geographer of the new cities and the urban life and problems that have accompanied the rapid industrialization in the postwar era. The concern is chiefly with Congolese centers, though Father Denis includes some cities of neighboring territories. He has used material from over 400 sources listed in his bibliography.

A more specialized study is the author's LES YAKA DU KWANGO: CONTRIBUTION A UNE ETUDE ETHNO-DEMOGRAPHIQUE (Tervuren, Musée Royale de l'Afrique Centrale, 1964, xi, 107 p., maps, tables; Annales, Sér. in-8°, Sciences humaines, no. 53), an account of the diffusion of the Bayaka people over the territories of Popokabaka, Kasongo-Lunda, and Kenge.

See also no. 840.

2296. Dumont, Georges H. LA TABLE RONDE BELGO-CONGOLAISE (JANVIER-FEVRIER 1960). Paris, Editions Universitaires, 1961. 308 p. map, tables, fold. chart. (Encyclopédie universitaire)

At head of title: LE CONGO, DU REGIME COLONIAL A L'INDEPENDANCE, 1955-1960.

Description of the origins, composition, and proceedings of the Brussels Round Table. It was at this conference, attended by a Congolese delegation of almost 100 persons, representing some 15 different political groups, that the target date for Congo independence was eventually fixed for June 30, 1960. The resolutions of the conference are given in the body of the text and numerous documents appear in appendixes. Both an analytical index and an index of personal names are included.

2297. ENCYCLOPEDIE DU CONGO BELGE. Bruxelles, Bieleveld, 1950(?)-52. 3 v. 722, 668, 862 p. illus., col. plates, maps (part col.), diagrs.

Synthesis of then available knowledge about the Congo, prepared through the collaboration of about 50 specialists. Statistics are of 1948. Vol. I covers history, ethnology, geology, climate and soils, botany, colonial agricultural industries; Vol. II, forestry, fauna, animal husbandry, mines and mining; Vol. III, colonial hygiene, diseases of animals, plants, applied entomology,

economic life, political institutions, and education. At the end
of Vol. III is an alphabetical index plus an index of 60-odd maps.

2298. Epstein, Howard M., ed. REVOLT IN THE CONGO, 1960-64. New York,
         Facts on File, 1965. 187 p. ("An Interim History Book")

   A day-to-day record of the Congolese rebellion, from the
signing of the Congo independence agreement in 1960 to the U.S.-
Belgian airdrop in Nov. 1964. The text is taken from news materials
provided by Facts on File, which in turn derive from U.S. and
foreign newspapers and press services. An attempt is made to
provide straight news, avoiding bias. A concluding section, taken
from U.S. State Department Background Notes, describes the Congo
and its peoples.

2299. Ethnographic Survey of Africa: Central Africa, Belgian Congo
         [series]. London, International African Institute.

   For the general note on this series, see no. 980.

   The studies relating to Congolese peoples were also published
in the Annales du Musée Royal du Congo Belge, Tervuren, Sér. in-8°,
Sciences de l'homme, Monographies ethnographiques. Some that have
appeared are:

a)   Part 1.   LES TRIBUS BA-KUBA ET LES PEUPLADES APPARENTEES.
               By Jan Vansina. 1954. xiii, 64 p. fold.
               map. [Monographies ethnographiques, v. 1]

               Bibliography: p. 57-61.

b)   Part 2.   LES BIRA ET LES PEUPLADES LIMITROPHES. By H. van
               Geluwe. 1957. xiii, 165 p. fold. map.
               [Monographies ethnographiques, v. 2]

               Bibliography: p. 155-161.

c)   Part 3.   MAMVU-MANGUTU ET BALESE-MVUBA. By H. van Geluwe.
               1957. xv, 195 p. fold. map. [Monographies
               ethnographiques, v. 3]

               Bibliography: p. 175-182.

d)   Part 4.   LES PEUPLADES DE L'ENTRE CONGO-UBANGI (NGBANDI,
               NGBAKA, MBANDJA, NGOMBE ET GENS D'EAU). By
               H. Burssens. 1958. 219 p. fold. map.
               [Monographies ethnographiques, v. 4]

               Bibliography: p. 175-198.

e)   Part 5.   LES BALI ET LES PEUPLADES APPARENTEES (NDAKA, MBO,
                 BEKE, LIKA, BUDU, NYARI). By H. van Geluwe.
                 1960. 130 p. fold. map. [Monographies
                 ethnographiques, v. 5]

         Bibliography: p. 115-122.

     See also THE LELE OF THE KASAI, by Mary Douglas (1963, xiv,
286 p., fold. map; bibliography: p. 280-282. [I.A.I. Series]

     An earlier study was issued in 1935 by the Musée Royal du
Congo Belge (Publications du Bureau de documentation ethno-
graphique, Sér. 2, Monographies idéologiques, v. 1): LES PEUPLADES
DU CONGO BELGE: NOM ET SITUATION GEOGRAPHIQUE, by Joseph Maes and
Olga Boone (Bruxelles, Impr. Veuve Monnom, 379 p., maps). This
work presented an inventory of tribes and groupings, with geographic
locations, variant names, etc., and included bibliographical notes
and an index of place and tribal names. A more recent work by
Olga Boone is her CARTE ETHNIQUE DU CONGO: QUART SUD-EST (Tervuren,
Musée Royal de l'Afrique Centrale, 1961, xvi, 271 p., maps [1 fold.
in pocket]; Annales, Sér. in-8°, Sciences humaines, no. 37), in
which she surveys each of some 55 peoples of the southeastern Congo
by the use of the following format: name, geographical situation,
demography, bibliography, map.

2300. European Economic Community. Mission Congo. MISSION C.E.E.--
       CONGO. Bruxelles, 1963. 5 fasc. maps (part col.).
       Processed.

     A report prepared for the Congolese government by a 21-man
mission to the Congo. The fascicles comprising the economic survey
are:

     Fasc. I.   EXPOSES GENERAUX: ESSAI DE SYNTHESE: ASPECTS
                 ECONOMIQUES: SITUATION FINANCIERE ET MONETAIRE.
                 189 p.

     Fasc. II.   SECTEUR PRIMAIRE: AGRICULTURE-MINES. 99 p.

     Fasc. III. SECTEUR SECONDAIRE: INDUSTRIE-ENERGIE-EAU. 264 p.

     Fasc. IV.   SECTEUR TERTIARE: TRANSPORT ET VOIES DE COMMUNICATIONS:
                 TELECOMMUNICATIONS. 173 p.

     Fasc. V.   PROBLEMES HUMAINS: SANTE-ENSEIGNEMENT. 118 p.

2301.   Franck, Louis. LE CONGO BELGE. Bruxelles, La Renaissance du
           Livre, 1928. 2 v. 379; 489 p. maps.

       A monumental work, profusely illustrated with large folding
maps. The book covers every aspect of Belgian colonization in the
Congo.

2302.   Ganshof van der Meersch, W. J. FIN DE LA SOUVERAINETE BELGE AU
           CONGO: DOCUMENTS ET REFLEXIONS. Bruxelles, Institut Royal
           des Relations Internationales; La Haye, M. Nijhoff, 1963.
           684 p. plates, maps, charts.

       "Bibliographie": p. 671-676; "Notice bibliographique de
       l'auteur": p. 678-679.

       The author, a lawyer and professor, was named Ministre des
Affaires Générales en Afrique (Resident Minister in the Congo)
without portfolio in May 1960 and resigned his post in July 1960.
The tumultuous events in which he was involved during this two-
month period are documented and his thoughts on them recorded in
this useful volume of source material which was largely inspired
by his official report, CONGO MAI-JUIN 1960: RAPPORT DU MINISTRE
CHARGE DES AFFAIRES GENERALES EN AFRIQUE (Bruxelles, 1960, 482 p.,
maps, fold. charts, tables). A chronology from Jan. 4, 1959, to
Apr. 6, 1962, is provided, with page references given for events
covered in the volume. Included are 10 appendixes and an index.

2303.   Gérard-Libois, Jules. KATANGA SECESSION. Translated by Rebecca
           Young. Madison, University of Wisconsin Press, 1966. 377 p.

       The best of the Katanga secession studies of the period. The
author, director of the Center for Socio-Political Research and
Information (CRISP) at Brussels, has drawn on a wealth of unpublished
material supplemented by personal information. He sketches in the
background of preindependence Katanga politics, analyzes the up-
heavals in the Katanga, the part played by the UN, and ends with
an interesting chapter entitled "Concluding Observations," cast
in the form of questions and answers. Full attention is given to
the complex ethnic struggles within Katanga, and also to the role
of the local Europeans.

2304.   Gevaerts, Franz. VADE-MECUM A L'USAGE DES FONCTIONNAIRES ET
           AGENTS TERRITORIAUX DU CONGO BELGE. Costermansville, Belgian
           Congo, 1953. 585 p.

       Important source for an assessment of Belgian colonization in
Congo. The work contains the legislation on most subjects needed
by the colonial officials in the different provinces of the Congo.

2305. Gilis, Charles-André. KASA-VUBU AU COEUR DU DRAME CONGOLAIS. Paris,
       Editions Europe-Afrique (exclusive distributor, Office Inter-
       national de Librairie, Bruxelles), 1964. 349 p.

       "Sources de l'ouvrage": p. 345-349.

       A biography of the former president of the Congo, leader of
       ABAKO, published the year before he was deposed (Nov. 25, 1965) in
       a coup by General Mobutu.

2306. Goffart, Ferdinand. LE CONGO: GEOGRAPHIE PHYSIQUE, POLITIQUE ET
       ECONOMIQUE. 2d ed. rev. and published by George Monissens.
       Bruxelles, 1908. 502 p. maps.

       This excellent standard work is one of the most detailed sources
       for Congolese ethnology, ethnography, political structure, and
       economy of the period.

2307. Hempstone, Smith. REBELS, MERCENARIES, AND DIVIDENDS: THE KATANGA
       STORY. New York, Praeger, 1962. 250 p. illus. (Books That
       Matter)

       Journalistic account of the secession of the Katanga from the
       Congo Republic in 1960, deploring the U.S. and UN involvement in its
       repression.

       Another account, even more controversial than Mr. Hempstone's,
       TO KATANGA AND BACK: A UN CASE HISTORY (New York, Simon & Schuster,
       1963, 371 p., illus., maps), was written by Conor Cruise O'Brien,
       an Irish officer who had served as UN representative in Katanga
       from June to Nov. 1961 and had resigned in protest against UN policy.

       A documentary study was issued by CRISP: SECESSION AU KATANGA,
       by J. Gérard-Libois (Bruxelles, 1963, 363 p.; Les études du CRISP);
       English edition, KATANGA SECESSION. This is the outstanding work
       on the secession (see no. 2303 above).

2308. Hostelet, Georges. L'OEUVRE CIVILISATRICE DE LA BELGIQUE AU CONGO,
       DE 1885 A 1945: Vol. I, L'OEUVRE ECONOMIQUE ET SOCIALE.
       Bruxelles, Institut Royal Colonial Belge, 1954. 512 p. maps
       (1 fold. in pocket), tables. (Section des sciences morales et
       politiques, Mémoires in-8°, v. 33, fasc. unique)

       _____. L'OEUVRE CIVILISATRICE DE LA BELGIQUE AU CONGO, DE 1885
       A 1953: Vol. II, LES AVANTAGES DONT LES BLANCS ET LES NOIRS
       ONT BENEFICIE ET BENEFICIERONT DE L'OEUVRE CIVILISATRICE DE

LA BELGIQUE AU CONGO. Bruxelles, Académie Royale des Sciences
Coloniales, 1954. 411 p. tables. (Section des sciences
morales et politiques, Mémoires in-8°, v. 37, fasc. 2)

"Ouvrages consultés (Tomes I et II)": v. 2, p. 400-403.

In these two volumes the author, former director of the Institut
de Sociologie Solvay, presents a review and appreciation of Belgian
colonization in the Congo from the economic and social standpoint.
The introduction to the first volume includes a summary of Congolese
conditions of life before the arrival of the Belgians. The text
then outlines the political, administrative, economic, and social
situation before and during World War II. In the second volume
Hostelet first describes what he considers the many advantages
gained by both the black man and the white man up to the eve of
World War II, and then comments on the potential benefits to be
derived from the 10-year plan decreed in 1949. Although the tenor
of both volumes is essentially optimistic, Hostelet points out the
serious possibility of racial and social conflicts as of 1953 and
stresses the means by which a catastrophe might be avoided.

2309. Jadot, J. M. LES ECRIVAINS AFRICAINS DU CONGO BELGE AND DU RUANDA-
URUNDI: UNE HISTOIRE--UN BILAN--DES PROBLEMES. Bruxelles,
Académie Royale des Sciences Coloniales, 1959. 167 p. (Classe
des sciences morales et politiques, Mémoires in-8°, n.s. v.
17, fasc. 2)

Bibliography: p. 152-156.

A literary history covering the period 1885 to the late 1950's.
Jadot traces the evolution of an oral literature into a written
literature, reviews the various literary genres, and analyzes the
problems facing new African writers.

2310. Kinshasa, Congo. Université Lovanium. Institut de Recherches
Economiques et Sociales. Centre de Recherches Economiques.
INDEPENDANCE, INFLATION, DEVELOPPEMENT: L'ECONOMIE CONGOLAISE
DE 1960 A 1965. Paris, Mouton, 1968. 865 p. fold. maps
(in pocket), tables, diagrs. (Recherches africaines, 5)

2311. Kitchen, Helen, ed. FOOTNOTES TO THE CONGO STORY: AN "AFRICA
REPORT" ANTHOLOGY. New York, Walker, 1967. xiv, 175 p.
map.

Eighteen essays by scholars and statesmen which appeared in
AFRICA REPORT from June 1960 to Nov. 1966. A chronology of events,
1960 through 1966, is provided.

2312. Lacroix, Jean Louis. INDUSTRIALISATION AU CONGO: LA TRANSFORMATION
        DES STRUCTURES ECONOMIQUES. Paris and La Haye, Mouton, 1967.
        358 p. map, tables, graphs. (Institut de Recherches
        Economiques et Sociales, Université Lovanium de Kinshasa,
        Recherches africaines, 1)

        Bibliographical footnotes.

        A technical analysis in which Dr. Lacroix details and appraises
three major shifts which have taken place in the process of the
Congo's industrialization: the transformation of (1) methods of
production, (2) the rapport between various sectors of the national
economy, and (3) international economic relations. The principal
sectors of Congolese industry are reviewed in a 50-page appendix.

2313. Langenhove, Fernand van. CONSCIENCES TRIBALES ET NATIONALES EN
        AFRIQUE NOIRE. Bruxelles, Institut Royal des Relations Inter-
        nationales, 1960. 465 p. illus.

        The author, director of the Institut, is a political scientist
and a former representative of Belgium to the United Nations. His
study of nationalism and politics in the new states of Africa
analyzes the interplay of surviving traditional values with new
cultural standards as background to the situation in the Congo and
Ruanda-Urundi.

2314. Lefever, Ernest W. UNCERTAIN MANDATE: POLITICS OF THE U.N. CONGO
        OPERATION. Baltimore, Johns Hopkins Press, 1967. xvi, 254 p.
        illus., map.

        Bibliography: p. 239-246.

        An analysis of the achievements and failures of the UN peace-
keeping mission to the Congo, which lasted four years, cost $411
million (41 percent of which was paid by the United States), and
involved a force of 93,000 men from 34 countries. Professor Lefever
contends that although the UN intervention helped to tone down the
violence among the conflicting groups, it also extended both the
magnitude and, probably, the duration of the crisis. Most of the
entries in the selected bibliography are briefly annotated. Ten
appendixes and an analytical index are included. The volume relies
strongly on materials used and insights gained by Lefever in doing
research for the work described in the next entry and for his CRISIS
IN THE CONGO: A UNITED NATIONS FORCE IN ACTION (Washington, D.C.,
Brookings Institution, 1965, xii, 212 p., map; Studies of U.S.
Policy and the U.N.), which places the peacekeeping experience within
the larger context of international politics, stressing the role of
the United States.

2315. Lefever, Ernest W., and Wynfred Joshua. UNITED NATIONS PEACE-
KEEPING IN THE CONGO, 1960-1964: AN ANALYSIS OF POLITICAL,
EXECUTIVE AND MILITARY CONTROL. Prepared for the U.S. Arms
Control and Disarmament Agency. Washington, D.C., Brookings
Institution, 1966. 4 v. Processed.

Vol. I.   SUMMARY AND CONCLUSIONS. 46 p. (includes index).

Vol. II.   FULL TEXT. 454 p. (includes index).

Vol. III. APPENDIXES. various pagings.

Vol. IV.   A CONGO CHRONOLOGY, 1960-1964. 98 p.

Bibliography: v. 3 [15 p.].

A major objective of this study was "to identify precedents
and pitfalls for possible future peacekeeping operations." The
full text contains material on the internationalization of the
Congo crisis, legal and constitutional aspects; the Secretary-General
and executive control; the host state; the roles of the United States,
the Soviet Union, France, Great Britain, Belgium, Canada, and the
Afro-Asian donor states; and various aspects of the UN force (e.g.,
recruitment and maintenance, command and control, logistical support,
financing).

A critical examination of the UN operation is Paul-Henry
Gendebien's L'INTERVENTION DES NATIONS UNIES AU CONGO, 1960-1964
(Paris, La Haye, Mouton, 1967, 292 p.; bibliography: p. 284-288;
Institut de Recherches Economiques et Sociales, Université Lovanium
de Kinshasa, Recherches africaines, 2), in which the author concludes
that the UN's peacekeeping role should not be to boost the direct
intervention of the great powers but to prevent and eliminate the
essentially economic and social causes of such conflicts as that
which occurred in the Congo. A more specialized study is by Fernand
van Langenhove, former permanent Belgian representative to the UN,
LE ROLE PROEMINENT DU SECRETAIRE GENERAL DANS L'OPERATION DES NA-
TIONS UNIES AU CONGO (Bruxelles, Institut Royal des Relations Internationales; La Haye, M. Nijhoff, 1964, 260 p.; bibliography: p. 243-
235).

2316. Lemarchand, René. POLITICAL AWAKENING IN THE BELGIAN CONGO. Berkeley, University of California Press; London, Cambridge University Press, 1964. xi, 357 p. plates, ports., maps.

Bibliographical footnotes.

Survey of the factors in the Belgian-controlled territory that made for "fragmentation," tribal and linguistic divisions, different patterns of administration, centralization which undermined chiefly authority, etc., in detail that gives damning evidence of Belgian mistakes.

A very good book by Catherine Hoskyns, THE CONGO SINCE INDEPENDENCE, JANUARY 1960--DECEMBER 1961 (issued under the auspices of the Royal Institute of International Affairs, London, New York Oxford University Press, 1965, xii, 518 p.), is complementary, particularly regarding Katanga.

2317.   Leopoldville. Université Lovanium. Institut de Recherches Economiques et Sociales. LES PROVINCES DU CONGO: STRUCTURE ET FONCTIONNEMENT. Léopoldville, 1964-65. 5 v. maps, tables. (Cahiers économiques et sociaux, Collection d'études politiques, nos. 1-5)

The five studies in this IRES collection are as follows (nos. 1-4 were prepared under the direction of Benoît Verhaegen):

No. 1.   KWILU--LULUABOURG--NORD KATANGA--UBANGI. By J. C. Willame. May 1964. 184, 27 p.

No. 2.   SUD KASAI--UELE--KONGO CENTRAL. By L. Monnier and J. C. Willame. July 1964. 340 p.

          Bibliography: p. 313-318.

No. 3.   NORD-KIVU--LAC LEOPOLD II. By J. C. Willame. Oct. 1964. 172 p.

          Bibliography: p. 157-161.

No. 4.   LOMAMI--KIVU CENTRAL. By J. C. Willame. Dec. 1964. 198 p.

          Bibliography: p. 181-186.

No. 5.   MOYEN CONGO--SANKURU. By J. C. Willame. Oct. 1965. 148 p.

          Bibliography: p. 135-139.

For each of the provinces studied a beginning section provides basic data on the economy, demography, ethnography, administration, politics, and history. Following this are sections on problems concerning territorial formation of the new province and the operation of the province's institutions. In appendixes are legislative texts and biographical notes on political personalities. Each study includes an index, with identifying notes accompanying the entries, and there are numerous maps.

2318. Lumumba, Patrice. CONGO, MY COUNTRY. Translated by Graham Heath. London, Pall Mall Press with Barrie and Rockliff, 1962. xxxii, 195 p. ports., facsim.

_____. LA PENSEE POLITIQUE DE PATRICE LUMUMBA. Texts and documents collected and presented by Jean Van Lierde. Paris, Présence Africaine, 1963. xlvi, 406 p. port.

CONGO, MY COUNTRY was written by Lumumba during 1956-57 and first published posthumously in 1961 in Belgium under the title LE CONGO, TERRE D'AVENIR--EST'IL MENACE? A notable historical document, it not only provides a record of Lumumba's ideas (some of which he later discarded) and of his political development, but also offers valuable insight into the attitudes of the Congolese évolués toward Belgian rule and the attitudes of the Congolese leaders on the eve of independence. The volume is enhanced by Colin Legum's thoughtful foreword, "The Life and Death of Patrice Lumumba."

The second reference provides an excellent supplement to the first since it records the important discourses and conferences of Lumumba between Dec. 1958 (two months after he had formed his supra-tribal Mouvement National Congolais) and Jan. 1961, the month of his assassination. Jean-Paul Sartre has contributed a long and compassionate preface. See also Serge Michel, UHURU LUMUMBA (Paris, R. Juillard, 1962, 269 p.), and Pierre Vos, VIE ET MORT DE LUMUMBA (Paris, Calmann-Lévy, 1961, 259 p.).

2319. Merriam, Alan P. CONGO: BACKGROUND OF CONFLICT. Evanston, Ill., Northwestern University Press, 1961. 368 p. illus. (Northwestern University African Studies, no. 6)

Includes bibliography.

Detailed study of the development of the national movement in the Congo, the parties and their leaders, and the Belgian background for relinquishing authority.

2320. Michiels, Albert, and N. Laude. CONGO BELGE ET RUANDA-URUNDI: GEOGRAPHIE ET NOTICE HISTORIQUE. 18th ed., rev. and enl., of NOTRE COLONIE. Bruxelles, Edition Universelle, 1957. 370 p. illus., maps.

A comprehensive survey, originally published in the early
1920's and revised to include later statistics. Its arrangement
follows the usual order: physical geography, anthropology, economics,
and politics and administration. Ruanda-Urundi is treated in a
separate section following the same order, and the very brief outline
of chief historical events takes up the last 30 pages. There are
chapter bibliographies, with references mostly in French.

2321. Monheim, Francis. MOBUTU, L'HOMME SEUL. Bruxelles, Editions
       Actuelles, 1962. 251 p.

2322. Morel, Edmund Dene. HISTORY OF THE CONGO REFORM MOVEMENT. Completed
       by Wm. Roger Louis and Jean Stengers. Oxford, Clarendon Press,
       1968. 289 p. illus.

       Bibliography: p. 274-277.

       Valuable survey of the reform movement which forced the Belgian
government to take over the Congo Free State from Leopold II. See
also Morel's RED RUBBER: THE STORY OF THE RUBBER SLAVE TRADE ... ON
THE CONGO ... (London, Unwin, 1906; new and rev. ed., Manchester,
National Labour Press, 1919), the major exposé of the conditions in
Leopold's Congo.

2323. Musée Royal de l'Afrique Centrale, Tervuren, Belgium. INVENTARIA
       ARCHAEOLOGICA AFRICANA: CONGO (LEOPOLDVILLE). Tervuren, 1964.

       Not available for examination.

2324. Pauwels, Johan M. REPERTOIRE DE DROIT COUTUMIER CONGOLAIS: JURIS-
       PRUDENCE ET DOCTRINE, 1954-1967. Kinshasa, O.N.R.D., 1970.
       443 p.

2325. Robert, Maurice. LE CONGO PHYSIQUE. 3d ed., rev. and completed.
       Liège, H. Vaillant-Carmanne, 1946. 449 p. illus., maps.

       Supplements: 1948, 83 p.; 1954, 15 p.

       Bibliography: p. 417-427.

       By a professor of geology at the Université Libre of Brussels,
author of many studies of Central Africa, this work was first published in 1919; it was brought up to date with a synthesis of
existing information in two later editions and two supplements.
Its coverage includes geology, mineralogy, climatology, hydrology,
soils, and biogeography.

2326. Robert, Maurice. GEOLOGIE ET GEOGRAPHIE DU KATANGA, Y COMPRIS
           L'ETUDE DES RESSOURCES ET DE LA MISE EN VALEUR. Published
           under the auspices of the Union Minière du Haut-Katanga.
           Bruxelles, 1956. xvi, 620 p. illus., fold. maps.

       Bibliography: p. 589-601.

       Folio volume prepared in honor of the 50th anniversary of the
    founding of the Union Minière. The author, an authority on develop-
    ment of Central Africa, describes it as a synthesis of available
    knowledge about this territory which was perhaps the largest single
    contributor to Belgian prosperity. (He was himself responsible for
    about 30 of the studies recorded in the bibliography.) Part 1 is on
    the physical and biological geography of the area; Part 2 tells
    briefly the history of European penetration; and Part 3 (p. 359-588)
    covers in detail the development of the Katanga's resources (mineral,
    vegetable, and animal) and "sources of energy," including hydro-
    electric power and communications.

       An anniversary volume, UNION MINIERE DU HAUT KATANGA, 1906-1956:
    EVOLUTION DES TECHNIQUES ET DES ACTIVITES SOCIALES, appeared in 1957
    (Bruxelles, L. Cuypers, 355 p., plates, col. maps, col. diagrs.,
    tables). It contained papers by members of the Union, some of
    which were presented at scientific congresses. The RAPPORTS DU
    CONSEIL D'ADMINISTRATION of the Union Minière are issued annually
    in Brussels, providing important information on the economy of the
    Katanga and the country as a whole.

2327. Ryckmans, Pierre. DOMINER POUR SERVIR. New and rev. ed. Bruxelles,
           L'Edition Universelle, 1948. 189 p.

       _____. LA POLITIQUE COLONIALE. Louvain, Editions Rex, 1934.
       117 p.

       Ryckmans was a Governor General of the Belgian Congo. These
    works represent a defense of the Belgian colonial policy, com-
    parable in many respects, and similar in inspiration to Lord
    Lugard's famous THE DUAL MANDATE IN TROPICAL AFRICA (see no.
    1248).

2328. Slade, Ruth N. ENGLISH-SPEAKING MISSIONS IN THE CONGO INDEPENDENT
           STATE (1878-1908). Bruxelles, Académie Royale des Sciences
           Coloniales, 1959. 432 p. maps. (Classe des sciences
           morales et politiques, Mémoires in-8°, n.s. v. 16, fasc. 2)

       Bibliography: p. 409-414.

_____. KING LEOPOLD'S CONGO: ASPECTS OF THE DEVELOPMENT OF
RACE RELATIONS IN THE CONGO INDEPENDENT STATE. London, New
York, Oxford University Press, 1962. xi, 230 p. illus., ports.,
maps.

Bibliography: p. 215-219.

By an English scholar who had done extensive research in
archival material, particularly that relating to the missionary
activities which are studied in detail in the first-mentioned work.
In her 1962 book, issued under the auspices of the Institute of
Race Relations, Dr. Slade examines the first European contacts with
the Congo, the acquisition and rule of the Congo by Leopold II,
and the founding of the Congo Free State. Her account is carried
through the annexation by Belgium in 1908 and up to World War I.

2329. Sohier, Jean. REPERTOIRE GENERAL DE LA JURISPRUDENCE ET DE LA
DOCTRINE COUTUMIERES DU CONGO ET DU RUANDA-URUNDI JUSQU'AU
31 DECEMBRE 1953. Bruxelles, Maison F. Larcier, 1957. 975 p.

Standard compilation of the customary law of the Belgian
colonies. A condensed version by Antoine Sohier was also issued
by the same publisher: TRAITE ELEMENTAIRE DE DROIT COUTUMIER DU
CONGO BELGE (2d ed., rev. and enl., 1954, 206 p.).

2330. Stengers, Jean. BELGIQUE ET CONGO: L'ELABORATION DE LA CHARTE
COLONIALE. Bruxelles, Renaissance du Livre, 1963. 251 p.
("Notre passé")

Bibliography: p. 237-240.

The book outlines the steps and the work of the commission
leading to the promulgation of the Charte Coloniale in 1908, when
the territory became a formal colony of Belgium. Excerpts from
the text of the charter are on p. 229-236.

2331. Turnbull, Colin M. THE FOREST PEOPLE. New York, Simon & Schuster,
1961. 288 p. illus.

In this book by an anthropologist writing from personal experience, scholarly ethnological data on the pygmies of the Congo
forest are set in a narrative so readable that it made the best-
seller lists. See also his THE LONELY AFRICAN (New York, Simon &
Schuster, 1962, 251 p., illus.).

The standard works on the pygmies of Africa are those of
Father Paul Schebesta, originally written in German and brought
out in English translation by Hutchinson, London: AMONG CONGO
PYGMIES (1932, 287 p.), MY PYGMY AND NEGRO HOSTS (1936, 287 p.),
and REVISITING MY PGYMY HOSTS (1936, 288 p.). They were given
definitive publication in more scholarly form in the ARSOM Mémoires
series (Coll. in-4°, v. 1, 2, 4, 5): DIE BAMBUTI-PYGMAEN VON ITURI:
ERGEBNISSE ZWEIER FORSCHUNGSREISEN ZU DEN ZENTRAL-AFRIKANISCHEN
PYGMAEN (Bruxelles, Hayez, 1938-50, 2 v. in 4, illus.).

2332. U.S. Department of the Interior. Office of Geography. REPUBLIC
       OF THE CONGO (LEOPOLDVILLE): OFFICIAL STANDARD NAMES APPROVED
       BY THE UNITED STATES BOARD ON GEOGRAPHIC NAMES. Washington,
       U.S. Govt. Print. Off., Apr. 1964. 426 p. map. (30,400
       names) (Gazetteer no. 80)

       This publication was issued shortly before the name of the
country was officially designated the Democratic Republic of the
Congo (Aug. 1964).

       For note on series see no. 484.

2333. Vanhove, Julien. HISTOIRE DU MINISTERE DES COLONIES. Bruxelles,
       Académie Royale des Sciences d'Outre-Mer, 1968. 168 p. illus.
       (Académie Royale des Sciences d'Outre-Mer, Classe des sciences
       morales et politiques, 35, no. 3)

       Bibliography: p. 163-166.

       Account of the history of the Ministère des Colonies from its
founding in October 1908 through its development into the Ministère
du Congo Belge et du Ruanda-Urundi, the Ministère des Affaires
Africaines, and finally into the Ministère des Affaires Etrangeres.
There is a name index.

2334. Vansina, Jan. INTRODUCTION A L'ETHNOGRAPHIE DU CONGO. Kinshasa,
       Université Lovanium; Kisangani, Université Libre du Congo;
       Lubumbashi, Université Officiel du Congo; Bruxelles, CRISP,
       1966. 228 p. maps. (Editions universitaires du Congo, 1)

       Includes bibliographies.

       A concise study of the peoples of the Congo, describing their
history, languages, economies, social and political structure,
religion, and art. The four main sections of the volume are arranged
by region--the northern savannas, the forest area, the southern

savannas, and the eastern Congo--with each of 15 chapters devoted
to an ethnographic subregion. There are 15 ethnographic maps.

2335. Vansina, Jan. KINGDOMS OF THE SAVANNA. Madison, University of
Wisconsin Press, 1966. 364 p.

Bibliography: p. 305-332.

History of the little-studied precolonial past of the grasslands south of the Congo forest, running into Angola and Zambia.
Written records for the development of the Luba, Lunda, Kongo, and
other kingdoms of 1600 to 1900 are mainly Portuguese, and Dr.
Vansina has combined their evidence with extensive dependence on
oral tradition. This work is likely to become a classic of African
historiography.

2336. Vansina, Jan. LE ROYAUME KUBA. Tervuren, Musée Royal de l'Afrique
Centrale, 1964. 196 p. plates, maps (part fold.), tables,
diagrs. (Annales, Sér. in-8°, Sciences Humaines, no. 49)

Bibliography: p. 186-189.

An ethnographic study of the Kuba (or Bushongo) people, who
live in the territoire of Mweka between the Kasai and Sankuru
rivers. The main object of Dr. Vansina's description and analysis
is to point out a distinctive feature of Kuba society--the subordinate
role of the weakly developed social structures, which serve largely
to fulfill the functions of the political structure.

2337. Weiss, Herbert F. POLITICAL PROTEST IN THE CONGO: THE PARTI
SOLIDAIRE AFRICAIN DURING THE INDEPENDENCE STRUGGLE. Princeton, N.J., Princeton University Press, 1967. xxiv, 326 p.
maps, tables.

Bibliography: p. 313-317.

Based on official party documents and the author's personal
observations, this volume constitutes the first detailed study of
the Parti Solidaire Africain. Part 1 is a general analysis of
recent preindependence history. The history of the PSA is covered
in Part 2, and Part 3 concerns the phenomenon of "rural radicalism"
and the role of the masses in the independence struggle and their
relationship with the PSA leadership. Of value in conjunction with
this study is PARTI SOLIDAIRE AFRICAIN (P.S.A.): DOCUMENTS, 1959-
1960 (Bruxelles, CRISP, 1963, 315 p., maps, tables; Les dossiers
du CRISP), co-edited by Weiss and Benoît Verhaegen.

2338. Willequet, Jacques. LE CONGO BELGE ET LA WELTPOLITIK, 1894-1914.
      Bruxelles, Presses Universitaires de Bruxelles, 1962. 499 p.
      plates, maps. (Travaux de la Faculté de Philosophie et
      Lettres, 22)

      Bibliography: p. 451-466.

      Detailed study of German, Belgian, and British policies toward
the Congo and Portuguese Africa. Its thesis is that the Belgian
Congo was never the primary concern of German foreign policy. This
is an indispensable work for the study of the period.

2339. Wing, Joseph van. ETUDES BAKONGO: SOCIOLOGIE, RELIGION ET MAGIE.
      2d ed. Bruges, Desclée, De Brouwer, 1959. 512 p. illus.
      (Museum Lessianum, Section missiologique, no. 39)

      Bibliography: p. 15-17.

      A celebrated study, published first in 1930-37, by a Jesuit
priest who had been a missionary in Kisantu. The revision includes
a number of additions. Other studies by Father van Wing have been
published in the Mémoires series of ARSOM (see its CATALOGUE, no.
2209).

2340. Young, Crawford. POLITICS IN THE CONGO: DECOLONIZATION AND
      INDEPENDENCE. Princeton, N.J., Princeton University Press,
      1965. xii, 659 p. maps, tables.

      Bibliography: p. 609-644.

      A lucid and readable analysis of the nature of an African
political system that, in the author's words, "slowly emerged out
of the rubble of decolonization which went awry." The snarl of
politics involved in the sudden and calamitous transfer of power in
the Congo is examined in detail as Professor Young first describes
the colonial power structure and then successively discusses the
Belgian vision of decolonization and the disintegration of the power
structure, the Congolese response to colonialism, and the trends
and forces emerging in the years of independence and strife 1960-
63. An interim assessment of the events of 1964 is offered in an
epilogue.

RWANDA AND BURUNDI

Note: On July 1, 1962, the UN trust territory known as Ruanda-Urundi and administered by Belgium was divided into two parts, one becoming the Republic of Rwanda and the other the Kingdom of Burundi. Since much of the material below deals with them before independence, it is presented under a single heading.

For further specific references, see also the Congo section, above, wherein are listed so many materials which also apply to Ruanda-Urundi that their repetition here is precluded.

Bibliographies

2341. Boston University. African Studies Program. RWANDA AND BURUNDI: SELECTED BIBLIOGRAPHY. Boston, 1964. 5 l. Processed.

2342. Clément, Joseph R. A. M. ESSAI DE BIBLIOGRAPHIE DU RUANDA-URUNDI. [Usumbara, Service des Affaires Indigènes] 1959. 201, xxii p.

Published under the auspices of IRSAC (Institut pour la Recherche Scientifique en Afrique Centrale), this classed listing of books and periodicals covers ethnology, history, government, geography, agriculture, etc. An author index is included.

2343. Walraet, Marcel. LES SCIENCES AU RWANDA: BIBLIOGRAPHIE (1894-1965). Bruxelles, Bibliotheque Royale de Belgique, 1966. 211 p. (Académie Royale des Sciences d'Outre-Mer, Classe des sciences morales et politiques, Mémoires in-8°, n.s. v. 34, fasc. 5)

This volume, the first extensive bibliography on Rwanda, was compiled by the "conservateur adjoint" and head of the Centre de Documentation Africaine of the Bibliothèque Royale de Belgique. The 1,934 books and articles listed appear under five main sections: general bibliographies and documentation (including geography and scientific research); the humanities; physical sciences; life sciences (e.g., conservation, botany, zoology, medicine); and agronomic sciences. Arrangement is alphabetical by author. There is an index of authors, tribal names, and place names, as well as a brief chronological index.

Reference Works

2344. Belgium. Office de l'Information et des Relations Publiques pour
          le Congo Belge et le Ruanda-Urundi. LE RUANDA-URUNDI.
          Bruxelles, 1959. 377 p. 18 col. maps (6 in pocket), diagrs.,
          tables.

        A general survey prepared by specialists, a number of them
connected with IRSAC. The five parts treat geography, history,
governmental organization, economic life, and social life. A
translation into English by Goldie Blankoff-Scarr was issued in
several parts by this office in 1960, all with the main title
RUANDA-URUNDI: ECONOMY (2 v.), SOCIAL ACHIEVEMENTS (79 p.), and
GEOGRAPHY AND HISTORY (79 p.).

2345. Bourgeois, R. BANYARWANDA ET BARUNDI. Bruxelles, Académie Royale
          des Sciences Coloniales, 1954- illus., maps. (Classe des
          sciences morales et politiques, Mémoires in-8o)

        Includes bibliographies.

        The Banyarwanda are the peoples of Rwanda, the Barundi those
of Burundi. Four volumes have been published of this exhaustive
anthropological study in the Mémoires series. Vol. I, ETHNOGRAPHIE
(790 p.; n.s. v. 15), appearing in 1957, was not the first issued.
The other volumes are Vol. II, LA COUTUME (1954, 472 p.; v. 35);
Vol. III, RELIGION ET MAGIE (1956, 376 p.; n.s. v. 4); Vol. IV,
L'EVOLUTION DU CONTRAT DE BAIL A CHEPTEL AU RUANDA-URUNDI (1958,
60 p.; n.s. v. 9, fasc. 4).

2346. CARREFOUR D'AFRIQUE. v. 1- July 1962- Kigali, Rwanda, Ministère
          des Affaires Etrangères. Semimonthly, July 1962-July 1963;
          monthly, Aug. 1963-

        A well-presented illustrated leaflet chronicling events in
Rwanda; from July 1962 to July 1963 titled ACTUALITES: BULLETIN
D'INFORMATION.

2347. Centre de Recherche et d'Information Socio-Politiques. RWANDA
          POLITIQUE, 1958-1960. Documents presented by F. Nkundabagenzi.
          Bruxelles, 1961. 423 p. map. (Les dossiers du CRISP)

        Bibliography: p. 407-412.

The first complete assemblage of facts and documents (many unpublished) relating to the political changes as the Batutsi-dominated feudal society broke down under the voting weight of the formerly suppressed Bahutu majority.

2348.   DECOLONISATION ET INDEPENDANCE DU RWANDA ET DU BURUNDI. Bruxelles, Institut Royal des Relations Internationales, 1963. 309 p. (CHRONIQUE DE POLITIQUE ETRANGERE, v. 16, no. 4-6, July-Nov. 1963: p. 439-748)

Survey with complete documentation from official sources.

2349.   Hertefelt, Marcel d', and André Coupez, eds. LA ROYAUTE SACREE DE L'ANCIEN RWANDA: TEXTE, TRADUCTION ET COMMENTAIRE DE SON RITUEL. Tervuren, Musée Royal de l'Afrique Centrale, 1964. 520 p. illus., maps. (Annales, Sér. in-8°, Sciences humaines, no. 52)

This text is cited as the first of its kind for the whole of Africa. The reader is guided through the complex, symbolic Kinyarwanda text and French translation by abundant linguistic and anthropological commentary on the secret royal ritual of ancient Rwanda.

Another Kinyarwanda text in the Annales series of the Musée Royal is Clement Gakaniisha, RECITS HISTORIQUES RWANDA, DANS LA VERSION DE C. GAKANIISHA, edited by André Coupez and Th. Kamanzi (1962, 327 p., illus., fold. map; Sciences humaines, no. 43), in which the editors first comment on the main aspects of Rwandese social life and culture and then present historical narratives in the Kinyarwanda language, with accompanying French translation and linguistic notes.

2350.   Hertefelt, Marcel d', A. Trouwborst, and J. Scherer. LES ANCIENS ROYAUMES DE LA ZONE INTERLACUSTRE MERIDIONALE (RWANDA, BURUNDI, BUHA). London, International African Institute, 1962. 252 p. maps. (Ethnographic Survey of Africa, East Central Africa, pt. 14)

Bibliographies: Rwanda, p. 99-111; Burundi, p. 165-169; Buha (of Tanganyika), p. 221-223.

See note on series, nos. 980 and 1670.

2351.   Heusch, Luc de. LE RWANDA ET LA CIVILISATION INTERLACUSTRE:
         ETUDES D'ANTHROPOLOGIE HISTORIQUE ET STRUCTURALE. Bruxelles,
         Institut de Sociologie, Université Libre de Bruxelles, 1966.
         471 p. maps. (Collection du Centre National des Problèmes
         Sociaux de l'Industrialisation en Afrique Noire)

         Bibliography: p. 460-468.

         In this interesting study of the emergence of the state in an
    archaic society, the author begins with points of reference for a
    history of the interlacustrine civilizations and then examines the
    establishment and expansion of the Rwanda kingdom, describing the
    formation of a caste society founded on the totemic clan. He then
    analyzes the general mythology of the interlacustrine civilizations
    (legends, narratives, cults, and rites), and concludes with a dis-
    cussion of clan, caste, and the feudal system in the regions of
    Rwanda, Ankole, Burundi, Bunyoro, and Buhaya.

2352.   INFOR BURUNDI. 1962- Bujumbura, Office National de Presse du
         Burundi. Weekly.

         A weekly information bulletin published by the new govern-
    ment and begun some months before the independence date.

2353.   Kagame, Alexis. LA PHILOSOPHIE BANTU-RWANDAISE DE L'ETRE.
         Bruxelles, Académie Royale des Sciences d'Outre-Mer, 1955.
         64 p. maps. (Classe des sciences morales et politiques,
         Mémoires in-8°, n.s. v. 6, fasc. 1)

         Abbé Kagame is perhaps the best known of Rwandaise scholars.
    This volume, one of several he has had published in the ARSOM
    Mémoires, is a study of Bantu religion, consisting of extracts
    from his thesis presented at the Université Pontificale Grégorienne
    in Rome.

2354.   Leurquin, Philippe. LE NIVEAU DE VIE DES POPULATIONS RURALES DU
         RUANDA-URUNDI. Louvain, Institut de Recherches Economiques
         et Sociales, 1960. 420 p. illus., maps, diagrs., tables.
         (Publications de l'Université Lovanium de Léopoldville, no. 6)

         Bibliography: p. 353-376.

         Excellent study by an outstanding Belgian economist.

2355. Louis, William Roger. RUANDA-URUNDI, 1884-1919. Oxford, Clarendon
          Press, 1963. xvii, 290 p. maps.

       Bibliographical note: p. 261-272; notes: p. 272-278.

       A diplomatic and administrative history of the two countries,
       which the author calls by the joint name under which they were
       administered until independence in 1962. During most of the period
       covered in this study, the kingdoms formed part of German East
       Africa.

2356. Maquet, Jacques J. THE PREMISE OF INEQUALITY IN RUANDA: A STUDY
          OF POLITICAL RELATIONS IN A CENTRAL AFRICAN KINGDOM. London,
          Published for the International African Institute by the Oxford
          University Press, 1961. 199 p. illus., ports., maps.

       Bibliography: p. 186-194.

       Professor Maquet, a highly trained social anthropologist, was
       director of IRSAC in Elisabethville. This book, a synthesis of
       research carried out over some years, was published in part at
       Tervuren (Musée du Congo Belge) in 1954 as LE SYSTEME DES RELATIONS
       SOCIALES DANS LE RUANDA ANCIEN. It is regarded as an authoritative
       analysis of the respective roles of the ruling Batutsi and the sub-
       ject Bahutu in the former society of Ruanda-Urundi.

2357. Maquet, Jacques J., and Marcel d'Hertefelt. ELECTIONS EN SOCIETE
          FEODALE: UNE ETUDE SUR L'INTRODUCTION DU VOTE POPULAIRE AU
          RUANDA-URUNDI. Bruxelles, Académie Royale des Sciences
          Coloniales, 1959. 231 p. (Classe des sciences morales et
          politiques, Mémoires in-8°, n.s. v. 21, fasc. 2)

       A study reflecting the changes in the society of Ruanda-
       Urundi as shown in the elections even several years before the UN-
       supervised elections of Sept. 1961 in which the voters of Ruanda,
       some 84 percent of the population, abolished the already over-
       thrown Batutsi monarchy.

       A succinct account of the culture and society of Rwanda is
       provided by d'Hertefelt's "The Rwanda of Rwanda," in PEOPLES OF
       AFRICA, edited by James L. Gibbs (see no. 984).

2358. REVUE DU DROIT ADMINISTRATIF. 1968- Bujumbura, Ecole Nationale
          d'Administration. Frequency unknown.

       Not available for examination.

2359.   Syracuse University. Maxwell Graduate School of Citizenship and
            Public Affairs. Program of Eastern African Studies. THE
            POLITICAL DEVELOPMENT OF RWANDA AND BURUNDI. By John B.
            Webster. Syracuse, N.Y., 1966. 121 p. (Occasional Paper,
            no. 16)

        Bibliography: p. 101-121.

        An ethnopolitical history based primarily on resources
        available at Syracuse University. The author traces the develop-
        ment of the two countries from precolonial Tutsi rule to the mid-
        1960's.

2360.   U.S. Department of the Interior. Office of Geography. BURUNDI:
            OFFICIAL STANDARD NAMES APPROVED BY THE UNITED STATES BOARD
            ON GEOGRAPHIC NAMES. Washington, U.S. Govt. Print. Off.,
            Oct. 1964. 44 p. map. (3,000 names) (Gazetteer no. 84)

        See note on series, no. 484.

2361.   U.S. Department of the Interior. Office of Geography. RWANDA:
            OFFICIAL STANDARD NAMES APPROVED BY THE UNITED STATES BOARD
            ON GEOGRAPHIC NAMES. Washington, U.S. Govt. Print. Off.,
            Oct. 1964. 44 p. map. (3,000 names) (Gazetteer no. 85)

        See note on series, no. 484.

2362.   Vansina, Jan. L'EVOLUTION DU ROYAUME RWANDA DES ORIGINES A 1900.
            Bruxelles, Académie Royale des Sciences d'Outre-Mer, 1962.
            100 p. (Classe de sciences morales et politiques, Mémoires
            in-8°, n.s. v. 26, fasc. 2)

        Professor Vansina first delineates the problems inherent in
        the historiography of Rwanda, in terms of sources and chronology,
        and presents an evaluation of Rwanda oral tradition. He then
        concisely reviews the expansion of the ancient kingdom and traces
        the country's institutional developments from the fifteenth to the
        twentieth century.

CHAPTER 39

EAST AFRICA

<u>Note</u>: This section lists works relating to the region usually interpreted
to comprise the three (formerly four) countries of what had been British
East Africa. There are also a few works that cover the neighboring regions of Northeastern Africa (Ethiopia, Somalia, Sudan) and/or Central
Africa. It was decided that Mauritius and the Seychelles would be included
in this section as well.

Bibliographies

2363.   BIBLIOGRAPHY OF AFRICAN LAW: Part I, EAST AFRICA. Edited by
        Antony N. Allott. London, School of Oriental and African
        Studies, University of London, 1961. 83 p. Mimeographed.

        The first part of the comprehensive bibliography on
    customary laws of former British Africa (see Allott, no. 684).
    It includes many references to unpublished documentary material
    in East African archives.

2364.   Butterfield, Harry R. F., comp. INDEX DIGEST OF THE REPORTED
        CASES DETERMINED BY THE COURT OF APPEAL FOR EASTERN AFRICA
        AND ON APPEAL THEREFROM BY THE JUDICIAL COMMITTEE OF THE
        PRIVY COUNCIL, 1900-1952. Nairobi, Govt. Printer, 1954.
        135 p.

2365.   East Africa High Commission (from 1962, East African Common Services
        Organization). East African Agriculture and Forestry Research
        Organisation. AN EAST AFRICAN FOREST BIBLIOGRAPHY. Compiled
        by A. L. Griffith and B. E. St. L. Stuart. Nairobi, 1955.
        118 p.

        Includes many official papers and reports, articles from
    scientific journals, etc.

2366.   East Africa High Commission. East African Statistical Department.
            BIBLIOGRAPHY OF ECONOMICS IN EAST AFRICA (KENYA, TANGANYIKA,
            UGANDA AND ZANZIBAR). Nairobi, 1958. 30 l.

        The many official documents cited are covered in the Library of
Congress bibliography described below.

2367.   East African Literature Bureau. CATALOGUE. Nairobi. Issued occasionally.

        List of books and pamphlets published by the Bureau in English,
Swahili, and vernaculars. The majority of the titles are for students.
The Bureau has a series of Early Travellers in East Africa, with short
accounts of the first explorers, and also issues works on East African
history, customs, and languages.

2368.   East African Research Information Centre (EARIC). SOURCES FOR THE STUDY
            OF EAST AFRICAN CULTURES AND DEVELOPMENT: A BIBLIOGRAPHY OF SOCIAL
            SCIENTIFIC BIBLIOGRAPHIES, ABSTRACTS, REFERENCE WORKS, CATALOGUES,
            DIRECTORIES, WRITINGS ON ARCHIVES, BIBLIOGRAPHIES, BOOK PRODUCTION,
            LIBRARIES, AND MUSEUMS; WITH SPECIAL REFERENCE TO KENYA, TANZANIA,
            AND UGANDA, 1946-1966 (1967-1968). Compiled by Angela Molnos.
            Nairobi, Sept. 1968. 54 p. Mimeographed. 32 cm. (EARIC
            Information Circular no. 1)

        This first publication of EARIC, a new center sponsored by the East
African Academy, is a comprehensive, unclassified listing which
constitutes a substantially enlarged version of the fourth bibliography
which appears in the appendix of the volume by Dr. Molnos described
below (no. 2375). The 796 entries are arranged alphabetically by
author. A list of selected addresses of organizations and agencies
relevant to African studies concludes the bibliography.

2369.   Great Britain. Colonial Office. INVENTORY OF MATERIALS DEALING
            WITH EAST AFRICA. Compiled by Cyril Ehrlich. [London, 1965?]
            2 v. 22 x 33 cm. (Pamphlet Series)

        This unique, valuable collection was gradually assembled by the
Colonial Office from around 1890 to 1948 and includes reprints from
journals, newspaper clippings, political ephemera, government documents, memoranda, committee reports, etc. It covers Abyssinia,
Somaliland, Belgian Congo, East Africa, Kenya, Uganda, Tanganyika,
Zanzibar, the Rhodesias and Nyasaland. Copies are available from
the Center for Research Libraries, Chicago. There are series for
West Africa and South Africa as well but inventories for these
collections are not yet available.

2370.   International African Institute. EAST AFRICA: GENERAL, ETHNOGRAPHY,
            SOCIOLOGY, LINGUISTICS. Compiled by Ruth Jones, librarian, with

the assistance of a panel of consultants. London, 1960. 62 l. (Africa Bibliography Series, Ethnography, Sociology, Linguistics, and Related Subjects)

See note on series, no. 970.

Covers ethnic groups of Kenya, Tanganyika, Uganda, and Zanzibar.

2371. Jacobs, Alan H. "Bibliography of the Masai." AFRICAN STUDIES BULLETIN, v. 8, no. 3, Dec. 1965: 40-60.

A useful list, revised from one compiled several years ago and circulated privately.

2372. Langlands, B. W. RESEARCH IN GEOGRAPHY AT MAKERERE 1947-1967. Kampala, Makerere University College, 1967. 87 p.

See also his bibliography, no. 1166.

2373. McLoughlin, Peter F. M. RESEARCH ON AGRICULTURAL DEVELOPMENT IN EAST AFRICA. New York, Agricultural Development Council, 1967. 111 p.

Emphasis is on the economics of agricultural development in this monograph which classifies and evaluates research on rural development and also indicates areas and priorities of future research in East Africa. The major portion of the volume consists of two bibliographies: Appendix 1 contains a bibliography of books, articles, government documents, reports, theses, dissertations, and research in progress on East Africa, Kenya, Tanzania, and Uganda; Appendix 2 consists of major bibliographies.

2374. Mezger, Dorothea, and Eleonore Littich. WIRTSCHAFTSWISSENSCHAFTLICHE VEROFFENTLICHUNGEN UBER OSTAFRIKA IN ENGLISCHER SPRACHE: EINE BIBLIOGRAPHIE DES NEUEREN ENGLISCHSPRACHIGEN SCHRIFTTUMS MIT INHALTSANGABEN. München, IFO-Institut für Wirtschaftsforschung, 1967. 3 v.

Vols. I and II list 638 items including articles, monographs, government publications, unpublished papers, and chapters from books on East African economics (including Zanzibar). Arrangement is by subject, then alphabetical by author. Almost all items are annotated (in German). Subjects covered include population, development planning, finance, agriculture, land tenure, industry, trade and transport, labour, co-operatives, and inter African trade. Vol. III contains a bibliography of government publications and an author index.

2375. Molnos, Angela, comp. DEVELOPMENT IN AFRICA, PLANNING AND IMPLEMENTA-
TION: A BIBLIOGRAPHY (1946-1969) AND OUTLINE, WITH SOME EMPHASIS
ON KENYA, TANZANIA, AND UGANDA. Nairobi, East African Academy
Research Information Centre, 1970. 120 p. (Information Circular
no. 3)

The guide has four parts: an essay for the general reader on aims
and problems of development in Africa; bibliographies; list of
periodicals; and names and addresses of institutions. There is no index.

2376. Molnos, Angela, comp. LANGUAGE PROBLEMS IN AFRICA: A BIBLIOGRAPHY
(1946-1967) AND SUMMARY OF THE PRESENT SITUATION, WITH SPECIAL
REFERENCE TO KENYA, TANZANIA, AND UGANDA. Nairobi, East African
Academy Research Information Centre, 1969. 62 p. (Information
Circular no. 2)

2377. Molnos, Angela, comp. DIE SOZIALWISSENSCHAFTLICHE ERFORSCHUNG OSTAFRIKAS
1954-1963 (KENYA, TANGANYIKA/SANSIBAR, UGANDA). Berlin, New
York, Springer-Verlag, 1965. xv, 304 p. fold. maps, tables.
(Afrika-Studien, no. 5)

A fine survey and bibliography of social and economic research in
East Africa. Following a survey of research centers is a research
review first by ethnic group and region and then by topic (history,
politics, law, demography, health, economics, sociology and psychology,
general works). A section on methodology concludes the survey material.
A long appendix consists of four bibliographies and four lists: the
bibliographies (p. 148-256) complement specific chapters and total 2,019
entries; the lists cover periodicals appearing in the bibliographies,
group the tribes and districts of Kenya, Tanzania, and Uganda, and
include selected addresses of institutes and institutions. There is an
insert in English on how to use the volume, with the table of contents
annexed.

2378. Nye, J. S. UNITY AND DIVERSITY IN EAST AFRICA: A BIBLIOGRAPHICAL
ESSAY. Durham, N.C., Committee on African Studies, Commonwealth
Studies Center, Duke University, 1966. [20 p.]

Reprint from SOUTH ATLANTIC QUARTERLY, v. 65, no. 1, Winter 1966:
104-123.

A wide-ranging, evaluative bibliographic essay which brings in
education, political ideas of East African leaders, religion, ethnic
groups, language, internal disunity, and PAFMECA (Pan-African Freedom
Movement of East, Central and Southern Africa).

2379. PERIODICALS IN EAST AFRICAN LIBRARIES: A UNION LIST. 3d ed. Morgantown,
West Virginia University Library, 1969. 465 p.

For annotation see no. 389.

2380. Shields, James J., comp. A SELECTED BIBLIOGRAPHY ON EDUCATION IN EAST
      AFRICA, 1941-1961. Kampala, Uganda, Makerere University College,
      1962. 39 p. (Makerere Library Publications, no. 2)

      Compiled by a research assistant to the American Teachers' East
African Project, Columbia University, an effort to help provide
teachers for East African secondary schools. The items in the bibliography are all in the Makerere Library with the exception of some of the
older publications of the Education Departments.

2381. Spaandonck, Marcel van, comp. PRACTICAL AND SYSTEMATICAL SWAHILI
      BIBLIOGRAPHY: LINGUISTICS, 1850-1963. Leiden, E. J. Brill, 1965.
      xxiv, 61 p.

      Prepared by the director of African languages and history at the
University of Ghent. This valuable bibliography, arranged by topic
and by country, surveys Swahili grammars, instruction books, phrase
books, exercises, vocabularies, dictionaries, and linguistic articles
published since 1850.

2382. Syracuse University. Maxwell Graduate School of Citizenship and Public
      Affairs. Program of Eastern African Studies. A BIBLIOGRAPHY ON
      ANTHROPOLOGY AND SOCIOLOGY IN TANZANIA AND EAST AFRICA. Compiled
      by Lucas Kuria and John Webster. Syracuse, N.Y., 1966. 91 l.
      (Occasional Bibliography, no. 4)

      Arrangement is alphabetical by author; information is not always
complete. German, French, Italian, and Portuguese entries are included,
with coverage from the late nineteenth century on. See also A BIBLIOG-
RAPHY ON KENYA (no. 2469). Section A is devoted to East Africa in
general and there are listed 141 entries containing significant
bibliographies as well.

2383. Syracuse University. Maxwell Graduate School of Citizenship and Public
      Affairs. Program of Eastern African Studies. Occasional Biblio-
      graphies [series]. Syracuse, N.Y., 1965-

      The Bibliographic Section of the Program of Eastern African Studies
at Syracuse University is bringing out a series of bibliographies
relating to East Africa and neighboring areas; although primarily for
use in the Program, they are in a form to be made available to other
libraries. These are extensive lists of books and articles, in straight
author arrangement, prepared by John Webster and others of the Program's
staff (see preceding entry). They are processed on loose-leaf pages,
in a binder with bright red cover pages. See, for example, Barbara

Skapa, A SELECT PRELIMINARY BIBLIOGRAPHY ON URBANISM IN EASTERN AFRICA
(1967, 42 l.).

2384. U.S. Library of Congress. National Program for Acquisitions and Cata-
        loging. ACCESSIONS LIST: EASTERN AFRICA. v. 1, no. 1- Jan.
        1968- Nairobi, Library of Congress Office. Quarterly.

        Available to libraries upon request to the Field Director,
Library of Congress Office, East Africa, P.O. Box 30598, Nairobi, Kenya.

        The aim of this new quarterly is to advise other libraries of
current materials available in and near Eastern Africa. Arrangement is
alphabetical by country, by languages in which the country's
publications appear, and by author. The first issue (40 p.) covered
publications of Ethiopia, French Somaliland, Kenya, Malagasy, Malawi,
Mauritius, Somalia, Sudan, Tanzania, Uganda, and Zambia.

2385. U.S. Library of Congress. General Reference and Bibliography Division.
        OFFICIAL PUBLICATIONS OF BRITISH EAST AFRICA: Part 1, THE EAST
        AFRICA HIGH COMMISSION AND OTHER REGIONAL DOCUMENTS. Compiled by
        Helen F. Conover, African Section. Washington, 1960. 67 p.

        Covering as extensively as possible from printed sources the
documents of the East African interterritorial official bodies. The
East Africa High Commission, between the preparation of this guide
and its appearance in print, had become the East African Common Services
Organization. This list includes its documents from its inception and
also those of several predecessors. The other three parts of the set
of official publications of former British East Africa follow in the
country sections.

2386. Vaughan, John H., and George H. Paterson. INDEX-DIGEST OF THE REPORTED
        CASES DETERMINED BY THE COURT OF APPEAL FOR EASTERN AFRICA AND AN
        APPEAL THEREFROM BY THE JUDICIAL COMMITTEE OF THE PRIVY COUNCIL,
        1900 to 1938. Nairobi, 1939. 129, xv p. (200 entries)

2387. Whiteley, W. H., and A. E. Gutkind. A LINGUISTIC BIBLIOGRAPHY OF EAST
        AFRICA. Rev. ed. Kampala, Uganda, East African Swahili Committee
        and East African Institute of Social Research, 1958. 1 v. Loose-
        leaf.

        Supplement. no. 1, Apr. 1960-

        The first edition attempted to bring together "in one easily
accessible publication a list of all that was known to have been written
on the grammar and lexicon of the East African languages." The revised

edition incorporates the listings from the 1954 volume and its
supplements with additional material: books, periodical articles,
and manuscripts. Sections are devoted to the languages of
Tanganyika, Kenya, and Uganda, with a special section for Swahili.

The East African Inter-Territorial Language Committee issued its
first report in 1930, its headquarters then being in Arusha, Tanganyika.
In 1948 it came under the East Africa High Commission and in 1952 was
transferred to Makerere College and renamed East African Swahili
Committee. In 1962 it was again transferred, this time to the new
University College in Dar es Salaam, and renamed Institute of Swahili
Research. The Institute sponsors a number of publications in
Swahili, including its journal, SWAHILI (see no. 2401). The standard
dictionaries of the Swahili language spoken by the mixed Arab-Bantu
Swahilis of Zanzibar, which has become the lingua franca of the East
African coast, are those of the Inter-Territorial Language (Swahili)
Committee, STANDARD SWAHILI-ENGLISH DICTIONARY and STANDARD ENGLISH-
SWAHILI DICTIONARY (London, Oxford University Press, 1939, 2 v., 538,
635 p.). The old standard grammar was by Ethel O. Ashton: SWAHILI
GRAMMAR, INCLUDING INTONATION (London, New York, Longmans, Green,
1944, 398 p.). A handy little book available in the United States is
by T. L. Gilmore and S. O. Kwasa, SWAHILI PHRASE BOOK FOR TRAVELERS
(New York, F. Ungar, 1963, 90 p.).

2388. Young, Roland, and J. Gus Liebenow. "Survey of Background Material
for the Study of the Governments of East Africa." AMERICAN
POLITICAL SCIENCE REVIEW, v. 48, Mar. 1964: 187-203.

Highly informative critical bibliography on East African political
developments.

Serials

2389. AZANIA: JOURNAL OF THE BRITISH INSTITUTE OF HISTORY AND ARCHAEOLOGY
IN EAST AFRICA. v. 1- 1966- Edited by Neville Chittick. Nairobi,
Published on behalf of the Institute by Oxford University Press.
plates, maps. Annual.

The journal's name stems from that used for the eastern coasts of
Africa in Greco-Roman times. Not only are Kenya, Tanzania, and Uganda
covered in articles on archaeology and precolonial history but also
the great central region of Africa; articles may be in French, German,
or Italian, although most are in English. There are sections of notes
and book reviews and one on research work in progress. The Institute is
formally connected with the University of East Africa.

2390. EAST AFRICA AND RHODESIA. 1924- London, Published by East Africa, Ltd.
(66 Great Russell Street, W.C.1). Weekly.

The leading conservative organ for political and economic news. The editor, F. S. Joelson, is known for a number of books on East Africa. The chief daily of Nairobi, which formerly represented the white settlers' viewpoint, is the well-known EAST AFRICAN STANDARD.

2391. EAST AFRICA JOURNAL. v. 1, no. 1- Apr. 1964- Nairobi, East African Institute of Social and Cultural Affairs.

A journal "dedicated to the free and open discussion of topics significant to the East African region." Mr. Odinge Odera is the editor of this journal, which is published 10 times yearly (Uniafric Bldg., Koinange St., P.O. Box 30492, Nairobi, Kenya). Patrons of the East African Institute are the Hon. Jomo Kenyatta, President of the Republic of Kenya, the Hon. Dr. Julius Nyerere, President of the United Republic of Tanzania, and the Hon. Dr. Milton Obote, President of Uganda.

2392. East African Academy. PROCEEDINGS OF THE . . . SYMPOSIUM. 1963- Nairobi, Longmans, Green.

2393. EAST AFRICAN ECONOMIC REVIEW. 1954-63; n.s. 1964- Nairobi, Oxford University Press. Semiannual.

2394. EAST AFRICAN GEOGRAPHICAL REVIEW. Apr. 1963- Kampala, Uganda Geographical Association. Annual.

2395. EAST AFRICAN JOURNAL OF RURAL DEVELOPMENT. Nairobi, East African Publishing House (P.O. Box 30571). Semiannual.

2396. THE EAST AFRICAN MEDICAL JOURNAL. 1924- Nairobi. Monthly.

2397. EAST AFRICAN TRADE AND INDUSTRY. 1954- Nairobi, D. A. Hawkins. Monthly.

2398. EASTERN AFRICA LAW REIVEW. Apr. 1968- Dar es Salaam, Faculty of Law, University of East Africa. Quarterly.

2399. REPORTER: EAST AFRICA'S FORTNIGHTLY NEWSMAGAZINE. 1961- Nairobi, News Publishers.

2400. Survey of Language Use and Language Training in Eastern Africa. BULLETIN. v. 1- Nov. 1967- Nairobi. Quarterly.

Useful newsletter describing language work in East Africa. Bibliographical suggestions are included.

2401. SWAHILI: JOURNAL OF THE INSTITUTE OF SWAHILI RESEARCH. v. 1, no. 1-
        Oct. 1930- Dar es Salaam, Institute of Swahili Research,
        University College. Semiannual.

        This journal was first issued as the BULLETIN and then the
JOURNAL of the East African Inter-Territorial Language (Swahili)
Committee (see no. 2387n); it then appeared as SWAHILI: JOURNAL OF
THE EAST AFRICAN SWAHILI COMMITTEE from 1959 through 1964, adopting
its present subtitle with the Mar. 1965 issue. The editor is W. H.
Whiteley. Most articles are in Swahili or English, but French or
German contributions may also appear. In addition to linguistic
studies, the journal includes books reviews, reports on projects
and workshops, and bibliographical materials.

2402. TRANSITION: A JOURNAL OF THE ARTS, CULTURE AND SOCIETY. Nov. 1961-
        Kampala (P.O. Box 20026). Irregular.

        For annotation see no. 1067.

Reference Works

2403. Beck, Ann. A HISTORY OF THE BRITISH MEDICAL ADMINISTRATION OF EAST
        AFRICA, 1900-1950. Cambridge, Mass., Harvard University Press,
        1970. 271 p. (Commonwealth Fund Book)

2404. Belton, E. J., comp. DIRECTORY OF EAST AFRICAN LIBRARIES. Kampala,
        Makerere University College, 1961. 76 p. (Makerere Library
        Publications, no. 1)

        Contains over 90 entries for specialized and larger general
libraries in East Africa.

        The recently formed East African Library Association in 1962
began publication of a quarterly BULLETIN (Kampala, Makerere College
Library).

2405. Cameron, John. THE DEVELOPMENT OF EDUCATION IN EAST AFRICA. New
        York, Teachers College Press, 1970. 148 p. (Publications of
        the Center for Education in Africa)

2406. CATHOLIC DIRECTORY OF EASTERN AFRICA, 1965. Tabora, Tanzania, T.M.P.
        Book Dept., 1965. 512 p. illus., col. maps.

Covers not only Kenya, Tanzania, Uganda, and the Seychelles but
also Malawi, Zambia, the Somali Republic, Sudan, French Somaliland
(Djibouti), Arabia, and Kuwait--all of which are ecclesiastical
jurisdictions served by the Apostolic Delegation in Nairobi. Part 1
offers selected data on the Catholic Church and on the areas under
concern. Part 2 lists each jurisdiction, providing concise data on
its districts (dioceses, etc.), conferences, and associations, plus
a historical note. Part 3 comprises alphabetical lists of orders,
congregations, Catholic serials, clergy, etc., and indexes of jurisdictions and missions. Advertising is included.

2407. Clark, Paul G. DEVELOPMENT PLANNING IN EAST AFRICA. Nairobi, East
        African Publishing House for the East African Institute of Social
        Research, 1965. 154 p. tables. (East African Studies, no. 21)

        Bibliographical footnotes.

        An academic economist's analysis of recent economic problems in
Kenya, Uganda, and Tanzania and his presentation of development
techniques to accelerate material progress. Included is a statistical
projection model for the three economies, along with a discussion of
goals for Uganda in 1981 and of the new plans of each country.

2408. Cole, Sonia M. THE PREHISTORY OF EAST AFRICA. Rev. and enl. ed.
        New York, Macmillan, 1963. 382 p. illus., maps, diagrs.,
        drawings. Paperback ed., New York, New American Library, 1965.
        384 p. (Mentor Books)

        Bibliography: p. 357-369 (hardcover ed.)

        Summarization of archaeological knowledge regarding early man and
prehistoric cultures of Kenya, Uganda, Tanganyika, Somaliland, and
Ethiopia. This study was first published in 1954; the present edition
has been reworked to take into account the results of archaeological
investigations through 1962.

        See also works in Part III on Prehistory, nos. 518-530.

2409. Coupland, Sir Reginald. THE EXPLOITATION OF EAST AFRICA, 1856-1890: THE
        SLAVE TRADE AND THE SCRAMBLE. Evanston, Ill., Northwestern
        University Press, 1967. xiii, 507 p. plates, ports., fold. col.
        map, geneal. table.

        Bibliographical footnotes.

        A classic study, first published in 1939, of East Africa and the
European powers in the nineteenth century. Coupland's work has not
been tampered with; no attempt has been made to update it, for, as Jack

Simmons states in his introduction to this edition, "It stands, with its virtues and faults, as a work of its age, and it will continue to be read: not only by students of East African history, but by connoisseurs of good historical writing." See also his EAST AFRICA AND ITS INVADERS, FROM THE EARLIEST TIMES TO THE DEATH OF SEYYID SAID IN 1856 (New York, Russell and Russell, 1965, 584 p., maps; first published in 1938).

2410. Cox, Richard. PAN-AFRICANISM IN PRACTICE: AN EAST AFRICAN STUDY, PAFMECSA, 1958-1964. Written under the auspices of the Institute of Race Relations. London, New York, Oxford University Press, 1964. 95 p. map.

Summary history and analysis of the regional organization which began in 1958 as the Pan-African Freedom Movement of East and Central Africa and in 1962 became the Pan-African Freedom Movement of Eastern, Central, and Southern Africa. The hope of development into a working federation declined in 1963, after the establishment of the OAU. By 1964, particularly in face of Ghana's attacks on the idea of federation, PAFMECSA had ceased to function effectively.

2411. Diamond, Stanley, and Fred G. Burke, eds. THE TRANSFORMATION OF EAST AFRICA: STUDIES IN POLITICAL ANTHROPOLOGY. New York, London, Basic Books, 1966. 623 p. maps, tables.

Includes bibliographies.

Sixteen essays prepared by distinguished Africanists for a faculty-student seminar on "Problems of Nation-Building in East Africa" at the Program of Eastern African Studies, Maxwell Graduate School of Citizenship and Public Affairs, Syracuse University. The studies cover the precolonial and colonial setting (including racial minorities); race relations in Mozambique; political development in the three East African countries as well as in Malawi, Zambia, Sudan, and Ethiopia; the African élite of East Africa; the growth of urban societies; education; religion; economic development; and East African federation. Most papers include 2- to 3-page bibliographies, and there is an index.

2412. East African Academy, 3d Symposium, Dar es Salaam, Sept. 1965. RE-SEARCH AND DEVELOPMENT IN EAST AFRICA: SEVEN PAPERS PRESENTED AT A PLENARY SESSION AT THE THIRD SYMPOSIUM OF THE EAST AFRICAN ACADEMY, DAR ES SALAAM, SEPTEMBER, 1965. Edited by D. F. Owen. Nairobi, East African Publishing House, 1966. 106 p.

Seven papers dealing, in order, with scientific and technological research, administration of research, industrial research, and research in civil engineering, in the biological sciences, in geography, and in linguistics. The authors are, respectively, Olu Ibukun, D. M. Wako, M. G. Edwards, R. Jones, David P. S. Wasawo, L. Berry, and W. H. Whiteley.

2413.   EAST AFRICAN ANNUAL. 1941- Nairobi, East African Standard. illus. (part col.). Includes advertising. (1963-64 ed., 88 p.)

   Well-illustrated slick-paper magazine published once a year by East Africa's leading daily. Contents are feature articles on many phases of East African life.

2414.   East African Common Services Organization. TREATY FOR EAST AFRICAN COOPERATION, SIGNED AT KAMPALA, UGANDA, ON 6TH JUNE 1967, ON BEHALF OF THE GOVERNMENTS OF THE UNITED REPUBLIC OF TANZANIA, THE SOVEREIGN STATE OF UGANDA AND THE REPUBLIC OF KENYA; COMING INTO FORCE: 1ST DECEMBER 1967. Nairobi, Govt. Printer, 1967. 125 p.

   Text of the treaty which established the East African Community and Common Market between Kenya, Tanzania, and Uganda. An East African Development Bank was also set up. Two of the provisions of the treaty are eventual abolishment of internal tariffs on East African goods and establishment of a common external customs tariff.

2415.   East African Institute of Social and Cultural Affairs. PROBLEMS OF ECONOMIC DEVELOPMENT IN EAST AFRICA: TEN PAPERS ON ECONOMIC PLANNING, MANPOWER UTILIZATION AND REGIONAL DEVELOPMENT. Nairobi, East African Publishing House, 1965. 107 p. (Contemporary African Monographs Series, no. 2)

   A collection of most of the papers presented at a seminar in Sept. 1964 by experts and practitioners in the field of economic development. Topics include economic trends and prospects, the role of economic planning in African socialism, planning for agricultural development, industrial location, tax structure, the central bank, and wages and employment.

2416.   East African Institute of Social and Cultural Affairs. RESEARCH PRIORI- TIES FOR EAST AFRICA. Nairobi, East African Publishing House, 1966. 102 p. (Contemporary African Monographs Series, no. 5)

   A volume comprising the 14 papers given at the conference on Priorities in Biological Research, Feb. 1966, in Nairobi. Following the lead paper by T. J. Mboya on scientific progress in East Africa, representative topics are: the case for pure research, problems of livestock development, and research on tropical diseases, public health, agriculture, wildlife management, and oceanography.

2417.   East African Studies. no. 1- Kampala, Makerere Institute of Social
        Research, Makerere University College, 1953-

        A series of valuable pamphlets and conference proceedings result-
ing from field research carried out by the fellows of the Makerere
Institute of Social Research (formerly the East African Institute of
Social Research). Typical studies are no. 13, TRIBAL MAPS OF EAST
AFRICA AND ZANZIBAR, by J. E. Goldthorpe and F. B. Wilson (1960, 14 p.,
8 l. of sketch maps), and no. 21, P. G. Clark, DEVELOPMENT PLANNING IN
EAST AFRICA (1965, 154 p.). The Institute also issues an annual bibliography, RESEARCH AND PUBLICATIONS (1969 ed., 104 p.), which describes
current projects of its members and lists publicatons of present and
recent members. It also issues EAST AFRICAN LINGUISTIC STUDIES.

2418.   The Economist, London. THE ECONOMY OF EAST AFRICA: A STUDY OF TRENDS.
        Prepared by the Economist Intelligence Unit for the East African
        Railways and Harbours Administration. Nairobi, East African
        Railways and Harbours Administration, 1955. 237 p.

        Requested as an independent opinion from skilled investigators to
aid future planning with regard to prospects for large capital investments. The report reviewed the activities of over a half-century of
the Railways and Harbours Administration and then studied likely trends
in trade, agriculture, and industry, analyzing them by specific products
and aspects of development. See also no. 741 on quarterly surveys of
East Africa by the Economist Intelligence Unit.

2419.   Ethnographic Survey of Africa: East Central Africa. London, Interna-
        tional African Institute.

        For the general note on this series, see no. 980. The following
volumes relate to the peoples of Kenya, Tanganyika, and Uganda.

   a)   Part 3.   THE COASTAL TRIBES OF THE NORTH-EASTERN BANTU (POKOMO,
                  NYIKA AND TEITA). By A. H. J. Prins. 1952. 138 p.
                  fold. map. (Bibliography: p. 133-134; Index of Tribes:
                  p. 135-138.)

   b)   Part 4.   THE NILOTES OF THE ANGLO-EGYPTIAN SUDAN AND UGANDA. By
                  Audrey J. Butt. 1952. 198 p. fold. map. (Bibliography:
                  p. 182-198.)

   c)   Part 5.   THE KIKUYU AND KAMBA OF KENYA. By John Middleton. 1953.
                  107 p. fold. map. (Bibliography: p. 96-102.)

   d)   Part 6.   THE NORTHERN NILO-HAMITES. By G. W. B. Huntingford. 1953.
                  108 p. fold. map. (Bibliography: p. 99-102.)

   e)   Part 7.   THE CENTRAL NILO-HAMITES. By Pamela Gulliver and P. H.

Gulliver. 1953. 106 p. fold. map. (Bibliography: p. 100-101.)

f) Part 8. THE SOUTHERN NILO-HAMITES. By G. W. B. Huntingford. 1953. 152 p. fold. map. (Bibliography: p. 140-146.)

g) Part 10. THE GISU OF UGANDA. By J. S. La Fontaine. 1959. 68 p. fold. map. (Bibliography: p. 62-63.)

h) Part 11. THE EASTERN LACUSTRINE BANTU (GANDA, SOGA [ETC.]). By Margaret Chave Fallers. 1960. 86 p. fold. map. (Bibliography: p. 74-81.)

i) Part 12. THE SWAHILI-SPEAKING PEOPLES OF ZANZIBAR AND THE EAST AFRICAN COAST (ARABS, SHIRAZI AND SWAHILI). By A. H. J. Prins. 1961. 143 p. fold. map. (Bibliography: p. 116-138.)

j) Part 13. THE WESTERN LACUSTRINE BANTU (NYORO, TORO [ETC.]). By Brian K. Taylor. 1962. 159 p. fold. map. (Bibliography: p. 149-152.)

k) Part 14. LES ANCIENS ROYAUMES DE LA ZONE INTERLACUSTRE MERIDIONALE (RWANDA, BURUNDI, BUHA). By Marcel d'Hertefelt, A. Trouwborst, and J. Scherer. 1962. 252 p. fold. map. (Bibliographies at end of sections; Buha of Tanganyika: p. 221-223.) Also issued as Musée Royal de l'Afrique Centrale, Monographies ethnographiques, no. 6.

2420. Freeman-Grenville, G. S. P., ed. THE EAST AFRICAN COAST: SELECT DOCU-MENTS FROM THE FIRST TO THE EARLIER NINETEENTH CENTURY. Oxford, Clarendon Press, 1962. 314 p. maps (1 fold.).

Valuable information on the life of the coast and its commerce is presented in translations from Greek, Arabic, Chinese, French, Portu-guese, Italian, Dutch, and Swahili as well as some English originals, many inaccessible or out of print. The author eschews a general intro-duction on the period (he suggests works to be consulted) but provides an informative note preceding each of the 48 documents.

2421. Ghai, Dharam P., ed. PORTRAIT OF A MINORITY: ASIANS IN EAST AFRICA. Nairobi, London, Oxford University Press, 1965 [i.e., 1966]. 154 p.

Consists of six essays by five prominent "Asian" East Africans and an Austrian-born professor of Indian studies at Syracuse University. A chapter of historical background is followed by social, political, economic, and educational surveys of the Asian community, with a con-cluding analysis of the future prospects of Asians in East Africa.

2422. Great Britain. East Africa Royal Commission. REPORT [1953-55].
       London, H.M. Stationery Off., 1955. xiv, 482 p. (Cmd. 9475)
       Chairman, Sir Hugh Dow.

       Report of a commission appointed at the request of the Governors
of East Africa to inquire into measures to increase national income and
to raise the standards of living of the people of the East African
territories, Africans, Europeans, and Indians alike. Its central
thesis was that restrictions to free competition of the races as to
goods, services, and land must be done away with, notably as regards
rights of African landholders outside tribal areas. The commissioners
recommended that barriers to the free exchange of land be progressively
removed and called for establishment of Development Boards to plan the
use of land and the rehabilitation of overcrowded areas.

2423. Great Britain. East African Economic and Fiscal Commission. EAST
       AFRICA: REPORT. London, H.M. Stationery Off., 1961. 83 p.
       tables. Chairman, J. Raisman.

       The Raisman Report, prepared in connection with the discussions of
the future of the East African Common Services Organization, is concerned chiefly with arrangements for a common market area in East Africa.

       For other official documents, see the Library of Congress bibliogra-
phy, no. 2385 above.

2424. Haight, Mabel V. Jackson. EUROPEAN POWERS AND SOUTH-EAST AFRICA: A
       STUDY OF INTERNATIONAL RELATIONS ON THE SOUTH-EAST COAST OF AFRICA,
       1796-1856. Rev. ed. London, Routledge & Kegan Paul, 1967. xv,
       368 p. maps, charts, graph.

       Bibliography: p. 343-357.

       An excellent study of the period which served as a prologue to the
"scramble." The author puts her emphasis on trade (both the slave trade
and lawful commerce) and deftly analyzes the intense commercial rivalry
which marked the course of international relations in Southeast Africa.
She successively discusses the place of Southeast Africa in ocean
strategy, the Portuguese possessions, the French and the East Coast, the
beginnings of British interest in East Africa, East Africa as an object
of British official policy, Portuguese East Africa and the slave trade,
and Portuguese East Africa's emergence from obscurity. An appendix is
comprised of 12 Portuguese documents with translations, 7 of them on the
Great Trek, 4 on Livingstone. The extensive bibliography is good, as is
the analytical index.

2425. Harries, Lyndon, ed. and tr. SWAHILI POETRY. Text transliterated and
       translated into English. Oxford, Clarendon Press, 1962. xi, 326 p.

Swahili poetry, which is still written in the traditional prosodic forms, is meaningful in the culture of East Africa. Obviously of close connection with Arabic poetry (it was written in the Swahili-Arabic script), its chief purpose up to the end of the nineteenth century was to express the spirit and practice of Islam. This volume is a broad selection of texts from the manuscripts in the library of the School of Oriental and African Studies, where Dr. Harries was a lecturer in Swahili. The representative poems are given in parallel transliteration from the script with English translation on facing pages, each explained in full scholarly commentary.

Dr. Harries has also edited and translated Carl Velten's compilation, SWAHILI PROSE TEXTS: A SELECTION FROM THE MATERIAL COLLECTED BY CARL VELTEN FROM 1893 TO 1896 (London, Oxford University Press, 1965, 298 p.), and a work by Ahmad Nassir bin Juma Bhalo, POEMS FROM KENYA: GNOMIC VERSES IN SWAHILI (Madison, University of Wisconsin Press, 1966, 244 p.).

2426.   HIGHER EDUCATION IN EAST AFRICA. Entebbe, Govt. Printer, 1958. 123 p.

A white paper issued jointly by Kenya, Tanganyika, Uganda, and Zanzibar in which a University of East Africa was proposed, with the planned University Colleges in Kenya and Tanganyika as well as the then Royal Technical College of East Africa in Nairobi to be component parts of the new university. Included are the Carr-Saunders, Keir, Harlow, etc., report of the working party on Higher Education in East Africa, 1955, and the report by Giffen and Alexander on a visit to the Royal Technical College, 1956.

2427.   HISTORY OF EAST AFRICA. Oxford, Clarendon Press, 1963-

Vol. I, edited by Roland A. Oliver and Gervase Mathew. 1963. 500 p. maps. (Bibliography: p. 457-480.)

Vol. II, edited by Vincent T. Harlow and E. M. Chilver, assisted by Alison Smith. 1965. li, 766 p. maps. (Bibliography: p. 700-736.)

The first two volumes of an authoritative history of East Africa, projected in three volumes. The editors have been joined by a group of specialist contributors for individual chapters. The first volume carries the history from the Stone Age up to 1890; the second ends with the year 1945. Included in the appendixes to Vol. II is a reprint of the British Mandate for East Africa. The select bibliographies cover published and unpublished materials, government documents, and serials.

An earlier historical study by Dr. Oliver was THE MISSIONARY FACTOR IN EAST AFRICA, first published in 1962 (2d ed., 1965, xv, 302 p., maps; bibliography: p. 293-297).

The Royal Commonwealth Society (London) maintains a dictionary file with over 5,000 names of East African biographies. The aim

is to collect data on individuals who played a significant part
in the history of East Africa prior to 1900.

2428. Hoyle, B. S. THE SEAPORTS OF EAST AFRICA: A GEOGRAPHICAL STUDY.
        Written under the auspices of the Makerere Institute of Social
        Research, Kampala, Uganda. Nairobi, East African Publishing
        House, 1967. 137 p. maps. (East African Studies, no. 26)

        Bibliography: p. 134-137.

        A geographical analysis of the development of the ports of Mombasa,
Tanga, Zanzibar, Dar es Salaam, and Mtwara and of their role in the
expanding economies of the countries of East Africa. Included are
discussions of facilities, traffic, and the hinterlands of the ports.

2429. Hughes, Anthony J. EAST AFRICA: THE SEARCH FOR UNITY; KENYA, TAN-
        GANYIKA, UGANDA, AND ZANZIBAR. Harmondsworth, Middlesex, and
        Baltimore, Md., Penguin Books, 1963. 278 p. (Penguin African
        Library)

        The writer, a political reporter in East Africa, acted as press
liaison and public relations officer of KANO in 1963. In this condensed
history of the political development of the four countries of former
British East Africa he examines the factors favoring federation--which
at the time of his writing seemed imminent. In the appendix is a
reprint of the declaration of federation stated in Nairobi on June 5,
1963, by President Julius Nyerere of Tanganyika, Prime Minister M. A.
Obote of Uganda, and Prime Minister Jomo Kenyatta of Kenya.

        A strong argument for federation of Tanganyika, Uganda, and Kenya
was presented by two American political scientists, Carl G. Rosberg,
Jr., and Aaron Segal: AN EAST AFRICAN FEDERATION (New York, Carnegie
Endowment for International Peace, 1963, 72 p.; INTERNATIONAL CON-
CILIATION, no. 543, May 1963).

2430. Ingham, Kenneth. A HISTORY OF EAST AFRICA. London, Longmans, Green,
        1962; New York, Praeger, 1963. xii, 456 p. illus., maps.

        Select bibliography: p. 443-448.

        By the author of a notable study of Uganda, this is at present one
of the most comprehensive modern works covering the entire history of
East Africa.

2431. KENYA, UGANDA, TANZANIA, ZAMBIA, MALAWI AND ETHIOPIA DIRECTORY; TRADE
        AND COMMERCIAL INDEX, 1968 EDITION. Nairobi, East African Directory
        Co., [1968?]. 1 v. various pagings. illus., maps.

        A business directory, expanding on the earlier KENYA, UGANDA AND
TANZANIA DIRECTORY.

2432.   Kirkman, James S. MEN AND MONUMENTS ON THE EAST AFRICAN COAST. New
York, Praeger, 1966 [c1964]. 224 p. plates, maps, plans.

Bibliography: p. 219-221.

Kirkman, an archaeologist who has worked in Kenya for more than 16
years, tells the story of East Africa's coastal strip through its
monuments. His treatment, intended for the general reader, excludes
prehistoric sites such as Olorgesaillie. Areas covered are Somalia,
the Lamu Archipelago, the Tana Basin, Malindi and the north mainland,
Gedi, Mombasa, Fort Jesus, Zanzibar and Pemba, Tanganyika, the Comoros,
Madagascar, and Mozambique.

2433.   Lugard, Frederick J. D. Lugard, baron. THE DIARIES OF LORD LUGARD.
Edited by Margery Perham; assistant editor, Mary Bull. Evanston,
Ill., Northwestern University Press, 1959-63. 4 v. ports., maps,
facsims. (Northwestern University African Studies, no. 3)

The first three volumes cover East Africa (especially in what was
to become Uganda) from Nov. 1889 to Dec. 1890, Dec. 1890 to Dec. 1891,
and Jan. 1892 to Aug. 1892, respectively; the fourth volume deals with
the Nigerian area, in 1894-95 and again in 1897-98.

See also Dame Perham's two-volume biography, LUGARD. Lord Lugard's
own narrative of his campaigns as representative of the Imperial East
African Company in suppression of the slave trade is a primary source
for the history of this period: THE RISE OF OUR EAST AFRICAN EMPIRE:
EARLY EFFORTS IN NYASALAND AND UGANDA (Edinburgh, London, W. Blackwood,
1893, 2 v., illus., maps, plans).

2434.   Lury, D. A. THE TRADE STATISTICS OF THE COUNTRIES OF EAST AFRICA,
1945-1964, AND POPULATION ESTIMATES: BACK PROJECTIONS OF RECENT
CENSUS RESULTS. Nairobi, Institute for Development Studies,
University College, 1965. [5 p.] (Reprint Series, no. 13)

Reprinted from East African Statistical Department, ECONOMIC AND
STATISTICAL REVIEW, Mar. and Sept. 1965.

The first part gives trade statistics for Uganda, Kenya, and
Tanganyika; in the second part are estimates of population for 1921,
1931, 1939, 1948, and 1963 for the three countries plus Zanzibar.

2435.   Macpherson, Margaret. THEY BUILT FOR THE FUTURE: A CHRONICLE OF
MAKERERE UNIVERSITY COLLEGE, 1922-1962. Cambridge, Eng.,
University Press, 1964. xiii, 212 p. illus. (1 col.), ports.

Bibliographic references included in "Notes": p. 190-206.

Account of the chief center for learning in East Africa.

2436. Mangat, J. S.   A HISTORY OF THE ASIANS IN EAST AFRICA, C. 1886 TO 1945.
       Oxford, Clarendon Press, 1969.   216 p.

       Bibliography: p. 179-204.

       The first detailed, historical survey on Asians in East Africa.
       Based on extensive research into original sources, the book examines
       fully the economic, political, and social implications of Asian immigra-
       tion into East Africa during the colonial period.

2437. Marsh, Zoë, ed.   EAST AFRICA THROUGH CONTEMPORARY RECORDS.   Cambridge,
       Eng., University Press, 1961.   214 p.   illus.

       Selected extracts from primary sources for the history of East
       Africa. A prelude is Dr. Leakey's announcement in 1959 of the finding
       of the skull of Zinjanthropus, considered the oldest human skull yet
       found. There follow the first written reference, in Herodotus, references
       in Arabic sources, accounts of Portuguese voyages of the sixteenth
       century, etc., ending with reports of the Kenya Land Commission in 1932.

2438. Marsh, Zoë, and George William Kingsnorth.   AN INTRODUCTION TO THE HISTORY
       OF EAST AFRICA.   3d ed.   New York, Cambridge University Press,
       1965.   xxi, 254 p.   maps.

       Bibliography: p. 236-242.

       An outline history of the peoples and territories of East Africa,
       designed both for the student and for the general reader. Beginning with
       East Africa's early history, the authors then cover the slave trade and
       the abolition movement; the period of European exploration; missionary
       societies and East African development; the "scramble" for Africa and the
       first partition of East Africa; Ugandan history up to 1890; kingdoms and
       leaders, Zanzibar under British influence; the railway and the economic,
       social, and constitutional development of Kenya; and the later history
       of Uganda and of Tanganyika.

2439. Matheson, J. K., and E. W. Bovill, eds.   EAST AFRICAN AGRICULTURE: A
       SHORT SURVEY OF THE AGRICULTURE OF KENYA, UGANDA, TANGANYIKA,
       AND ZANZIBAR AND OF ITS PRINCIPAL PRODUCTS.   London, New York,
       Oxford University Press, 1950.   xvi, 332 p.

       Lucid and still useful description by a number of specialists. The
       first 60 pages, by Mr. Matheson, give a general geographical introduction
       on land, population, land tenure, white settlement, native labor, native
       welfare, soil conservation problems, and agricultural research institutes.
       Part 2 describes in detail the agriculture of the European settlers,
       explaining practices and conditions regarding the chief crops. Part 3
       considers agriculture by territorial division. There are short lists of
       sources at the end of the sections. Appendixes tabulate statistics.

2440. Middleton, John, and E. H. Winter, eds. WITCHCRAFT AND SORCERY IN
          EAST AFRICA. London, Routledge & Kegan Paul; New York, Praeger,
          1963. 302 p.

      A collection of intriguing anthropological papers by 10 writers,
including the two editors. The various beliefs in and techniques of
witchcraft and sorcery in 10 East African societies are described in
language understandable to the lay reader.

2441. Morgan, D. J. BRITISH PRIVATE INVESTMENT IN EAST AFRICA: REPORT OF
          A CONFERENCE. London, Overseas Development Institute, 1965. 63 p.

      An inquiry into the nature of obstacles to British investment in
the developing countries of East Africa. The booklet ends with the
general conclusions of the conference (held June 22, 1965, in London)
and appends a statement by the Tanzanian government on Africanizing the
economy.

2442. Müller, Fritz F. DEUTSCHLAND, ZANZIBAR, OSTAFRIKA: GESCHICHTE EINER
          DEUTSCHEN KOLONIALEROBERUNG, 1884-1890. Berlin, Rutten & Loening,
          1959. 581 p. illus.

      Bibliography: p. 555-567.

      Well-documented Marxist interpretation of the German conquest in
East Africa, covering diplomatic moves in Berlin and London and
containing a detailed account of actions of Carl Peters and the Deutsche
Ost-Afrikanische Gesellschaft in East Africa. Events are carried up to
the establishment in 1891 of the crown colony of German East Africa
(Tanganyika).

2443. Ndegwa, Philip. THE COMMON MARKET AND DEVELOPMENT IN EAST AFRICA.
          Nairobi, East African Publishing House for the East African
          Institute of Social Research, 1965. 150 p. tables. (East African
          Studies, no. 22)

      The author, Senior Planning Officer in the Kenya Ministry of
Economic Planning and Development, examines the role of expanded inter-
state trade and import substitution within the framework of a customs
union or a common market among underdeveloped countries. The major
features of East African trade and the prospect for a larger East African
trading area are analyzed, and policy recommendations are made.

2444. Nyerere, Julius Kambarage. FREEDOM AND UNITY--UHURU NA UMOJA: A
          SELECTION FROM WRITINGS AND SPEECHES, 1952-65. London, Oxford
          University Press, 1967. xii, 366 p. plates, ports.

An introduction is followed by some 70 statements, ranging from a pamphlet on the race problem in East Africa written by Nyerere as an Edinburgh University student to speeches made and articles written while President of Tanzania (including a reprint of his 1962 pamphlet UJAMAA: THE BASIS OF AFRICAN SOCIALISM). Topics covered are: African unity, international affairs, socialism, democracy, equality and human rights, economic development, methods and aims of independence, education, national purposes and the national ethic, and security and the rule of law. See no. 2511 for further comment.

2445. O'Connor, A. M. AN ECONOMIC GEOGRAPHY OF EAST AFRICA. New York, Praeger, 1966. 292 p. maps, tables. (Praeger Surveys in Economic Geography)

Includes bibliographies.

The first comprehensive study of the economic geography of Kenya, Tanzania, and Uganda, by a lecturer in geography at Makerere University College. The book is somewhat unusual in format in that the concluding rather than the opening chapters deal with the physical, demographic, economic, and political factors which determine the pattern of economic activities. It begins with a regional survey and then covers agriculture, livestock, fisheries, forestry, mining, manufacturing, power and transport, tourism, and internal and external trade. There are 20 helpful distribution maps, and references follow each chapter except the "Conclusion." An index is included.

2446. Ogot, Bethwell A. HISTORY OF THE SOUTHERN LUO: Vol. I, MIGRATION AND SETTLEMENT, 1500-1900. Nairobi, East African Publishing House, 1967. 250 p. illus., maps, tables. (Peoples of East Africa, v. 1)

Bibliography: p. 241-245.

A study of the Padhola and Kenya Luo which also functions as an outline history of eastern Uganda and western Kenya. The author carefully examines the traditions of these peoples, notes possible links with other Nilotic groups, and speculates on how their societies evolved.

2447. Ogot, B. A., and J. A. Kiernan, eds. ZAMANI: A SURVEY OF EAST AFRICAN HISTORY. Nairobi, East African Publishing House, 1968. 407 p. maps.

Eighteen leading scholars reassess the last 2,000 years of East African history.

2448. Paulus, Margarete. DAS GENOSSENSCHAFTSWESEN IN TANGANYIKA UND UGANDA: MOGLICHKEITEN UND AUFGABEN. Berlin, New York, Springer-Verlag, 1967. xiii, 156 p. illus., maps. (Afrika-Studien, no. 15)

Bibliography: p. 132-143.

2449. Political and Economic Planning (PEP). NEW COMMONWEALTH STUDENTS IN
       BRITAIN, WITH SPECIAL REFERENCE TO STUDENTS FROM EAST AFRICA.
       London, G. Allen & Unwin, 1965. 253 p.

       Selective bibliography: p. 246-248.

       The report was written by Jean Currie and Timothy Leggatt; research
included an interview survey and a survey by mail questionnaire. The
work is divided into four parts which deal with (1) trends in admission
of overseas students to institutions of higher education in Britain and
an estimate of future demand from East Africa, (2) policies and problems
relating to the academic and formal educational side of the students'
lives, (3) their experiences in the nonacademic life of Britain, and
(4) conclusions and recommendations.

2450. Polomé, Edgar C. SWAHILI LANGUAGE HANDBOOK. Washington, D.C., Center
       for Applied Linguistics, 1967. xvii, 232 p. map. (Language
       Handbook Series)

       The book, directed to the nonspecialist, gives comprehensive
information about the language, including cultural background. There is
a chapter on Swahili literature, as well as bibliographical references.

2451. RESEARCH SERVICES IN EAST AFRICA. Compiled for the East African Academy.
       Nairobi, East African Publishing House, 1966. 239 p.

       A guide to research facilities in Kenya, Tanzania, and Uganda up
to the end of 1964. Field work for the survey was conducted by Marco
Surveys, Ltd. Academic, commercial, private, and public services are
described first by region and then by country in more than 30 fields of
research, e.g., agriculture, antiquities, chemistry, economics, game,
housing, library services, medicine, political science, religious studies,
and zoology. For each center the data given are: location, facilities,
date established, staff, sources of finance, scope of research, and
publications. There is an index.

2452. Richards, Audrey I., ed. EAST AFRICAN CHIEFS: A STUDY OF POLITICAL
       DEVELOPMENT IN SOME UGANDA AND TANGANYIKA TRIBES. New York,
       Praeger, 1960. 419 p. illus. (Books That Matter)

       Bibliography: p. 398-409.

       A comparative study of political development begun in 1952 under
the auspices of the East African Institute of Social Research and
carried out by anthropologists on the staff and other researchers, with

the final writing by Dr. Richards, then head of the Institute. A collection was made of career histories of over 1,100 chiefs of varying types, kings, paramount chiefs, clan elders, and so on, with data about their age, education, religion, service, outside training, genealogy, and economic position within the community.

2453. Richards, Charles G., and James Place, eds. EAST AFRICAN EXPLORERS. London, Oxford University Press, 1960. 356 p. illus. (World's Classics, no. 572)

Compilation in a pocket-size volume of outstanding passages from the books and journals of the nineteenth-century explorers of East Africa: Krapf and Rebmann, Charles New, Livingstone and Stanley, Burton, Speke and Grant, Samuel W. Baker, Joseph Thomson, Gaetano Casati, Count Teleki and L. von Höhnel, J. W. Gregory, Lord Lugard, J. R. L. Macdonald, Herbert Austin. The works from which the extracts are taken are noted, but there is no combined listing of the well-known sources, most of which are available in large American libraries in the original editions or as reprints.

2454. Russell, Edward Walter, ed. THE NATURAL RESOURCES OF EAST AFRICA. Nairobi, East African Literature Bureau, 1962. 144 p. illus., maps.

A handbook on the natural resources of East Africa by 18 contributors. Topics include history, archaeology, populations, soils, climate, agriculture, and forestry to imports and exports. There is also a section on recent research. No political articles are included.

2455. Strandes, Justus. THE PORTUGUESE PERIOD IN EAST AFRICA. Translated from the German by Jean F. Wallwork; edited, with topographical notes, by J. S. Kirkman. Nairobi, Published for the Kenya History Society by East African Literature Bureau, 1961. 373 p. illus., fold. map in pocket. (Transactions of the Kenya History Society, v. 2)

Bibliography: p. 365-369.

The first English version of a major work originally published in 1899 in Germany and long out of print. Strandes' account of the Portuguese domination of the East African coast from the early sixteenth to the late seventeenth century was based on his skillful gleaning of the abundant material in Portuguese chronicles and in Portuguese archives. The editor has added a bibliography of works published since 1899.

2456. TRAVELLERS' GUIDE TO EAST AFRICA: A CONCISE GUIDE TO THE REPUBLICS OF KENYA, TANZANIA, AND UGANDA, THEIR WILDLIFE AND THEIR TOURIST

FACILITIES. New York, London, House & Maxwell [1966]. 175 p.
illus., maps.

2457. Tucker, A. N., and M. A. Bryan. LINGUISTIC SURVEY OF THE NORTHERN
        BANTU BORDERLAND: Vol. IV, LANGUAGES OF THE EASTERN SECTION,
        GREAT LAKES TO INDIAN OCEAN. London, New York, Published for
        the International African Institute by Oxford University Press,
        1957. 89 p. fold. map.

        _____. THE NON-BANTU LANGUAGES OF NORTH-EASTERN AFRICA. With a
        supplement on the non-Bantu languages of Southern Africa by
        E. O. J. Westphal. London, New York, Published for the Interna-
        tional African Institute by Oxford University Press, 1956. xv,
        228 p. illus., 2 fold. maps (1 col. in pocket). (Handbook of
        African Languages, pt. 3)

        The volume on non-Bantu languages covers the Nilo-Hamitic lan-
        guages of certain tribes (Masai, Nandi, etc.) of Kenya, Uganda, and
        Tanganyika, as well as those of southern Sudan, Somalia, and Ethiopia.
        The LINGUISTIC SURVEY volume indicated covers languages of the Bantu
        tribes of the same regions.

2458. United Nations. Economic Commission for Africa. Industrial Co-
        ordination Mission to East and Central Africa. REPORT.
        New York, Dec. 1963. 67 p. and annexes. (E/CN.14/247)

        Bibliographical footnotes.

        Like the report for West Africa (no. 1312), this has three parts:
        economic setting, industrial development of large-scale industries,
        and industrial development of small-scale industries.

2459. U.S. Department of the Interior. Office of Geography. BRITISH EAST
        AFRICA: OFFICIAL STANDARD NAMES APPROVED BY THE UNITED STATES
        BOARD ON GEOGRAPHIC NAMES. Washington, U.S. Govt. Print. Off.,
        Apr. 1955. 601 p. (24,700 names) (Gazetteer no. 1)

        See note on series, no. 484.

2460. Welbourn, Frederick B. EAST AFRICAN REBELS: A STUDY OF SOME INDE-
        PENDENT CHURCHES. London, SCM Press, 1961. 258 p. maps.
        (World Mission Studies)

        The author, a clergyman connected with Makerere University Col-
        lege, studies the movements of four separatist churches, three in
        Uganda and one in Kenya. His work, based on unpublished material as
        well as printed sources, is at once church history and social

psychology. See also his EAST AFRICAN CHRISTIAN (London, Oxford University Press, 1965, 226 p., illus.).

2461. WHO'S WHO IN EAST AFRICA, 1967-1968. Nairobi, Marco Publishers (Africa), Ltd., 1968. 120, 9 p. ports.

Divided into three country sections--Kenya, Tanzania, and Uganda. Biographies are based on interviews. A list of government ministers precedes each country section. Most entries give name, date and place of birth, education, positions held, membership in organizations, and address. Some portraits are included. At the back is a list of abbreviations of political parties, organizations, titles, degrees, etc. This is the second edition of WHO'S WHO IN EAST AFRICA (first published in 1964).

Marco Surveys, Ltd., Kenwood House, P. O. Box 5837, Nairobi, another member of the Marco group, issues a series of politico-economic pamphlets, Public Opinion Poll (1960-). No. 14 is COMPARATIVE CHANGE IN PUBLIC OPINION, 1964-1966, NAIROBI, DAR ES SALAAM, KAMPALA (Nairobi, June 1966, 41 p.).

2462. Williams, John George. A FIELD GUIDE TO THE BIRDS OF EAST AND CENTRAL AFRICA. Boston, Houghton Mifflin, 1964 [c.1963]. 288 p. illus., plates (part col.), map, index.

2463. Worthington, Stella, and E. B. Worthington. INLAND WATERS OF AFRICA: THE RESULT OF TWO EXPEDITIONS TO THE GREAT LAKES OF KENYA AND UGANDA, WITH ACCOUNTS OF THEIR BIOLOGY, NATIVE TRIBES AND DEVELOPMENT. London, New York, Macmillan, 1933. xix, 259 p.

Bibliography: p. 246-253.

Dr. E. B. Worthington, who was scientific secretary of CSA from 1951 to 1955, had been scientific adviser for Lord Hailey's African Survey and in 1946 was development adviser for Uganda. This book records expeditions made with his wife to the African lakes from 1927 to 1931, with much geographical and biological information on fisheries. The bibliography refers to the publications arising from the various lake fishery expeditions.

2464. THE YEAR BOOK AND GUIDE TO EAST AFRICA. 1950- London, S. Low, Marston; Robert Hale, 1951-. Edited by A. Gordon-Brown and issued by the Union-Castle Mail Steamship Co. Annual. (1965 ed., 320 p., 16 maps, 72 p. of advertising)

Handy volume of general information for travelers, with historical sections, handbook analysis by territories, chapters on safaris and

mountaineering, travel sections in baedeker style, and various chapters
of miscellaneous information. Separately indexed notes on fauna were
discontinued after 1957. There are indexes of geographical names and
subjects at the beginning of the book.

KENYA

Atlas

2465. Kenya Colony and Protectorate. Survey of Kenya. ATLAS OF KENYA: A
         COMPREHENSIVE SERIES OF NEW AND AUTHENTIC MAPS PREPARED FROM THE
         NATIONAL SURVEY AND OTHER GOVERNMENTAL SOURCES, WITH GAZETTEER
         AND NOTES ON PRONUNCIATION AND SPELLING. Nairobi, Printed by the
         Survey of Kenya, 1959. 44 l. of maps (part col.). Page size,
         20" x 18".

         Text on verso of a few maps.

         Maps covering geology, physical features, soil, meteorology,
agriculture, population, economy, administration, and history (scales,
1:1,000,000 to 1:3,000,000). Also included are a town plan of Mombasa
and interesting reproductions of early maps. From 1,500 to 2,000 names
appear in the gazetteer.

Bibliographies

2466. African Bibliographic Center, Washington, D.C. A SELECTED AND BRIEF
         GUIDE TO KENYA POLITICS AND GOVERNMENT, 1965-1967. Washington,
         1968. 10 l. (Current Reading List Series, v. 6, no. 1)

2467. DuPré, Carole E. THE LUO OF KENYA: AN ANNOTATED BIBLIOGRAPHY.
         Washington, D.C., Institute for Cross-Cultural Research, 1968.
         164 p. (ICR Studies, 3).

         The first section contains an introductory essay to Kenya and the
Luo with particular reference to contemporary problems in Luoland. This
is followed by a bibliographic essay on Luo materials. The main bibliography is annotated and divided into three parts. Part 1 contains
material on East Africa and Kenya. Part 2 covers references to the Luo,
and Part 3 includes works containing information relevant to the Luo.
Each part is further divided by subject. The over 130 references cited
include documents, maps, articles, conference papers, theses, and books.
Some Luo language works are included.

2468. Hakes, Jay E. A STUDY GUIDE FOR KENYA. Boston, Development Program, African Studies Center, Boston University, 1969. 76 p. Includes bibliography.

2469. Syracuse University. Maxwell Graduate School of Citizenship and Public Affairs. Program of Eastern African Studies. A BIBLIOGRAPHY OF KENYA. Compiled by John B. Webster and others. Syracuse, N.Y., 1967. xviii, 461 p. (Syracuse University, Eastern African Bibliographical Series, no. 2)

The 7,210 entries on Kenya and East Africa include books, articles, government publications, dissertations, and conference papers in many European and East African languages. Arrangement is by subject. There is a large section on language and literature which has works on and in Swahili and other East African languages. The bibliogrpahy, second in the series of national bibliographies by Syracuse University (the first is the 1965 BIBLIOGRAPHY OF MALAWI), was originally compiled to aid development of the Kenya Institute of Administration and its library. It attempts to update the Library of Congress guide, Part 3 of which is described in the next entry.

2470. U.S. Library of Congress. General Reference and Bibliography Division. OFFICIAL PUBLICATIONS OF BRITISH EAST AFRICA: Part 3, KENYA AND ZANZIBAR. Compiled by Audrey A. Walker, African Section. Washington, 1963. 162 p.

Contains 994 entries (p. 1-120) for official publications of Kenya Colony and Protectorate and of the East African Common Services Organization and Great Britain relating to Kenya. The documents published by the colony under its earlier name, East Africa Protectorate (1899-1920), are included without differentiation. Many of the reports of the agencies are continued virtually unchanged under the independent government of Kenya.

Reference Works

2471. AFRICAN LAND DEVELOPMENT IN KENYA. 1945/50- Nairobi. illus., photos., fold. maps. Irregular.

Issued from 1945/50 to 1952 by the African Land Utilization and Settlement Board, with title AFRICAN LAND UTILIZATION AND SETTLEMENT REPORT; to 1955/56, with present title, by the African Land Development Board; and from 1956/57 by the Land Development Board (Non-scheduled Areas). The publication consists of progress reports on government-supported land reclamation and development schemes in the African areas of Kenya under British colonial administration. This basic source includes statistics.

2472. American University, Washington, D.C. Foreign Area Studies. AREA
         HANDBOOK FOR KENYA. By Irving Kaplan and others. Washington, U.S.
         Govt. Printing Off., 1967. xii, 707 p. map, tables. (Department
         of the Army Pamphlet no. 550-56)

      Bibliography: p. 663-689.

         Similar to others of the series, this is a comprehensive survey
      of the country. The volume is comprised of four main sections: social
      (including physical environment and historical setting), political,
      economic, and military. Arrangement of the bibliography is also by
      these four divisions. A glossary and an analytical index are included.

2473. Bennett, George. KENYA, A POLITICAL HISTORY: THE COLONIAL PERIOD.
         London, Oxford University Press, 1963. 190 p. maps.
         (Students' Library)

         Although hardly more than a brief summary, this political history
      is perhaps the most useful single work on the British administration of
      Kenya. It contains broad coverage of political developments from 1900--
      the Colonial Office take-over, the role of the European settlers, the
      development of racism and African nationalism, the Mau Mau Emergency,
      changing multiracial policies, and the last stages of the road to
      independence. Bibliographical notes refer chiefly to newspapers and
      official documents.

2474. Bolton, Kenneth. THE LION AND THE LILY--A GUIDE TO KENYA. With
         specialist contributions. London, G. Bles, 1962. 241 p. illus.,
         fold. map.

         In this popular guidebook slanted for the tourist trade the author
      attempts to explain the various aspects of the country, excluding
      politics, to its own inhabitants. Chapters on several topics--e.g.,
      archaeology, wildlife--are contributed by well-known Kenyan authorities.

2475. Corfield, F. D. HISTORICAL SURVEY OF THE ORIGINS AND GROWTH OF MAU MAU.
         London, H.M. Stationery Off., 1960. 321 p. (Cmnd. 1030)

         The official study resulting from the trial of Kenyatta and pre-
      senting what appeared to be complete proof of his responsibility for
      the Mau Mau "emergency." According to most critics, by the time of
      publication the work was outdated and much of the evidence had been
      disproved. Delf (below) speaks of it as "history composed by the
      patient himself," though he admits that it was a reliable chronicle
      of government information at the time it was being written. For an
      opposite interpretation of the "emergency," see Carl G. Rosberg, Jr.,
      and John Nottingham, THE MYTH OF "MAU MAU": NATIONALISM IN KENYA (New
      York, Published by Praeger for the Hoover Institution, 1966, 427 p.).

Rosberg and Nottingham do not see "Mau Mau" as primarily an atavistic
Kikuyu movement but rather as part of the growth and development of
Kenya's African nationalism.

2476. Delf, George. JOMO KENYATTA: TOWARDS TRUTH ABOUT "THE LIGHT OF KENYA."
           London, V. Gollancz, 1961. 223 p. illus.

       U.S. ed., Garden City, N.Y., Doubleday, 1961. 215 p.

       Includes bibliography.

       An attempt to trace Kenyatta's career as the eventual logical
leader of Kenya. The writer alludes to the widespread belief among
Africans that the trial of Kenyatta for association with Mau Mau was
"rigged." His argument is that Mau Mau was "the inexorable product of
a seriously distorted social system" and could have been prevented by
a less weak British government.

2477. Huxley, Elspeth. WHITE MAN'S COUNTRY: LORD DELAMERE AND THE MAKING
           OF KENYA. London, New York, Macmillan, 1935. 2 v.

       This biography of the leader who was largely responsible for
attracting Europeans to the colony for permanent residence as farmers in
the Highlands is also a history of white settlement in Kenya. Its
author is an expert on East Africa.

2478. International Bank for Reconstruction and Development. THE ECONOMIC
           DEVELOPMENT OF KENYA. Baltimore, Md., Johns Hopkins Press, 1963.
           380 p.

       Bibliographical footnotes.

       Prepared by the Economic Survey Mission to Kenya subsequent to a
field survey of resources--agricultural, manufacturing, mining, transport and communications, tourist trade, educational system, monetary
system, etc. It begins with a general examination of the economy and
ends with recommendations made by the Mission.

2479. Kenya. Government Archives. ARCHIVES MICROFILMING PROGRAMME: Sec. I,
           PROVINCIAL AND DISTRICT ANNUAL [AND QUARTERLY] REPORTS. Nairobi,
           Mar. 1964. 75 1. fold. map. 33 cm. Mimeographed.

       Details of a projected program, with the general introduction
signed by Derek Charman, archivist, the technical adviser appointed by
the U.K. Department of Technical Co-operation. In the introduction to
Sec. I the form of the reports is described and subject headings are
listed (the earliest for Nandi District, 1904/5, and Nyanza Province,
1905/6). For each province and district a historic account is provided,

followed by the list of reports available. The large map is of the
East Africa Protectorate--the original name of Kenya. A microfilm
copy of the archives is held by Syracuse University in New York.

2480. KENYA WEEKLY NEWS. 1928- Nakuru, Nakura Press. Weekly.

    Pro-settler journal, valuable for local whites' views and opinions.

2481. Kenyatta, Jomo. FACING MOUNT KENYA: THE TRIBAL LIFE OF THE GIKUYU.
    London, Secker and Warburg, 1938. xxv, 339 p.

    Reprint, New York, Vintage Books, 1962. 326 p.

    Detailed ethnosociological study of the writer's people. As general
secretary of the Kikuyu Central Association in the 1920's, Kenyatta had
led the agitation against European settlement in the Kenya Highlands,
which the Kikuyu claimed as their land. In this book, written after he
studied under Professor Malinowski at the London School of Economics,
Kenyatta attempted to show the evil effects of this culture contact for
the Kikuyu.

2482. Kenyatta, Jomo. HARAMBEE! THE PRIME MINISTER OF KENYA'S SPEECHES,
    1963-1964, FROM THE ATTAINMENT OF INTERNAL SELF-GOVERNMENT TO THE
    THRESHOLD OF THE KENYA REPUBLIC. Text edited and arranged by
    Anthony Cullen. Nairobi, Oxford University Press, 1964. 115 p.
    ports.

    Published in Dec. 1964, on the first anniversary of Kenya's
independence, this volume marks the formal institution of the Republic
of Kenya, with Jomo Kenyatta as President. Some 100 speeches delivered
by Kenyatta during his tenure of office as the first and only Prime
Minister of Kenya (June 1963-Dec. 1964) are presented here. The editor
has transformed the speeches into a narrative by condensing them or
splitting them into subject components (some speeches appear in full);
he has also provided introductory notes. The aims and philosophy of
Kenya's unifying, forward-looking leader are neatly conveyed in this
book, the title of which translates "Let's all pull together"--the
national slogan adopted by Kenyatta to succeed the preindependence
nationalist slogan Uhuru ("Freedom"). Also important is his paper presented to the Kenya Parliament, AFRICAN SOCIALISM AND ITS APPLICATION
TO PLANNING IN KENYA (1965).

2483. Mboya, Tom. FREEDOM AND AFTER. Boston, Little, Brown, 1963. 288 p.
    illus., ports., map.

    The story of the late Kenyan labor leader during the formative
years of Kenyan independence is of importance as source material. In an
appendix Mr. Mboya gives the text of Kenya's industrial relations charter,
signed in Nairobi on Oct. 15, 1962.

2484. Mungeam, G. H. BRITISH RULE IN KENYA, 1895-1912: THE ESTABLISHMENT OF ADMINISTRATION IN THE EAST AFRICA PROTECTORATE. Oxford, Clarendon Press, 1966. xii, 329 p. plates, ports., maps. (Oxford Studies in African Affairs)

Bibliography: p. 290-307.

A detailed introduction to Kenyan history in the 17 formative years of British administration. Emphasis is on the relationship between the district officer, the commissioner or governor, and the officials at Whitehall. The book ends at the point at which growing signs of African resentment and opposition began to appear. An analytical index is included.

2485. Ruthenberg, Hans. AFRICAN AGRICULTURAL PRODUCTION DEVELOPMENT POLICY IN KENYA, 1952-1965. Berlin, New York, Springer-Verlag, 1966. xv, 164 p. maps. (Afrika-Studien, 10).

Bibliography: p. 154-164.

2486. Sorrenson, M. P. K. LAND REFORM IN THE KIKUYU COUNTRY: A STUDY IN GOVERNMENT POLICY. Nairobi, Oxford University Press, 1967. 266 p.

Bibliography: p. 253-256.

Thorough historical study based largely on official files of the Kenya government on the question of land policy. See also Hanfried Fliedner, DIE BODENRECHTSREFORM IN KENYA: STUDIE UBER DIE ANDERUNG DER BODENRECHTSVERHALTNISSE IM ZUGE DER AGRARREFORM UNTER BESONDERER BERUCKSICHTIGUNG DES KIKUYU-STAMMESGEBIETES (Berlin, New York, Springer-Verlag, 1965, 114 p.).

2487. U.S. Department of the Interior. Office of Geography. KENYA: OFFICIAL STANDARD NAMES APPROVED BY THE UNITED STATES BOARD ON GEOGRAPHIC NAMES. Washington, U.S. Govt. Print. Off., Mar. 1964. 367 p. map. (26,000 names) (Gazetteer no. 78)

See note on series, no. 484.

TANZANIA (TANGANYIKA AND ZANZIBAR)

Note: On Apr. 27, 1964, thw two recently independent republic of Tanganyika (independence date, Dec. 9, 1961; became a republic Dec. 9, 1962) and Zanzibar (independence date, Dec. 10, 1963) merged to become a single United Republic of Tanganyika and Zanzibar, which in Oct. 1964 changed its name to United Republic of Tanzania. Since there is as yet little literature relating to Tanzania as such except in periodicals, most of the references in this section appear under the headings Tanganyika and Zanzibar below.

Atlas

2488.   Jensen, S. REGIONAL ECONOMIC ATLAS, MAINLAND TANZANIA. Dar es
             Salaam, Bureau of Resource Assessment and Land Use Planning,
             University College, 1968. 70 p.

         Eighteen maps illustrating population, employment, industrial
location, trade, tax rates, cooperatives, schools, hospitals, crop
production, etc. Each map is accompanied by a "brief analysis,
tabular material, references, and critical evaluation of the sources
used." The atlas is useful as a source to review growth and development during the colonial period.

Bibliographies

2489.   Bates, Margaret L. A STUDY GUIDE FOR TANZANIA. Boston, African
             Studies Center, Boston University, 1969. 83 p.

2489A.   Decalo, Samuel, comp. TANZANIA: AN INTRODUCTORY BIBLIOGRAPHY.
             [Kingston] University of Rhode Island, 1968. 57 l. (University
             of Rhode Island Occasional Papers in Political Science, N-4)

         Emphasis is on political developments in Tanzania (including
Zanzibar) between 1960 and 1968. Listed are books, articles, chapters from composite works, conference papers, theses, and other
unpublished papers.

2490.   Langlands, Bryan W. "Tanzania Bibliography--1965 Publications--Part
             I." TANZANIA NOTES AND RECORDS, no. 65, Mar. 1966: 113-122.

         Continued: "1965 Publications--Part II; 1966 Publications--
Part I," no. 66, Dec. 1966: 231-238; "Tanzania Bibliography--
1966, Part II," no. 67, June 1967: 79-88; "Tanzania Bibliog-
raphy--1966-1967," no. 68, Feb. 1968: 117-124.

         A continuing compilation of publications, including articles,
appearing both in Tanzania and abroad. "A Bibliography of Tanganyika, 1959-1964," by Andrew Roberts, appeared in TANZANIA NOTES AND
RECORDS, June 1967.

2490A.   Roberts, Andrew D. A BIBLIOGRAPHY OF PRIMARY SOURCES FOR TANZANIA,
             1799-1899; BOOKS ONLY. Lusaka, 1969. 46 l.

Reference Works

2491. American University, Washington, D.C. Foreign Area Studies. AREA
        HANDBOOK FOR TANZANIA. Washington, U.S. Govt. Print. Off.,
        1968. 522 p. illus. tables, maps.

        Bibliography: p. 481-498.

        Similar to others of the series, this is a comprehensive survey of
the country.

2492. Bienen, Henry. TANZANIA: PARTY TRANSFORMATION AND ECONOMIC DEVELOPMENT.
        Princeton, N.J., Princeton University Press, 1967. 446 p.

        Bibliography: p. 429-440.

        Case study of the Tanganyika African National Union relating
economic development to TANU growth and development; mainly concerned
with events prior to the 1964 union of Tanganyika and Zanzibar. Part 1
is the history of TANU before independence, and Part 2 concerns
organization, recruitment, and ideology. Part 3 discusses TANU and
economic development. The work concludes with a chapter on the significance of the Jan. 1964 army mutiny for TANU and one on the Sept. 1965
elections.

2493. Cliffe, Lionel, ed. ONE PARTY DEMOCRACY: THE 1965 TANZANIA GENERAL
        ELECTIONS. Nairobi, East African Publishing House, 1967. 470 p.
        illus., maps, diagrs. (EAPH Political Studies Series, no. 3)

        Analysis of the Sept. 1965 parliamentary elections conducted under
a new electoral system for "single-party democracy." There are chapters
on the candidates and the new legislators elected, the voter and his
perceptions and attitudes, the factors and issues which helped determine
the election results, and the impact of the elections on the nation's
political system. Seven case studies reveal the workings of the election
in Buhaya, Ugogo, Kilimanjaro, Rungwe, Arusha, Sukumaland, and Dar es
Salaam. Appendixes contain presidential and parliamentary election
results, a constituency survey, two papers on the role of symbols in the
elections, and extracts from the report of the commission on the
establishment of a democratic one-party state.

        This is the third volume in the EAPH Political Studies Series,
of which the first two volumes were POLITICIANS AND POLICIES (1967),
by Colin Leys, and the work by Tordoff described below.

2494. Tordoff, William. GOVERNMENT AND POLITICS IN TANZANIA: A COLLECTION
        OF ESSAYS COVERING THE PERIOD FROM SEPTEMBER 1960 TO JULY 1966.

Nairobi, East African Publishing House, 1967.   xviii, 257 p.
maps. (EAPH Political Studies Series, no. 2)

Bibliographical footnotes.

Primarily concerned with the problems facing the government and
the Tanganyika African National Union (TANU) following independence
in Dec. 1961, particularly after the Republic was inaugurated a year
later. Emphasis is on mainland Tanzania. The Interim Constitution
of Tanzania and the Constitution of TANU are included as documentary
appendixes. There is an analytical index. An important party publication of TANU is THE ARUSHA DECLARATION AND TANU'S POLICY ON
SOCIALISM AND SELF-RELIANCE (Dar es Salaam, 1967).

2495. U.S. Department of the Interior. Office of Geography. TANZANIA:
OFFICIAL STANDARD NAMES APPROVED BY THE UNITED STATES BOARD ON
GEOGRAPHIC NAMES. Washington, U.S. Govt. Print. Off., June
1965. 236 p. map. (16,500 names) (Gazetteer no. 92)

See note on series, no. 484.

Tanganyika

Atlas

2496. Tanganyika. Department of Lands and Mines. Survey Division. ATLAS
OF TANGANYIKA, EAST AFRICA. 4th ed. Dar es Salaam, 1969. 29
col. plates of maps, tables.

Maps (uniformly 1:3,000,000) covering physical geography, biogeography, human geography, industry and commerce, and town plans.
Appended are a statistical section and gazetteer. A transparent
population overlay is provided for use with the individual maps.

Bibliographies

2497. Hall, R. de Z. "A Bibliography of Ethnological Literature for Tanganyika Territory." TANGANYIKA NOTES AND RECORDS, no. 7, 1939:
75-83.

2498. Taylor, Barbara. CATALOGUE OF EARLY GERMAN MATERIAL RELATING TO TAN-
ZANIA IN THE LIBRARY OF THE MINERAL RESOURCES DIVISION, DODOMA.
Dodoma, Mineral Resources Division, 1968. 26 p. (Report No.
BMT/4)

Lists works published up to and including 1940 in fields of physiography, climate, hydrology, vegetation, ethnography, geology, palaeontology, and archaeology. Books, articles, maps, and periodicals are covered.

2499. Tanganyika Territory. Laws, statutes, etc. INDEX TO THE LAWS OF THE
TANGANYIKA TERRITORY IN FORCE ON THE 31ST DAY OF DECEMBER 1940, WITH
A TABLE SHOWING THE EFFECT OF AMENDING LEGISLATION, 1929-40. Compiled by G. M. Pillai. Dar es Salaam, Govt. Printer, 1941. xxv,
88 p. (3,000 entries)

An earlier edition, compiled by H. R. F. Butterfield, was published
in 1935 (xii, 94 p.), with some 3,000 entries on laws in Dec. 1933, with
references to amending legislation enacted in 1934.

2500. U.S. Library of Congress. General Reference and Bibliography Division.
OFFICIAL PUBLICATIONS OF BRITISH EAST AFRICA: Part 2, TANGANYIKA.
Compiled by Audrey A. Walker, African Section. Washington, 1962.
134 p.

List of 715 numbered entries and index of subjects and personal
names. Arrangement is by name of issuing agency. The coverage is of
former German East Africa, of Tanganyika Territory under British administration, and of British and UN documents relating to Tanganyika.

Reference Works

2501. American University, Washington, D.C. Foreign Area Studies Division.
AREA HANDBOOK FOR TANZANIA. Washington, 1968. 522 p.

Bibliography: p. 481-498.

Like others in this series, this volume offers a comprehensive country survey.

2502. Bee, David. OUR FATAL SHADOWS. London, G. Bles, 1964. 414 p.

History of Tanganyika from the German past up to the date of
independence, Dec. 9. 1961.

2503. Chidzero, Bernard T. G. TANGANYIKA AND INTERNATIONAL TRUSTEESHIP.
London, New York, Oxford University Press, 1961. 286 p. maps
(2 fold. col. in pocket).

Bibliography: p. 277-282.

History and analysis of the part played by the United Nations trusteeship in the progress of Tanganyika toward independence. This scholarly and comprehensive study had been prepared by the Rhodesian author for his doctoral thesis at McGill University in 1958 and was subsequently worked on at Nuffield College, Oxford, for two years, being published just before the Tanganyika Constitutional Conference of Mar. 1961.

2504. Clyde, D. F. HISTORY OF THE MEDICAL SERVICES OF TANGANYIKA. Dar es Salaam, Govt. Press, 1962. 223 p. illus., ports., maps.

Bibliography: p. 207-209.

Valuable history of medical services and public health problems.

See also no. 1173.

2505. Cole, J. S. R., and W. N. Denison. TANGANYIKA: THE DEVELOPMENT OF ITS LAWS AND CONSTITUTION. London, Stevens, 1964. 339 p. (The British Commonwealth: The Development of Its Laws and Constitutions, v. 12)

Describes the constitutional structure of Tanganyika and gives an account of the laws by which the state regulates its internal affairs. It is for the general reader as well as the legal expert. Part 1 gives general background information on the country; Part 2, the laws of Tanganyika. Appendixes contain the constitution and various agreements.

2506. Freeman-Grenville, G. S. P. THE MEDIEVAL HISTORY OF THE COAST OF TANGANYIKA, WITH SPECIAL REFERENCE TO RECENT ARCHAEOLOGICAL DISCOVERIES. London, New York, Oxford University Press, 1962. 238 p. illus.

Bibliography: p. 13-17; and footnote references.

_____, ed. THE EAST AFRICAN COAST: SELECT DOCUMENTS FROM THE FIRST TO THE EARLIER NINETEENTH CENTURY. Oxford, Clarendon Press, 1962. 314 p. maps (1 fold.).

The history, based largely on Arabia and other Asian sources as well as archaeological evidence, is supported by the selection of documents presented in the second book (see no. 2420 for annotation).

2507. HANDBOOK OF TANGANYIKA. Edited by J. P. Moffett. 2d ed. Dar es Salaam, Govt. Printer, 1958. xi, 703 p. illus., plates, maps.

Bibliography: p. 567-677.

Completely superseding a first edition of the HANDBOOK OF TANGANYIKA published in 1930, this work complements the 1955 TANGANYIKA: A REVIEW OF ITS RESOURCES AND THEIR DEVELOPMENTS (no. 2514) and like it was edited by the Commissioner for Social Development although it was not an official publication. The first 150 pages are devoted to an outline of history from paleolithic times to the mid-1950's. There follow detailed descriptions of the country, province by province, and chapters on peoples, government, economic and social services, natural history, sports, and miscellaneous information for visitors. The long bibliography contains about 2,000 entries, including articles in periodicals. Arrangement is by topic.

2508. International Bank for Reconstruction and Development. THE ECONOMIC DEVELOPMENT OF TANGANYIKA: REPORT. Baltimore, Md., Johns Hopkins Press, 1961. xxviii, 548 p. fold. maps, diagrs., tables.

This volume results from an Economic Survey Mission organized at the request of the Tanganyika and British governments. The field survey was carried out in the summer of 1959 and the study prepared the following winter, with additional data gathered in Tanganyika in the summer of 1960. The extended report begins with a general and budgetary examination of the Tanganyika economy and continues with analyses of specific economic aspects. Several annexes provide background information, supplementary statistical tables, and a summary of the recommendations made by the Mission. A full subject index is included.

2509. Listowel, Judith. THE MAKING OF TANGANYIKA. London, Chatto & Windus; New York, British Book Centre, 1965. xix, 451 p. plates, maps.

Bibliography: p. 441-443.

A readable political history of Tanganyika by a perceptive observer rather than a professional historian.

2510. Morris-Hale, Walter. BRITISH ADMINISTRATION IN TANGANYIKA FROM 1920 TO 1945; WITH SPECIAL REFERENCES TO THE PREPARATION OF AFRICANS FOR ADMINISTRATIVE POSITIONS. Genève, Imprimo, 1969. 352 p. (Université de Genève, Institut Universitaire de Hautes Etudes Internationales, Thèse no. 192)

Includes bibliography.

2511. Nyerere, Julius Kambarage. FREEDOM AND UNITY--UHURU NA UMOJA: A SELECTION FROM WRITINGS AND SPEECHES, 1952-65. London, Oxford University Press, 1967. xii, 366 p. plates, ports.

By the President of Tanzania and one of Africa's more able leaders and political thinkers. His views are a blend of Catholicism,

socialism, and humanism imposed on a basic foundation of his African-
ness. The book stresses unity, self-help, rural development, and independence for all Africans. See no. 2444 for further comment.

2512. Redeker, Dietrich. DIE GESCHICHTE DER TAGESPRESSE DEUTSCH-OSTAFRIKAS
            (1899-1916). Berlin, Triltsch & Huther, 1937. 135 p.

        Survey of the German daily press in Germany and German East Africa
dealing with the former German colonies.

2513. Stephens, Hugh W. THE POLITICAL TRANSFORMATION OF TANGANYIKA: 1920-67.
            New York, Praeger, 1968. xii, 225 p. maps, charts, tables.
            (Praeger Special Studies in International Politics and Public
            Affairs)

        Bibliography: p. 217-225.

        A delineation and analysis of the effects of basic social changes
upon politics in Tanganyika from the colonial era to the present.
Following an introduction, the study is divided into six parts: background of political change; the "mothball phase," 1920-40; the development phase, 1950-54; the nationalist phase, 1954-61; and the post-
colonial quest for political stability. Included are a statistical
appendix and an appendix presenting social mobilization indicators.

2514. Tanganyika. TANGANYIKA: A REVIEW OF ITS RESOURCES AND THEIR DEVELOP-
            MENT. Prepared under the direction of J. F. R. Hill; edited by
            J. P. Moffett. Dar es Salaam, Govt. Printer, 1955. xviii, 924
            p. maps, tables.

        Bibliography: p. 861-868.

        Edited by the Commissioner for Social Development of Tanganyika,
this big volume surveyed resources and requirements of the territory in
close detail. The various sections, covering widely the land, people,
political structure, social services, communications, and all phases
of production and economic life, were prepared largely by the heads of
departments concerned. There are maps and tables throughout, a select
bibliography (listing mainly documentary sources), and an extensive
index.

2515. Tanganyika. Department of Commerce and Industry. COMMERCE AND INDUSTRY
            IN TANGANYIKA. Dar es Salaam, 1961. 106 p. illus.

        Well-illustrated pamphlet prepared to coincide with independence
and addressed to prospective investors and others interested in the
economic future of the new nation.

2516.   TANZANIA NOTES AND RECORDS (formerly TANGANYIKA NOTES AND RECORDS).   no.
        1- Mar. 1936- Dar es Salaam. illus., ports., maps, diagrs.

        The journal of the Tanzania (earlier Tanganyika) Society, published
semiannually except for a period in the 1950's. It is an organ for
scholarly research in all disciplines relating to Tanzania. Issues
carry a number of reviews of pertinent books. Since 1965 an annual
bibliography on Tanzania has appeared.

2517.   TANZANIA ZAMANI, A BULLETIN OF RESEARCH ON PRE-COLONIAL HISTORY. no. 1-
        July 1967- Dar es Salaam, History Department, University College.

        Information on research in progress in fields of oral history,
archaeology, anthropology; includes some post-1870 historical research.
The bulletin also carries news, notes, and a bibliography of books and
articles.

2518.   Taylor, J. Clagett. THE POLITICAL DEVELOPMENT OF TANGANYIKA.   Stanford,
        Calif., Stanford University Press, 1963. 254 p. map.

        Bibliography: p. 243-248.

        Readable political history of period before and under the British
mandate and trusteeship and the achievement of independence.

                                Zanzibar

Bibliographies

2519.   Crossey, John M. D., and John A. Braswell. [Comprehensive Bibliography
        of Zanzibar, Pemba, and Adjacent Islands]. New Haven, Yale
        University Library.

        Classified bibliography now in course of compilation, to include
books, articles, maps, manuscript collections. (Information from note
in AFRICAN STUDIES BULLETIN, v. 8, no. 1, Apr. 1965: 90.)

2520.   U. S. Library of Congress. General Reference and Bibliography Division.
        OFFICIAL PUBLICATIONS OF BRITISH EAST AFRICA: Part 3, KENYA AND
        ZANZIBAR. Compiled by Audrey A. Walker, African Section. Washington,
        1963. 162 p.

        The 254 official publications of Zanzibar and of Great Britain
relating to Zanzibar here catalogued (p. 121-149) are put in a two-part
bibliography together with Kenya because, as stated in the introduction,

"of the administrative tie held between Kenya and Zanzibar during the early years of British control and because of their mutual interest in the mainland strip." The bibliography was published just prior to the announcement of the union of independent Zanzibar with Tanganyika.

2521. Zanzibar Protectorate. Laws, statutes, etc. CHRONOLOGICAL INDEX OF ENACTMENTS ISSUED 1863-1911, AND TEXT OF ENACTMENTS IN FORCE DECEMBER 31, 1911. Compiled by John H. Sinclair. [n.p.] 1912. 307 p.

2522. Zanzibar Protectorate. Laws, statutes, etc. INDEX TO THE LAWS OF THE ZANZIBAR PROTECTORATE IN FORCE ON THE 1ST DAY OF MARCH 1955. Compiled by F. J. Jasavala. Zanzibar, 1955. 47 p.

2523. Zanzibar Protectorate. Laws, statutes, etc. LIST OF ZANZIBAR DECREES ENACTED UP TO...1940. Zanzibar, 1941. 8 p. (250 entries)

Reference Works

2524. Gray, Sir John Milner. HISTORY OF ZANZIBAR, FROM THE MIDDLE AGES TO 1856. London, Oxford University Press, 1962. 314 p. illus.

"Authorities" (chapter notes): p. 281-299; bibliography: p. 300-309.

The writer, late master of Jesus College, is a barrister who closed his long career in the Colonial Service as Chief Justice of Zanzibar from 1943 to 1952. He is also a historian and in East Africa has specialized in studies making heavy use of Portuguese sources. This interesting narrative history gives a full account of Zanzibar and Pemba from the earliest archaeological evidences through the death of Seyyid Said. See also Coupland, no. 2409, which has much information on Zanzibar.

2525. Ingrams, William Harold. ZANZIBAR: ITS HISTORY AND PEOPLE. London, Witherby, 1931. 527 p.

Bibliography: p. 515-519.

The most complete, authoritative history of Zanzibar, by a British expert on the Arab world, who had been an official at Zanzibar from 1919 to 1927. The book begins with geography and people, covers the history from early times, and devotes its major part to ethnology, surveying the Arabs, the detribalized and mixed-blood Swahilis, and various African people, in a well-rounded anthropological study.

2526. Lofchie, Michael F. ZANZIBAR: BACKGROUND TO REVOLUTION. Princeton,
       N.J., Princeton University Press, 1965. 316 p. maps, tables.

       Bibliography: p. 288-301.

       The author's aim in this political study is to provide some explana-
       tion of why Zanzibar's multiparty parliamentary system collapsed in a
       violent revolutionary change. Mr. Lofchie had done field research in
       Zanzibar in 1962-63 and bases his information in part on his many con-
       tacts with the Zanzibari, particularly with political leaders. He goes
       back to the establishment of the Arab state and British colonial policy
       in his beginning sketch of historical and social background and then
       examines the origins of the conflict between Arab and African in party
       politics. He is lavish in his inclusion of tables--population, land-
       ownership, election results, and many other features reducible to statis-
       tics. An appendix reproduces "The Articles of Union between the Republic
       of Tanganyika and the Peoples' Republic of Zanzibar."

2527. Middleton, John, and Jane Campbell. ZANZIBAR: ITS SOCIETY AND ITS
       POLITICS. Issued under the auspices of the Institution of Race
       Relations, London. London, Oxford University Press, 1965. 71 p.

       Describes historical and social conditions in Zanzibar before
       independence and relates these to recent events on the island.

2528. Prins, Adriaan H. J. THE SWAHILI-SPEAKING PEOPLES OF ZANZIBAR AND THE
       EAST AFRICAN COAST (ARABS, SHIRAZI AND SWAHILI). London, Inter-
       national African Institute, 1961. 143 p. illus. (Ethnographic
       Survey of Africa, East Central Africa, pt. 12)

       Combined bibliography: p. 116-138.

       See general note on this series (no. 980). In the exceptionally
       comprehensive bibliography, the author notes many historical and
       descriptive works and official documents in addition to ethnographical
       studies.

2529. Shelswell-White, Geoffrey H. A GUIDE TO ZANZIBAR: A DETAILED ACCOUNT
       OF ZANZIBAR TOWN AND ISLAND, INCLUDING GENERAL DESCRIPTION OF
       ITINERARIES FOR THE USE OF VISITORS. 4th rev. ed. Zanzibar,
       Govt. Printer, 1952. 146 p. illus., maps (part fold.).

       A handbook for tourists that was originally prepared by an adminis-
       trative officer and "private secretary of His Highness the Sultan" in
       1932, with additions by other hands. It contains general articles and
       practical information on miscellaneous topics, a baedeker of tours, and
       appendixes on such special features of Zanzibar as fishing, bullfighting,
       the carved Arab doorways, and Arab chests.

2530.   U.S. Department of the Interior. Office of Geography. ZANZIBAR:
        OFFICIAL STANDARD NAMES APPROVED BY THE UNITED STATES BOARD ON
        GEOGRAPHIC NAMES. Washington, U.S. Govt. Print. Off., Jan.
        1964. 36 p. map. (2,400 names) (Gazetteer no. 76)

        See note on series, no. 484.

                                UGANDA

Atlas

2531.   Uganda. Department of Lands and Surveys. ATLAS OF UGANDA. 1st ed.
        Entebbe, 1962. 83 p. illus., col. maps. 48 cm.

Bibliographies

2532.   Hopkins, Terence K. A STUDY GUIDE FOR UGANDA. Boston, African
        Studies Center, Boston University, 1969. 162 p.

2532A. Langlands, Bryan W. "Uganda Bibliography, 1961-1962." UGANDA JOUR-
        NAL, v. 27, no. 2, Sept. 1963: 245-260.

        Continued: "1962-1963," v. 28, no. 1, Mar. 1964: 115-124;
        "1963-1964," v. 28, no. 2, Sept. 1964: 233-242; "1964," v. 29,
        pt. 1, 1965: 115-132; "1965," v. 30, pt. 1, 1966: 119-136;
        "1965-1966," v. 30, pt. 2, 1966: 241-257; "1966," v. 31, pt. 1,
        1967: 139-154; "1967," v. 32, pt. 1, 1968: 101-117.

        This journal of the Uganda Society regularly carried a number of
        book reviews, and its scholarly articles are frequently followed by
        long subject reading lists. Langlands' record of current publishing
        on Uganda has been appearing as a regular feature of the journal.

2533.   Manyangenda, Salome. A SELECTED AND ANNOTATED BIBLIOGRAPHY OF SOCIAL
        SCIENCE MATERIALS IN ENGLISH ON UGANDA FROM 1860 TO THE PRESENT.
        Washington, D.C., 1966. 82 p.

        In this master's thesis (Catholic University of America), en-
        tries are arranged by subject (anthropology, economics, geography,
        history, language, politics, sociology). There are author and title
        indexes.

2534.   Syracuse University. Maxwell Graduate School of Citizenship and
        Public Affairs. Program of Eastern African Studies. A

BIBLIOGRAPHY ON ANTHROPOLOGY AND SOCIOLOGY IN UGANDA. Compiled by Robert Peckham, Isis Ragheb, and others. Syracuse, N.Y., 1965. 60 l. (Occasional Bibliography, no. 3)

Lists books, articles, conference papers, government documents, and a few dissertations alphabetically by author. Works are in German, English, Italian, and vernacular languages, from the late nineteenth century to 1965.

2535. Syracuse University. Maxwell Graduate School of Citizenship and Public Affairs. Program of Eastern African Studies. A BIBLIOGRAPHY ON POLITICS AND GOVERNMENT IN UGANDA. Compiled by Lucas Kuria and others. Syracuse, N.Y., 1965. 31 l. (Occasional Bibliography, no. 2)

2536. Uganda. Ministry of Lands and Mineral Development. BIBLIOGRAPHY OF LAND TENURE. Entebbe, 1957. 57 p.

Many of the references cited are official documents which are covered in the Library of Congress bibliography, below.

2537. Uganda Protectorate. Laws, statutes, etc. CHRONOLOGICAL TABLE AND INDEX TO THE LAWS OF THE UGANDA PROTECTORATE. New ed. Entebbe, 1909. xi, 61 p. (3,000 entries)

2538. Uganda Protectorate. Laws, statutes, etc. INDEX TO THE LAWS OF THE UGANDA PROTECTORATE IN FORCE ON THE 1ST DAY OF MAY 1947; WITH A TABLE OF REFERENCES TO AMENDING LEGISLATION ENACTED FROM 1936 TO 1946. Compiled by L. Mendonça. Entebbe, Govt. Printer, 1947. 92 p.

2539. U.S. Library of Congress. General Reference and Bibliography Division. OFFICIAL PUBLICATIONS OF BRITISH EAST AFRICA: Part 4, UGANDA. Compiled by Audrey A. Walker, African Section. Washington, 1963. 100 p.

Bibliography of documents of the Uganda government and of British governmental agencies concerned with Uganda, totaling 764 numbered items, with index of subjects and personal names. As in others of this series, arrangement is alphabetical by agency, with separate sections for publications of Uganda, the East African Common Services Organization, and Great Britain.

Reference Works

2540. Brown, Douglas. AN INTRODUCTION TO THE LAW OF UGANDA. London, Sweet & Maxwell; Lagos, African Universities Press, 1968. 136 p.

2541.   Clark, Ralph, in association with Tom Soper and Peter Williams. AID IN
        UGANDA--PROGRAMMES AND POLICIES. London, Overseas Development
        Institute (ODI), 1966. 101 p. tables.

        This slim volume is Part I of a three-part OWI study concerned
with the impact of aid in Uganda and the problems of aid as seen by the
recipient country. Development planning in the colonial era, the first
Uganda five-year plan, and aid vis-à-vis the influence of political
factors are first given consideration; the author then focuses on
British aid, American aid, and problems of technical assistance. He
concludes with specific proposals regarding future aid. An analytical
index is included.

        Part II of this series is Peter Williams' AID IN UGANDA--EDUCATION
(1966, 152 p., tables), and Part III Hal Mettrick's AID IN UGANDA--
AGRICULTURE (1967, 135 p., fold. map, tables). Both outline progress to
date, problems remaining, and the pros and cons of aid programs.

2542.   Diplomatic Press. UGANDA TRADE DIRECTORY, 1966-67, INCLUDING CLASSIFIED
        TRADE INDEX. London, Diplomatic Press and Publishing Co., 1967.
        72 p. illus.

        The first edition of a directory providing basic information on
Uganda's economy. Main sections cover the economy and government
policies in 1966, exports and imports, tourism, and foreign relations.
Advertising is included.

2543.   Fallers, Lloyd A. BANTU BUREAUCRACY: A STUDY OF INTEGRATION AND CONFLICT
        IN THE POLITICAL INSTITUTIONS OF AN EAST AFRICAN PEOPLE. Cambridge,
        Eng., Published for the East African Institute of Social Research
        by W. Heffer, 1956. xiv, 283 p. illus., maps, diagrs., tables.

        1965. With new subtitle, A CENTURY OF POLITICAL EVOLUTION AMONG THE
        BASOGA OF UGANDA, and "Preface to the 1965 Edition." Chicago and
        London, University of Chicago Press. xix, 283 p.

        Bibliographical footnotes.

        _____,ed. THE KING'S MEN: LEADERSHIP AND STATUS IN BUGANDA ON THE
        EVE OF INDEPENDENCE. London, New York, Published on behalf of
        the East African Institute of Social Research by Oxford University
        Press, 1964. 414 p. illus., ports., fold. map.

        Bibliography: p. 401-409.

        Professor Fallers, an American social anthropologist, had been
director of the East African Institute of Social Research for some years
after 1956. His BANTU BUREAUCRACY is a highly professional analysis of
the Soga people of Uganda. THE KING'S MEN contains essays by Professor
Fallers, Dr. Audrey I. Richards, C. C. Wrigley, Martin Southwold,

Leonard W. Doob, and others, on traditional social structures and changing patterns in Buganda. It is one of a series of studies of political and economic leadership in East Africa resulting from field research carried out under the auspices of the East African Institute of Social Research.

2544. Haydon, Edwin S. LAW AND JUSTICE IN BUGANDA. London, Butterworth, 1960. 342 p. illus. (Butterworth's African Law Series, no. 2)

See note on series, no. 684.

2545. Ingham, Kenneth. THE MAKING OF MODERN UGANDA. London, G. Allen and Unwin, 1958. 303 p. illus.

Bibliogaphy: p. 285-294.

Straightforward history of Uganda from the first European penetration in the 1860's to the present. The author has been a history professor at Makerere.

2546. Ingrams, William Harold. UGANDA: A CRISIS OF NATIONHOOD. London, H.M. Stationery Off., 1960. 365 p. illus. (Corona Library)

Bibliography: p. 347-353.

One of a series prepared under Colonial Office auspices as authoritative popular presentations of specific countries. In addition to published and unpublished works, the author made use of oral source material gathered during long visits to the country.

2547. International Bank for Reconstruction and Development. THE ECONOMIC DEVELOPMENT OF UGANDA. Baltimore, Md., Johns Hopkins Press, 1962. xviii, 475 p. maps, charts, tables.

Report of an Economic Survey Mission, requested by the Uganda and British governments and organized by the World Bank, which surveyed and analyzed the economy of Uganda, making recommendations for a five-year development program, 1961/62-1965/66, with particular attention to priorities for expenditure. The nine-man team was headed by Professor Edward S. Mason of Harvard University and included expert advisers from five nations on economics, health, industry, transport, agriculture, and education. Except for a 10-page introduction, the entire focus is on present economic conditions, priorities, and approaches for development. There are statistical annexes and a few footnotes indicating sources of statistics.

2548. Johnston, Sir Harry H. THE UGANDA PROTECTORATE: AN ATTEMPT TO
GIVE SOME DESCRIPTION OF THE PHYSICAL GEOGRAPHY, BOTANY,
ZOOLOGY, ANTHROPOLOGY, LANGUAGES, AND HISTORY OF THE TERRI-
TORIES UNDER BRITISH PROTECTION IN EAST CENTRAL AFRICA,
BETWEEN THE CONGO FREE STATE AND THE RIFT VALLEY AND BETWEEN
THE FIRST DEGREE OF SOUTH LATITUDE AND THE FIFTH DEGREE OF
NORTH LATITUDE. 2d ed., with prefatory chapter giving addi-
tional matter. With 510 illustrations from drawings and
photographs by the author and others, 48 full-page colored
plates by the author, and 9 maps by J. G. Bartholomew and
the author. New York, Dodd, Mead, 1904. 2 v. 1018 p. col.
front., illus., col. plates, ports., fold. maps.

Old standard work on Uganda by the explorer, naturalist, and
empire-building administrator who served as Special Commissioner to
the Uganda Protectorate from 1899 to 1902. Sir Harry Johnston nego-
tiated the agreement of 1900 with Buganda which provided for the
kingdom's administrative autonomy.

The appendix to chap. xiii, "Anthropology," and that to chap.
xiv, "Pygmies and Forest Negroes," are by Dr. F. C. Shrubsall.

2549. Morris, H. F., and James S. Read. UGANDA: THE DEVELOPMENT OF ITS
LAWS AND CONSTITUTION. London, Stevens, 1966. 448 p. map.
(British Commonwealth: The Development of Its Laws and
Constitutions, 13)

Bibliography: p. 412-416.

Part 1 traces the development of the constitution from the
tribal organizations of the second half of the nineteenth century
through the colonial period to the year of independence, 1962.
Part 2 deals with the constitution and its "quasi-federal" structure,
and includes a section on the prospect of an East African federation
in the light of the functions of the East African Common Services
Organization. In Part 3 the most important branches of law in
Uganda are analyzed. A table of legislation and one of cases are
included.

2550. Scott, Roger. THE DEVELOPMENT OF TRADE UNIONS IN UGANDA. Nairobi,
East African Publishing House, 1966. 200 p. fold. map.

Bibliography: p. 182-187.

The early development of trade unions, effect of colonial
labor policy on unions, international influences, and the role of
unions in independent Uganda are among the subjects treated.
Included also are case studies of individual unions such as the

Railway African Union, National Union of Plantation Workers, and Uganda Public Employees Union. In appendixes are a reprint of the Uganda Industrial Relations Charter and biographical notes on union-connected individuals.

2551. Snowden, J. D. THE GRASS COMMUNITIES AND MOUNTAIN VEGETATION OF UGANDA. London, Crown Agents for Government of Uganda, 1953. 94 p. map.

Important source on the vegetation of Uganda, with a provisional vegetation map and a list of relevant references.

2552. Taylor, John Vernon. THE GROWTH OF THE CHURCH IN BUGANDA: AN ATTEMPT AT UNDERSTANDING. London, SCM Press, 1958. Distributed by Friendship Press, New York. 288 p. illus. (World Mission Studies)

Includes bibliographical references.

2553. Thomas, Harold B., and Robert Scott. UGANDA. London, Oxford University Press, H. Milford, 1935. xx, 559 p. plates, ports., fold. maps.

Reprint, without change, 1949.

Bibliography: p. 480-502.

Comprehensive reference work on Uganda by two administrative officers, published by authority of the Government of the Protectorate. This historical chapter which opens the handbook is prefaced by a chronology of 50 guiding dates, from Speke's discovery of Lake Victoria to the first regular airmail from London in 1931. There follow well-written expositions of all aspects of the country, including its life, administration, and economy. A short final chapter on nineteenth-century writing about Uganda precedes a select list of references and statistical appendixes.

2554. Tothill, John D., ed. AGRICULTURE IN UGANDA. By the Staff of the Department of Agriculture of Uganda. London, Oxford University Press, 1940. xvi, 551 p.

Officially sponsored specialist work beginning with an account of Uganda agriculture in general aspects and then covering climate, native agriculture and land tenure, crop rotation, plowing, soils and soil erosion problems, fertilizers, experiment stations, native food crops, and (in a long analysis) the export crops--cotton, coffee, sugar, etc.

2555. Trowell, Margaret, and K. P. Wachsmann. TRIBAL CRAFTS OF UGANDA. London, New York, Oxford University Press, 1953. xxi, 422 p. illus.

Bibliography: p. 279-280.

Ethnological survey of the material culture of the tribes of Uganda, including drawings and an appendix with tabulation of objects described. The book is based on studies undertaken at the Uganda Museum, of which Mrs. Trowell was curator from 1941 to 1946, and during her work as head of the School of Art of Makerere College. She contributed two-thirds of the text, covering domestic and cultural arts and crafts. Her collaborator, Dr. Wachsmann, curator of the Uganda Museum at the time of writing, wrote the section on sound instruments. The volume ends with a section of plates--drawings of the instruments and photographs of the musicians in action. There are separate indexes for the two parts. The short bibliography lists about a hundred references to books, pamphlets, and periodical articles.

2556. Uganda. National Parks Trustees. UGANDA NATIONAL PARKS: HANDBOOK. 3d ed. Kampala, 1962. 120 p.

2557. UGANDA JOURNAL. v. 1- 1934- Kampala, Uganda Society. Semiannual.

A distinguished review, published for some years by Oxford University Press but now issued in Kampala. Contributors are scholars, many of whom had worked in the British administration of Uganda or had been connnected with Makerere University College.

2558. U.S. Department of Health, Education, and Welfare. EDUCATION IN UGANDA. By David G. Scanlon. Washington, U.S. Govt. Print. Off., 1965. 115 p. (U.S. Office of Education, Bulletin 1964, no. 32; OE-14103)

Various levels and types of education in Uganda are described, with emphasis on curriculum and course content. Documents published or issued by the Uganda government or schools from 1953 through 1962 are heavily relied on. There are sections on the examination system, teachers and teacher education, technical and agricultural education, and community development. The appendix includes a summary of the 1963 recommendations of the Uganda Education Commission.

2559. U.S. Department of the Interior. Office of Geography. UGANDA: OFFICIAL STANDARD NAMES APPROVED BY THE UNITED STATES BOARD ON

GEOGRAPHIC NAMES. Washington, U.S. Govt. Print. Off., 1964.
167 p. map. (11,900 names) (Gazetteer no. 82)

See note on series, no. 484.

MAURITIUS

Bibliographies

2560. Hahn, Lorna, with Robert Edison. MAURITIUS: A STUDY AND ANNOTATED
        BIBLIOGRAPHY. Washington, D.C., The American University, Cen-
        ter for Research in Social Systems, 1969. 44 p.

        A brief up-to-date study of the sociological, economic, and
political conditions of Mauritius, to provide basic understanding of
the country as it approached independence on March 12, 1968. It
consists of an essay and a comprehensive annotated bibliography of
books, periodicals, government documents, and other publications.

2561. Lalouette, Gérard. THE MAURITIUS DIGEST: BEING A DIGEST OF THE
        REPORTED DECISIONS OF THE SUPREME COURT OF MAURITIUS TO THE END
        OF 1950. Port Louis, Mauritius Printing Co. [195-].

        Supplement, 1951-1955. Port Louis, 1957. xi, 191 p.

2562. Mauritius. Archives Department. MEMORANDUM OF BOOKS PRINTED IN
        MAURITIUS AND REGISTERED IN THE ARCHIVES OFFICE. Port Louis.
        Quarterly.

        _____. _____. REPORT. 1950- Port Louis, Govt. Printer. Annual.

        The second reference was previously issued as REPORT of the
Archives Branch. It lists not only Mauritius publications but also
works on Mauritius published abroad. The 1967 REPORT had a 23-page
supplement of books on Mauritius.

2563. Toussaint, Auguste. BIBLIOGRAPHIE DE MAURICE, 1502-1954. Port Louis,
        Esclapon, 1956. 884 p.

        _____. SELECT BIBLIOGRAPHY OF MAURITIUS. Port Louis, Printed by
        Henry, 1951. 60 p. (Société de l'Histoire de l'Ile Maurice
        Publication)

        The French history of Mauritius, the former Ile de France, goes back to 1715. Bernardin de Saint-Pierre's VOYAGE A L'ILE DE FRANCE (1773, 2 v.) and, still more, his famous Rousseauian novel, PAUL ET VIRGINIE (1789), established the island's reputation as an earthly paradise. A large body of literature, mostly in French, has been recorded exhaustively by the Chief Archivist of Mauritius, M. Toussaint. His huge bibliography of 1956 (8,865 items) covers printed works, manuscripts, archivalia, and cartographic materials. Supplements appear in the annual REPORT of the Archives Department which is presented by M. Toussaint. He collaborated earlier with Patrick J. Barnwell in A SHORT HISTORY OF MAURITIUS (London, New York, Published for the Government of Mauritius by Longmans, Green, 1949, 268 p., illus.).

Reference Works

2564. Benedict, Burton. INDIANS IN THE PLURAL SOCIETY: A REPORT ON MAURITIUS. London, H.M. Stationery Off., 1961. 168 p. plates. (Colonial Research Studies, no. 34)

Socioanthropological study of the Muslim and Hindu groups who came to Mauritius from 1835 to 1907 and who now form two-thirds of the population.

2565. d'Unienville, J. R. M. LAST YEARS OF THE ISLE OF FRANCE (1800-1814) THROUGH TEXTS. Port Louis, Printed by Claude M. d'Unienville, Mauritius Printing Co., 1959. 244 p. illus.

History assembled from primary texts and documents which the author, a Mauritian who studied law in London, consulted in the British Public Record Office and elsewhere. The extracts are given indifferently in French or English, bearing witness to the bilingual character of the island in spite of a century and a half of British domination.

A more general history, covering a longer period, is in French: Pierre de Sornay's ILE DE FRANCE, ILE MAURICE: SA GEOGRAPHIE, SON HISTOIRE, SON AGRICULTURE, SES INDUSTRIES, SES INSTITUTIONS (Port Louis, General Printing and Stationery Co., 1950, 550 p., illus., maps; bibliography: p. 547-550).

2566. Great Britain. Colonial Office. ANNUAL REPORT ON MAURITIUS. 1946- London, H.M. Stationery Off. illus., maps. (Colonial Annual Reports)

One of the very few Colonial Office annual reports still being published in the 1960's. The 1965 edition was published in 1967 (176 p., illus., maps, tables; reading list, classed: p. 166-176).

See general note on this series, no. 1233.

2567. Mauritius. Chamber of Agriculture. THE MAURITIUS CHAMBER OF AGRI-
        CULTURE, 1853-1953. Port Louis, General Printing and Station-
        ery Co., 1953. 377 p. illus., tables.

        Includes bibliography.

2568. Mauritius. Chamber of Commerce and Industry. MAURITIUS GUIDE,
        1968-1969. Port Louis, 1968. 87 p.

        Useful survey of past and present in Mauritius.

2569. Mauritius. Ministry of Industry, Commerce and External Communica-
        tions. COMMERCE AND INDUSTRY IN MAURITIUS. Port Louis, 1964.
        98 p.

        Contains information on various aspects of the national economy
        and trade, including chapters on labor, factory, and commercial
        legislation and on incentives to investment.

2570. Mauritius Sugar Industry Research Institute, Réduit. REPORT.
        1953- Réduit. Annual.

        The primary place of the sugar industry in Mauritius is evidenced
        in the handsomely presented centenary volume of the Chamber of Agri-
        culture, with text in English and French, and in the annual report
        of the research institute. The difficulties attending the industry
        were discussed in a long article by H. C. Brookfield, "Problems of
        Monoculture and Diversification in a Sugar Island--Mauritius"
        (ECONOMIC GEOGRAPHY, v. 35, Jan. 1959: 25-40).

2571. Meade, James E., ed. THE ECONOMIC AND SOCIAL STRUCTURE OF MAURITIUS:
        A REPORT TO THE GOVERNOR OF MAURITIUS. London, Methuen, 1961.
        xviii, 264 p. maps, diagrs., tables. (Mauritius, Legislative
        Council, Sessional Papers, no. 7, 1961)

        By several writers, these papers uniformly warn of critical
        conditions in the economy due to the rate of population increase.
        Included are studies on education and governmental structure. A short
        summary stresses that the only answer to the problems of Mauritius
        is birth control.

2572. Scott, Sir Robert. LIMURIA: THE LESSER DEPENDENCIES OF MAURITIUS.

London, New York, Oxford University Press, 1961. 308 p.
illus.

"Bibliographical note and selected bibliography": p. 295-300.

The author was Governor of Mauritius from 1954 to 1959. He
presents here a full account of the islands in the Indian Ocean to
the north and northeast of Mauritius, from 245 to almost 1,200 miles
away, which are known as the Lesser Dependencies: St. Brandon (a
fishing-fleet island, where women are not allowed), Agalega, and the
Chagos Archipelago. The total land area of these islands and islets,
both inhabited and uninhabited, is given as some 47 square miles.
The islanders are mostly descendants of slaves brought from the East
African coast or the larger islands. The book, one of the few full-
length works on the region, is in two parts. The first covers
geography and history; the second, island-by-island description.

2573. Société de l'Histoire de l'Ile Maurice. DICTIONNAIRE DE BIOGRAPHIE
        MAURICIENNE. DICTIONARY OF MAURITIUS BIOGRAPHY. Port Louis,
        1941-52. 2 v.

2574. Titmuss, Richard Morris, Brian Abel-Smith, and Tony Lynes. SOCIAL
        POLICIES AND POPULATION GROWTH IN MAURITIUS: A REPORT TO THE
        GOVERNOR OF MAURITIUS. London, Methuen, 1961. xviii, 308 p.
        diagrs., tables.

        The authors are British population experts. They warn that
under present policies the island faces disaster from overpopulation
and that the government must back a campaign for family planning,
as well as economic programs for higher employment. See also report
by Meade (no. 2571, above).

SEYCHELLES

Bibliography

2575. U.S. Library of Congress. General Reference and Bibliography Divi-
        sion. MADAGASCAR AND ADJACENT ISLANDS.... Compiled by
        Julian W. Witherell, African Section. Washington, U.S. Govt.
        Print. Off., 1965. xiii, 58 p.

        For annotation see no. 2038.

Reference Works

2576. Benedict, Burton. PEOPLE OF THE SEYCHELLES. London, H.M. Stationery Off., 74 p. fold. map, tables. (Ministry of Overseas
Development, Overseas Research Publication no. 14)

Covers history, occupations, marriage and family relations,
social status, religion, the domestic economy, and development
problems.

2577. Bulpin, Thomas V. ISLANDS IN A FORGOTTEN SEA. Cape Town, Howard
Timmins, 1959. 435 p.

Popular account of Mauritius, Madagascar, the Seychelles, and
other Indian Ocean islands. See also William Travis, BEYOND THE
REEFS (London, George Allen & Unwin, 1959, 221 p.).

2578. Great Britain. Colonial Office. REPORT ON SEYCHELLES. 1946-
London, H.M. Stationery Off.

2579. Hawtrey, S. H. C. HANDBOOK OF SEYCHELLES; COMPILED FROM OFFICIAL
AND OTHER RELIABLE SOURCES. Mahé, 1928. 55 p.

2580. Tyack, Maurice. MAURITIUS AND ITS DEPENDENCIES, THE SEYCHELLES,
TREASURES OF INDIAN OCEAN. Lausanne, L. A. M. Tyack, Frana
Inter Presse, 1965. 191 p. illus., maps, ports.

Includes bibliographies.

CHAPTER 40

NORTHEAST AFRICA

Note: This area, comprising Ethiopia, Somalia, French Somaliland, and the Southern Sudan, is sometimes omitted from studies of Africa south of the Sahara on the grounds that it belongs instead to the Middle Eastern region. It is, in fact, included in both categories, as some of the references in this section indicate.

See also earlier section on French Territory of the Afars and the Issas. A separate section of this Guide lists works on the area by Italian experts dealing primarily with the period of Italian colonialism (see nos. 3062-3126).

Bibliographies

2581. Haile Sellassie I University. REGISTER OF CURRENT RESEARCH ON ETHIOPIA AND THE HORN OF AFRICA. Addis Ababa, 1963- Annual.

    The first 44-page issue of this list, edited by S. Chojnacki, Richard Pankhurst, and William A. Slack, contained classified entries for 341 research projects on various aspects of Ethiopia and Ethiopian culture being carried out in that country and abroad. The record "is concerned essentially with research in progress rather than with completed and published research."

2582. International African Institute. NORTH-EAST AFRICA: GENERAL, ETHNOGRAPHY, SOCIOLOGY, LINGUISTICS. Compiled by Ruth Jones, librarian, with the assistance of a panel of consultants. London, 1959. 51 l. (Africa Bibliography Series, Ethnography, Sociology, Linguistics, and Related Subjects)

    See note on series, no. 970. Included are ethnic groups of Ethiopia, Somalia, and the Sudan.

2583. MIDDLE EAST JOURNAL. v. 1- Jan. 1947- Washington, Middle
       East Institute. maps. Quarterly.

       In the quarterly chronology, the book review section, and the
       "Bibliography of Periodical Literature" (also issued as a separate),
       material is covered relating to the Arab world, including Ethi-
       opia, the Sudan, and Somalia.

2584. U.S. Library of Congress. General Reference and Bibliography
       Division. NORTH AND NORTHEAST AFRICA: A SELECTED, ANNOTATED
       LIST OF WRITINGS, 1951-1957. Compiled by Helen F. Conover.
       Washington, 1957. 182 p.

       The first annotated list on Africa prepared in the Library of
       Congress was the INTRODUCTION TO AFRICA, compiled in 1951 and cover-
       ing the whole continent. When revised in 1956, the extent of new
       writing necessitated division into two parts, and NORTH AND NORTH-
       EAST AFRICA was interpreted to include Ethiopia and Eritrea, Somalia,
       and the Sudan, as well as the Mediterranean littoral. The sections
       on these countries occupy pages 124-173, with some 87 references,
       many of them annotated at considerable length.

Reference Works

2585. Hurst, Harold E. THE NILE: A GENERAL ACCOUNT OF THE RIVER AND
       THE UTILIZATION OF ITS WATERS. London, Constable, 1952.
       326 p. illus.

       Rev. ed. London, Constable, 1957. xv, 331 p. illus.

       This book, by a leading scientist concerned with control of
       the Nile, is a basic work for layman and specialists alike. Dr.
       Hurst's account of the river, its history, and irrigation systems
       follows the Nile from Egypt through its entire course--the main
       Nile in the northern Sudan, the Blue Nile in the central Sudan
       and Ethiopia, the White Nile in central and southern Sudan, and
       its sources in the great lakes--Lakes Albert, Edward, and Victoria.
       Climate, health, and vegetation, history of the peoples of the
       Nile Basin and their origin, and exploration in modern times are
       given attention before the author turns to more specific hydrology,
       outlining the major Nile projects undertaken and proposed.

       For technical studies of the Nile, essential sources are the
       PAPERS of the Egyptian Physical Department published by the Min-
       istry of Public Works (1920-). These include the important series
       titled THE NILE BASIN, by Dr. Hurst and others (Cairo, Govt. Press,
       1931-), which contain all the measurements of the discharge of the
       river and its tributaries, its levels, and the rainfall in its basin.

More popular works on the Nile and its exploration are the two recent books by Alan Moorehead, THE WHITE NILE and THE BLUE NILE (New York, Harper & Row, 1960, 1962, 385, 308 p., illus., maps).

2586. Società Geográfica Italiana. L'AFRICA ORIENTALE. Edited by C. Zoli. Bologna, Zanichelli, 1935. 407 p. fold. maps (1 in pocket).

A full and reliable account of the geography and geology of the Horn of Africa and Ethiopia.

2587. Tucker, A. N., and M. A. Bryan. LINGUISTIC SURVEY OF THE NORTHERN BANTU BORDERLAND: Vol. IV, LANGUAGES OF THE EASTERN SECTION, GREAT LAKES TO INDIAN OCEAN. London, International African Institute, 1957. 89 p. fold. map (in pocket).

Besides the partly Bantu languages of Kenya, Uganda, and the Sudan, this volume includes Nilotic, Nilo-Hamitic, and Cushitic languages of Northeast Africa, among them Galla and Somali.

Vol. I, Part 2, of this linguistic survey, OUBANGUI TO NILE, by G. van Bulck and Peter Hackett, includes tribes of the southern Sudan.

2588. Tucker, A. N., and M. A. Bryan. THE NON-BANTU LANGUAGES OF NORTH-EASTERN AFRICA. With a supplement on the non-Bantu languages of Southern Africa, by E. O. J. Westphal. London, Published for the International African Institute by Oxford University Press, 1956. 228 p. (Handbook of African Languages)

See note on series, no. 1011.

Includes Nilo-Hamitic and Cushitic languages of Somalia, Ethiopia, and the Sudan. Another volume in part 3 of the Handbook by the same authors is LINGUISTIC ANALYSES: THE NON-BANTU LANGUAGES OF NORTH-EASTERN AFRICA, with a supplement on the Ethiopic languages by Wolf Leslau (London, New York, Published for the International African Institute by the Oxford University Press, 1966, 627 p., plate, tables, diagrs.; Handbook of African Languages, pt. 3). It deals mainly with morphemes and with grammatical and syntactic behavior; the sections in the main follow those of THE NON-BANTU LANGUAGES (1956) above.

2589. Usoni, Luigi. RISORSE MINERARIE DELL'AFRICA ORIENTALE: ERITREA, ETIOPIA, SOMALIA. Roma, Jandi Sapi, 1952. 553 p. illus. (part col.), maps.

Bibliography: p. 521-532.

Comprehensive and heavily statistical study, arranged by
types of minerals--metals, nonmetallic substances (including oil),
materials for construction and cement, mineral waters and hot
mineral springs. Many references and authorities, mainly Italian,
are cited. Good plates and a full index are included.

ETHIOPIA

Bibliographies

2590. African Bibliographic Center, Washington, D.C. A CURRENT BIBLI-
        OGRAPHY ON ETHIOPIAN AFFAIRS. Compiled by Daniel G. Matthews.
        Washington, Mar. 1965. 46 p. (Special Bibliographic Series,
        v. 3, no. 3)

        Supersedes two earlier bibliographies, ETHIOPIA, 1950-1962
(1962, 7 l.) and ETHIOPIAN SURVEY (compiled by Annette Delaney, Jan.
1964, 12 l.). Although emphasis is on English-language publications,
included also are those in Russian (titles transliterated and translated), French, German, Italian, and other languages. Entries are
arranged by subject, and there is an author index. See also note on
African Bibliographic Center series, no. 292, and ETHIOPIAN OUTLINE:
A BIBLIOGRAPHIC RESEARCH GUIDE, compiled by Daniel G. Matthews
(Washington, D.C., 1966, 17 l.; Special Bibliographic Series, v. 4,
no. 3).

2591. Baylor, Jim, comp. ETHIOPIA: A LIST OF WORKS IN ENGLISH. Berkeley,
        Calif. (privately circulated), Mar. 1966. 60, 6 l. Mimeo-
        graphed.

        2d ed., 1967. 60, 10 l.

        Works are grouped by subject. No periodical articles are in-
cluded unless separately printed. There are selected governmental
publications. Addenda in the first edition consists of 2 pages of
"Additions, Changes, and Deletions" and a four-page author index; in
the second edition, additional entries only are included.

2592. Chojnacki, S., and Ephraim Haile Sellassie, comps. ETHIOPIAN PUB-
        LICATIONS: BOOKS, PAMPHLETS, ANNUALS, AND PERIODICAL ARTICLES
        PUBLISHED IN .... 1963/64- Addis Ababa, Institute of Ethiopian
        Studies, Haile Sellassie I University, 1965- Annual.

In Part 1 works in Ethiopian languages are arranged alphabetically. Part 2 lists works in foreign languages, classified
according to an adaptation of the Dewey decimal system, and includes an index of authors and their works. The third issue
(ETHIOPIAN PUBLICATIONS . . . PUBLISHED IN 1958 ETHIOPIAN AND
1966 GREGORIAN CALENDAR) had 58 pages and 551 entries (380 in
foreign languages, 171 in Ethiopian languages).

2593. Comba, Pierre. LIST OF BOOKS IN AMHARIC IN THE ETHIOPIAN COL-
LECTION OF THE UNIVERSITY COLLEGE OF ADDIS ABABA. Addis
Ababa, University College Press, 1961. 133 p.

Introduction in French and English; list in Amharic and
French. In this bibliography 529 works, original and translated,
are described.

2594. Ethiopia. Ministry of Foreign Affairs. BIBLIOGRAPHY OF ETHIOPIA.
With an introduction by H. E. Ato Ketema Yifru, Minister of
Foreign Affairs of the Imperial Ethiopian Government. Addis
Ababa, Ethiopia, 1968. 46 p.

Short list of titles on various aspects of Ethiopian history
and culture in Western languages.

2595. Fumagalli, Giuseppe. BIBLIOGRAFIA ETIOPICA: CATALOGO DESCRITTIVO
E RAGIONATO DEGLI SCRITTI PUBBLICATI DALLA INVENZIONE DELLA
STAMPA FINO A TUTTO IL 1891. INTORNO ALLA ETIOPIA E REGIONI
LIMITROFE. Milano, U. Hoepli, 1893. xi, 288 p.

Usually cited as the most comprehensive and renowned bibliography of Ethiopica and Amharica from the earliest records to the
end of the nineteenth century.

This work was supplemented by Silvio Zanutto in his BIBLI-
OGRAFIA ETIOPICA, IN CONTINUAZIONE ALLA "BIBLIOGRAFIA ETIOPICA"
DI G. FUMAGALLI (Roma, Published for the Ministry of Colonies by
the Sindicato Italiano Arti Grafiche, 1929, 2 v.). The first volume,
1. CONTRIBUTO (54 p.), which was reprinted in a 1936 edition, was
a bibliography of bibliographies, general and by broad subject
fields, including catalogues and reading lists in published studies.
The second CONTRIBUTO (1932, 178 p.) listed "Manoscritti etiopici"--
presumably those discovered since 1891.

In the chief nineteenth-century English work on Ethiopia, published following the punitive expedition against the Emperor Theodore in 1867, ABYSSINIA AND ITS PEOPLE; OR, LIFE IN THE LAND OF
PRESTER JOHN, edited by John Camden Hotten (London, 1868, 384 p.),
the last 15 pages were given to a "Bibliography of All the Known

Works Relating to Abyssinia," comprising, according to the editor,
"a tolerably perfect list of the books and tracts which have been
published upon that country." Comparison by length alone shows the
superiority of Italian to British knowledge of Ethiopia.

2596.   Laborde, Marquis Léon E. S. J. de. VOYAGES EN ABYSSINIE: ANALYSE
          CRITIQUE DES VOYAGES QUI ONT ETE FAITS DANS CE PAYS ET DES
          OUVRAGES QU'ON A PUBLIE [SIC] SUR SON HISTOIRE, SA RELIGION ET
          SES MOEURS. [n.p.] 1938. 87 p. (150 entries)

2597.   Leslau, Wolf. AN ANNOTATED BIBLIOGRAPHY OF THE SEMITIC LANGUAGES
          OF ETHIOPIA. The Hague, Mouton, 1965. 336 p. map. (Bibli-
          ographies on the Near East, 1)

      The author is well known as a philologist specializing in
Ethiopian and Middle East languages. In this excellent bibliography he first lists works on Semitic languages and on Ethiopian
languages in general and then covers linguistic studies and texts
of the various Semitic languages of Ethiopia--Ge'ez, Tigre,
Tigrinya, Amharic, Argobba, Gafat, Gurage, and Harari. Annotations are provided for works in languages other than English
and when an English title is not self-explanatory. Occasionally
grammars and dictionaries receive critical evaluation. For each
language analytical tables are presented first; these are followed
by a bibliography broken down into several categories, e.g.,
grammatical outlines, grammars, grammatical studies, special problems of grammar and lexicography, dictionaries and vocabularies,
text collections and phrase books. The volume concludes with an
index of authors and their works, an index of reviewers, and an
analytical subject index. Mr. Leslau has contributed a "List of
Publications on the History and Language of Ethiopia" to the
ETHIOPIA INFORMATION BULLETIN (issued also in French; Paris, 1963-).

2598.   LIST OF CURRENT PERIODICAL PUBLICATIONS IN ETHIOPIA. Addis Ababa,
          Institute of Ethiopian Studies, Haile Sellassie I University,
          Oct. 1964-

      The first two issues (the second appeared in 1965) were com-
piled by S. Chojnacki and Ephraim Haile Sellassie; the third, compiled by S. Chojnacki and Kifle Markos, was published in July 1968
(29 p.; 285 entries). This series of bibliographies includes all
current titles published in Ethiopia and those produced abroad by
Ethiopian nations; also listed are periodicals of the UN Economic
Commission for Africa as well as those of diplomatic missions to
Ethiopia. All categories of serials (newspapers, periodicals,
annual reports, series) are listed, even those of very limited
circulation. Amharic titles are transliterated and sometimes
translated into English. An index of English titles and one of
Ethiopian titles are included.

2599. Selassie, Sergew Hable. BIBLIOGRAPHY OF ANCIENT AND MEDIEVAL ETHI-
      OPIAN HISTORY. Addis Ababa, Star Print. Press, 1969. 76 p.

      Covers period from ancient times to 1270 and imprints up to
      1965 with a few for post-1965. The book contains 918 items (mono-
      graphs and articles) arranged under the following headings: major
      bibliographic works, prehistory, geography, archaeology, in-
      scriptions, numismatic, history (general, specific), architecture
      and art, Ethiopian church history, textual and related titles,
      travel and commerce. Publications in French, Italian, English,
      German, Latin are included. There is an index of authors.

2600. Simon, J. "Bibliographie éthiopienne, 1946-1951." ORIENTALIA,
      v. 21, 1952: 47-66, 209-230.

      This list of 411 references is a continuation of Carlo Conti
      Rossini's "Pubblicazioni etiopici dal 1936 al 1945," RASSEGNA DI
      STUDI ETIOPICI, 1944, p. 1-132.

2601. Wright, Stephen G., comp. ETHIOPIAN INCUNABULA [A BIBLIOGRAPHY OF
      PRE-1936 PRINTED MATERIAL PRODUCED IN ETHIOPIA]. Compiled
      from the collections in the National Library of Ethiopia
      and the Haile Sellassie I University. Addis Ababa, Commer-
      cial Printing Press, 1967. 107 p.

      "Incunabula" is defined in this case as all books printed in
      Ethiopia before the Italian occupation of 1936-41. Newspapers and
      other serials are excluded and only books found in the National
      Library and the University Library are covered by the 223 items.
      Section 1 consists of a subject index. In the body of the bibli-
      ography, Section 2, entries are arranged by town of printing, then
      further by printing press. Detailed bibliographical data are given
      for the entries, virtually all of which are in Amharic (others are
      in Italian). Section 3 is a rough chronological listing of the
      books. A second, more comprehensive edition is planned.

Serials

2602. Addis Ababa. University College. Ethnological Society. BULLETIN.
      no. 1- May 1953- Addis Ababa. Irregular. English and
      Amharic.

2603. ETHIOPIA OBSERVER: JOURNAL OF INDEPENDENT OPINION, ECONOMICS,
      HISTORY AND THE ARTS. v. 1, no. 1- Dec. 1956- Edited by
      Richard and Rita Pankhurst. Addis Ababa. illus. Quarterly.

The NEW TIMES AND ETHIOPIA NEWS, which had been edited by Miss
E. Sylvia Pankhurst from May 5, 1936, was terminated on May 5, 1956,
and succeeded by this larger illustrated magazine published monthly
during the editor's life and revived as a quarterly under the editorship of her son after her death in 1960. Articles on a wide range
of topics concerned with Ethiopia are sometimes of monograph length.
A chronology, "Ethiopian Record," occupies the last pages.

Among the most important organs for study of Ethiopian culture
and Ethiopica is the journal founded by the late Italian Ethiopicist,
Carlo Rossini, RASSEGNA DI STUDI ETIOPICA (1941-, published by
Istituto Studi Orientali, Centro di Studi Etiopici e Christiano-
Orientali, Università di Roma).

2604. ETHIOPIAN ECONOMIC REVIEW. no. 1- Dec. 1959- Issued by the Im-
       perial Ethiopian Government Ministry of Commerce and Industry.
       Addis Ababa. tables. Irregular.

Official journal reviewing the economic life of Ethiopia. A
large, well-printed magazine, its text is equally divided between
articles on general and specific aspects of economic life and
statistical tables of external trade, industry, finances, etc. In
no. 5, Feb. 1962, an inserted green-paper section lists businesses
in the Empire of Ethiopia. The periodical follows and supersedes
an ECONOMIC HANDBOOK, Dec. 1958 (93, 119 p.), published by the
Ministry of Commerce and Industry, which in turn superseded an
illustrated volume, ECONOMIC PROGRESS OF ETHIOPIA (Addis Ababa,
1955, 171 p.).

2605. ETHIOPIAN GEOGRAPHICAL JOURNAL. v. 1, no. 1- June 1963- Addis
       Ababa. Semiannual.

Scholarly journal published by the Mapping and Geography
Institute of Ethiopia. The text is in Amharic and English.

2606. ETHIOPIAN TRADE JOURNAL. v. 1, no. 1- 1960- Addis Ababa.
       Chamber of Commerce. Semiannual.

2607. JOURNAL OF ETHIOPIAN LAW. v. 1- 1964- Addis Ababa, Faculty of
       Law, Haile Sellassie I University, in cooperation with the
       Ministry of Justice. Semiannual.

Each issue of the journal includes a table of cases reported,
case reports, current issues, articles commenting on various
aspects of Ethiopian law, and a book review section first appearing in 1966. The last issue each year has an annual index to
cases reported and index of laws cited.

2608. JOURNAL OF ETHIOPIAN STUDIES. no. 1- 1963- Addis Ababa, Insti-
           tute of Ethiopian Studies, Haile Sellassie I University.
           Semiannual.

           The Institute, established in Jan. 1963 and directed by Dr.
    Richard Pankhurst, serves as the University's principal insti-
    tution for research in all fields relating to Ethiopia. It is
    described in the AFRICAN STUDIES BULLETIN (v. 6, no. 2, May 1963:
    15-16). The journal superseded the COLLEGE REVIEW, published by
    University College (one number only, Spring 1961).

Reference Works

2609. Addis Ababa. Chamber of Commerce. Information, Documentation and
           Press Department. TRADE DIRECTORY & GUIDE BOOK TO ETHIOPIA,
           1967. Addis Ababa [1967?] 397 p. fold. map.

           Contains general information plus data on trade, industry,
    agriculture, transportation, and tourism. There is a list of
    Chamber of Commerce members and one of importers and exporters
    (listed under commodity traded in). Also provided is a directory
    of miscellaneous business firms (e.g., agricultural concerns, con-
    sulting engineers, insurance companies) and one of industrialists
    and manufacturers.

           The Chamber of Commerce also publishes the notable Western-
    style semiannual periodical, ETHIOPIAN TRADE JOURNAL.

2610. American University, Washington, D.C. Foreign Areas Study Division.
           AREA HANDBOOK FOR ETHIOPIA. By George A. Lipsky and others.
           2d ed. Washington, June 1964. xi, 621 p. maps, tables,
           charts, graphs.

           Includes bibliographies.

           One of the series of country surveys, this handbook was
    originally published in Oct. 1960 and the 1964 edition appears to
    be an unaltered reprint. It presents basic background information
    in four sections: social (including physical setting and his-
    torical data), economic, political, and military. Each section is
    followed by a bibliography, the longest running eight pages.

2611. Beckingham, Charles F., and G. W. B. Huntingford, eds. and trs.
           SOME RECORDS OF ETHIOPIA, 1593-1646: BEING EXTRACTS FROM THE
           HISTORY OF HIGH ETHIOPIA OR ABASSIA, BY MANOEL DE ALMEIDA,
           TOGETHER WITH BAHREY'S HISTORY OF THE GALLA. London, Printed

for the Hakluyt Society, 1954. xcviii, 267 p. illus., maps.
(Works Issued by the Hakluyt Society, 2d ser., no. 107)

The Hakluyt Society has long done invaluable work in publishing source materials. The present publication has translations from two works on the medieval history of Abyssinia--i.e., the central highlands which formed the ancient Semitic and Christian country, in contrast to the present extended empire of Ethiopia. The editors have contributed useful notes. This supplements the monumental work of Budge (below).

A later portion, the ROYAL CHRONICLE OF ABYSSINIA, 1769-1840, was published with translation and notes by H. Weld Blundell (Cambridge, Eng., University Press, 1922, 548 p.). This is an impressive work of scholarship, giving the text in Ge'ez (or Ethiopic, the literary language of Ethiopia) and following it with a complete translation and appendixes containing explanatory notes on chronology, church ritual, geographical index, etc. The chronicle by court historians is in the epic style, to the glory of the Negus.

2612. Bruce, James. TRAVELS TO DISCOVER THE SOURCES OF THE NILE IN THE
        YEARS 1768, 1769, 1770, 1771, 1772, and 1773. By James
        Bruce of Kinnaird. Edinburgh, G. G. J. & J. Robinson, 1790.
        5 v. plates, maps.

        Reprint. Edinburgh, Edinburgh University Press; New York, Horizon
            Press, 1964. 281 p. illus., maps, fold. geneal. tables.

The most famous of early accounts in English of Abyssinia, used as a source by all later writers and now available in a modern edition.

2613. Budge, Sir E. A. Wallis. A HISTORY OF ETHIOPIA, NUBIA AND ABYS-
        SINIA (ACCORDING TO THE HIEROGLYPHIC INSCRIPTIONS OF EGYPT
        AND NUBIA, AND THE ETHIOPIAN CHRONICLES). London, Methuen,
        1928. 2 v.

        Bibliography: v. 2, p. 631-644.

Monumental work by the keeper of Egyptian and Assyrian antiquities of the British Museum. It brings together the results of scholarship in translations of classical inscriptions and medieval and modern Ethiopic chronicles regarding the legends and facts of history of Ethiopia from the time of the Pharaohs to the twentieth century.

An equally detailed history in French is by T. B. Coulbeaux, HISTOIRE POLITIQUE ET RELIGIEUSE DE L'ABYSSINIE DEPUIS LES TEMPS LES PLUS RECULES JUSQU'A L'AVENEMENT DE MENELICK II (Paris, Geuthner, 1929, 3 v.).

2614. Cerulli, Enrico. STORIA DELLA LETTERATURA ETIOPICA. Milan, Nuova
Accademia, Editrice, 1956. 279 p.

_____. STUDI ETIOPICI. Roma, Istituto per l'Oriente, 1936-67.

Basic sources.

2615. Cerulli, Ernesta. PEOPLES OF SOUTH-WEST ETHIOPIA AND ITS BORDER-
LAND. London, International African Institute, 1956. 148 p.
maps, tables. (Ethnographic Survey of Africa, North-eastern
Africa, pt. 3)

Bibliography: p. 133-142.

Handbook on the odd groups of hill peoples, mainly Negroid,
of the area of Ethiopia bordering the Sudan. According to H. E.
Hurst (THE NILE, no. 2585), 70 languages are spoken in Ethiopia;
a good many of them are accounted for by these tribes, Ingassana-Mao,
Suri-Surma-Mekan, Burji-Konso, Sidama, etc. A long bibliography
ends this volume, which follows the pattern of the series (see
no. 980). Many of the references are to Italian sources.

2616. Clapham, Christopher. HAILE SELASSIE'S GOVERNMENT. New York,
Praeger, 1969. 218 p.

Bibliography: p. 206-208.

Recent general survey.

2617. Conti Rossini, Carlo. ETIOPIA E GENTI DI ETIOPIA. Firenze, R.
Bemporad, 1937. 402 p. plates, maps.

_____. STORIA D'ETIOPIA: Vol. I, DELLE ORIGINI ALL'AVVENTO
DELLA DINASTIA SALOMONIDE. Milano, A. Lucini, 1928.
(Africa italiana, no. 3)

The late Professor Conti Rossini of the Academia dei Lincei
at the University of Rome began his publications on languages
and literature of Northeast Africa before the turn of the century
and was considered the leading Italian exponent of Ethiopian studies. The first of the two books here mentioned is a broad ethnological survey. Only the first volume of the history was published; it covers the Ethiopian past from Biblical times to the
re-establishment of the Solomonic dynasty in 1270.

Among the writer's numerous works, another important volume
is his comprehensive account of customary laws of the peoples of
Eritrea, PRINCIPI DI DIRITTO CONSUETUDINARIO DELLA COLONIA ERITREA

(Rome, Tipografia dell'Unione Editrice, 1916, 802 p.).

2618. Diplomatic Press. TRADE DIRECTORY OF THE EMPIRE OF ETHIOPIA,
          INCLUDING CLASSIFIED TRADE INDEX. 1965- London, Diplo-
          matic Press and Publishing Co.

       The 1965 edition (64 p.) has brief sections on history,
agriculture and animal resources, mining, and foreign relations
(including a list of diplomatic and consular missions in Ethiopia), among others. The second part is the trade index, classified as to agricultural produce, coffee, hides and skins, petroleum products, etc. There is an index to advertisers.

2619. Doresse, Jean. L'EMPIRE DU PRETRE-JEAN. Paris, Plon, 1957.
          2 v. illus. (D'un monde à l'autre, La collection des
          découvertes)

       Bibliographies: v. 1, p. 283-296; v. 2, p. 333-351.

       A history of ancient and medieval Ethiopia, based on study
of the many existent manuscripts of Ethiopic literature. The
author is a French specialist in Coptic literature and Ethiopica
who has been in the country as director of archaeological research.
The chief art treasures of Ethiopia are described and illustrated
in his 1956 book, AU PAYS DE LA REINE DE SABA: L'ETHIOPIE,
ANTIQUE ET MODERNE (Paris, Guillot, 171 p., plates). It was
translated into English by Elsa Colt: ETHIOPIA (London, Elek
Books; New York, Putnam, 1959, 239 p., illus.).

2620. Ethiopia. THE HANDBOOK FOR ETHIOPIA. Nairobi, Published for . . .
          Ministry of Information, Imperial Ethiopian Government by
          University Press of Africa, 1969. 328 p. illus., maps.

       Information on geography, government, communications, the
economy, history and tourism. Appendices cover Amharic conver-
sation vocabulary, secondary school directory, business directory,
diplomatic roster, and economic statistics. There is an index and
advertisers' index.

2621. Ethiopia. Institute of Public Administration. ADMINISTRATIVE
          DIRECTORY. 6th ed. Addis Ababa, Nov. 1966. 101 p. Mimeo-
          graphed.

       Directory giving location and postal addresses of the agen-
cies of the Imperial Government, of foreign ministries and missions, and of units of local government, with name and telephone
number of top officials.

2622. Ethiopia. Ministry of Finance. Central Statistical Office.
           STATISTICAL ABSTRACT. Addis Ababa, Commercial Printing
           Press, 1963-

2623. Ethiopia. Ministry of Mines. MINERAL OCCURRENCES OF ETHIOPIA.
           Addis Ababa, 1966. 720 p.

2624. ETHIOPIA TRADE AND ECONOMIC REVIEW, 1967-68. n.p., n.d. 212 p.
           [Annual?]

           Contains short descriptions of latest developments in banks,
       businesses, and factories. There are also short articles on the
       history of Ethiopian airlines, the growth of electrical power in
       Ethiopia, the Awash Valley Authority, development of telecommuni-
       cations, and the Ethiopian merchant marine.

2625. Food and Agriculture Organization of the United Nations. AGRI-
           CULTURE IN ETHIOPIA. Compiled by H. P. Huffnagel, consultant
           to FAO. Rome, 1961. xv, 484 p. illus., maps (part fold.),
           tables.

           Bibliography: p. 481-484.

           Exhaustive survey of Ethiopian agriculture, covering phy-
       sical characteristics, economic conditions, agricultural prac-
       tices, production of specific crops, animal husbandry, marketing
       and processing, forestry, fisheries, agricultural administration,
       research and education, and agricultural credit.

2626. Greenfield, Richard. ETHIOPIA: A NEW POLITICAL HISTORY. New
           York, Praeger, 1965. 515 p. illus., maps, tables. (Praeger
           Library of African Affairs)

           Bibliography: p. 475-482.

           An interpretative, readable account by a former dean and
       assistant to the president of Haile Sellassie I University.
       Ethiopia's complicated history is carefully traced from earliest
       times to the 1960's (Ethiopian roots, Ethiopia emergent, war with
       Italy, etc.). Appendixes include the Ethiopian calendar, Ethio-
       pian titles and modes of address, and statistical tables. An
       index is included.

2627. Haile Selassie I, Emperor of Ethiopia. SPEECHES DELIVERED ON
           VARIOUS OCCASIONS, MAY 1957-DECEMBER 1959. Addis Ababa,
           Ministry of Information, 1960. 183 p. illus.

Of the 50-odd addresses by the Emperor brought together in
this collection, over a third are concerned with education and
almost as many with the economic progress of his country. Several
others involve international relations.

2628. Huntingford, George W. B. THE GALLA OF ETHIOPIA: THE KINGDOMS OF
KAFA AND JANJERO. London, International African Institute,
1955. 156 p. (Ethnographic Survey of Africa, North-eastern
Africa, pt. 2)

Bibliography: p. 145-147.

See general note on this series, no. 980.

The Galla, a pastoral Hamitic people whose original home was
in British Somaliland, invaded and have spread widely over southern
and eastern Ethiopia during the past 400 years and now form one of
the more important racial stocks of that country. For this handbook the main sources were the important older works of French,
German, and Italian authorities. The author readily admitted that
because of the difficult nature of the Galla country and the lack
of recent studies, it was impossible to say whether the mores he
described were still prevalent. For more recent works see Herbert
S. Lewis, A GALLA MONARCHY: JEMMA ABBA JIFAR, ETHIOPIA, 1830-1932
(Madison, University of Wisconsin Press, 1965, 148 p., illus.,
maps; bibliography: p. 135-142); and Eike Haberland, GALLA SUD-
AETHIOPIENS (Stuttgart, W. Kohlhammer, 1959, xix, 815 p., illus.,
plates, maps; Frobenius Institut, Frankfurt am Main, Völker Süd-
Aetiopiens, v. 2), which includes an English summary.

2629. International Conference of Ethiopian Studies, 2d, Manchester
University, 1963. ETHIOPIAN STUDIES: PAPERS READ AT THE
SECOND INTERNATIONAL CONFERENCE OF ETHIOPIAN STUDIES, MAN-
CHESTER UNIVERSITY, JULY 1963. Under the patronage of His
Imperial Majesty the Emperor of Ethiopia. Manchester, Eng.,
Manchester University Press, 1964. xv, 264 p. (JOURNAL
OF SEMITIC STUDIES, v. 9, no. 1)

Thirty-one articles in English, French, German, and Italian,
more than half of them concerned with archaeology and linguistics.
The Proceedings of the 3d International Conference, Addis Ababa,
1966, were at the press in 1969.

2630. Jäger, Otto A. ANTIQUITIES OF NORTH ETHIOPIA: A GUIDE. Stuttgart,
F. A. Brockhaus, Abt. Antiquarium 1965. 129 p. illus. (part
col.), maps, plans.

Bibliography: p. 125-129.

Brief history of and guide to the churches, monasteries, wall paintings, icons, and manuscript illuminations of Ethiopia. There is a timetable of historical dates and events--known and legendary.

2631. Levine, Donald Nathan. WAX & GOLD: TRADITION AND INNOVATION IN ETHIOPIAN CULTURE. Chicago, University of Chicago Press, 1965. xvi, 315 p. plates, map, tables.

Bibliographical footnotes.

A thorough, well-written account of Amharic culture rather than of Ethiopian society. A brief historical summary from 1270 is followed by a detailed discussion of Amharic life and of the many and great contradictions between tradition and modernity in present-day Ethiopia. A four-page glossary and an index are included.

2632. Lipsky, George A. ETHIOPIA: ITS PEOPLE, ITS SOCIETY, ITS CULTURE. By George A. Lipsky, in collaboration with Wendall Blanchard, Abraham M. Hirsch, and Bela C. Maday. New Haven, Conn., HRAF Press, 1962. 376 p. maps, diagrs., tables. (Survey of World Cultures, no. 9)

Bibliography: p. 343-357.

Intended to meet the need for a "comprehensive reliable volume" synthesizing the most authoritative materials on Ethiopia in all aspects of behavioral sciences. The presentation is encyclopedic, with chapters divided into sections with subheadings, the writing in easy narrative style. The book concludes with tabulated statistical data, a selected bibliography, and a full index.

2633. Marein, Nathan. THE ETHIOPIAN EMPIRE: FEDERATION AND LAWS. Rotterdam, Royal Netherlands Print. & Lithographing Co., 1955. 456 p. port.

A compendium for the use of Ethiopian lawyers and judges and for foreigners concerned with laws relating to Ethiopian commerce and finance, by the Advocate General and General Adviser to the Imperial Ethiopian Government. This 1955 volume superseded two earlier guides, HANDBOOK TO THE LAWS OF ETHIOPIA (Addis Ababa, 1949, 207 p.) and THE JUDICIAL SYSTEM AND THE LAWS OF ETHIOPIA (Rotterdam, Royal Netherlands Print. & Lithographing Co., 1951, 288 p.).

2634. Pankhurst, Estelle Sylvia. ETHIOPIA: A CULTURAL HISTORY. Essex, Eng., Lalibela House, 1955. xxxviii, 747 p. illus. (part col.), ports.

Monumental tome presenting a "comprehensive" survey of Ethiopian history and culture. Based on careful study and including much good archaeological and artistic material, as exemplified in the plates, it is a basic account in English, despite the enormous amount of detail. Much of this is in the form of long quotations from Ethiopian records, papers, and documents testifying to the glories of the past and the virtuous accomplishments of the present.

2635. Pankhurst, Richard. "The Foundations of Education, Printing, Newspapers, Book Production, Libraries and Literature in Ethiopia." ETHIOPIA OBSERVER, v. 6, no. 3, 1962: 241-290.

Includes names of many organizations and individual scholars.

2636. Pankhurst, Richard. AN INTRODUCTION TO THE ECONOMIC HISTORY OF ETHIOPIA FROM EARLY TIMES TO 1800. London, Sidgwick & Jackson, 1961. 454 p. illus.

Bibliography: p. 429-436.

By the director of the new Institute of Ethiopian Studies at Haile Sellassie I University, editor of the ETHIOPIA OBSERVER, and a leading authority on Ethiopian history and culture. A reviewer speaks of Dr. Pankhurst as "an impassioned defender of values and institutions Amharan." This book was intended as the first of a series, to be followed by a volume covering the contemporary scene. A number of preliminary articles have appeared in the ETHIOPIA OBSERVER. A volume covering 1800-1935 is in press. See also his THE ETHIOPIAN ROYAL CHRONICLES (London, Oxford University Press, 1967, 210 p., illus., maps), extracts from accounts from the 4th to the 20th century. A useful survey by Pankhurst is AN INTRODUCTION TO THE HISTORY OF THE ETHIOPIAN ARMY (Addis Ababa, Imperial Air Force, 1967, 183 p., illus.).

2637. Perham, Margery. THE GOVERNMENT OF ETHIOPIA. London, Faber & Faber, 1948. xxiii, 481 p.

Reprint, 1969.

Bibliography: p. 457-464.

Standard work on Ethiopian government and political history up to the postwar Restoration. In the introduction of her skillful, far-ranging study, the author commented that the book was designed to offset the distortions of propaganda regarding Ethiopia, which since the Italian aggression had become the subject for an emotional approach little backed by "serious information."

2638. RERUM AETHIOPICARUM SCRIPTORES OCCIDENTALES INEDITI A SAECULO XVI
         AD XIX CURANTE C. BECCARI, S.I. Edited by Camillo Beccari.
         Roma, Excudebat C. de Luigi, 1903-17. 15 v.

         Voluminous compilation of the writings of the Jesuit priests
    and other European visitants to Ethiopia from the sixteenth to
    the eighteenth century. The first volume is bibliographical:
    NOTIZIA E SAGGI DI OPERE E DOCUMENTI INEDITI RIGUARDANTI LA
    STORIA DI ETIOPIA DURANTE I SECOLI XVI, XVII, E XVIII, CON OTTO
    FACSIMILI E DUE CARTE GEOGRAFICHE. Besides the listing of writ-
    ings, it includes analysis of the major manuscripts.

2639. Trimingham, John S. ISLAM IN ETHIOPIA. London, New York,
         Oxford University Press, 1952. xv, 299 p. maps.

         Reissue, New York, Barnes & Noble, 1965. xv, 299 p.

         A major contribution to Islamic studies, surveying Islam,
    its history and extent in the entire region of the Horn of Africa,
    including Eritrea and the Somalilands as well as the highland
    kingdom, which is designated as Abyssinia. Canon Trimingham
    begins with an account of the region, its peoples, and distri-
    bution of religions and then considers in historic terms the
    centuries-old conflict of Islam with the Christian religion that
    had been brought to Abyssinia in the days of the Early Church.
    His third part is a detailed analysis of the tribal distribution
    of Islam in Ethiopia--Beni Amir, Danakil, Galla, Somali, and many
    minor groups, including Negroid tribes. Last, the special char-
    acteristics of Islam in Ethiopia are examined, as well as the
    interplay of influence with paganism and Westernism.

         A booklet by this author, THE CHRISTIAN CHURCH AND MISSIONS
    IN ETHIOPIA (INCLUDING ERITREA AND THE SOMALILANDS) (London and
    New York, World Dominion Press, 1950, 73 p., fold. maps; Survey
    Series), contains a short statement of the general religious back-
    ground and of the National Church of Ethiopia, which since 1951
    has been distinct from the Coptic Church in Egypt and has an
    Ethiopian Copt archbishop. There follows a systematic examination
    of missions and their work in the Horn of Africa before, during,
    and since the Italian occupation, their connection with the
    Ethiopian National Church, and their proselytizing efforts among
    pagans and Muslims.

         The standard work on the Ethiopian Coptic church is by Harry
    M. Hyatt, THE CHURCH OF ABYSSINIA (London, Luzac, 1928, 302 p.).

2640. Trudeau, E. HIGHER EDUCATION IN ETHIOPIA. Montreal, 1964.
       195 l. tables, graphs. Processed.

       Bibliography: p. 186-195.

       This doctoral project first surveys the overall development
of education in Ethiopia and the foundations and progress (1951-
61) of higher education. The author then describes Haile Sellassie
I University and concludes with a discussion of problems and
prospects in planning the future development of higher education.

2641. Ullendorff, Edward. THE ETHIOPIANS: AN INTRODUCTION TO COUNTRY
       AND PEOPLE. London, New York, Oxford University Press,
       1960. 232 p. illus.

       Rev. ed., 1964.

       Bibliography: p. 207-213.

       By an Ethiopicist who has spent over 20 years in the study
of Ethiopian languages and civilizations. His survey begins with
a review of explorations and studies, followed by a background of
country and people and then by an outline of history. The focus
is on cultural factors, explained in chapters on religion, languages, literature, art and music, daily life and customs; only
the last chapter, "Ethiopia Today," touches on modern politico-
economic matters. The work is dedicated to Haile Selassie, by
whose "high example . . . no one living in Ethiopia can fail to
be inspired."

       A new book on the Emperor, by Leonard O. Mosley, a British
writer of popular histories and biographies, is HAILE SELASSIE:
THE CONQUERING LION (Englewood Cliffs, N.J., Prentice-Hall,
1965, 288 p., illus.).

2642. Virginia Legal Studies. THE LEGAL SYSTEMS OF AFRICA SERIES:
       Vol. I, THE LEGAL SYSTEM OF ETHIOPIA. By Kenneth R. Redden.
       Charlottesville, Va., The Michie Company, 1969. 290 p.

2643. Wohlgemuth, Lennart. ETIOPIENS EKONOMI. Uppsala, Nordiska Afrika-
       Institutet, 1967.

       Not available for examination.

SOMALIA

Bibliographies

2644. African Bibliographic Center, Washington, D.C. SOMALIAN PANORAMAS:
       A SELECT BIBLIOGRAPHICAL SURVEY, 1960-1966. Washington, 1967.
       17 p. Processed. (Special Bibliographical Series, v. 5, no. 3)

2645. Somalia. Laws, statutes, etc. INDEX TO THE LAWS IN FORCE IN THE
       NORTHERN REGION ON 15TH AUGUST 1960. Compiled by Iqbal Singha.
       Hargeisa, Govt. Printer, 1960. 46 l.

2646. U.S. Library of Congress. General Reference and Bibliography
       Division. OFFICIAL PUBLICATIONS OF SOMALILAND, 1941-1959:
       A GUIDE. Compiled by Helen F. Conover. Washington, 1960.
       41 p.

       This bibliography is out of print, but a positive microfilm
       can be obtained from the Photoduplication Service of the Library
       of Congress. It will be useful for anyone doing serious research
       on Somalia and on the former British and French Somalilands. The
       first seven items, descriptively annotated, name published bibli-
       ographies in which unofficial literature in Italian and other
       languages regarding the Horn of Africa is exhaustively covered.
       The list gives detailed attention to United Nations documents
       relating to the trust territory of Somaliland under Italian
       administration.

2647. Viney, N. M. A BIBLIOGRAPHY OF BRITISH SOMALILAND. Hargeisa, 1947.
       36 p. Mimeographed.

       Bibliography compiled under the military government by a for-
       mer assistant director of the General Survey of British Somaliland
       and revised by John A. Hunt in his survey of the Somaliland pro-
       tectorate (see no. 2652). It is in classified arrangement by sub-
       jects and includes a scattering of material on both Italian and
       French Somaliland.

Reference Works

2648. Andrzejewski, B. W., and I. M. Lewis. SOMALI POETRY: AN INTRO-
       DUCTION. Oxford, Clarendon Press, 1964. 167 p. (Oxford
       Library of African Literature)

       Important source for Somali literature, history, and values.

2649. Castagno, Alphonso A. SOMALIA. New York, Carnegie Endowment for
      International Peace, 1959. 62 p. (INTERNATIONAL CONCILIATION,
      no. 522, p. 339-400)

      Concentrated review of the stages of political, educational,
and economic development of the trust territory of Somalia during
the decade after the United Nations decision in 1949 to give the
country its independence in 1960. Emphasis is on relations of the
Amministrazione Fiduciaria Italiana della Somalia (AFIS) with the
United Nations. A chapter on "International Problems" considers
the boundary dispute with Ethiopia and the "Greater Somalia" issue.
Documents are cited in footnotes. See also his more up-to-date essay
on Somalia in Coleman and Rosberg, eds., POLITICAL PARTIES AND
NATIONAL INTEGRATION IN TROPICAL AFRICA (no. 612).

2650. Cerulli, Enrico. SOMALIA: SCRITTI VARI EDITI ED INEDITI. Roma,
      Published for the Amministrazione Fiduciaria Italiana della
      Somalia by Istituto Poligrafico dello Stato, 1957-64. 3 v.

      Bibliographical footnotes.

      By an Italian colonial administrator and scholar noted for
his studies of Northeastern African peoples and letters. These
three volumes bring together writings on many aspects of Somalia.
In the first volume are essays on history and legend, Islam,
religious literature and astronomy, and the Arab text and translation in Italian of a Somali chronicle, "The Book of Zengi."
The second volume is on customary law, ethnography, linguistics,
and the tribal way of life. The third volume deals with Somali
peoples and poetry and writings in Arabic.

2651. Drysdale, John. THE SOMALI DISPUTE. New York, Praeger, 1964.
      183 p. maps.

      Study of the "Greater Somalia" issue by a former adviser to
the Prime Minister of Somalia. References to many primary sources
are given in "Notes" (p. 168-177).

      Another study of this question, prepared as a doctoral thesis
and based on extensive research and firsthand knowledge, is by
Saadia Touval, SOMALI NATIONALISM: INTERNATIONAL POLITICS AND
THE DRIVE FOR UNITY IN THE HORN OF AFRICA (Cambridge, Mass.,
Harvard University Press, 1963, 241 p.; "Notes," p. 185-205).

2652. Hunt, John A. A GENERAL SURVEY OF THE SOMALILAND PROTECTORATE,
      1944-1950: FINAL REPORT ON "AN ECONOMIC SURVEY AND RE-
      CONNAISSANCE OF THE BRITISH SOMALILAND PROTECTORATE, 1944-

1950," COLONIAL DEVELOPMENT AND WELFARE SCHEME D. 484.
Hargeisa, To be purchased from the Chief Secretary, 1951.
203 p. maps, tables.

Bibliography: p. 180-201.

Publication recording the results of the seven-year geographical survey carried out under a Colonial Development and
Welfare scheme. Special attention is given to topography,
meteorology, geology, and ecology of the nomadic stock-herding
tribesmen, and recommendations are made for various lines of
development. The text, printed on folio pages and illustrated
with sketch maps, is divided between expository paragraphs and
tables of many varieties, among which are a gazetteer of place
names, tables of road mileages, rainfall records, temperatures,
genealogies, and summaries of the tribes. A long bibliography
compiled by N. M. Viney in 1947 (see no. 2647) was revised by
Mr. Hunt in 1950 and serves as the bibliography for this survey.

2653. International Bank for Reconstruction and Development. THE
        ECONOMY OF THE TRUST TERRITORY OF SOMALILAND: REPORT OF
        A MISSION ORGANIZED AT THE REQUEST OF THE GOVERNMENT OF
        ITALY. Washington, D.C., 1957. 99 l. maps, diagrs.,
        tables.

        A report issued as "a working paper . . . for those who will
have to determine what has to be done" in economic development to
prepare Somalia for independence. The character of the economy,
recent plans, prospects, and problems are analyzed and conclusions
presented stressing the need for continuing financial aid in the
foreseeable future.

2654. Lewis, I. M. THE MODERN HISTORY OF SOMALILAND: FROM NATION TO
        STATE. New York, Praeger, 1965. xi, 234 p. plates, maps.
        (Praeger Asia-Africa Series)

        Bibliographical footnotes.

        A well-written narrative of the historical events which led
Somalia from cultural to political nationalism. The book is
based in part on unpublished traditional source materials obtained
by Dr. Lewis in Somalia during 1955-57 and 1962. Two brief opening chapters describe the physical and social framework and summarize Somalia's long centuries of history before partition. Next
is an account of the European establishment in East Africa, the
Italian East African empire, the restoration of colonial frontiers,
and the period from trusteeship to independence. The book concludes with an analysis of the problems of independence as of mid-
1964. An analytical index is included.

2655. Lewis, I. M. A PASTORAL DEMOCRACY: A STUDY OF PASTORALISM AND
          POLITICS AMONG THE NORTHERN SOMALI OF THE HORN OF AFRICA.
          London, New York, Published for the International African
          Institute by the Oxford University Press, 1961. 320 p.
          illus., maps.

       Bibliography: p. 307-312.

       Study in "pastoral habits and political institutions" by one
of the few English-speaking authorities on Somaliland. It is
mostly confined to the northern Somali, the tribes of the former
British protectorate--nomads with herds of camel, sheep, and
goats--whose political system "lacks to a remarkable degree all
the machinery of centralized government." Dr. Lewis focuses his
work on the political organization, which is based on kinship and
lineage, but he also includes background material on economy,
ecology, and residence patterns. In his last chapter he reviews
the modern political scene in Somalia and its repercussions in
the protectorate. The long bibliography covers material on the
entire Horn.

2656. Lewis, I. M. PEOPLES OF THE HORN OF AFRICA: SOMALI, AFAR, AND
          SAHO. London, International African Institute, 1955. 200 p.
          maps, tables. (Ethnographic Survey of Africa, North-
          eastern Africa, pt. 1)

       Bibliography: p. 177-194.

       Summary of available information about the Somali, Afar (Dana-
kil), and Saho, closely related nomadic peoples of camel culture and
Mohammedan faith, who are spread through the three (former) countries
of the Horn of Africa--Somalia (Italian Somaliland), the British
Somaliland protectorate, and French Somaliland. The Afar and Saho
are also distributed across the borders in Eritrea and Ethiopia, and
the Somali in Ethiopia and northern Kenya. For his survey made from
library sources the writer used many Italian and French works as well
as English, which are listed in the bibliography.

       Dr. Lewis supplemented the bibliography of this book with a
bibliographical essay, "Recent Progress in Somali Studies," which
was presented as a paper at the Second International Conference of
Ethiopian Studies at Manchester University in 1963 and published in
ETHIOPIAN STUDIES (Manchester, Eng., Manchester University Press,
1964, p. 122-134).

2657. Somalia. Information Services. THE SOMALI PENINSULA: A NEW LIGHT
          ON IMPERIAL MOTIVES. Mogadiscio, 1962. xiii, 137 p. maps.
          Printed by Staples, St. Albans, Herts.

       Bibliography: p. 131-134.

An official publication summarizing Somali history to justify the claim to the Ogaden District of Ethiopia and the Somali pocket in the Northern Frontier of Kenya as "Greater Somalia." Many government documents are cited.

2658. Somali Republic. Ministry of Foreign Affairs. THE SOMALI PEOPLES' QUEST FOR UNITY. Mogadiscio, 1965. 32 p. map, tables.

Official statement of "Greater Somalia" issues in border disputes with Ethiopia and Kenya.

2659. Somali Republic. Presidency of the Council of Ministers. GOVERNMENT ACTIVITIES FROM INDEPENDENCE UNTIL TODAY (JULY 1, 1960-DECEMBER 31, 1963). Mogadiscio, 1964. 199 l. [i.e., 50] p. illus. Printed by Artigrafiche Stella, Rome.

Handsome and sophisticated report of what was accomplished in its first three years by the government of independent Somalia in the fields of legislation, economics, education, and social welfare. The 50 pages in Roman numbering at the end give texts of addresses by the Prime Minister, Hon. Dr. Abdirashid Ali Shermarke.

2660. Technical Assistance Mission to the Trust Territory of Somaliland under Italian Administration. THE TRUST TERRITORY OF SOMALILAND UNDER ITALIAN ADMINISTRATION. Report prepared jointly for the Government of Italy by an expert appointed by the United Nations Technical Assistance Administration and by experts appointed respectively by the Food and Agriculture Organization of the United Nations, the United Nations Educational, Scientific, and Cultural Organization, and the World Health Organization. New York, 1952. 343 p. illus., maps, tables. (United Nations [Document] ST/TAA/K Somaliland/1)

Includes bibliographies.

Processed publication of the United Nations. Six experts had spent three months making an extended survey of the economic needs of the territory, touring the country widely, talking with local officials and representatives on all levels, visiting all institutions. They reported in great detail, offering advice on many points. Their impressions were not optimistic regarding a viable economy.

2661. Thompson, Virginia, and Richard Adloff. DJIBOUTI AND THE HORN OF AFRICA. Stanford, Calif., Stanford University Press, 1968. 246 p.

See no. 2094 for annotation.

2662. U.S. Operations Mission to Italy. [Reports] Rome, 1950-

This mission, later under the International Cooperation
Administration, began operations in 1950 as the ECA [Economic
Cooperation Administration] Special Mission to Italy. In that
year the United States suggested to the Italian Foreign Office
that Somaliland be included in the Dependent Overseas Territory
Program, and visits of inspection to Somaliland by American
technicians were undertaken at once. Their reports were brought
out as mimeographed pamphlets, in limited editions. Among them
are the following:

a) SOMALIA AGRICULTURAL PROJECTS. By W. E. Corfitzen and
     Grover Kinsey. Rome, Sept. 1950. 36 l.

b) A RECONNAISSANCE GROUND-WATER SURVEY OF SOMALIA, EAST AFRICA.
     By Thomas P. Ahrens. Rome, 1951. 270 p. illus.

c) ROAD STUDY IN SOMALIA, EAST AFRICA. By H. A. Van Dyke.
     Rome, Dec. 31, 1953. 105 l.

d) PORT SURVEY IN SOMALIA, EAST AFRICA. By Frederick G.
     Reinicke. Rome, Jan. 10, 1954. 40 l.

e) THE MINERAL DEPOSITS OF SOMALIA. By Ralph J. Holmes. Rome,
     Mar. 1954. 56 l. illus.

f) PLANS AND SCHEDULES FOR SOMALIA ECONOMIC DEVELOPMENT. By
     W. E. Corfitzen. Rome, June 28, 1954. 34 p.

g) PROPOSED PROGRAM FOR AGRICULTURAL TECHNICAL ASSISTANCE FOR
     SOMALIA. By W. W. Worzella and A. L. Musson. Rome,
     Aug. 9, 1954. 17 l.

h) A FISHERIES RECONNAISSANCE, SOMALIA, EAST AFRICA. By Ralph
     L. Johnson. Rome, June 18, 1956. 29 l.

i) LIVESTOCK SURVEY, SOMALIA, EAST AFRICA. By C. L. McColloch.
     Rome, Feb. 1, 1957. 15 l.

j) FORESTRY AND RANGE MANAGEMENT SURVEY, SOMALIA, EAST AFRICA.
     By Marvin Klemme. Rome, Feb. 28, 1957. 23 l. map.

2663. U.S. Operations Mission to the Somali Republic. INTER-RIVER
     ECONOMIC EXPLORATION: THE SOMALI REPUBLIC. Washington,
     1961. xxxi, 347 p. illus., maps, diagrs., tables.

The Mission has continued under the new name after the independence date of Somalia, through 1961 under the International
Cooperation Administration, from 1962 under AID (Agency for Inter-

national Development). This big report contains economic data and estimates for development by irrigation and other measures of the land between the Giuba and Uebi Scebeli rivers (these names have varied spellings) in southern Somalia. There are somewhat optimistic forecasts of what might be accomplished in a 20-year program with large investment. Other reports are submitted, often in working-paper form. One more paper of 1961 available for distribution is TWENTY QUESTIONS AND ANSWERS REGARDING THE SOMALI REPUBLIC (18 p.).

SUDAN

Note: In selecting references on the Sudan, the choice has not been restricted to works entirely or in large part on the southern Sudan. The general works are chiefly concerned with the North whose culture belongs more to the Middle East.

Bibliographies

2664. African Bibliographic Center, Washington, D.C. A CURRENT BIBLIOGRAPHY
       ON SUDANESE AFFAIRS: A SELECT BIBLIOGRAPHY FROM 1960-1964. Compiled by Daniel G. Matthews. Washington, 1965. 28 p. (Special
       Bibliographic Series, v. 3, no. 4)

2665. Andrew, G. S. SOURCES OF INFORMATION ON THE GEOLOGY OF THE ANGLO-
       EGYPTIAN SUDAN. Khartoum, 1946. 36 p. (Geological Survey
       Department Bulletin no. 3)

2666. Dagher, Joseph Assaad. SUDANESE BIBLIOGRAPHY, ARABIC SOURCES, 1875-
       1967. Beirut, 1968. 1 v. In Arabic.

       The first bibliography of Arabic language writings and translations by Sudanese writers, this work contains approximately 2,000 entries covering books and periodical articles. There is an author index.

2667. Hill, Richard L. A BIBLIOGRAPHY OF THE ANGLO-EGYPTIAN SUDAN, FROM
       THE EARLIEST TIMES TO 1937. London, Oxford University Press,
       H. Milford, 1939. xi, 213 p.

       A justly celebrated area bibliography by an officer of the Sudan Civil Service. The list, covering books, periodical articles, and documents in Western languages and Arabic from Herodotus, ca. 457 B.C., to the year of its completion, is classified under disciplines and sub-disciplines according to a five-page table of contents. Within

the subsections the entries, set down in the briefest identifiable
form, are arranged in chronological order. There are indexes of
persons and subjects.

2668. Ibrahim, Asma, and Abdel Rahman el-Nasri. "Sudan Bibliography,
           1959-1963." SUDAN NOTES AND RECORDS, no. 46, 1965: 130-166.

        A comprehensive "Sudan Bibliography" was carried regularly
(1921-56) in the semiannual SUDAN NOTES AND RECORDS (see no. 2706).

2669. Ibrahim-Hilmy, Prince. THE LITERATURE OF EGYPT AND THE SOUDAN FROM
           THE EARLIEST TIMES TO THE YEAR 1885 [i.e., 1887] INCLUSIVE;
           A BIBLIOGRAPHY: COMPRISING PRINTED BOOKS, PERIODICAL WRITINGS,
           AND PAPERS OF LEARNED SOCIETIES; MAPS AND CHARTS; ANCIENT
           PAPYRI, MANUSCRIPTS, DRAWINGS, ETC. London, Trübner & Co.,
           1886-88. 2 v. 398, 459 p.

        A massive compilation, this basic bibliography for the early
period gives complete data for roughly 20,000 titles. Arrangement
is by author, with some subject and form headings.

2670. Khartoum. University. Library. THESES ON THE SUDAN AND BY SUDANESE
           ACCEPTED FOR HIGHER DEGREES. No. 2. Compiled by Maymouna Mir-
           ghani Hamza, assisted by the library staff. Khartoum, 1966.
           63 p.

2671. Knight, R. L., and B. M. Boyns. AGRICULTURAL SCIENCE IN THE SUDAN:
           A BIBLIOGRAPHY WITH ABSTRACTS. Arbroath, Scotland, T. Buncle,
           1950. 251 p.

        Survey of all publications in the field of agricultural science
having direct relation to the Sudan, bringing together the research
carried out in the country over 50 years under British administration. Many of the contributions had been previously published
in obscure journals. Abstracts of the less readily accessible papers
are included.

2672. Köhler, Oswin. GESCHICHTE DER ERFORSCHUNG DER NILOTISCHEN SPRACHEN.
           Berlin, D. Reimer, 1955. 85 p. (Afrika and Ubersee, Beiheft 28)

        A full bibliography including earlier sources for Nilotic and
related languages.

2673. el-Nasri, Abdel Rahman. A BIBLIOGRAPHY OF THE SUDAN, 1938-1958.
           London, Published on behalf of the University of Khartoum by
           Oxford University Press, Nov. 1962. 171 p.

Compiled by the librarian of the University of Khartoum. This
bibliography containing 2,763 numbered entries updates Hill's work
(above) and follows the same arrangement by subject: agriculture
(general, by provinces and localities, crops, irrigation, soil conservation and rural water development, agricultural research);
anthropology (general, by tribes); bibliography (items 630-651);
biography, etc. There are subject and author indexes.

2674. Santandrea, Stefano. BIBLIOGRAFIA DI STUDI AFRICANI DELLA MISSIONE
DELL'AFRICA CENTRALE. Verona, Istituto Missioni Africane,
1948. 167 p. (Museum combonianum, no. 1)

Most entries are annotated and are for works published from the
middle 1800's, with Italian and German works predominating. Part 1
deals with archaeology, Mahdism, travels, agriculture, people and
customs, religion, schools, slavery, music, art, and folklore. Part
2 covers ethnic groups arranged by area, and Part 3 traces the history of the Central African mission from 1840 to 1948. There is a
name index.

2675. SUDAN BIBLIOGRAPHY BULLETIN. 1967-? Khartoum. [Annual?]

Not available for consultation.

2676. Twining, W. L., and others. "Bibliography of Sudan Law, 1." SUDAN
LAW JOURNAL AND REPORT, 1960: 313-334.

Reference Works

2677. American University, Washington, D.C. Special Operations Research
Office. AREA HANDBOOK FOR THE REPUBLIC OF THE SUDAN. 2d ed.
By John A. Cookson and others. Washington, U.S. Govt. Print.
Off., 1964. 473 p. map, tables. (Department of the Army
Pamphlet no. 550-27)

Includes bibliographies.

Background study in the country series being prepared at
American University. Bibliographies of sources follow comprehensive surveys of anthropological, sociological, political, economic,
and military aspects.

2678. Barbour, Kenneth M. THE REPUBLIC OF THE SUDAN: A REGIONAL GEOGRAPHY.
London, University of London Press, 1961. 292 p. illus.,
maps.

Bibliographical footnotes.

Physical and economic geography, emphasizing regional variation in agriculture and animal husbandry and the spread of cash
economy.

2679. Beshir, Mohamed Omer. THE SOUTHERN SUDAN: BACKGROUND TO CONFLICT.
New York, Praeger, 1968. 192 p. maps.

Defense of government program to pacify and integrate the
pagan and Catholic peoples of the South.

2680. Bonfanti, Adriano, ed. TESTIMONIANZE SULLA VIOLAZIONE DEI DIRITTI
UMANI DA PARTE DEI SOLDATI E POLIZIOTTI DEL SUDAN SETTENTIONALE
CONTRO LA POPULAZIONE NERA DEL SUDAN MERIDIONALE DALLA FINE
DEL 1963 AI PRIMI MESI DEL 1964: DEPOSIZIONI DEI MISSIONARI
COMBONIANA ESPULSI DAN SUDAN MERIODIONALE AI PRIMI DEL MARZO
1964. Verona, 1964. 1 v. (unpaged). fascims. 34 cm.

Missionaries' complaints against oppression of the South by the
Muslim-dominated North.

2681. Collins, Robert O. THE SOUTHERN SUDAN, 1883-1898: A STRUGGLE FOR
CONTROL. New Haven, Yale University Press, 1962. 212 p.
(Yale Historical Publications, Miscellany, no. 76)

Bibliography: p. 192-198.

By an American scholar who has done exhaustive work in the
Sudanese archives at Khartoum among the documents of the Mahdist
State. He examines in detail all actions of the Mahdiya in the
southern Sudan from the first appearance of the agents in the Bahr
el Ghazal in 1882 to raise the tribes for the "holy war" to the
time of Kitchener's defeat of the Khalifa and the end of the era.
The bibliography carries evaluative annotations of many items.

2682. Collins, Robert O., and Robert L. Tignor. EGYPT AND THE SUDAN.
Englewood Cliffs, N.J., Prentice-Hall, 1967. 180 p. (The
Modern Nations in Historical Perspective)

Bibliography: p. 165-171.

Covers the period from 1800 to the present and provides a
background to contemporary Sudan and Egypt.

2683. Diplomatic Press. SUDAN TRADE DIRECTORY. 1957/58- London, Diplo-
       matic Press and Publishing Co. illus., ports.

         Like the other directories issued for African countries (e.g.,
       Nigeria, Ghana) by the Diplomatic Press, this volume is prepared
       with the cooperation of the information services of the Sudan
       government. The eighth edition covers 1966-67 (108 p.). Besides
       encylopedic information on all phases of the government and economic
       life of the country, it includes a classified trade index and an
       index of advertisers. Earlier editions had material on the cultural
       life and a biographical section; the title varies. The Diplomatic
       Press and Publishing Co. has also issued a smaller SUDAN TRADE AND
       INVESTMENT GUIDE (1960, 84 p.).

2684. Ethnographic Survey of Africa: East Central Africa. London, Inter-
       national African Institute.

         For the general note on this series, see no. 980. The follow-
       ing volumes relate to tribes of the Sudan:

       a)   Part 4.   THE NILOTES OF THE ANGLO-EGYPTIAN SUDAN AND UGANDA.
                       By Audrey J. Butt. 1952. 198 p.

       b)   Part 6.   THE NORTHERN NILO-HAMITES. By G. W. B. Huntingford.
                       1953. 108 p.

                       Includes the Bari, Lotuko, and Lokoya.

       c)   Part 9.   THE AZANDE AND RELATED PEOPLES OF THE ANGLO-EGYPTIAN
                       SUDAN AND BELGIAN CONGO. By P. T. W. Baxter and
                       Audrey Butt. 1953. 152 p.

         All ethnological studies of the southern Sudan are indebted for
       their foundations to the pioneer work by Charles G. and Brenda Z.
       Seligman: PAGAN TRIBES OF THE NILOTIC SUDAN (London, Routledge,
       1932, xxiv, 565 p., illus., 60 plates, maps, fold. geneal. table;
       Ethnology of Africa).

2685. Evans-Pritchard, E. E. THE NUER.... Oxford, Clarendon Press, 1940.
       271 p. illus., plates, maps, diagr.

       _____. WITCHCRAFT, ORACLES AND MAGIC AMONG THE AZANDE. Oxford,
       Clarendon Press, 1937. 558 p.

         Outstanding works by the leading anthropologist of the Sudan.

2686. Gaitskell, Arthur. GEZIRA: A STORY OF DEVELOPMENT IN THE SUDAN.
       London, Faber and Faber, 1959. 372 p. illus., ports., maps.
       (Colonial and Comparative Studies)

"References": p. 358-368.

By the first chairman and managing director of the Sudan Gezira Board. This is the standard account of the great irrigation scheme in the area called the Gezira, below the confluence of the Blue and the White Nile at Khartoum, by which there have been brought into production a million acres of the long-staple cotton that is the Sudan's chief export crop.

2687. Gray, Richard. A HISTORY OF THE SOUTHERN SUDAN, 1839-1889. London, Oxford University Press, 1961. 219 p. maps.

Bibliography: p. 204-211.

A valuable history. The chapters cover background and the first Egyptian expeditions, 1839-41; the contest and deadlock between European ivory traders, slave traders, and the first Christian missionaries; administration for the Khedive Isma'il by Baker and Gordon; the fight against the slave trade; the Mahdiya; and British interests and the southern Sudan.

2688. Hasan, Yūsuf Fadl. THE ARABS AND THE SUDAN: FROM THE SEVENTH TO THE EARLY SIXTEENTH CENTURY. Edinburgh, University Press, 1967. xiii, 298 p. plates, map, geneal. tables.

Bibliography: p. 265-274.

An enlightening readable study by a Sudanese professor at the University of Khartoum of the geographic, political, and economic forces that shaped the Sudan. Based largely on Arab sources, the work constitutes the first truly comprehensive examination of the two major aspects of Sudanese history: the relations between the Muslims and the Christian kingdoms of Nuba and 'Alwa (and the Beja country); and the Arab penetration into the Sudan which led ultimately to the Arabization and Islamization of the country. In a valuable appendix the author presents a survey of the major Arab sources of the history of the Sudan in the Middle Ages. Included is an analytical index.

2689. Henderson, Kenneth D. D. SUDAN REPUBLIC. London, E. Benn, 1965; New York, Praeger, 1966. 256 p. maps (1 fold.). (Nations of the Modern World)

Bibliography: p. 229-233.

The author, who spent 36 years in the political service of the Sudan, offers "a personal, but not, I hope, a subjective" account of the new Sudan. The opening chapters provide a geo-

graphic, ethnic, and historical framework for the core of the
book, which deals with the political and administrative training
period and preliminary trials. The text ends with a chapter on
the problem of the South (several documents are included) and
one on the Oct. 1964 revolution. The bibliography is expository
and there is an analytical index.

2690. Hill, Richard Leslie. A BIOGRAPHICAL DICTIONARY OF THE SUDAN.
London, Cass, 1967. 409 p.

This second edition includes a list of notes and corrections
(p. 395-409). The first edition, entitled A BIOGRAPHICAL DIC-
TIONARY OF THE ANGLO-EGYPTIAN SUDAN, appeared in 1951. There are
over 1,900 biographies of people who died before 1948; inclusion
has been based primarily on availability of information. Among
them are the foreign born who have played a significant part in
Sudanese history. Included are a wide range of personalities,
from Diocletian, a Roman emperor of the third century, to Logan
Pasha, a British officer in the Egyptian army in Khartoum in the
early 1900's. A glossary gives Arabic and Turkish ranks, titles,
and other designations.

2691. Hill, Richard Leslie. EGYPT IN THE SUDAN, 1820-1881. Issued under
the auspices of the Royal Institute of International Affairs.
London, New York, Oxford University Press, 1959. xi,
188 p. fold. map. (Middle Eastern Monographs, no. 2)

Bibliography: p. 171-177.

_____. SUDAN TRANSPORT: A HISTORY OF RAILWAY, MARINE AND RIVER
SERVICES IN THE REPUBLIC OF THE SUDAN. London, Oxford University Press, 1965. 188 p. illus., maps, ports.

Bibliography: p. 173-182.

The first volume is a concentrated history covering the period
of Turko-Egyptian conquest and rule (or misrule) of the Sudan up to
the beginning of the Mahdist rebellion. The second study is a good
historical survey of the transportation system of the Sudan.

2692. Holt, Peter M. THE MAHDIST STATE IN THE SUDAN, 1881-1898: A STUDY
OF ITS ORIGINS, DEVELOPMENT, AND OVERTHROW. Oxford, Clarendon
Press, 1958. 264 p. illus.

Bibliography: p. 248-252.

_____. A MODERN HISTORY OF THE SUDAN, FROM THE FUNJ SULTANATE TO
THE PRESENT DAY. New York, Grove Press, 1961. 241 p. illus.,
maps.

Bibliography: p. 221-227.

Two books by a specialist in Sudanese studies who was formerly archivist of the Sudanese government and then a professor at the University of Khartoum. In the first study he examines the history of the Mahdiya less from the "romantic" reporting on the European side than from the archives of the Mahdist State, to which he had access. Dr. Holt's second history, covering as it does the Turko-Egyptian period, the Mahdist revolution, the condominium, and the first years of the republic, is necessarily highly compressed. The theme is the interplay in the Sudan of Arab-African indigenous tradition and Egyptian and British influence. Sketch maps, notes, a select bibliography, and an index add to the usefulness of the work.

2693. MacMichael, Sir Harold A. THE ANGLO-EGYPTIAN SUDAN. London, Faber
        & Faber, 1934. 288 p.

Comprehensive standard work by a former colonial official in the Sudan (1905-34). This is an account of the country from Gordon's death--the Kitchener campaign, the final British conquest, the establishment of the condominium which gave Britain charge of government, and the evolution of the savage and war-torn country into what the author considered a near model of peaceful administration and agricultural experimentation. Sources are cited in footnotes.

2694. MacMichael, Sir Harold A. A HISTORY OF THE ARABS IN THE SUDAN; AND
        SOME ACCOUNT OF THE PEOPLE WHO PRECEDED THEM AND OF THE TRIBES
        INHABITING DARFUR. Cambridge, Eng., University Press, 1922.
        2 v. xx, 347; viii, 488 p. tables.

Reissue, London, Cass; New York, Barnes & Noble, 1967.

Bibliography: v. 1, p. xiii-xxii.

A scholarly basic study, going deeply into classical authorities and technical anthropology. The entire second volume is devoted to Sudanese manuscripts, which are for the most part genealogies.

Another reissue brought out by Cass and by Barnes & Noble in 1967 is Sir Harold's THE TRIBES OF NORTHERN AND CENTRAL KORDOFAN (Cambridge, Eng., University Press, 1912, xv, 259 p.).

2695. El Mahdi, Mandour. A SHORT HISTORY OF THE SUDAN. London, Oxford
University Press, 1965. 154 p. plates, maps.

An outline history of the Sudan from earliest times to independence in 1962. Intended for the layman, the book emphasizes emergent social and political patterns. The author is principal of the Institute of Education at Bakht er Ruda.

2696. Oduho, Joseph, and William Deng. THE PROBLEM OF THE SOUTHERN
        SUDAN. Issued under the auspices of the Institute of Race
        Relations. London, Oxford University Press, 1963. 60 p.

An indictment of the government of Sudan and a statement of the case for Southern Sudan by two leaders of the south.

2697. Santandrea, Stefano. AGGIORNAMENTI SUL GRUPPO NDOGO DEL BAHR EL
        GHAZAL (SUDAN); TRIBU: NDOGO, SERE, BAI, BVIRI E GOLO.
        Ritmo e musica dei balli Bor e Bviri [di] Filiberto Giorgetti.
        Bologna, Editrice Nigrizia, 1966. 45, 242 p. illus., fold.
        col. map. (Museum combonianum, no. 19)

In addition to this ethnological work by Father Santandrea, another recent title pertaining to the peoples in the Bahr el Ghazal is one on the Dinka by Arturo Nebel: I DINCA SONO COSI: RICORDI DI UNA VITA FRA I DINCA DEL BAHR EL GHAZAL SUDAN (Bologna, Editrice Nigrizia, 1968, 266 p., illus.; Museum combonianum, no. 21).

2698. Shinnie, P. L. MEROE: A CIVILIZATION OF THE SUDAN. New York,
        Praeger, 1967. 229 p. illus., maps.

Valuable survey of the ancient and relatively unstudied history of the kingdom of Meroe which played such an important role in the cultural development of Black Africa.

2699. Squires, H. C. THE SUDAN MEDICAL SERVICE: AN EXPERIMENT IN
        SOCIAL MEDICINE. London, Heinemann, 1958. 138 p. illus.,
        maps.

The author was associated with the Sudan Medical Service for almost 43 years as doctor, teacher and consultant. Provides a history of the medical services and training and a description of diseases endemic to the Sudan and of epidemics.

2700. Sudan. Commission of Inquiry into the Disturbances in the South-
        ern Sudan. SOUTHERN SUDAN DISTURBANCES, AUGUST 1955: REPORT.
        [Khartoum] 1956. 127 p. fold. maps.

The mistrust of the tribes in the southern Sudan for policies of the northern Sudan leaders and parties came to a head a few months before the independence date with "incidents of mutiny and disorder," particularly in Equatoria province and among the Southern Police Corps. This is the detailed report of the Commission of Inquiry, which was submitted to the new Minister of the Interior of the Sudan Republic--a rare document, a copy of which has been secured by the Library of Congress.

2701. Sudan. Jonglei Investigation Team. THE EQUATORIAL NILE PROJECT AND ITS EFFECT IN THE ANGLO_EGYPTIAN SUDAN: BEING THE REPORT OF THE JONGLEI INVESTIGATION TEAM. [Khartoum?] 1954. 5 v. (v.1-3, p. 1-1077; v. 4, 8 maps, about 240 figs.; v. 5, lxix p.).

Includes bibliographies.

Report on effects to be expected from the project for drainage of the Sudd--the great swampy, weed-infested areas of the southern Sudan. This had been outlined by Dr. Harold E. Hurst and his colleagues of the Egyptian Physical Department in one volume of their series of papers, THE NILE BASIN (Cairo, Govt. Press, 1931-; Vol. VII, THE FUTURE CONSERVATION OF THE NILE). Modifications were made in 1948. The Jonglei Investigation Team of engineers, agricultural specialists, and other officials of the Sudan Political Service was appointed in 1946 to study the White Nile system in detail, ignoring political concerns, in order to determine the best form of river control for the benefit of all inhabitants of the Nile Valley. The report, issued following interim reports in 1946, 1947, and 1948, was prepared under the chairmanship of P. P. Howell. It is in five volumes: I, A SURVEY OF THE AREA AFFECTED; II, THE EQUATORIAL NILE PROJECT: ITS EFFECTS AND REMEDIES; III, SPECIAL INVESTIGATIONS AND EXPERIMENTAL DATA; IV, MAPS AND DIAGRAMS; V, INTRODUCTION AND SUMMARY. The recommendations in the final volume called for a revised operation of the Egyptian-sponsored project to reduce the losses in riverine pasture and fisheries which would seriously affect the way of life of the 660,000 pastoral tribesmen of the area.

2702. Sudan. Southern Development Investigation Team. NATURAL RESOURCES AND DEVELOPMENT POTENTIAL IN THE SOUTHERN PROVINCES OF THE SUDAN: A PRELIMINARY REPORT, 1954. London, Sudan Govt., 1955. xxii, 262 p. tables.

Includes bibliographies.

This group, under the chairmanship of Dr. P. P. Howell of the Sudan Political Service and comprising officials of various branches of the Service in the southern Sudan, functioned in the spring of 1954. Their report is wider in scope than that of the Jonglei Investigation Team, on which a number of the same specialists, including the chairman, had served; it covers the entire physical and economic picture, present and possible future, of the three provinces of the southern Sudan (Upper Nile, Bahr el Ghazal, Equatoria). The 32-page introduction is a summarization of the development problems, under the same headings as the following technical appendixes (p. 35-262), which are in two groups, "The Present Position" and "Potential Development." Aspects covered in factual text and tables are physical environment, ecology, inhabitants, crop husbandry, animal husbandry, fisheries, water resources, communications and trade, and other services. In the second group there are also examined the potential development of forestry, big-game hunting and tourist trade, and possible exploitation of the estimated (exaggeratedly, the reports say) 5,000 square miles of papyrus.

2703. SUDAN ALMANAC: AN OFFICIAL HANDBOOK. 1903- Khartoum, Govt. Printing Press. Annual. (1967 ed., 312 p., fold. map, tables; bibliography: p. 307-309)

Originally compiled by the Intelligence Department, Cairo, now by the Central Office of Information of the Republic of the Sudan. It contains a vast store of information about all aspects of administration, history, ethnology and religion, geology and climate (including data on the Nile water levels), agriculture, economy, health and welfare, and many other matters of interest.

2704. SUDAN DIRECTORY. Khartoum. Annual.

Conventional trade directory, published by Editions Fischer in Cairo, with text in English and Arabic. The Library of Congress has issues from 1921 (incomplete).

2705. SUDAN JOURNAL OF ADMINISTRATION AND DEVELOPMENT. v. 1, no. 1- Jan. 1965- Khartoum. illus. Annual.

Journal of the Institute of Public Administration, Republic of the Sudan. Contents, in English and Arabic, cover not only the Sudan but also other areas of Africa and sometimes pertain simply to the art and science of administration in general. The first issue totaled 142 pages, including 34 in Arabic. The Institute also publishes various series: Annual Reports, Proceedings, Handbooks, Occasional Papers.

2706. SUDAN NOTES AND RECORDS. no. 1- 1918- Khartoum. Semiannual.

Journal of the Sudan Philosophical Society and important organ for the many scholars who participated in the British civil service in the Anglo-Egyptian Sudan. It has been continued under the independent state. Contributions are in many disciplines, including natural sciences, history, and social sciences. Important also is SUDAN LAW JOURNAL, 1966- (Faculty of Law, University of Khartoum).

2707. Tothill, John D., ed. AGRICULTURE IN THE SUDAN: BEING A HAND-
        BOOK OF AGRICULTURE AS PRACTISED IN THE ANGLO-EGYPTIAN SUDAN.
        By numerous authors. London, Oxford University Press, 1948.
        xviii, 974 p. illus., maps.

        Includes bibliographies.

        Articles by a group of high-ranking specialists, in a sym-
        posium edited by the former director of the Sudan Department of
        Agriculture and Forests. The chapters are on general and specific
        aspects of agriculture; many are followed by selective reading
        lists.

2708. Trimingham, J. Spencer. ISLAM IN THE SUDAN. London, New York,
        Oxford University Press, 1949. 280 p.

        Reissue, New York, Barnes & Noble, 1965.

        Useful background study of the entire country, its history
        and culture, by the former secretary of the Church Mission Society
        in the Sudan. The writer's aim was to give a composite picture
        of the people both as Moslems and as Sudanese, with emphasis on
        the role of Islam in shaping present-day society. In the same year
        Mr. Trimingham published THE CHRISTIAN CHURCH IN THE POST-WAR
        SUDAN (London, World Dominion Press, 1949, 44 p.), a survey of the
        educational work of the Christian missions in this country of
        devoted Moslems, a large number of whom are animated by Pan-
        Arabism. Another of his works is a useful grammar and phrase
        book, SUDAN COLLOQUIAL ARABIC (London, Oxford University Press,
        1946, 176 p.).

2709. Tucker, A. N. THE EASTERN SUDANIC LANGUAGES, Vol. I. London,
        Published for the International African Institute by the
        Oxford University Press, 1940. 434 p.

        Study of the Azande, Moru-Madi, Bongo-Baka-Bagirmi, and
        Ndogo-Sere groups of the Sudan and the Belgian Congo. It begins
        with a short section on "distribution" and history, to which three
        chapters (55 p.) are devoted. The second section contains in-
        tensive linguistic studies of these groups. There are two indexes,
        a "Tribal and Historical Index" (p. 419-427) and a "Linguistic
        Index" (p. 428-434).

2710. U.S. Department of the Interior. Office of Geography. SUDAN:
        OFFICIAL STANDARD NAMES APPROVED BY THE UNITED STATES BOARD
        ON GEOGRAPHIC NAMES. Washington, U.S. Govt. Print. Off., June
        1962. xi, 358 p. map. (25,000 names) (Gazetteer no. 68)

        See note on series, no. 484.

CHAPTER 41

PORTUGUESE AFRICA

Atlases

2711. Portugal. Junta de Investigações do Ultramar. ATLAS DE PORTUGAL
        ULTRAMARINO E DAS GRANDES VIAGENS PORTUGUESAS DE DESCOBRIMENTO
        E EXPANSAO. Lisboa, 1948. 8 p. 110 col. maps.

        The Junta, the leading center for all studies of overseas
Portugal, was established as the Junta das Missões Geográficas
e de Investigações do Ultramar. The shorter name has come into
official use during the last few years.

2712. Portugal. Junta de Investigações do Ultramar. ATLAS MISSIONARIO
        PORTUGUES. Prepared by the Missão para o Estudo da Missiono-
        logia Africana. 2d ed. Lisboa, 1964. 184 p. fold. maps,
        charts.

        Handsomely printed, with 46 maps and charts of Roman Catholic
and Protestant missions in the Portuguese overseas possessions.
Included are locations of stations and descriptions of the dioceses.

2713. Portugal. Junta de Investigações do Ultramar. CARTAS E PLANOS
        HIDROGRAFICOS DE PROVINCIAS ULTRAMARINOS PORTUGUESAS. Lisboa,
        1959. 33 p. (chiefly col. maps).

        Separate from GARCIA DE ORTA, v. 7, no. 1, 1959.

        See also nos. 2758 and 2854.

828

Bibliographies

2714.   Carvalho Dias, Fernando de.   "O Ultramar português e a expansão
            na Africa e no Oriente: Breve notícia dos documentos manu-
            scritos de Fundo Geral da Biblioteca Nacional de Lisboa;
            extracto do fíchero geral." GARCIA DE ORTA, v. 3, no. 3-4,
            1955; v. 4, nos. 1, 2, 3, 4, 1956.

2715.   Carvalho Dias, Fernando de.   "Notícias dos documentos da Secçao
            dos Reservados, Fundo Geral, da Biblioteca Nacional de
            Lisboa respeitantes às províncias ultramarinas de Angola,
            Cabo Verde, Guiné, Macau, Moçambique, S. Tomé e Príncipe e
            Timor." GARCIA DE ORTA, v. 5, nos. 2, 3, 1957.

2716.   Chilcote, Ronald H.   EMERGING NATIONALISM IN PORTUGUESE AFRICA:
            A BIBLIOGRAPHY OF DOCUMENTARY EPHEMERA THROUGH 1965.
            Stanford, Calif., Hoover Institution, Stanford University,
            1969. 114 p. (Hoover Institution Bibliographical Series,
            no. 36)

        This bibliography presents a wide range of viewpoints, in-
cluding the official Portuguese position, the various African
nationalist movements, and Portuguese in opposition. It covers
Portuguese Africa in general, the various territories, and United
Nations documents on Portuguese Africa, as well as other sources.
The publication distinguishes between ephemera and other material.
This major bibliographical work will soon be supplemented by the
author's EMERGING NATIONALISM IN PORTUGUESE AFRICA: DOCUMENTARY
EPHEMERA THROUGH 1965. This will be a major collection of
documents on African nationalism in the Portuguese colonies, and
the most extensive publication of its kind.

2717.   "Documenting Portuguese Africa." AFRICANA NEWSLETTER, v. 1, no.
            3, Summer 1963: 16-36.

        This survey of sources, archives, and movements concerned
with the Portuguese in Africa is in four main parts: serial
publications of Portugal and Portuguese Africa; archives, libraries,
and institutes, with country subdivisions; general works published
since 1945; political groups in Portuguese Africa, with country
subdivisions.

2718. Gonçalves, Francisco, and Jaime Caseiro. BIBLIOGRAFIA GEOLOGICA
DO ULTRAMAR PORTUGUES. Lisboa, Junta de Investigações do
Ultramar, 1959. lxxiii, 272 p.

2719. Gonçalves, José Júlio. "Bibliografia antropológica do Ultramar
português." In Portugal, Agência Geral do Ultramar.
BOLETIM GERAL DO ULTRAMAR, ano 37, 1961: Mar.-Apr., p. 483-
499; Oct.-Dec., p. 431-471.

A set of references printed in the form of cards that might
be clipped for use in a file, though the entries appear on both
sides of the pages.

2720. Pélissier, René. "Eléments de bibliographie: L'Afrique portugaise
dans les publications de la Junta de Investigações do Ultramar
(Lisbonne)." GENEVE-AFRIQUE, v. 4, no. 2, 1965: 249-270.

Excellent critical review of major publications of the Junta.
Arrangement is by subject and by territory.

2721. Portugal. Agência Geral do Ultramar. CATALOGO DAS EDICOES. Lisboa,
1966. 249 p.

Supplement, 1969. 49 p.

2722. Portugal. Centro de Estudos de Antrobiología. BIBLIOGRAFIA DO
CENTRO DE ESTUDOS DE ETHNOLOGIA DO ULTRAMAR. By M. Emília de
Castro e Almeida, M. Cecilia de Castro, and José D. Lampreria.
Lisboa, 1964. 163 p.

Text in Portuguese, English, and French.

2723. Portugal. Instituto Nacional de Estatística. BIBLIOGRAFIA SOBRE
ECONOMIA PORTUGUESA, 1948/49-. Lisboa, 1958- Annual.

Covers fully Portuguese overseas provinces.

2724. Portugal. Junta de Investigações du Ultramar. CATALOGO DIDASCALICO
DAS PUBLICACOES EDITADAS E SUBSIDIADAS PELA JUNTA DE INVESTI-
GACOES DO ULTRAMAR. Lisboa, 1959. 45 p.

Supplement to Dec. 1960. 17 p. (Separate from GARCIA DE ORTA,
v. 8, 1960)

This comprehensive catalogue of the many works published or
sponsored by the Junta is supplemented from time to time in GARCIA

830

DE ORTA. Its contents include: ANAIS (analytics of v. 1, 1946-
v. 12, 1957, in the 1959 catalogue)--titles in history, zoology,
legislation, geography, botany, technology, meteorology, anthropology and ethnology, geology and paleontology, marine biology,
phytosanitation, etc.; Coloquios; Estudos de ciências políticas e
sociais; Estudos, ensaios e documentos; GARCIA DE ORTA (analytics
of contents of all issues).

2725. Portugal. Junta de Investigações do Ultramar. Centro de Documenta-
            cão Científica Ultramarina. BIBLIOGRAFIA CIENTIFICA DA JUNTA DE
            INVESTIGACOES DO ULTRAMAR. v. 1- 1958- Lisboa, 1960- Annual.

        As complete as possible a list of studies and papers, along
with analytics of contents of the journal GARCIA DE ORTA. The
first compilation, covering the period 1936-58, contained 1,697
references, based on the card file of the Centro, printed on one
side only (371 l.) and suitable for clipping for a card file. The
volume for publications of 1959 added 382 card references. Entries
are classed by the Universal Decimal Classification, mainly in the
social sciences, pure and applied sciences, and geography. There
is an author index.

2726. Portugal. Junta de Investigações do Ultramar. Centro de
            Documentação Científica Ultramarina. BOLETIM ANALITICO.
            no. 1- 1959- Lisboa. Every 2 months.

2727. Portugal. Junta de Investigações do Ultramar. Centro de
            Documentação Científica Ultramarina. BOLETIM BIBLIOGRAFICO.
            no. 1- 1958- Lisboa. Mimeographed. Every 2 months.

2728. Portugal. Junta de Investigações do Ultramar. Centro de
            Documentação Científica Ultramarina. CATALOGO DAS PUBLICACOES
            PERIODICOS E SERIADOS EXISTENTES NA BIBLIOTECA DE JUNTA.
            Lisboa, 1958. 158 p.

2729. Portugal. Junta de Investigações do Ultramar. Centro de
            Documentação Científica Ultramarina. DOCUMENTACAO ESPECIAL
            ELABORADA PELO CENTRO DE DOCUM. CIENT. ULTRAM. (NOS. D1 A
            D199, 1957 A 1966). Lisboa, Dec. 31, 1966. 13 l.

2730. Portugal. Junta de Investigações du Ultramar. Centro de
            Documentação Científica Ultramarina. INSTITUICOES PORTUGUESAS
            DE INTERESSE ULTRAMARINO. Lisboa, 1964. 138 p. Processed.

_____. _____. _____. PERIODICOS PORTUGUESES DE
INTERESSE ULTRAMARINO ACTUALMENTE EM PUBLICACAO. 2d ed.
Lisboa, 1967. 59 p. Processed.

    Comprehensive listings of Portuguese institutions and period-
icals concerned with overseas development. Both are classified
according to the Dewey decimal system. The list of periodicals
includes official and unofficial serials published in Portugal
and overseas. Many items from this list are included in the Library
of Congress list SERIALS FOR AFRICAN STUDIES. Three indexes are
included in both these Junta publications. Their earlier editions
(1960 and 1959, respectively) were also published in nos. 2-5 of
the international journal INFORMATIONS EURAFDOC (Paris, Union
Eurafricaine de Documentation, Feb.-May 1960).

2731. U.S. Library of Congress. General Reference and Bibliography
        Division. Reference Department. PORTUGUESE AFRICA: A GUIDE
        TO OFFICIAL PUBLICATIONS. Compiled by Mary Jane Gibson,
        African Section. Washington, 1967. 217 p.

    An extensive listing of documents of Portuguese Africa from
1850 to 1964. Unfortunately, it is confined to documents published in Africa and leaves out much of the massive publication
program of the Imprensa Nacional in Lisbon. In addition to government documents, the guide includes municipal and provincial documents
as well as publications either attributed to or subsidized by
government agencies. Arrangement is in six parts: Angola, Cape
Verde Islands, Mozambique, Portuguese Guinea, São Tomé e Principe,
and Portugal. At the end of each part is an "Other Authors"
section which cites works written by individuals and issued by a
government agency or government-affiliated organization. Locations
in U.S. Libraries are indicated, and there is an index (primarily
of subjects and authors, but with a few titles).

Serials

Note: See no. 2717 for fuller listing of serials. See also no. 2759.

2732. Centro de Estudos Históricos Ultramarinos. STUDIA: REVISTA
        SEMESTRAL. 1958- Lisboa. Semiannual.

    A big volume usually on historical studies. Most of the
essays are furnished with footnote references or bibliographies.
Occasional articles, by English authors, are in English. The
Center also issues DOCUMENTACAO ULTRAMARINA PORTUGUESA, 1960-.

2733. ESTUDOS ULTRAMARINOS. no. 1- 1948- Lisboa, Instituto Superior de
Estudos Ultramarinos. Quarterly.

Review originally titled ESTUDOS COLONIAIS and carrying valuable
contributions on political, economic, and social aspects of overseas
Portugal. Issues are often centered on a single theme, e.g., 1960,
no. 3, "Problemas políticos" (the United Nations in relation to
Portuguese territories), and no. 4, "Problemas políticos-sociais";
1962, no. 2, "Política, economia e trabalho," no. 3, "Política e
ensino," and no. 4, "Diretto corporativo." Some issues include long
bibliographies, e.g., "Bibliografia sôbre economia ultramarina
portuguesa," 1959, no. 4, p. 255-281.

2734. GARCIA DE ORTA: REVISTA DA JUNTA DE INVESTIGACOES DO ULTRAMAR.
v. 1- 1953- Lisboa. illus. Quarterly.

The journal of this scholarly official body, carrying monograph-
length articles on natural and human sciences. The last pages often
given the impressive list of publications of the Junta, including
contents of earlier volumes of GARCIA DE ORTA.

In some issues in the 1950's the journal included lists of
"Publicações de interesse ultramarino entradas na Biblioteca
Nacional de Lisboa por abrigação de depósito legal" (v. 1, no. 1,
1953; v. 2, no. 3, 1954; v. 3, no. 1, 1955), as well as occasional
special bibliographies.

2735. Portugal. Agência Geral do Ultramar. BOLETIM GERAL DO ULTRAMAR.
no. 1- July 1925- Lisboa. illus., fold. col. maps.
Monthly.

This official journal is of first importance for study of
administrative matters relating to the overseas territories. It
also contains specialist articles of general coverage, a regular
review of missionary activity, a section of news and notes, a
review of the press, and other features, including summary sections
in English and French. Many issues contain bibliographies which in
some cases are complete listings of publications of the Agência
and records of books received and in other cases are specialized
bibliographical entries, "Fichas bibliográficas," printed in form
to be cut for files (see, for instance, the work by José Júlio
Gonçalves cited above, no. 2729).

The Agência, which was formerly known as the Agência Geral
das Colónias, operates under the Ministério do Ultramar, formerly
the Ministério das Colónias, at Lisbon. It has sponsored numerous
publications of a historical, legal and ethnographic nature. It
has also published a good many studies defending Portugal's colonial
record.

2736.   PORTUGAL COLONIAL: REVISTA MENSAL DE PROPAGANDA E EXPANSAO DO
          IMPERIO PORTUGUES. 1931- Lisboa. Monthly.

2737.   PORTUGAL EM AFRICA. 1894- Lisboa. Monthly, formerly 2 times a
          month.

          The former title of the journal was PORTUGAL EM AFRICA:
        REVISTA ILLUSTRADA E SCIENTIFICA. It is published under Catholic
        auspices and contains a wealth of information concerning the
        colonies, with special reference to missionary work.

2738.   Portugal. Ministério do Ultramar. ARQUIVO DAS COLONIAS. illus.
          Monthly July 1917-June 1919; quarterly April/June 1922-
          Publication suspended July 1919-March 1922. July 1922-1928.

          The earlier numbers were issued by the Ministry under its
        original name Ministério das Colónias. The Arquivo Histórico
        Ultramarino has issued since 1950 the BOLETIM.

          See also no. 2759.

Reference Works

2739.   ANUARIO CATOLICO DO ULTRAMAR PORTUGUES (1960). Lisboa, Centro de
          Estudos Políticos e Sociais, Junta de Investigações do
          Ultramar, 1962. 433 p. (Estudos de ciências políticas e
          sociais, no. 57)

          The Catholic yearbook of overseas Portugal, giving names and
        statistical data of missions and parishes in West Africa, East
        Africa, Asia, and Oceania.

          A significant missionary journal, PORTUGAL EM AFRICA: REVISTA
        DE CULTURA MISSIONARIA, carrying general articles on Portuguese
        Africa, is published bimonthly in Lisbon (1894-; 2d ser., 1942-).

2740.   ANUARIO ESTATISTICO DO ULTRAMAR. ANNUAIRE STATISTIQUE D'OUTRE-MER.
          Prepared by the Portuguese Instituto Nacional de Estatística.
          [1945?-] Lisboa, Tipografia Portuguesa.

          Annual volume covering in detailed tables all aspects of
        population and economic life in the Portuguese overseas territories.
        There is a full index with subject breakdown under each country.

The ANUARIO DO ULTRAMAR PORTUGUES (with which this is not to be confused), issued by the Anuário Comercial de Portugal in Lisbon, is a business directory, with data on regions and administration (29th ed., 1963/64, 1056 p.).

2741.   Brásio, Antônio D., ed. Monumenta missionaria africana: Africa ocidental [series]. 2d ser., v. 1- Lisboa, Divisão de Publicações e Biblioteca, Agência Geral do Ultramar, 1958-. illus.

A collection of source accounts for Portuguese missions, in Latin and Portuguese. The first series was published in nine volumes, 1952-56. The first volume of the second series covers the earliest years, 1342-1499 (746 p.).

2742.   Caetano, Marcelo. COLONIZING TRADITIONS, PRINCIPLES AND METHODS OF THE PORTUGUESE. [Translation from the Portuguese; translation also in French] Lisboa, Agência Geral do Ultramar, 1951. 54 p.

Official statement of Portuguese colonial policy. The writer, a distinguished professor of law and later Rector at the University of Lisbon was at one time Minister of Colonies; he is now Prime Minister.

A later study by Professor Caetano was on the question of African labor in Mozambique and Angola, OS NATIVOS NA ECONOMIA AFRICANA (Coimbra, Coimbra Editora, 1954, 144 p.).

2743.   Chilcote, Ronald H. PORTUGUESE AFRICA. Englewood Cliffs, N.J. Prentice-Hall, 1967. 149 p. maps. (A Spectrum Book: The Modern Nations in Historical Perspective)

Bibliography: p. 129-141.

A short and readable introduction sympathetic to African nationalist aspirations. There is an excellent bibliographical guide.

2744.   Duffy, James. PORTUGAL IN AFRICA. Cambridge, Mass., Harvard University Press, 1962. 240 p.

Paperback ed., Harmondsworth, Middlesex, Penguin Books, 1962. (Penguin African Library, AP3)

Bibliography: p. 230-232.

_____. PORTUGUESE AFRICA. Cambridge, Mass., Harvard Univer-
Press, 1959. 389 p. illus.

Bibliographical references in chapter cnotes: p. 345-378.

The book PORTUGUESE AFRICA is the most comprehensive and
balanced work in English on the subject, covering politico-
economic history from the earliest times to the late 1950's.
The shorter book of 1962 outlines the past and analyzes more
fully the "theory and reality" of contemporary Portuguese Africa
under the Salazar government, ending with consideration of the
changes during the 1950's and the beginning of the nationalist
revolt. Its very brief bibliography is limited to recent works
in English.

Other works by Duffy on the same area are PORTUGAL'S AFRICAN
TERRITORIES: PRESENT REALITIES (New York, 1962, 39 p.), in the
Carnegie Endowment for International Peace Occasional Paper (no.
1) series, and A QUESTION OF SLAVERY (Oxford, Clarendon Press,
1967, 240 p.).

2745. Galvão, Henrique, and Carlos Selvagem. IMPERIO ULTRAMARINO POR-
TUGUES (MONOGRAFIA DO IMPERIO). Lisboa, Empresa Nacional
de Publicidade, 1950-53. 4 v. illus., maps, tables.

Includes brief bibliographies.

Survey of the Portuguese overseas territories, with emphasis
on political and economic geography. The two writers are both
literary men who have written extensively in the fields of drama,
history, and colonial literature. Senhor Galvão was at the time
of writing Inspector Superior of Colonial Administration. (He is
known now as an opponent of the Salazar government, especially in
regard to the incident of the seizure of the liner Santa Maria in
1961. A report he had made in 1947 on conditions in Angola,
which was a violent denunciation of the government, had been
suppressed; he reprinted portions of it in his SANTA MARIA: MY
CRUSADE FOR PORTUGAL [Cleveland, New York, World Pub. Co., 1961,
211 p.].)

2746. Gersdorff, Ralph von. WIRTSCHAFTSPROBLEME PORTUGIESISCH-AFRIKAS.
Bielefeld, Verlag Ernst und Werner Gieseking, 1962. 359 p.

By a consulting economist who has also written on Spanish
West Africa. He presents fully the Portuguese economic argument
for their administration of the African territories.

2747.   Hammond, Richard James. PORTUGAL AND AFRICA, 1815-1910: A STUDY
            IN UNECONOMIC IMPERIALISM. Stanford, Calif., Stanford
            University Press, 1966. xv, 384 p. illus., maps. (Stanford
            University, Food Research Institute, Studies in Tropical
            Development)

        Bibliographical footnotes.

        A narrative and interpretive history of Portugal's African
    activities, beginning with the early nineteenth century but with
    more emphasis on Angola and on the period 1870-1910. The book
    attempts to make intelligible the Portuguese view on imperial
    questions, a matter usually neglected except by Portuguese his-
    torians.

        Another work by Hammond in that same general area is PORTUGAL'S
    AFRICAN PROBLEM: SOME ECONOMIC FACETS (New York, 1962, 39 p.), in
    the Carnegie Endowment for International Peace Occasional Paper (no.
    2) series.

2748.   Lopes de Lima, José Joaquim. ENSAIOS SOBRE A STATISTICA DAS
            POSSESSOES PORTUGUEZAS NA AFRICA OCIDENTAL E ORIENTAL: NA
            ASIA OCIDENTAL: NA CHINA, E NA OCEANIA: ESCRIPTOS. [Begun
            by José Joaquim Lopes de Lima and continued by Francisco
            Maria Bordalo] Ordenados em seis livros (livros 1-5, pte. 1).
            Lisboa, Imprensa Nacional, 1844-62. 5 v. fold. maps, tables.

        Libro 1, Ilhas de Cabo Verde, e suas dependencias; libro 2,
    Ilhas de S. Thomé e Príncipe, e suas dependencias; libro 3,
    Angola, Benguella, e suas dependencias; libro 4, Moçambique,
    e suas dependencias; libro 5 (pte. 1), Goa, Damão, Diu, e
    suas dependencias.

        This first detailed survey of overseas Portuguese territories
    is still of value in studying development since the nineteenth
    century.

2749.   Mendes Corrêa, Antônio Augusto. ULTRAMAR PORTUGUES: Vol. I,
            SINTESE DA AFRICA. Lisboa, Divisão de Publicações e
            Biblioteca, Agência Geral das Colonías, 1949. 437 p. maps.

        The first volume of a projected general survey of all Portuguese
    territory (for Vol. II, see no. 2826). Among the subjects covered
    are physiography, climate, ethnography, and economy. The book
    contains good maps and bibliographies and summaries of each chapter
    in French and English.

2750. Moreira, Adriano. PORTUGAL'S STAND IN AFRICA. New York, University
Publishers, 1962. 265 p.

Explanation of Portugal's overseas policy, prepared in an
English-language edition to counter what the author considered
American misunderstanding of trends that led to unrest and nationalist
revolt in Portugal's African territories. The author, Overseas
Minister of Portugal, is also a professor at the Instituto Superior
de Estudos Ultramarinos in Lisbon. His book is largely made up of
addresses delivered in various Portuguese institutions from 1958 to
1961 and includes texts of the major colonial decrees of 1961 that
were intended to ameliorate conditions. Portugal's multiracial
concepts are emphasized.

Another expression of the Portuguese position is by the Foreign
Minister Dr. Franco Nogueira, THE UNITED NATIONS AND PORTUGAL: A
STUDY IN ANTICOLONIALISM (London, Sidgwick & Jackson, 1963, 188 p.).

2751. Moser, Gerald M. "African Literature in Portuguese: The First
Written, the Last Discovered." AFRICAN FORUM, v. 2, no. 4,
Spring 1967: 78-96.

An interpretive essay and bibliographic survey.

2752. Portugal. Agência Geral do Ultramar. BASES ORGANICAS DA
ADMINISTRACAO, CIVIL E FINANCEIRA DAS COLONIAS. Codificadas
for J. M. L. Prazeres da Costa. Lisboa, Agência Geral das
Colonias, 1926. 48 p.

2753. Portugal. Agência Geral do Ultramar. Vicente Ferreira. ESTUDOS
ULTRAMARINOS. Preface by Prof. Doutor Marcello Caetano.
Lisboa, Divisão de Publicações e Biblioteca, Agência Geral do
Ultramar, 1953-55. 4 v.

The first volume deals mainly with financial questions; the
second and third with Angola; and the fourth with miscellaneous
problems.

2754. Portugal. Agência Geral do Ultramar. José Júlio Gonçalves, comp.
CRIACAO E REORGANIZACOES DO INSTITUTO SUPERIOR DE ESTUDOS
ULTRAMARINOS, 1906-1961. Lisboa, Agência Geral do Ultramar,
1962. 2 v. illus.

An essential work concerning Portuguese colonial studies.

2755. Portugal. Agência Geral do Ultramar. Adriano Moreira. ADMINIS-
TRACAO DA JUSTICIA AOS INDIGENAS. Lisboa, Divisão de
Publicações e Biblioteca, Agência Geral do Ultramar, 1955.
275 p.

Bibliography: p. 273-275.

This study deals with both customary and statutory law respecting Africans in the Portuguese colonies.

2756. Portugal. Agência Geral do Ultramar. NOVA LEGISLACAO ULTRAMARINA.
Lisboa, Divisão de Publicações e Biblioteca, Agência Geral do
Ultramar. 1953-

2757. Portugal. Agência Geral do Ultramar. Francisco José Vieira Machado,
ed. COLONIZACAO, PROJECTOS DE DECRETOS. Lisboa, Agência Geral
das Colónias, 1940. 376 p.

2758. Portugal. Comissão Executiva das Comemorações do V Centenário
da Morte do Infante D. Henrique. PORTUGALIAE MONUMENTA
CARTOGRAPHICA. By Armando Cortesão and Avelino Teixeira da
Mota. Lisboa, 1960. 5 v. plus index vol. illus., col.
plates, maps (part fold., part col.), facsims., tables. 62 cm.
(except index).

Handsome and monumental work, issued by the Portuguese government commemorating the 500th anniversary of the death of Henry the
Navigator; in Portuguese and English. Two eminent authorities have
provided, besides the general introduction and the introductions to
each volume, studies on the hundreds of charts and maps illustrating
the history of Portuguese cartography from the late fifteenth to
the seventeenth century.

2759. Portugal. Junta das Missões Geográficas e de Investigações do
Ultramar.

This body was earlier known as the Junta das Missões Geográficas
e de Investigações Coloniais, and also as the Junta de Investigações
do Ultramar. It was first established in 1936 at Lisbon and operates
under the Ministério do Ultramar, formerly the Ministério das
Colónias. It administers numerous research institutes and centers.
These include the following, whose respective founding dates are
given in parentheses: Instituto de Investigação Científica de Angola
(1955), Luanda; Instituto de Investigação Científica de Moçambique
(1955), Lourenço Marques; Centro de Biologia Piscatoria (1959),

Lisbon; Centro de Botânica (1948), Lisbon; Centro de Documentação Científica Ultramarina (1957), Lisbon; Centro de Estudos de Etnologia do Ultramar (1954), Lisbon; Centro de Estudos Históricos Ultramarinos (1955), Lisbon; Centro de Estudos de Pedologia Tropical (1960), Tapada d'Ajuda; Centro de Estudos Políticos e Sociais (1956), Lisbon; Centro de Geografia do Ultramar (1946, 1955), Lisbon; Centro de Investigação das Ferrugens do Cafeeiro (1955), Oeiras; and the Centro de Zoologia (1948), Lisbon. Smaller research centers, missions, and laboratories have also been established by the Junta.

The Junta is also responsible for an extensive publications program covering natural sciences, social sciences, history, and so forth. The studies in the natural sciences include the following ESTUDOS:

a)   ESTUDOS DE BIOLOGIA MARITIMA. 1958-

b)   ESTUDOS SOBRE A ANTROPOLOGIA FISICA DO ULTRAMAR PORTUGUES. 1959-

c)   ESTUDOS DE ZOOLOGIA. 1959-

d)   ESTUDOS DE BOTANICA. 1960-

e)   ESTUDOS SOBRE A ETNOLOGIA DO ULTRAMAR PORTUGUES. 1960-

The Junta likewise issued several series of Memórias. Initially these were published in separate runs, known respectively as Série de agronomía tropical, Série antropológica ..., Série geológica, and so forth. In 1958 the earlier Memórias were united into a single set known as Memórias, 2d ser.

The Junta's publications include the following serials:

f)   ANAIS. v. 1- 1946-

g)   Estudos, ensaios e documentos. 1950-

h)   Estudos de ciencias políticas e sociais. 1956-

2760. Portugal. Junta de Investigações do Ultramar. ESTUDOS SOBRE A
       ETNOLOGIA DO ULTRAMAR PORTUGUES. Lisboa, 1960-63. 3 v.
       plates, maps. (Estudos, ensaios e documentos, nos. 81, 84,
       102)

       Includes bibliographies.

       A collection of scholarly papers on many aspects of ethnology
in Portuguese Africa, by leading scholars. The first volume (188 p.)

contains essays on the Angolares of São Tomé, the Quioco of Angola, Angolan concepts of death, and medicine of tribes of Portuguese Guinea. Vol. II (361 p.) contains a monograph-length paper by Eduardo dos Santos on pictographs and ideographs of the Quioco, as well as articles on the study of ethnosociology and ethnolinguistics, on animals in overseas ethnology, and on Negro ethnoreligion. Vol. III (240 p.) begins with a monograph on the weaving technology of Portuguese Guinea (bibliography, p. 83-87). All the articles in this series are followed by sections of plates, many have short reading lists, and for all there are résumés in French and English. In Vol. III the list of titles of the 100-odd publications in the series is given on five prefatory pages.

In the same form, with plates, short reading lists, and summaries in English and French following the articles, is a work in the Junta's Memórias, 2d ser., no. 13, ESTUDOS SOBRE A ANTROPOLOGIA FISICA DO ULTRAMAR PORTUGUES, by A. A. Mendes Corrêa and others (Lisboa, 1959, 153 p.). Tables of anthropometric data are included on the natives of São Tomé, Portuguese Guinea, and Angola.

2761. Portugal. Junta de Investigações do Ultramar. JUNTA DE INVESTI-GACOES DO ULTRAMAR: SEUS ORGANISMOS, PESSOAL CIENTIFICO, TECNICO E AUXILIAR. 7th ed. Lisboa, Centro de Documentação Científica Ultramarina, 1968. 153 p.

Directory of the Junta, including the Executive Commission and Secretariat, research groups, personnel of research institutes, scientific missions, etc., with indexes of institutions, of personal names, and of scientific organizations (p. 83-84) and subject indexes. The headings in Portuguese are repeated in French and English translation. Research groups include those in fields of engineering, geography and cartography, etc. Study groups include centers for phytosanitary research, Biological Center for Fisheries, Botanical Center, Overseas Scientific Documentation Center, Research Center for Anthropobiology, Cultural Anthropology Center, Cabo Verde Research Center, Community Development Research Center, Overseas History Research Center, Missionary Research Center, Tropical Pedology Center, Political and Social Research Center, Overseas Geography Center, Coffee Rust Research Center, Zoological Center.

2762. Portugal. Ministério do Ultramar. LEGISLACAO MANDADA APLICAR AO ULTRAMAR PORTUGUES, 1926 A 1963. Lisboa, Agência Geral do Ultramar, 1965-66. 2 v. 585, 501 p.

2763. Rego, António da Silva. CURSO DA MISSIONOLOGIA. Preface by
          Adriano Moreira. Lisboa, Agência Geral do Ultramar, 1956.
          700 p.

          Bibliography: p. xxvii-xlv.

          The standard work by a distinguished colonial historian who
is a clergyman and sympathizes with the Portuguese colonial record.

2764. Rego, António da Silva. O ULTRAMAR PORTUGUES NO SECULO XIX, 1834-
          1910.... Lisbon, Agência Geral do Ultramar, 1966. 446 p.

2765. United Nations. General Assembly. Special Committee on Territories
          under Portuguese Administration. REPORT, 15 AUG. 1962. New
          York, 1962. 144 p. annexes. (A/5160)

          The Committee, consisting of representatives from Bulgaria, Cey-
long, Colombia, Cyprus, Guatemala, Guinea, and Nigeria, had received
no cooperation from the Portuguese government, which had supplied no
reports as directed for Administering Power in the Charter. After
obtaining all possible information from sources outside the territories, they concluded that the situation "warrants the serious concern of the international community in every respect" and called for
United Nations action against Portugal. See also more recent reports: A/AC.109/L.451/Add.1.2: 1968 and A/AC.109/L.538: 1969.

          For many other papers of the United Nations relating to the
overseas possessions of Portugal, see the UNITED NATIONS DOCUMENTS
INDEX. For example:

          United Nations. General Assembly. Special Committee on the
             Situation with Regard to the Implementation of the Declara-
             tion on the Granting of Independence to Colonial Countries
             and Peoples. Sub-committee I. SUPPLEMENTARY REPORT: THE
             ACTIVITIES OF FOREIGN ECONOMIC AND OTHER INTERESTS WHICH
             ARE IMPEDING THE IMPLEMENTATION OF THE DECLARATION ON THE
             GRANTING OF INDEPENDENCE IN THE TERRITORIES UNDER PORTU-
             GUESE ADMINISTRATION. New York, 1966. 278 p. (A/AC.109/
             L.334/Add.1)

                              ANGOLA

Bibliographies

Note: Several brief reading lists on Angola were put out in the early
1960's, consisting mainly of periodical articles on the revolt and now

somewhat outdated by events, e.g., United Nations, Secretariat, ANGOLA: A
BIBLIOGRAPHY, 1963 (New York, 1963, 11 p.; ST/LIB/10). For bibliographical
references other than those cited below, see the general bibliographies on
Portuguese Africa cited above. The BOSTON UNIVERSITY PAPERS ON AFRICA,
Vol. IV, is to have a chapter by D. Wheeler, "Towards a History of
Angola: Problems and Sources."

2766. Angola. Comissão para a Exposição Histórica da Ocupação, 1st,
      Lisboa, 1937. CATALOGO DO DOCUMENTARIO COLIGIDO PELA
      COMISSAO DE LUANDA PARA A EXPOSICAO HISTORICA DA OCUPACAO A
      REALIZER EM LISBOA, EM 1937. Remetido pelo govêrno geral de
      Angola. Luanda, Imprensa Nacional, 1937. 107 p. plates,
      ports., maps, facsims.

2767. Borchardt, Paul. BIBLIOGRAPHIE DE L'ANGOLA (BIBLIOTHECA ANGOLENSIS),
      1500-1910. Bruxelles, Institut de Sociologie, 1912. 61 p.
      (Monographies bibliographiques, no. 2)

      Cites some 1,000 references concerned primarily with geography
and economics.

2768. Greenwood, Margaret Joan. ANGOLA: A BIBLIOGRAPHY. Cape Town,
      Cape Town University School of Librarianship, 1967. 52 p.
      (Bibliographical Series)

2769. Werner, Manfred W. ANGOLA: A SELECTED BIBLIOGRAPHY 1960-1965.
      Washington, U.S. Library of Congress, 1965.

      A useful list of articles in English.

Serials

2770. Angola. Instituto de Angola. BOLETIM INFORMATIVO. 1953-
      Luanda. Monthly.

2771. Angola. Instituto de Investigação Cientifica. MEMORIAS E TRABALHOS.
      1960- Luanda, Imprensa Nacional de Angola. Irregular.

2772. Angola. Instituto de Investigação Cientifica. RELATORIOS E
      COMUNICACOES. 1962- Luanda.

2773. Angola. Museu de Angola. ARQUIVOS DE ANGOLA and BOLETIM CULTURAL. 1933- Luanda. Irregular.

2774. BOLETIM CULTURAL DA CAMARA MUNICIPAL DE LUANDA. Luanda. 5-6 times a year.

2775. TRABALHO. 1963- Luanda. Providência e Acção Social, Instituto do Trabalho, Quarterly.

Reference Works

2776. Albuquerque Felner, Alfredo de. ANGOLA: APONTAMENTOS SOBRE A COLONIZACAO DOS PLANALTOS E LITORAL DO SUL DE ANGOLA; EXTRAIDOS DE DOCUMENTOS HISTORICOS. Lisboa, Divisão de Publicações e Biblioteca, Agência Geral dos Colonias, 1940. 3 v. illus.

Documentary history of European settlement in the highlands and littoral of the south of Angola, in continuation of the author's earlier-published work (see next entry). Vol. I deals with colonization and the indigenous people; Vol. II has documents for the period 1801-55; Vol. III covers the period 1856-93.

2777. Albuquerque Felner, Alfredo de. ANGOLA: APONTAMENTOS SOBRE A OCUPACAO E INICIO DO ESTABELECIMENTO DOS PORTUGUESES NO CONGO, ANGOLA E BENGUELA; EXTRAIDOS DE DOCUMENTOS HISTORICOS. Coimbra, Imprensa da Universidade, 1933. xv, 596 p. fold. map, facsims.

Deals with the early occupation of Zaïre and the Congo and Angola up to the end of the seventeenth century. Texts and documents are on pages 375-585.

2778. American University, Washington, D.C. Foreign Area Studies. AREA HANDBOOK FOR ANGOLA. By Allison Butler Herrick and others. Washington, Aug. 1967. xii, 439 p. maps, tables. (DA PAM no. 550-59)

Bibliography: p. 391-424.

One of a series of comprehensive surveys of various countries, this volume establishes the historical background of Angola and then presents a balanced compilation of basic facts on social, economic, political, and military conditions through 1966. In addition to the extensive bibliography, there is a glossary and an analytical index.

2779. Associação Industrial de Angola. GUIA INDUSTRIAL DE ANGOLA: EDICAO UNICA COMMEMORATIVA DO 30.º ANNIVERSARIO DA ASSOCIACAO INDUSTRIAL DE ANGOLA. Luanda, 1960. 740 p.

A large volume of business addresses. The Association publishes a quarterly (irregular) BOLETIM, contents of which are analyzed in the "Reseña de revistas" carried in AFRICA (Madrid).

2780. Birmingham, David. TRADE AND CONFLICT IN ANGOLA: THE MBUNDU AND THEIR NEIGHBOURS UNDER THE INFLUENCE OF THE PORTUGUESE 1483-1790. Oxford, Clarendon Press, 1966. 178 p. map, tables.

Bibliography: p. 164-168.

See also his THE PORTUGUESE CONQUEST OF ANGOLA (Oxford University Press, 1965, 50 p.). A valuable pamphlet is Douglas L. Wheeler, "Portuguese Expansion in Angola since 1836: A Re-examination" (Salisbury, Central Africa Historical Association, 1967).

2781. Boavida, Américo. ANGOLA: CINCO SECULOS DE EXPLORACAO PORTUGUESA. Rio de Janeiro, Civilização Brasileira, 1967. 138 p.

A Marxist-Leninist, Fanonesque attack, this work is fully documented from Portuguese sources and is a kind of historical document in itself. No other systematic work of this size written by an Angola nationalist has yet appeared.

2782. Childs, Gladwyn M. UMBUNDU KINSHIP AND CHARACTER.... London, Oxford University Press for the International African Institute, 1949. 245 p. illus., map.

2783. Companhia de Diamantes de Angola [Diamang]. ANGOLA DIAMOND COMPANY: A SHORT REPORT. Lisbon, The Company, 1963. 168 p. illus., map.

English-language public-relations report on the rich company which plays a preponderant part in the economy of Angola. The company also issues its annual RAPPORTS (French and Portuguese editions) and sponsors a series prepared by the Museu do Dundo, Luanda, Angola: Publicações culturais (1946-).

2784. Estermann, Carlos. ETNOGRAFIA DO SUDOESTE DE ANGOLA. 2d ed., corr. Lisboa, 1960- illus., fold. col. map. (Junta de Investigações do Ultramar, Memórias, Série antropológica e etnológica, nos. 4-5)

These comprehensive scholarly volumes are the first two of a trilogy concerned with peoples of southeastern Angola. Vol. I takes in the Bushmen and kindred tribes and the ethnic group of the Ambo (Ovambo). In Vol. II Father Estermann studies the Nhaneca-Humbe group, covering all phases of history, tribal and family life, mores, art, and religious beliefs and practices. The third volume will deal with the northern Herero. At the end of each volume is a short list of sources used. A 15-page list of the writings of this anthropologist, BIBLIOGRAFIA DO ETNOLOGO PADRE CARLOS ESTERMANN, S.SP., compiled by Afonso Costa, was published by the Instituto de Angola in Luanda in 1961.

2785. Gonzaga, Norberto. ANGOLA: PEQUENA MONOGRAFIA. Lisboa, Centro de Informação e Turismo de Angola, Agência Geral do Ultramar, 1965. 286 p. illus., fold. map.

2786. Lopo, Júlio Castro de. JORNALISMO DE ANGOLA: SUBSIDIOS PARA A SUA HISTORIA. Luanda, Centro de Informação e Turismo de Angola, 1964. 127 p. illus., ports., facsims.

Valuable survey of the press in Angola in the nineteenth and twentieth centuries. There are useful lists of journals published. Also included is a section on African journalists.

2787. McCulloch, Merran. THE OVIMBUNDU OF ANGOLA. London, International African Institute, 1952. 50 p. (Ethnographic Survey of Africa, West Central Africa, pt. 2)

Bibliography: p. 48-50.

_____. THE SOUTHERN LUNDA AND RELATED PEOPLES (NORTHERN RHODESIA, BELGIAN CONGO, ANGOLA). London, International African Institute, 1951. 110 p. (Ethnographic Survey of Africa, West Central Africa, pt. 1)

Bibliography: p. 101-109.

Two monographs in this authoritative series (see no. 980), synthesizing existing studies. The Southern Lunda and related peoples occupy most of the eastern half of Angola, spreading over its borders into northwestern Rhodesia (Zambia) and the Katanga province of the Congo (Leopoldville). Their total population in the early 1950's was estimated at around 63,000, of whom 10,000 lived in Angola, 10,000 in the Congo, and the rest in two districts of what was then Northern Rhodesia. The Ovimbundu are the dominant autochthonous race of Angola, their homeland being the Benguela Highland in the west-central part of the country, though they are found as far as the coast. It is estimated that more than a third of Angola's total population of about four million are Ovimbundu.

A more recent specialized study is by Adrian C. Edwards, THE OVIMBUNDU UNDER TWO SOVEREIGNTIES: A STUDY OF SOCIAL CONTROL AND SOCIAL CHANGE AMONG A PEOPLE OF ANGOLA (London, Published for the International African Institute by the Oxford University Press, 1962, 169 p.).

2788. Okuma, Thomas Masaji. AFRICA IN FERMENT: THE BACKGROUND AND PRO-
        SPECTS OF AFRICAN NATIONALISM. Boston, Beacon Press, 1962.
        137 p. illus.

Bibliography: p. 127-131.

In 1961-62 there was a spate of books, mainly from the nationalist viewpoint, regarding the Angola revolt. This work, by a writer who had been for some years a missionary in Angola, is among the best-balanced reviews of the background of Portuguese repression and events of early 1961.

A useful pamphlet was ANGOLA: A SYMPOSIUM (London, Published for the Institute of Race Relations by Oxford University Press, 1962, 160 p.); in a collection of views there were included the official Portuguese statement, the impressions of Protestant missionaries, reports from the Catholic press, etc. Another work is by two Swedish authors, Anders Ehnmark and Per Wästerberg, ANGOLA AND MOZAMBIQUE: THE CASE AGAINST PORTUGAL, translated by Paul Britten-Austin (New York, Roy, 1963, 176 p.).

2789. Portugal. Agência Geral do Ultramar. Alberto de Almeida Teixeira.
        LUANDA: SUA ORGANIZACAO E OCUPACAO. Lisboa, Divisão de
        Publicações e Biblioteca, Agência Geral das Colónias, 1948.
        258 p. illus., ports., map.

2790. Santos, Rui Martins dos. A HISTORIA DE ANGOLA ATRAVES DOS SEUS
          PERSONAGENS PRINCIPAIS. Lisboa, Agência Geral do Ultramar,
          1967. 476 p. illus.

          A history of Angola, written from a strictly Portuguese point
     of view. The author seeks to cover his subject by a series of
     biographies that take the story from the early discovery to the
     present. The book is divided into two parts. The first deals
     with early Luso-African relations, as well as specific topics such
     as mission work and administrative reforms. The second part
     attempts to do justice to great names of Angola history not initially
     covered; it also presents what the author calls "panoramic visions"
     of Angolan history. These embrace issues as different as "The
     Terrorism" of the early 1960's and "The Adolescence of Angola,"
     including Angola's frontiers, its railways, the port of Luanda,
     Angola's fighting records in the Great War, and so forth. There
     is an index of names.

2791. Sousa Dias, Gastão. PIONEIROS DE ANGOLA: EXPLORACOES PORTUGUESAS
          NO SUL DE ANGOLA (SECULOS XVII & XVIII). Lisboa, 1937. 56 p.
          plates, maps.

          _____. OS PORTUGUESES EM ANGOLA. Lisboa, Agência Geral do
          Ultramar, 1959. 329 p. illus.

          Posthumously edited and published history of Portuguese
     discovery, exploration, and settlement of Angola, covering the
     period from 1482 to 1815. The author, a former officer in the
     Angolan service, died in 1942. A long list of his other books
     and papers regarding Angolan history is given on flyleaves.

2792. U.S. Department of the Interior. Office of Geography. ANGOLA:
          OFFICIAL STANDARD NAMES APPROVED BY THE UNITED STATES BOARD
          ON GEOGRAPHIC NAMES. Washington, U.S. Govt. Print. Off.,
          June 1956. 234 p. (Gazetteer no. 20)

          See note on series, no. 484.

2793. Vansina, Jan. KINGDOMS OF THE SAVANNA. Madison, University of
          Wisconsin Press, 1966. 364 p.

          For annotation see no. 2335.

MOZAMBIQUE

Atlas

2794. Mozambique. Direcção dos Serviços de Agrimensura. ATLAS DE
MOCAMBIQUE. Lourenço Marques, Empresa Moderna, 1960. 43 p.
chiefly col. maps (part fold.). 38 cm. ("Exemplar no. 4697")

Scale of maps 1:1,000,000 or 1:6,000,000.

Bibliographies

2795. Almeida de Eça, Felipe Gastão de Moura Coutinho de. ACHEGAS
PARA A BIBLIOGRAFIA DE MOCAMBIQUE: NOVOS SUBSIDIOS PARA
UM ESTUDO COMPLETO. Lisboa, Agência Geral das Colónias,
1949. 134 p.

List of 428 numbered entries for books and separately issued
papers, including many works of the nineteenth century. Arrangement is alphabetical, and indexes of names and subjects are included.

See also bibliographies in the serial MOCAMBIQUE: DOCUMENTARIO
TRIMESTRAL (no. 2810).

2796. Carrazola, J. da Silva Rodriques, comp. LEGISLACAO DA METROPOLE
EM VIGOR NA PROVINCIA DE MOCAMBIQUE, PUBLICADA NO "BOLETIM
OFICIAL," 1900 A 1964. Lourenço Marques, Imprensa Nacional de
Moçambique, 1965. 414 p.

2797. Costa, Mário Augusto da. BIBLIOGRAFIA GERAL DE MOCAMBIQUE (CON-
TRIBUICAO PARA UM ESTUDO COMPLETO), Vol. I. Lisboa, Divisão
de Publicações e Biblioteca, Agência Geral das Colónias,
1946-. 359 p.

A long bibliography classed under 35 alphabetical headings
(administration, agriculture . . . veterinary sciences, voyages
and travels, etc.), some with from 2 to 20 subdivisions. A
detailed table of contents is complemented by indexes of personal
and organizational names (onomástico) and of subjects. References
are to monographic publications and separates from reviews or
collected volumes.

2798.   International African Institute. SOUTH-EAST CENTRAL AFRICA AND
        MADAGASCAR: GENERAL, ETHNOGRAPHY, SOCIOLOGY, LINGUISTICS.
        Compiled by Ruth Jones, librarian, with the assistance of a
        panel of consultants. London, 1961. 53 l. (Africa Bibli-
        ography Series, Ethnography, Sociology, Linguistics, and
        Related Subjects)

        Mozambique: p. 28-37.

        See note on series, no. 970.

2799.   Rita-Ferreira, Antônio. BIBLIOGRAFIA ETNOLOGICA DE MOCAMBIQUE
        (DAS ORIGENS A 1954). Lisboa, Junta de Investigações do
        Ultramar, 1962. 254 p.

        Bibliography of 968 numbered entries for books and articles
        in all languages on the ethnology of the races of Mozambique and
        of Southeastern Africa in general. Introductory chapters are on
        South and East Africa (p. 1-61), Republic of South Africa (p. 62-
        64), Rhodesia and Nyasaland (p. 65-79), and Tanganyika (p. 80-91).
        Then division is by tribal groups living within Mozambique and
        also in the rest of the area (p. 92-230). Ethnology is broadly
        interpreted here and includes references on music, medicine, and
        travel, as well as folklore, customs, magic, religion, and language.
        Some entries are briefly annotated. There are indexes of authors
        and of periodicals cited.

2800.   SINOPSE DAS MATERIAS OFICIAIS PUBLICADAS NO "BOLETIM OFICIAL"
        DA PROVINCIA DE MOCAMBIQUE. By Josué Knopfli Júnior.
        1923- Lourenço Marques. Annual.

Reference Works

2801.   American University, Washington, D.C. Foreign Areas Study
        Division. AREA HANDBOOK FOR MOZAMBIQUE. Washington,
        D.C., 1969. XIV, 351 p. maps, tables.

        Bibliography: p. 315-338.

        The most up-to-date compendium in English, with separate
        sections on social, political, economic and military problems
        respectively. The bibliography is similarly subdivided by
        topics.

2802. ANNUARIO DA PROVINCIA DE MOCAMBIQUE. 43d ed. Lourenço Marques,
A. W. Bayly & Co., 1962. 1268, 84 p. maps, plans. Annual.

Comprehensive business register of the city of Lourenço
Marques and other districts of Mozambique, including an encyclopedic
survey of the colony as well as a directory by towns and districts.
It begins with indexes of subjects, addresses of government offices,
business and industries, local names, and economic activities (the
latter in English translation also). The main text includes folded
maps, town plans, etc. (interspersed with advertisements). The
separately numbered pages at the end are an index of advertisers.
There is also an English edition, begun in 1899 as DELAGOA DIRECTORY
and since 1943 titled LOURENCO MARQUES DIRECTORY.

2803. Axelson, Eric V. PORTUGUESE IN SOUTH-EAST AFRICA, 1600-1700.
Johannesburg, Witwatersrand University Press, 1960. 226 p.
illus.

Bibliography: p. 211-215; and footnote references.

_____. SOUTH-EAST AFRICA, 1488-1530. London, New York,
Longmans, Green, 1940. 306 p. illus., maps, facsims.

Bibliography: p. 284-297.

SOUTH-EAST AFRICA is concerned with the Portuguese acquisition
of the Arab States along the southeast African coast after Vasco da
Gama's landing at Mozambique in 1498. A long description of
documentary materials held in the archives of Torre do Tombo and
in other Portuguese archives is given in Appendix V. The 1960
book continues the history through the seventeenth century.
See also his PORTUGAL AND THE SCRAMBLE FOR AFRICA, 1875-1891
(Johannesburg, Witwatersrand University Press, 1967, 318 p.,
illus., maps).

2804. BOLETIM OFICIAL DA COLONIA DE MOCAMBIQUE. May 1854- Moçambique,
later Lourenço Marques. Irregular, later weekly.

The BOLETIM first began publication in Mozambique on May 13,
1854. From January 5, 1855 it appeared as a regular weekly. At
first it contained articles of general interest, reports submitted
by senior officials, details concerning agricultural production,
missionary work, statistical information, and so forth, in addition
to legislation. Gradually it became more specialized in content
and confined itself to laws.

The earlier numbers were indexed in great detail in Alberto
Cota Mesquita, INDICE ALFABETICO E CRONOLOGICO DA PRINCIPAL
LEGISLACAO PUBLICADA NOS "BOLETIMS OFICIAIS" DA COLONIA DE MOCAMBIQUE,
DESDE 1854 A 1920... (Lourenço Marques, Imprensa Nacional, 1941,
63 p.). The first part contains a subject index arranged alphabetically. The second is a chronological index, listing all
legislation concerning the colony between 1761 and 1920.

2805. Costa, Mário Augusto da. VOLUNTARIOS DE LOURENCO MARQUES.
Lourenço Marques, Imprensa Nacional, 1928. 90 p. illus.

Provides a military history of Mozambique.

2806. DOCUMENTS ON THE PORTUGUESE IN MOZAMBIQUE AND CENTRAL AFRICA,
1497-1840. [Title also in Portuguese] Lisbon, National
Archives of Rhodesia and Nyasaland and Centro de Estudos
Históricos Ultramarinos, 1962-

For annotation see no. 2109.

2807. Freitas, Antônio Joaquim de. A GEOLOGIA E O DESENVOLVIMENTO
ECONOMICO E SOCIAL DE MOCAMBIQUE. Lourenço Marques, Imprensa
Nacional de Moçambique, 1959. 396 p. illus., fold. maps,
tables.

Includes bibliographies.

Extended economic and technical survey of geology and mining
developments in Mozambique. The author was formerly Chief of the
Services of Industry and Geology of the province.

2808. Liesegang, Gerhard Julius. "Beiträge zur Geschichte der Gaza
Nguni im südlichen Moçambique 1820-1895." Doctoral dissertation, Cologne University, 1967. 292 p. illus., map,
tables.

Bibliography: p. 254-287.

A pioneer study based on unpublished archival sources. It
traces the growth and destruction of the Gaza kingdom in Moçambique.
The bibliography contains a detailed description of the archival
sources which the author consulted in the Arquivo Histórico
Ultramarino at Lisbon, the Biblioteca da Sociedade de Geografía
at Lisbon, and the Royal Geographical Society and the Public Records
Office in London.

2809. Mousinho de Albuquerque, Joaquim Augosto. ESCRITOS SOBRE
        MOCAMBIQUE. Lisboa, Biblioteca Colonial Portuguesa, 1934-35.
        2 v. plates, ports., plans.

        Mousinho de Albuquerque was a Royal Commissioner in Moçambique,
where he succeeded António Ennes in 1896. He played an important
part in the history of modern Portuguese colonization.

2810. Mozambique. MOCAMBIQUE: DOCUMENTARIO TRIMESTRAL. 1935- Lourenço
        Marques. illus., plates (part col.), maps, music.

        This official quarterly, which carries excellent articles on
many aspects of history, economy, and culture, is a valuable source
for information on Mozambique. The issues include regular bibliographies of works published in Mozambique and received on legal
deposit by the Arquivo Histórico. See also Sociedade de Estudos
de Moçambique, BOLETIM, 1931-.

2811. Oliveira Boleo, José de. MOCAMBIQUE. Lisboa, Divisão de Publicações
        e Biblioteca, Agência Geral do Ultramar, 1951. 562 p. plates,
        maps. (Monografias dos territórios do Ultramar)

        Bibliography: p. 539-558.

        Like others of the series, this study surveys factors of
physical geography, geology, climate, flora and fauna, anthropo-
geography, history, politics, and social welfare under the Portuguese,
and economic development. Chapters are followed by résumés in
French and English. In conclusion there is a long bibliography,
arranged by subject field and including writings in various languages.

2812. Pinto, Frederico da Silva. ROTEIRO HISTORICO-BIOGRAFICO DA CIDADE
        DE LOURENCO MARQUES. Lourenço Marques, Moçambique Editora,
        1965. 206 p.

        A biographical survey of important men in the history of
Lourenço Marques.

2813. Portugal. Agência Geral do Ultramar. Joaquim Moreira da Silva
        Cunha. O TRABALHO INDIGENA: ESTUDO DE DIREITO COLONIAL.
        Lisboa, Divisão de Publicações e Biblioteca, Agência Geral
        das Colónias, 1949. 295 p.

        Bibliography: p. 279-289.

Standard study of Portuguese labor legislation in the colonies before the period of post-war reform.

2814.   Portugal. Agência Geral do Ultramar. Filipe Gastão de Moura Coutinho de Almeida de Eça. HISTORIA DAS GUERRAS NO ZAMBEZE, CHICOA E MASSANGANO, 1807-1888. Lisboa, Divisão de Publicações e Biblioteca, Agência Geral do Ultramar, 1953-54. 2 v. illus., ports., map, facsims., plan.

Bibliography: v. 1, p. 471-75; v. 2, p. 683-684.

2815.   Portugal. Agência Geral do Ultramar. António Ennes. MOCAMBIQUE: RELATORIO APRESENTADO AO GOVERNO. 3d ed. Lisboa, Divisão de Publicações e Biblioteca, Agência Geral das Colónias, 1946. 625 p.

This report was first published in 1893. Its author, a Royal Commissioner in the colony at the time, played an important part in the affairs of Mozambique.

2816.   Portugal. Laws, statutes, etc. PRINCIPAL LEGISLACAO APLICAVEL AOS INDIGENAS DA PROVINCIA DE MOCAMBIQUE. Lourenço Marques, Imprensa Nacional de Moçambique, 1960. 385 p.

2817.   Santos, Joaquim Rodrigues dos. CONTRIBUICAO PARA O ESTUDO DA ANTROPOLOGIA DE MOCAMBIQUE: ALGUMAS TRIBOS DO DISTRITO DE TETE. Pôrto, Tipografia Mendonça, 1944. 412 p. illus., fold. maps, tables. (República Portuguêsa, Ministério das Colónias, Junta das Missões Geográficas e de Investigações do Ultramar, Memórias, Série Antropológica, no. 2)

Bibliographical notes: p. 361-387; bibliography: p. 389-397.

This scholar, a professor at the University of Pôrto, was a noted anthropologist and author of many works relating to East Africa. In the 1930's he conducted Portuguese expeditions studying and photographing tribes of Mozambique, an account of which was published by the Agência Geral das Colónias in 1940 (Portugal, MISSAO ANTROPOLOGICA DE MOCAMBIQUE . . . 2A. CAMPANHA, AGOSTO DE 1937 A JANEIRO DE 1938, por J. R. dos Santos Júnior, Lisboa, 1940, 91 p., 95 plates on 48 l.). The present book is an extensive study of the physical anthropology of tribes of Zambesia, particularly of the district of Tete. It ends with anthropometric tables and almost 40 pages of bibliographical notes, in which the author's own contributions are entered under the name Santos Júnior (J. R. dos).

2818. Santos, Rui Martins dos. UMA CONTRIBUICAO PARA A ANALISE DA
ECONOMIA DE MOCAMBIQUE. Lisboa, Companhia de Cimentos de
Moçambique, 1959. 373 p. tables, diagrs.

Full-scale statistical study of all phases of economic life
in Mozambique.

2819. Silva, Carlos A. Vieira da, ed. THE CITY OF LOURENCO MARQUES
GUIDE. Lourenço Marques, 1956. 221 p. illus.

Guidebook to the port city of Lourenço Marques on Delagoa Bay
(Baía da Lagoa, Bay of the Lagoon), which is a favorite visiting
place for the British residents of the interior of Southern Africa.
Illustrated with many photographs of the landscape, architecture,
and monuments, the book devotes equal space to culture and to
travel information. A smaller guide by Alfredo Pereira de Lima,
LOURENCO MARQUES, appeared in 1963.

2820. Spence, C. F. MOCAMBIQUE (EAST AFRICAN PROVINCE OF PORTUGAL).
Cape Town, Timmins, 1963. 147 p. illus.

An overall picture of Mozambique by an experienced travel
writer and interpreter of Southern Africa. Mr. Spence had published in 1951 an economic survey of Mozambique, which this supersedes and covers more broadly. His informative chapters cover
historical background, geographical information, game, the tsetse
fly and its influence on the economy, population, government and
citizenship (the rate of assimilação has been notoriously slow),
education, health, and many aspects of the economy.

2821. Teixeira Botelho, José Justino. HISTORIA MILITAR E POLITICA
DOS PORTUGUESES EM MOCAMBIQUE DE 1833 AOS NOSSOS DIAS. 2d
ed. Lisboa, Centro Tipográfico Colonial, 1936. 742 p.
illus.

This work is a continuation of the author's standard work
HISTORIA MILITAR E POLITICA DOS PORTUGUESES EM MOCAMBIQUE DA
DESCOBERTA A 1833 (Lisboa, Centro Tipográfico Colonial, 1934, 637 p.,
illus.). Both are rigidly Eurocentric in conception.

2822. U.S. Department of the Interior. Army Topographic Command. Geographic Names Division. MOZAMBIQUE: OFFICIAL STANDARD NAMES
APPROVED BY THE UNITED STATES BOARD ON GEOGRAPHIC NAMES. Washington, 1969. 505 p. map. (Gazetteer no. 109)

See note on series, no. 484.

PORTUGUESE GUINEA, CAPE VERDE ISLANDS, SAO TOME AND PRINCIPE

Note: For the other countries of overseas Portugal on the west coast of Africa--the Cape Verde Islands, Portuguese Guinea, and São Tomé and Principé--recent books on current events and conditions are conspicuous by their absence, modern history being treated either in overall studies of the Portuguese African possessions or in short news articles.

Bibliographies

2823. Lampreia, José D. CATALOGO-INVENTARIO DE SECCAO DE ETNOGRAFIA DO MUSEU DA GUINE PORTUGUESA. Lisboa, Junta de Investigações do Ultramar, 1962. 91 p. illus.

2824. Tenreiro, Francisco. "Bibliografia geográfica de Guiné." GARCIA DE ORTA, v. 2, no. 1, 1954.

Reference Works

2825. BOLETIM CULTURAL DA GUINE PORTUGUESA. v. 1- 1946- Bissau, Centro de Estudos da Guiné Portuguesa. illus. Quarterly.

A distinguished review, organ of the prominent center for study and research on Portuguese Guinea, edited at its headquarters in the Museu Guiné Portuguesa in Bissau. The numbers carry substantial articles on "what is considered of interest . . . of an historical, ethnographic, scientific, literary, or artistic character." There are also regular sections of chronicle of the province, economic statistics, notes and news, and list of publications received at the museum. On the back cover are titles of the Centro's monographic publications (Memórias).

2826. Mendes Corrêa, Antônio A. ULTRAMAR PORTUGUES: Vol. II, ILHAS DE CABO VERDE. Lisboa, Divisão de Publicações e Biblioteca, Agência Geral do Ultramar, 1954. 262 p. illus., maps.

Detailed coverage of the physical and human geography of the Cape Verde Islands. The first eight chapters are on natural science, the remaining seven on ethnology, demography, social conditions, languages, culture and education, politics and government, and economy. Each chapter is followed by résumés in French and English. An earlier work by Professor Mendes Corrêa (anthro-

pology, University of Pôrto) is concerned with ethnology of the
tribes of Portuguese Guinea: UMA JORNADA CIENTIFICA NA GUINE
PORTUGUESA (Lisboa, Divisão de Publicações e Biblioteca, Agência
Geral das Colónias, 1947, 193 p.)

2827. Portugal. Agência Geral do Ultramar. ESTATUTO POLITICO-ADMINIS-
        TRATIVO DA PROVINCIA S. TOME E PRINCIPLE. Lisboa, 1965.
        40 p.

2828. Portugal. Agência Geral do Ultramar. PORTUGAL OVERSEAS PROVINCES:
        FACTS AND FIGURES. Lisboa, 1965. 175 p. illus., maps.

        The first half of this work is devoted to Portugal's African
        provinces. For each province succinct information is given on geo-
        graphical location and area, relief and river system, climate, pop-
        ulation, main towns, history, and government and administration.

2829. Portugal. Agência Geral do Ultramar. S. TOME E PRINCIPE: PEQUENA
        MONOGRAFIA. Lisboa, 1964. 108 p. plates, ports., maps.

2830. Portugal. Junta de Investigações do Ultramar. Centro de Estudos
        Políticos e Sociais. COLOQUIOS CABO-VERDIANOS. Lisboa,
        1959. 182 p. (Estudos de ciências políticas e sociais,
        no. 22)

        Proceedings of a conference on Cape Verde studies held by
        the Centro. The papers covered a broad perspective. Eight are
        reproduced here: an opening discussion of literary trends in
        Cape Verde, talks on creole society, bilinguism, education and
        culture, and the problem of emigration, an essay on demography,
        a glance at the importance of spiritual values, and final con-
        siderations on fundamental problems of Cape Verde.

2831. Silva, Hélder Lains e. SAO TOME E PRINCIPE E A CULTURA DO CAFE.
        By Hélder Lains e Silva, with the collaboration, on soil
        studies, of José Carvalho Cardoso. Lisboa, Junta de
        Investigações do Ultramar, 1958. 499 p. plates, fold. map
        (in pocket), tables. (Memórias, 2d ser., no. 1)

        Bibliography: p. 391-403.

        Scholarly ecological study beginning with a general account
        of the province in geographical, geological, climatological, and

economic aspects and then analyzing in detail its agriculture generally and the coffee culture specifically. A summary in English is
given on pages 353-387.

2832. Teixeira da Mota, Avelino. GUINE PORTUGUESA. Lisboa, Divisão de
        Publicações e Biblioteca, Agência Geral do Ultramar, 1954. 2 v.
        plates, maps, diagrs. (Monografias dos territórios do Ultramar)

        Bibliography (by subject classes): v. 2, p. 251-286.

        An impressive survey giving wide coverage to physical features--
        geology, hydrography, climate, flora and fauna, etc.--and to ethno-
        logical aspects of Portuguese Guinea and the islands of São Tomé and
        Príncipe, as well as to economic and social development under the
        Portuguese administration. All chapters are followed by summaries
        in French and English and some also by bibliographies.

        A well-presented illustrated brochure offering a short factual
        survey was published by the Agência Geral do Ultramar in 1967:
        GUINE: PEQUENA MONOGRAFIA, 2d ed. (Lisboa, 80 p.). A companion
        brochure treats the Cape Verde Islands: CABO VERDE: PEQUENA MONO-
        GRAFIA, 2d ed. (Lisboa, 1966, 80 p.).

2833. Tenreiro, Francisco. A ILHA DE SAO TOME. Lisboa, Junta de Investi-
        gações do Ultramar, 1961. 279 p. 73 plates, maps, diagrs.
        (Memórias, 2d ser., no. 24)

        Bibliography: p. 243-278.

        A comprehensive geographical survey, with chapters on climate
        and soils, colonization and agriculture, peoples, socioeconomics,
        and economic position with particular reference to the export crops
        of coffee and cocoa. There is a long classifed bibliography, largely
        of articles in Portuguese journals but including a handful of writ-
        ings in English.

2834. U.S. Department of the Interior. Army Map Service. Geographic
        Names Division. PORTUGUESE GUINEA: OFFICIAL STANDARD NAMES
        APPROVED BY THE UNITED STATES BOARD ON GEOGRAPHIC NAMES. Wash-
        ington, May 1968. 122 p. map. (8,700 names) (Gazetteer
        no. 105)

        See note on series, no. 484.

CHAPTER 42

SPANISH AFRICA

EQUATORIAL GUINEA (SPANISH GUINEA)

Note: The only Spanish possession in sub-Saharan Africa was this region
of two territories under one governorship, the mainland Río Muni and the
large island of Fernando Po (Fernando Póo in Spanish) some 20 miles from
the coast. The latter administration included four smaller islands,
Annobón, Corisco, and Great and Little Elobey. The seat of government was
at Santa Isabel on Fernando Po.

    "Spanish Guinea" has been, since 12 October 1968, the independent
republic of Equatorial Guinea. It retains as a republic the basic structure
of the last years of Spanish control, viz.: two provinces--Fernando Po
(including the island of Annobón), and Río Muni (including the islands of
Corisco, and Great and Little Elobey). Santa Isabel remains the capital but
since independence increasing numbers of government functions are being
carried out at Bata in Río Muni.

Atlas

2835. Spain. Dirección General de Marruecos y Colonias. ATLAS HISTORICO
        Y GEOGRAFICO DE AFRICA ESPANOLA. Madrid, 1955. 197 p. maps
        (part col.).

        The preface of this folio atlas is signed by J. Dias de Villegas,
    director general of the Dirección General de Marruecos y Colonias
    (later the Dirección General de Plazas y Provincias Africanas) and
    the Instituto de Estudios Africanos, both of which organizations were
    responsible for preparation and publication of the atlas. It is in
    two parts, historical (p. 13-67) and geographical. In the first
    section 31 maps in color showing stages of the history of Spain in
    Africa are interspersed with explanatory text. In the geographical
    atlas the maps--physical, geological, and political-administrative

on double-page spreads with following sections of explanatory text--
cover practically all details of geographical information about
Spanish African possessions. There is a comprehensive index of place
names.

Bibliographies

2836. Berman, Sanford. SPANISH GUINEA: AN ANNOTATED BIBLIOGRAPHY.
        Washington, D.C., Catholic University of America, 1961. 597 l.
        Typescript.

        A unique contribution to African studies, invaluable for research
on Spanish Guinea. Microfilm copies of this master's thesis in
library science may be obtained from the Catholic University of
America. After an introductory essay on the literature relating to
the region, the bibliography proper, occupying more than 330 pages,
is arranged under alphabetical subject headings, with a preliminary
section of general works. Mr. Berman has analyzed practically all
entries in evaluative annotations, often of several hundred words.
He follows this list, which he speaks of as "a representative core of
current and retrospective Guineana," with a supplementary bibliography
of works useful for African studies and then gives titles for "A
Basic Library of Guineana" (p. 430-433). Next are provided an
extended glossary (p. 434-490), a chronology (p. 491-527), a directory
of publishers, periodicals, and institutions, and finally a full
index of authors and subject matter.

2837. Guinea, Spanish. Laws, statutes, etc. INDICE LEGISLATIVO DE GUINEA.
        [Prepared by Francisco Martos Avila] Madrid, Instituto de
        Estudios Políticos, 1944. xxii, 249 p.

        An index to legislation published in the BOLETIN OFICIAL from
1907 to 1944. Entries total roughly 3,500.

2838. Pélissier, René. "Spanish Africa: A Bibliographical Survey."
        AFRICANA NEWSLETTER, v. 2, no. 2, 1964: 13-22.

        By a French authority on Spanish Africa (see no. 2846), this
bibliographical survey is based on the "monumental work" by Sanford
Berman, giving in extremely simplified form the most prominent titles
from that bibliography as well as a supplementary summary of works
published after 1961. Titles cited relate to Spanish Africa as a
whole or specifically to Spanish Guinea.

Reference Works

2839. AFRICA [REVISTA DE ACCION ESPANOLA]. v. 1- Jan. 1942- Madrid,
        Instituto de Estudios Africanos [IDEA]. illus., maps.
        Monthly.

        IDEA, an institute of the official Spanish Consejo Superior de
Investigaciones Científicas, took over publication of this review
from a non-governmental organization, the Instituto de Estudios
Políticos, in 1950. In 1960 the subtitle was dropped and the subject matter broadened in line with wider Spanish interest in other
parts of Africa. The journal is the most ready source of information about the remaining Spanish possessions in Africa, now limited
to Spanish West Africa (Spanish Sahara and Ifni). Equatorial
Guinea's laws and decrees are no longer cited. Besides articles
and news notes, AFRICA carries a regular section on "Actividades
communistas en el mundo afroasiático," a press review, a list of
new publications including contents of periodicals, and a section
of laws and decrees.

2840. Alvarez García, Heriberto R. HISTORIA DE LA ACCION CULTURAL EN LA
        GUINEA ESPANOLA, CON NOTAS SOBRE LA ENSENANZA EN EL AFRICA
        NEGRA. Madrid, Instituto de Estudios Africanos, 1948. 557 p.
        illus., maps, diagrs.

        Bibliography: p. 543-545.

        Study of Spanish educational work in West Africa by the Chief
Inspector of Education of these tropical colonies. The account is
largely historical.

2841. Crespo Gil-Delgado, Carlos, conde de Castillo Fiel. NOTAS PARA UN
        ESTUDIO ANTROPOLOGICO Y ETNOLOGICO DEL BUBI DE FERNANDO POO.
        Madrid, Instituto de Estudios Africanos y Instituto Bernardino
        de Sahagún, de Antropología y Etnología, 1949. xi, 290 p.
        illus.

        Bibliography: p. 271-283.

        Comprehensive ethnological and anthropometrical treatise on the
Bubi, based on two years of field research and presented as a
doctoral thesis. The work was published jointly by two institutes
of the Consejo Superior de Investigaciones Científicas.

2842. FERNANDO POO. 1961- Santa Isabel. illus. Bimonthly, 1961; quar-
        terly, 1962-

The Library of Congress receives this "Revista de la Deputación Provincial." Its contents have been analyzed in the "Reseña de revistas" in the IDEA monthly AFRICA. Also noted in AFRICA are occasional articles from the information bulletin LA GUINEA ECUATORIAL (formerly LA GUINEA ESPANOLA, 1903-) published semiweekly in Santa Isabel by the Misioneros Hijos del Immaculado Corazón de María.

2843. France. Direction de la Documentation. LES TERRITOIRES ESPAGNOLS D'AFRIQUE. By René Pélissier. Paris, La Documentation Française, 1963. 40 p. (Notes et études documentaires, no. 2951, Jan. 3, 1963)

Spanish ed., LOS TERRITORIOS ESPANOLES DE AFRICA. Madrid, 1964.

Part of the official French series of background documentation, this brochure gives a concise survey of the three remaining territories held by Spain: Ifni (p. 7-12); Le Sahara espagnol (p. 13-19); La Guinée espagnole (p. 20-37). A short reading list is given on pages 38-39. Aspects of Guinea considered are general conditions with outline of geography, history, and people; evolution of political and administrative institutions; economic and financial development; cultural and social evolution. The two short paragraphs of conclusions speak hopefully of equality of civil rights officially recognized since 1959-60, of active efforts toward literacy, and of improvement of living conditions. They are less hopeful about the climate, depopulation, and the unfortunate export dependence on cocoa, coffee, and tropical wood which require price supports from the metropole.

An article by R. Pélissier, "Spain Changes Course in Africa," appeared in AFRICA REPORT, v. 8, Dec. 1963: 8-11.

2844. Guinea, Spanish. Laws, statutes, etc. LEYES COLONIALES. Edited by Agustín Miranda Junco. Madrid, Imprenta Sucesores de Rivadeneyra, 1945. 1462 p.

Compilation in chronological order of all legislation of the Territorios Españoles del Golfo de Guinea from the acquisition by Spain in 1778 through the year 1944. The new constitution and some of the material from the Constitutional Conference appear in: TEXTOS FUNDAMENTALES DE GUINEA ECUATORIAL (Madrid, Servicio Informativo Español, 1968, 150 p., illus.; "Documentos históricos," no. 5). See also no. 2837, above.

2845. Martínez García, Tomás. FERNANDO POO: GEOGRAFIA, HISTORIA, PAISAJE, LA GUINEA ESPANOLA. Santa Isabel, Ediciones Instituto "Claret" de Africanistas, 1968. 119 p. illus., map, plan.

Includes bibliography.

2846. Pélissier, René. "Spanish Guinea: An Introduction." RACE
        (London), v. 6, Oct. 1964: 117-128.

        By the author of the monograph on Spanish territories in
        Africa (no. 2843), this article in the journal of the Institute of
        Race Relations describes the political and economic situation in
        Guinea in mid-1964. An earlier account, "La Guinée espagnole," by
        M. Pélissier appeared in the REVUE FRANCAISE DE SCIENCE POLITIQUE
        (v. 13, Sept. 1963: 624-644). Both these articles are available
        as offprints. He also contributed an article on "Spain's Dis-
        creet Decolonization" to FOREIGN AFFAIRS (v. 43, Apr. 1965: 519-
        527). See also his ETUDES HISPANO-GUINEENNES (Paris, n.p., 1969,
        unpaginated [61 p.]).

2847. Prothero, G. W., general ed. SPANISH GUINEA. London, H.M. Sta-
        tionery Off., 1920. 60 p. (Handbooks Prepared under the
        Direction of the Historical Section of the Foreign Office,
        no. 125)

        Useful older work.

2848. Spain. Consejo Superior de Investigaciones Científicas. Instituto
        de Estudios Africanos. ARCHIVOS. 1947-66. Madrid. illus.,
        maps. Quarterly.

        _____. _____. _____. CATALOGO DE PUBLICACIONES. Madrid,
            1965. 51 p.

        ARCHIVOS was the scholarly review of IDEA, carrying articles by
        experts in varied subject fields. Most numbers contain the list of
        300-odd monographs published by the Institute since its establish-
        ment in the early 1940's, together with titles of articles in pre-
        vious issues of ARCHIVOS. Among the latter there appear many items
        on Spanish Guinea in varied fields of human and physical sciences.
        The CATALOGO DE PUBLICACIONES, which is revised periodically, is
        available from the Institute. Replacing ARCHIVOS is a series of
        pamphlets "Colección monográfica africana."

2849. Spain. Consejo Superior de Investigaciones Científicas. Instituto
        de Estudios Africanos. RESUMENES ESTADISTICOS DEL GOBIERNO
        GENERAL DE LA REGION ECUATORIAL, PROVINCIAS DE FERNANDO POO Y
        RIO MUNI, 1959-60. Madrid, 1962. 479 p. maps, diagrs.
        (Publicaciones)

        A joint publication of IDEA and the Dirección General de Plazas
        y Provincias Africanas. This is separate from the overall RESUMEN
        ESTADISTICO DEL AFRICA ESPANOLA, which has appeared periodically
        since 1954 (1963-64 ed. published in 1965, 528 p., map); until 1958

this section was entitled RESUMENES...DE LOS TERRITORIOS DEL GOLFO
DE GUINEA. The overall volume includes official data relating to
Ifni, the Spanish Sahara, and the "plazas" of Ceuta and Melilla,
as well as the two provinces of Spanish Guinea. Subjects treated
include climatology, population, industry, commerce, transportation, public and private finance, labor and social activities,
health, charity, culture, justice, and religion.

2850. Spain. Oficina de Información Española. SPAIN IN EQUATORIAL AFRICA.
        Madrid, SIE (Servicio Informativo Español), 1964. 91 p.
        illus., maps. (Political Documents, 2)

        Descriptive survey of economic, social, and political condi-
        tions in Spanish Guinea.

2851. Terán, Manuel de. SINTESIS GEOGRAFICA DE FERNANDO POO. Madrid,
        Instituto de Estudios Africanos, Consejo Superior de Investi-
        gaciones Científicas, 1962. 116 p. illus., maps. (Ediciones
        de IDEA)

        Bibliography: p. 111-116.

        Specialist study by a prominent Spanish geographer.

2852. U.S. Department of the Interior. Office of Geography. RIO MUNI,
        FERNANDO PO, AND SAO TOME E PRINCIPE: OFFICIAL STANDARD NAMES
        APPROVED BY THE UNITED STATES BOARD ON GEOGRAPHIC NAMES. Wash-
        ington, U.S. Govt. Print. Off., Apr. 1962. 95 p. map. (6,500
        names) (Gazetteer no. 63)

        See note on series, no. 484.

2853. Unzueta y Yuste, Abelardo de. GEOGRAFIA HISTORICA DE LA ISLA DE
        FERNANDO POO. Madrid, Instituto de Estudios Africanos, 1947.
        494 p. illus., maps.

        Bibliography: p. 435-462.

        _____. GUINEA CONTINENTAL ESPANOLA. Madrid, Instituto de
        Estudios Políticos, 1944. 394 p. illus., maps.

        Bibliography: p. 381-384.

        _____. ISLAS DE GOLFO DE GUINEA (ELOBEYES, CORISCO, ANNOBON,
        PRINCIPE Y SANTO TOME). Madrid, Instituto de Estudios Políticos,
        1945. 386 p. illus., maps.

        Bibliography: p. 373-378.

Standard encyclopedic surveys of the Spanish possessions in West Africa by an authority on colonial trade, professor of economic geography at the Institute of Political Studies. The coverage includes historical, physical, and human geography as well as ethnology, social welfare, political administration, and economy.

2854. Zamora Loboc, Miguel. NOTICIA DE ANNOBON: SU GEOGRAFIA, HISTORIA Y COSTUMBRES. Madrid, Papelería Madrileña, 1962. 88 p. illus. (chiefly col.), plates, maps (part col.). (Publicaciones de la Deputación Provincial de Fernando Póo)

Reviewed in AFRICA (Madrid), no. 247, July 1962: 357. The author, a Spanish writer and artist, was brought up and lives in Annobón, where he directs an educational center.

CHAPTER 43

SOUTHERN AFRICA

Note: The majority of the items in this Southern Africa section have been
provided by Reuben Musiker, Deputy University Librarian, Rhodes University,
Grahamstown, South Africa. Mr. Musiker has very kindly agreed to forego the
librarian's usual arrangement and follow the simplified order used throughout the preceding sections of Part IV and in Part III as well: Atlases
first, then Bibliographies, Serials, and finally Reference Works.

     A few of the items included have been added by the Editors of the
Guide; we have placed "Eds." at the end of the entry so added.

REPUBLIC OF SOUTH AFRICA

Atlases

2855. South Africa. Department of Planning. ONTWIKKELINGSATLAS.
          DEVELOPMENT ATLAS. Pretoria, Govt. Printer, 1966- illus.,
          maps (part col.). 51 x 57 cm.

          Includes bibliographies.

          Major new atlas, loose-leaf in form and issued in sections.
       Complemented by a brief but factual text in Afrikaans and English,
       it covers such topics as physical features, administration, water
       resources, and minerals.

2856. Talbot, A. M., and W. J. Talbot. ATLAS OF THE UNION OF SOUTH
          AFRICA. Prepared in collaboration with the Trigonometrical
          Survey Office and under the aegis of the National Council
          for Social Research. Pretoria, Govt. Printer, 1960. [vii],
          lxiv, 177 p. maps (part col.), tables, diagrs.

A comprehensive atlas with maps showing relief, geology, mining, soils, vegetation, climate and water resources, population, agriculture, industries and occupations, transportation, and trade. The introduction has much useful descriptive and statistical information.

The National Advisory Survey Council has compiled a CATALOGUE OF MAPS PUBLISHED IN THE REPUBLIC OF SOUTH AFRICA (Pretoria, Govt. Printer, 1966, 23 p.). This catalogue includes maps produced by the Bureau of Census and Statistics, Water Affairs Department, Geological Survey, and Natural Resources Development Council.

Bibliographies

2857.   AFRICANA NOVA: A QUARTERLY BIBLIOGRAPHY OF BOOKS CURRENTLY PUBLISHED IN AND ABOUT THE REPUBLIC OF SOUTH AFRICA, BASED ON THE ACCESSIONS TO THE AFRICANA DEPARTMENT...AND INCLUDING MATERIAL RECEIVED BY LEGAL DEPOSIT. 1958- Cape Town, South African Public Library.

This current national bibliography issued by South Africa's second national library (there are two) complements S.A.N.B. (see no. 2866, below), the major difference being that AFRICANA NOVA includes material about South Africa published abroad, whereas S.A.N.B. is limited to South African imprints. Arranged under broad subject headings in the order of the Dewey decimal classification, with alphabetical author index in each quarterly issue and a cumulative annual index in the last number for each year. Includes a list of publishers' names and addresses. From Mar. 1962 includes government and provincial publications. See also no. 277 for information on two important bibliographic series.

2858.   INDEX TO SOUTH AFRICAN PERIODICALS. 1940- Johannesburg, Public Library. Annual.

An invaluable guide to the contents of more than 250 significant and useful periodicals. Two decennial cumulations covering 1940-49 (4 v.) and 1950-59 (3 v.) are available. Author entries are combined with Library of Congress subject entries in a single sequence. Particular attention has been paid to the selection of articles which may in the future contribute to the history of any aspect of South Africa. Among the periodicals indexed in the African studies sphere are AFRICAN MUSIC, AFRICAN STUDIES, AFRICANA NOTES AND NEWS, BANTU EDUCATION JOURNAL, JOURNAL OF RACIAL AFFAIRS, OPTIMA, and SOUTH AFRICAN JOURNAL OF ECONOMICS.

An index of similar scope for the period 1900-1909 is in preparation at the Johannesburg Public Library.

An index to Afrikaans periodical articles (which are also well covered in the INDEX TO SOUTH AFRICAN PERIODICALS) has also been published since 1947: P. J. Nienaber, BRONNEGIDS BY DIE STUDIE VAN DIE AFRIKAANSE TAAL EN LETTERKUNDE (Johannesburg, The Author, 1947-53, 3 v.; Addenda, 2 v.), supplemented by annual reprints from TYDSKRIF VIR GEESTESWETENSKAPPE, in which journal this work is kept up to date.

2859. Johannesburg. Public Library. Strange Collection of Africana.
       CATALOGUE OF BANTU, KHOISAN AND MALAGASY IN THE STRANGE
       COLLECTION OF AFRICANA. Edited by Anna H. Smith. Johannes-
       burg, The Library, 1942. 232 p.

There are 1,671 entries arranged according to language and subdivided into three groups: language, pure literature, and subject literature. An alphabetical index of languages, authors, translators, editors, and titles is included.

Another useful bibliography of African languages, by Dorothea Elizabeth Rossouw, CATALOGUE OF AFRICAN LANGUAGES (1858-1900) IN THE GREY COLLECTION OF THE SOUTH AFRICAN LIBRARY, CAPE TOWN (Cape Town, University School of Librarianship, 1947, 67 p.), contains 379 entries arranged by language and classified by a scheme used in the University of Cape Town libraries.

2860. Mendelssohn, Sidney. SOUTH AFRICAN BIBLIOGRAPHY. London, Kegan
       Paul, 1910. 2 v.

Reprint, London, Holland Press, 1957, 1968.

The standard and best-known retrospective South African bibliography covering the period prior to 1910. Supplementary work containing entries to 1925 and omissions from the original work, totalling over 30,000 items, is in preparation at the South African Library, Cape Town. The major part of the work consists of an alphabetically arranged author catalogue with very full annotations. Included in Vol. II are bibliographies of South African Imperial Blue Books (chronologically arranged) and of periodical articles, drawn from English, French, German, and American sources.

Another retrospective bibliography is the SOUTH AFRICAN CATALOGUE OF BOOKS, edited by N. S. Coetzee, fourth edition, covering 1900-1950 (Johannesburg, The Editor, 1952, 2 v.). Vol.

I (A-K) of a projected fifth edition covering 1900-1954 was published by Technibooks, P.O. Box 1881, Johannesburg, in 1956. Vol. II of this edition has not been published. This work is an author-title list of books published in South Africa, excluding government publications and mission presses.

2861. Muller, C. F. J., F. A. van Jaarsveld, and T. van Wyk, eds. A SELECT BIBLIOGRAPHY OF SOUTH AFRICAN HISTORY. Pretoria, University of South Africa, 1966. xii, 215 p.

A useful, unannotated checklist of 2,521 items. It begins with general aids--bibliographies, periodicals, atlases, guides to archives, and general histories. The second part is arranged by periods, from prehistory to the present, and the third part by subject. An author index and index to persons is included.

2862. Musiker, Reuben. GUIDE TO SOUTH AFRICAN REFERENCE BOOKS. 4th rev. ed. Cape Town, Balkema, 1965. 110 p.

5th ed. scheduled for publication in 1970.

Contains more than 500 entries of the more important works of reference on South African topics, limited to works published in South Africa. The first edition appeared in 1955. Arrangement is by subject headings in the sequence of the Dewey decimal classification and, within sections, alphabetically by author or title. English is used for collation, notes, and annotations. There is an index of authors, titles, and subject. Supplements to the work were published annually in the Hoover Institution's AFRICANA NEWSLETTER and now appear annually in the AFRICAN STUDIES BULLETIN of the African Studies Association of the United States. A companion work to the GUIDE, SOUTH AFRICAN BIBLIOGRAPHY by R. Musiker, is scheduled for publication by Crosby Lockwood, London, in 1969. This is a survey of retrospective and current national bibliographies, periodical and newspaper lists and indexes, archives and manuscripts, official publications and offers the first evaluative guide to South African subject bibliographies.

2863. Niemandt, J. J. BIBLIOGRAFIE VAN DIE BANTOETALE IN DIE UNIE VAN SUID-AFRIKA. v. 1-6. Pretoria, 1959-63.

v. 4- have title BIBLIOGRAPHY OF THE BANTU LANGUAGES IN THE REPUBLIC OF SOUTH AFRICA.

2864. Nienaber, Petrus Johannes. BIBLIOGRAFIE VAN AFRIKAANSE BOEKE. Johannesburg, The Author [24 Kafue Road, Emmarentia, Johannesburg] 1943-67. 6 v.

A most important bibliography of books in the Afrikaans language, providing a record of books published in Afrikaans between 1861 and 1966. Full author, title, and subject lists are included in each volume, complemented by authors' and publishers' addresses.

A comprehensive bibliography of subject literature in the Afrikaans language was published in 1958: G. R. Morris, DIE AFRIKAANSE VAKLITERATUUR (Pretoria, Transvaal Provincial Library, 1958). This is a classified list complemented by an alphabetical index of authors, titles, and subjects. The period since 1958 is well covered in the current national bibliographies.

2865. PERIODICALS IN SOUTH AFRICAN LIBRARIES: A REVISED EDITION OF THE CATALOGUE OF UNION PERIODICALS. Pretoria, South African Council for Scientific and Industrial Research and National Council for Social Research, 1961-

A union list of serials based on P. Freer's CATALOGUE OF UNION PERIODICALS, which it will supersede when complete. The work is still in progress (letter P was published in 1969) and subject to continuous revision. It is commonly referred to as PISAL. Arrangement is alphabetical by title of periodical.

2866. S.A.N.B.: SOUTH AFRICAN NATIONAL BIBLIOGRAPHY: PUBLICATIONS RECEIVED IN TERMS OF COPYRIGHT ACT NO. 9 OF 1916. 1959- Pretoria, State Library. Quarterly with annual cumulations.

Formerly issued as an annual list: PUBLICATIONS RECEIVED IN TERMS OF COPYRIGHT ACT NO. 9 OF 1916, 1933-58.

Lists all publications received by this national library, including government and provincial publications, as well as new periodicals. The arrangement of entries is according to the Dewey decimal classification. Included are lists of publishers and authors writing under pseudonyms.

2867. Schapera, Isaac, comp. SELECT BIBLIOGRAPHY OF SOUTH AFRICAN NATIVE LIFE AND PROBLEMS. Compiled for the Inter-university Committee for African Studies under the direction of I. Schapera. London, Oxford University Press, 1941. xii, 249 p.

A valuable bibliography, which includes government reports and periodical articles and is critically annotated. Contents cover physical anthropology, archaeology, ethnography, and modern status and conditions, including administration, law, economics, education, religion, health and social services.

Three supplements to this work have been published by the University of Cape Town School of Librarianship in its Bibliographical Series: M. A. Holden and A. Jacoby, FIRST SUPPLEMENT, 1934-1949; R. Giffen and J. Back, SECOND SUPPLEMENT, 1950-1958; and C. Solomon, THIRD SUPPLEMENT, 1958-1963. These three supplements cover only the section on modern status and conditions.

The main work and the supplements have been reprinted by Kraus Periodicals, Inc., New York.

See also Shelagh M. Willet, THE BUSHMAN: A SELECT BIBLIOGRAPHY, 1952-1962 (Johannesburg, Department of Bibliography, Librarianship and Typography, University of the Witwatersrand, 1965, 35 l.).

2868. South Africa. House of Assembly. INDEX TO THE MANUSCRIPT ANNEXURES AND PRINTED PAPERS OF THE HOUSE OF ASSEMBLY, INCLUDING SELECT COMMITTEE REPORTS AND BILLS, AND ALSO TO PRINCIPAL MOTIONS AND RESOLUTIONS AND COMMISSION REPORTS, INCLUDING DEPARTMENTAL COMMITTEES, 1910-1961. Cape Town, Govt. Printer, 1963. 631 p.

An invaluable index to government publications for the period 1910-61. Current lists of official publications are given in AFRICANA NOVA and S.A.N.B. (the two national bibliographies), in the GOVERNMENT GAZETTE, and in the monthly LIST OF OFFICIAL PUBLICATIONS (Pretoria, Govt. Printer).

A useful American work in this category is Yale University's SOUTH AFRICAN OFFICIAL PUBLICATIONS HELD BY YALE UNIVERSITY: A LIST OF HOLDINGS IN YALE UNIVERSITY LIBRARIES OF OFFICIAL PUBLICATIONS OF THE COLONIAL, UNION AND REPUBLICAN GOVERNMENTS OF SOUTH AFRICA AND OF ALL TERRITORIES WITHIN THE PRESENT BORDERS OF SOUTH AFRICA, INCLUDING THE HIGH COMMISSION TERRITORIES AND SOUTHWEST AFRICA. (New Haven, Conn., May 1966, 64 p.; processed), which is a list of 631 entries in geographical arrangement.

2869. Spohr, Otto H., comp., assisted by Manfred R. Poller. GERMAN AFRICANA: GERMAN PUBLICATIONS ON SOUTH- AND SOUTH WEST AFRICA. Pretoria, State Library, 1968. 332 p. (Pretoria, State Library, Bibliographies, no. 14)

This bibliography, the most complete of its kind, covers 3,423 entries arranged in alphabetical order by author. There is also an index for personal names (including joint authors, illustrators, and editors), plus a subject index for South-West Africa and one for South Africa. Readers are also provided with an indication as to which South African library holds any particular book. The subjects covered include every conceivable topic--ethnography, history, geography, mining, agriculture, linguistic studies, and so forth.

The entries are confined to published material; archival sources are not included.

See also Gerhard Tötemeyer, SUDAFRIKA-SUDWESTAFRIKA: EINE BIBLIOGRAPHIE, 1945-1963 (Freiburg, Arnold-Bergsträsser-Institut für Kulturwissenschaftliche Forschung, 1964, 284 p.). [Eds.]

2870. State Library, Pretoria. CURRENT SOUTH AFRICAN PERIODICALS, JULY 1965. Pretoria, 1966. 167 p.

A comprehensive directory of South African periodicals in classified order with an alphabetical index. Annual supplements have been issued since 1966.

Two other useful lists showing serials published in South Africa were published by the South African Public Library in 1951: CLASSIFIED LIST OF SOUTH AFRICAN ANNUAL PUBLICATIONS (Grey Bibliographies, no. 4) and HANDLIST OF SOUTH AFRICAN PERIODICALS (Grey Bibliographies, no. 5). These lists are supplemented in the QUARTERLY BULLETIN of the South African Public Library.

2871. United Nations. Dag Hammarskjöld Library. APARTHEID: A SELECTIVE BIBLIOGRAPHY ON THE RACIAL POLICIES OF THE GOVERNMENT OF THE REPUBLIC OF SOUTH AFRICA. New York, May 15, 1968. 52 p. (ST/LIB/22)

The UN library's acquisition of works concerned exclusively or primarily with apartheid are cited here. Many periodical articles are included. The list is arranged under 12 broad categories, each denoting a different aspect of the problem (e.g., treatment of people of Indo-Pakistan origin, economic aspects of racial policies, the Tomlinson report, the treason trial, biographies and personal narratives). [Eds.]

2872. Van Riebeeck Festival. Book Exhibition Committee. SOUTH AFRICA IN PRINT ...: CATALOGUE OF AN EXHIBITION OF BOOKS, ATLASES AND MAPS HELD IN THE SOUTH AFRICAN LIBRARY. Cape Town, The Committee, 1952. xii, 187 p. illus., maps.

An important bibliography issued in conjunction with a national exhibition to mark the Van Riebeeck tercentenary and forming an excellent select list of Africana. Arrangement is in broad subject groups, e.g., discovery and travel, South African English literature, language and literature of native peoples, fauna, flora, historical work. The introductions to each section are good, as are the annotations.

THE BOOK IN SOUTH AFRICA: EXHIBITION OF SOUTH AFRICAN PUB-
LICATIONS was a bibliography issued in 1960 to mark the Union
Festival (Bloemfontein, Union Festival Committee). The emphasis
in this bibliography is on literary works, the first half consisting of Afrikaans books and the second comprising a select
bibliography of books in English by South African writers (1789-
1960), as well as German, Hebrew, and Yiddish books by South
African writers since 1910.

Serials

Note: There are so many serial publications in South Africa that only a
few can be mentioned here. See the preceding section on bibliographies
for references to periodical lists, indexes to periodicals, etc.

2873. HISTORIA: AMPTELIKE ORGAAN VAN DIE HISTORIESE GENOOTSKAP VAN SUID-
        AFRIKA. [1955?-] Pretoria, University of Pretoria. Quarterly.

2874. HISTORIESE STUDIES. 1939- Pretoria, University of Pretoria.
        Quarterly.

2875. SOUTH AFRICAN GEOGRAPHICAL JOURNAL. 1917- Johannesburg. Annual.

2876. South African Institute of Race Relations, Johannesburg. FACT
        PAPER. 1958- Irregular.

        SURVEY OF RACE RELATIONS IN SOUTH AFRICA. 1951/52- Annual.

        RACE RELATIONS JOURNAL. 1933-62. Quarterly.

        See also no. 2950.

2877. SOUTH AFRICAN JOURNAL OF ECONOMICS: THE QUARTERLY JOURNAL OF THE
        ECONOMIC SOCIETY OF SOUTH AFRICA. 1933- Johannesburg.
        Quarterly.

2878. SOUTH AFRICAN LAW JOURNAL. 1900- Cape Town. Quarterly.

2879. TYDSKRIF VIR RASSE-AANGELEENTHEDE. JOURNAL OF RACIAL AFFAIRS.
        1949- Pretoria, South African Bureau of Racial Affairs.
        Quarterly.

Reference Works
_____

2880.   AFRIKAANSE KINDERENSIKLOPEDIE. Onder redaksie van C. F. Albertyn.
            Kaapstad, Nasionale Boekhandel, 1963-64. 10 v.

        A major South African encyclopedia in the Afrikaans language;
a revised edition of a work first published in 1943-55. Although
intended primarily for juvenile audiences, it is invaluable for
information on South African history, literature, biography, and
culture in the absence of a comprehensive English-language encylco-
pedia for South Africa. Well illustrated and clearly written,
the volumes are arranged according to broad topics with indexes in
each volume and in the final volume.

        A major multi-volume adult South African encyclopedia in
separate English and Afrikaans editions is in preparation by
Nasionale Boekhandel.

2881.   Andrews, H. T., and others, eds. SOUTH AFRICA IN THE SIXTIES: A
            SOCIO-ECONOMIC SURVEY. Cape Town, South Africa Foundation,
            1962. xii, 216 p. front., illus., maps.

        A descriptive and statistical résumé of the economic scene in
the Republic. Three other up-to-date surveys are D. H. Houghton,
THE SOUTH AFRICAN ECONOMY (2d ed., Cape Town, Oxford University
Press, 1967, 280 p., maps, tables, diagrs.; bibliography: p. 264-
272); N. Hurwitz and O. Williams, THE ECONOMIC FRAMEWORK OF SOUTH
AFRICA (Pietermaritzburg, Shuter and Shooter, 1962, 148 p., maps,
tables, diagrs.; bibliography); Union Acceptances, Ltd., THE SCOPE
FOR INVESTMENT IN SOUTH AFRICA (Johannesburg, The Firm, 1964, 59 p.),
a concise statistical and factual review of recent economic developments.

        The following survey is a basic work, a classic analysis of
African economic history, with South Africa given special attention:
S. Herbert Frankel, CAPITAL INVESTMENT IN AFRICA: ITS COURSE AND
EFFECTS (London, New York, Oxford University Press, 1938, xvi, 487 p.,
2 maps, tables; bibliography: p. 435-462).

2282.   Antonissen, Rob J. K. E. DIE AFRIKAANSE LETTERKUNDE VAN AANVANG TOT
            HEDE. 3de hersiene dr. Kaapstad, Nasou, 1965. 358 p. plates.

        A comprehensive history of Afrikaans literature.

        Another work of similar scope is Gerrit Dekker, AFRIKAANSE
LITERATUURGESKIEDENIS (7de dr., Kaapstad, Nasionale Boekhandel, 1963,
416 p.).

No comparable works exist for South African English literature, but the SOUTH AFRICAN P.E.N. YEAR BOOK (1954-1956/57, 1960, Johannesburg, South African Centre of the International P.E.N. Club) is of great value for its essays and surveys of South African English literature, especially the 1960 volume, which features 50-year surveys.

2883. ARCHIVES YEARBOOK FOR SOUTH AFRICAN HISTORY. 1938- Pretoria, Govt. Printer. illus., maps.

This important series consists of original contributions, some in English and some in Afrikaans, on various aspects of South African history, e.g., N. H. MacKenzie, SOUTH AFRICAN TRAVEL LITERATURE IN THE SEVENTEENTH CENTURY (1955). Many of the earlier volumes are out of print; a full list showing prices and availability may be had on application to the Government Archivist, Private Bag 236, Pretoria. The publications themselves are obtainable from the Government Printer, Bosman Street, Pretoria.

Archival records for the provinces have also been published (Pretoria, Govt. Printer) at irregular intervals: Cape, nos. 1-5, 1651-1719; Orange Free State, nos. 1-4, 1854-9, Transvaal, nos. 1-7, 1845-68; Natal, nos. 1-5, 1838-59.

2884. Automobile Association of South Africa. ROAD ATLAS AND TOURING GUIDE OF SOUTHERN AFRICA. 2d ed. Johannesburg, The Association, 1963. 200 p. maps, diagrs.

In addition to detailed maps, includes diagrams of exits and entrances for over 200 towns, as well as a wealth of general information for the motorist.

2885. Axelson, Eric V., ed. SOUTH AFRICAN EXPLORERS. London, Oxford University Press, 1954. xxv, 346 p. fold. map. (The World's Classics, no. 538)

Professor Axelson has specialized in early South African history. Among his other books are THE PORTUGUESE IN SOUTH-EAST AFRICA, 1600-1600 and SOUTH-EAST AFRICA, 1488-1530 (see no. 2803 for annotations).

2886. Beerman, R., firm, publishers. CITY OF CAPE TOWN: OFFICIAL GUIDE. 4th ed. Cape Town, Beerman, 1957. 238 p. illus., maps.

This same firm has also published guides of similar scope for the following cities: East London (2d ed., 1953), Kimberley (2d ed., 1957), Durban (1953), Pietermaritzburg (1952), Bloemfontein (1950), Germiston (1957), Johannesburg (3d ed., 1962), Pretoria (1951).

Contents of these guides include sporting facilities, clubs, social organizations, medical services, newspapers, transportation, hotels, motoring, and cultural entertainments.

2887. Beerman, R., firm, publishers. OFFICIAL GUIDE TO THE PROVINCE OF THE CAPE OF GOOD HOPE. Cape Town, Beerman, 1953. 262 p. illus., maps.

Provincial guides have also been published for the other provinces: Natal (1959), Orange Free State (1956), Transvaal (1960).

These guides give short descriptions of each town in the province, as well as information on history, churches, universities, geographical features, fishing, flora, monuments, mining, and industry.

2888. BEERMAN'S ALL MINING YEARBOOK: A CYCLOPAEDIA OF ALL MINING UNDER- TAKINGS IN THE REPUBLIC OF SOUTH AFRICA AND THE PROTECTORATES. 1956- Cape Town, Beerman.

This directory of mining companies, arranged alphabetically under the ore produced, gives full directory and production infor- mation for each mine, including capital, property, and location. An outline of South-West Africa mining law is included.

A current official source is MINERALS: QUARTERLY INFORMATION CIRCULAR, compiled by the Mineral Development Section (Pretoria, Govt. Printer). Gives data on production and exports of gold, silver, diamonds, and other minerals. Includes a summary of pro- duction, sale, and exports of minerals of South-West Africa, as well as information on mining in Basutoland, Bechuanaland, and Swaziland.

2889. BEERMAN'S FINANCIAL YEARBOOK OF SOUTHERN AFRICA. 1947/48- Cape Town, Beerman.

From 1961 issued in two volumes. For each company are given directors, address, capital, assets, and liabilities. Arranged alphabetically with a classified index. Includes general infor- mation on taxation, stock exchange procedures, and a who's who of South African company directors. Title changed in 1963 from SOUTH AFRICAN FINANCIAL YEARBOOK: INVESTOR'S MANUAL AND CYCLOPAEDIA OF SOUTH AFRICAN PUBLIC COMPANIES.

2890. Benson, Mary. SOUTH AFRICA: THE STRUGGLE FOR A BIRTHRIGHT.
           Completely rev. ed. London, Penguin, 1966. 314 p. map.
       (African Library)

           Originally published as THE AFRICAN PATRIOTS (London, Faber &
       Faber, 1963), this is a sympathetic account of African nationalist
       movements by a white, liberal activist in the movement to secure more
       political rights for Africans. [Eds.]

2891. Border Regional Survey [series]. 1961- Cape Town, Oxford University
           Press for Rhodes University, Institute of Social and Economic
           Research. Irregular.

           This series deals with economic and sociological problems in
       the Eastern Cape. The series includes a triology--Xhosa in Town--
       the three volumes being as follows: Vol. 1, D. H. Reader, THE
       BLACK MAN'S PORTION: HISTORY, DEMOGRAPHY AND LIVING CONDITIONS IN
       THE NATIVE LOCATIONS OF EAST LONDON, CAPE PROVINCE (1961, 180 p.);
       Vol. 2, P. Mayer, TOWNSMEN OR TRIBESMEN: CONSERVATISM AND THE
       PROCESS OF URBANIZATION IN A SOUTH AFRICAN CITY (1961, 306 p.);
       Vol. 3, B. A. Pauw, THE SECOND GENERATION (1963, 238 p.).

           A basic work in this series is C. Board, THE BORDER REGION:
       NATURAL ENVIRONMENT AND LAND USE IN THE EASTERN CAPE (1962, 2 v.),
       which presents the results of a land-use survey of the East London
       (Cape) and King William's Town districts.

2892. Bosman, Daniel Brink, and others. TWEETALIGE WOORDEBOEK: ENGELS-
           AFRIKAANS; AFRIKAANS-ENGELS. 6de verbeterde nitgawe deur D.
           B. Bosman, I. W. van der Merwe en L. W. Hiemstra. Kaapstad,
       Nasionale Boekhandel, 1962. xvii, 1906 p.

           The most comprehensive Afrikaans-English dictionary available.
       Another good bilingual dictionary is M. S. Kritzinger and others,
       GROOT WOORDEBOEK: AFRIKAANS-ENGELS: ENGLISH-AFRIKAANS (9de verbeterde
       en belangrik uitgebreide uitgawe, Pretoria, van Schaik, 1963, 1340 p.).

2893. CAMBRIDGE HISTORY OF THE BRITISH EMPIRE. Cambridge, Eng.,
           University Press. Vol. VIII, SOUTH AFRICA, RHODESIA AND THE
           HIGH COMMISSION TERRITORIES. General editor, Eric A. Walker;
           2d ed. 1963. xxviii, 1087 p.

           The previous edition was published in 1936. This is a basic
       work covering Southern Africa from ancient times to date. Aspects
       covered include social, economic, and cultural development and
       native inhabitants. The bibliography (p. 917-1017) includes a
       detailed list of manuscripts, official sources, and other works.

2894. Carnegie Commission of Investigation on the Poor White Question in
        South Africa. THE POOR WHITE PROBLEM IN SOUTH AFRICA: REPORT
        OF THE CARNEGIE COMMISSION. Stellenbosch, Pro-Ecclesia
        Drukkery, 1932. 5 v. plates, fold. maps, diagrs.

        Includes bibliography.

        A comprehensive report by specialists on economic, psychological,
health, and sociological aspects of the problem.

2895. Carter, Gwendolen M. THE POLITICS OF INEQUALITY: SOUTH AFRICA
        SINCE 1948. Rev. ed. New York, Praeger, 1959. 541 p. maps,
        diagrs.

        2d printing, 1962.

        Bibliography: p. 497-524.

        A valuable contribution surveying the South African political
scene, with an extensive annotated bibliography, including many
official documents. This expanded edition includes a brief appendix
(p. 491-495) on voting returns in the 1958 election and a reference
to H. F. Verwoerd as Prime Minister following the death of J. G.
Strijdom (p. 238). [Eds.]

        Of equal importance is the sequel to this work: FIVE AFRICAN
STATES, edited by Gwendolen M. Carter (Ithaca, N.Y., Cornell
University Press, 1963; London, Pall Mall Press, 1964); chap. vi,
South Africa, by Thomas Karis. A valuable, critically annotated
bibliography (p. 607-616) includes official publications, newspapers
and periodicals, pamphlets, and other material chiefly of a political
nature.

2896. Clark, John Desmond. THE PREHISTORY OF SOUTHERN AFRICA. Harmonds-
        worth, Middlesex, Penguin Books, 1959. xxvi, 341 p. illus.,
        maps, tables, diagrs. (Pelican Archaeological Series)

        Bibliography: p. 315-330.

        Contents: Man-apes, fossil remains in South Africa, early and
late stone ages, prehistoric art, miners, metalwork, and builders
in stone.

2897. Cluver, Eustace Henry. MEDICAL AND HEALTH LEGISLATION IN THE UNION
        OF SOUTH AFRICA. 2d ed. Johannesburg, Central News Agency,
        1960. xvi, 813 p.

Gives a commentary on the acts, as well as the texts of the acts and regulations. Also deals with rules and regulations of the South African Medical and Dental Council, ethical rules, medical degrees entitled to registration, and history of public health acts.

A useful complementary volume is E. H. Cluver, PUBLIC HEALTH IN SOUTH AFRICA (6th ed., Johannesburg, Central News Agency, 1959, 364 p.). This gives information on malnutrition in South Africa, housing, slum elimination, refuse disposal, diseases and their distribution, and vital statistics.

2898. Cole, Monica M. SOUTH AFRICA. 2d ed. London, Methuen; New York, Dutton, 1966. xxx, 706 p. plates, maps, diagrs.

Includes bibliographies.

This extensive study by a geographer (formerly at the University of Witwatersrand) contains chapters on physical background, occupation, water supply and irrigation, agriculture, mineral resources, power, communication and trade, Bantu economy, major regions, population, and the future.

2899. Cope, John Patrick. SOUTH AFRICA. 2d ed. New York, Praeger, 1967. xvii, 238 p. maps (part fold.). (Nations of the Modern World)

Useful, popular account. [Eds.]

2900. De Kiewiet, C. W. A HISTORY OF SOUTH AFRICA, SOCIAL AND ECONOMIC. London, Oxford University Press, 1941. xii, 292 p. maps, diagrs.

Bibliography: p. xi-xii.

One of the standard histories of South Africa.

2901. De Villiers, Christoffel Coetzee. GENEALOGIES OF OLD SOUTH AFRICAN FAMILIES. Completely rev. ed., augmented and rewritten by C. Pama. Cape Town, Balkema, 1966. 3 v.

Title page and preliminary matter in English and Afrikaans; text in Afrikaans.

An important source for retrospective biography, with genealogical information on early Cape families. The original edition in Dutch (Kaapstad, Van de Sandt de Villiers, 1893-94, 3 v.) was

supplemented in J. Hoge, BYRDRAES TOT DIE GENEALOGIE VAN OU
AFRIKAANSE FAMILIES (Kaapstad, Balkema, 1958, 224 p.).

2902. DICTIONARY OF SOUTH AFRICAN BIOGRAPHY. Vol. I. W. J. de Kock,
Editor-in-chief. Cape Town, Published for the National
Council for Social Research, Department of Higher Education,
by Nasionale Boekhandel BPK, 1968- 894 p.

The first volume in a basic series which will contain biographies of persons who died before the end of 1950; succeeding
series will cover persons who died after 1950. The second and
each succeeding volume will have a cumulative index. Coverage
includes individuals from the former High Commission territories
and South-West Africa, those who were either born in South Africa
or spent considerable time there and achieved distinction abroad,
non-South Africans whose lives and activities have had a "considerable influence" on South Africa, and "scoundrels" and "frauds."
The first volume contains 568 biographies, many quite lengthy,
from A to Z. Each sketch is accompanied by a bibliography of
books and articles about the biographies. [Eds.]

2903. DIRECTORY OF SOUTHERN AFRICA AND BUYERS' GUIDE. 1933- Cape Town,
Cape Times. Annual.

The title was changed in 1964 from CAPE TIMES DIRECTORY OF
SOUTHERN AFRICA. This comprehensive professional and business
directory, arranged alphabetically by town, is fuller for the Cape
province than for the other provinces. It also has a classified
trade directory for the larger centers and lists of telegraphic
addresses and post-office-box renters. The directory is prefaced
by a section listing diplomatic, official, and legal personnel.
South-West Africa, Basutoland, Bechuanaland, and Swaziland are
included.

A work of similar scope is BRABY'S COMMERCIAL DIRECTORY OF
SOUTH, EAST AND CENTRAL AFRICA (1924/25-, Durban, Braby, annual).
It is published in two parts: an alphabetical section and a
classified trades section. Included, too, are sections on
Basutoland, Bechuanaland, Swaziland, and South-West Africa. Braby
also publishes separate business directories for each province
and for some of the larger cities. A detailed list is available
from the publishers, P.O. Box 731, Durban.

2904. Doke, Clement Martyn, and Benedict Wallet Vilakazi. ZULU-ENGLISH
DICTIONARY. 2d ed. rev. Johannesburg, Witwatersrand University
Press, 1958. xxvi, 918 p.

Most comprehensive Zulu-English dictionary. A companion volume to this work is ENGLISH AND ZULU DICTIONARY, compiled by C. M. Doke, D. McK. Malcolm, and J. M. A. Sikakana (Johannesburg, Witwatersrand University Press, 1958, 2 v. in 1). Part 1 of this work is an English-Zulu dictionary; Part 2, Zulu-English vocabulary, is an abridgment of the author's Zulu-English dictionary.

Numerous dictionaries of other African languages in South Africa are also available. A few of the more important ones are T. J. Kriel, THE NEW ENGLISH-SESOTHO DICTIONARY (rev. ed., Johannesburg, Afrikaanse Pers, 1958, 339 p.); A. Mabille and H. Dieterlen, SOUTHERN SOTHO-ENGLISH DICTIONARY (rev. and enl. 8th ed., Morija, Sesuto Book Depot, 1961, 445 p.); J. McLaren, A NEW CONCISE XHOSA-ENGLISH DICTIONARY (London, Longmans, 1963, xviii, 194 p.).

2905.   Duggan-Cronin, A. M.   BANTU TRIBES OF SOUTH AFRICA: REPRODUCTIONS OF PHOTOGRAPHIC STUDIES. Cambridge, Eng., Deighton, Bell, 1938-41. 4 v.

The excellent photographic studies are prefaced by introductions and bibliographies compiled by specialists. The peoples covered are the Bavenda, Bechuana, Bapedi, Basotho, Nguni, M'Pondo, M'Pondomise, Zulu, Swazi, Baca, Hlubi and Xesibe, Vathonga, and Vachopi, and those of the Ciskei and Southern Transkei. [Eds.]

2906.   Du Plessis, Johannes.   A HISTORY OF CHRISTIAN MISSIONS IN SOUTH AFRICA. London, Longmans, 1911. xx, 494 p. map.

Bibliography: p. 466-479.

A well-documented historical account of missionary history in South Africa, especially good for the period before 1850. It deals with the missions of the Dutch colonists, Dominican Fathers, Moravians, Wesleyans, Scottish, French, Rhenish, Dutch Reformed Church, Roman Catholics, and Scandinavians, as well as the early London missionaries, Berlin mission, Swiss Romane mission, American Zulu mission, and Church of England mission.

2907.   Du Toit, Alexander Logie. THE GEOLOGY OF SOUTH AFRICA. 3d ed. Edinburgh, Oliver & Boyd, 1954. 611 p. col. map.

The standard work on the subject. In addition to detailed descriptions of formations, there are chapters on primitive man, soils, economic geology, and geological history of South Africa. An excellent, concise, and recent work in this field is: E. D. Mountain, GEOLOGY OF SOUTHERN AFRICA (Cape Town, Books of Africa, 1968, 249 p., illus., maps).

A work which deals with each mineral and its distribution in South Africa has been issued by the Geological Survey: MINERAL RESOURCES OF THE UNION OF SOUTH AFRICA (4th ed., Pretoria, Govt. Printer, 1959, 622 p., maps). A briefer more recent work is R. A. Pelletier, MINERAL RESOURCES OF SOUTH-CENTRAL AFRICA (Cape Town, Oxford University Press, 1964, 277 p., illus., maps). It is arranged regionally, giving for each territory descriptions of minerals (location, production, prices). Statistical data cover the period 1950-59. There is a bibliography.

2908. EDUCATION AND THE SOUTH AFRICAN ECONOMY: THE 1961 EDUCATION PANEL
          SECOND REPORT. Johannesburg, Witwatersrand University Press,
          1966. 152 p. tables, charts. Chairman: O. D. Schreiner.

     This report, which deals only with educational changes required from an economic viewpoint, discusses the expansion in the quantity of education which will have to take place by 1980 and makes recommendations for primary, secondary, university, and technical education.

2909. EDUCATIONAL INSTITUTIONS IN SOUTH AFRICA. Johannesburg, Erudite
          Publications, 1967. 425 p.

     A descriptive and statistical work giving information about education for the various race groups, as well as lists of schools.

2910. ENCYCLOPAEDIA OF SOUTHERN AFRICA. Compiled and edited by Eric
          Rosenthal. 4th ed. London, New York, Warne, 1967. 638 p.
          illus., plates (part col.), maps.

     Useful encyclopedia though limited in detail; first published in 1961. Arrangement is alphabetical by topic, but the volume is not indexed. There are some 5,000 short articles and over 20 longer ones on such topics as Bantu languages, Afrikaans, and English literature.

     A comprehensive STANDARD ENCYCLOPAEDIA OF SOUTHERN AFRICA is in preparation by Nasionale Boekhandel.

2911. Fagan, Brian M. SOUTHERN AFRICA DURING THE IRON AGE. New York,
          Praeger, 1965. 222 p. illus., maps. (Ancient Peoples and
          Places Series)

     Bibliography: p. 173-177.

This is a professional archaeologist's survey of the Iron Age in Southern Africa through the recent--historically documented-- past to the present century. The first part of the book deals briefly with the later Stone Age indicating the way of life into which the Iron Age economy was introduced by the first farmers. The main part surveys the succession of Iron Age cultures in Central and South Africa with the emphasis increasingly historical as the book approaches the final chapter on the nineteenth century. This is a basic book to understanding the Iron Age in Africa. [Eds.]

2912. Fitzsimons, Vivian F. M. SNAKES OF SOUTH AFRICA. Cape Town, Purnell, 1962. 423 p. illus., plates, maps.

Bibliography: p. 383-406.

An important, comprehensive work giving systematic descriptions of 137 snakes. Included are chapters on feeding habits, venoms, longevity, courtship, and dangerous species.

The same author has written a comprehensive work on South African lizards: LIZARDS OF SOUTH AFRICA (Pretoria, Transvaal Museum, 1943, xv, 528 p., illus., plates, map). A useful reference work covering South African reptiles as a whole is Walter Rose, THE REPTILES AND AMPHIBIANS OF SOUTHERN AFRICA (rev. and enl. ed., Cape Town, Maskew Miller, 1962, xxxii, 494 p., illus.).

2913. Gordon-Brown, Alfred. PICTORIAL ART IN SOUTH AFRICA DURING THREE CENTURIES TO 1875, WITH NOTES ON OVER FOUR HUNDRED ARTISTS. London, Sawyer, 1952. 172 p. illus., plates.

Includes bibliography.

Addenda in AFRICANA NOTES AND NEWS (Johannesburg, Africana Society, Africana Museum), v. 12, Sept. 1957: 229-269.

An outstanding work on the history of art in South Africa. Gives short biographies of 400 artists who painted pictures of South African interest. An appendix includes a chronological list of South African lithographers and engravers. A revised edition is to be published by Balkema, Cape Town.

The more recent period is well covered by several publications: F. L. Alexander, ART IN SOUTH AFRICA: PAINTING, SCULPTURE AND GRAPHIC WORK SINCE 1900 (Cape Town, Balkema, 1962, 171 p.); H. Jeppe, SOUTH AFRICAN ARTISTS, 1900-1962 (Johannesburg, Afrikaanse Pers, 1963, 172 p., illus., some col.); OUR ART (Pretoria, Lantern, in collaboration with South African Broadcasting Corp., 1959-60, 2 v.).

2914.   Grossert, J. W., ed. THE ART OF AFRICA. Pietermaritzburg, Shuter
        & Shooter, 1958. 140 p. illus., maps, diagrs.

       Contributions by Walter W. Battiss and other specialists on
the art of the Bushman, Bavenda, Basuto, Ndebele, and Zulu peoples.

2915.   GUIDE TO SOUTHERN AFRICA: REPUBLIC OF SOUTH AFRICA, SOUTH-WEST
        AFRICA, RHODESIA, ZAMBIA, MALAWI, ETC. Edited by A. Gordon
        Brown for the Union-Castle Mail Steamship Co., Ltd. 1967 ed.
        London, Robert Hale, 1966. 576 p. illus. (part col.), fold.
        maps.

       From 1901 to 1949 the volume was published as the SOUTH AND EAST
AFRICAN YEAR BOOK AND GUIDE: from 1950 to 1966 as the YEARBOOK AND
GUIDE TO SOUTHERN AFRICA. Beginning with the 1967 edition this
work became a biannual rather than an annual publication, and
greater emphasis was given to travel. There is still a substantial
section of general information; statistical information is no longer
included though sources of such data are supplied. Additional
sections are on Lesotho (Basutoland), Botswana (Bechuanaland),
Swaziland, and Angola, as well as the Canaries, Madeira, Ascension,
and St. Helena. There are geographical and subject indexes.

2916.   Hahlo, H. R., and Ellison Kahn. SOUTH AFRICA: THE DEVELOPMENT OF
        ITS LAWS AND CONSTITUTION. Cape Town, Juta, 1960. xxx,
        900 p.

       A compendium of the whole field of South African law, giving
a general picture of the basic doctrines and institutions of South
Africa's laws and constitution. Contents include the genesis of
South African law, seventeenth to eighteenth century, constitutional
development to 1910, administration of justice, criminal law, native
law and native courts, mercantile law, economic and racial legislation.
It has a very useful bibliography (p. 815-829). A supplement covering the transition of the country to a republic was published in
1962: E. Kahn, THE NEW CONSTITUTION (Cape Town, Juta).

       The ANNUAL SURVEY OF SOUTH AFRICAN LAW (1947- , Cape Town,
Juta for the Faculty of Law, University of the Witwatersrand) is
a valuable summary review covering numerous aspects of law, including administration of justice. ACTA JURIDICA (Cape Town,
Balkema for the Faculty of Law, University of Cape Town), also
published annually, has articles and reviews on various aspects
of South African law. The 1960 volume was a special issue tracing
the development of South African government and law from 1910 to
1960.

2917. Hellmann, Ellen, ed. HANDBOOK ON RACE RELATIONS IN SOUTH AFRICA.
Cape Town, Oxford University Press for South African Institute
of Race Relations, 1949. xii, 778 p. fold. map, tables (some
fold.).

Contributions by 31 specialists on numerous aspects: population,
government and administration, law, trade unions, land and agriculture
in and outside the reserves, Indian land legislation and agriculture,
pass laws, taxation, African education, health services, social
welfare, African cooperative societies, African press, religion,
literature of Africans, Indians, Cape Malays, race attitudes.

2918. Hill, Christopher R. BANTUSTANS: THE FRAGMENTATION OF SOUTH AFRICA.
Issued under the asupices of the Institute of Race Relations,
London. London, New York, Oxford University Press, 1964.
114 p. maps.

Based largely on materials gathered by the author (assistant
director of the Institute of Race Relations) in South Africa in
late 1963, this is a critical appraisal of the Bantustans--the
self-governing black states created or proposed by the South
African government in the Republic's African reserve areas. The
Transkei, the first reserve area to obtain self-government, is
given special consideration, along with a discussion of the
economics of the reserve areas, the new universities for non-
whites, and conditions in Zululand. [Eds.]

2919. Kirby, Percival Robson. THE MUSICAL INSTRUMENTS OF THE NATIVE
RACES OF SOUTH AFRICA. 2d ed. Johannesburg, Witwatersrand
University Press, 1965. xxiii, 293 p. front., plates, map.

An authoritative, standard work covering historical aspects,
distribution, and description of a wide variety of musical instruments; first published in 1934.

2920. Kuper, Leo. AN AFRICAN BOURGEOISIE: RACE, CLASS, AND POLITICS IN
SOUTH AFRICA. New Haven, Yale University Press, 1965.
xviii, 452 p. illus.

Bibliography: p. [439]-443.

The author of this valuable new work is a South African sociologist now teaching at the University of California at Los Angeles.

2921. Legum, Colin, and Margaret Legum. SOUTH AFRICA: CRISIS FOR THE
        WEST. New York, London, Praeger, 1964. 333 p. (A Praeger
        World Affairs Special)

        In this survey of the South African situation, internal and
in world aspects, the authors begin with the statement that South
Africa is the most urgent crisis of the day. In the first part
the power and weapons of Afrikaners are examined, then those of
English-speaking South Africans and of the Africans. Part 2
examines international power in relation to South Africa. There
is a chapter of conclusions. References are to British and South
African newspapers. [Eds.]

2922. Marloth, Rudolf. THE FLORA OF SOUTH AFRICA, WITH SYNOPTICAL TABLES
        OF THE GENERA OF THE HIGHER PLANTS. Cape Town, Darter, 1913-
        32. 4 v. in 6. illus., plates, diagrs.

        Bibliography at end of each volume.

        A classic of South African botany, superbly illustrated with
photographs, drawings, and paintings. Each volume contains a
general index and an index of plant names.

        Floral studies for each of the provinces also exist. Among
the most comprehensive of these is Robert Stephen Adamson and T.
M. Salter, FLORA OF THE CAPE PENINSULA (Cape Town, Juta, 1950,
xix, 889 p., maps). This deals with 2,622 species and gives full
descriptions.

2923. Marquard, Leo. THE PEOPLES AND POLICIES OF SOUTH AFRICA. Rev.
        3d ed. London, Oxford University Press, 1962. 284 p.

        The previous edition was published in 1960. A discussion
of present-day conditions and policies, with a brief historical
background. Contents include the people, government, administration,
the color bar, politics, policies, parties, education, race relations, and a chapter on South-West Africa and the High Commission
Territories.

2924. MEN OF THE TIMES: OLD COLONISTS OF THE CAPE COLONY AND ORANGE
        RIVER COLONY. Johannesburg, Transvaal Publishing Co., 1906.
        645 p. illus., plates.

        An important biographical dictionary for retrospective biography.
An index to this work was published by the University of Cape Town
libraries in 1960. A companion work for the Transvaal province is

MEN OF THE TIMES: PIONEERS OF THE TRANSVAAL AND GLIMPSES OF SOUTH
AFRICA (Johannesburg, Transvaal Publishing Co., 1905, 390 p.,
illus.). A dictionary of South African biography is now being
published (see no. 2902, above).

The following are a few examples of outstanding biographies
of some famous South Africans: Sir W. Keith Hancock, SMUTS (Cambridge,
University Press, 1962-68. 2 v.); John G. Lockhart and C. M.
Woodhouse, RHODES (London, Hodder and Stoughton, 1963, 511 p.);
Albert J. Luthuli, LET MY PEOPLE GO: AN AUTOBIOGRAPHY (New York,
McGraw-Hill, 1962, 255 p.); M. Nathan, PAUL KRUGER: HIS LIFE AND
TIMES (Durban, Knox, 1941, 510 p.); A. Paton, HOFMEYR (Cape Town,
Oxford University Press, 1964, 545 p.)

2925. Meredith, Dudley B. D., ed. THE GRASSES AND PASTURES OF SOUTH
        AFRICA. Johannesburg, Central News Agency, 1955. xvi, 771 p.
        illus., fold. maps, diagrs.

Gives descriptions of indigenous and some introduced South
African grasses, with notes on the ecology of grasslands and a
brief history of botanical survey in South Africa. Includes a
guide to identification, pasture management, and an index of
botanical and common names.

2926. Musiker, Reuben. GUIDE TO SOURCES OF INFORMATION IN THE HUMANITIES.
        Potchefstroom, Potchefstroom University in collaboration with
        the South African Library Association, 1962. 100 p.

A directory of libraries and special collections in non-
scientific and nontechnical fields. Special attention has been
paid to libraries of Africana. Alphabetically arranged with
subject and geographical indexes. A supplement was published
in 1965.

The State Library has published a DIRECTORY OF SOUTH AFRICAN
LIBRARIES (Pretoria, 1965) giving details of about 340 scientific
and research libraries in South and South-West Africa, Rhodesia,
Zambia, and Malawi. An up-to-date directory of all South African
libraries will appear in the State Library's HANDBOOK OF SOUTH
AFRICAN LIBRARIANSHIP which is in preparation.

2927. Natal Regional Survey [series]. 1951- Cape Town, New York, Pub-
        lished for the University of Natal by Oxford University Press.
        illus., maps, diagrs., tables.

General series edited by H. R. Burrows. The following volumes were among those in print in 1969:

a) ARCHAEOLOGY AND NATURAL RESOURCES OF NATAL. 1951. 140 p.

b) Alsop, M. H. THE POPULATION OF NATAL. 1953. 144 p.

c) Fair, J. D. THE DISTRIBUTION OF POPULATION IN NATAL. 1955. 99 p.

d) ELECTRICITY UNDERTAKINGS IN NATAL. 1954. 100 p.

e) BAUMANNVILLE: A STUDY OF AN URBAN AFRICAN COMMUNITY. Edited by the Institute for Social Research. 1959. 79 p.

f) Brookes, Edgar H., and Nathaniel Hurwitz. THE NATIVE RESERVES OF NATAL. 1957. 195 p.

g) Woods, C. A. THE INDIAN COMMUNITY OF NATAL. 1954. 102 p.

h) Palmer, Mabel. THE HISTORY OF THE INDIANS IN NATAL. 1958. 197 p.

i) STUDIES OF INDIAN EMPLOYMENT IN NATAL. 1961. 167 p.

j) Hurwitz, Nathaniel. AGRICULTURE IN NATAL, 1860-1950. 1957. 123 p.

k) AGRICULTURE IN NATAL: RECENT DEVELOPMENTS. 1957. 205 p.

l) THE UNGERI-UNBILO-UMLAZI RIVERS CATCHMENT AREAS. Part 1. 1967. 179 p.

m) THE PORT OF DURBAN. 1969. 150 p.

The Oxford University Press publishes also a series of numbered reports for various departments of the University of Natal, e.g.:

Natal. University, Pietermaritzburg. Department of Economics. THE AFRICAN FACTORY WORKER: A SAMPLE STUDY OF THE LIFE AND LABOUR OF THE URBAN AFRICAN WORKER. 1950. 221 p. illus., maps, tables. (Durham Economic Research Committee, Report no. 2)

A four-volume research study of an African reserve in the same province was published in 1952: THE KEISKAMMAHOEK RURAL SURVEY (Pietermaritzburg, Shuter & Shooter).

2928.   OFFICIAL SOUTH AFRICAN MUNICIPAL YEAR BOOK. 1909- Pretoria,
        South African Association of Municipal Employees.

        1967-68 ed., 464 p.

        A comprehensive and important yearbook prefaced by a general
statistical review of South African municipalities. Comparative
statistics of municipalities (population, finance) followed by a
directory of municipalities arranged alphabetically within each
province and giving population statistics, rateable value, area,
outline of development, brief description and features, members of
town councils and officials. Included is a separate section on
the municipalities of South-West Africa.

2929.   Omer-Cooper, John D. THE ZULU AFTERMATH: A NINETEENTH-CENTURY
        REVOLUTION IN BANTU AFRICA. London, Longmans; Evanston, Ill.,
        Northwestern University Press, 1966. 208 p. illus., maps.
        (Ibadan History Series)

        Bibliography: p. 183-192.

        The author, professor of History at the University of Zambia,
offers a detailed account of the emergence of the militaristic Zulu
kingdom and of its weighty impact on neighboring peoples. Emphasis
is on the precolonial period, but when deemed necessary events are
carried down to modern times.

        See also Donald Morris, THE WASHING OF THE SPEARS: A HISTORY
OF THE RISE OF THE ZULU NATION UNDER SHAKA AND ITS FALL IN THE
ZULU WAR OF 1879 (New York, Simon and Schuster, 1965, 655 p.).
[Eds.]

2930.   Palmer, Eve, and Norah Pitman. TREES OF SOUTH AFRICA. Cape
        Town, Balkema, 1961. 352 p. illus., col. plates, maps,
        tables.

        Bibliography: p. 330-332.

        A comprehensive work on indigenous South African trees, well
illustrated, with detailed descriptions of 170 trees, including
distribution, habits, foliage, fruit and timber properties,
legends and historic associations, key to identification, and
notes on cultivation.

2931.   Pettman, Charles. AFRICANDERISMS: A GLOSSARY OF SOUTH AFRICAN
        COLLOQUIAL WORDS AND PHRASES AND OF PLACES AND OTHER NAMES.
        London, Longmans, 1913. xviii, 579 p.

        Reprint. Detroit, Gale Research Co., 1969.

Bibliography: p. vii-xvii.

An invaluable dictionary of its kind. In addition to the explanation of terms, sources and quotations to illustrate their South African usage are given. Many foreign words introduced into South Africa are included, as well as words in the vernacular, e.g., Malay, Dutch, Basuto.

This work was supplemented by C. P. Swart, "Africanderisms" (unpublished M.A. thesis, University of South Africa, Pretoria, 1934), and further supplemented by M. D. W. Jeffreys, "Africanderisms," AFRICANA NOTES AND NEWS, v. 16, no. 2, June 1964, p. 43-95, and v. 17, no. 5, Mar. 1967, p. 216-220.

2932. Pettman, Charles. SOUTH AFRICAN PLACE NAMES, PAST AND PRESENT. Queenstown, Daily Representative, 1931. 194 p.

A valuable work which includes origins and correct forms of Bushman, Hottentot, Portuguese, Bantu, French, Dutch, English, and German place names found in South Africa.

The Place Names Committee of the Republic's Department of Education, Arts, and Science has compiled a list of OFFICIAL PLACE NAMES IN THE UNION OF SOUTH AFRICA AND SOUTH WEST AFRICA, APPROVED TO 1948 (Pretoria, Govt. Printer, 1952, 376 p.). A supplementary list was published in 1952 covering the years 1949-52 (54 p.). These alphabetical lists provide guidance with regard to correct spelling of South African place names.

2933. Ploeger, Jan, and Anna H. Smith. PICTORIAL ATLAS OF THE HISTORY OF THE UNION OF SOUTH AFRICA. Pretoria, Van Schaik, 1949. 196 p. illus., maps.

A history of South Africa in pictures, taken mostly from the period they illustrate.

Pictorial histories are important for an understanding of the cultural history and background of the South African nation. Two other works in this category are Victor de Kock, OUR THREE CENTURIES (Cape Town, Central Committee for the Van Riebeeck Festival, 1952, 264 p., illus., plates, 450 pictures recording 300 years of development), and C. van Riet Lowe and B. D. Malan, THE MONUMENTS OF SOUTH AFRICA (2d rev. and enl. ed., Pretoria, Govt. Printer, 1949, 179 p., illus., maps).

2934. Roberts, Austin. BIRDS OF SOUTH AFRICA. Revised by G. R. McLaghlan and R. Liversidge. Johannesburg, Central News Agency, 1957. 504 p. col. illus.

A comprehensive and important work on South African birds. Descriptions of each bird include identification, distribution, habits, nests, and eggs. Indexes of English, Latin, Afrikaans, and African names.

Another work of wider scope is C. W. Mackworth-Praed and C. H. B. Grant, BIRDS OF THE SOUTHERN THIRD OF AFRICA (London, Longmans, 1962-63, 2 v., col. illus.; African Handbook of Birds, ser. 2). Systematic name, distinguishing characteristics, habits, nest and eggs, recorded breeding, and call are given for each bird.

Other recent books on South African birds include: P. A. Clancey, GAMEBIRDS OF SOUTHERN AFRICA (Cape Town, Purnell, 1967); K. Newman, GARDEN BIRDS OF SOUTH AFRICA (Cape Town, Purnell, 1967); C. J. Skead, SUNBIRDS OF SOUTHERN AFRICA (Cape Town, Balkema, 1967).

2935. Roberts, Austin. THE MAMMALS OF SOUTH AFRICA. Edited by R. Bigalke [and others]; col. plates by P. J. Smit. 2d ed. Johannesburg, Mammals of South Africa Book Fund, 1954. xlviii, 700 p. illus., map.

A comprehensive work, giving chief characteristics of South African animals in each species and genus and their distribution.

2936. Schapera, Isaac, ed. THE BANTU-SPEAKING TRIBES OF SOUTH AFRICA: AN ETHNOGRAPHICAL SURVEY. London, Routledge, 1937. xv, 453 p. plate, map, tables. Reprinted 1953.

Bibliography: p. 435-444.

A basic work by specialist contributors on African customs, languages, and cultural life. Contents include racial origins, habitat, grouping and ethnic history, social organization, the native in the towns, the Bantu on European-owned farms, cultural changes in tribal life, traditional literature, religious beliefs and practice, magic and medicine, law and justice, political institutions, work and wealth, domestic and communal life.

AFRICAN STUDIES (1942- Johannesburg, Witwatersrand University Press), published quarterly, is a valuable periodical, indexed in the INDEX TO SOUTH AFRICAN PERIODICALS since its inception. It was preceded by BANTU STUDIES (1921-41).

2937. Smit, Bernard. INSECTS IN SOUTHERN AFRICA: HOW TO CONTROL THEM;
        A HANDBOOK FOR STUDENTS, HEALTH OFFICERS, GARDENERS, FARMERS.
        Cape Town, Oxford University Press, 1964. xiv, 399 p. illus.,
        plates (part col.).

        Bibliography: p. 379-384.

        A useful guide to the harmful and harmless insects, its gives
information on classification, life history, and habits.

2938. Smith, James Leonard Brierley. SEA FISHES OF SOUTHERN AFRICA. With
        illustrations by Margaret M. Smith and other artists. 4th rev.
        ed. Johannesburg, Central News Agency, 1961. xvi, 580 p.
        col. front., illus., col. plates, col. map.

        The most comprehensive and important work on South African
fishes, brilliantly illustrated. Gives descriptions of the structure,
habits, and habitat of each fish, with composite and common name
indexes. There is a bibliography.

2939. South Africa. Bureau of Census and Statistics. OFFICIAL YEARBOOK
        OF THE REPUBLIC AND OF BASUTOLAND, BECHUANALAND PROTECTORATE
        AND SWAZILAND. 1910-60. Pretoria, Govt. Printer. Annual.

        An important yearbook giving detailed statistical and descriptive
information on numerous topics, e.g., history, constitution and
government, health, social conditions, labor and industrial
conditions, education, justice, Bantu administration and development, state finance. Earlier volumes contain important source
material not repeated in later volumes, e.g., no. 12, 1929-30,
gives a bibliography of government reports since 1910; no. 30,
1960, was greatly condensed and contains only descriptive material.
A separate chapter on South-West Africa is included.

        Publication of the yearbook was discontinued with the 1960
edition. Thereafter the statistical content was published as
STATISTICAL YEAR BOOK [no. 1] 1964-1966. (See no. 2941, below.)
A successor to the descriptive part of the OFFICIAL YEARBOOK is
still awaited.

2940. South Africa. Bureau of Census and Statistics. UNION STATISTICS
        FOR FIFTY YEARS. Pretoria, Govt. Printer, 1960. 1 v.
        various pagings.

        On cover: Jubilee issue, 1910-60.

More than 400 pages of statistical tables on all phases of the Republic's social and economic development, giving a résumé of the country's development over a 50-year period. Topics covered include population, health, education, crime, labor, agriculture, mining, industry, trade, communications, and finance.

The current official source of statistical information is the QUARTERLY BULLETIN OF STATISTICS (formerly MONTHLY BULLETIN OF STATISTICS) (Pretoria, Govt. Printer) compiled by the Bureau of Statistics; frequency changed with v. 46, no. 3 (Mar. 1967). It contains data on demography, labor, agriculture, mining, manufacturing, construction, trade, transport, and finance.

2941.   South Africa. Bureau of Statistics. STATISTICAL YEAR BOOK. 1964-66, 1968- Pretoria, Govt. Printer.

The yearbook for 1964 contains more than 600 pages of statistical tables for the period 1945-63 on the following subjects: population, migration, vital statistics, health, education, social security, judicial statistics, labor, prices, agriculture, fisheries, mining, industry, internal and foreign trade, transport, communications, public finance, statistics of large towns, currency, banking and general finance, national accounts, balance of payments, foreign liabilities and assets. The yearbooks for 1965 and following years did not include the cumulative information for 1945-63 given in the 1964 yearbook. A 1967 edition was not published, and the title was changed to SOUTH AFRICAN STATISTICS with the 1968 yearbook.

2942.   South Africa. Bureau of Statistics. STATISTICS OF SCHOOLS: 1963 AND EARLIER YEARS: WHITES. Pretoria, Govt. Printer, 1965. xviii, 204 p. (Report no. 285)

Covers the years 1957-63 and gives comprehensive statistics for provincial and private primary and secondary schools, as well as teacher training and technical colleges. A similar compilation for the nonwhite population is in preparation.

The Department of Bantu Education has compiled BULLETIN: STATISTICS AND OTHER INFORMATION ABOUT BANTU EDUCATION (Pretoria, Govt. Printer, 1964, 157 p.). This has an appendix on the Transkei.

Current educational statistics are given in Cape of Good Hope (Province), Department of Public Education, EDUCATIONAL STATISTICS (1922-, Cape Town, The Department). Data are given on number of schools, pupils, and teachers and on age and standard of pupils, for both white and colored population in the Cape province. The equivalent work for the Natal province is issued as a triannual supplement to the report of the director of education and also includes information on white, colored, and Indian population. Similar information for the provinces of Transvaal and the Orange Free State is to be found in the annual reports of the provincial education departments.

The Department of Education, Arts, and Science issues an irregular BULLETIN OF EDUCATIONAL STATISTICS (1939-, Pretoria, Govt. Printer), giving data on primary, secondary, and university education, as well as African, Coloured, and Indian education.

2943. South Africa. Commission for the Socio-Economic Development of the Bantu Areas within the Union. SUMMARY OF THE REPORT. Pretoria, Govt. Printer, 1955. xviii, 213 p. maps, diagrs. (U.G. 61/1955) Chairman: F. R. Tomlinson.

In 1950 the South African government appointed a commission headed by Professor Frederik Rothman Tomlinson to inquire into South Africa's Bantu policy. The report of the commission's findings and recommendations constitutes one of the most comprehensive modern sources in existence for conditions in the African areas of South Africa. The full report of this basic statement of government policy was published in mimeographed form in 17 volumes plus an atlas volume of 66 maps. The text, most of which is in Afrikaans, totaled 3,755 pages. The summary report is in English. The Tomlinson report was issued in a limited edition, but copies are in the possession of South African university libraries, the Library of Congress (microfilm), and the Hoover Institution.

In 1956, the government published a white paper on the report: GOVERNMENT DECISIONS ON THE RECOMMENDATIONS (16 p.; W.P. F-56), and in the same year the South African Institute of Race Relations published its own summary: D. H. Houghton, THE TOMLINSON REPORT: A SUMMARY OF THE FINDINGS AND RECOMMENDATIONS (Johannesburg, The Institute, 1956, 76 p.). [Eds.]

2944. South Africa. Department of Agriculture. HANDBOOK FOR FARMERS IN SOUTH AFRICA. Pretoria, Govt. Printer, 1957-60. 3 v.

An encyclopedic handbook on all aspects of South African agriculture. Contents: Vol. I, Agriculture and related services; Vol. II, Agronomy and horticulture; Vol. III, Stock farming and pasture.

The Department of Agricultural Economics and Marketing has compiled a HANDBOOK OF AGRICULTURAL STATISTICS, 1904-1950 (Pretoria, Govt. Printer, 1961, xv, 186 p.). This gives comprehensive statistics on land use, farm labor, livestock, agricultural crops, forestry, imports and exports, price, and price indexes.

A useful ABSTRACT OF AGRICULTURAL STATISTICS was published by the Division of Agricultural Economic Research in 1958 and contained statistics since 1936. 1st Supplement, Jan. 1966; 2d Supplement, Jan. 1968.

2945. South Africa. Department of Bantu Administration and Development. Ethnological Publications Series. 1930- Pretoria, Govt. Printer.

To date 49 monographs have been published, covering tribal studies in various parts of South Africa, e.g., no. 23, VENDA LAW (1948-49, 4 v.); no. 27, LANGUAGE MAP OF SOUTH AFRICA, by N. J. van Warmelo (1952); no. 35, TRIBES OF UMTATA DISTRICT (1956). A full list of the series is given in the publications.

2946. South Africa. Department of Customs and Excise. FOREIGN TRADE STATISTICS. 1956- Pretoria, Govt. Printer. Annual.

From 1906 to 1955 published as ANNUAL STATEMENT OF TRADE AND SHIPPING, with varying titles. Since 1956 issued in four volumes annually: Vol. I, Imports; Vol. II, Exports; Vol. III, Supplementary trade statistics; Vol. IV, Standard internal trade classification and supplementary tables. These volumes show quantities and value of imports and exports by articles and countries of origin and destination. The trade statistics for Basutoland, Bechuanaland, Swaziland, and South-West Africa are integrated in the South African tables and not shown separately. The current official trade statistical source is the MONTHLY ABSTRACT OF TRADE STATISTICS, compiled by the Department of Customs and Excise (Pretoria, Govt. Printer). This gives monthly totals of imports and exports in value, imports by country of origin, and exports by country of destination.

2947. South Africa. Statutes. UNION STATUTES: CLASSIFIED AND ANNOTATED REPRINT. Durban, Butterworth, 1949. 13 v.

A consolidated compilation of South African law from 1910 to 1947, basic to any legal library. An annual cumulative supplement, giving references to new acts since 1948, is also published by Butterworth. The texts of new acts since 1948 are included in the annual volume of STATUTES OF THE REPUBLIC OF SOUTH AFRICA (Pretoria, Govt. Printer). The 1949 compilation will be superseded by a new loose-leaf consolidated set: STATUTES OF THE REPUBLIC OF SOUTH AFRICA, 1910-1967 (Durban, Butterworth, 19 v.), published in 1967-68, and revised continuously. The annual cumulative supplement to the 1949 publication and the annual volume of STATUTES will no longer be published in their present form.

A useful index to statutes is C. H. Blaine, NEW CONSOLIDATED INDEX TO PRE-UNION AND UNION STATUTES AND PROVINCIAL ORDINANCES AND THE REGULATIONS, ETC., THEREUNDER, UP TO 31ST DECEMBER 1936 (Durban, Prentice-Hall, 1937), supplemented annually by an alphabetical subject index, INDEX OF STATUTE LAW AND REGULATIONS.

2948.   South Africa. University. Bureau of Market Research. A GUIDE TO STATISTICAL SOURCES IN THE REPUBLIC OF SOUTH AFRICA. Compiled by G. Geertseme, assisted by J. R. Klerck. Pretoria, The Bureau, 1962. 2 v. (Report no. 4)

Does not contain actual statistics but is a useful guide to sources. Contents: Vol. I, Part 1, a product and subject index to subjects for which statistical data are available; Part 2, a list of institutional sources for the data, arranged alphabetically, with a brief description of the publication listed (e.g., under Bureau of Census and Statistics are listed 63 publications with a brief description of each); Vol. II, reprints of 60 different statistical questionnaires currently used by seven institutional sources.

Other reports published by the Bureau deal with research into consumer expenditure of Bantu and Coloured households and related matters.

2949.   South African Council for Scientific and Industrial Research. DIRECTORY OF SCIENTIFIC RESOURCES IN SOUTH AFRICA. Pretoria, The Council, 1961- Loose-leaf binder.

A work planned for continuous revision and comprising the following parts: Part 1, Scientific research organizations in South Africa--a list of scientific institutes, government departments, museums, etc., giving nature of research and special facilities; Part 2, Guide to sources of scientific, technical, and medical information in South African libraries--the scientific counterpart of R. Musiker's GUIDE TO SOURCES OF INFORMATION IN THE HUMANITIES; Part 3, Scientific and technical societies in South Africa--gives addresses, objects, publications, etc.; Part 4, Scientific and technical periodicals published in South Africa; Part 5, Acronyms.

As of 1967, Parts 1, 3, and 4 of this DIRECTORY are published separately. Parts 2 and 5 have been discontinued.

Parts 1, 2, and 3 of this directory supersede the South African entries in the Scientific Council for Africa South of the Sahara, DIRECTORY OF SCIENTIFIC AND TECHNICAL LIBRARIES (1954) and DIRECTORY OF SCIENTIFIC INSTITUTES, ORGANISATIONS AND SERVICES (1954).

In 1968, the South African Council for Scientific and Industrial
Research issued A BRIEF GUIDE TO SOURCES OF TECHNICAL INFORMATION
IN THE REPUBLIC OF SOUTH AFRICA (57 p.).

2950. South African Institute of Race Relations. SURVEY OF RACE RELATIONS
       IN SOUTH AFRICA. 1951/52- Johannesburg, The Institute.
       Annual.

       Valuable summary review of developments and trends in legis-
       lation, government action, and opposition. The Institute also
       publishes a monthly periodical, RACE RELATIONS NEWS, and a pamphlet
       series. Among important pamphlets published are D. H. Houghton,
       LIFE IN THE CISKEI (1955, 72 p.), and M. Horrell, THE NEW LOOK IN
       THE AFRICAN RESERVES (1964, 45 p.), reprinted from the 1963 SURVEY
       OF RACE RELATIONS and forming an excellent compendium of facts and
       figures about the Transkei.

       An earlier handbook, still useful, is edited by Ellen Hellman,
       (see no. 2917). [Eds.]

2951. SOUTHERN AFRICAN DICTIONARY OF NATIONAL BIOGRAPHY. Compiled by
       Eric Rosenthal. London, Warne, 1966. xxxix, 430 p.

       Contains over 2,000 biographies of notable persons, of what-
       ever race, in South Africa, South-West Africa, Rhodesia, Zambia,
       Malawi, Mozambique, Swaziland, Botswana, and Lesotho from the time
       of Bartholomew Diaz to the twentieth century. No living person
       is included. The biographies attempt to "assess [the individuals']
       place in history and their achievements, be they soldiers, writers,
       statesmen, explorers, sportsmen, inventors, financiers--sometimes
       even criminals." There is a classified list of personalities by
       field from "Adventurers" to those in "Zoology and Biology." [Eds.]

2952. State Library, Pretoria. DIRECTORY OF SOUTH AFRICAN LIBRARIES.
       Pretoria, The Library, 1965. (Contributions to Library
       Science, no. 6)

       Comprehensive loose-leaf directory covering libraries in the
       Republic of South Africa, South-West Africa, Rhodesia, Malawi,
       and Zambia. Part 1 (1965) consists of scientific and technical
       libraries and has 339 entries, with geographic and subject indexes.

2953. STATE OF SOUTH AFRICA: PICTORIAL, SOCIAL, ECONOMIC, FINANCIAL,
       STATISTICAL. 1957- Johannesburg, Da Gama Publications. Annual.

       1968 ed., 396 p.

An up-to-date and useful annual, comprising a comprehensive survey of the Republic's present state of development in numerous fields: constitution and government, defense, external affairs, population, education, housing, mineral resources, mining, agriculture, commerce, trade, industry. Title changed in 1964 from STATE OF SOUTH AFRICA YEARBOOK: ECONOMIC, FINANCIAL AND STATISTICAL YEARBOOK FOR THE REPUBLIC OF SOUTH AFRICA.

2954. Sundkler, Bengt G. M. BANTU PROPHETS IN SOUTH AFRICA. 2d ed. London, Oxford University Press for the International African Institute, 1961. 381 p. illus., ports.

Bibliography: p. 338-339.

A study of the Bantu separatist or independent churches in many aspects, e.g., leader and followers, worship, government policy.

2955. Theal, George McCall. HISTORY OF SOUTH AFRICA, 1505-1884. London, Allen and Unwin, 1919-26. 11 v.

Reprinted Cape Town, Struik, 1964. 11 v. plates, maps.

Editions earlier than that of Allen and Unwin were published by Swan Sonnenschein, London, 1888-93 (5 v.) and 1907-10 (8 v.).

This most comprehensive standard work on South African history is a pioneering work of its kind based largely on original sources and archives. Vol. I covers ethnography and conditions of South Africa before 1505; Vols. II-IV, history of South Africa before 1795; Vols. V-IX, history of South Africa since 1795; Vols. X-XI, history of South Africa, 1873-84.

Another important work which draws on Theal to a large extent but which is nevertheless invaluable for the Eastern Cape is Sir G. E. Cory, THE RISE OF SOUTH AFRICA (London, Longmans, 1910-30, 5 v., fronts., plates, maps). A sixth volume was published in ARCHIVES YEAR BOOK FOR SOUTH AFRICAN HISTORY, 1939, Part 1. Reprint: Cape Town, Struik, 1965, 6 v.

2956. Tylden, G. THE ARMED FORCES OF SOUTH AFRICA. Johannesburg, Africana Museum, 1954. xvi, 239 p.

Gives a short account of the armed forces in South African history from 1659 to 1946. Armed forces are listed alphabetically by regiments or corps. Included are a useful tabulation of wars waged in the four provinces and a bibliography. Addenda and corrigenda have appeared in AFRICANA NOTES AND NEWS, Mar. 1955, Dec. 1958, and Sept. 1960.

The work which describes the campaigns and battle honors of the regiments is Herbert Henry Curson, COLOURS AND HONOURS IN SOUTH AFRICA, 1783-1948 (Pretoria, The Author, 1948, xv, 123 p., illus.).

2957. United Nations. Economic Commission for Africa. ECONOMIC SURVEY OF AFRICA: Vol. I, WESTERN SUB-REGION; REPUBLIC OF SOUTH AFRICA. New York, 1966- xi, 230 p. tables. (E/CN. 14/370)

Bibliographical footnotes.

The section on South Africa (p. 171-230) provides detailed data, accompanied by 56 statistical tables, on the socioeconomic structure, recent economic trends, and development problems and politics of the Republic. Included is an analysis of development programs. [Eds.]

2958. Van Riebeeck Society. Publications. 1918- Cape Town, The Society.

A series of great value for historical research. It contains mostly transcriptions of manuscript records, e.g., Vol. XXXI, D. J. Kotze, ed., LETTERS OF THE AMERICAN MISSIONARIES, 1835-1838 (1950). Vol. XLVIII was published in 1967. A detailed list of the publications is given in each volume and is available from The Society, c/o South African Public Library, Queen Victoria Street, Cape Town.

In 1952 the Society published the JOURNAL OF JAN VAN RIEBEECK, edited and with an introduction and footnotes by H. B. Thom (Cape Town, Balkema for the Van Riebeeck Society, 2 v., illus., maps., facsim.).

2959. Walker, Eric Anderson. A HISTORY OF SOUTHERN AFRICA. 3d ed. London, Longmans, 1957. xxiv, 973 p. maps.

Bibliography: p. 925-945.

This is a standard work on South African history, very well documented and maintaining a high level of objectivity. The bibliography draws on many official sources, and there is a useful list of executive officers, from the earliest times onward.

2960.   Wellington, John Harold. SOUTHERN AFRICA: A GEOGRAPHICAL STUDY.
            Cambridge, Eng., University Press, 1955. 2 v. plates, maps,
            tables, diagrs.

        Standard work on South African geography. Vol. I covers
physical geography, climate, vegetation and soils, hydrography;
Vol. II, land utilization, minerals and other industries, the
people. South-West Africa is dealt with in many chapters.

2961.   WHO'S WHO OF SOUTHERN AFRICA, INCLUDING MAURITIUS AND INCORPORATING
            SOUTH AFRICAN WHO'S WHO AND THE CENTRAL AFRICAN WHO'S WHO:
            AN ILLUSTRATED BIOGRAPHICAL SKETCH BOOK OF PERSONALITIES IN
            SOUTHERN AFRICA. 1907- Johannesburg, Wootton & Gibson,-1964;
            Johannesburg, Combined Publishers, 1965- illus., ports.
            Irregular; then annual.

        A major source of current biography. The 1969 volume (52d
ed., 1,296 p.) included roughly 8,000 entries. It has a directory
of diplomatic, civil service, and university personnel and includes
a separate section of some 250 entries on South-West Africa. The
title and incorporation of the publication have varied.

        WIE IS WIE IN SUID-AFRIKA (1958-, Johannesburg, Vitae
Uitgewers) is an annual biographical work which is bilingual,
with some of the biographies in English and others in Afrikaans.
The biographies of cabinet ministers are very full. South-West
African personalities are included among the South African entries.

        A who's who of leading Jewish personalities is included in
SOUTH AFRICAN JEWRY (2d ed., Johannesburg, Fieldhill, 1968, 480 p.;
first published in 1965).

        AFRICAN WHO'S WHO: AN ILLUSTRATED CLASSIFIED AND NATIONAL
BIOGRAPHICAL DICTIONARY OF THE AFRICANS IN THE TRANSVAAL, edited
and compiled by T. D. Mweli Skota, with contributions by leading
Africans (Johannesburg, Central News Agency [1963?] 393 p.), gives
biographical notes on non-white personalities. Although awkwardly
arranged, the work is also of value for information on African
churches, lists of university graduates and writers, and
directories of schools, hospitals, societies, and institutions.

2962.   Wilson, Monica, and Leonard Thompson. THE OXFORD HISTORY OF SOUTH
            AFRICA. vol. 1, SOUTH AFRICA TO 1870. London, Oxford
            University Press, 1969. 528 p.

        First of a two-volume history of South Africa. Chapters treat
of pre colonial history to the beginning of the diamond-mining
industry. [Eds.]

SOUTH-WEST AFRICA

Bibliographies

2963. De Jager, Theo, comp. SOUTH WEST AFRICA. SUIDWES-AFRIKA. Edited
        by Brigitte Klaas. Pretoria, State Library, 1964. 216 p.
        (Bibliographies, no. 7)

   About 2,000 references on South-West Africa, all to books or
pamphlets; periodicals are included only when available in pamphlet
reprints. The arrangement is alphabetical by author or title, with
a detailed subject index. A good many items are nineteenth-century
publications. A second edition is planned, after the library stock
has been checked against the bibliography; it will also include
periodical articles, government publications, and books in the
vernacular.

   A consolidated bibliography of German Africana relating to
both South-West Africa and South Africa, compiled by O. H. Spohr
covering the period from the seventeenth century to 1965, has been
published by the State Library, Pretoria. (See no. 2869 for
details.)

2964. Roukens de Lange, E. J., comp. SOUTH WEST AFRICA, 1946-1960:
        A SELECTIVE BIBLIOGRAPHY. Cape Town, School of Librarianship,
        University of Cape Town, 1961. 51 p. (Bibliographical
        Series).

   This compilation of 332 references to books, pamphlets, and
substantial periodical articles relating in whole or major part
to South-West Africa complements an earlier publication of the
University of Cape Town School of Librarianship, Floretta J.
Welch's SOUTH-WEST AFRICA: A BIBLIOGRAPHY (Cape Town, 1946, 33 l.),
which covered comparable literature from 1919 to 1946.

2965. Voigts, Barbara. SOUTH WEST AFRICAN IMPRINTS: A BIBLIOGRAPHY.
        Cape Town, School of Librarianship, University of Cape Town,
        1964. 58 p. (Bibliographical Series)

   Other lists in this series relating to South-West Africa are
by L. S. E. Loening, BIBLIOGRAPHY OF THE STATUS OF SOUTH-WEST AFRICA
UP TO JUNE 30TH, 1951 (1951), and E. R. Kahn, KARAKUL SHEEP IN SOUTH
WEST AFRICA AND SOUTH AFRICA (1959).

Reference Works

2966.   ARCHIVES YEARBOOK FOR SOUTH AFRICAN HISTORY. 1938- Pretoria,
            Govt. Printer.

        Several of the volumes in this series have dealt with South-
West African history: 1942, Part 2, J. Davies, PALGRAVE AND
DAMARALAND, and E. A. Nobbs, WILLIAM DUCKITT'S DIARY and A NOTE
ON THE HISTORY OF THE KARAKUL BREEDS OF SHEEP IN SOUTH WEST AFRICA;
1948, Part 2, G. P. J. Truempelmann, DIE BOER IN SUIDWES-AFRIKA
(deals with immigration of Afrikaner farmers); 1959, Part 1, W. B.
Campbell, THE SOUTH AFRICAN FRONTIER, 1865-1885, a study in ex-
pansion.

2967.   CAMBRIDGE HISTORY OF THE BRITISH EMPIRE: Vol. VIII, SOUTH AFRICA,
            RHODESIA AND THE HIGH COMMISSION TERRITORIES. General
            editor, Eric A. Walker. 2d ed. Cambridge, Eng., University
            Press, 1963. xxviii, 1087 p.

        Bibliography: p. 917-1017.

        Includes a history of German Southwest Africa, 1883-1914
(chap. xxvi). The previous edition was dated 1936.

2968.   Esterhuyse, J. H. SOUTH WEST AFRICA, 1880-1894: THE ESTABLISHMENT
            OF GERMAN AUTHORITY IN SOUTH WEST AFRICA. Cape Town, Struik,
            1968. xii, 282 p.

        Bibliography: p. 240-251.

        An important contribution to the earlier history of South West
Africa.

2969.   Goldblatt, I. THE MANDATED TERRITORY OF SOUTH WEST AFRICA IN
            RELATION TO THE UNITED NATIONS. Cape Town, C. Struik,
            1961. 67 p.

        Essay by a Windhoek lawyer, examining objectively the question
of South West Africa from 1919, when it was made a C Mandate of
the League of Nations under the trusteeship of South Africa. He
reviews South Africa's de facto annexation of the territory and
refusal to submit reports to the Trusteeship Council, as well as
United Nations action through the Oct.-Nov. session of 1959.

        Two later studies of this question are Ruth First's SOUTH
WEST AFRICA (Harmondsworth, Middlesex, Penguin Books 1963, 269 p.,
maps; Penguin African Library) and Allard K. Lowenstein's BRUTAL
MANDATE: A JOURNEY TO SOUTH WEST AFRICA (New York, Macmillan,
1962, 257 p). [Eds.]

2970. Hailey, William Malcolm Hailey, 1st baron. AN AFRICAN SURVEY: A STUDY OF PROBLEMS ARISING IN AFRICA SOUTH OF THE SAHARA. Rev. 1956. London, Oxford University Press, 1957. xxviii, 1676 p. plates, maps, tables.

Contains copious references to South-West Africa, the most important being political and social objectives, p. 169-175; systems of government, p. 268-271; and administration of African affairs, p. 435-438.

2971. Hellmann, Ellen, ed. HANDBOOK ON RACE RELATIONS IN SOUTH AFRICA. Cape Town, Oxford University Press for South African Institute of Race Relations, 1949. xii, 778 p. map, tables.

Chap. XXXV (p. 742-758): The Mandated Territory of South West Africa.

2972. International Conference on South West Africa, Oxford, 1966. SOUTH WEST AFRICA: TRAVESTY OF TRUST: THE EXPERT PAPERS AND FINDINGS OF THE INTERNATIONAL CONFERENCE ON SOUTH WEST AFRICA, OXFORD, 23-26 MARCH 1966, WITH A POSTSCRIPT BY IAIN MACGIBBON ON THE 1966 JUDGEMENT OF THE INTERNATIONAL COURT OF JUSTICE. Edited by Ronald Segal and Ruth First. London, Deutsch, 1967. 352 p. tables.

Includes bibliographies. [Eds.]

2973. Logan, Richard Fink. THE CENTRAL NAMIB DESERT, SOUTH WEST AFRICA. Washington, D.C., National Academy of Sciences, National Research Council, 1960. 162 p. illus., maps, diagrs., tables. (National Research Council, Division of Earth Sciences, Foreign Field Research Program, Report no. 9; National Research Council, Publication no. 758)

Includes bibliography.

A work dealing with the physical geography and natural history of the region.

2974. MEINERT'S TRADE AND FARMS DIRECTORY OF SOUTH WEST AFRICA. 1923/24- Windhoek, Meinert.

Formerly MEINERT'S DIRECTORY OF SOUTH WEST AFRICA. The title varies.

2975. THE NATIVE TRIBES OF SOUTH WEST AFRICA. Cape Town, Cape Times,
           1928. 211 p. plates.

       The Foreword is signed by H. P. Smit, Secretary for South
West Africa.

       The volume was prepared for submission to the League of
Nations as a sketch of the tribes in the territory administered
by South Africa as a C Mandate. The five main tribal divisions
are briefly sketched as to history, customs, beliefs, and manners.
Mr. C. H. L. Hahn, representative of the Administration in Ovam-
boland, wrote the first essay on the Ovambo. The Bushmen were
analyzed by Dr. L. Fourie, Medical Officer for South West Africa;
the Berg Damara, the Nama, a branch of the Hottentots, and the
Herero by Dr. Heinrich Vedder, a missionary who had lived among
and was known as an authority on the Herero. Each section is
followed by a bibliography.

       The standard anthropological work on the Bushmen and the
Hottentots of Cape province and Bechuanaland as well as South-West
Africa is Dr. Isaac Schapera's THE KHOISAN PEOPLES OF SOUTH AFRICA
(London, Routledge, 1930, xi, 450 p.; bibliography: p. 439-445).

2976. Shortridge, Guy Chester. THE MAMMALS OF SOUTH WEST AFRICA: A
           BIOLOGICAL ACCOUNT OF THE FORMS OCCURRING IN THAT REGION.
           London, Heinemann, 1934. 2 v. fronts., plates, maps (1
           fold.).

       Bibliography: v. 2, p. 775-779.

       Descriptions of each species, including bibliographic
references, distribution, habits, appearance, and structure.
English, Afrikaans, Latin, and native names are given for each
species. Vol. II has a useful appendix of field measurements of
mammals.

2977. South Africa. REPORTS PRESENTED BY THE GOVERNMENT OF THE UNION
           OF SOUTH AFRICA TO THE COUNCIL OF THE LEAGUE OF NATIONS
           CONCERNING THE ADMINISTRATION OF SOUTH WEST AFRICA. 1918-
           Pretoria, Govt. Printer.

       The title varies.

       The Government Printer also publishes UNITED NATIONS, SOUTH
WEST AFRICA: PROCEEDINGS AT THE UNITED NATIONS (Dec. 1949-, annual).

2978.   South Africa. Commission of Enquiry into South West African
           Affairs, 1962-63. REPORT. Pretoria, Govt. Printer, 1964.
           li, 557 p. illus., 49 maps, tables, diagrs. Chairman:
           F. H. Odendaal.

           Bibliography: p. 552-557.

           Text in English and Afrikaans. Includes much factual and
       statistical information on history, topography, natural resources,
       land utilization, population, government and administration, health
       services, social development and welfare services, education,
       agriculture, economic and industrial development.

           An earlier government survey dealing with general conditions,
       administration, and policy is South Africa, South West Africa
       Commission, REPORT (Pretoria, Govt. Printer, 1936, 104 p.; UG 26/36,
       Chairman, H. S. van Zyl).

2979.   South Africa. Department of Bantu Administration and Development.
           Ethnological Publications Series. Pretoria, Govt. Printer, 1930-

           The following monographs in this series by O. Köhler deal
       with various parts of South-West Africa: no. 40, KARIBIB DISTRICT
       (1958, 116 p.); no. 42, GOBABIS DISTRICT (1959, 108 p.); no. 43,
       OMARURU DISTRICT (1959, 113 p.); no. 44, OTJIWARONGO DISTRICT
       (1959, 98 p.); no. 45, GROOTFONTEIN DISTRICT (1959, 85 p.).

2980.   South West Africa. Statutes. UNION LEGISLATION AFFECTING SOUTH
           WEST AFRICA AND PROCLAMATIONS, ORDINANCES AND PRINCIPAL
           GOVERNMENT NOTICES ISSUED IN SOUTH WEST AFRICA, 1915-. 1916-
           Windhoek, Administration of South West Africa.

           The following annotated reprint covers the years 1915-28:
       LAW OF SOUTH WEST AFRICA, edited and prepared for publication by
       R. E. G. Rosenow (Parow, Cape Times, 1957, 3 v.). Further
       consolidated volumes of the laws have appeared since then.

2981.   SOUTH WEST AFRICA ANNUAL. 1946- Windhoek, South West Africa
           Publications.

           Does not give much statistical information but has articles
       of general interest on many South-West African subjects.

2982.   United Nations. General Assembly. Committee on South West Africa.
           REPORT. 1954- New York.

Issued as Supplements to the Official Records of the General Assembly (GAOR).

Following discussions of the question of South-West Africa, both in the Trusteeship Council and before the General Assembly from 1946 on, this seven-member committee was established in 1953 to study the question of the area considered by the UN a trusteeship but by South Africa a territory under its sole administration, "until such time as an agreement is reached." Annual reports have presented petitions and recommendations including the request that the case be referred to the International Court. For extended summaries of discussions and resolutions relating to South-West Africa in the Fourth (Trusteeship) Committee and the General Assembly of the UN, see the annual volumes of the YEARBOOK OF THE UNITED NATIONS.

A brief survey of the situation in South-West Africa was issued in 1965 under the auspices of the Institute of Race Relations, London: R. W. Imishue, SOUTH WEST AFRICA: AN INTERNATIONAL PROBLEM (London, Pall Mall, 80 p.). Its purpose was to provide background material for the impending International Court decision. It covers South-West Africa from the time of the granting of the mandate in 1919 through the demise of the League, the subsequent UN concern with the South African administration, and the effects of emerging African nationalism. Further studies in article or book form are to be expected following the International Court decision against consideration of the case (brought by Ethiopia and Liberia against South Africa) and General Assembly action in 1966. [Eds.]

2983. Vedder, Heinrich. SOUTH WEST AFRICA IN EARLY TIMES: BEING THE STORY OF SOUTH WEST AFRICA UP TO THE DATE OF MAHARERO'S DEATH IN 1890. Translated by Cyril G. Hall. London, Oxford University Press, 1938. 525 p. illus., fold. maps.

Reprint, New York, Barnes & Noble, 1966.

Bibliography: p. 508-510.

An abridged translation of DAS ALTE SUDWESTAFRIKA (Berlin, Warneck, 1934, xvi, 666 p.); a comprehensive history of the early period. [Eds.]

2984. Wellington, John H. SOUTH WEST AFRICA AND ITS HUMAN ISSUES. Oxford, Clarendon Press, 1967. xxiv, 461 p. plates, maps, tables.

Bibliographical footnotes.

A full geographical survey of the area, with good sections on history during the German period. The work attempts to cover the League of Nations and the United Nations controversy with the government of South Africa. [Eds.]

BOTSWANA (BECHUANALAND), LESOTHO (BASUTOLAND), SWAZILAND
(FORMER HIGH COMMISSION TERRITORIES)

Note: The High Commission Territories have recently become independent:
Bechuanaland became Botswana on Sept. 30, 1966, Basutoland became Lesotho
on Oct. 4, 1966, and Swaziland gained independence on Sept. 6, 1968.

Bibliographies

2985. Arnheim, J. SWAZILAND: A BIBLIOGRAPHY. Cape Town, School of
        Librarianship, University of Cape Town, 1950. 20 [v.] p.

        There are 150 entries arranged under subject headings, in-
cluding administration, agriculture, botany, education, ethnology,
geology, history, land and labor, language, medicine, and missions.
A list of South African imperial blue books is given, and there is
author index. The bibliography is complemented and updated by the
Wallace work described below (see no. 2991).

2986. Botswana National Library Service. ONE HUNDRED BOOKS ON BOTSWANA:
        AN ANNOTATED LIST OF BOOKS, ARTICLES AND PAMPHLETS. Supple-
        ment to KUTLWANO, Nov. 1969. Gaberone, 1969. 1 v.

        The entries, most of which are annotated, are arranged by the
following subjects: general works, missions and missionaries, travel
and exploration, social anthropology, biography, administration and
development, language, literature, natural history. Publications
from 1842 through 1969 are covered.

2987. Groen, Julie te. BIBLIOGRAPHY OF BASUTOLAND. Cape Town, School of
        Librarianship, University of Cape Town, 1946. 30 p.

        The 288 entries are classified under broad subject headings,
e.g., administration, agriculture, botany, Christian missions,
crafts, education, geology, law, history, literature, medicine,
music, and native races. An author index is included.

        The list will be complemented by a bibliography for the period
1947 onwards, being compiled by L. Gordon at the University of the
Witwatersrand Department of Bibliography, Librarianship and Typography.

2988. Middleton, Coral. BECHUANALAND: A BIBLIOGRAPHY. Cape Town, School
        of Librarianship, University of Cape Town, 1965. 37 p.
        (Bibliographical Series)

Complements and supplements the Stevens bibliography described
in the next entry. Arranged by subject, the partially annotated
list excludes periodical articles and works in vernacular languages
but includes reprints from newspapers and periodicals. References
cited were found in three African libraries and location of each
work is indicated. There is an author index.

2989. Stevens, Pamela E. BIBLIOGRAPHY OF BECHUANALAND. Cape Town, School
of Librarianship, University of Cape Town, 1949. 27 p.

Consists of 305 entries including official publications,
arranged under subject headings with an author index. Aspects
covered include administration, botany, boundaries, Christian
missions, climate, education, geology, history, law, medicine,
native races, railways, and zoology.

2990. Syracuse University. Maxwell Graduate School of Citizenship and
Public Affairs. Program of Eastern African Studies. A
BIBLIOGRAPHY ON BECHUANALAND. Compiled by Paulus Mohome and
John B. Webster. Syracuse, N.Y., 1966. 58 l. (Occasional
Bibliography, no. 5)

Books, articles, pamphlets, and some government publications
are covered; emphasis is on social science topics. Entries are
arranged by categories, e.g., general, bibliography, agriculture,
education, politics, traditional religion. [Eds.]

2991. Wallace, Charles Stewart, comp. SWAZILAND: A BIBLIOGRAPHY.
Johannesburg, Department of Bibliography, Librarianship and
Typography, University of the Witwatersrand, 1967. 87 p.
Processed.

Adds to and continues the 1950 bibliography of Johanna
Arnheim (see no. 2985, above) and brings coverage up to the end of
1965. The 1,191 entries are arranged by subject and include monographs, books, articles, newspaper supplements (but no newspaper
articles), government publications, unpublished papers, and theses.
Most entries are in the humanities and social sciences and geology,
with special attention being given to the latter and to philately.
There are author, geographical, mineral, and biographical indexes.

Reference Works

2992. Africa Institute. LESOTHO. Pretoria, The Institute [1968?]. 38 p.
       illus. 26 x 39 cm. (Africa at a Glance, no. 2)

       _____. LESOTHO: A GEOGRAPHICAL STUDY. By P. Smit. Pretoria,
       The Institute, 1967. 44 p. illus., maps (part fold., part
       col.). (Communications, no. 6)

       _____. LESOTHO: A POLITICAL STUDY. By A. J. van Wyk. Preto-
       ria, The Institute, 1967. 61 p. illus., map. (Communica-
       tions, no. 7)

       _____. LESOTHO: ECONOMIC STRUCTURE AND GROWTH. By G. M. E.
       Leistner. Pretoria, The Institute, 1966. 56 p. illus., map.
       (Communications, no. 5)

2993. Ashton, Hugh. THE BASUTO. London, Oxford University Press for the
       International African Institute, 1952. xi, 355 p. illus.,
       tables.

       Bibliography: p. 346-349.

       An important anthropological monograph on the Basuto peoples
       covering the following aspects: social background, education,
       religious beliefs, animal husbandry, land tenure, political and
       judicial organization, law, medicine, and magic and sorcery.

2994. BASUTOLAND RED CROSS YEAR BOOK AND DIARY. Maseru, Basutoland Red
       Cross. illus., fold. maps. Annual.

       This annual diary is a valuable reference book for the terri-
       tory. The text includes articles on postal services, architecture
       (mostly by James Walton), government, the Anglican church in Basuto-
       land, history, and common wild flowers, as well as a fisherman's
       guide. The articles are not repeated from year to year, and the
       set as a whole forms a valuable reference file.

2995. Botswana. Information Services. CENTRAL GOVERNMENT ORGANIZATION
       CHART. Gaberones, 1969. 71 p.

2996. Coates, Austin. BASUTOLAND. London, H.M. Stationery Off., 1966.
       135 p. (Corona Library)

       Part of a series sponsored by the Colonial Office dealing with
       the United Kingdom dependent territories. The brief survey covers
       history, economic situation (including agricultural problems), tra-
       ditional life, education, religion, and politics. [Eds.]

2997.   Great Britain.   BASTUOLAND, BECHUANALAND PROTECTORATE AND SWAZILAND:
        REPORT OF AN ECONOMIC SURVEY MISSION.   London, H.M. Stationery
        Off., 1960.   2 v.   v. 1: text, 555 p.; v. 2: maps.   Chairman:
        Chandler Morse.

        A comprehensive survey of the political, administrative, and
        fiscal background and the economic situation, including cattle,
        crops, water, minerals, power, communications, industry and commerce,
        and education.   An appendix gives statistics of population, area,
        finance, and imports and exports.

        An earlier survey was conducted in 1951:   Great Britain, Colo-
        nial Office, AN ECONOMIC SURVEY OF THE COLONIAL TERRITORIES, 1951
        (London, H.M. Stationery Off., 1952, 7 v.; Colonial nos. 281-287).
        Vol. I included the High Commission Territories (see no. 1237).

2998.   Great Britain.   Central Office of Information.   Reference Division.
        BOTSWANA.   New York, British Information Services, 1966.   32 p.
        illus. (1 col.), fold. col. map.

        Brief general description of the former Bechuanaland Protec-
        torate.   [Eds.]

2999.   Great Britain.   Central Office of Information.   Reference Division.
        LESOTHO.   New York, British Information Services, 1966.   32 p.
        illus., fold. col. map.

        A general information pamphlet on former Basutoland.   [Eds.]

3000.   Great Britain.   Commonwealth Office.   ANNUAL REPORT ON BASUTOLAND.
        1946-[65?]   London, H.M. Stationery Off.   illus., map.   (Colo-
        nial Annual Reports)

        1962.   126 p.   Reading list: p. 124-126.

        _____.   _____.   ANNUAL REPORT ON THE BECHUANALAND PROTECTORATE.
        1946-66.   London, H.M. Stationery Off.   (Colonial Annual Re-
        ports)

        1961 and 1962.   1964.   116 p.

        _____.   _____.   ANNUAL REPORT ON SWAZILAND.   1946-   London,
        H.M. Stationery Off.   map.   (Colonial Annual Reports)

        1962.   125 p.   Reading list: p. 119-122 (classed).

Until Dec. 1961 the annual reports of the three High Commission Territories were submitted to the Office of Commonwealth Relations (now the Commonwealth Office) by the High Commissioner, who was also High Commissioner of the Union of South Africa. After the Republic of South Africa withdrew from the Commonwealth, the office in South Africa was changed to that of Ambassador, responsible as High Commissioner of the Territories to the Colonial Office. The annual reports were then published by the Colonial Office. They were in systematic style, containing short summaries of the chief events of the past year and handbook and statistical information on the territories. They included reading lists citing official publications as well as unofficial writings.

3001. Great Britain. Commonwealth Office. BASUTOLAND, THE BECHUANALAND PROTECTORATE AND SWAZILAND: HISTORY OF DISCUSSIONS WITH THE UNION OF SOUTH AFRICA, 1909-1939. London, H.M. Stationery Off., 1952. 135 p. map. (Cmd. 8707)

Historical review of the consistent and oft-repeated refusal of the United Kingdom to consider incorporation of its High Commission Territories for South Africa, "except with the full consent of the peoples concerned."

3002. Hailey, William M. Hailey, 1st baron. NATIVE ADMINISTRATION IN THE BRITISH AFRICAN TERRITORIES: Part 5, THE HIGH COMMISSION TERRITORIES: BASUTOLAND, THE BECHUANALAND PROTECTORATE AND SWAZILAND. London, H.M. Stationery Off., 1953. 447 p. tables.

For comment, see no. 1240.

3003. Hailey, William M. Hailey, 1st baron. THE REPUBLIC OF SOUTH AFRICA AND THE HIGH COMMISSION TERRITORIES. London, New York, Oxford University Press, 1963. 136 p.

Based on material collected from 1960 to bring the 1953 study up to date, but changed into a review and analysis of past and present aspects of the relations of the three territories with the Union and the Republic.

3004. THE HIGH COMMISSION TERRITORIES LAW REPORTS: DECISIONS OF THE HIGH COURTS AND SPECIAL COURTS OF BASUTOLAND, THE BECHUANA-LAND PROTECTORATE AND SWAZILAND, 1926-1953. Edited by Sir Harold Willan. Maseru, High Court, 1955. xxiv, 328 p.

Annual volume, 1954-.

3005. Holleman, J. F., ed. EXPERIMENT IN SWAZILAND: REPORT OF THE
       SWAZILAND SAMPLE SURVEY, 1960. By the Institute of Social
       Research, University of Natal, for the Swaziland Administra-
       tion. Cape Town, Oxford University Press, 1964. xi, 352 p.
       maps.

       Bibliography: p. 346-347.

       A socioeconomic survey covering the following aspects: land
   use, demography, rural economy, wage employment and labor resources,
   and urbanization.

3006. Kuper, Hilda. AN AFRICAN ARISTOCRACY: RANK AMONG THE SWAZI.
       London, Oxford University Press for the International African
       Institute, 1947. xii, 251 p. illus., plates, diagrs., maps.

       A full study of the traditional Swazi political system and
   its economic and related institutions.

3007. Kuper, Hilda. THE UNIFORM OF COLOUR: A STUDY OF BLACK AND WHITE
       RELATIONSHIPS IN SWAZILAND. Johannesburg, Witwatersrand
       University Press, 1948. 160 p. plates.

       A continuation of AN AFRICAN ARISTOCRACY, analyzing the
   influence of Western civilization on the traditional society.

3008. Kuper, Hilda. THE SWAZI. London, International African Institute,
       1952. 89 p. map, tables. (Ethnographic Survey of Africa,
       Southern Africa, pt. 1)

       A concise survey of Swazi social conditions, political and
   economic structure, religious beliefs and practices, technology,
   and art.

3009. Kuper, Hilda. THE SWAZI: A SOUTH AFRICAN KINGDOM. New York,
       Holt, 1963. 87 p. illus., maps. (Case Studies in Cultural
       Anthropology)

       Bibliography: p. 85-87.

A concise up-to-date description of Swazi kinship, political structure, work and wealth, age and education, religion, and magic and sorcery.

These above four references are major anthropological studies of the Swazi people by a specialist in her field.

Another well-known work is B. A. Marwick, THE SWAZI: AN ETHNOGRAPHICAL ACCOUNT OF THE NATIVES OF SWAZILAND PROTECTORATE (Cambridge Eng., University Press, 1940, 320 p., plates, diagrs., map).

3010. Munger, Edwin S. BECHUANALAND: PAN-AFRICAN OUTPOST OR BANTU
           HOMELAND? London, New York, Oxford University Press,
           1965. 114 p.

3011. Natal. University. Institute for Social Research. [Swaziland
           Surveys] Series. 1962- Durban.

A series of socioeconomic studies of Swaziland, issued by the Institute in large processed pamphlets, lavishly furnished with illustrations, maps, charts, etc. The following have been published:

   Daniel, J. B. McI. THE GEOGRAPHY OF THE RURAL ECONOMY OF
        SWAZILAND. 1962. pt. $\underline{1}$: text, 353 $\underline{1}$.; pt. 2: atlas,
        59 figs., maps.

   Hughes, A. J. B. SWAZI LAND TENURE. 1964. 313 p.

   Jones, Sonya M. A STUDY OF SWAZI NUTRITION. Prepared for
        the Swaziland Government. 1963. 264 p.

   Report of the Swaziland Nutrition Survey, 1961-62.

3012. Royal Institute of International Affairs. THE HIGH COMMISSION
           TERRITORIES AND THE REPUBLIC OF SOUTH AFRICA. By G. V. Doxey.
           London, Distributed for the Royal Institute of International
           Affairs by the Oxford University Press, 1963. 51 p. (Chatham
           House Memoranda)

Supersedes earlier memoranda of 1956 and 1957. A general description of the three territories and their economic, political, and social development is followed by a discussion of their relations with South Africa.

3013. Schapera, Isaac. THE TSWANA. London, International African
            Institute, 1953. 80 p. map. (Ethnographic Survey of Africa,
            Southern Africa, pt. 3)

        Professor Schapera is the recognized authority on the Tswana,
Bakgatla, and other tribes of the Bechuanaland Protectorate. This
volume in the Ethnographic Survey Series is of the reference-guide
nature, and its bibliography includes titles of many other books
and articles by his hand. Among them are HANDBOOK OF TSWANA LAW
AND CUSTOM (2d ed., London, Published for the International
African Institute by Oxford University Press, 1955, 328 p.),
MARRIED LIFE IN AN AFRICAN TRIBE [the Bakgatla] (London, Faber &
Faber, 1940, 364 p.), and MIGRANT LABOUR AND TRIBAL LIFE: A STUDY
OF CONDITIONS IN THE BECHUANALAND PROTECTORATE (London, Oxford
University Press, 1947, 248 p.).

3014. Sheddick, Vernon G. J. THE SOUTHERN SOTHO. London, International
            African Institute, 1953. 87 p. map. (Ethnographic Survey
            of Africa, Southern Africa, pt. 2)

        Bibliography: p. 80-84.

        Standard ethnographical survey. Another work by Dr. Sheddick,
LAND TENURE IN BASUTOLAND (London, H.M. Stationery Off., 1954,
196 p., illus., fold. maps; Colonial Research Studies, no. 13),
was a full field survey, analyzing and suggesting remedies for
land shortage in Basutoland.

3015. Silberbauer, George B. REPORT TO THE GOVERNMENT OF BECHUANALAND
            ON THE BUSHMAN SURVEY. Gaberones, Bechuanaland Govt., 1965.
            138 p. illus., map.

        An investigation into the present state of the Bushman popu-
lation of the Bechuana Protectorate. It covers geographical
disposition, interracial contacts, social structure and organization,
law and justice, economics, material, culture, and languages. [Eds.]

3016. Sillery, A. THE BECHUANALAND PROTECTORATE. Cape Town, Oxford
            University Press, 1952. xii, 236 p. maps.

        Bibliography: p. 219-222.

        An important general work covering history from the beginning
of the nineteenth century, the traditions and history of the tribes,
and an account of contemporary conditions--topography, the towns,
lands and cattle posts, animal husbandry and agriculture, and
migrant labor.

A more specialized work is the author's recent FOUNDING A
PROTECTORATE: HISTORY OF BECHUANALAND, 1885-1895 (London, Mouton,
1965, 267 p., illus., maps; Studies in African History, Anthropology
and Ethnology, 3), a very detailed account, much of it taken from
the unpublished correspondence of the missionaries and traders
who were the first Europeans in the region. The style of writing
is easy and anyone deeply concerned with the period will find the
book interesting reading. [Eds.]

3017. South Africa. Bureau of Census and Statistics. OFFICIAL YEARBOOK OF
        THE REPUBLIC OF SOUTH AFRICA. 1910- Pretoria, Govt. Printer.

        Each issue of the yearbook has separate chapters on Basutoland,
Bechuanaland, and Swaziland, covering the following topics: history,
description, game, administration, population, vital statistics, public health, education, labor, justice, land and agriculture, commerce, communications, public finance, and taxation. (See also no.
2939.)

3018. Spence, J. E. LESOTHO: THE POLITICS OF DEPENDENCE. London,
        Published for the Institute of Race Relations [by] Oxford
        University Press, 1968. 88 p. map.

        By a political scientist who in 1965 visited what was then
Basutoland. The historical background is established and
developments are carried up to 1966 in this readable discussion
of the country's economic and political difficulties, with particular
reference to dependence on South Africa. [Eds.]

3019. Stevens, Richard P. LESOTHO, BOTSWANA, AND SWAZILAND: THE FORMER
        HIGH COMMISSION TERRITORIES IN SOUTHERN AFRICA. New York,
        Praeger, 1967. 294 p. (Praeger Library of African Affairs)

        Bibliography: p. 277-285.

        Account of political and constitutional development in the
three countries. H. George Henry has contributed chapters on the
economy of each. [Eds.]

3020. Swaziland. Government Information Service. A HANDBOOK TO THE
        KINGDOM OF SWAZILAND. Mbabane, 1968. 126 p. Cover title:
        THE KINGDOM OF SWAZILAND.

A survey of the history, geography, population, government, finance, agriculture, mining, medical services, education, communications, traditional ceremonies, tourism, among other data. [Eds.]

3021. Theal, G. McCall. BASUTOLAND RECORDS. Cape Town, W. A. Richard, 1883. 3 v.

Reprinted Cape Town, Struik, 1964. 3 v. in 4. maps.

A pioneer work which lists chronologically 2,194 documents and letters (among them many missionary and official reports), relating to the history of Basutoland during the period 1833-68. Three further volumes relating to 1868 and 1869 were never printed and exist only in manuscript form in the Cape Archives.

3022. Tylden, G. THE RISE OF THE BASUTO. Cape Town, Juta, 1950. xi, 270 p. illus., ports., maps.

A concise history of Basutoland from 1824, well documented throughout the text, with a valuable bibliography (p. 241-246) which includes government publications and maps.

Two standard histories, especially good for the earlier period, are D. F. Ellenberger and J. C. MacGregor, HISTORY OF THE BASUTO, ANCIENT AND MODERN (London, Caxton, 1912), and Sir G. Lagden, THE BASUTOS (London, Hutchinson, 1909, 2 v.).

3023. Winchester-Gould, G. A. THE GUIDE TO BOTSWANA. Gaberones, Winchester Press, 1968. 213 p. illus., maps.

Tourist-oriented, describes tourist attractions, and gives information on photography and hunting safaris. The work briefly describes the government (including list of cabinet members, members of the House of Chiefs). Included is a short history of Botswana, economic information, and a short list of Tswana words and phrases. [Eds.]

CHAPTER 44

FORMER GERMAN AFRICA

<u>Note</u>: For material on individual countries see also country sections of
the Guide.

Bibliographies

3024. African Law Association in America, Inc. NEWSLETTER NUMBER 5.
          April 15, 1967.

          Contains a detailed bibliography concerning German colonial
       law, indexes to compilations and series. The bibliography is
       divided into general works and works concerning particular colonies.

3025. Bridgman, Jon, and David E. Clarke. GERMAN AFRICA: A SELECT
          ANNOTATED BIBLIOGRAPHY. Stanford, Calif., Hoover Institution,
          Stanford University, 1965. (Hoover Institution Bibliographical
          Series, no. 19)

          A detailed bibliography going up to 1964. The work contains a
       general note on German official and semiofficial publications,
       annotated lists of general works, and annotated lists on each of
       the German African colonies. The authors provide nearly 1,000
       titles. They also give a description of material dealing with
       German Africa contained in the British Confidential Prints prepared
       by the Colonial Office and the Foreign Office between the years
       1888 and 1906, as well as an alphabetical list of serials and news-
       papers, respectively.

3026. Köhler, Jochen, ed. DEUTSCHE DISSERTATIONEN UBER AFRIKA: EIN
          VERZEICHNIS FUR DIE JAHRE 1919-1959. Bonn, K. Schroeder,
          1962. 1 v. (unpaged)

Published under the auspices of the Deutsche Afrika-Gesellschaft, Bonn. It lists 795 items.

3027.   Pogge von Strandmann, Hartmut.   "The German Empire in Africa and
           British Perspectives: A Historiographical Essay." In BRITAIN
        AND GERMANY IN AFRICA: IMPERIAL RIVALRY AND COLONIAL RULE,
        edited by Prosser Gifford and Wm. Roger Louis with the assistance
        of Alison Smith. New Haven, Conn., Yale University Press, 1967:
        p. 709-795.

        A detailed and up-to-date essay which gives a general review of
the printed literature concerning Anglo-American rivalry in the colonies, Germany's bid for the colonies, local aspects of German-British
rivalry, the Heligoland-Zanzibar treaty, Anglo-German relations respecting the Transvaal, the Portuguese colonies, and the Congo, as
well as German and British war aims during and after World War I.
The author then discusses the literature concerning German as well as
British administration; the study of the colonial period in general
and of the German colonial period in particular. He also provides a
great deal of information concerning German archival sources, printed
material of official provenance, and so on. The essay also explains
the structure of the German Colonial Office, lists the principal
officials concerned with colonial affairs, and finally gives a list
of titles extending over more than 20 pages. See also Schramm,
DEUTSCHLAND UND UBERSEE (no. 3046); pages 476-600 contain a detailed
bibliography illustrating various German connections with Africa.

Reference Works

3028.   Cornevin, Robert.   HISTOIRE DE LA COLONISATION ALLEMANDE. Paris,
        Presses Universitaires de France, 1969. 128 p. maps. ("Que
        sais-je?" Le point des connaissances actuelles, no. 1331)

        Bibliography: p. 123-126.

        A useful, short, popular account by a distinguished French his-
torian.

3029.   DENKSCHRIFTEN ZUM KOLONIAL-ETAT. Berlin, Reichstagdruck, 1885-
        [1918?]. Annual; later, every 2 years.

        These memoranda were published by the Kolonial Abteilung of the
Auswärtiges Amt and its successors in order to assist members of the
Reichstag in framing the colonial budgets. The series also includes
special reports. The annual reports formed the continuation of the
original WEISSBUCHER (see no. 3047). The annual reports appeared as
supplements to the DEUTSCHES KOLONIALBLATT (no. 3032).

3030. DIE DEUTSCHE KOLONIALGESETZGEBUNG: SAMMLUNG DER AUF DIE DEUTSCHEN
SCHUTZGEBIETE BEZUGLICHEN GESETZE, VERORDNUNGEN, ERLASSE
UND INTERNATIONALEN VEREINBARUNGEN, MIT ANMERKUNGEN UND
SACHREGISTER.... Berlin, E. S. Mittler, 1893-1910. 13 v.

A collection of the legislation and international treaties
concerning the German colonies. The editors include authorities
such as A. Zimmermann, E. Schmidt-Dargitz, O. M. Köbner, J. Gerst-
meyer, and T. Riebow. The volumes are annotated, and there is a
subject index. Vol. I goes up to 1892. Vols. II to XIII go up to
1910. Lists of laws subsequent to 1909 were published in the
ZEITSCHRIFT FUR KOLONIALPOLITIK and elsewhere.

3031. DEUTSCHE KOLONIALZEITUNG. 1884-1942. Berlin. Irregular.

Published from 1884 by the Deutscher Kolonialverein (German
Colonial League, Frankfurt, later Berlin), and from 1887 by the
Deutsche Kolonialgesellschaft. The journal expressed the views of
various colonial lobbies, and also provided information concerning
the colonies. It ceased publication in 1922. It appeared first of
all as a semimonthly and later as a weekly journal. The Deutsche
Kolonialgesellschaft also published various other journals,
including the KOLONIALES JAHRBUCH (1889-99), the BEITRAGE ZUR
KOLONIALPOLITIK UND KOLONIALWIRTSCHAFT, which became known in 1904
as ZEITSCHRIFT FUR KOLONIALPOLITIK, KOLONIALRECHT UND KOLONIAL-
WIRTSCHAFT, and in 1913 as KOLONIALE MONATSBLATTER. The Colonial
Economic Committee (Kolonialwirtschaftliches Komitee) became
affiliated to the Colonial League and issued DER TROPENPFLANZER:
ZEITSCHRIFT FUR TROPISCHE LANDWIRTSCHAFT, an agricultural journal.

3032. DEUTSCHES KOLONIALBLATT: AMTSBLATT DES REICHSKOLONIALAMTES.
1890-1921. Berlin, E. S. Mittler und Sohn.

This was the official German government gazette for the colonial
empire as a whole. It was issued originally under the auspices of
the Auswärtige Amt (the German Foreign Ministry). In 1907 an
independent Reichskolonialamt came into existence, which continued
to publish the journal. In 1919 the ministry became known as
Reichskolonialministerium, but this ceased to exist in 1920. Subsequently the journal was published by the Kolonialzentralverwaltung
im Reichsministerium für Wiederaufbau (the colonial section within
the German Ministry of Reconstruction), and only stopped publication
in 1921.

The name of the journal changed several times. From 1890 to
1904 it was known as the AMTSBLATT FUR DIE SCHUTZGEBIETE DES
DEUTSCHEN REICHES. In 1905 it became the AMTSBLATT FUR DIE SCHUTZ-
GEBIETE IN AFRIKA UND IN DER SUDSEE.

The KOLONIALBLATT published not only official legislation, but
also a great deal of additional information derived from scholars,
travelers, missionaries, planters, and so forth, especially in its
earlier numbers. From 1898 it also issued supplementary volumes
giving official reports for annual submission to the Reichstag.
These contained an account of the development of each colony, together with numerous statistics. These reports were later issued
independently by the Reichskolonialamt.

3033. Dove, Karl, et al., eds. DAS UBERSEEISCHE DEUTSCHLAND IN WORT UND
    BILD.... Stuttgart, Union Deutsche Verlagsgesellschaft, 1911.
    2 v., illus., plates, maps (part col., fold.).

The first volume relates to Kamerun, South-West Africa, and
Germany's Pacific possessions. The second volume deals with Togo,
German East Africa, and Samoa. The book were compiled by persons
considered experts at the time, many of them naval or military
officers.

3034. Germany. Reichskolonialamt. DIE DEUTSCHEN SCHUTZGEBIETE IN AFRIKA
    UND DER SUDSEE. Berlin, 1906-13. Annual.

These were official publications giving a general review of
German colonial development. Earlier titles were: 1906/7, JAHRES-
BERICHT UBER DIE ENTWICKLUNG DER DEUTSCHEN SCHUTZGEBIETE; 1908/9,
DENKSCHRIFT UBER DIE ENTWICKLUNG DER SCHUTZGEBIETE IN AFRIKA UND
DER SUDSEE. These appeared as supplements to the DEUTSCHES KOLO-
NIALBLATT.

Before the Kolonialamt was set up as an independent agency in
1907, colonial affairs were handled under the auspices of the Auswärtiges Amt, the German Foreign Office, which also issued the
KOLONIALBLATT. The KOLONIALBLATT, which also printed a good deal
of information derived from missionaries, travelers, and soldiers,
likewise issued annual reports as annual supplements, starting with
1891/92, ENTWICKLUNG UNSERER KOLONIEN.

3035. Germany. Reichskolonialamt. MITTEILUNGEN AUS DEN DEUTSCHEN SCHUTZ-
    GEBIETEN MIT BENUTZUNG AMTLICHER QUELLEN. Berlin, 1888-1919.
    illus., plates, maps (part fold.). Annual.

These were issued by official German agencies, mainly the
Reichskolonialamt, as long as this office remained in existence.
The compilers included Freiherr von Danckelmann and H. Marquandsen.
The MITTEILUNGEN were supplemented by ERGANZUNGSHEFTE, starting
from 1909. The series provides extensive information concerning
expeditions in the German colonies, and geographical, geological,
and agronomic data.

3036. Germany. Reichskolonialamt. VEROFFENTLICHUNGEN. Jena, G. Fischer, 1911-17. 9 v. illus., maps (part fold.).

The Reichskolonialamt published a series of detailed monographs concerning cotton cultivation, forestry, veterinary science, irriga-tion, domestic slavery, company concessions, and similar questions. All are of considerable academic value and all were compiled by leading experts of the time.

3037. Germany. Reichstag. STENOGRAPHISCHE BERICHTE UBER DIE VERHANDLUNGEN DES DEUTSCHEN REICHSTAGES. Berlin, 1871-1938.

The Reichstag formed the lower house in the legislature of the German Reich. Its debates (VERHANDLUNGEN), the material placed before the House (ANLAGEBANDE), and official papers (DRUCKSACHEN) are an essential source, as the powers of the Reichstag in colonial matters were relatively great. This material and the BEILAGEN to the DEUTSCHES KOLONIALBLATT include not only all the debates on colonial questions but also numerous documents, committee reports, correspondence, and the official reports on the colonies given by the Colonial Office.

The material dealing with the colonies as a whole has never been reprinted. There is, however, one valuable publication entitled DIE LETZTEN KOLONIALDEBATTEN IM AUFGELOSTEN REICHSTAG, NOVEMBER UND DE-ZEMBER, 1906 (Berlin, E. S. Mittler, 1907, 295 p.). These debates, in which the Catholic Center Party and the Social Democrats opposed the government's policy in South-West Africa, provide a great deal of material containing real and alleged abuses committed under the German colonial regime. (They also contributed both to German colo-nial reforms and to the "Hottentot elections" of 1907, in which a conservative-liberal coalition defeated the Center and the Social-ists.)

3038. Gifford, Prosser, and William Roger Louis, eds., assisted by Alison Smith. BRITAIN AND GERMANY IN AFRICA: IMPERIAL RIVALRY AND COLONIAL RULE. New Haven, Conn., and London, Yale University Press, 1967. xvii, 825 p. maps.

Bibliography: p. 709-795.

For full annotation of this detailed comparative study, see nos. 550 and 3037.

3039. Kolonialinstitut. ABHANDLUNGEN. Hamburg, L. Friederichsen, 1910-21. 43 v.

The ABHANDLUNGEN, monographs of the highest scientific value, concern mainly Africa. They deal with subjects as varied as African linguistics, ethnography, hydrology, economics, education, folklore, agriculture, and colonial legislation. The publications are remarkable for their objectivity and completeness.

3040. Kolonialinstitut. BERICHT UBER DAS STUDIENJAHR. Hamburg, 1908-21. Annual.

The Kolonialinstitut carried on investigations into various German colonial problems and issued regular reports concerning its work.

3041. MARINE RUNDSCHAU: MONATSSCHRIFT FUR SEEWESEN. 1890- Berlin, later Frankfurt.

The official organ of the German Navy, issued by the Reichsmarineamt, later by the Marineleitung im Reichswehrministerium and its successors. It now continues as a non-official publication under the title of MARINE RUNDSCHAU: ZEITSCHRIFT FUR SEEWESEN, put out by the Arbeitskreis für Wehrforschung, published by E. S. Mittler und Sohn, Frankfurt. The journal was primarily concerned with matters of naval interest, but there are references to colonial affairs during the imperial period.

3042. Meyer, Hans Heinrich Joseph, ed. DAS DEUTSCHE KOLONIALREICH: EINE LANDERKUNDE DER DEUTSCHEN SCHUTZGEBIETE. Leipzig, Bibliographisches Institut, 1909-10. 2 v. illus., maps, diagrs.

An encyclopedic work which summarizes the geographical, ethnographic, geological, and related information available at the time concerning the German colonies. There is also some reference to economic and administrative matters. Meyer, himself an expert on railways and economic development in the colonies, called on leading experts to assist him in his work. The first volume, dealing with East Africa and Kamerun, was compiled by Meyer himself and by Siegfried Passarge. The second volume, which treats Togo, South-West Africa, and Germany's Pacific possessions, was put together by Passarge, Leonhard Schultze, Wilhelm Sievers, and Georg Wegener.

3043. Schack, Friedrich. DAS DEUTSCHE KOLONIALRECHT IN SEINER ENTWICKLUNG BIS ZUM WELTKRIEG: DIE ALLGEMEINEN LEHREN; EINE BERICHTENDE DARSTELLUNG DER THEORIE UND PRAXIS NEBST KRITISCHER BEMERKUNGEN. Hamburg, L. Friederichsen, 1923. 434 p. (Abhandlungen aus dem Gebiet der Auslandkunde, no. 12)

Bibliography: p. 395-431.

An exhaustive study of German colonial law. Included is an
extensive bibliography on German colonial law.

3044.   Schmokel, Wolfe W. DREAM OF EMPIRE: GERMAN COLONIALISM, 1919-1945.
        New Haven, Conn., Yale University Press, 1964. 204 p. illus.

        Bibliography: p. 185-196.

        Reviews German colonial revisionist claims until the end of the
Second World War. The author concludes that colonialism was
primarily the casualty of the Second World War, and might have
lasted longer, had the British and French decided on a policy of
greater appeasement.

3045.   Schnee, Heinrich, ed. DEUTSCHES KOLONIAL-LEXIKON. Leipzig, Quelle
        und Meyer, 1920. 3 v. 776, 698, 778 p. illus., maps,
        tables.

        This massive work forms an exhaustive summary of the knowledge
available at the time concerning the German colonies and also puts
forward revisionist claims.

3046.   Schramm, Percy. DEUTSCHLAND UND UBERSEE: DER DEUTSCHE HANDEL MIT
        DEN ANDEREN KONTINENTEN, INSBESONDERE AFRIKA, VON KARL V. BIS
        ZU BISMARCK; EIN BEITRAG ZUR GESCHICHTE DER RIVALITAT IM
        WIRTSCHAFTSLEBEN. Braunschweig, Westermann, 1950. 639 p.
        fold. maps.

        Bibliography: p. 476-600.

        A history of German overseas trade with special reference to
Africa, from the sixteenth to the late nineteenth century.

3047.   WEISSBUCHER UBER KOLONIALANGELEGENHEITEN. Berlin, Reichdruckerei,
        1883-85. 13 v.

        These were published by the Kolonial Abteilung des Auswärtigen
Amts, and dealt with a great variety of African matters of interest
to German parliamentarians. The series was continued later as
DENKSCHRIFTEN ZUM KOLONIAL-ETAT (see no. 3029).

3048.   ZEITSCHRIFT FUR EINGEBORENEN-SPRACHEN. 1910-20. Berlin. Irregu-
        lar.

A valuable linguistic journal. In 1920 it was superseded by the
ZEITSCHRIFT FUR KOLONIALSPRACHEN, and in 1952 by AFRIKA UND
UBERSEE: SPRACHEN, KULTUREN.

3049.   ZEITSCHRIFT FUR ETHNOLOGIE. Berlin, 1869-1944; Braunschweig, 1950-
Semiannual.

Published until 1944 as the organ of the Berliner Gesellschaft
für Anthropologie, Ethnologie und Urgeschichte. In 1944 it was suspended with vol. 7. In 1950 it was revived with vol. 75, as the
organ of the Deutsche Gesellschaft für Völkerkunde. A major ethnographic source for Africa and other regions.

3050.   ZEITSCHRIFT FUR KOLONIALPOLITIK, KOLONIALRECHT UND KOLONIALWIRTSCHAFT:
HERAUSGEGEBEN VON DER DEUTSCHEN KOLONIALGESELLSCHAFT. Berlin,
W. Süsserott, 1899-1914. 16 v.

Each volume of this major source contains much information concerning the most varied aspects of German colonization, including
a good deal of legal material. Vols. 15 and 16 were bound
separately under the title ZEITSCHRIFT FUR KOLONIALRECHT, with
separate pagination.

EAST AFRICA

3051.   Austen, Ralph Albert. NORTHWEST TANZANIA UNDER GERMAN AND BRITISH
RULE: COLONIAL POLICY AND TRIBAL POLITICS, 1889-1939. New
Haven, Conn., Yale University Press, 1968. 307 p. map.

Case study of German and subsequent British colonial policy
and indigenous responses in one area of a German colony. Based
on detailed archival research, the work is important both for its
knowledgeable treatment of the German background and its comparative
data on British colonial rule.

3052.   Great Britain. Naval Staff. Naval Intelligence Division. A HAND-
BOOK OF GERMAN EAST AFRICA. Compiled by the Geographical Section of the Naval Intelligence Division, Naval Staff, Admiralty.
London, H.M. Stationery Off. [printed by Frederick Hall], 1923.
440 p. illus., plans, diagrs.

An account with special emphasis on geographical and related
features.

3053.   Iliffe, John. TANGANYIKA UNDER GERMAN RULE, 1905-1912. London,
Cambridge University Press, 1969. 236 p. map.

Bibliography: p. 211-223.

A detailed study based on extensive archival sources. It eluci-
dates the causes and effects of the Maji Maji rising, the impact of
German settlement, attempts at administrative and social reform, and
the various contradictions that beset German policy. There is an
excellent, detailed bibliography which contains a short description
of relevant material in the Tanzania National Archives at Dar es
Salaam; University College, Dar es Salaam; Tanzania Area Offices;
Makerere University College, Kampala; as well as in the Deutsches
Zentralarchiv, Potsdam, and in the archives of the United Society
for the Propagation of the Gospel, London.

3054. Meyer, Hans Heinrich Joseph, ed. DAS DEUTSCHE KOLONIALREICH: EINE
        LANDERKUNDE DER DEUTSCHEN SCHUTZGEBIETE: Vol. I, OSTAFRIKA UND
        KAMERUN. Leipzig, Bibliographisches Institut, 1909. 909 p.
        illus., maps, diagrs.

        A detailed account, with special reference to geographic, eco-
logical, and geological features. The portion on German East Africa
was compiled by the editor himself. See no. 3042 for further comment.

3055. Redeker, Dietrich. DIE GESCHICHTE DER TAGESPRESSE DEUTSCH-OSTAFRIKAS
        (1899-1916).... Berlin, Triltsch und Huther, 1937. 135 p.

        A history of the German daily press in German East Africa, pre-
pared as a doctoral dissertation for the University of Berlin. It
contains a description of the sources used.

KAMERUN AND TOGO

3056. Rudin, Harry Rudolph. GERMANS IN THE CAMEROONS, 1884-1914: A CASE
        STUDY IN MODERN IMPERIALISM. New Haven, Yale University Press,
        1938. 456 p. fold. map. (Yale Historical Publications, Stud-
        ies, no. 12)

        Bibliographical note: p. 427-437.

        A classical work on German Kamerun written by an American his-
torian. The book is based on extensive source material and is provided with a detailed bibliography. In its original form (later
extensively amended before going into print) the work won the John
Addison Porter Prize at Yale University.

3057. Stoecker, Helmuth, ed. KAMERUN UNTER DEUTSCHER KOLONIALHERRSCHAFT.
        Berlin, Rütten und Loening, 1960. 2 v. illus., maps, tables.

A cooperative project which seeks to interpret the history of Kamerun from the Marxist-Leninist point of view. The collaborators include Hans-Peter Jaeck, Adolf Rüger, Hella Winkler, Rudi Kaeselitz, and Hartmut and Ellen Mehls. Despite its marked political bias, the work provides an extensive amount of information on subjects as varied as the German annexation, the development of the local black proletariat, indigenous resistance against the Germans, and the German concession companies. The work is based on detailed archival re-research. Included is a geographic index.

SOUTH-WEST AFRICA

3058. Bley, Helmut. KOLONIALHERRSCHAFT UND SOZIALSTRUKTUR IN DEUTSCH-SUD-WEST AFRIKA 1894-1914. Hamburg, Leibniz-Verlag, 1968. 390 p. (Hamburger Beiträge zur Zeitgeschichte, v. 5)

Bibliography: p. 377-386.

Based on extensive archival and published material. Bley's study is influenced by the socio-psychological theories elaborated by Fanon and Mannoni; the author argues that German colonial governance possessed some of the features that distinguish modern totalitarianism and that German colonialism in turn helped to poison the political climate at home. Little reference, however, is made to the more positive aspects of German colonization. The book has a detailed bibliography and an index of persons.

3059. Germany. Reichskolonialamt. DIE BEHANDLUNG DER EINHEIMISCHEN BE-VOLKERUNG IN DEN KOLONIALEN BESITZUNGEN DEUTSCHLANDS UND ENG-LANDS: EINE ERWIDERUNG AUF DAS ENGLISCHE BLAUBUCH VOM AUGUST 1918: REPORT ON THE NATIVES OF SOUTH-WEST AFRICA AND THEIR TREATMENT BY GERMANY. Berlin, Kommissionsverlag H. R. Engelmann, 1919. 201 p. plates.

An official German defense of Germany's colonial record against what the Germans called die Kolonialschuldlüge, the lie of colonial guilt. The official British case was embodied in Great Britain, Parliament, Accounts and Papers, UNION OF SOUTH-AFRICA--REPORT ON THE NATIVES OF SOUTH-WEST AFRICA AND THEIR TREATMENT BY GERMANY, prepared by the Administrator's Office, Windhoek, South-West Africa, Jan. 1918 (Cmd. 9146).

3060. Hintrager, Oskar. SUDWESTAFRIKA IN DER DEUTSCHEN ZEIT. München, Kommissionsverlag R. Oldenbourg, 1955. 261 p. illus., map.

Written by a senior German colonial official in retirement. Hintrager writes from the German colonial point of view, stressing the positive aspects of German colonial rule and providing a good deal of statistical material to substantiate his interpretation. The book contains a chronology, an index of places, and an index of names.

3061. Lenssen, H. E. CHRONIK VON DEUTSCH-SUDWESTAFRIKA: EINE KURZ GE-
        FASSTE AUFZAHLUNG GESCHICHTLICHER EREIGNISSE AUS DER DEUTSCHEN
        KOLONIALZEIT VON 1883-1915. Windhoek, Verlag der S.W.A. Hissen-
        schaftlichen Gesellschaft, 1966. 246 p. ports.

        A useful chronological history of German South-West Africa.

CHAPTER 45

FORMER ITALIAN AFRICA: THE NORTHEAST COLONIES

Note: The colonies of former Northeast Italian Africa were Eritrea, Ethiopia, and Italian Somaliland. After World War II the Italian government
lost power over Eritrea and Ethiopia. Eritrea was reunited with the free
kingdom of Ethiopia by the United Nations. Italy was allowed to administer
Somaliland until July 1, 1960, when British Somaliland and Italian Somaliland were joined to form the independent nation of Somalia.

     For specific references see also the country sections of this Guide.

Atlases

3062. Agostini, Giovanni de. ITALY AND HER EMPIRE: PERFORATED POCKET
          ATLAS, WITH 16 COLORED MAPS AND EXPLANATORY TEXT. Translated
          by E. Cope. Genoa, E. E. Ortelli, 1937. 34 p. col. illus.,
          col. maps.

3063. Traversi, Carlo. STORIA DELLA CARTOGRAFIA COLONIALE ITALIANA.
          Roma, Istituto Poligrafico dello Stato, 1964. 294 p. plates,
          facsims., maps (part fold., part col.). (Comitato per la Docu-
          mentazione dell'Opera dell'Italia in Africa, L'Italia in
          Africa, Serie scientifico-culturale)

          Bibliography: p. 247-257.

Bibliographies

3064. GUIDE BIBLIOGRAFICHE DELL'ISTITUTO COLONIALE FASCISTA. Roma, Isti-
          tuto Coloniale Fascista, 1928.

3065. Hess, Robert I. ITALIAN COLONIALISM IN SOMALIA. Chicago, Chicago
       University Press, 1966. 234 p. maps, tables.

       Bibliography: p. 213-226.

       For full annotation of this work, which contains an excellent
bibliography on Italian Africa, see no. 3119.

3066. Istituto Italiano per l'Africa. BIBLIOGRAFIA DELL'ISTITUTO FASCISTA
       DELL'AFRICA ITALIANA: ELENCO COMPLETO DI TUTTE LE OPERE PUBBLI-
       CATE DALL'I.F.A.I. DALLA SUA FONDAZIONE (1906) AL GENNAIO 1939
       (XVII) E DEGLI ARTICOLI APPARSI NELLE RIVISTE EDITE DALL'ISTI-
       TUTO (RIVISTA COLONIALE--L'OTREMARE--AFRICA ITALIANA). Roma,
       1939. 89 p.

       Catalogue of publications of the Institute (first Istituto Colo-
niale Italiano, then Istituto Coloniale Fascista) from its founding
in 1906 to January 1939. Part 1 is a listing of periodicals, conference proceedings, and monographs. Part 2 lists articles appearing
in periodicals of the Institute, arranged by geographical area and
topic. Geographic areas covered include Eritrea, Somalia, Ethiopia,
and the Belgian Congo.

3067. Istituto Nazionale per le Relazioni Culturali con l'Estero. Centro
       Studi di Diritto e Politica Coloniale Fascista. BIBLIOGRAFIA
       DELL'ITALIA D'OLTREMARE: ANNO 1939-40. Roma, 1940-42. (Bib-
       liographie, ser. 2)

3068. Italy. Ministero degli Affari Esteri. RACCOLTA DI PUBBLICAZIONI
       COLONIALI ITALIANI. Roma, Tipografia della Camera dei Deputati,
       1911.

3069. U.S. Library of Congress. General Reference and Bibliographical
       Division. NORTH AND NORTHEAST AFRICA: A SELECTED, ANNOTATED
       LIST OF WRITINGS, 1951-1957. Compiled by Helen F. Conover.
       Washington, 1957. 182 p.

       Contains separate sections respectively on "Ethiopia and Eri-
trea" and on "The Somalilands," as well as "Libya." See no. 2584
for full annotation.

3070. Varley, Douglas H. A BIBLIOGRAPHY OF ITALIAN COLONISATION IN AFRICA,
       WITH A SECTION ON ABYSSINIA. London, Royal Empire Society and
       the Royal Institute of International Affairs, 1936. 92 p.

       Prepared in connection with the international interest occasioned
by the Italo-Abyssinian war in 1936, which added Ethiopia to the

former Italian possessions in Africa--Libya, Eritrea, and Somaliland.
There was subsequently set up the central administration of Italian
East Africa, combining Ethiopia, Eritrea, and Somalia. This list,
pages 72-92 of which relate to Ethiopia, cites books and periodical
material, particularly those relating to modern political developments.

3071. Zanutto, Silvio. "Bibliografia dell'Africa orientale Italiana."
        ANNALI DELL'AFRICA ITALIANA, v. 3, no. 2, 1940: 1269-1313.

3072. Zanutto, Silvio. PUBBLICAZIONI EDITE DALL'AMMINISTRAZIONE COLONIALE
        E SOTTO I SUOI AUSPICI, 1882-1937. Roma, Società Anonima Ita-
        liana, 1938.

        Not available for examination. See nos. 3094-3096 and 3105-3110
for bibliographies on individual colonies, and Martineau, no. 1536.

Reference Works

3073. Agostino Orsini, Paolo d'. LA COLONIZZAZIONE AFRICANA NELL SISTEMA
        FASCISTA, I PROBLEMI DELLA COLONIZZAZIONE NELL'AFRICA ITALIANA.
        Milano, Fratelli Bocca, 1941. 164 p.

        Bibliography: p. 157-161.

        An overview of Italian colonization from the Fascist viewpoint.

3074. ANNUARIO DELLE COLONIE ITALIANE (E DEI PAESI VICINI). Roma, Coopera-
        tiva Tipografica "Castaldi" [etc.], 1926-39. 13 v. plates,
        maps, facsims.

        This annual publication was issued by the Istituto Coloniale
Italiano (later known as Istituto Coloniale Fascista) in Rome. The
title varies: 1926/36, ANNUARIO DELLE COLONIE ITALIANE ...; 1937,
ANNUARIO DELL'IMPERO ITALIANO; 1938/39, ANNUARIO DELL'AFRICA ITALIANA.
The yearbook is valuable for a study of Fascist policies and precon-
ceptions.

3075. Becker, George H. THE DISPOSITION OF THE ITALIAN COLONIES, 1941-1951.
        Annemasse, 1952. 270 p.

        Bibliography: p. 265-270.

        Prepared as a thesis at the Institut Universitaire des Hautes
Etudes Internationales in Geneva, this work reviews the postwar
settlements for the former Italian colonies, Eritrea, Somaliland,

and Libya. A short background section on prewar and wartime
administration is followed by a discussion of the economic, strategic, and prestige value of the colonies and the efforts of the
Council of Foreign Ministers, the Paris Peace Conference, and
finally the UN General Assembly to settle the problems.

3076. Centro di Studi Coloniali. ATTI DEL PRIMO CONGRESSO DI STUDI
        COLONIALI. Florence, 1931. 6 v.

3077. ENCICLOPEDIA ITALIANA DI SCIENZE, LETTERE E ARTI. Pubblicata
        sotto l'Alto Patronato di S. M. il Re d'Italia. 36 v. Milano,
        Istituto Giovanni Treccani, 1927-37.

        The first volume of appendices came out in 1938. Two more
volumes, covering all letters from A to Z, appeared in 1949. These
cover the years 1938 to 1948 under the auspices of the Istituto
della Enciclopedia Italiana.

        The encyclopedia is much vaster in extent than comparable con-
temporary publications like the ENCYCLOPAEDIA BRITANNICA or DER
GROSSE BROCKHAUS. There are headings like "Somalia," "Eritrea,
colonia," etc., together with many maps, illustrations, tables,
etc.

3078. Gaibi, Agostino. MANUALE DI STORIA POLITICO-MILITARE DELLE COLONIE
        ITALIANE. Roma, Provveditoria generale dello stato, Libreria,
        1928. 579 p. illus., plans, fold. tables.

        Published under the auspices of the Ministry of War to give
a general account of the political and military problems of the
empire. The author was official historian of the General Staff.

3079. GUIDA DELL'AFRICA ORIENTALE ITALIANA. Milano, 1938. maps.

        An excellent work--much more than just a guide. Coverage
includes Ethiopia, Eritrea, and former Italian Somaliland.

3080. L'ITALIA COLONIALE: ORGANO DELLE NOSTRE COLONIE DI DIRITTO
        DOMINIO E DELLA GENTE ITALIANA NEGLI ALTRI PAESI. 1924-
        Milano, later Roma. Monthly.

        Presents the Fascist point of view, both on colonies under
direct Italian rule, and on Italians in other countries.
Copiously illustrated and popular in style, it contains biographical, statistical, and other types of information, as well
as Fascist propaganda.

3081. Italy. Comitato per la Documentazione dell'Opera dell'Italia in
         Africa. L'ITALIA IN AFRICA. Roma, Istituto Poligrafico dello
         Stato, 1955-

         This publication, issued under the auspices of the Italian
Ministry of Foreign Affairs, provides a great deal of detailed information, though some of it tends to be apologetic in character
and cannot be relied upon for a more critical appraisal of Italian
colonialism. Some 20 volumes are projected. There are numerous
bibliographical and archival references. L'ITALIA IN AFRICA is
divided into several series. These in turn are composed of several
volumes. In some cases the so-called volumes comprise several
parts, which in fact rank as separate publications.

a) L'ITALIA IN AFRICA. Roma, Istituto Poligrafico dello Stato, 1955.
       2 v.

       Covers early exploration, the acquisition of Assab, economic
penetration of East Africa in the second part of the nineteenth
century, etc. Original documents are appended.

b) L'ITALIA IN AFRICA. SERIE CIVILE. Roma, Istituto Poligrafico
       dello Stato, 1965-

       Two volumes have appeared up to now; they deal with sanitary
and veterinary administration and include bibliographies.

c) L'ITALIA IN AFRICA. SERIE GIURIDICHO-AMMINISTRATIVA. Roma, Isti-
       tuto Poligrafico dello Stato, 1963-

       The first volume covers certain aspects of judicial and civil
administration in the Italian colonies (later trusteeship territories) between 1869 and 1955. There is information regarding the
central organs of government, the civil service, and other aspects.

d) L'ITALIA IN AFRICA. SERIE SCIENTIFICO-CULTURALE. Roma, Istituto
       Poligrafico dello Stato, 1963-

       The first volume concerns the contribution made by Italy to
world knowledge of Africa. An additional volume published in 1964
deals with the development of colonial cartography (see no. 3063).

e) L'ITALIA IN AFRICA. SERIE STORICA. Roma, Istituto Poligrafico
       dello Stato, 1958-

       The series comprises an extensive number of documents, ex-
cerpts from parliamentary debates, private letters, and so forth.

There is also a great deal of bibliographical information, as well as editorial annotation.

f) L'ITALIA IN AFRICA. SERIE STORICO-MILITARE. Roma, Istituto Poligrafico dello Stato, 1960-64.

Covers the history of the army in the colonies from 1885 to 1943; naval operations connected with the colonies between 1868 and 1943; operations of the air force from 1888 to 1932 in Libya and Eritrea; and the army's part in civil administration.

3082. Italy. Commissione per la Pubblicazione dei Documenti Diplomatici. I DOCUMENTI DIPLOMATICI ITALIANI. Roma, Libreria dello Stato, 1952-

The Italians began to publish their diplomatic documents only well after the Germans and British had done so. They hope to produce a complete collection dating from the foundation of the kingdom of Italy to 1943. This collection will naturally include a great deal of information concerning colonial diplomacy and other related matters. But so far, only a limited number of volumes have appeared; they cover only selected periods, and there are as yet many gaps. The arrangement is purely chronological. The documents are useful for an understanding of Italian imperialism, though they do not throw much light on the colonies as such.

The collection as a whole is divided into several series, each covering a specific period. Each series in turn is subdivided into several volumes. The first series covers the period Jan. 8, 1861-Sept. 20, 1870; the fifth, Aug. 2, 1914-Oct. 16, 1914; the sixth, Nov. 4, 1918-Jan. 17, 1919; the seventh, Oct. 31, 1922-Sept. 23, 1928; the eighth, May 23, 1939-Sept. 3, 1939; the ninth, Sept. 4, 1939-June 10, 1940.

3083. Italy. Ministero degli Affari Esteri. L'AFRICA ITALIANA. 1882-1905.

This is useful as a summary and as a reference on debates on Africa in the Italian parliament. Indexes are by subject and name of speaker.

3084. Italy. Ministero dell'Africa Italiana. GLI ANNALI DELL'AFRICA ITALIANA. Roma, Casa Editrice A Mondadori, 1938-43. 20 v. plates, ports., maps, diagr.

Includes bibliographies.

This series deals with subjects as varied as administration, agriculture, colonial history, settlement in Italian Africa, etc. There are also articles of a more general propagandistic kind extolling the virtues of Fascist policy. The series is nevertheless a valuable historical source.

3085. Italy. Ministero delle Colonie. BOLLETTINO DI INFORMAZIONI. 1913-22. Roma.

   Title changes and series added: BOLLETTINO DI INFORMAZIONI ECONOMICHE, 1923-27; RASSEGNA ECONOMICA DELLE COLONIE, 1928-37; RASSEGNA ECONOMICA DELL'AFRICA ITALIANA, 1937-[41?].

   One of the most valuable series for information on Italian colonialism.

3086. Italy. Senato. MEMORANDUM SULLA SITUAZIONE ECONOMICA E FINANZARIA DEI TERRITORI ITALIANI IN AFRICA. Roma, 1946. 53 p.

3087. Micus, Ingeborg. DIE PRESSE DES ITALIENISCHEN KOLONIALREICHES. Würzburg, K. Triltsch, 1941. 64 p. plates, facsims.

   Bibliographical footnotes.

   A general account of the colonial press.

3088. Mondaini, Genuaro. LA LEGISLAZIONE COLONIALE ITALIANA NEL SUO SVILUPPO STORICO E NEL SUO STATO ATTUALE (1881-1940). 2 v. Milano, Istituto per gli Studi di Política Internazionale, 1941. (Manuali di Política Internazionale, no. 30)

   Reviews the colonial legislation within their historical context. This is a revised edition of the author's MANUALE DI STORIA E LEGISLAZIONE COLONIALE DEL REGNO D'ITALIA (1924-1927) (Roma, 1927, 2 v.), which includes bibliographies.

3089. Parpagliolo, A. RACCOLTA DEI PRINCIPALI ORDINAMENTI LEGISLATIVI DELLE COLONIE ITALIANE. Roma, Ministero delle Colonie, 1930-32. 2 v.

3090. Piccioli, Angelo. LA NUOVA ITALIA D'OLTREMARE, L'OPERA DEL FASCISMO NELLE COLONIE ITALIANE. 2d ed. Verona, Mondadori, 1934. 2 v. illus., plates, maps, tables, diagrs.

This work was commissioned by the colonial ministry and is the official history of the colonial accomplishments of Fascism in the first decade of Mussolini's rule.

3091. RIVISTA COLONIALE: ORGANO DELL'ISTITUTO COLONIALE ITALIANO. 1906-27. Roma. Monthly.

The 1920 volume contains an index for the years 1906-20. The early issues especially contain interesting articles by colonial pioneers.

The Italians subsequently published the illustrated monthly RIVISTA DELLA COLONIE: RASSEGNA DEI POSSEDIMENTI ITALIANI E STRA-NIERI D'OLTREMARE, 1927-43. The journal was published for the first eight years by the Ministero delle Colonie under the title OLTREMARE, and then RIVISTA DELLE COLONIE ITALIANE.

3092. Società Geográfica Italiana. MEMORIE DELLA REALE SOCIETA GEOGRAFICA ITALIANA. v. 1- 1878- Roma, Reale Società Geográfica Italiana.

Useful accounts by travelers, geographers, colonial officials, and missionaries. See Enrico de Agostini, LA REALE SOCIETA GEOGRA-FICA ITALIANA E LA SUA OPERA DALLA FONDAZIONE AD OGGI (1887-1936) (Roma, Reale Società Geográfica Italiana, 1937), which is an official history of the Italian Geographical Society.

3093. Villari, Luigi. THE EXPANSION OF ITALY. London, Faber & Faber, 1930. 290 p.

ETHIOPIA AND ERITREA

Bibliographies

3094. Dainelli, Giotto, Marinelli Olinto, and Attilio Mori. "Bibliografia geografia della colonia Eritrea, 1891-1906." RIVISTA GEOGRAFICA ITALIANA, v. 4, 1907: 72 p.

3095. Haskell, Daniel Carl, comp. ETHIOPIA AND THE ITALO-ETHIOPIAN CON-FLICT, 1936: A SELECTED LIST OF REFERENCES. New York, New York Public Library, 1936. 13 p.

3096. Italy. Ministero degli Affari Esteri. Istituto Agronomico per
l'Africa Italiana. CONTRIBUTION TO AN ITALIAN BIBLIOGRAPHY ON
ETHIOPIA, 1935-1950 (AGRICULTURE AND ARGUMENTS RELATIVE TO).
Translated from Italian by P. Gemma. Florence, n.d. 154 <u>1</u>.

Translation of a work published in Florence by the Istituto
Agronómico in 1953 (84 p.; 1,500 entries).

Reference Works

3097. Baer, George W. THE COMING OF THE ITALO-ETHIOPIAN WAR. Cambridge,
Mass., Harvard University Press, 1967. 404 p. map.

Bibliography: p. 379-400.

A standard work.

3098. Becker, George H. THE DISPOSITION OF THE ITALIAN COLONIES, 1941-
1951. Annemasse, 1952. 270 p.

Bibliography: p. 265-270.

For annotation see no. 3075.

3099. Conti Rossini, Carlo. ITALIA ED ETIOPIA: DAL TRATTATO D'UCCIALI
ALLA BATTAGLIA DI ADUA. Roma, Pubblicazioni dell'Istituto per
l'Oriente, 1935. 494 p. maps.

A history of Italo-Ethiopian relations compiled by one of the
most distinguished Italian authorities on Ethiopia, who had previously written many works on the early history, languages and the
ethnography of Abyssinia.

3100. Greenfield, Richard. ETHIOPIA: A NEW POLITICAL HISTORY. New York,
Praeger, 1965. 515 p. illus., maps, tables. (Praeger Library
of African Affairs)

Bibliography: p. 475-482.

A thorough study, but not primarily concerned with Italian colonialism. For full annotation see no. 2626.

3101. Longrigg, Stephen Hemsley. A SHORT HISTORY OF ERITREA. Oxford,
Clarendon Press, 1945. 188 p. illus., maps.

The author, a former brigadier-general in the British army, saw extensive service in Iraq and other parts of the Middle East. After the British conquest of Eritrea, he became Chief Administrator of the occupied area.

3102. Quaranta di San Severino, Ferdinando, barone. ETHIOPIA, AN EMPIRE IN THE MAKING. With a foreword by the Rt. Hon. Lord Hailey.... London, P. S. King and Son, 1939. 120 p. illus., plates, fold. maps.

A review of economic and social development during the first three years of Italian civil administration written by an official in the Ministry of Italian East Africa. A more technical analysis of Italy's administrative organization in conquered Ethiopia appears in an article by an American political scientist, Arthur H. Steiner, "The Government of Italian East Africa," AMERICAN POLITICAL SCIENCE REVIEW, v. 30, Oct. 1936, p. 884-902.

3103. Rennell, Francis James Rennell Rodd, baron. BRITISH MILITARY ADMINISTRATION OF OCCUPIED TERRITORIES IN AFRICA DURING THE YEARS 1941-1947. London, H.M. Stationery Off., 1948. 637 p. maps.

The official British account. The author was a recognized authority on the Sahara, the Tuareg people, and other aspects of Africa.

3104. Trevaskis, Gerald Kennedy Nicholas. ERITREA: A COLONY IN TRANSITION, 1941-1952. London, Oxford University Press, 1960. 137 p. maps.

Written by a former official in the British occupation service, this book briefly describes the period of transition from Italian Fascist to British military rule, and finally to semi-independence within a greater Ethiopian federation.

SOMALIA

Bibliographies

3105. Camera di Commercio Industria ed Agricoltura della Somalia. Sezione Fiere e Mostre, Mogadiscio. BIBLIOGRAFIA SOMALA. Mogadishu, Scuola Tipografica Missione Cattolica, 1958. 135 p. illus., map, facsims.

This bibliography, prepared under the auspices of the Mogadiscio Chamber of Commerce, "aims at being a complete bibliography of Somalia." The work was compiled by Professor Apollonio, head of the Dipartimento Studi of the Somalia Government, and by Dr. Pirone, Administrative Director of the Istituto Superiore di Diritto ed Economia della Somalia, with the assistance of various outside scholars and institutions. The bibliography lists over 2,000 items and is divided into two main sections. The first covers books and monographs. The second lists articles and similar material. The sections are subdivided by topics, including agriculture and related subjects; anthropology and other social studies; bibliography; hunting, fishing, and zoology; accounts of journeys; economics and statistics; geology and related subjects; military affairs; education and linguistics; legislation and law; literature; medicine and nutrition; history, politics, and religion; works of general interest; veterinary sciences; maps. The work has a general index, and forms the most extensive bibliography of the country available.

3106. Caroselli, Francisco Saverio. CATALOGO DEL MUSEO NELLA GARESA A MOGADISCIO. Mogadishu, Stampa della Colonia, 1934. 727 p.

A descriptive list of Arabic literature in Somalia and of documents pertaining to the Filonardi Company. The author wrote on numerous aspects of Italian colonial history (see, e.g., no. 3112).

3107. Italy. Ministero degli Affari Esteri. Istituto Agronomico per l'Africa Italiana. CONTRIBUTO AD UNA BIBLIOGRAFIA ITALIANA SU ERITREA E SOMALIA CON PARTICOLARE RIFERIMENTO ALL'AGRICOLTURA ED ARGOMENTI AFFINI. Firezne, 1953. 239 p. (4,000 entries)

3108. Papieri, Mario. CONTRIBUTO ALLA BIBLIOGRAFIA E CARTOGRAFIA DELLA SOMALIA ITALIANA. Roma, Istituto Coloniale Fascista, 1932. 90 p.

3109. U.S. Library of Congress. General Reference and Bibliographical Division. OFFICIAL PUBLICATIONS OF SOMALILAND, 1941-1959: A GUIDE. Compiled by Helen Conover. Washington, 1960. 41 p.

Covers works on British and French as well as Italian Somaliland. Most of the literature cited is, however, in Italian. For full annotation see no. 2646. See also Hess, no. 3119.

Reference Works

3110. Angeloni, Renato. PRINCIPI DIRITTO AMMINISTRATIVO SOMALO. Milano, A. Giuffrè, 1965. 390 p. (Istituto Universitario della

Somalia, Facoltà di Diritto ed Economia, Collana scientifica, 10)

3111. Bono, E. VADE MECUM DEL R. RESIDENTE IN SOMALIA. Mogadishu, Stamperia della Colonia, 1930.

Intended as a manual of regulations for local administrators in Somalia.

3112. Caroselli, Francisco Saverio. FERRO E FUOCO NELLA SOMALIA. Roma, Arti Grafiche, 1931. 333 p. plates, maps, plans, facsims.

A narrative on the career of Muhammad Abdullah Hassan, a famous dervish revolutionary, known to the British as the "Mad Mullah." See also the account by Douglas Jardine, Secretary of the Protectorate during the last campaigns against the long anti-British revolt of the "Mad Mullah" and his followers, THE MAD MULLAH OF SOMALILAND (London, H. Jenkins, 1923, 336 p.).

3113. Castagno, Alphonso A. SOMALIA. New York, Carnegie Endowment for International Peace, 1959. 61 p. tables. (INTERNATIONAL CONCILIATION, no. 522)

Bibliographical footnotes.

Useful survey.

3114. Cerulli, Enrico. SOMALIA: SCRITTI VARI EDITI ED INEDITI. Roma, Published for the Amministrazione Fiduciaria Italiana della Somalia by Istituto Poligrafico dello Stato, 1957-64. 3 v.

For annotation see no. 2650.

3115. Constanzo, Giuseppe A. PROBLEMI CONSTITUZIONALI DELLA SOMALIA NELLA PREPARAZIONE ALL'INDIPENDENZA (1957-1960). Milano, A. Giuffrè, 1962. 146 p.

Concerns work on constitutional problems in anticipation of Somalia's independence. Among the many aspects covered are the agreement on fiduciary administration, the establishment and work of the political and technical committees, the legislative assembly, the constituent assembly, the plan for gradual transformation of powers, and the question of Somalia before the United Nations. The work concludes with the proclamation of independence.

3116. Convegno di Studi Coloniali, 2d, Florence, 1947. AMMINISTRAZIONE
          FIDUCIARIA ALL'ITALIA IN AFRICA, ATTI DEL SECONDO CONVEGNO
          DI STUDI COLONIALI, FIRENZE, 12-15 MAGGRO. Firenze, 1947.
          415 p.

3117. Corni, Guido, ed. SOMALIA ITALIANA. Milano, Editoriale Arte e
          Storia, 1937. 2 v. illus. (part col.), maps.

          A large general survey of Italian Somaliland under the Fascist
       government, lavishly produced in two volumes of articles by Italian
       specialists. The first volume has a general sketch and papers on
       history, geology, flora and fauna, peoples, primitive agriculture,
       stock raising and diseases, and fishing. The second volume is on
       the Fascist administration and its measures of physical and economic
       development.

          The editor was a former Governor of Italian Somaliland who had
       himself written a book PROBLEMI COLONIALI (Milano, 1933).

3118. Great Britain. Foreign Office. Historical Section. ITALIAN SOMA-
          LILAND. London, H.M. Stationery Off., 1920. (Handbooks...,
          no. 128)

          There is a list of authorities on p. 26-27.

3119. Hess, Robert I. ITALIAN COLONIALISM IN SOMALIA. Chicago, Chicago
          University Press, 1966. 234 p. maps, tables.

          Bibliography: p. 213-226.

          A brief but extremely well-documented account with an "anno-
       tated bibliography," which is in fact an excellent bibliographical
       essay. Hess provides much detail, for instance, regarding official
       Italian reports.

3120. Istituto Agricolo Coloniale. PER LE NOSTRE COLONIE. Firenze,
          Vallecchi, 1927.

          A collection of essays on a high intellectual level by
       Antalupo, Mangini, De Celles, Cavazza, etc.

3121. Istituto Coloniale Italiano. ATTI DEL 2º CONGRESSO DEGLI ITALIANI
          ALL'ESTERO (11-20 GIUGNO 1911). Roma, 1912. 4 v.

3122. Italy. Ministero degli Affari Esteri. RAPPORT DU GOUVERNEMENT
       ITALIEN A L'ASSEMBLEE GENERALE DES NATIONS UNIES SUR L'ADMIN-
       ISTRATION DE TUTELLE DE LA SOMALIE. 1950- Roma. illus.,
       maps. Annual.

3123. Pankhurst, Estelle Sylvia. EX-ITALIAN SOMALILAND. London, Watts
       and Co., 1951. 460 p. illus., ports., maps.

       A partisan publication written by a veteran British suffragette
       leader who later became a militant advocate of Ethiopian claims.
       The author also wrote on many other aspects of history and politics
       in the Horn of Africa. Her works include a massive book, ETHIOPIA:
       A CULTURAL HISTORY (with a foreword by Canon John A. Douglas; Essex,
       Eng., Lalibela House, 1955), which also touches on adjacent areas.

3124. Rossetti, Carlo. MANUALE DI LEGISLAZIONE DELLA SOMALIA ITALIANA.
       Roma, Ministero delle Colonie, 1912-14. 3 v.

       A general compendium of Italian legislation on Somalia.

3125. Technical Assistance Mission to the Trust Territory of Somaliland
       under Italian Administration. THE TRUST TERRITORY OF SOMALI-
       LAND UNDER ITALIAN ADMINISTRATION. Report prepared jointly
       for the Government of Italy by an expert appointed by the
       United Nations Technical Assistance Administration and by
       experts appointed respectively by the Food and Agriculture
       Organization of the United Nations, the United Nations Edu-
       cational, Scientific, and Cultural Organization, and the World
       Health Organization. New York, 1952. 343 p. illus., maps,
       tables. (United Nations [Document] ST/TAA/K Somaliland/1)

       Includes bibliographies.

       Processed publication of the United Nations. Six experts
       spent three months making an extended survey of the economic needs
       of the territory, touring the country widely, talking with local
       officials and representatives on all levels, and visiting all
       institutions. They reported in great detail, offering advice on
       many points. They were not optimistic regarding the possibility
       of a viable economy.

3126. U.S. Operations Mission to Italy. [Reports] Rome, 1950-

       For listing and annotation, see no. 2662.

3127. U.S. Operations Mission to the Somali Republic. INTER-RIVER
ECONOMIC EXPLORATIONS: THE SOMALI REPUBLIC. Washington,
1961. xxxi, 347 p. illus., maps, diagrs., tables.

For annotation see no. 2663.

INDEX

INDEX

Note: An index of authors, editors, compilers, and titles is combined here with a subject and geographic index. Numbers refer to items, with a few exceptions in which pages are specified for works mentioned in notes unrelated to individual entries. An "n" following the number indicates reference not in the entry but in the annotation or related note. The broad subject entries pertain to Africa in general; therefore the user should refer to the geographic entries for selected subject breakdown for a specific region or country. Cross references are held to a minimum; thus for the specific, there is usually no cross reference to the general--e.g., "Archaeology" is not cross-referred to the general discipline of "History"; also, Nigeria is not cross-referred to West Africa, or Katanga to Congo. Names of peoples are given in accordance with the author's spelling. The current names of the countries and major regions of Africa are underscored, as are the designations for areas of the former colonial powers.

LE ROYAUME KUBA, 2336
LA ROYAUTE SACREE DE L'ANCIEN
    RWANDA: TEXTE, TRADUCTION ET
    COMMENTAIRE DE SON RITUEL, 2349
Ruanda-Urundi, see Burundi; Rwanda
RUANDA-URUNDI, 2344n
LE RUANDA-URUNDI, 2344
RUANDA-URUNDI (1884-1919), 2355
Rubadiri, David, Note, p. 351
Rubbens, A., 1000
Rubin, Edward, 739n
Rubin, Leslie, 694n, 1381
Rudd, Charles Dunnell, 2123(d)
Rudin, Harry R., 1952, 3056
Rüger, Adolf, 3057n
Rumeau, A., 428, 1128n
Rupp, Brigitta, 14, 27, 413, 1616n
RURAL AFRICANA: RESEARCH NOTES ON
    LOCAL POLITICS AND POLITICAL AN-
    THROPOLOGY (East Lansing), 583,
    850
Russell, Edward Walter, 2454
Russell, Ronald S., 1226
Russian literature on Africa, see
    Soviet African studies
RUSSIAN MATERIALS ON AFRICA: A SE-
    LECTIVE BIBLIOGRAPHY, 352
Ruth Sloan Associates, Washington,
    D.C., 391, 912
Ruthenberg, Hans, 2485
Rutherfoord, Peggy, 1064
Rwanda, Note, p. 732
    ancient kingdoms, 2349-2351, 2356,
      2419
    archives on, 62, 65, 108
    atlases, 2206, 2208
    bibliographies, 2210, 2211, 2215-
      2219, 2227, 2341-2343
    customary law, 2329
    directory of colonial institu-
      tions, 2286
    economy, 2277, 2354
    ethnography, 2289, 2345, 2349-2351
    gazetteer, 2361
    geography, 2320
    guide, 2279
    history, 2346-2348, 2255, 2362
    linguistic research, 2285
    literature, 2309
    politics, 2347, 2348, 2356, 2357,
      2359
    the press, 2211

Rwanda--continued
    reference works, 2277, 2279, 2289,
      2309, 2344-2351, 2353-57, 2359,
      2361, 2362
    religion, 2353
    serials, 371
    survey, 2344
RWANDA AND BURUNDI: SELECTED BIBLI-
    OGRAPHY, 2341
LE RWANDA ET LA CIVILISATION INTER-
    LACUSTRE ..., 2351
"The Rwanda of Rwanda," 2357n
RWANDA: OFFICIAL STANDARD NAMES ...,
    2361
Rwanda people, 2357
RWANDA POLITIQUE (1958-1960), 2347
Ryckmans, Pierre, 2327
Ryder, A. F. C., 48(b)
Ryder, Alan, 528n
Rydings, H. A., 1259, 1330n

S.A. ARCHIVES JOURNAL (Pretoria),
    246
S.A. ARGIEFBLAD (Pretoria), 246
S.A.N.B.: SOUTH AFRICAN NATIONAL
    BIBLIOGRAPHY ..., 2866, 2868n
SCAUL, see Standing Committee on Af-
    rican University Libraries
SCAUL NEWSLETTER (Dar es Salaam),
    114; Note, p. 18
SCOLMA, see Standing Conference on
    Library Materials on Africa
THE SCOLMA DIRECTORY OF LIBRARIES
    AND SPECIAL COLLECTIONS ON
    AFRICA, 93
SEDES, see Société d'Etudes pour le
    Développement Economique et
    Social
SERESA, see Société d'Etudes et de
    Réalisations Economiques et So-
    ciales dans l'Agriculture
SESAF, see Société Anonyme pour les
    Echanges entre la Suisse et
    l'Afrique
SESAF INFORMATIONS, 766n
Sachs, Moshe Y., 459
Sadler, Sir Michael Ernest, 1308
Sahara, 1763, 1779, 1780; Note,
    p. 564
    development planning, 1765
    ethnography, 1762, 1781, 1979,
      1988